CENSUS OF INDIA 1931

Census of India 1871-1951, 9 Sets In 384 Bindings (9788121258876) Rs. 700000

Census of India 1931, 28 Vols. In 52 Bindings (9788121271233) Rs. 102000

1. India - Report (9788121276153) Rs. 2820 (Vol. I, Pt. 1)
2. India - Imperial Tables (9788121276139) Rs. 3210 (Vol. I, Pt. 2)
3. India - Ethnographical and Administration Report (9788121276115) Rs. 2900 (Vol. I, Pt. 3 & 5)
4. The Andaman And Nicobar Islands - Report, Tables (9788121276078) Rs. 720 (Vol. II, Pt. 1, Pt. 2)
5. Assam - Report (9788121276054) Rs. 1340 (Vol. III, Pt. 1)
6. Assam - Tables and Administrative Report (9788121276030) Rs. 1830 (Vol. III, Pt. 2 & 3)
7. Baluchistan - Report, Imeprial and Provincial Tables and Administrative Report (9788121276016) Rs. 2320 (Vol. IV, Pt. 1 & 2 & 3)
8. Bengal & Sikkim - Report (9788121275972) Rs. 2860 (Vol. V, Pt. 1)
9. Bengal & Sikkim - Tables (9788121275958) Rs. 1660 (Vol. V, Pt. 2)
10. Calcutta (9788121275910) Rs. 960 (Vol. VI, Pt. 1 & 2)
11. Bengal, Sikkim And Calcutta - Administrative Report (9788121275934) Rs. 580 (Vol. V & VI, Pt. 3)
12. Bihar And Orissa - Report (9788121275897) Rs. 1780 (Vol. VII, Pt. 1)
13. Bihar And Orissa - Tables and Administrative Report (9788121275873) Rs. 1190 (Vol. VII, Pt. 2 & 3)
14. Bombay Presidency - General Report (9788121275835) Rs. 3620 (Vol. VIII, Pt. 1)
15. Bombay - Statistical tables (9788121275811) Rs. 3060 (Vol. VIII, Pt. 2)
16. Bombay Presidency Aden - report and tables and Administrative report (9788121275798) Rs. 520 (Vol. VIII, Pt. 3 & 4)
17. Cities of the Bombay Presidency Report & Statistical tables (9788121275750) Rs. 2020 (Vol. IX, Pt. 1 & 2)
18. The Western India States Agency, In Two Parts - The Report & The Statistical Tables (9788121275736) Rs. 2560 (Vol. X, Pt. 1 & 2)
19. Burma - Report (9788121275712) Rs. 1860 (Vol. XI, Pt. 1)
20. Burma - Tables and Administrative Report (9788121275699) Rs. 1690 (Vol. XI, Pt. 2 & 3)
21. Central Provinces & Berar - Report (9788121275651) Rs. 2340 (Vol. XII, Pt. 1)
22. Central Provinces & Berar - Tables and Administrative Report (9788121275637) Rs. 3120 (Vol. XII, Pt. 2 & 3)
23. Coorg - Report And Tables and Madras - Report (9788121275613) Rs. 2680 (Vol. XIV, Pt. 1)
24. Madras - Imperial And Provincial Tables and The Administration Report (9788121275576) Rs. 1950 (Vol. XIV, Pt. 2 & 4)
25. North - West Frontier Province - Report & Tables (9788121275538) Rs. 2300 (Vol. XV, Pt. 1 & 2)
26. Delhi - Report & Tables (9788121275514) Rs. 1180 (Vol. XVI, Pt. 1 & 2)
27. Punjab - Report (9788121275491) Rs. 2070 (Vol. XVII, Pt. 1)
28. Punjab - Tables (9788121275477) Rs. 1690 (Vol. XVII, Pt. 2)
29. United Provinces of Agra And Oudh - Report (9788121275453) Rs. 3380 (Vol. XVIII, Pt. 1)
30. United Provinces of Agra And Oudh - Imperial And Provincial Tables and Administrative (9788121275439) Rs. 3600 (Vol. XVIII, Pt. 2 & 3)
31. Baroda - Report (9788121275415) Rs. 2800 (Vol. XIX, Pt. 1)
32. Baroda - Tables (9788121275392) Rs. 730 (Vol. XIX, Pt. 2)
33. Baroda - Administrative (9788121275378) Rs. 780 (Vol. XIX, Pt. 3)
34. Central India Agency - Report (9788121275354) Rs. 1690 (Vol. XX, Pt. 1)
35. Central India Agency - Tables and Administrative Volume (9788121275330) Rs. 2260 (Vol. XX, Pt. 2 & 3)
36. Cochin - Report & Tables (9788121275293) Rs. 2460 (Vol. XXI, Pt. 1 & 2 - A & B.)
37. Gwalior - Report (9788121275279) Rs. 1470 (Vol. XXII, Pt. 1)
38. Gwalior - Tables (9788121275255) Rs. 980 (Vol. XXII, Pt. 2)
39. H. E. H. The Nizam's Dominions (Hyderabad State) - Report (9788121275231) Rs. 1540 (Vol. XXIII, Pt. 1)
40. H. E. H. The Nizam's Dominions (Hyderabad State) - Tables (9788121275217) Rs. 1510 (Vol. XXIII, Pt. 2)
41. Jammu & Kashmir State - Report (9788121275194) Rs. 2060 (Vol. XXIV, Pt. 1)
42. Jammu & Kashmir State - Imperial & State Tables (9788121275170) Rs. 1940 (Vol. XXIV, Pt. 2 & 3)
43. Mysore - Report (9788121275156) Rs. 1950 (Vol. XXV, Pt. 1)
44. Mysore - Tables (9788121275132) Rs. 1380 (Vol. XXV, Pt. 2)
45. Ajmer-Merwara - Report And Tables (9788121275118) Rs. 780 (Vol. XXVI)
46. Rajputana Agency And Ajmer-Merwara - Report and Tables and Administrative (9788121275095) Rs. 2380 (Vol. XXVII, Pt. 1 & 2)
47. Travancore - Report (9788121276092) Rs. 2960 (Vol. XXVIII, Pt. 1)
48. Travancore - Tables & Administrative (9788121275996) Rs. 1360 (Vol. XXVIII, Pt. 2 & 4)
49. Jaipur State- Report (9788121275859) Rs. 1280 (Pt. 1)
50. Jaipur State- Tables (9788121275774) Rs. 2030 (Pt. 2)
51. Mayurbhanj state- Report (9788121275675) Rs. 3180 (Pt. 1)
52. Mayurbhanj state- Tables (9788121275552) Rs. 3070 (Pt. 2)

Owing to the antiquity and rarity of this book, certain pages are regrettably absent, and readability is compromised due to the blurring of the original text. If you possess any insights regarding the availability of these missing sections, kindly inform us. Your assistance is crucial in ensuring the completion of this significant work for the benefit of future generations.

CENSUS OF INDIA, 1931

BOOK - 22: VOLUME - XII

CENTRAL PROVINCES & BERAR

PART II - TABLES
PART III - ADMINISTRATIVE REPORT

W. H. SHOOBERT

GYAN

Published by

Gyan Publishing House
5, Ansari Road
Daryaganj, New Delhi-110002
Phone: 011-47034999, 9811692060
E-mail: books@gyanbooks.com

Distribution Network
gyanbooks.com
India, USA, Canada, UK, Australia

ISBN: 978-81-212-7123-3 (Set) 28 Vols. In 52 Bindings

ISBN: 978-81-212-7563-7 (PB) Vol. XII, Pt. II, III

First Published, 1932

2nd Impression 2024

Printed at: Gyan Press, Delhi.

CENSUS OF INDIA 1931

Census of India, 1931

VOLUME XII

CENTRAL PROVINCES & BERAR

PART II—TABLES

BY

W. H. SHOOBERT

_F THE INDIAN CIVIL SERVICE

Superintendent of Census Operations, Central Provinces and Berar

NAGPUR

GOVERNMENT PRINTING, C.P.

1932

AGENTS FOR THE SALE OF PUBLICATIONS ISSUED BY THE CENTRAL PROVINCES GOVERNMENT

[NOTE.—Appointments of all official Agents in the United Kingdom and on the Continent for the sale of Government Publications have been terminated with effect from the 1st April 1925.

All publications in future are obtainable either direct from the High Commissioner for India, India House, Aldwych, London, W. C. 2, or through any bookseller.]

INDIA

AKOLA :
The Proprietor, Shri Ramdas Stores, Tajnapeth.

ALLAHABAD :
Mr. Ram Narain Lal, Publisher, etc., 1, Bank Road.
The Superintendent, Nazair Kanun Hind Press.

AMRAOTI :
Thakur & Co., Booksellers.

BARODA.
Mr. M. C. Kothari, Bookseller and Publisher, Raopura Road.

BILASPUR :
Mr. M. A. Subhan, Bookseller and Publisher.

BOMBAY :
D. B. Taraporevala, Sons & Co., 190, Hornby Road, Fort.
Radhabai Atmaram Sagoon.
Sunder Pandurang, 25, Kalbadevi Road.
Thacker & Co., Ltd.

CALCUTTA :
The Book Company, 4/4-A, College Street.
Butterworth & Co. (India), Ltd., 8-2, Hastings Street.
The Indian School Supply Depôt.
M. C. Sircar & Sons, 75 Harriton Road.
Newman& Co :
R. Cambray & Co.
S. K. Lahiri & Co.
Thacker, Spink & Co.

COOCH BEHAR :
Babu S. C. Taluqdar, Proprietor, Students & Co.

DELHI :
The Oxford Book and Stationery Co.

JUBBULPORE :
The Manager, General Book Depôt.

KARACHI :
The Standard Bookstall.

LAHORE :
Rai Sahib M. Gulab Singh & Sons.

LUCKNOW :
The Punjab Sansk Book Depôt
The Proprietor, Newal Kishore Press.
The Upper India Publishing House, Ltd., 41, Aminabad Park.

MADRAS :
Higginbotham & Co.
S. Murthy & Co., Post Box No. 152.
The Proprietor, The City Book Co., Post Box No. 283.

NAGPUR :
Aidan Binzani, Proprietors, Karmavir Book Depôt, Mahal.
Mr. G. G. Khot, Walker Road.
Mr. G. A. Shastri, Bookseller and Publisher, Hislop College Road.
The Manager, General Book Depôt.
The Manager, " The Hitavada ".
The Proprietor, Bhisey Brothers, Booksellers and Publishers.
Mr. D. M. Dhumal, Manager, Experimental Book Binding Depot.

PATNA :
The Patna Law Press Co.

POONA :
The Proprietor, New Kitabkhana.

RANGOON :
The Superintendent, American Baptis Mission Press.

SIMLA :
Thacker, Spink & Co

YEOTMAL:
V. N. Saraswat.

CENSUS TABLES OF 1931

ERRATA

Page.	Table.	Unit or serial number.	Column.	*For*	*Read*
16	IV	67	5	Blank space	7,053
27	V	115	13	Blank space	4
40	VI	(ii) States and Agencies ..	41	46	946
44	VI	Gwalior ..	62	154	159
49	VI	(*c*) French and Portuguese Settlements ..	7	33	133
58	VII	All religions—0—5 ..	6	53,873	58,373
70	VII	All religions—0—1 ..	3	9,172	9,772
85	VIII	Barhai—Male ..	25	1,96	1,967
87	VIII	Darzi—Female ..	14	1,707	1,797
88	VIII	Ghasia—Total—Male ..	9	3,222	322
88	VIII	Ghasia—Total—Female ..	9	10	102
104	X	21	4	244,095	224,095
104	X	Heading ..	11	Males	Females
105	X	37	17	Blank space	31
281	XI	Dahayat—Jubbulpore ..	22	76	576
281	XI	Dhanwar—Bilaspur ..	24	3	31
307	XI	Indian Christians ..	47	7	1
320	XIII	Bhandara district all Religions—0—5 ..	10	61,841	61,843
322	XIII	Bilaspur district Hindus—5—10 ..	7	2,755	2,355
322	XIII	Bilaspur district Hindus—0—5 ..	9	216,708	216,108
326	XIII	Nagpur—Christians ..	14	331	1,331
326	XIII	Nagpur—Christians—0—5 ..	14	1,176	176
343	XV	Serial number below 16 ..	..	1	17
359	XV	50	13	..	18
359	XV	51	13	81	..
381	XVII	Bhuinhar, Tribal Religions—Korea ..	4	1,314	1,514
392	XVII	Kharia, Hindu—Central Provinces States ..	2	9 0	9,210
394	XVII	Korku, Tribal,—Betul ..	2	2,972	29,972
403	XVII	Pardhi,—Balaghat ..	4	9	96
403	XVII	Pardhi—Raipur ..	4	28	282
433	XVIII	Kol, Hindu—Narsinghpur ..	19	3	333
501	XX	16	22	100	199
505	Provincial Table I.	Gondia Tahsil Khalsa ..	7	47,348	47,548
506	Provincial Table I.	Yeotmal Town ..	12	11	181
521	Provincial Table II.	Wun Taluk ..	13	7	37

FOREWORD

The figures set out in this volume have been tabulated from the returns made at the Census held on the 26th February 1931.

The statistics have been examined in Part I of the Report and anything which appears unusual in them has been discussed there.

Owing to the masses of material involved, printing errors have occurred in some of the tables. Officials and others are therefore advised to refer to the *errata*, and to correct in manuscript any mistakes shown therein to have been made in the following pages, before using the figures for any purpose.

W. H. SHOOBERT,

Superintendent of Census Operations,
Central Provinces and Berar.

NAGPUR :
The 16*th November* 1932.

TABLE OF CONTENTS

TABLE I

Area, Houses and Population

1. This table shows for each district the area, the number of towns and villages, the number of occupied houses and the total urban and rural population, male and female. Similar figures are given for the States.

2. The difference between some of the areas here shown and those in the corresponding Table of 1921 is due to inter-district transfers and recalculation of areas, as explained on the title page of Table II.

3. For the purpose of column 3 (number of towns) cantonments have at this census for the first time been treated as separate towns and have not been regarded as forming part of the Municipalities which they adjoin.

4. The main statistics for tahsils or taluqs will be found in Provincial Tables I and II at the end of the volume.

5. The areas given in this Table and in Provincial Table I are subject to some revision in light of the results of the latest survey which were not available in detail when the Tables were printed. The newly calculated district areas will in most cases vary only slightly from those now shown.

TABLE I — Area, Houses

Serial No.	District or State.	Area in square miles.	Towns.	Villages.	Occupied houses. Total.	Occupied houses. In towns.	Occupied houses. In villages.
	1	2	3	4	5	6	7
	Central Provinces and Berar	**131,095**	**122**	**48,722**	**3,592,022**	**367,796**	**3,224,226**
	C. P. British districts and Berar.	**99,920**	**112**	**39,762**	**3,168,788**	**351,815**	**2,816,973**
	C. P. British districts ..	**82,153**	**70**	**33,827**	**2,439,990**	**243,733**	**2,196,257**
	Jubbulpore Division ..	*18,956*	*13*	*8,992*	*517,616*	*67,652*	*449,964*
1	Saugor ..	3,964	6	1,860	107,656	26,763	80,893
2	Damoh ..	2,807	1	1,148	68,065	2,348	65,717
3	Jubbulpore ..	3,912	4	2,382	169,520	33,603	135,917
4	Mandla ..	5,057	1	2,020	88,473	1,795	86,678
5	Seoni ..	3,216	1	1,582	83,902	3,143	80,759
	Nerbudda Division ..	*18,386*	*18*	*6,650*	*482,879*	*42,685*	*440,194*
6	Narsinghpur ..	1,978	3	992	69,732	5,100	64,632
7	Hoshangabad ..	3,693	8	1,335	123,351	10,820	112,531
8	Nimar ..	4,227	2	1,141	92,101	15,440	76,661
9	Betul ..	3,910	2	1,252	77,449	3,222	74,227
10	Chhindwara ..	4,578	3	1,930	120,246	8,103	112,143
	Nagpur Division ..	*22,760*	*31*	*7,690*	*696,085*	*105,462*	*590,623*
11	Wardha ..	2,434	7	939	108,224	18,532	89,692
12	Nagpur ..	3,834	13	1,644	184,097	62,788	121,309
13	Chanda ..	9,312	6	2,385	148,382	11,524	136,858
14	Bhandara ..	3,623	4	1,498	154,070	10,451	143,619
15	Balaghat ..	3,557	1	1,224	101,312	2,167	99,145
	Chhattisgarh Division ..	*22,051*	*8*	*10,495*	*743,410*	*27,934*	*715,476*
16	Raipur ..	9,717	4	4,481	304,367	15,162	289,205
17	Bilaspur ..	7,618	3	3,439	271,514	9,874	261,640
18	Drug ..	4,716	1	2,575	167,529	2,898	164,631
	Berar ..	**17,767**	**42**	**5,935**	**728,798**	**108,082**	**620,716**
19	Amraoti ..	4,691	14	1,612	202,415	39,536	162,879
20	Akola ..	4,091	11	1,492	187,100	30,545	156,555
21	Buldana ..	3,766	9	1,206	160,225	20,573	139,652
22	Yeotmal ..	5,219	8	1,625	179,058	17,428	161,630
	Central Provinces States ..	**31,175**	**10**	**8,960**	**423,234**	**15,981**	**407,253**
23	Makrai ..	155	..	69	3,266	..	3,266
24	Bastar ..	13,062	1	2,442	91,143	2,358	88,785
25	Kanker ..	1,431	1	549	19,254	967	18,287
26	Nandgaon ..	871	1	523	34,566	3,275	31,291
27	Khairagarh ..	931	2	492	31,957	2,867	29,090
28	Chhuikhadan ..	153	..	104	5,894	..	5,894
29	Kawardha ..	798	1	384	16,114	1,302	14,812
30	Sakti ..	138	1	124	9,412	693	8,719
31	Raigarh ..	1,486	2	795	48,181	3,287	44,894
32	Sarangarh ..	540	1	456	19,186	1,232	17,954
33	Changbhakar ..	906	..	128	5,076	..	5,076
34	Korea ..	1,631	..	317	17,131	..	17,131
35	Surguja ..	6,055	..	1,654	72,488	..	72,488
36	Udaipur ..	1,055	..	284	16,853	..	16,853
37	Jashpur ..	1,963	..	639	32,713	..	32,713

Note 1.—The population (1,313 males, 1,395 females) of the villages of Lalipur and Maharajpur and of Maharajpur railway station, which lie within the limits of Mandla Municipality, has been classed as rural and not as urban.

Population.									
Persons.			Males.			Females.			
Total.	Urban.	Rural.	Total.	Urban.	Rural.	Total.	Urban.	Rural.	Serial No.
8	9	10	11	12	13	14	15	16	
17,990,937	**1,754,611**	**16,236,326**	**8,997,203**	**928,157**	**8,069,046**	**8,993,734**	**826,454**	**8,167,280**	
15,507,723	**1,679,546**	**13,828,177**	**7,761,818**	**890,796**	**6,871,022**	**7,745,905**	**788,750**	**6,957,155**	
12,065,885	**1,157,649**	**10,908,236**	**6,002,239**	**612,852**	**5,389,387**	**6,063,646**	**544,797**	**5,518,849**	
2,463,466	*277,453*	*2,186,013*	*1,240,655*	*149,024*	*1,091,631*	*1,222,811*	*128,429*	*1,094,382*	
544,589	80,542	464,047	280,385	42,195	238,190	264,204	38,347	225,857	1
305,568	20,728	284,840	154,791	10,726	144,065	150,777	10,002	140,775	2
773,811	152,105	621,706	391,649	83,783	307,866	382,162	68,322	313,840	3
445,766	7,997	437,769	221,359	4,115	217,244	224,407	3,882	220,525	4
393,732	16,081	377,651	192,471	8,205	184,266	201,261	7,876	193,385	5
2,254,566	*216,879*	*2,037,687*	*1,137,806*	*114,631*	*1,023,175*	*1,116,760*	*102,248*	*1,014,512*	
321,481	23,825	297,656	161,417	12,350	149,067	160,064	11,475	148,589	6
486,630	64,805	421,825	248,226	34,802	213,424	238,404	30,003	208,401	7
466,931	78,688	388,243	242,042	42,116	199,926	224,889	36,572	188,317	8
406,252	14,992	391,260	201,114	7,783	193,331	205,138	7,209	197,929	9
573,272	34,569	538,703	285,007	17,580	267,427	288,265	16,989	271,276	10
3,602,108	*532,379*	*3,069,729*	*1,809,541*	*281,270*	*1,528,271*	*1,792,567*	*251,109*	*1,541,458*	
516,266	85,283	430,983	261,394	45,340	216,054	254,872	39,943	214,929	11
940,049	323,345	616,704	481,246	172,250	308,996	458,803	151,095	307,708	12
759,695	59,865	699,830	381,204	30,413	350,791	378,491	29,452	349,039	13
824,496	54,281	770,215	408,799	28,219	380,580	415,697	26,062	389,635	14
561,602	9,605	551,997	276,898	5,048	271,650	284,704	4,557	280,147	15
3,745,745	*130,938*	*3,614,807*	*1,814,237*	*67,927*	*1,746,310*	*1,931,508*	*63,011*	*1,868,497*	
1,527,573	71,365	1,456,208	739,950	37,214	702,736	787,623	34,151	753,472	16
1,400,248	46,401	1,353,847	683,920	23,838	660,082	716,328	22,563	693,765	17
817,924	13,172	804,752	390,367	6,875	383,492	427,557	6,297	421,260	18
3,441,838	**521,897**	**2,919,941**	**1,759,579**	**277,944**	**1,481,635**	**1,682,259**	**243,953**	**1,438,306**	
941,604	183,404	758,200	485,593	97,625	387,968	456,011	85,779	370,232	19
876,362	151,693	724,669	448,896	80,566	368,330	427,466	71,127	356,339	20
766,584	104,792	661,792	388,966	55,470	333,496	377,618	49,322	328,296	21
857,288	82,008	775,280	436,124	44,283	391 841	421,164	37,725	383,439	22
2,483,214	**75,065**	**2,408,149**	**1,235,385**	**37,361**	**1,198,024**	**1,247,829**	**37,704**	**1,210,125**	
15,516	..	15,516	7,900	..	7,900	7,616	..	7,616	23
524,721	10,128	514,593	263,248	5,041	258,207	261,473	5,087	256,386	24
136,101	5,305	130,796	67,132	2,652	64,480	68,969	2,653	66,316	25
182,380	15,977	166,403	87,886	8,206	79,680	94,494	7,771	86,723	26
157,400	12,692	144,708	75,647	6,260	69,387	81,753	6,432	75,321	27
31,668	..	31,668	15,238	..	15,238	16,430	..	16,430	28
72,820	5,052	67,768	35,098	2,366	32,732	37,722	2,686	35,036	29
48,489	3,240	45,249	23,571	1,574	21,997	24,918	1,666	23,252	30
277,569	15,625	261,944	136,723	7,815	128,908	140,846	7,810	133,036	31
128,967	7,046	121,921	62,443	3,447	58,996	66,524	3,599	62,925	32
23,322	..	23,322	11,987	..	11,987	11,335	..	11,335	33
90,886	..	90,886	46,748	..	46,748	44,138	..	44,138	34
501,939	..	501,939	254,923	..	254,923	247,016	..	247,016	35
97,738	..	97,738	49,425	..	49,425	48,313	..	48,313	36
193,698	..	193,698	97,416	..	97,416	96,282	..	96,282	37

Note 2.—The population (3,173 males and 3,043 females) of four villages of Amraoti district, which are now included within the Municipality of Anjangaon, has been classed as rural and not urban.

TABLE II

Variation in Population since 1881

1. The table compares the population of each district and State in the Central Provinces and Berar as ascertained at the Census of 1931 with that of the five previous censuses. The figures for the latter differ from those shown in the previous Census Reports. This is due to subsequent transfers of territory from one district or State to another within the province and also to the recalculation of areas. The effect of these changes on the population of the districts or States concerned has been calculated and the figures have been adjusted accordingly.

2. The following are the districts and States of which transfers of territory have taken place :—

Between 1881 *and* 1891.

Mandla, Balaghat, Seoni.

Between 1891 *and* 1901.

Nagpur, Seoni, Chhindwara, Hoshangabad, Nimar, Betul, Mandla, Balaghat.

Between 1901 *and* 1911.

Saugor, Narsinghpur, Mandla, Balaghat, Hoshangabad, Nimar, Betul, Chhindwara, Chanda, Drug, Raipur, Bilaspur, Amraoti, Akola, Buldana, Yeotmal.

Between 1911 *and* 1921.

Damoh, Seoni, Hoshangabad, Chhindwara, Wardha, Nagpur, Bhandara, Balaghat, Raipur, Amraoti, Akola, Buldana, Yeotmal, Kanker State.

Between 1921 *and* 1931.

Drug, Raipur, Amraoti, Akola, Buldana, Chhuikhadan State.

3. Between 1901 and 1911 Berar and the Chhota Nagpur States (Changbhakar, Korea, Surguja, Udaipur and Jashpur) were added to the province, almost the whole of the Sambalpur district and the Oriya States (Bamra, Rairakhol, Sonpur, Patna and Kalahandi) were transferred to Bengal and a portion of Chanda was transferred to Madras.

TABLE II — **Variation in**

Serial Number.	District or State.	Persons. 1931.	1921.	1911.	1901.	1891.	1881.	1921 to 1931.
	1	2	3	4	5	6	7	8
	Central Provinces and Berar ..	**17,990,937**	**15,979,660**	**16,033,310**	**13,602,592**	**14,761,534**	**13,330,657**	**+2,011,277**
	C. P. British Districts and Berar	**15,507,723**	**13,912,760**	**13,916,158**	**11,971,328**	**13,048,845**	**11,943,251**	**+1,594,963**
	C. P. British Districts ..	**12,065,885**	**10,837,444**	**10,858,996**	**9,217,312**	**10,151,354**	**9,270,578**	**+1,228,441**
	Jubbulpore Division ..	*2,463,466*	*2,296,508*	*2,421,748*	*2,082,052*	*2,375,485*	*2,200,771*	***+166,958***
1	Saugor	544,589	528,380	541,410	469,479	589,837	562,829	+16,209
2	Damoh	305,568	287,126	333,047	285,326	325,613	312,957	+18,442
3	Jubbulpore	773,811	745,685	745,892	680,585	748,146	687,233	+28,126
4	Mandla	445,766	386,446	405,234	318,381	340,443	301,377	+59,320
5	Seoni	393,732	348,871	396,165	328,281	371,446	336,375	+44,661
	Nerbudda Division ..	*2,254,566*	*2,013,021*	*2,081,638*	*1,785,142*	*1,883,204*	*1,765,363*	***+241,545***
6	Narsinghpur	321,481	315,162	325,677	315,518	368,932	367,294	+6,319
7	Hoshangabad	486,630	445,733	457,395	446,645	493,941	464,384	+40,897
8	Nimar	466,931	396,554	391,071	327,173	286,176	253,921	+70,377
9	Betul	406,252	363,737	390,386	287,807	326,581	306,796	+42,515
10	Chhindwara	573,272	491,835	517,109	407,999	407,574	372,968	+81,437
	Nagpur Division	*3,602,108*	*3,146,228*	*3,108,993*	*2,658,580*	*2,908,492*	*2,696,514*	***+455,880***
11	Wardha	516,266	463,696	460,775	386,012	401,770	388,063	+52,570
12	Nagpur	940,049	792,521	808,922	750,935	756,946	696,514	+147,528
13	Chanda	759,695	660.630	677,544	533,887	625,495	589,000	+99,065
14	Bhandara	824,496	717,747	685,828	587,812	658,519	606,145	+106,749
15	Balaghat	561,602	511,634	475,924	399,934	465,762	416,792	+49,968
	Chhattisgarh Division ..	*3,745,745*	*3,381,687*	*3,246,617*	*2,691,538*	*2,984,173*	*2,607,930*	***+364,058***
16	Raipur	1,527,573	1,392,768	1,310,584	1,082,433	1,109,010	980,783	+134,805
17	Bilaspur	1,400,248	1,231,765	1,146,223	918,491	1,046,606	880,878	+168,483
18	Drug	817,924	757,154	789,810	690,614	828,557	746,269	+60,770
	Berar	**3,441,838**	**3,075,316**	**3,057,162**	**2,754,016**	**2,897,491**	**2,672,673**	**+366,522**
19	Amraoti	941,604	827,867	873,012	806,859	847,187	775,560	+113,737
20	Akola	876,362	794,847	786,042	752,066	756,555	732,504	+81,515
21	Buldana	766,584	703,643	673,698	617,990	682,501	646,341	+62,941
22	Yeotmal	857,288	748,959	724,410	577,101	611,248	518,268	+108.329
	Central Provinces States ..	**2,483,214**	**2,066,900**	**2,117,152**	**1,631,264**	**1,712.689**	**1,387,406**	**+416,314**
23	Makrai	15,516	12,803	15,021	13,035	18,549	16,764	+2,713
24	Bastar	524,721	464,407	433,310	306,501	310,884	196,248	+60,314
25	Kanker	136,101	124,928	127,164	103,660	82,506	63,722	+11,173
26	Nandgaon	182,380	147,906	167,362	126,365	183,866	164,339	+34,474
27	Khairagarh	157,400	124,008	155,471	137,554	181,184	166,178	+33,392
28	Chhuikhadan	31,668	26,122	31,150	26,368	36,288	32,979	+5,546
29	Kawardha	72,820	61,783	77,654	57,474	91,813	86,362	+11,037
30	Sakti	48,489	41,554	34,547	22,301	25,374	22,819	+6,935
31	Raigarh	277,569	241,634	218,860	174,929	168,525	128,943	+35,935
32	Sarangarh	128,967	117,781	102,071	79.900	83,210	71,274	+11,186
33	Changbhakar	23,322	21,826	24,421	19,548	18,526	13,466	+1,496
34	Korea	90,886	79,189	62,107	35,113	36,240	29,846	+11,697
35	Surguja	501,939	377,679	428,703	351,011	324,552	270,311	+124,260
36	Udaipur	97,738	71,124	64,853	45,391	37,536	33,955	+26,614
37	Jashpur	193,698	154,156	174,458	132,114	113,636	90,240	+39,542

Population since 1881. **TABLE II**

Variation, Increase (+), Decrease (—). 1911 to 1921.	1901 to 1911.	1891 to 1901.	1881 to 1891.	Net variation in period 1881—1931. Increase (+), Decrease (—).	Males. 1931.	1921.	1911.	1901.	Serial Number.
9	10	11	12	13	14	15	16	17	
—53,650	**+2,430,718**	**—1,158,942**	**+1,430,877**	**+4,660,280**	**8,997,203**	**7,980,797**	**7,984,022**	**6,738,327**	
—3,398	**+1,944,830**	**—1,077,517**	**+1,105,594**	**+3,564,472**	**7,761,818**	**6,951,399**	**6,930,315**	**5,926,293**	
—21,552	**+1,641,684**	**—934,042**	**+880,776**	**+2,795,307**	**6,002,239**	**5,385,525**	**5,379,701**	**4,531,993**	
—125,240	*+339,696*	*—293,433*	*+174,714*	*+262,695*	*1,240,655*	*1,158,885*	*1,211,318*	*1,032,756*	
—13,030	+71,931	—120,358	+27,008	—18,240	280,385	272,298	276,233	237,972	1
—45,921	+47,721	—40,287	+12,656	—7,389	154,791	146,914	168,060	143,488	2
—207	+65,307	—67,561	+60,913	+86,578	391,649	376,959	373,173	335,552	3
—18,788	+86,853	—22,062	+39,066	+144,389	221,359	192,083	200,872	157,050	4
—47,294	+67,884	—43,165	+35,071	+57,357	192,471	170,631	192,980	158,694	5
—68,617	*+296,496*	*—98,062*	*+117,841*	*+489,203*	*1,137,806*	*1,012,760*	*1,043,317*	*886,093*	
—10,515	+10,159	—53,414	+1,638	—45,813	161,417	158,345	161,795	154,694	6
—11,662	+10,750	—47,296	+29,557	+22,246	248,226	226,632	230,632	222,893	7
+5,483	+63,898	+40,997	+32,255	+213,010	242,042	205,444	200,765	167,994	8
—26,649	+102,579	—38,774	+19,785	+99,456	201,114	179,591	194,163	141,113	9
—25,274	+109,110	+425	+34,606	+200,304	285,007	242,748	255,962	199,399	10
+37,235	*+450,413*	*—249,912*	*+211,978*	*+905,594*	*1,809,541*	*1,573,219*	*1,548,321*	*1,312,465*	
+2,921	+74,763	—15,758	+13,707	+128,203	261,394	235,074	232,351	194,258	11
—16,401	+57,987	—6,011	+60,432	+243,535	481,246	402,869	408,363	377,169	12
—16,914	+143,657	—91,608	+36,495	+170,695	381,204	328,964	337,540	263,562	13
+31,919	+98,016	—70,707	+52,374	+218,351	408,799	354,509	336,424	283,823	14
+35,710	+75,990	—65,828	+48,970	+144,810	276,898	251,803	233,643	193,653	15
+135,070	*+555,079*	*—292,635*	*+376,243*	*+1,137,815*	*1,814,237*	*1,640,661*	*1,576,745*	*1,300,679*	
+82,184	+228,151	—26,577	+128,227	+546,790	739,950	677,772	638,381	525,798	16
+85,542	+227,732	—128,115	+165,728	+519,370	683,920	601,761	558,477	446,405	17
—32,656	+99,196	—137,943	+82,288	+71,655	390,367	361,128	379,887	28,476	18
+18,154	**+303,146**	**—143,475**	**+224,818**	**+769,165**	**1,759,579**	**1,565,874**	**1,550,614**	**1,394,300**	
—45,145	+66,153	—40,328	+71,627	+166,044	485,593	423,802	445,739	411,663	19
+8,805	+33,976	—4,489	+24,051	+143,858	448,896	405,923	399,504	382,070	20
+29,945	+55,708	—64,511	+36,160	+120,243	388,966	355,604	339,459	310,300	21
+24,549	+147,309	—34,147	+92,980	+339,020	436,124	380,545	365,912	290,267	22
—50,252	**+485,888**	**—81,425**	**+325,283**	**+1,095,808**	**1,235,385**	**1,029,398**	**1,053,707**	**812,034**	
—2,218	+1,986	—5,514	+1,785	—1,248	7,900	6,573	7,530	6,492	23
+31,097	+126,809	—4,383	+114,636	+328,473	263,248	234,824	218,015	155,683	24
—2,236	+23,504	+21,154	+18,784	+72,379	67,132	61,513	63,087	51,660	25
—19,456	+40,997	—57,501	+19,527	+18,041	87,886	70,661	80,293	60,110	26
—31,463	+17,917	—43,630	+15,046	—8,738	75,647	58,970	74,742	65,699	27
—5,028	+4,782	—9,920	+3,309	—1,311	15,238	12,452	15,117	12,596	28
—15,871	+20,180	—34,339	+5,451	—13,542	35,098	29,454	37,488	27,962	29
+7,007	+12,246	—3,073	+2,555	+25,670	23,571	20,250	16,871	10,885	30
+22,774	+43,931	+6,404	+39,582	+148,626	136,723	119,454	107,850	86,543	31
+15,710	+22,171	—3,310	+11,936	+57,693	62,443	57,103	49,851	38,738	32
—2,595	+4,873	+1,022	+5,060	+9,856	11,987	11,308	12,462	10,003	33
+17,082	+26,994	—1,127	+6,394	+61,040	46,748	40,531	31,856	17,948	34
—51,024	+77,692	+26,459	+54,241	+231,628	254,923	192,547	217,749	177,961	35
+6,271	+19,462	+7,855	+3,581	+63,783	49,425	35,897	32,790	23,107	36
—20,302	+42,344	+18,478	+23,396	+103,458	97,416	77,861	88,006	66,647	37

TABLE II.—Variation in Population since 1881—*concld.*

Serial Number.	District or State.	Males—*concld.* 1891.	1881.	Females. 1931.	1921.	1911.	1901.	1891.	1881
	1	18	19	20	21	22	23	24	25
	Central Provinces and Berar.	**7,436,060**	**6,757,203**	**8,993,734**	**7,998,863**	**8,049,288**	**6,864,265**	**7,325,474**	**6,573,454**
	C. P. British Districts and Berar.	**6,573,493**	**6,056,252**	**7,745,905**	**6,961,361**	**6,985,843**	**6,045,035**	**6,475,352**	**5,886,999**
	C. P. British Districts	**5,081,667**	**4.675,760**	**6,063,646**	**5,451,919**	**5,479,295**	**4,685,319**	**5,069,687**	**4,594,818**
	Jubbulpore Division ..	*1,205.032*	*1,127,610*	*1,222,811*	*1,137,623*	*1,210,430*	*1,049,296*	*1,170,453*	*1,073,161*
1	Saugor ..	304.737	293,684	264,204	256.082	265,177	231.507	285,100	269,145
2	Damoh ..	167.329	162, 70	150.777	140,212	164,987	141,838	158,284	150,387
3	Jubbulpore ..	375,964	349,251	382,162	368,726	372,719	345,033	372,182	337,982
4	Mandla ..	171,822	153,343	224,407	194,363	204.362	161,331	168.621	148,034
5	Seoni ..	185,180	168,762	201,261	178,240	203,185	169,587	186,266	167,613
	Nerbudda Division ..	*951,747*	*901,909*	*1,116,760*	*1,000,261*	*1,038,321*	*899,049*	*931,457*	*863 454*
6	Narsinghpur ..	185,032	187,746	160,064	156,817	163,882	160,824	183,900	179,548
7	Hoshangabad ..	252,048	239,480	238,404	219,101	226,763	223,752	241,893	224,904
8	Nimar ..	148,215	133,076	224,889	191,110	190,306	159,179	137,961	120,845
9	Betul ..	164,287	155,407	205,138	184,146	196,223	146,694	162,294	151,389
10	Chhindwara .	202,165	186,200	288,265	249,087	261,147	208,600	205,409	186,768
	Nagpur Division ..	*1,457,116*	*1,352,267*	*1,792,567*	*1,573,009*	*1 560,672*	*1,346,115*	*1,451,376*	*1,344 247*
11	Wardha ..	203,735	195,975	254,872	228,622	228,424	191,754	198,035	192,088
12	Nagpur ..	382,414	351,345	458,803	389,652	400,559	373,766	374,552	345,169
13	Chanda ..	314,605	296,012	378,491	331,666	340,064	270,325	310,890	292,988
14	Bhandara ..	324,600	301,702	415,697	363,238	349,464	303,989	333,919	304,443
15	Balaghat ..	231.762	207,233	284,704	259,831	242,281	206,281	234.000	209,559
	Chhattisgarh Division ..	*1,467,772*	*1,293,474*	*1,931,508*	*1,741,026*	*1,066,272*	*1,390,559*	*1,516,401*	*1,313,956*
16	Raipur ..	548,119	488,832	787,623	714,996	672,203	556,635	560,891	491,951
17	Bilaspur ..	515,267	436,853	716,528	630 004	587,746	472,086	531,339	444,025
18	Drug ..	404,386	368,289	427,557	396,026	409,925	362,138	424,171	377,980
	Berar ..	**1,491,826**	**1,380,492**	**1,682,259**	**1,509,442**	**1,506,548**	**1,359,716**	**1,405,665**	**1,292,181**
19	Amraoti ..	438,566	401,712	456,011	404,065	427,273	395,196	408,621	373,848
20	Akola ..	390,570	379,976	427,466	388,924	386,538	369,996	365,985	352,528
21	Buldana ..	349,605	332,675	377,618	348,039	334,239	307,690	332,896	313,666
22	Yeotmal ..	313,085	266,129	421,164	368,414	358,498	286,834	298,163	252,139
	Central Provinces States.	**862,567**	**700,951**	**1,247,829**	**1,037,502**	**1,063,445**	**819,230**	**850.122**	**686,455**
23	Makrai ..	9,339	8,521	7,616	6,230	7,491	6,543	9,210	8,243
24	Bastar ..	159,656	103.046	261,473	229,583	215,295	150,818	151,228	93,202
25	Kanker ..	42,372	32,190	68,969	63,415	64,077	52.000	40,134	31,532
26	Nandgaon ..	90,558	81,717	94,494	77,245	87,069	66,255	93,308	82.622
27	Khairagarh ..	89.076	82,677	81,753	65,038	80,729	71,855	92,108	83,461
28	Chhuikhadan ..	17,672	16,267	16,430	13,670	16,033	13,772	18,616	16,712
29	Kawardha ..	46.063	42,706	37,722	32,329	40,166	29,512	45,750	43,656
30	Sakti ..	12,582	11,352	24,918	21,304	17,676	11,416	12,792	11,467
31	Raigarh ..	84,227	64,767	140,846	122,180	111,010	88,386	84,298	64,176
32	Sarangarh ..	41,034	35,221	66,524	60,678	52,220	41,162	42,176	36,053
33	Changbhakar ..	9,708	6,826	11,335	10,518	11,959	9,545	8,818	6,640
34	Korea ..	18,586	15,162	44,138	38,658	30,251	17,165	17,654	14,684
35	Surguja ..	165,294	137,389	247,016	185,132	210,954	173,050	159,258	132,922
36	Udaipur ..	19,121	17,111	48,313	35,227	32,063	22,284	18,415	16,844
37	Jashpur ..	57,279	45,999	96,282	76,295	86,452	65,467	56,357	44,241

TABLE III

Towns and Villages Classified by Population

In this table as in Table I, Cantonments have been treated as separate towns.

Serial number.	District or State.	Total number of inhabited towns and villages.	Population.	Under 500. Number.	Under 500. Population.	500—1,000. Number.	500—1,000. Population.	1,000—2,000. Number.	1,000—2,000. Population.
	1	2	3	4	5	6	7	8	9
	Central Provinces and Berar.	**48,844**	**17,990,937**	**39,591**	**7,961,869**	**6,898**	**4,684,544**	**1,828**	**2,428,141**
	C. P. British Districts and Berar.	**39,874**	**15,507,723**	**31,835**	**6,476,894**	**5,865**	**4,001,849**	**1,670**	**2,223,676**
	C. P. British Districts.	**33,897**	**12,065,885**	**27,809**	**5,550,661**	**4,576**	**3,086,373**	**1,182**	**1,557,637**
	Jubbulpore Division ..	*9,005*	*2,463,466*	*8,105*	*1,433,340*	*705*	*469,021*	*153*	*198,268*
1	Saugor ..	1,866	544,589	1,643	277,174	166	110,701	46	60,051
2	Damoh ..	1,149	305,568	1,010	161,641	104	68,768	30	40,564
3	Jubbulpore ..	2,386	773,811	2,106	382,391	216	146,538	48	60,337
4	Mandla ..	2,021	445,766	1,916	354,141	91	58,091	8	10,825
5	Seoni ..	1,583	393,732	1,430	257,993	128	84,923	21	26,491
	Nerbudda Division ..	*6,668*	*2,254,566*	*5,576*	*1,081,841*	*827*	*554,692*	*200*	*273,758*
6	Narsinghpur ..	995	321,481	829	152,908	114	75,267	41	51,626
7	Hoshangabad ..	1,343	486,630	1,099	213,582	185	126,780	42	58,763
8	Nimar ..	1,143	466,931	916	187,785	174	116,999	41	56,078
9	Betul —	1,254	406,252	1,043	209,355	165	111,188	38	52,191
10	Chhindwara ..	1,933	573,272	1,689	318,211	189	124,458	38	55,100
	Nagpur Division ..	*7,721*	*3,602,108*	*5,703*	*1,142,538*	*1,405*	*976,662*	*467*	*624,844*
11	Wardha ..	946	516,266	647	146,109	208	144,218	64	83,792
12	Nagpur ..	1,657	940,049	1,317	283,924	234	158,948	66	88,673
13	Chanda ..	2,391	759,695	1,989	312,856	286	196,825	84	119,872
14	Bhandara ..	1,502	824,496	943	215,384	361	259,539	165	216,516
15	Balaghat ..	1,225	561,602	807	184,265	316	217,132	88	115,991
	Chhattisgarh Division ..	*10,503*	*3,745,745*	*8,425*	*1,892,942*	*1,639*	*1,085,998*	*362*	*460,767*
16	Raipur ..	4,485	1,527,573	3,671	802,821	651	430,979	130	169,439
17	Bilaspur ..	3,442	1,400,248	2,606	587,179	609	417,066	188	246,213
18	Drug ..	2,576	817,924	2,148	502,942	379	237,953	44	54,115
	Berar ..	**5,977**	**3,441,838**	**4,026**	**926,233**	**1,289**	**915,476**	**488**	**666,039**
19	Amraoti ..	1,626	941,604	1,164	226,358	286	206,029	115	160,685
20	Akola ..	1,503	876,362	1,034	244,841	294	206,507	130	178,648
21	Buldana ..	1,215	766,584	752	183,524	295	209,950	125	166,448
22	Yeotmal ..	1,633	857,288	1,076	271,510	414	292,990	118	160,256
	Central Provinces States.	**8,970**	**2,483,214**	**7,756**	**1,484,975**	**1,033**	**682,695**	**158**	**204,465**
23	Makrai ..	69	15,516	62	9,090	6	4,595	1	1,831
24	Bastar ..	2,443	524,721	2,201	313,875	194	131,562	42	55,418
25	Kanker ..	550	136,101	503	100,427	45	29,245	1	1,124
26	Nandgaon ..	524	182,380	439	105,665	76	49,785	8	10,953
27	Khairagarh ..	494	157,400	422	97,170	65	39,841	4	5,043
28	Chhuikhadan ..	104	31,668	96	23,130	7	4,914	..	..
29	Kawardha ..	385	72,820	361	51,344	21	13,422	2	2,699
30	Sakti ..	125	48,489	95	22,008	24	16,116	4	4,914
31	Raigarh ..	797	277,569	653	157,299	127	83,623	14	18,977
32	Sarangarh ..	457	128,967	404	79,163	36	22,583	16	20,175
33	Changbhakar ..	128	23,322	121	19,070	7	4,252	..	..
34	Korea ..	317	90,886	272	52,903	35	24,203	10	13,780
35	Surguja ..	1,654	501,939	1,372	288,104	245	163,357	36	45,634
36	Udaipur ..	284	97,738	214	46,871	63	40,898	5	5,380
37	Jashpur ..	639	193,698	541	118,856	82	54,299	15	18,537

Classified by Population

TABLE III

2,000—5,000.		5,000—10,000.		10,000—20,000.		20,000—50,000.		50,000—100,000.		100,000 and over.		Encampment, Boats and Railway population unclassified.	Serial number.
Number.	Population.	Number.	Population.	Number.	Population.	Number.	Population.	Number.	Population.	Number.	Population.		
10	11	12	13	14	15	16	17	18	19	20	21	22	
403	**1,119,954**	**71**	**500,838**	**35**	**473,429**	**16**	**496,533**	..	..	**2**	**319,482**	**6,147**	
387	**1,074,097**	**67**	**475,354**	**32**	**434,512**	**16**	**496,533**	..	..	**2**	**319,482**	**5,326**	
263	**711,456**	**36**	**256,164**	**18**	**249,932**	**11**	**329,048**	..	..	**2**	**319,482**	**5,132**	
29	*83,226*	*6*	*43,632*	*2*	*26,930*	*4*	*102,574*	...	...	*1*	*104,317*	*2,158*	
5	16,092	4	29,871	1	10,849	1	39,822	..	..	..	..	29	1
4	13,189	..	..	..	..	1	20,728	..	..	..	..	678	2
12	32,024	1	5,764	..	..	2	42,024	..	..	1	104,317	416	3
5	13,885	1	7,997	..	..	..	..	..	..	..	..	827	4
3	8,036	..	..	1	16,081	..	..	..	..	..	..	208	5
51	*140,314*	*6*	*44,539*	*6*	*79,877*	*2*	*78,688*	..	...	...	...	*857*	
9	21,526	1	9,077	1	11,077	..	..	..	..	..	..	..	6
12	32,778	2	14,551	3	40,150	..	..	..	..	..	..	26	7
10	26,867	..	..	..	..	2	78,688	..	..	..	..	514	8
6	18,427	2	14,992	..	..	..	..	..	..	..	..	99	9
14	40,716	1	5,919	2	28,650	..	..	..	..	..	..	218	10
115	*322,573*	*19*	*129,401*	*8*	*118,958*	*3*	*71,526*	..	...	*1*	*215,165*	*441*	
20	56,759	4	26,818	2	35,864	1	22,601	..	..	..	..	105	11
23	88,693	8	55,032	2	28,813	1	20,787	..	..	1	215,165	14	12
26	69,200	5	32,524	..	..	1	28,138	..	..	..	..	280	13
29	78,761	..	..	4	54,281	..	..	..	..	..	..	15	14
12	29,160	2	15,027	..	..	..	..	..	..	..	..	27	15
68	*165,343*	*5*	*38,592*	*2*	*24,167*	*2*	*76,260*	...	...	...	...	*1,676*	
28	52,740	3	23,607	1	11,505	1	45,338	..	..	..	..	144	16
56	103,017	2	14,985	..	..	1	30,922	..	..	..	..	866	17
4	9,586	..	..	1	12,662	..	..	..	..	..	..	666	18
124	**362,641**	**31**	**219,190**	**14**	**184,580**	**5**	**167,485**	..	..	..	..	**194**	
39	117,316	16	110,251	4	45,541	2	75,424	..	..	..	..	..	19
33	89,138	6	37,093	5	72,503	1	47,632	..	..	..	..	..	20
34	101,870	4	27,391	4	53,939	1	23,462	..	..	..	..	..	21
18	54,317	5	44,455	1	12,597	1	20,967	..	..	..	..	194	22
16	**45,857**	**4**	**25,484**	**3**	**38,917**	..	..	..	..	..	..	**821**	
5	13,738	..	..	1	10,128	..	..	..	..	..	..	..	23
..	..	1	5,305	..	..	..	..	..	..	..	..	..	24
..	..	..	..	1	15,969	..	..	..	..	..	..	..	25
2	6,793	1	8,081	..	..	..	..	..	..	..	..	8	26
1	3,624	..	..	..	..	..	..	..	..	..	..	472	27
..	..	1	5,052	..	..	..	..	..	..	..	..	..	28
2	5,413	..	..	..	..	..	..	..	..	..	..	303	29
2	4,850	..	..	1	12,820	..	..	..	..	..	..	38	30
..	..	1	7,046	..	..	..	..	..	..	..	..	..	31
..	..	..	..	..	..	..	..	..	..	..	..	..	32
..	..	..	..	..	..	..	..	..	..	..	..	..	33
1	4,844	..	..	..	..	..	..	..	..	..	..	..	34
2	4,589	..	..	..	..	..	..	..	..	..	..	..	35
1	2,006	..	..	..	..	..	..	..	..	..	..	..	36
		..	..	..	..	..	..	..	..	..	..	..	37

Note.—A reference is invited to the note on page 16 regarding Saugor Cantonment and Mandla Municipality.

TABLE IV

Towns classified by population with variation since 1881

1. The population of Cantonments has been shown separately from that of the towns adjoining them.

2. Amraoti and Amraoti Camp have, as at previous censuses, been shown separately because each is a Municipality. If the two were treated as a single unit Amraoti Town would fall in class II. The Municipalities of Ellichpur and Ellichpur Camp have also been shown separately as before.

3. The figures of Railway settlements not lying within Municipal limits but clearly forming part of the place concerned have been included with those of the Municipalities of Jubbulpore, Bilaspur and Etawah. The population of the Gun Carriage Factory area has also been added to that of Jubbulpore. The number of those actually living within Municipal limits is :—

Jubbulpore	..	97,468
Bilaspur	..	25,735
Etawah	..	7,430

4. Travellers enumerated in encampments, trains, etc., and shown in column 22 of Table III have, in this Table and Table V, been included in the population of any town adjoining which the place of enumeration is situated.

5. As the Table is intended to show the purely urban population, the figures for towns have not been adjusted so as to allow for changes of area since the Census of 1921, and except for 1931 the class totals are not the totals of the figures given below them but represent the whole urban population recorded at each census. The population in former decades of places not previously classed as towns has been entered in brackets when known for purposes of comparison.

6. Ten places treated as towns at the last census have now been omitted as they have entirely ceased to possess urban characteristics. Eight new towns have been included in the Table, either because they have become Municipalities during the decade or on account of their growing commercial importance. Full details of all these places are given in the statement below showing the effect of these adjustments upon the size of the urban population.

Statement showing the net variation in population owing to reclassification of urban areas during the decade 1921-31.

District or State.	Places now treated as towns which were not so treated in 1921.		Places treated as towns in 1921 but now omitted.			Net variation in decade 1921-31.
	Name of place.	Population in 1931.	District or State.	Name of place.	Population in 1921.	
1	2	3	4	5	6	7
Hoshangabad ..	Piparia ..	3,968	Chhindwara	Mohgaon ..	4,455	
Amraoti ..	Pathrot ..	5,218	Bilaspur ..	Ratanpur ..	4,751	
	Daryapur Banosa ..	8,556				
Yeotmal ..	Pandharkaoda ..	7,577	Amraoti ..	Talegaon-Dashasahasra ..	5,971	
	Ghatanji ..	3,989		Shendurjana ..	5,950	
				Ner-Pinglai ..	5,376	
Raigarh ..	Kharsia ..	2,805		Kholapur ..	4,306	
				Pusla ..	4,947	
Sakti ..	Sakti ..	3,240		Mangrul Dastgir ..	5,511	
				Balgaon Jagir ..	4,926	
Bastar ..	Jagdalpur ..	10,128		Chandur Railway ..	5,391	
	Total ..	45,481		Total ..	51,584	
						—6,103

TABLE IV Towns classified by population

Serial No.	Town.	District or State.	Town, Municipality or Cantonment.	Population. 1931.	1921	1911.	1901.	1891.	1881.
	1	2	3	4	5	6	7	8	9
	Central Provinces and Berar ..		**122 Towns ..**	**1,754,611**	**1,441,430**	**1,213,049**	**1,316,533**	**1,138,959**	**1,006,763**
	C. P. British Districts and Berar		**112 Towns ..**	**1,679,546**	**1,393,267**	**1,176,225**	**1.240,269**	**1,100,303**	**981,758**
	Class I—100,000 and over ..		**2 Towns ..**	**319,482**	**253,986**	**202,066**	**127,734**	**117,014**	..
1	Nagpur ..	Nagpur ..	Municipality ..	215,165	145,193	101,415	127,734	117,014	98,299
2	Jubbulpore ..	Jubbulpore ..	Do. ..	104,317	86,796	79,009	77,376	73,356	(a)76,023
	Class II—50,000 to 100,000 ..		**None ..**	..	..	..	**90,316**	**84,481**	**224,991**
	Class III—20,000 to 50,000 ..		**16 Towns ..**	**497,037**	**310,337**	**185,720**	**236,260**	**220,897**	**149,659**
3	Akola ..	Akola ..	Municipality ..	47,632	37,864	25,826	29,289	21,470	16,614
4	Amraoti ..	Amraoti ..	Do. ..	46,832	40,694	34,270	34,216	28,946	23,550
5	Raipur ..	Raipur ..	Do. ..	45,390	38,341	35,335	32,114	23,759	24,948
6	Burhanpur ..	Nimar ..	Do. ..	44,066	35,916	22,777	33,341	32,252	30,017
7	Saugor ..	Saugor ..	Do. ..	39,822	28,571	34,876	31,412	32,736	(b)44,416
8	Khandwa ..	Nimar ..	Do. ..	34,622	26,602	21,604	19,401	15,589	15,142
9	Bilaspur ..	Bilaspur ..	Municipality and Railway Settlement.	31,374	24,295	19,850	18,937	11,122	7,775
10	Ellichpur ..	Amraoti ..	Municipality ..	28,592	23,899	13,909	26,082	26,637	26,728
11	Chanda ..	Chanda ..	Do. ..	28.138	22,981	19,866	17,803	16,175	16,137
12	Khamgaon ..	Buldana ..	Do. ..	23,462	19,962	10,123	18,341	15,598	12,390
13	Hinganghat ..	Wardha ..	Do. ..	22,601	17,200	14,943	12,662	10,964	9,000
14	Murwara ..	Jubbulpore ..	Do. ..	21,959	19,682	15,812	14,137	9,460	8,612
15	Yeotmal ..	Yeotmal ..	Do. ..	20,967	17,238	13,525	10,545	6,464	4,445
16	Kamptee ..	Nagpur ..	Do. ..	20,787	17,531	14,869	(c)38,888	(d)43,159	(e)50,987
17	Damoh ..	Damoh ..	Do. ..	20,728	15,296	17,042	13,355	11,753	8,665
18	Jubbulpore ..	Jubbulpore ..	Cantonment.	20,065	21,997	21,642	13,157	11,326	..
	Class IV—10,000 to 20,000 ..		**32 Towns ..**	**435,022**	**356,181**	**301,002**	**352,190**	**268,693**	**229,875**
19	Wardha ..	Wardha ..	Municipality ..	19,571	16,044	10,541	9,872	8,322	5,816
20	Akot ..	Akola ..	Do. ..	18,693	16.887	12,583	18,252	15,995	16,137
21	Umrer ..	Nagpur ..	Do. ..	17,913	15,061	17,630	15,943	15,180	14,247
22	Malkapur ..	Buldana ..	Do. ..	17,565	14,947	12,391	13,112	9,222	8,152
23	Chhindwara ..	Chhindwara ..	Do. ..	17,080	13.383	12,872	9,736	8,973	8,220
24	Bhandara ..	Bhandara ..	Do. ..	16,738	13,399	7,414	14,023	13,348	11,150
25	Karanja ..	Akola ..	Do. ..	16,615	13,645	12,647	16,535	14,436	10,923
26	Arvi ..	Wardha ..	Do. ..	16,293	13,248	11,902	10,676	8,615	8,072
27	Seoni ..	Seoni ..	Do. ..	16,081	12,772	13,839	11,864	11,976	10,203
28	Harda ..	Hoshangabad ..	Do. ..	16,031	11,077	8,341	16,300	13,556	11,203
29	Gondia ..	Bhandara ..	Do. ..	14,957	10,617	5,847	4,457	2,770	..
30	Shegaon ..	Buldana ..	Do. ..	14,699	14,531	11,962	15,057	11,422	11,079
31	Basim ..	Akola ..	Do. ..	14,409	10,970	9,068	13,823	12,389	11,576
32	Badnera ..	Amraoti ..	Town	13,666	12,372	11,098	10,859	9,916	6,460
33	Drug ..	Drug ..	Municipality ..	13,172	11,274	7,048	4,002	4,151	3,797
34	Wun ..	Yeotmal ..	Do. ..	12,597	6,841	6,282	6,109	4,856	4,206
35	Pauni ..	Bhandara ..	Do. ..	12,525	10,481	10,222	9,366	9,869	9,773
36	Hoshangabad ..	Hoshangabad ..	Do. ..	12,332	12,048	5,503	14,940	13,495	15,863
37	Itarsi ..	Do. ..	Do. ..	11,787	7,007	4,430	5,769	3,090	2,138
38	Anjangaon ..	Amraoti ..	Do. ..	11,597	9,338	8,628	8,783	10,593	9,842
39	Pandhurna ..	Chhindwara ..	Do. ..	11,570	8,611	7,058	8,904	8,172	7,469
40	Murtizapur ..	Akola ..	Do. ..	11,541	10,552	5,101	6,156	4,438	4,887

(a) Includes the figures of Jubbulpore Cantonment now shown separately below in Class No. III.
(b) Includes the figures of Saugor Cantonment now shown separately below in Class No. V.
(c), (d), (e) Include the figures of Kamptee Cantonment now shown separately below in Class No. V.

Note.—See note 2 on page 1 regarding Anjangaon Municipality.

with variation since 1881. **TABLE IV**

Variation—Increase (+) Decrease (−).					Variation in period 1881 to 1931. Increase (+) Decrease (−).	Males.			Females.			Serial No.
1921 to 1931.	1911 to 1921.	1901 to 1911.	1891 to 1901.	1881 to 1891.		1931.	1921.	1911.	1931.	1921.	1911.	
10	11	12	13	14	15	16	17	18	19	20	21	
+313,181	**+228,381**	**−103,484**	**+177,574**	**+132,196**	**+747,848**	**928,157**	**754,989**	**628,375**	**826,454**	**686,441**	**584,674**	
+286,279	**+217,042**	**−64,044**	**+139,966**	**+118,545**	**+697,788**	**890,796**	**731,877**	**610,417**	**788,750**	**661,390**	**565,808**	
+65,496	**+51,920**	**+74,332**	**+10,720**	..	..	**173,016**	**139,660**	**109,731**	**146,466**	**114,326**	**93,335**	
+69,972	+43,778	−26,319	+10,720	+18,715	+116,866	116,403	77,906	53,696	96,762	67,287	47,719	1
+17,521	+7,787	+1,633	+4,020	−2,667	+28,294	56,613	46,883	41,783	47,704	39,913	37,226	2
..	..	..	**+5,835**	**−140,510**	..	..	..	..	..	..	..	
+186,700	**+124,617**	**−50,540**	**+15,363**	**+71,238**	**+347,378**	**266,736**	**164,118**	**7,656**	**230,301**	**146,219**	**88,064**	
+9,768	+12,038	−3,463	+7,819	+4,856	+31,018	26,401	20,718	14,006	21,231	17,146	11,820	3
+6,138	+6,424	+54	+5,270	+5,396	+23,282	25,746	21,802	18,147	21,086	18,892	16,123	4
+7,049	+3,006	+3,221	+8,355	−1,189	+20,442	24,060	19,910	18,038	21,330	18,431	17,297	5
+8,150	+13,139	−10,564	+1,089	+2,235	+14,049	23,056	18,886	11,624	21,010	17,030	11,153	6
+11,251	−6,305	+3,464	−1,324	−11,680	−4,594	20,723	14,965	17,820	19,099	13,606	17,056	7
+7,820	+5,198	+2,203	+3,812	+447	+19,480	19,060	14,423	11,511	15,562	12,379	10,093	8
+7,079	+4,445	+913	+7,815	+3,347	+23,599	16,366	12,454	9,983	15,008	11,841	9,867	9
+4,693	+9,990	−12,173	−555	−91	+1,864	14,822	12,183	7,027	13,770	11,716	6,882	10
+5,157	+3,115	+2,063	+1,628	+38	+12,001	14,394	11,539	10,077	13,744	11,442	9,789	11
+3,500	+9,839	−8,218	+2,743	+3,208	+11,072	13,113	10,664	5,545	10,349	9,298	4,578	12
+5,401	+2,257	+2,281	+1,698	+1,964	+13,601	11,812	8,887	7,690	10,789	8,313	7,253	13
+2,277	+3,870	+1,675	+4,677	+848	+13,347	11,572	0,359	8,173	10,387	9,323	7,639	14
+3,729	+3,713	+2,980	+4,081	+2,019	+16,522	11,434	9,298	7,249	9,533	7,940	6,276	15
+3,256	+2,662	−24,019	−4,271	−7,828	−30,200	10,806	8,601	7,617	9,981	8,930	7,252	16
+5,432	−1,746	+3,687	+1,602	+3,088	+12,063	10,726	7,993	8,732	10,002	7,303	8,310	17
−1,932	+355	+8,485	+1,831	..	..	12,645	14,871	14,252	7,420	7,126	7,390	18
+78,841	**+55,179**	**−51,188**	**+83,497**	**+38,818**	**+205,147**	**228,369**	**185,632**	**154,864**	**206,653**	**170,549**	**146,138**	
+3,527	+5,503	+669	+1,550	+2,506	+13,755	10,790	8,845	5,719	8,781	7,199	4,822	19
+1,806	+4,304	−5,669	+2,257	−142	+2,556	9,637	8,630	6,523	9,056	8,257	6,060	20
+2,852	−2,569	+1,687	+763	+933	+3,666	8,857	7,353	8,600	9,056	7,708	9,030	21
+2,618	+2,556	−721	+3,890	+1,070	+9,413	9,350	7,851	6,463	8,215	7,096	5,928	22
+3,697	+511	+3,136	+763	+753	+8,860	8,729	6,833	6,503	8,351	6,550	6,369	23
+3,339	+5,985	−6,609	+675	+2,198	+5,588	8,562	6,867	3,787	8,176	6,532	3,627	24
+2,970	+998	−3,888	+2,099	+3,513	+5,692	8,776	7,180	6,556	7,839	6,465	6,091	25
+3,045	+1,346	+1,226	+2,061	+543	+8,221	8,823	6,918	6,134	7,470	6,330	5,768	26
+3,309	−1,067	+1,975	−112	+1,773	+5,878	8,205	6,521	6,740	7,876	6,251	7,099	27
+4,954	+2,736	−7,959	+2,744	+2,353	+4,828	8,601	5,754	4,303	7,430	5,323	4,038	28
+4,340	+4,770	+1,390	+1,687	..	..	9,201	5,550	3,115	6,756	5,067	2,732	29
+168	+2,569	−3,095	+3,635	+343	+3,620	7,583	7,519	6,290	7,116	7,012	5,672	30
+3,439	+1,902	−4,755	+1,434	+813	+2,833	7,594	5,716	4,562	6,815	5,254	4,506	31
+1,294	+1,274	+239	+943	+3,456	+7,206	7,197	6,505	5,898	6,469	5,867	5,200	32
+1,898	+4,226	+3,046	−149	+354	+9,375	6,875	5,731	3,589	6,297	5,543	3,459	33
+5,756	+559	+173	+1,253	+650	+8,391	7,003	3,451	3,273	5,594	3,390	3,009	34
+2,044	+259	+856	−503	+96	+2,752	6,339	5,253	5,037	6,186	5,228	5,185	35
+284	+6,545	−9,437	+1,445	−2,368	−3,531	6,564	6,471	2,993	5,768	5,577	2,510	36
+4,780	+2,577	−1,339	+2,679	+952	+9,649	6,496	3,891	2,506	5,291	3,116	1,924	37
+2,259	+710	−155	−1,810	+751	+1,755	6,065	4,931	4,394	5,532	4,407	4,234	38
+2,959	+1,553	−1,846	+732	+703	+4,101	5,842	4,329	3,507	5,728	4,282	3,551	39
+989	+5,451	−1,055	+1,718	−449	+6,654	6,420	6,047	2,988	5,121	4,505	2,113	40

TABLE IV

Towns classified by population

Serial No.	Town.	District or State.	Town, Municipality, or Cantonment.	Population. 1931.	1921.	1911.	1901.	1891.	1881.
	1	2	3	4	5	6	7	8	9
41	Dhamtari ..	Raipur ..	Municipality.	11,505	12,721	10,460	9,151	6,726	6,647
42	Balapur ..	Akola ..	Town ..	11,245	10,567	5,953	10,486	10,250	11,244
43	Nandura ..	Buldana ..	Municipality..	11,212	6,667	6,794	6,669	6,471	6,743
44	Narsinghpur ..	Narsinghpur ..	Do. ..	11,077	9,839	10,630	11,233	10,220	10,222
45	Katol ..	Nagpur ..	Do. ..	10,900	9,795	6,269	7,313	4,560	4,137
46	Bina Etawah ..	Saugor ..	Municipality and Railway Settlement.	10,849	9,226	8,968	6,418	3,982	2,177
47	Jalgaon ..	Buldana ..	Municipality..	10,463	10,207	7,552	8,487	9,307	10,392
48	Amraoti Camp ..	Amraoti ..	Do. ..	10,268	4,775	6,340	5,295	4,709	..
49	Tumsar ..	Bhandara ..	Do. ..	10,061	6,692	4,378	8,116	7,566	7,388
50	Warud ..	Amraoti ..	Town ..	10,010	7,465	7,089	7,179	7,291	6,607
	Class V—5,000 to 10,000 ..		**54 Towns** ..	**395,971**	**394,229**	**411,979**	**403,004**	**404,509**	**377,233**
51	Pusad ..	Yeotmal ..	Municipality..	9,862	7,510	6,862	6,742	5,144	5,047
52	Warora ..	Chanda ..	Do. ..	9,811	8,809	6,174	10,626	10,018	8,022
53	Dattapur-Dhamangaon.	Amraoti ..	Town ..	9,807	8,638	4,776	5,187	3,225	1,090
54	Ellichpur Camp or Paratwada.	Do. ..	Municipality..	9,799	7,743	4,001	10,410	9,603	9,445
55	Darwha ..	Yeotmal ..	Town ..	9,661	7,460	3,910	5,168	4,972	4,052
56	Betul ..	Betul ..	Municipality..	9,614	6,954	7,454	5,566	5,014	2,881
57	Balaghat ..	Balaghat ..	Do. ..	9,605	7,300	7,400	6,223	5,138	4,136
58	Morsi ..	Amraoti ..	Town ..	9,523	7,732	6,336	8,313	7,104	5,592
59	Digras ..	Yeotmal ..	Municipality..	9,398	7,857	6,479	6,034	5,081	4,235
60	Gadarwara ..	Narsinghpur ..	Do. ..	9,077	8,539	4,715	8,198	8,815	8,100
61	Saugor ..	Saugor ..	Cantonment ..	9,040	10,748	11,032	10,918	11,938	..
62	Ramtek ..	Nagpur ..	Municipality..	8,939	8,580	9,806	8,732	7,584	7,814
63	Daryapur-Banosa	Amraoti ..	Town ..	8,556	(6,420)	(5,668)	(5,304)	(5,261)	..
64	Champa ..	Bilaspur ..	Notified Area	8,362	6,344	5,627	..	..	..
65	Garhakota ..	Saugor ..	Town ..	8,242	5,864	8,180	8,508	9,525	11,414
66	Khapa ..	Nagpur ..	Municipality..	8,191	7,510	8,233	7,615	9,383	8,465
67	Sohagpur ..	Hoshangabad ..	Do. ..	8,141		7,239	7,420	7,306	7,027
68	Narkhed ..	Nagpur ..	Town ..	8,139	7,130	6,203	7,726	8,256	7,061
69	Mandla ..	Mandla ..	Municipality..	7,997	8,784	9,379	5,428	5,057	4,732
70	Bhatapara ..	Raipur ..	Notified Area	7,974	4,714	2,456	..	..	..
71	Saoner ..	Nagpur ..	Municipality..	7,969	7,078	6,636	5,821	5,555	5,023
72	Umerkhed ..	Yeotmal ..	Notified Area	7,957	6,442	5,822	4,570	6,414	5,959
73	Pulgaon ..	Wardha ..	Municipality..	7,845	7,443	5,466	4,710	1,979	..
74	Pandharkaoda ..	Yeotmal ..	Do. ..	7,577	(6,044)	(2,621)	(1,992)	(1,613)	..
75	Buldana ..	Buldana ..	Do. ..	7,504	5,691	3,820	4,137	3,243	2,979
76	Chikhli ..	Do. ..	Do. ..	7,041	6,093	4,731	5,889	4,672	4,396
77	Mehkar ..	Do. ..	Do. ..	7,009	5,831	4,423	5,330	5,102	4,374
78	Khurai ..	Saugor ..	Do. ..	6,951	6,078	6,868	6,012	6,272	5,370
79	Hiwarkhed ..	Akola ..	Town ..	6,914	6,297	6,404	6,143	6,520	7,300
80	Sindi ..	Wardha ..	Notified Area	6,883	5,444	5,981	4,533	5,463	4,644
81	Sirasgaon Kasba	Amraoti ..	Town ..	6,880	5,884	6,039	6,537	5,776	5,408
82	Karasgaon ..	Do ..	Do. ..	6,853	6,569	5,581	7,456	6,846	7,330
83	Patur ..	Akola ..	Do ..	6,838	5,734	5,500	5,990	6,156	7,219
84	Mungeli ..	Bilaspur ..	Do. ..	6,665	6,536	5,881	5,907	4,755	4,757
85	Armori ..	Chanda ..	Do. ..	6,522	5,429	5,445	..	..	..
86	Arang ..	Raipur ..	Do. ..	6,496	6,052	5,820	6,499	5,250	4,608
87	Seoni-Malwa ..	Hoshangabad ..	Municipality..	6,410	6,004	6,568	7,531	6,779	6,998
88	Mangrul Pir ..	Akola ..	Town ..	6,386	5,492	6,072	5,793	5,241	4,900
89	Deoli ..	Wardha ..	Municipality..	6,209	5,991	5,575	5,008	5,450	5,126
90	Wadegaon ..	Akola ..	Town ..	5,965	5,520	4,890	5,825	5,872	6,096

Note 1.—The inclusion of the population of the strictly military area of Saugor in the figures of the Cantonment would raise it from class V to class IV. See fly sheet of Table V.

with variation since 1881—*contd.*

TABLE IV

Variation—Increase (+) Decrease (−).					Variation in period 1881 to 1931. Increase (+). Decrease (−).	Males.			Females.			Serial No.
1921 to 1931.	1911 to 1921.	1901 to 1911.	1891 to 1901.	1881 to 1891.		1931.	1921.	1911.	1931.	1921.	1911.	
10	11	12	13	14	15	16	17	18	19	20	21	
−1,216	+2,261	+1,309	+2,425	+79	+4,858	5,786	6,341	5,170	5,719	6,380	5,290	41
+678	+4,614	−4,533	+236	—994	+1	5,753	5,365	2,939	5,492	5,202	3,014	42
+4,545	−127	+125	+198	−272	+4,469	5,675	3,353	3,464	5,537	3,314	3,330	43
+1,238	−791	−603	+1,013	−2	+855	5,794	5,193	5,407	5,283	4,646	5,223	44
+1,105	+3,526	−1,044	+2,753	+423	+6,763	5,675	5,022	3,252	5,225	4,773	3,017	45
+1,623	+258	+2,550	+2,436	+1,805	+8,672	5,952	5,140	4,897	4,897	4,086	4,071	46
+256	+1,655	−935	−820	−1,085	+71	5,248	5,181	3,851	5,215	5,026	3,701	47
+5,493	−1,565	+1,045	+586	..	..	5,509	2,541	3,334	4,759	2,234	3,006	48
+3,369	+2,314	−3,738	+550	+178	+2,673	5,117	3,348	2,123	4,944	3,344	2,255	49
+2,545	+376	−90	−112	+684	+3,403	5,351	3,850	3,634	4,659	3,615	3,455	50
+1,742	−17,750	+8,975	−1,505	+27,276	+18,738	205,614	202,640	208,932	190,357	191,589	203,047	
+2,352	+648	+120	+1,598	+97	+4,815	5,180	3,840	3,448	4,682	3,670	3,414	51
+1,002	+2,635	−4,452	+608	+1,996	+1,789	5,031	4,525	3,196	4,780	4,284	2,978	52
+1,169	+3,862	−411	+1,962	+2,135	+8,717	5,274	4,636	2,631	4,533	4,002	2,145	53
+2,056	+3,742	−6,409	+807	+158	+354	5,256	3,911	2,136	4,543	3,832	1,865	54
+2,201	+3,550	—1,258	+196	+920	+5,609	5,136	3,889	2,007	4,525	3,571	1,903	55
+2,660	−500	+1,888	+552	+2,133	+6,733	5,207	3,596	3,839	4,407	3,358	3,615	56
+2,305	−100	+1,177	+1,085	+1,002	+5,469	5,048	3,788	3,665	4,557	3,512	3,735	57
+1,791	+1,396	−1,977	+1,209	+1,512	+3,931	4,915	3,895	3,229	4,608	3,837	3,107	58
+1,541	+1,378	+445	+953	+846	+5,163	4,954	4,235	3,355	4,444	3,622	3,124	59
+538	+3,824	−3,483	−617	+715	+977	4,709	4,548	2,350	4,368	3,991	2,365	60
−1,708	−284	+114	−1,020	..	..	4,583	6,596	6,510	4,457	4,152	4,522	61
+359	−1,226	+1,074	+1,148	−230	+1,125	4,424	4,310	4,840	4,515	4,270	4,966	62
+2,136	+752	+364	+43	..	..	4,775	3,375	3,030	3,781	3,045	2,638	63
+2,018	+717	..	..	..	..	4,191	3,175	2,762	4,171	3,169	2,865	64
+2,378	−2,316	−328	−1,017	−1,889	−3,172	4,681	2,913	4,590	3,561	2,951	3,590	65
+681	−723	+618	−1,768	+918	−274	4,129	3,789	4,140	4,062	3,721	4,093	66
+1,088	−186	−181	+114	+279	+1,114	4,059	3,509	3,513	4,082	3,544	3,726	67
+1,009	+927	−1,523	−530	+1,195	+1,078	4,122	3,630	3,065	4,017	3,500	3,138	68
−787	−595	+3,951	+371	+325	+3,265	4,115	4,322	4,640	3,882	4,462	4,739	69
+3,260	+2,258	..	..	..	..	4,271	2,364	1,302	3,703	2,350	1,154	70
+891	+442	+815	+266	+532	+2,946	4,162	3,795	3,425	3,807	3,283	3,211	71
+1,515	+620	+1,252	−1,844	+455	+1,998	4,092	3,237	2,908	3,865	3,205	2,914	72
+402	+1,977	+756	+2,731	..	..	4,281	4,056	2,870	3,564	3,387	2,596	73
+1,533	+3,423	+629	+379	..	..	4,175	3,261	1,375	3,402	2,783	1,246	74
+1,813	+1,871	−317	+894	+264	+4,525	4,208	2,992	2,037	3,296	2,699	1,783	75
+948	+1,362	−1,158	+1,217	+276	+2,645	3,663	3,164	2,406	3,378	2,929	2,325	76
+1,178	+1,408	−907	+228	+728	+2,635	3,694	2,989	2,279	3,315	2,842	2,144	77
+873	−790	+856	−260	+902	+1,581	3,478	3,102	3,437	3,473	2,976	3,431	78
+617	−107	+261	−377	−780	−386	3,520	3,166	3,209	3,394	3,131	3,195	79
+1,439	−537	+1,448	−930	+819	−2,239	3,529	2,734	2,950	3,354	2,710	3,031	80
+996	−155	−498	+761	+368	+1,472	3,486	3,030	3,048	3,394	2,854	2,991	81
+284	+988	−1,875	+610	−484	−477	3,570	3,381	2,808	3,283	3,188	2,773	82
+1,104	+234	−490	−166	−1,063	−381	3,425	2,955	2,818	3,413	2,779	2,682	83
+129	+655	−26	+1,152	−2	+1,908	3,281	3,273	2,839	3,384	3,263	3,042	84
+1,093	−16	..	..	..	..	3,341	2,735	2,705	3,181	2,694	2,740	85
+444	+232	−679	+1,249	+642	+1,888	3,097	3,008	2,831	3,399	3,044	2,989	86
+406	−564	−963	+752	−219	−588	3,276	3,008	3,396	3,134	2,996	3,172	87
+894	−580	+279	+552	+341	+1,486	3,237	2,779	3,074	3,149	2,713	2,998	88
+218	+416	+567	−442	+324	+1,083	3,112	3,222	2,808	3,097	2,769	2,767	89
+445	+630	−935	−47	−224	−131	3,015	2,827	2,532	2,950	2,693	2,358	90

Note 2.—See note 1 on page 3. Mandla Municipality should strictly be in class IV.

TABLE IV — **Towns classified by population**

Serial No.	Town.	District or State.	Town, Municipality or Cantonment.	Population. 1931.	1921.	1911.	1901.	1891.	1881.
	1	2	3	4	5	6	7	8	9
91	Sausar	Chhindwara	Municipality	5,919	5,318	5,442	4,785	4,707	4,311
92	Ashti	Wardha	Town	5,881	5,706	6,257	5,237	5,898	5,245
93	Deolgaon Raja	Buldana	Notified Area	5,837	5,176	6,026	6,293	7,382	7,025
94	Chandur Bazar	Amraoti	Town	5,803	4,701	3,850	5,208	4,974	4,816
95	Sihora	Jubbulpore	Municipality	5,764	6,387	5.432	5,595	5,798	5,736
96	Deori	Saugor	Do.	5,638	5,369	5,739	4,980	6,306	7,414
97	Kamptee	Nagpur	Cantonment	5,554	2,695	2,286	..	..	..
98	Barsi Takli	Akola	Town	5,455	5,405	5,696	6,288	5,046	5,377
99	Betul Bazar	Betul	Notified Area	5,378	5,773	5,473	4,739	5,260	4,693
100	Nawargaon	Chanda	Town	5,330	3,919	5,087	4,100	5,086	4,304
101	Pathrot	Amraoti	Do.	5,218	(5,267)	(4,773)	(4,510)	(4,857)	..
102	Brahmapuri	Chanda	Do.	5,216	4,706	5,359	4,328	4,885	4,818
103	Mowar	Nagpur	Municipality	5,206	4,795	4,719	4,799	4,581	4,054
104	Kelod	Nagpur	Town	5,160	4,887	5,785	5,141	5,200	4,481
	Class VI.—Under 5,000		**8 Towns**	**32,034**	**78,534**	**75,458**	**30,765**	**4,709**	..
105	Chimur	Chanda	Town	4,848	4,519	5,218	4,085	5,096	4,846
106	Mohpa	Nagpur	Do.	4,757	4,878	5,477	5,336	5,638	5,515
107	Pachmarhi	Hoshangabad	Cantonment	4,699	4,114	3,287	..	..	(*f*) 2,054
108	Kalmeshwar	Nagpur	Municipality	4,665	4,851	5,575	5,340	5,921	5,318
109	Ghatanji	Yeotmal	Town	3,989	(1,887)	(1,800)	(1,119)	(801)	..
110	Piparia	Hoshangabad	Notified Area	3,968	(1,726)	(2,406)	(1,834)	(1,414)	..
111	Chhota Chhindwara.	Narsinghpur	Municipality	3,671	3,836	3,404	4,216	3,814	3,519
112	Pachmarhi	Hoshangabad	Do.	1,437	454	535	(*g*) 3,020	(*h*) 1,823	..
	Central Provinces States		**10 Towns**	**75,065**	**48,163**	**36,824**	**76,264**	**38,656**	**25,005**
	Class IV.—10,000 to 20,000		**3 Towns**	**38,925**	**12,631**	**11,979**	**11,094**	..	..
113	Rajnandgaon	Nandgaon	Municipality	15,977	12,631	11,979	11,094	8,850	5,849
114	Raigarh	Raigarh	Do.	12,820	8,667	8,041	6,764	4,552	4,860
115	Jagdalpur	Bastar	Nominated Town Committee.	10,128	(7,313)	(6,068)	(4,762)	(5,044)	(4,294)
	Class V.—5,000 to 10,000		**4 Towns**	**25,936**	**22,178**	**24,845**	**32,436**	**38,656**	**25,005**
116	Dongargarh	Khairagarh	Municipality	8,533	7,120	6,249	5,856	5,675	5,543
117	Sarangarh	Sarangarh	Do.	7,046	6,391	5,375	5,227	4,393	4,220
118	Kanker	Kanker	Do.	5,305	4,536	..	..	..	..
119	Kawardha	Kawardha	Town	5,052	4,773	5,180	4,372	5,349	5,685
	Class VI.—Under 5,000		**3 Towns**	**10,204**	**13,354**	..	**32,734**	..	..
120	Khairagarh	Khairagarh	Town	4,159	4,045	..	..	..	..
121	Sakti	Sakti	Municipality	3,240	(2,935)	(2,513)	(1,791)	(1,228)	..
122	Kharsia	Raigarh	Do.	2,805	(2,318)	(1,872)	(1,260)	..	..

(*f*) Includes the figures of Civil Lines for which separate figures could not be obtained.
(*g*), (*h*) Include the figures of Pachmarhi Cantonment now shown separately above in the same class.

with variation since 1881—*concld.* **TABLE IV**

Variation—Increase (+) Decrease (—).					Variation in period 1881 to 1931. Increase (+). Decrease (—).	Males.			Females.			Serial No.
1921 to 1931.	1911 to 1921.	1901 to 1911.	1891 to 1901.	1881 to 1891.		1931.	1921.	1911.	1931.	1921.	1911.	
10	11	12	13	14	15	16	17	18	19	20	21	
+601	−124	+657	+78	+396	+1,608	3,009	2,683	2,729	2,910	2,635	2,713	91
+175	−551	+1,020	−661	+653	+636	2,993	2,914	3,144	2,888	2,792	3,113	92
+661	−850	−267	−1,089	+357	−1,188	2,936	2,563	3,012	2,901	2,613	3,014	93
+1,102	+851	−1,358	+234	+158	+987	3,008	2,414	1,998	2,795	2,287	1,852	94
−623	+955	−163	−203	+62	+28	2,953	3,119	2,620	2,811	3,268	2,812	95
+269	−370	+759	−1,326	−1,108	−1,776	2,778	2,741	2,882	2,860	2,628	2,857	96
+2,859	+409	..	..	..	..	3,704	2,041	1,731	1,850	654	555	97
+50	−291	−592	+1,242	−331	+78	2,788	2,765	2,889	2,667	2,640	2,807	98
−395	+300	+734	−521	+567	+685	2,576	2,756	2,622	2,802	3,017	2,851	99
+1,411	−1,168	+987	−986	+782	+1,026	2,662	1,955	2,435	2,668	1,964	2,652	100
−49	+494	+263	−347	..	..	2,651	2,716	2,379	2,567	2,551	2,394	101
+510	−653	+1,031	−557	+67	+398	2,612	2,359	2,585	2,604	2,347	2,774	102
+411	+76	−80	+218	+527	+1,152	2,594	2,368	2,307	2,612	2,427	2,412	103
+273	−898	+644	−59	+719	+679	2,648	2,440	2,945	2,512	2,447	2,840	104
−46,500	**+3,076**	**+44,693**	**+26,056**	..	..	**17,061**	**39,827**	**39,234**	**14,973**	**38,707**	**36,224**	
+329	−699	+1,133	−1,011	+250	+2	2,373	2,256	2,520	2,475	2,263	2,698	105
−121	−599	+141	−302	+123	−758	2,337	2,460	2,702	2,420	2,418	2,775	106
+585	+827	..	..	..	+2,645	2,564	2,339	1,842	2,135	1,775	1,445	107
−186	−724	+235	−581	+603	−653	2,389	2,474	2,868	2,276	2,377	2,707	108
+2,102	+87	+681	+318	..	..	2,309	1,067	980	1,680	820	820	109
+2,242	−680	+572	+420	..	..	2,171	1,343	1,166	1,797	383	1,240	110
−165	+432	−812	+402	+295	+152	1,847	1,923	1,687	1,824	1,913	1,717	111
+983	−81	−2,485	+1,197	..	..	1,071	267	320	366	187	215	112
+26,902	**+11,339**	**−39,440**	**+37,608**	**+13,651**	**+50,060**	**37,361**	**23,112**	**17,958**	**37,704**	**25,051**	**18,866**	
+26,294	**+652**	**+885**	..	..	..	**19,601**	**6,258**	**6,041**	**19,324**	**6,373**	**5,938**	
+3,346	+652	+885	+2,244	+3,001	+10,128	8,206	6,258	6,041	7,771	6,373	5,938	113
+4,153	+626	+1,277	+2,212	−308	+7,960	6,354	4,201	3,986	6,466	4,466	4,055	114
+2,815	+1,245	+1,306	−282	+750	+5,834	5,041	3,603	3,049	5,087	3,710	3,019	115
+3,758	**−2,667**	**−7,591**	**−6,220**	**+13,651**	**+931**	**12,665**	**10,662**	**11,917**	**13,271**	**11,516**	**12,928**	
+1,413	+871	+393	+181	+132	+2,990	4,200	3,390	2,965	4,333	3,730	3,284	116
+655	+1,016	+148	+834	+173	+2,826	3,447	3,071	2,625	3,599	3,320	2,750	117
+769	..	..	..	..	..	2,652	2,116	..	2,653	2,420	..	118
+279	−407	+808	−977	−336	−633	2,366	2,172	2,341	2,686	2,601	2,839	119
−3,150	..	..	..	..	..	**5,095**	**6,192**	..	**5,109**	**7,162**	..	
+114	..	..	..	..	..	2,060	1,904	..	2,099	2,141	..	120
+305	+422	+722	+563	..	..	1,574	1,397	..	1,666	1,538	..	121
+487	+446	+612	..	..	..	1,461	1,203	952	1,344	1,115	920	122

TABLE V

Towns arranged territorially with Population by Religion

1. In this table as in Table IV travellers enumerated in encampments, trains, etc., and shown in column 22 of Table III have been included in the population of any town adjoining which the place of enumeration is situated.

2. Below are given separate figures for the Military and Civil population of each cantonment. The third column shows only the figures obtained from the census of the strictly military area, and those for the civil population may contain a certain number properly to be reckoned military.

Serial No.	Name of Cantonment.	Population.	
		Military.	Civil.
1	2	3	4
1	Saugor	*1,305	9,040
2	Jubbulpore	7,794	12,271
3	Pachmarhi	137	4,562
4	Kamptee	1,855	3,699

*In all tables the strictly military population of Saugor (988 males and 317 females) has been included in the figures of the Municipality instead of in those of the Cantonment. The mistake was detected after the tables were printed. See fly sheet of Provincial Table I.

TABLE V

Towns arranged territorially

Serial No.	District or State and name of Town.	Municipality, Cantonment or Town.	Population. Persons.	Population. Males.	Population. Females.	Hindus. Persons.	Hindus. Males.	Hindus. Females.	Muslims. Persons.	Muslims. Males.	Muslims. Females.
	1	2	3	4	5	6	7	8	9	10	11
	Central Provinces and Berar. 122 towns.	..	**1,754,611**	**928,157**	**826,454**	**1,371,229**	**723,099**	**648,130**	**313,574**	**167,402**	**146,172**
	C. P. British Districts and Berar. 112 towns.	..	**1,679,546**	**890,796**	**788,750**	**1,306,204**	**690,938**	**615,266**	**307,597**	**164,407**	**143,190**
	C. P. British Districts 70 towns.	..	**1,157,649**	**612,852**	**544,797**	**917,488**	**483,210**	**434,278**	**186,005**	**100,184**	**85,821**
	Jubbulpore Division—13 towns.		*277,453*	*149,024*	*128,429*	*200,193*	*106,876*	*93,317*	*57,124*	*30,920*	*26,204*
	SAUGOR DISTRICT										
1	Saugor ..	M.	39,822	20,723	19,099	29,885	15,435	14,450	7,632	4,036	3,596
2	Do. ..	C.	9,040	4,583	4,457	6,191	3,193	2,998	2,518	1,229	1,289
3	Deori ..	M.	5,638	2,778	2,860	4,690	2,317	2,373	581	282	299
4	Khurai ..	M.	6,951	3,478	3,473	4,915	2,494	2,421	1,291	642	649
5	Garhakota ..	T.	8,242	4,681	3,561	6,481	3,643	2,838	1,351	811	540
6	Bina-Etawah ..	M.	10,849	5,952	4,897	7,505	4,091	3,414	2,061	1,165	896
	DAMOH DISTRICT										
7	Damoh ..	M.	20,728	10,726	10,002	15,416	7,952	7,464	3,759	1,923	1,836
	JUBBULPORE DISTRICT										
8	Jubbulpore ..	M.	104,317	56,613	47,704	73,704	40,239	33,465	24,647	13,325	11,322
9	Do.	C.	20,065	12,645	7,420	11,835	6,885	4,950	4,375	2,862	1,513
10	Murwara ..	M.	21,959	11,572	10,387	17,799	9,422	8,377	3,135	1,742	1,393
11	Sihora ..	M.	5,764	2,953	2,811	4,965	2,546	2,419	650	333	317
	MANDLA DISTRICT										
12	Mandla ..	M.	7,997	4,115	3,882	6,417	3,298	3,119	1,335	688	647
	SEONI DISTRICT										
13	Seoni ..	M.	16,081	8,205	7,876	10,390	5,361	5,029	3,789	1,882	1,907
	Nerbudda Division—18 towns.	..	*216,879*	*114,631*	*102,248*	*157,270*	*83,002*	*74,268*	*50,342*	*26,658*	*23,684*
	NARSINGHPUR DISTICT										
14	Narsinghpur ..	M.	11,077	5,794	5,283	8,078	4,216	3,862	2,170	1,126	1,044
15	Chhota Chhindwara ..	M.	3,671	1,847	1,824	2,678	1,355	1,323	325	163	162
16	Gadarwara	M.	9,077	4,709	4,368	7,631	3,984	3,647	1,075	542	533
	HOSHANGABAD DISTRICT										
17	Hoshangabad ..	M.	12,332	6,564	5,768	9,907	5,270	4,637	2,031	1,062	969
18	Itarsi ..	M.	11,787	6,496	5,291	8,431	4,650	3,781	2,126	1,183	943
19	Harda ..	M.	16,031	8,601	7,430	12,240	6,532	5,708	3,350	1,834	1,516
20	Sohagpur ..	M.	8,141	4,059	4,082	5,701	2,921	2,780	2,072	1,000	1,072
21	Seoni-Malwa ..	M.	6,410	3,276	3,134	5,122	2,609	2,513	1,049	535	514
22	Pachmarhi ..	M	1,437	1,071	366	801	587	214	319	255	64
23	Do. ..	C.	4,699	2,564	2,135	3,273	1,774	1,499	1,221	659	562
24	Piparia ..	*	3,968	2,171	1,797	3,393	1,864	1,529	495	262	233
	NIMAR DISTRICT										
25	Khandwa ..	M.	34,622	19,060	15,562	23,595	13,147	10,448	9,572	5,166	4,406
26	Burhanpur ..	M.	44,066	23,056	21,010	26,001	13,511	12,490	17,675	9,328	8,347

*N. A. C. = Notified Area Committee.

Note 1.—Regarding the population of Saugor Municipality and that of Saugor Cantonment seefly sheet.

with Population by Religion — TABLE V

Christians. Persons.	Males.	Females.	Tribal religion. Persons.	Males.	Females.	Sikhs. Persons.	Males.	Females.	Zoroastrians. Persons.	Males.	Females.	Jains. Persons.	Males.	Females.	Others. Persons.	Males.	Females.	Serial No.
12	13	14	15	16	17	18	19	20	21	22	23	24	25	26	27	28	29	
30,743	**16,593**	**14,150**	**8,710**	**4,639**	**4,071**	**2,315**	**1,624**	**691**	**1,968**	**1,032**	**936**	**25,878**	**13,654**	**12,224**	**194**	**114**	**80**	
29,344	**15,944**	**13,400**	**7,085**	**3,676**	**3,409**	**2,265**	**1,584**	**681**	**1,953**	**1,022**	**931**	**24,907**	**13,112**	**11,795**	**191**	**113**	**78**	
26,299	**14,442**	**11,857**	**6,538**	**3,401**	**3,137**	**2,018**	**1,439**	**579**	**1,726**	**894**	**832**	**17,409**	**9,182**	**8,227**	**166**	**100**	**66**	
9,430	*5,450*	*3,980*	*1,427*	*721*	*706*	*828*	*617*	*211*	*341*	*168*	*173*	*8,016*	*4,214*	*3,802*	*94*	*58*	*36*	
507	258	249	..	..	..	29	23	6	17	9	8	1,752	962	790	..	..	..	1
290	139	151	..	..	..	38	21	17	..	..	..	3	1	2	..	..	..	2
8	3	5	..	..	..	..	..	..	..	..	..	359	176	183	..	..	..	3
..	..	..	..	..	..	1	1	..	..	..	..	744	341	403	..	..	..	4
6	5	1	..	..	..	..	..	..	..	..	..	404	222	182	..	..	..	5
510	281	229	1	1	..	26	16	10	102	49	53	644	349	295	..	..	..	6
455	301	154	94	52	42	9	5	4	8	3	5	985	489	496	2(a)	1	1	7
3,716	1,848	1,868	251	132	119	6	4	2	199	101	98	1,702	907	795	92(b)	57	35	8
3,008	2,284	724	4	2	2	682	529	153	..	..	..	161	83	78	..	..	..	9
509	118	391	..	..	..	24	14	10	9	3	6	483	273	210	..	..	..	10
4	2	2	..	..	..	3	1	2	..	..	..	142	71	71	..	..	..	11
151	82	69	30	14	16	10	3	7	..	..	..	54	30	24	..	..	..	12
266	129	137	1,047	520	527	..	..	..	6	3	3	583	310	273	.	..	..	13
3,423	*1,801*	*1,622*	*2,011*	*1,094*	*917*	*216*	*163*	*53*	*232*	*122*	*110*	*3,378*	*1,787*	*1,591*	*7*	*4*	*3*	
174	104	70	268	146	122	..	..	..	..	..	..	387	202	185	..	..	..	14
8	4	4	281	133	148	..	..	..	..	..	..	379	192	187	..	..	..	15
40	23	17	85	42	43	..	..	..	..	..	..	246	118	128	..	..	..	16
123	77	46	34	27	7	24	17	7	..	..	..	213	111	102	..	..	..	17
554	302	252	375	198	177	12	8	4	41	21	20	248	134	114	..	..	..	18
196	105	91	65	32	33	..	..	..	..	..	..	180	98	82	..	..	..	19
320	111	209	2	2	..	2	1	1	2	2	..	42	22	20	..	..	..	20
36	19	17	77	43	34	7	7	..	..	..	..	119	63	56	..	..	..	21
253	176	77	..	..	..	64	53	11	..	..	..	..	..	..	..	..	..	22
117	73	44	39	22	17	33	26	7	..	..	..	16	10	6	..	..	..	23
17	9	8	4	3	1	6	4	2	5	2	3	48	27	21	..	..	..	24
746	365	381	11	5	6	21	16	5	88	37	51	588	323	265	1(c)	1	..	25
47	21	26	7	6	1	..	..	..	74	45	29	262	145	117	..	..	..	26

(a) All Jews.
(b) Buddhists—m. 18; f. 7 and Jews—m. 39; f. 28.
(c) Buddhist.

Note 2.—The correct population of Mandla Municipality is 10,705. See note 1 on page 3.

TABLE V — Towns arranged territorially

Serial No.	District or State and name of Town.	Municipality, Cantonment or Town.	Population.			Hindus.			Muslims.		
			Persons.	Males.	Females.	Persons.	Males.	Females.	Persons.	Males.	Females.
	1	2	3	4	5	6	7	8	9	10	11
	Betul District										
27	Betul ..	M.	9,614	5,207	4,407	7,652	4,144	3,508	1,610	863	747
28	Betul Bazar ..	*	5,378	2,576	2,802	5,056	2,416	2,640	274	133	141
	Chhindwara District										
29	Chhindwara ..	M.	17,080	8,729	8,351	12,119	6,153	5,966	3,405	1,745	1,660
30	Sausar ..	M.	5,919	3,009	2,910	5,316	2,709	2,607	445	219	226
31	Pandhurna ..	M.	11,570	5,842	5,728	10,276	5,160	5,116	1,128	583	545
	Nagpur Division 31 towns.		*532,379*	*281,270*	*251,109*	*450,976*	*236,929*	*214,047*	*62,755*	*34,173*	*28,582*
	Wardha District										
32	Wardha ..	M.	19,571	10,790	8,781	16,710	9,206	7,504	1,968	1,113	855
33	Hinganghat ..	M.	22,601	[illegible]812	10,789	19,213	10,010	9,203	2,729	1,466	1,263
34	Arvi ..	M.	16,293	8,823	7,470	13,780	7,494	6,286	1,811	959	852
35	Deoli ..	M.	6,209	3,112	3,097	5,791	2,893	2,898	378	199	179
36	Pulgaon ..	M.	7,845	4,281	3,564	6,604	3,599	3,005	817	456	361
37	Sindi ..	*	6,883	3,529	3,354	6,026	3,082	2,944	683	367	316
38	Ashti ..	T.	5,881	2,993	2,888	4,697	2,411	2,286	1,124	552	572
	Nagpur District										
39	Nagpur ..	M.	215,165	116,403	98,762	176,237	95,077	81,160	28,042	15,628	12,414
40	Kamptee ..	M.	20,787	10,806	9,981	13,673	7,045	6,628	6,959	3,678	3,281
41	Do. ..	C.	5,554	3,704	1,850	2,820	1,636	1,184	965	717	248
42	Umrer ..	M.	17,913	8,857	9,056	17,007	8,396	8,611	860	440	420
43	Ramtek ..	M.	8,939	4,424	4,515	8,345	4,125	4,220	529	262	267
44	Khapa ..	M.	8,191	4,129	4,062	7,661	3,845	3,816	505	268	237
45	Narkhed ..	T.	8,139	4,122	4,017	7,403	3,751	3,652	697	352	345
46	Saoner ..	M.	7,969	4,162	3,807	7,366	3,832	3,534	579	317	262
47	Kelod ..	T.	5,160	2,648	2,512	4,826	2,460	2,366	309	174	135
48	Mohpa ..	T.	4,757	2,337	2,420	4,497	2,210	2,287	260	127	133
49	Kalmeshwar ..	M.	4,665	2,389	2,276	4,407	2,250	2,157	240	131	109
50	Mowar ..	M.	5,206	2,594	2,612	4,753	2,360	2,393	450	233	217
51	Katol ..	M.	10,900	5,675	5,225	9,723	5,061	4,662	1,014	535	479
	Chanda District										
52	Chanda ..	M.	28,138	14,394	13,744	25,203	12,889	12,314	2,157	1,100	1,057
53	Warora ..	M.	9,811	5,031	4,780	8,104	4,176	3,928	1,350	674	676
54	Brahmapuri ..	T.	5,216	2,612	2,604	4,710	2,340	2,370	387	205	182
55	Chimur ..	T.	4,848	2,373	2,475	4,356	2,128	2,228	492	245	247
56	Armori ..	T.	6,522	3,341	3,181	6,135	3,115	3,020	189	107	82
57	Nawargaon ..	T.	5,330	2,662	2,668	4,946	2,475	2,471	143	73	70
	Bhandara District										
58	Bhandara ..	M.	16,738	8,562	8,176	14,596	7,446	7,150	1,978	1,033	945
59	Gondia ..	M.	14,957	8,201	6,756	12,723	6,926	5,797	1,953	1,130	823
60	Pauni ..	M.	12,525	6,339	6,186	11,464	5,792	5,672	1,061	547	514
61	Tumsar ..	M.	10,061	5,117	4,944	9,300	4,721	4,579	686	356	330
	Balaghat District										
62	Balaghat ..	M.	9,605	5,048	4,557	7,900	4,178	3,722	1,440	729	711
	Chhattisgarh Division 8 towns.		*130,938*	*67,927*	*63,011*	*109,049*	*56,403*	*52,646*	*15,784*	*8,433*	*7,351*
	Raipur District										
63	Raipur ..	M.	45,390	24,060	21,330	36,491	19,412	17,079	7,227	3,798	3,429
64	Dhamtari ..	M.	11,505	5,786	5,719	9,405	4,584	4,821	1,171	652	519
65	Bhatapara ..	*	7,974	4,271	3,703	7,097	3,787	3,310	737	402	335
66	Arang ..	T.	6,496	3,097	3,399	6,256	2,972	3,284	210	105	105
	Bilaspur District										
67	Bilaspur ..	M.	31,374	16,366	15,008	25,372	13,232	12,140	4,213	2,265	1,948
68	Champa ..	*	8,362	4,191	4,171	7,346	3,717	3,629	401	227	174
69	Mungeli ..	T.	6,665	3,281	3,384	5,676	2,815	2,861	427	215	212
	Drug District										
70	Drug ..	M.	13,172	6,875	6,297	11,406	5,884	5,522	1,398	769	629

* N. A. C.=Notified Area Committee.

Christians.			Tribal religion.			Sikhs.			Zoroastrians.			Jains.			Others.			
Persons.	Males.	Females.	Persons.	Males.	Females.	Persons.	Males.	Females.	Persons.	Males.	Females.	Persons.	Males.	Females.	Persons.	Males.	Females.	Serial No.
12	13	14	15	16	17	18	19	20	21	22	23	24	25	26	27	28	29	30
180	105	75	..	..	..	16	13	3	4	4	..	152	78	74	..	..	..	27
1	1	..	..	..	..	..	..	..	..	..	..	47	26	21	..	..	..	28
603	302	301	530	302	228	31	18	13	13	6	7	373	200	173	6(d)	3	3	29
7	3	4	127	66	61	..	..	..	3	3	..	21	9	12	..	..	..	30
1	1	..	106	67	39	..	..	..	2	2	..	57	29	28	..	..	..	31
9,062	*5,095*	*3,967*	*2,971*	*1,494*	*1,477*	*758*	*516*	*242*	*1,107*	*584*	*523*	*4,712*	*2,455*	*2,257*	*38*	*24*	*14*	
198	128	70	121	57	64	16	9	7	21	10	11	537	267	270	..	..	..	32
31	15	16	229	111	118	..	..	..	1	1	..	394	207	187	4(e)	2	2	33
..	..	..	363	186	177	..	..	..	..	..	..	339	184	155	..	..	..	34
..	..	..	..	..	..	..	..	..	..	..	..	40	20	20	..	..	..	35
19	13	6	138	70	68	..	..	..	16	7	9	251	136	115	..	..	..	36
6	2	4	77	39	38	..	..	..	4	2	2	87	37	50	..	..	..	37
..	..	..	2	2	..	..	..	..	..	..	..	58	28	30	..	..	..	38
6,449	3,359	3,090	1,163	572	591	444	274	170	963	516	447	1,833	955	878	34(f)	22	12	39
91	48	43	..	..	..	15	12	3	3	3	..	46	20	26	..	..	..	40
1,495	1,134	361	4	2	2	200	181	19	41	19	22	29	15	14	..	..	..	41
23	1	12	..	..	..	..	..	..	2	1	1	21	9	12	..	..	..	42
15	10	5	..	..	..	..	..	..	..	..	..	50	27	23	..	..	..	43
2	1	1	7	5	2	..	..	..	..	..	..	16	10	6	..	..	..	44
..	..	..	..	..	..	..	..	..	..	..	..	39	19	20	..	..	..	45
9	4	5	..	..	..	..	..	..	6	4	2	9	5	4	..	..	..	46
..	..	..	..	..	..	..	..	..	..	..	..	25	14	11	..	..	..	47
..	..	..	..	..	..	..	..	..	..	..	..	..	..	..	..	..	..	48
1	1	..	..	..	..	..	..	..	..	..	..	17	7	10	..	..	..	49
..	..	..	..	..	..	..	..	..	..	..	..	3	1	2	..	..	..	50
11	3	8	..	..	..	5	2	3	13	9	4	134	65	69	..	..	..	51
401	210	191	161	72	89	6	3	3	13	6	7	197	114	83	..	..	..	52
36	20	16	41	20	21	..	..	..	21	6	15	259	135	124	..	..	..	53
13	6	7	103	58	45	..	..	..	..	..	..	3	3	..	..	..	..	54
..	..	..	..	..	..	..	..	..	..	..	..	..	..	..	..	..	..	55
..	..	..	195	118	77	..	..	..	..	..	..	3	1	2	..	..	..	56
..	..	..	241	114	127	..	..	..	..	..	..	..	..	..	..	..	..	57
82	36	46	38	23	15	7	2	5	..	..	..	37	22	15	..	..	..	58
116	62	54	45	22	23	44	24	20	..	..	..	76	37	39	..	..	..	59
..	..	..	..	..	..	..	..	..	..	..	..	..	..	..	..	..	..	60
..	..	..	38	21	17	..	..	..	..	..	..	37	19	18	..	..	..	61
64	32	32	5	2	3	21	9	12	3	..	3	172	98	74	..	..	..	62
4,384	*2,096*	*2,288*	*129*	*92*	*37*	*216*	*143*	*73*	*46*	*20*	*2*	*1,303*	*726*	*577*	*27*	*14*	*13*	
959	440	519	73	51	22	108	68	40	27	11	16	496	274	222	9(g)	6	3	63
589	374	215	1	1	..	3	1	2	1	1	..	335	173	162	..	..	..	64
57	35	22	3	3	..	2	2	..	..	..	..	78	42	36	..	..	..	65
3	3	..	24	14	10	1	1	..	1	1	..	1	1	..	..	..	..	66
1,645	773	872	26	23	3	80	56	24	7	3	4	13	6	7	18(h)	8	10	67
609	245	364	..	..	..	6	2	4	..	..	..	..	..	..	..	..	..	68
474	196	278	..	..	..	2	2	..	..	..	..	86	53	33	..	..	..	69
48	30	18	2	..	2	14	11	3	10	4	6	294	177	112		..	..	70

(*d*) All Jews. (*e*) All Jews. (*f*) Jews—m. 20; f. 11 and Buddhists—m. 2; f. Buddhists— m. 6 f. 5.

TABLE V — **Towns arranged territorially**

Serial No.	District or State and name of Town.	Municipality, Cantonment or town.	Population. Persons.	Population. Males.	Population. Females.	Hindus. Persons.	Hindus. Males.	Hindus. Females.	Muslims. Persons.	Muslims. Males.	Muslims. Females.
	1	2	3	4	5	6	7	8	9	10	11
	Berar—42 towns	..	**521,897**	**277,944**	**243,953**	**388,716**	**207,728**	**180,988**	**121,592**	**64,223**	**57,369**
	AMRAOTI DISTRICT										
71	Amraoti	M.	46,832	25,746	21,086	36,529	20,087	16,442	9,582	5,272	4,310
72	Amraoti Camp	M.	10,268	5,509	4,759	8,067	4,356	3,711	1,648	946	702
73	Badnera	T.	13,666	7,197	6,469	10,312	5,417	4,895	2,893	1,552	1,341
74	Anjangaon	M.	11,597	6,065	5,532	8,028	4,246	3,782	3,295	1,687	1,608
75	Ellichpur	M.	28,592	14,822	13,770	19,792	10,317	9,475	8,606	4,406	4,200
76	Ellichpur Camp Paratwada.	M.	9,799	5,256	4,543	6,891	3,733	3,158	2,528	1,314	1,214
77	Dattapur Dhamangaon	T.	9,807	5,274	4,533	8,790	4,694	4,096	864	490	374
78	Morsi	T.	9,523	4,915	4,608	7,843	4,056	3,787	1,643	840	803
79	Warud	T.	10,010	5,351	4,659	8,567	4,573	3,994	1,225	661	564
80	Karasgaon	T.	6,853	3,570	3,283	5,702	2,959	2,743	1,045	560	485
81	Shirasgaon-kasba	T.	6,880	3,486	3,394	5,567	2,840	2,727	1,190	596	594
82	Chandur Bazar	T.	5,803	3,008	2,795	4,161	2,144	2,017	1,522	799	723
83	Pathrot	T.	5,218	2,651	2,567	4,621	2,341	2,280	556	292	264
84	Daryapur Banosa	T.	8,556	4,775	3,781	6,842	3,820	3,022	1,541	865	676
	AKOLA DISTRICT										
85	Akola	M.	47,632	26,401	21,231	35,202	19,612	15,590	11,208	6,118	5,090
86	Akot	M.	18,693	9,637	9,056	14,016	7,380	6,636	4,551	2,193	2,358
87	Basim	M.	14,409	7,594	6,815	9,788	5,186	4,602	4,121	2,139	1,982
88	Murtizapur	M.	11,541	6,420	5,121	8,678	4,815	3,863	2,421	1,358	1,063
89	Karanja	M.	16,615	8,776	7,839	9,982	5,296	4,686	5,374	2,838	2,536
90	Barsi-Takli	T.	5,455	2,788	2,667	3,071	1,559	1,512	2,354	1,213	1,141
91	Balapur	T.	11,245	5,753	5,492	4,897	2,519	2,378	5,871	3,011	2,860
92	Patur	T.	6,838	3,425	3,413	4,069	2,074	1,995	2,757	1,343	1,414
93	Wadegaon	T.	5,965	3,015	2,950	5,307	2,653	2,654	646	355	291
94	Hiwarkhed	T.	6,914	3,520	3,394	5,453	2,778	2,675	1,344	679	665
95	Mangrulpir	T.	6,386	3,237	3,149	3,393	1,711	1,682	2,916	1,486	1,430
	BULDANA DISTRICT										
96	Buldana	M.	7,504	4,208	3,296	5,769	3,231	2,538	1,420	790	630
97	Chikhli	M.	7,041	3,663	3,378	5,145	2,670	2,475	1,774	927	847
98	Mehkar	M.	7,009	3,694	3,315	5,418	2,860	2,558	1,582	831	751
99	Malkapur	M.	17,565	9,350	8,215	10,624	5,695	4,929	6,445	3,396	3,049
100	Nandura	M.	11,212	5,675	5,537	8,854	4,440	4,414	2,291	1,202	1,089
101	Khamgaon	M.	23,462	13,113	10,349	17,916	10,012	7,904	4,976	2,847	2,129
102	Shegaon	M.	14,699	7,583	7,116	12,265	6,315	5,950	2,315	1,196	1,119
103	Jalgaon	M.	10,463	5,248	5,215	8,066	4,060	4,006	2,358	1,170	1,188
104	Deolgaon Raja	*	5,837	2,936	2,901	4,504	2,252	2,252	1,013	510	503
	YEOTMAL DISTRICT										
105	Yeotmal	M.	20,967	11,434	9,533	17,858	9,691	8,167	2,430	1,376	1,054
106	Digras	M.	9,398	4,954	4,444	6,894	3,663	3,231	2,413	1,246	1,167
107	Pusad	M.	9,862	5,180	4,682	7,190	3,835	3,355	2,402	1,201	1,201
108	Darwha	M.	9,661	5,136	4,525	6,526	3,470	3,056	2,944	1,564	1,380
109	Wun	M.	12,597	7,003	5,594	10,888	6,018	4,870	1,518	877	641
110	Umerkhed	*	7,957	4,092	3,865	5,634	2,938	2,696	2,237	1,111	1,126
111	Pandharkaoda	M.	7,577	4,175	3,402	5,937	3,300	2,637	1,513	807	706
112	Ghatanji	T.	3,989	2,309	1,680	3,660	2,112	1,548	260	159	101
	C. P. States 10 towns.	..	**75,065**	**37,361**	**37,704**	**65,025**	**32,161**	**32,864**	**5,977**	**2,995**	**2,982**
	NANDGAON										
113	Rajnandgaon	M.	15,977	8,206	7,771	13,563	6,938	6,625	1,549	817	732
	RAIGARH										
114	Raigarh	M.	12,820	6,354	6,466	11,674	5,742	5,932	1,094	574	520
115	Kharsia	M.	2,805	1,461	1,344	2,730	1,425	1,305	62	28	34
	BASTAR										
116	Jagdalpur	†	10,128	5,041	5,087	7,644	3,717	3,927	722	325	397

*N. A. C.-Notified Area Committee. -† N. T. C. Nominated Town Committee.

Note.—**The correct population of Anjangaon Municipality is 17,813. See note 2 on page 3.**

Christians. Persons.	Christians. Males.	Christians. Females.	Tribal religion. Persons.	Tribal religion. Males.	Tribal religion. Females.	Sikhs. Persons.	Sikhs. Males.	Sikhs. Females.	Zoroastrians. Persons.	Zoroastrians. Males.	Zoroastrians. Females.	Jains. Persons.	Jains. Males.	Jains. Females.	Others. ns.	Others. Males.	Others. Females.	Serial No.
12	13	14	15	16	17	18	19	20	21	22	23	24	25	26	27	28	29	
3,045	**1,502**	**1,543**	**547**	**275**	**272**	**247**	**145**	**102**	**227**	**128**	**99**	**7,498**	**3,930**	**3,568**	**25**	**13**	**12**	
69	38	31	1	..	1	6	4	2	6	5	1	639	340	299	..	..	..	71
504	176	328	2	2	..	21	15	6	14	9	5	10	4	6	2 (*i*)	1	1	72
249	116	133	..	..	..	..	..	..	77	39	38	135	73	62	..	..	..	73
21	11	10	1	1	..	..	..	..	..	..	..	252	120	132	..	..	..	74
19	9	10	8	3	5	..	..	..	5	2	3	162	85	77	..	..	..	75
235	128	107	27	13	14	18	11	7	8	5	3	92	52	40	..	..	..	76
7	7	..	..	..	..	..	..	..	..	..	..	146	83	63	..	..	..	77
..	..	..	25	13	12	..	..	..	..	..	..	12	6	[illegible]	..	..	..	78
6	4	2	106	56	50	..	..	..	3	3	..	103	54	49	..	..	..	79
..	..	..	24	12	12	..	..	..	..	..	..	82	39	43	..	..	..	80
..	..	..	22	6	16	..	..	..	..	..	..	101	44	57	..	..	..	81
2	2	..	5	4	1	..	..	..	2	2	..	111	57	54	..	..	..	82
29	14	15	..	..	..	..	..	..	..	..	..	12	4	8	..	..	..	83
19	9	10	..	..	..	3	2	1	..	..	..	151	79	72	..	..	..	84
521	286	235	15	7	8	41	20	21	45	23	22	590	330	260	10 (*j*)	5	5	85
21	10	11	2	1	1	..	..	..	4	2	2	99	51	48	..	..	..	86
218	113	105	..	..	..	6	3	3	..	..	..	271	151	120	5 (*k*)	2	3	87
163	99	64	29	13	16	16	10	6	15	5	10	219	120	99	..	..	..	88
10	6	4	6	3	3	5	5	..	5	5	..	1,238	625	613	1 (*l*)	1	..	89
..	..	..	..	..	..	..	..	..	..	..	..	24	13	11	..	..	..	90
..	..	..	..	..	..	..	..	..	..	..	..	477	223	254	..	..	..	91
..	..	..	..	..	..	..	..	..	..	..	..	12	8	4	..	..	..	92
..	..	..	..	..	..	..	..	..	..	..	..	12	7	5	..	..	..	93
..	..	..	5	5	..	..	..	..	..	..	..	112	58	54	..	..	..	94
12	6	6	1	..	1	..	..	..	..	..	..	64	34	30	..	..	..	95
99	114	85	..	..	..	..	..	..	..	..	..	116	73	43	..	..	..	96
41	23	18	..	..	..	6	3	3	..	..	..	75	40	35	..	..	..	97
2	..	2	..	..	..	..	..	..	..	..	..	7	3	4	..	..	..	98
30	14	16	..	..	..	19	8	11	..	..	..	447	237	210	..	..	..	99
..	..	..	..	..	..	4	1	3	..	..	..	63	32	31	..	..	..	100
78	39	139	..	..	..	67	40	27	23	12	11	302	163	139	..	..	..	101
17	10	7	..	..	..	2	2	..	9	8	1	91	52	39	..	..	..	102
2	..	2	..	..	..	8	4	4	..	..	..	29	14	15	..	..	..	103
1	1	..	..		..	..	..	..	..	..	..	319	173	146	..	..	..	104
2[illegible]	158	118	186	95	91	3	3	..	10	7	3	198	101	97	6 (*m*)	3	3	105
23	15	8	..	..	..	..	..	..	..	..	..	68	30	38	..	..	..	106
51	30	21	2	1	1	..	..	..	1	1	..	216	112	104	..	..	..	107
40	24	16	14	6	8	9	7	2	..	..	..	128	65	63	..	..	..	108
54	27	27	12	5	7	2	2	..	..	..	..	122	73	49	1 (*n*)	1	..	109
[illegible]	10	10	..	..	..	..	..	..	..	..	..	66	33	33	..	..	..	110
[illegible]	2	3	25	15	10	5	4	1	..	..	..	92	47	45	..	..	..	111
	1	..	29	14	15	6	1	5	..	..	..	33	22	11	..	..	..	112
1,39[illegible]	**649**	**750**	**1,625**	**963**	**662**	**50**	**40**	**10**	**15**	**10**	**5**	**971**	**542**	**429**	**3**	**1**	**2**	
29[illegible]	125	174	47	29	18	5	4	1	3	2	1	511	291	220	..	..	..	113
1[illegible]	6	6	..	..	..	20	19	1	3	3	..	17	10	7	..	..	..	114
		3	..	..	..	1	1	..	..	..	..	5	3	2	..	..	..	115
639	290	349	1,016	646	370	..	..	..	2	1	1	105	62	43	..	..	..	116

(*i*) Buddhists. (*j*) Jews—m. 3; f. 3. and Buddhists—m. 2. (*k*) All Jews. (*l*) Jew. (*m*) All Jews. (*n*) Jew.

TABLE V

Towns arranged territorially

Serial No.	District or State and name of Town.	Municipality, Cantonment or town.	Population.			Hindus.			Muslims.		
			Persons.	Males.	Females.	Persons.	Males.	Females.	Persons.	Males.	Females.
	1	2	3	4	5	6	7	8	9	10	11
	KHAIRAGARH										
117	Dongargarh ..	M.	8,533	4,200	4,333	6,983	3,431	3,552	1,063	520	543
118	Khairagarh ..	T.	4,159	2,060	2,099	3,767	1,857	1,910	265	131	134
	SARANGARH										
119	Sarangarh ..	M.	7,046	3,447	3,599	6,752	3,297	3,455	271	137	134
	KANKER										
120	Kanker ..	M.	5,305	2,652	2,653	4,412	2,182	2,230	311	173	138
	KAWARDHA										
121	Kawardha ..	T.	5,052	2,366	2,686	4,519	2,128	2,391	419	182	237
	SAKTI										
122	Sakti ..	M.	3,240	1,574	1,666	2,981	1,444	1,537	221	108	113

with Population by Religion—*concluded* **TABLE V**

Christians.			Tribal religion.			Sikhs.			Zoroastrians.			Jains.			Others.			
Persons.	Males.	Females.	Persons.	Males.	Females.	Persons.	Males.	Females.	Persons.	Males.	Females.	Persons.	Males.	Females.	Persons.	Males.	Females.	Serial No.
12	13	14	15	16	17	18	19	20	21	22	23	24	25	26	27	28	29	
387	198	189	..	..	..	5	2	3	5	2	3	90	47	43	..	..	..	117
8	4	4	..	..	..	8	6	2	..	..	..	111	62	49	..	..	..	118
20	10	10	..	..	..	1	1	..	2	2	..	..	..	..	..	..	..	119
16	8	8	542	276	266	..	..	..	..	..	..	24	13	11	..	..	..	120
6	2	4	..	..	..	..	..	..	..	..	..	108	54	54	..	..	..	121
5	2	3	20	12	8	10	7	3	..	..	..	..	..	..	3 (*o*)	1	2	122

(*o*) All Buddhists.

TABLE VI

Birthplace

1. **This table is divided into two parts :—**

Part A contains the statistics of birthplace for the province as a whole, for each district and for all the Central Provinces States combined.

Part B contains similar information for cities.

2. The phrase "Within British Dominions" occurring in column 1 has been taken to mean "within the British Empire and Mandated Territories," but the figures of those born in Iraq have been included with those against "Outside British Dominions".

TABLE VI **Birthplace**

District, State, Province or Country where born.	District where enumerated.								
	Total population.			Saugor.			Damoh.		
	Persons.	Males.	Females.	Persons.	Males.	Females.	Persons.	Males.	Females.
1	2	3	4	5	6	7	8	9	10
Total Population ..	**17,990,937**	**8,997,203**	**8,993,734**	**544,589**	**280,385**	**264,204**	**305,568**	**154,791**	**150,77[illegible]**
A.—Born in India ..	**17.984,427**	**8,992,252**	**8,992,175**	**544,293**	**280,183**	**264,110**	**305,535**	**154,768**	**150,76[illegible]**
I.—In Central Provinces and Berar.	**17,335,363**	**8,651,046**	**8,684,317**	**504,702**	**262.413**	**242,289**	**290,151**	**147,943**	**142,20[illegible]**
(i) British Territory ..	**15,032,035**	**7,497,882**	**7,534,153**	**504,692**	**262,406**	**242,286**	**290,142**	**147,937**	**142,205**
District of enumeration ..	*13,873,895*	*6,988,683*	*6,885,212*	*493,058*	*257,512*	*235,546*	*274,503*	*142,475*	*132,028*
Other districts of British C. P. and Berar.	*1,158,140*	*509,199*	*648,941*	*11,634*	*4,894*	*6,740*	*15,639*	*5,462*	*10,177*
C. P. and Berar unspecified ..	..	..	..	..	..	..	..	..	..
(ii) Central Provinces States	**2,303,328**	**1,153.164**	**1,150,164**	**10**	**7**	**3**	**9**	**6**	**3**
Makrai	12,600	6,912	5,688	1	1	..	2	2	..
Bastar	509,674	255,400	254,274	9	6	3	..	..	..
Kanker	109,478	54,595	54,883	..	..	..	..	..	..
Nandgaon	164,535	78,954	85,581	..	..	..	1	1	..
Khairagarh	151,692	75,603	76,089	..	..	..	3	1	2
Chhuikhadan ..	30,286	14,943	15,343	..	..	..	..	..	..
Kawardha	66,996	32,449	34,547	..	..	..	..	..	..
Sakti	33,039	17,332	15,707	..	..	..	..	..	..
Raigarh	266,841	132,801	134,040	..	..	..	2	1	1
Sarangarh	122,161	60,192	61,969	..	..	..	..	..	..
Changbhakar ..	18,271	9,397	8,874	..	..	..	..	..	..
Korea	69,276	35,101	34,175	..	..	..	1	1	..
Surguja	485,407	245,888	239,519	..	..	..	..	..	..
Udaipur	82,028	41,978	40,050	..	..	..	..	..	..
Jashpur	181,044	91,619	89,425	..	..	..	..	..	..
II.—Provinces and States beyond C. P. and Berar.	**649,064**	**341,206**	**307.858**	**39,591**	**17,770**	**21,821**	**15,384**	**6,825**	**8,559**
(a) Provinces and States adjacent to C. P. and Berar.	*553,975*	*281,412*	*272,563*	*37,627*	*16,383*	*21,244*	*15,090*	*6,622*	*8,468*
(i) British Territory ..	**277,302**	**152,965**	**124,337**	**18,001**	**8,811**	**9,190**	**1,437**	**861**	**576**
Bihar and Orissa ..	47,082	21,922	25,160	35	21	14	21	11	10
United Provinces of Agra and Oudh.	118,473	72,577	45,898	17,361	8,456	8,905	1,298	776	522
Bombay (including Aden) ..	98,867	51,455	47,412	522	290	232	109	68	41
Madras	12,878	7,011	5,867	83	44	39	9	6	3
(ii) States and Agencies ..	**276,673**	**128,447**	**148,226**	**19,626**	**7,572**	**12,054**	**13,653**	**5,761**	**7,892**
Central India (Agency) ..	176,802	84,780	92,022	14,259	5,611	8,648	13,552	5,699	7,853
Rewa	*84,048*	*44,500*	*39,548*	*153*	*102*	*51*	*126*	*79*	*47*
Panna	*20,467*	*8,754*	*11,713*	*2,392*	*828*	*1,564*	*7,835*	*2,995*	*4,840*
Bhopal	*26,664*	*10,155*	*16,509*	*4,919*	*1,760*	*3,159*	*116*	*47*	*69*
Indore	*15,535*	*6,655*	*8.880*	*95*	*44*	*51*	*108*	*62*	*46*
Other States ..	*30,088*	*14,716*	*15,372*	*6,700*	*2,877*	*3,823*	*5,367*	*2,516*	*2,851*
Hyderabad	91,065	39,738	51,327	66	49	17	3	2	1
Gwalior	8,806	3.929	4,877	5,301	1,912	3,389	98	60	38
(b) Other Provinces and States in India.	*94,468*	*59,452*	*35,016*	*1,964*	*1,387*	*577*	*294*	*203*	*91*
(i) British Territory ..	**28,970**	**19,627**	**9,343**	**1,079**	**840**	**239**	**132**	**74**	**58**
Ajmer-Merwara ..	3,429	2,157	1.272	84	76	8	6	3	3
Andamans and Nicobar ..	96	73	23	1	1	..	..	..	..
Assam	581	310	271	8	6	2	3	1	2
Baluchistan	709	599	110	10	7	3	..	..	..
Bengal	6,771	3,564	3,207	78	40	38	32	13	19
Burma	156	90	66	3	2	1	2	..	2
Coorg	254	35	219	..	..	..	..	..	..
Delhi	795	547	248	26	12	14	6	4	2
North-West Frontier Province	1,158	1,000	158	37	35	2	4	3	1
Punjab	15,021	11,252	3,769	832	661	171	79	50	29
(ii) States and Agencies ..	**65,498**	**39,825**	**25,673**	**885**	**547**	**338**	**162**	**129**	**33**
Assam States ..	6	3	3	..	..	..	..	..	..
Baroda	509	279	230	5	4	1	2	..	2
Bihar and Orissa States ..	4,837	2,272	2,565	..	..	..	..	..	..
Bengal States ..	175	165	10	..	..	..	..	..	..
Bombay States ..	6,146	3,971	2,175	..	..	..	..	..	..
Kashmir	273	249	24	..	..	..	4	4	..
Madras States (including Cochin and Travancore).	167	111	56	..	..	..	..	..	..
Mysore	711	378	333	3	..	3	3	1	2
North-West Frontier Province (Agencies and Tribal areas).	9	8	1	..	..	..	..	..	..
Punjab States ..	754	484	270	3	3	..	2	..	2
Rajputana Agency ..	51,621	31,722	19,899	866	534	332	151	124	27
Sikkim	12	12	..	..	..	..	..	..	..
United Provinces States ..	278	171	107	8	6	2	..	..	..
Baluchistan States ..	..	..	..	..	..	..	..	..	..

Part A.—Districts and States

TABLE VI

District, State, Province or Country where born.	District where enumerated.								
	Total population.			Saugor.			Damob		
	Persons.	Males.	Females.	Persons.	Males.	Females.	Persons.	Males.	Females.
1	2	3	4	5	6	7	8	9	10
(c) French and Portuguese Settlements.	**528**	**298**	**230**	..	..	..	..	..	..
(d) India unspecified ..	**93**	**44**	**49**	..	..	..	..	..	..
B.—Born in other Asiatic Countries.	**1,905**	**1,406**	**499**	**124**	**93**	**31**	**17**	**15**	**2**
(i) Within British Dominions ..	*158*	*89*	*69*	2	*1*	*1*	..	..	..
Ceylon	52	36	16	1	1	..	..	..	..
Straits Settlements and Malaya	1	1	..	..	..	..	..	..	..
Elsewhere	105	52	53	1	..	1	..	..	..
(ii) Outside British Dominions ..	*1,630*	*1,217*	*413*	*121*	*92*	*29*	*17*	*15*	*2*
Afghanistan	834	773	61	30	26	4	14	14	..
China	31	26	5	*1*	*1*	..	..	..	..
Nepal	683	360	323	90	65	25	3	1	2
Elsewhere	82	58	24	..	..	..	..	..	..
(iii) Asia, unspecified ..	*117*	*100*	*17*	*1*	..	*1*	..	..	..
C.—Born in Europe ..	**4,206**	**3,353**	**853**	**166**	**105**	**61**	**3**	**3**	..
(i) United Kingdom and Ireland.	4,021	3,253	768	156	100	56	3	3	..
(ii) British possessions in Europe	3	1	2	..	..	..	..	..	..
(iii) Continental Europe ..	104	48	56	10	5	5	..	..	..
(iv) Europe, unspecified ..	*78*	*51*	*27*	..	..	..	..	..	..
D.—Born in Africa ..	**87**	**56**	**31**	..	..	..	..	..	..
(i) Within British Dominions ..	*18*	*8*	*10*	..	..	..	..	..	..
Cape Colony ..	..	..	..	..	..	..	..	..	..
Kenya (British East Africa) ..	8	4	4	..	..	..	..	..	..
Mauritius	..	..	..	..	..	..	..	..	..
Natal	3	2	1	..	..	..	..	..	..
Nyasaland	..	..	..	..	..	..	..	..	..
Tanganyika	..	..	..	..	..	..	..	..	..
Transvaal	..	..	..	..	..	..	..	..	..
Uganda	..	..	..	..	..	..	..	..	..
Zanzibar	..	..	..	..	..	..	..	..	..
Elsewhere	7	2	5	..	..	..	..	..	..
(ii) Outside British Dominions ..	*1*	..	*1*	..	..	..	..	..	..
Mozambique ..	..	..	..	..	..	..	..	..	..
Elsewhere	1	..	1	..	..	..	..	..	..
(iii) Africa, unspecified ..	*68*	*48*	*20*	..	..	..	..	..	..
E.—Born in America ..	**279**	**119**	**160**	**2**	**1**	**1**	**13**	**5**	**8**
(i) Within British Dominions ..	*12*	*9*	*3*	..	..	..	*1*	*1*	..
British Guiana ..	..	..	..	..	..	..	..	..	..
British Honduras ..	..	..	..	..	..	..	..	..	..
Canada	10	7	3	..	..	..	..	..	..
Elsewhere	2	2	..	..	..	..	1	1	..
(ii) Outside British Dominions ..	*109*	*38*	*71*	..	..	..	*12*	*4*	*8*
United States ..	109	38	71	..	..	..	12	4	8
Elsewhere	..	..	..	..	..	..	..	..	..
(iii) America, unspecified ..	*158*	*72*	*86*	*2*	*1*	*1*	..	..	..
F.—Born in Australasia ..	**21**	**13**	**8**	**4**	**3**	**1**	..	..	..
(i) Within British Dominions ..	*19*	*11*	*8*	*4*	*3*	*1*	..	..	..
Australia	12	7	5	4	3	1	..	..	..
Fiji Islands	2	1	1	..	..	..	..	..	..
New Zealand ..	2	..	2	..	..	..	..	..	..
Tasmania	3	3	..	..	..	..	..	..	..
Other British possessions in Australasia.	..	..	..	..	..	..	..	..	..
(ii) Outside British Dominions ..	..	..	..	..	..	..	..	..	..
(iii) Australasia, unspecified ..	*2*	*2*	..	..	..	..	..	..	..
G.—Born at Sea ..	**1**	**1**	..	..	..	..	..	..	..
H.—Birth place unspecified or not returned.	**11**	**3**	**8**	..	..	..	..	..	..

TABLE VI

District, State, Province or Country where born.	District where enumerated.								
	Jubbulpore.			Mandla.			Seoni.		
	Persons.	Males.	Females.	Persons.	Males.	Females.	Persons.	Males.	Females.
1	11	12	13	14	15	16	17	18	19
Total Population ..	**773,811**	**391,649**	**382,162**	**445,766**	**221,359**	**224,407**	**393,732**	**192,471**	**201,261**
A.—Born in India ..	**771,346**	**389,657**	**381,689**	**445,698**	**221,308**	**224,390**	**393,685**	**192,435**	**201,250**
I.—In Central Provinces and Berar.	**698,770**	**350,750**	**348,020**	**436,673**	**216,517**	**220,156**	**391,146**	**190,932**	**200,214**
(i) British Territory ..	**698,687**	**350,710**	**347,977**	**436,599**	**216,479**	**220,120**	**391,126**	**190,923**	**200,203**
District of enumeration ..	*659,036*	*331,353*	*327,653*	*414,915*	*205,450*	*209,465*	*367,332*	*181,228*	*186,104*
Other districts of British C. P. and Berar.	*39,651*	*19,327*	*20 324*	*21,684*	*11,029*	*10,655*	*23,794*	*9,695*	*14,099*
C. P. and Berar unspecified ..	.	..	..	..	..	..	..	..	..
(ii) Central Provinces States	**83**	**40**	**43**	**74**	**38**	**36**	**20**	**9**	**11**
Makrai ..	2	2	..	1	1	..	4	3	1
Bastar ..	29	11	18	16	10	6	..	..	..
Kanker ..	..	..	..	1	..	1	..	..	..
Nandgaon ..	24	13	11	3	2	1	8	..	8
Khairagarh ..	8	4	4	6	1	5	..	..	..
Chhuikhadan	..	..	..	..	..	..	1	..	1
Kawardha ..	5	1	4	36	18	18	2	1	1
Sakti ..	..	..	..	3	1	2	..	..	..
Raigarh ..	9	5	4	..	..	..	..	..	..
Sarangarh ..	5	3	2	..	..	..	..	..	..
Changbhakar	..	..	..	..	..	..	..	..	..
Korea	..	..	..	1	1	..	..	..	..
Surguja ..	1	1	..	7	4	3	5	5	..
Udaipur ..	..	..	..	..	..	..	..	..	..
Jashpur ..	..	..	..	..	..	..	..	..	..
II.—Provinces and States beyond C. P. and Berar.	**72,576**	**38,907**	**33,669**	**9,025**	**4,791**	**4,234**	**2,539**	**1,503**	**1,036**
(a) Provinces and States adjacent to C. P. and Berar.	*66,493*	*34,510*	*31,983*	*8,506*	*4,466*	*4,040*	*1,925*	*1,114*	*811*
(i) British Territory ..	**20,756**	**12,592**	**8,164**	**1,757**	**1,173**	**584**	**1,184**	**711**	**473**
Bihar and Orissa ..	342	172	170	103	78	25	31	16	15
United Provinces of Agra and Oudh.	16,785	10,255	6,530	1,329	896	433	984	584	400
Bombay (including Aden) ..	2,297	1,418	879	192	137	55	135	95	40
Madras ..	1,332	747	585	133	62	71	34	16	18
(ii) States and Agencies ..	**45,737**	**21,918**	**23,819**	**6,749**	**3,293**	**3,456**	**741**	**403**	**338**
Central India (Agency) ..	44,998	21,465	23,533	6,700	3,262	3,438	714	398	316
Rewa ..	*26,857*	*13,007*	*13,850*	*5,993*	*2,796*	*3,197*	*363*	*216*	*147*
Panna ..	*6,916*	*3,057*	*3,859*	*333*	*226*	*107*	*71*	*24*	*47*
Bhopal ..	*507*	*271*	*236*	*58*	*35*	*23*	*71*	*27*	*44*
Indore ..	*548*	*306*	*242*	*27*	*16*	*11*	*29*	*21*	*8*
Other States ..	*10,170*	*4,824*	*5,346*	*289*	*189*	*100*	*150*	*110*	*70*
Hyderabad ..	361	223	138	11	5	6	6	2	4
Gwalior ..	378	230	148	38	26	12	21	3	18
(b) Other Provinces and States in India.	*6,030*	*4 397*	*1,633*	*511*	*320*	*191*	*614*	*389*	*225*
(i) British Territory ..	**5,110**	**3,819**	**1,291**	**409**	**259**	**150**	**313**	**215**	**98**
Ajmer-Merwara ..	49	21	28	4	2	2	10	3	7
Andamans and Nicobar ..	9	2	7	1	..	1	3	3	..
Assam ..	80	41	39	25	14	11	22	16	6
Baluchistan ..	58	17	41	3	3	..	25	25	..
Bengal ..	833	449	384	152	80	72	70	37	33
Burma ..	40	19	21	1	..	1	..	..	..
Coorg ..	..	..	..	..	..	..	..	..	..
Delhi ..	20	14	6	6	4	2	14	7	7
North-West Frontier Province	353	317	36	7	6	1	4	4	..
Punjab ..	3,668	2,939	729	210	150	60	165	120	45
(ii) States and Agencies ..	**920**	**578**	**342**	**102**	**61**	**41**	**301**	**174**	**127**
Assam States ..	..	..	..	..	..	..	..	..	..
Baroda ..	..	..	..	5	4	1	4	..	4
Bihar and Orissa States ..	..	..	..	..	..	..	..	..	..
Bengal States ..	..	..	..	..	..	..	..	..	..
Bombay States ..	22	11	11	..	..	..	18	13	5
Kashmir ..	62	54	8	..	..	..	1	1	..
Madras States (including Cochin and Travancore).	..	..	..	..	..	..	..	..	..
Mysore ..	52	27	25	2	2	..	..	..	..
North-West Frontier Province (Agencies and Tribal areas).	..	..	..	..	..	..	1	1	..
Punjab States ..	23	6	17	..	..	..	19	13	6
Rajputana Agency ..	757	480	277	95	55	40	258	146	112
Sikkim ..	..	..	..	..	..	..	..	..	..
United Provinces States ..	4	..	4	..	..	..	..	..	..
Baluchistan States ..	..	..	..	..	..	..	..	..	..

District, State, Province or Country where born.	District where enumerated.								
	Jubbulpore.			Mandla.			Seoni.		
	Persons.	Males.	Females.	Persons.	Males.	Females.	Persons.	Males.	Females.
1	11	12	13	14	15	16	17	18	19
(c) French and Portuguese Settlements.	**53**	..	**53**	**8**	**5**	**3**	..	..	..
(d) India unspecified	..	..	..	..	..	..	..	..	..
B.—Born in other Asiatic Countries.	**178**	**134**	**44**	**47**	**41**	**6**	**33**	**31**	**2**
(i) Within British Dominions	*22*	*11*	*11*	*1*	*1*	..	..	..	..
Ceylon	17	10	7	1	1	..	..	..	..
Straits Settlements and Malaya	..	..	..	..	..	..	..	..	..
Elsewhere	5	1	4	..	..	..	..	..	..
(ii) Outside British Dominions	*152*	*119*	*33*	*45*	*39*	*6*	*33*	*31*	*2*
Afghanistan	70	65	5	36	34	2	27	27	..
China	13	11	2	..	..	..	1	1	..
Nepal	57	38	19	8	5	3	5	3	2
Elsewhere	12	5	7	1	..	1	..	..	..
(iii) Asia, unspecified	*4*	*4*	..	*1*	*1*	..	..	..	..
C.—Born in Europe	**2,236**	**1,835**	**401**	**20**	**10**	**10**	**10**	**4**	**6**
(i) United Kingdom and Ireland.	2,212	1,827	385	13	8	5	10	4	6
(ii) British possessions in Europe	..	..	..	..	..	..	..	..	..
(iii) Continental Europe	24	8	16	7	2	5	..	..	..
(iv) Europe, unspecified	..	..	..	..	..	..	..	..	..
D.—Born in Africa	**17**	**10**	**7**	**1**	..	**1**	**1**	..	**1**
(i) Within British Dominions	..	..	..	*1*	..	*1*	*1*	..	*1*
Cape Colony	..	..	..	..	..	..	..	..	..
Kenya (British East Africa)	..	..	..	1	..	1	..	..	..
Mauritius	..	..	..	..	..	..	..	..	..
Natal	..	..	..	..	..	..	..	..	..
Nyasaland	..	..	..	..	..	..	..	..	..
Tanganyika	..	..	..	..	..	..	..	..	..
Transvaal	..	..	..	..	..	..	..	..	..
Uganda	..	..	..	..	..	..	..	..	..
Zanzibar	..	..	..	..	..	..	..	..	..
Elsewhere	..	..	..	..	..	..	1	..	1
(ii) Outside British Dominions	*1*	..	*1*	..	..	..	..	..	..
Mozambique	..	..	..	..	..	..	..	..	..
Elsewhere	1	..	1	..	..	..	..	..	..
(iii) Africa, unspecified	*16*	*10*	*6*	..	..	..	..	..	..
E.—Born in America	**32**	**12**	**20**	..	..	..	**2**	**1**	**1**
(i) Within British Dominions	*2*	*2*	..	..	..	..	..	..	..
British Guiana	..	..	..	..	..	..	..	..	..
British Honduras	..	..	..	..	..	..	..	..	..
Canada	2	2	..	..	..	..	..	..	..
Elsewhere	..	..	..	..	..	..	..	..	..
(ii) Outside British Dominions	*26*	*9*	*17*	..	..	..	..	..	..
United States	26	9	17	..	..	..	..	..	..
Elsewhere	..	..	..	..	..	..	..	..	..
(iii) America, unspecified	*4*	*1*	*3*	..	..	..	*2*	*1*	*1*
F.—Born in Australasia	**2**	**1**	**1**	..	..	..	**1**	..	**1**
(i) Within British Dominions	*2*	*1*	*1*	..	..	..	*1*	..	*1*
Australia	1	1	..	..	..	..	..	..	..
Fiji Islands	..	..	..	..	..	..	..	..	..
New Zealand	1	..	1	..	..	..	1	..	1
Tasmania	..	..	..	..	..	..	..	..	..
Other British possessions in Australasia.	..	..	..	..	..	..	..	..	..
(ii) Outside British Dominions	..	..	..	..	..	..	..	..	..
(iii) Australasia, unspecified	..	..	..	..	..	..	..	..	..
G.—Born at Sea	..	..	..	..	..	..	..	..	..
H.—Birthplace unspecified or not returned.	..	..	..	..	..	..	..	..	..

District, State, Province or Country where born.	District where enumerated. Narsinghpur. Persons.	Narsinghpur. Males.	Narsinghpur. Females.	Hoshangabad. Persons.	Hoshangabad. Males.	Hoshangabad. Females	Nimar. Persons.	Nimar. Males	Nimar. Females.
1	20	21	22	23	24	25	26	27	28
Total Population ..	**321,481**	**161,417**	**160,064**	**486,630**	**248,226**	**238,404**	**466,931**	**242,042**	**224,889**
A.—Born in India ..	**321,464**	**161,403**	**160,061**	**486,322**	**247,998**	**238,324**	**466,826**	**241,953**	**224,873**
I.—In Central Provinces and Berar.	**316,640**	**159,325**	**157,315**	**457,583**	**234,433**	**223,150**	**407,859**	**211,730**	**196,129**
(i) British Territory ..	**316,630**	**159,322**	**157,308**	**456,732**	**234,110**	**222,622**	**406,367**	**211,013**	**195,354**
District of enumeration ..	*296,871*	*150,819*	*146,052*	*432,325*	*223,237*	*209,088*	*358,547*	*186,882*	*171,665*
Other districts of British C. P. and Berar.	*19,759*	*8,503*	*11,256*	*24,407*	*10,873*	*13,534*	*47,820*	*24,131*	*23,689*
C. P. and Berar unspecified ..	..	..	..	..	..	..	..	..	..
(ii) Central Provinces States	10	3	7	851	323	528	1,492	717	775
Makrai	..	..	..	831	311	520	1,479	711	768
Bastar	3	1	2	4	4	..	6	3	3
Kanker	4	..	4	..	..	..	..	..	..
Nandgaon	1	1	..	2	2	..	7	3	4
Khairagarh	..	..	..	..	..	..	..	..	..
Chhuikhadan ..	..	..	..	..	..	..	..	..	..
Kawardha	1	..	1	..	..	..	..	..	..
Sakti	..	..	..	..	..	..	..	..	..
Raigarh	..	..	..	13	5	8	..	..	..
Sarangarh	..	..	..	..	..	..	..	..	..
Changbhakar ..	..	..	..	..	..	..	..	..	..
Korea	1	1	..	1	1	..	..	..	..
Surguja	..	..	..	..	..	..	..	..	..
Udaipur	..	..	..	..	..	..	..	..	..
Jashpur	..	..	..	..	..	..	..	..	..
II.—Provinces and States beyond C. P. and Berar.	**4,824**	**2,078**	**2,746**	**28,739**	**13,565**	**15,174**	**58,967**	**30,223**	**28,744**
(a) *Provinces and States adjacent to C. P. and Berar.*	*4,662*	*1,979*	*2,683*	*25,208*	*11,178*	*14,030*	*53,945*	*27,011*	*26,934*
(i) British Territory ..	**922**	**624**	**298**	**6,667**	**4,046**	**2,621**	**35,401**	**18,215**	**17,186**
Bihar and Orissa ..	12	9	3	58	40	18	34	22	12
United Provinces of Agra and Oudh.	748	512	236	4,770	2,881	1,889	8,651	5,606	3,045
Bombay (including Aden) ..	144	90	54	1,679	1,023	656	26,620	12,528	14,092
Madras	18	13	5	160	102	58	96	59	37
(ii) States and Agencies ..	**3,740**	**1,355**	**2,385**	**18,541**	**7,132**	**11,409**	**18,544**	**8,796**	**9,748**
Central India (Agency) ..	3,672	1,312	2,360	17,517	6,602	10,915	16,677	7,808	8,869
Rewa	*262*	*151*	*111*	*937*	*435*	*502*	*590*	*407*	*183*
Panna	*97*	*58*	*39*	*84*	*51*	*33*	*173*	*104*	*69*
Bhopal	*3,008*	*945*	*2,063*	*12,468*	*4,293*	*8,175*	*3,599*	*1,863*	*1,736*
Indore	*62*	*27*	*35*	*3,116*	*1,211*	*1,905*	*9,736*	*4,035*	*5,701*
Other States ..	*243*	*131*	*112*	*912*	*612*	*300*	*2,579*	*1,399*	*1,180*
Hyderabad	10	7	3	141	85	56	857	423	434
Gwalior	58	36	22	883	445	438	1,010	565	445
(b) *Other Provinces and States in India.*	*162*	*99*	*63*	*3,471*	*2,351*	*1,120*	*5,022*	*3,212*	*1,810*
(i) British Territory ..	**110**	**71**	**39**	**1,125**	**846**	**279**	**1,149**	**797**	**352**
Ajmer-Merwara ..	8	6	2	67	37	30	139	79	60
Andamans and Nicobars ..	..	..	..	..	..	..	..	..	..
Assam	3	1	2	11	8	3	1	..	1
Baluchistan	..	..	..	47	41	6	116	87	29
Bengal	22	10	12	102	48	54	117	65	52
Burma	..	..	..	14	9	5	3	..	3
Coorg	..	..	..	..	..	..	..	..	..
Delhi	2	2	..	32	22	10	70	38	32
North-West Frontier Province	3	3	..	65	49	16	16	12	4
Punjab	72	49	23	787	632	155	687	516	171
(ii) States and Agencies ..	**52**	**28**	**24**	**2,346**	**1,505**	**841**	**3,873**	**2,415**	**1,458**
Assam States ..	..	..	..	..	..	..	..	..	..
Baroda	..	..	..	27	12	15	21	8	13
Bihar and Orissa States ..	..	..	..	..	..	..	..	..	..
Bengal States ..	..	..	..	..	..	..	..	..	..
Bombay States ..	..	..	..	..	..	..	..	..	..
Kashmir	..	..	..	7	7	..	5	3	2
Madras States (including Cochin and Travancore).	..	..	..	1	1	..	..	..	..
Mysore	..	..	..	40	19	21	35	21	14
North-West Frontier Province (Agencies and Tribal areas).	..	..	..	..	..	..	..	..	..
Punjab States ..	..	..	..	1	1	..	..	..	..
Rajputana Agency ..	51	27	24	2,260	1,457	803	3,812	2,383	1,429
Sikkim	..	..	..	..	..	..	..	..	..
United Provinces States ..	1	1	..	10	8	2	..	..	..
Baluchistan States ..	..	..	..	..	..	..	..	..	..

Part A.—Districts and States—*continued*. **TABLE VI**

District State, Province or Country where born.	District where enumerated.								
	Narsinghpur.			Hoshangabad.			Nimar.		
	Persons.	Males.	Females.	Persons.	Males.	Females.	Persons.	Males.	Females.
1	20	21	22	23	24	25	26	27	28
(c) French and Portuguese Settlements.	..	..	..	**60**	**36**	**24**	..	..	..
(d) India unspecified ..	..	..	..	..	..	..	..	..	..
B.—Born in other Asiatic Countries.	**13**	**12**	**1**	**73**	**62**	**11**	**55**	**51**	**4**
(i) Within British Dominions ..	..	..	..	*4*	*3*	*1*	*2*	*2*	..
Ceylon	..	..	..	3	2	1	2	2	..
Straits Settlements and Malaya	..	..	..	1	1	..	..	..	..
Elsewhere	..	..	..	..	..	..	..	..	..
(ii) Outside British Dominions ..	*13*	*12*	*1*	*69*	*59*	*10*	*53*	*49*	*4*
Afghanistan	12	11	1	8	8	..	32	32	..
China	..	..	..	..	..	..	..	..	..
Nepal	1	1	..	59	49	10	14	10	4
Elsewhere	..	..	..	2	2	..	7	7	..
(iii) Asia, unspecified ..	..	..	..	..	..	..	..	..	..
C.—Born in Europe ..	**3**	**2**	**1**	**223**	**160**	**63**	**22**	**18**	**4**
(i) United Kingdom and Ireland.	1	1	..	216	155	61	18	14	4
(ii) British possessions in Europe	..	..	..	..	..	..	..	..	..
(iii) Continental Europe ..	1	..	1	7	5	2	2	2	..
(iv) Europe, unspecified ..	*1*	*1*	..	..	..	..	*2*	*2*	..
D.—Born in Africa ..	..	..	..	**3**	**2**	**1**	**19**	**17**	**2**
(i) Within British Dominions ..	..	..	..	*3*	*2*	*1*	..	..	..
Cape Colony ..	..	..	..	..	..	..	..	..	..
Kenya (British East Africa) ..	..	..	..	..	..	..	..	..	..
Mauritius	..	..	..	..	..	..	..	..	..
Natal	..	..	..	..	..	..	..	..	..
Nyasaland	..	..	..	..	..	..	..	..	..
Tanganyika	..	..	..	..	..	..	..	..	..
Transvaal	..	..	..	..	..	..	..	..	..
Uganda	..	..	..	..	..	..	..	..	..
Zanzibar	..	..	..	..	..	..	..	..	..
Elsewhere	..	..	..	3	2	1	..	..	..
(ii) Outside British Dominions ..	..	..	..	..	..	..	..	..	..
Mozambique ..	..	..	..	..	..	..	..	..	..
Elsewhere	..	..	..	..	..	..	..	..	..
(iii) Africa, unspecified ..	..	..	..	..	..	..	*19*	*17*	*2*
E.—Born in America ..	**1**	..	**1**	**6**	**3**	**3**	**7**	**2**	**5**
(i) Within British Dominions ..	..	..	..	*2*	*2*	..	..	..	..
British Guiana ..	..	..	..	..	..	..	..	..	..
British Honduras ..	..	..	..	..	..	..	..	..	..
Canada	..	..	..	..	..	..	..	..	..
Elsewhere	..	..	..	2	2	..	..	..	..
(ii) Outside British Dominions ..	..	..	..	..	..	..	..	..	..
United States ..	..	..	..	..	..	..	..	..	..
Elsewhere	..	..	..	..	..	..	..	..	..
(iii) America, unspecified ..	*1*		*1*	*4*	*1*	*3*	*7*	*2*	*5*
F.—Born in Australasia ..	..	..	..	**2**	..	**2**	**2**	**1**	**1**
(i) Within British Dominions ..	..	..	..	*2*	..	*2*	*2*	*1*	*1*
Australia	..	..	..	2	..	2	..	..	..
Fiji Islands	..	..	..	..	..	..	2	1	1
New Zealand ..	..	..	..	..	..	..	..	..	..
Tasmania	..	..	..	..	..	..	..	..	..
Other British possessions in Australasia.	..	..	..	..	..	..	..	..	..
(ii) Outside British Dominions ..	..	..	..	..	..	..	..	..	..
(ii) Australasia, unspecified ..	..	..	..	..	..	..	..	..	..
G.—Born at Sea ..	..	..	..	**1**	**1**	..	..	..	—
H.—Birthplace unspecified or not returned.	..	..	..	..	..	..	..	..	—

District, State, Province or Country where born.	District where enumerated.								
	Betul.			Chhindwara.			Wardha.		
	Persons.	Males.	Females.	Persons.	Males.	Females.	Persons.	Males.	Females.
1	29	30	31	32	33	34	35	36	37
Total Population ..	**406,252**	**201,114**	**205,138**	**573,272**	**285,007**	**288,265**	**516,266**	**261,394**	**254,872**
A.—Born in India ..	**406,211**	**201,091**	**205,120**	**573,007**	**284,804**	**288,203**	**516,239**	**261,373**	**254,866**
I.—In Central Provinces and Berar.	**402,843**	**199,027**	**203,816**	**564,352**	**279,052**	**285,300**	**502,854**	**252,859**	**249,995**
(i) British Territory ..	**402,838**	**199,026**	**203,812**	**564,341**	**279,045**	**285,296**	**502,824**	**252,844**	**249,980**
District of enumeration ..	*384,977*	*190,701*	*194,276*	*529,374*	*264,196*	*265,178*	*418,598*	*217,777*	*200,821*
Other districts of British C. P. and Berar.	*17,861*	*8,325*	*9,536*	*34,967*	*14,849*	*20,118*	*84,226*	*35,067*	*49,159*
C. P. and Berar unspecified ..	..	..	..	..	..	..	..	..	..
(ii) Central Provinces States	**5**	**1**	**4**	**11**	**7**	**4**	**30**	**15**	**15**
Makrai	2	1	1	1	..	1	..	..	..
Bastar	..	..	..	..	..	..	12	8	4
Kanker	..	..	..	..	..	..	3	..	3
Nandgaon	2	..	2	5	4	1	8	1	7
Khairagarh	..	..	..	5	3	2	..	..	..
Chhuikhadan ..	..	..	..	.	..	..	..	..	..
Kawardha	..	..	..	..	..	..	1	1	..
Sakti	..	..	..	..	..	..	..	..	..
Raigarh	1	..	1	..	..	..	..	..	..
Sarangarh	..	..	..	..	..	..	..	..	..
Changbhakar ..	..	..	..	..	..	..	..	..	..
Korea	..	..	..	..	..	..	..	..	..
Surguja	..	..	..	..	..	..	..	..	..
Udaipur	..	..	..	..	..	..	6	5	1
Jashpur	..	..	..	..	..	..	..	..	..
II.—Provinces and States beyond C. P. and Berar.	**3,368**	**2,064**	**1,304**	**8,655**	**5,752**	**2,903**	**13,385**	**8,514**	**4,871**
(a) Provinces and States adjacent to C. P. and Berar.	*2,667*	*1,593*	*1,074*	*7,507*	*4,972*	*2,535*	*9,403*	*6,107*	*3,296*
(i) British Territory ..	**1,905**	**1,161**	**744**	**4,146**	**2,889**	**1,257**	**4,963**	**3,104**	**1,859**
Bihar and Orissa ..	3	2	1	92	48	44	10	9	1
United Provinces of Agra and Oudh.	1,400	857	543	3,247	2,322	925	2,863	1,896	967
Bombay (including Aden) ..	458	279	179	663	429	234	1,972	1,121	851
Madras	44	23	21	144	90	54	118	78	40
(ii) States and Agencies ..	**762**	**432**	**330**	**3,361**	**2,083**	**1,278**	**4,440**	**3,003**	**1,437**
Central India (Agency) ..	665	376	289	3,235	2,005	1,230	3,719	2,581	1,138
Rewa	*157*	*112*	*45*	*2,046*	*1,301*	*745*	*3,154*	*2,234*	*920*
Panna	*12*	*8*	*4*	*154*	*98*	*56*	*163*	*101*	*62*
Bhopal	*260*	*122*	*138*	*379*	*208*	*171*	*56*	*33*	*23*
Indore	*84*	*40*	*44*	*41*	*25*	*16*	*121*	*75*	*46*
Other States ..	*152*	*94*	*58*	*615*	*373*	*242*	*225*	*138*	*87*
Hyderabad	36	18	18	50	29	21	637	372	265
Gwalior	61	38	23	76	49	27	84	50	34
(b) Other Provinces and States in India.	*694*	*465*	*229*	*1,148*	*780*	*368*	*3,974*	*2,399*	*1,575*
(i) British Territory ..	**282**	**217**	**65**	**635**	**480**	**155**	**319**	**208**	**111**
Ajmer-Merwara ..	33	26	7	8	7	1	59	26	33
Andamans and Nicobars ..	..	..	..	..	..	..	..	..	..
Assam	4	4	..	7	5	2	4	3	1
Baluchistan	9	8	1	18	15	3	34	31	3
Bengal	38	19	19	136	71	65	54	26	28
Burma	1	1	..	11	7	4	13	8	5
Coorg	..	..	..	..	..	..	..	..	..
Delhi	..	..	..	9	4	5	10	3	7
North-West Frontier Province	27	26	1	120	114	6	12	12	..
Punjab	170	133	37	326	257	69	133	99	34
(ii) States and Agencies ..	**412**	**248**	**164**	**513**	**300**	**213**	**3,655**	**2,191**	**1,464**
Assam States ..	..	..	..	..	..	..	1	..	1
Baroda	2	1	1	..	..	..	53	31	22
Bihar and Orissa States ..	..	..	..	..	..	..	14	10	4
Bengal States ..	..	..	..	..	..	..	..	..	..
Bombay States ..	..	..	..	10	10	..	713	422	291
Kashmir	5	5	..	2	..	2	2	1	1
Madras States (including Cochin and Travancore).	..	..	..	3	3	..	96	79	17
Mysore	6	4	2	9	7	2	23	15	8
North-West Frontier Province (Agencies and Tribal areas).	..	..	..	2	2	..	..	..	..
Punjab States ..	8	..	8	4	2	2	11	6	5
Rajputana Agency ..	391	238	153	483	276	207	2,733	1,623	1,110
Sikkim	..	..	..	..	..	..	..	..	..
United Provinces States ..	..	..	..	..	..	..	..	..	..
Baluchistan States ..	..	..	..	..	..	..	9	4	5

District, State, Province or Country where born.	District where enumerated								
	Betul.			Chhindwara.			Wardha.		
	Persons.	Males.	Females.	Persons.	Males.	Females.	Persons.	Males.	Females.
1	29	30	31	32	33	34	35	36	37
(c) French and Portuguese Settlements.	7	6	1	..	..	..	8	8	..
(d) India, unspecified ..	..	..	..	..	..	..	..	..	..
B.—Born in other Asiatic Countries.	13	11	2	205	171	34	18	16	2
(i) Within British Dominions ..	..	..	..	*1*	*1*	..	*2*	*1*	*1*
Ceylon	..	..	..	1	1	..	2	1	1
Straits Settlements and Malaya	..	..	..	..	..	..	..	..	..
Elsewhere	..	..	..	..	..	..	..	..	..
(ii) Outside British Dominions ..	*12*	*10*	*2*	*199*	*166*	*33*	*16*	*15*	*1*
Afghanistan	7	7	..	193	165	28	14	13	1
China	..	..	..	..	..	..	..	..	..
Nepal	5	3	2	6	1	5	..	..	..
Elsewhere	..	..	..	..	..	..	2	2	..
(iii) Asia, unspecified ..	*1*	*1*	..	*5*	*4*	*1*	..	..	..
C.—Born in Europe ..	24	9	15	60	32	28	7	5	2
(i) United Kingdom and Ireland.	14	5	9	42	26	16	7	5	2
(ii) British possessions in Europe	..	..	..	..	..	..	..	..	..
(iii) Continental Europe ..	8	3	5	15	3	12	..	..	..
(iv) Europe, unspecified ..	*2*	*1*	*1*	*3*	*3*	..	..	..	..
D.—Born in Africa ..	..	..	..	..	..	..	..	..	..
(i) Within British Dominions ..	..	..	..	..	..	..	..	..	..
Cape Colony ..	..	..	..	..	..	..	..	..	..
Kenya (British East Africa) ..	..	..	..	..	..	..	..	..	..
Mauritius	..	..	..	..	..	..	..	..	..
Natal	..	..	..	..	..	..	..	..	..
Nyasaland	..	..	..	..	..	..	..	..	..
Tanganyika	..	..	..	..	..	..	..	..	..
Transvaal	..	..	..	..	..	..	..	..	..
Uganda	..	..	..	..	..	..	..	..	..
Zanzibar	..	..	..	..	..	..	..	..	..
Elsewhere	..	..	..	..	..	..	..	..	..
(ii) Outside British Dominions ..	..	..	..	..	..	..	..	..	..
Mozambique ..	..	..	..	..	..	..	..	..	..
Elsewhere	..	..	..	..	..	..	..	..	..
(iii) Africa, unspecified ..	..	..	..	..	..	..	..	..	..
E.—Born in America ..	3	2	1	..	..	..	2	..	2
(i) Within British Dominions ..	*1*	..	*1*	..	..	..	..	..	..
British Guiana ..	..	..	..	..	..	..	..	..	..
British Honduras ..	..	..	..	..	..	..	..	..	..
Canada	1	..	1	..	..	..	..	..	..
Elsewhere	..	..	..	..	..	..	..	..	..
(ii) Outside British Dominions ..	..	..	..	..	..	..	*2*	..	*2*
United States ..	..	..	..	..	..	..	2	..	2
Elsewhere . ..	..	..	..	..	..	..	..	..	..
(iii) America, unspecified ..	*2*	*2*	..	..	..	..	..	..	..
F.—Born in Australasia ..	1	1	..	..	..	..	..	..	..
(i) Within British Dominions ..	..	..	..	..	..	..	..	..	..
Australia	..	..	..	..	..	..	..	..	..
Fiji Islands	..	..	..	..	..	..	..	..	..
New Zealand ..	..	..	..	..	..	..	..	..	..
Tasmania	..	..	..	..	..	..	..	..	..
Other British possessions in Australasia.	..	..	..	..	..	..	..	..	..
(ii) Outside British Dominions ..	..	..	..	..	..	..	..	..	..
(iii) Australasia, unspecified ..	*1*	*1*	..	..	..	..	..	..	..
G.—Born at Sea ..	..	..	..	..	..	..	..	..	..
H.—Birthplace unspecified or not returned.	..	..	..	..	..	..	..	..	..

District, State, Province or Country where born.	District where enumerated.								
	Nagpur.			Chanda.			Bhandara.		
	Persons.	Males.	Females.	Persons.	Males.	Females.	Persons.	Males.	Females.
1	38	39	40	41	42	43	44	45	46
Total Population ..	**940,049**	**481,246**	**458,803**	**759,695**	**381,204**	**378,491**	**824,496**	**408,799**	**415,697**
A.—Born in India	**938,655**	**480,080**	**458,575**	**759,623**	**381,149**	**378,474**	**824.357**	**408,693**	**415,664**
I.—In Central Provinces and Berar.	**905,439**	**459,131**	**446,308**	**742,872**	**372,243**	**370,629**	**818,550**	**404,912**	**413,638**
(i) British Territory ..	**904,591**	**458,678**	**445,913**	**741,139**	**371,391**	**369,748**	**818,213**	**404,778**	**413,435**
District of enumeration ..	*805,276*	*414,300*	*390,976*	*708,119*	*356,705*	*351,414*	*758,305*	*385,665*	*372,640*
Other districts of British C. P. and Berar.	*99,315*	*44,378*	*54,937*	*33,020*	*14,686*	*18,334*	*59,908*	*19,113*	*40,795*
C. P. and Berar unspecified ..	..	..	..	..	..	..	..	..	..
(ii) Central Provinces States.	**848**	**453**	**395**	**1,733**	**852**	**881**	**337**	**134**	**203**
Makrai	..	..	..	..	..	..	1	..	1
Bastar	48	22	26	1,490	694	796	1	..	1
Kanker	9	4	5	68	35	33	5	2	3
Nandgaon	482	254	228	146	106	40	189	81	108
Khairagarh	227	128	99	26	14	12	108	39	69
Chhuikhadan ..	2	1	1	..	..	..	18	..	18
Kawardha	9	5	4	..	..	..	..	..	..
Sakti	6	..	6	..	..	..	..	..	..
Raigarh	21	10	11	..	..	..	2	1	1
Sarangarh	4	2	2	2	2	..	2	..	2
Changbhakar ..	..	..	..	..	..	..	2	2	..
Korea	4	1	3	..	..	..	..	..	..
Surguja	5	3	2	..	..	..	..	..	..
Udaipur	27	23	4	1	1	..	9	9	..
Jashpur	4	..	4	..	..	..	..	..	..
II.—Provinces and States beyond C. P and Berar.	**33,216**	**20,949**	**12,267**	**16,751**	**8,906**	**7,845**	**5,807**	**3,781**	**2,026**
(a) *Provinces and States adjacent to C. P. and Berar.*	*25,186*	*15,719*	*9,467*	*15,386*	*7,971*	*7,415*	*3,869*	*2,548*	*1,321*
(i) British Territory ..	**19,369**	**12,116**	**7,253**	**2,608**	**1,766**	**842**	**2,531**	**1,763**	**768**
Bihar and Orissa ..	131	86	45	19	8	11	73	47	26
United Provinces of Agra and Oudh.	10,011	6,313	3,698	1,376	1,044	332	1,456	1,033	423
Bombay (including Aden) ..	6,717	4,228	2,489	858	498	360	735	497	238
Madras	2,510	1,489	1,021	355	216	139	267	186	81
(ii) States and Agencies ..	**5,817**	**3,603**	**2,214**	**12,778**	**6,205**	**6,573**	**1,338**	**785**	**553**
Central India (Agency) ..	4,717	3,022	1,695	349	245	104	1,186	697	489
Rewa	*3,157*	*2,057*	*1,100*	*281*	*197*	*84*	*986*	*582*	*404*
Panna	*289*	*209*	*80*	*7*	*6*	*1*	*55*	*35*	*20*
Bhopal	*303*	*168*	*135*	*17*	*11*	*6*	*15*	*3*	*12*
Indore	*348*	*200*	*148*	*31*	*19*	*12*	*32*	*21*	*11*
Other States ..	*620*	*388*	*232*	*13*	*12*	*1*	*98*	*56*	*42*
Hyderabad ..	961	492	469	12,412	5,948	6,464	119	59	60
Gwalior	139	89	50	17	12	5	33	29	4
(b) *Other Provinces and States in India.*	*7,640*	*5,009*	*2,631*	*1,356*	*928*	*428*	*1,936*	*1,231*	*705*
(i) British Territory ..	**4,997**	**3,441**	**1,556**	**410**	**268**	**142**	**593**	**381**	**212**
Ajmer-Merwara ..	829	508	321	129	70	59	19	17	2
Andamans and Nicobars ..	12	..	12	4	3	1	1	1	..
Assam ..	16	11	5	4	2	2	6	5	1
Baluchistan	61	54	7	39	35	4	2	1	1
Bengal . ..	1,333	700	633	66	39	27	248	150	98
Burma	26	15	11	2	1	1	4	4	..
Coorg	..	..	..	..	..	..	..	..	..
Delhi	263	218	45	3	2	1	41	35	6
North-West Frontier Province	97	90	7	30	22	8	39	27	12
Punjab	2,360	1,845	515	133	94	39	233	141	92
(ii) States and Agencies ..	**2,643**	**1,568**	**1,075**	**46**	**660**	**286**	**1,343**	**850**	**493**
Assam States ..	..	..	..	..	..	..	1	1	..
Baroda	103	59	44	17	11	6	17	9	8
Bihar and Orissa States ..	56	8	48	3	1	2	2	2	..
Bengal States ..	4	3	1	22	21	1	2	1	1
Bombay States ..	492	326	166	400	277	123	159	78	81
Kashmir	1	1	..	6	2	4	165	165	..
Madras States (including Cochin and Travancore).	22	9	13	15	4	11	4	4	..
Mysore	146	110	36	10	5	5	7	6	1
North-West Frontier Province (Agencies and Tribal areas).	..	..	..	..	..	..	1	..	1
Punjab States ..	110	94	16	8	6	2	25	15	10
Rajputana Agency ..	1,707	956	751	465	333	132	956	566	390
Sikkim	2	2	..	..	..	..	3	3	..
United Provinces States ..	..	..	..	..	..	..	1	..	1
Baluchistan States ..	..	..	..	..	..	..	..	..	..

District, State, Province or Country where born.	District where enumerated.								
	Nagpur.			Chanda.			Bhandara.		
	Persons.	Males.	Females	Persons.	Males.	Females.	Persons.	Males.	Females.
1	38	39	40	41	42	43	44	45	46
(c) French and Portuguese Settlements.	**344**	**202**	**142**	**7**	**7**	..	..	..	..
(d) India Unspecified ..	**46**	**19**	**27**	**2**	..	**2**	**2**	**2**	..
B.—Born in other Asiatic Countries.	**137**	**111**	**26**	**49**	**44**	**5**	**121**	**94**	**27**
(i) Within British Dominions ..	..	..	..	*2*	*1*	*1*	..	..	..
Ceylon ..	..	..	..	2	1	1	..	..	..
Straits Settlements and Malaya	..	..	..	..	..	..	..	..	..
Elsewhere	..	..	..	..	..	..	..	..	..
(ii) Outside British Dominions ..	*137*	*111*	*26*	*40*	*39*	*1*	*74*	*48*	*26*
Afghanistan	78	73	5	31	31	..	17	15	2
China	5	3	2	1	..	1	..	..	..
Nepal	41	23	18	..	..	..	57	33	24
Elsewhere	13	12	1	8	8	..	..	..	..
(iii) Asia, Unspecified ..	..	..	..	*7*	*4*	*3*	*47*	*46*	*1*
C.—Born in Europe ..	**1,212**	**1,029**	**183**	**20**	**11**	**9**	**14**	**10**	**4**
(i) United Kingdom and Ireland.	1,212	1,029	183	..	..	..	..	..	..
(ii) British possessions in Europe.	..	..	..	..	..	..	..	..	..
(iii) Continental Europe ..	..	..	..	..	..	..	..	..	..
(iv) Europe, Unspecified ..	..	..	..	*20*	*11*	*9*	*14*	*10*	*4*
D.—Born in Africa ..	**25**	**18**	**7**	..	..	..	**2**	..	**2**
(i) Within British Dominions ..	..	..	..	..	..	..	*2*	..	*2*
Cape Colony ..	..	..	..	..	..	..	..	..	..
Kenya (British East Africa) ..	..	..	..	..	..	..	..	..	..
Mauritius	..	..	..	..	..	..	..	..	..
Natal	..	..	..	..	..	..	..	..	..
Nyasaland	..	..	..	..	..	..	..	..	..
Tanganyika ..	..	..	..	..	..	..	..	..	..
Transvaal	..	..	..	..	..	..	..	..	..
Uganda	..	..	..	..	..	..	..	..	..
Zanzibar	..	..	..	..	..	..	..	..	..
Elsewhere	..	..	..	..	..	..	2	..	2
(ii) Outside British Dominions ..	..	..	..	..	..	..	..	..	..
Mozambique ..	..	..	..	..	..	..	..	..	..
Elsewhere	..	..	..	..	..	..	..	..	..
(iii) Africa, Unspecified ..	*25*	*18*	*7*	..	..	..	..	..	..
E.—Born in America ..	**19**	**7**	**12**	**3**	..	**3**	**2**	**2**	..
(i) Within British Dominions ..	..	..	..	..	..	..	..	..	..
British Guiana ..	..	..	..	..	..	..	..	..	..
British Honduras ..	..	..	..	..	..	..	..	..	..
Canada ..	..	..	..	..	..	..	..	..	..
Elsewhere ...	..	..	..	..	..	..	..	..	..
(ii) Outside British Dominions ..	..	..	..	..	..	..	*2*	*2*	..
United States ..	..	..	..	..	..	..	2	2	..
Elsewhere	..	..	..	..	..	..	..	..	..
(iii) America, Unspecified ..	*19*	*7*	*12*	*3*	..	*3*	..	..	..
F.—Born in Australasia ..	..	..	..	..	..	..	..	..	..
(i) Within British Dominions ..	..	..	..	..	..	..	..	..	..
Australia ..	..	..	..	..	..	..	..	..	..
Fiji Islands	..	..	..	..	..	..	..	..	..
New Zealand ..	..	..	..	..	..	..	..	..	..
Tasmania	..	..	..	..	..	..	..	..	..
Other British possessions in Australasia	..	..	..	..	..	..	..	..	..
(ii) Outside British Dominions ..	..	..	..	..	..	..	..	..	..
(iii) Australasia, Unspecified ..	..	..	..	..	..	..	..	..	..
G.—Born at Sea ..	..	..	..	..	..	..	..	..	..
H.—Birthplace unspecified or not returned.	**1**	**1**	..	..	..	..	..	..	—

TABLE VI

District, State, Province or Country where born.	District where enumerated.								
	Balaghat.			Raipur.			Bilaspur.		
	Persons.	Males.	Females.	Persons.	Males.	Females.	Persons.	Males	Females.
1	47	48	49	50	51	52	53	54	55
Total Population ..	**561,602**	**276,898**	**284,704**	**1,527,573**	**739,950**	**787,623**	**1,400,248**	**683,920**	**716,328**
A.—Born in India ..	**561,544**	**276,854**	**284,690**	**1,527,380**	**739,811**	**787,569**	**1,400,047**	**683,777**	**716,270**
I.—In Central Provinces and Berar.	**557,717**	**274,482**	**283,235**	**1,491,558**	**721,089**	**770,469**	**1,365,278**	**666,415**	**698,863**
(i) British Territory ..	**557,481**	**274,360**	**283,121**	**1,479,432**	**715,309**	**764,123**	**1,347,662**	**659,999**	**687,663**
District of enumeration ..	*508,649*	*252,055*	*256,594*	*1,436,800*	*692,432*	*744,368*	*1,321,656*	*646,600*	*675,056*
Other districts of British C. P. and Berar.	*48,832*	*22,305*	*26,527*	*42,632*	*22,877*	*19,755*	*26,006*	*13,399*	*12,607*
C. P. and Berar, Unspecified ..	..	..	..	..	..	..	..	..	..
(ii) Central Provinces States	**236**	**122**	**114**	**12,126**	**5,780**	**6,346**	**17,616**	**6,416**	**11,200**
Makrai ..	..	..	..	..	..	..	..	..	..
Bastar	31	24	7	935	433	502	55	19	36
Kanker	7	2	5	4,942	2,374	2,568	133	70	63
Nandgaon	12	2	10	920	432	488	201	73	128
Khairagarh	9	2	7	910	440	470	300	164	136
Chhuikhadan	..	..	..	187	87	100	44	18	26
Kawardha	169	88	81	176	86	90	2,587	866	1,721
Sakti	..	..	..	46	23	23	971	344	627
Raigarh	2	..	2	461	241	220	5,560	1,679	3,881
Sarangarh	..	..	..	3,520	1,647	1,873	2,537	676	1,861
Changbhakar ..	..	..	..	..	..	..	28	10	18
Korea	5	4	1	2	..	2	747	338	409
Surguja	1	..	1	13	6	7	2,878	1,413	1,465
Udaipur ..	..	..	..	6	4	2	1,554	739	815
Jashpur	..	..	..	8	7	1	21	7	14
II.—Provinces and States beyond C. P. and Berar.	**3,827**	**2,372**	**1,455**	**35,822**	**18,722**	**17,100**	**34,769**	**17,362**	**17,407**
(*a*) *Provinces and States adjacent to C. P. and Berar.*	2,749	1,686	1,063	29,067	14,804	14,263	30,308	15,076	15,232
(*i*) **British Territory** ..	**1,473**	**1,000**	**473**	**26,679**	**13,608**	**13,071**	**15,529**	**8,181**	**7,348**
Bihar and Orissa ..	118	91	27	18,786	9,023	9,763	4,421	1,785	2,636
United Provinces of Agra and Oudh.	1,025	689	336	5,181	3,137	2,044	8,822	5,238	3,584
Bombay (including Aden) ..	278	175	103	853	546	307	1,088	613	475
Madras	52	45	7	1,859	902	957	1,198	545	653
(ii) States and Agencies ..	**1,276**	**686**	**590**	**2,388**	**1,196**	**1,192**	**14,779**	**6,895**	**7,884**
Central India (Agency) ..	1,200	643	557	2,204	1,080	1,124	14,663	6,802	7,861
Rewa	*874*	*458*	*416*	*704*	*442*	*262*	*13,902*	*6,407*	*7,495*
Panna	*35*	*23*	*12*	*1,345*	*593*	*752*	*273*	*181*	*92*
Bhopal	*36*	*18*	*18*	*71*	*11*	*60*	*71*	*31*	*40*
Indore ..	*39*	*17*	*22*	*41*	*20*	*21*	*50*	*31*	*19*
Other States ..	*216*	*127*	*89*	*43*	*14*	*29*	*367*	*152*	*215*
Hyderabad	38	20	18	131	82	49	95	77	18
Gwalior	38	23	15	53	34	19	21	16	5
(*b*) *Other Provinces and States in India.*	*1,078*	*686*	*392*	*6,747*	*3,911*	*2,836*	*4,434*	*2,269*	*2,165*
(i) British Territory ..	**480**	**327**	**153**	**1,846**	**1,181**	**665**	**2,413**	**1,156**	**1,257**
Ajmer-Merwara ..	22	17	5	13	10	3	182	99	83
Andamans and Nicobars ..	..	..	..	..	..	..	2	1	1
Assam	58	32	26	51	35	16	60	21	39
Baluchistan	8	8	..	..	..	..	1	1	..
Bengal ..	76	43	33	816	436	380	905	401	504
Burma ..	1	..	1	4	3	1	4	1	3
Coorg	..	..	..	..	..	..	251	35	216
Delhi	9	4	5	8	2	6	..	..	..
North-West Frontier Province	20	15	5	35	24	11	25	22	3
Punjab	286	208	78	919	671	248	983	575	408
(ii) States and Agencies ..	**598**	**359**	**239**	**4,901**	**2,730**	**2,171**	**2,021**	**1,113**	**908**
Assam States ..	..	..	..	..	..	..	1	1	..
Baroda	16	5	11	17	15	2	21	20	1
Bihar and Orissa States ..	..	..	..	769	354	415	127	52	75
Bengal States ..	..	..	..	1	1	..	..	..	..
Bombay States ..	23	16	7	668	437	231	90	65	25
Kashmir	..	..	..	..	..	..	1	..	1
Madras States (including Cochin and Travancore).	3	3	..	..	..	..	3	2	1
Mysore	..	..	..	1	1	..	246	59	187
North-West Frontier Province (Agencies and Tribal areas).	..	..	..	..	..	..	..	..	..
Punjab States ..	3	2	1	30	21	9	164	110	54
Rajputana Agency ..	553	333	220	3,286	1,816	1,470	1,350	792	558
Sikkim	..	..	..	..	..	..	..	..	..
United Provinces States ..	..	..	..	129	85	44	18	12	6
Baluchistan States ..	..	..	..	..	..	..	..	..	..

Part A.—Districts and States—*continued.*

TABLE VI

District, State, Province or Country where born.	District where enumerated.								
	Balaghat.			Raipur.			Bilaspur.		
	Persons.	Males.	Females.	Persons.	Males.	Females.	Persons.	Males.	Females.
1	47	48	49	50	51	52	53	54	55
(c) French and Portuguese Settlements.	..	..	..	1	1	..	6	5	1
(d) India, Unspecified	..	..	..	7	6	1	21	12	9
B.—Born in other Asiatic countries.	**33**	**32**	**1**	**111**	**96**	**15**	**102**	**89**	**13**
(i) Within British Dominions	*4*	*3*	*1*	*3*	*3*	..	*10*	*7*	*3*
Ceylon	4	3	1	3	3	..	10	7	3
Straits Settlements and Malaya.	..	..	..	..	..	..	..	..	..
Elsewhere	..	..	..	..	..	..	..	..	..
(ii) Outside British Dominions	*29*	*29*	..	*103*	*88*	*15*	*91*	*82*	*9*
Afghanistan	25	25	..	53	53	..	72	71	1
China	..	..	..	..	..	..	..	..	..
Nepal	4	4	..	46	33	13	18	11	7
Elsewhere	..	..	..	4	2	2	1	..	1
(iii) Asia, Unspecified	...	..	..	*5*	*5*	..	*1*	..	*1*
C.—Born in Europe	**22**	**12**	**10**	**17**	**9**	**8**	**51**	**34**	**17**
(i) United Kingdom and Ireland.	20	11	9	11	6	5	42	28	14
(ii) British possessions in Europe.	..	..	..	..	..	..	..	..	..
(iii) Continental Europe	2	1	1	5	2	3	9	6	3
(iv) Europe, Unspecified	..	..	..	*1*	*1*	..	..	..	..
D.—Born in Africa	**1**	..	**1**	..	..	..	**2**	**2**	..
(i) Within British Dominions	..	..	..	..	..	..	*2*	*2*	..
Cape Colony	..	..	..	..	..	..	..	..	..
Kenya (British East Africa)	..	..	..	..	..	..	..	..	..
Mauritius	..	..	..	..	..	..	..	..	..
Natal	..	..	..	..	..	..	..	..	..
Nyasaland	..	..	..	..	..	..	2	2	..
Tanganyika	..	..	..	..	..	..	..	..	..
Transvaal	..	..	..	..	..	..	..	..	..
Uganda	..	..	..	..	..	..	..	..	..
Zanzibar	..	..	..	..	..	..	..	..	..
Elsewhere	..	..	..	..	..	..	..	..	..
(ii) Outside British Dominions	..	..	..	..	..	..	..	..	..
Mozambique	..	..	..	..	..	..	..	..	..
Elsewhere	..	..	..	..	..	..	..	..	..
(iii) Africa, Unspecified	*1*	..	*1*	..	..	..	..	..	..
E.—Born in America	**2**	..	**2**	**64**	**34**	**30**	**45**	**18**	**27**
(i) Within British Dominions	..	..	..	..	..	..	*4*	*2*	*2*
British Guiana	..	..	..	..	..	..	..	..	..
British Honduras	..	..	..	..	..	..	..	..	..
Canada	..	..	..	..	..	..	..	..	..
Elsewhere	..	..	..	..	..	..	4	2	2
(ii) Outside British Dominions	..	..	..	*27*	*8*	*19*	*7*	*1*	*6*
United States	..	..	..	27	8	19	7	1	6
Elsewhere	..	..	..	..	..	..	..	..	..
(iii) America, Unspecified	*2*	..	*2*	*37*	*26*	*11*	*34*	*15*	*19*
F.—Born in Australasia	..	..	..	**1**	..	**1**	**1**	..	**1**
(i) Within British Dominions	..	..	..	*1*	..	*1*	*1*	..	*1*
Australia	..	..	..	1	..	1	1	..	1
Fiji Islands	..	..	..	..	..	..	..	..	..
New Zealand	..	..	..	..	..	..	..	..	..
Tasmania	..	..	..	..	..	..	..	..	..
Other British possessions in Australasia.	..	..	..	..	..	..	..	..	..
(ii) Outside British Dominions	..	..	..	..	..	..	..	..	..
(iii) Australasia, Unspecified	..	..	..	..	..	..	..	..	..
G.—Born at Sea	..	..	..	..	..	..	..	..	..
H.—Birth place unspecified or not returned.	..	..	..	..	..	..	..	..	..

District, State, Province or Country where born.	District where enumerated.								
	Drug.			Amraoti.			Akola.		
	Persons.	Males.	Females.	Persons.	Males.	Females.	Persons.	Males.	Females.
1	56	57	58	59	60	61	62	63	64
Total Population ..	**817,924**	**390,367**	**427,557**	**941,604**	**485,593**	**456,011**	**876,362**	**448,896**	**427,466**
A.—Born in India	**817,863**	**390,329**	**427,534**	**941,429**	**485,490**	**455,939**	**876,279**	**448,834**	**427,445**
I.—In Central Provinces and Berar.	**814,017**	**387,821**	**426,196**	**907,855**	**464,963**	**442,892**	**825,738**	**420,337**	**405,401**
(i) British Territory ..	**784,752**	**376,597**	**408,155**	**907,816**	**464,939**	**442,877**	**825,688**	**420,296**	**405,392**
District of enumeration ..	*763,292*	*366,645*	*396,647*	*807,200*	*420,800*	*386,400*	*745,949*	*385,726*	*360,223*
Other districts of British C. P. and Berar.	*21,460*	*9,952*	*11,508*	*100,616*	*44,139*	*56,477*	*79,739*	*34,570*	*45,169*
C. P. and Berar, Unspecified ..	..	..	..	..	..	..	..	..	..
(ii) Central Provinces States	**29,265**	**11,224**	**18,041**	**39**	**24**	**15**	**50**	**41**	**9**
Makrai	..	..	..	1	1	..	..	..	..
Bastar	*561*	*300*	*261*	*10*	*5*	*5*	..	..	..
Kanker	4,127	1,873	2,254	1	1	..	..	..	..
Nandgaon	10,022	3,563	6,459	12	6	6	4	3	1
Khairagarh	7,957	3,030	4,927	1	..	1	..	..	..
Chhuikhadan ..	3,518	1,208	2,310	2	1	1	..	..	..
Kawardha	2,994	1,232	1,762	..	..	..	..	..	..
Sakti	..	..	..	..	..	..	..	..	..
Raigarh	63	6	57	6	5	1	7	5	2
Sarangarh	8	4	4	2	1	1	2	2	..
Changbhakar ..	..	..	..	..	..	..	..	..	..
Korea	4	..	4	..	..	..	..	..	..
Surguja	..	..	..	..	..	..	..	..	..
Udaipur	..	..	..	4	4	..	37	31	6
Jashpur	11	8	3	..	..	..	..	..	..
II.—Provinces and States beyond C. P. and Berar.	**3,846**	**2,508**	**1,338**	**33,574**	**20,527**	**13,047**	**50,541**	**28,497**	**22,044**
(a) Provinces and States adjacent to C. P. and Berar.	*1,956*	*1,342*	*614*	*24,398*	*14,758*	*9,640*	*37,568*	*19,632*	*17,936*
(i) British Territory ..	**1,617**	**1,115**	**502**	**17,431**	**10,701**	**6,730**	**20,068**	**11,916**	**8,152**
Bihar and Orissa ..	120	87	33	..	..	..	5	5	..
United Provinces of Agra and Oudh	1,242	863	379	9,182	6,192	2,990	6,108	4,284	1,824
Bombay (including Aden) ..	231	150	81	8,051	4,398	3,653	13,614	7,403	6,211
Madras	24	15	9	198	111	87	341	224	117
(ii) States and Agencies ..	**339**	**227**	**112**	**6,967**	**4,057**	**2,910**	**17,500**	**7,716**	**9,784**
Central India (Agency) ..	305	202	103	4,829	2,960	1,869	1,615	1,056	559
Rewa	*250*	*166*	*84*	*3,448*	*2,285*	*1,163*	*1,118*	*816*	*302*
Panna	*17*	*11*	*6*	*84*	*58*	*26*	*42*	*31*	*11*
Bhopal	*25*	*14*	*11*	*253*	*134*	*119*	*93*	*43*	*50*
Indore	*8*	*7*	*1*	*249*	*131*	*118*	*278*	*122*	*156*
Other States ..	*5*	*4*	*1*	*795*	*352*	*443*	*84*	*44*	*40*
Hyderabad ..	14	11	3	1,972	993	979	15,726	6,570	9,156
Gwalior	20	14	6	166	104	62	154	90	69
(b) Other Provinces and States in India.	*1,888*	*1,166*	*722*	*9,175*	*5,769*	*3,406*	*12,961*	*8,855*	*4,106*
(i) British Territory ..	**546**	**354**	**192**	**823**	**566**	**257**	**1,445**	**1,028**	**417**
Ajmer-Merwara ..	6	6	..	210	118	92	688	467	221
Andamans and Nicobars ..	..	..	..	..	..	..	2	1	1
Assam	40	22	18	3	3	..	19	10	9
Baluchistan	..	..	..	75	69	6	122	119	3
Bengal	264	151	113	73	51	22	70	41	29
Burma	1	1	..	11	7	4	4	4	..
Coorg	..	..	..	..	..	..	..	..	..
Delhi	2	1	1	86	48	38	60	50	10
North-West Frontier Province	1	1	..	40	34	6	46	34	12
Punjab ..	232	172	60	325	236	89	434	302	132
(ii) States and Agencies ..	**1,342**	**812**	**530**	**8,352**	**5,203**	**3,149**	**11,516**	**7,827**	**3,689**
Assam States ..	..	..	..	3	1	2	..	..	..
Baroda ..	..	..	..	58	29	29	72	38	34
Bihar and Orissa States ..	10	1	9	42	32	10	..	..	..
Bengal States ..	..	..	..	134	134	..	1	1	..
Bombay States ..	13	11	2	390	225	165	2,343	1,586	757
Kashmir	..	..	..	5	3	2	4	1	3
Madras States (including Cochin and Travancore).	..	..	..	10	..	10	5	5	..
Mysore	3	3	..	85	73	12	8	5	3
North-West Frontier Province (Agencies and Tribal areas).	..	..	..	5	5	..	..	..	..
Punjab States ..	7	7	..	45	36	9	64	54	10
Rajputana Agency ..	1,301	782	519	7,548	4,648	2,900	9,009	6,128	2,881
Sikkim	..	..	..	7	7	..	..	..	..
United Provinces States ..	8	8	..	20	10	10	10	9	1
Baluchistan States ..	..	..	..	..	..	..	..	..	..

District, State, Province or Country where born.	District where enumerated.								
	Drug.			Amraoti.			Akola.		
	Persons.	Males.	Females.	Persons.	Males.	Females.	Persons.	Males.	Females.
1	56	57	58	59	60	61	62	63	64
(c) French and Portuguese Settlements.	..	..	..	..	..	..	12	10	2
(d) India Unspecified ..	2	..	2	1	..	1	..	..	..
B.—Born in other Asiatic Countries.	33	26	7	138	79	59	53	51	2
(i) *Within British Dominions* ..	..	..	..	*97*	*49*	*48*	..	..	..
Ceylon ..	..	..	..	..	..	..	..	..	..
Straits Settlements and Malaya	..	..	..	..	..	..	..	..	..
Elsewhere	..	..	..	97	49	48	..	..	..
(ii) *Outside British Dominions*	*33*	*26*	*7*	*27*	*21*	*6*	*48*	*46*	*2*
Afghanistan ..	27	23	4	2	..	2	41	40	1
China	..	..	..	10	10	..	..	..	..
Nepal	1	1			3	3	5	4	1
Elsewhere	5	2			8	1	2	2	..
(iii) *Asia, Unspecified* ..	..	..	..	*14*	*9*	*5*	*5*	*5*	..
C.—Born in Europe ..	3	2	1	23	13	10	.	2	2
(i) United Kingdom and Ireland.	3	2	1	..	..	..		2	1
(ii) British possessions in Europe.	..	..	..	2	1	1	1	..	1
(iii) Continental Europe ..	..	..	..	..	..	..	..	..	..
(iv) *Europe, Unspecified* ..	..	..	..	*21*	*12*	*9*	..	..	..
D.—Born in Africa ..	..	..	..	7	4	3	7	3	4
(i) *Within British Dominions* ..	..	..	..	*7*	*4*	*3*	*1*	..	*1*
Cape Colony ..	..	..	..	..	..	..	..	..	..
Kenya (British East Africa) ..	..	..	..	7	4	3	..	..	..
Mauritius ..	..	..	..	..	..	..	..	..	..
Natal	..	..	..	..	..	..	1	..	1
Nyasaland	..	..	..	..	..	..	..	..	..
Tanganyika	..	..	..	..	..	..	..	..	..
Transvaal	..	..	..	..	..	..	..	..	..
Uganda	..	..	..	..	..	..	..	..	..
Zanzibar	..	..	..	..	..	..	..	..	..
Elsewhere	..	..	..	..	..	..	..	..	..
(ii) *Outside British Dominions*	..	..	..	..	..	..	..	..	..
Mozambique ..	..	..	..	..	..	..	..	..	..
Elsewhere	..	..	..	..	..	..	..	..	..
(iii) *Africa, Unspecified* ..	..	..	..	..	..	..	*6*	*3*	*3*
E.—Born in America ..	25	10	15	1	1	..	9	4	5
(i) *Within British Dominions* ..	..	..	..	*1*	*1*	..	*1*	*1*	..
British Guiana ..	..	..	..	..	..	..	..	..	..
British Honduras ..	..	..	..	..	..	..	..	..	..
Canada	..	..	..	1	1	..	1	1	..
Elsewhere	..	..	..	..	..	..	..	..	..
(ii) *Outside British Dominions*	*25*	*10*	*15*	..	..	..	..	..	..
United States ..	25	10	15	..	..	..	..	..	..
Elsewhere	..	..	..	..	..	..	..	..	..
(iii) *America, Unspecified* ..	..	..	..	..	..	..	8	3	*5*
F.—Born in Australasia ..	..	..	..	6	6	..	..	..	..
(i) *Within British Dominions* ..	..	..	..	*6*	*6*	..	..	..	..
Australia	..	..	..	3	3	..	..	..	..
Fiji Islands	..	..	..	..	..	..	..	..	..
New Zealand ..	..	..	..	..	..	..	..	..	..
Tasmania ..	..	..	..	3	3	..	..	..	..
Other British possessions in Australasia ..	..	..	..	..	..	..	..	..	..
(ii) *Outside British Dominions*	..	..	..	..	..	..	..	..	..
(iii) *Australasia, Unspecified* ..	..	..	..	..	..	..	..	..	..
G.—Born at Sea	..	..	..	..	..	..	..	..	..
H.—Birthplace unspecified or not returned.	..	..	..	..	..	..	10	2	8

District, State, Province or Country where born.	District where enumerated.								
	Buldana.			Yeotmal.			Central Provinces States.		
	Persons.	Males.	Females.	Persons.	Males.	Females.	Persons.	Males.	Females.
1	65	66	67	68	69	70	71	72	73
Total Population ..	**766.584**	**388,966**	**377,618**	**857,288**	**436,124**	**421,164**	**2.483,214**	**1,235,385**	**1,247,829**
A.—Born in India ..	**766,520**	**388,922**	**377,598**	**857,254**	**436,103**	**421,151**	**2,482,850**	**1,235,237**	**1,247,613**
I.—In Central Provinces and Berar.	***711,571***	***365,114***	***346,457***	***802,083***	***406,878***	***395,205***	***2,419,112***	***1,202,680***	***1,216,432***
(i) British Territory ..	**711,554**	**365,098**	**346,456**	**801,961**	**406,769**	**395,192**	**180,768**	**75,853**	**104,915**
District of enumeration ..	*682,728*	*353,265*	*329,463*	*706,385*	*362,830*	*343,555*	..	..	..
Other districts of British C. P. and Berar	*28,826*	*11,833*	*16,993*	*95,576*	*43,939*	*51,637*	*180,768*	*75,853*	*104,915*
C. P. and Berar Unspecified ..	..	..	..	..	..	..	..	..	..
(ii) Central Provinces States	**17**	**16**	**1**	**122**	**109**	**13**	**2,238,344**	**1,126,827**	**1,111,517**
Makrai	..	..	..	..	..	..	10,275	5,879	4,396
Bastar	..	..	..	7	7	..	506,457	253,853	252,604
Kanker	..	..	..	2	2	..	100,176	50,232	49,944
Nandgaon	..	..	..	17	13	4	152,469	74,394	78,075
Khairagarh	..	..	..	17	12	5	142,115	71,765	70,350
Chhuikhadan ..	..	..	..	..	..	..	26,514	13,628	12,886
Kawardha ..	..	..	..	..	..	..	61,016	30,151	30,865
Sakti	1	..	1	..	..	..	32,012	16,964	15,048
Raigarh	..	..	..	26	25	1	260,668	130,818	129,850
Sarangarh	..	..	..	..	..	..	116,079	57,855	58,224
Changbhakar ..	..	..	..	..	..	..	18,241	9,385	8,856
Korea ..	..	..	..	..	..	..	68,510	34,754	33,756
Surguja	..	..	..	..	..	..	482,502	244,461	238,041
Udaipur ..	16	16	..	45	42	3	80,318	41,099	39,219
Jashpur	..	..	..	8	8	..	180,992	91,589	89,403
II.—Provinces and States beyond C. P. and Berar.	**54,949**	**23,808**	**31,141**	**55,171**	**29,225**	**25,946**	**63,738**	**32,557**	**31,181**
(a) Provinces and States adjacent to C. P. and Berar.	*47,641*	*19,218*	*28,423*	*49,739*	*25,861*	*23,878*	*53,075*	*26,862*	*26,213*
(i) British Territory ..	**22,900**	**10,030**	**12,870**	**15,172**	**9,492**	**5,680**	**34,786**	**17,090**	**17,696**
Bihar and Orissa ..	9	7	2	34	32	2	22,625	10,323	12,302
United Provinces of Agra and Oudh.	1,668	1,104	564	4,621	2,850	1,771	8,347	4,789	3,558
Bombay (including Aden) ..	21,099	8,821	12,278	10,107	6,383	3,724	445	265	180
Madras	124	98	26	410	227	183	3,369	1,713	1,656
(ii) States and Agencies ..	**24,741**	**9,188**	**15,553**	**34,567**	**16,369**	**18,198**	**18,289**	**9,772**	**8,517**
Central India (Agency) ..	527	287	240	1,602	1,112	490	17,897	9,555	8,342
Rewa	*175*	*122*	*53*	*1,180*	*842*	*338*	*17,335*	*9,286*	*8,049*
Panna	*12*	*6*	*6*	*25*	*20*	*5*	*53*	*31*	*22*
Bhopal	*77*	*33*	*44*	*49*	*13*	*36*	*213*	*72*	*141*
Indore	*204*	*87*	*117*	*151*	*99*	*52*	*137*	*39*	*98*
Other States ..	*59*	*39*	*20*	*197*	*138*	*59*	*159*	*127*	*32*
Hyderabad ..	24,176	8,875	15,301	32,921	15,228	17,693	322	168	154
Gwalior ..	38	26	12	44	29	15	70	49	21
(b) Other Provinces and States in India.	*7,299*	*4,582*	*2,717*	*5,419*	*3,355*	*2,064*	*10,651*	*5,689*	*4,962*
(i) British Territory ..	**787**	**576**	**211**	**1,060**	**783**	**277**	**2,907**	**1,740**	**1,167**
Ajmer-Merwara ..	396	256	140	419	268	151	49	35	14
Andamans and Nicobars ..	57	57	..	..	..	..	4	4	..
Assam ..	3	2	1	4	2	2	149	66	83
Baluchistan	63	63	..	18	15	3	..	..	..
Bengal	38	24	14	35	11	24	1,213	659	554
Burma	1	1	..	1	1	..	9	6	3
Coorg	..	..	..	..	..	..	3	..	3
Delhi	17	8	9	71	48	23	40	21	19
North-West Frontier Province	34	29	5	94	88	6	49	33	16
Punjab ..	178	136	42	418	350	68	1,391	916	475
(ii) States and Agencies ..	**6,512**	**4,006**	**2,506**	**4,359**	**2,572**	**1,787**	**7,744**	**3,949**	**3,795**
Assam States ..	..	..	..	..	..	..	..	..	..
Baroda	38	15	23	23	13	10	8	5	3
Bihar and Orissa States ..	6	2	4	2	2	..	3,806	1,808	1,998
Bengal States ..	11	4	7	..	..	..	..	..	..
Bombay States ..	362	242	120	150	80	70	293	172	121
Kashmir	..	..	..	..	..	..	3	2	1
Madras States (including Cochin and Travancore).	..	..	..	5	1	4	.	..	..
Mysore	4	3	1	8	3	5	20	14	6
North-West Frontier Province (Agencies and Tribal areas).	..	..	..	..	..	..	..	..	..
Punjab States ..	12	7	5	40	11	29	175	90	85
Rajputana Agency ..	6,021	3,705	2,316	4,131	2,462	1,669	3,437	1,858	1,579
Sikkim	..	..	..	..	..	..	..	..	..
United Provinces States ..	58	28	30	..	..	..	2	..	2
Baluchistan States ..	.	..	..	..	..	..	..	..	..

Part A.—Districts and States—*concluded.* **TABLE VI**

District, State, Province or Country where born.	District where enumerated.								
	Buldana.			Yeotmal.			Central Provinces States.		
	Persons.	Males.	Females.	Persons.	Males.	Females.	Persons.	Males.	Females.
1	65	66	67	68	69	70	71	72	73
(c) French and Portuguese Settlements.	9	8	1	10	8	2	3	2	1
(d) India, unspecified ..	..	..	..	3	1	2	9	4	5
B.—Born in other Asiatic Countries.	42	34	8	13	10	3	297	103	194
(i) Within British Dominions ..	*1*	*1*	..	*3*	*3*	..	*4*	*2*	*2*
Ceylon	1	1	..	1	1	..	4	2	2
Straits Settlements and Malaya	..	..	..	..	..	..	..	..	..
Elsewhere	..	..	..	2	2	..	..	..	..
(ii) Outside British Dominions	*22*	*19*	*3*	*3*	..	*3*	*293*	*101*	*192*
Afghanistan	20	17	3	1	..	1	24	23	1
China	..	..	..	..	..	..	..	..	..
Nepal	1	1	..	..	..	..	256	71	185
Elsewhere	1	1	..	2	..	2	13	7	6
(iii) Asia, unspecified ..	*19*	*14*	*5*	*7*	*7*	..	..	..	..
C.—Born in Europe ..	7	4	3	5	5	..	54	39	15
(i) United Kingdom and Ireland.	..	..	..	..	..	..	38	27	11
(ii) British possessions in Europe.	..	..	..	..	..	..	..	..	..
(iii) Continental Europe ..	..	..	..	..	..	..	14	11	3
(iv) Europe, unspecified ..	*7*	*4*	*3*	*5*	*5*	..	*2*	*1*	*1*
D.—Born in Africa ..	1	..	1	1	..	1	..	..	..
(i) Within British Dominions ..	..	..	..	*1*	..	*1*	..	..	..
Cape Colony ..	..	..	..	..	..	..	..	..	..
Kenya (British East Africa). ..	..	..	..	..	..	..	..	..	..
Mauritius	..	..	..	..	..	..	..	..	..
Natal	..	..	..	..	..	..	..	..	..
Nyasaland	..	..	..	..	..	..	..	..	..
Tanganyika	..	..	..	..	..	..	..	..	..
Transvaal ..	..	..	..	..	..	..	..	..	..
Uganda	..	..	..	..	..	..	..	..	..
Zanzibar	..	..	..	..	..	..	..	..	..
Elsewhere	..	..	..	1	..	1	..	..	..
(ii) Outside British Dominions ..	..	..	..	..	..	..	..	..	..
Mozambique ..	..	..	..	..	..	..	..	..	..
Elsewhere	..	..	..	..	..	..	..	..	..
(iii) Africa, unspecified ..	*1*	..	*1*	..	..	..	..	..	..
E.—Born in America ..	13	5	8	15	6	9	13	6	7
(i) Within British Dominions ..	..	..	..	..	..	..	..	..	..
British Guiana ..	..	..	..	..	..	..	..	..	..
British Honduras ..	..	..	..	..	..	..	..	..	..
Canada	..	..	..	..	..	..	..	..	..
Elsewhere	..	..	..	..	..	..	..	..	..
(ii) Outside British Dominions	..	..	..	..	..	..	*8*	*4*	*4*
United States ..	..	..	..	..	..	..	8	4	4
Elsewhere	..	..	..	..	..	..	..	..	..
(iii) America, unspecified ..	*13*	*5*	*8*	*15*	*6*	*9*	*5*	*2*	*3*
F.—Born in Australasia ..	1	1	..	..	..	..	..	..	..
(i) Within British Dominions ..	..	..	..	..	..	..	..	..	..
Australia	..	..	..	..	..	..	..	..	..
Fiji Islands	..	..	..	..	..	..	..	..	..
New Ze lan ..	..	..	..	..	..	..	..	..	..
Tasmania	..	..	..	..	..	..	..	..	..
Other British possessions in Australasia.	..	..	..	..	..	..	..	..	..
(ii) Outside British Dominions	..	..	..	..	..	..	..	..	..
(iii) Australasia, unspecified ..	*1*	*1*	..	..	..	..	..	..	..
G.—Born at Sea ..	..	..	..	..	..	..	..	..	..
H.—Birthplace unspecified or no returned.	..	..	..	..	..	..	..	..	..

District, State, Province or Country where born.	Total population.			City where enumerated. Nagpur.			Jubbulpore.		
	Persons.	Males.	Females.	Persons.	Males	Females.	Persons.	Males.	Females.
1	2	3	4	5	6	7	8	9	10
Total Population ..	**339,547**	**185,661**	**153,886**	**215,165**	**116,403**	**98,762**	**124,382**	[illegible]	**55,124**
A.—Born in India ..	**336,838**	**183,523**	**153,315**	**214,808**	**116,188**	**98,620**	**122,030**	[illegible]	**54,695**
I.—In Central Provinces and Berar.	**279,670**	**148,350**	**131,320**	**191,886**	**101,853**	**90,033**	**87,734**	[illegible]	**41,287**
(i) British Territory ..	**278,977**	**147,952**	**131,025**	**191,246**	**101,481**	**89,765**	**87,731**	[illegible]	**41,260**
District of enumeration ..	*224,983*	*119,313*	*105,670*	*170,258*	[illegible]	*70,197*	*74,125*	[illegible]	*35,473*
Other districts of British C. P. and Berar.	*53,994*	*28,639*	*25,355*	*40,988*	*21,420*	*19,568*	*13,606*	*7,219*	*5,787*
Central Provinces and Berar, unspecified.	..	..	..	..	..	..	..	..	..
(ii) Central Provinces States	693	398	295	640	372	268	53	26	27
Makrai	..	..	..	..	..	..	..	..	..
Bastar	38	16	22	26	13	13	12	3	9
Kanker	8	3	5	6	3	5	..	..	..
Nandgaon	363	217	146	345	206	139	18	11	7
Khairagarh ..	191	111	80	183	107	76	8	4	4
Chhuikhadan ..	2	1	1	2	1	1	..	..	..
Kawardha	10	5	5	9	5	4	1	..	1
Sakti	6	..	6	6	..	6	..	..	..
Raigarh	30	15	15	21	10	11	9	5	4
Sarangarh	8	4	4	4	2	2	4	2	2
Changbhakar ..	..	..	..	..	..	..	..	..	..
Korea	3	..	3	3	..	3	..	..	..
Surguja	3	3	..	2	2	..	1	1	..
Udaipur	27	23	4	27	23	4	..	..	..
Jashpur	4	..	4	4	..	4	..	..	..
II.—Provinces and States beyond C. P. and Berar.	**57,168**	**35,173**	**21,995**	**22,922**	**14,335**	**8,587**	**34,246**	**20,838**	**13,408**
(a) Provinces and States adjacent to Central Provinces and Berar.	*47,029*	*28,248*	*18,781*	*17,864*	*11,171*	*6,693*	*29,165*	*17,077*	*12,088*
(i) British Territory ..	**29,991**	**18,581**	**11,410**	**14,581**	**9,147**	**5,434**	**15,410**	**9,434**	**5,976**
Bihar and Orissa ..	260	136	124	59	36	23	201	100	101
United Provinces of Agra and Oudh.	18,818	11,798	7,020	6,739	4,300	2,439	12,079	7,498	4,581
Bombay (including Aden) ..	7,539	4,644	2,895	5,616	3,479	2,137	1,923	1,165	758
Madras	3,374	2,003	1,371	2,167	1,332	835	1,207	671	536
(ii) States and Agencies ..	**17,038**	**9,667**	**7,371**	**3,283**	**2,024**	**1,259**	**13,755**	**7,643**	**6,112**
Central India (Agency) ..	15,750	8,932	6,818	2,529	1,624	905	13,221	7,308	5,913
Rewa	*9,453*	*5,312*	*4,141*	*1,398*	*918*	*480*	*8,045*	*4,393*	*3,652*
Panna	*1,807*	*1,031*	*776*	*215*	*156*	*59*	*1,592*	*875*	*717*
Bhopal	*594*	*332*	*262*	*239*	*140*	*99*	*355*	*192*	*163*
Indore	*816*	*463*	*353*	*304*	*175*	*129*	*512*	*288*	*224*
Other States ..	*3,080*	*1,794*	*1,286*	*363*	*234*	*129*	*2,717*	*1,560*	*1,157*
Hyderabad	987	544	443	667	345	322	320	199	121
Gwalior	301	191	110	67	35	32	214	136	78
(b) Other Provinces or States in India.	*9,769*	*6,734*	*3,035*	*4,734*	*2,972*	*1,762*	*5,035*	*3,761*	*1,274*
(i) British Territory ..	**7,437**	**5,401**	**2,036**	**3,059**	**2,049**	**1,010**	**4,378**	**3,352**	**1,026**
Ajmer-Merwara ..	224	135	89	188	123	65	36	12	24
Andamans and Nicobars ..	20	5	15	10	..	10	10	5	5
Assam	53	26	27	10	8	2	43	18	25
Baluchistan ..	59	36	23	27	21	6	32	15	17
Bengal	1,785	949	836	1,174	620	554	611	329	282
Burma	59	32	27	22	14	8	37	18	19
Coorg	..	..	..	..	..	..	..	..	..
Delhi	246	205	41	246	205	41	..	..	..
North-West Frontier Province.	403	366	37	61	59	2	342	308	34
Punjab	4,588	3,647	941	1,321	1,000	321	3,267	2,647	620
(ii) States and Agencies ..	**2,332**	**1,333**	**999**	**1,673**	**922**	**751**	**657**	**409**	**248**
Assam States ..	..	..	..	..	..	..	..	..	..
Baroda	96	53	43	96	53	43	..	..	..
Bihar and Orissa States ..	23	4	19	23	4	19	..	..	..
Bengal States ..	4	3	1	4	3	1	..	..	..
Bombay States ..	312	174	138	298	167	131	14	7	7
Kashmir	63	55	8	1	1	..	62	54	8
Madras States (including Cochin and Travancore).	22	9	13	22	9	13	..	..	..
Mysore	176	124	52	131	101	30	45	23	22
North-West Frontier Province (Agencies and Tribal areas).	..	..	..	..	..	..	..	..	..
Punjab States ..	64	33	31	41	27	14	23	6	17
Rajputana Agency ..	1,568	878	690	1,059	559	500	509	319	190
Sikkim	..	..	..	..	..	..	..	..	..
United Provinces States ..	4	..	4	..	..	..	4	..	4
Baluchistan States ..	..	..	..	..	..	..	..	..	..

TABLE VI

District. State, Province or Country where born.	Total population.			City where enumerated.					
				Nagpur.			Jubbulpore.		
	Persons.	Males.	Females.	Persons.	Males.	Females.	Persons.	Males.	Females.
1	2	3	4	5				9	10
(c) French and Portuguese Settlements.	370	191	179	324	191	33	46	..	46
(d) India, unspecified ..	..	..	..	..	..	..	..	..	..
B.—Born in other Asiatic Countries.	186	145	41	85	63	22	101	82	19
(i) Within British Dominions ..	*17*	*12*	*5*	*3*	*3*	..	*14*	*9*	*5*
Ceylon	17	12	5	3	3	..	14	9	5
Straits Settlements and Malaya.	..	..	..	..	..	..	..	..	..
Elsewhere ..	..	..	..	..	..	..	..	..	..
(ii) Outside British Dominions	*169*	*133*	*36*	*82*	*60*	*22*	*87*	*73*	*14*
Afghanistan ..	78	70	8	32	29	3	46	41	5
China	17	13	4	4	2	2	13	11	2
Nepal	56	36	20	36	20	16	20	16	4
Elsewhere ..	18	14	4	10	9	1	8	5	3
(iii) Asia, unspecified ..	..	..	..	..	..	..	..	..	..
C.—Born in Europe ..	2,445	1,952	493	237	134	103	2,208	1,818	390
(i) United Kingdom and Ireland.	*2,425*	*1,944*	*481*	*237*	*134*	*103*	*2,188*	*1,810*	*378*
(ii) British possessions in Europe.	..	..	..	..	..	..	..	..	..
(iii) Continental Europe ..	20	8	12	..	..	..	20	8	12
(iv) Europe, unspecified ..	..	..	..	..	..	..	..	..	..
D.—Born in Africa ..	25	19	6	17	12	5	8	7	1
(i) Within British Dominions ..	..	..	..	..	..	..	..	..	..
Cape Colony ..	..	..	..	..	..	..	..	..	..
Kenya (British East Africa)	..	..	..	..	..	..	..	..	..
Mauritius ..	..	..	..	..	..	..	..	..	..
Natal ..	..	..	..	..	..	..	..	..	..
Nyasaland ..	..	..	..	..	..	..	..	..	..
Tanganyika ..	..	..	..	..	..	..	..	..	..
Transvaal ..	..	..	..	..	..	..	..	..	..
Uganda ..	..	..	..	..	..	..	..	..	..
Zanzibar ..	..	..	..	..	..	..	..	..	..
Elsewhere ..	1	..	1	..	..	..	1	..	1
(ii) Outside British Dominions	..	..	..	..	..	..	..	..	..
Mozambique ..	..	..	..	..	..	..	..	..	..
Elsewhere ..	..	..	..	..	..	..	..	..	..
(iii) Africa, unspecified ..	*24*	*19*	*5*	*17*	*12*	*5*	*7*	*7*	..
E.—Born in America .	51	21	30	18	6	12	33	15	18
(i) Within British Dominions ..	*2*	*2*	..	..	..	..	*2*	*2*	..
British Guiana .	..	..	..	..	..	..	..	..	..
British Honduras ..	..	..	..	..	..	..	..	..	..
Canada ..	2	2	..	..	..	..	..	..	..
Elsewhere ..	..	..	..	..	..	..	2	2	..
(ii) Outside British Dominions	*26*	*9*	*17*	..	..	..	*26*	*9*	*17*
United States ..	26	9	17	..	..	..	26	9	17
Elsewhere ..	..	..	..	..	..	..	..	..	..
(iii) America, unspecified ..	*23*	*10*	*13*	*18*	*6*	*12*	*5*	*4*	*1*
F.—Born in Australasia ..	2	1	1	..	..	..	2	1	1
(i) Within British Dominions ..	*2*	*1*	*1*	..	..	..	*2*	*1*	*1*
Australia ..	1	1	..	..	..	..	1	1	..
Fiji Islands ..	..	..	..	..	..	..	..	..	..
New Zealand ..	1	..	1	..	..	..	1	..	1
Tasmania ..	..	..	..	..	..	..	..	..	..
Other British possessions in Australasia	..	..	..	..	..	..	..	..	..
(ii) Outside British Dominions	..	..	..	..	..	..	..	..	..
(iii) Australasia, unspecified ..	..	..	..	..	..	..	..	..	..
G.—Born at Sea ..	..	..	..	..	..	..	..	..	..
H.—Birthplace unspecified or not returned.	..	..	..	..	..	..	..	..	..

TABLE VII

Age, Sex and Civil Condition

1. This Table is divided into three parts. Part A shows the distribution for the Province as a whole of the total population and of each religion by age, sex and civil condition. Part B shows the distribution in Districts and States of the total population and of the main religions by age, sex and civil condition, but in this part the age statistics have been given in less detail than in the Provincial Summary. Part C gives similar details for cities.

2. Detailed information for the age periods not shown in Parts B and C, can be obtained from the manuscript Compilation Registers which have been preserved.

3. The method of grouping ages is that recommended by the Actuary to the Government of India, and age groups have been smoothed in order to secure greater accuracy, according to the system laid down in the Imperial Census Code.

TABLE VII.—Age, Sex and Civil Condition.

Part A—Provincial Summary.

Religion.	Age.	Population.			Unmarried.			Married.			Widowed.		
		Persons.	Males.	Females.	Persons.	Males	Females.	Persons.	Males.	Females.	Persons.	Males.	Females.
	1	2	3	4	5	6	7	8	9	10	11	12	13
ALL RELIGIONS	0—1 ..	634,294	313,927	320,367	624,732	309,216	315,516	9,284	4,593	4,691	278	118	160
	1—2 ..	544,912	260,121	284,791	534,639	255,708	278,931	9,922	4,251	5,671	351	162	189
	2—3 ..	569,670	274,694	294,976	553,077	268,839	284,238	16,063	5,630	10,433	530	225	305
	3—4 ..	576,526	289,106	287,420	544,494	279,184	265,310	31,128	9,596	21,532	904	326	578
	4—5 ..	549,688	270,551	279,137	506,221	257,502	248,719	42,129	12,576	29,553	1,338	473	865
	0—5 ..	*2,875,090*	*1,408,399*	*1,466,691*	*2,763,163*	*1,370,449*	*1,392,714*	*108,526*	*36,646*	*71,880*	*3,401*	*1,304*	*2,097*
	5—10..	2,303,905	1,175,395	1,128,510	1,786,209	1,003,963	782,246	508,082	168,389	339,693	9,614	3,043	6,571
	10—15..	2,039,504	1,051,893	987,611	1,231,255	768,006	463,249	793,836	279,251	514,585	14,413	4,636	9,777
	15—20..	1,599,713	779,121	820,592	331,231	273,553	57,678	1,237,041	493,856	743,185	31,441	11,712	19,729
	20—25..	1,680,781	813,986	866,795	173,799	151,736	22,063	1,455,952	642,719	813,233	51,030	19,531	31,499
	25—30..	1,527,861	771,892	755,969	59,763	51,064	8,699	1,380,051	690,968	689,083	88,047	29,860	58,187
	30—35..	1,370,925	696,767	674,158	37,178	31,104	6,074	1,218,509	631,208	587,301	115,238	34,455	80,783
	35—40..	1,109,832	561,043	548,789	22,024	17,990	4,034	915,638	501,346	414,292	172,170	41,707	130,463
	40—45..	955,917	490,020	465,897	17,020	13,658	3,362	745,394	430,939	314,455	193,503	45,423	148,080
	45—50..	756,213	396,867	359,346	10,720	8,601	2,119	520,273	337,251	183,022	225,220	51,015	174,205
	50—55..	585,047	301,876	283,171	7,390	6,018	1,372	373,590	249,978	123,612	204,067	45,880	158,187
	55—60..	425,241	204,100	221,141	4,650	3,658	992	222,619	158,712	63,907	197,972	41,730	156,242
	60—65..	348,726	161,538	187,188	3,991	3,143	848	165,671	121,403	44,268	179,064	36,992	142,072
	65—70..	159,182	72,766	86,416	1,975	1,566	409	68,086	51,098	17,078	89,121	20,192	68,929
	70 and over.	253,000	111,540	141,460	2,993	2,126	867	91,867	71,569	20,298	158,140	37,845	120,295
	Total ..	*17,990,937*	*8,997,203*	*8,993,734*	*6,453,361*	*3,706,635*	*2,746,726*	*9,805,135*	*4,865,243*	*4,939,892*	*1,732,441*	*425,325*	*1,307,116*
HINDU (BRAHMANIC AND SATNAMIS)	0—1 ..	535,156	264,710	270,446	526,792	260,618	266,174	8,130	3,989	4,141	234	103	131
	1—2 ..	452,202	215,092	237,110	443,062	211,242	231,820	8,826	3,705	5,121	314	145	169
	2—3 ..	469,740	226,828	242,912	454,591	221,641	232,950	14,668	4,980	9,688	481	207	274
	3—4 ..	476,096	240,175	235,921	446,118	231,152	214,966	29,135	8,713	20,422	843	310	533
	4—5 ..	454,506	223,164	231,342	413,786	211,271	202,515	39,543	11,472	28,071	1,177	421	756
	0—5 ..	**2,387,700**	**1,169,969**	**1,217,731**	**2,284,349**	**1,135,924**	**1,148,425**	**100,302**	**32,859**	**67,443**	**3,049**	**1,186**	**1,863**
	5—10..	1,924,787	981,974	942,813	1,437,457	820,380	617,077	478,407	158,764	319,643	8,923	2,830	6,093
	10—15..	1,714,418	884,516	829,902	971,827	619,487	352,340	729,417	260,791	468,626	13,174	4,238	8,936
	15—20..	1,346,635	656,758	689,877	241,859	206,271	35,588	1,077,267	440,182	637,085	27,509	10,305	17,204
	20—25..	1,413,844	684,637	729,207	123,958	110,337	13,621	1,245,739	557,404	688,335	44,147	16,896	27,251
	25—30..	1,280,332	647,009	633,323	43,397	37,311	6,086	1,161,591	584,263	577,328	75,344	25,435	49,909
	30—35..	1,152,686	585,451	567,235	27,947	23,597	4,350	1,025,813	532,490	493,323	98,926	29,364	69,562
	35—40..	935,436	471,030	464,406	16,725	13,651	3,074	771,087	421,739	349,348	147,624	35,640	111,984
	40—45..	808,442	412,416	396,026	13,171	10,533	2,638	629,030	362,929	266,101	166,241	38,954	127,287
	45—50..	643,786	336,371	307,415	8,621	6,939	1,682	441,678	285,619	156,059	193,487	43,813	149,674
	50—55..	499,185	256,486	242,699	5,906	4,852	1,054	317,531	212,066	105,465	175,748	39,568	136,180
	55—60..	364,334	174,102	190,232	3,732	2,974	758	189,953	135,199	54,754	170,649	35,929	134,720
	60—65..	298,721	137,811	160,910	3,267	2,618	649	141,327	103,474	37,853	154,127	31,719	122,408
	65—70..	137,870	62,692	75,178	1,683	1,369	314	58,834	43,929	14,905	77,353	17,394	59,959
	70 and over.	216,590	95,175	121,415	2,507	1,804	703	78,309	61,014	17,295	135,774	32,357	103,417
	Total ..	*15,124,766*	*7,556,397*	*7,568,369*	*5,186,406*	*2,998,047*	*2,188,359*	*8,446,285*	*4,192,722*	*4,253,563*	*1,492,075*	*365,628*	*1,126,447*
HINDU (ARYA)	0—1 ..	67	36	31	66	35	31	1	1	..	..	..	..
	1—2 ..	60	36	24	60	36	24	..	..	..	..	..	..
	2—3 ..	66	34	32	64	34	30	1	..	1	1	..	1
	3—4 ..	46	22	24	46	22	24	..	..	..	..	..	..
	4—5 ..	67	37	30	65	36	29	1	1	..	1	..	1
	0—5 ..	*306*	*165*	*141*	*301*	*163*	*138*	*3*	*2*	*1*	*2*	..	*2*
	5—10..	242	144	98	208	124	84	31	19	12	3	1	2
	10—15..	245	146	99	179	117	62	66	29	37	..	..	..
	15—20..	191	107	84	76	61	15	111	44	67	4	2	2
	20—25..	173	94	79	38	31	7	131	60	71	4	3	1
	25—30..	154	83	71	16	11	5	129	70	59	9	2	7
	30—35..	123	74	49	7	5	2	105	65	40	11	4	7
	35—40..	107	64	43	4	4	..	88	53	35	15	7	8
	40—45..	105	60	45	7	5	2	78	47	31	20	8	12
	45—50..	65	38	27	6	5	1	36	27	9	23	6	17
	50—55..	46	22	24	2	1	1	21	16	5	23	5	18
	55—60..	33	19	14	..	..	..	18	17	1	15	2	13
	60—65..	26	20	6	2	2	..	14	14	..	10	4	6
	65—70..	14	9	5	2	2	..	6	6	..	6	1	5
	70 and over.	12	4	8	..	..	..	2	2	..	10	2	8
	Total ..	*1,842*	*1,049*	*793*	*848*	*531*	*317*	*839*	*471*	*368*	*155*	*47*	*108*

TABLE VII—Part A—Provincial Summary—*contd.*

Religion.	Age.	Population.			Unmarried.			Married.			Widowed.		
		Persons.	Males.	Females.	Persons.	Males.	Females.	Persons.	Males.	Females.	Persons.	Males.	Females.
	1	2	3	4	5	6	7	8	9	10	11	12	13
HINDU (BRAHMO).	0—1 ..	..	..	..	..	..	..	..	..	..	..	..	..
	1—2 ..	..	..	..	..	..	..	..	..	..	..	..	..
	2—3 ..	..	..	..	..	..	..	..	..	..	..	..	..
	3—4 ..	..	..	..	..	..	..	..	..	..	..	..	..
	4—5 ..	2	..	2	2	..	2	..	..	..	..	..	..
	0—5 ..	*2*	..	*2*	*2*	..	*2*	..	..	..	..	..	..
	5—10 ..	3	..	3	3	..	3	..	..	..	..	..	..
	10—15 ..	2	..	2	1	..	1	1	..	1	..	..	..
	15—20 ..	1	1	..	..	..	..	1	1	..	..	..	..
	20—25 ..	1	..	1	..	..	..	1	..	1	..	..	..
	25—30 ..	2	..	2	..	..	..	2	..	2	..	..	..
	30—35 ..	1	..	1	..	..	..	1	..	1	..	..	..
	35—40 ..	2	1	1	..	..	..	2	1	1	..	..	..
	40—45 ..	..	..	..	..	..	..	..	..	..	..	..	..
	45—50 ..	1	..	1	..	..	..	..	..	..	1	..	1
	50—55 ..	..	..	..	..	..	..	..	..	..	..	..	..
	55—60 ..	..	..	..	..	..	..	..	..	..	..	..	..
	60—65 ..	..	..	..	..	..	..	..	..	..	..	..	..
	65—70 ..	..	..	..	..	..	..	..	..	..	..	..	..
	70 and over.	1	1	..	1	1	..	..	..	..	..	..	..
	Total ..	*16*	*3*	*13*	*7*	*1*	*6*	*8*	*2*	*6*	*1*	..	*1*
SIKH.	0—1 ..	140	74	66	140	74	66	..	..	..	..	..	..
	1—2 ..	116	59	57	115	59	56	1	..	1	..	..	..
	2—3 ..	116	61	55	116	61	55	..	..	..	..	..	..
	3—4 ..	92	53	39	91	52	39	1	1	..	..	..	..
	4—5 ..	133	67	66	127	66	61	6	1	5	..	..	..
	0—5 ..	*597*	*314*	*283*	*589*	*312*	*277*	*8*	*2*	*6*	..	..	..
	5—10 ..	452	256	196	416	247	169	36	9	27	..	..	..
	10—15 ..	432	278	154	319	210	109	112	67	45	1	1	..
	15—20 ..	568	398	170	238	222	16	323	173	150	7	3	4
	20—25 ..	629	438	191	214	207	7	405	224	181	10	7	3
	25—30 ..	493	341	152	76	74	2	399	255	144	18	12	
	30—35 ..	418	303	115	46	45	1	358	249	109	14	9	5
	35—40 ..	299	216	83	18	16	2	262	191	71	19	9	10
	40—45 ..	230	172	58	8	8	..	203	154	49	19	10	9
	45—50 ..	160	123	37	4	4	..	132	110	22	24	9	15
	50—55 ..	88	63	25	3	3	..	67	54	13	18	6	12
	55—60 ..	63	40	23	2	2	..	37	28	9	24	10	14
	60—65 ..	39	25	14	1	1	..	24	19	5	14	5	9
	65—70 ..	22	13	9	2	2	..	7	7	..	13	4	9
	70 and over.	30	23	7	3	3	..	13	12	1	14	8	6
	Total ..	*4,520*	*3,003*	*1,517*	*1,939*	*1,356*	*583*	*2,386*	*1,551*	*832*	*195*	*93*	*102*
JAIN	0—1 ..	2,824	1,508	1,316	2,806	1,500	1,306	16	8	8	2	..	2
	1—2 ..	2,147	1,053	1,094	2,126	1,043	1,083	20	10	10	1	..	1
	2—3 ..	2,222	1,055	1,167	2,175	1,035	1,140	47	20	27	..	..	..
	3—4 ..	2,177	1,045	1,132	2,120	1,026	1,094	57	19	38	..	..	..
	4—5 ..	2,129	1,051	1,078	2,030	1,022	1,008	92	27	65	7	2	5
	0—5 ..	*11,499*	*5,712*	*5,787*	*11,257*	*5,626*	*5,631*	*232*	*84*	*148*	*10*	*2*	*8*
	5—10 ..	9,330	4,818	4,512	8,291	4,574	3,717	1,013	237	776	26	7	19
	10—15 ..	8,688	4,589	4,099	6,508	4,112	2,396	2,121	463	1,658	59	14	45
	15—20 ..	7,770	4,083	3,687	2,445	2,250	195	5,113	1,791	3,322	212	42	170
	20—25 ..	8,092	4,192	3,900	1,505	1,470	35	6,214	2,647	3,567	373	75	298
	25—30 ..	6,890	3,628	3,262	563	545	18	5,640	2,918	2,722	687	165	522
	30—35 ..	6,122	3,325	2,797	393	378	15	4,866	2,733	2,133	863	214	649
	35—40 ..	4,850	2,530	2,320	227	213	14	3,459	2,053	1,406	1,164	264	900
	40—45 ..	4,405	2,316	2,089	164	155	9	2,923	1,826	1,097	1,318	335	983
	45—50 ..	3,683	1,986	1,697	123	116	7	2,031	1,412	619	1,529	458	1,071
	50—55 ..	2,949	1,585	1,364	90	85	5	1,477	1,075	402	1,382	425	957
	55—60 ..	2,067	1,018	1,049	52	48	4	895	661	234	1,120	309	811
	60—65 ..	1,609	759	850	32	31	1	647	481	166	930	247	683
	65—70 ..	798	388	410	13	11	2	277	227	50	508	150	358
	70 and over.	1,103	487	616	14	12	2	290	252	38	799	223	576
	Total ..	*79,855*	*41,416*	*38,439*	*31,677*	*19,626*	*12,051*	*37,198*	*18,860*	*18,338*	*10,980*	*2,930*	*8,050*

TABLE VII.—Part A—Provincial Summary—*contd.*

Religion.	Age.	Population. Persons.	Population. Males.	Population. Females.	Unmarried. Persons.	Unmarried. Males.	Unmarried. Females.	Married. Persons.	Married. Males.	Married. Females.	Widowed. Persons.	Widowed. Males.	Widowed. Females.
	1	2	3	4	5	6	7	8	9	10	11	12	13
BUDDHIST	0—1 ..	4	2	2	4	2	2	..	..	..	..	..	..
	1—2 ..	2	1	1	2	1	1	..	..	..	..	..	..
	2—3 ..	2	1	1	2	1	1	..	..	..	..	..	..
	3—4 ..	..	..	..	..	..	..	..	..	..	..	..	..
	4—5 ..	4	2	2	4	2	2	..	..	..	..	..	..
	0—5 ..	*12*	*6*	*6*	*12*	*6*	*6*	..	..	..	..	..	..
	5—10..	6	4	2	5	4	1	1	..	1	..	..	..
	10—15..	5	4	1	5	4	1	..	..	..	..	..	..
	15—20..	14	8	6	7	6	1	7	2	5	..	..	..
	20—25..	5	1	4	..	..	..	5	1	4	..	..	..
	25—30..	10	9	1	4	4	..	6	5	1	..	..	..
	30—35..	6	5	1	3	3	..	3	2	1	..	..	..
	35—40..	2	1	1	..	..	..	2	1	1	..	..	..
	40—45..	3	1	2	1	1	..	2	..	2	..	..	..
	45—50..	2	2	..	..	..	..	2	2	..	..	..	..
	50—55..	1	1	..	..	..	..	1	1	..	..	..	..
	55—60	2	1	1	..	..	..	1	1	..	1	..	1
	60—65..	..	..	..	..	..	..	..	..	..	..	..	..
	65—70..	..	..	..	..	..	..	..	..	..	..	..	..
	70 and over.	1	1	..	..	..	..	1	1	..	..	..	..
	Total ..	*69*	*44*	*25*	*37*	*28*	*9*	*31*	*16*	*15*	*1*	..	*1*
ZOROASTRIAN	0—1 ..	59	29	30	59	29	30	..	..	..	..	..	..
	1—2 ..	46	24	22	46	24	22	..	..	..	..	..	..
	2—3 ..	45	20	25	45	20	25	..	..	..	..	..	..
	3—4 ..	40	19	21	40	19	21	..	..	..	..	..	..
	4—5 ..	68	29	39	68	29	39	..	..	..	..	..	..
	0—5 ..	*258*	*121*	*137*	*258*	*121*	*137*	..	..	..	..	..	..
	5—10..	231	105	126	230	104	126	1	1	..	..	..	..
	10—15..	198	92	106	197	91	106	1	1	..	..	..	..
	15—20..	168	77	91	139	67	72	27	9	18	2	1	1
	20—25..	167	85	82	114	72	42	52	13	39	1	..	1
	25—30..	197	102	95	74	58	16	119	42	77	4	2	2
	30—35	188	99	89	49	34	15	135	62	73	4	3	1
	35—40..	174	98	76	24	16	8	141	78	63	9	4	5
	40—45..	152	95	57	18	13	5	125	77	48	9	5	4
	45—50..	123	84	39	9	6	3	100	71	29	14	7	7
	50—55..	91	60	31	6	5	1	75	52	23	10	3	7
	55—60..	63	40	23	2	2	..	45	31	14	16	7	9
	60—65..	41	22	19	..	..	..	28	18	10	13	4	9
	65—70..	30	24	6	..	..	..	20	18	2	10	6	4
	70 and over.	28	15	13	2	1	1	14	10	4	12	4	8
	Total ..	*2,109*	*1,119*	*990*	*1,122*	*590*	*532*	*888*	*483*	*400*	*104*	*46*	*58*
MUSLIM	0—1 ..	22,694	11,355	11,339	22,440	11,234	11,206	236	115	121	18	6	12
	1—2 ..	21,290	10,525	10,765	21,036	10,410	10,626	244	111	133	10	4	6
	2—3 ..	22,366	10,803	11,563	22,067	10,660	11,407	294	141	153	5	2	3
	3—4 ..	22,314	10,886	11,428	21,910	10,712	11,198	392	170	222	12	4	8
	4—5 ..	21,812	10,877	10,935	21,243	10,639	10,604	523	223	300	46	15	31
	0—5 ..	*110,476*	*54,446*	*56,030*	*108,696*	*53,655*	*55,041*	*1,689*	*760*	*929*	*91*	*31*	*60*
	5—10..	92,966	47,938	45,028	86,326	46,051	40,275	6,463	1,834	4,629	177	53	124
	10—15..	81,904	43,009	38,895	66,853	39,684	27,169	14,750	3,237	11,513	301	88	213
	15—20..	66,693	34,620	32,073	25,230	21,329	3,901	40,363	12,880	27,483	1,100	411	689
	20—25..	70,639	36,873	33,766	15,531	14,167	1,364	53,103	21,871	31,232	2,005	835	1,170
	25—30..	59,155	32,080	27,075	4,400	3,917	483	51,288	26,787	24,501	3,467	1,376	2,091
	30—35..	51,604	28,475	23,129	2,298	1,952	346	44,903	25,011	19,892	4,403	1,512	2,891
	35—40..	41,720	22,399	19,321	1,080	848	232	34,040	19,856	14,184	6,600	1,695	4,905
	40—45..	35,334	19,107	16,227	735	567	168	27,185	16,742	10,443	7,414	1,798	5,616
	45—50..	27,872	15,473	12,399	505	403	102	18,917	13,123	5,794	8,450	1,947	6,503
	50—55..	21,433	11,867	9,566	366	288	78	13,579	9,846	3,733	7,488	1,733	5,755
	55—60..	15,863	8,553	7,310	178	123	55	8,482	6,727	1,755	7,203	1,703	5,500
	60—65..	13,425	6,993	6,432	154	101	53	6,602	5,294	1,308	6,669	1,598	5,071
	65—70..	6,194	3,306	2,888	75	44	31	2,728	2,306	422	3,391	956	2,435
	70 and over	10,830	5,494	5,336	140	81	59	4,043	3,491	552	6,647	1,922	4,725
	Total ..	*706,108*	*370,633*	*335,475*	*312,567*	*183,210*	*129,357*	*328,135*	*169,765*	*158,370*	*65,406*	*17,658*	*47,748*

TABLE VII.—Part A—Provincial Summary—*concld.*

Religion.	Age.	Population.			Unmarried.			Married.			Widowed.		
		Persons.	Males.	Females.	Persons.	Males.	Females.	Persons.	Males.	Females.	Persons.	Males.	Females.
	1	2	3	4	5	6	7	8	9	10	11	12	13
CHRISTIAN	0—1 ..	4,046	2,058	1,988	4,042	2,056	1,986	4	2	2	..	..	..
	1—2 ..	3,491	1,734	1,757	3,487	1,730	1,757	3	3	..	1	1	..
	2—3 ..	3,761	1,830	1,931	3,754	1,825	1,929	5	3	2	2	2	.
	3—4 ..	3,718	1,833	1,885	3,708	1,827	1,881	10	6	4	..	..	..
	4—5 ..	3,468	1,752	1,716	3,445	1,739	1,706	22	12	10	1	1	..
	0—5 ..	*18,484*	*9,207*	*9,277*	*18,436*	*9,177*	*9,259*	*44*	*26*	*18*	*1*	*4*	..
	5—10..	14,357	7,343	7,014	14,053	7,232	6,821	298	108	190	6	3	3
	10—15..	12,657	6,501	6,156	11,687	6,231	5,456	948	261	687	22	9	13
	15—20..	9,882	4,979	4,903	5,654	3,556	2,098	4,138	1,394	2,744	90	29	61
	20—25..	9,951	5,274	4,677	3,787	2,756	1,031	6,002	2,457	3,545	162	61	101
	25—30..	8,386	4,515	3,871	1,360	1,126	234	6,735	3,281	3,454	291	108	183
	30—35..	7,192	3,644	3,548	618	452	166	6,176	3,066	3,110	398	126	272
	35—40..	5,846	3,064	2,782	421	311	110	4,782	2,599	2,183	643	154	489
	40—45..	4,931	2,646	2,285	319	227	92	3,910	2,252	1,658	702	167	535
	45—50..	3,458	1,872	1,586	126	65	61	2,572	1,628	944	760	179	581
	50—55..	2,692	1,445	1,247	103	50	53	1,887	1,232	655	702	163	539
	55—60..	1,793	857	936	60	25	35	1,005	685	320	728	147	581
	60—65..	1,357	618	739	43	14	29	673	483	190	639	119	520
	65—70..	525	244	281	28	11	17	213	162	51	284	71	213
	70 and over	774	331	443	37	2	25	[illegible]	206	80	451	113	338
	Total ..	*102,285*	*52,540*	*49,715*	*56,732*	*31,215*	*25,187*	*39,671*	*19,842*	*19,829*	*5,882*	*1,453*	*4,429*
JEW	0—1 ..	9	5	4	9	5	4	..	..	..	..	..	..
	1—2 ..	2	1	1	2	1	1	..	..	..	..	..	..
	2—3 ..	5	3	2	5	3	2	..	..	..	..	..	..
	3—4 ..	3	1	2	3	1	2	..	..	..	..	..	..
	4—5 ..	11	5	6	9	4	5	2	1	1	..	..	..
	0—5 ..	*30*	*15*	*15*	*28*	*14*	*14*	*2*	*1*	*1*	..	..	..
	5—10..	25	14	11	24	14	10	1	..	1	..	..	..
	10—15..	19	14	5	19	14	5	..	..	..	..	..	..
	15—20..	18	12	6	15	11	4	3	1	2	..	..	..
	20—25..	12	6	6	9	6	3	3	..	3	..	..	..
	25—30..	15	4	11	3	1	2	12	3	9	..	..	..
	30—35..	7	4	3	..	..	..	7	4	3	..	..	..
	35—40..	10	7	3	..	..	..	9	7	2	1	..	1
	40—45..	6	6	..	..	..	..	6	6	..	..	..	..
	45—50..	6	3	3	..	..	..	5	3	2	1	..	1
	50—55..	3	1	2	..	..	..	2	1	1	1	..	1
	55—60..	..	..	..	..	..	..	..	..	..	..	..	..
	60—65..	1	1	..	..	..	..	1	1	..	..	..	..
	65—70..	1	1	..	..	..	..	..	..	..	1	1	..
	70 and over.	..	..	..	..	..	..	..	..	..	..	..	..
	Total ..	*153*	*88*	*65*	*95*	*60*	*35*	*51*	*27*	*24*	*4*	*1*	3
TRIBAL	0—1 ..	69,295	34,150	35,145	68,374	33,663	34,711	897	478	419	24	9	15
	1—2 ..	65,556	31,596	33,960	64,703	31,162	33,541	828	422	406	25	12	13
	2—3 ..	71,347	34,059	37,288	70,258	33,559	36,699	1,048	486	562	41	14	27
	3—4 ..	72,040	35,072	36,968	70,458	34,373	36,085	1,533	687	846	49	12	37
	4—5 ..	67,488	33,567	33,921	65,442	32,694	32,748	1,940	839	1,101	106	34	72
	0—5 ..	*345,726*	*168,444*	*177,282*	*339,235*	*165,151*	*173,784*	*6,216*	*2,912*	*3,334*	*245*	*81*	*164*
	5—10..	261,506	132,799	128,707	239,196	125,233	113,963	21,831	7,417	14,414	479	149	330
	10—15..	220,936	112,744	108,192	173,660	98,056	75,604	46,420	14,402	32,018	856	286	570
	15—20..	167,773	78,078	89,695	55,568	39,780	15,788	109,688	37,379	72,309	2,517	919	1,598
	20—25..	177,268	82,386	94,882	28,643	22,690	5,953	144,297	58,042	86,255	4,328	1,654	2,674
	25—30..	172,227	84,121	88,106	9,870	8,017	1,853	154,130	73,344	80,786	8,227	2,760	5,467
	30—35..	152,578	75,387	77,191	5,817	4,638	1,179	136,142	67,526	68,616	10,619	3,223	7,396
	35—40..	121,386	61,633	59,753	3,525	2,931	594	101,766	54,768	46,998	16,095	3,934	12,161
	40—45..	102,309	53,201	49,108	2,597	2,149	448	81,932	46,906	35,026	17,780	4,146	13,634
	45—50..	77,057	40,915	36,142	1,326	1,063	263	54,800	35,256	19,544	20,931	4,596	16,335
	50—55..	58,559	30,346	28,213	914	734	180	38,950	25,635	13,315	18,695	3,977	14,718
	55—60..	41,023	19,470	21,553	624	484	140	22,183	15,363	6,820	18,216	3,623	14,593
	60—65..	33,507	15,289	18,218	492	376	116	16,353	11,617	4,736	16,662	3,296	13,366
	65—70..	13,728	6,089	7,639	172	127	45	6,001	4,353	1,648	7,555	1,609	5,946
	70 and over.	23,631	10,009	13,622	289	212	77	8,909	6,581	2,328	14,433	3,216	11,217
	Total ..	*1,969,214*	*970,911*	*998,303*	*861,928*	*471,941*	*389,987*	*949,648*	*461,501*	*488,147*	*157,638*	*37,469*	*120,169*

TABLE VII.—Part B—Details for Districts.

District.	Age.	Population.			Unmarried.			Married.			Widowed.		
		Persons.	Males.	Females.	Persons.	Males.	Females.	Persons.	Males.	Females.	Persons.	Males.	Females.
	1	2	3	4	5	6	7	8	9	10	11	12	13
SAUGOR	ALL RELIGIONS ..	*544,589*	*280,385*	*264,204*	*228,177*	*138,591*	*89,586*	*254,653*	*126,295*	*128,358*	*61,759*	*15,499*	*46,260*
	0—1 ..	16,634	8,523	8,111	16,607	8,508	8,099	26	15	11	1	..	1
	1—2 ..	13,293	6,701	6,592	13,235	6,668	6,567	58	33	25	..	..	..
	2—3 ..	15,110	7,440	7,670	15,016	7,388	7,628	93	52	41	1	..	1
	3—4 ..	16,778	8,411	8,367	16,666	8,350	8,316	107	60	47	5	1	4
	4—5 ..	16,055	8,234	7,821	15,924	8,168	7,756	118	63	55	13	3	10
	Total 0—5 ..	*77,870*	*39,309*	*38,561*	*77,148*	*39,082*	*38,366*	*402*	*223*	*179*	*20*	*4*	*16*
	5—10 ..	70,718	37,218	33,500	66,128	36,510	29,618	4,491	690	3,801	99	18	81
	10—15 ..	66,274	35,637	30,637	52,312	32,939	19,373	13,665	2,644	11,021	297	54	243
	15—20 ..	55,506	29,086	26,420	17,412	15,786	1,626	36,887	12,950	23,937	1,207	350	857
	20—30 ..	104,509	54,007	50,502	11,030	10,643	387	87,447	41,652	45,795	6,032	1,712	4,320
	30—40 ..	73,763	37,253	36,510	2,107	1,999	108	59,338	32,473	26,865	12,318	2,781	9,537
	40—50 ..	53,099	27,026	26,073	1,138	1,078	60	34,038	21,633	12,405	17,923	4,315	13,608
	50—60 ..	28,119	14,070	14,049	439	407	32	13,521	9,965	3,556	14,159	3,698	10,461
	60 and over ..	14,731	6,779	7,952	163	147	16	4,864	4,065	799	9,704	2,567	7,137
	HINDUS ..	*480,121*	*247,101*	*233,020*	*200,376*	*121,822*	*78,554*	*224,935*	*111,671*	*113,264*	*54,810*	*13,608*	*41,202*
	0—1 ..	14,665	7,524	7,141	14,647	7,515	7,132	18	9	9	..	..	..
	1—2 ..	11,592	5,839	5,753	11,546	5,815	5,731	46	24	22	..	..	..
	2—3 ..	13,191	6,504	6,687	13,113	6,461	6,652	77	43	34	1	..	1
	3—4 ..	14,769	7,422	7,347	14,672	7,368	7,304	92	53	39	5	1	4
	4—5 ..	14,124	7,255	6,869	14,022	7,201	6,821	92	52	40	10	2	8
	Total 0—5 ..	*68,341*	*34,544*	*33,797*	*68,000*	*34,360*	*33,640*	*325*	*181*	*144*	*16*	*3*	*13*
	5—10 ..	62,403	32,878	29,525	58,420	32,249	26,171	3,896	615	3,281	87	14	73
	10—15 ..	58,687	31,600	27,087	46,174	29,125	17,049	12,245	2,429	9,816	268	46	222
	15—20 ..	49,245	25,857	23,388	15,118	13,837	1,281	33,044	11,711	21,333	1,083	309	774
	20—30 ..	92,603	47,788	44,815	9,419	9,154	265	77,800	37,152	40,648	5,384	1,482	3,902
	30—40 ..	65,151	32,790	32,361	1,781	1,706	75	52,283	28,643	23,640	11,087	2,441	8,646
	40—50 ..	46,582	23,630	22,952	962	921	41	29,651	18,886	10,765	15,969	3,823	12,146
	50—60 ..	24,483	12,237	12,246	370	348	22	11,616	8,615	3,001	12,497	3,274	9,223
	60 and over ..	12,626	5,777	6,849	132	122	10	4,075	3,439	636	8,419	2,216	6,203
	MUSLIMS ..	*25,746*	*13,655*	*12,091*	*11,266*	*6,776*	*4,490*	*11,938*	*6,128*	*5,810*	*2,542*	*751*	*1,791*
	0—1	805	399	406	798	394	404	7	5	2	..	..	..
	1—2 ..	711	353	358	703	348	355	8	5	3	..	..	..
	2—3 ..	847	406	441	839	403	436	8	3	5	..	..	..
	3—4 ..	864	421	443	855	418	437	9	3	6	..	..	..
	4—5 ..	782	387	395	767	382	385	14	5	9	1	..	1
	Total 0—5 .	*4,009*	*1,996*	*2,013*	*3,962*	*1,945*	*2,017*	*46*	*21*	*25*	*1*	..	*1*
	5—10 ..	3,404	1,799	1,605	3,171	1,756	1,415	227	41	186	6	2	4
	10—15 ..	3,105	1,685	1,420	2,481	1,569	912	611	112	499	13	4	9
	15—20 .	2,605	1,377	1,228	877	785	92	1,678	569	1,109	50	23	27
	20—30 ..	4,794	2,635	2,159	629	592	37	3,933	1,931	2,002	232	112	120
	30—40 ..	3,300	1,777	1,523	92	83	9	2,762	1,552	1,210	446	142	304
	40—50 ..	2,407	1,323	1,084	33	29	4	1,669	1,111	558	705	183	522
	50—60 ..	1,315	689	626	14	12	2	704	531	173	597	146	451
	60 and over	807	404	403	7	5	2	308	260	48	492	139	353
	JAINS ..	*17,136*	*8,910*	*8,226*	*7,358*	*4,587*	*2,771*	*7,317*	*3,616*	*3,701*	*2,461*	*707*	*1,754*
	0—1 ..	587	308	279	586	308	278	..	..	..	1	..	1
	1—2 ..	471	253	218	467	249	218	4	4	..	..	..	..
	2—3 ..	498	248	250	490	242	248	8	6	2	..	..	..
	3—4 ..	506	246	260	501	243	258	5	3	2	..	..	..
	4—5 ..	493	253	240	483	248	235	8	4	4	2	1	1
	Total 0—5 ..	*2,555*	*1,308*	*1,247*	*2,527*	*1,290*	*1,237*	*25*	*17*	*8*	*3*	*1*	*2*
	5—10 ..	2,101	1,102	999	1,993	1,077	916	104	24	80	4	1	3
	10—15 ..	1,881	1,010	871	1,544	960	584	326	47	279	11	3	8
	15—20 ..	1,594	848	746	544	522	22	1,009	318	691	41	8	33
	20—30 ..	3,195	1,668	1,527	476	471	5	2,459	1,133	1,326	260	64	196
	30—40 ..	2,273	1,219	1,054	134	132	2	1,684	968	716	455	119	336
	40—50 ..	1,758	903	855	84	82	2	988	621	367	686	200	486
	50—60 .	1,086	539	547	38	36	2	478	321	157	570	182	388
	60 and over ..	693	313	380	18	17	1	244	167	77	431	129	302

TABLE VII.—Part B—Details for Districts—*contd.*

District.	Age.	Population. Persons.	Population. Males.	Population. Females.	Unmarried. Persons.	Unmarried. Males.	Unmarried. Females.	Married. Persons.	Married. Males.	Married. Females.	Widowed. Persons.	Widowed. Males.	Widowed. Females.
1	1	2	3	4	5	6	7	8	9	10	11	12	13
SAUGOR—*concld.*	TRIBAL RELIGION	*19,415*	*9,583*	*9,832*	*7,883*	*4,685*	*3,198*	*9,705*	*4,502*	*5,203*	*1,827*	*396*	*1,431*
	0—1 ..	495	247	248	494	246	248	1	1	..	..	..	..
	1—2 ..	456	224	232	456	224	232	..	..	..	..	..	..
	—3 .	506	250	256	506	250	256	.	..	..	..	..	..
	3—4 ..	578	293	285	577	292	285	1	1	..	..	..	..
	4—5 ..	588	302	286	584	300	284	4	2	2	..	..	..
	Total 0—5 .	*2,623*	*1,316*	*1,307*	*2,617*	*1,312*	*1,305*	*6*	*4*	*2*	..	..	..
	5—10 ..	2,537	1,295	1,242	2,273	1,284	989	262	10	252	2	1	1
	10—15 ..	2,359	1,229	1,130	1,875	1,172	703	480	56	424	4	1	3
	15—20 ..	1,843	901	942	718	557	161	1,096	336	760	29	8	21
	20—30 ..	3,479	1,680	1,799	332	301	31	3,005	1,332	1,673	142	47	95
	30—40 ..	2,721	1,288	1,433	35	30	5	2,379	1,190	1,189	307	68	239
	40—50 ..	2,145	1,051	1,094	23	21	2	1,592	933	659	530	97	433
	50—60 ..	1,150	561	589	9	7	2	672	461	211	469	93	376
	60 and over ..	558	262	296	1	1	..	213	180	33	344	81	263
DAMOH	ALL RELIGIONS ..	*305,568*	*154,791*	*150,777*	*127,244*	*75,327*	*51,917*	*141,616*	*70,734*	*70,882*	*36,708*	*8,730*	*27,978*
	0—1 ..	14,596	7,383	7,213	14,585	7,378	7,207	10	4	6	1	1	..
	1—2 ..	6,962	3,500	3,462	6,954	3,496	3,458	7	3	4	1	1	..
	2—3 ..	7,908	3,939	3,969	7,895	3,932	3,963	13	7	6	..	..	..
	3—4 ..	8,480	4,228	4,252	8,461	4,219	4,242	19	9	10	..	..	..
	4—5 ..	7,849	3,955	3,894	7,816	3,941	3,875	30	13	17	3	1	2
	Total 0—5 ..	*45,795*	*23,005*	*22,790*	*45,711*	*22,966*	*22,745*	*79*	*36*	*43*	*5*	*3*	*2*
	5—10 ..	36,744	19,138	17,606	34,699	18,625	16,074	2,005	507	1498	40	6	34
	10—15 ..	35,526	19,055	16,471	28,499	17,274	11,225	6,862	1,747	5,115	165	34	131
	15—20 ..	30,796	15,827	14,969	9,478	8,184	1,294	20,559	7,453	13,106	759	190	569
	20—30 ..	60,466	30,405	30,061	6,378	5,937	441	50,106	23,518	26,588	3,982	950	3,032
	30—40 ..	42,818	21,198	21,620	1,444	1,366	78	33,696	18,218	15,478	7,678	1,614	6,064
	40—50 ..	29,563	14,907	14,656	699	663	36	18,459	11,765	6,694	10,405	2,479	7,926
	50—60 ..	15,833	7,673	8,160	237	223	14	7,301	5,400	1,901	8,295	2,050	6,245
	60 and over ..	8,027	3,583	4,444	99	89	10	2,549	2,090	459	5,379	1,404	3,975
	HINDUS ..	*265,708*	*134,626*	*131,082*	*109,974*	*65,442*	*44,532*	*123,375*	*61,501*	*61,874*	*32,359*	*7,683*	*24,676*
	0—1 ..	12,868	6,406	6,462	12,864	6,404	6,460	3	1	2	1	1	..
	1—2 ..	5,993	3,037	2,956	5,987	3,034	2,953	5	2	3	1	1	..
	2—3 ..	6,782	3,399	3,383	6,771	3,393	3,378	11	6	5	..	..	..
	3—4 ..	7,290	3,633	3,657	7,271	3,624	3,647	19	9	10	..	..	..
	4—5 ..	6,758	3,405	3,353	6,732	3,394	3,338	24	10	14	2	1	1
	Total 0—5 ..	*39,691*	*19,880*	*19,811*	*39,625*	*19,849*	*19,776*	*62*	*28*	*34*	*4*	*3*	*1*
	5—10 ..	31,866	16,603	15,263	30,000	16,136	13,864	1,832	463	1,369	34	4	30
	10—15 ..	31,032	16,649	14,383	24,681	15,027	9,654	6,203	1,592	4,611	148	30	118
	15—20 ..	27,149	13,948	13,201	8,038	7,125	913	18,418	6,647	11,771	693	176	517
	20—30 ..	53,063	26,754	26,309	5,421	5,205	216	44,003	20,691	23,312	3,639	858	2,781
	30—40 ..	37,076	18,372	18,704	1,265	1,204	61	28,945	15,739	13,206	6,866	1,429	5,437
	40—50 ..	25,441	12,827	12,614	640	611	29	15,681	10,041	5,640	9,120	2,175	6,945
	50—60 ..	13,600	6,581	7,019	213	202	11	6,139	4,570	1,569	7,248	1,809	5,439
	60 and over ..	6,790	3,012	3,778	91	83	8	2,092	1,730	362	4,607	1,199	3,408
	MUSLIMS ..	*10,516*	*5,439*	*5,077*	*4,657*	*2,781*	*1,876*	*4,896*	*2,434*	*2,462*	*963*	*224*	*739*
	0—1 ..	489	248	241	488	248	240	1	..	1	..	..	..
	1—2 ..	271	134	137	270	134	136	1	..	1	..	..	..
	2—3 ..	310	159	151	310	159	151	..	..	..	..	..	..
	3—4 ..	328	172	156	328	172	156	..	..	..	..	..	..
	4—5 ..	308	158	150	304	156	148	3	2	1	1	..	1
	Total 0—5 ..	*1,706*	*871*	*835*	*1,700*	*869*	*831*	*5*	*2*	*3*	*1*	..	*1*
	5—10 ..	1,339	704	635	1,277	688	589	59	15	44	3	1	2
	10—15 ..	1,217	659	558	1,020	617	403	191	40	151	6	2	4
	15—20 ..	992	533	459	360	319	41	616	210	406	16	4	12
	20—30 ..	1,945	1,018	927	239	233	6	1,633	763	870	73	22	51
	30—40 ..	1,448	734	714	40	37	3	1,234	655	579	174	42	132
	40—50 ..	1,020	514	506	14	12	2	709	422	287	297	80	217
	50—60 ..	533	256	277	4	4	..	307	214	93	222	38	184
	60 and over ..	316	150	166	3	2	1	142	113	29	171	35	136

TABLE VII.—Part B—Details for Districts—*contd.*

District.	Age.	Population.			Unmarried.			Married.			Widowed.		
		Persons.	Males.	Females.	Persons.	Males.	Females.	Persons.	Males.	Females.	Persons.	Males.	Females.
	1	2	3	4	5	6	7	8	9	10	11	12	13
DAMOH—*concld.*	TRIBAL RELIGION	*21,331*	*10,555*	*10,776*	*9,090*	*1,863*	*4,227*	*10,061*	*5,175*	*4,886*	*2,180*	*517*	*1,663*
	0—1 ..	795	423	372	789	420	369	6	3	3	..	..	..
	1—2 ..	513	246	267	512	245	267	1	1	..	..	..	..
	2—3 ..	614	295	319	612	294	318	2	1	1	..	..	..
	3—4 ..	663	337	326	663	337	326	.	..	..	..	..	..
	4—5 ..	600	315	285	597	314	283	3	1	2	..	..	..
	Total 0—5 ..	*3,185*	*1,616*	*1,569*	*3,173*	*1,610*	*1,563*	*12*	*6*	*6*	..	..	..
	5—10 ..	2,594	1,333	1,261	2,514	1,307	1,207	79	26	53	1	..	1
	10—15 ..	2,357	1,225	1,132	2,030	1,129	901	321	95	226	6	1	5
	15—20 ..	1,914	937	977	805	481	324	1,085	449	636	24	7	17
	20—30 ..	3,979	1,889	2,090	472	259	213	3,361	1,581	1,780	146	49	97
	30—40 ..	3,170	1,503	1,667	65	54	11	2,698	1,359	1,339	407	90	317
	40—50 ..	2,274	1,145	1,129	24	19	5	1,603	992	611	647	134	513
	50—60 ..	1,222	614	608	6	4	2	665	479	186	551	131	420
	60 and over ..	636	293	343	1	..	1	237	188	49	398	105	293
JUBBULPORE	ALL RELIGIONS ..	*773,811*	*391,649*	*382,162*	*305,981*	*178,196*	*127,485*	*388,861*	*194,567*	*194,294*	*78,969*	*18,586*	*60,383*
	0—1 ..	24,928	12,499	12,429	24,821	12,441	12,380	105	57	48	2	1	1
	1—2 ..	22,588	11,033	11,555	22,325	10,900	11,425	257	132	125	6	1	5
	2—3 ..	24,668	11,860	12,808	24,075	11,697	12,378	581	160	421	12	3	9
	3—4 ..	25,055	12,298	12,757	24,270	12,072	12,198	763	220	543	22	6	16
	4—5 ..	22,971	11,547	11,424	22,260	11,263	10,997	677	277	400	34	7	27
	Total 0—5 ..	*120,210*	*59,237*	*60,973*	*117,751*	*53,873*	*59,378*	*2,383*	*846*	*1,537*	*76*	*18*	*58*
	5—10 ..	94,476	48,875	45,601	83,247	45,083	38,164	10,964	3,707	7,257	265	85	180
	10—15 ..	85,795	45,356	40,439	61,432	37,324	24,108	23,821	7,841	15,980	542	191	351
	15—20 ..	76,421	39,241	37,180	21,410	18,051	3,359	53,313	20,534	32,779	1,698	656	1,042
	20—30 ..	154,476	78,172	76,304	16,237	14,706	1,531	129,913	60,927	68,986	8,326	2,539	5,787
	30—40 ..	112,409	57,034	55,375	3,546	3,023	523	92,749	50,314	42,435	16,114	3,697	12,417
	40—50 ..	73,857	37,630	36,227	1,522	1,265	257	50,207	31,551	18,656	22,128	4,814	17,314
	50—60 ..	36,935	17,837	19,098	549	448	101	18,870	13,588	5,282	17,516	3,801	13,715
	60 and over ..	19,232	8,267	10,965	287	223	64	6,641	5,259	1,382	12,304	2,785	9,519
	HINDUS ..	*697,355*	*350,708*	*346,647*	*271,752*	*158,014*	*113,738*	*353,419*	*175,933*	*177,486*	*72,184*	*16,761*	*55,423*
	0—1 ..	22,638	11,339	11,299	22,545	11,288	11,257	91	50	41	2	1	1
	1—2 ..	20,417	9,962	10,455	20,178	9,841	10,337	233	120	113	6	1	5
	2—3 ..	22,296	10,722	11,574	21,733	10,574	11,159	551	145	406	12	3	9
	3—4 ..	22,756	11,182	11,574	22,008	10,974	11,034	726	202	524	22	6	16
	4—5 ..	20,831	10,485	10,346	20,161	10,222	9,939	639	257	382	31	6	25
	Total 0—5 ..	*108,938*	*53,690*	*55,248*	*106,625*	*52,899*	*53,726*	*2,240*	*774*	*1,466*	*73*	*17*	*56*
	5—10 ..	85,387	44,215	41,172	74,819	40,644	34,175	10,316	3,491	6,825	252	80	172
	10—15 ..	77,455	40,982	36,473	54,668	33,424	21,244	22,269	7,376	14,893	518	182	336
	15—20 ..	68,403	34,827	33,576	18,070	15,408	2,662	48,794	18,838	29,956	1,539	581	958
	20—30 ..	138,202	68,871	69,331	12,743	11,571	1,172	117,827	55,048	62,779	7,632	2,252	5,380
	30—40 ..	101,730	51,151	50,579	2,864	2,429	435	84 048	45,377	38,671	14,818	3,345	11,473
	40—50 ..	66,907	33.838	33,069	1,242	1,039	203	45,365	28,417	16,948	20,300	4,382	15,918
	50—60 ..	33,277	15,877	17,400	475	402	73	16,784	12,043	4,741	16,018	3,432	12,586
	60 and over ..	17,056	7,257	9,799	246	198	48	5,776	4,569	1,207	11,034	2,490	8,544
	MUSLIMS ..	*47,614*	*25,763*	*21,851*	*20,051*	*11,999*	*8,052*	*23,405*	*12,584*	*10,821*	*4,158*	*1,180*	*2,978*
	0—1 ..	1,473	753	720	1,465	749	716	8	4	4	..	..	..
	1—2 ..	1,448	709	739	1,430	700	730	18	9	9	..	..	..
	2—3 ..	1,568	751	817	1,543	739	804	25	12	13	..	..	..
	3—4 ..	1,472	713	759	1,440	697	743	32	16	16	..	..	..
	4—5 ..	1,388	680	708	1,352	661	691	34	18	16	2	1	1
	Total 0—5 ..	*7,349*	*3,606*	*3,713*	*7,230*	*3,546*	*3,684*	*117*	*59*	*58*	*2*	*1*	*1*
	5—10 ..	5,834	3,055	2,779	5,331	2,882	2,449	495	169	326	8	4	4
	10—15 ..	5,179	2,821	2,358	4,082	2,512	1,570	1,082	303	779	15	6	9
	15—20 ..	4,816	2,633	2,183	1,700	1,485	215	3,025	1,108	1,917	91	40	51
	20—30 ..	9,764	5,425	4,339	1,402	1,313	89	7,942	3,925	4,017	420	187	233
	30—40 ..	6,782	3,923	2,859	196	174	22	5,806	3,502	2,304	780	247	533
	40—50 ..	4,277	2,399	1,878	70	55	15	3,090	2,076	1,014	1,117	268	849
	50—60 ..	2,229	1,231	998	27	22	5	1,286	982	304	916	227	689
	60 and over ..	1,384	670	714	13	10	3	562	460	102	809	200	609

TABLE VII.—Part B—Details for Districts—*contd.*

District.	Age.	Population. Persons.	Population. Males.	Population. Females	Unmarried. Persons.	Unmarried. Males.	Unmarried. Females	Married. Persons.	Married. Males.	Married. Females.	Widowed Persons.	Widowed Males.	Widowed Females.
	1	2	3	4	5	6	7	8	9	10	11	12	13
JUBBULPORE—concld.	**CHRISTIANS** ..	*7,697*	*4,494*	*3,203*	*5,276*	*3,401*	*1,875*	*2,131*	*1,012*	*1,122*	*287*	*81*	*206*
	0—1 ..	181	96	83	181	98	83	..	..	..	..	..	..
	1—2 ..	160	85	75	160	85	75	..	..	..	..	..	..
	2—3 ..	165	87	78	165	87	78	..	..	..	..	..	..
	3—4 ..	156	82	74	156	82	74	..	..	..	..	..	..
	4—5 ..	150	74	76	150	74	76	..	..	..	..	..	..
	Total 0—5 ..	*812*	*426*	*386*	*812*	*426*	*386*	..	.	..	..	..	..
	5—10 ..	770	347	423	759	336	423	11	11	..	..	..	..
	10—15 ..	819	343	476	792	329	463	26	13	13	1	1	..
	15—20 ..	985	585	400	829	534	295	151	50	101	5	1	4
	20—30 ..	2,361	1,716	645	1,509	1,310	199	821	390	431	31	16	15
	30—40 ..	914	497	417	358	312	46	501	169	332	55	16	39
	40—50 ..	572	329	243	165	134	31	336	176	160	71	19	52
	50—60 ..	282	159	123	30	10	20	193	135	58	59	14	45
	60 and over ..	182	92	90	22	10	12	95	68	27	65	14	51
	TRIBAL RELIGION	*13,261*	*6,405*	*6,856*	*5,471*	*2,983*	*2,488*	*6,484*	*3,128*	*3,356*	*1,306*	*294*	*1,012*
	0—1 ..	387	188	199	381	185	196	6	3	3	..	..	..
	1—2 ..	366	180	186	360	177	183	6	3	3	..	..	..
	2—3 ..	425	201	224	420	198	222	5	3	2	..	..	..
	3—4 ..	446	211	235	441	209	232	5	2	3	..	..	..
	4—5 ..	410	206	204	405	204	201	4	2	2	1	..	1
	Total 0—5 ..	*2,034*	*986*	*1,018*	*2,007*	*973*	*1,034*	*26*	*13*	*13*	*1*	..	*1*
	5—10 ..	1,673	841	832	1,546	804	742	123	36	87	4	1	3
	10—15 ..	1,523	763	760	1,193	670	523	325	92	233	5	1	4
	15—20 ..	1,278	623	655	410	296	114	825	298	527	43	29	14
	20—30 ..	2,448	1,173	1,275	240	189	51	2,083	926	1,157	125	58	67
	30—40 ..	1,877	863	1,014	42	28	14	1,601	797	804	234	38	196
	40—50 ..	1 354	671	683	20	14	6	970	587	383	364	70	294
	50—60 ..	711	346	365	10	7	3	399	277	122	302	62	240
	60 and over ..	363	139	224	3	2	1	132	102	30	228	35	193
MANDLA	**ALL RELIGIONS** ..	*445,766*	*221,359*	*224,407*	*170,933*	*97,282*	*73,651*	*241,150*	*115 977*	*124,173*	*33,683*	*7,100*	*26,583*
	0—1 ..	15,867	7,810	8,057	15,764	7,768	7,996	103	42	61	..	..	..
	1—2 ..	15,058	7,352	7,706	14,858	7,286	7,572	199	65	134	1	1	..
	2—3 ..	15,632	7,528	8,104	15,194	7,339	7,855	435	188	247	3	1	2
	3—4 ..	15,852	7,787	8,055	15,129	7,505	7,674	717	282	435	6	..	6
	4—5 ..	15,221	7,669	7,552	14,387	7 405	6,982	819	261	558	15	3	12
	Total 0—5 ..	*77,630*	*38,146*	*39,484*	*75,332*	*37,303*	*38,029*	*2,273*	*838*	*1,435*	*25*	*5*	*20*
	5—10 ..	57,426	29,643	27,783	47,678	26,424	21,254	9,631	3,190	6 441	117	29	88
	10—15 ..	49,733	25,671	24,062	31,283	19,421	11,862	18,208	6,172	12,036	242	78	164
	15—20 ..	41,283	19,450	21,833	8,336	6,911	1,425	32,334	12,304	20,030	613	235	378
	20—30 ..	83,131	40,268	42,863	5,521	4,891	630	75,073	34,474	40,599	2,537	903	1,634
	30—40 ..	60,991	30,716	30,275	1,517	1,275	242	53,884	28,087	25,797	5,590	1,354	4,236
	40—50 ..	41,103	21,375	19,728	784	654	130	31,343	18,993	12,350	8,976	1,728	7,248
	50—60 ..	21,937	10,845	11,092	341	288	53	13,289	9,079	4,210	8,307	1,478	6,829
	60 and over ..	12,532	5,245	7,287	141	115	26	5,115	3,840	1,275	7,276	1,290	5,986
	HINDUS ..	*237,934*	*118,713*	*119,221*	*91,667*	*52,537*	*39,130*	*126,652*	*62,004*	*64,658*	*19,605*	*4,172*	*15,433*
	0—1 ..	8,690	4,295	4,395	8,654	4,287	4,367	36	8	28	..	..	..
	1—2 ..	8,104	3,993	4,111	8,011	3,968	4,043	92	24	68	1	1	..
	2—3 ..	8,256	4,014	4,242	7.975	3,875	4,100	279	138	141	2	1	1
	3—4 ..	8,263	4,064	4,199	7,824	3,879	3,945	436	185	251	3	.	3
	4—5 ..	7,872	3,973	3,899	7,430	3,846	3,584	435	126	309	7	1	6
	Total 0—5 ..	*41,185*	*20,339*	*20,845*	*39,894*	*19,855*	*20,039*	*1,278*	*481*	*797*	*13*	*3*	*10*
	5—10 ..	30,405	15,645	14,760	25,280	14,051	11,229	5,056	1,578	3,478	69	16	53
	10—15 ..	26,758	13,782	12 976	17.021	10,583	6,438	9,594	3,158	6,436	143	41	102
	15—20 ..	22,680	10,878	11,802	4,688	3,918	770	17,612	6,822	10,790	380	138	242
	20—30 .	45,115	22,220	22,895	3,164	2,814	350	40,340	18,859	21,481	1,611	547	1,064
	30—40 ..	32,690	16,684	16,006	877	721	156	28,224	15,115	13,109	3,589	848	2,741
	40—50 ..	21,793	11,334	10,459	465	371	94	15,905	9,878	6,027	5,423	1,085	4,338
	50—60 ..	11,142	5,354	5,788	194	158	36	6,348	4,367	1,981	4,600	829	3,771
	60 and over	6,166	2,477	3,689	84	66	18	2,305	1,746	559	3,777	665	3,112

TABLE VII.—Part B—Details for Districts—*contd.*

District.	Age.	Population Persons.	Population Males.	Population Females.	Unmarried. Persons.	Unmarried. Males.	Unmarried. Females.	Married. Persons.	Married. Males.	Married. Females.	Widowed. Persons.	Widowed. Males.	Widowed. Females.
	1	2	3	4	5	6	7	8	9	10	11	12	13
MANDLA—*concld.*	**TRIBAL RELIGION** ..	*199,310*	*98,123*	*101,187*	*75,508*	*42,491*	*33,017*	*110,498*	*52,878*	*57,620*	*13,304*	*2,754*	*10,550*
	0—1 ..	6,857	3,346	3,511	6,794	3,315	3,479	63	31	32	..	..	..
	1—2 ..	6,678	3,223	3,455	6,574	3,183	3,391	104	40	64	..	..	..
	2—3 ..	7,118	3,392	3,726	6,963	3,342	3,621	154	50	104	1	..	1
	3—4 ..	7,333	3,590	3,743	7,052	3,494	3,558	278	96	182	3	..	3
	4—5 ..	7,079	3,548	3,531	6,694	3,414	3,280	377	132	245	8	2	6
	Total 0—5 ..	*35,065*	*17,099*	*17,966*	*34,077*	*16,748*	*17,329*	*976*	*349*	*627*	*12*	*2*	*10*
	5—10 ..	25,976	13,425	12,551	21,418	11,823	9,595	4,510	1,589	2,921	48	13	35
	10—15 ..	22,066	11,396	10,670	13,516	8,390	5,126	8,454	2,971	5,483	96	35	61
	15—20 ..	17,761	8,123	9,638	3,323	2,728	595	14,217	5,302	8,915	221	93	128
	20—30 .	36,375	17,173	19,202	2,093	1,847	246	33,419	14,990	18,429	863	336	527
	30—40 ..	27,079	13,384	13,695	581	506	75	24,655	12,412	12,243	1,843	466	1,377
	40—50 ..	18,481	9,599	8,882	308	276	32	14,854	8,727	6,127	3,319	596	2,723
	50—60 ..	10,379	5,261	5,118	138	125	13	6,698	4,523	2,175	3,543	613	2,930
	60 and over ..	6,128	2,663	3,465	54	48	6	2,715	2,015	700	3,359	600	2,759
SEONI	**ALL RELIGIONS** ..	*393,732*	*192,471*	*201,261*	*149,413*	*84,224*	*65,189*	*204,236*	*99,072*	*105,164*	*40,083*	*9,175*	*30,908*
	0—1 ..	14,108	6,903	7,205	14,073	6,889	7,184	33	13	20	2	1	1
	1—2 ..	11,701	5,692	6,009	11,649	5,665	5,984	50	26	24	2	1	1
	2—3 ..	12,400	5,856	6,544	12,309	5,819	6,490	89	36	53	2	1	1
	3—4 ..	12,353	5,940	6,413	12,124	5,859	6,265	224	78	146	5	3	2
	4—5 ..	11,545	5,738	5,807	11,195	5,618	5,577	339	116	223	11	4	7
	Total 0—5 ..	*62,107*	*30,129*	*31,978*	*61,350*	*29,850*	*31,500*	*735*	*269*	*466*	*22*	*10*	*12*
	5—10 ..	46,995	23,883	23,112	41,029	22,065	18,964	5,900	1,797	4,103	66	21	45
	10—15 ..	42,264	21,818	20,446	30,107	18,078	12,029	12,007	3,691	8,316	150	49	101
	15—20 ..	36,142	17,507	18,635	9,563	7,714	1,849	26,060	9,594	16,466	519	199	320
	20—30 ..	72,961	35,086	37,875	5,599	4,997	602	64,568	29,077	35,491	2,794	1,012	1,782
	30—40 ..	55,697	27,411	28,286	1,078	940	138	47,954	24,673	23,281	6,665	1,798	4,867
	40—50 ..	40,113	19,929	20,184	444	377	67	28,841	17,166	11,675	10,828	2,386	8,442
	50—60 ..	22,652	10,744	11,908	166	144	22	12,653	8,650	4,003	9,833	1,950	7,883
	60 and over ..	14,801	5,964	8,837	77	59	18	5,518	4,155	1,363	9,206	1,750	7,456
	HINDUS ..	*215,865*	*106,813*	*109,052*	*78,468*	*45,071*	*33,397*	*115,522*	*56,515*	*59,007*	*21,875*	*5,227*	*16,648*
	0—1 ..	8,206	4,066	4,140	8,192	4,059	4,133	13	6	7	1	1	..
	1—2 ..	6,531	3,233	3,298	6,497	3,215	3,282	32	17	15	2	1	1
	2—3 ..	6,759	3,206	3,553	6,699	3,184	3,515	58	21	37	2	1	1
	3—4 ..	6,757	3,264	3,493	6,567	3,203	3,364	186	59	127	4	2	2
	4—5 ..	6,347	3,184	3,163	6,041	3,083	2,958	301	100	201	5	1	4
	Total 0—5 ..	*34,600*	*16,953*	*17,647*	*33,996*	*16,744*	*17,252*	*590*	*203*	*387*	*14*	*6*	*8*
	5—10 ..	26,293	13,355	12,938	21,497	11,880	9,617	4,748	1,462	3,286	48	13	35
	10—15 ..	23,702	12,205	11,497	15,093	9,438	5,655	8,508	2,734	5,774	101	33	68
	15—20 ..	19,972	9,912	10,060	4,363	3,762	601	15,309	6,031	9,278	300	119	181
	20—30 ..	39,829	19,525	20,304	2,630	2,452	178	35,624	16,502	19,122	1,575	571	1,004
	30—40 ..	29,994	15,090	14,904	557	504	53	25,769	13,563	12,206	3,668	1,023	2,645
	40—50 ..	21,204	10,643	10,561	222	197	25	15,179	9,102	6,077	5,803	1,344	4,459
	50—60 ..	12,088	5,800	6,288	76	67	9	6,728	4,615	2,113	5,284	1,118	4,166
	60 and over ..	8,183	3,330	4,853	34	27	7	3,067	2,303	764	5,082	1,000	4,082
	MUSLIMS ..	*18,506*	*9,152*	*9,354*	*8,330*	*4,732*	*3,598*	*8,334*	*4,052*	*4,282*	*1,842*	*368*	*1,474*
	0—1 ..	639	321	318	638	321	317	1	..	1	..	..	..
	1—2 ..	562	270	292	561	270	291	1	..	1	..	..	..
	2—3 ..	644	299	345	641	299	342	3	..	3	..	..	..
	3—4 ..	637	316	321	634	315	319	3	1	2	..	..	..
	4—5 ..	603	308	295	598	306	292	4	2	2	1	..	1
	Total 0—5 ..	*3,085*	*1,514*	*1,571*	*3,072*	*1,511*	*1,561*	*12*	*3*	*9*	*1*	..	*1*
	5—10 ..	2,361	1,224	1,137	2,276	1,201	1,075	84	23	61	1	..	1
	10—15 ..	2,026	1,058	968	1,739	996	743	283	61	222	4	1	3
	15—20 ..	1,718	829	889	669	523	146	1,030	300	730	19	6	13
	20—30 ..	3,481	1,699	1,782	472	417	55	2,866	1,241	1,625	143	41	102
	30—40 ..	2,505	1,237	1,268	72	60	12	2,097	1,099	998	336	78	258
	40—50 ..	1,728	864	864	24	19	5	1,201	750	451	503	95	408
	50—60 ..	984	480	504	6	5	1	543	394	149	435	81	354
	60 and over ..	618	247	371	..	..	..	218	181	37	400	66	334

TABLE VII.—Part B—Details for Districts—*contd.*

District.	Age.	Population.			Unmarried.			Married.			Widowed.		
		Persons.	Males.	Females.	Persons.	Males	Females.	Persons.	Males.	Females.	Persons.	Males	Females
	1	2	3	4	5	6	7	8	9	10	11	12	13
SEONI—*concld.*	TRIBAL RELIGION ..	*157,194*	*75,407*	*81,787*	*61,627*	*33,841*	*27,786*	*79,462*	*38,052*	*41,410*	*16,105*	*3,514*	*12,591*
	0—1 ..	5,190	2,483	2,707	5,170	2,476	2,694	19	7	12	1	..	1
	1—2 ..	4,552	2,162	2,390	4,535	2,153	2,382	17	9	8	..	..	..
	2—3 ..	4,930	2,318	2,612	4,903	2,304	2,599	27	14	13	..	..	..
	3—4 ..	4,895	2,328	2,567	4,860	2,310	2,550	34	17	17	1	1	..
	4—5 ..	4,535	2,211	2,324	4,496	2,194	2,302	34	14	20	5	3	2
	Total 0—5 ..	*24,102*	*11,502*	*12,600*	*23,964*	*11,437*	*12,527*	*131*	*61*	*70*	*7*	*4*	*3*
	5—10 ..	18,061	9,154	8,907	16,992	8,838	8,154	1,053	308	745	16	8	8
	10—15 ..	16,270	8,421	7,849	13,055	7,516	5,539	3,171	890	2,281	44	15	29
	15—20 ..	14,234	6,664	7,570	4,451	3,365	1,086	9,595	3,227	6,368	188	72	116
	20—30 ..	29,262	13,671	15,591	2,423	2,070	353	25,791	11,206	14,585	1,048	395	653
	30—40 ..	22,924	10,942	11,982	426	355	71	19,876	9,898	9,978	2,622	689	1,933
	40—50 ..	16,969	8,304	8,665	194	159	35	12,320	7,216	5,104	4,455	929	3,526
	50—60 ..	9,457	4,400	5,057	81	70	11	5,317	3,596	1,721	4,059	734	3,325
	60 and over ..	5,915	2,349	3,566	41	31	10	2,208	1,650	558	3,666	668	2,998
NARSINGHPUR	ALL RELIGIONS ..	*321,481*	*161,417*	*160,064*	*125,274*	*73,991*	*51,283*	*159,653*	*78,247*	*81,406*	*36,554*	*9,179*	*27,375*
	0—1 ..	11,189	5,722	5,467	11,136	5,708	5,428	52	14	38	1	..	1
	1—2 ..	9,151	4,382	4,769	9,095	4,362	4,733	54	19	35	2	1	1
	2—3 ..	9,555	4,587	4,968	9,486	4,557	4,929	66	29	37	3	1	2
	3—4 ..	9,409	4,680	4,729	9,318	4,647	4,671	89	32	57	2	1	1
	4—5 ..	8,910	4,578	4,332	8,782	4,538	4,244	120	36	84	8	4	4
	Total 0—5 ..	*48,214*	*23,949*	*24,265*	*47,817*	*23,812*	*24,005*	*381*	*130*	*251*	*16*	*7*	*9*
	5—10 ..	39,979	20,781	19,198	35,541	19,688	15,853	4,354	1,071	3,283	84	22	62
	10—15 ..	37,292	19,606	17,686	26,952	16,799	10,153	10,126	2,743	7,383	214	64	150
	15—20 ..	30,027	15,193	14,834	7,771	6,945	826	21,597	7,985	13,612	659	263	396
	20—30 ..	59,956	30,106	29,850	5,170	4,874	296	51,690	24,088	27,602	3,096	1,144	1,952
	30—40 ..	45,249	22,582	22,667	1,140	1,055	85	37,432	19,740	17,692	6,677	1,787	4,890
	40—50 ..	32,967	16,550	16,417	590	556	34	22,157	13,618	8,539	10,220	2,376	7,844
	50—60 ..	18,020	8,621	9,399	217	201	16	8,779	6,340	2,439	9,024	2,080	6,944
	60 and over ..	9,777	4,029	5,748	76	61	15	3,137	2,532	605	6,564	1,436	5,128
	HINDUS ..	*264,233*	*133,214*	*131,019*	*102,687*	*61,087*	*41,598*	*130,847*	*64,225*	*66,622*	*30,699*	*7,900*	*22,799*
	0—1 ..	9,301	4,799	4,502	9,285	4,796	4,489	16	3	13	..	..	..
	1—2 ..	7,562	3,640	3922	7,523	3,628	3,895	37	11	26	2	1	1
	2—3 ..	7,870	3,811	4,059	7,823	3,792	4,031	45	18	27	2	1	1
	3—4 ..	7,756	3,894	3,862	7,685	3,871	3,814	69	22	47	2	1	1
	4—5 ..	7,345	3,793	3,552	7,246	3,766	3,480	95	26	69	..	1	3
	Total 0—5 ..	*39,834*	*19,937*	*19,897*	*39,562*	*19,853*	*19,709*	*262*	*80*	*182*	*10*	*4*	*6*
	5—10 ..	33,121	17,275	15,846	29,225	16,326	12,897	3,825	930	2,895	71	17	54
	10—15 ..	30,805	16,241	14,564	21,921	13,799	8,122	8,703	2,389	6,314	181	53	128
	15—20 ..	24,629	12,517	12,112	6,097	5,546	551	17,970	6,747	11,223	562	224	338
	20—30 ..	49,088	24,719	24,369	4,164	3,958	206	42,286	19,769	22,517	2,638	992	1,646
	30—40 ..	36,970	18,584	18,386	963	903	60	30,335	16,119	14,216	5,672	1,562	4,110
	40—50 ..	26,896	13,492	13,404	504	478	26	17,803	10,970	6,833	8,589	2,044	6,545
	50—60 ..	14,769	7,086	7,683	182	170	12	7,086	5,139	1,947	7,501	1,777	5,724
	60 and over ..	8,121	3,363	4,758	69	54	15	2,577	2,082	495	5,475	1,227	4,248
	MUSLIMS ..	*11,404*	*5,802*	*5,602*	*4,905*	*2,921*	*1,981*	*5,322*	*2,607*	*2,715*	*1,177*	*271*	*906*
	0—1 ..	412	204	208	410	203	207	2	1	1	..	..	..
	1—2 ..	332	162	170	329	160	169	3	2	1	..	..	..
	2—3 ..	357	165	192	353	162	191	4	3	1	..	..	..
	3—4 ..	349	167	182	346	165	181	3	2	1	..	..	..
	4—5 ..	330	173	157	324	170	154	5	2	3	1	1	..
	Total 0—5 ..	*1,780*	*871*	*909*	*1,762*	*860*	*902*	*17*	*10*	*7*	*1*	*1*	..
	5—10 ..	1,480	784	696	1,350	749	601	125	33	92	5	2	3
	10—15 ..	1,381	742	639	1,071	666	405	302	74	228	8	2	6
	15—20 ..	1,113	589	524	379	338	41	715	244	471	19	7	12
	20—30 ..	2,028	1,051	977	263	243	20	1,667	776	891	98	32	66
	30—40 ..	1,459	702	757	44	36	8	1,228	626	602	187	40	147
	40—50 ..	1,106	562	544	20	18	2	777	476	301	309	68	241
	50—60 ..	634	310	324	14	12	2	333	236	97	287	62	225
	60 and over ..	423	191	232	2	2	..	158	132	26	263	57	206

TABLE VII.—Part B—Details for Districts—*contd.*

District.	Age.	Population. Persons	Males	Females	Unmarried. Persons.	Males.	Females.	Married. Persons.	Males.	Females.	Widowed. Persons.	Males.	Females.
	1	2	3	4	5	6	7	8	9	10	11	12	13
NARSINGHPUR—*concld.*	TRIBAL RELIGION..	*42,890*	*20,845*	*22,045*	*16,328*	*9,156*	*7,172*	*22,231*	*10,783*	*11,448*	*4,331*	*906*	*3,425*
	0—1 ..	1,335	649	686	1,300	639	661	34	10	24	1	..	1
	1—2 ..	1,168	537	631	1,154	531	623	14	6	8	..	..	..
	2—3 ..	1,242	570	672	1,224	562	662	17	8	9	1	..	1
	3—4 ..	1,214	573	641	1,197	565	632	17	8	9	..	..	..
	4—5 ..	1,145	566	579	1,122	556	566	20	8	12	3	2	1
	Total 0—5 ..	*6,104*	*2,895*	*3,209*	*5,997*	*2,553*	*3,141*	*102*	*40*	*62*	*5*	*2*	*3*
	5—10 ..	4,994	2,516	2 478	4,603	2,412	2,191	384	101	283	7	3	4
	10—15 ..	4,765	2,437	2,328	3,680	2,160	1,520	1,063	269	794	22	8	14
	15—20 ..	4,022	1,947	2,075	1,198	971	227	2,755	946	1,809	69	30	39
	20—30 ..	8,303	4,062	4,241	664	595	69	7,313	3,355	3,958	326	112	214
	30—40 ..	6,407	3,078	3,329	108	94	14	5,543	2,813	2,730	756	171	585
	40—50 ..	4,706	2,345	2,361	56	51	5	3,408	2,052	1,356	1,242	242	1,000
	50—60 ..	2,462	1,139	1,323	18	16	2	1,293	914	379	1,151	209	942
	60 and over ..	1,127	426	701	4	4		370	293	77	753	129	624
HOSHANGABAD	ALL RELIGIONS ..	*436,630*	*248,226*	*238,404*	*185,806*	*111,893*	*74,913*	*245,531*	*122,174*	*123,357*	*54,293*	*14,159*	*40,134*
	0—1 ..	16,534	8,169	8,365	16,504	8,154	8,350	28	14	14	2	1	1
	1—2 ..	14,099	6,919	7,180	14,043	6,901	7,142	53	18	35	3	..	3
	2—3 ..	14,422	6,989	7,433	14,352	6,966	7,386	69	23	46	1	..	1
	3—4 ..	13,995	6,932	7,063	13,865	6,891	6,974	127	41	86	3	..	3
	4—5 ..	13,115	6,716	6,399	12,920	6,657	6,263	187	58	129	8	1	7
	Total 0—5 ..	*72,165*	*35,725*	*36,440*	*71,684*	*35,569*	*36,115*	*464*	*154*	*310*	*17*	*2*	*15*
	5—10 ..	58,956	30,926	28,030	52,265	29,591	22,674	6,580	1,308	5,272	111	27	84
	10—15 ..	54,350	28,829	25,521	39,591	25,393	14,198	14,502	3,368	11,134	257	68	189
	15—20 ..	44,397	22,447	21,950	11,957	10,752	1,205	31,587	11,377	20,210	853	318	535
	20—30 ..	90,052	45,745	44,307	8,270	7,796	474	77,324	36,299	41,025	4,458	1,650	2,808
	30—40 ..	69,178	36,203	32,975	1,749	1,608	141	58,298	31,989	26,309	9,131	2,606	6,525
	40—50 ..	49,121	25,591	23,530	775	716	59	34,406	21,364	13,042	13,940	3,511	10,429
	50—60 ..	29.440	14,431	15,009	347	321	26	15,547	10,928	4,619	13,546	3,182	10,364
	60 and over ..	18,971	8,329	10,642	168	147	21	6,823	5,387	1,436	11,980	2,795	9,185
	HINDUS ..	*413 303*	*210,599*	*202,404*	*156,180*	*94,100*	*62,080*	*210,161*	*104,559*	*105,602*	*46,962*	*12,240*	*34,722*
	0—1 ..	14,159	6,990	7,169	14,140	6,982	7,158	19	8	11	..	..	..
	1—2 ..	11,958	5,896	6,062	11,916	5,884	6,032	41	12	29	1	..	1
	2—3 ..	12,173	5,939	6,234	12,119	5,924	6,195	53	15	38	1	..	1
	3—4 ..	11,796	5,881	5,915	11,684	5,849	5,835	109	32	77	3	..	3
	4—5 ..	11,056	5,684	5,372	10,890	5,640	5,250	160	43	117	6	1	5
	Total 0—5 ..	*61,142*	*30.390*	*30,752*	*60,749*	*30,279*	*30.470*	*382*	*110*	*272*	*11*	*1*	*10*
	5—10 ..	50,092	26,343	23,749	44,027	25,106	18,921	5,965	1,212	4,753	100	25	75
	10—15 ..	46,359	24,604	21,755	32,984	21,406	11,578	13,136	3,135	10,001	239	63	176
	15—20 ..	37,782	19,132	18,650	9,365	8,688	677	27,654	10,167	17,487	763	277	486
	20—30 ..	76,521	38,837	37,684	6,512	6,236	276	66,123	31,213	34,910	3,886	1.388	2,498
	30—40 ..	58,640	30,710	27,930	1,424	1,328	96	49,231	27,128	22,103	7,985	2,254	5,731
	40—50 ..	41,547	21,571	19,976	659	625	34	28.789	17,876	10,913	12,099	3,070	9,029
	50—60 ..	25,146	12,276	12,870	306	292	14	13,127	9.216	3,911	11,713	2,768	8,945
	60 and over ..	16.074	7,036	9,038	154	140	14	5,754	4,502	1,252	10,166	2,394	7,772
	MUSLIMS ..	*23,475*	*12,368*	*11,107*	*10.103*	*6,052*	*4,051*	*10,930*	*5,628*	*5,302*	*2,442*	*688*	*1,754*
	0—1 ..	760	373	387	756	371	385	3	1	2	1	1	..
	1—2 ..	656	319	337	652	318	334	3	1	2	1	..	1
	2—3 ..	696	328	368	693	326	367	3	2	1	..	..	..
	3—4 ..	699	332	367	695	330	365	4	2	2	..	..	..
	4—5 ..	672	341	331	662	336	326	9	5	4	1	..	1
	Total 0—5 ..	*3,483*	*1,692*	*1,790*	*3,458*	*1,681*	*1,777*	*22*	*11*	*11*	*3*	*1*	*2*
	5—10 ..	2,992	1,566	1,426	2,797	1,531	1,266	192	34	158	3	1	2
	10—15 ..	2,067	1,428	1,239	2,201	1,345	856	459	81	378	7	2	5
	15—20 ..	2,192	1,168	1,024	841	742	99	1,313	411	902	38	15	23
	20—30 ..	4,372	2,365	2,007	665	630	35	3,488	1,635	1,853	219	100	119
	30—40 ..	3,199	1,747	1,452	100	91	9	2,704	1,525	1,179	395	131	264
	40—50 ..	2,255	1,220	1,035	26	21	5	1,650	1,055	595	579	144	435
	50—60 ..	1,290	691	599	8	6	2	729	550	179	553	135	418
	60 and over ..	1,025	490	535	7	5	2	373	326	47	645	159	486

TABLE VII.—Part B—Details for Districts—*contd.*

District.	Age.	Population. Persons.	Population. Males.	Population. Females.	Unmarried. Persons.	Unmarried. Males.	Unmarried. Females.	Married. Persons.	Married. Males.	Married. Females.	Widowed. Persons.	Widowed. Males.	Widowed. Females.
	1	2	3	4	5	6	7	8	9	10	11	12	13
HOSHANGABAD—*concld.*	TRIBAL RELIGION	*45,150*	*22,567*	*22,883*	*18,369*	*10,461*	*7,908*	*22,615*	*11,005*	*11,610*	*4,466*	*1,101*	*3,365*
	0—1 ..	1,476	734	742	1,472	731	741	3	3	..	1	..	1
	1—2 ..	1,357	646	711	1,347	641	706	9	5	4	1	..	1
	2—3 ..	1,431	669	762	1,418	663	755	13	6	7	..	..	..
	3—4 ..	1,381	662	719	1,367	655	712	14	7	7	..	..	..
	4—5 ..	1,258	628	630	1,239	618	621	18	10	8	1	..	1
	Total 0—5 ..	*6,903*	*3,339*	*3,564*	*6,813*	*3,308*	*3,535*	*57*	*31*	*26*	*3*	..	*3*
	5—10 ..	5,340	2,746	2,594	4,926	2,687	2,239	407	58	349	7	1	6
	10—15 ..	4,845	2,547	2,298	3,973	2,399	1,574	862	145	717	10	3	7
	15—20 ..	4,017	1,924	2,093	1,523	1,154	369	2,448	746	1,702	46	24	22
	20—30 ..	8,345	4,069	4,276	853	720	133	7,176	3,194	3,982	316	155	161
	30—40 ..	6,674	3,370	3,304	148	119	29	5,847	3,054	2,793	679	197	482
	40—50 ..	4,855	2,517	2,338	75	57	18	3,621	2,199	1,422	1,159	261	898
	50—60 ..	2,766	1,329	1,437	23	16	7	1,559	1,064	495	1,184	249	935
	60 and over ..	1,705	726	979	5	1	4	638	514	124	1,062	211	851
NIMAR	ALL RELIGIONS ..	*466,931*	*242,042*	*224,889*	*173,291*	*103,351*	*69,910*	*247,183*	*124,996*	*122,487*	*46,157*	*13,695*	*32,462*
	0—1 ..	16,070	8,055	8,015	15,914	8,001	7,913	154	53	101	2	1	1
	1—2 ..	13,888	6,807	7,081	13,654	6,708	6,946	231	97	134	3	2	1
	2—3 ..	14,262	6,864	7,398	14,025	6,755	7,270	232	108	124	5	1	4
	3—4 ..	14,243	6,989	7,254	13,852	6,871	6,981	383	117	266	8	1	7
	4—5 ..	13,299	6,750	6,549	12,795	6,633	6,162	491	113	378	13	4	9
	Total 0—5 ..	*71,762*	*35,465*	*36,297*	*70,240*	*34,968*	*35,272*	*1,491*	*488*	*1,003*	*31*	*9*	*22*
	5—10 ..	58,388	30,403	27,985	48,379	27,836	20,543	9,878	2,526	7,352	131	41	90
	10—15 ..	53,491	27,841	25,650	34,556	22,529	12,027	18,654	5,235	13,419	281	77	204
	15—20 ..	46,016	22,576	23,440	9,941	8,884	1,057	35,190	13,371	21,819	885	321	564
	20—30 ..	91,433	47,066	44,367	7,185	6,670	515	79,759	38,654	41,105	4,489	1,742	2,747
	30—40 ..	64,679	35,396	29,283	1,530	1,370	160	54,360	31,236	23,124	8,789	2,790	5,999
	40—50 ..	41,303	22,586	18,717	895	611	284	28,865	18,763	10,102	11,543	3,212	8,331
	50—60 ..	23,550	12,579	10,971	388	346	42	12,820	9,429	3,391	10,342	2,804	7,538
	60 and over ..	16,309	8,130	8,179	177	137	40	6,466	5,294	1,172	9,666	2,699	6,967
	HINDUS ..	*372,583*	*193,412*	*179,171*	*131,449*	*79,390*	*52,059*	*202,649*	*102,659*	*99,990*	*38,485*	*11,353*	*27,122*
	0—1 ..	12,722	6,387	6,335	12,631	6,351	6,280	90	36	54	1	..	1
	1—2 ..	10,777	5,292	5,485	10,616	5,221	5,395	159	70	89	2	1	1
	2—3 ..	11,059	5,332	5,727	10,878	5,255	5,623	176	76	100	5	1	4
	3—4 ..	11,074	5,446	5,628	10,744	5,360	5,384	322	85	237	8	1	7
	4—5 ..	10,277	5,254	5,023	9,837	5,166	4,671	430	86	344	10	2	8
	Total 0—5 ..	*55,909*	*27,711*	*28,198*	*54,706*	*27,353*	*27,353*	*1,177*	*353*	*824*	*26*	*5*	*21*
	5—10 ..	45,820	23,907	21,913	36,666	21,564	15,102	9,039	2,307	6,732	115	36	79
	10—15 ..	42,365	22,072	20,293	25,660	17,231	8,429	16,463	4,775	11,688	242	66	176
	15—20 ..	36,838	18,139	18,699	6,960	6,459	501	29,135	11,423	17,712	743	257	486
	20—30 ..	73,629	37,964	35,665	5,148	4,867	281	64,713	31,685	33.028	3,768	1,412	2,356
	30—40 ..	52,541	28,829	23,712	1,200	1,108	92	43,918	25,398	18,520	7,423	2,323	5,100
	40—50 ..	33,381	18,206	15,175	701	446	255	23,013	15,057	7,956	9,667	2,703	6,964
	50—60 ..	19,097	10,159	8,938	269	243	26	10,213	7,559	2,654	8,615	2,357	6,258
	60 and over ..	13,003	6,425	6,578	139	119	20	4,978	4,102	876	7,886	2,204	5,682
	MUSLIMS ..	*50,925*	*26,839*	*24,086*	*22,692*	*13,397*	*9,295*	*23,632*	*11,961*	*11,671*	*4,601*	*1,481*	*3,120*
	0—1 ..	1,629	824	805	1,586	813	773	42	10	32	1	1	..
	1—2 ..	1,550	778	772	1,493	759	734	56	18	38	1	1	..
	2—3 ..	1,638	788	850	1,600	767	833	38	21	17	..	..	..
	3—4 ..	1,622	794	828	1,579	772	807	43	22	21	..	..	..
	4—5 ..	1,557	790	767	1,515	769	746	39	19	20	3	2	1
	Total 0—5 ..	*7,996*	*3,974*	*4,022*	*7,773*	*3,880*	*3,893*	*218*	*90*	*128*	*5*	*4*	*1*
	5—10 ..	6,922	3,627	3,295	6,417	3,487	2,930	493	137	356	12	3	9
	10—15 ..	6,209	3,275	2,934	5,022	3,029	1,993	1,161	237	924	26	9	17
	15—20 ..	4,933	2,491	2,442	1,726	1,458	268	3,119	988	2,131	88	45	43
	20—30 ..	9,492	5,002	4,490	1,276	1,149	127	7,770	3,626	4,144	446	227	219
	30—40 ..	6,554	3,600	2,954	209	165	44	5,513	3,128	2,385	832	307	525
	40—50 ..	4,286	2,417	1,869	147	131	16	3,076	1,976	1.100	1,063	310	753
	50—60 ..	2,525	1,398	1,127	97	88	9	1,407	1,047	360	1,021	263	758
	60 and over ..	2,008	1,055	953	25	10	15	875	732	143	1,108	313	795

Betul

TABLE VII.—Part B—Details for Districts—*contd.*

District.	Age.	Population.			Unmarried.			Married.			Widowed.		
		Persons.	Males	Females.	Persons.	Males.	Females.	Persons.	Males.	Females.	Persons.	Males.	Females.
	1	2	3	4	5	6	7	8	9	10	11	12	13
NIMAR—concld.	TRIBAL RELIGION	*35,429*	*17,659*	*17,770*	*15,858*	*8,641*	*7,217*	*17,226*	*8,378*	*8,848*	*2,345*	*640*	*1,705*
	0—1 ..	1,453	707	746	1,433	700	733	20	7	13	..	..	..
	1—2 ..	1,321	620	701	1,306	611	695	15	9	6	..	..	..
	2—3 ..	1,316	626	690	1,301	615	686	15	11	4	..	..	..
	3—4 ..	1,302	634	668	1,286	624	662	16	10	6	..	..	..
	4—5 ..	1,221	590	631	1,204	582	622	17	8	9	..	..	..
	Total 0—5 ..	*6,613*	*3,177*	*3,436*	*6,530*	*3,132*	*3,398*	*83*	*45*	*38*	..	..	..
	5—10 ..	4,611	2,342	2,269	4,419	2,296	2,123	189	45	144	3	1	2
	10—15 ..	3,957	1,987	1,970	3,219	1,851	1,368	728	135	593	10	1	9
	15—20 ..	3,439	1,539	1,900	1,009	781	228	2,384	742	1,642	46	16	30
	20—30 ..	6,767	3,328	3,439	568	500	68	5,996	2,748	3,248	203	80	123
	30—40 ..	4,484	2,357	2,127	68	54	14	4,037	2,186	1,851	379	117	262
	40—50 ..	2,948	1,581	1,367	25	16	9	2,300	1,420	880	623	145	478
	50—60 ..	1,566	831	735	9	5	4	1,003	686	317	554	140	414
	60 and over ..	1,044	517	527	11	6	5	506	371	135	527	140	387
BETUL	ALL RELIGIONS .	*406,252*	*201,114*	*205,138*	*172,236*	*95,898*	*76,338*	*196,445*	*96,168*	*100,277*	*37,571*	*9,048*	*28,523*
	0—1 ..	15,848	7,952	7,896	15,757	7,879	7,878	89	72	17	2	1	1
	1—2 ..	13,575	6,655	6,920	13,444	6,559	6,885	129	95	34	2	1	1
	2—3 ..	13,856	6,676	7,180	13,743	6,624	7,119	112	51	61	1	1	..
	3—4 ..	13,443	6,606	6,837	13,211	6,534	6,677	229	72	157	3	..	3
	4—5 ..	12,716	6,386	6,330	12,389	6,296	6,093	317	89	228	10	1	9
	Total 0—5 ..	*69,438*	*34,275*	*35,163*	*68,544*	*33,892*	*34,652*	*876*	*379*	*497*	*18*	*4*	*14*
	5—10 ..	52,980	26,861	26,119	47,109	25,197	21,912	5,766	1,638	4,128	105	26	79
	10—15 ..	47,402	24,180	23,222	35,613	20,608	15,005	11,586	3,502	8,084	203	70	133
	15—20 ..	36,181	17,408	18,773	11,741	8,609	3,132	23,896	8,566	15,330	544	233	311
	20—30 ..	71,311	34,611	36,700	7,111	5,870	1,241	61,556	27,759	33,797	2,644	982	1,662
	30—40 ..	53,382	26,813	26,569	1,252	1,039	213	46,286	24,261	22,025	5,844	1,513	4,331
	40—50 ..	37,199	18,974	18,225	526	425	101	27,406	16,453	10,953	9,267	2,096	7,171
	50—60 ..	22,120	10,735	11,385	210	161	49	12,653	8,538	4,115	9,257	2,036	7,221
	60 and over ..	16,239	7,257	8,982	130	97	33	6,420	5,072	1,348	9,689	2,088	7,601
	HINDUS ..	*275,093*	*136,689*	*138,404*	*107,924*	*61,596*	*46,328*	*140,497*	*69,005*	*71,492*	*26,672*	*6,088*	*20,584*
	0—1 ..	10,645	5,314	5,331	10,560	5,242	5,318	83	71	12	2	1	1
	1—2 ..	9,025	4,443	4,582	8,909	4,352	4,557	115	91	24	1	..	1
	2—3 ..	8,990	4,330	4,660	8,900	4,285	4,615	89	44	45	1	1	..
	3—4 ..	8,628	4,185	4,443	8,432	4,132	4,300	193	53	140	3	..	3
	4—5 .	8,067	3,982	4,085	7,793	3,923	3,870	267	58	209	7	1	6
	Total 0—5 ..	*45,355*	*22,254*	*23,101*	*44,594*	*21,931*	*22,660*	*747*	*317*	*430*	*14*	*3*	*11*
	5—10 ..	35,041	17,768	17,273	29,701	16,347	13,354	5,248	1,399	3,849	92	22	70
	10—15 ..	31,994	16,506	15,488	21,893	13,478	8,415	9,941	2,984	6,957	160	44	116
	15—20 ..	24,660	12,066	12,594	6,402	5,200	1,202	17,876	6,728	11,148	382	138	244
	20—30 ..	48,874	23,995	24,879	3,956	3,456	500	43,003	19,882	23,121	1,915	657	1,258
	30—40 ..	36,265	18,354	17,911	773	689	84	31,453	16,682	14,771	4,039	983	3,056
	40—50 ..	25,496	12,875	12,621	363	304	59	18,669	11,178	7,491	6,464	1,393	5,071
	50—60 ..	15,492	7,512	7,980	150	120	30	8,803	5,993	2,810	6,539	1,399	5,140
	60 and over .	11,916	5,359	6,557	92	68	24	4,757	3,842	915	7,067	1,449	5,618
	TRIBAL RELIGION	*121,883*	*59,642*	*62,241*	*60,225*	*31,971*	*28,254*	*51,648*	*24,936*	*26,712*	*10,010*	*2,735*	*7,275*
	0—1 ..	4,893	2,490	2,403	4,887	2,489	2,398	6	1	5	..	..	..
	1—2 ..	4,257	2,067	2,190	4,246	2,064	2,182	11	3	8	..	..	..
	2—3 ..	4,576	2,203	2,373	4,555	2,196	2,359	21	7	14	..	..	..
	3—4 ..	4,537	2,283	2,254	4,502	2,264	2,238	35	19	16	..	..	..
	4—5 ..	4,374	2,265	2,109	4,327	2,235	2,092	46	30	16	1	..	1
	Total 0—5 ..	*22,637*	*11,308*	*11,329*	*22,517*	*11,248*	*11,269*	*119*	*60*	*59*	*1*	..	*1*
	5—10 ..	16,788	8,523	8,265	16,349	8,298	8,051	430	221	209	9	4	5
	10—15 ..	14,413	7,185	7,228	12,904	6,678	6,226	1,470	483	987	39	24	15
	15—20 ..	10,651	4,912	5,739	4,979	3,142	1,837	5,525	1,683	3,842	147	87	60
	20—30 ..	20,690	9,695	10,995	2,846	2,154	692	17,180	7,247	9,933	664	294	370
	30—40 ..	15,801	7,720	8,081	412	294	118	13,722	6,932	6,790	1,667	494	1,173
	40—50 ..	10,842	5,636	5,206	138	101	37	8,124	4,878	3,246	2,580	657	1,923
	50—60 ..	6,111	2,944	3,167	50	34	16	3,561	2,326	1,235	2,500	584	1,916
	60 and over ..	3,950	1,719	2,231	30	22	8	1,517	1,106	411	2,403	591	1,812

TABLE VII.—Part B—Details for Districts—*contd.*

District.	Age.	Population.			Unmarried.			Married.			Widowed.		
		Persons.	Males.	Females	Persons.	Males.	Females.	Persons.	Males.	Females.	Persons.	Males.	Females.
	1	2	3	4	5	6	7	8	9	10	11	12	13
CHHINDWARA	**ALL RELIGIONS** ..	*573,272*	*285,007*	*288 265*	*231,931*	*131,071*	*100,860*	*289,822*	*141,851*	*147,971*	*51,519*	*12,085*	*39,434*
	0—1 ..	21,115	10,312	10,803	20,859	10,203	10,656	253	107	146	3	2	1
	1—2 ..	19,649	9,482	10,167	19,415	9,374	10,041	227	104	123	7	4	3
	2—3 ..	19,758	9,416	10,342	19,448	9,303	10,145	303	110	193	7	3	4
	3—4 ..	18,921	9,214	9,707	18,444	9,082	9,362	471	131	340	6	1	5
	4—5 ..	17,564	8,786	8,778	16,945	8,627	8,318	607	156	451	12	3	9
	Total 0—5 ..	*97,007*	*47,210*	*49,797*	*95,111*	*46,589*	*48,522*	*1,861*	*608*	*1,253*	*35*	*13*	*22*
	5—10 ..	72,096	36,558	35,538	62,984	33,971	29,013	8,948	2,545	6,403	164	42	122
	10—15 ..	63,002	32,439	30,563	45,887	27,149	18,738	16,840	5,204	11,636	275	86	189
	15—20 ..	50,272	24,383	25,889	14,118	11,133	2,985	35,485	12,966	22,519	669	284	385
	20—30 ..	104,337	51,040	53,297	9,903	8,741	1,162	90,860	40,932	49,928	3,574	1,367	2,207
	30—40 ..	77,975	39,516	38,459	2,136	1,902	234	67,773	35,530	32,243	8,066	2,084	5,982
	40—50 ..	53,552	27,522	26,030	990	865	125	39,725	23,818	15,907	12,837	2,839	9,998
	50—60 ..	31,544	15,702	15,842	467	416	51	18,566	12,730	5,836	12,511	2,556	9,955
	60 and over ..	23,487	10,637	12,850	335	305	30	9,764	7,518	2,246	13,388	2,814	10,574
	HINDUS ..	*349,600*	*175,768*	*173,832*	*132,281*	*76,222*	*56,059*	*185,594*	*91,830*	*93,764*	*31,725*	*7,716*	*24,009*
	0—1 ..	13,084	6,400	6,684	12,914	6,329	6,585	168	70	98	2	1	1
	1—2 ..	11,823	5,758	6,065	11,665	5,688	5,977	153	68	85	5	2	3
	2—3 ..	11,828	5,660	6,168	11,605	5,591	6,014	220	69	151	3	..	3
	3—4 ..	11,340	5,532	5,808	10,934	5,434	5,500	402	98	304	4	..	4
	4—5 ..	10,487	5,298	5,189	9,948	5,174	4,774	529	121	408	10	3	7
	Total 0—5 ..	*58,562*	*28,648*	*29,914*	*57,066*	*28,216*	*28,850*	*1,472*	*426*	*1,046*	*24*	*6*	*18*
	5—10 ..	44,170	22,491	21,679	36,291	20,279	16,012	7,738	2,174	5,564	141	38	103
	10—15 ..	38,723	20,066	18,657	25,386	15,778	9,608	13,109	4,216	8,893	228	72	156
	15—20 ..	30,586	15,142	15,444	6,775	5,768	1,007	23,371	9,182	14,189	440	192	248
	20—30 ..	63,688	31,626	32,062	5,005	4,608	397	56,480	26,176	30,304	2,203	842	1,361
	30—40 ..	47,186	24,321	22,865	966	866	100	41,346	22,153	19,193	4,874	1,302	3,572
	40—50 ..	32,526	16,769	15,757	411	361	50	24,266	14,611	9,655	7,849	1,797	6,052
	50—60 ..	19,541	9,921	9,620	184	164	20	11,637	8,103	3,534	7,720	1,654	6,066
	60 and over ..	14,618	6,784	7,834	197	182	15	6,175	4,789	1,386	8,246	1,813	6,433
	MUSLIMS ..	*20,183*	*10,550*	*9,633*	*9,126*	*5,328*	*3,798*	*9,328*	*4,769*	*4,559*	*1,729*	*453*	*1,276*
	0—1 ..	725	353	372	720	349	371	5	4	1	..	..	..
	1—2 ..	676	329	347	669	324	345	7	5	2	..	..	..
	2—3 ..	679	333	346	671	328	343	8	-	3	..	..	..
	3—4 ..	655	328	327	650	326	324	5	2	3	..	..	..
	4—5 ..	629	319	310	619	315	304	10	4	6	..	..	..
	Total 0—5 ..	*3,364*	*1,662*	*1,702*	*3,329*	*1,642*	*1,687*	*35*	*20*	*15*	..	..	..
	5—10 ..	2,583	1,323	1,260	2,456	1,289	1,167	123	33	90	4	1	3
	10—15 ..	2 186	1,145	1,041	1,880	1,086	794	302	58	244	4	1	3
	15—20 ..	1,825	960	865	723	619	104	1,081	333	748	21	8	13
	20—30 ..	3,758	1,983	1,775	574	541	33	3,068	1,391	1,677	116	51	65
	30—40 ..	2,706	1,471	1,235	103	97	6	2,323	1,298	1,025	280	76	204
	40—50 ..	1,855	987	868	37	33	4	1,374	860	514	444	94	350
	50—60 ..	1,089	580	509	13	11	2	666	473	193	410	96	314
	60 and over ..	817	439	378	11	10	1	356	303	53	450	126	324
	TRIBAL RELIGION	*200,173*	*96,986*	*103,187*	*88,938*	*48,618*	*40,320*	*93,509*	*44,539*	*48,970*	*17,726*	*3,829*	*13,897*
	0—1 ..	7,190	3,499	3,691	7,110	3,465	3,645	79	33	46	1	1	..
	1—2 ..	7,053	3,347	3,706	6,985	3,314	3,671	66	31	35	2	2	..
	2—3 ..	7,166	3,374	3,792	7,088	3,335	3,753	74	36	38	4	3	1
	3—4 ..	6,841	3,306	3,535	6,775	3,274	3,501	64	31	33	2	1	1
	4—5 ..	6,342	3,118	3,224	6,274	3,088	3,186	66	30	36	2	..	2
	Total 0—5 ..	*34,592*	*16,644*	*17,948*	*34,232*	*16,476*	*17,756*	*349*	*161*	*188*	*11*	*7*	*4*
	5—10 ..	24,920	12,527	12,393	23,829	12,191	11,638	1,073	333	740	18	3	15
	10—15 ..	21,689	11,016	10,673	18,264	10,082	8,182	3,383	921	2,462	42	13	29
	15—20 ..	17,523	8,111	9,412	6,444	4,631	1,813	10,878	3,397	7,481	201	83	118
	20—30 ..	36,341	17,157	19,184	4,212	3,513	699	30,908	13,179	17,729	1,221	465	756
	30—40 ..	27,650	13,514	14,136	1,042	916	126	23,755	11,903	11,852	2,853	695	2,158
	40—50 ..	18,826	9,580	9,246	528	462	66	13,832	8,192	5,640	4,466	926	3,540
	50—60 ..	10,719	5,099	5,620	263	237	26	6,150	4 073	2,077	4,306	789	3,517
	60 and over ..	7,913	3,338	4,575	124	110	14	3,181	2,380	801	4,608	848	3,760

TABLE VII.—Part B—Details for Districts—*contd.*

District.	Age.	Population.			Unmarried.			Married.			Widowed.		
		Persons.	Males.	Females.	Persons.	Males.	Females.	Persons.	Males.	Females.	Persons.	Males.	Females.
	1	2	3	4	5	6	7	8	9	10	11	12	13
WARDHA	ALL RELIGIONS ..	*516,266*	*261,394*	*254,872*	*172,654*	*102,274*	*70,380*	*289,926*	*145,149*	*144,777*	*53,686*	*13,971*	*39,715*
	0—1 ..	17,495	8,768	8,727	17,296	8,664	8,632	195	101	94	4	3	1
	1—2 ..	15,525	7,660	7,865	15,340	7,574	7,766	181	81	97	4	2	2
	2—3 ..	15,324	7,406	7,916	15,074	7,335	7,739	244	72	172	6	1	5
	3—4 ..	14,741	7,234	7,507	14,215	7,130	7,085	518	101	417	8	3	5
	4—5 ..	14,056	7,041	7,015	13,276	6,894	6,382	763	141	622	17	6	11
	Total 0—5 ..	*77,111*	*38,111*	*39,030*	*75,201*	*37,597*	*37,604*	*1,901*	*499*	*1,402*	*39*	*15*	*24*
	5—10 ..	63,745	32,088	31,657	48,937	28,691	20,246	14,571	3,348	11,223	237	49	188
	10—15 ..	58,532	29,641	28,891	33,691	22,522	11,169	24,396	7,030	17,366	445	89	356
	15—20 ..	45,901	22,275	23,626	7,758	7,115	643	37,340	14,937	22,403	803	223	580
	20—30 ..	88,348	43,838	44,510	4,867	4,464	403	79,747	38,213	41,534	3,734	1,161	2,573
	30—40 ..	69,873	35,707	34,166	1,178	1,025	153	60,350	32,593	27,757	8,345	2,089	6,256
	40—50 ..	52,158	27,961	24,197	574	483	91	39,126	24,382	14,744	12,458	3,096	9,362
	50—60 ..	33,326	17,933	15,393	279	239	40	20,367	14,470	5,897	12,680	3,224	9,456
	60 and over ..	27,242	13,840	13,402	169	138	31	12,128	9,677	2,451	14,945	4,025	10,920
	HINDUS ..	*452,285*	*229,234*	*223,051*	*148,367*	*88,539*	*59,828*	*256,899*	*128,375*	*128,524*	*47,019*	*12,320*	*34,699*
	0—1 ..	15,393	7,716	7,677	15,225	7,630	7,595	165	84	81	3	2	1
	1—2 ..	13,640	6,725	6,915	13,479	6,652	6,827	157	71	86	4	2	2
	2—3 ..	13,407	6,470	6,937	13,180	6,410	6,770	222	59	163	5	1	4
	3—4 ..	12,862	6,308	6,554	12,369	6,219	6,150	486	87	399	7	2	5
	4—5 ..	12,235	6,139	6,096	11,510	6,015	5,495	711	119	592	14	5	9
	Total 0—5 ..	*67,537*	*33,358*	*34,179*	*65,763*	*32,926*	*32,837*	*1,741*	*420*	*1,321*	*33*	*12*	*21*
	5—10 ..	55,812	28,182	27,630	41,986	25,072	16,914	13,606	3,063	10,543	220	47	173
	10—15 ..	51,470	26,127	25,343	28,557	19,514	9,043	22,501	6,531	15,970	412	82	330
	15—20 ..	40,388	19,596	20,792	6,286	5,800	486	33,381	13,593	19,788	721	203	518
	20—30 ..	77,475	38,530	38,945	3,897	3,573	324	70,290	33,945	36,345	3,288	1,012	2,276
	30—40 ..	61,064	31,216	29,848	987	882	105	52,737	28,491	24,246	7,340	1,843	5,497
	40—50 ..	45,569	24,476	21,093	498	428	70	34,225	21,323	12,902	10,846	2,725	8,121
	50—60 ..	29,197	15,685	13,512	249	218	31	17,860	12,613	5,247	11,088	2,854	8,234
	60 and over ..	23,773	12,064	11,709	144	126	18	10,558	8,396	2,162	13,071	3,542	9,529
	MUSLIMS ..	*20,928*	*11,046*	*9,882*	*9,379*	*5,506*	*3,873*	*9,590*	*4,959*	*4,631*	*1,959*	*581*	*1,378*
	0—1 ..	660	338	322	647	332	315	13	6	7	..	..	..
	1—2 ..	642	330	312	631	325	306	11	5	6	..	..	..
	2—3 ..	670	337	333	661	331	330	9	6	3	..	..	..
	3—4 ..	674	340	334	663	334	329	10	5	5	1	1	..
	4—5 ..	653	326	327	638	320	318	15	6	9	..	..	..
	Total 0—5 ..	*3,299*	*1,671*	*1,628*	*3,240*	*1,642*	*1,598*	*58*	*28*	*30*	*1*	*1*	..
	5—10 ..	2,735	1,343	1,392	2,568	1,313	1,255	163	29	134	4	1	3
	10—15 ..	2,390	1,201	1,189	1,998	1,147	851	385	51	334	7	3	4
	15—20 ..	1,927	1,026	901	787	694	93	1,123	326	797	17	6	11
	20—30 .	3,677	1,953	1,724	621	580	41	2,917	1,311	1,606	139	62	77
	30—40 .	2,717	1,504	1,213	104	86	18	2,311	1,330	981	302	88	214
	40—50 ..	1,952	1,100	852	41	31	10	1,420	930	490	491	139	352
	50—60 ..	1,191	680	511	15	10	5	722	551	171	454	119	335
	60 and over ..	1,040	568	472	5	3	2	491	403	88	544	162	382
	TRIBAL RELIGION	*39,789*	*19,408*	*20,381*	*13,694*	*7,469*	*6,225*	*21,754*	*10,948*	*10,806*	*4,341*	*991*	*3,350*
	0—1 ..	1,346	664	682	1,328	652	676	17	11	6	1	1	..
	1—2 ..	1,160	566	594	1,148	559	589	12	7	5	..	..	..
	2—3 ..	1,161	560	601	1,149	554	595	11	6	5	1	..	1
	3—4 ..	1,121	543	578	1,102	535	567	19	8	11	..	..	..
	4—5 ..	1,069	523	546	1,038	510	528	29	13	16	2	..	2
	Total 0—5 ..	*5,857*	*2,856*	*3,001*	*5,765*	*2,810*	*2,955*	*88*	*45*	*43*	*4*	*1*	*3*
	5—10 ..	4,812	2,349	2,463	4,048	2,104	1,944	752	244	508	12	1	11
	10—15 ..	4,331	2,126	2,205	2,890	1,695	1,195	1,416	427	989	25	4	21
	15—20 ..	3,260	1,491	1,769	597	542	55	2,604	936	1,668	59	13	46
	20—30 ..	6,584	3,054	3,530	274	248	26	6,035	2,726	3,309	275	80	195
	30—40 ..	5,634	2,736	2,898	69	42	27	4,920	2,545	2,375	645	149	496
	40—50 ..	4,308	2,201	2,107	26	17	9	3,248	1,976	1,272	1,034	208	826
	50—60 ..	2,720	1,459	1,261	9	6	3	1,675	1,224	451	1,036	229	807
	60 and over ..	2,283	1,136	1,147	16	5	11	1,016	825	191	1,251	306	945

TABLE VII.—Part B—Details for Districts—*contd.*

District.	Age.	Population.			Unmarried.			Married.			Widowed.		
		Persons.	Males.	Females	Persons.	Males.	Females	Persons	Males.	Females.	Persons	Males	Females.
	1	2	3	4	5	6	7	8	9	10	11	12	13
NAGPUR	ALL RELIGIONS ..	*940,049*	*481,246*	*458,803*	*325,947*	*194,415*	*131,532*	*520,833*	*264,168*	*256,665*	*93,269*	*22,663*	*70,606*
	0—1 ..	30,754	15,194	15,560	30,518	15,101	15,417	192	81	111	44	12	32
	1—2 ..	27,880	13,784	14,096	27,547	13,665	13,882	264	100	164	69	19	50
	2—3 ..	27,760	13,492	14,268	27,266	13,323	13,943	427	149	278	67	20	47
	3—4 ..	26,948	13,325	13,623	25,969	13,098	12,871	911	206	705	68	21	47
	4—5 ..	25,653	13,099	12,554	24,282	12,845	11,437	1,297	231	1,066	74	23	51
	Total 0—5 ..	*138,995*	*68,894*	*70,101*	*135,582*	*68,032*	*67,550*	*3,091*	*767*	*2,324*	*322*	*95*	*227*
	5—10 ..	116,156	59,071	57,085	90,967	53,426	37,541	24,584	5,481	19,103	605	164	441
	10—15 ..	105,604	54,256	51,348	64,227	42,219	22,008	40,473	11,818	28,655	904	219	685
	15—20 ..	84,826	42,498	42,328	17,761	15,384	2,377	65,425	26,637	38,788	1,640	477	1,163
	20—30 ..	167,555	85,281	82,274	12,651	11,435	1,216	148,190	71,610	76,580	6,714	2,236	4,478
	30—40 ..	129,726	67,845	61,881	2,659	2,302	357	112,616	61,973	50,643	14,451	3,570	10,881
	40—50 ..	92,144	49,030	43,114	1,177	939	238	69,402	43,415	25,987	21,565	4,676	16,889
	50—60 ..	56,939	30,267	26,672	519	392	127	35,174	25,089	10,085	21,246	4,785	16,460
	60 and over ..	48,104	24,104	24,000	404	286	118	21,878	17,378	4,500	25,822	6,440	19,382
	HINDUS ..	*862,519*	*439,201*	*423,318*	*291,133*	*173,665*	*117,468*	*484,419*	*244,585*	*239,834*	*86,967*	*20,951*	*66,016*
	0—1 ..	28,688	14,131	14,557	28,471	14,050	14,421	174	70	104	43	11	32
	1—2 ..	25,756	12,723	13,033	25,452	12,618	12,834	236	86	150	68	19	49
	2—3 ..	25,545	12,429	13,116	25,079	12,275	12,804	400	135	265	66	19	47
	3—4 ..	24,753	12,262	12,491	23,817	12,056	11,761	871	187	684	65	19	46
	4—5 ..	23,532	12,049	11,483	22,228	11,820	10,408	1,236	208	1,028	68	21	47
	Total 0—5 ..	*128,274*	*63,594*	*64,680*	*125,047*	*62,819*	*62,228*	*2,917*	*686*	*2,231*	*310*	*89*	*221*
	5—10 ..	106,543	54,185	52,358	82,079	48,714	33,365	23,879	5,314	18,565	585	157	428
	10—15 ..	96,805	49,704	47,101	56,946	37,994	18,952	38,996	11,504	27,492	863	206	657
	15—20 ..	77,206	38,333	38,873	14,238	12,614	1,624	61,433	25,277	36,156	1,535	442	1,093
	20—30 ..	152,536	76,741	75,795	9,127	8,400	727	137,180	66,300	70,880	6,229	2,041	4,188
	30—40 ..	119,016	61,723	57,293	2,117	1,773	244	103,551	56,696	46,855	13,448	3,254	10,194
	40—50 ..	84,851	44,856	39,995	947	782	165	63,810	39,763	24,047	20,094	4,311	15,783
	50—60 ..	52,658	27,803	24,855	409	324	85	32,427	23,009	9,418	19,822	4,470	15,352
	60 and over ..	44,630	22,262	22,368	323	245	78	20,226	16,036	4,190	24,081	5,981	18,100
	MUSLIMS ..	*53,809*	*29,366*	*24,443*	*23,571*	*14,022*	*9,549*	*25,799*	*14,085*	*11,714*	*4,439*	*1,259*	*3,180*
	0—1 ..	1,393	716	677	1,377	706	671	16	10	6	..	..	..
	1—2 ..	1,515	762	753	1,489	750	739	25	12	13	1	..	1
	2—3 ..	1,587	759	828	1,563	747	816	23	11	12	1	1	..
	3—4 ..	1,591	770	821	1,559	753	806	29	15	14	3	2	1
	4—5 ..	1,531	760	771	1,488	740	748	38	18	20	5	2	3
	Total 0—5 ..	*7,617*	*3,767*	*3,850*	*7,476*	*3,696*	*3,780*	*131*	*66*	*65*	*10*	*5*	*5*
	5—10 ..	6,857	3,485	3,372	6,372	3,356	3,016	471	124	347	14	5	9
	10—15 ..	6,164	3,196	2,968	5,110	2,973	2,137	1,025	214	811	29	9	20
	15—20 ..	5,143	2,815	2,328	2,175	1,822	353	2,895	964	1,931	73	29	44
	20—30 ..	10,241	5,801	4,440	1,929	1,749	180	7,969	3,894	4,075	343	158	185
	30—40 ..	7,407	4,348	3,059	321	284	37	6,387	3,829	2,558	699	235	464
	40—50 ..	4,943	2,885	2,058	109	85	24	3,806	2,540	1,266	1,028	260	768
	50—60 ..	2,936	1,709	1,227	45	34	11	1,887	1,448	439	1,004	227	777
	60 and over ..	2,501	1,360	1,141	34	23	11	1,228	1,006	222	1,239	331	908
	CHRISTIANS ..	*8,558*	*4,810*	*3,748*	*5,508*	*3,300*	*2,208*	*2,632*	*1,406*	*1,226*	*418*	*104*	*314*
	0—1 ..	229	123	106	229	123	106	..	..	..	..	..	..
	1—2 ..	206	104	102	206	104	102	..	..	..	..	..	..
	2—3 ..	215	108	107	215	108	107	..	..	..	..	..	..
	3—4 ..	204	97	107	204	97	107	..	..	..	..	..	..
	4—5 ..	198	94	104	198	94	104	..	..	..	..	..	..
	Total 0—5 ..	*1,052*	*526*	*526*	*1,052*	*526*	*526*	..	..	..	..	..	..
	5—10 ..	1,030	523	507	1,016	523	493	12	..	12	2	..	2
	10—15 ..	1,035	531	504	984	524	460	48	6	42	3	1	2
	15—20 ..	1,064	629	435	889	572	317	170	57	113	5	..	5
	20—30 ..	1,886	1,209	677	1,183	919	264	670	282	388	33	8	25
	30—40 ..	1,107	603	504	217	163	54	813	423	390	77	17	60
	40—50 ..	757	440	317	80	42	38	568	370	198	109	28	81
	50—60 ..	386	221	165	48	20	28	253	184	69	85	17	68
	60 and over ..	241	128	113	39	11	28	98	84	14	104	33	71
	TRIBAL RELIGION	*9,784*	*4,972*	*4,812*	*3,644*	*2,125*	*1,519*	*5,203*	*2,605*	*2,598*	*937*	*242*	*695*
	0—1 ..	301	151	150	298	149	149	2	1	1	1	1	..
	1—2 ..	289	142	147	286	140	146	3	2	1	..	..	..
	2—3 ..	287	138	149	283	135	148	4	3	1	..	..	..
	3—4 ..	273	135	138	263	131	132	10	4	6	..	..	..
	4—5 ..	264	134	130	245	130	115	18	4	14	1	..	1
	Total 0—5 ..	*1,414*	*700*	*714*	*1,375*	*685*	*690*	*37*	*14*	*23*	*2*	*1*	*1*
	5—10 ..	1,132	579	553	1,006	553	453	124	25	99	2	1	1
	10—15 ..	1,031	531	500	788	473	315	238	56	182	5	2	3
	15—20 ..	854	415	439	252	211	41	589	201	388	13	3	10
	20—30 ..	1,775	899	876	173	161	12	1,533	716	817	69	22	47
	30—40 ..	1,414	714	700	27	21	6	1,238	647	591	149	46	103
	40—50 ..	1,028	530	498	14	12	2	809	471	338	205	47	158
	50—60 ..	628	356	272	4	4	..	406	302	104	218	50	168
	60 and over ..	508	248	260	5	5	..	229	173	56	274	70	204

TABLE VII.—Part B—Details for Districts—*contd.*

District.	Age.	Population. Persons.	Population. Males.	Population. Females.	Unmarried. Persons.	Unmarried. Males.	Unmarried. Females.	Married. Persons.	Married. Males.	Married. Females.	Widowed. Persons.	Widowed. Males.	Widowed. Females.
	1	2	3	4	5	6	7	8	9	10	11	12	13
CHANDA	**ALL RELIGIONS** ..	*759,695*	*381,204*	*375,491*	*272,387*	*157,421*	*114,966*	*413,853*	*205,990*	*207,863*	*73,455*	*17,793*	*55,662*
	0—1 ..	25,699	12,744	12,955	24,874	12,127	12,747	819	614	205	6	3	3
	1—2 ..	23,977	11,743	12,234	23,053	11,139	11,914	913	598	315	11	6	5
	2—3 ..	23,498	11,169	12,329	22,312	10,548	11,764	1,161	612	549	25	9	16
	3—4 ..	23,587	11,387	12,200	21,585	10,581	11,004	1,950	789	1,161	52	17	35
	4—5 ..	23,594	11,713	11,881	20,913	10,730	10,183	2,602	954	1,648	79	29	50
	Total 0—5 ..	*120,355*	*58,756*	*61,599*	*112,737*	*55,125*	*57,612*	*7,445*	*3,567*	*3,878*	*173*	*64*	*109*
	5—10 ..	100,063	50,225	49,838	72,356	41,053	31,303	27,114	8,975	18,139	593	197	396
	10—15 ..	89,270	44,971	44,299	49,452	31,224	18,228	39,037	13,507	25,530	781	240	541
	15—20 ..	67,024	31,930	35,094	15,183	11,389	3,794	50,653	20,192	30,461	1,188	349	839
	20—30 ..	133,110	65,172	67,938	13,617	10,523	3,094	114,043	53,034	61,009	5,450	1,615	3,835
	30—40 ..	100,661	51,843	48,818	4,631	4,209	422	84,262	44,889	39,373	11,768	2,745	9,023
	40—50 ..	70,384	37,733	32,651	2,322	2,077	245	50,875	31,824	19,051	17,187	3,832	13,355
	50—60 ..	43,684	23,129	20,555	1,252	1,100	152	25,282	18,083	7,199	17,150	3,946	13,204
	60 and over ..	35,144	17,445	17,699	837	721	116	15,142	11,919	3,223	19,165	4,805	14,360
	HINDUS	*630,517*	*317,050*	*313,467*	*214,783*	*126,226*	*88 557*	*353,670*	*176,600*	*177,610*	*62,064*	*14,824*	*47,240*
	0—1 ..	21,824	10,801	11,023	21,095	10,229	10,866	726	570	156	3	2	1
	1—2 ..	20,073	9,847	10,226	19,252	9,295	9,957	811	547	264	10	5	5
	2—3 ..	19,294	9,198	10,096	18,228	8,646	9,582	1,044	545	499	22	7	15
	3—4 ..	19,102	9,233	9,869	17,248	8,509	8,739	1,809	710	1,099	45	14	31
	4—5 ..	19,090	9,513	9,577	16,596	8,623	7,973	2,427	866	1,561	67	24	43
	Total 0—5 ..	*99,383*	*48,592*	*50,791*	*92,419*	*45,302*	*47,117*	*6,817*	*3,238*	*3,579*	*147*	*52*	*95*
	5—10 ..	82,896	41,859	41,037	56,855	33,277	23,578	25,507	8,411	17,096	534	171	363
	10—15 ..	74,458	37,893	36,565	37,850	25,080	12,770	35,905	12,601	23,904	703	212	491
	15—20 ..	55,221	26,439	28,782	10,413	8,165	2,248	43,800	17,981	25,819	1,008	293	715
	20—30 ..	109,728	53,784	55,944	9,800	7,476	2,324	95,430	44,998	50,432	4,498	1,310	3,188
	30—40 ..	83,080	42,719	40,361	3,768	3,515	253	69,583	37,012	32,571	9,729	2,192	7,537
	40—50 ..	58,731	31,360	27,371	1,922	1,790	132	42,394	26,394	16,000	14,415	3,176	11,239
	50—60 ..	36,930	19,468	17,462	1,049	971	78	21,288	15,181	6,107	14,593	3,316	11,277
	60 and over ..	30,090	14,936	15,154	707	650	57	12,946	10,184	2,762	16,437	4,102	12,335
	MUSLIMS ..	*13,556*	*7,045*	*6,511*	*5,798*	*3,394*	*2,404*	*6,322*	*3,315*	*3,007*	*1,436*	*336*	*1,100*
	0—1 ..	386	197	189	373	186	187	13	11	2	..	..	..
	1—2 ..	346	170	176	339	163	176	7	7	..	..	..	..
	2—3 ..	353	169	184	345	162	183	8	7	1	..	..	..
	3—4 ..	379	187	192	369	179	190	10	8	2	..	..	..
	4—5 ..	378	194	184	362	182	180	15	12	3	1	..	1
	Total 0—5 ..	*1,842*	*917*	*925*	*1,788*	*872*	*916*	*53*	*45*	*8*	*1*	..	*1*
	5—10 ..	1,713	866	847	1,565	798	767	144	67	77	4	1	3
	10—15 ..	1,582	797	785	1,277	708	569	299	87	212	6	2	4
	15—20 ..	1,290	671	619	509	418	91	758	244	514	23	9	14
	20—30 ..	2,517	1,354	1,163	431	397	34	1,991	927	1,064	95	30	65
	30—40 ..	1,839	1,012	827	125	113	12	1,481	838	643	233	61	172
	40—50 ..	1,306	705	601	64	56	8	894	576	318	348	73	275
	50—60 ..	805	414	391	27	23	4	449	323	126	329	68	261
	60 and over ..	662	309	353	12	9	3	253	208	45	397	92	305
	TRIBAL RELIGION	*113,327*	*55,916*	*57,411*	*50,657*	*27,159*	*23,498*	*52 907*	*26,167*	*26,740*	*9,763*	*2,590*	*7,173*
	0—1 ..	3,418	1,704	1,714	3,337	1,672	1,665	78	31	47	3	1	2
	1—2 ..	3,500	1,698	1,802	3,404	1,653	1,751	95	44	51	1	1	..
	2—3 ..	3,794	1,779	2,015	3,684	1,718	1,966	107	59	48	3	2	1
	3—4 ..	4,051	1,943	2,108	3,915	1,870	2,045	129	70	59	7	3	4
	4—5 ..	4,055	1,972	2,083	3,890	1,894	1,996	154	73	81	11	5	6
	Total 0—5 ..	*18,818*	*9,096*	*9,722*	*18,230*	*8,807*	*9,423*	*563*	*277*	*286*	*25*	*12*	*13*
	5—10 ..	15,147	7,347	7,800	13,653	6,832	6,821	1,439	490	949	55	25	30
	10—15 ..	12,931	6,125	6,806	10,065	5,290	4,775	2,795	809	1,986	71	26	45
	15—20 ..	10,252	4,686	5,566	4,110	2,711	1,399	5,990	1,930	4,060	152	45	107
	20—30 ..	20,426	9,816	10,610	3,271	2,569	702	16,314	6,978	9,336	841	269	572
	30—40 ..	15,432	7,948	7,484	712	561	151	12,961	6,902	6,059	1,759	485	1,274
	40—50 ..	10,135	5,535	4,600	326	224	102	7,436	4,737	2,699	2,373	574	1,799
	50—60 ..	5,850	3,189	2,661	172	103	69	3,488	2,534	954	2,190	552	1,638
	60 and over ..	4,336	2,174	2,162	118	62	56	1,921	1,510	411	2,297	602	1,695

TABLE VII.—Part B—Details for Districts—*contd.*

District.	Age	Population			Unmarried			Married.			Widowed.		
		Persons.	Males.	Females.	Persons.	Males.	Females.	Persons.	Males.	Females.	Persons.	Males.	Females.
	1	2	3	4	5	6	7	8	9	10	11	12	13
BHANDARA	**ALL RELIGIONS** ..	*824,496*	*408,799*	*415,697*	*280,425*	*160,270*	*120,155*	*469,874*	*230,604*	*239,270*	*74,197*	*17,925*	*56,272*
	0—1 ..	28,565	14,046	14,519	25,774	12,623	13,151	2,737	1,396	1,341	54	27	27
	1—2 ..	24,276	11,755	12,521	22,327	10,861	11,466	1,869	846	1,023	80	48	32
	2—3 ..	25,245	12,072	13,173	23,075	11,084	11,991	2,058	929	1,129	112	59	53
	3—4 ..	24,574	12,103	12,471	22,346	11,237	11,109	2,117	811	1,306	111	55	56
	4—5 ..	23,414	11,867	11,547	21,253	11,191	10,064	2,046	619	1,427	113	57	56
	Total 0—5 ..	*126,074*	*64,843*	*61,231*	*114,777*	*56,996*	*57,781*	*10,827*	*4,601*	*6,226*	**470**	**246**	**224**
	5—10 ..	102,136	52,074	50,062	77,666	43,875	33,791	23,951	8,010	15,941	519	189	330
	10—15 ..	92,619	47,254	45,365	54,744	33,463	21,281	37,200	13,577	23,623	675	214	461
	15—20 ..	71,303	34,909	36,394	15,327	11,806	3,521	54,650	22,626	32,024	1,326	477	849
	20—30 ..	143,657	69,913	73,744	10,824	9,024	1,800	127,301	59,291	68,010	5,532	1,598	3,934
	30—40 ..	113,853	55,859	57,994	3,274	2,303	971	99,170	50,979	48,191	11,409	2,577	8,832
	40—50 ..	78,580	40,688	37,892	1,377	1,055	322	60,924	35,775	25,149	16,279	3,858	12,421
	50—60 ..	49,698	24,906	24,792	850	600	250	32,263	20,646	11,617	16,585	3,660	12,925
	60 and over ..	46,576	21,353	25,223	1,586	1,148	438	23,588	15,099	8,489	21,402	5,106	16,296
	HINDUS ..	*767,373*	*380,517*	*386,856*	*257,950*	*147,782*	*110,168*	*440,707*	*216,170*	*224,537*	*68,716*	*16,565*	*52,151*
	0—1 ..	26,782	13,156	13,626	24,156	11,821	12,335	2,591	1,313	1,278	35	22	13
	1—2 ..	22,703	10,990	11,713	20,863	10,150	10,713	1,777	797	980	63	43	20
	2—3 ..	23,551	11,281	12,270	21,506	10,352	11,154	1,954	874	1,080	91	55	36
	3—4 ..	22,927	11,316	11,611	20,810	10,504	10,306	2,017	758	1,259	100	54	46
	4—5 ..	21,823	11,105	10,718	19,763	10,474	9,289	1,954	579	1,375	106	52	54
	Total 0—5 ..	*117,786*	*57,848*	*59,938*	*107,098*	*53,301*	*53,797*	*10,293*	*4,321*	*5,972*	**395**	**226**	**169**
	5—10 ..	95,445	48,765	46,680	71,655	40,792	30,863	23,305	7,797	15,508	485	176	309
	10—15 ..	86,492	44,177	42,315	49,906	30,768	19,138	35,964	13,210	22,754	622	199	423
	15—20 ..	66,276	32,428	33,848	13,409	10,411	2,998	51,624	21,571	30,053	1,243	446	797
	20—30 ..	133,811	65,141	68,670	9,462	7,907	1,555	119,181	55,758	63,423	5,168	1,476	3,692
	30—40 ..	105,746	51,792	53,954	3,029	2,124	905	92,104	47,294	44,810	10,613	2,374	8,239
	40—50 ..	72,680	37,576	35,104	1,217	919	298	56,354	33,070	23,284	15,109	3,587	11,522
	50—60 ..	46,113	23,058	23,055	757	532	225	29,952	19,134	10,818	15,404	3,392	12,012
	60 and over ..	43,024	19,732	23,292	1,417	1,028	389	21,930	14,015	7,915	19,677	4,689	14,988
	MUSLIMS ..	*15,484*	*8,134*	*7,350*	*6,853*	*3,986*	*2,867*	*7,272*	*3,817*	*3,455*	**1,359**	**331**	**1,028**
	0—1 ..	474	239	235	437	222	215	28	15	13	9	2	7
	1—2 ..	436	223	213	410	214	196	23	9	14	3	..	3
	2—3 ..	484	237	247	457	228	229	27	9	18	..	..	..
	3—4 ..	472	233	239	451	225	226	21	8	13	..	..	..
	4—5 ..	439	217	222	420	210	210	17	6	11	2	1	1
	Total 0—5 ..	*2,305*	*1,149*	*1,156*	*2,175*	*1,099*	*1,076*	*116*	*47*	*69*	*14*	*3*	*11*
	5—10 ..	1,912	969	943	1,794	930	864	112	37	75	6	2	4
	10—15 ..	1,696	878	818	1,457	812	645	232	63	169	7	3	4
	15—20 ..	1,430	755	675	613	483	130	794	262	532	23	10	13
	20—30 ..	2,927	1,566	1,361	530	468	62	2,298	1,060	1,238	99	38	61
	30—40 ..	2,115	1,185	930	113	85	28	1,790	1,038	752	212	62	150
	40—50 ..	1,393	767	626	54	44	10	1,028	657	371	311	66	245
	50—60 ..	877	476	401	42	27	15	530	378	152	305	71	234
	60 and over ..	829	389	440	75	38	37	372	275	97	382	76	306
	TRIBAL RELIGION .	*39,600*	*19,156*	*20,444*	*14,818*	*8,040*	*6,778*	*20,862*	*10,131*	*10,731*	*3,920*	*985*	*2,935*
	0—1 ..	1,240	613	627	1,112	542	570	118	68	50	10	3	7
	1—2 ..	1,081	515	566	999	470	529	68	40	28	14	5	9
	2—3 ..	1,155	529	626	1,058	479	579	76	46	30	21	4	17
	3—4 ..	1,119	529	590	1,033	485	548	75	43	32	11	1	10
	4—5 ..	1,086	513	573	1,014	478	536	67	31	36	5	4	1
	Total 0—5 ..	*5,681*	*2,699*	*2,982*	*5,216*	*2,454*	*2,762*	*404*	*228*	*176*	*61*	*17*	*44*
	5—10 ..	4,517	2,218	2,299	4,012	2,045	1,967	477	162	315	28	11	17
	10—15 ..	4,191	2,085	2,106	3,230	1,799	1,431	916	274	642	45	12	33
	15—20 ..	3,401	1,630	1,771	1,225	849	376	2,118	761	1,357	58	20	38
	20—30 ..	6,561	3,045	3,516	766	591	175	5,543	2,373	3,170	252	81	171
	30—40 ..	5,718	2,744	2,974	124	90	34	5,051	2,524	2,527	543	130	413
	40—50 ..	4,317	2,234	2,083	106	92	14	3,392	1,945	1,447	819	197	622
	50—60 ..	2,592	1,314	1,278	49	39	10	1,711	1,084	627	832	191	641
	60 and over ..	2,622	1,187	1,435	90	81	9	1,250	780	470	1,282	326	956

TABLE VII.—Part B—Details for Districts—*contd.*

District.	Age.	Population.			Unmarried.			Married.			Widowed.		
		Persons.	Males.	Females.	Persons.	Males.	Females.	Persons.	Males.	Females.	Persons.	Males.	Females.
	1	2	3	4	5	6	7	8	9	10	11	12	13
BALAGHAT	ALL RELIGIONS ..	*561,602*	*276,898*	*284,704*	*195,915*	*110,455*	*85,460*	*311,987*	*153,457*	*158,530*	*53,700*	*12,986*	*40,714*
	0—1 ..	19,699	9,172	9,927	19,620	9,729	9,891	79	43	36	..	..	..
	1—2 ..	14,787	7,275	7,512	14,618	7,191	7,427	164	81	83	5	3	2
	2—3 ..	15,751	7,627	8,124	15,479	7,533	7,946	267	92	175	5	2	3
	3—4 ..	15,667	7,661	8,00[illegible]	15,081	7,479	7,602	573	180	393	13	2	11
	4—5 ..	14,904	7,418	7,486	14,042	7,139	6,903	834	272	562	28	7	21
	Total 0—5 ..	*80,808*	*39,753*	*41,055*	*78,840*	*39,071*	*39,769*	*1,917*	*668*	*1,249*	*51*	*14*	*37*
	5—10 ..	69,921	35,331	34,590	55,630	30,258	25,372	14,104	5,029	9,075	187	44	143
	10—15 ..	65,995	33,587	32,408	41,297	24,376	16,921	24,381	9,130	15,251	317	81	236
	15—20 ..	51,725	25,377	26,348	11,188	8,797	2,391	39,824	16,338	23,486	713	242	471
	20—30 ..	99,158	48,829	50,329	6,622	5,923	699	89,193	41,729	47,464	3,343	1,177	2,166
	30—40 ..	76,376	37,398	38,978	1,283	1,109	174	67,253	34,119	33,134	7,840	2,170	5,670
	40—50 ..	54,885	27,893	26,992	617	543	74	42,164	24,363	17,801	12,104	2,987	9,117
	50—60 ..	32,737	15,866	16,871	249	222	27	20,376	13,014	7,362	12,112	2,630	9,482
	60 and over ..	29,997	12,864	17,133	189	156	33	12,775	9,067	3,708	17,033	3,641	13,392
	HINDUS ..	*481,520*	*237,728*	*243,792*	*163,118*	*92,234*	*70,884*	*272,504*	*134,406*	*138,098*	*45,898*	*11,088*	*34,810*
	0—1 ..	17,206	8,570	8,636	17,141	8,533	8,608	65	37	28	..	..	..
	1—2 ..	12,797	6,329	6,468	12,639	6,252	6,387	156	76	80	2	1	1
	2—3 ..	13,560	6,582	6,978	13,303	6,497	6,806	254	85	169	3	..	3
	3—4 ..	13,441	6,582	6,859	12,874	6,408	6,466	555	172	383	12	2	10
	4—5 ..	12,732	6,353	6,379	11,911	6,094	5,817	798	254	544	23	5	18
	Total 0—5 ..	*69,736*	*34,416*	*35,320*	*67,868*	*33,784*	*34,084*	*1,828*	*624*	*1,204*	*40*	*8*	*32*
	5—10 ..	60,122	30,368	29,754	46,387	25,480	20,907	13,563	4,849	8,714	172	39	133
	10—15 ..	56,907	28,945	27,962	33,646	20,110	13,536	22,972	8,762	14,210	289	73	216
	15—20 ..	44,487	21,882	22,605	8,451	6,802	1,649	35,429	14,871	20,558	607	209	398
	20—30 ..	85,107	42,024	43,083	4,902	4,437	465	77,387	36,595	40,792	2,818	992	1,826
	30—40 ..	64,989	31,965	33,024	1,018	875	143	57,332	29,259	28,073	6,639	1,831	4,808
	40—50 ..	46,525	23,596	22,929	493	440	53	35,696	20,621	15,075	10,336	2,535	7,801
	50—60 ..	27,878	13,440	14,438	198	177	21	17,326	11,023	6,303	10,354	[illegible],240	8,114
	60 and over ..	25,769	11,092	14,677	155	129	26	10,971	7,802	3,169	14,643	3,161	11,482
	TRIBAL RELIGION	*67,404*	*32,884*	*34,520*	*27,122*	*14,938*	*12,184*	*33,875*	*16,314*	*17,561*	*6,407*	*1,632*	*4,775*
	0—1 ..	2,045	983	1,062	2,032	977	1,055	13	6	7	..	..	..
	1—2 ..	1,653	776	877	1,643	770	873	8	5	3	2	1	1
	2—3 ..	1,831	867	964	1,821	862	959	10	5	5	..	..	..
	3—4 ..	1,859	896	963	1,840	888	952	18	8	10	1	..	1
	4—5 ..	1,805	876	929	1,772	860	912	29	14	15	4	2	2
	Total 0—5 ..	*9,193*	*4,398*	*4,795*	*9,108*	*4,357*	*4,751*	*78*	*38*	*40*	*7*	*3*	*4*
	5—10 ..	8,205	4,137	4,068	7,714	3,974	3,740	478	159	319	13	4	9
	10—15 ..	7,659	3,910	3,749	6,400	3,570	2,830	1,235	333	902	24	7	17
	15—20 ..	6,068	2,918	3,150	2,237	1,616	621	3,747	1,274	2,473	84	28	56
	20—30 ..	11,734	5,655	6,079	1,289	1,098	191	10,031	4,403	5,628	414	154	260
	30—40 ..	9,594	4,562	5,032	204	180	24	8,428	4,094	4,334	962	288	674
	40—50 ..	7,134	3,674	3,460	96	79	17	5,605	3,203	2,402	1,433	392	1,041
	50—60 ..	4,168	2,090	2,078	43	38	5	2,678	1,717	961	1,447	335	1,112
	60 and over ..	3,649	1,540	2,109	31	26	5	1,595	1,093	502	2,023	421	1,602
RAIPUR	ALL RELIGIONS ..	*1,527,573*	*739,950*	*787,623*	*518,764*	*287,867*	*230,897*	*868,863*	*425,721*	*443,142*	*139,946*	*26,362*	*113,584*
	0—1 ..	54,499	26,564	27,935	53,618	26,238	27,380	866	326	540	15	..	15
	1—2 ..	46,814	22,599	24,215	46,065	22,293	23,772	734	300	434	15	6	9
	2—3 ..	47,780	22,751	25,029	46,452	22,277	24,175	1,296	463	833	32	11	21
	3—4 ..	49,061	23,724	25,337	45,996	22,627	23,369	2,998	1,081	1,917	67	16	51
	4—5 ..	46,659	23,170	23,489	42,259	21,553	20,706	4,290	1,591	2,699	110	26	84
	Total 0—5 ..	*244,813*	*118,808*	*126,005*	*234,390*	*114,988*	*119,402*	*10,184*	*3,761*	*6,423*	*239*	*59*	*180*
	5—10 ..	196,535	100,388	96,147	146,740	81,191	65,549	49,301	19,027	30,274	494	170	324
	10—15 ..	169,211	87,712	81,499	96,390	58,786	37,604	72,183	28,686	43,497	638	240	398
	15—20 ..	129,212	61,362	67,850	21,087	16,740	4,347	106,237	43,816	62,421	1,888	806	1,082
	20—30 ..	266,029	127,750	138,279	13,281	10,951	2,330	243,614	113,526	130,088	9,134	3,273	5,861
	30—40 ..	218,156	106,517	111,639	3,818	2,950	868	193,135	98,649	94,486	21,203	4,918	16,285
	40—50 ..	148,701	73,039	75,662	1,802	1,381	421	113,858	65,664	48,194	33,041	5,994	27,047
	50—60 ..	87,802	39,330	48,472	790	571	219	52,753	33,568	19,185	34,259	5,191	29,068
	60 and over ..	67,114	25,044	42,070	466	309	157	27,598	19,024	8,574	39,050	5,711	33,339

TABLE VII.—Part B—Details for Districts—*contd.*

District.	Age.	Population. Persons.	Males.	Females.	Unmarried. Persons.	Males.	Females.	Married. Persons.	Males.	Females.	Widowed. Persons.	Males.	Females
	1	2	3	4	5	6	7	8	9	10	11	12	13
RAIPUR—*contd.*	HINDUS ..	*1,403,879*	*679,436*	*724,443*	*468,163*	*259,832*	*208,331*	*807,067*	*395,260*	*411,807*	*128,649*	*24,344*	*104,305*
	0—1 ..	50,728	24,745	25,983	49,879	24,436	25,443	835	309	526	14	..	14
	1—2 ..	43,233	20,887	22,346	42,512	20,598	21,914	706	283	423	15	6	9
	2—3 ..	44,110	21,011	23,099	42,817	20,552	22,265	1,263	449	814	30	10	20
	3—4 ..	45,199	21,870	23,329	42,221	20,799	21,422	2,912	1,055	1,857	66	16	50
	4—5 ..	42,855	21,314	21,541	38,596	19,740	18 856	4,155	1,549	2,606	104	25	79
	Total 0—5 ..	*226,125*	*109,827*	*116,298*	*216,025*	*106,125*	*109,900*	*9,871*	*3,645*	*6,226*	*229*	*57*	*172*
	5—10 ..	180,513	92,130	88,383	132,122	73,440	58,682	47,912	18,524	29,388	479	166	313
	10—15 ..	155,369	80,406	74,963	85,346	52,431	32,915	69,412	27,741	41,671	611	234	377
	15—20 ..	118,543	56,259	62,284	17,715	14,250	3,465	99,069	41,239	57,830	1,759	770	989
	20—30 ..	244,168	117,111	127,057	10,977	9,095	1,882	224,779	104,974	119,805	8,412	3,042	5,370
	30—40 ..	200,338	97,685	102,653	3,291	2,523	768	177,556	90,615	86,941	19,491	4,547	14,944
	40—50 ..	136,652	67,023	69,629	1,546	1,169	377	104,755	60,325	44,430	30,351	5,529	24,822
	50—60 ..	80,765	36,097	44,668	714	516	198	48,504	30,811	17,693	31,547	4,770	26,777
	60 and over ..	61,406	22,898	38,508	427	283	144	25,209	17,386	7,823	35,770	5,229	30,541
	MUSLIMS ..	*19,992*	*10,251*	*9,741*	*8,059*	*4,753*	*3,306*	*9,837*	*5,137*	*4 700*	*2,096*	*361*	*1,735*
	0—1 ..	593	303	290	581	295	286	12	8	4	..	..	..
	1—2 ..	503	246	257	494	241	253	9	5	4	..	..	..
	2—3 ..	529	262	267	521	257	264	8	5	3	..	..	..
	3—4 ..	537	262	275	527	258	269	10	4	6	..	..	..
	4—5 ..	521	249	272	506	244	262	14	5	9	1	..	1
	Total 0—5 ..	*2,683*	*1,322*	*1,361*	*2,629*	*1,295*	*1,334*	*53*	*27*	*26*	*1*	..	*1*
	5—10 ..	2,332	1,210	1,122	2,160	1,150	1,010	169	59	110	3	1	2
	10—15 ..	2,139	1,143	996	1,756	1,047	709	378	96	282	5	..	5
	15—20 ..	1,918	982	936	746	602	144	1,145	374	771	27	6	21
	20—30 ..	3,867	2,033	1,834	613	538	75	3,080	1,437	1,643	174	58	116
	30—40 ..	2,956	1,556	1,400	104	85	19	2,474	1,386	1,088	378	85	293
	40—50 ..	2,025	1,024	1,001	30	24	6	1,463	930	533	532	70	462
	50—60 ..	1,187	587	600	13	9	4	683	511	172	491	67	424
	60 and over ..	885	394	491	8	3	5	392	317	75	485	74	411
	TRIBAL RELIGION	*95,393*	*45,954*	*49,439*	*38,493*	*21,052*	*17,441*	*48,319*	*23,424*	*24,895*	*8,581*	*1,478*	*7,103*
	0—1 ..	2,902	1,374	1,528	2,884	1,366	1,518	17	8	9	1	..	1
	1—2 ..	2,834	1,344	1,490	2,818	1,335	1,483	16	9	7	..	..	..
	2—3 ..	2,896	1,365	1,531	2,873	1,358	1,515	21	6	15	2	1	1
	3—4 ..	3,087	1,479	1,608	3,015	1,460	1,555	71	19	52	1	..	1
	4—5 ..	3,045	1,494	1,551	2,927	1,458	1,469	113	35	78	5	1	4
	Total 0—5 ..	*14 764*	*7,056*	*7,708*	*14,517*	*6,977*	*7,540*	*238*	*77*	*161*	*9*	*2*	*7*
	5—10 ..	12,660	6,527	6,133	11,469	6,094	5,375	1,179	430	749	12	3	9
	10—15 ..	10,702	5,643	5,059	8,375	4,812	3,563	2,308	826	1,482	19	5	14
	15—20 ..	7,812	3,654	4,158	2,137	1,574	563	5,584	2,052	3,532	91	28	63
	20—30 ..	16,479	7,808	8,671	1,369	1,078	291	14,610	6,577	8,033	500	153	347
	30—40 ..	13,733	6,664	7,069	366	301	65	12,132	6,107	6,025	1,235	256	979
	40—50 ..	9,232	4,547	4,685	192	166	26	7,053	4,029	3,024	1,987	352	1,635
	50—60 ..	5,456	2,435	3,021	47	34	13	3,329	2,083	1,246	2,080	318	1,762
	60 and over ..	4,555	1,620	2,935	21	16	5	1,886	1,243	643	2,648	361	2,287
BILASPUR	ALL RELIGIONS ..	*1,400,248*	*683,920*	*716,328*	*447,078*	*250,956*	*196,122*	*829,270*	*407,651*	*421,619*	*123,900*	*25,313*	*98,587*
	0—1 ..	50,393	25,012	25,381	49,314	24,538	24,776	1,059	464	595	20	10	10
	1—2 ..	44,192	21,510	22,682	43,057	21,033	22,024	1,105	457	648	30	20	10
	2—3 ..	45,903	21,907	23,996	43,769	21,127	22,642	2,058	751	1,307	76	29	47
	3—4 ..	47,382	22,924	24,458	42,515	21,194	21,321	4,721	1,690	3,031	146	40	106
	4—5 ..	44,480	22,163	22,317	37,608	19,738	17,870	6,687	2,374	4,313	185	51	134
	Total 0—5 ..	*232,350*	*113,516*	*118,834*	*216,263*	*107,630*	*108,633*	*15,630*	*5,736*	*9,894*	*457*	*150*	*307*
	5—10 ..	187,554	95,094	92,460	123,357	70,377	52,980	62,604	24,379	38,225	1,593	338	1,255
	10—15 ..	159,057	81,629	77,428	75,326	47,571	27,755	81,840	33,618	48,222	1,891	440	1,451
	15—20 ..	120,483	56,734	63,749	14,508	12,025	2,483	103,093	43,754	59,339	2,882	955	1,927
	20—30 ..	247,933	118,084	129,849	10,869	8,880	1,989	226,115	105,848	120,267	10,949	3,356	7,593
	30—40 ..	193,108	94,194	98,914	3,517	2,444	1,073	168,755	87,199	81,556	20,836	4,551	16,285
	40—50 ..	130,480	65,611	64,869	1,832	1,194	638	99,986	58,938	41,048	28,662	5,479	23,183
	50—60 ..	76,058	36,308	39,750	856	515	341	47,240	30,899	16,341	27,962	4,894	23,068
	60 and over ..	53,225	22,750	30,475	550	320	230	24,007	17,280	6,727	28,668	5,150	23,518

TABLE VII.—Part B—Details for Districts—*contd.*

District.	Age.	Population. Persons.	Population. Males	Population. Females.	Unmarried. Persons.	Unmarried. Males.	Unmarried. Females.	Married. Persons.	Married. Males	Married. Females.	Widowed. Persons.	Widowed. Males.	Widowed. Females.
	1	2	3	4	5	6	7	8	9	10	11	12	13
BILASPUR—*concld.*	HINDUS ..	*1,306,899*	*637,289*	*659,610*	*408,536*	*229,669*	*178,867*	*781,471*	*383,817*	*397,654*	*116,892*	*23,803*	*93,089*
	0—1 ..	47,153	23,440	23,713	46,165	23,005	23,160	971	426	545	17	9	8
	1—2 ..	41,094	20,031	21,063	40,025	19,587	20,438	1,040	424	616	29	20	9
	2—3 ..	42,565	20,339	22,226	40,538	19,611	20,927	1,953	699	1,254	74	29	45
	3—4 ..	43,985	21,295	22,690	39,256	19,626	19,630	4,586	1,629	2,957	143	40	103
	4—5 ..	41,311	20,603	20,708	34,589	18,234	16,355	6,545	2,320	4,225	177	49	128
	Total 0—5 ..	*216,108*	*105,708*	*110,400*	*200,573*	*100,063*	*100,510*	*15,095*	*5,498*	*9,597*	*440*	*147*	*293*
	5—10 ..	175,151	88,762	86,389	112,591	64,616	47,975	61,006	23,823	37,183	1,554	323	1,231
	10—15 ..	148,723	76,247	72,476	67,854	43,173	24,681	79,033	32,656	46,377	1,836	418	1,418
	15—20 ..	112,390	52,908	59,482	12,304	10,346	1,958	97,321	41,655	55,666	2,765	907	1,858
	20—30 ..	230,884	109,735	121,149	9,151	7,492	1,659	211,352	99,091	112,261	10,381	3,152	7,229
	30—40 ..	180,252	87,526	92,726	3,119	2,158	961	157,436	81,114	76,322	19,697	4,254	15,443
	40—50 ..	122,272	61,239	61,033	1,654	1,066	588	93,586	55,021	38,565	27,032	5,152	21,880
	50—60 ..	71,283	33,926	37,357	782	464	318	44,202	28,853	15,349	26,299	4,609	21,690
	60 and over ..	49,836	21,238	28,598	508	291	217	22,440	16,106	6,334	26,888	4,841	22,047
	MUSLIMS ..	*18,673*	*9,495*	*9,178*	*7,145*	*4,123*	*3,022*	*9,854*	*5,093*	*4,761*	*1,674*	*279*	*1,395*
	0—1 ..	593	268	325	569	259	310	21	8	13	3	1	2
	1—2 ..	509	246	263	492	238	254	16	8	8	1	..	1
	2—3 ..	537	256	281	508	243	265	27	13	14	2	..	2
	3—4 ..	542	253	289	514	242	272	27	11	16	1	..	1
	4—5 ..	528	252	276	498	242	256	28	9	19	2	1	1
	Total 0—5 ..	*2,709*	*1,275*	*1,434*	*2,581*	*1,224*	*1,357*	*119*	*49*	*70*	*9*	*2*	*7*
	5—10 ..	2,202	1,119	1,083	1,931	1,031	900	265	85	180	6	3	3
	10—15 ..	1,960	1,032	928	1,467	887	580	486	143	343	7	2	5
	15—20 ..	1,789	877	912	556	467	89	1,205	404	801	28	6	22
	20—30 ..	3,709	1,916	1,793	455	401	54	3,121	1,470	1,651	133	45	88
	30—40 ..	2,790	1,517	1,273	99	73	26	2,402	1,381	1,021	289	63	226
	40—50 ..	1,804	948	856	37	25	12	1,340	860	480	427	63	364
	50—60 ..	990	486	504	13	10	3	588	432	156	389	44	345
	60 and over ..	720	325	395	6	5	1	328	269	59	386	51	335
	TRIBAL RELIGION ..	*65,672*	*34,231*	*31,441*	*28,289*	*15,554*	*12,735*	*35,505*	*17,559*	*17,946*	*4,878*	*1,118*	*3,760*
	0—1 ..	2,453	1,205	1,248	2,386	1,175	1,211	67	30	37	..	..	..
	1—2 ..	2,421	1,155	1,266	2,372	1,130	1,242	49	25	24	..	..	..
	2—3 ..	2,618	1,232	1,386	2,540	1,193	1,347	78	39	39	..	..	..
	3—4 ..	2,675	1,283	1,392	2,565	1,233	1,332	108	50	58	2	..	2
	4—5 ..	2,457	1,208	1,249	2,339	1,162	1,177	113	45	68	5	1	4
	Total 0—5 ..	*12,624*	*6,083*	*6,541*	*12,202*	*5,893*	*6,309*	*415*	*189*	*226*	*7*	*1*	*6*
	5—10 ..	9,432	4,831	4,601	8,078	4,349	3,729	1,321	470	851	33	12	21
	10—15 ..	7,663	4,015	3,648	5,322	3,180	2,142	2,294	815	1,479	47	20	27
	15—20 ..	5,679	2,660	3,019	1,252	994	258	4,345	1,626	2,719	82	40	42
	20—30 ..	12,299	5,938	6,361	972	802	170	10,920	4,989	5,931	407	147	260
	30—40 ..	9,254	4,738	4,516	256	184	72	8,228	4,348	3,880	770	206	564
	40—50 ..	5,798	3,107	2,691	124	93	31	4,577	2,778	1,799	1,097	236	861
	50—60 ..	3,478	1,753	1,725	52	36	16	2,252	1,495	757	1,174	222	952
	60 and over ..	2,445	1,106	1,339	31	23	8	1,153	849	304	1,261	234	1,027
DRUG	ALL RELIGIONS ..	*817,924*	*390,367*	*427,557*	*229,819*	*126,944*	*102,875*	*505,980*	*248,067*	*258,913*	*81,125*	*15,356*	*65,769*
	0—1 ..	33,279	16,010	17,269	32,860	15,819	17,041	412	191	221	7	..	7
	1—2 ..	27,021	12,912	14,109	26,378	12,704	13,674	632	206	426	11	2	9
	2—3 ..	25,705	11,975	13,730	24,394	11,596	12,798	1,297	376	921	14	3	11
	3—4 ..	25,238	12,101	13,137	22,331	11,103	11,228	2,878	988	1,890	29	10	19
	4—5 ..	23,089	11,542	11,547	19,032	10,060	8,972	4,002	1,464	2,538	55	18	37
	Total 0—5 ..	*134,332*	*64,540*	*69,792*	*124,995*	*61,282*	*63,713*	*9,221*	*3,225*	*5,996*	*116*	*33*	*83*
	5—10 ..	98,785	50,696	48,089	58,350	34,128	24,222	40,154	16,457	23,697	281	111	170
	10—15 ..	86,152	44,389	41,763	33,135	21,621	11,514	52,644	22,598	30,046	373	170	203
	15—20 ..	68,142	32,106	36,036	6,240	4,611	1,629	60,949	27,039	33,910	953	456	497
	20—30 ..	138,400	66,022	72,378	4,718	3,564	1,154	129,066	60,588	68,478	4,616	1,870	2,746
	30—40 ..	115,906	55,239	60,667	1,232	994	238	103,371	51,334	52,037	11,303	1,911	8,392
	40—50 ..	84,910	40,894	44,016	764	448	316	64,874	36,921	27,953	19,272	3,525	15,747
	50—60 ..	51,222	22,127	29,095	237	179	58	30,533	18,934	11,599	20,452	3,014	17,438
	60 and over ..	40,075	14,354	25,721	148	117	31	16,168	10,971	5,197	23,759	3,266	20,493

TABLE VII.—Part B—Details for Districts—*contd.*

District.	Age.	Population.			Unmarried.			Married.			Widowed.		
		Persons.	Males.	Females.	Persons.	Males.	Females.	Persons.	Males.	Females.	Persons.	Males.	Females
	1	2	3	4	5	6	7	8	9	10	11	12	13
DRUG—concld.	HINDUS ..	*794,949*	*378,958*	*115,991*	*219,527*	*121,210*	*98,317*	*498,155*	*212,839*	*253,629*	*78,954*	*14,909*	*64,045*
	0—1 ..	32,551	15,645	16,906	32,136	15,457	16,679	408	188	220	7	..	7
	1—2 ..	26,346	12,568	13,778	25,707	12,362	13,345	628	204	424	11	2	9
	2—3 ..	24,944	11,623	13,321	23,640	11,245	12,395	1,292	375	917	12	3	9
	3—4 ..	24,452	11,728	12,724	21,554	10,732	10,822	2,869	986	1,883	29	10	19
	4—5 ..	22,353	11,172	11,181	18,315	9,696	8,619	3,986	1,458	2,528	52	18	34
	Total 0—5 ..	*130,646*	*62,736*	*67,910*	*121,352*	*59,492*	*61,860*	*9,183*	*3,211*	*5,972*	*111*	*33*	*78*
	5—10 ..	95,845	49,184	46,661	55,591	32,669	22,922	39,978	16,405	23,573	276	110	166
	10—15 ..	83,640	43,099	40,541	31,032	20,453	10,579	52,243	22,476	29,767	365	170	195
	15—20 ..	66,195	31,181	35,014	5,428	4,063	1,365	59,844	26,671	33,173	923	447	476
	20—30 ..	134,418	64,044	70,374	3,996	2,987	1,009	125,954	59,243	66,711	4,468	1,814	2,654
	30—40 ..	112,533	53,574	58,959	1,054	856	198	100,569	49,897	50,672	10,910	2,821	8,089
	40—50 ..	82,633	39,691	42,942	719	413	306	63,181	35,863	27,318	18,733	3,415	15,318
	50—60 ..	49,934	21,509	28,425	220	168	52	29,774	18,421	11,353	19,940	2,920	17,020
	60 and over ..	39,105	13,940	25,165	135	109	26	15,742	10,652	5,090	23,228	3,179	20,049
	MUSLIMS ..	*7,539*	*3,651*	*3,688*	*2,797*	*1,668*	*1,129*	*3,759*	*1,867*	*1,892*	*783*	*116*	*667*
	0—1 ..	246	128	118	245	127	118	1	1	..	..	..	..
	1—2 ..	205	113	92	205	113	92	..	..	..	..	..	..
	2—3 ..	213	104	109	211	104	107	1	..	1	1	..	1
	3—4 ..	214	104	110	211	104	107	3	..	3	..	..	..
	4—5 ..	198	102	96	189	100	89	8	2	6	1	..	1
	Total 0—5 ..	*1,076*	*551*	*525*	*1,061*	*548*	*513*	*13*	*3*	*10*	*2*	..	*2*
	5—10 ..	845	432	413	754	409	345	88	22	66	3	1	2
	10—15 ..	741	387	354	557	329	228	180	58	122	4	..	4
	15—20 ..	669	338	331	186	161	25	471	174	297	12	3	9
	20—30 ..	1,401	705	696	189	179	10	1,160	510	650	52	16	36
	30—40 ..	1,126	576	550	41	36	5	966	519	447	119	21	98
	40—50 ..	717	351	366	7	5	2	511	317	194	199	29	170
	50—60 ..	415	177	238	1	..	1	229	157	72	185	20	165
	60 and over ..	349	134	215	1	1	.	141	107	34	207	26	181
	TRIBAL RELIGION	*12,155*	*6,140*	*6,018*	*5,985*	*3,313*	*2,672*	*5,323*	*2,589*	*2,734*	*850*	*238*	*612*
	0—1 ..	379	182	197	376	180	196	3	2	1	..	..	..
	1—2 ..	384	185	199	381	184	197	3	1	2	..	..	..
	2—3 ..	458	210	248	453	209	244	4	1	3	1	..	1
	3—4 ..	491	236	255	485	234	251	6	2	4	..	..	..
	4—5 ..	460	233	227	451	230	221	7	3	4	2	..	2
	Total 0—5 ..	*2,172*	*1,046*	*1,126*	*2,146*	*1,037*	*1,109*	*23*	*9*	*14*	*3*	..	*3*
	5—10 ..	1,742	907	835	1,661	882	779	79	25	54	2	..	2
	10—15 ..	1,423	737	686	1,235	685	550	183	52	133	3	..	3
	15—20 ..	954	458	496	454	311	143	489	142	347	11	5	6
	20—30 ..	2,014	1,011	1,003	378	312	66	1,573	666	907	63	33	30
	30—40 ..	1,649	830	819	74	60	14	1,440	721	719	135	49	86
	40—50 ..	1,085	601	484	16	12	4	881	534	347	188	55	133
	50—60 ..	638	323	315	11	8	3	410	262	148	217	53	164
	60 and over ..	481	227	254	10	6	4	243	178	65	228	43	185
AMRAOTI	ALL RELIGIONS ..	*941,604*	*485,593*	*456,011*	*329,673*	*197,143*	*132,530*	*505,013*	*251,945*	*250,068*	*106,918*	*33,505*	*73,413*
	0—1 ..	32,143	16,159	15,984	32,005	16,100	15,905	129	55	74	9	4	5
	1—2 ..	27,824	13,762	14,062	27,593	13,685	13,908	223	73	150	8	4	4
	2—3 ..	27,852	13,504	14,348	27,406	13,378	14,028	439	123	316	7	3	4
	3—4 ..	26,489	12,960	13,529	25,498	12,759	12,739	972	195	777	19	6	13
	4—5 ..	25,134	12,655	12,479	23,732	12,412	11,320	1,365	231	1,134	37	12	25
	Total 0—5 ..	*139,442*	*69,040*	*70,402*	*136,234*	*68,334*	*67,900*	*3,128*	*677*	*2,451*	*80*	*29*	*51*
	5—10 ..	114,417	57,557	56,860	89,540	51,841	37,699	24,436	5,593	18,843	441	123	318
	10—15 ..	105,271	53,330	51,941	63,870	41,826	22,044	40,697	11,311	29,386	704	193	511
	15—20 ..	87,214	43,411	43,803	18,606	16,585	2,021	66,726	26,156	40,570	1,882	670	1,212
	20—30 ..	164,251	84,090	80,161	14,019	12,747	1,272	141,585	67,692	73,893	8,647	3,651	4,996
	30—40 ..	127,372	67,607	59,765	3,933	3,284	649	105,899	58,474	47,425	17,540	5,849	11,691
	40—50 ..	93,153	50,203	42,950	2,026	1,337	689	66,342	41,646	24,696	24,785	7,220	17,565
	50—60 ..	59,640	33,334	26,306	737	608	129	34,441	25,481	8,960	24,462	7,245	17,217
	60 and over ..	50,844	27,021	23,823	708	581	127	21,759	17,915	3,844	28,377	8,525	19,852

TABLE VII.—Part B—Details for Districts—*contd.*

District.	Age.	Population. Persons.	Population. Males.	Population. Females.	Unmarried. Persons.	Unmarried. Males.	Unmarried. Females.	Married. Persons.	Married. Males.	Married. Females.	Widowed. Persons.	Widowed. Males.	Widowed. Females.
	1	2	3	4	5	6	7	8	9	10	11	12	13
AMRAOTI—concld.	HINDUS ..	*835,409*	*430,034*	*405,375*	*281,414*	*168,960*	*112,454*	*457,421*	*230,584*	*226,837*	*96,574*	*30,490*	*66,084*
	0—1 ..	28,701	14,449	14,252	28,568	14,391	14,177	124	54	70	9	4	5
	1—2 ..	24,511	12,114	12,397	24,286	12,041	12,245	218	70	148	7	3	4
	2—3 ..	24,428	11,827	12,601	23,998	11,709	12,289	423	115	308	7	3	4
	3—4 ..	23,197	11,357	11,840	22,246	11,170	11,076	933	181	752	18	6	12
	4—5 ..	21,860	11,030	10,830	20,529	10,809	9,720	1,298	210	1,088	33	11	22
	Total 0—5 ..	*122,697*	*60,777*	*61,920*	*119,627*	*60,120*	*59,507*	*2,996*	*630*	*2,366*	*74*	*27*	*47*
	5—10 ..	100,274	50,302	49,972	76,351	44,807	31,544	23,502	5,378	18,124	421	117	304
	10—15 ..	92,532	46,758	45,774	53,458	35,674	17,784	38,403	10,899	27,504	671	185	486
	15—20 ..	76,999	38,201	38,798	14,517	13,199	1,318	60,747	24,381	36,366	1,735	621	1,114
	20—30 ..	145,750	74,377	71,373	10,927	9,999	928	127,003	61,036	65,967	7,820	3,342	4,478
	30—40 ..	114,099	60,518	53,581	3,414	2,879	535	94,869	52,301	42,568	15,816	5,338	10,478
	40—50 ..	83,685	44,39[illegible]	38,692	1,831	1,197	634	59,520	37,220	22,300	22,334	6,576	15,758
	50—60 ..	53,720	29,929	23,791	654	547	107	30,914	22,766	8,148	22,152	6,616	15,536
	60 and over ..	45,653	24,179	21,474	635	538	97	19,467	15,973	3,494	25,551	7,668	17,883
	MUSLIMS	*86,498*	*45,714*	*40,784*	*40,146*	*23,714*	*16,432*	*37,968*	*19,534*	*18,434*	*8,384*	*2,466*	*5,918*
	0—1 ..	2,796	1,388	1,408	2,791	1,387	1,404	5	1	4	..	..	..
	1—2 ..	2,725	1,361	1,364	2,720	1,358	1,362	4	2	2	1	1	..
	2—3 ..	2,791	1,377	1,414	2,779	1,371	1,408	12	6	6	..	..	..
	3—4 ..	2,696	1,319	1,377	2,669	1,307	1,362	26	12	14	1	..	1
	4—5 ..	2,693	1,348	1,345	2,649	1,330	1,319	41	17	24	3	1	2
	Total 0—5 ..	*13,701*	*6,793*	*6,908*	*13,608*	*6,753*	*6,855*	*88*	*38*	*50*	*5*	*2*	*3*
	5—10 ..	11,660	6,055	5,605	11,011	5,898	5,113	635	154	481	14	3	11
	10—15 ..	10,387	5,483	4,904	8,712	5,200	3,512	1,651	278	1,373	24	5	19
	15—20 ..	8,327	4,346	3,981	3,474	2,944	530	4,727	1,358	3,369	126	44	82
	20—30 ..	15,106	7,988	7,118	2,670	2,413	257	11,758	5,309	6,449	678	266	412
	30—40 ..	10,667	5,734	4,933	418	328	90	8,871	4,986	3,885	1,378	420	958
	40—50 ..	7,628	4,236	3,392	144	102	42	5,505	3,604	1,901	1,979	530	1,449
	50—60 ..	4,732	2,727	2,005	55	41	14	2,836	2,185	651	1,841	501	1,340
	60 and over ..	4,290	2,352	1,938	54	35	19	1,897	1,622	275	2,339	695	1,644
	TRIBAL RELIGION	*11,871*	*5,810*	*6,061*	*5,014*	*2,712*	*2,302*	*5,720*	*2,783*	*2,937*	*1,137*	*315*	*822*
	0—1 ..	423	210	213	423	210	213	..	..	..	..	..	..
	1—2 ..	379	178	201	378	177	201	1	1	..	..	..	..
	2—3 ..	398	183	215	395	182	213	3	1	2	..	..	..
	3—4 ..	386	180	206	378	179	199	8	1	7	..	..	..
	4—5 ..	378	181	197	363	179	184	14	2	12	1	..	1
	Total 0—5 ..	*1,964*	*932*	*1,032*	*1,937*	*927*	*1,010*	*26*	*5*	*21*	*1*		*1*
	5—10 ..	1,556	737	819	1,404	714	690	148	21	127	4	2	2
	10—15 ..	1,465	649	816	1,087	596	491	374	52	322	4	1	3
	15—20 ..	1,091	479	612	359	271	88	719	205	514	13	3	10
	20—30 ..	1,959	972	987	184	163	21	1,689	784	905	86	25	61
	30—40 ..	1,528	787	741	24	23	1	1,314	710	604	190	54	136
	40—50 ..	1,099	585	514	10	10	..	814	508	306	275	67	208
	50—60 ..	700	391	309	6	6	..	410	315	95	284	70	214
	60 and over ..	509	278	231	3	2	1	226	183	43	280	93	187
	ALL RELIGIONS ..	*876,362*	*448,896*	*427,466*	*272,932*	*163,674*	*109,258*	*506,950*	*256,022*	*250,928*	*96,480*	*29,200*	*67,280*
	0—1 ..	28,011	13,729	14,282	27,792	13,649	14,143	197	74	123	22	6	16
	1—2 ..	26,295	12,723	13,572	25,886	12,623	13,263	385	90	295	24	10	14
	2—3 ..	26,621	12,724	13,897	25,730	12,554	13,176	850	146	704	41	24	17
	3—4 ..	25,966	12,560	13,406	23,655	12,166	11,489	2,235	356	1,879	76	38	38
	4—5 ..	25,196	12,477	12,719	21,754	11,884	9,870	3,337	546	2,791	105	47	58
	Total 0—5 ..	*132,089*	*64,213*	*67,876*	*124,817*	*62,876*	*61,941*	*7,004*	*1,212*	*5,792*	*268*	*125*	*143*
	5—10 ..	110,246	55,669	54,577	73,511	44,577	28,934	35,910	10,755	25,155	825	337	488
	10—15 ..	99,015	50,325	48,690	47,493	32,485	15,008	50,402	17,395	33,007	1,120	445	675
	15—20 ..	79,184	38,656	40,528	12,331	10,987	1,344	64,880	26,853	38,027	1,973	816	1,157
	20—30 ..	153,952	78,593	75,359	9,537	8,574	963	136,665	66,717	69,948	7,750	3,302	4,448
	30—40 ..	119,175	63,432	55,743	2,794	2,269	525	100,438	55,849	44,589	15,943	5,314	10,629
	40—50 ..	86,378	46,394	39,984	1,330	1,099	231	61,907	39,001	22,906	23,141	6,294	16,847
	50—60 ..	53,981	29,577	24,404	575	451	124	31,383	23,195	8,188	22,023	5,931	16,092
	60 and over ..	42,342	22,037	20,305	544	356	188	18,361	15,045	3,316	23,437	6,636	16,801

TABLE VII.—Part B—Details for Districts—*contd.*

District.	Age.	Population.			Unmarried.			Married.			Widowed.		
		Persons.	Males.	Females.	Persons.	Males.	Females.	Persons.	Males.	Females.	Persons.	Males.	Females.
	1	2	3	4	5	6	7	8	9	10	11	12	13
AKOLA—*concld.*	**HINDUS**	*778,451*	*397,460*	*380,991*	*228,697*	*138,009*	*90,688*	*462,392*	*232,923*	*229,469*	*87,362*	*26,528*	*60,834*
	0—1 ..	24,901	12,180	12,721	24,716	12,113	12,603	166	62	104	19	5	14
	1—2 ..	23,211	11,201	12,010	22,839	11,115	11,724	350	77	273	22	9	13
	2—3 ..	23,379	11,159	12,220	22,540	11,009	11,531	799	127	672	40	23	17
	3—4 ..	22,710	10,976	11,734	20,477	10,609	9,868	2,159	330	1,829	74	37	37
	4—5 ..	21,947	10,864	11,083	18,618	10,313	8,305	3,233	509	2,724	96	42	54
	***Total* 0—5** ..	*116,148*	*56,380*	*59,768*	*109,190*	*55,159*	*51,031*	*6,707*	*1,105*	*5,602*	*251*	*116*	*135*
	5—10 ..	96,794	48,801	47,993	61,108	37,998	23,110	34,892	10,479	24,413	794	324	470
	10—15 ..	87,436	44,304	43,132	38,077	26,933	11,144	48,285	16,940	31,345	1,074	431	643
	15—20 ..	70,271	34,072	36,199	8,929	8,103	826	59,539	25,214	34,325	1,803	755	1,048
	20—30 ..	136,540	69,481	67,059	6,931	6,229	702	122,701	60,278	62,423	6,908	2,974	3,934
	30—40 ..	106,575	56,523	50,052	2,316	1,890	426	89,888	49,796	40,092	14,371	4,837	9,534
	40—50 ..	77,853	41,619	36,234	1,154	974	180	55,697	34,912	20,785	21,002	5,733	15,269
	50—60 ..	48,841	26,602	22,239	501	401	100	28,302	20,814	7,488	20,038	5,387	14,651
	60 and over ..	37,993	19,678	18,315	491	322	169	16,381	13,385	2,996	21,121	5,971	15,150
	MUSLIMS ..	*59,185*	*16,903*	*42,282*	*10,731*	*23,577*	*17,154*	*40,353*	*20,925*	*19,428*	*8,101*	*2,401*	*5,700*
	0—1 ..	2,835	1,429	1,406	2,807	1,420	1,387	26	8	18	2	1	1
	1—2 ..	2,813	1,394	1,419	2,786	1,385	1,401	26	8	18	1	1	..
	2—3 ..	2,953	1,432	1,521	2,914	1,416	1,498	38	15	23	1	1	..
	3—4 ..	2,990	1,457	1,533	2,929	1,435	1,494	59	21	38	2	1	1
	4—5 ..	2,980	1,477	1,503	2,891	1,443	1,448	82	30	52	7	4	3
	***Total* 0—5** ..	*14,571*	*7,189*	*7,382*	*14,327*	*7,099*	*7,228*	*231*	*82*	*149*	*13*	*8*	*5*
	5—10 ..	12,338	6,274	6,064	11,488	6,047	5,441	825	217	608	25	10	15
	10—15 ..	10,569	5,463	5,106	8,699	5,091	3,608	1,833	362	1,471	37	10	27
	15—20 ..	8,119	4,166	3,953	3,120	2,654	466	4,848	1,456	3,392	151	56	95
	20—30 ..	15,898	8,348	7,550	2,415	2,173	242	12,738	5,870	6,868	745	305	440
	30—40 ..	11,423	6,308	5,115	426	342	84	9,599	5,528	4,071	1,398	438	960
	40—50 ..	7,667	4,294	3,373	150	104	46	5,632	3,698	1,934	1,885	492	1,393
	50—60 ..	4,642	2,690	1,952	62	40	22	2,812	2,169	643	1,768	481	1,287
	60 and over ..	3,958	2,171	1,787	44	27	17	1,835	1,543	292	2,079	601	1,478
BULDANA	**ALL RELIGIONS** ..	*760,584*	*388,966*	*377,618*	*234,123*	*141,235*	*92,888*	*452,405*	*225,494*	*226,911*	*80,056*	*22,237*	*57,819*
	0—1 ..	25,433	12,678	12,755	25,147	12,543	12,604	274	131	143	12	4	8
	1—2 ..	23,631	11,475	12,156	23,172	11,348	11,824	440	118	322	19	9	10
	2—3 ..	23,663	11,279	12,384	22,724	11,134	11,590	916	133	783	23	12	11
	3—4 ..	23,129	11,145	11,984	20,683	10,815	9,868	2,398	312	2,086	48	18	30
	4—5 ..	22,527	11,116	11,411	18,855	10,591	8,264	3,595	499	3,096	77	26	51
	***Total* 0—5** ..	*118,383*	*57,693*	*60,690*	*110,581*	*56,431*	*54,150*	*7,623*	*1,193*	*6,430*	*179*	*69*	*110*
	5—10 ..	100,528	50,547	49,981	62,824	38,954	23,870	36,931	11,314	25,617	773	279	494
	10—15 ..	90,686	46,252	44,434	39,841	27,675	12,166	49,744	18,147	31,597	1,101	430	671
	15—20 ..	70,071	34,412	35,659	9,888	8,805	1,083	58,541	24,879	33,662	1,642	728	914
	20—30 ..	132,196	67,562	64,634	7,424	6,637	787	118,625	58,265	60,360	6,147	2,660	3,487
	30—40 ..	100,904	52,684	48,220	1,833	1,438	395	86,103	47,254	38,849	12,968	3,992	8,976
	40—50 ..	73,077	38,183	34,894	991	774	217	52,906	32,722	20,184	19,180	4,687	14,493
	50—60 ..	45,486	24,149	21,337	446	326	120	26,608	19,380	7,228	18,432	4,443	13,989
	60 and over ..	35,253	17,484	17,769	295	195	100	15,324	12,340	2,984	19,634	4,949	14,685
	HINDUS ..	*689,152*	*348,531*	*340,621*	*198,404*	*120,583*	*77,821*	*417,138*	*207,395*	*209,743*	*73,610*	*20,553*	*53,057*
	0—1 ..	22,795	11,359	11,436	22,535	11,240	11,295	249	115	134	11	4	7
	1—2 ..	21,108	10,263	10,845	20,667	10,145	10,522	424	110	314	17	8	9
	2—3 ..	21,121	10,064	11,057	20,210	9,933	10,277	888	119	769	23	12	11
	3—4 ..	20,546	9,897	10,649	18,155	9,587	8,568	2,345	292	2,053	46	18	28
	4—5 ..	19,903	9,827	10,076	16,313	9,328	6,985	3,520	474	3,046	70	25	45
	***Total* 0—5** ..	*105,473*	*51,410*	*54,063*	*97,880*	*50,233*	*47,647*	*7,426*	*1,110*	*6,316*	*167*	*67*	*100*
	5—10 ..	89,523	44,877	44,646	52,690	33,517	19,173	36,085	11,086	24,999	748	274	474
	10—15 ..	81,150	41,239	39,911	32,143	23,047	9,096	47,939	17,768	30,171	1,068	424	644
	15—20 ..	62,885	30,752	32,133	7,226	6,559	667	54,126	23,499	30,627	1,533	694	839
	20—30 ..	118,802	60,545	58,257	5,431	4,869	562	107,714	53,200	54,514	5,657	2,476	3,181
	30—40 ..	91,311	47,411	43,900	1,510	1,194	316	77,853	42,511	35,342	11,948	3,706	8,242
	40—50 ..	66,648	34,673	31,975	860	688	172	48,131	29,656	18,475	17,657	4,329	13,328
	50—60 ..	41,523	21,966	19,557	396	295	101	24,192	17,582	6,610	16,935	4,089	12,846
	60 and over ..	31,837	15,658	16,179	268	181	87	13,672	10,983	2,689	17,897	4,494	13,403

TABLE VII.—Part B—Details for Districts—*contd.*

District.	Age.	Population.			Unmarried.			Married.			Widowed.		
		Persons.	Males.	Females.	Persons.	Males.	Females.	Persons.	Males.	Females.	Persons.	Males.	Females.
	1	2	3	4	5	6	7	8	9	10	11	12	13
BULDANA—concld.	MUSLIMS ..	*71,766*	*37,474*	*34,292*	*33,510*	*19,324*	*14,186*	*32,457*	*16,662*	*15,795*	*5,799*	*1,488*	*4,311*
	0—1 ..	2,437	1,217	1,220	2,411	1,201	1,210	25	16	9	1	..	1
	1—2 ..	2,350	1,135	1,215	2,334	1,127	1,207	16	8	8	..	..	..
	2—3 ..	2,380	1,133	1,247	2,357	1,122	1,235	23	11	12	..	..	..
	3—4 ..	2,433	1,168	1,265	2,389	1,152	1,237	42	16	26	2	..	2
	4—5 ..	2,468	1,211	1,257	2,402	1,188	1,214	60	22	38	6	1	5
	Total 0—5 ..	*12,068*	*5,864*	*6,204*	*11,893*	*5,790*	*6,103*	*166*	*73*	*93*	*9*	*1*	*8*
	5—10 ..	10,325	5,319	5,006	9,583	5,124	4,459	721	192	529	21	3	18
	10—15 ..	8,896	4,687	4,209	7,263	4,360	2,903	1,603	322	1,281	30	5	25
	15—20 ..	6,615	3,378	3,237	2,485	2,107	378	4,031	1,239	2,792	99	32	67
	20—30 ..	12,371	6,474	5,897	1,848	1,644	204	10,091	4,663	5,428	432	167	265
	30—40 ..	8,821	4,854	3,967	279	206	73	7,637	4,396	3,241	905	252	653
	40—50 ..	5,882	3,217	2,665	102	64	38	4,416	2,839	1,577	1,364	314	1,050
	50—60 ..	3,625	1,994	1,631	34	17	17	2,243	1,667	576	1,348	310	1,038
	60 and over ..	3,163	1,687	1,476	23	12	11	1,549	1,271	278	1,591	404	1,187
YEOTMAL	ALL RELIGIONS ..	*857,288*	*436,124*	*421,164*	*282,757*	*164,840*	*117,917*	*489,750*	*246,329*	*243,421*	*84,781*	*24,955*	*59,826*
	0—1 ..	29,734	14,659	15,075	29,483	14,555	14,928	243	99	144	8	5	3
	1—2 ..	28,221	13,628	14,593	27,614	13,444	14,170	586	173	413	21	11	10
	2—3 ..	27,317	12,985	14,332	26,013	12,663	13,350	1,259	302	957	45	20	25
	3—4 ..	26,174	12,580	13,594	23,543	11,947	11,596	2,519	574	1,945	112	59	53
	4—5 ..	25,731	12,693	13,038	22,130	11,807	10,323	3,429	789	2,640	172	97	75
	Total 0—5 ..	*137,177*	*66,545*	*70,632*	*128,783*	*64,416*	*64,367*	*8,036*	*1,937*	*6,099*	*358*	*192*	*166*
	5—10 ..	110,121	55,094	55,027	76,604	44,455	32,149	32,457	10,174	22,283	1,060	465	595
	10—15 ..	98,703	49,477	49,226	50,626	32,742	17,884	46,774	16,191	30,583	1,303	544	759
	15—20 ..	76,884	36,858	40,026	12,360	10,609	1,751	62,707	25,455	37,252	1,817	794	1,023
	20—30 ..	148,631	74,791	73,840	8,609	7,651	958	133,293	64,423	68,870	6,729	2,717	4,012
	30—40 ..	111,608	57,993	53,615	2,651	2,220	431	95,857	51,723	44,134	13,100	4,050	9,050
	40—50 ..	80,671	44,467	36,204	1,480	1,295	185	60,123	38,172	21,951	19,068	5,000	14,068
	50—60 ..	50,651	28,175	22,476	854	750	104	30,801	22,505	8,296	18,996	4,920	14,076
	60 and over ..	42,842	22,724	20,118	790	702	88	19,702	15,749	3,953	22,350	6,273	16,077
	HINDUS	*763,475*	*387,945*	*375,530*	*242,297*	*141,311*	*100,986*	*445,367*	*224,319*	*221,048*	*75,811*	*22,315*	*53,496*
	0—1 ..	26,521	13,064	13,457	26,279	12,966	13,313	234	93	141	8	5	3
	1—2 ..	25,138	12,099	13,039	24,546	11,922	12,624	572	166	406	20	11	9
	2—3 ..	24,279	11,505	12,774	23,010	11,201	11,809	1,226	285	941	43	19	24
	3—4 ..	23,164	11,113	12,051	20,593	10,508	10,085	2,460	546	1,914	111	59	52
	4—5 ..	22,701	11,182	11,519	19,185	10,329	8,856	3,351	758	2,593	165	95	70
	Total 0—5 ..	*121,803*	*58,963*	*62,840*	*113,613*	*56,926*	*56,687*	*7,843*	*1,848*	*5,995*	*347*	*189*	*158*
	5—10 ..	97,687	48,749	48,938	65,381	38,436	26,945	31,279	9,855	21,424	1,027	458	569
	10—15 ..	87,906	43,946	43,960	42,455	27,845	14,610	44,208	15,573	28,635	1,243	528	715
	15—20 ..	68,553	32,754	35,799	9,779	8,452	1,327	57,117	23,558	33,559	1,657	744	913
	20—30 ..	132,613	66,660	65,953	6,571	5,850	721	119,999	58,332	61,667	6,043	2,478	3,565
	30—40 ..	99,607	51,846	47,761	2 052	1,683	369	85,842	46,492	39,350	11,713	3,671	8,042
	40—50 ..	72,009	39,816	32,193	1,132	972	160	53,769	34,308	19,461	17,108	4,536	12,572
	50—60 ..	45,242	25,142	20,100	643	553	90	27,608	20,204	7,404	16,991	4,385	12,606
	60 and over ..	38,055	20,069	17,986	671	594	77	17,702	14,149	3,553	19,682	5,326	14,356
	MUSLIMS ..	*52,231*	*27,457*	*24,774*	*23,630*	*13,643*	*9,987*	*23,527*	*12,172*	*11,355*	*5,074*	*1,642*	*3,432*
	0—1 ..	1,715	860	855	1,713	858	855	2	2	..	..	..	..
	1—2 ..	1,703	848	855	1,699	845	854	4	3	1	..	..	..
	2—3 ..	1,723	844	879	1,712	836	876	11	8	3	..	..	..
	3—4 ..	1,725	842	883	1,696	827	869	28	15	13	1	..	1
	4—5 ..	1,735	864	871	1,690	844	846	41	19	22	4	1	3
	Total 0—5 ..	*8,601*	*4,258*	*4,343*	*8,510*	*4,210*	*4,300*	*86*	*47*	*39*	*5*	*1*	*4*
	5—10 ..	7,220	3.705	3,515	6,651	3,528	3,123	550	173	377	19	4	15
	10—15 ..	6,233	3,225	3,008	4,958	2,926	2,032	1,242	288	954	33	11	22
	15—20 ..	4,860	2,484	2,376	1,756	1,462	294	3,008	989	2,019	96	33	63
	20—30 ..	9,184	4,846	4,338	1,390	1,217	173	7,374	3,474	3,900	420	155	265
	30—40 ..	6,369	3,385	2,984	236	193	43	5,340	2,971	2,369	793	221	572
	40—50 ..	4,351	2,391	1,960	74	65	9	3,199	2,069	1,130	1,078	257	821
	50—60 ..	2,668	1,526	1,142	33	26	7	1,594	1,213	381	1,041	287	754
	60 and over ..	2,745	1,637	1,108	22	16	6	1,134	948	186	1,589	673	916

TABLE VII.—Part B—Details for Districts—*contd.*

District.	Age.	Population.			Unmarried.			Married.			Widowed.		
		Persons.	Males.	Females.	Persons.	Males	Females.	Persons.	Males.	Females.	Persons.	Males.	Females.
	1	2	3	4	5	6	7	8	9	10	11	12	13
YEOTMAL—*concld.*	TRIBAL RELIGION	*36,739*	*15,251*	*18,488*	*14,859*	*8,733*	*6,106*	*18,595*	*8,685*	*9,910*	*3,305*	*833*	*2,472*
	0—1 ..	1,339	662	677	1,335	658	677	4	4	..	..	..	..
	1—2 ..	1,240	620	620	1,232	616	616	7	4	3	1	..	1
	2—3 ..	1,180	570	610	1,164	562	602	14	7	7	2	..	1
	3—4 ..	1,156	565	591	1,134	554	580	22	11	11	..	1	..
	4—5 ..	1,157	589	568	1,128	578	550	26	10	16	3	1	2
	Total 0—5 ..	*6,072*	*3,006*	*3,066*	*5,993*	*2,968*	*3,025*	*73*	*36*	*37*	*6*	*2*	*4*
	5—10 ..	4,614	2,358	2,256	4,050	2,227	1,823	552	129	423	12	2	10
	10—15 ..	3,998	2,022	1,976	2,787	1,718	1,069	1,188	300	888	23	4	19
	15—20 ..	2,985	1,368	1,617	656	555	101	2,277	797	1,480	52	16	36
	20—30 ..	5,968	2,828	3,140	512	464	48	5,243	2,291	2,952	213	73	140
	30—40 ..	4,973	2,403	2,570	326	311	15	4,161	1,958	2,203	486	134	352
	40—50 ..	3,831	1,987	1,844	251	238	13	2,844	1,592	1,252	736	157	579
	50—60 ..	2,449	1,350	1,099	172	165	7	1,462	987	475	815	198	617
	60 and over ..	1,849	929	920	92	87	5	795	595	200	962	247	715
C. P. STATES	ALL RELIGIONS ..	*2,483,214*	*1,235,385*	*1,247,829*	*1,019,600*	*559,016*	*460,584*	*1,269,980*	*630,564*	*639,416*	*193,634*	*45,805*	*147,829*
	0—1 ..	91,703	45,264	46,439	90,411	44,601	45,810	1,231	627	604	61	36	25
	1—2 ..	84,502	40,771	43,731	83,316	40,228	43,088	1,159	533	626	27	10	17
	2—3 ..	89,680	44,646	45,034	87,840	43,907	43,933	1,798	718	1,080	42	21	21
	3—4 ..	89,039	46,317	42,722	85,737	45,018	40,719	3,209	1,271	1,938	93	28	65
	4—5 ..	96,017	43,239	52,778	91,681	41,513	50,168	4,177	1,683	2,494	159	43	116
	Total 0—5 ..	*450,941*	*220,237*	*230,704*	*438,985*	*215,267*	*223,718*	*11,574*	*4,832*	*6,742*	*382*	*138*	*244*
	5—10 ..	344,941	177,276	167,665	290,668	156,147	134,521	53,448	20,868	32,580	825	261	564
	10—15 ..	284,259	148,637	135,622	194,931	113,982	80,949	87,794	34,096	53,698	1,534	559	975
	15—20 ..	200,754	95,536	105,218	47,328	35,792	11,536	149,107	58,073	91,034	4,319	1,671	2,648
	20—30 ..	432,731	209,388	223,343	34,050	27,242	6,808	380,270	175,371	204,899	18,411	6,775	11,636
	30—40 ..	347,902	177,373	170,529	8,900	6,971	1,929	305,170	161,000	144,170	33,832	9,402	24,430
	40—50 ..	214,728	112,696	102,032	3,083	2,421	662	167,731	100,241	67,490	43,914	10,034	33,880
	50—60 ..	118,915	57,638	61,277	1,035	768	267	74,989	48,779	26,210	42,891	8,091	34,800
	60 and over ..	88,043	36,604	51,439	620	426	194	39,897	27,304	12,593	47,526	8,874	38,652
	HINDUS ..	*1,788,401*	*886,123*	*902,278*	*682,113*	*375,275*	*306,838*	*957,947*	*476,619*	*481,328*	*148,341*	*34,229*	*114,112*
	0—1 ..	65,004	31,970	33,034	64,060	31,529	32,531	888	407	481	56	34	22
	1—2 ..	58,867	28,257	30,610	58,006	27,894	30,112	836	355	481	25	8	17
	2—3 ..	60,419	30,457	29,962	58,990	29,901	29,089	1,392	538	854	37	18	19
	3—4 ..	59,373	31,757	27,616	56,723	30,753	25,970	2,579	982	1,597	71	22	49
	4—5 ..	69,070	29,738	39,332	65,601	28,418	37,183	3,358	1,290	2,068	111	30	81
	Total 0—5 ..	*312,733*	*152,179*	*160,554*	*303,380*	*148,495*	*154,885*	*9,053*	*3,572*	*5,481*	*300*	*112*	*188*
	5—10 ..	243,829	125,474	118,355	196,946	107,102	89,844	46,261	18,168	28,093	622	204	418
	10—15 ..	203,897	107,110	96,787	129,256	77,293	51,963	73,452	29,371	44,081	1,189	446	743
	15—20 ..	145,469	69,643	75,826	27,365	21,858	5,507	114,765	46,420	68,345	3,339	1,365	1,974
	20—30 ..	312,064	151,353	160,711	18,075	15,055	3,020	280,424	131,070	149,354	13,565	5,228	8,337
	30—40 ..	251,505	127,238	124,267	4,439	3,448	991	222,224	116,953	105,271	24,842	6,837	18,005
	40—50 ..	160,515	82,779	77,736	1,660	1,288	372	125,383	74,130	51,253	33,472	7,361	26,111
	50—60 ..	90,879	43,201	47,678	649	495	154	56,693	36,667	20,026	33,537	6,039	27,498
	60 and over ..	67,510	27,146	40,364	343	241	102	29,692	20,268	9,424	37,475	6,637	30,838
	MUSLIMS ..	*23,254*	*11,733*	*11,521*	*8,824*	*5,070*	*3,754*	*12,139*	*6,229*	*5,910*	*2,291*	*434*	*1,857*
	0—1 ..	752	356	396	748	353	395	3	3	..	1	..	1
	1—2 ..	611	283	328	609	281	328	2	2	..	..	..	..
	2—3 ..	673	306	367	659	303	356	14	3	11	..	..	..
	3—4 ..	690	332	358	665	326	339	24	6	18	1	..	1
	4—5 ..	683	340	343	648	325	323	33	15	18	2	..	2
	Total 0—5 ..	*3,409*	*1,617*	*1,792*	*3,329*	*1,588*	*1,741*	*76*	*29*	*47*	*4*	..	*4*
	5—10 .	2,809	1,470	1,339	2,435	1,320	1,115	362	145	217	12	5	7
	10—15 ..	2,446	1,298	1,148	1,784	1,068	716	638	222	416	24	8	16
	15—20 ..	2,073	1,007	1,066	606	497	109	1,421	493	928	46	17	29
	20—30 ..	4,545	2,340	2,205	525	477	48	3,812	1,796	2,016	208	67	141
	30—40 ..	3,599	1,855	1,744	119	102	17	3,060	1,663	1,397	420	90	330
	40—50 ..	2,230	1,167	1,063	17	13	4	1,659	1,061	598	554	93	461
	50—60 ..	1,263	607	656	3	1	2	745	533	212	515	73	442
	60 and over ..	880	372	508	6	4	2	366	287	79	508	81	427

TABLE VII.—Part B—Details for Districts—*concld.*

District.	Age.	Population.			Unmarried.			Married.			Widowed.		
		Persons.	Males.	Females.	Persons.	Males.	Females.	Persons.	Males.	Females.	Persons.	Males.	Females.
	1	2	3	4	5	6	7	8	9	10	11	12	13
C. P. STATES—*concld.*	CHRISTIANS ..	*51,701*	*26,102*	*25,599*	*27,852*	*15,039*	*12,813*	*20,958*	*10,351*	*10,607*	*2,891*	*712*	*2,179*
	0—1 ..	2,514	1,270	1,244	2,514	1,270	1,244	..	..	..	..	..	..
	1—2 ..	2,092	1,039	1,053	2,092	1,039	1,053	..	..	..	..	..	..
	2—3 ..	2,301	1,130	1,171	2,301	1,130	1,171	..	..	..	..	..	..
	3—4 ..	2,304	1,141	1,163	2,301	1,136	1,163	3	3	..	..	..	..
	4—5 ..	2,046	1,040	1,006	2,040	1,034	1,006	6	6	..	..	..	..
	Total 0—5 ..	*11,257*	*5,620*	*5,637*	*11,248*	*5,611*	*5,637*	*9*	*9*	..	..	..	..
	5—10 ..	7,924	4,130	3,794	7,874	4,111	3,763	49	19	30	1	..	1
	10—15 ..	6,438	3,437	3,001	5,974	3,341	2,633	456	94	362	8	2	6
	15—20 ..	4,231	2,075	2,156	1,794	1,266	528	2,385	789	1,596	52	20	32
	20—30 ..	8,120	3,963	4,157	831	629	202	7,061	3,248	3,813	228	86	142
	30—40 ..	6,290	3,234	3,056	80	46	34	5,774	3,063	2,711	436	125	311
	40—50 ..	3,798	1,944	1,854	28	20	8	3,116	1,767	1,349	654	157	497
	50—60 ..	2,334	1,146	1,188	14	11	3	1,518	951	567	802	184	618
	60 and over ..	1,309	553	756	9	4	5	590	411	179	710	138	572
	TRIBAL RELIGION	*617,599*	*310,156*	*307,443*	*299,819*	*163,018*	*136,831*	*277,886*	*136,788*	*141,098*	*39,864*	*10,350*	*29,514*
	0—1 ..	23,357	11,628	11,729	23,013	11,409	11,604	340	217	123	4	2	2
	1—2 ..	22,871	11,158	11,713	22,548	10,980	11,568	321	176	145	2	2	..
	2—3 ..	26,224	12,722	13,502	25,827	12,542	13,285	392	177	215	5	3	2
	3—4 ..	26,617	13,062	13,555	25,993	12,776	13,217	603	280	323	21	6	15
	4—5 ..	24,150	12,087	12,063	23,325	11,702	11,623	779	372	407	46	13	33
	Total 0—5 ..	*123,219*	*60,657*	*62,562*	*120,705*	*59,409*	*61,297*	*2,435*	*1,222*	*1,213*	*78*	*26*	*52*
	5—10 ..	90,125	46,069	44,056	83,170	43,484	39,686	6,765	2,533	4,232	190	52	138
	10—15 ..	71,240	36,662	34,578	57,726	32,160	25,566	13,202	4,399	8,803	312	103	209
	15—20 ..	48,738	22,673	26,065	17,474	12,087	5,387	30,388	10,318	20,070	876	268	608
	20—30 ..	107,553	51,475	56,078	14,542	11,005	3,537	88,625	39,086	49,539	4,386	1,384	3,002
	30—40 ..	86,170	44,835	41,335	4,233	3,346	887	73,852	39,156	34,696	8,085	2,333	5,752
	40—50 ..	47,954	26,664	21,290	1,370	1,092	278	37,421	23,174	14,247	9,163	2,398	6,765
	50—60 ..	24,327	12,613	11,709	366	258	108	15,975	10,584	5,391	7,986	1,776	6,210
	60 and over ..	18,273	8,503	9,770	262	177	85	9,223	6,316	2,907	8,788	2,010	6,778

Jubbulpore]

TABLE VII.—Part C—Details for Cities.

City.	Age.	Population.			Unmarried.			Married.			Widowed.		
		Persons.	Males.	Females.	Persons.	Males.	Females.	Persons.	Males.	Females.	Persons.	Males.	Females.
	1	2	3	4	5	6	7	8	9	10	11	12	13
JUBBULPORE CITY (including Cantonment).	ALL RELIGIONS ..	*124,332*	*69,258*	*55,124*	*50,852*	*31,622*	*19,230*	*62,082*	*34,142*	*27,940*	*11,448*	*3,494*	*7,954*
	0—1 ..	3,972	1,958	2,014	3,940	1,940	2,000	30	17	13	2	1	1
	1—2 ..	3,524	1,708	1,816	3,463	1,674	1,789	58	33	25	3	1	2
	2—3 ..	3,579	1,704	1,875	3,513	1,671	1,842	62	32	30	4	1	3
	3—4 ..	3,420	1,683	1,737	3,354	1,651	1,703	65	32	33	1	..	1
	4—5 ..	3,171	1,606	1,565	3,094	1,567	1,527	72	37	35	5	2	3
	Total 0—5 ..	*17,666*	*8,659*	*9,007*	*17,364*	*8,503*	*8,861*	*287*	*151*	*136*	*15*	*5*	*10*
	5—10 ..	13,574	7,284	6,290	12,464	6,924	5,540	1,092	354	738	18	6	12
	10—15 ..	12,578	6,943	5,635	9,802	6,156	3,646	2,720	762	1,958	56	25	31
	15—20 ..	12,986	7,239	5,747	4,739	4,117	622	7,985	3,000	4,985	262	122	140
	20—30 ..	28,104	16,360	11,744	5,041	4,675	366	21,763	11,108	10,655	1,300	577	723
	30—40 ..	19,026	11,429	7,597	953	859	94	15,785	9,762	6,023	2,288	808	1,480
	40—50 ..	11,289	6,593	4,696	332	284	48	7,958	5,500	2,458	2,999	809	2,190
	50—60 ..	5,758	3,127	2,631	91	60	31	3,158	2,424	734	2,509	643	1,866
	60 and over ..	3,401	1,624	1,777	66	44	22	1,334	1,081	253	2,001	499	1,502
	HINDUS ..	*85,539*	*47,124*	*38,415*	*32,276*	*19,852*	*12,424*	*44,690*	*24,652*	*20,038*	*8,573*	*2,620*	*5,953*
	0—1 ..	2,798	1,352	1,446	2,772	1,337	1,435	24	14	10	2	1	1
	1—2 ..	2,437	1,167	1,270	2,388	1,138	1,250	46	28	18	3	1	2
	2—3 ..	2,420	1,141	1,279	2,373	1,115	1,258	43	25	18	4	1	3
	3—4 ..	2,339	1,149	1,190	2,293	1,126	1,167	45	23	22	1	..	1
	4—5 ..	2,145	1,100	1,045	2,088	1,072	1,016	54	27	27	3	1	2
	Total 0—5 ..	*12,139*	*5,909*	*6,230*	*11,914*	*5,788*	*6,126*	*212*	*117*	*95*	*13*	*4*	*9*
	5—10 ..	9,130	4,970	4,160	8,293	4,707	3,586	823	259	564	14	4	10
	10—15 ..	8,421	4,693	3,728	6,366	4,127	2,239	2,008	546	1,462	47	20	27
	15—20 ..	8,690	4,696	3,994	2,646	2,389	257	5,847	2,214	3,633	197	93	104
	20—30 ..	19,103	10,708	8,395	2,408	2,261	147	15,717	8,024	7,693	978	423	555
	30—40 ..	13,668	8,221	5,447	439	400	39	11,476	7,196	4,280	1,753	625	1,128
	40—50 ..	8,034	4,708	3,326	131	118	13	5,645	3,964	1,681	2,258	626	1,632
	50—60 ..	4,056	2,154	1,902	43	35	8	2,118	1,644	474	1,895	475	1,420
	60 and over ..	2,298	1,065	1,233	36	27	9	844	688	156	1,418	350	1,068

TABLE VII.—Part C—Details for Cities—*contd.*

City.	Age.	Population.			Unmarried.			Married.			Widowed.		
		Persons.	Males.	Females.	Persons.	Males.	Females.	Persons.	Males.	Females.	Persons.	Males.	Females.
	1	2	3	4	5	6	7	8	9	10	11	12	13
JUBBULPORE CITY—*contd.*	MUSLIMS ..	*29,022*	*16,187*	*12,835*	*12,571*	*7,688*	*4,883*	*14,121*	*7,783*	*6,338*	*2,330*	*716*	*1,614*
	0—1 ..	915	468	447	909	465	444	6	3	3	..	..	..
	1—2 ..	875	427	448	863	422	441	12	5	7	..	..	..
	2—3 ..	943	454	489	924	447	477	19	7	12	..	..	..
	3—4 ..	874	428	446	854	419	435	20	9	11	..	..	..
	4—5 ..	826	407	419	806	396	410	18	10	8	2	1	1
	Total 0—5 ..	*4,433*	*2,184*	*2,249*	*4,356*	*2,149*	*2,207*	*75*	*34*	*41*	*2*	*1*	*1*
	5—10 ..	3,518	1,857	1,661	3,263	1,771	1,492	252	84	168	3	2	1
	10—15 ..	3,165	1,741	1,424	2,554	1,581	973	605	157	448	6	3	3
	15—20 ..	3,035	1,714	1,321	1,179	1,050	129	1,804	639	1,165	52	25	27
	20—30 ..	6,087	3,536	2,551	1,013	963	50	4,812	2,441	2,371	262	132	130
	30—40 ..	4,119	2,513	1,606	135	121	14	3,552	2,237	1,315	432	155	277
	40—50 ..	2,478	1,438	1,040	40	30	10	1,843	1,264	579	595	144	451
	50—60 ..	1,318	764	554	20	15	5	800	616	184	498	133	365
	60 and over ..	869	440	429	11	8	3	378	311	67	480	121	359
	CHRISTIANS ..	*6,724*	*4,132*	*2,592*	*4,656*	*3,195*	*1,461*	*1,819*	*865*	*954*	*249*	*72*	*177*
	0—1 ..	158	83	75	158	83	75	..	..	..	..	..	..
	1—2 ..	140	71	69	140	71	69	..	..	..	..	..	..
	2—3 ..	144	74	70	144	74	70	..	..	..	..	..	..
	3—4 ..	136	72	64	136	72	64	..	..	..	..	..	..
	4—5 ..	130	64	66	130	64	66	..	..	..	..	..	..
	Total 0—5 ..	*708*	*364*	*344*	*708*	*364*	*344*	..	..	..	..	..	
	5—10 ..	634	309	325	623	298	325	11	11	..	..	..	..
	10—15 ..	656	312	344	633	298	335	22	13	9	1	1	..
	15—20 ..	831	552	279	721	507	214	105	44	61	5	1	4
	20—30 ..	2,174	1,646	528	1,431	1,276	155	717	357	360	26	13	13
	30—40 ..	815	446	369	343	306	37	427	127	300	45	13	32
	40—50 ..	503	290	213	151	128	23	291	145	146	61	17	44
	50—60 ..	244	135	109	27	9	18	165	112	53	52	14	38
	60 and over ..	159	78	81	19	9	10	81	56	25	59	13	46
NAGPUR CITY	ALL RELIGIONS ..	*215,165*	*116,403*	*98,762*	*81,268*	*49,149*	*32,119*	*115,041*	*62,601*	*52,440*	*18,856*	*4,653*	*14,203*
	0—1 ..	5,501	2,783	2,718	5,411	2,743	2,668	67	29	38	23	11	12
	1—2 ..	5,724	2,884	2,840	5,563	2,807	2,756	120	58	62	41	19	22
	2—3 ..	5,877	2,907	2,970	5,665	2,800	2,865	172	88	84	40	19	21
	3—4 ..	5,685	2,822	2,863	5,451	2,713	2,738	195	91	104	39	18	21
	4—5 ..	5,419	2,744	2,675	5,160	2,641	2,519	215	84	131	44	19	25
	Total 0—5 ..	*28,206*	*14,140*	*14,066*	*27,250*	*13,704*	*13,546*	*769*	*350*	*419*	*187*	*86*	*101*
	5—10 ..	24,545	12,792	11,753	21,248	11,780	9,468	3,114	934	2,180	183	78	105
	10—15 ..	23,167	12,345	10,822	16,949	10,373	6,576	6,020	1,889	4,131	198	83	115
	15—20 ..	22,531	11,971	10,560	7,442	6,093	1,349	14,751	5,750	9,001	338	128	210
	20—30 ..	44,590	24,377	20,213	6,209	5,495	714	36,837	18,306	18,531	1,544	576	968
	30—40 ..	31,927	18,619	13,308	1,265	1,072	193	27,530	16,684	10,846	3,132	863	2,269
	40—50 ..	20,353	11,746	8,607	489	365	124	15,188	10,368	4,820	4,676	1,013	3,663
	50—60 ..	11,405	6,243	5,162	232	155	77	6,928	5,228	1,700	4,245	860	3,385
	60 and over ..	8,441	4,170	4,271	184	112	72	3,904	3,092	812	4,353	966	3,387
	HINDUS ..	*176,237*	*95,077*	*81,160*	*63,502*	*38,659*	*24,843*	*96,870*	*52,574*	*44,296*	*15,865*	*3,844*	*12,021*
	0—1 ..	4,563	2,298	2,265	4,487	2,266	2,221	53	21	32	23	11	12
	1—2 ..	4,708	2,386	2,322	4,565	2,318	2,247	103	49	54	40	19	21
	2—3 ..	4,811	2,398	2,413	4,617	2,300	2,317	155	80	75	39	18	21
	3—4 ..	4,649	2,324	2,325	4,437	2,227	2,210	176	81	95	36	16	20
	4—5 ..	4,393	2,241	2,152	4,171	2,155	2,016	183	69	114	39	17	22
	Total 0—5 ..	*23,124*	*11,647*	*11,477*	*22,277*	*11,266*	*11,011*	*670*	*300*	*370*	*177*	*81*	*96*
	5—10 ..	19,814	10,370	9,444	16,836	9,446	7,390	2,808	850	1,958	170	74	96
	10—15 ..	18,694	9,997	8,697	13,164	8,180	4,984	5,356	1,743	3,613	174	74	100
	15—20 ..	18,524	9,787	8,737	5,425	4,597	828	12,824	5,084	7,740	275	106	169
	20—30 ..	36,916	20,088	16,828	4,286	3,940	346	31,355	15,675	15,680	1,275	473	802
	30—40 ..	26,395	15,376	11,019	882	769	113	22,862	13,890	8,972	2,651	717	1,934
	40—50 ..	16,605	9,494	7,111	341	263	78	12,304	8,402	3,902	3,960	829	3,131
	50—60 ..	9,321	5,024	4,297	155	109	46	5,582	4,194	1,388	3,584	721	2,863
	60 and over ..	6,844	3,294	3,550	136	89	47	3,109	2,436	673	3,599	769	2,830

TABLE VII.—Part C—Details for Cities—concld.

City.	Age.	Population.			Unmarried.			Married.			Widowed.		
		Persons.	Males	Females.	Persons.	Males.	Females.	Persons.	Males.	Females.	Persons.	Males.	Females.
	1	2	3	4	5	6	7	8	9	10	11	12	13
NAGPUR CITY—concld.	MUSLIMS ..	*28,042*	*15,628*	*12,414*	*12,085*	*7,336*	*4,749*	*13,697*	*7,649*	*6,048*	*2,260*	*643*	*1,617*
	0—1 ..	630	327	303	617	319	298	13	8	5	..	..	..
	1—2 ..	742	362	380	724	353	371	17	9	8	1	..	1
	2—3 ..	777	366	411	760	357	403	16	8	8	1	1	..
	3—4 ..	767	369	398	746	357	389	18	10	8	3	2	1
	4—5 ..	757	376	381	727	361	366	25	13	12	5	2	3
	Total 0—5 ..	*3,673*	*1,800*	*1,873*	*3,574*	*1,747*	*1,827*	*89*	*48*	*41*	*10*	*5*	*5*
	5—10 ..	3,416	1,744	1,672	3,182	1,673	1,509	223	67	156	11	4	7
	10—15 ..	3,158	1,660	1,498	2,630	1,542	1,088	508	110	398	20	8	12
	15—20 ..	2,805	1,580	1,225	1,236	1,049	187	1,522	512	1,010	47	19	28
	20—30 ..	5,609	3,237	2,372	1,161	1,064	97	4,247	2,084	2,163	201	89	112
	30—40 ..	4,011	2,414	1,597	193	172	21	3,460	2,124	1,336	358	118	240
	40—50 ..	2,644	1,620	1,024	61	53	8	2,056	1,428	628	527	139	388
	50—60 ..	1,487	891	596	26	22	4	963	761	202	498	108	390
	60 and over ..	1,239	682	557	22	14	8	629	515	114	588	153	435
	CHRISTIANS ..	*6,149*	*3,359*	*3,090*	*3,943*	*2,123*	*1,820*	*2,144*	*1,152*	*992*	*362*	*84*	*278*
	0—1 ..	186	105	81	186	105	81	..	..	..	..	..	..
	1—2 ..	172	86	86	172	86	86	..	..	..	..	..	..
	2—3 ..	181	92	89	181	92	89	..	..	..	..	..	..
	3—4 ..	166	80	86	166	80	86	..	..	..	..	..	..
	4—5 ..	161	77	84	161	77	84	..	..	..	..	..	..
	Total 0—5 ..	*866*	*440*	*426*	*866*	*440*	*426*	..	..	..	..	..	..
	5—10 ..	834	435	399	820	435	385	12	..	12	2	..	2
	10—15 ..	845	444	401	802	437	365	40	6	34	3	1	2
	15—20 ..	740	366	374	603	317	286	132	49	83	5	..	5
	20—30 ..	1,133	563	570	584	344	240	520	212	308	29	7	22
	30—40 ..	854	448	406	136	90	46	655	344	311	63	14	49
	40—50 ..	647	372	275	67	36	31	483	311	172	97	25	72
	50—60 ..	333	184	149	42	17	25	217	155	62	74	12	62
	60 and over ..	197	107	90	23	7	16	85	75	10	89	25	64

TABLE VIII

Civil condition by age for selected castes.

This table repeats the information given in Table VII in respect of civil condition with this difference that, whereas in that table, the population is distributed by age and religion, it is here arranged according to caste or tribe. Moreover, in Table VII, the whole population is dealt with, while this table refers only to selected castes and tribes; the minor castes and tribes have been left out of account altogether and even those selected have been taken only for the localities where they are specially numerous. The arrangement of the corresponding table of 1921 has been generally followed. To save space, figures have been given not for each district separately, but for groups of districts the local conditions of which may be presumed to be fairly uniform. These natural divisions for the purpose of this and Tables XI (Occupation by selected castes) and XIV (Literacy by selected castes) are constituted as follows:--

Nerbudda Valley Division ..	Saugor, Damoh, Jubbulpore, Narsinghpur, Hoshangabad, Nimar and Makrai State.
Maratha Plain Division ..	Nagpur, Wardha, Bhandara, Chanda, Balaghat, Amraoti, Akola, Buldana and Yeotmal.
Plateau Division ..	Betul, Chhindwara, Seoni and Mandla.
Chhattisgarh Plain Division ..	Raipur, Bilaspur, Drug, Bastar, Kanker, Nandgaon, Kawardha, Khairagarh, Raigarh, Sarangarh, Sakti and Chhuikhadan.
Chhota Nagpur States ..	Changbhakar, Korea, Surguja, Udaipur and Jashpur.

In the 1921 Table Balaghat was included in the Plateau Division, and not in the Maratha Plain Division as now.

The caste figures in this table agree with those in Table XVII.

Caste, tribe or race.	Locality.	Sex.	Population dealt with.	Unmarried. Total.	0—6.	7—13.	14—16.	17—23.	24—43.	44 and over.
1	2	3	4	5	6	7	8	9	10	11
Ahir ..	Province ..	Male ..	(a) 406,993	162,964	81,435	54,626	12,400	8,664	4,778	1,061
		Female ..	(b) 411,112	127,005	81,139	38,542	4,104	1,908	999	313
(Hindu)..	Do. ..	Male ..	404,826	161,937	80,977	54,306	12,295	8,574	4.734	1,051
		Female ..	408,709	126,168	80.667	38,270	4,054	1,877	989	311
(Tribal) ..	Do. ..	Male ..	2,164	1,027	458	320	105	90	44	10
		Female ..	2,395	834	472	272	50	28	10	2
Andh ..	Berar ..	Male ..	29,801	12,368	6,275	4,344	738	398	453	160
		Female ..	28,718	8,864	6,284	2,237	92	98	85	68
Baiga ..	Total ..	Male ..	14,075	6,743	3,338	2,094	575	390	294	52
		Female ..	14,168	5,337	3,486	1,505	188	83	61	14
(Hindu)..	..	Male ..	3,996	1,935	942	589	171	133	87	13
		Female ..	4,089	1,524	937	464	60	20	36	7
	Jubbulpore ..	Male ..	1,173	612	295	178	52	56	29	2
		Female ..	1,167	476	266	146	32	13	16	3
	Mandla ..	Male ..	2,704	1,273	647	396	110	66	47	7
		Female ..	2,803	1,029	671	305	26	6	18	3
	Balaghat ..	Male ..	119	50	..	15	9	11	11	4
		Female ..	119	19	..	13	2	1	2	1
(Tribal) ..	..	Male ..	10,079	4,808	2,396	1,505	404	257	207	39
		Female ..	10,079	3,813	2,549	1,041	128	63	25	7
	Jubbulpore ..	Male ..	150	81	32	17	16	13	3	..
		Female ..	175	79	41	27	..	6	4	1
	Mandla ..	Male ..	7,266	3,328	1,698	1,063	258	157	128	24
		Female ..	7,165	2,579	1,770	687	74	32	12	4
	Balaghat ..	Male ..	2,663	1,399	666	425	130	87	76	15
		Female ..	2,739	1,155	738	327	54	25	9	2
Bairagi ..	Province ..	Male ..	(c) 19,408	8,169	3,222	2,486	653	615	735	458
		Female ..	19,066	5,476	3,283	1,724	214	111	86	58
Balahi ..	Total ..	Male ..	27,529	10,438	5,365	3,695	769	406	186	17
		Female ..	27,481	7,404	5,317	2,030	27	14	15	1
(Hindu and Tribal.)	..	Male ..	26,271	9,917	5,085	3,502	738	394	182	16
		Female ..	26,222	7,002	5,020	1,927	25	14	15	1
	Hoshangabad ..	Male ..	10,044	3,740	1,848	1,419	307	121	38	7
		Female ..	10,270	2,522	1,791	706	13	8	4	..
	Nimar ..	Male ..	15,245	5,796	3,049	1,947	391	262	140	7
		Female ..	14,956	4,222	3,043	1,152	10	6	10	1
	Makrai ..	Male ..	982	381	188	136	40	11	4	2
		Female ..	996	258	186	69	2	..	1	..
(Christian..)	Nimar ..	Male ..	1,258	521	280	193	31	12	4	1
		Female ..	1,259	402	297	103	2	..	..	..
Bania ..	Province ..	Male ..	(d) 122,156	54,731	20,466	16,816	5,739	6,145	4,392	1,173
		Female ..	111,505	33,922	20,047	11,958	845	308	512	252
Banjara ..	Total ..	Male ..	76,718	37,868	16,832	12,386	3,359	2,926	1,309	1,056
		Female ..	75,443	28,789	16,730	9,203	1,356	751	506	243
(Hindu and Tribal.)	..	Male ..	76,660	37,833	16,822	12,372	3,355	2,920	1,308	1,056
		Female ..	75,388	28,763	16,713	9,196	1,354	751	506	243
	Plateau Division ..	Male ..	3,282	1,737	664	492	179	209	164	29
		Female ..	3,187	1,162	718	362	57	16	8	1
	Maratha Division ..	Male ..	57,450	27,726	12,980	9,028	2,302	1,827	642	947
		Female ..	56,972	22,253	12,908	6,981	1,083	651	421	209
	Chhattisgarh Administrative Division.	Male ..	4,423	2,125	830	775	212	163	117	28
		Female ..	4,958	1,634	906	569	82	42	22	13
	8 States of Chhattisgarh Plain Division.	Male ..	1,018	448	184	150	41	43	26	4
		Female ..	1,089	351	177	100	37	10	20	7
	Bastar ..	Male ..	1,555	796	303	275	60	71	77	10
		Female ..	1,572	577	314	188	29	13	22	11
	Nimar ..	Male ..	8,932	5,001	1,861	1,652	561	607	282	38
		Female ..	7,610	2,786	1,690	996	66	19	13	2

(a) Includes 3 Christians. (b) Includes 8 Christians. (c) Includes 1 Christian. (d) Includes 1 Christian.

Married.							Widowed.						
Total.	0—6.	7—13.	14—16.	17—23.	24—43.	44 and over.	Total.	0—6.	7—13.	14—16.	17—23.	24—43.	44 and over.
12	13	14	15	16	17	18	19	20	21	22	23	24	25
223,476 227,606	2,673 5,530	16,710 26,868	14,653 22,087	35,744 47,821	107,433 99,459	46,263 25,841	20,553 56,501	113 120	254 345	441 452	1,444 1,593	7,708 16,469	10,593 37,522
222,428 226,391	2,671 5,528	16,689 26,826	14,620 22,002	35,631 47,595	106,847 98,765	45,970 25,675	20,461 56,150	113 120	254 345	441 452	1,441 1,589	7,677 16,378	10,535 37,266
1,046 1,211	2 2	21 42	32 85	113 225	585 691	293 166	91 350	.. ..	.. ..	.. ..	3 4	31 90	57 256
16,429 15,787	174 403	1,324 2,434	1,148 1,851	2,979 3,625	7,241 6,071	3,563 1,403	1,004 4,067	13 11	20 60	19 94	48 189	313 1,206	591 2,507
6,951 7,502	44 63	229 527	365 758	928 1,683	3,659 3,631	1,726 840	381 1,329	.. 4	.. 5	6 8	28 26	147 354	200 932
1,953 *2,132*	*9* *13*	*62* *167*	*104* *207*	*266* *489*	*1,051* *1,046*	*461* *210*	*108* *133*	.. ..	.. *1*	*2* *1*	*7* *9*	*38* *122*	*61* *300*
526 557	.. 1	10 41	27 42	70 130	307 296	112 47	35 134	.. ..	.. ..	.. 1	3 3	14 49	18 81
1,362 1,495	7 12	52 114	67 151	184 346	712 714	340 158	69 279	.. ..	.. ..	2 ..	4 6	23 69	40 204
65 80	2 ..	.. 12	10 14	12 13	32 36	9 5	4 20	.. ..	.. 1	.. ..	.. ..	1 4	3 15
4,998 *5,370*	*35* *50*	*167* *360*	*261* *551*	*662* *1,194*	*2,608* *2,585*	*1,265* *630*	*273* *396*	.. *4*	.. *4*	*4* *7*	*21* *17*	*109* *232*	*139* *632*
63 69	.. 1	.. 2	1 4	7 18	37 37	18 7	6 27	.. ..	.. ..	.. ..	.. ..	2 11	4 16
3,742 3,971	34 47	136 288	223 420	518 891	1,923 1,863	908 462	196 615	.. ..	.. 4	3 6	15 12	80 164	98 429
1,193 1,330	1 2	31 70	37 127	137 285	648 685	339 161	71 254	.. 4	.. ..	1 1	6 5	27 57	37 187
9,900 10,154	110 196	513 1,025	523 880	1,506 2,180	4,784 4,558	2,464 1,315	1,339 3,436	5 4	17 13	15 14	64 88	442 935	796 2,382
15,806 *16,093*	*26* *224*	*697* *2,540*	*1,244* *1,794*	*3,103* *3,894*	*7,762* *6,522*	*2,974* *1,119*	*1,285* *3,984*	.. ..	*9* *26*	*13* *31*	*43* *64*	*565* *1,368*	*655* *2,475*
15,123 *15,393*	*26* *224*	*657* *2,416*	*1,193* *1,730*	*2,948* *3,736*	*7,410* *6,218*	*2,859* *1,069*	*1,231* *3,827*	.. ..	*8* *26*	*13* *30*	*39* *81*	*542* *1,304*	*629* *2,386*
5,848 6,086	7 150	253 897	415 641	1,100 1,451	2,938 2,467	1,135 480	456 1,662	.. ..	5 7	3 7	13 22	160 524	275 1,102
8,738 8,753	19 65	386 1,426	739 1,016	1,733 2,177	4,251 3,516	1,610 553	711 1,981	.. ..	3 17	10 22	25 57	363 707	310 1,178
537 554	.. 9	18 93	39 73	115 108	251 235	114 36	64 184	.. ..	.. 2	.. 1	1 2	19 73	44 106
683 700	.. ..	40 124	51 64	155 158	322 304	115 50	54 157	.. ..	1 ..	.. 1	4 3	23 64	26 89
58,348 55,122	398 918	1,928 4,982	2,136 6,308	9,643 13,760	30,373 23,940	13,870 5,214	9,077 22,461	35 20	64 100	104 194	364 774	2,848 7,783	5,662 13,590
35,067 *36,816*	*359* *484*	*1,503* *3,291*	*1,907* *4,018*	*5,650* *9,012*	*17,601* *15,363*	*8,047* *4,648*	*3,783* *9,838*	*7* *20*	*75* *84*	*78* *191*	*284* *498*	*1,136* *2,936*	*2,203* *6,109*
35,046 *36,795*	*359* *484*	*1,503* *3,290*	*1,907* *4,017*	*5,646* *9,003*	*17,586* *15,355*	*8,045* *4,646*	*3,781* *9,830*	*7* *20*	*75* *84*	*78* *191*	*284* *498*	*1,136* *2,935*	*2,201* *6,102*
1,384 1,472	11 4	35 35	34 108	158 336	799 861	347 128	161 553	.. ..	2 ..	.. 2	6 9	59 157	94 385
26,884 27,960	305 412	1,274 2,888	1,628 3,255	4,558 6,688	12,965 10,959	6,154 3,758	2,840 6,759	6 17	70 78	73 170	217 404	759 1,977	1,715 4,113
2,068 2,331	19 37	118 118	94 185	274 586	1,057 1,047	506 358	230 993	1 1	2 2	1 9	30 37	77 242	119 702
512 537	4 13	19 38	44 53	73 114	249 234	123 85	58 201	.. ..	.. ..	.. 3	12 6	18 63	28 129
652 704	1 3	19 34	21 48	81 171	360 381	170 67	107 291	.. 1	.. 2	2 2	3 9	56 144	46 133
3,546 3,791	19 15	38 177	86 368	502 1,108	2,156 1,873	745 250	385 1,033	.. 1	1 2	2 5	16 33	167 352	199 640

Caste, tribe or race.	Locality.	Sex.	Population dealt with.	Unmarried. Total.	0—6.	7—13.	14—16.	17—23.	24—43.	44 and over.
1	2	3	4	5	6	7	8	9	10	11
Banjara—*concld.* (Muslim)	..	Male	58	35	10	14	4	6	1	..
		Female	55	26	17	7	2	..	..	..
	Plateau Division ..	Male	4	1	1	..	..	..	..	..
		Female	4	1	1	..	..	..	..	..
	Maratha Division ..	Male	..	..	..	..	..	..	..	..
		Female	..	..	..	..	..	..	..	..
	Chhattisgarh Administrative Division.	Male	..	..	..	..	..	..	..	..
		Female	..	..	..	..	..	..	..	..
	8 States of Chhattisgarh Plain Division.	Male	..	..	..	..	..	..	..	..
		Female	..	..	..	..	..	..	..	..
	Bastar ..	Male	..	..	..	..	..	..	..	..
		Female	..	..	..	..	..	..	..	..
	Nimar ..	Male	54	34	9	14	4	6	1	
		Female	51	33	16	7	2	..	..	..
Barhai ..	Province ..	Male	(e) 58,097	22,037	9,972	7,357	1,976	1,341	784	157
		Female	(f) 53,893	14,687	9,957	4,180	223	169	102	56
Basor ..	Nerbudda Valley ..	Male	(g) 16,142	7,448	3,430	2,575	698	448	228	69
		Female	(h) 15,590	5,257	3,174	1,886	140	33	19	5
Beldar ..	Total ..	Male	2,691	1,150	475	429	106	94	39	7
		Female	2,824	819	529	252	17	4	13	4
	Saugor ..	Male	266	141	41	60	19	14	7	..
		Female	293	98	55	34	9	..	..	..
	Jubbulpore ..	Male	524	229	73	84	33	26	11	2
		Female	510	140	94	42	3	1	..	..
	Nimar ..	Male	612	258	118	88	21	20	9	2
		Female	669	206	144	60	1	1	..	..
	Wardha ..	Male	946	365	171	143	22	22	5	2
		Female	955	244	161	70	3	2	4	4
	Nagpur ..	Male	343	157	72	54	11	12	7	1
		Female	397	131	75	46	1	..	9	..
Bhaina .	Bilaspur ..	Male	7,561	3,134	1,642	1,084	208	119	69	12
		Female	7,670	2,796	1,821	838	80	30	25	2
Bhamta ..	Wardha ..	Male	593	234	141	69	12	9	3	..
		Female	583	134	110	21	1	1	1	..
Bharia—Bhumia	Total ..	Male	18,523	8,746	4,291	2,831	790	557	222	55
		Female	19,827	7,196	4,258	2,316	397	108	74	13
(Hindu)..		Male	14,411	6,696	3,272	2,239	595	408	147	35
		Female	15,672	5,636	3,277	1,878	339	75	59	8
	Jubbulpore ..	Male	13,877	6,448	3,143	2,163	574	393	142	33
		Female	15,108	5,450	3,138	1,841	335	70	58	8
	Narsinghpur ..	Male	481	227	120	69	21	12	3	2
		Female	511	169	129	30	4	5	1	..
	Chhindwara ..	Male	53	21	9	7	..	3	2	..
		Female	53	17	10	7	..	..	..	..
(Tribal)..	..	Male	4,112	2,050	1,019	592	195	149	75	20
		Female	4,155	1,560	981	468	58	33	15	5
	Jubbulpore ..	Male	10	4	2	..	..	2	..	..
		Female	11	4	1	3	..	..	..	..
	Narsinghpur ..	Male	640	309	140	89	30	33	13	4
		Female	513	208	138	56	8	6	..	..
	Chhindwara ..	Male	3,462	1,737	877	503	165	114	62	16
		Female	3,631	1,348	842	409	50	27	15	5
Bhil ..	Nimar ..	Male	(i) 12,568	5,085	2,497	1,994	360	169	48	17
		Female	(j) 12,425	3,891	2,531	1,325	14	11	9	1
Bhilala ..	Total ..	Male	8,177	3,602	1,502	1,329	359	302	98	12
		Female	7,654	2,460	1,568	851	14	10	14	3
	Hoshangabad ..	Male	1,249	509	195	182	55	52	23	2
		Female	1,297	382	261	113	3	2	3	..

(e) Includes 13 Christians. (f) Includes 13 Christians. (g) Includes 1 Christian. (h) Includes 1 Christian
(i) Includes 28 Muslims. (j) Includes 18 Muslims.

Married.							Widowed.						
Total.	0—6.	7—13.	14—16.	17—23.	24—43.	44 and over.	Total.	0—6	7—13.	14—16.	17—23	24—43.	44 and over
12	13	14	15	16	17	18	19	20	21	22	23	24	25
21	..	..	..	*4*	*15*	*2*	*2*	..	..	..	..	..	*2*
21	..	*1*	*1*	*9*	*8*	*2*	*5*	..	..	..	..	*1*	*7*
2	..	..	..	1	1	..	1	..	..	..	..	..	1
3	..	..	..	2	1	..	..	..	..	..	..	..	..
..	..	..	..	..	..	..	..	..	..	..	..	..	..
..	..	..	..	..	..	..	..	..	..	..	..	..	..
..	..	..	..	..	..	..	..	..	..	..	..	..	..
..	..	..	..	..	..	..	..	..	..	..	..	..	..
..	..	..	..	..	..	..	..	..	..	..	..	..	..
..	..	..	..	..	..	..	..	..	..	..	..	..	..
..	..	..	..	..	..	..	..	..	..	..	..	..	..
..	..	..	..	..	..	..	..	..	..	..	..	..	..
19	..	..	..	3	14	2	1	..	..	..	..	..	1
18	..	1	1	7	7	2	8	..	..	..	..	1	7
31,907	207	1,573	1,796	5,058	15,311	7,962	**4,103**	7	473	367	196	1,093	1,96
30,907	598	4,485	2,987	6,423	13,212	3,202	**8,299**	16	66	68	218	2,288	5,643
8,074	66	290	380	1,513	4,294	1,531	**620**	..	6	19	40	246	309
8,274	44	651	907	2,064	4,002	606	**2,059**	1	13	25	75	751	1,194
1,412	*2*	*55*	*51*	*240*	*748*	*316*	*129*	..	*1*	*3*	*6*	*42*	*77*
1,480	*8*	*182*	*151*	*355*	*659*	*125*	*525*	..	*5*	..	*22*	*177*	*321*
118	..	..	..	17	68	33	**7**	..	..	..	..	4	3
131	..	1	14	39	66	11	**64**	..	..	..	3	21	40
263	..	3	3	45	174	38	**32**	..	..	2	2	15	13
261	1	12	17	77	126	28	**109**	..	1	..	4	45	59
328	1	14	18	74	169	52	**26**	..	1	1	2	9	13
357	2	41	52	89	157	16	**106**	..	2	..	3	39	62
533	1	35	22	80	246	149	**48**	..	..	..	2	9	37
554	5	103	50	106	239	51	**157**	..	2	..	8	42	105
170	..	3	8	24	91	44	**16**	..	..	..	..	5	11
177	..	25	18	44	71	19	**89**			..	3	36	55
4,168	36	208	248	716	2,098	862	**259**	..	4	5	10	98	142
4,057	50	348	307	1,011	1,844	497	**817**	3	3	4	20	265	522
335	1	21	49	85	105	74	**24**	..	..	..	.	13	11
347	8	73	27	49	156	32	**102**	.	3	3	..	27	69
9,23[illegible]	*40*	*213*	*434*	*1,526*	[illegible]	*1,065*	[illegible]	*1*	*2*	*11*	*32*	*153*	*312*
9,772	*96*	*315*	*904*	*2,175*	[illegible]	*955*	*2,[illegible]*	*76*	*55*	*131*	*91*	*855*	*1,618*
7,303	*30*	*176*	*335*	*1,231*	*3,973*	*1,556*	[illegible]	*1*	*2*	*10*	*26*	*132*	*211*
7,729	*91*	*391*	*661*	*1,[illegible]*	*3,930*	*751*	*2,307*	*79*	*55*	*129*	*73*	*725*	*1,246*
7,036	28	173	331	1,149	3,811	1,404	**393**	1	2	10	24	123	233
7,479	91	288	639	1,953	3,789	728	**2,179**	79	55	129	44	694	1,178
236	2	3	3	29	143	56	**18**	..	.	..	2	9	7
224	..	13	21	30	138	22	**118**	..	..	..	29	27	62
31	.	..	1	3	21	6	**1**	..	.	.	..	.	1
26	..	..	1	9	12	4	**10**	..	..	..	..	4	6
1,93[illegible]	*10*	*37*	*99*	*29[illegible]*	*1,08[illegible]*	*409*	[illegible]	..	..	*1*	*6*	*51*	*71*
2,0[illegible]	*5*	[illegible]	*213*	[illegible]*6*	*951*	*231*	*552*	..	..	*2*	*18*	*160*	*372*
4	..	..	1	3	..	..	**2**	..	..	..	..	1	1
7	..	1	1	2	3	.	..	..	..	..	..	..	..
309	..	2	11	41	201	54	**22**	..	..	..	..	9	13
258	..	12	23	64	150	29	**47**	..	..	..	4	15	28
1,620	10	35	87	251	882	355	**105**	..	..	1	6	41	57
1,778	5	81	219	420	851	202	**505**	..	..	2	14	145	344
6,864	17	188	394	1,22[illegible]	3,716	1,324	**619**	..	5	3	18	242	351
7,001	42	810	759	1,724	3,163	503	**1,583**	3	11	21	58	541	899
4,010	*12*	*60*	*105*	*652*	*2,[illegible]*	*915*	*565*	*1*	..	*3*	*18*	*206*	*337*
3,973	*4*	*336*	*458*	*967*	*1,858*	*320*	*1,221*	*1*	*4*	*14*	*28*	*439*	*735*
630	1	4	15	86	362	162	**110**	..	..	..	5	36	69
667	..	62	70	145	318	72	**248**	..	2	2	4	65	175

Caste, tribe or race.	Locality.	Sex.	Population dealt with.	Unmarried. Total.	0—6.	7—13.	14—16	17—23.	24—43.	44 and over.
1	2	3	4	5	6	7	8	9	10	11
Bhilala—*concld.*	Nimar	Male	**6,928**	**3,093**	1,307	1,147	304	250	75	10
		Female	**6,357**	**2,078**	1,307	738	11	8	11	3
Bhoyar	Total	Male	*34,766*	*13,148*	*7,402*	*4,316*	*812*	*417*	*145*	*26*
		Female	*35,744*	*9,885*	*7,252*	*2,474*	*101*	*26*	*17*	*16*
	Betul	Male	**12,884**	**5,423**	2,761	1,872	393	271	108	18
		Female	**13,452**	**4,259**	2,914	1,237	72	15	13	8
	Chhindwara	Male	**12,863**	**4,329**	2,658	1,311	227	96	31	6
		Female	**13,188**	**3,224**	2,478	719	12	9	2	4
	Wardha	Male	**7,030**	**2,637**	1,565	899	145	28	..	..
		Female	**7,198**	**1,878**	1,473	387	14	2	..	2
	Nagpur	Male	**1,989**	**759**	418	264	47	22	6	2
		Female	**1,906**	**524**	386	131	3	..	2	2
Bhulia	Raipur	Male	**2,077**	**833**	433	265	73	44	17	1
		Female	**2,051**	**666**	337	230	64	35	..	..
Bhunjia	Raipur	Male	**3,586**	**1,822**	823	577	158	130	124	10
		Female	**3,672**	**1,491**	850	399	127	66	44	5
Binjhwar	Total	Male	*26,589*	*11,796*	*5,223*	*4,057*	*1,267*	*790*	*326*	*133*
		Female	*27,216*	*9,641*	*5,063*	*3,298*	*661*	*305*	*170*	*144*
	Bhandara	Male	**1,842**	**787**	396	203	66	38	58	26
		Female	**1,895**	**631**	379	118	25	99	8	2
	Balaghat	Male	**4,027**	**1,677**	656	597	174	194	34	22
		Female	**4,232**	**1,397**	570	422	147	82	68	108
	Raipur	Male	**14,330**	**6,576**	2,771	2,371	829	404	158	43
		Female	**14,893**	**5,548**	2,821	2,122	415	96	69	25
	Bilaspur	Male	**6,390**	**2,7[illegible]6**	1,400	886	198	154	76	42
		Female	**6,196**	**2,065**	1,293	636	74	28	25	9
Bohra (Muslim.)	Nimar	Male	**1,206**	**777**	164	263	155	162	30	3
		Female	**1,407**	**678**	286	250	83	51	7	1
Brahman	Province	Male	(*k*) **277,936**	**131,768**	43,905	39,236	14,311	19,184	12,188	2,944
		Female	(*l*) **239,829**	**78,905**	43,478	30,108	3,214	1,119	789	197
Chadar	Total	Male	*13,392*	*6,224*	*2,447*	*2,268*	*803*	*491*	*170*	*45*
		Female	*13,014*	*4,215*	*2,225*	*1,769*	*141*	*53*	*10*	*17*
	Saugor	Male	**7,300**	**3,490**	1,306	1,310	489	288	74	23
		Female	**6,982**	**2,203**	1,179	911	66	40	5	2
	Damoh	Male	**3,407**	**1,468**	601	540	176	100	44	7
		Female	**3,380**	**1,104**	530	510	53	9	1	1
	Jubbulpore	Male	**1,270**	**591**	255	198	64	40	30	4
		Female	**1,264**	**465**	271	179	8	2	4	1
	Narsinghpur	Male	**1,415**	**675**	285	220	74	63	22	11
		Female	**1,388**	**443**	245	169	14	2	..	13
Chamar	Province	Male	(*m*) **305,693**	**116,965**	61,521	38,209	9,227	5,199	2,096	713
		Female	(*n*) **309,999**	**94,786**	61,835	25,966	3,380	1,649	1,363	593
Daraiha	Bilaspur	Male	**222**	**81**	47	22	5	3	3	1
		Female	**376**	**94**	65	25	3	1	..	..
Dahayat	Jubbulpore	Male	**4,311**	**1,815**	818	597	158	145	71	26
		Female	**4,467**	**1,382**	876	438	44	9	11	4
Darzi	Province	Male	(*o*) **26,210**	**10,498**	4,639	3,635	986	782	368	88
		Female	(*p*) **25,019**	**6,966**	4,597	2,142	132	43	35	17
Deswali	Total	Male	*3,554*	*1,550*	*562*	*588*	*192*	*16[illegible]*	*68*	*6*
		Female	*3,407*	*1,043*	*618*	*112*	*9*	*2*	*2*	..
	Hoshangabad	Male	**2,405**	**1,086**	399	400	129	111	43	4
		Female	**2,304**	**737**	439	292	6	..	..	..
	Nimar	Male	**1,149**	**494**	163	188	63	53	25	2
		Female	**1,103**	**306**	179	120	3	2	2	..
Dhanuk	Narsinghpur	Male	**2,534**	**1,180**	560	411	119	73	13	4
		Female	**2,652**	**952**	562	351	28	7	4	..
Dhanwar	Bilaspur	Male	**6,368**	**3,143**	1,470	1,092	248	179	114	40
		Female	**6,403**	**2,601**	1,627	771	70	51	62	20

(*k*) Includes 9 Christians (*l*) Includes 7 Christians. (*m*) Includes 13 Christians. (*n*) Includes 12 Christians.
(*o*) Includes 12 Muslims. (*p*) Includes 4 Muslims.

Married.							Widowed.						
Total.	0—6.	7—13.	14—16.	17—23.	24—43.	44 and over.	Total.	0—6.	7—13.	14—16.	17—23.	24—43.	44 and over.
12	13	14	15	16	17	18	19	20	21	22	23	24	25
3,380	11	56	90	566	1,904	753	455	1		3	13	170	268
3,306	4	2[illegible]	3[illegible]8	822	1,570	[illegible]48	973	1	2	12	24	374	560
20,281	212	1,740	1,447	3,125	9,100	4,657	1,337	7	18	23	49	371	869
21,440	669	3,297	1,790	4,514	8,497	2,673	4,41[illegible]	2	56	38	89	1,110	3 124
6,894	26	417	427	1,020	3,356	1,648	567	2	6	7	25	172	355
7,197	79	819	711	1,653	3,126	809	1,9[illegible]	2	15	18	28	538	1,395
8,045	179	915	576	1,197	3,432	1,746	489	5	12	14	17	125	316
8,221	461	1,489	620	1,011	3,164	876	1,743	..	32	11	37	427	1,236
4,179	6	332	352	691	1,804	994	214	..	.	..	5	62	147
4,883	113	794	329	1,009	1,784	854	437	..	6	5	24	86	316
1,163	1	76	92	217	508	269	67	..	.	2	2	12	51
1,139	16	195	130	241	423	134	243	..	3	4	..	59	177
1,186	19	200	144	230	443	150	58	..	..	..	5	26	27
1,196	9	28	332	313	388	126	189	..	..	3	13	52	121
1,573	23	67	108	235	786	354	191	..	5	13	24	57	92
1,702	16	98	232	426	748	192	479	..	2	5	20	177	275
13,223	145	597	572	1,97[illegible]	6,659	3,298	1,570	2	27	79	141	527	794
13,803	220	975	1,129	3,264	6,139	2,076	3,772	8	68	97	148	1,040	2,411
854	7	75	65	116	353	238	201	2	22	21	7 35	45	74
974	27	131	123	174	404	115	290	1	32	16	1	78	148
2,139	47	45	95	314	1,052	586	211	..	1	5	12	56	137
2,107	56	145	215	501	878	312	728	..	25	42	42	205	414
6,821	28	145	190	1,073	3,667	1,718	933	..	..	48	80	348	457
7,320	36	214	543	1,934	3,356	1,237	2,025	3	7	28	60	547	1,380
3,409	63	332	222	469	1,567	756	225	..	4	5	12	78	126
3,402	101	485	248	655	1,501	412	729	4	4	11	31	210	469
375	6	7	16	32	165	149	54	..	..	..	1	20	33
582	..	11	19	170	311	71	147	..	..	1	1	25	120
126,319	607	2,506	3,560	17,790	69,949	31,907	19,849	35	150	109	650	6,141	12,764
111,010	976	7.405	10,903	28,692	50,986	12,048	49,914	30	298	517	2,145	17,744	29,180
6,495	5	64	156	1,252	3,604	1,415	673	1	.	3	29	252	388
6,569	16	289	697	1,738	3,255	574	2.230	1	2	9	71	898	1,249
3,439	5	16	85	607	1,978	748	371	1	..	1	11	139	219
3,549	3	175	404	94[illegible]	1,729	298	1,230	1	.	7	25	514	683
1,764	..	24	34	412	919	375	175	..	..	1	9	65	100
1,708	..	40	164	456	888	160	568	..	..	1	35	223	309
617	..	17	16	126	327	131	62	.	..	1	5	21	35
605	13	37	55	156	286	58	194	..	2	1	6	74	111
675	..	7	20	107	380	161	65	..	..	..	4	27	34
707	..	37	74	186	352	58	238	.	.	..	5	87	146
177,[illegible]90	4,127	16,295	11,821	29,648	79.249	35,960	11,[illegible]38	25	183	237	796	3,844	6,553
177,404	5.148	22,850	17,829	37,114	73,783	20,680	378,09	118	339	449	1,091	11,549	24,263
131	..	5	14	24	54	34	10	.	..	..	2	56	3
200	1	21	11	54	96	17	32	..	..	..	..	12	20
2,291	20	71	115	422	1,320	343	205	.	2	5	26	80	92
2,359	9	160	226	586	1,222	156	726	2	2	4	15	251	452
11,178	86	525	798	2,4[illegible]0	6,[illegible]19	3,400	1,534	2	15	8	92	484	933
13,955	228	1,7[illegible]7	1,506	3,212	5,852	1,360	1,098	5	27	31	109	1,222	2,704
1,752	1	25	69	322	952	383	222	..	1	1	6	2 85	129
1,762	4	136	183	429	840	170	602	..	4	1	12	157	398
1,1[illegible]0	1	16	43	196	643	261	159	..	.	1	5	56	97
1,174	2	79	125	230	[illegible]61	127	393	.	..	.	9	129	255
592	..	9	26	126	309	122	63	..	1	..	1	29	32
588	2	57	58	149	279	43	209	..	4	1	3	58	143
1,245	..	24	58	207	682	274	1[illegible]9	.	.	..	6	49	54
1,305	1	5	121	324	682	102	395	.	..	1	9	115	270
3,068	41	104	116	412	1,610	785	157	2	1	3	12	60	79
3,259	31	187	277	723	1,675	366	543	1	6	3	15	170	348

TABLE VIII

Caste, tribe or race.	Locality.	Sex.	Population dealt with.	Unmarried. Total.	0—6.	7—13.	14—16.	17—23.	24—43.	44 and over.
1	2	3	4	5	6	7	8	9	10	11
Dhimar ..	Province ..	Male ..	(q) 161,064	68,216	33,105	23,450	5,891	3,929	1,404	437
		Female ..	161,754	51,646	33,779	16,616	1,388	458	305	100
Dhobi ..	Province ..	Male ..	(r) 92,245	33,962	17,843	11,368	2,345	1,387	800	219
		Female ..	(s) 95,361	26,443	18,189	7,143	526	277	209	99
Dohor ..	Buldana ..	Male ..	1,523	598	347	171	51	20	6	3
		Female ..	1,453	405	313	63	16	4	6	3
Ganda ..	Total ..	Male ..	*(t) 84,572*	*36,565*	*18,545*	*12,331*	*2,819*	*1,657*	*977*	*236*
		Female ..	*(u) 89,392*	*31,270*	*18,068*	*10,519*	*1,329*	*909*	*367*	*78*
	Chhattisgarh Administrative Division.	Male ..	52,293	23,277	11,709	7,932	1,803	983	713	137
		Female ..	56,252	19,384	10,947	6,798	783	502	293	61
	9 States of Chhattisgarh Plain Division.	Male ..	24,929	9,629	5,047	3,256	637	450	161	78
		Female ..	25,793	8,730	5,345	2,627	362	334	47	15
	Surguja ..	Male ..	1,827	916	463	311	59	33	41	9
		Female ..	1,781	692	456	208	13	9	6	..
	Jashpur ..	Male ..	5,523	2,743	1,326	832	320	191	62	12
		Female ..	5,566	2,464	1,320	886	171	64	21	2
Ghasia ..	Total ..	Male ..	*(v) 16,015*	*6,626*	*3,177*	*2,439*	*416*	*3,222*	*225*	*47*
		Female ..	*17,591*	*5,633*	*[illegible]*	*1,874*	*191*	*10*	*101*	*19*
	Chhattisgarh Administrative Division	Male ..	11,092	4,495	2,130	1,687	288	216	139	35
		Female ..	12,315	3,596	2,180	1,188	102	46	69	11
	9 States of Chhattisgarh Plain Division	Male ..	4,922	2,131	1,047	752	128	106	86	12
		Female ..	5,579	2,037	1,166	686	89	56	32	8
Golar ..	Yeotmal ..	Male ..	1,038	225	170	35	9	2	8	1
		Female ..	1,130	153	140	10	1	1	1	..
Gond ..	Province ..	Male ..	(w) 1,104,178	490,531	222,954	164,865	48,187	34,177	15,950	4,398
		Female ..	(x) 1,156,960	407,603	233,096	136,036	22,342	9,043	5,658	1,428
(Hindu) ..	Do. ..	Male ..	504,710	213,372	100,397	73,795	19,273	12,623	5,911	1,373
		Female ..	531,963	176,705	105,496	57,026	7,900	3,084	2,309	890
(Tribal) ..	Do. ..	Male ..	599,456	277,152	122,556	91,069	28,914	21,551	10,038	3,024
		Female ..	624,985	230,898	127,600	79,010	14,442	5,959	3,349	538
Gosain ..	Total ..	Male ..	*[illegible]*	*4,812*	*2,003*	*1,546*	*415*	*368*	*323*	*137*
		Female ..	*10,846*	*3,261*	*2,030*	*983*	*96*	*33*	*11*	*18*
	Balaghat ..	Male ..	809	379	136	129	32	46	24	12
		Female ..	803	264	165	87	4	3	3	2
	Narsimhpur ..	Male ..	741	369	139	116	42	41	24	7
		Female ..	659	209	114	86	4	3	2	..
	Jubbulpore ..	Male ..	[illegible]	452	167	140	50	54	28	13
		Female	877	306	165	83	24	..	4	10
	Hoshangabad	Male ..	1,337	614	251	213	66	46	32	26
		Female	1,254	373	249	118	4	..	2	..
	Nagpur ..	Male ..	1,471	620	261	207	46	36	41	29
		Female ..	1,357	351	250	88	5	2	6	..
	Wardha	Male	832	383	136	101	28	50	44	24
		Female ..	792	234	131	71	8	3	1	..
	Bhandara ..	Male ..	828	386	203	78	30	28	39	8
		Female ..	823	274	184	76	7	3	2	2
	Raipur ..	Male ..	1,285	520	217	175	39	29	50	10
		Female	1,331	357	226	111	9	5	6	..
	Bilaspur ..	Male ..	1,900	775	373	270	57	42	28	5
		Female ..	2,045	599	358	194	23	9	11	4
	Drug ..	Male ..	812	314	140	117	25	16	13	3
		Female ..	925	234	148	69	8	5	4	..
Gowari ..	Maratha Division	Male ..	82,082	32,163	15,267	11,835	2,720	1,647	552	142
		Female ..	81,473	24,740	14,932	8,120	902	419	300	67
Halba	Total ..	Male ..	*[illegible]*	*8,019*	*3,452*	*2,675*	*805*	*629*	*368*	*70*
		Female ..	*17,015*	*6,110*	*3,729*	*1,941*	*269*	*121*	*67*	*10*
	Chanda ..	Male ..	1,739	806	303	261	95	78	65	4
		Female ..	1,548	522	305	170	27	9	10	1

(q) Includes 2 Christians. (r) Includes 5 Christians and 13 Muslims. (s) Includes 7 Christians and 18 Muslims.
(t) Includes 98 Christians. (u) Includes 83 Christians. (v) Includes 13 Christians. (w) Includes 9 Christians and 3 Muslims.
(x) Includes 11 Christians and 1 Muslim.

Married.							Widowed.						
Total.	0—6.	7—13.	14—16.	17—23.	24—43	44 and over.	Total.	0—6.	7—13.	14—16.	17—23.	24—43.	44 and over.
12	13	14	15	16	17	18	19	20	21	22	23	24	25
85,354	736	4,271	4,596	13,683	42,748	19,320	7,494	25	99	141	354	2,474	4,401
88,309	1,514	9,962	9,134	19,312	39,463	8,924	21,799	31	132	220	639	6,953	13,824
54,068	854	4,482	3,680	9,041	24,552	11,459	4,215	44	68	66	242	1,350	2,445
55,394	1,629	8,400	5,000	11,766	22,673	5,926	13,524	37	117	119	385	3,975	8,891
869	19	110	86	129	361	164	56	2	14	7	5	13	15
866	40	178	106	168	304	70	182	10	13	16	2	45	96
44,502	567	2,720	3,685	6,772	21,105	9,653	3,505	47	60	225	291	1,210	1,672
47,612	1,211	3,860	4,551	10,983	19,964	7,043	10,510	40	66	139	361	2,998	6,906
27,095	301	1,525	2,349	4,225	13,115	5,580	1,921	34	18	32	150	689	998
30,040	857	2,378	2,985	7,136	12,858	3,826	6,828	29	44	45	192	1,957	4,561
14,141	223	1,132	1,028	2,014	6,379	3,365	1,159	13	14	160	76	377	519
14,009	348	1,358	1,185	3,068	5,430	2,620	3,054	11	16	75	130	864	1,949
835	22	26	31	122	427	207	76	..	3	6	5	30	32
940	5	58	73	213	471	120	149	..	2	12	6	31	98
2,431	21	37	277	411	1,184	501	349	..	25	27	60	114	123
2,623	1	66	308	566	1,205	477	479	..	4	7	24	146	298
8,772	156	514	409	1,268	4,339	1,996	617	14	5	5	85	205	303
9,985	294	844	785	2,016	4,595	1,451	2,276	12	23	28	94	629	1,490
6,192	125	375	320	928	3,080	1,364	405	12	5	3	41	144	200
7,126	231	635	572	1,401	3,298	989	1,593	10	21	13	43	428	1,078
2,580	31	139	179	340	1,259	632	212	2	..	2	44	61	103
2,859	63	209	213	615	1,297	462	683	2	2	15	51	201	412
751	31	158	61	99	301	101	62	2	3	1	..	20	36
750	94	154	64	131	262	45	227	2	5	3	1	78	138
565,731	4,786	22,004	25,204	79,365	294,381	139,991	47,916	107	345	488	2,355	16,582	28,039
594,544	7,167	41,383	49,064	128,448	290,793	77,689	154,813	219	724	1,152	3,599	42,233	106,886
269,861	2,416	13,197	13,376	38,143	136,165	66,564	21,477	54	219	295	1,395	7,412	12,102
281,024	3,761	24,084	24,351	59,721	131,888	37,219	74,234	124	400	752	1,941	20,013	51,004
295,865	2,370	8,806	11,828	41,222	158,213	73,426	26,439	53	126	193	960	9,170	15,937
313,516	3,406	17,299	24,712	68,727	158,902	40,470	80,571	95	324	400	1,658	22,219	55,875
5,460	35	217	292	891	2,690	1,326	630	4	3	3	32	237	351
5,744	54	639	478	1,278	2,565	730	1,901	3	20	9	58	519	1,292
387	1	12	25	56	198	95	43	..	..	..	1	14	28
401	2	28	29	103	194	45	138	1	1	1	1	27	107
317	1	3	14	54	172	73	55	..	1	1	2	23	28
329	1	25	33	90	144	36	121	..	..	1	..	32	88
377	4	6	22	54	220	71	58	..	..	..	4	27	27
390	1	28	46	92	203	20	181	..	1	..	8	55	117
637	1	7	23	107	357	142	86	..	..	..	4	38	44
628	1	64	66	122	329	46	233	..	..	3	11	61	158
754	..	26	30	94	372	232	97	1	..	..	5	33	58
779	8	129	49	164	338	91	227	1	12	1	4	51	158
396	1	6	8	55	210	116	53	..	..	1	1	16	35
404	3	49	32	108	159	53	154	..	2	1	4	57.	90
412	1	13	21	67	203	107	30	2	1	..	1	10	16
459	1	24	22	79	192	141	90	..	..	1	1	21	67
680	15	24	36	121	313	171	85	1	..	1	3	28	52
713	10	88	73	160	283	99	261	..	1	1	11	68	180
1,041	11	88	83	200	438	221	84	..	..	..	9	32	43
1,130	16	136	104	242	508	124	316	1	2	..	16	101	196
459	..	32	30	83	216	98	39	..	1	..	2	16	20
511	11	68	24	118	215	75	180	..	1	..	2	46	131
45,273	324	1,872	2,568	7,026	21,228	12,255	4,646	18	43	65	243	1,206	3,071
45,446	767	5,309	4,502	9,328	19,395	6,145	11,287	62	181	138	382	3,029	7,495
8,421	63	503	500	1,350	4,086	1,919	742	..	2	19	41	306	374
8,478	100	961	872	1,944	3,683	918	2,397	3	10	15	72	922	1,375
843	3	32	31	111	455	211	90	..	..	..	1	29	60
739	9	104	110	133	318	65	287	1	2	4	10	118	152

TABLE VIII — Civil condition by

Caste, tribe or race.	Locality.	Sex.	Population dealt with.	Unmarried.						
				Total.	0—6.	7—13.	14—16.	17—23.	24—43.	44 and over.
1	2	3	4	5	6	7	8	9	10	11
Halba—*concld.*	Bastar ..	Male ..	8,291	4,196	1,702	1,353	468	399	251	23
		Female ..	7,861	3,132	1,855	980	158	87	49	3
	Kanker ..	Male ..	4,260	1,848	805	706	149	98	51	39
		Female ..	4,430	1,434	894	454	60	18	4	4
	Raipur ..	Male ..	2,892	1,169	642	355	93	54	21	4
		Female ..	3,176	1,052	675	337	24	10	4	2
Kahar ..	Total ..	Male ..	*6,510*	*2,950*	*1,314*	*1,146*	*281*	*157*	*46*	*6*
		Female ..	*6,477*	*2,218*	*1,504*	*681*	*20*	*7*	*3*	*3*
	Narsinghpur ..	Male ..	1,029	475	210	192	47	20	5	1
		Female ..	1,024	366	250	109	5	1	1	..
	Hoshangabad ..	Male ..	3,759	1,749	791	676	163	88	26	5
		Female ..	3,748	1,310	874	415	14	3	1	3
	Nimar ..	Male ..	1,722	726	313	278	71	49	15	..
		Female ..	1,705	542	380	157	1	3	1	..
Kalar ..	Province ..	Male ..	(y) 108,656	41,872	20,161	13,974	3,501	2,464	1,361	411
		Female ..	110,512	31,608	20,721	9,168	878	381	323	137
Katia ..	Plateau Division ..	Male ..	13,653	6,416	2,845	2,159	698	453	231	30
		Female ..	14,090	5,017	3,059	1,625	220	71	33	9
Kawar (Hindu)	Total ..	Male ..	*85,635*	*37,363*	*18,090*	*12,803*	*2,952*	*2,115*	*1,071*	*332*
		Female ..	*92,069*	*31,985*	*19,052*	*10,377*	*1,260*	*622*	*371*	*303*
	Chanda ..	Male ..	952	426	201	172	25	18	7	3
		Female ..	879	315	159	132	7	7	9	1
	Chhattisgarh Administrative Division.	Male ..	52,377	23,468	11,332	8,191	1,739	1,413	649	144
		Female ..	54,943	19,955	11,743	6,646	728	472	267	99
	9 States of Chhattisgarh Plain Division.	Male ..	35,306	13,469	6,557	4,440	1,188	684	415	185
		Female ..	36,247	11,715	7,150	3,599	525	143	95	203
Kayasth ..	Province ..	Male ..	(z) 20,333	10,572	3,436	3,151	1,205	1,736	920	124
		Female ..	18,496	6,903	3,502	2,657	454	156	86	48
Kewat ..	Total ..	Male ..	*6,240*	*2,600*	*1,283*	*857*	*219*	*103*	*47*	*91*
		Female ..	*6,167*	*1,812*	*1,336*	*425*	*37*	*5*	*7*	*2*
	Jubbulpore ..	Male ..	2,972	1,322	643	417	120	66	34	42
		Female ..	2,887	912	652	229	23	5	3	..
	Narsinghpur ..	Male ..	144	62	31	23	3	5	..	..
		Female ..	134	46	26	20	..	..	..	..
	Chanda ..	Male ..	3,124	1,216	609	417	96	32	13	49
		Female ..	3,146	854	658	176	14	..	4	2
Khangar ..	Total ..	Male ..	*5,546*	*2,631*	*926*	*895*	*387*	*286*	*114*	*23*
		Female ..	*5,438*	*1,826*	*992*	*751*	*66*	*7*	*8*	*2*
	Saugor ..	Male ..	2,955	1,387	494	496	206	141	43	7
		Female ..	2,827	968	539	392	31	3	3	..
	Damoh ..	Male ..	870	415	133	149	67	40	20	6
		Female ..	884	289	142	134	10	2	1	..
	Jubbulpore ..	Male ..	1,298	637	234	186	88	82	40	7
		Female ..	1,280	411	222	161	22	2	3	1
	Narsinghpur ..	Male ..	423	195	65	64	26	23	14	3
		Female ..	447	158	89	64	3	..	1	1
Kol ..	Total ..	Male ..	*37,885*	*16,447*	*8,456*	*5,167*	*1,561*	*808*	*369*	*86*
		Female ..	*38,750*	*14,068*	*8,540*	*4,517*	*612*	*216*	*150*	*33*
(Hindu) ..	..	Male ..	*30,547*	*13,667*	*6,780*	*4,499*	*1,290*	*731*	*294*	*73*
		Female ..	*31,778*	*11,618*	*6,850*	*3,867*	*556*	*182*	*131*	*32*
	Jubbulpore ..	Male ..	28,215	12,705	6,243	4,194	1,230	698	270	70
		Female ..	29,528	10,897	6,334	3,682	548	179	124	30
	Mandla ..	Male ..	1,244	527	290	160	46	17	11	3
		Female ..	1,200	370	274	85	4	1	5	1
	Chhota Nagpur States ..	Male ..	1,088	435	247	145	14	16	13	..
		Female ..	1,050	351	242	100	4	2	2	1
(Tribal) ..	..	Male ..	*7,338*	*2,780*	*1,676*	*668*	*271*	*77*	*75*	*13*
		Female ..	*6,972*	*2,450*	*1,690*	*650*	*56*	*34*	*19*	*1*

(y) Includes 3 Christians.

(z) Includes 2 Christians.

Married.							Widowed.						
Total.	0—6.	7—13.	14—16.	17—23.	24—43.	44 and over	Total.	0—6.	7—13.	14—16.	17—23.	24—43.	44 and over.
12	13	14	15	16	17	18	19	20	21	22	23	24	25
3,645 **3,578**	14 34	175 347	219 369	621 832	1,822 1,589	794 307	**450** **1,151**	.. 1	2 8	15 10	34 49	207 493	192 590
2,289 **2,518**	42 46	152 242	148 215	344 611	1,098 1,077	505 327	**123** **478**	.. 1	.. ..	4 1	6 9	53 186	60 281
1,644 **1,643**	4 11	144 268	102 17[illegible]	274 308	711 599	409 219	**79** **481**	.. ..	.. ..	.. ..	.. 4	17 125	62 352
3,274 *3,37[illegible]*	*4* *35*	*59* *315*	*152* *377*	*5[illegible]3* *790*	*1,75[illegible]* *1,575*	*690* *286*	*236* *583*	.. *2*	*1* *4*	*1* *4*	*14* *28*	*127* *2[illegible]1*	*143* *594*
505 **522**	2 2	18 49	23 43	66 105	280 269	116 53	**49** **136**	.. ..	.. ..	1 1	2 5	14 37	32 93
1,874 **1,938**	2 4	35 159	87 246	328 451	1,015 911	407 167	**136** **500**	.. 2	1 3	.. 3	4 14	47 127	84 351
895 **916**	.. 29	16 107	42 88	179 233	43[illegible] 593	167 65	**101** **247**	.. ..	.. 1	.. ..	8 9	66 87	27 150
61,167 **62,234**	841 1,482	4,303 8,391	3,819 5,862	10,023 13,124	28,464 26,405	13,717 6,970	**5,617** **16,670**	39 40	70 110	80 192	267 497	1,906 4,860	3,2[illegible] 10,971
6,688 **7,126**	22 26	175 414	282 636	1,026 1,702	3,7[illegible]8 3,60[illegible]	1,445 665	**549** **1,947**	.. ..	3 3	7 14	25 30	195 580	319 1,320
16,12[illegible] *18,37[illegible]*	*652* *741*	*[illegible],483* *4,253*	*3,758* *1,798*	*7,357* *10[illegible]*	*21,1[illegible]* *[illegible]*	*10,[illegible]* *[illegible]*	*[illegible]* *11,705*	*13* *19*	*17* *[illegible]2*	*255* *151*	*496* *733*	*1,533* *3,515*	*2,484* *7,322*
490 **439**	6 7	18 50	25 44	90 102	217 136	154 50	**36** **125**	.. ..	.. 1	2 1	2 7	8 37	24 79
26,[illegible] **28,134**	406 477	1,817 2,[illegible]	1,560 2,459	4,1[illegible] 5,552	12,7[illegible] 13,[illegible]	5,925 4,05[illegible]	**2,508** **6,[illegible]54**	10 13	19 39	22 45	124 177	786 2,222	1,347 4,358
19,[illegible] **19,[illegible]**	240 257	1,646 1,031	2,167 2,[illegible]	3,090 4,442	[illegible],226 7,747	3,9[illegible]2 3,334	**2,50[illegible]** **4,[illegible]6**	3 6	18 22	261 108	370 549	739 1,256	1,113 2,785
8,[illegible] **8,024**	59 71	119 236	190 695	962 2,040	4,91[illegible] 3,954	2,231 928	**1,290** **3,569**	.. 8	.. 14	7 31	28 156	441 1,225	814 2,135
3,37[illegible] *3,[illegible]*	*17* *55*	*221* *144*	*235* *106*	*[illegible]* *724*	*[illegible]* *1,52[illegible]*	*[illegible]* *25[illegible]*	*[illegible]79* *[illegible]11*	*2* *1*	*5* *9*	*6* *10*	*11* *29*	*79* *317*	*164* *519*
1,525 **1,515**	3 5	107 147	123 168	234 34[illegible]	327 741	239 114	**125** **163**	1 ..	6 6	4 7	7 16	43 179	64 252
75 **73**	.. ..	.. 2	6 7	17 21	38 41	14 7	**7** **10**	.. ..	.. ..	.. ..	.. ..	.. ..	7 10
1,770 **1,321**	13 50	114 295	106 231	273 368	904 746	360 131	**133** **471**	1 1	2 3	2 3	4 13	36 164	93 287
2,511 *2,587*	6 7	*14* *110*	*58* *277*	*[illegible]58* *563*	*1,155* *1,318*	*553* *212*	*[illegible]* *1,02[illegible]*	.. *1*	.. *1*	.. *10*	*11* *24*	*115* *429*	*211* *569*
1,365 **1,381**	2 1	6 71	36 165	265 373	755 656	301 115	**203** **478**	.. ..	.. ..	.. 5	7 11	83 191	113 271
383 **399**	.. ..	2 11	5 37	72 104	212 214	92 33	**72** **196**	.. ..	.. 1	.. 2	2 2	25 85	45 106
587 **599**	2 5	3 20	14 58	95 145	363 324	110 47	**74** **270**	.. 1	.. ..	.. 3	2 10	31 121	41 135
209 **208**	2 1	3 8	3 17	26 41	125 124	50 17	**19** **81**	.. ..	.. ..	.. ..	.. 1	7 23	12 57
20,071 *19,997*	*152* *169*	*1,077* *1,141*	*966* *1,720*	*3,324* *4,572*	*10,716* *10,618*	*3,836* *1,777*	*1,367* *4,685*	*2* *3*	*13* *13*	*79* *25*	*97* *116*	*477* *1,733*	*699* *2,795*
15,726 *16,170*	*96* *95*	*492* *801*	*769* *1,355*	*2,726* *3,711*	*8,148* *8,739*	*3,195* *1,466*	*1,154* *3,990*	*2* *2*	*5* *9*	*19* *21*	*82* *77*	*428* *1,465*	*618* *2,416*
14,439 **14,909**	90 88	378 668	674 1,220	2,524 3,418	7,809 8,129	2,964 1,386	**1,071** **3,722**	2 2	3 8	17 18	78 64	387 1,362	584 2,268
685 **666**	3 7	27 63	39 90	127 166	365 309	124 31	**32** **164**	.. ..	2 ..	2 2	1 8	11 71	16 83
602 **595**	3 ..	87 70	56 45	75 130	274 301	107 49	**51** **104**	.. ..	.. 1	.. 1	3 5	30 32	18 65
4,345 *3,827*	*56* *71*	*585* *340*	*197* *365*	*598* *858*	*2,268* *1,879*	*641* *311*	*213* *695*	.. *1*	*8* *4*	*50* *4*	*15* *39*	*49* *268*	*81* *379*

TABLE VIII

Caste, tribe or race.	Locality.	Sex.	Population dealt with.	Unmarried. Total.	0—6.	7—13	14—16.	17—23.	24—43.	44 and over.
1	2	3	4	5	6	7	8	9	10	11
(Tribal)—*concld.*	Jubbulpore ..	Male ..	45	16	7	7	1	1	..	..
		Female ..	39	13	7	5	1	..	..	..
	Mandla ..	Male ..	4,296	1,739	998	537	118	45	35	6
		Female ..	4,184	1,314	980	314	11	7	2	..
	Chhota Nagpur States ..	Male ..	2,997	1,025	671	124	152	31	40	7
		Female ..	2,749	1,123	703	331	44	27	17	1
Koli ..	Berar ..	Male ..	19,418	7,006	3,612	2,386	502	290	170	46
		Female ..	18,651	4,698	3,542	959	83	54	43	17
Kolta ..	Raigarh ..	Male ..	6,973	2,286	1,309	801	106	54	14	2
		Female ..	7,244	2,262	1,472	711	58	18	3	..
Komti ..	Chanda ..	Male ..	1,719	723	284	229	74	53	64	19
		Female ..	1,827	423	299	118	2	..	3	1
Kori ..	Nerbudda Valley ..	Male ..	(a[1]) 14,246	5,973	2,517	1,987	666	510	175	118
		Female ..	14,319	4,419	2,717	1,428	106	67	52	49
Korku ..	Total ..	Male ..	*(a[2]) 72,529*	*37,287*	*17,315*	*11,879*	*3,886*	*2,991*	*1,085*	*131*
		Female ..	*(a[3]) 72,990*	*31,169*	*17,948*	*10,305*	*1,844*	*716*	*296*	*60*
(Hindu) ..	..	Male ..	*38,005*	*19,379*	*9,073*	*6,220*	*1,972*	*1,514*	*538*	*62*
		Female ..	*37,790*	*16,075*	*9,330*	*5,280*	*902*	*352*	*181*	*30*
	Hoshangabad ..	Male ..	6,127	3,057	1,319	1,006	338	270	115	9
		Female ..	6,022	2,350	1,276	908	102	38	22	4
	Amraoti ..	Male ..	15,103	7,773	3,666	2,384	780	654	248	41
		Female ..	14,767	6,675	3,919	2,010	431	186	113	16
	Nimar ..	Male ..	13,092	6,533	3,156	2,214	642	417	97	7
		Female ..	13,192	5,340	3,211	1,775	242	75	30	7
	Betul ..	Male ..	3,683	2,016	932	616	212	173	78	5
		Female ..	3,809	1,710	924	587	127	53	16	3
(Tribal) ..	..	Male ..	*34,518*	*17,907*	*8,242*	*5,689*	*1,913*	*1,477*	*517*	*69*
		Female ..	*35,190*	*15,088*	*8,617*	*5,025*	*938*	*364*	*115*	*29*
	Hoshangabad ..	Male ..	5,012	2,482	983	786	352	258	94	9
		Female ..	4,853	1,949	1,080	657	116	67	22	7
	Amraoti ..	Male ..	1,925	953	463	301	100	67	16	6
		Female ..	2,058	790	514	223	38	9	5	1
	Nimar ..	Male ..	12,849	6,431	3,081	2,088	637	480	120	25
		Female ..	13,039	5,504	3,335	1,803	268	67	20	11
	Betul ..	Male ..	14,732	8,041	3,715	2,484	824	672	317	29
		Female ..	15,240	6,845	3,688	2,342	516	221	68	10
Kumhar ..	Province ..	Male ..	(a[4]) 66,320	25,489	12,590	8,485	2,072	1,441	761	140
		Female ..	64,991	19,683	12,805	5,843	592	226	139	78
Kunbi ..	Total ..	Male ..	*(a[5]) 649,839*	*218,036*	*111,718*	*74,288*	*14,839*	*9,251*	*5,930*	*2,010*
		Female ..	*623,217*	*139,015*	*100,756*	*32,529*	*2,057*	*2,022*	*1,276*	*375*
	Maratha Division ..	Male ..	595,533	198,641	101,684	67,672	13,484	8,388	5,485	1,928
		Female ..	570,212	126,244	91,226	29,449	1,980	1,991	1,240	358
	Chhindwara ..	Male ..	15,435	5,152	2,765	1,864	281	137	87	18
		Female ..	15,308	3,353	2,673	646	16	11	5	2
	Nimar ..	Male ..	9,837	3,490	1,650	1,163	293	239	128	17
		Female ..	8,710	2,152	1,500	634	9	1	6	2
	Betul ..	Male ..	29,034	10,753	5,619	3,589	781	487	230	47
		Female ..	28,987	7,266	5,357	1,800	52	19	25	13
Kurmi ..	Total ..	Male ..	*155,021*	*56,348*	*28,373*	*17,832*	*4,205*	*3,528*	*1,909*	*501*
		Female ..	*159,483*	*42,062*	*29,539*	*11,214*	*597*	*342*	*229*	*141*
	Nerbudda Valley ..	Male ..	59,726	24,897	10,284	8,483	2,522	2,300	1,019	289
		Female ..	57,206	16,456	10,357	5,484	326	188	75	26
	Plateau Division ..	Male ..	9,256	3,994	1,788	1,355	391	266	137	57
		Female ..	10,165	3,159	2,045	996	81	23	9	5
	Chhattisgarh Administrative Division	Male ..	77,647	24,772	14,756	7,221	1,179	854	623	139
		Female ..	82,867	20,266	15,534	4,279	153	82	111	107
	9 States of Chhattisgarh Plain Division.	Male ..	8,392	2,685	1,545	773	113	108	130	16
		Female ..	9,245	2,181	1,603	455	37	49	34	3

(a[1]) Includes 1 Christian. (a[2]) Includes 6 Christians (a[3]) Includes 10 Christians. (a[4]) Includes 2 Christians.
(a[5]) Includes 5 Christians.

Married.							Widowed.						
Total.	0—6.	7—13.	14—16.	17—23.	24—43.	44 and over.	Total.	0—6.	7—13	14—16.	17—23.	24—43	44 and over
12	13	14	15	16	17	18	19	20	21	22	23	24	25
26	..	.	.	5	11	10	3	.				2	1
24	.	1	3	..	7	5	2	.	.	.	..	.	2
2,469	45	171	149	380	1,268	456	88	.	2	..	..	23	63
2,452	63	271	224	541	1,136	217	418	1	3	..	7	174	283
1,850	11	414	48	213	989	175	122	..	6	60	15	24	17
1,351	11	68	138	309	736	89	275	..	1	4	32	144	94
11,286	91	783	735	1,834	4,943	2,900	1,176	9	29	14	115	320	639
11,065	300	2,148	1,181	2,283	3,961	1,192	2,888	3	30	40	99	786	1,930
4,292	7	237	536	1,057	1,746	709	395	..	25	6	12	170	182
3,429	23	482	323	798	1,101	702	1,553	..	12	15	28	946	552
861	2	13	43	140	444	219	135	.	1	1	2	38	93
831	6	128	110	201	307	79	573	..	2	6	34	202	329
7,491	18	164	376	1,299	4,174	1,460	[illegible]	..	7	16	57	318	384
7,475	31	574	785	1,889	3,626	570	2,425	2	7	18	78	819	1,501
32,630	*202*	*352*	*799*	*4,269*	*18,975*	*8,033*	*2,512*	*2*	*8*	*16*	*109*	*867*	*1,610*
34,743	*169*	*1,171*	*3,193*	*8,659*	*17,594*	*3,854*	*7,078*	*5*	*16*	*33*	*169*	*1,929*	*4,926*
17,382	*112*	*245*	*473*	*2,319*	*10,117*	*4,116*	*1,244*	*2*	*5*	*7*	*62*	*424*	*744*
17,971	*96*	*603*	*1,744*	*4,539*	*9,071*	*1,918*	*3,741*	*5*	*6*	*18*	*100*	*1,064*	*2,551*
2,818	5	18	46	317	1,705	727	252	1	..	..	8	92	151
2,941	13	97	212	616	1,664	339	731	..	..	3	12	182	534
6,855	77	156	206	988	3,761	1,667	475	1	4	4	26	163	277
6,816	55	232	713	1,751	3,275	790	1,276	4	2	4	52	373	841
6,190	26	56	195	851	3,764	1,298	369	.	1	2	22	131	213
6,486	25	244	697	1,781	3,167	572	1,366	1	4	11	30	421	899
1,519	4	15	26	163	887	424	148	..	..	1	6	38	103
1,728	3	30	122	391	965	217	371	..	..	..	6	88	277
15,243	*90*	*107*	*326*	*1,950*	*8,856*	*3,914*	*1,568*	..	*2*	*9*	*47*	*443*	*866*
16,770	*73*	*571*	*1,449*	*4,118*	*8,623*	*1,936*	*3,332*	..	*10*	*15*	*69*	*863*	*2,378*
2,289	18	10	39	266	1,376	580	241	..	..	3	7	103	128
2,358	18	72	158	616	1,228	266	546	..	6	1	10	143	386
893	2	22	19	132	469	249	79	..	2	..	2	20	55
1,125	2	190	109	204	504	116	143	..	2	1	6	39	95
5,981	48	42	171	936	3,414	1,370	437	..	..	2	17	154	264
6,383	33	199	702	1,734	3,034	681	1,152	..	2	9	29	329	783
6,080	22	33	97	616	3,597	1,715	611	..	1	4	21	166	419
6,904	20	110	480	1,564	3,857	873	1,491	..	..	4	24	352	1,111
37,392	518	2,735	2,622	6,213	17,665	7,639	3,439	14	96	48	237	1,120	1,924
36,134	913	4,896	3,459	7,941	15,173	3,752	9,174	15	82	85	266	2,740	5,986
388,032	*3,478*	*32,749*	*27,988*	*62,514*	*162,793*	*98,510*	*43,772*	*222*	*1,016*	*865*	*1,951*	*12,766*	*26,951*
386,356	*15,060*	*70,110*	*35,857*	*73,276*	*144,869*	*47,184*	*97,846*	*329*	*1,425*	*1,453*	*2,773*	*25,759*	*66,107*
356,298	3,296	30,488	25,819	57,544	148,099	91,052	40,594	220	972	772	1,815	11,815	25,000
354,490	14,322	64,605	32,882	67,106	131,868	43,707	89,478	314	1,319	1,394	2,632	23,546	60,273
9,376	67	813	702	1,514	3,964	2,316	907	1	6	17	44	270	569
9,557	406	1,978	740	1,717	3,670	1,046	2,398	9	41	19	42	593	1,694
5,578	22	219	335	937	2,907	1,158	769	..	13	34	22	243	457
5,216	19	691	559	1,245	2,291	411	1,342	1	8	5	18	449	861
16,780	93	1,229	1,132	2,519	7,823	3,984	1,501	1	25	42	70	438	925
17,093	313	2,836	1,676	3,208	7,040	2,020	4,628	5	57	35	81	1,171	3,279
90,066	*1 725*	*8,259*	*6,181*	*15,267*	*40,893*	*17,741*	*8,607*	*45*	*123*	*135*	*649*	*3,136*	*4,519*
92,328	*2,870*	*13 055*	*8,715*	*20,083*	*38,062*	*9,543*	*25,093*	*82*	*256*	*169*	*645*	*7,768*	[illegible]
31,055	142	1,395	1,940	5,495	16,066	6,017	3,774	5	27	62	229	1,451	2,000
31,131	310	3,019	3,455	7,626	14,114	2,607	9,619	7	60	87	353	3,337	5,775
4,787	6	126	244	939	2,530	942	475	..	1	3	21	175	275
5,233	23	487	489	1,249	2,551	434	1,773	..	5	5	27	589	1,147
48,829	1,390	6,116	3,656	8,190	19,856	9,621	4,046	36	85	66	359	1,414	2,086
50,246	2,281	8,600	4,402	10,262	19,046	5,655	12,355	72	187	68	245	3,498	8.285
5,395	187	622	341	643	2,441	1.161	312	4	10	4	40	96	158
5,718	256	949	369	946	2,351	847	1,346	3	4	9	20	344	966

Caste, tribe or race.	Locality.	Sex.	Population dealt with.	Unmarried. Total.	0—6.	7—13	14—16	17—23.	24—43.	44 and over.
1	2	3	4	5	6	7	8	9	10	11
Lodhi	Province	Male	(a^{4}) 158,675	68,795	30,470	23,209	6,704	5,015	2,800	597
		Female	159,902	48,657	30,170	16,543	1,388	301	193	62
Lohar	Do	Male	(a^{5}) 102,194	42,079	19,938	14,156	3,635	2,657	1,290	403
		Female	(a^{8}) 101,109	31,740	20,287	9,725	865	371	365	127
Madgi	Chanda	Male	2,973	1,234	553	420	114	79	57	11
		Female	2,499	816	539	210	36	24	4	3
Majhwar	Total	Male	*4,793*	*2,552*	*1,250*	*870*	*212*	*177*	*38*	*5*
		Female	*4,397*	*2,179*	*1,155*	*811*	*78*	*118*	*14*	*3*
	Surguja	Male	2,757	1,496	821	480	99	61	31	4
		Female	2,679	1,138	744	336	22	23	10	3
	Udaipur	Male	2,036	1,056	429	390	113	116	7	1
		Female	1,718	1,041	411	475	56	95	4	..
Mala	Chanda	Male	..	..	..	..	..	..	..	..
		Female	..	..	..	..	..	..	..	..
Mali	Province	Male	(a^{9}) 313,186	105,124	56,935	35,532	6,007	3,864	2,123	663
		Female	(a^{10}) 313,383	76,752	55,208	17,928	1,726	937	657	296
Mana	Nagpur Division	Male	24,456	9,100	4,684	3,354	710	239	83	30
		Female	24,923	6,541	4,667	1,747	63	25	31	8
Mang	Maratha Division	Male	(b^{1}) 46,661	17,898	9,765	6,043	962	604	415	109
		Female	(b^{2}) 47,791	13,519	9,605	3,092	379	196	166	81
Maratha	Province	Male	(b^{3}) 145,576	54,953	24,150	18,850	5,028	4,132	2,293	500
		Female	(b^{4}) 141,613	36,007	22,577	10,808	1,174	701	487	260
Maria	Total	Male	*90,534*	*48,259*	*22,767*	*14,156*	*3,687*	*4,073*	*3,300*	*276*
		Female	*90,312*	*40,867*	*22,870*	*11,921*	*2,616*	*2,001*	*1,266*	*193*
	Chanda	Male	17,128	8,930	3,965	2,738	738	852	594	43
		Female	17,648	8,279	4,[illegible]87	2,562	707	453	232	38
	Bastar State	Male	73,406	39,329	18,802	11,418	2,949	3,221	2,706	233
		Female	72,664	32,588	18,583	9,359	1,909	1,548	1,034	155
Mehra or Mahar	Province	Male	(b^{5}) 646,521	261,949	128,144	90,823	21,651	14,172	5,772	1,387
		Female	(b^{6}) 661,441	203,014	130,241	61,333	6,086	2,842	1,707	805
Hindu, Muslim and Tribal).	Do.	Male	646,152	261,762	128,084	90,754	21,633	14,166	5,767	1,358
		Female	661,200	202,90[illegible]	130,191	61,300	6,086	2,820	1,707	805
(Christian)	Do.	Male	369	187	60	69	18	6	5	29
		Female	241	105	50	33	..	22	..	..
Mehtar	Total	Male	*(b^{7}) 9,981*	*4,764*	*2,005*	*1,603*	*425*	*462*	*234*	*35*
		Female	*(b^{8}) 9,247*	*3,385*	*1,964*	*1,149*	*118*	*68*	*62*	*24*
	Nerbudda Valley	Male	7,275	3,575	1,441	1,206	357	369	174	28
		Female	6,641	2,485	1,405	849	94	54	59	24
	Nagpur	Male	2,314	1,039	495	348	55	82	53	6
		Female	2,175	799	505	267	16	8	3	..
	Raipur	Male	392	150	69	49	13	11	7	1
		Female	431	101	54	33	8	6	..	..
Mhali	Maratha Division	Male	31,907	11,320	5,575	3,982	842	529	290	102
		Female	30,121	7,256	5,182	1,798	126	79	51	20
Nai	Province	Male	(b^{9}) 66,804	26,334	12,479	9,100	2,205	1,657	744	149
		Female	(b^{10}) 66,452	18,796	12,214	5,909	367	188	93	25
Oraon	Total	Male	*[illegible]*	*28,598*	*11,537*	*9,420*	*2,547*	*1,534*	*430*	*130*
		Female	*[illegible]*	*24,908*	*14,591*	*8,271*	*1,142*	*451*	*321*	*132*
(Christian)	Raigarh	Male	18	8	5	3	..	..	..	..
		Female	20	8	7	1	..	..	..	..
(Tribal)	Chota Nagpur States	Male	[illegible]	1[illegible],634	7,800	4,643	1,113	666	293	119
		Female	25,686	1[illegible],114	7,895	4,095	495	232	270	127
(Christian)	Jashpur	Male	24,629	13,956	6,732	4,774	1,434	868	137	11
		Female	23,450	11,786	6,689	4,175	647	219	51	5
Paik	Raipur	Male	2,392	1,415	583	455	152	110	95	20
		Female	2,309	889	483	322	50	21	13	..
Panka	Total	Male	*(c^{1}) 83,37[illegible]*	*30,195*	*15,773*	*10,030*	*1,958*	*1,277*	*952*	*205*
		Female	*(c^{2}) [illegible]*	*24,047*	*16,099*	*6,494*	*708*	*401*	*219*	*126*

(a^{4}) Includes 5 Christians. (a^{5}) Includes 182 Christians and 22 Muslims. (a^{8}) Includes 188 Christians and 43 Muslims. (a^{9}) Includes 1 Christian (a^{10}) Includes 2 Christians. (b^{1}) Includes 16 Christians. (b^{2}) Includes 21 Christians. (b^{3}) Includes 1 Christian. (b^{4}) Includes 2 Christians. (b^{5}) Incudes 14 Muslims. (b^{6}) Includes 9 Muslims. (b^{7}) Includes 16 Christians and 102 Muslims (b^{8}) Includes 10 Christians and 113 Muslims. (b^{9}) Includes 3 Christians and 50 Muslims. (b^{10}) Includes 53 Muslims. (c^{1}) Includes 2 Christians. (c^{2}) Includes 6 Christians.

Married. Total.	0—6.	7—13.	14—16.	17—23.	24—43.	44 and over.	Widowed. Total.	0—6.	7—13.	14—16.	17—23.	24—43.	44 and over.
12	13	14	15	16	17	18	19	20	21	22	23	24	25
81,906	681	4,744	4,673	13,893	41,468	16,447	**7,974**	24	48	85	346	2,822	4,649
84,137	1,099	8,867	7,984	19,198	38,425	8,564	**27,108**	34	125	196	737	9,271	16,745
55,420	617	2,807	3,009	8,857	27,329	12,801	**4,695**	23	72	59	228	1,676	2,637
55,332	922	6,325	5,257	11,673	24,979	6,176	**14,037**	25	111	132	375	3,880	9,514
1,602	18	51	100	233	883	317	**137**	..	..	11	7	46	73
1,411	22	186	143	344	632	84	**272**	1	7	4	10	94	156
2,078	*14*	*54*	*69*	*242*	*1,427*	*272*	*163*	*1*	*1*	*1*	*12*	*103*	*45*
1,886	*6*	*84*	*171*	*360*	*1,016*	*219*	*332*	*2*	*2*	*4*	*12*	*120*	*192*
1,168	14	45	58	150	765	136	**93**	1	1	..	8	52	31
1,297	6	79	147	281	652	132	**244**	2	2	3	6	80	151
910	..	9	11	92	662	136	**70**	..	..	1	4	51	14
589	..	5	24	79	364	117	**88**	..	..	1	6	40	41
..	..	..	..	..	.	..	..	..	..	..	..	..	..
..	..	..	..	..	..	..	..	..	..	..	..	..	..
189,532	2,169	18,534	14,348	19,375	81,657	43,449	**18,530**	143	372	480	944	5,953	10,638
190,746	6,711	33,068	17,591	36,451	73,888	23,037	**45,885**	179	529	485	1,238	12,015	31,439
14,342	77	797	887	2.120	6,530	3,931	**1,014**	4	8	12	21	233	736
14,568	214	2,498	1,429	2,852	5,940	1,635	**3,814**	11	38	29	68	999	2,669
27,035	291	2,185	1,883	4,617	12,265	5,794	**1,728**	18	61	34	105	515	995
28,168	1,005	4,936	3,004	5,812	10,420	2,991	**6,104**	48	91	75	209	1,841	3,840
80,258	542	4,500	4,689	13,263	36,461	20,803	**10,365**	27	136	226	512	3,411	6,053
80,382	2,879	11,494	8,431	17,999	30,550	9,029	**25,224**	46	244	208	992	7,656	16,078
39,040	*370*	*1,935*	*2,065*	*5,555*	*21,452*	*7,663*	*3,235*	*8*	*24*	*62*	*126*	*1,288*	*1,727*
41,589	*411*	*3,086*	*3,659*	*9,254*	*21,023*	*4,156*	*7,856*	*15*	*57*	*222*	*239*	*2,939*	*4,384*
7,452	98	289	241	939	4,244	1,641	**746**	4	7	6	26	294	409
7,504	84	301	574	1,631	4,234	680	**1,865**	5	4	17	40	642	1,157
31,588	272	1,646	1,824	4,616	17,208	6,022	**2,489**	4	17	56	100	994	1,318
34,085	327	2,785	3,085	7,623	16,789	3,476	**5,991**	10	53	205	199	2,297	3,227
356,034	3,464	20,851	21,102	55,495	167,727	87,395	**28,538**	177	456	582	1,384	8,248	17,69[illegible]
369,134	7,803	47,422	37,559	79,310	155,641	41,399	**89,293**	604	1,171	975	2,502	24,794	59,247
355,862	3,464	20,839	21,087	55,458	167,641	87,373	**28,528**	177	456	582	1,384	8,243	17,686
369,026	7,803	47,408	37,545	79,293	155,589	41,388	**89,265**	604	1,171	975	2,500	24,780	59,235
172	..	12	15	37	86	22	**10**	..	..	..	..	5	5
108	..	14	14	17	52	11	**28**	..	..	..	2	14	12
4,739	*42*	*152*	*212*	*771*	*2,647*	*915*	*478*	*1*	*6*	*15*	*36*	*199*	*221*
4,703	*39*	*369*	*475*	*1,172*	*2,240*	*408*	*1,159*	*3*	*13*	*16*	*14*	*416*	*667*
3,324	19	71	147	558	1,903	626	**376**	1	2	14	29	158	172
3,247	10	193	357	842	1,585	260	**909**	2	8	11	38	332	518
1,185	13	71	54	177	635	235	**90**	..	4	1	6	38	41
1,180	26	150	84	277	522	121	**196**	1	5	5	4	71	110
230	10	10	11	36	109	54	**12**		.	.	1	3	8
276	3	26	34	53	133	27	**54**	.	..	.	2	13	39
18,680	176	1,234	1,288	3,330	8,235	4.417	**1,907**	6	31	33	154	599	1,084
17,998	467	3,276	1,773	3,585	7,010	1,887	**4,867**	21	53	43	105	1,343	3,302
36,935	491	2,364	2,089	6,486	18.037	7,468	**3,535**	12	35	62	244	1,217	1,965
37,181	741	4,575	3,477	8,254	16,359	3,775	**10,475**	15	58	73	273	3,178	6,878
20,595	*351*	*375*	*624*	*2,765*	*12,035*	*4,445*	*1,403*	*2*	*7*	*33*	*76*	*455*	*530*
20,741	*384*	*634*	*1,704*	*4,646*	*10,718*	*2,655*	*3,507*	..	*10*	*41*	*93*	*915*	*2,445*
10	..	.	..	..	8	2	.	..	..	..	..	.	..
10	..	..	..	1	9	.	**2**	..	..	..	.	.	*2*
11,163	351	344	481	1,464	6,186	2,337	**752**	2	7	30	42	245	426
11,033	384	592	1,069	2,344	5,356	1,288	**1,539**	..	10	30	48	406	1,045
9,422	..	31	143	1,301	5,841	2,106	**651**	..	..	3	34	210	404
9,698	..	42	635	2,301	5,353	1,367	**1,966**	..	..	11	45	509	1,401
914	2	6	22	149	512	223	**63**	..	..	1	3	27	32
1,169	2	35	134	316	515	167	**251**	..	..	10	18	103	120
49,204	*823*	*3,951*	*3,004*	*7,393*	*22,108*	*11,925*	*3,975*	*28*	*57*	*99*	*304*	*1,525*	[illegible]
52,279	*1,468*	*5,901*	*4,199*	*9,986*	*23,068*	*7,657*	*13,300*	*35*	*130*	*76*	*322*	*3,285*	[illegible]

Caste, tribe or race.	Locality.	Sex.	Population dealt with.	Unmarried. Total.	0—6.	7—13.	14—16.	17—23.	24—43.	44 and over.
1	2	3	4	5	6	7	8	9	10	11
Panka— *concld.*	Mandla	Male	9,399	4,364	2,050	1,396	403	305	174	36
		Female	9,640	3,157	2,016	964	102	43	26	6
	Seoni	Male	855	383	192	108	43	19	17	4
		Female	903	297	208	80	6	1	2	..
	Balaghat	Male	1,610	757	319	236	88	82	28	4
		Female	1,671	563	300	225	26	9	3	..
	Chhattisgarh Administrative Division.	Male	54,662	18,861	10,128	6,334	1,031	734	501	133
		Female	59,393	14,981	10,475	3,685	416	158	143	104
	9 States of Chhattisgarh Plain Division.	Male	16,848	5,830	3,084	1,956	393	137	232	28
		Female	18,019	5,049	3,100	1,540	158	190	45	16
Rajjhar or Lajjhar.	Total	Male	*1,735*	*787*	*373*	*260*	*85*	*11*	*22*	*6*
		Female	*1,858*	*674*	*386*	*228*	*37*	*14*	*6*	*3*
	Seoni	Male	512	204	95	62	31	7	6	3
		Female	534	202	114	65	14	6	2	1
	Hoshangabad	Male	631	319	155	105	27	21	8	3
		Female	682	284	169	97	14	1	2	1
	Betul	Male	592	264	123	93	27	13	8	..
		Female	642	188	103	66	9	7	2	1
Rajput	Province	Male	(c[3]) 258,231	106,632	44,702	34,134	10,231	9,820	6,273	1,472
		Female	(c[4]) 247,856	71,538	43,757	23,495	2,545	870	635	236
(Muslim)	Do.	Male	151	73	8	4	3	51	7	..
		Female	30	12	9	3	..	..	..	..
Sawara or Saonr. (Hindu)	Total	Male	*41,126*	*18,294*	*8,456*	*6,505*	*1,862*	*1,101*	*300*	*70*
		Female	*42,576*	*15,574*	*8,813*	*5,640*	*669*	*226*	*147*	*79*
	Saugor	Male	10,834	5,263	2,137	1,895	684	429	98	20
		Female	10,983	4,161	2,254	1,662	189	39	14	3
	Damoh	Male	3,023	1,421	578	458	194	139	48	4
		Female	3,101	1,226	615	507	84	19	1	..
	Chhattisgarh Administrative Division.	Male	18,287	8,317	3,858	3,190	752	372	115	30
		Female	19,286	7,340	4,134	2,721	329	76	65	15
	9 States of Chhattisgarh Plain Division.	Male	8,982	3,293	1,883	962	232	161	39	16
		Female	9,506	2,847	1,810	750	67	92	67	61
ɔunar	Province	Male	72,550	30,527	13,701	10,272	2,839	2,295	1,209	211
		Female	69,991	20,000	12,887	6,327	373	179	150	84
Teli	Do.	Male	(c[5]) 501,952	165,527	97,770	51,910	8,115	4,433	2,481	818
		Female	(c[6]) 520,929	126,585	93,626	28,051	1,849	1,331	1,304	424
(Muslim)	Do.	Male	35	11	..	9	2	..	..	..
		Female	85	24	17	5	..	1	1	..
Waddar	Yeotmal	Male	2,951	1,409	765	444	88	79	29	4
		Female	3,467	1,376	821	446	35	23	31	20
Wanjari	Berar	Male	23,175	9,639	5,031	2,850	737	641	303	77
		Female	22,733	7,134	4,696	1,846	260	124	168	40
Anglo-Indians or Eurasians	Province	Male	2,640	1,708	476	469	187	309	234	33
		Female	2,425	1,408	485	404	166	210	104	39
Indian Christians. (Excluding those who returned their original caste.)	Do.	Male	(c[7]) 19,581	11,162	3,758	3,514	1,439	1,682	623	146
		Female	(c[8]) 20,220	10,421	3,711	3,583	1,463	1,235	349	80

(c[3]) Includes 10 Christians. (c[4]) Includes 17 Christians. (c[5]) Includes 14 Christians. (c[6]) Includes 11 Christians.
(c[7] and (c[8]) Include 4 male and 4 female Indian Christians who returned caste as Satnami.

age for selected castes—*concld.* **TABLE VIII**

Married.							Widowed.						
Total.	0—6.	7—13.	14—16.	17—23.	24—43.	44 and over.	Total.	0—6.	7—13.	14—16.	17—23.	24—43.	44 and over.
12	13	14	15	16	17	18	19	20	21	22	23	24	25
4,806	31	156	252	774	2,513	1,080	**229**	..	**2**	4	13	104	**106**
5,295	73	388	486	1,209	2,567	572	**1,188**	..	9	9	15	310	**845**
441	3	12	15	73	247	91	**31**	..	..	1	2	14	**14**
456	..	24	50	107	242	33	**150**	..	..	..	6	47	**97**
771	2	26	24	113	414	192	**82**	1	1	2	8	31	**39**
847	10	44	71	202	438	79	**261**	..	..	..	5	82	**174**
33,005	598	2,865	2,041	5,929	14,512	7,960	**2,796**	15	41	47	220	1,091	**1,382**
35,177	1,026	4,254	2,768	6,649	15,450	5,030	**9,235**	20	108	44	234	2,236	**6,593**
10,181	189	892	672	1,404	4,422	2,602	**837**	12	13	45	61	285	**421**
10,504	359	1,191	821	1,819	4,371	1,943	**2,466**	15	13	23	62	610	**1,743**
816	*1*	*11*	*47*	*105*	*457*	*195*	*132*	..	..	..	*6*	*43*	***83***
869	*4*	*29*	*75*	*226*	*453*	*81*	*315*	*1*	..	*1*	*9*	*101*	***203***
230	..	6	35	22	99	68	**78**	..	..	..	5	24	**49**
235	..	5	30	61	119	20	**97**	..	..	..	7	33	**57**
284	1	..	..	34	190	59	**28**	..	..	..	..	13	**15**
316	2	6	18	80	183	27	**82**	..	..	..	..	22	**60**
302	..	5	12	49	168	68	**26**	..	..	..	1	6	**19**
318	2	18	28	85	151	34	**136**	1	..	1	2	46	**86**
136,658	1,160	8,281	7,923	22,204	65,982	31,108	**14,941**	31	132	154	639	4,885	9,100
133,466	2,193	15,544	13,418	29,341	57,951	15,019	**42,852**	46	333	498	1,433	13,394	27,148
77	..	..	..	36	41	..	**1**	..	..	..	..	1	..
16	..	..	9	7	..	..	**2**	..	..	..	..	..	**2**
21,212	*311*	*729*	*1,110*	*3,534*	*10,473*	*5,075*	*1,620*	*6*	*3*	*15*	*88*	*579*	***929***
22,142	*159*	*1,451*	*2,004*	*4,971*	*10,387*	*3,160*	*5,160*	*6*	*16*	*44*	*182*	*1,947*	***2,965***
5,235	4	43	146	890	2,918	1,234	**336**	..	1	5	23	108	**199**
5,535	2	243	547	1 440	2,790	513	**1,287**	1	1	7	30	498	**750**
1,504	..	9	34	183	862	416	**98**	..	..	..	1	33	**64**
1,534	..	41	141	367	796	189	**341**	..	..	2	10	122	**207**
9,208	269	368	641	1 564	4,338	2,028	**762**	6	2	7	36	276	**435**
9,556	66	550	865	2 265	4,452	1,358	**2,390**	5	13	14	74	897	**1,387**
5,265	38	309	289	897	2,335	1,397	**424**	..	..	3	28	162	**231**
5,517	101	617	451	899	2,349	1,100	**1,142**	..	2	21	68	430	**621**
38,012	368	1,629	1,930	6,612	18,325	9,148	**4,011**	8	41	101	211	1,403	**2,247**
38,288	760	4,941	3,933	8,880	15,586	4,188	**11,703**	12	69	95	391	3,680	**7,456**
312,864	6,180	37,095	25,627	49,981	129,285	64,696	**23,561**	92	440	442	1,291	7,308	13,988
324,384	13,348	58,319	29,300	52,498	124,561	36,358	**69,960**	159	612	420	1,516	17,648	49,605
18	2	2	..	3	10	1	**6**	..	..	..	2	2	**2**
56	1	12	6	13	22	2	**5**	..	..	..	..	..	**5**
1,422	18	101	85	235	687	296	**120**	1	3	5	15	33	**63**
1,736	23	311	212	381	605	204	**355**	..	10	13	34	90	**208**
11,829	119	1,060	758	1,908	5,274	2,710	**1,707**	32	97	107	181	483	**807**
12,910	586	1,892	1,477	2,710	4,937	1,308	**2,689**	28	40	38	97	707	**1,779**
849	..	3	2	36	538	270	**83**	..	..	..	2	23	**58**
810	..	4	11	128	523	144	**207**	..	..	1	12	54	**140**
7,715	9	129	174	873	4,147	2,383	**704**	1	3	3	11	278	**408**
7,746	4	109	309	1,866	4,408	1,050	**2,053**	..	1	4	59	675	**1,314**

TABLE IX

Infirmities

1. This table is divided into two parts. Part I shows the distribution of persons afflicted according to age, and Part II their distribution according to Districts and States.

2. Persons who were returned as suffering from more than one infirmity have been shown as suffering from each. Consequently the totals entered under " Total afflicted " in columns 2, 3 and 4 do not agree with the totals for each separate infirmity, since those three columns give the number of the infirm and columns 5 to 16 give the number of actual infirmities.

The following statement shows the number of persons afflicted with more than one infirmity :—

No	Combination of infirmities.	Persons afflicted.	Males.	Females.
1	Insanity and Deaf-muteness	151	86	65
2	Insanity and Blindness	30	12	18
3	Insanity and Leprosy	10	6	4
4	Deaf-muteness and Blindness	153	76	77
5	Deaf-muteness and Leprosy	24	17	7
6	Blindness and Leprosy	86	43	43
	Total ..	454	240	214

The above figures include 2 males suffering from three infirmities, *viz.*, Insanity, Deaf-muteness and Blindness.

TABLE IX.—Infirmities. Part I.—Distribution by Age.

Age.	Population afflicted.			Insane.			Deaf-mutes.			Blind.			Lepers.		
	Persons.	Males.	Females.	Persons.	Males.	Females.	Persons.	Males.	Females.	Persons.	Males.	Females.	Persons.	Males.	Females.
1	2	3	4	5	6	7	8	9	10	11	12	13	14	15	16
0—1 ..	165	91	74	2	..	2	18	12	6	135	76	59	10	3	7
1—2 ..	228	131	97	3	2	1	23	12	11	190	112	78	13	6	7
2—3 ..	319	180	139	7	5	2	73	39	34	230	132	98	12	6	6
3—4 ..	481	279	202	18	12	6	179	104	75	270	155	115	15	8	7
4—5 ..	612	356	256	32	18	14	250	146	104	311	182	129	26	14	12
Total 0—5 ..	*1,805*	*1,037*	*768*	*62*	*37*	*25*	*543*	*313*	*230*	*1,136*	*657*	*479*	*76*	*37*	*39*
5—10 ..	3,462	2,049	1,413	325	189	136	1,387	826	561	1,552	935	617	228	117	111
10—15 ..	3,861	2,299	1,562	453	263	190	1,447	880	567	1,624	980	644	367	194	173
15—20 ..	3,770	2,231	1,539	497	294	203	1,175	734	442	1,531	869	662	596	353	243
20—25 ..	4,096	2,442	1,654	550	344	206	1,157	726	431	1,668	910	758	755	483	272
25—30 ..	4,616	2,687	1,929	608	420	188	1,116	701	415	1,879	879	1,000	1,045	705	340
30—35 ..	5,049	2,807	2,242	589	407	182	1,103	678	425	2,078	875	1,203	1,315	864	451
35—40 ..	5,875	3,013	2,862	507	328	179	979	573	406	2,805	1,095	1,710	1,613	1,029	584
40—45 ..	6,105	3,087	3,018	435	277	158	885	517	368	3,210	1,264	1,946	1,601	1,043	558
45—50 ..	6,555	3,148	3,407	318	203	115	802	476	326	4,010	1,538	2,472	1,456	950	506
50—55 ..	6,033	2,796	3,237	239	154	85	689	406	283	3,956	1,491	2,465	1,180	762	418
55—60 ..	6,782	2,788	3,994	158	97	61	693	384	309	5,103	1,785	3,318	859	535	324
60—65 ..	6,485	2,551	3,934	132	77	55	652	357	295	5,035	1,707	3,328	693	422	271
65—70 ..	4,211	1,565	2,646	63	31	32	384	205	179	3,466	1,134	2,332	320	206	114
70 and over ..	9,432	3,518	5,914	97	40	57	957	485	472	8,018	2,768	5,250	415	251	164
Total ..	*78,137*	*38,018*	*40,119*	*5,033*	*3,161*	*1,872*	*13,970*	*8,261*	*5,709*	*47,071*	*18,887*	*28,184*	*12,519*	*7,951*	*4,568*

TABLE IX.—Infirmities. Part II.—Distribution by Districts

Serial number.	District or state.	Population afflicted.			Insane.			Deaf-mutes.			Blind.			Lepers.		
		Persons.	Males.	Females.	Persons.	Males.	Females.	Persons.	Males.	Females.	Persons.	Males.	Females.	Persons.	Males.	Females.
	1	2	3	4	5	6	7	8	9	10	11	12	13	14	15	16
	Central Provinces and Berar ..	**78,137**	**38,018**	**40,119**	**5,033**	**3,161**	**1,872**	**13,970**	**8,261**	**5,709**	**47,071**	**18,887**	**28,184**	**12,519**	**7,951**	**4,568**
	C. P. British Districts and Berar ..	**71,224**	**34,704**	**36,520**	**4,526**	**2,844**	**1,682**	**12,703**	**7,550**	**5,153**	**42,924**	**17,201**	**25,723**	**11,506**	**7,341**	**4,165**
	C. P. British Districts ..	**52,446**	**24,422**	**28,024**	**3,266**	**2,088**	**1,178**	**8,626**	**5,165**	**3,461**	**33,458**	**12,885**	**20,573**	**7,344**	**4,415**	**2,929**
	JUBBULPORE DIVISION ..	*9,561*	*4,268*	*5,293*	*530*	*314*	*216*	*1,616*	*991*	*625*	*7,154*	*2,808*	*4,346*	*273*	*164*	*109*
1	Saugor ..	1,963	948	1,015	99	68	31	365	223	142	1,452	627	825	52	35	17
2	Damoh ..	1,492	657	835	69	43	26	296	176	120	1,104	427	677	23	11	12
3	Jubbulpore ..	3,630	1,547	2,083	191	108	83	424	260	164	2,931	1 130	1,801	90	53	37
4	Mandla ..	1,278	623	655	110	64	46	277	181	96	807	329	478	85	49	36
5	Seoni ..	1,198	493	705	61	31	30	254	151	103	860	295	565	23	16	7
	NERBUDDA DIVISION ..	*9,014*	*4,203*	*4,811*	*453*	*278*	*175*	*1,919*	*1,127*	*792*	*6,303*	*2,577*	*3 726*	*356*	*232*	*124*
6	Narsinghpur ..	1,658	719	939	66	37	29	367	203	164	1,194	460	734	31	19	12
7	Hoshangabad	2,061	916	1,145	93	57	36	304	192	112	1,618	640	978	50	30	20
8	Nimar ..	2.024	997	1.027	110	72	38	406	251	155	1,349	560	789	162	115	47
9	Betul ..	1,259	637	622	81	54	27	328	187	141	833	387	446	23	14	9
10	Chhindwara ..	2,012	934	1,078	103	58	45	514	294	220	1,309	530	779	90	54	36
	NAGPUR DIVISION.	*14,021*	*7,651*	*6,373*	*1,379*	*927*	*452*	*3,379*	*2,031*	*1,348*	*6,476*	*2,860*	*3,616*	*2,885*	*1,879*	*1,006*
11	Wardha ..	2,540	1,425	1,115	122	65	57	493	286	207	1,163	544	619	767	531	236
12	Nagpur ..	3,881	2,235	1,646	687	503	184	850	517	333	1,678	793	885	699	437	262
13	Chanda ..	3,405	1,809	1,596	176	107	69	830	509	321	1,513	636	877	903	568	335
14	Bhandara ..	2,541	1,393	1,148	244	159	85	753	455	298	1,150	511	639	433	285	148
15	Balaghat ..	1,654	789	865	150	93	57	453	264	189	972	376	596	83	58	25
	CHHATTISGARH DIVISION ..	*19,850*	*8,300*	*11,550*	*904*	*569*	*335*	*1,712*	*1,016*	*696*	*13,525*	*4,640*	*8,885*	*3,830*	*2,140*	*1,690*
16	Raipur ..	8,691	3,518	5,173	415	262	153	794	465	329	6,118	1,995	4,123	1,408	822	586
17	Bilaspur ..	6,424	2,823	3,601	356	219	137	609	362	247	4,221	1,557	2,664	1,273	703	570
18	Drug ..	4,735	1.959	2,776	133	88	45	309	189	120	3,186	1,088	2,098	1,149	615	534
	Berar ..	**18,778**	**10,282**	**8,496**	**1,260**	**756**	**504**	**4,077**	**2,385**	**1,692**	**9,466**	**4,316**	**5,150**	**4,162**	**2,926**	**1,236**
19	Amraoti ..	5,888	3,288	2,600	419	247	172	1,220	717	503	2.801	1,292	1,509	1,522	1,073	449
20	Akola ..	4,577	2,512	2,065	350	207	143	923	541	382	2,395	1,085	1,310	942	695	247
21	Buldana ..	4,042	2.156	1,886	245	156	89	835	467	368	2,219	1.017	1,202	770	528	242
22	Yeotmal ..	4,271	2,326	1,945	246	146	100	1.099	660	439	2,051	922	1,129	928	630	298
	C. P. States ..	**6,913**	**3,314**	**3,599**	**507**	**317**	**190**	**1,267**	**711**	**556**	**4,147**	**1,686**	**2,461**	**1,013**	**610**	**403**
23	Makrai ..	96	39	57	10	6	4	20	13	7	60	16	44	6	4	2
24	Bastar ..	1,074	537	537	99	53	46	191	113	78	452	191	261	333	180	153
25	Kanker ..	460	196	264	31	21	10	80	51	29	294	94	200	60	32	28
26	Nandgaon ..	744	303	441	30	22	8	65	41	24	521	178	343	131	65	66
27	Khairagarh ..	597	233	364	23	14	9	53	23	30	438	143	295	83	53	30
28	Chhuikhadan ..	245	83	162	13	10	3	9	6	3	190	44	146	34	24	10
29	Kawardha ..	520	197	323	12	7	5	43	25	18	402	121	281	67	45	22
30	Sakti ..	202	82	120	19	10	9	57	24	33	113	42	71	13	6	7
31	Raigarh ..	538	290	248	57	41	16	138	79	59	278	123	155	68	48	20
32	Sarangarh ..	283	148	135	16	9	7	87	54	33	154	66	88	27	20	7
33	Changbhakar ..	72	35	37	17	8	9	13	8	5	40	18	22	2	1	1
34	Korea ..	181	106	75	17	12	5	9	..	9	130	73	57	25	21	4
35	Surguja ..	1,106	626	480	91	60	31	270	151	119	654	351	303	93	64	29
36	Udaipur ..	247	137	110	22	13	9	66	37	29	145	78	67	14	9	5
37	Jashpur ..	548	302	246	50	31	19	166	86	80	276	148	128	57	38	19

TABLE X

Occupation or means of livelihood

The scheme of occupations presented in this table is that approved by the Government of India. In the following groups there were no returns in the Central Provinces and Berar and they have therefore not been shown in the Table :—

8. Cultivators of jhum, taungya and shifting areas.
9. Cinchona cultivation.
31. *Exploitation of lead, silver and zinc.*
33. Exploitation of tin and wolfram.
36. Exploitation of petroleum.
38. Exploitation of mica.
39. Exploitation of precious and semi-precious stones.
79. Manufacturers of opium.
80. Manufacturers of ganja.
101. Persons concerned with aerodromes and aeroplanes.
155. Navy.

2. Under sub-order (*a*) in place of the groups of 1921 for " Income from rent of agricultural land ", and " Ordinary cultivators ",—the groups for " Non-cultivating proprietors taking rent in money or kind ", " Cultivating owners ", and " Tenant cultivators " have been substituted. " Farm servants " and " Field labourers " appear under " Agricultural labourers ", or any other head more appropriate to the specific form of occupation. Comparison with the figures of 1921 in these groups should therefore be made with caution. It may be explained that the instructions were to class as " cultivating owners " all those personally cultivating land over which they have permanent rights of occupation, and under " Cultivating tenants " all those who take land on temporary contract or lease. The figures are examined in Part I of the Report.

TABLE X Occupation or means of

Serial No.	District, City, or State.	Total of all classes. Total population. Total population.	Total earners (principal occupations). Males.	Total earners (principal occupations). Females.	Total. Working dependants. Males.	Total. Working dependants. Females.	Total. Non-working dependants. Males.	Total. Non-working dependants. Females.	Total following occupation Subsidiary to other. Males.	Males.
1	2	3	4	5	6	7	8	9	10	11
	Central Provinces and Berar.	**17,990,937**	**5,114,115**	**2,436,147**	**519,517**	**1,431,652**	**3,363,571**	**5,125,935**	**469,891**	**130,208**
	C. P. British Districts and Berar	**15,507,723**	**4,501,317**	**2,272,140**	**358,448**	**1,125,561**	**2,902,053**	**4,348,204**	**427,081**	**122,039**
	C. P. British Districts ..	**12,065,885**	**3,457,225**	**1,682,961**	**293,409**	**1,005,150**	**2,251,605**	**3,375,535**	**343,044**	**102,790**
	Jubbulpore Division ..	*2,463,466*	*703,641*	*286,366*	*40,374*	*148,100*	*496,640*	*788,345*	*85,259*	*16,472*
1	Saugor ..	544,58[illegible]	154,119	55,586	11,057	23,608	115,209	185,010	16,600	2,628
2	Damoh ..	305,568	92,437	39,467	3,616	12,848	58,738	98,462	14,121	2,267
3	Jubbulpore ..	773,811	226,670	91,154	10 880	37,653	154,099	253,355	36,457	5,921
	Jubbulpore City ..	*124,382*	*40,333*	*8,200*	*523*	*655*	*28,402*	*46,269*	*2,797*	*107*
4	Mandla ..	445,766	106,623	28,019	4,544	23,598	110,192	172,790	7,184	913
5	Seoni ..	393,732	123,792	72,140	10,277	50,393	58,402	78,728	10,897	4,743
	Nerbudda Division ..	*2,254,566*	*647,284*	*238,546*	*65,952*	*209,304*	*424,570*	*668,910*	*62,841*	*15,807*
6	Narsinghpur ..	321,481	88,034	41,564	6,223	21,502	67,160	96,998	9,782	2,892
7	Hoshangabad ..	486,630	144,513	55,126	11,835	23,612	91,878	159,666	17,281	3,329
8	Nimar ..	466,931	131,998	41,626	19,100	42,905	90,944	140,358	9,633	995
9	Betul ..	406,252	124,124	48,757	6,937	36,614	70,053	119,767	11,845	5,641
10	Chhindwara ..	573,272	158,615	51,473	21,857	84,671	104,535	152,121	14,300	2,950
	Nagpur Division ..	*3,602,108*	*1,104,382*	*649,213*	*59,759*	*234,253*	*645,400*	*909,101*	*102,511*	*44,130*
11	Wardha ..	516,266	164,733	118,338	4,723	11,307	91,938	125,227	12,375	4,842
12	Nagpur ..	940,049	297,684	180,380	7,459	27,438	176,103	250,985	18,520	5,017
	Nagpur City ..	*215,165*	*64,128*	*15,848*	*1,185*	*2,563*	*51,090*	*80,351*	*1,465*	*76*
13	Chanda ..	759,695	225,544	126,860	11,653	49,264	144,007	202,367	32,068	14,120
14	Bhandara ..	824,496	251,490	174,928	14,784	55,217	142,525	185,552	26,238	16,531
15	Balaghat ..	561,602	164,931	48,707	21,140	91,027	90,827	144,970	13,310	3,620
	Chhattisgarh Division ..	*3,745,745*	*1,001,918*	*508,836*	*127,324*	*413,493*	*684,995*	*1,009,179*	*92,433*	*26,381*
16	Raipur .	1,527,573	430,287	216,614	41,675	180,621	267,988	390,388	33,554	10,708
17	Bilaspur ..	1,400,248	383,217	204,390	21,571	89,941	279,132	421,997	46,349	13,896
18	Drug ..	817,924	188,414	87,832	64,078	142,931	137,875	196,794	12,530	1,777
	Berar .	**3,441,838**	**1,044,092**	**589,179**	**65,939**	**120,411**	**650,448**	**972,669**	**84,037**	**19,249**
19	Amraoti ..	941,604	286,360	151,385	15,294	26,967	183,939	277,659	32,149	5,132
20	Akola ..	876,362	270,187	145,238	14,739	17,362	163,970	264,866	20,764	3,452
21	Buldana ..	766,584	244,095	123,063	16,818	30,543	148,053	224,012	18,537	3,773
22	Yeotmal ..	857,288	263,450	169,493	18,188	45,539	154,486	206,132	12,587	6,892
	Central Provinces States	**2,483,214**	**612,798**	**164,007**	**161,069**	**306,091**	**461,518**	**777,731**	**42,810**	**8,169**
23	Makrai ..	15,516	5,029	996	116	993	2,755	5,627	323	41
24	Bastar ..	524,721	114,525	27,516	46,650	88,847	102,073	145,110	4,318	274
25	Kanker ..	136,101	31,946	15,315	12,505	23,158	22,681	30,496	2,814	1,114
26	Nandgaon ..	182,380	46,584	19,366	14,865	32,350	26,437	42,778	1,964	188
27	Khairagarh ..	157,400	37,778	18,572	12,506	28,033	25,363	35,148	2,255	612
28	Chhuikhadan ..	31,668	6,732	3,303	3,038	5,404	5,468	7,723	604	165
29	Kawardha ..	72,820	23,093	20,496	751	1,369	11,254	15,857	3,034	986
30	Sakti ..	48,489	12,273	4,372	3,973	10,582	7,325	9,964	882	343
31	Raigarh ..	277,569	62,390	9,872	23,648	33,653	50,685	97,321	5,031	188
32	Sarangarh ..	128,967	29,806	6,692	6,123	3,873	26,514	55,959	2,590	4,026
33	Changbhaker ..	23,322	7,246	5,323	150	702	4,591	5,310	413	22
34	Korea ..	90,886	26,363	4,699	886	1,019	19,499	38,420	1,518	25
35	Surguja ..	501,939	128,267	20,720	27,985	53,237	98,671	173,059	7,804	124
36	Udaipur ..	97,738	27,235	890	265	119	21,925	47,304	1,209	6
37	Jashpur	193,698	53,531	5,875	7,608	22,752	36,277	67,655	8,051	55

Livelihood—General Distribution. **TABLE X**

Class A.—Production of raw materials. Total of class A. Total earners (principal occupation.) Males.	Females.	Total working dependants. Males.	Females.	Total following occupation as subsidiary to other. Males.	Females.	Serial No.
12	13	14	15	16	17	
3,958,193	**2,048,085**	**473,125**	**1,289,274**	**252,875**	**80,789**	
3,432,509	**1,914,978**	**321,217**	**1,011,748**	**232,020**	**74,994**	
2,639,012	**1,383,865**	**265,309**	**912,746**	**185,770**	**62,335**	
508,839	*220,461*	*35,090*	*132,876*	*44,481*	*9,185*	
107,948	42,524	9,836	19,439	9,872	1,107	1
68,600	31,192	2,895	10,629	7,450	906	2
142,071	59,258	8,329	31,731	17,742	2,817	3
2,522	*549*	*81*	*96*	*2,078*	*18*	
88,695	23,470	4,300	22,703	2,822	289	4
101,525	64,017	9,730	48,374	6,595	4,066	5
479,417	*192,370*	*60,498*	*190,802*	*32,953*	*6,956*	
63,211	31,694	5,626	17,316	5,132	1,328	6
96,629	41,768	10,105	19,737	9,259	1,671	7
91,907	34,366	17,676	40,797	3,718	656	8
100,470	40,020	6,693	32,211	6,108	1,699	9
127,200	44,522	20,398	80,741	8,736	1,602	10
784,340	*536,866*	*51,736*	*202,020*	*60,127*	*31,371*	
123,858	109,110	4,170	10,122	7,985	4,085	11
172,465	145,326	5,425	17,132	10,469	2,854	12
3,147	*597*	*140*	*47*	*581*	*25*	
173,465	106,365	10,273	41,932	20,763	9,940	13
197,140	134,736	11,999	49,115	13,821	11,491	14
137,412	41,329	19,869	83,719	7,089	3,001	15
866,416	*434,168*	*117,985*	*387,048*	*48,209*	*14,823*	
367,299	176,608	38,079	170,401	16,724	6,392	16
335,068	179,943	19,458	83,260	24,479	7,313	17
164,049	77,617	60,448	133,387	7,006	1,118	18
793,497	**531,113**	**55,908**	**99,002**	**46,250**	**12,659**	
212,654	137,593	12,785	22,465	17,651	2,993	19
202,334	132,087	13,112	14,385	11,342	1,777	20
176,057	112,559	15,500	28,335	10,338	2,121	21
202,452	148,874	14,511	33,817	6,919	5,768	22
525,684	**133,107**	**151,908**	**277,526**	**20,855**	**5,795**	
3,839	790	84	892	180	19	23
101,844	23,898	44,774	83,875	1,777	137	24
27,009	13,880	11,679	21,398	1,791	390	25
35,618	15,552	14,309	30,706	782	26	26
31,548	15,696	11,812	26,443	1,309	515	27
5,275	2,286	2,652	4,788	302	67	28
20,173	17,944	737	1,235	1,735	359	29
10,234	2,887	3,404	9,868	333	130	30
51,429	5,305	21,714	28,384	2,041	63	31
25,737	5,035	5,510	2,584	975	3,998	32
6,072	4,632	129	675	233	9	33
22,664	3,416	866	1,004	793	11	34
114,000	18,285	26,941	47,383	2,604	39	35
24,254	358	229	113	459	1	36
45,988	3,143	7,068	18,178	5,541	1	37

TABLE X Occupation or means of

Serial No.	Class ..	Class A.—Production					
	Sub-class ..	Sub-class I.—Exploitation of animals					
	Order ..	Total of sub-class I.					
	Sub-order ..						
	Group ..						
	District, City or State.	Total earners (principal occupations)		Total working dependants.		Total following occupation as subsidiary to other.	
		Males.	Females	Males.	Females.	Males.	Females.
1	2	18	19	20	21	22	23
	Central Provinces and Berar ..	**3,944,119**	**2,040,113**	**472,984**	**1,288,908**	**251,693**	**79,979**
	C. P. British Districts and Berar ..	**3,418,557**	**1,907,067**	**321,084**	**1,011,476**	**230,884**	**74,205**
	C. P. British Districts ..	**2,627,130**	**1,376,656**	**265,217**	**912,597**	**184,715**	**61,580**
	Jubbulpore Division ..	*508,606*	*220,395*	*35,089*	*132,870*	*44,375*	*9,182*
1	Saugor ..	107,877	42,510	9,836	19,435	9,775	1,104
2	Damoh ..	68,584	31,192	2,895	10,629	7,450	906
3	Jubbulpore ..	141,929	59,206	8,328	31,729	17,734	2,817
	Jubbulpore City ..	*2,504*	*549*	*81*	*96*	*2,078*	*18*
4	Mandla ..	88,695	23,470	4,300	22,703	2,821	289
5	Seoni ..	101,521	64,017	9,730	48,374	6,595	4,066
	Nerbudda Division ..	*476,281*	*190,619*	*60,482*	*190,789*	*32,482*	*6,901*
6	Narsinghpur ..	63,154	31,654	5.626	17,316	5,130	1,328
7	Hoshangabad ..	96,141	41,591	10,102	19.737	9,233	1,671
8	Nimar ..	91,771	34,364	17,673	40,797	3,650	652
9	Betul ..	100,418	39,975	6,693	32,210	6,096	1,688
10	Chhindwara ..	124,797	43,035	20,388	80,729	8,373	1,562
	Nagpur Division ..	*776,012*	*531,526*	*51,678*	*201,908*	*59,691*	*30,695*
11	Wardha ..	123,676	108,976	4,170	10,122	7,966	4,085
12	Nagpur ..	169,691	143,270	5,417	17,092	10,424	2,840
	Nagpur City ..	*3,109*	*584*	*140*	*47*	*580*	*25*
13	Chanda ..	171,803	106,090	10,269	41,931	20,712	9,937
14	Bhandara ..	175,288	133,231	11,988	49,113	13,623	10,892
15	Balaghat ..	135,554	39,959	19,834	83,650	6,966	2,941
	Chhattisgarh Division ..	*866,231*	*434,116*	*117,968*	*387,030*	*48,167*	*14,802*
16	Raipur ..	367,167	176,580	38,066	170,394	16,710	6,375
17	Bilaspur ..	335,036	179,921	19,457	83,260	24,461	7,309
18	Drug ..	164,028	77,615	60,445	133,376	6,996	1,118
	Berar ..	**791,427**	**530,411**	**55,867**	**98,879**	**46,169**	**12,625**
19	Amraoti ..	212,364	137,383	12,780	22,463	17,613	2,988
20	Akola ..	201,878	131,834	13,104	14,375	11,333	1,752
21	Buldana ..	175,455	112,475	15,481	28,331	10,322	2,119
22	Yeotmal ..	201,730	148,719	14,502	33,710	6,901	5,766
	Central Provinces States ..	**525,562**	**133,046**	**151,900**	**277,432**	**20,809**	**5,774**
23	Makrai ..	3,833	779	84	892	180	19
24	Bastar ..	101,827	23,890	44,766	83,856	1,774	137
25	Kanker ..	27,007	13,880	11,679	21,398	1,789	390
26	Nandgaon ..	35,612	15,552	14,309	30,706	780	26
27	Khairagarh ..	31,533	15,696	11,812	26,429	1,309	515
28	Chhuikhadan ..	5,275	2,286	2,652	4,788	302	67
29	Kawardha ..	20,173	17,944	737	1,235	1,735	359
30	Sakti ..	10,234	2,887	3,404	9,868	333	130
31	Raigarh ..	51,429	5,305	21,714	28,384	2,041	63
32	Sarangarh ..	25,720	5,035	5,510	2,584	975	3,998
33	Changbhakar ..	6,072	4,632	129	675	233	9
34	Korea ..	22,660	3,416	866	1,004	793	11
35	Surguja ..	113,974	18,278	26,941	47,382	2,604	39
36	Udaipur ..	24,254	353	229	113	459	1
37	Jashpur ..	45,959	3,113	7,068	18,118	5,502	10

Livelihood—General Distribution—*contd.*

TABLE X

of raw materials—*contd.*

and vegetation—*contd.*

Order I.—Pasture and Agriculture. Total of order I.						Sub-order (*a*).—Cultivation. Total of sub-order (*a*).						Serial No.
Total earners (principal occupations).		Total working dependants.		Total following occupation as subsidiary to other.		Total earners (principal occupations).		Total working dependants.		Total following occupation as subsidiary to other.		
Males.	Females.	Males.	Females.	Males.	Females.	Males.	Females.	Males.	Females.	Males	Females.	
24	25	26	27	28	29	30	31	32	33	34	35	
3,903,105	**2,033,818**	**470,900**	**1,286,928**	**239,483**	**78,546**	**3,700,784**	**2.013,835**	**412,384**	**1,268,615**	**213,088**	**74,496**	
3,379,183	**1,900,986**	**319,262**	**1,009,812**	**219,500**	**72,780**	**3,204,436**	**1,884,331**	**270,919**	**998,030**	**197,092**	**68,954**	
2,593,116	**1,371,815**	**263,700**	**911,124**	**174,969**	**60,565**	**2,445,347**	**1,357,072**	**225,038**	**900,693**	**154,780**	**57,018**	
505,897	*220,241*	*34,626*	*132,762*	*43,572*	*9,145*	*477,687*	*217,326*	*29,381*	*131,463*	*40,601*	*8,766*	
107,725	42,494	9,821	19,425	9,717	1,104	101,951	42,191	7,524	19,227	9,374	1,080	1
67,942	31,189	2,665	10,628	7,372	903	64,068	30,294	2,148	10,467	6,809	743	2
141,272	59,159	8,117	31,669	17,365	2.803	135,170	58,083	7,495	31,185	16,034	2,656	3
2,405	*520*	*81*	*96*	*2,011*	*18*	*1,595*	*300*	*60*	*79*	*1,993*	*8*	
88,365	23,426	4,296	22,689	2,653	284	83,644	23,117	3,996	22,540	2,161	257	4
100,593	63,973	9,727	48,351	6,465	4,051	92,854	63,641	8,218	48,044	6,223	4,030	5
473,819	*190,498*	*60,423*	*190.665*	*31,807*	*6,886*	*445,426*	*188,772*	*48,067*	*189,135*	*27,774*	*6,625*	
63,012	31,647	5,623	17,310	5,002	1,327	60,442	31,275	4,016	16,931	4,721	1,283	6
95,467	41,586	10,092	19,733	9,075	1,669	87,321	40,934	7,253	19,376	7,713	1,593	7
91,233	34,351	17,664	40,796	3,496	649	87.345	34,232	15,795	40,665	3,196	641	8
99,956	39,917	6,684	32,174	5,984	1,685	92,269	39,678	4,170	32,015	4,384	1,584	9
124,151	42,997	20,360	80,652	8,250	1,556	118,049	42,653	16,833	80,148	7,760	1,524	10
752,998	*528,410*	*51,188*	*201,216*	*56,540*	*30,121*	*702,982*	*525,615*	*38,314*	*200,416*	*53,474*	*29.474*	
121,668	108,498	4,150	10,039	7,638	4,006	115,934	108,271	3,459	10,005	7,475	3,965	11
166,696	142,663	5,392	17,056	9,986	2,768	151,514	141,972	3,281	16,839	9,561	2,709	12
2,946	*567*	*138*	*47*	*569*	*25*	*2,060*	*489*	*94*	*46*	*535*	*25*	
163,251	105,099	10,129	41,643	19,347	9,756	149,709	104,111	7,208	41,405	18,345	9,491	13
169,833	132,623	11,794	48,995	12,929	10,757	158,907	131,931	7,350	48,793	11,997	10,695	14
131,550	39,527	19.723	83,483	6,640	2,834	126,918	39,330	17,016	83,374	6,096	2,614	5
860.402	*432,666*	*117,463*	*386,481*	*43,050*	*14,413*	*819,252*	*425,359*	*109,276*	*379,679*	*32,931*	*12,153*	
364,448	175.519	37,835	170,212	14,605	6,109	344,456	170,776	34,397	166,764	10,691	5,095	16
333,495	179,617	19,390	83,171	22,131	7,204	322,906	177,949	17,851	82,323	17,403	6,276	17
162,459	77,530	60,238	133,098	6,314	1,100	151,890	76,634	57,028	130,592	4,837	782	18
786,067	**529,171**	**55,562**	**98,688**	**44,531**	**12,215**	**759,089**	**527,259**	**45,881**	**97,337**	**42,312**	**11,936**	
210.681	136,790	12,697	22,336	16,819	2,676	203,514	135,784	11,099	21,736	15,927	2,612	19
201,223	131,759	13,096	14,363	10,968	1,721	196,045	131,346	10,892	14,226	10,535	1,619	20
175,165	112,437	15.480	28,326	10,147	2,096	169.457	112,244	,704	28,142	9,663	2,056	21
198,998	148,185	14,289	33,663	6,597	5,722	190,073	147,885	11,186	33,233	6,187	5,649	22
523,922	**132,832**	**151,638**	**277,116**	**19,983**	**5,766**	**496,348**	**129,504**	**141,465**	**270,585**	**15,996**	**5,542**	
3,833	779	84	892	167	15	3,600	774	51	886	163	15	23
101,573	23,857	44,716	83,776	1,677	135	98,222	23,148	43,979	82,453	1,361	128	24
26,901	13,875	11,640	21,342	1,661	390	25,309	13,724	11,226	20,843	1,023	347	25
35,207	15,521	14,285	30,643	729	25	32,541	15,385	13,828	30,106	516	18	26
31,301	15,637	11,785	26,381	1,251	515	27,664	15,232	11,346	25,812	977	502	27
5,231	2,278	2,652	4,786	276	66	4,605	2,222	2,120	4,601	209	54	28
19,986	17,943	736	1,235	1,674	359	18,195	17,412	157	1,103	966	284	29
10,227	2,884	3,402	9,839	296	130	9,691	2,727	3,169	9,599	200	108	30
51,259	5,294	21,613	28,371	2,015	63	49,823	5,208	20,442	27,893	1,766	60	31
25,586	5,035	5,494	2,584	768	3,998	24,596	4,972	5,033	2,506	584	3.997	32
6,063	4,626	129	674	213	9	5,380	4,509	84	585	152	3	33
22,653	3,416	866	1,004	782	11	21,556	3.322	816	1,000	640	2	34
113,964	18,278	26,940	47,380	2,588	39	109,680	17,997	24,560	46,384	1,790	13	35
24.236	353	229	113	443	1	22,849	295	221	113	323	1	36
45,902	3,056	7,067	18,096	5,443	10	42,637	2,577	4,433	16.701	5,326	10	37

TABLE X — Occupation or means of

Serial No.	Class ..	Class A.—Production					
	Sub-class ..	Sub-class I.—Exploitation					
	Order ..	Order 1.—Pasture					
	Sub-order ..	Sub-order (a).—					
	Group ..	1.—Non-cultivating proprietors taking rent in money or kind.					
	District, City or State.	Total earners (principal occupations).		Total working dependants.		Total following occupation as subsidiary to other.	
		Males	Females	Males	Females.	Males.	Females.
1	2	36	37	38	39	40	41
	Central Provinces and Berar	**44,699**	**9,356**	**1,013**	**2,998**	**21,785**	**1,450**
	C. P. British Districts and Berar	**43,385**	**9,139**	**991**	**503**	**21,445**	**1,441**
	C. P. British Districts	**32,749**	**6,086**	**660**	**232**	**18,324**	**1,149**
	Jubbulpore Division	*4,591*	*876*	*88*	*34*	*4,211*	*281*
1	Saugor	1,081	319	30	6	1,224	82
2	Damoh	523	176	8	6	796	41
3	Jubbulpore	1,356	241	44	19	1,083	92
	Jubbulpore City	*167*	*22*	*8*	*5*	*20*	*1*
4	Mandla	209	30	1	3	423	19
5	Seoni	1,422	110	5	..	685	47
	Nerbudda Division	*9,193*	*2,801*	*307*	*52*	*6,604*	*423*
6	Narsinghpur	2,243	641	15	14	708	70
7	Hoshangabad	2,924	1,096	92	9	1,457	65
8	Nimar	720	226	13	5	682	29
9	Betul	1,249	509	166	13	1,255	108
10	Chhindwara	2,057	329	21	11	2,502	151
	Nagpur Division	*15,111*	*1,989*	*229*	*128*	*5,612*	*349*
11	Wardha	3,530	667	8	10	1,387	67
12	Nagpur	4,937	362	27	9	1,626	102
	Nagpur City	*288*	*40*	*16*	*2*	*19*	..
13	Chanda	3,164	248	10	9	802	29
14	Bhandara	2,846	455	182	86	1,016	115
15	Balaghat	634	257	2	14	781	36
	Chhattisgarh Division	*3,854*	*420*	*36*	*18*	*1,897*	*96*
16	Raipur	1,196	101	5	3	775	45
17	Bilaspur	1,608	149	14	4	964	41
18	Drug	1,050	170	17	11	158	10
	Berar	**10,636**	**3,053**	**331**	**271**	**3,121**	**292**
19	Amraoti	3,434	929	53	26	1,240	67
20	Akola	2,704	958	60	56	950	70
21	Buldana	1,946	763	57	31	525	19
22	Yeotmal	2,552	403	161	158	406	136
	Central Provinces States	**1,314**	**217**	**22**	**2,495**	**340**	**9**
23	Makrai	14	3	..	..	1	2
24	Bastar	99	38	..	..	54	..
25	Kanker	83	7	5	..	73	2
26	Nandgaon	15	6	2	1	35	..
27	Khairagarh	177	42	7	..	11	..
28	Chhuikhadan	..	7	..	..	..	..
29	Kawardha	13	12	..	..	4	5
30	Sakti	109	23	..	..	..	..
31	Raigarh	51	3	..	..	23	..
32	Sarangarh	29	..	..	..	2	..
33	Chhangbhakar	1	..	..	..	19	..
34	Korea	16	3	..	..	13	..
35	Surguja	655	26	8	1	69	..
36	Udaipur	16	..	..	..	26	..
37	Jashpur	36	41	..	2,493	10	..

Livelihood—General Distribution—*contd.* TABLE X

of Raw materials—*contd.*

of animals and vegetation—*contd.*

and agriculture—*contd.*

cultivation—*contd.*

Serial No	2.—Estate agents and managers of owners. Total earners (principal occupations). Males.	Total earners (principal occupations). Females.	Total working dependants. Males.	Total working dependants. Females.	Total following occupation as subsidiary to other. Males.	Total following occupation as subsidiary to other. Females	3.—Estate agents and managers of Government. Total earners (principal occupations). Males.	Total earners (principal occupations). Females.	Total working dependants. Males.	Total working dependants. Females	Total following occupation as subsidiary to other. Males.	Total following occupation as subsidiary to other. Females.
	42	43	44	45	46	47	48	49	50	51	52	53
	151	2	10	..	33	..	204	8	..	5	11	..
	149	2	10	..	33	..	199	8	..	5	11	..
	90	1	..	..	27	..	189	8	..	5	11	..
	6	*1*	..	..	*1*	..	*70*	*1*	..	..	*2*	..
1	..	1	..	..	..	..	10	..	..	..	..	..
2	..	..	..	..	..	..	1	..	..	..	..	..
3	6	..	..	..	1	..	23	..	..	..	..	..
	1	..	..	..	..	..	*3*	..	..	..	..	..
4	..	..	..	..	..	..	..	..	..	..	..	..
5	..	..	..	..	..	..	36	1	..	..	2	..
	22	..	..	..	*2*	..	*42*	*1*	..	..	*4*	..
6	..	..	..	..	..	..	..	..	..	..	..	..
7	..	..	..	..	..	..	4	1	..	..	..	..
8	..	..	..	..	..	..	2	..	..	..	..	..
9	..	..	..	..	..	..	..	..	..	..	..	..
10	22	..	..	..	2	..	36	..	..	..	4	..
	61	..	..	..	*24*	..	*23*	*1*	..	..	*1*	..
11	20	..	..	..	10	..	5	..	..	..	..	..
12	29	..	..	..	14	..	13	1	..	..	..	..
	4	..	..	..	..	..	*10*	*1*	..	..	..	..
13	10	..	..	..	..	..	1	..	..	..	..	..
14	2	..	..	..	..	..	..	..	..	..	..	..
15	..	..	..	..	..	..	4	..	..	..	1	..
	1	..	..	..	..	..	*54*	*5*	..	*5*	*4*	..
16	..	..	..	..	..	..	3	..	..	..	1	..
17	..	..	..	..	..	..	25	..	..	3	3	..
18	1	..	..	..	..	..	26	5	..	2	..	..
	59	1	10	..	6	..	10	..	..	..	..	..
19	50	..	7	..	3	..	..	..	..	..	..	..
20	3	..	..	..	1	..	10	..	..	..	..	..
21	3	1	3	..	1	..	..	..	..	..	..	..
22	3	..	..	..	1	..	..	..	..	..	..	..
	2	..	..	..	..	..	5	..	..	..	..	..
23	2	..	..	..	..	..	3	..	..	..	..	..
24	..	..	..	..	..	..	1	..	..	..	..	..
25	..	..	..	..	..	..	..	..	..	..	..	..
26	..	..	..	..	..	..	..	..	..	..	..	..
27	..	..	..	..	..	..	..	..	..	..	..	..
28	..	..	..	..	..	..	..	..	..	..	..	..
29	..	..	..	..	..	..	..	..	..	..	..	..
30	..	..	..	..	..	..	..	..	..	..	..	..
31	..	..	..	..	..	..	..	..	..	..	..	..
32	..	..	..	..	..	..	..	..	..	..	..	..
33	..	..	..	..	..	..	..	..	..	..	..	..
34	..	..	..	..	..	..	1	..	..	..	..	..
35	..	..	..	..	..	..	..	..	..	..	..	..
36	..	..	..	..	..	..	..	..	..	..	..	..
37	..	..	..	..	..	..	..	..	..	..	..	..

TABLE X — Occupation or means of

Serial No.	Class .. / Sub-class .. / Order ... / Sub-order . / Group ..	Class A.—Production / Sub-class I.—Exploitation / Order I.—Pasture / Sub-order (a).— / 4.—Rent collectors, clerks, etc.					
	District, City or State.	Total earners (principal occupations).		Total working dependants.		Total following occupation as subsidiary to other.	
		Males.	Females.	Males.	Females.	Males.	Females.
1	2	54	55	56	57	58	59
	Central Provinces and Berar ..	**7,212**	**183**	**60**	**5**	**881**	**13**
	C. P. British Districts and Berar ..	**6,993**	**178**	**60**	**5**	**876**	**13**
	C. P. British Districts ..	**6,893**	**167**	**60**	**5**	**867**	**13**
	Jubbulpore Division ..	*957*	*28*	*17*	*1*	*238*	*1*
1	Saugor	57	2	1	..	14	..
2	Damoh	110	..	4	..	20	..
3	Jubbulpore	420	16	8	..	165	1
	Jubbulpore City ..	*22*	..	*7*	..	*1*	..
4	Mandla	259	10	2	1	20	..
5	Seoni	111	..	2	..	19	..
	Nerbudda Division	*4,407*	*54*	*31*	*3*	*347*	*7*
6	Narsinghpur	69	27	1	1	25	*1*
7	Hoshangabad	3,851	18	28	1	201	..
8	Nimar ..	106	1	2	..	68	..
9	Betul	152	3	..	1	41	..
10	Chhindwara	229	5	..	..	12	6
	Nagpur Division ..	*574*	*3*	*9*	*1*	*144*	..
11	Wardha	3	..	..	..	..	..
12	Nagpur	141	..	..	..	4	..
	Nagpur City ..	*61*	..	..	..	..	..
13	Chanda	51	1	1	..	2	..
14	Bhandara	64	..	..	..	30	..
15	Balaghat	315	2	8	1	108	..
	Chhattisgrah Division ..	*955*	*82*	*3*	..	*138*	*5*
16	Raipur	420	33	..	..	26	5
17	Bilaspur	151	33	3	..	76	..
18	Drug	384	16	..	..	36	..
	Berar	**100**	**11**	..	..	9	..
19	Amraoti	6	..	..	..	..	..
20	Akola	31	5	..	..	..	..
21	Buldana	10	..	..	..	2	..
22	Yeotmal	53	6	..	..	7	..
	Central Provinces States	**219**	**5**	..	..	**5**	..
23	Makrai ..	..	..	..	..	..	..
24	Bastar	60	..	..	..	..	..
25	Konker	..	..	..	..	..	..
26	Nandgaon . ..	..	..	..	..	..	..
27	Khairagarh . ..	..	..	..	..	..	..
28	Chhuikhadan . ..	2	..	..	..	..	..
29	Kawardha	2	..	..	..	..	..
30	Sakti	..	..	..	..	..	..
31	Raigarh	5	..	..	..	..	..
32	Sarangarh	..	..	..	..	..	..
33	Changbhakar	..	..	..	..	..	..
34	Korea	1	..	..	..	..	..
35	Surguja	135	5	..	..	5	..
36	Udaipur	1	..	..	..	..	..
37	Jashpur	13	..	..	..	..	..

Livelihood—General Distribution—*contd.*

TABLE X

of raw materials—*contd*

of animals and vegetation—*contd*

and agriculture—*contd.*

Cultivation—*contd.*

5.—Cultivating owners.						6.—Tenant-cultivators.						Serial No.
Total earners (principal occupations).		Total working dependants.		Total following occupation as subsidiary to other		Total earners (principal occupations).		Total working dependants.		Total following occupation as subsidiary to other.		
Males.	Females	Males.	Females	Males.	Females	Males	Females.	Males	Females.	Males	Females.	
60	61	62	63	64	65	66	67	68	69	70	71	
2,056,454	319,254	294,412	778,467	85,756	24,186	105,097	21,096	4,565	16,974	16,758	897	
1,707,248	288,105	170,522	553,216	73,386	19,307	90,136	20,419	3,532	7,286	16,004	889	
1,455,574	260,134	143,282	509,847	64,511	16,769	42,983	18,187	2,085	5,920	7,566	648	
291,777	*22,988*	*11,753*	*43,160*	*17,051*	*2,325*	*2,540*	*281*	*7*	*6*	*381*	*16*	
55,795	2,771	1,937	2,357	2,978	66	1,220	26	1	..	117	2	1
38,161	2,163	1,487	3,249	2,755	115	219	158	1	..	13	6	2
84,204	9,623	3,219	7,962	8,579	481	467	68	5	6	70	6	3
1,175	*145*	*45*	*59*	*1,953*	*6*	*9*	*1*	..	..	*7*	..	
60,751	2,227	1,538	6,185	1,022	35	77	6	..	..	7	..	4
52,866	6,204	3,572	23,407	1,717	1,628	557	23	..	..	174	2	5
247,416	*10,550*	*12,096*	*37,819*	*9,098*	*590*	*5,829*	*3,033*	*250*	*2,836*	*1,123*	*49*	
30,432	1,923	1,109	2,382	1,501	36	110	22	..	..	42	1	6
42,925	3,429	3,223	7,182	1,936	49	1,348	39	30	2	362	3	7
47,800	1,713	3,094	5,777	1,470	211	410	43	90	136	99	3	8
58,044	1,458	875	13,432	1,512	61	1,842	1,005	..	2,412	371	5	9
68,215	2,027	3,795	8,646	2,679	233	2,119	1,924	130	286	249	37	10
363,179	*78,793*	*18,956*	*84,054*	*21,103*	*9,546*	*13,406*	*1,561*	*499*	*124*	*4,293*	*258*	
34,247	3,027	928	1,012	2,021	1,834	3,326	237	39	14	785	35	11
66,103	6,925	1,068	4,454	3,005	249	3,578	562	32	15	1,558	95	12
1,088	*161*	*49*	*31*	*482*	*23*	*82*	*6*	*3*	*6*	*23*	..	
89,980	23,090	4,638	21,126	7,901	1,376	2,244	225	16	2	932	34	13
94,412	40,064	4,884	40,970	5,105	5,027	3,647	486	400	83	855	92	14
78 437	5,687	7,438	16,492	3,071	1,060	611	51	12	10	163	2	15
553,202	*147,803*	*100,477*	*345,214*	*17,259*	*4,308*	*21,208*	*13,312*	*1,329*	*2,954*	*1,769*	*325*	
219,947	46,440	33,766	156,222	7,379	2,560	5,053	2,891	355	906	189	55	16
245,660	93,122	14,726	76,375	7,025	1,298	15,610	10,287	966	2,040	1,467	263	17
87,595	8,241	51,985	112,617	2,855	450	545	134	8	8	113	7	18
251,674	**27,971**	**27,240**	**43,369**	**8,875**	**2,538**	**47,153**	**2,232**	**1,447**	**1,366**	**8,438**	**241**	
53,879	5,571	4,153	4,344	3,027	411	11,881	543	129	61	3,724	87	19
64,207	7,689	8,040	6,844	2,130	151	9,430	486	119	46	2,477	32	20
66,529	7,982	10,171	21,882	2,097	325	7,725	455	83	86	1,525	52	21
67,059	6,729	4,876	10,299	1,621	1,651	18,117	748	1,116	1,173	712	70	22
349,206	**31,149**	**123,890**	**225,251**	**12,370**	**4,881**	**14,961**	**677**	**1,033**	**9,688**	**754**	**8**	
2,343	51	51	197	83	1	..	..	..	..	..	..	23
70,435	2,701	36,896	64,977	946	59	567	17	90	2,634	19	..	24
15,625	4,251	7,739	12,855	753	322	56	329	6	1,286	8	..	25
17,186	350	12,722	28,682	397	15	118	91	11	101	39	2	26
16,881	2,222	11,339	25,792	377	192	..	..	..	..	..	..	27
2,444	270	1,279	3,969	188	36	5	..	..	..	..	..	28
13,566	7,731	156	1,098	504	192	110	19	..	..	74	..	29
7,277	291	2,761	8,877	76	6	106	..	..	..	..	..	30
36,652	1,283	19,675	26,968	1,550	52	47	9	..	..	11	1	31
13,371	634	4,678	1,921	447	3,992	15	..	..	..	16	..	32
4,367	3,383	84	585	101	2	..	..	..	..	..	..	33
16,923	1,092	801	170	545	..	24	15	..	817	63	1	34
79,425	5,906	21,772	37,328	1,238	10	8,828	167	897	3,398	201	..	35
19,875	12	218	113	286	1	4	..	..	..	2	..	36
32,836	972	3,719	11,719	4,879	1	5,081	30	29	1,452	321	4	37

TABLE X Occupation or means of

Serial No.	Class .. / Sub-class .. / Order .. / Sub-order .. / Group .. / District, City or State.	Class A.—Production / Sub-class I.—Exploitation / Order 1.—Pasture / Sub-order (a).—Cultivation—concld. / 7.—Agricultural labourers. Total earners (principal occupations). Males.	Females.	Total working dependants. Males.	Females.	Total following occupation as subsidiary to other. Males.	Females.	Sub-order (b).—Cultivation of special / Total sub- Total earners (principal occupations). Males.	Females.	Total working dependants. Males.	Females
1	2	72	73	74	75	76	77	78	79	80	81
	Central Provinces and Berar	**1,486,967**	**1,663,936**	**112,324**	**470,166**	**87,864**	**47,948**	**9,884**	**2,873**	**1,570**	**2,969**
	C. P British Districts and Berar.	**1,356,326**	**1,566,480**	**95,804**	**437,015**	**85,337**	**47,304**	**8,931**	**2,548**	**1,003**	**2,071**
	C. P. British Districts ..	**906,869**	**1,072,489**	**78,951**	**384,684**	**63,474**	**38,439**	**6,988**	**1,708**	**844**	**1,466**
	Jubbulpore Division ..	*177,746*	*193,151*	*17,516*	*88,262*	*18,717*	*6,143*	*2,482*	*293*	*81*	*101*
1	Saugor	43,788	39,072	5,555	16,864	5,041	930	332	46	24	27
2	Damoh	25,054	27,797	648	7,212	3,225	581	375	22	4	3
3	Jubbulpore .. .	48,694	48,135	4,219	23,198	6,136	2,076	991	148	31	55
	Jubbulpore City ..	*218*	*132*	..	*15*	*12*	*1*	*450*	*38*	*5*	*7*
4	Mandla	22,348	20,844	2,455	16,351	689	203	213	62	15	6
5	Seoni	37,862	57,303	4,639	24,637	3,626	2,353	571	15	7	10
	Nerbudda Division ..	*178,517*	*172,333*	*35,383*	*148,825*	*10,596*	*•5,556*	*636*	*55*	*52*	*91*
6	Narsinghpur	27,588	28,662	2,891	14,534	2,445	1,175	39	4	9	3
7	Hoshangabad	36,269	36,351	3,880	12,182	3,757	1,476	251	31	35	73
8	Nimar	38,307	32,249	12,596	34,747	877	398	225	13	8	15
9	Betul	30,982	36,703	3,129	16,157	1,205	1,410	80	1	..	..
10	Chhindwara	45,371	38,368	12,887	71,205	2,312	1,097	41	6	..	..
	Nagpur Division ..	*310,628*	*443,268*	*18,621*	*116,109*	*22,297*	*19,321*	*1,340*	*156*	*30*	*42*
11	Wardha	74,803	104,340	2,484	8,969	3,272	2,029	118	13	1	3
12	Nagpur	76,713	134,122	2,154	12,361	3,354	2,263	784	95	7	16
	Nagpur City	*527*	*281*	*26*	*7*	*11*	*2*	*222*	*43*	..	..
13	Chanda	54,259	80,547	2,543	20,268	8,708	8,052	233	37	..	12
14	Bhandara	57,936	90,926	1,884	7,654	4,991	5,461	143	11	14	1
15	Balaghat	46,917	33,333	9,556	66 857	1,972	1,516	62	..	8	10
	Chhattisgarh Division ..	*239,978*	*263,737*	*7,431*	*31,488*	*11,864*	*7,419*	*2,530*	*1,204*	*681*	*1,232*
16	Raipur	117,837	121,311	271	9,633	2,321	2,430	1,319	932	400	687
17	Bilaspur	59,852	74,358	2,142	3,901	7,868	4,674	304	206	6	80
18	Drug	62,289	68,068	5,018	17,954	1,675	315	907	66	275	465
	Berar	**449,457**	**493,991**	**16,853**	**52,331**	**21,863**	**8,865**	**1,943**	**840**	**159**	**605**
19	Amraoti	134,264	128,741	6,757	17,305	7,933	2,047	1,341	602	90	425
20	Akola	119,660	122,208	2,673	7,280	4,977	1,366	332	171	31	57
21	Buldana	93,244	103,043	2,390	6,143	5,513	1,660	97	35	32	122
22	Yeotmal	102,289	139,999	5,033	21,603	3,440	3,792	173	32	6	1
	Central Provinces States ..	**130,641**	**97,456**	**16,520**	**33,151**	**2,527**	**644**	**953**	**325**	**567**	**898**
23	Makrai	1,238	720	..	689	79	12	1	..	..	..
24	Bastar	27,060	20,392	6,993	14,842	342	69	95	28	29	36
25	Kanker	9,545	9,137	3,476	6,702	189	23	131	20	60	100
26	Nandgaon	15,222	14,938	1,093	1,322	45	1	154	50	62	156
27	Khairagarh	10,606	12,968	..	20	589	310	172	104	69	318
28	Chhuikhadan	2,154	1,945	841	632	21	18	6	..	300	..
29	Kawardha	4,504	9,650	1	5	384	87	103	35	4	..
30	Sakti	2,199	2,407	408	722	124	102	211	67	39	202
31	Raigarh	13,068	3,913	767	925	182	7	1	..	..	..
32	Sarangarh	11,181	4,338	355	585	119	5	1	13	2	67
33	Changbhakar	1,012	1,126	..	..	32	1	1	1	1	..
34	Korea	4,591	2,212	15	13	19	1	4	..	..	..
35	Surguja	20,637	11,893	1,883	5,657	277	3	25	1	1	19
36	Udaipur	2,953	283	3	..	9	..	17	1	..	..
37	Jashpur	4,671	1,534	685	1,037	116	5	31	5	..	..

...of raw materials—*contd.*

...ot animals and vegetation—*contd.*

...and agriculture—*contd.*

...crops, fruits, etc. (planters, managers, clerks and labourers).

...order (*b*).		10.—Coconut.						11.—Coffee.						Serial No.
Total following occupation as subsidiary to other.		Total earners (principal occupations).		Total working dependants.		Total following occupation as subsidiary to other.		Total earners (principal occupations).		Total working dependants.		Total following occupation as subsidiary to other.		
Males.	Females.	Males.	Females.	Males.	Females.	Males.	Females.	Males.	Females.	Males.	Females.	Males.	Females	
82	83	84	85	86	87	88	89	90	91	92	93	94	95	
5,945	**1,289**	**83**	**2**	..	..	**45**	..	**41**	**21**	..	..	..	..	
4,975	**1,258**	**83**	**2**	..	..	**45**	..	**41**	**21**	..	..	..	..	
4,535	**1,206**	**83**	**2**	..	..	**45**	..	**15**	..	..	..	..	..	
897	*47*	*8*	..	..	..	..	..	*14*	..	..	..	..	..	
78	5	..	..	..	..	..	..	..	..	..	..	..	..	1
123	4	..	..	..	..	..	..	..	..	..	..	..	..	2
578	33	..	..	..	..	..	..	14	..	..	..	..	..	3
6	*3*	..	..	..	..	..	..	*13*	..	..	..	..	..	
93	3	8	..	..	..	..	..	..	..	..	..	..	..	4
25	2	..	..	..	..	..	..	..	..	..	..	..	..	5
441	*12*	*75*	*2*	..	..	*45*	..	*1*	..	..	..	..	..	
10	..	..	..	..	..	6	..	1	..	..	..	..	..	6
312	8	..	..	..	..	..	..	..	..	..	..	..	..	7
30	4	51	2	..	..	5	..	..	..	..	..	..	..	8
49	..	3	..	..	..	2	..	..	..	..	..	..	..	9
40	..	21	..	..	..	32	..	..	..	..	..	..	..	10
313	*37*	..	..	..	..	..	..	..	..	..	..	..	..	
30	5	..	..	..	..	..	..	..	..	..	..	..	..	11
66	10	..	..	..	..	..	..	..	..	..	..	..	..	12
2	..	..	..	..	..	..	..	..	..	..	..	..	..	
92	21	..	..	..	..	..	..	..	..	..	..	..	..	13
56	..	..	..	..	..	..	..	..	..	..	..	..	..	14
69	1	..	..	..	..	..	..	..	..	..	..	..	..	15
2,884	*1,110*	..	..	..	..	..	..	..	..	..	..	..	..	
965	254	..	..	..	..	..	..	..	..	..	..	..	..	16
1,058	580	..	..	..	..	..	..	..	..	..	..	..	..	17
861	276	..	..	..	..	..	..	..	..	..	..	..	..	18
440	**52**	..	..	..	..	..	..	**26**	**21**	..	..	..	..	
294	37	..	..	..	..	..	..	26	21	..	..	..	..	19
75	9	..	..	..	..	..	..	..	..	..	..	..	..	20
52	6	..	..	..	..	..	..	..	..	..	..	..	..	21
19	..	..	..	..	..	..	..	..	..	..	..	..	..	22
970	**31**	..	..	..	..	..	..	..	..	..	..	..	..	
..	..	..	..	..	..	..	..	..	..	..	..	..	..	23
38	1	..	..	..	..	..	..	..	..	..	..	..	..	24
118	..	..	..	..	..	..	..	..	..	..	..	..	..	25
88	1	..	..	..	..	..	..	..	..	..	..	..	..	26
134	4	..	..	..	..	..	..	..	..	..	..	..	..	27
20	..	..	..	..	..	..	..	..	..	..	..	..	..	28
426	10	..	..	..	..	..	..	..	..	..	..	..	..	29
11	10	..	..	..	..	..	..	..	..	..	..	..	..	30
..	..	..	..	..	..	..	..	..	..	..	..	..	..	31
128	1	..	..	..	..	..	..	..	..	..	..	..	..	32
1	4	..	..	..	..	..	..	..	..	..	..	..	..	33
..	..	..	..	..	..	..	..	..	..	..	..	..	..	34
1	..	..	..	..	..	..	..	..	..	..	..	..	..	35
2	..	..	..	..	..	..	..	..	..	..	..	..	..	36
3	..	..	..	..	..	..	..	..	..	..	..	..	..	37

TABLE X Occupation or means of

Serial No.	Class .. Sub-class .. Order .. Sub-order .. Group ..	Class A.—Production; Sub-class I.—Exploitation; Order I.—Pasture; Sub-order (b).—Cultivation of special crops, fruits, etc.; 12.—Ganja.					
	District, City or State.	Total earners (principal occupations).		Total working dependants.		Total following occupation as subsidiary to other.	
		Males.	Females.	Males.	Females.	Males.	Females.
1	2	96	97	98	99	100	101
	Central Provinces and Berar	25	..	..	..	..	..
	C. P. British Districts and Berar	25	..	..	..	..	..
	C. P. British Districts	25	..	..	..	..	..
	Jubbulpore Division	..	..	..	..	..	..
1	Saugor	..	..	..	..	..	..
2	Damoh	..	..	..	..	..	..
3	Jubbulpore	..	..	..	..	..	..
	Jubbulpore City	..	..	..	..	..	..
4	Mandla	..	..	..	..	..	..
5	Seoni	..	..	..	..	..	..
	Nerbudda Division	25	..	..	..	..	..
6	Narsinghpur	..	..	..	..	..	..
7	Hoshangabad	..	..	..	..	..	..
8	Nimar	25	..	..	..	..	..
9	Betul	..	..	..	..	..	..
10	Chhindwara	..	..	..	..	..	..
	Nagpur Division	..	..	..	..	..	..
11	Wardha	..	..	..	..	..	..
12	Nagpur	..	..	..	..	..	..
	Nagpur City	..	..	..	..	..	..
13	Chanda	..	..	..	..	..	..
14	Bhandara	..	..	..	..	..	..
15	Balaghat	..	..	..	..	..	..
	Chhattisgarh Division	..	..	..	..	..	..
16	Raipur	..	..	..	..	..	..
17	Bilaspur	..	..	..	..	..	..
18	Drug	..	..	..	..	..	..
	Berar	..	..	..	..	..	..
19	Amraoti	..	..	..	..	..	..
20	Akola	..	..	..	..	..	..
21	Buldana	..	..	..	..	..	..
22	Yeotmal	..	..	..	..	..	..
	Central Provinces States	..	..	..	..	..	..
23	Makrai	..	..	..	..	..	..
24	Bastar	..	..	..	..	..	..
25	Kanker	..	..	..	..	..	..
26	Nandgaon	..	..	..	..	..	..
27	Khairagarh	..	..	..	..	..	..
28	Chhuikhadan	..	..	..	..	..	..
29	Kawardha	..	..	..	..	..	..
30	Sakti	..	..	..	..	..	..
31	Raigarh	..	..	..	..	..	..
32	Sarangarh	..	..	..	..	..	..
33	Changbhakar	..	..	..	..	..	..
34	Korea	..	..	..	..	..	..
35	Surguja	..	..	..	..	..	..
36	Udaipur	..	..	..	..	..	..
37	Jashpur	..	..	..	..	..	..

Livelihood—General Distribution—*contd.*

TABLE X

of raw materials—*contd.*

of animals and vegetation—*contd.*

and agriculture—*contd.*

(planters, managers, clerks and labourers)—*contd.*

13.—Pan-vine.						14.—Rubber.						Serial No.
Total earners (principal occupations.)		Total working dependants.		Total following occupation as subsidiary to other.		Total earners (principal occupations.)		Total working dependants.		Total following occupation as subsidiary to other.		
Males.	Females.	Males.	Females.	Males.	Females.	Males.	Females.	Males.	Females.	Males.	Females.	
102	103	104	105	106	107	108	109	110	111	112	113	
1,840	866	152	599	366	44	..	1	..	..	..	..	
1,818	866	148	598	364	44	..	1	..	..	..	..	
408	113	27	43	39	18	..	1	..	..	..	..	
104	*38*	7	7	*24*	*1*	..	..	..	..	..	..	
34	6	..	..	13	..	..	..	..	..	..	..	1
..	..	..	2	..	..	..	..	..	..	..	..	2
7	15	3	5	2	..	..	..	..	..	..	..	3
5	*3*	..	..	*1*	..	..	..	..	..	..	..	
63	17	4	..	9	1	..	..	..	..	..	..	4
..	..	..	..	..	..	..	..	..	..	..	..	5
90	*11*	*14*	*20*	..	*1*	..	..	..	..	..	..	
19	..	9	3	..	..	..	..	..	..	..	..	6
19	10	..	5	..	1	..	..	..	..	..	..	7
49	1	5	12	..	..	..	..	..	..	..	..	8
..	..	..	..	..	..	..	..	..	..	..	..	9
3	..	..	..	..	..	..	..	..	..	..	..	10
203	*29*	*6*	*10*	*1*	..	..	..	..	..	..	..	
..	..	..	..	..	..	..	..	..	..	..	..	11
123	29	6	10	1	..	..	..	..	..	..	..	12
..	..	..	..	..	..	..	..	..	..	..	..	
77	..	..	..	..	..	..	..	..	..	..	..	13
3	..	..	..	..	..	..	..	..	..	..	..	14
..	..	..	..	..	..	..	..	..	..	..	..	15
11	*35*	..	*6*	*14*	*16*	..	*1*	..	..	..	..	
..	..	..	..	..	..	..	1	..	..	..	..	16
5	31	..	3	11	16	..	..	..	..	..	..	17
6	4	..	3	3	..	..	..	..	..	..	..	18
1,410	753	121	555	325	26	..	..	..	..	..	..	
1,175	567	90	422	267	17	..	..	..	..	..	..	19
215	153	3	23	25	5	..	..	..	..	..	..	20
9	18	28	110	26	4	..	..	..	..	..	..	21
11	15	..	..	7	..	..	..	..	..	..	..	22
22	..	4	1	2	..	..	..	..	..	..	..	
..	..	..	..	..	..	..	..	..	..	..	..	23
1	..	..	..	..	..	..	..	..	..	..	..	24
7	..	1	..	2	..	..	..	..	..	..	..	25
3	..	3	..	..	..	..	..	..	..	..	..	26
11	..	..	1	..	..	..	..	..	..	..	..	27
..	..	..	..	..	..	..	..	..	..	..	..	28
..	..	..	..	..	..	..	..	..	..	..	..	29
..	..	..	..	..	..	..	..	..	..	..	..	30
..	..	..	..	..	..	..	..	..	..	..	..	31
..	..	..	..	..	..	..	..	..	..	..	..	32
..	..	..	..	..	..	..	..	..	..	..	..	33
..	..	..	..	..	..	..	..	..	..	..	..	34
..	..	..	..	..	..	..	..	..	..	..	..	35
..	..	..	..	..	..	..	..	..	..	..	..	36
..	..	..	..	..	..	..	..	..	..	..	..	37

TABLE X — Occupation or means of

Serial No.	Class .. / Sub-class .. / Order .. / Sub-order .. / Group ..	Class A.—Production / Sub-class I.—Exploitation / Order 1.—Pasture / Sub-order (b).—Cultivation of special crops, fruits, / 15.—Tea.					
	District, City or State.	Total earners (principal occupations).		Total working dependants.		Total following occupation as subsidiary to other.	
		Males.	Females.	Males.	Females.	Males.	Females.
1	2	114	115	116	117	118	119
	Central Provinces and Berar ..	213	12	..	..	50	..
	C. P. British Districts and Berar	194	7	..	..	49	..
	C. P. British Districts ..	178	7	..	..	44	..
	Jubbulpore Division	*47*	*1*	..	..	*2*	..
1	Saugor ..	15	..	..	..	..	..
2	Damoh ..	6	..	..	..	2	..
3	Jubbulpore ..	21	..	..	..	..	..
	Jubbulpore City ..	*20*	..	..	..	..	..
4	Mandla ..	3	1	..	..	..	..
5	Seoni ..	2	..	..	..	..	..
	Nerbudda Division ..	*81*	..	..	..	*41*	..
6	Narsinghpur ..	..	..	..	..	..	..
7	Hoshangabad ..	16	..	..	..	..	..
8	Nimar ..	1	..	..	..	..	..
9	Betul ..	64	..	..	..	41	..
10	Chhindwara ..	..	..	..	..	..	..
	Nagpur Division ..	*2*	*4*	..	..	*1*	..
11	Wardha ..	..	..	..	..	..	..
12	Nagpur ..	..	..	..	..	..	..
	Nagpur City ..	..	..	..	..	..	..
13	Chanda ..	2	4	..	..	1	..
14	Bhandara ..	..	..	..	..	..	..
15	Balaghat ..	..	..	..	..	..	..
	Chhattisgarh Division ..	*48*	*2*	..	..	..	..
16	Raipur ..	26	1	..	..	..	..
17	Bilaspur ..	21	1	..	..	..	..
18	Drug ..	1	..	..	..	..	..
	Berar ..	16	..	..	..	5	..
19	Amraoti ..	16	..	..	..	5	..
20	Akola ..	..	..	..	..	..	..
21	Buldana ..	..	..	..	..	..	..
22	Yeotmal ..	..	..	..	..	..	..
	Central Provinces States ..	19	5	..	..	1	..
23	Makrai ..	..	..	..	..	..	..
24	Bastar ..	2	..	..	..	..	..
25	Kanker ..	..	..	..	..	..	..
26	Nandgaon ..	..	..	..	..	..	..
27	Khairagarh ..	..	..	..	..	..	..
28	Chhuikhadan ..	..	..	..	..	..	..
29	Kawardha ..	..	..	..	..	..	..
30	Sakti ..	..	..	..	..	..	..
31	Raigarh ..	..	..	..	..	..	..
32	Sarangarh ..	..	..	..	..	..	..
33	Changbhakar ..	..	..	..	..	..	..
34	Korea ..	..	..	..	..	..	..
35	Surguja ..	..	..	..	..	..	..
36	Udaipur ..	..	..	..	..	..	..
37	Jashpur ..	17	5	..	..	1	..

of raw materials—*contd.*

of animals and vegetation—*contd.*

and agriculture—*contd.*

etc. (planters, managers, clerks and labourers)—*concld.* | Sub-order (*c*).—Forestry.

16.—Market gardeners, flower and fruit growers. | Total sub-order (*c*).

16. Total earners (principal occupations). Males.	Females.	Total working dependants. Males.	Females.	Total following occupation as subsidiary to other. Males.	Females.	Total sub-order (c). Total earners (principal occupations). Males.	Females.	Total working dependants Males.	Females.	Total following occupation as subsidiary to other. Males.	Females.	Serial No.
120	121	122	123	124	125	126	127	128	129	130	131	
7,682	**1,971**	**1,418**	**2,370**	**5,484**	**1,245**	**10,975**	**3,849**	**472**	**1,338**	**5,083**	**1,058**	
6,770	**1,651**	**855**	**1,473**	**4,517**	**1,214**	**9,723**	**3,370**	**355**	**1,034**	**4,608**	**1,022**	
6,279	**1,585**	**817**	**1,423**	**4,407**	**1,188**	**8,629**	**3.114**	**280**	**953**	**4,220**	**907**	
2,309	*254*	*74*	*94*	*871*	*46*	*1,946*	*1,029*	*53*	*281*	*699*	*267*	
283	40	24	27	65	5	379	137	13	88	121	14	1
369	22	4	1	121	4	247	155	4	[illegible]	169	145	2
949	133	28	50	576	33	525	503	33	130	251	78	3
412	*35*	*5*	*7*	*5*	*3*	*199*	*175*	*10*	*10*	*6*	*2*	
139	44	11	6	84	2	449	129	1	12	128	20	4
569	15	7	10	25	2	346	105	2	25	30	10	5
364	*42*	*38*	*71*	*355*	*11*	*2,873*	*583*	*120*	*361*	*2,391*	*195*	
19	4	..	..	4	..	137	84	..	12	85	31	6
216	21	35	68	312	7	929	301	27	146	715	54	7
99	10	3	3	25	4	435	8	18	6	85	2	8
13	1	..	..	6	..	1,123	105	17	69	1,246	99	9
17	6	..	..	8	..	249	85	58	128	260	9	10
1,135	*123*	*24*	*32*	*311*	*37*	*2,660*	*1,132*	*70*	*269*	*720*	*319*	
118	13	1	3	30	5	168	99	1	20	9	23	11
661	66	1	6	65	10	508	285	6	146	68	46	12
222	*43*	..	..	*2*	..	*231*	*15*	*2*	*1*	*20*	.	
154	33	..	12	91	21	1,164	688	27	92	402	228	13
140	11	14	1	56	..	300	34	4	3	164	21	14
62	..	8	10	69	1	520	26	32	8	77	1	15
2,471	*1,166*	*681*	*1,226*	*2,870*	*1,094*	*1,150*	*370*	*37*	*42*	*410*	*126*	
1,293	930	400	687	965	254	628	285	30	17	246	98	16
278	174	6	77	1,047	564	370	61	7	20	142	26	17
900	62	275	462	858	276	152	24	..	5	22	2	18
491	**66**	**38**	**50**	**110**	**26**	**1,094**	**256**	**75**	**81**	**388**	**115**	
124	14	..	3	22	20	468	132	53	76	247	9	19
117	18	28	34	50	4	318	44	3	3	53	81	20
88	17	4	12	26	2	152	28	19	..	80	25	21
162	17	6	1	12	..	156	52	..	2	8	..	22
912	**320**	**563**	**897**	**967**	**31**	**1,252**	**479**	**117**	**304**	**475**	**36**	
1	..	..	..	..	..	23	1	..	..	..	..	23
92	28	29	36	38	1	264	31	1	7	7	1	24
124	20	59	100	116	..	96	1	7	..	5	..	25
151	50	59	156	88	1	56	4	1	..	..	..	26
161	104	69	317	134	4	65	51	14	1	48	..	27
6	..	300	..	20	..	19	22	..	15	2	6	28
103	35	4	..	426	10	47	80	35	92	136	17	29
211	67	39	202	11	10	..	..	..	..	..	..	30
1	..	..	..	..	..	87	17	11	9	11	2	31
..	13	2	67	128	1	29	37	..	..	1	..	32
1	1	1	..	1	4	129	40	6	80	43	2	33
4	..	..	..	..	..	100	73	..	2	70	8	34
25	1	1	19	1	..	135	39	41	98	129	..	35
17	1	..	..	2	..	105	37	1	..	18	..	36
14	..	..	..	2	..	97	46	..	..	5	..	37

TABLE X — **Occupation or means of**

Serial No.	Class .. / Sub-class .. / Order .. / Sub-order . / Group ..	Class A —Production / Sub-class I.— Exploitation / Order 1.—Pasture / Sub-order (c).— / 17.—Forest officers, rangers, guards, etc.					
	District, City or State.	Total earners (principal occupations).		Total working dependants.		Total following occupation as subsidiary to other.	
		Males.	Females.	Males.	Females.	Males.	Females.
1	2	132	133	134	135	136	137
	Central Provinces and Berar	**5,336**	**178**	**69**	**31**	**569**	**96**
	C. P. British Districts and Berar ..	**4,811**	**170**	**67**	**31**	**547**	**96**
	C. P. British Districts	**4,330**	**169**	**66**	**31**	**473**	**96**
	Jubbulpore Division .. .	*991*	*6*	*1*	*8*	*66*	..
1	Saugor .. .	176	1	..	1	6	..
2	Damoh .. .	211	.	.	..	1	..
3	Jubbulpore	102	1	.	..	11	..
	Jubbulpore City	*28*	..	.	..	..	..
4	Mandla	320	4	1	7	33	..
5	Seoni	182	..	..	.	15	..
	Nerbudda Division .. .	*1,661*	*32*	*60*	*14*	*297*	*65*
6	Narsinghpur	69	12	..	..	7	..
7	Hoshangabad	219	5	..	..	5	26
8	Nimar	256	..	2	..	9	..
9	Betul	923	15	6	14	71	39
10	Chhindwara	194	..	52	..	205	..
	Nagpur Division	*1,165*	*5*	*5*	..	*72*	..
11	Wardha	65	..	..	..	..	..
12	Nagpur	161	..	..	..	1	..
	Nagpur City	*22*	..	..	..	..	..
13	Chanda	287	3	..	..	8	..
14	Bhandara .. .	173	1	2	..	7	..
15	Balaghat	479	1	3	..	56	..
	Chhattisgarh Division .. .	*513*	*126*	..	*9*	*38*	*31*
16	Raipur .. .	311	126	.	9	11	31
17	Bilaspur	72	..	..	..	16	..
18	Drug	130	..	..	..	11	..
	Berar	**481**	**1**	**1**	..	**74**	..
19	Amraoti	202	1	1	..	14	..
20	Akola .. .	90	..	..	..	2	..
21	Buldana	57	..	..	..	50	..
22	Yeotmal	132	..	..	..	8	..
	Central Provinces States	**525**	**8**	**2**	..	**22**	..
23	Makrai	21	1	..	..	..	..
24	Bastar	144	7	..	..	4	..
25	Kanker	56	..	..	..	1	..
26	Nandgaon	49	..	1	..	..	..
27	Khairagarh	29	..	..	..	..	..
28	Chhuikhadan	19	..	..	..	2	..
29	Kawardha	38	..	..	..	2	..
30	Sakti	..	..	..	..	..	..
31	Raigarh	35	..	..	..	4	..
32	Sarangarh	17	..	..	..	1	..
33	Changbhakar	..	..	..	..	..	..
34	Korea	8	..	..	..	..	..
35	Surguja	3	..	..	..	3	..
36	Udaipur	17	..	1	..	..	..
37	Jashpur	89	..	..	..	5	..

of raw materials—*contd.*

of animals and vegetation—*contd*

and agriculture *contd.*

Forestry - *contd*

18 —Wood-cutters and charcoal burners.						19 —Collectors of forest produce.						Serial No.
Total earners (principal occupations)		Total working dependants.		Total following occupation as sub-sidiary to other		Total earners (principal occupations).		Total working dependants.		Total following occupation as sub-sidiary to other.		
Males	Females	Males	Females	Males	Females	Males	Females	Males.	Females	Males.	Females.	
138	139	140	141	142	143	144	145	146	147	148	149	
3,041	**314**	**161**	**234**	**2,937**	**133**	**2,549**	**3,260**	**242**	**1,069**	**1,369**	**784**	
2,697	**233**	**133**	**111**	**2,725**	**130**	**2,191**	**2,875**	**155**	**858**	**1,186**	**758**	
2,241	**214**	**81**	**139**	**2,483**	**93**	**2,034**	**2,639**	**133**	**779**	**1,112**	**680**	
512	*150*	*14*	*31*	*270*	*47*	*429*	*832*	*38*	*241*	*260*	*208*	
64	20	.	1	16	.	133	114	13	86	87	14	1
11	3	..	.	20		21	118	4	26	57	138	2
301	48	14	16	166	42	118	449	19	113	74	31	3
162	*1*	6	..	*6*		*9*	*174*	*4*	*9*	..	*2*	
19	4	..	5	63	3	110	121	.	..	27	17	4
117	75	.	9	..	2	47	30	2	16	15	8	5
945	*54*	*48*	*106*	*1,896*	*35*	*258*	*446*	*12*	*238*	*149*	*69*	
27	11	.	3	14	.	35	56	..	9	15	14	6
566	27	23	49	655	4	142	225	4	97	57	15	7
147	2	16	3	69	2	32	6	..	3	7	..	8
183	14	9	51	1,158	29	17	76	2	1	17	31	9
22	..	.	..	2	.	32	83	6	128	53	9	10
468	*9*	..	*2*	*112*	*4*	*1,026*	*1,118*	*65*	*267*	*536*	*315*	
80	4	..	2	9	4	23	95	1	18	..	19	11
303	3	.	.	49	..	44	282	6	146	18	46	12
190	*2*	..	.	*19*	..	*19*	*13*	*2*	*1*	*1*	..	
71	2	..	..	52	..	806	683	27	92	342	228	13
4	..	.	.	.	.	122	33	2	3	157	21	14
10	..	..	.	2	.	31	25	29	8	19	1	15
316	*1*	*19*	..	*205*	*7*	*321*	*243*	*18*	*33*	*167*	*88*	
177	.	19	.	195	7	140	159	11	8	40	60	16
120	1	..	.	1	..	178	60	7	20	125	26	17
19		.	.	9	.	3	24	..	5	2	2	18
456	**19**	**52**	**2**	**240**	**37**	**157**	**236**	**22**	**79**	**74**	**78**	
209	.	51	..	211	.	57	131	1	76	22	9	19
188	14	1	2	13	37	40	30	2	1	38	44	20
35	..	..	..	16	.	60	28	19	..	14	25	21
24	5	..	..	..	..	..	47	.	2	..	..	22
344	**81**	**28**	**93**	**214**	**3**	**358**	**385**	**87**	**211**	**183**	**26**	
2	..	..	..	..	.	..	..	..	..	..	..	23
105	..	1	6	3	.	12	23	..	1	..	1	24
22	..	7	..	..	.	.	..	..	..	..	..	25
6	..	..	..	..	.	1	4	..	..	..	..	26
35	..	14	..	48	.	1	51	..	1	..	..	27
..	..	..	..	..	..	..	22	..	15	..	6	28
..	..	..	.	97	..	9	80	35	92	37	17	29
..	..	..	..	..	..	..	..	..	..	..	..	30
..	..	..	..	..	..	52	17	11	9	7	2	31
..	..	..	..	..	..	12	37	..	..	..	..	32
129	40	6	80	43	2	..	..	..	..	..	..	33
44	40	..	2	14	1	44	30	..	..	4	..	34
..	1	..	5	9	..	132	38	41	93	117	..	35
..	..	..	..	..	..	88	37	..	..	18	..	36
1	..	..	..	..	..	7	46	..	..	..	..	37

TABLE X — Occupation or means of

Serial No.	Class .. / Sub-class .. / Order .. / Sub-order .. / Group .. / District, City or State.	Class A.—Production / Sub-class I.—Exploitation / Order 1.—Pasture / Sub-order (c) Forestry—concld. / 20.—Collectors of lac. Total earners (principal occupations). Males.	Total earners (principal occupations). Females.	Total working dependants. Males.	Total working dependants. Females.	Total following occupation as subsidiary to other. Males.	Total following occupation as subsidiary to other. Females.
1	2	150	151	152	153	154	155
	Central Provinces and Berar	49	97	..	4	208	45
	C. P. British Districts and Berar	24	92	..	4	152	38
	C. P. British Districts	24	92	..	4	152	38
	Jubbulpore Division	*14*	*41*	..	*1*	*103*	*12*
1	Saugor	6	2	..	..	12	..
2	Damoh	4	34	..	..	91	7
3	Jubbulpore	4	5	..	1	..	5
	Jubbulpore City	..	..	..	*1*	..	..
4	Mandla	..	..	..	..	..	..
5	Seoni	..	..	..	..	..	..
	Nerbudda Division	*9*	*51*	..	*3*	*49*	*26*
6	Narsinghpur	6	5	..	..	49	17
7	Hoshangabad	2	44	..	..	..	9
8	Nimar	..	..	..	..	..	..
9	Betul	..	..	..	3	..	..
10	Chhindwara	1	2	..	..	..	..
	Nagpur Division	*1*	..	..	..	..	..
11	Wardha	..	..	..	..	..	..
12	Nagpur	..	..	..	..	..	..
	Nagpur City	..	..	..	..	..	..
13	Chanda	..	..	..	..	..	..
14	Bhandara	1	..	..	..	..	..
15	Balaghat	..	..	..	..	..	..
	Chhattisgarh Division	..	..	..	..	..	..
16	Raipur	..	..	..	..	..	..
17	Bilaspur	..	..	..	..	..	..
18	Drug	..	..	..	..	..	..
	Berar	..	..	..	..	..	..
19	Amraoti	..	..	..	..	..	..
20	Akola	..	..	..	..	..	..
21	Buldana	..	..	..	..	..	..
22	Yeotmal	..	..	..	..	..	..
	Central Provinces States	25	5	..	..	56	7
23	Makrai	..	..	..	..	..	..
24	Bastar	3	1	..	..	..	..
25	Kanker	18	1	..	..	4	..
26	Nandgaon	..	..	..	..	..	..
27	Khairagarh	..	..	..	..	..	..
28	Chhuikhadan	..	..	..	..	..	..
29	Kawardha	..	..	..	..	..	..
30	Sakti	..	..	..	..	..	..
31	Raigarh	..	..	..	..	..	..
32	Sarangarh	..	..	..	..	..	..
33	Changbhakar	..	..	..	..	..	..
34	Korea	4	3	..	..	52	7
35	Surguja	..	..	..	..	..	..
36	Udaipur	..	..	..	..	..	..
37	Jashpur	..	..	..	..	..	..

Livelihood—General Distribution—*contd.*

TABLE X

of raw materials—*contd.*

of animals and vegetation—*contd.*

and agriculture—*contd.*

Sub-order (*d*).—Stock-raising.

Total sub-order (*d*).						21.—Cattle and buffalo breeders and keepers.						Serial No.
Total earners (principal occupations).		Total working dependants.		Total following occupation as subsidiary to other.		Total earners (principal occupation).		Total working dependants.		Total following occupation as subsidiary to other.		
Males.	Females.	Males.	Females.	Males.	Females.	Males.	Females.	Males.	Females.	Males.	Females.	
156	157	158	159	160	161	162	163	164	165	166	167	
180,525	**12,799**	**56,455**	**13,847**	**13,911**	**1,425**	**45,971**	**6,856**	**11,692**	**8,403**	**7,022**	**986**	
155,396	**10,322**	**46,979**	**8,663**	**12,008**	**1,318**	**31,536**	**4,878**	**5,904**	**4,735**	**5,560**	**896**	
131,456	**9,506**	**37,533**	**7,998**	**10,617**	**1,206**	**31,233**	**4,789**	**5,862**	**4,686**	**5,505**	**891**	
23,748	*1,590*	*5,110*	*912*	*1,240*	*63*	*1*	*1*	..	..	*1*	..	
5,061	120	2,260	83	144	5	1	..	..	..	..	..	1
3,248	715	509	132	204	11	..	..	..	..	..	..	2
4,582	425	558	294	499	34	..	1	..	..	1	..	3
161	*7*	*6*	..	*6*	*5*	..	..	..	..	..	..	
4,035	118	283	131	206	4	..	..	..	..	..	..	4
6,822	212	1,500	272	187	9	..	..	..	..	..	..	5
24,644	*923*	*12,180*	*1,075*	*1,081*	*50*	*18*	..	*1*	..	*6*	..	
2,373	284	1,598	364	185	13	..	..	..	..	..	..	6
6,780	155	2,775	137	264	12	..	..	..	..	..	..	7
3,226	98	1,843	110	185	2	18	..	1	..	6	..	8
6,484	133	2,497	90	305	2	..	..	..	..	..	..	9
5,781	253	3,467	374	142	21	..	..	..	..	..	..	10
45,926	*1,381*	*12,774*	*487*	*1,791*	*73*	*473*	*48*	*22*	*11*	*105*	..	
5,446	115	689	11	124	13	10	..	..	..	1	..	11
13,886	311	2,098	55	291	3	284	10	13	..	11	..	12
433	*20*	*42*	..	*12*	..	*279*	*10*	*13*	..	*9*	..	
12,143	248	2,894	133	508	14	86	33	5	11	1	..	13
10,483	647	4,426	198	712	41	87	5	4	..	91	..	14
3,968	60	2,667	90	156	2	6	..	..	..	1	..	15
37,138	*5,612*	*7,469*	*5,524*	*6,505*	*1,020*	*30,741*	*4,740*	*5,839*	*4,675*	*5,393*	*891*	
17,850	3,469	3,008	2,743	2,408	658	14,034	3,072	2,317	2,408	2,017	636	16
9,778	1,337	1,526	745	3,503	322	8,243	1,001	1,183	640	2,873	217	17
9,510	806	2,935	2,036	594	40	8,464	667	2,339	1,627	503	38	18
23,940	**816**	**9,446**	**665**	**1,391**	**112**	**303**	**89**	**42**	**49**	**55**	**5**	
5,357	272	1,454	99	351	18	257	58	34	10	11	3	19
4,528	198	2,170	77	305	12	31	24	2	9	21	1	20
5,459	130	2,725	62	352	9	8	..	6	2	9	..	21
8.596	216	3,097	427	383	73	7	7	..	28	14	1	22
25,129	**2,477**	**9,476**	**5,184**	**1,903**	**107**	**14,435**	**1,978**	**5,788**	**3,668**	**1,462**	**90**	
209	4	33	6	4	..	..	..	..	..	..	..	23
2,985	649	707	1,280	270	5	2,024	558	501	806	222	..	24
1,365	130	347	399	193	23	771	86	281	353	17c	20	25
2,456	82	394	381	124	6	1,470	49	213	244	84	6	26
3.400	246	356	218	92	9	822	202	79	112	66	5	27
601	34	232	170	45	6	587	34	219	170	44	6	28
1,633	416	540	40	61	39	1,592	401	516	24	54	38	29
325	90	194	38	85	12	325	90	194	38	85	12	30
1,342	68	1,160	469	238	1	757	54	904	461	193	1	31
960	13	459	11	55	..	741	13	413	11	37	..	32
553	76	38	9	17	..	553	76	38	9	17	..	33
993	21	50	2	67	1	902	18	42	2	66	1	34
3,906	200	2,325	766	443	5	1,650	122	432	353	255	1	35
1,264	20	7	..	100	..	1,188	19	7	..	98	..	36
3,137	428	2,634	1,395	109	..	1,053	256	1,949	1,085	65	..	37

TABLE X | Occupation or means of

Serial No.	Class .. / Sub-class .. / Order .. / Sub-order .. / Group .. — District, City or State.	Class A.—Production / Sub-class I.—Exploitation / Order 1.—Pasture / Sub-order (d).—Stock / 22.—Breeders of transport animals. Total earners (principal occupations). Males.	Females.	Total working dependants. Males.	Females.	Total following occupation as subsidiary to other. Males.	Females.
1	2	168	169	170	171	172	173
	Central Provinces and Berar ..	**148**	**3**	**11**	**7**	**4**	..
	C. P. British Districts and Berar ..	**126**	**3**	**11**	**7**	**4**	..
	C. P. British Districts	**118**	**3**	**10**	**4**	**3**	..
	Jubbulpore Division .. .	*44*	..	..	..	*1*	..
1	Saugor .. .	30	..	..	..	..	..
2	Damoh .. .	3	..	..	..	..	..
3	Jubbulpore	5	..	..	..	..	..
	Jubbulpore City . ..	*1*	..	..	..	..	..
4	Mandla	2	..	..	..	..	..
5	Seoni	4	..	..	..	1	..
	Nerbudda Division . ..	*25*	..	..	*2*	*1*	..
6	Narsinghpur	7	..	..	..	1	..
7	Hoshangabad	2	..	..	2	..	..
8	Nimar	..	..	..	..	..	..
9	Betul	5	..	..	..	..	..
10	Chhindwara . .	11	..	..	..	..	..
	Nagpur Division	*25*	*2*	*10*	*2*	*1*	..
11	Wardha	5	1	6	2	1	..
12	Nagpur	4	1	4	..	..	..
	Nagpur City	..	..	..	..	..	..
13	Chanda	..	..	..	..	..	..
14	Bhandara . ..	..	..	..	..	..	..
15	Balaghat	10	..	..	..	..	..
	Chhattisgarh Division	*24*	*1*	..	..	..	..
16	Raipur	..	1	..	..	..	..
17	Bilaspur	17	..	..	..	..	..
18	Drug	7	..	..	..	..	..
	Berar	**8**	..	**1**	**3**	**1**	..
19	Amraoti	2	..	..	..	1	..
20	Akola	3	..	1	..	..	..
21	Buldana	..	..	..	..	..	..
22	Yeotmal	3	..	..	3	..	..
	Central Provinces States	**22**	..	..	..	..	..
23	Makrai	..	..	..	..	..	..
24	Bastar	1	..	..	..	..	..
25	Kanker	..	..	..	..	..	..
26	Nandgaon	..	..	..	..	..	..
27	Khairagarh	..	..	..	..	..	..
28	Chhuikhadan	..	..	..	..	..	..
29	Kawardha	1	..	..	..	..	..
30	Sakti	..	..	..	..	..	..
31	Raigarh	..	..	..	..	..	..
32	Sarangarh	..	..	..	..	..	..
33	Changbhakar	..	..	..	..	..	..
34	Korea	..	..	..	..	..	..
35	Surguja	..	..	..	..	..	..
36	Udaipur	7	..	..	..	..	..
37	Jashpur	13	..	..	..	..	..

of raw materials—*contd.*

of animals and vegetation—*contd.*

and agriculture—*contd.*

raising—*concld.*						**Sub-order (*e*).—Raising of small animals and insects.**						
23.—Herdsmen, shepherds and breeders of other animals.						**Total sub-order (*e*).**						**Serial No.**
Total earners (principal occupations).		Total working dependants.		Total following occupation as subsidiary to other.		Total earners (principal occupations)		Total working dependants.		Total following occupation as subsidiary to other.		
Males.	Females.	Males	Females.	Males.	Females.	Males.	Females.	Males.	Females.	Males.	Females.	
174	175	176	177	178	179	180	181	182	183	184	185	
134,406	**5,940**	**44,752**	**5,437**	**6,885**	**439**	**937**	**462**	**19**	**159**	**1,456**	**278**	
123,734	**5,441**	**41,064**	**3,921**	**6,444**	**422**	**697**	**415**	**6**	**14**	**817**	**228**	
100,105	**4,714**	**31,661**	**3,308**	**5,109**	**315**	**696**	**415**	**5**	**14**	**817**	**228**	
23,703	*1,589*	*5,110*	*912*	*1,238*	*63*	*34*	*3*	*1*	*5*	*135*	*2*	
5,030	120	2,260	83	144	5	2	..	..	..	..	..	
3,245	715	509	132	204	11	4	3	..	..	67	..	2
4,577	424	558	294	498	34	4	..	..	5	3	2	3
160	*7*	*6*	..	*6*	*5*	..	..	..	..	..	..	
4,033	118	283	131	206	4	24	..	1	..	65	..	4
6,818	212	1,500	272	186	9	..	..	..	..	..	..	5
24,601	*923*	*12,179*	*1,073*	*1,074*	*50*	*240*	*165*	*4*	*3*	*120*	*4*	
2,366	284	1,598	364	184	13	21	..	..	..	1	..	6
6,778	155	2,775	135	264	12	186	165	2	1	71	2	7
3,208	98	1,842	110	179	2	2	..	..	..	..	..	8
6,479	133	2,497	90	305	2	..	..	..	..	..	..	9
5,770	253	3,467	374	142	21	31	..	2	2	48	2	10
45,428	*1,331*	*12,742*	*474*	*1,685*	*73*	*90*	*126*	..	*2*	*242*	*218*	
5,431	114	683	9	122	13	2	..	..	..	..	..	11
13,598	300	2,081	55	280	3	4	..	..	..	..	..	12
154	*10*	*29*	..	*3*	..	..	..	..	..	..	..	
12,057	215	2,889	122	507	14	2	15	..	1	..	2	13
10,396	642	4,422	198	621	41	..	..	..	..	..	..	14
3,946	60	2,667	90	155	2	82	111	..	1	242	216	15
6,373	*871*	*1,630*	*849*	*1,112*	*129*	*332*	*121*	..	*4*	*320*	*4*	
3,816	396	691	335	391	22	195	57	..	1	295	4	16
1,518	336	343	105	630	105	137	64	..	3	25	..	17
1,039	139	596	409	91	2	..	..	..	..	..	..	18
23,629	**727**	**9,403**	**613**	**1,335**	**107**	**1**	..	**1**	..	..	..	
5,098	214	1,420	89	339	15	1	..	1	..	..	..	19
4,494	174	2,167	68	284	11	..	..	..	..	..	..	20
5,451	130	2,719	60	343	9	..	..	..	..	..	..	21
8,586	209	3,097	396	369	72	..	..	..	..	..	..	22
10,672	**499**	**3,688**	**1,516**	**441**	**17**	**240**	**47**	**13**	**145**	**639**	**50**	
209	4	33	6	4	..	..	..	..	..	..	..	23
960	91	206	474	48	5	7	1	..	..	1	..	24
594	44	66	46	17	3	..	..	..	..	322	20	25
986	33	181	137	40		..	..	..	..	1	..	26
2,578	44	277	106	26	4	..	4	..	32	..	..	27
14	..	13	..	1	..	..	..	..	..	..	..	28
40	15	24	16	7	1	8	..	..	..	85	9	29
..	..	..	..	..	..	..	..	..	..	..	..	30
585	14	256	8	45	..	6	1	..	..	..	..	31
219	..	46	..	18	..	..	..	..	..	..	..	32
..	..	..	..	..	..	..	..	..	..	..	..	33
91	3	8	..	1	..	..	..	..	..	5	..	34
2,256	78	1,893	413	188	4	218	41	13	113	225	21	35
69	1	..	..	2	..	1	..	..	..	..	..	36
2,071	172	685	310	44	..	..	..	..	..	..	..	37

TABLE X — **Occupation or means of**

Serial No.	Class .. / Sub-class .. / Order .. / Sub-order .. / Group ..	Class A.—Production / Sub-class I.—Exploitation / Order 1.—Pasture / Sub-order (e).—Raising of / 24.—Birds, bees, etc.					
	District, City or State.	Total earners (principal occupations).		Total working dependants.		Total following occupation as subsidiary to other.	
		Males.	Females.	Males.	Females.	Males.	Females.
1	2	186	187	188	189	190	191
	Central Provinces and Berar ..	57	2	3	..	102	..
	C. P. British Districts and Berar ..	57	2	3	..	102	..
	C. P. British Districts	56	2	2	..	102	..
	Jubbulpore Division	*24*	..	*1*	..	*65*	..
1	Saugor	..	..	..	..	..	..
2	Damoh	..	..	..	..	..	..
3	Jubbulpore	..	..	..	..	..	..
	Jubbulpore City	..	..	..	..	..	..
4	Mandla	24	..	1	..	65	..
5	Seoni	..	..	..	..	..	..
	Nerbudda Division	*26*	..	*1*	..	*34*	..
6	Narsinghpur	..	..	..	..	..	..
7	Hoshangabad	26	..	1	..	34	..
8	Nimar	..	..	..	..	..	..
9	Betul	..	..	..	..	..	..
10	Chhindwara	..	..	..	..	..	..
	Nagpur Division	*6*	..	..	..	..	..
11	Wardha	2	..	..	..	..	..
12	Nagpur	4	..	..	..	..	..
	Nagpur City ..	..	..	..	..	..	..
13	Chanda	..	..	..	..	..	..
14	Bhandara	..	..	..	..	..	..
15	Balaghat	..	..	..	..	..	..
	Chhattisgarh Division	..	*2*	..	..	*3*	..
16	Raipur	..	..	..	..	..	..
17	Bilaspur	..	2	..	..	3	..
18	Drug	..	..	..	..	..	..
	Berar	*1*	..	*1*	..	..	..
19	Amraoti	1	..	1	..	..	..
20	Akola	..	..	..	..	..	..
21	Buldana	..	..	..	..	..	..
22	Yeotmal	..	..	..	..	..	..
	Central Provinces States	..	..	..	..	..	..
23	Makrai	..	..	..	..	..	..
24	Bastar	..	..	..	..	..	..
25	Kanker	..	..	..	..	..	..
26	Nandgaon	..	..	..	..	..	..
27	Khairagarh	..	..	..	..	..	..
28	Chhuikhadan	..	..	..	..	..	..
29	Kawardha	..	..	..	..	..	..
30	Sakti	..	..	..	..	..	..
31	Raigarh	..	..	..	..	..	..
32	Sarangarh	..	..	..	..	..	..
33	Changbhakar	..	..	..	..	..	..
34	Korea	..	..	..	..	..	..
35	Surguja	..	..	..	..	..	..
36	Udaipur	..	..	..	..	..	..
37	Jashpur	..	..	..	..	..	..

of raw materials—*contd*

of animals and vegetation—*contd.*

and agriculture—*contd*

small animals and insects—*concld*

25.—Silk-worms. Total earners (principal occupations). Males	Females	Total working dependants. Males.	Females	Total following occupation as subsidiary to other. Males	Females	26.—Lac cultivation. Total earners (principal occupations). Males	Females	Total working dependants. Males.	Females	Total following occupation as subsidiary to other. Males.	Females.	Serial No.
192	193	194	195	196	197	198	199	200	201	202	203	
..	4	..	32			880	456	16	127	1,354	278	
..	..	..	..	..	..	640	413	3	14	715	228	
..	..	..	..	..	..	640	413	3	14	715	228	
..	..	..	..	..	..	*10*	*3*	..	*5*	*70*	*2*	
..	..	..	..	..	..	2	..	..		..	..	1
..	..	..	..	..	..	4	3	..	..	67	..	2
..	..	..	..	..	..	4	..	..	5	3	2	3
..	..	..	..	..	..	..	..	..	..		..	
..	..	..	..	..	..	..	..	..		..	..	4
..	..	..	..	..	..		..	..		..	..	5
..	..	..	..	..	..	*214*	*165*	*3*	*3*	*86*	*4*	
..	..	..	..	..	..	21	..	..	..	1	..	6
..	..	..	..	..	..	160	165	1	1	37	2	7
..	..	..	..	..	..	2	..	..	..	..	..	8
..	..	..	..	..	..	..	..	..	..	..	..	9
..	..	..	..	..	..	31	..	2	2	48	2	10
..	..	..	..	..	..	*84*	*126*	..	*2*	*242*	*218*	
..	..	..	..	..	..	..	..	..	..	..	..	11
..	..	..	..	..	..	..	..	..	..	..	..	12
..	..	..	..	..	..	..	..	..	..	..	..	
..	..	..	..	..	..	2	15	..	1	..	2	13
..	..	..	..	..	..	..	..	..	..	..	..	14
..	..	..	..	..	..	82	111	..	1	242	216	15
..	..	..	..	..	..	*332*	*119*	..	*4*	*317*	*4*	
..	..	..	..	..	..	195	57	..	1	295	4	16
..	..	..	..	..	..	137	62	..	3	22	..	17
..	..	..	..	..	..	..	..	..	..	..	..	18
..	..	..	..	..	..	..	..	..	..	..	..	
..	..	..	..	..	..	..	..	..	..	..	..	19
..	..	..	..	..	..	..	..	..	..	..	..	20
..	..	..	..	..	..	..	..	..	..	..	..	21
..	..	..	..	..	..	..	..	..	..	..	..	22
..	4	..	32	..	..	240	43	13	113	639	50	
..	..	..	..	..	..	..	..	..	..	..	..	23
..	..	..	..	..	..	7	1	..	..	1	..	24
..	..	..	..	..	..	..	..	..	..	322	20	25
..	..	..	..	..	..	..	..	..	..	1	..	26
..	4	..	32	..	..	..	..	..	..	..	..	27
..	..	..	..	..	..	..	..	..	..	..	..	28
..	..	..	..	..	..	8	..	..	..	85	9	29
..	..	..	..	..	..	..	..	..	..	..	..	30
..	..	..	..	..	..	6	1	..	..	..	..	31
..	..	..	..	..	..	..	..	..	..	..	..	32
..	..	..	..	..	..	..	..	..	..	..	..	33
..	..	..	..	..	..	..	..	..	..	5	..	34
..	..	..	..	..	..	218	41	13	113	225	21	35
..	..	..	..	..	..	1	..	..	..	..	..	36
..	..	..	..	..	..	..	..	..	..	..	..	37

TABLE X — Occupation or means of

Serial No.	Class .. / Sub-class .. / Order .. / Sub-order .. / Group ..	Class A.—Production					
		Sub-class I.—Exploitation					
		Order 2.—Fishing					
		Total order 2.					
	District, City or State.	Total earners (principal occupations)		Total working dependants.		Total following occupation as subsidiary to other.	
		Males.	Females.	Males.	Females.	Males.	Females.
1	2	204	205	206	207	208	209
	Central Provinces and Berar ..	**41,014**	**6,295**	**2,084**	**1,980**	**12,210**	**1,433**
	C. P. British Districts and Berar ..	**39,374**	**6,081**	**1,822**	**1,664**	**11,384**	**1,425**
	C. P. British Districts	**34,014**	**4,841**	**1,517**	**1,473**	**9,746**	**1,015**
	Jubbulpore Division	*2,709*	*154*	*463*	*108*	*803*	*37*
1	Saugor	152	16	15	10	58	..
2	Damoh	642	3	230	1	78	3
3	Jubbulpore	657	47	211	60	369	14
	Jubbulpore City	*99*	*29*	..	..	*67*	..
4	Mandla	330	44	4	14	168	5
5	Seoni	928	44	3	23	130	15
	Nerbudda Division	*2,462*	*121*	*59*	*124*	*675*	*15*
6	Narsinghpur	142	7	3	6	128	1
7	Hoshangabad	674	5	10	4	158	2
8	Nimar	538	13	9	1	154	3
9	Betul	462	58	9	36	112	3
10	Chhindwara	646	36	28	77	123	6
	Nagpur Division	*23,014*	*3,116*	*490*	*692*	*3,151*	*574*
11	Wardha	2,008	478	20	83	328	79
12	Nagpur	2,995	607	25	36	438	72
	Nagpur City	*163*	*17*	*2*	..	*11*	..
13	Chanda	8,552	991	140	288	1,365	181
14	Bhandara	5,455	608	194	118	694	135
15	Balaghat	4,004	432	111	167	326	107
	Chhattisgarh Division	*5,829*	*1,450*	*505*	*549*	*5,117*	*389*
16	Raipur	2,719	1,061	231	182	2,105	266
17	Bilaspur	1,541	304	67	89	2,330	105
18	Drug	1,569	85	207	278	682	18
	Berar	**5,360**	**1,240**	**305**	**191**	**1,638**	**410**
19	Amraoti	1,683	593	83	127	794	312
20	Akola	655	75	8	12	365	31
21	Buldana	290	38	1	5	175	23
22	Yeotmal	2,732	534	213	47	304	44
	Central Provinces States	**1,640**	**214**	**262**	**316**	**826**	**8**
23	Makrai	..	..	..	..	13	4
24	Bastar	254	33	50	80	97	2
25	Kanker	106	5	39	56	128	..
26	Nandgaon	405	31	24	63	51	1
27	Khairagarh	232	59	27	48	58	..
28	Chhuikhadan	44	8	..	2	26	1
29	Kawardha	187	1	1	..	61	..
30	Sakti	7	3	2	29	37	..
31	Raigarh	170	11	101	13	26	..
32	Sarangarh	134	..	16	..	207	..
33	Changbhakar	9	6		1	20	..
34	Korea	7	..	..	..	11	..
35	Surguja	10	..	1	2	16	..
36	Udaipur	18	..	..	..	16	..
37	Jashpur	57	57	1	22	59	..

Livelihood—General distribution—*contd.*

TABLE X

…of raw materials—*contd.*

…of animals and vegetation—*concld.*

…and hunting.

27.—Fishing and pearling						28.—Hunting.						Serial No.
Total earners (principal occupations).		Total working dependants.		Total following occupation as subsidiary to other		Total earners (principal occupations).		Total working dependants		Total following occupation as subsidiary to other		
Males.	Females.	Males.	Females	Males	Females	Males	Females.	Males	Females	Males.	Females	
210	211	212	213	214	215	216	217	218	219	220	221	
37,522	**6,015**	**1,661**	**1,847**	**11,097**	**1,390**	**3,492**	**280**	**423**	**133**	**1,113**	**43**	
36,006	**5,804**	**1,402**	**1,557**	**10,360**	**1,383**	**3,368**	**277**	**420**	**107**	**1,024**	**42**	
31,537	**4,690**	**1,117**	**1,379**	**8,855**	**993**	**2,477**	**151**	**400**	**94**	**891**	**22**	
1,603	*115*	*97*	*40*	*706*	*33*	*1,106*	*39*	*366*	*68*	*77*	*4*	
65	1	14		49	.	87	15	1	10	9		1
33	..	..	.	46		609	3	230	1	32	3	2
292	34	76	3	330	13	365	13	135	57	39	1	3
92	*29*	.	..	*67*		*7*	.		.	..		
303	44	4	14	157	5	27	..	.	.	11		4
910	36	3	23	124	15	18	8			6		5
2,273	*113*	*54*	*124*	*461*	*14*	*189*	*8*	*5*		*214*	*1*	
130	7	3	6	125	1	12				3	.	6
613	4	9	4	107	1	61	1	1		51	1	7
450	7	7	1	135	3	88	6	2	..	19		8
455	58	9	36	24	3	7	.	.	.	88		9
625	37	26	77	70	6	21	1	2	..	53	.	10
22,419	*3,068*	*482*	*666*	*2,939*	*573*	*595*	*48*	*8*	*24*	*212*	*1*	
1,864	465	19	59	310	78	144	13	1	24	18	1	11
2,700	580	21	36	341	72	295	27	4		97		12
124	..	*2*		*11*		*30*	*17*			.	.	
8,427	989	137	288	1,314	181	125	2	3		51		13
5,445	603	194	118	664	135	10	5		.	30		14
3,983	431	111	167	310	107	21	1		..	16		15
5,212	*1,394*	*484*	*547*	*4,749*	*373*	*587*	*56*	*21*	*2*	*368*	*16*	
2,322	1,032	220	182	1,865	254	397	29	11	.	240	12	16
1,447	278	62	87	2,223	101	94	26	5	2	107	4	17
1,473	84	202	278	661	18	96	1	5		21		18
4,469	**1,114**	**285**	**178**	**1,505**	**390**	**891**	**126**	**20**	**13**	**133**	**20**	
1,506	574	82	125	743	299	177	19	1	2	51	13	19
402	37	3	4	326	30	253	38	5	8	39	1	20
239	35	1	5	155	23	51	3	.		20	.	21
2,322	468	199	44	281	38	410	66	14	3	25	6	22
1,516	**211**	**259**	**290**	**737**	**7**	**124**	**3**	**3**	**26**	**59**	**1**	
..	..	.	..	.	4			.		13	.	23
234	33	47	76	81	1	20		3	4	16	1	24
102	5	39	54	101		4		..	2	27		25
365	31	24	63	51	1	40						26
216	59	27	28	57		16						27
32	8	.	2	26	1	12	.		20	1		28
172	1	1	..	60		15	.					29
7	3	2	29	37				.		1		30
166	11	101	13	26	..	4			.			31
134	..	16		207			..				.	32
9	6		1	.	.	.					.	33
5	..	..	.		.				.	20	.	34
10	..	1	2	16	..	2	.	.		11	.	35
13	..	.	.	16		..	.	.				36
51	54	1	22	59	..	5		..	..	.		
						6	3	..	.	.		37

TABLE X Occupation or means of

Serial No.	Class .. / Sub-class .. / Order .. / Sub-order .. / Group ..	Class A.—Production / Sub-class II.—Exploitation / Total sub-class II.					
	District, City or State.	Total carriers (principal occupations).		Total working dependants.		Total following occupation as subsidiary to other.	
		Males.	Females.	Males.	Females.	Males.	Females.
1	2	222	223	224	225	226	227
	Central Provinces and Berar	**14,074**	**7,972**	**141**	**366**	**1,182**	**810**
	C. P. British Districts and Berar ..	**13,952**	**7,911**	**133**	**272**	**1,136**	**789**
	C. P. British Districts	**11,882**	**7,209**	**92**	**149**	**1,055**	**755**
	Jubbulpore Division	*233*	*66*	*1*	*6*	*106*	*3*
1	Saugor	71	14	..	4	97	3
2	Damoh	16	..	..	..	..	..
3	Jubbulpore	142	52	1	2	8	..
	Jubbulpore City	*18*	..	..	..	..	..
4	Mandla	..	..	..	..	1	..
5	Seoni	4	..	..	..	..	..
	Nerbudda Division	*3,136*	*1,751*	*16*	*13*	*471*	*55*
6	Narsinghpur	57	40	..	..	2	..
7	Hoshangabad	488	177	3	..	26	..
8	Nimar	136	2	3	..	68	4
9	Betul	52	45	..	1	12	11
10	Chhindwara	2,403	1,487	10	12	363	40
	Nagpur Division	*8,328*	*5,340*	*58*	*112*	*436*	*676*
11	Wardha	182	134	..	..	19	..
12	Nagpur	2,774	2,056	8	40	45	14
	Nagpur City	*38*	*13*	..	..	*1*	..
13	Chanda	1,662	275	4	1	51	3
14	Bhandara	1,852	1,505	11	2	198	599
15	Balaghat	1,858	1,370	35	69	123	60
	Chhattisgarh Division	*185*	*52*	*17*	*18*	*42*	*21*
16	Raipur	132	28	13	7	14	17
17	Bilaspur	32	22	1	..	18	4
18	Drug	21	2	3	11	10	..
	Berar	**2,070**	**702**	**41**	**123**	**81**	**34**
19	Amraoti	290	210	5	2	38	5
20	Akola	456	253	8	10	9	25
21	Buldana	602	84	19	4	16	2
22	Yeotmal	722	155	9	107	18	2
	Central Provinces States	**122**	**61**	**8**	**94**	**46**	**21**
23	Makrai	6	11	..	..	..	..
24	Bastar	17	8	8	19	3	..
25	Kanker	2	..	..	..	2	..
26	Nandgaon	6	..	..	..	2	..
27	Khairagarh	15	..	..	14	..	..
28	Chhuikhadan	..	..	..	..	..	..
29	Kawardha	..	..	..	..	..	..
30	Sakti	..	..	..	..	..	..
31	Raigarh	..	..	..	..	..	..
32	Sarangarh	17	..	..	..	..	..
33	Changbhakar	..	..	..	..	..	..
34	Korea	4	..	..	..	..	..
35	Surguja	26	7	..	1	..	..
36	Udaipur	..	5	..	..	..	..
37	Jashpur	29	30	..	60	39	21

of raw materials—*contd.*

of minerals—*contd.*

Order 3.—Metallic minerals.

Total order 3.						29.—Gold.						
Total earners (principal occupations).		Total working dependants.		Total following occupation as subsidiary to other.		Total earners (principal occupations).		Total working dependants.		Total following occupation as subsidiary to other.		Serial No.
Males.	Females.	Males.	Females.	Males.	Females.	Males.	Females.	Males.	Females.	Males.	Females.	
228	229	230	231	232	233	234	235	236	237	238	239	
5,644	**4,469**	**51**	**180**	**356**	**692**	**79**	**51**	**10**	**103**	**47**	**23**	
5,558	**4,426**	**43**	**87**	**312**	**671**	**18**	**15**	**3**	**16**	**6**	**2**	
5,558	**4,426**	**43**	**87**	**312**	**671**	**18**	**15**	**3**	**16**	**6**	**2**	
9	..	.	*2*	*2*	..	..	..	.	..	..	..	
7	..	..	2	2	.	..	..	..	..	.	..	1
..	..	..	..	..	.	..	..	..	..	..	..	2
1	..	..	..	..	..	..	..	..	..	..	..	3
..	..	..	.	.	.	..	..	..	..	..	..	
..	..	..	.	..	..	..	..	..	..	..	..	4
1	..	..	..	..	.	..	..	..	..	..	..	5
14	*1*	..	..	..	..	..	..	..	..	..	..	
..	..	..	.	..	..	..	..	..	..	..	..	6
..	1	..	..	..	..	..	..	..	..	..	..	7
..	..	..	..	..	..	..	..	..	..	..	..	8
..	..	..	.	.	..	.	..	..	..	..	..	9
14	..	..	..	..	..	..	..	..	..	.	..	10
5,517	*4,410*	*40*	*69*	*304*	*669*	..	.	..	..	..	..	
..	..	..	..	..	..	..	..	..	..	..	..	11
1,857	1,548	.	..	7	11	..	..	..	..	..	..	12
25	..	..	.	..	..	..	..	..	..	..	..	
..	..	..	..	..	..	..	..	..	..	..	..	13
1,840	1,492	11	2	177	598	..	..	..	..	..	..	14
1,820	1,370	29	67	120	60	..	..	..	.	..	..	15
18	*15*	*3*	*16*	*6*	*2*	*18*	*15*	*3*	*16*	*6*	*2*	
1	15	..	7	..	2	1	15	..	7	..	2	16
6	..	..	..	..	..	6	..	..	..	..	..	17
11	..	3	9	6	..	11	..	3	9	6	..	18
.	..	..	..	.	..	..	..	..	..	..	..	
..	..	..	..	..	..	..	..	..	..	..	..	19
..	..	..	..	..	..	..	..	..	..	..	..	20
..	..	..	..	..	..	..	..	..	..	..	..	21
..	..	..	..	..	..	..	..	..	..	..	..	22
86	**43**	**8**	**93**	**44**	**21**	**61**	**36**	**7**	**87**	**41**	**21**	
..	..	..	..	..	..	..	..	..	..	..	..	23
17	8	8	19	3	..	15	1	7	13	..	..	24
2	..	..	..	2	..	2	..	..	..	2	..	25
..	..	..	..	..	..	..	..	..	..	..	..	26
15	..	..	14	..	..	15	..	..	14	..	..	27
..	..	..	..	.	..	..	..	..	..	..	..	28
.	..	..	..	..	..	..	..	..	..	..	..	29
..	..	..	.	..	..	..	..	..	..	..	..	30
..	..	.	..	..	..	..	..	..	..	..	..	31
.	..	..	..	..	..	..	..	..	.	..	..	32
..	..	..	..	..	..	..	..	..	..	..	..	33
..	..	..	..	..	..	..	..	..	..	..	..	34
23	..	..	..	..	..	..	..	..	..	..	..	35
..	5	..	..	..	..	..	5	..	..	..	..	36
29	30	..	60	39	21	29	30	..	60	39	21	37

TABLE X — Occupation or means of

Serial No.	District, City or State.	Class A.—Production; Sub-class II.—Exploitation; Order 3.—Metallic; Group 30.—Iron. Total earners (principal occupations). Males.	Females.	Total working dependants. Males	Females.	Total following occupation as subsidiary to other. Males.	Females.	Group 32.—Man- Total earners (principal occupations). Males.	Females.	Total working dependants. Males.	Females.
1	2	240	241	242	243	244	245	246	247	248	249
	Central Provinces and Berar	9	7	1	6	3	..	5,532	4,411	40	69
	C. P. British Districts and Berar.	7	..	..	..	..	..	5,532	4,411	40	69
	C. P. British Districts	7	..	..	..	..	..	5,532	4,411	40	69
	Jubbulpore Division	7	..	..	..	..	..	*1*	..	..	..
1	Saugor	7	..	..	..	..	..	..	..	..	..
2	Damoh	..	..	..	..	..	..	..	..	..	..
3	Jubbulpore	..	..	..	..	..	..	..	..	..	..
	Jubbulpore City	..	..	..	..	..	..	..	..	..	..
4	Mandla	..	..	..	..	..	..	..	..	..	..
5	Seoni	..	..	..	..	..	..	1	..	..	..
	Nerbudda Division	..	..	..	..	..	..	*14*	*1*	..	..
6	Narsinghpur	..	..	..	..	..	..	..	..	..	..
7	Hoshangabad	..	..	..	..	..	..	..	1	..	..
8	Nimar	..	..	..	..	..	..	..	..	..	..
9	Betul	..	..	..	..	..	..	..	..	..	..
10	Chhindwara	..	..	..	..	..	..	14	..	..	..
	Nagpur Division	..	..	..	..	..	..	*5,517*	*4,410*	*40*	*69*
11	Wardha	..	..	..	..	..	..	..	..	..	..
12	Nagpur	..	..	..	..	..	..	1,857	1,548	..	..
	Nagpur City	..	..	..	..	..	..	*25*	..	..	..
13	Chanda	..	..	..	..	..	..	..	..	..	..
14	Bhandara	..	..	..	..	..	..	1,840	1,492	11	2
15	Balaghat	..	..	..	..	..	..	1,820	1,370	29	67
	Chhattisgarh Division	..	..	..	..	..	..	..	..	..	..
16	Raipur	..	..	..	..	..	..	..	..	..	..
17	Bilaspur	..	..	..	..	..	..	..	..	..	..
18	Drug	..	..	..	..	..	..	..	..	..	..
	Berar	..	..	..	..	..	..	..	..	..	..
19	Amraoti	..	..	..	..	..	..	..	..	..	..
20	Akola	..	..	..	..	..	..	..	..	..	..
21	Buldana	..	..	..	..	..	..	..	..	..	..
22	Yeotmal	..	..	..	..	..	..	..	..	..	..
	Central Provinces States	2	7	1	6	3	..	..	..	..	..
23	Makrai	..	..	..	..	..	..	..	..	..	..
24	Bastar	2	7	1	6	3	..	..	..	..	..
25	Kanker	..	..	..	..	..	..	..	..	..	..
26	Nandgaon	..	..	..	..	..	..	..	..	..	..
27	Khairagarh	..	..	..	..	..	..	..	..	..	..
28	Chhuikhadan	..	..	..	..	..	..	..	..	..	..
29	Kawardha	..	..	..	..	..	..	..	..	..	..
30	Sakti	..	..	..	..	..	..	..	..	..	..
31	Raigarh	..	..	..	..	..	..	..	..	..	..
32	Sarangarh	..	..	..	..	..	..	..	..	..	..
33	Changbhakar	..	..	..	..	..	..	..	..	..	..
34	Korea	..	..	..	..	..	..	..	..	..	..
35	Surguja	..	..	..	..	..	..	..	..	..	..
36	Udaipur	..	..	..	..	..	..	..	..	..	..
37	Jashpur	..	..	..	..	..	..	..	..	..	..

of raw materials—*contd.*

of minerals—*contd.*

minerals—*concld.* | Order 4.—Non-Metallic minerals.

ganese.		34.—Other metallic minerals.						Total order 4.						Serial No.
Total following occupation as subsidiary to other.		Total earners (principal occupations).		Total working dependants.		Total following occupation as subsidiary to other.		Total earners (principal occupations)		Total working dependants.		Total following occupation as subsidiary to other.		
Males.	Females.	Males.	Females.	Males.	Females	Males.	Females	Males	Females.	Males.	Females.	Males.	Females.	
250	251	252	253	254	255	256	257	258	259	260	261	262	263	
304	**669**	**24**	..	..	**2**	**2**	..	**8,430**	**3,503**	**90**	**186**	**826**	**118**	
304	**669**	**1**	..	..	**2**	**2**	..	**8,394**	**3,485**	**90**	**185**	**824**	**118**	
304	**669**	**1**	..	..	**2**	**2**	..	**6,324**	**2,783**	**49**	**62**	**743**	**84**	
..	..	*1*	..	..	*2*	*2*	..	*224*	*66*	*1*	*4*	*104*	*3*	
..	..	..	..	..	2	2	..	64	14	..	2	95	3	1
..	..	..	..	..	..	..	..	16	..	..	..	..	..	2
..	..	1	..	..	..	..	..	141	52	1	2	8	..	3
..	..	..	..	..	..	..	..	*18*	..	..	..	..	..	
..	..	..	..	..	..	..	..	..	..	..	..	1	..	4
..	..	..	..	..	..	..	..	3	..	..	..	..	..	5
..	..	..	..	..	..	..	..	*3,122*	*1,750*	*16*	*13*	*471*	*55*	
..	..	..	..	..	..	..	..	57	40	..	..	2	..	6
..	..	..	..	..	..	..	..	488	176	3	..	26	..	7
..	..	..	..	..	..	..	..	136	2	3	..	68	4	8
..	..	..	..	..	..	..	..	52	45	..	1	12	11	9
..	..	..	..	..	..	..	..	2,389	1,487	10	12	363	40	10
304	*669*	..	..	..	..	..	..	*2,811*	*930*	*18*	*43*	*132*	*7*	
..	..	..	..	..	..	..	..	182	134	..	..	19	..	11
7	11	..	..	..	..	..	..	917	508	8	40	38	3	12
..	..	..	..	..	..	..	..	*13*	*13*	..	..	*1*	..	
..	..	..	..	..	..	..	..	1,662	275	4	1	51	3	13
177	598	..	..	..	..	..	..	12	13	..	..	21	1	14
120	60	..	..	..	..	..	..	38	..	6	2	3	..	15
..	..	..	..	..	..	..	..	*167*	*37*	*14*	*2*	*36*	*9*	
..	..	..	..	..	..	..	..	131	13	13	..	14	15	16
..	..	..	..	..	..	..	..	26	22	1	..	18	4	17
..	..	..	..	..	..	..	..	10	2	..	2	4	..	18
..	..	..	..	..	..	..	..	**2,070**	**702**	**41**	**123**	**81**	**34**	
..	..	..	..	..	..	..	..	290	210	5	2	38	5	19
..	..	..	..	..	..	..	..	456	253	8	10	9	25	20
..	..	..	..	..	..	..	..	602	84	19	4	16	2	21
..	..	..	..	..	..	..	..	722	155	9	107	18	2	22
..	..	**23**	..	..	..	..	..	**36**	**18**	..	**1**	**2**	..	
..	..	..	..	..	..	..	..	6	11	..	..	..	..	23
..	..	..	..	..	..	..	..	..	..	..	..	..	..	24
..	..	..	..	..	..	..	..	..	..	..	..	..	..	25
..	..	..	..	..	..	..	..	6	..	..	..	2	..	26
..	..	..	..	..	..	..	..	..	..	..	..	..	..	27
..	..	..	..	..	..	..	..	..	..	..	..	..	..	28
..	..	..	..	..	..	..	..	..	..	..	..	..	..	29
..	..	..	..	..	..	..	..	..	..	..	..	..	..	30
..	..	..	..	..	..	..	..	..	..	..	..	..	..	31
..	..	..	..	..	..	..	..	17	..	..	..	..	..	32
..	..	..	..	..	..	..	..	..	..	..	..	..	..	33
..	..	..	..	..	..	..	..	4	..	..	..	..	..	34
..	..	23	..	..	..	..	..	3	7	..	1	..	..	35
..	..	..	..	..	..	..	..	..	..	..	..	..	..	36
..	..	..	..	..	..	..	..	..	..	..	..	..	..	37

TABLE X — Occupation or means of

Serial No.	Class ..	Class A.—Production					
	Sub-class ..	Sub-class II.—Exploitation					
	Order ..	Order 4.—Non-metallic					
	Sub-order ..						
	Group	35.—Coal.					
	District, City or State.	Total earners (principal occupations).		Total working dependants.		Total following occupation as subsidiary to other.	
		Males.	Females.	Males.	Females.	Males.	Females.
1	2	264	265	266	267	268	269
	Central Provinces and Berar ..	**4,741**	**2,068**	**32**	**51**	**565**	**58**
	C. P. British Districts and Berar ..	**4,728**	**2,050**	**32**	**50**	**565**	**58**
	C. P. British Districts	**4,712**	**2,050**	**32**	**50**	**564**	**58**
	Jubbulpore Division	*116*	*44*	..	*3*	*87*	*3*
1	Saugor	40	14	..	2	85	3
2	Damoh	16	..	..	..	..	..
3	Jubbulpore	57	30	..	1	1	..
	Jubbulpore City	*6*	..	..	..	..	..
4	Mandla	..	..	..	..	1	..
5	Seoni	3	..	..	..	..	..
	Nerbudda Division	*2,659*	*1,599*	*14*	*13*	*439*	*55*
6	Narsinghpur	46	40	..	..	2	..
7	Hoshangabad	155	28	1	..	10	..
8	Nimar	66	..	3	..	56	4
9	Betul	26	45	..	1	10	11
10	Chhindwara	2,366	1,486	10	12	361	40
	Nagpur Division	*1,935*	*406*	*18*	*34*	*38*	..
11	Wardha	1	..	..	..	..	..
12	Nagpur	380	203	8	31	15	..
	Nagpur City	*1*	..	..	..	..	..
13	Chanda	1,516	203	4	1	20	..
14	Bhandara	..	..	..	..	..	..
15	Balaghat	38	..	6	2	3	..
	Chhattisgarh Division	*2*	*1*	..	..	..	..
16	Raipur	..	1	..	..	..	..
17	Bilaspur	..	..	..	..	..	..
18	Drug	2	..	..	..	..	..
	Berar	**16**	..	..	..	**1**	..
19	Amraoti	..	..	..	..	..	..
20	Akola	1	..	..	..	..	..
21	Buldana	7	..	..	..	1	..
22	Yeotmal	8	..	..	..	..	..
	Central Provinces States	**13**	**18**	..	**1**	..	..
23	Makrai	6	11	..	..	..	..
24	Bastar	..	..	..	..	..	..
25	Kanker	..	..	..	..	..	..
26	Nandgaon	..	..	..	..	..	..
27	Khairagarh	..	..	..	..	..	..
28	Chhuikhadan	..	..	..	..	..	..
29	Kawardha	..	..	..	..	..	..
30	Sakti	..	..	..	..	..	..
31	Raigarh	..	..	..	..	..	..
32	Sarangarh	..	..	..	..	..	..
33	Changbhakar	..	..	..	..	..	..
34	Korea	4	..	..	..	..	..
35	Surguja	3	7	..	1	..	..
36	Udaipur	..	..	..	..	..	..
37	Jashpur	..	..	..	..	..	..

of raw materials—*contd.*

of minerals—*contd.*

minerals—*contd.*

37.—Building materials (including stone, materials for cement-manufactured and clays).						40.—Salt, saltpetre and other saline substances.						Serial No.
Total earners (principal occupations).		Total working dependants.		Total following occupation as subsidiary to other.		Total earners (principal occupations).		Total working dependants.		Total following occupation as subsidiary to other.		
Males.	Females.	Males.	Females.	Males.	Females.	Males.	Females.	Males.	Females.	Males.	Females.	
270	271	272	273	274	275	276	277	278	279	280	281	
3,472	**1,435**	**57**	**135**	**246**	**60**	**11**	..	..	..	..	..	
3,449	**1,435**	**57**	**135**	**244**	**60**	**11**	..	..	..	..	..	
1,395	**733**	**16**	**12**	**164**	**26**	**11**	..	..	..	..	..	
89	*22*	*1*	*1*	*17*	..	..	..	..	..	..	..	
16	..	..	..	10	..	..	..	..	..	..	..	1
..	..	..	..	..	..	..	..	..	..	..	..	2
73	22	1	1	7	..	..	..	..	..	..	..	3
1	..	..	..	..	..	..	..	..	..	..	..	
..	..	..	..	..	..	..	..	..	..	..	..	4
..	..	..	..	..	..	..	..	..	..	..	..	5
265	*151*	*1*	..	*17*	..	*11*	..	..	..	..	..	
..	..	..	..	..	..	11	..	..	..	..	..	6
146	148	1	..	1	..	..	..	..	..	..	..	7
70	2	..	..	12	..	..	..	..	..	..	..	8
26	..	..	..	2	..	..	..	..	..	..	..	9
23	1	..	..	2	..	..	..	..	..	..	..	10
876	*524*	..	*9*	*94*	*7*	..	..	..	..	..	..	
181	134	..	..	19	..	..	..	..	..	..	..	11
537	305	..	9	23	3	..	..	..	..	..	..	12
12	*13*	..	..	*1*	..	..	..	..	..	..	..	
146	72	..	..	31	3	..	..	..	..	..	..	13
12	13	..	..	21	1	..	..	..	..	..	..	14
..	..	..	..	..	..	..	..	..	..	..	..	15
165	*36*	*14*	*2*	*36*	*19*	..	..	..	..	..	..	
131	12	13	..	14	15	..	..	..	..	..	..	16
26	22	1	..	18	4	..	..	..	..	..	..	17
8	2	..	2	4	..	..	..	..	..	..	..	18
2,054	**702**	**41**	**123**	**80**	**34**	..	..	..	..	..	..	
290	210	5	2	38	5	..	..	..	..	..	..	19
455	253	8	10	9	25	..	..	..	..	..	..	20
595	84	19	4	15	2	..	..	..	..	..	..	21
714	155	9	107	18	2	..	..	..	..	..	..	22
23	..	..	..	**2**	..	..	..	..	..	..	..	
..	..	..	..	..	..	..	..	..	..	..	..	23
..	..	..	..	..	..	..	..	..	..	..	..	24
6	..	..	..	2	..	..	..	..	..	..	..	25
..	..	..	..	..	..	..	..	..	..	..	..	26
..	..	..	..	..	..	..	..	..	..	..	..	27
..	..	..	..	..	..	..	..	..	..	..	..	28
..	..	..	..	..	..	..	..	..	..	..	..	29
..	..	..	..	..	..	..	..	..	..	..	..	30
17	..	..	..	..	..	..	..	..	..	..	..	31
..	..	..	..	..	..	..	..	..	..	..	..	32
..	..	..	..	..	..	..	..	..	..	..	..	33
..	..	..	..	..	..	..	..	..	..	..	..	34
..	..	..	..	..	..	..	..	..	..	..	..	35
..	..	..	..	..	..	..	..	..	..	..	..	36
..	..	..	..	..	..	..	..	..	..	..	..	37

TABLE X

Occupation or means of

Serial No.	Class ..	Class A.—Production of raw materials—*concld.*					
	Sub-class ..	Sub-class II.—Exploitation of minerals—*concld.*					
	Order ..	Order 4.—Non-metallic mineral—*concld.*					
	Sub-order ..						
	Group ..	41.—Other non-metallic minerals.					
	District, City or State.	Total earners (principal occupations).		Total working dependants.		Total following occupation as subsidiary to other.	
		Males.	Females.	Males.	Females.	Males.	Females.
1	2	282	283	284	285	286	287
	Central Provinces and Berar ..	206	..	1	..	15	..
	C. P. British Districts and Berar ..	206	..	1	..	15	..
	C. P. British Districts	206	..	1	..	15	..
	Jubbulpore Division	*19*	..	..	..	..	..
1	Saugor	8	..	..	..	..	..
2	Damoh	..	..	..	..	..	..
3	Jubbulpore	11	..	..	..	..	..
	Jubbulpore City	*11*	..	..	..	..	..
4	Mandla	..	..	..	..	..	..
5	Seoni	..	..	..	..	..	..
	Nerbudda Division	*187*	..	*1*	..	*15*	..
6	Narsinghpur	..	..	..	..	..	..
7	Hoshangabad	187	..	1	..	15	..
8	Nimar	..	..	..	..	..	..
9	Betul	..	..	..	..	..	..
10	Chhindwara	..	..	..	..	..	..
	Nagpur Division	..	..	..	..	..	..
11	Wardha	..	..	..	..	..	..
12	Nagpur	..	..	..	..	..	..
	Nagpur City	..	..	..	..	..	..
13	Chanda	..	..	..	..	..	..
14	Bhandara	..	..	..	..	..	..
15	Balaghat	..	..	..	..	..	..
	Chhattisgarh Division	..	..	..	..	..	..
16	Raipur	..	..	..	..	..	..
17	Bilaspur	..	..	..	..	..	..
18	Drug	..	..	..	..	..	..
	Berar	..	..	..	..	..	..
19	Amraoti	..	..	..	..	..	..
20	Akola	..	..	..	..	..	..
21	Buldana	..	..	..	..	..	..
22	Yeotmal	..	..	..	..	..	..
	Central Provinces States	..	..	..	..	..	..
23	Makrai	..	..	..	..	..	..
24	Bastar	..	..	..	..	..	..
25	Kanker	..	..	..	..	..	..
26	Nandgaon	..	..	..	..	..	..
27	Khairagarh	..	..	..	..	..	..
28	Chhuikhadan	..	..	..	..	..	..
29	Kawardha	..	..	..	..	..	..
30	Sakti	..	..	..	..	..	..
31	Raigarh	..	..	..	..	..	..
32	Sarangarh	..	..	..	..	..	..
33	Changbhakar	..	..	..	..	..	..
34	Korea	..	..	..	..	..	..
35	Surguja	..	..	..	..	..	..
36	Udaipur	..	..	..	..	..	..
37	Jashpur	..	..	..	..	..	..

Livelihood—General Distribution—*contd.*

TABLE X

Class B.—Preparation and supply of material substances.												
Total class B						Sub-class III.—Industry.						Serial No.
						Total sub-class III.						
Total earners (principal occupations).		Total working dependants.		Total following occupation as subsidiary to other		Total earners (principal occupations).		Total working dependants.		Total following occupation as subsidiary to other.		
Males	Females	Males.	Females	Males.	Females.	Males.	Females	Males.	Females	Males	Females	
288	289	290	291	292	293	294	295	296	297	298	299	
797,887	**252,848**	**36,065**	**113,072**	**167,305**	**41,376**	**488,058**	**138,995**	**25,847**	**82,745**	**85,293**	**16,922**	
738,196	**233,118**	**27,672**	**85,932**	**149,624**	**39,185**	**447,204**	**128,282**	**19,213**	**61,986**	**73,287**	**16,260**	
578,004	**204,187**	**22,416**	**76,721**	**122,189**	**33,999**	**357,824**	**109,967**	**16,063**	**56,013**	**63,555**	**13,854**	
137,691	*39,954*	*3,872*	*11,335*	*32,411*	*5,729*	*77,183*	*17,846*	*2,090*	*6,547*	*16,145*	*1,796*	
35,489	9,109	996	2,919	5,455	1,184	20,053	3,757	641	1,505	2,862	441	1
18,922	6,198	549	1,645	5,393	1,085	11,848	3,297	229	918	2,826	464	2
53,649	15,474	1,814	4,162	14,920	2,365	32,285	7,768	880	2,202	1,925	600	3
22,590	*3,575*	*152*	*345*	*533*	*72*	*12,926*	*2,114*	*97*	*208*	*216*	*44*	
13,266	3,537	190	782	3,177	575	4,738	650	114	495	1,042	77	4
16,365	5,636	323	1,827	3,466	520	8,259	2,374	226	1,427	1,490	214	5
123,141	*34,995*	*4,266*	*14,394*	*23,020*	*7,947*	*68,693*	*15,927*	*2,765*	*9,990*	*7,966*	*2,356*	
18,811	7,138	462	3,542	3,562	1,317	11,060	3,260	304	2,466	1,437	332	6
34,710	9,720	1,268	3,097	5,644	1,248	18,919	4,581	877	2,090	1,512	390	7
29,084	5,536	1,189	1,863	4,638	296	15,921	3,381	660	1,334	1,597	184	8
16,165	7,495	154	2,209	4,678	3,872	9,458	2,655	107	1,432	1,686	1,140	9
24,371	5,106	1,193	3,683	4,498	1,214	13,335	2,050	817	2,668	1,734	310	10
230,418	*82,105*	*6,224*	*26,824*	*33,245*	*10,722*	*160,269*	*53,094*	*4,795*	*21,755*	*18,551*	*5,389*	
29,712	6,871	428	1,101	3,379	578	19,134	4,763	192	822	1,413	308	11
84,992	22,420	1,645	9,538	6,167	1,780	57,609	14,709	1,318	8,665	2,412	588	12
38,749	*7,995*	*816*	*2,188*	*504*	*32*	*25,357*	*5,473*	*609*	*2,063*	*176*	*5*	
37,592	14,407	824	4,412	8,099	3,446	27,446	7,865	666	2,939	4,601	1,478	13
57,010	32,397	2,170	5,028	10,448	4,368	41,915	23,058	1,805	3,987	6,941	2,825	14
21,112	6,010	1,157	6.745	5,152	550	14,165	2,699	814	5,342	3,184	190	15
86,754	*47,133*	*8,054*	*24,168*	*33,513*	*9,601*	*51,679*	*23,100*	*6,413*	*17,721*	*20,893*	*1,313*	
42,045	28,867	3,051	9,560	13,472	4,029	24,724	15,101	2,411	7,391	8,142	1,461	16
28,193	13,139	1,598	5,463	15,792	5,022	15,505	5,930	1,152	3,670	9,860	2,599	17
16,516	5,127	3,405	9,145	4,249	550	11,450	2,069	2,850	6,660	2,891	253	18
160,192	**28,931**	**5,256**	**9,211**	**27,435**	**5,186**	**89,380**	**18,315**	**3,150**	**5,973**	**9,732**	**2,406**	
49,523	8,956	1,615	3,405	10,952	1,743	28,142	5,646	859	2,179	3,382	761	19
43,591	7,273	954	1,979	6,543	1,430	23,354	4,911	519	1,445	2,575	743	20
31,239	6,655	954	1,875	6,307	1,447	17,174	4,223	514	1,373	2,486	598	21
35,839	6,047	1,733	1,952	3,633	566	20,710	3,535	1,258	976	1,289	304	22
59,691	**19,730**	**8,393**	**27,140**	**17,681**	**2,191**	**40,854**	**10,713**	**6,634**	**20,759**	**12,006**	**662**	
813	165	24	101	113	22	435	37	24	37	27	9	23
8,883	2,228	1,655	4,819	1,911	125	6,608	1,270	1,451	4,022	1,276	54	24
3,064	1,036	777	1,726	870	669	1,704	529	566	1,072	494	132	25
8,059	2,512	506	1,510	924	137	5,780	1,538	388	1,216	578	43	26
3,872	1,658	661	1,573	805	95	2,123	798	566	1,474	590	42	27
768	445	382	572	220	73	474	250	367	378	103	63	28
1,927	1,758	12	126	1,179	586	1,365	905	11	106	513	84	29
1,482	1,291	548	714	450	211	463	484	95	341	170	107	30
7,623	2,886	1,811	5,012	2,498	123	4,546	1,305	1,543	4,042	1,824	27	31
2,317	1,286	551	1,139	1,300	27	1,599	623	363	886	889	16	32
469	90	10	27	88	9	349	62	4	17	65	7	33
1,850	258	15	10	553	9	1,308	206	15	8	414	6	34
10,022	1,306	900	5,319	4,269	80	7,380	806	724	3,026	3,086	52	35
2,322	459	17	6	603	5	1,986	313	14	3	487	4	36
6,220	2,352	524	4,486	1,898	20	4,734	1,587	503	4,131	1,490	16	37

TABLE X Occupation or means of

Serial No.	Class .. / Sub-class .. / Order .. / Sub-order .. / Group ..	Class B.—Preparation and supply / Sub-class III.— / Order 5.— / Total order 5.					
	District, City or State.	Total earners (principal occupations).		Total working dependants.		Total following occupation as subsidiary to other.	
		Males.	Females.	Males.	Females.	Males.	Females.
1	2	300	301	302	303	304	305
	Central Provinces and Berar ..	**122,992**	**34,467**	**9,157**	**42,067**	**18,645**	**3,379**
	C. P. British Districts and Berar ..	**109,899**	**32,292**	**6,271**	**32,461**	**14,162**	**3,245**
	C. P. British Districts	**94,658**	**27,429**	**5,924**	**30,653**	**13,174**	**2,826**
	Jubbulpore Division	*7,354*	*1,681*	*255*	*1,542*	*1,623*	*289*
1	Saugor	1,944	353	83	422	214	53
2	Damoh	896	304	46	112	206	66
3	Jubbulpore	2,694	759	50	269	634	99
	Jubbulpore City	*1,516*	*264*	*13*	*14*	*14*	*1*
4	Mandla	858	70	25	112	324	4
5	Seoni	962	195	51	627	245	67
	Nerbudda Division	*13,740*	*3,091*	*559*	*2,649*	*1,632*	*355*
6	Narsinghpur	1,392	472	50	687	333	123
7	Hoshangabad	2,046	646	58	333	308	37
8	Nimar	5,444	1,240	180	560	392	47
9	Betul	2,064	596	19	417	267	56
10	Chhindwara	2,794	137	252	652	332	92
	Nagpur Division	*57,923*	*16,144*	*2,038*	*15,589*	*3,686*	*990*
11	Wardha	5,871	2,157	36	406	206	75
12	Nagpur	27,542	7,138	758	7,420	384	148
	Nagpur City	*16,492*	*3,780*	*308*	*1,771*	*40*	..
13	Chanda	9,939	3,141	282	1,794	1,658	446
14	Bhandara	8,004	3,127	543	2,691	704	275
15	Balaghat	5,567	581	419	3,278	734	46
	Chhattisgarh Division	*15,641*	*6,513*	*3,072*	*10,873*	*6,233*	*1,192*
16	Raipur	8,012	4,774	1,213	4,689	2,327	439
17	Bilaspur	4,213	1,606	570	2,053	2,958	723
18	Drug	3,416	133	1,289	4,131	948	30
	Berar	**15,241**	**4,863**	**347**	**1,808**	**988**	**419**
19	Amraoti	6,560	1,609	160	943	485	204
20	Akola	4,942	1,647	59	291	230	71
21	Buldana	1,406	954	58	505	160	89
22	Yeotmal	2,333	653	70	69	113	55
	Central Provinces States	**13,093**	**2,175**	**2,886**	**9,606**	**4,483**	**134**
23	Makrai	51	6	2	..	2	8
24	Bastar	3,067	506	737	2,241	676	6
25	Kanker	511	74	195	484	116	35
26	Nandgaon	1,693	325	175	717	181	12
27	Khairagarh	518	23	306	699	92	5
28	Chhuikhadan	247	60	64	165	10	15
29	Kawardha	337	292	4	57	73	14
30	Sakti	81	14	24	91	48	11
31	Raigarh	1,323	144	1,007	1,594	838	4
32	Sarangarh	592	28	137	242	264	..
33	Changbhakar	15	1	..	..	9	..
34	Korea	97	..	..	2	107	..
35	Surguja	2,115	101	122	601	979	14
36	Udaipur	774	151	4	1	306	..
37	Jashpur	1,672	450	109	2,712	782	10

of material substances—*contd.*

Industry—*contd.*

Textiles.

42.—Cotton ginning, cleaning and pressing.						43.—Cotton spinning, sizing and weaving.						Serial No
Total earners (principal occupations).		Total working dependants.		Total following occupation as subsidiary to other.		Total earners (principal occupations).		Total working dependants.		Total following occupation as subsidiary to other.		
Males.	Females.	Males.	Females.	Males.	Females.	Males.	Females.	Males.	Females.	Males.	Females.	
306	307	308	309	310	311	312	313	314	315	316	317	
13,127	**5,667**	**151**	**580**	**1,414**	**444**	**98,930**	**24,704**	**3,225**	**38,361**	**14,955**	**2,357**	
13,109	**5,664**	**151**	**580**	**1,413**	**442**	**86,310**	**22,811**	**5,423**	**29,021**	**10,624**	**2,248**	
6,465	**2,750**	**82**	**398**	**931**	**192**	**79,028**	**21,169**	**5,207**	**27,727**	**10,320**	**2,161**	
941	*177*	*18*	*25*	*326*	*28*	*5,157*	*1,147*	*184*	*1,242*	*967*	*202*	
363	51	14	13	100	16	1,130	235	53	248	57	36	1
199	38	..	4	111	10	454	170	37	85	44	29	2
286	69	3	5	89	2	2,036	557	31	192	388	69	3
106	*58*	*1*	..	*2*	..	*1,327*	*173*	*12*	*13*	*7*	*1*	
21	4	..	1	1	..	792	46	24	109	313	2	4
72	15	1	2	25	..	745	139	39	608	165	66	5
2,562	*738*	*33*	*233*	*436*	*44*	*9,600*	*1,734*	*420*	*1,837*	*876*	*185*	
277	49	4	30	50	9	780	214	26	415	195	30	6
553	184	6	90	67	2	989	250	34	173	142	23	7
1,432	466	11	91	269	31	3,596	676	124	431	59	11	8
26	3	..	..	1	..	1,907	529	13	223	222	32	9
274	36	12	22	49	2	2,328	65	223	595	258	89	10
2,958	*1,797*	*31*	*139*	*167*	*120*	*49,852*	*12,401*	*1,733*	*14,593*	*2,938*	*712*	
1,885	1,219	15	24	76	51	4,754	895	19	367	53	16	11
738	409	7	88	81	57	23,425	6,458	540	7,149	211	76	12
359	*162*	*2*	*16*	*4*	..	*15,876*	*3,550*	*304*	*1,736*	*33*	..	
265	153	..	10	4	10	9,058	2,084	262	1,592	1,361	327	13
48	9	8	..	1	2	7,185	2,423	498	2,267	628	254	14
22	7	1	17	5	..	5,430	541	414	3,218	685	39	15
4	*38*	..	*1*	*2*	..	*14,419*	*5,887*	*2,870*	*10,055*	*5,539*	*1,062*	
..	3	..	1	..	..	7,624	4,539	1,192	4,448	2,104	421	16
3	35	..	..	2	..	3,734	1,266	496	1,877	2,747	628	17
1	..	..	..	..	..	3,061	82	1,182	3,730	688	13	18
6,644	**2,914**	**69**	**182**	**482**	**250**	**7,282**	**1,642**	**216**	**1,294**	**304**	**87**	
2,591	648	35	91	276	129	3,538	889	112	817	139	44	19
2,257	1,048	17	40	105	23	2,338	506	32	219	79	33	20
527	677	6	18	54	66	598	179	19	225	40	7	21
1,269	541	11	33	47	32	808	68	53	33	46	3	22
18	**3**	..	..	**1**	**2**	**12,620**	**1,893**	**2,802**	**9,340**	**4,331**	**109**	
18	3	..	..	1	2	22	1	..	..	1	4	23
..	..	..	..	..	..	3,019	503	723	2,201	654	6	24
..	..	..	..	..	..	509	72	194	484	114	34	25
..	..	..	..	..	..	1,594	309	143	612	144	..	26
..	..	..	..	..	..	477	16	287	655	75	4	27
..	..	..	..	..	..	237	54	64	142	10	14	28
..	..	..	..	..	..	252	176	4	39	29	9	29
..	..	..	..	..	..	81	14	24	91	48	11	30
..	..	..	..	..	..	1,272	134	1,000	1,579	823	3	31
..	..	..	..	..	..	592	28	137	238	261	..	32
..	..	..	..	..	..	15	1	..	..	9	..	33
..	..	..	..	..	..	97	..	..	2	107	..	34
..	..	..	..	..	..	2,084	80	122	601	975	14	35
..	..	..	..	..	..	733	146	4	..	306	..	36
..	..	..	..	..	..	1,636	359	100	2,696	775	10	37

TABLE X — Occupation or means

Serial No.	Class .. / Sub-class .. / Order .. / Sub-order .. / Group ..	Class B.—Preparation and supply / Sub-class III.— / Order 5.— / 44.—Jute pressing, spinning and weaving.					
	District, City or Stat.	Total earners (principal occupations).		Total working dependants.		Total following occupation as subsidiary to other.	
		Males.	Females.	Males.	Females.	Males.	Females.
1	2	318	319	320	321	322	323
	Central Provinces and Berar ..	**535**	**331**	**26**	**174**	**241**	**61**
	C. P. British Districts and Berar ..	**471**	**329**	**23**	**148**	**188**	**58**
	C. P. British Districts	**317**	**274**	**19**	**138**	**152**	**45**
	Jubbulpore Division	*35*	*6*	..	*1*	*21*	*1*
1	Saugor	8	..	..	..	11	..
2	Damoh	..	1	..	..	..	1
3	Jubbulpore	..	4	..	1	..	..
	Jubbulpore City	..	..	..	..	..	..
4	Mandla	..	1	..	..	..	..
5	Seoni	27	..	..	..	10	..
	Nerbudda Division	*127*	*143*	*17*	*102*	*19*	*22*
6	Narsinghpur	47	42	..	44	3	10
7	Hoshangabad	19	35	..	20	3	7
8	Nimar	45	66	16	18	13	5
9	Betul	..	..	..	20	..	..
10	Chhindwara	16	..	1	..	..	..
	Nagpur Division	*134*	*125*	*2*	*8*	*33*	*20*
11	Wardha	38	9	..	5	6	4
12	Nagpur	36	24	..	..	1	1
	Nagpur City	*1*	*2*	..	..	..	..
13	Chanda	40	32	2	3	9	3
14	Bhandara	20	60	..	..	17	12
15	Balaghat	..	..	..	..	..	..
	Chhattisgarh Division	*21*	..	..	*27*	*79*	*2*
16	Raipur	2	..	..	..	30	..
17	Bilaspur	..	..	..	..	33	2
18	Drug	19	..	..	27	16	..
	Berar . ..	**154**	**55**	**4**	**10**	**36**	**13**
19	Amraoti	59	8	3	1	24	..
20	Akola	59	30	1	6	11	13
21	Buldana	26	17	..	3	1	..
22	Yeotmal	10	..	..	..	..	..
	Central Provinces States	**64**	**2**	**3**	**26**	**53**	**3**
23	Makrai	..	..	..	..	..	..
24	Bastar	6	..	..	5	20	..
25	Kanker	..	..	..	..	..	..
26	Nandgaon	22	..	3	21	..	3
27	Khairagarh	..	..	..	..	..	..
28	Chhuikhadan	4	..	..	..	..	..
29	Kawardha	7	2	..	..	33	..
30	Sakti	..	..	..	..	..	..
31	Raigarh	..	..	..	..	..	..
32	Sarangarh	..	..	..	..	..	..
33	Changbhakar	..	..	..	..	..	..
34	Korea	..	..	..	..	..	..
35	Surguja	25	..	..	..	..	..
36	Udaipur	..	..	..	..	..	..
37	Jashpur	..	..	..	..	..	..

of material substances—*contd.*

Industry—*contd.*

Textiles—*contd.*

45.—Rope, twine, string and other fibres. Total earners (principal occupations). Males.	Females.	Total working dependants. Males.	Females.	Total following occupation as subsidiary to other. Males.	Females.	46.—Wool carding, spinning and weaving. Total earners (principal occupations). Males.	Females.	Total working dependants. Males.	Females.	Total following occupation as subsidiary to other. Males.	Females.	Serial No.
324	325	326	327	328	329	330	331	332	333	334	335	
1,354	**851**	**87**	**417**	**614**	**165**	**1,702**	**1,231**	**177**	**1,089**	**992**	**179**	
1,224	**751**	**71**	**387**	**585**	**164**	**1,565**	**1,086**	**148**	**981**	**944**	**164**	
1,112	**717**	**62**	**257**	**570**	**153**	**1,374**	**1,014**	**138**	**892**	**847**	**135**	
250	*132*	*18*	*50*	*115*	*8*	*312*	*72*	*15*	*116*	*84*	*18*	
97	11	5	24	34	..	154	12	1	65	1	1	1
24	45	..	1	11	4	41	15	9	9	26	5	2
48	48	4	9	26	3	73	26	5	41	47	10	3
14	*16*	..	..	..	..	*7*	..	..	..	..	..	
5	..	1	..	2	..	30	19	..	..	7	2	4
76	28	8	16	42	1	14	..	..	1	3	..	5
543	*254*	*33*	*89*	*174*	*20*	*83*	*36*	*4*	*126*	*53*	*18*	
135	80	6	61	59	17	24	12	1	33	13	13	6
236	124	8	14	55	..	11	7	2	10	23	2	7
83	8	17	3	24	..	..	..	..	..	..	..	8
52	25	1	5	33	3	22	15	1	80	2	3	9
37	17	1	6	3	..	26	2	..	3	15	..	10
220	*260*	*4*	*60*	*259*	*104*	*299*	*752*	*5*	*134*	*196*	*21*	
9	25	1	3	22	2	82	2	1	4	42	1	11
40	26	..	..	8	..	73	73	1	34	49	8	12
19	*11*	..	..	*1*	..	..	*2*	..	*2*	..	..	
118	133	3	27	185	90	106	547	2	85	84	12	13
27	56	..	6	12	6	31	129	1	10	21	..	14
26	20	..	24	32	6	7	1	..	1	..	..	15
99	*71*	*7*	*58*	*22*	*21*	*680*	*154*	*114*	*516*	*514*	*78*	
51	48	6	10	18	1	233	80	13	204	150	16	16
45	23	1	36	4	6	159	35	1	38	125	59	17
3	..	..	12	..	14	288	39	100	274	239	3	18
112	**34**	**9**	**130**	**15**	**11**	**191**	**72**	**10**	**89**	**97**	**29**	
27	9	1	3	7	4	18	10	..	5	16	3	19
37	8	2	2	2	..	69	23	2	5	19	2	20
38	13	5	125	4	7	80	34	7	79	54	5	21
10	4	1	..	2	..	24	5	1	..	8	19	22
130	**100**	**16**	**30**	**29**	**1**	**137**	**145**	**29**	**108**	**48**	**15**	
..	..	..	..	..	..	..	..	..	..	..	..	23
..	..	..	..	2	..	..	..	..	..	..	..	24
..	..	..	..	..	..	2	..	1	..	2	..	25
..	..	..	..	..	..	65	9	28	61	36	9	26
..	..	..	..	..	..	..	..	..	..	..	..	27
3	..	..	..	..	..	..	3	..	9	..	1	28
4	3	..	..	1	..	69	107	..	17	10	5	29
..	..	..	..	..	..	..	..	..	..	..	..	30
41	8	7	14	15	1	..	..	..	..	..	..	31
..	..	..	..	..	..	..	..	..	..	..	..	32
..	..	..	..	..	..	..	..	..	..	..	..	33
5	2	..	..	..	..	..	..	..	..	..	..	34
41	..	..	..	4	..	1	19	..	..	..	..	35
..	..	..	..	..	..	..	5	..	1	..	..	36
36	87	9	16	7	..	..	2	..	..	..	..	37

TABLE X — Occupation or means

Serial No.	Class .. / Sub-class .. / Order .. / Sub-order .. / Group ..	Class B.—Preparation and supply / Sub-class III.— / Order 5.— / 47.—Silk spinning and weaving.					
	District, City or State.	Total earners (principal occupations).		Total working dependants.		Total following occupation as subsidiary to other.	
		Males.	Females.	Males.	Females.	Males.	Females.
1	2	336	337	338	339	340	341
	Central Provinces and Berar ..	**4,043**	**870**	**340**	**686**	**124**	**21**
	C. P. British Districts and Berar ..	**3,962**	**864**	**307**	**604**	**104**	**20**
	C. P. British Districts	**3,950**	**856**	**307**	**603**	**104**	**20**
	Jubbulpore Division	*24*	..	..	..	*49*	..
1	Saugor	2	..	..	..	..	..
2	Damoh	2	..	..	..	..	..
3	Jubbulpore	20	..	..	..	49	..
	Jubbulpore City	*6*	..	..	..	..	..
4	Mandla	..	..	..	..	..	..
5	Seoni	..	..	..	..	..	..
	Nerbudda Division	*85*	*7*	*2*	*1*	..	..
6	Narsinghpur	2	2	..	..	..	..
7	Hoshangabad	..	..	..	..	..	..
8	Nimar	83	2	2	1	..	..
9	Betul	..	..	..	..	..	..
10	Chhindwara	..	3	..	..	..	..
	Nagpur Division	*3,608*	*610*	*238*	*519*	*42*	*4*
11	Wardha	..	..	..	..	..	..
12	Nagpur	2,782	17	197	64	12	1
	Nagpur City	..	*5*	..	..	..	..
13	Chanda	230	165	11	57	9	2
14	Bhandara	590	428	30	394	21	1
15	Balaghat	6	..	..	4	..	..
	Chhattisgarh Division	*233*	*239*	*67*	*83*	*13*	*16*
16	Raipur	33	51	2	7	3	..
17	Bilaspur	200	188	65	76	10	16
18	Drug	..	..	..	..	..	..
	Berar	**12**	**8**	..	**1**	..	..
19	Amraoti	3	..	..	..	..	..
20	Akola	1	..	..	1	..	..
21	Buldana	..	7	..	..	..	..
22	Yeotmal	8	1	..	..	..	..
	Central Provinces States	**81**	**6**	**33**	**82**	**20**	**1**
23	Makrai	..	..	..	..	..	..
24	Bastar	42	2	14	35	..	..
25	Kanker	..	..	..	..	..	..
26	Nandgaon	..	..	..	..	..	..
27	Khairagarh	38	4	19	43	17	1
28	Chhuikhadan	..	..	..	..	..	..
29	Kawardha	..	..	..	..	..	..
30	Sakti	..	..	..	..	..	..
31	Raigarh	1	..	..	..	..	..
32	Sarangarh	..	..	..	4	3	..
33	Changbhakar	..	..	..	..	..	..
34	Korea	..	..	..	..	..	..
35	Surguja	..	..	..	..	..	..
36	Udaipur	..	..	..	..	..	..
37	Jashpur	..	..	..	..	..	..

of Livelihood—General Distribution—*contd.* **TABLE X**

of material substances.—*contd.*

Industry —*contd.*

Textiles.—*contd*

48.—Hair (Horse-hair), etc						49.—Dyeing, bleaching, printing, preparation and sponging of textiles.						Serial No.
Total earners (principal occupations)		Total working dependants		Total following occupation as subsidiary to other		Total earners (principal occupations).		Total working dependants.		Total following occupation as subsidiary to other.		
Males.	Females	Males.	Females	Males	Females	Males.	Females.	Males.	Females.	Males	Females.	
342	343	344	345	346	347	348	349	350	351	352	353	
20	**3**	..	**2**	..		**2,779**	**561**	**130**	**448**	**199**	**91**	
20	**3**	..	**2**	.	.	**2,761**	**557**	**128**	**447**	**198**	**89**	
20	**3**	..	**2**	..	..	**1,963**	**438**	**89**	**393**	**147**	**86**	
11	.	..	.	.	..	*558*	*137*	*20*	*106*	*60*	*32*	
6	..	..	..	..	..	168	40	10	72	11	..	1
..	..	..	..	..	.	143	31	..	13	14	17	2
..	.	..	..	..	..	218	53	7	19	34	15	3
..	..	..	..	.	.	*53*	*17*	..	..	*5*	..	
5	..	..	..	.	.	5	..	..	2	1	..	4
..	..	..	..	..	..	24	13	3	..	..	..	5
9	*3*	..	*2*	..	..	*642*	*153*	*43*	*180*	*44*	*48*	
..	..	..	.	..	..	122	72	13	101	13	44	6
..	3	..	2	..	..	223	37	6	24	17	3	7
..	..	..	..	..	..	145	15	9	14	5	..	8
..	..	..	..	..	..	48	22	..	15	2	..	9
9	..	..	.	..	..	104	7	15	26	7	1	10
..	..	..	..	.	..	*761*	*148*	*25*	*107*	*43*	*6*	
..	..	..	.	..	..	77	4	..	3	4	..	11
..	..	..	..	.	..	396	90	13	62	20	5	12
..	.	..	..	..	..	*201*	*23*	*2*	*10*	*1*	..	
..	..	..	..	..	..	121	21	2	16	3	..	13
..	..	..	..	.	..	95	22	6	12	4	..	14
..	..	..	..	.	.	72	11	4	14	12	1	15
..	.	..	..	..	..	*2*	..	*1*	..	..	..	
..	..	..	..	..	..	..	..	..	..	..	..	16
..	..	..	..	..	..	1	..	..	..	..	..	17
..	..	..	.	..	..	1	..	1	..	..	..	18
..	..	..	.	..	..	**798**	**119**	**39**	**54**	**51**	**3**	
..	..	..	..	..	.	306	32	9	20	23	2	19
..	..	..	..	..	.	162	28	5	17	12	..	20
..	..	..	..	..	..	132	26	21	14	7	..	21
..	..	..	..	..	.	198	33	4	3	9	1	22
..	..	..	..	..	..	**18**	**4**	**2**	**1**	**1**	**2**	
..	..	..	..	..	..	9	2	2	..	..	2	23
..	..	..	..	..	..	..	..	..	..	..	..	24
..	..	..	..	..	..	..	..	..	..	..	..	25
..	..	..	..	..	..	7	1	..	..	1	..	26
..	..	..	..	..	..	..	..	..	..	..	..	27
..	..	..	..	..	..	..	..	..	..	..	..	28
..	..	..	..	..	..	2	..	..	1	..	..	29
..	..	..	..	..	..	..	..	..	..	..	..	30
..	..	..	..	..	..	..	1	..	..	..	..	31
..	..	..	..	..	..	..	..	..	..	..	..	32
..	..	..	..	..	..	..	..	..	..	..	..	33
..	..	..	..	..	..	..	..	..	..	..	..	34
..	..	..	..	..	..	..	..	..	..	..	..	35
..	..	..	..	..	..	..	..	..	..	..	..	36
..	..	..	..	..	..	..	..	..	..	..	..	37

TABLE X **Occupation or means**

Serial No.	District, City or State.	Total earners (principal occupations). Males.	Total earners (principal occupations). Females.	Total working dependants. Males.	Total working dependants. Females.	Total following occupation as subsidiary to othe.. Males.	Total following occupation as subsidiary to othe.. Females.
	Class ..	Class B.—Preparation and supply					
	Sub-class ..	Sub-class III.—					
	Order .	Order 5.—Textiles.—*concld.*					
	Sub-order ..						
	Group ..	50.—Lace, crepe, embroideries, fringes, etc., and insufficiently described textile industries.					
1	2	354	355	356	357	358	359
	Central Provinces and Berar ..	**502**	**249**	**21**	**310**	**106**	**61**
	C. P. British Districts and Berar ..	**477**	**227**	**20**	**291**	**106**	**60**
	C. P. British Districts	**429**	**208**	**20**	**243**	**103**	**34**
	Jubbulpore Division	66	*10*	..	*2*	*1*	..
1	Saugor	16	4	..	..	..	..
2	Damoh	33	4	..	..	..	..
3	Jubbulpore	13	2	..	2	1	..
	Jubbulpore City	*3*	..	..	*1*	..	..
4	Mandla	..	..	..	..	..	..
5	Seoni	4	..	..	..	..	..
	Nerbudda Division	*89*	*23*	*7*	*79*	*30*	*18*
6	Narsinghpur	5	1	..	3	..	..
7	Hoshangabad	15	6	2	..	1	..
8	Nimar	60	7	1	2	22	..
9	Betul	9	2	4	74	7	18
10	Chhindwara	..	7	..	..	..	..
	Nagpur Division	*91*	*51*	..	*29*	*8*	*3*
11	Wardha	26	3	..	..	3	1
12	Nagpur	52	41	..	23	2	..
	Nagpur City	*36*	*25*	..	*7*	*1*	..
13	Chanda	1	6	..	4	3	2
14	Bhandara	8	..	..	2	..	..
15	Balaghat	4	1	..	..	..	..
	Chhattisgarh Division	*183*	*124*	*13*	*133*	*64*	*13*
16	Raipur	69	53	..	19	22	1
17	Bilaspur	71	59	7	26	37	12
18	Drug	43	12	6	88	5	..
	Berar	**48**	**19**	..	**48**	**3**	**26**
19	Amraoti	18	13	..	6	..	22
20	Akola	19	4	..	11	2	..
21	Buldana	5	1	..	41	..	4
22	Yeotmal	6	1	..	..	1	..
	Central Provinces States	**25**	**22**	**1**	**19**	..	**1**
23	Makrai	2	..	..	..	..	..
24	Bastar	..	1	..	..	..	..
25	Kanker	..	2	..	..	..	1
26	Nandgaon	5	6	1	3	..	..
27	Khairagarh	3	3	..	1	..	..
28	Chhuikhadan	3	3	..	14	..	..
29	Kawardha	3	4	..	..	..	..
30	Sakti	..	..	..	..	..	..
31	Raigarh	9	1	..	1	..	..
32	Sarangarh	..	..	..	..	..	..
33	Changbhakar	..	..	..	..	..	..
34	Korea	..	..	..	..	..	..
35	Surguja	..	..	..	..	..	..
36	Udaipur	..	..	..	..	..	..
37	Jashpur	..	2	..	..	..	..

of materials substances—*contd.*

Industry—*contd.*

Order 6.—Hides, skins and hard materials from the animal kingdom.												Serial No.
Total order 6.						51.—Working in leather.						
Total earners (principal occupations).		Total working dependants.		Total following occupation as subsidiary to other.		Total earners (principal occupations).		Total working dependants.		Total following occupation as subsidiary to other.		
Males.	Females.	Males.	Females.	Males.	Females.	Males.	Females.	Males.	Females.	Males.	Females.	
360	361	362	363	364	365	366	367	368	369	370	371	
14,726	**2,370**	**579**	**1,339**	**1,651**	**221**	**14,618**	**2,295**	**578**	**1,335**	**1,621**	**212**	
14,093	**2,331**	**521**	**1,268**	**1,493**	**212**	**13,985**	**2,256**	**520**	**1,264**	**1,463**	**203**	
11,053	**1,840**	**432**	**1,120**	**1,151**	**155**	**10,982**	**1,794**	**431**	**1,116**	**1,129**	**146**	
1,116	*146*	*15*	*186*	*201*	*7*	*1,062*	*146*	*14*	*186*	*179*	*7*	
240	14	1	15	61	1	187	14	..	15	39	1	1
6	..	..	..	8	..	6	..	..	..	8	..	2
60	9	..	39	89	1	59	9	..	39	89	1	3
19	..	..	..	..	..	*18*	..	..	..	..	..	
59	9	..	22	1	..	59	9	..	22	1	..	4
751	114	14	110	42	5	751	114	14	110	42	5	5
4,772	*529*	*230*	*510*	*268*	*53*	*4,772*	*495*	*230*	*510*	*268*	*49*	
912	133	22	121	91	18	912	133	22	121	91	18	6
2,411	304	145	260	84	16	2,411	304	145	260	84	16	7
38	9	6	4	10	8	38	9	6	4	10	8	8
339	29	5	64	23	..	339	29	5	64	23	..	9
1,072	54	52	61	60	11	1,072	20	52	61	60	7	10
4,163	*874*	*67*	*252*	*339*	*70*	*4,146*	*862*	*67*	*248*	*339*	*65*	
620	146	6	9	26	1	620	146	6	9	26	1	11
1,048	327	7	79	58	26	1,035	317	7	75	58	21	12
7	*81*	..	*30*	..	..	*2*	*81*	..	*30*	..	..	
1,607	128	17	31	121	14	1,603	128	17	31	121	14	13
667	235	20	24	90	27	667	233	20	24	90	27	14
221	38	17	109	44	2	221	38	17	109	44	2	15
1,002	*291*	*120*	*172*	*343*	*25*	*1,002*	*291*	*120*	*172*	*343*	*25*	
349	199	22	96	89	18	349	199	22	96	89	18	16
379	61	42	20	197	7	379	61	42	20	197	7	17
274	31	56	56	57	..	274	31	56	56	57	..	18
3,040	**491**	**89**	**148**	**342**	**57**	**3,003**	**462**	**89**	**148**	**334**	**57**	
969	161	31	37	138	19	937	156	31	37	130	19	19
575	95	13	30	51	18	573	71	13	30	51	18	20
844	91	36	43	136	19	844	91	36	43	136	19	21
652	144	9	38	17	1	649	144	9	38	17	1	22
633	**39**	**58**	**71**	**158**	**9**	**633**	**39**	**58**	**71**	**158**	**9**	
..	..	..	..	..	..	..	..	..	..	..	..	23
40	10	8	21	4	2	40	10	8	21	4	2	24
22	4	4	15	7	..	22	4	4	15	7	..	25
..	..	..	..	..	..	..	..	..	..	..	..	26
40	..	5	23	6	..	40	..	5	23	6	..	27
..	..	..	..	..	..	..	..	..	..	..	..	28
..	1	..	..	..	1	..	1	..	..		1	29
18	..	1	..	..	..	18	..	1	..	..	..	30
69	4	5	10	15	3	69	4	5	10	15	3	31
11	1	13	..	..	..	11	1	13	..	..	..	32
128	18	3	..	15	3	128	18	3	..	15	3	33
45	..	4	..	41	..	45	..	4	..	41	..	34
180	1	15	..	58	..	180	1	15	..	58	..	35
52	..	..	..	4	..	52	..	..	..	4	..	36
28	..	..	2	8	..	28	..	..	2	8	..	37

TABLE X Occupation or means

Serial No.	District, City or State.	Class B.—Preparation and supply / Sub-class III.— / Order 6.—Hides, skins and hard materials / 52.—Furriers and persons occupied with feathers and bristles; brush makers. Total earners (principal occupations). Males.	Total earners (principal occupations). Females.	Total working dependants. Males.	Total working dependants. Females.	Total following occupation as subsidiary to other. Males.	Total following occupation as subsidiary to other. Females.
1	2	372	373	374	375	376	377
	Central Provinces and Berar	20	63	..	..	..	4
	C. P. British Districts and Berar	20	63	..	..	..	4
	C. P. British Districts	14	34	..	..	..	4
	Jubbulpore Division	..	..	..	..	..	..
1	Saugor	..	..	..	..	..	..
2	Damoh	..	..	..	..	..	..
3	Jubbulpore	..	..	..	..	..	..
	Jubbulpore City	..	..	..	..	..	..
4	Mandla	..	..	..	..	..	..
5	Seoni	..	..	..	..	..	..
	Nerbudda Division	..	34	..	..	..	4
6	Narsinghpur	..	..	..	..	..	..
7	Hoshangabad	..	..	..	..	..	..
8	Nimar	..	..	..	..	..	..
9	Betul	..	..	..	..	..	..
10	Chhindwara	..	34	..	..	..	4
	Nagpur Division	14	..	..	..	..	..
11	Wardha	..	..	..	..	..	..
12	Nagpur	10	..	..	..	..	..
	Nagpur City	5	..	..	..	..	..
13	Chanda	4	..	..	..	..	..
14	Bhandara	..	..	..	..	..	..
15	Balaghat	..	..	..	..	..	..
	Chhattisgarh Division	..	..	..	..	..	..
16	Raipur	..	..	..	..	..	..
17	Bilaspur	..	..	..	..	..	..
18	Drug	..	..	..	..	..	..
	Berar	6	29	..	..	..	..
19	Amraoti	4	5	..	..	..	..
20	Akola	2	24	..	..	..	..
21	Buldana	..	..	..	..	..	..
22	Yeotmal	..	..	..	..	..	..
	Central Provinces States	..	..	..	..	..	..
23	Makrai	..	..	..	..	..	..
24	Bastar	..	..	..	..	..	..
25	Kanker	..	..	..	..	..	..
26	Nandgaon	..	..	..	..	..	..
27	Khairagarh	..	..	..	..	..	..
28	Chhuikhadan	..	..	..	..	..	..
29	Kawardha	..	..	..	..	..	..
30	Sakti	..	..	..	..	..	..
31	Raigarh	..	..	..	..	..	..
32	Sarangarh	..	..	..	..	..	..
33	Changbhakar	..	..	..	..	..	..
34	Korea	..	..	..	..	..	..
35	Surguja	..	..	..	..	..	..
36	Udaipur	..	..	..	..	..	..
37	Jashpur	..	..	..	..	..	..

of materials substances—*contd.* Industry—*contd.* from the animal kingdom—*concld.* 53.—Bone, ivory, horn, shell, etc., workers (except buttons).						Order 7.—Wood. Total order 7.						Serial No.
Total earners (principal occupations).		Total working dependants.		Total following occupation as subsidiary to other.		Total earners (principal occupations).		Total working dependants.		Total following occupation as subsidiary to other.		
Males.	Females.	Males.	Females.	Males.	Females.	Males.	Females.	Males.	Females.	Males.	Females.	
378	379	380	381	382	383	384	385	386	387	388	389	
88	**12**	**1**	**4**	**30**	**5**	**59,616**	**19,145**	**2,148**	**6,125**	**12,593**	**3,222**	
88	**12**	**1**	**4**	**30**	**5**	***54,300***	***17,748***	**1,624**	**4,622**	**11,421**	**3,119**	
57	**12**	**1**	**4**	**22**	**5**	**39,863**	**15,283**	**1,281**	**4,199**	**9,365**	**2,434**	
54	..	*1*	..	*22*	..	*9,240*	*3,055*	*221*	*792*	*1,809*	*270*	
53	..	1	..	22	..	2,267	695	93	54	290	66	1
..	..	..	..	..	..	1,857	378	31	135	404	82	2
1	..	..	..	..	..	3,354	1,406	79	343	513	84	3
1	..	..	..	..	..	*1,384*	*290*	*3*	*9*	*41*	*27*	
..	..	..	..	..	..	614	160	10	94	265	17	4
..	..	..	..	..	..	1,148	416	8	166	337	21	5
..	..	..	..	..	..	*8,126*	*2,545*	*341*	*1,472*	*2,056*	*1,255*	
..	..	..	..	..	..	1,016	505	42	520	185	37	6
..	..	..	..	..	..	2,584	815	139	426	416	137	7
..	..	..	..	..	..	1,291	376	89	184	262	51	8
..	..	..	..	..	..	1,645	563	11	217	853	994	9
..	..	..	..	..	..	1,590	286	60	125	340	36	10
3	*12*	..	*4*	..	*5*	*17,803*	*6,017*	*503*	*1,414*	*3,041*	*514*	
..	..	..	..	..	..	2,739	355	19	37	349	62	11
3	10	..	4	..	5	6,210	1,451	155	199	618	149	12
..	..	..	..	..	..	*1,638*	*331*	*76*	*76*	*27*	*2*	
..	..	..	..	..	..	4,139	1,595	91	282	727	33	13
..	2	..	..	..	..	3,468	2,074	187	270	840	231	14
..	..	..	..	..	..	1,247	542	51	626	507	39	15
..	..	..	..	..	..	*4,694*	*3,666*	*216*	*521*	*2,459*	*395*	
..	..	..	..	..	..	2,484	2,514	66	173	1,455	59	16
..	..	..	..	..	..	1,405	874	67	38	885	330	17
..	..	..	..	..	..	805	278	83	310	119	6	18
31	..	..	..	**8**	..	**14,437**	**2,465**	**343**	**423**	**2,056**	**685**	
28	..	..	..	8	..	3,977	697	101	163	663	208	19
..	..	..	..	..	..	3,407	590	76	58	597	276	20
..	..	..	..	..	..	3,237	856	78	54	508	171	21
3	..	..	..	..	..	3,816	322	88	148	288	30	22
..	..	..	..	..	..	**5,316**	**1,397**	**524**	**1,503**	**1,172**	**103**	
..	..	..	..	..	..	17	3	5	22	..	..	23
..	..	..	..	..	..	672	107	47	163	227	13	24
..	..	..	..	..	..	146	56	37	27	23	..	25
..	..	..	..	..	..	229	102	10	35	7	..	26
..	..	..	..	..	..	169	54	16	66	20	3	27
..	..	..	..	..	..	33	40	1	14	15	5	28
..	..	..	..	..	..	77	24	1	6	184	25	29
..	..	..	..	..	..	113	119	20	33	45	27	30
..	..	..	..	..	..	575	154	48	344	108	9	31
..	..	..	..	..	..	189	116	17	12	39	..	32
..	..	..	..	..	..	3	..	..	..	..	..	33
..	..	..	..	..	..	330	144	1	..	18	..	34
..	..	..	..	..	..	1,526	120	171	693	299	21	35
..	..	..	..	..	..	304	78	4	..	67	..	36
..	..	..	..	..	..	933	280	146	88	120	..	37

TABLE X — Occupation or means of

Serial No.	Class .. / Sub-class .. / Order .. / Sub-order .. / Group ..	Class B.—Preparation and supply / Sub-class III.— / Order 7.— / 54.—Sawyers.					
	District, City or State.	Total earners (principal occupations).		Total working dependants.		Total following occupation as subsidiary to other.	
		Males.	Females.	Males.	Females.	Males.	Females.
1	2	390	391	392	393	394	395
	Central Provinces and Berar ..	**3,186**	**232**	**29**	**47**	**904**	**17**
	C. P. British Districts and Berar ..	**2,792**	**220**	**13**	**7**	**854**	**17**
	C. P. British Districts	**2,445**	**217**	**10**	**7**	**734**	**17**
	Jubbulpore Division	*953*	*184*	*2*	*1*	*291*	*17*
1	Saugor	133	109	..	..	5	..
2	Damoh	..	..	..	..	..	..
3	Jubbulpore	316	10	..	1	16	..
	Jubbulpore City	*263*	*9*	..	*1*	*6*	..
4	Mandla	337	64	2	..	251	17
5	Seoni	167	1	..	..	19	..
	Nerbudda Division	*244*	..	*1*	..	*135*	..
6	Narsinghpur	8	..	..	..	3	..
7	Hoshangabad	44	..	1	..	102	..
8	Nimar	22	..	..	..	2	..
9	Betul	52	..	..	..	3	..
10	Chhindwara	118	..	..	..	25	..
	Nagpur Division	*892*	*29*	*5*	*6*	*265*	..
11	Wardha	67	..	..	..	13	..
12	Nagpur	298	..	..	..	14	..
	Nagpur City	*209*	..	..	..	..	..
13	Chanda	219	..	1	..	50	..
14	Bhandara	140	..	4	..	48	..
15	Balaghat	168	29	..	6	140	..
	Chhattisgarh Division	*356*	*4*	*2*	..	*43*	..
16	Raipur	273	3	2	..	30	..
17	Bilaspur	56	..	..	..	9	..
18	Drug	27	1	..	..	4	..
	Berar	**347**	**3**	**3**	..	**120**	..
19	Amraoti	144	3	1	..	86	..
20	Akola	60	..	..	..	8	..
21	Buldana	70	..	2	..	14	..
22	Yeotmal	73	..	..	..	12	..
	Central Provinces States	**394**	**12**	**16**	**40**	**50**	..
23	Makrai	..	..	..	..	..	..
24	Bastar	287	11	16	40	38	..
25	Kanker	2	..	..	..	1	..
26	Nandgaon	9	..	..	..	..	..
27	Khairagarh	8	..	..	..	1	..
28	Chhuikhadan	..	..	..	..	..	..
29	Kawardha	6	..	..	..	10	..
30	Sakti	..	..	..	..	..	..
31	Raigarh	23	..	..	..	..	..
32	Sarangarh	18	..	..	..	..	..
33	Changbhakar	..	..	..	..	..	..
34	Korea	..	..	..	..	..	..
35	Surguja	..	..	..	..	..	..
36	Udaipur	..	..	..	..	..	..
37	Jashpur	41	1	..	..	..	..

material substances—*contd.*

Industry—*contd.*

Wood—*concld.*

55.—Carpenters, turners and joiners, etc.						56.—Basket makers, and other industries of woody materials, including leaves and thatchers and binders working with bamboo reeds or similar materials.						Serial No.
Total earners (principal occupations).		Total working dependants.		Total following occupation as subsidiary to other.		Total earners (principal occupations).		Total working dependants.		Total following occupation as subsidiary to other.		
Males.	Females.	Males.	Females.	Males.	Females.	Males.	Females.	Males.	Females.	Males.	Females.	
396	397	398	399	400	401	402	403	404	405	406	407	
34,479	**366**	**727**	**227**	**5,520**	**66**	**21,951**	**18,547**	**1,392**	**5,851**	**6,169**	**3,139**	
33,614	**363**	**700**	**207**	**5,362**	**65**	**17,894**	**17,165**	**911**	**4,408**	**5,205**	**3,037**	
21,878	**238**	**434**	**176**	**4,161**	**57**	**15,540**	**14,828**	**837**	**4,016**	**4,470**	**2,360**	
3,499	*59*	*60*	*46*	*838*	*4*	*4,788*	*2,812*	*159*	*745*	*680*	*249*	
918	32	8	38	122	3	1,216	554	85	16	163	63	1
689	8	10	..	237	..	1,168	370	21	135	167	82	2
1,241	17	37	8	265	1	1,797	1,379	42	334	232	83	3
783	*5*	*3*	*5*	*11*	..	*338*	*276*	..	*3*	*24*	*27*	
135	1	1	..	8	..	142	95	7	94	6	..	4
516	1	4	..	206	.	465	414	4	166	112	21	5
5,340	*53*	*181*	*31*	*900*	*1*	*2,542*	*2,492*	*159*	*1,441*	*1,021*	*1,254*	
530	3	2	3	34	..	478	502	40	517	148	37	6
1,759	1	85	7	143	1	781	814	53	419	171	136	7
843	27	39	7	143	..	426	349	50	177	117	51	8
1,002	8	4	12	288	.	591	555	7	205	562	994	9
1,206	14	51	2	292	..	266	272	9	123	23	36	10
11,821	*84*	*174*	*38*	*1,805*	*37*	*5,090*	*5,904*	*324*	*1,370*	*971*	*477*	
2,421	7	19	3	244	..	251	348	..	34	92	62	11
4,708	30	92	10	354	..	1,204	1,421	63	189	250	149	12
1,035	*13*	*20*	*2*	*19*	..	*391*	*318*	*56*	*74*	*8*	*2*	
2,274	16	23	4	539	.	1,646	1,579	67	278	138	33	13
2,074	31	34	4	471	37	1,254	2,043	149	266	321	194	14
344	..	6	17	197	..	735	513	45	603	170	39	15
1,218	*42*	*19*	*61*	*618*	*15*	*3,120*	*3,620*	*195*	*460*	*1,798*	*380*	
591	16	3	59	197	14	1,620	2,495	61	114	1,228	45	16
392	26	11	1	347	1	957	848	56	37	529	329	17
235	..	5	1	74	..	543	277	78	309	41	6	18
11,736	**125**	**266**	**31**	**1,201**	**8**	**2,354**	**2,337**	**74**	**392**	**735**	**677**	
3,342	25	84	8	406	2	491	669	16	155	171	206	19
2,800	20	45	4	295	3	547	570	31	54	294	273	20
2,435	50	60	7	276	.	732	806	16	47	218	171	21
3,159	30	77	12	224	3	584	292	11	136	52	27	22
865	**3**	**27**	**20**	**158**	**1**	**4,057**	**1,382**	**481**	**1,443**	**964**	**102**	
1	..	..	..	.	..	16	3	5	22	.	..	23
175	1	4	17	28	1	210	95	27	106	161	12	24
36	..	15	..	4	..	108	56	22	27	18	..	25
89	..	3	..	3	..	131	102	7	35	4	..	26
129	..	1	..	19	..	32	54	15	66	.	3	27
17	..	.	..	13	..	16	40	1	14	2	5	28
23	.	..	..	24	..	48	24	1	6	150	25	29
24	.	2	..	..	..	89	119	18	33	45	27	30
95	.	2	..	22	..	457	154	46	344	86	9	31
32	..	..	..	17	..	139	116	17	12	22	..	32
3	.	.	..	..	..	..	..	..	..	..	..	33
8	..	..	..	2	..	322	144	1	.	16	..	34
182	2	..	3	22	..	1,344	118	171	690	277	21	35
4	..	..	..	..	..	300	78	4	..	67	..	36
47	..	..	..	4	..	845	279	146	88	116	..	37

TABLE X

Occupation or means of

Serial No.	Class .. / Sub-class .. / Order .. / Sub-order .. / Group ..	Class B.—Preparation and supply / Sub-class III.— / Order 8.— / Total order 8.					
	District, City or State.	Total earners (principal occupations).		Total working dependants.		Total following occupation as subsidiary to other.	
		Males.	Females.	Males.	Females.	Males.	Females.
1	2	408	409	410	411	412	413
	Central Provinces and Berar	**43,467**	**2,995**	**2,852**	**4,335**	**6,290**	**326**
	C. P. British Districts and Berar ..	**36,763**	**2,538**	**1,747**	**1,905**	**5,180**	**312**
	C. P. British Districts	**30,603**	**1,993**	**1,411**	**1,652**	**4,779**	**274**
	Jubbulpore Division	*7,468*	*205*	*132*	*172*	*1,195*	*16*
1	Saugor	1,324	23	46	34	280	..
2	Damoh	807	46	7	30	146	5
3	Jubbulpore	3,127	94	35	29	480	10
	Jubbulpore City	*2,058*	*25*	*3*	*2*	*10*	..
4	Mandla	1,005	19	23	54	121	..
5	Seoni	1,205	23	21	25	168	1
	Nerbudda Division	*6,474*	*391*	*292*	*514*	*527*	*53*
6	Narsinghpur	1,299	51	14	45	154	2
7	Hoshangabad	1,243	22	90	28	66	2
8	Nimar	986	34	47	62	89	2
9	Betul	1,358	263	27	207	62	38
10	Chhindwara	1,588	21	114	172	156	9
	Nagpur Division	*10,765*	*538*	*280*	*303*	*1,251*	*71*
11	Wardha	1,044	50	30	80	59	7
12	Nagpur	2,504	202	61	79	139	21
	Nagpur City	*472*	*36*	*20*	..	*9*	..
13	Chanda	2,589	134	57	65	261	17
14	Bhandara	2,981	118	74	42	484	16
15	Balaghat	1,647	34	58	37	308	10
	Chhattisgarh Division	*5,896*	*859*	*707*	*663*	*1,806*	*134*
16	Raipur	2,687	505	281	378	639	28
17	Bilaspur	1,620	311	93	120	963	106
18	Drug	1,589	43	333	165	204	..
	Berar	**6,160**	**545**	**336**	**253**	**401**	**38**
19	Amraoti	1,751	88	68	79	120	5
20	Akola	1,490	158	48	57	117	4
21	Buldana	1,056	134	47	63	74	13
22	Yeotmal	1,863	165	173	54	90	16
	Central Provinces States	**6,704**	**457**	**1,105**	**2,430**	**1,110**	**14**
23	Makrai ..	17	1	..	6	6	..
24	Bastar	1,272	130	345	853	117	..
25	Kanker	273	20	77	67	91	3
26	Nandgaon	424	15	49	29	68	..
27	Khairagarh	283	27	52	9	41	..
28	Chhuikhadan	3	..	..	2	..	5
29	Kawardha	185	38	1	4	8	..
30	Sakti	39	..	11	..	15	..
31	Raigarh	727	32	185	451	103	..
32	Sarangarh	112	6	22	4	43	3
33	Changbhakar	109	17	..	10	13	2
34	Korea	379	29	3	3	77	..
35	Surguja	1,435	70	157	331	419	1
36	Udaipur	451	..		..	15	..
37	Jashpur	995	72	203	661	94	..

of material substances.—*contd.*

Industry.—*contd.*

Metals.

57.—Smelting, forging and rolling of iron and other metals.						58.—Makers of arms, guns, etc.						Serial No.
Total earners (principal occupations).		Total working dependants.		Total following occupation as subsidiary to other.		Total earners (principal occupations).		Total working dependants.		Total following occupation as subsidiary to other.		
Males.	Females.	Males.	Females.	Males.	Females.	Males.	Females.	Males.	Females.	Males.	Females.	
414	415	416	417	418	419	420	421	422	423	424	425	
787	**161**	**79**	**67**	**77**	**2**	**1,834**	**65**	**109**	**1**	**9**	**5**	
596	**109**	**32**	**9**	**23**	**2**	**1,833**	**65**	**109**	**1**	**9**	**5**	
490	**105**	**31**	**5**	**16**	**2**	**1,825**	**65**	**109**	**1**	**7**	**5**	
19	*1*	..	..	..	..	*1,697*	*50*	*3*	..	*5*	*5*	
19	1	..	..	..	..	5	..	..	..	..	..	1
..	..	..	..	..	..	2	..	..	..	..	..	2
..	..	..	..	..	..	1,684	50	3	..	5	5	3
..	..	..	..	..	..	*1,507*	*17*	*3*	..	*5*	..	
..	..	..	..	..	..	1	..	..	..	..	..	4
..	..	..	..	..	..	5	..	..	..	..	..	5
395	..	*15*	..	*8*	..	*14*	*8*	..	..	*2*	..	
174	..	..	..	..	..	4	..	..	..	..	..	6
218	..	15	..	8	..	2	..	..	..	..	..	7
..	..	..	..	..	..	2	..	..	..	1	..	8
3	..	..	..	..	..	..	..	..	..	..	..	9
..	..	..	..	..	..	6	8	..	..	1	..	10
61	*29*	*16*	*2*	*8*	..	*2*	*7*	..	*1*	..	..	
..	..	1	..	..	..	..	..	..	..	..	..	11
15	8	..	1	1	..	1	..	..	..	..	..	12
..	*7*	..	..	..	..	*1*	..	..	..	..	..	
26	9	2	1	2	..	..	7	..	1	..	..	13
20	10	13	..	5	..	..	..	..	..	..	..	14
..	2	..	..	..	..	1	..	..	..	..	..	15
15	*75*	..	*3*	..	*2*	*112*	..	*106*	..	..	..	
2	48	..	2	..	2	109	..	106	..	..	..	16
13	27	..	1	..	..	3	..	..	..	..	..	17
..	..	..	..	..	..	..	..	..	..	..	..	18
106	**4**	**1**	**4**	**7**	..	**8**	..	..	..	**2**	..	
29	1	..	..	1	..	..	..	..	..	..	..	19
27	1	..	..	1	..	8	..	..	..	2	..	20
31	2	..	4	1	..	..	..	..	..	..	..	21
19	..	1	..	4	..	..	..	..	..	..	..	22
191	**52**	**47**	**58**	**54**	..	**1**	..	..	..	..	..	
..	..	..	..	..	..	1	..	..	..	..	..	23
79	43	27	40	9	..	..	..	..	..	..	..	24
3	..	2	..	..	..	..	..	..	..	..	..	25
..	..	..	..	..	..	..	..	..	..	..	..	26
..	..	..	..	..	..	..	..	..	..	..	..	27
..	..	..	..	..	..	..	..	..	..	..	..	28
..	..	..	..	..	..	..	..	..	..	..	..	29
12	..	4	..	15	..	..	..	..	..	..	..	30
..	..	..	..	..	..	..	..	..	..	..	..	31
..	..	..	..	..	..	..	..	..	..	..	..	32
..	..	..	..	..	..	..	..	..	..	..	..	33
1	..	..	..	..	..	..	..	..	..	..	..	34
95	9	14	18	30	..	..	..	..	..	..	..	35
..	..	..	..	..	..	..	..	..	..	..	..	36
1	..	..	..	..	..	..	..	..	..	..	..	37

TABLE X

Occupation or means of

Serial No.	District, City or State.	Total earners (principal occupations). Males	Total earners (principal occupations). Females	Total working dependants. Males	Total working dependants. Females	Total following occupation as subsidiary to other. Males	Total following occupation as subsidiary to other. Females
	Class ..	Class B.—Preparation and supply					
	Sub-class ..	Sub-class III.—					
	Order ..	Order 8.—					
	Sub-order ..						
	Group ..	59.—Blacksmiths, other workers in iron, makers of implements.					
1	2	426	427	428	429	430	431
	Central Provinces and Berar	**35,004**	**2,125**	**2,333**	**3,808**	**5,603**	**285**
	C. P. British Districts and Berar ..	**29,446**	**1,930**	**1,352**	**1,708**	**4,726**	**274**
	C. P. British Districts ..	**24,396**	**1,415**	**1,056**	**1,463**	**4,436**	**238**
	Jubbulpore Division ..	*4,882*	*84*	*105*	*110*	*1,149*	*10*
1	Saugor ..	1,037	13	31	21	268	..
2	Damoh ..	699	17	7	5	144	4
3	Jubbulpore ..	1,183	25	29	25	461	5
	Jubbulpore City ..	*430*	*2*	..	*2*	*4*	..
4	Mandla ..	836	15	21	40	108	..
5	Seoni ..	1,127	14	17	19	168	1
	Nerbudda Division ..	*4,907*	*301*	*233*	*451*	*465*	*52*
6	Narsinghpur ..	864	10	13	22	137	2
7	Hoshangabad ..	774	19	50	27	52	1
8	Nimar ..	736	28	33	46	78	2
9	Betul ..	1,165	233	27	204	54	38
10	Chhindwara ..	1,368	11	110	152	144	9
	Nagpur Division ..	*9,851*	*405*	*230*	*273*	*1,162*	*66*
11	Wardha ..	969	42	28	78	50	7
12	Nagpur ..	2,289	148	49	77	121	21
	Nagpur City ..	*349*	*10*	*8*	..	*1*	..
13	Chanda ..	2,405	115	55	63	234	16
14	Bhandara ..	2,651	81	45	33	456	12
15	Balaghat ..	1,537	19	53	22	301	10
	Chhattisgarh Division ..	*4,756*	*625*	*488*	*629*	*1,660*	*110*
16	Raipur ..	2,106	360	128	373	565	22
17	Bilaspur ..	1,315	240	76	110	901	88
18	Drug ..	1,335	25	284	146	194	..
	Berar ..	**5,050**	**515**	**296**	**245**	**290**	**36**
19	Amraoti ..	1,344	78	59	76	92	5
20	Akola ..	1,106	150	30	56	69	2
21	Buldana ..	851	127	42	59	47	13
22	Yeotmal ..	1,749	160	165	54	82	16
	Central Provinces States ..	**5,558**	**195**	**981**	**2,100**	**877**	**11**
23	Makrai ..	10	1		6	6	..
24	Bastar ..	993	51	292	710	92	..
25	Kanker ..	259	20	71	57	90	3
26	Nandgaon ..	380	2	48	17	66	..
27	Khairagarh ..	262	11	51	9	41	..
28	Chhuikhadan ..			..	2	..	5
29	Kawardha ..	162	38	1	4	4	..
30	Sakti ..	27		7	..	..	..
31	Raigarh ..	504	10	160	402	75	..
32	Sarangarh ..	92	..	20	3	37	..
33	Changbhakar ..	109	17	..	10	13	2
34	Korea ..	262	5	3	3	65	..
35	Surguja ..	1,224	40	126	264	284	1
36	Udaipur ..	395	..	..	..	14	..
37	Jashpur ..	879	..	202	613	90	..

Livelihood—General Distribution—*contd.*

TABLE X

of material substances—*contd.*

Industry—*contd.*

Metals—*contd*

60.—Workers in brass, copper and bell metals.						61.—Workers in other metals (except precious metals).						Serial No.
Total earners (principal occupations).		Total working dependants.		Total following occupation as subsidiary to other.		Total earners (principal occupations).		Total working dependants.		Total following occupation as subsidiary to other.		
Males.	Females.	Males	Females.	Males.	Females.	Males.	Females.	Males.	Females.	Males	Females.	
432	433	434	435	436	437	438	439	440	441	442	443	
4,331	**448**	**291**	**408**	**378**	**18**	**1,510**	**194**	**39**	**51**	**223**	**16**	
3,467	**280**	**219**	**168**	**233**	**15**	**1,420**	**152**	**34**	**19**	**189**	**16**	
3,003	**272**	**198**	**166**	**188**	**13**	**888**	**134**	**16**	**17**	**132**	**16**	
756	*64*	*23*	*61*	*37*	*1*	*113*	*4*	..	*1*	*4*	..	
234	9	15	13	9	..	28	..	..	..	3	..	1
106	29	..	25	2	1	..	..	..	..	..	..	2
185	13	3	4	13	..	75	4	..	..	1	..	3
72	*4*	..	..	.	..	*49*	..	..	..	*1*	..	
162	4	1	13	13	.	6	..	..	1	..	..	4
69	9	4	6	..	..	4	..	..	..	..	..	5
975	*79*	*44*	*63*	*33*	*1*	*183*	*3*	..	..	*19*	..	
244	41	1	23	17	..	13	..	..	..	..	..	6
219	1	25	1	5	1	30	2	..	..	1	..	7
163	6	14	16	1	..	85	..	.	..	9	..	8
174	30	..	3	6	..	16	..	..	..	2	..	9
175	1	4	20	4	.	39	1	..	..	7	..	10
466	*60*	*19*	*24*	*40*	*4*	*385*	*37*	*15*	*3*	*41*	*1*	
5	4	..	..	1	.	70	4	1	2	8	..	11
46	21	..	..	3	..	153	25	12	1	14	..	12
32	*3*	..	..	1	..	*90*	*6*	*12*	..	*7*	..	
88	3	..	..	13	..	70	..	..	..	12	1	13
233	20	14	9	18	4	77	7	2	.	5	..	14
94	12	5	15	5	..	15	1	.	..	2	..	15
806	*69*	*112*	*18*	*78*	*7*	*207*	*90*	*1*	*13*	*68*	*15*	
362	31	46	..	44	1	108	66	1	3	30	3	16
210	32	17	..	26	6	79	12	..	9	36	12	17
234	6	49	18	8	..	20	12	..	1	2	..	18
464	**8**	**21**	**2**	**45**	**2**	**532**	**18**	**18**	**2**	**57**	..	
155	2	3	2	4	..	223	7	6	1	23	..	19
178	..	11	..	32	2	171	7	7	1	13	..	20
91	3	2	..	9	..	83	2	3	.	17	..	21
40	3	5	..	..	..	55	2	2	.	4	..	22
864	**168**	**72**	**240**	**145**	**3**	**90**	**42**	**5**	**32**	**34**	..	
4	..	..	..	..	..	2	..	..	..	..	..	23
191	29	26	103	14	..	9	7	..	..	2	..	24
11	..	4	10	1	..	..	..	..	..	..	..	25
23	..	1	..	1	..	21	13	.	12	1	..	26
17	16	1	.	.	..	4	.	..	..	..	..	27
3	..	..	.	..	..	..	..	.	..	..	..	28
19	..	..	..	4	..	4	..	..	..	..	..	29
..	..	..	..	..	..	..	..	..	..	..	..	30
206	13	24	49	26	..	17	9	1	..	2	..	31
20	6	2	1	5	3	..	..	..	.	1	..	32
..	..	..	..	..	..	..	..	..	..	..	..	33
114	24	..	..	12	..	2	..	..	..	..	..	34
85	8	13	29	77	..	31	13	4	20	28	..	35
56	..	..	..	1	..	..	.	..	..	.	..	36
115	72	1	48	4	..	..	..	..	..	..	..	37

TABLE X **Occupation or means of**

Serial No.	Class .. / Sub-class .. / Order .. / Sub-order .. / Group ..	Class B.—Preparation and supply / Sub-class III.— / Order 8—Metals—*concld.* / 62.—Workers in mints, die-sinkers, etc.					
	District, City or State.	Total earners (principal occupations).		Total working dependants.		Total following occupation as subsidiary to other.	
		Males.	Females.	Males.	Females.	Males.	Females.
1	2	444	445	446	447	448	449
	Central Provinces and Berar ..	1	2	1	..	..	..
	C. P. British Districts and Berar ..	1	2	1	..	..	..
	C. P. British Districts ..	1	2	1	..	..	..
	Jubbulpore Division ..	*1*	*2*	*1*	..	..	..
1	Saugor ..	1	..	..	..	..	..
2	Damoh ..	..	..	..	..	..	..
3	Jubbulpore ..	..	2	..	..	..	..
	Jubbulpore City ..	..	2	..	..	..	..
4	Mandla ..	..	..	1	..	..	..
5	Seoni ..	..	..	..	..	..	..
	Nerbudda Division ..	..	..	..	..	..	..
6	Narsinghpur ..	..	..	..	..	..	..
7	Hoshangabad ..	..	..	..	..	..	..
8	Nimar ..	..	..	..	..	..	..
9	Betul ..	..	..	..	..	..	..
10	Chhindwara ..	..	..	..	..	..	..
	Nagpur Division ..	..	..	..	..	..	..
11	Wardha ..	..	..	..	..	..	..
12	Nagpur ..	..	..	..	..	..	..
	Nagpur City ..	..	..	..	..	..	..
13	Chanda ..	..	..	..	..	..	..
14	Bhandara ..	..	..	..	..	..	..
15	Balaghat ..	..	..	..	..	..	..
	Chhattisgarh Division ..	..	..	..	..	..	..
16	Raipur ..	..	..	..	..	..	..
17	Bilaspur ..	..	..	..	..	..	..
18	Drug ..	..	..	..	..	..	..
	Berar ..	..	..	..	..	..	..
19	Amraoti ..	..	..	..	..	..	..
20	Akola ..	..	..	..	..	..	..
21	Buldana ..	..	..	..	..	..	..
22	Yeotmal ..	..	..	..	..	..	..
	Central Provinces States ..	..	..	..	..	..	..
23	Makrai ..	..	..	..	..	..	..
24	Bastar ..	..	..	..	..	..	..
25	Kanker ..	..	..	..	..	..	..
26	Nandgaon ..	..	..	..	..	..	..
27	Khairagarh ..	..	..	..	..	..	..
28	Chhuikhadan ..	..	..	..	..	..	..
29	Kawardha ..	..	..	..	..	..	..
30	Sakti ..	..	..	..	..	..	..
31	Raigarh ..	..	..	..	..	..	..
32	Sarangarh ..	..	..	..	..	..	..
33	Changbhakar ..	..	..	..	..	..	..
34	Korea ..	..	..	..	..	..	..
35	Surguja ..	..	..	..	..	..	..
36	Udaipur ..	..	..	..	..	..	..
37	Jashpur ..	..	..	..	..	..	..

Livelihood—General Distribution—*contd.*

TABLE X

of material substances—*contd.*

Industry—*contd.*

Order 9.—Ceramics.

Total order 9.						63.—Potters and makers of earthen wares.						Serial No.
Total earners (principal occupations).		Total working dependants.		Total following occupation as subsidiary to other.		Total earners (principal occupations).		Total working dependants.		Total following occupation as subsidiary to other.		
Males.	Females.	Males.	Females.	Males.	Females.	Males.	Females.	Males.	Females.	Males.	Females.	
450	451	452	453	454	455	456	457	458	459	460	461	
26,020	**11,745**	**2,009**	**7,751**	**4,969**	**1,087**	**19,487**	**8,858**	**1,829**	**7,178**	**3,938**	**804**	
23,366	**10,796**	**1,372**	**5,575**	**3,802**	**1,009**	**17,175**	**8,030**	**1,207**	**5,038**	**2,871**	**729**	
18,362	**8,738**	**1,153**	**4,812**	**3,308**	**847**	**12,867**	**6,152**	**1,004**	**4,326**	**2,473**	**618**	
5,076	*2,297*	*238*	*1,171*	*537*	*159*	*3,631*	*1,669*	*191*	*1,010*	*486*	*137*	
820	291	47	223	86	15	783	270	47	200	85	13	1
705	299	35	85	68	70	692	298	35	85	65	70	2
2,659	1,438	139	678	314	52	1,669	996	101	604	294	47	3
909	*439*	*36*	*81*	*12*	*1*	*166*	*88*	*9*	*20*	*7*	..	
335	88	6	62	23	6	187	27	3	21	8	6	4
557	181	11	123	46	16	300	78	5	100	34	1	5
3,571	*1,681*	*206*	*947*	*457*	*124*	*1,964*	*1,016*	*141*	*753*	*115*	*18*	
510	248	54	244	74	44	326	151	48	216	9	8	6
1,140	549	59	312	72	21	663	304	44	281	42	4	7
791	410	38	137	170	13	464	281	35	99	45	1	8
396	219	4	62	33	4	173	124	2	37	5	4	9
734	255	51	192	108	42	338	156	12	120	14	1	10
5,376	*2,463*	*130*	*605*	*732*	*170*	*3,410*	*1,415*	*98*	*517*	*367*	*76*	
732	302	10	64	63	19	459	269	8	63	36	9	11
1,955	1,058	18	199	98	19	717	303	7	157	27	8	12
520	*226*	*9*	*26*	*1*	..	*57*	*16*	..	..	..	..	
946	303	24	90	169	63	780	250	19	79	90	39	13
1,212	628	40	67	294	56	956	446	32	49	176	17	14
531	172	38	185	108	13	498	147	32	169	38	3	15
4,339	*2,297*	*579*	*2,089*	*1,582*	*394*	*3,862*	*2,052*	*574*	*2,046*	*1,505*	*387*	
2,030	1,625	200	743	780	213	1,743	1,429	200	728	771	210	16
1,526	598	57	401	649	177	1,402	565	55	397	617	173	17
783	74	322	945	153	4	717	58	319	921	117	4	18
5,004	**2,058**	**219**	**763**	**494**	**162**	**4,308**	**1,878**	**203**	**712**	**398**	**111**	
1,858	659	73	222	251	61	1,621	595	67	207	184	35	19
1,365	522	66	290	140	49	1,120	467	66	274	120	47	20
781	405	45	161	96	27	742	390	44	159	78	26	21
1,000	472	35	90	27	25	825	426	26	72	16	3	22
2,654	**949**	**637**	**2,176**	**1,167**	**78**	**2,312**	**825**	**622**	**2,140**	**1,067**	**75**	
6	2	3	..	1	..	3	2	3	..	..	..	23
579	123	169	293	134	18	512	90	164	260	125	18	24
119	75	55	144	18	22	119	75	55	144	18	22	25
378	81	23	183	11	..	157	28	20	180	9	..	26
141	99	77	86	24	1	139	93	74	86	21	1	27
25	64	..	147	25	9	24	64	..	147	8	9	28
57	47	..	..	41	9	55	47	..	..	10	6	29
18	1	7	33	3	13	15	1	7	33	3	13	30
282	17	131	288	149	..	241	15	131	288	148	..	31
94	15	46	63	128	1	93	15	46	63	128	1	32
20	13	1	4	5	..	20	13	1	4	5	..	33
56	18	6	2	76	1	56	18	6	2	76	1	34
432	156	73	482	325	4	432	135	69	482	292	4	35
121	2	3	..	25	..	120	2	3	..	24	..	36
326	236	43	451	202	..	326	227	43	451	200	..	37

TABLE X — Occupation or means of

Serial No.	Class ..	Class B.—Preparation and supply					
	Sub-class ..	Sub-class III.—					
	Order ..	Order 9.—					
	Sub-order ..						
	Group ..	64.—Brick and tile makers.					
	District, City or State.	Total earners (principal occupations).		Total working dependants.		Total following occupation as subsidiary to other.	
		Males.	Females.	Males.	Females.	Males.	Females.
1	2	462	463	464	465	466	467
	Central Provinces and Berar	**5,582**	**2,506**	**174**	**531**	**1,023**	**282**
	C. P. British Districts and Berar ..	**5,278**	**2,390**	**159**	**517**	**923**	**279**
	C. P. British Districts	**4,582**	**2,210**	**143**	**466**	**827**	**228**
	Jubbulpore Division	*728*	*295*	*44*	*161*	*51*	*21*
1	Saugor	36	21	..	23	1	2
2	Damoh	13	1	..	..	3	..
3	Jubbulpore	274	109	35	74	20	4
	Jubbulpore City	*212*	*38*	*26*	*61*	*5*	*1*
4	Mandla	148	61	3	41	15	..
5	Seoni	257	103	6	23	12	15
	Nerbudda Division	*1,594*	*648*	*65*	*176*	*337*	*106*
6	Narsinghpur	178	82	6	10	65	36
7	Hoshangabad	472	245	15	31	25	17
8	Nimar	327	127	3	38	125	12
9	Betul	221	95	2	25	28	..
10	Chhindwara	396	99	39	72	94	41
	Nagpur Division	*1,796*	*1,032*	*29*	*87*	*364*	*94*
11	Wardha	273	33	2	1	27	10
12	Nagpur	1,119	744	10	42	70	11
	Nagpur City	*363*	*201*	*8*	*26*	..	..
13	Chanda	138	52	5	10	79	24
14	Bhandara	233	178	6	18	118	39
15	Balaghat	33	25	6	16	70	10
	Chhattisgarh Division	*464*	*235*	*5*	*42*	*75*	*7*
16	Raipur	276	191	..	15	7	3
17	Bilaspur	122	33	2	4	32	4
18	Drug	66	11	3	23	36	..
	Berar	**696**	**180**	**16**	**51**	**96**	**51**
19	Amraoti	237	64	6	15	47	26
20	Akola	245	55	..	16	20	2
21	Buldana	39	15	1	2	18	1
22	Yeotmal	175	46	9	18	11	22
	Central Provinces States	**304**	**116**	**15**	**14**	**100**	**3**
23	Makrai	3	..	..	..	1	..
24	Bastar	66	31	5	13	9	..
25	Kanker	..	..	..	..	..	..
26	Nandgaon	221	49	3	1	2	..
27	Khairagarh	2	6	3	..	3	..
28	Chhuikhadan	1	..	..	..	17	..
29	Kawardha	2	..	..	..	31	3
30	Sakti	3	..	..	..	..	..
31	Raigarh	4	2	..	..	1	..
32	Sarangarh	1	..	..	..	..	..
33	Changbhakar	..	..	..	..	..	..
34	Korea	..	..	..	..	..	..
35	Surguja	..	19	4	..	33	..
36	Udaipur	1	..	..	..	1	..
37	Jashpur	..	9	..	..	2	..

of material substances—*contd.*

Industry—*contd.*

Ceramics—*concld.*						Order 10.—Chemical products properly so called and analogous.						
65.—Other workers in ceramics.						Total order 10.						Serial No.
Total earners (principal occupations).		Total working dependants.		Total following occupation as subsidiary to other.		Total earners (principal occupations).		Total working dependants.		Total following occupation as subsidiary to other.		
Males.	Females.	Males.	Females.	Males.	Females.	Males.	Females.	Males.	Females.	Males.	Females	
468	469	470	471	472	473	474	475	476	477	478	479	
951	**384**	**6**	**42**	**8**	**1**	**9,102**	**5,209**	**901**	**3,193**	**3,761**	**698**	
913	**376**	**6**	**20**	**8**	**1**	**8,256**	**4,122**	**461**	**1,958**	**2,963**	**624**	
913	**376**	**6**	**20**	**8**	**1**	**7,663**	**4,087**	**431**	**1,949**	**2,901**	**620**	
717	*333*	*3*	..	..	*1*	*1,667*	*800*	*50*	*355*	*586*	*101*	
1	..	..	..	..	..	373	120	11	74	43	13	1
..	..	..	..	..	..	573	287	9	119	89	37	2
716	333	3	..	..	1	443	214	13	75	286	40	3
531	*313*	*1*	..	..	..	*69*	*10*	..	..	*2*	..	
..	..	..	..	..	..	79	41	1	26	90	2	4
..	..	..	..	..	..	199	138	16	61	78	9	5
13	*17*	..	*18*	*5*	..	*2,077*	*1,023*	*136*	*620*	*362*	*55*	
6	15	..	18	..	..	295	192	18	80	63	22	6
5	..	..	..	5	..	445	142	30	88	39	10	7
..	2	..	..	..	..	311	30	7	17	67	2	8
2	..	..	..	..	..	534	330	9	192	71	11	9
..	..	..	..	..	..	492	329	72	243	122	10	10
170	*16*	*3*	*1*	*1*	..	*2,652*	*503*	*50*	*143*	*779*	*78*	
..	..	..	..	..	..	41	..	..	..	16	..	11
119	11	1	..	1	..	614	60	16	18	66	4	12
100	*9*	*1*	..	*1*	..	*133*	*2*	*10*	*1*	*4*	..	
28	1	..	1	..	..	512	106	9	51	175	7	13
23	4	2	..	..	..	872	235	16	33	220	57	14
..	..	..	..	..	..	613	102	9	41	302	10	15
13	*10*	..	*1*	*2*	..	*1,267*	*1,761*	*195*	*831*	*1,174*	*386*	
11	5	..	..	2	..	683	1,074	121	372	407	120	16
2	..	..	..	..	..	177	411	32	239	473	229	17
..	5	..	1	..	..	407	276	42	220	294	37	18
..	..	..	..	..	..	**593**	**35**	**30**	**9**	**62**	**4**	
..	..	..	..	..	..	163	5	11	..	39	..	19
..	..	..	..	..	..	140	10	5	..	12	1	20
..	..	..	..	..	..	156	6	5	2	7	1	21
..	..	..	..	..	..	134	14	9	7	4	2	22
38	**8**	..	**22**	..	..	**846**	**1,087**	**440**	**1,235**	**798**	**74**	
..	..	..	..	..	..	18	..	2	..	3	..	23
1	2	..	20	..	..	33	46	20	130	14	3	24
..	..	..	..	..	..	56	89	34	189	92	38	25
..	4	..	2	..	..	277	290	6	35	52	6	26
..	..	..	..	..	..	66	186	8	314	128	9	27
..	..	..	..	..	..	12	..	302	..	28	..	28
..	..	..	..	..	..	18	115	2	3	67	11	29
..	..	..	..	..	..	11	40	1	40	5	4	30
37	..	..	..	..	..	120	168	8	340	135	2	31
..	..	..	..	..	..	17	76	43	99	110	1	32
..	..	..	..	..	..	27	9	..	1	1	..	33
..	..	..	..	..	..	25	..	..	..	16	..	34
..	2	..	..	..	..	102	10	14	80	133	..	35
..	..	..	..	..	..	3	..	..	..	4	..	36
..	..	..	..	..	..	61	58	..	4	10	..	37

TABLE X — Occupation or means of

Serial No.	Class .. / Sub-class .. / Order .. / Sub-order .. / Group ..	Class B.—Preparation and supply / Sub-class III.— / Order 10.—Chemical products / 66.—Manufacture of matches, fire works and other explosives.					
	District, City or State.	Total earners (principal occupations).		Total working dependants.		Total following occupation as subsidiary to other.	
		Males.	Females.	Males.	Females.	Males.	Females.
1	2	480	481	482	483	484	485
	Ceutral Provinces and Berar ..	**292**	**43**	**7**	**8**	**44**	..
	C. P. British Districts and Berar ..	**287**	**43**	**4**	**8**	**44**	..
	C. P. British Districts	**275**	**39**	**3**	**8**	**42**	..
	Jubbulpore Division	*85*	*8*	*2*	*5*	*2*	..
1	Saugor	27	2	1	2	..	..
2	Damoh	23	1	..	3	..	..
3	Jubbulpore	30	5	1	..	2	..
	Jubbulpore City	*10*	..	..	..	..	..
4	Mandla	..	..	..	..	..	..
5	Seoni	5	..	..	..	..	..
	Nerbudda Division	*135*	*30*	..	*3*	*22*	..
6	Narsinghpur	19	7	..	3	6	..
7	Hoshangabad	28	17	..	..	5	..
8	Nimar	69	3	..	..	10	..
9	Betul	11	2	..	..	1	..
10	Chhindwara	8	1	..	..	..	..
	Nagpur Divinon	*3*	..	..	..	*8*	..
11	Wardha	..	..	..	..	..	..
12	Nagpur	2	..	..	..	1	..
	Nagpur City	..	..	..	..	..	..
13	Chanda	..	..	..	..	..	..
14	Bhandara	1	..	..	..	7	..
15	Balaghat	..	..	..	..	..	..
	Chhattisgarh Division	*52*	*1*	*1*	..	*10*	..
16	Raipur	10	..	..	..	1	..
17	Bilaspur	38	..	1	..	7	..
18	Drug	4	1	..	..	2	..
	Berar	**12**	**4**	**1**	..	**2**	..
19	Amraoti	1	3	..	..	1	..
20	Akola ..	10	1	1	..	1	..
21	Buldana	1	..	..	..	..	..
22	Yeotmal	..	..	..	..	..	..
	Central Provinces States	**5**	..	**3**	..	..	..
23	Makrai	..	..	..	..	..	..
24	Bastar	..	..	..	..	..	..
25	Kanker	1	..	3	..	..	..
26	Nandgaon	2	..	..	..	..	..
27	Khairagarh	..	..	..	..	..	..
28	Chhuikhadan	..	..	..	..	..	..
29	Kawardha	..	..	..	..	..	..
30	Sakti	..	..	..	..	..	..
31	Raigarh	1	..	..	..	..	..
32	Sarangarh	..	..	..	..	..	..
33	Changbhakar	..	..	..	..	..	..
37	Korea	1	..	..	..	..	..
35	Surguja	..	..	..	..	..	..
36	Udaipur	..	..	..	..	..	..
37	Jashpur	..	..	..	..	..	..

of material substances—*contd.*

Industry—*contd.*

properly so called and analogous—*contd.*

67.—Manufacture of aerated and mineral waters and ice.						68.—Manufacture and refining of vegetable oils.						Serial No.
Total earners (principal occupations).		Total working dependants.		Total following occupation as subsidiary to other.		Total earners (principal occupations).		Total working dependants.		Total following occupation as subsidiary to other		
Males.	Females.	Males.	Females.	Males.	Females.	Males	Females.	Males.	Females.	Males.	Females.	
486	487	488	489	490	491	492	493	494	495	496	497	
70	..	..	..	**10**	..	**6,731**	**4,096**	**844**	**2,803**	**3,460**	**598**	
65	..	..	..	**4**	..	**6,122**	**3,260**	**407**	**1,570**	**2,671**	**531**	
53	..	..	..	**2**	..	**5,567**	**3,232**	**379**	**1,561**	**2,614**	**530**	
..	..	..	..	..	..	*1,253*	*684*	*38*	*280*	*500*	*66*	
..	..	..	..	..	..	185	74	2	22	24	5	1
..	..	..	..	..	..	542	282	8	116	89	37	2
..	..	..	..	..	..	275	164	12	67	236	20	3
..	..	..	..	..	..	*12*	*4*	..	..	*1*	..	
..	..	..	..	..	..	60	29	..	14	77	1	4
..	..	..	..	..	..	191	135	16	61	74	3	5
..	..	..	..	..	..	*1,068*	*452*	*98*	*320*	*225*	*27*	
..	..	..	..	..	..	165	102	12	59	30	7	6
..	..	..	..	..	..	181	115	6	78	19	9	7
..	..	..	..	..	..	205	24	7	16	57	2	8
..	..	..	..	..	..	80	74	2	19	6	6	9
..	..	..	..	..	..	437	137	71	148	113	3	10
29	..	..	..	..	..	*2,081*	*341*	*50*	*130*	*733*	*51*	
2	..	..	..	..	..	39	..	..	..	16	..	11
19	..	..	..	..	..	523	57	16	18	64	4	12
18	..	..	..	..	..	*46*	..	*10*	*1*	*4*	..	
5	..	..	..	..	..	506	106	9	51	175	7	13
3	..	..	..	..	..	426	130	16	20	185	31	14
..	..	..	..	..	..	587	48	9	41	293	9	15
24	..	..	..	*2*	..	*1,165*	*1,755*	*193*	*831*	*1,156*	*386*	
20	..	..	..	..	..	637	1,069	121	372	400	120	16
4	..	..	..	2	..	126	411	30	239	464	229	17
..	..	..	..	..	..	402	275	42	220	292	37	18
12	..	..	..	**2**	..	**555**	**28**	**28**	**9**	**57**	**1**	
5	..	..	..	..	..	153	1	11	..	38	..	19
1	..	..	..	1	..	128	9	4	..	10	..	20
..	..	..	..	..	..	150	5	5	2	6	1	21
6	..	..	..	1	..	124	13	8	7	3	..	22
5	..	..	..	**6**	..	**609**	**836**	**437**	**1,233**	**789**	**67**	
..	..	..	..	..	..	18	..	2	..	3	..	23
..	..	..	..	..	..	33	45	20	139	14	2	24
2	..	..	..	..	..	55	62	31	189	92	33	25
..	..	..	..	5	..	46	68	6	33	47	5	26
..	..	..	..	..	..	66	186	8	314	128	9	27
..	..	..	..	..	..	12	..	302	..	28	..	28
..	..	..	..	..	..	18	115	2	3	67	11	29
2	..	..	..	..	..	11	40	1	40	5	4	30
1	..	..	..	..	..	117	167	8	340	132	2	31
..	..	..	..	1	..	16	76	43	99	109	1	32
..	..	..	..	..	..	27	9	..	1	1	..	33
..	..	..	..	..	..	24	..	..	..	16	..	34
..	..	..	..	..	..	102	10	14	80	133	..	35
..	..	..	..	..	..	3	..	..	..	4	..	36
..	..	..	..	..	..	61	58	..	4	10	..	37

TABLE X — **Occupation or means of**

	Class ..	Class B.—Preparation and supply					
	Sub-class ..	Sub-class III.—					
	Order ..	Order 10.—Chemical products					
Serial No.	Sub-order ..						
	Group ..	69.—Manufacture and refining of mineral oils.					
	District, City or State.	Total earners (principal occupations).		Total working dependants.		Total following occupation as subsidiary to other.	
		Males.	Females.	Males.	Females.	Males.	Females.
1	2	498	499	500	501	502	503
	Central Provinces and Berar ..	888	355	47	255	125	24
	C. P. British Districts and Berar ..	888	355	47	255	125	24
	C. P. British Districts	888	355	47	255	125	24
	Jubbulpore Division	*151*	*67*	*9*	*62*	*40*	*15*
1	Saugor	138	40	8	49	18	4
2	Damoh	..	..	..	..	..	..
3	Jubbulpore	1	15	..	1	10	4
	Jubbulpore City	..	2	..	..	..	..
4	Mandla	12	12	1	12	12	1
5	Seoni	..	..	..	..	..	6
	Nerbudda Division	*728*	*288*	*37*	*193*	*85*	*9*
6	Narsinghpur	111	27	6	15	24	3
7	Hoshangabad	178	9	24	6	7	1
8	Nimar	6	..	..	..	..	..
9	Betul	433	251	7	172	54	5
10	Chhindwara	..	1	..	..	..	..
	Nagpur Division	..	..	..	..	..	..
11	Wardha	..	..	..	..	..	..
12	Nagpur	..	..	..	..	..	..
	Nagpur City	..	..	..	..	..	..
13	Chanda	..	..	..	..	..	..
14	Bhandara	..	..	..	..	..	..
15	Balaghat	..	..	..	..	..	..
	Chhattisgarh Division	*9*	..	*1*	..	..	..
16	Raipur	..	..	..	..	..	..
17	Bilaspur	9	..	1	..	..	..
18	Drug	..	..	..	..	..	..
	Berar ..	..	..	..	..	..	..
19	Amraoti	..	..	..	..	..	..
20	Akola	..	..	..	..	..	..
21	Buldana	..	..	..	..	..	..
22	Yeotmal	..	..	..	..	..	..
	Central Provinces States ..	..	..	..	..	..	..
23	Makrai	..	..	..	..	..	..
24	Bastar	..	..	..	..	..	..
25	Kanker	..	..	..	..	..	..
26	Nandgaon	..	..	..	..	..	..
27	Khairagarh	..	..	..	..	..	..
28	Chhuikhadan	..	..	..	..	..	..
29	Kawardha	..	..	..	..	..	..
30	Sakti	..	..	..	..	..	..
31	Raigarh	..	..	..	..	..	..
32	Sarangarh	..	..	..	..	..	..
33	Changbhakar	..	..	..	..	..	..
34	Korea	..	..	..	..	..	..
35	Surguja	..	..	..	..	..	..
36	Udaipur	..	..	..	..	..	..
37	Jashpur	..	..	..	..	..	..

Livelihood—General Distribution—*contd.* **TABLE X**

of material substances—*contd.*												
Industry—*contd.*												
properly so called and analogous—*concld.*						Order 11.—Food Industries.						Serial No.
70.—Others.						Total order 11.						
Total earners (principal occupations).		Total working dependants.		Total following occupation as subsidiary to other.		Total earners (principal occupations).		Total working dependants.		Total following occupation as subsidiary to other.		
Males.	Females.	Males.	Females.	Males.	Females.	Males.	Females.	Males.	Females.	Males.	Females.	
504	505	506	507	508	509	510	511	512	513	514	515	
1,121	**715**	**3**	**127**	**122**	**76**	**38,747**	**29,809**	**1,595**	**4,962**	**6,977**	**3,828**	
894	**464**	**3**	**125**	**119**	**69**	**35,334**	**27,011**	**1,392**	**2,910**	**6,439**	**3,731**	
880	**461**	**2**	**125**	**118**	**66**	**31,584**	**26,183**	**1,286**	**2,692**	**6,096**	**3,656**	
178	*41*	*1*	*8*	*44*	*20*	*7,013*	*3,449*	*351*	*495*	*1,420*	*193*	
23	4	..	1	1	4	1,791	721	58	138	84	16	1
8	4	1	..	..	..	351	308	18	22	33	39	2
137	30	..	7	38	16	4,769	1,848	272	287	1,249	104	3
47	*4*	..	..	*1*	..	*2,091*	*462*	*4*	*48*	*94*	*14*	
7	..	..	..	1	..	18	80	1	16	4	9	4
3	3	..	..	4	..	84	492	2	32	50	25	5
146	*253*	*1*	*104*	*30*	*19*	*1,541*	*1,273*	*43*	*181*	*145*	*77*	
..	56	..	3	3	12	362	500	6	51	25	36	6
58	1	..	4	8	..	357	486	6	49	9	30	7
31	3	..	1	..	..	609	80	27	21	63	4	8
10	3	..	1	10	..	80	78	..	7	25	5	9
47	190	1	95	9	7	133	129	4	53	23	2	10
539	*162*	..	*13*	*38*	*27*	*20,178*	*17,748*	*789*	*1,463*	*3,814*	*2,732*	
..	..	..	..	..	..	612	100	8	8	50	4	11
70	3	..	..	1	..	2,331	1,247	17	46	65	9	12
69	*2*	..	..	..	..	*610*	*192*	*6*	*15*	*13*	..	
1	..	..	..	..	..	575	737	34	136	819	747	13
442	105	..	13	28	26	16,564	15,084	659	624	2,662	1,940	14
26	54	..	..	9	1	96	580	71	649	218	32	15
17	*5*	..	..	*6*	..	*2,852*	*3,713*	*103*	*553*	*717*	*654*	
16	5	..	..	6	..	1,601	2,485	24	248	254	186	16
..	..	..	..	..	..	780	613	33	212	396	429	17
1	..	..	..	..	..	471	615	46	93	67	39	18
14	**3**	**1**	..	**1**	**3**	**3,750**	**828**	**106**	**218**	**343**	**75**	
4	1	..	..	..	..	1,360	217	29	42	148	27	19
1	..	..	..	..	1	863	215	19	57	66	10	20
5	1	..	..	1	..	835	265	30	35	76	16	21
4	1	1	..	..	2	692	131	28	84	53	22	22
227	**251**	..	**2**	**3**	**7**	**3,413**	**2,798**	**203**	**2,052**	**538**	**97**	
..	..	..	..	..	..	3	2	1	..	..	..	23
..	1	..	..	..	1	151	161	34	145	29	8	24
..	27	..	..	..	5	265	126	108	84	57	3	25
227	222	..	2	..	1	1,673	553	14	37	24	1	26
..	..	..	..	..	..	85	205	..	56	4	17	27
..	..	..	..	..	..	30	57	..	8	1	5	28
..	..	..	..	..	..	48	143	..	1	4	5	29
..	1	..	..	..	..	10	245	..	71	7	32	30
..	..	..	..	3	..	533	509	37	631	142	8	31
..	..	..	..	..	..	157	244	3	355	69	8	32
..	..	..	..	..	..	13	3	..	1	6	2	33
..	..	..	..	..	..	8	1	..	..	..	..	34
..	..	..	..	..	..	251	189	6	533	69	..	35
..	..	..	..	..	..	62	58	..	2	8	3	36
..	..	..	..	..	..	124	302	..	128	118	5	37

TABLE X — Occupation or means of

Serial No.	Class .. / Sub-class .. / Order .. / Sub-order .. / Group .. — District, City or State.	Class B.—Preparation and supply — Sub-class III.— — Order 11.—Food — 71.—Rice pounders and huskers and flour grinders. — Total earners (principal occupations). Males.	Total earners (principal occupations). Females.	Total working dependants. Males.	Total working dependants. Females.	Total following occupation as subsidiary to other. Males.	Total following occupation as subsidiary to other. Females.
1	2	516	517	518	519	520	521
	Central Provinces and Berar ..	2,909	4,518	61	943	411	449
	C. P. British Districts and Berar ..	1,813	3,788	60	428	400	445
	C. P. British Districts	1,232	3,400	35	293	287	394
	Jubbulpore Division	*267*	*1,317*	*9*	*68*	*10*	*81*
1	Saugor	46	352	4	20	..	10
2	Damoh	54	248	..	9	..	36
3	Jubbulpore	146	504	4	33	5	20
	Jubbulpore City	*59*	*34*	.	..	*2*	..
4	Mandla	4	64	..	..	2	5
5	Seoni	17	149	1	6	3	10
	Nerbudda Division	*293*	*1,030*	*13*	*68*	*43*	*58*
6	Narsinghpur	79	448	6	39	7	32
7	Hoshangabad	82	368	1	9	5	18
8	Nimar	67	39	4	2	15	3
9	Betul	30	72	..	4	13	5
10	Chhindwara	35	103	2	14	3	..
	Nagpur Division	*317*	*506*	*11*	*119*	*47*	*131*
11	Wardha	112	40	2	2	18	1
12	Nagpur	111	68	4	17	14	6
	Nagpur City	*37*	*31*	*4*	*7*	*3*	..
13	Chanda	15	189	..	18	1	119
14	Bhandara	62	161	2	21	10	1
15	Balaghat	17	48	3	61	4	4
	Chhattisgarh Division	*355*	*547*	*2*	*38*	*187*	*124*
16	Raipur	127	356	1	6	19	7
17	Bilaspur	163	118	..	30	166	117
18	Drug	65	73	1	2	2	..
	Berar	581	388	25	135	113	51
19	Amraoti	251	89	12	17	55	23
20	Akola	176	146	5	43	26	9
21	Buldana	94	122	7	12	14	10
22	Yeotmal	60	31	1	63	18	9
	Central Provinces States	1,096	730	1	515	11	4
23	Makrai	..	2	..	..	..	..
24	Bastar	..	25	..	1	1	..
25	Kanker . ..	..	1	..	..	..	..
26	Nandgaon . ..	994	325	.	3	2	..
27	Khairagarh	..	..	.	..	..	..
28	Chhuikhadan	..	3	..	..	..	..
29	Kawardha	3	79	..	..	..	3
30	Sakti	..	..	..	..	..	..
31	Raigarh	90	79	1	13	8	..
32	Sarangarh	9	29	..	1	..	..
33	Changbhakar	..	..	..	..	..	..
34	Korea	..	..	..	..	..	..
35	Surguja	..	157	..	489	..	..
36	Udaipur	..	..	..	..	..	..
37	Jashpur	..	30	..	8	..	1

of material substances—*contd.*

Industry—*contd.*

Industries—*contd.*

72.—Grain parchers, etc.						73.—Butchers.						Serial No.
Total earners (principal occupations).		Total working dependants.		Total following occupation as subsidiary to other.		Total earners (principal occupations).		Total working dependants.		Total following occupation as subsidiary to other.		
Males.	Females.	Males.	Females.	Males.	Females.	Males.	Females.	Males.	Females.	Males.	Females.	
522	523	524	525	526	527	528	529	530	531	532	533	
2,572	**6,642**	**212**	**2,661**	**2,286**	**1,573**	**2,471**	**258**	**73**	**37**	**171**	**11**	
1,812	**4,884**	**150**	**1,247**	**1,872**	**1,485**	**2,454**	**254**	**72**	**37**	**171**	**11**	
1,601	**4,808**	**146**	**1,220**	**1,849**	**1,482**	**881**	**99**	**15**	**12**	**50**	**4**	
112	*373*	*1*	*30*	*44*	*16*	*67*	*57*	..	..	*4*	..	
27	9	..	5	..	1	24	54	..	..	..	..	1
..	48	..	1	..	..	..	3	..	..	..	..	2
35	20	..	..	2	..	35	..	..	..	4	..	3
19	*19*	..	..	..	..	*32*	..	..	..	..	..	
..	7	1	16	..	2	8	..	..	..	..	..	4
50	289	..	8	42	13	..	..	..	..	..	..	5
71	*106*	..	*48*	*24*	*11*	*222*	*5*	*14*	*3*	*15*	..	
25	33	..	9	2	3	10	3	..	..	2	..	6
9	47	..	9	1	7	11	..	..	..	..	..	7
20	8	..	5	12	1	133	1	12	3	11	..	8
1	3	..	..	..	..	39	..	..	..	1	..	9
16	15	..	25	9	..	29	1	2	..	1	..	10
821	*1,660*	*107*	*685*	*1,424*	*947*	*538*	*37*	*1*	*9*	*21*	*4*	
10	28	..	5	2	1	247	5	..	..	12	2	11
39	2	..	..	10	..	217	10	..	8	5	..	12
25	..	..	..	..	..	*83*	*5*	..	*2*	*2*	..	
448	530	33	116	796	627	30	..	..	..	1	..	13
272	582	8	25	414	291	34	20	..	1	3	2	14
52	518	66	539	202	28	10	2	1	..	..	..	15
597	*2,669*	*38*	*457*	*357*	*508*	*54*	..	..	..	*10*	..	
337	1,867	15	223	144	163	19	..	..	..	1	..	16
175	364	16	167	168	307	35	..	..	..	9	..	17
85	438	7	67	45	38	..	..	..	..	..	..	18
211	**76**	**4**	**27**	**23**	**3**	**1,573**	**155**	**57**	**25**	**121**	**7**	
33	3	..	8	3	..	627	56	7	6	65	4	19
16	9	..	4	..	..	354	29	11	6	18	..	20
135	58	4	14	20	3	311	48	13	6	14	3	21
27	6	..	1	..	..	281	22	26	7	24	..	22
760	**1,758**	**62**	**1,414**	**414**	**88**	**17**	**4**	**1**	..	..	..	
..	..	..	..	..	..	1	..	1	..	..	..	23
36	119	20	98	7	6	..	..	..	..	..	..	24
88	82	3	69	26	3	..	..	..	..	..	..	25
21	109	1	8	1	1	13	4	..	..	..	..	26
18	181	..	56	3	17	..	..	..	..	..	..	27
22	27	..	8	1	4	..	..	..	..	..	..	28
14	63	..	1	4	2	..	..	..	..	..	..	29
8	245	..	71	7	32	..	..	..	..	..	..	30
202	379	33	613	132	8	2	..	..	..	..	..	31
80	201	1	329	65	8	..	..	..	..	..	..	32
..	..	..	..	..	..	..	..	..	..	..	..	33
..	..	..	..	..	..	1	..	..	..	..	..	34
151	26	4	39	55	..	..	..	..	..	..	..	35
32	55	..	2	1	3	..	..	..	..	..	..	36
88	271	..	120	112	4	..	..	..	..	..	..	37

TABLE X

Occupation or means of

Serial No.	Class .. / Sub-class .. / Order .. / Sub-order .. / Group ..	Class B.—Preparation and / Sub-class / Order II.—											
		74.—Makers of sugar, molasses and gur.						75.—Sweetmeat and condiment makers.					
	District, City or State.	Total earners (principal occupations).		Total working dependants.		Total following occupation as subsidiary to other.		Total earners (principal occupations).		Total working dependants.		Total following occupation as subsidiary to other.	
		Males.	Females.	Males.	Females.	Males.	Females.	Males.	Females.	Males.	Females.	Males.	Females.
1	2	534	535	536	537	538	539	540	541	542	543	544	545
	Central Provinces and Berar ..	**29**	**4**	..	**2**	**13**	..	**2,525**	**227**	**51**	**78**	**199**	**9**
	C. P. British Districts and Berar ..	**29**	**4**	..	**2**	**13**	..	**2,323**	**186**	**44**	**54**	**188**	**9**
	C. P. British Districts ..	**8**	**4**	..	**2**	**12**	..	**1,363**	**140**	**33**	**45**	**114**	**8**
	Jubbulpore Division ..	*4*	*2*	..	*2*	*4*	..	*182*	*25*	*4*	*9*	*11*	*1*
1	Saugor ..	..	1	..	1	..	..	21	4	1	5	1	..
2	Damoh ..	..	..	..	1	..	..	27	4	..	2	2	1
3	Jubbulpore ..	4	1	..	..	2	..	134	13	3	2	8	..
	Jubbulpore City ..	*3*	..	..	..	*2*	..	*101*	*3*	..	..	*3*	..
4	Mandla ..	..	..	..	..	..	..	..	..	..	..	..	..
5	Seoni ..	..	..	..	..	2	..	..	4	..	..	..	..
	Nerbudda Division ..	*1*	..	..	..	*3*	..	*262*	*20*	*4*	*15*	*5*	*1*
6	Narsinghpur ..	..	..	..	..	..	..	1	..	..	..	..	..
7	Hoshangabad ..	..	..	..	..	..	..	133	4	4	3	1	..
8	Nimar ..	1	..	..	..	..	..	101	10	..	1	3	..
9	Betul ..	..	..	..	..	..	..	7	3	..	3	1	..
10	Chhindwara ..	..	..	..	..	3	..	20	3	..	8	..	1
	Nagpur Division ..	*3*	..	..	..	*5*	..	*438*	*36*	*7*	*2*	*43*	*2*
11	Wardha ..	..	..	..	..	..	..	171	9	5	1	14	..
12	Nagpur ..		..	..	..	..	..	190	3	1	..	7	..
	Nagpur City ..	..	*2*	..	..	..	..	*144*	..	..	..	*3*	..
13	Chanda ..	..	..	..	..	1	..	57	13	1	1	19	1
14	Bhandara ..	..	..	..	..	4	..	20	11	..	..	3	1
15	Balaghat ..	3	..	..	..	..	..	..	..	..	..	..	..
	Chhattisgarh Division ..	..	*2*	..	..	..	..	*481*	*59*	*18*	*19*	*55*	*4*
16	Raipur ..	..	2	..	..	..	..	380	22	2	9	28	1
17	Bilaspur ..	..	..	..	..	..	..	71	23	13	8	23	3
18	Drug ..	..	..	..	..	..	..	30	14	3	2	4	..
	Berar ..	**21**	..	..	..	**1**	..	**960**	**46**	**11**	**9**	**74**	**1**
19	Amraoti ..	2	..	..	..	1	..	310	13	5	2	20	..
20	Akola ..	16	..	..	..	..	..	241	16	..	3	22	1
21	Buldana ..	..	..	..	..	..	..	254	9	6	3	24	..
22	Yeotmal ..	3	..	..	..	..	..	155	8	..	1	8	..
	Central Provinces States ..	..	..	..	..	..	..	**202**	**41**	**7**	**24**	**11**	..
23	Makrai ..	..	..	..	..	..	..	..	..	..	..	..	..
24	Bastar ..	..	..	..	..	..	..	13	2	..	1	..	..
25	Kanker ..	..	..	..	..	..	..	6	..	..	..	1	..
26	Nandgaon ..	..	..	..	..	..	..	55	2	6	7	1	..
27	Khairagarh ..	..	..	..	..	..	..	24	11	..	..	..	..
28	Chhuikhadan ..	..	..	..	..	..	..	..	13	..	..	..	..
29	Kawardha ..	..	..	..	..	..	..	16	..	..	..	..	..
30	Sakti ..	..	..	..	..	..	..	..	..	..	..	..	..
31	Raigarh ..	..	..	..	..	..	..	37	2	..	3	..	..
32	Sarangarh ..	..	..	..	..	..	..	13	6	..	9	4	..
33	Changbhakar ..	..	..	..	..	..	..	..	..	..	..	..	..
34	Korea ..	..	..	..	..	..	..	1	..	..	..	..	..
35	Surguja ..	..	..	..	..	..	..	33	4	1	4	2	..
36	Udaipur ..	..	..	..	..	..	..	1	1	..	..	..	..
37	Jashpur ..	..	..	..	..	..	..	3	..	..	..	3	..

Livelihood—General Distribution—*contd.*

TABLE X

supply of material substances—*contd.*

III.—Industry—*contd.*

Food Industries—*contd.*

76.—Toddy drawers.						77.—Brewers and distillers.						78.—Manufacturers of tobacco.						Serial No.
Total earners (principal occupations).		Total working dependants.		Total following occupation as subsidiary to other.		Total earners (principal occupations).		Total working dependants.		Total following occupation as subsidiary to other.		Total earners (principal occupations).		Total working dependants.		Total following occupation as subsidiary to other.		
Males.	Females.	Males.	Females.	Males.	Females.	Males.	Females.	Males.	Females.	Males.	Females.	Males.	Females.	Males.	Females.	Males.	Females.	
546	547	548	549	550	551	552	553	554	555	556	557	558	559	560	561	562	563	
196	**4**	**1**	**2**	**4**	..	**393**	**35**	**117**	**54**	**78**	**4**	**27,416**	**17,961**	**1,073**	**1,109**	**3,748**	**1,768**	
194	**4**	**1**	**2**	**4**	..	**16**	**4**	..	**1**	**3**	..	**26,459**	**17,733**	**1,060**	**1,079**	**3,721**	**1,767**	
146	***1***	***1***	***2***	***2***	..	***16***	***4***	..	***1***	***3***	..	***26,122***	***17,574***	***1,051***	***1,057***	***3,713***	***1,754***	
..	..	..	..	..	..	*7*	..	..	..	..	..	*6,283*	*1,600*	*332*	*365*	*1,305*	*89*	
..	..	..	..	..	..	..	..	..	..	..	..	1,636	292	53	107	77	5	1
..	..	..	..	..	..	7	..	..	..	..	..	252	5	13	..	20	..	2
..	..	..	..	..	..	..	..	..	..	..	..	4,386	1,302	265	249	1,205	84	3
..	..	..	..	..	..	..	..	..	..	..	..	*1,876*	*406*	*4*	*48*	*87*	*14*	
..	..	..	..	..	..	..	..	..	..	..	..	2	..	..	..	..	..	4
..	..	..	..	..	..	..	..	..	..	..	..	7	1	1	9	3	..	5
8	..	..	*1*	..	..	..	..	..	..	..	..	*612*	*44*	*12*	*8*	*35*	..	
..	..	..	..	..	..	..	..	..	..	..	..	235	12	..	..	10	..	6
..	..	..	..	..	..	..	..	..	..	..	..	73	10	1	2	2	..	7
..	..	..	..	..	..	..	..	..	..	..	..	280	22	11	6	20	..	8
..	..	..	..	..	..	..	..	..	..	..	..	2	..	..	..	1	..	9
8	..	..	1	..	..	..	..	..	..	..	..	22	..	..	..	2	..	10
138	*1*	*1*	*1*	*2*	..	..	*1*	..	..	..	..	*17,889*	*15,504*	*662*	*646*	*2,271*	*1,647*	
59	..	1	..	..	..	..	..	..	..	..	..	12	18	..	..	4	..	11
64	..	..	..	2	..	..	..	..	..	..	..	1,678	1,162	12	20	26	2	12
..	..	..	..	..	..	..	..	..	..	..	..	*301*	*156*	*2*	*5*	*4*	..	
12	1	..	1	..	..	..	..	..	..	..	..	13	4	..	..	1	..	13
3	..	..	..	..	..	..	..	..	..	..	..	16,172	14,310	649	577	2,228	1,645	14
..	..	..	..	..	..	..	1	..	..	..	..	14	10	1	49	12	..	15
..	..	..	..	..	..	*9*	*3*	..	*1*	*3*	..	*1,338*	*426*	*45*	*38*	*102*	*18*	
..	..	..	..	..	..	7	1	..	1	..	..	721	236	6	9	59	15	16
..	..	..	..	..	..	1	..	..	..	2	..	327	102	4	7	28	2	17
..	..	..	..	..	..	1	2	..	..	1	..	290	88	35	22	15	1	18
48	**3**	..	..	**2**	..	..	..	..	..	..	..	**337**	**159**	**9**	**22**	**8**	**13**	
27	2	..	..	2	..	..	..	..	..	..	..	99	54	5	9	1	..	19
13	1	..	..	..	..	..	..	..	..	..	..	46	14	3	1	..	..	20
2	..	..	..	..	..	..	..	..	..	..	..	33	28	..	..	4	..	21
6	..	..	..	..	..	..	..	..	..	..	..	159	63	1	12	3	13	22
2	..	..	..	..	..	**377**	**31**	**117**	**53**	**75**	**4**	**957**	**228**	**13**	**30**	**27**	**1**	
..	..	..	..	..	..	..	..	..	..	..	..	..	..	..	..	..	..	23
..	..	..	..	..	..	54	11	11	40	19	2	48	2	3	5	2	..	24
..	..	..	..	..	..	158	11	105	11	27	..	13	32	..	4	3	..	25
..	..	..	..	..	..	2	..	..	..	..	..	588	112	7	19	20	..	26
..	..	..	..	..	..	5	..	..	..	1	..	38	13	..	..	..	..	27
..	..	..	..	..	..	..	..	..	..	..	..	8	14	..	..	..	1	28
..	..	..	..	..	..	7	..	..	..	..	..	8	1	..	..	..	..	29
2	..	..	..	..	..	..	..	..	..	..	..	..	..	..	..	..	..	30
..	..	..	..	..	..	3	..	..	..	..	..	199	49	3	2	2	..	31
..	..	..	..	..	..	..	..	..	..	..	..	55	5	..	..	..	..	32
..	..	..	..	..	..	13	3	..	1	6	2	..	..	..	..	..	..	33
..	..	..	..	..	..	6	1	..	..	..	..	..	..	..	..	..	..	34
..	..	..	..	..	..	67	2	1	1	12	..	..	..	..	..	..	..	35
..	..	..	..	..	..	29	2	..	..	7	..	..	..	..	..	..	..	36
..	..	..	..	..	..	33	1	..	..	3	..	..	..	..	..	..	..	37

TABLE X — Occupation or means of

Serial No.	Class ..	Class B.—Preparation and supply											
	Sub-class ..	Sub-class III.—											
	Order ..	Order 11.—Food Industries—*concld.*											
	Sub-order ..							Total order 12.					
	Group ..	81.—Others.											
	District, City or State.	Total earners (principal occupations.)		Total working dependants.		Total following occupation as subsidiary to other.		Total earners (principal occupations).		Total working dependants.		Total following occupation as subsidiary to other.	
		Males.	Females.	Males.	Females.	Males.	Females.	Males.	Females.	Males.	Females.	Males.	Females.
1	2	564	565	566	567	568	569	570	571	572	573	574	575
	Central Provinces and Berar	**236**	**160**	**7**	**76**	**67**	**14**	**106,565**	**20,899**	**4,471**	**11,013**	**21,627**	**3,102**
	C. P. British Districts and Berar.	**234**	**154**	**5**	**60**	**67**	**14**	**101,136**	**19,599**	**3,874**	**9,493**	**19,455**	**2,968**
	C. P. British Districts	**215**	**153**	**5**	**60**	**66**	**14**	**76,971**	**15,510**	**2,923**	**7,654**	**16,287**	**2,344**
	Jubbulpore Division ..	*91*	*75*	*5*	*21*	*42*	*6*	*24,100*	*3,239*	*596*	*1,472*	*6,518*	*466*
1	Saugor	37	9	..	..	6	..	7,599	861	206	463	1,551	135
2	Damoh	11	..	5	9	11	2	4,399	628	51	266	1,737	108
3	Jubbulpore	29	8	..	3	23	..	8,661	934	213	371	2,669	126
	Jubbulpore City ..	*1*	..	..	..	..	..	*2,074*	*245*	*20*	*39*	*27*	*1*
4	Mandla ..	4	9	..	..	2	2	1,284	164	43	106	163	36
5	Seoni	10	49	..	9	..	2	2,157	652	83	266	398	61
	Nerbudda Division ..	*72*	*68*	..	*38*	*20*	*7*	*17,876*	*3,416*	*685*	*2,754*	*1,642*	*297*
6	Narsinghpur	12	4	..	3	4	1	3,494	911	74	656	366	43
7	Hoshangabad	49	57	..	26	..	5	5,782	1,022	280	520	305	121
8	Nimar	7	..	..	4	2	..	3,388	360	170	245	366	18
9	Betul	1	..	..	..	9	..	1,898	411	27	253	213	15
10	Chhindwara	3	7	..	5	5	1	3,314	712	134	1,080	392	100
	Nagpur Division ..	*34*	*3*	..	*1*	*1*	*1*	*23,393*	*5,922*	*590*	*1,575*	*2,660*	*598*
11	Wardha	1	..	..	..	..	..	3,963	935	38	139	387	117
12	Nagpur ..	32	2	..	1	1	1	7,631	1,884	157	475	533	172
	Nagpur City ..	*20*	..	..	*1*	*1*	..	*2,331*	*296*	*98*	*111*	*27*	*3*
13	Chanda	..	..	..	..	..	..	3,973	1,338	92	383	331	106
14	Bhandara	1	..	..	..	..	..	5,039	1,211	184	211	911	168
15	Balaghat	..	1	..	..	..	..	2,787	554	119	367	498	35
	Chhattisgarh Division ..	*18*	*7*	..	..	*3*	..	*11,602*	*2,933*	*1,052*	*1,853*	*5,467*	*983*
16	Raipur	10	1	..	..	3	..	4,889	1,366	344	639	1,819	274
17	Bilaspur	8	6	..	..	..	..	3,774	1,112	200	536	2,736	572
18	Drug	..	..	..	..	..	..	2,939	455	508	678	912	137
	Berar	**19**	**1**	..	..	**1**	..	**24,165**	**4,089**	**951**	**1,839**	**3,168**	**624**
19	Amraoti	11	..	..	..	1	..	7,048	1,401	248	592	969	190
20	Akola	1	..	..	..	..	..	6,252	869	146	521	887	86
21	Buldana	6	..	..	..	..	..	5,022	733	120	332	896	138
22	Yeotmal	1	1	..	..	..	..	5,843	1,086	437	394	416	110
	Central Provinces States ..	**2**	**6**	**2**	**16**	..	..	**5,429**	**1,300**	**597**	**1,520**	**•2,172**	**134**
23	Makrai	2	..	..	..	..	..	201	10	11	9	10	1
24	Bastar	..	2	..	..	..	..	270	134	50	124	42	4
25	Kanker	..	..	..	..	..	..	231	67	48	46	76	31
26	Nandgaon	..	1	..	..	..	..	732	125	96	175	214	17
27	Khairagarh	..	..	..	..	..	..	619	178	80	220	254	7
28	Chhuikhadan	..	..	..	..	..	..	92	29	..	42	24	24
29	Kawardha	..	..	..	..	..	..	532	193	3	35	116	15
30	Sakti	..	..	..	..	..	..	126	54	30	70	45	20
31	Raigarh	..	..	..	..	..	..	544	101	81	334	278	..
32	Sarangarh	..	3	2	16	..	..	272	81	42	82	190	1
33	Changbhakar ..	..	..	..	..	..	..	13	1	..	1	7	..
34	Korea	..	..	..	..	..	..	280	13	1	1	74	..
35	Surguja	..	..	..	..	..	..	1,053	154	150	296	708	12
36	Udaipur	..	..	..	..	..	..	150	23	3	..	50	1
37	Jashpur	..	..	..	..	..	..	314	137	2	85	84	1

Livelihood—General Distribution—*contd.* **TABLE X**

of material substances—*contd.*

Industry—*contd.*

Order 12.—Industries of dress and the toilet.

82.—Boot, shoe, sandal and clog makers.						83.—Tailors, milliners, dress makers and darners.						84.—Embroiders, hat makers and makers of other articles of wear.						Serial No.
Total earners (principal occupations).		Total working dependants.		Total following occupation as subsidiary to other.		Total earners (principal occupations).		Total working dependants.		Total following occupation as subsidiary to other.		Total earners (principal occupations).		Total working dependants.		Total following occupation as subsidiary to other.		
Males.	Females.	Males.	Females.	Males.	Females.	Males.	Females.	Males.	Females.	Males.	Females.	Males.	Females.	Males.	Females.	Males	Females.	
576	577	578	579	580	581	582	583	584	585	586	587	588	589	590	591	592	593	
23,599	**2,154**	**1,025**	**2,261**	**6,044**	**508**	**22,563**	**4,388**	**1,008**	**2,524**	**2,594**	**466**	**476**	**59**	**20**	**281**	**61**	**3**	
22,039	**2,010**	**774**	**1,846**	**5,368**	**504**	**21,821**	**4,305**	**961**	**2,409**	**2,519**	**460**	**469**	**59**	**20**	**281**	**61**	**3**	
17,415	**1,528**	**576**	**1,561**	**4,791**	**410**	**15,558**	**3,482**	**640**	**1,915**	**1,660**	**321**	**163**	**4**	**13**	**15**	**26**	..	
8,303	*184*	*102*	*126*	*3,255*	*49*	*4,247*	*521*	*179*	*181*	*419*	*97*	*20*	*1*	*1*	..	*3*	..	
2,392	11	36	22	836	1	1,010	98	61	39	43	63	10	..	1	..	2	..	1
1,671	13	7	..	1,250	6	625	37	11	13	60	8	..	..	..	..	..	..	2
3,534	150	39	6	1,145	12	1,802	157	62	53	185	10	8	1	..	..	..	..	3
421	*23*	*7*	..	*11*	..	*857*	*66*	*8*	*13*	*9*	*1*	*8*	*1*	..	..	..	..	
434	10	11	69	2	27	371	54	19	12	36	..	..	..	..	..	..	..	4
272	..	9	29	22	3	439	175	26	64	95	16	2	..	..	..	1	..	5
3,761	*469*	*150*	*742*	*214*	*190*	*3,715*	*855*	*157*	*897*	*349*	*37*	*35*	*2*	..	*2*	*4*	..	
473	107	16	194	53	25	804	151	14	91	87	5	1	..	..	..	..	..	6
1,226	129	58	122	73	106	936	213	46	119	44	9	..	2	..	..	..	..	7
1,202	92	60	114	71	8	665	106	44	91	67	4	10	..	..	1	3	..	8
378	75	7	101	4	..	388	104	11	56	50	8	..	..	..	..	..	..	9
482	66	9	211	13	51	922	281	42	540	101	11	24	..	..	1	1	..	10
2,747	*602*	*43*	*205*	*218*	*71*	*6,168*	*1,869*	*241*	*766*	*707*	*153*	*97*	*1*	*12*	*13*	*11*	..	
399	71	3	13	21	10	1,166	248	21	68	125	34	15	..	..	..	1	..	11
800	361	2	102	21	25	2,238	508	81	228	151	45	63	1	12	13	8	..	12
319	*18*	..	*6*	*1*	..	*907*	*106*	*54*	*42*	*18*	*2*	*60*	*1*	*12*	*13*	..	..	
259	26	5	19	14	..	932	438	27	174	66	41	3	..	..	..	2	..	13
819	133	20	43	108	35	1,241	442	87	107	204	17	3	..	..	..	..	..	14
470	11	13	28	54	1	591	233	25	189	161	16	13	..	..	..	..	..	15
2,604	*273*	*281*	*488*	*1,104*	*100*	*1,428*	*237*	*63*	*71*	*185*	*34*	*11*	..	..	..	*8*	..	
936	61	62	108	375	15	646	106	10	17	57	11	5	..	..	..	3	..	16
1,016	190	63	155	506	78	585	112	26	19	112	23	..	..	..	..	..	..	17
652	22	156	225	223	7	197	19	27	35	16	..	6	..	..	..	5	..	18
4,624	**482**	**198**	**285**	**577**	**94**	**6,263**	**823**	**321**	**494**	**859**	**139**	**306**	**55**	**7**	**266**	**35**	**3**	
952	180	30	103	76	20	2,060	217	102	179	300	46	11	1	..	3	8	..	19
1,245	119	28	76	183	37	1,579	145	45	81	221	20	182	31	5	221	18	2	20
1,322	78	21	35	251	25	1,233	234	54	123	225	42	87	20	2	42	8	1	21
1,105	105	119	71	67	12	1,391	227	120	111	113	31	26	3	..	..	1	..	22
1,560	**144**	**251**	**415**	**676**	**4**	**742**	**83**	**47**	**115**	**75**	**6**	**7**	..	..	..	..	..	
105	..	9	..	..	..	24	2	..	..	1	..	..	..	..	..	..	..	23
89	4	18	52	8	..	54	15	..	10	10	..	..	..	..	..	..	..	24
31	1	19	2	7	..	59	5	4	..	..	..	..	..	..	..	..	..	25
180	10	44	84	24	..	56	11	9	29	1	..	4	..	..	..	..	..	26
150	32	37	130	135	3	82	11	8	19	2	1	3	..	..	..	..	..	27
16	11	..	..	..	..	8	2	..	..	..	..	..	..	..	..	..	..	28
183	61	..	20	19	1	95	8	2	13	2	3	..	..	..	..	..	..	29
9	..	2	..	..	..	5	..	..	..	..	1	..	..	..	..	..	..	30
30	1	8	8	20	..	85	2	5	29	7	..	..	..	..	..	..	..	31
31	1	4	1	27	..	30	8	7	..	3	..	..	..	..	..	..	..	32
..	..	..	..	..	..	4	..	..	..	1	..	..	..	..	..	..	..	33
136	2	..	1	33	..	64	4	..	..	3	..	..	..	..	..	..	..	34
518	21	109	111	399	..	134	9	12	15	40	1	..	..	..	..	..	..	35
5	..	..	..	3	..	21	1	..	..	2	..	..	..	..	..	..	..	36
77	..	1	6	1	..	21	5	..	..	3	..	..	..	..	..	..	..	37

TABLE X | Occupation or means of

Serial No.	Class .. / Sub-class .. / Order .. / Sub-order .. / Group ..	Class B.—Preparation and / Sub-class / Order 12.—Industries of / 85.—Washing and cleaning.					
	District, City or State.	Total earners (principal occupations).		Total working dependants.		Total following occupation as subsidiary to other.	
		Males.	Females.	Males.	Females.	Males.	Females.
1	2	594	595	596	597	598	599
	Central Provinces and Berar ..	**18,665**	**12,887**	**1,053**	**5,633**	**5,371**	**1,969**
	C. P. British Districts and Berar ..	**17,491**	**12,058**	**910**	**4,714**	**4,709**	**1,858**
	C. P. British Districts	**13,730**	**9,367**	**777**	**3,924**	**4,026**	**1,474**
	Jubbulpore District	*3,784*	*2,276*	*199*	*1,081*	*1,315*	*286*
1	Saugor	1,352	734	63	384	294	57
2	Damoh	729	510	31	227	221	88
3	Jubbulpore	1,091	555	51	285	620	97
	Jubbulpore City	*260*	*135*	*5*	*25*	*2*	..
4	Mandla	133	53	9	21	70	6
5	Seoni	479	424	45	164	110	38
	Nerbudda Division	*3,417*	*1,979*	*179*	*1,101*	*324*	*63*
6	Narsinghpur	1,170	609	28	362	87	8
7	Hoshangabad	1,260	651	97	279	66	6
8	Nimar	184	143	11	37	41	6
9	Betul	260	227	5	95	40	6
10	Chhindwara	543	349	38	328	90	37
	Nagpur Division	*4,010*	*3,116*	*145*	*562*	*594*	*343*
11	Wardha	629	603	7	58	75	64
12	Nagpur	1,225	993	31	132	107	102
	Nagpur City	*355*	*171*	*19*	*50*	*3*	*1*
13	Chanda	1,107	759	42	184	118	51
14	Bhandara	725	582	32	59	221	113
15	Balaghat	324	179	33	129	73	13
	Chhattisgarh Division	*2,519*	*1,996*	*254*	*1,180*	*1,793*	*782*
16	Raipur	1,112	967	106	445	553	243
17	Bilaspur	808	684	59	346	882	414
18	Drug	599	345	89	389	358	125
	Berar	**3,761**	**2,691**	**133**	**790**	**683**	**384**
19	Amraoti	1,168	994	35	307	273	123
20	Akola	897	567	19	142	220	124
21	Buldana	563	395	18	130	126	70
22	Yeotmal	1,133	735	61	211	64	67
	Central Provinces States	**1,174**	**829**	**143**	**919**	**662**	**111**
23	Makrai	14	7	2	9	3	1
24	Baster	67	69	19	62	13	4
25	Kanker	71	60	14	44	18	31
26	Nandgaon	110	84	6	48	92	16
27	Khairagarh	77	117	10	71	59	3
28	Chhuikhadan	17	7	..	42	23	24
29	Kawardha	50	107	..	2	75	8
30	Sakti	30	54	13	70	23	19
31	Raigarh	239	96	43	268	108	..
32	Sarangarh	115	72	18	81	84	1
33	Changbhakar	4	..	..	1	..	..
34	Korea	36	2	..	..	16	..
35	Surguja	174	88	16	154	79	2
36	Udaipur	78	22	2	..	19	1
37	Jashpur	92	44	..	67	50	1

supply of material substances—*contd*

III.—Industry—*contd.*

dress and the toilet—*concld.*

86.—Barbers, hair-dressers and wig-makers.						87.—Other industries connected with the toilet.						Serial No.
Total earners (principal occupations).		Total working dependants.		Total following occupation as subsidiary to other.		Total earners (principal occupations).		Total working dependants.		Total following occupation as subsidiary to other.		
Males.	Females.	Males.	Females.	Males.	Females.	Males.	Females.	Males.	Females.	Males.	Females.	
600	601	602	603	604	605	606	607	608	609	610	611	
40,806	**520**	**1,346**	**162**	**7,446**	**88**	**456**	**891**	**19**	**152**	**111**	**68**	
38,938	**469**	**1,203**	**127**	**6,713**	**77**	**378**	**698**	**6**	**116**	**85**	**66**	
29,744	**434**	**911**	**123**	**5,705**	**73**	**361**	**695**	**6**	**116**	**79**	**66**	
7,574	*90*	*113*	*29*	*1,515*	*8*	*172*	*167*	*2*	*55*	*11*	*26*	
2,733	1	43	..	372	..	102	17	2	18	4	14	1
1,348	56	2	26	203	3	26	12	..	..	3	3	2
2,207	28	61	3	717	5	19	43	..	24	2	2	3
526	*18*	..	*1*	*4*	..	*2*	*2*	..	..	*1*	..	
338	3	4	..	55	..	8	44	..	4	..	3	4
948	2	3	..	168	..	17	51	..	9	2	4	5
6,878	*40*	*198*	*6*	*749*	*6*	*70*	*71*	*1*	*6*	*2*	*1*	
1,037	23	16	4	138	5	9	21	..	5	1	..	6
2,353	2	79	..	122	..	7	25	..	..	..	..	7
1,301	1	55	2	184	..	26	18	..	..	..	..	8
872	..	4	..	119	..	..	5	..	1	..	1	9
1,315	14	44	..	186	1	28	2	1	..	1	..	10
10,346	*100*	*,48*	*7*	*1,129*	*14*	*25*	*234*	*1*	*22*	*1*	*17*	
1,754	1	7	..	165	.	..	12	..	..	..	9	11
3,302	10	31	..	246	..	3	11	..	..	..	..	12
687	..	*13*	..	*5*	.	*3*	..	..	..	..	..	
1,666	86	17	6	131	14	6	29	1	..	..	..	13
2,246	..	45	..	378	..	5	54	..	2	..	3	14
1,378	3	48	1	209	..	11	128	..	20	1	5	15
4,946	*204*	*452*	*81*	*2,312*	*45*	*94*	*223*	*2*	*33*	*65*	*22*	
2,129	109	166	63	785	3	61	123	..	6	46	2	16
1,347	85	52	8	1,220	42	18	41	..	8	16	15	17
1,470	10	234	10	307	..	15	59	2	19	3	5	18
9,194	**35**	**292**	**4**	**1,008**	**4**	**17**	**3**	..	..	**6**	..	
2,855	7	81	..	308	1	2	2	..	..	4	..	19
2,342	6	49	1	244	3	7	1	..	..	1	..	20
1,817	6	25	2	286	..	..	..	..	..	..	..	21
2,180	16	137	1	170	..	8	..	..	..	1	..	22
1,868	**51**	**143**	**35**	**733**	**11**	**78**	**193**	**13**	**36**	**26**	**2**	
58	1	..	.	6	..	..	..	..	..	..	..	23
60	3	3	..	11	..	..	43	10	..	..	..	24
70	1	11	..	51	..	..	..	..	..	..	..	25
382	..	37	..	95	..	..	20	..	14	2	1	26
307	10	25	..	58	..	..	8	..	..	..	..	27
51	9	..	..	..	..	..	..	..	..	1	..	28
198	15	1	..	19	3	6	2	..	..	1	..	29
82	..	15	..	22	..	..	..	..	..	..	..	30
184	1	25	29	143	..	6	1	..	..	..	..	31
94	..	13	..	69	..	2	..	..	..	7	..	32
5	..	..	..	6	..	..	1	..	..	..	..	33
43	..	1	..	22	..	1	5	..	..	..	..	34
216	6	10	6	190	8	11	30	3	10	..	1	35
38	..	1	..	18	..	8	..	..	..	8	..	36
80	5	1	..	23	..	44	83	..	12	7	..	37

TABLE X — Occupation or means of

Serial No.	Class ..	Class B.—Preparation and					
	Sub-class ..	Sub-class					
	Order ..	Order 13.—					
	Sub-order ..	Total order 13.					
	Group ..						
	District, City or State.	Total earners (principal occupations). Males.	Total earners (principal occupations). Females.	Total working dependants. Males.	Total working dependants. Females.	Total following occupation as subsidiary to other. Males.	Total following occupation as subsidiary to other. Females.
1	2	612	613	614	615	616	617
	Central Provinces and Berar	**2,730**	**187**	**83**	**99**	**1,568**	**18**
	C. P. British Districts and Berar	**2,579**	**170**	**73**	**78**	**1,560**	**18**
	C. P. British Districts	**2,506**	**108**	**72**	**71**	**1,550**	**10**
	Jubbulpore Division	*1,038*	*24*	*25*	*5*	*1,289*	*3*
1	Saugor	603	2	22	5	99	..
2	Damoh	..	13	..	..	..	2
3	Jubbulpore	341	5	3	..	1,143	..
	Jubbulpore City	*24*	..	..	..	*1*	..
4	Mandla	25	4	..	..	18	..
5	Seoni	69	..	..	..	29	1
	Nerbudda Division	*1,180*	*5*	*33*	*27*	*167*	..
6	Narsinghpur	421	..	15	11	47	..
7	Hoshangabad	464	1	2	..	56	..
8	Nimar	154	1	7	..	11	..
9	Betul	58	1	..	..	27	..
10	Chhindwara	83	2	9	16	26	..
	Nagpur Division	*272*	*57*	*14*	*38*	*37*	*6*
11	Wardha	20	29	..	17	..	2
12	Nagpur	61	19	1	21	3	4
	Nagpur City	*16*	..	..	*6*	*1*	..
13	Chanda	5	2	..	..	1	..
14	Bhandara	21	3	11	..	..	..
15	Balaghat	165	4	2	..	33	..
	Chhattisgarh Division	*16*	*22*	..	*1*	*57*	*1*
16	Raipur	13	21	..	1	57	1
17	Bilaspur	2	..	..	..	..	..
18	Drug	1	1	..	..	..	..
	Berar	**73**	**62**	**1**	**7**	**10**	**8**
19	Amraoti	24	36	..	1	1	3
20	Akola	19	5	..	1	6	3
21	Buldana	14	16	1	4	3	2
22	Yeotmal	16	5	..	1	..	..
	Central Provinces States	**151**	**17**	**10**	**21**	**8**	..
23	Makrai	54	..	..	..	1	..
24	Bastar	18	1	4	10	2	..
25	Kanker	..	..	1	..	3	..
26	Nandgaon	..	..	..	..	..	..
27	Khairagarh	10	16	..	..	..	..
28	Chhuikhadan	..	..	..	..	..	..
29	Kawardha	1	..	..	..	1	..
30	Sakti	..	..	..	..	..	..
31	Raigarh	..	..	..	11	..	..
32	Sarangarh	26	..	..	..	..	..
33	Changbhakar	..	..	..	..	..	..
34	Korea	..	..	..	..	..	..
35	Surguja	42	..	5	..	1	..
36	Udaipur	..	..	..	..	..	..
37	Jashpur	..	..	..	..	..	..

supply of material substances—*contd.*

III.—Industry—*contd.*

Furniture industries.

88.—Cabinet-makers, carriage painters, etc.						89.—Upholsterers, tent-makers, etc.						Serial No.
Total earners (principal occupations).		Total working dependants.		Total following occupation as subsidiary to other.		Total earners (principal occupations).		Total working dependants.		Total following occupation as subsidiary to other.		
Males.	Females.	Males.	Females.	Males.	Females.	Males.	Females.	Males.	Females.	Males.	Females.	
618	619	620	621	622	623	624	625	626	627	628	629	
2,538	**20**	**63**	**26**	**630**	..	**192**	**167**	**20**	**73**	**938**	**18**	
2,398	**19**	**53**	**5**	**623**	..	**181**	**151**	**20**	**73**	**937**	**18**	
2,388	**18**	**53**	**5**	**622**	..	**118**	**90**	**19**	**66**	**928**	**10**	
1,028	*10*	*25*	*5*	*421*	..	*10*	*14*	..	..	*868*	*3*	
603	2	22	5	99	..	..	..	..	..	..	..	1
..	3	..	..	..	..	..	10	..	..	..	2	2
338	5	3	..	282	..	3	..	..	..	861	..	3
24	..	..	..	*1*	..	..	..	..	..	..	..	
18	..	..	..	11	..	7	4	..	..	7	..	4
69	..	..	..	29	..	..	..	..	..	..	1	5
1,180	*2*	*25*	..	*167*	..	..	*3*	*8*	*27*	..	..	
421	..	7	..	47	..	..	..	8	11	..	..	6
464	1	2	..	56	..	..	..	..	..	..	..	7
154	1	7	..	11	..	..	..	..	..	..	..	8
58	..	..	..	27	..	..	1	..	..	..	..	9
83	..	9		26	..	..	2	..	16	..	..	10
170	*5*	*3*	..	*34*	..	*102*	*52*	*11*	*38*	*3*	*6*	
..	..	..	..	..	..	20	29	..	17	..	2	11
3	..	..	..	1	..	58	19	1	21	2	4	12
3	..	..	..	*1*	..	*13*	..	..	*6*	..	..	
..	1	..	..	..	..	5	1	..	..	1	..	13
2	..	1	..	..	..	19	3	10	..	..	..	14
165	4	2	..	33	..	..	..	..	..	..	..	15
10	*1*	..	..	..	..	*6*	*21*	..	*1*	*57*	*1*	
8	..	..	..	..	..	5	21	..	1	57	1	16
2	..	..	..	..	..	..	..	..	..	..	..	17
..	1	..	..	..	..	1	..	..	..	..	..	18
10	**1**	..	..	**1**	..	**63**	**61**	**1**	**7**	**9**	**8**	
2	..	..	..	..	..	22	36	..	1	1	3	19
3	..	..	..	1	..	16	5	..	1	5	3	20
..	..	..	..	..	..	14	16	1	4	3	2	21
5	1	..	..	..	..	11	4	..	1	..	..	22
140	**1**	**10**	**21**	**7**	..	**11**	**16**	..	..	**1**	..	
54	..	..	..	1	..	..	..	..	..	..	..	23
18	1	4	10	2	..	..	..	..	..	..	..	24
..	..	1	..	3	..	..	..	..	..	..	..	25
..	..	..	..	..	..	..	..	..	..	..	..	26
..	..	..	..	..	..	10	16	..	..	..	..	27
..	..	..	..	..	..	..	..	..	..	..	..	28
..	..	..	..	..	..	1	..	..	..	1	..	29
..	..	..	..	..	..	..	..	..	..	..	..	30
..	..	..	11	..	..	..	..	..	..	..	..	31
26	..	..	..	..	..	..	..	..	..	..	..	32
..	..	..	..	..	..	..	..	..	..	..	..	33
..	..	..	..	..	..	..	..	..	..	..	..	34
42	..	5	..	1	..	..	..	..	..	..	..	35
..	..	..	..	..	..	..	..	..	..	..	..	36
..	..	..	..	..	..	..	..	..	..	..	..	37

TABLE X — **Occupation or means of**

Serial No.	Class / Sub-class / Order / Sub-order / Group / District, City or State.	Class B.—Preparation and / Sub-class / Order 14.— / Total order 14. Total earners (principal occupations). Males.	Females.	Total working dependants. Males.	Females.	Total following occupation as subsidiary to other. Males.	Females.
1	2	630	631	632	633	634	635
	Central Provinces and Berar	**22,708**	**5,508**	**495**	**865**	**2,924**	**521**
	C. P. British Districts and Berar ..	**22,023**	**5,415**	**492**	**850**	**2,887**	**516**
	C. P. British Districts	**14,518**	**3,529**	**183**	**436**	**1,623**	**208**
	Jubbulpore Division	*5,371*	*1,105*	*52*	*36*	*397*	*40*
1	Saugor	997	127	3	7	103	2
2	Damoh	1,139	662	4	22	85	31
3	Jubbulpore	2,911	274	38	6	199	2
	Jubbulpore City	*885*	*68*	*5*	..	*5*	..
4	Mandla	168	5	4	..	8	..
5	Seoni	156	37	3	1	2	5
	Nerbudda Division ..	*2,523*	*754*	*40*	*105*	*223*	*32*
6	Narsinghpur	147	14	..	9	15	..
7	Hoshangabad	507	38	10	19	48	5
8	Nimar	1,354	615	26	57	72	14
9	Betul	257	50	..	1	49	5
10	Chhindwara	258	37	4	19	39	7
	Nagpur Division	*5,353*	*1,516*	*80*	*276*	*781*	*113*
11	Wardha	976	456	8	62	113	18
12	Nagpur	2,774	647	49	107	277	36
	Nagpur City	*1,054*	*177*	*43*	*9*	*37*	..
13	Chanda	911	275	15	102	202	36
14	Bhandara	607	134	6	5	167	22
15	Balaghat	85	4	2	..	22	1
	Chhattisgarh Division	*1,271*	*154*	*11*	*19*	*222*	*23*
16	Raipur	731	58	..	5	24	5
17	Bilaspur	382	73	1	8	158	18
18	Drug	158	23	10	6	40	..
	Berar	**7,505**	**1,886**	**309**	**414**	**1,264**	**308**
19	Amraoti	1,461	320	53	80	347	41
20	Akola	1,900	568	47	124	344	114
21	Buldana	1,938	584	29	161	403	120
22	Yeotmal	2,206	414	180	49	170	33
	Central Provinces States	**685**	**93**	**3**	**15**	**37**	**5**
23	Makrai	6	8	..	..	..	..
24	Bastar	251	1	1	1	2	..
25	Kanker	8	4	2	7	..	..
26	Nandgaon	69	5	..	..	5	..
27	Khairagarh	90	2	..	..	3	..
28	Chhuikhadan	..	..	..	..	..	..
29	Kawardha	14	23	..	..	13	4
30	Sakti	..	..	..	..	2	..
31	Raigarh	131	46	..	..	11	..
32	Sarangarh	31	..	..	..	..	..
33	Changbhakar	1	..	..	..	..	..
34	Korea	24	..	..	..	..	1
35	Surguja	21	4	..	7	..	..
36	Udaipur	24	..	..	..	..	..
37	Jashpur	15	..	..	..	1	..

supply of material substances—*contd.*

III.—Industry—*contd.*

Building Industries.						Order 15.—Construction of means of transport.						
90.—Lime burners, cement workers, excavators and well-sinkers, stone-cutters and dressers, brick-layers and masons, builders (other than buildings made of bamboos or similar materials), painters, decorators of houses, tilers, plumbers, etc.						Total order 15.						Serial No.
Total earners (principal occupations).		Total working dependants.		Total following occupation as subsidiary to other.		Total earners (principal occupations).		Total working dependants.		Total following occupation as subsidiary to other.		
Males.	Females.	Males.	Females.	Males.	Females.	Males.	Females.	Males.	Females.	Males.	Females.	
636	637	638	639	640	641	642	643	644	645	646	647	
22,708	**5,508**	**495**	**865**	**2,924**	**521**	**644**	**76**	**11**	**5**	**81**	**1**	
22,023	**5,415**	**492**	**850**	**2,887**	**516**	**623**	**76**	**11**	**4**	**71**	**1**	
14,518	**3,529**	**183**	**436**	**1623**	**208**	**467**	**72**	**10**	**3**	**60**	**1**	
5,371	*1,105*	*52*	*36*	*397*	*40*	*27*	*2*	..	*1*	*22*	..	
997	127	3	7	103	2	1	..	..	..	..	..	
1,139	662	1	22	85	31	2	..	..	..	..	..	
2,911	274	38	6	199	2	19	1	..	..	22	..	3
885	*68*	*5*	..	*5*	..	..	..	..	..	..	..	
168	5	4	..	8	..	..	..	..	..	..	..	4
156	37	3	1	2	5	5	1	..	1	..	..	5
2,523	*754*	*40*	*105*	*223*	*32*	*206*	*1*	*5*	..	*27*	..	
147	14	..	9	15	1	8	..	..	..	..	..	6
507	38	10	19	48	5	156	1	3	..	17	..	7
1,354	615	26	57	72	14	25	..	..	..	7	..	8
257	50	..	1	49	5	1	..	..	..	3	..	9
258	37	4	19	39	7	16	..	2	..	..	..	10
5,353	*1,516*	*80*	*276*	*781*	*113*	*175*	*52*	..	..	*7*	..	
976	456	8	62	113	18	40	..	..	..	2	..	11
2,774	647	49	107	277	36	122	52	..	..	1	..	12
1,054	*177*	*43*	*9*	*37*	..	*110*	*52*	..	..	..	..	
911	275	15	102	202	36	2	..	..	..	..	..	13
607	134	6	5	167	22	11	..	..	..	2	..	14
85	4	2	..	22	1	..	..	..	..	2	..	15
1,271	*154*	*11*	*19*	*222*	*23*	*59*	*17*	*5*	*2*	*4*	*1*	
731	58	..	5	24	5	33	17	5	2	3	1	16
382	73	1	8	158	18	15	..	..	..	..	..	17
158	23	10	5	40	..	11	..	..	..	1	..	18
7,505	**1,885**	**309**	**414**	**1,264**	**308**	**156**	**4**	**1**	**1**	**11**	..	
1,461	320	53	80	347	41	20	1	1	..	3	..	19
1,900	568	47	124	344	114	44	..	..	..	2	..	20
1,938	584	29	161	403	120	6	..	..	..	1	..	21
2,206	414	180	49	170	33	86	3	..	1	5	..	22
685	**93**	**3**	**15**	**37**	**5**	**21**	..	..	**1**	**10**	..	
6	8	..	..	..	..	..	..	..	..	..	..	23
251	1	1	1	2	..	11	..	..	1	10	..	24
8	4	2	7	..	..	..	..	..	..	..	..	25
69	5	..	..	5	..	1	..	..	..	..	..	26
90	2	..	..	3	..	..	..	..	..	..	..	27
..	..	..	..	..	..	..	..	..	..	..	..	28
14	23	..	..	13	4	..	..	..	..	..	..	29
..	..	..	..	2	..	3	..	..	..	..	..	30
31	46	..	..	11	..	4	..	..	..	..	..	31
31	..	..	..	..	..	..	..	..	..	..	..	32
1	..	..	..	..	..	..	..	..	..	..	..	33
24	..	..	..	..	1	..	..	..	..	..	..	34
21	4	..	7	..	..	..	..	..	..	..	..	35
24	..	..	..	..	..	..	..	..	..	..	..	36
15	..	..	..	1	..	2	..	..	..	..	..	37

TABLE X — Occupation or means of

Serial No.	Class .. / Sub-class .. / Order .. / Sub-order .. / Group ..	Class B.—Preparation and / Sub-class / Order 15.— / 91 —Persons engaged in making, assembling or repairing motor vehicles or cycles.					
	District, City or State.	Total earners (principal occupations).		Total working dependants.		Total following occupation as subsidiary to other.	
		Males.	Females.	Males	Females.	Males.	Females
1	2	648	649	650	651	652	653
	Central Provinces and Berar ..	**328**	**55**	**6**	**1**	**37**	..
	C. P. British Districts and Berar ..	**321**	**55**	**6**	**1**	**37**	..
	C. P. British Districts	**246**	**54**	**5**	**1**	**31**	..
	Jubbulpore Division	*8*	*1*	..	*1*	*20*	..
1	Saugor	..	..	..	..	..	..
2	Damoh	2	..	..	..	..	..
3	Jubbulpore	1	..	..	..	20	..
	Jubbulpore City	..	..	..	..	..	..
4	Mandla	..	..	..	..	..	..
5	Seoni	5	1	..	1	..	..
	Nerbudda Division	*12*	*1*	..	..	*3*	..
6	Narsinghpur	8	..	..	..	..	..
7	Hoshangabad ..	3	1	..	..	..	..
8	Nimar	..	..	..	..	..	..
9	Betul	1	..	..	..	3	..
10	Chhindwara	..	..	..	..	..	..
	Nagpur Division	*168*	*52*	..	..	*4*	..
11	Wardha	40	..	..	..	2	..
12	Nagpur	117	52	..	..	1	..
	Nagpur City	*106*	*52*	..	..	..	..
13	Chanda	2	..	..	..	..	..
14	Bhandara	9	..	..	..	1	..
15	Balaghat	..	..	..	..	..	..
	Chhattisgarh Division	*58*	..	*5*	..	*4*	..
16	Raipur	33	..	5	..	3	..
17	Bilaspur	14	..	..	..	..	..
18	Drug	11	..	..	..	1	..
	Berar	**75**	**1**	**1**	..	**6**	..
19	Amraoti	20	1	1	..	3	..
20	Akola	43	..	..	..	2	..
21	Buldana	6	..	..	..	1	..
22	Yeotmal	6	..	..	..	..	..
	Central Provinces States	**7**	..	..	..	..	..
23	Makrai	..	..	..	..	..	..
24	Bastar	..	..	..	..	..	..
25	Kanker	..	..	..	..	..	..
26	Nandgaon	1	..	..	..	..	..
27	Khairagarh	..	..	..	..	..	..
28	Chhuikhadan	..	..	..	..	..	..
29	Kawardha ..	..	..	..	..	..	..
30	Sakti ..	..	..	..	..	..	..
31	Raigarh	4	..	..	..	..	..
32	Sarangarh	..	..	..	..	..	..
33	Changbhakar	..	..	..	..	..	..
34	Korea	..	..	..	..	..	..
35	Surguja	..	..	..	..	..	..
36	Udaipur	..	..	..	..	..	..
37	Jashpur	2	..	..	..	..	..

Livelihood—General Distribution—*contd.* **TABLE X**

supply of material substances—*contd.*

III.—Industry—*contd.*

Construction of means of transport—*concld.*

92.—Carriage, cart, palki, etc., makers and wheel wrights.						93.—Ship, boat and aeroplane builders.						Serial No.
Total earners (principal occupations).		Total working dependants.		Total following occupation as subsidiary to other.		Total earners (principal occupations).		Total working dependants.		Total following occupation as subsidiary to other.		
Males.	Females.	Males.	Females.	Males.	Females.	Males.	Females.	Males.	Females.	Males.	Females.	
654	655	656	657	658	659	660	661	662	663	664	665	
153	**21**	**2**	**4**	**27**	**1**	**163**	..	**3**	..	**17**	..	
139	**21**	**2**	**3**	**17**	**1**	**163**	..	**3**	..	**17**	..	
65	**18**	**2**	**2**	**12**	**1**	**156**	..	**3**	..	**17**	..	
19	*1*	..	..	*2*	..	..	..	..	..	..	..	
1	..	..	..	..	..	..	..	..	..	..	..	1
..	..	..	..	..	..	..	..	..	..	..	..	2
18	1	..	..	2	..	..	..	..	..	..	..	3
..	..	..	..	..	..	..	..	..	..	..	..	
..	..	..	..	..	..	..	..	..	..	..	..	4
..	..	..	..	..	..	..	..	..	..	..	..	5
38	..	*2*	..	*7*	..	*156*	..	*3*	..	*17*	..	
..	..	..	..	..	..	..	..	..	..	..	..	6
..	..	..	..	..	..	153	..	3	..	17	..	7
25	..	..	..	7	..	..	..	..	..	..	..	8
..	..	..	..	..	..	..	..	..	..	..	..	9
13	..	2	..	..	..	3	..	..	..	..	..	10
7	..	..	..	*3*	..	..	..	..	..	..	..	
..	..	..	..	..	..	..	..	..	..	..	..	11
5	..	..	..	..	..	..	..	..	..	..	..	12
4	..	..	..	..	..	..	..	..	..	..	..	
..	..	..	..	..	..	..	..	..	..	..	..	13
2	..	..	..	1	..	..	..	..	..	..	..	14
..	..	..	..	2	..	..	..	..	..	..	..	15
1	*17*	..	*2*	..	*1*	..	..	..	..	..	..	
..	17	..	2	..	1	..	..	..	..	..	..	16
1	..	..	..	..	..	..	..	..	..	..	..	17
..	..	..	..	..	..	..	..	..	..	..	..	18
74	**3**	..	**1**	**5**	..	**7**	..	..	..	..	..	
..	..	..	..	..	..	..	..	..	..	..	..	19
1	..	..	..	..	..	..	..	..	..	..	..	20
..	..	..	..	..	..	..	..	..	..	..	..	21
73	3	..	1	5	..	7	..	..	..	..	..	22
14	..	..	**1**	**10**	..	..	..	..	..	..	..	
..	..	..	..	..	..	..	..	..	..	..	..	23
11	..	..	1	10	..	..	..	..	..	..	..	24
..	..	..	..	..	..	..	..	..	..	..	..	25
..	..	..	..	..	..	..	..	..	..	..	..	26
..	..	..	..	..	..	..	..	..	..	..	..	27
..	..	..	..	..	..	..	..	..	..	..	..	28
..	..	..	..	..	..	..	..	..	..	..	..	29
3	..	..	..	..	..	..	..	..	..	..	..	30
..	..	..	..	..	..	..	..	..	..	..	..	31
..	..	..	..	..	..	..	..	..	..	..	..	32
..	..	..	..	..	..	..	..	..	..	..	..	33
..	..	..	..	..	..	..	..	..	..	..	..	34
..	..	..	..	..	..	..	..	..	..	..	..	35
..	..	..	..	..	..	..	..	..	..	..	..	36
..	..	..	..	..	..	..	..	..	..	..	..	37

TABLE X — Occupation or means of

Serial No	District, City or State.	Total earners (principal occupations). Males.	Total earners (principal occupations). Females.	Total working dependants. Males.	Total working dependants. Females.	Total following occupation as subsidiary to other. Males.	Total following occupation as subsidiary to other. Females.
	Class ..	Class B.—Preparation and					
	Sub-class ..	Sub-class III.—					
	Order ..	Order 16.—Production and					
	Sub-order ..	Total order 16.					
	Group ..						
1	2	666	667	668	669	670	671
	Central Provinces and Berar	**436**	**6**	**2**	..	**8**	**1**
	C. P. British Districts and Berar	**415**	**6**	**2**	..	**7**	**1**
	C. P. British Districts	**344**	**6**	**2**	..	**7**	**1**
	Jubbulpore Division	*108*	..	..	..	*2*	..
1	Saugor	4	..	..	..	1	..
2	Damoh	..	..	..	..	..	..
3	Jubbulpore	104	..	..	..	1	..
	Jubbulpore City	*92*	..	..	..	*1*	..
4	Mandla	..	..	..	..	..	..
5	Seoni	..	..	..	..	..	..
	Nerbudda Division	*49*	..	*2*	..	*2*	..
6	Narsinghpur	3	..	..	..	..	..
7	Hoshangabad	2	..	..	..	1	..
8	Nimar	43	..	2	..	1	..
9	Betul	..	..	..	..	..	..
10	Chhindwara	1	..	..	..	..	..
	Nagpur Division	*154*	*6*	..	..	*3*	..
11	Wardha	24	..	..	..	..	..
12	Nagpur	130	6	..	..	2	..
	Nagpur City	*129*	*6*	..	..	*1*	..
13	Chanda	..	..	..	..	1	..
14	Bhandara	..	..	..	..	..	..
15	Balaghat	..	..	..	..	..	..
	Chhattisgarh Division	*33*	..	..	..	..	*1*
16	Raipur	25	..	..	..	..	1
17	Bilaspur	7	..	..	..	..	..
18	Drug	1	..	..	..	..	..
	Berar	**71**	..	..	..	..	..
19	Amraoti	18	..	..	..	..	..
20	Akola	45	..	..	..	..	..
21	Buldana	..	..	..	..	..	..
22	Yeotmal	8	..	..	..	..	..
	Central Provinces States	**21**	..	..	..	**1**	..
23	Makrai	..	..	..	..	..	..
24	Bastar	1	..	..	..	..	..
25	Kanker	..	..	..	..	..	..
26	Nandgaon	10	..	..	..	1	..
27	Khairagarh	..	..	..	..	..	..
28	Chhuikhadan	..	..	..	..	..	..
29	Kawardha	..	..	..	..	..	..
30	Sakti	..	..	..	..	..	..
31	Raigarh	7	..	..	..	..	..
32	Sarangarh	1	..	..	..	..	..
33	Chhangbhakar	..	..	..	..	..	..
34	Korea	..	..	..	..	..	..
35	Surguja	..	..	..	..	..	..
36	Udaipur	..	..	..	..	..	..
37	Jashpur	2	..	..	..	..	..

supply of material substances—*contd.*

Industry—*contd.*

transmission of physical force.						Order 17.—Miscellaneous and undefined industries.						
						Total order 17.						Serial No.
94.—Heat, light, electricity, motive power, etc., gas works and electric light and power.												
Total earners (principal occupations).		Total working dependants.		Total following occupation as subsidiary to other.		Total earners (principal occupations)		Total working dependants.		Total following occupation as subsidiary to other		
Males.	Females.	Males.	Females.	Males.	Females.	Males.	Females.	Males.	Females	Males.	Females.	
672	673	674	675	676	677	678	679	680	681	682	683	
436	**6**	**2**	..	**8**	**1**	**40,305**	**6,579**	**1,544**	**991**	**4,199**	**518**	
415	**6**	**2**	..	**7**	**1**	**38,417**	**6,178**	**1,373**	**862**	**3,847**	**504**	
344	**6**	**2**	..	**7**	**1**	**29,232**	**5,189**	**955**	**772**	**3,254**	**478**	
108	..	..	..	*2*	..	*7,605*	*1,843*	*155*	*320*	*546*	*252*	
4	..	..	..	1	..	2,090	550	71	70	50	140	1
..	..	..	..	..	..	1,113	372	28	127	50	24	2
104	..	..	..	1	..	3,143	786	38	105	326	82	3
92	..	..	..	1	..	*1,805*	*311*	*13*	*15*	*9*	..	
..	..	..	..	..	..	293	10	1	3	25	3	4
..	..	..	..	..	..	966	125	17	15	95	3	5
49	..	*2*	..	*2*	..	*6,558*	*1,218*	*193*	*211*	*458*	*55*	
3	..	..	..	..	..	1,201	234	9	42	84	6	6
2	..	..	..	1	..	1,782	555	55	55	91	11	7
43	..	2	..	1	..	1,487	226	61	47	87	25	8
..	..	..	..	..	..	828	115	5	12	60	12	9
1	..	..	..	..	..	1,260	88	63	55	136	1	10
154	*6*	..	..	*3*	..	*12,062*	*1,254*	*254*	*97*	*1,421*	*47*	
24	..	..	..	..	..	1,452	233	37	..	142	3	11
130	6	..	..	2	..	4,687	618	79	22	168	..	12
129	*6*	..	..	*1*	..	*1,845*	*304*	*39*	*18*	*16*	..	
..	..	..	..	1	..	2,248	106	45	5	136	9	13
..	..	..	..	..	..	2,469	209	65	20	567	33	14
..	..	..	..	..	..	1,206	88	28	50	408	2	15
33	..	..	..	..	*1*	*3,007*	*874*	*353*	*144*	*829*	*124*	
25	..	..	..	..	1	1,187	463	135	45	288	116	16
7	..	..	..	..	..	1,225	271	57	43	445	8	17
1	..	..	..	..	..	595	140	161	56	96	..	18
71	..	..	..	..	..	**9,185**	**989**	**418**	**90**	**593**	**26**	
18	..	..	..	..	..	2,933	452	84	20	238	3	19
45	..	..	..	..	..	2,312	232	40	16	123	11	20
..	..	..	..	..	..	1,879	179	65	13	126	2	21
8	..	..	..	..	..	2,061	126	229	41	106	10	22
21	..	..	..	**1**	..	**1,888**	**401**	**171**	**129**	**352**	**14**	
..	..	..	..	..	..	62	5	..	..	4	..	23
1	..	..	..	..	..	243	51	36	40	19	..	24
..	..	..	..	..	..	73	14	5	9	11	..	25
10	..	..	..	1	..	294	42	15	5	15	7	26
..	..	..	..	..	..	102	8	22	1	18	..	27
..	..	..	..	..	..	32	..	..	..	..	..	28
..	..	..	..	..	..	96	29	..	..	6	..	29
..	..	..	..	..	..	44	11	1	3	..	..	30
7	..	..	..	..	..	231	130	41	39	45	1	31
1	..	..	..	..	..	97	56	40	29	46	2	32
..	..	..	..	..	..	20	..	..	..	9	..	33
..	..	..	..	..	..	64	1	..	..	5	4	34
..	..	..	..	..	..	223	1	11	3	95	..	35
..	..	..	..	..	..	45	1	..	..	8	..	36
2	..	..	..	..	..	262	52	..	..	71	..	37

TABLE X — Occupation or means of

Serial No.	District, City or State.	Males.	Females.	Males.	Females.	Males.	Females.
	Class ..	Class B.—Preparation and					
	Sub-class ..	Sub-class III.—					
	Order ..	Order 17.—Miscellaneous					
	Sub-order ..						
	Group ..	95.—Printers, engravers, book-binders, etc.					
		Total earners (principal occupations).		Total working dependants.		Total following occupation as subsidiary to other.	
1	2	684	685	686	687	688	689
	Central Provinces and Berar ..	**1,144**	**36**	**3**	**1**	**26**	**12**
	C. P. British Districts and Berar ..	**1,129**	**36**	**3**	**1**	**23**	**12**
	C. P. British Districts	**981**	**22**	**3**	**1**	**16**	**12**
	Jubbulpore Division	*301*	*8*	*3*	*1*	*3*	*1*
1	Saugor	32	1	3	..	..	..
2	Damoh	35	2	..	..	..	..
3	Jubbulpore	209	5	..	..	1	1
	Jubbulpore City	*190*	*4*	..	..	..	..
4	Mandla	10	..	..	1	..	..
5	Seoni	15	..	..	..	2	..
	Nerbudda Division	*133*	*12*	..	..	*9*	..
6	Narsinghpur	17	..	..	..	..	..
7	Hoshangabad	47	11	..	..	1	..
8	Nimar	38	..	..	..	6	..
9	Betul	8	..	..	..	2	..
10	Chhindwara	23	1	..	..	..	..
	Nagpur Division	*506*	*2*	..	..	*4*	..
11	Wardha	44	1	..	..	2	..
12	Nagpur	422	1	..	..	1	..
	Nagpur City . ..	*376*	*1*	..	..	*1*	..
13	Chanda	10	..	..	..	..	..
14	Bhandara	24	..	..	..	..	..
15	Balaghat	6	..	..	..	1	..
	Chhattisgarh Division	*41*	..	..	..	..	*11*
16	Raipur	30	..	..	..	..	11
17	Bilaspur	5	..	..	..	..	..
18	Drug	6	..	..	..	..	..
	Berar	**148**	**14**	..	..	**7**	..
19	Amraoti	43	4	..	..	5	..
20	Akola	73	2	..	..	2	..
21	Buldana	7	..	..	..	..	..
22	Yeotmal	25	8	..	..	..	..
	Central Provinces States	**15**	..	..	..	**3**	..
23	Makrai	..	..	..	..	..	..
24	Bastar	..	..	..	..	..	..
25	Kanker	10	..	..	..	..	..
26	Nandgaon	2	..	..	..	2	..
27	Khairagarh	..	..	..	..	..	..
28	Chhuikhadan . ..	..	..	..	..	..	..
29	Kawardha	..	..	..	..	1	..
30	Sakti	..	..	..	..	..	..
31	Raigarh	..	..	..	..	..	..
32	Sarangarh	..	..	..	..	..	..
33	Chhangbhakar	..	..	..	..	..	..
34	Korea	..	..	..	..	..	..
35	Surguja	3	..	..	..	..	..
36	Udaipur	..	..	..	..	..	..
37	Jashpur	..	..	..	..	..	..

supply of material substances—*contd*.

Industry—*contd*.

and undefined industries—*contd*.

96.—Makers of musical instruments.						97.—Makers of clocks and surgical or scientific instruments, etc.						Serial No.
Total earners (principal occupations).		Total working dependants.		Total following occupation as subsidiary to other		Total earners (principal occupations).		Total working dependants.		Total following occupation as subsidiary to other.		
Males.	Females.	Males.	Females.	Males.	Females.	Males.	Females.	Males.	Females.	Males.	Females.	
690	691	692	693	694	695	696	697	698	699	700	701	
629	**59**	**32**	**32**	**200**	**2**	**267**	**1**	**2**	..	**15**	**1**	
383	**59**	**23**	**31**	**99**	**2**	**257**	**1**	**1**	..	**14**	**1**	
354	**58**	**20**	**28**	**94**	**2**	**198**	..	**1**	..	**8**	..	
54	*4*	..	*1*	*9*	..	*68*	..	..	..	..	..	
5	..	..	..	1	..	17	..	..	..	..	..	1
..	..	..	..	..	..	2	..	..	..	..	..	2
12	2	..	1	2	..	44	..	..	..	..	..	3
8	*2*	..	..	*1*	..	*36*	..	..	..	..	..	
32	1	..	..	4	..	1	..	..		..	..	4
5	1	..	..	2	..	4	..	..	..	..	..	5
10	..	..	..	*4*	..	*48*	..	*1*	..	*2*	..	
4	..	..	..	1	..	4	..	..	..	..	..	6
..	..	..	..	..	..	23	..	..	..	..	..	7
2	..	..	..	..	..	15	..	1	..	..	..	8
1	..	..	..	3	..	1	..	..	..	1	..	9
3	..	..	..	..	..	5	..	..	..	1	..	10
36	*4*	*3*	..	*5*	..	*60*	..	..	..	*2*	..	
6	1	..	..	1	..	10	..	..	..	1	..	11
24	2	2	..	4	..	37	..	..	..	1	..	12
22	..	*2*	..	*4*	..	*30*	..	..	..	*1*	..	
1	1	..	..	..	..	4	..	..	..	..	..	13
4	..	..	..	..	..	9	..	..	..	..	..	14
1	..	1	..	..	..	..	..	..	..	..	..	15
254	*50*	*17*	*27*	*76*	*2*	*22*	..	..	..	*4*	..	
127	30	14	12	18	..	9	..	..	..	3	..	16
126	20	3	1	57	2	10	..	..	..	..	..	17
1	..	..	14	1	..	3	..	..	..	1	..	18
29	**1**	**3**	**3**	**5**	..	**59**	**1**	..	..	**6**	**1**	
5	1	..	3	2	..	22	..	..	..	1	1	19
12	..	1	..	1	..	28	1	..	..	5	..	20
3	..	..	..	2	..	4	..	..	..	..	..	21
9	..	2	..	..	..	5	..	..	..	..	..	22
246	..	**9**	**1**	**101**	..	**10**	..	**1**	..	**1**	..	
..	..	..	..	..	..	..	..	..	..	1	..	23
1	..	..	..	..	..	2	..	1	..	..	..	24
..	..	..	..	..	..	..	..	..		..	..	25
..	..	..	..	..	..	6	..	..	..	..	..	26
..	..	..	..	..	..	..	..	..	..	..	..	27
..	..	..	..	..	..	..	..	..	..	..	..	28
..	..	..	..	1	..	..	..	..	..	..	..	29
2	..	..	..	..	..	..	..	..	..	..	..	30
17	..	5	..	1	..	1	..	..	..	..	..	31
9	..	..	..	..	..	1	..	..	..	..	..	32
7	..	..	..	7	..	..	..	..	..	..	..	33
10	..	..	..	2	..	..	..	..	..	..	..	34
55	..	4	1	50	..	..	..	..	..	..	..	35
2	..	..	..	2	..	..	..	..	..	..	..	36
143	..	..	..	38	..	..	..	..	..	..	..	37

TABLE X — Occupation or means of

Serial No.	District, City or State.	702 Total earners (principal occupations). Males.	703 Total earners (principal occupations). Females.	704 Total working dependants. Males.	705 Total working dependants. Females.	706 Total following occupation as subsidiary to other. Males.	707 Total following occupation as subsidiary to other. Females.	708 Total earners (principal occupations). Males.	709 Total earners (principal occupations). Females.	710 Total working dependants. Males.	711 Total working dependants. Females.	712 Total following occupations as subsidiary to other. Males.	713 Total following occupations as subsidiary to other. Females.
Class		Class B.—Preparation and											
Sub-class		Sub-class III.—Industry—*concld.*											
Order		Order 17.—Miscellaneous and undefined											
Group		98.—Makers of jewellery and ornaments.						99.—Other miscellaneous and undefined industries (toy-making, taxidermy, etc.).					
1	2	702	703	704	705	706	707	708	709	710	711	712	713
	Central Provinces and Berar	**29,893**	**629**	**1,347**	**203**	**3,627**	**100**	**1,372**	**321**	**38**	**163**	**115**	**184**
	C. P. British Districts and Berar.	**28,623**	**568**	**1,199**	**151**	**3,398**	**92**	**1,300**	**290**	**28**	**161**	**112**	**184**
	C. P. British Districts.	**20,891**	**447**	**800**	**105**	**2,846**	**81**	**1,074**	**234**	**28**	**144**	**106**	**181**
	Jubbulpore Division	*4,171*	*101*	*100*	*22*	*376*	*31*	*732*	*164*	*8*	*127*	*63*	*154*
1	Saugor	1,215	28	42	..	32	1	130	57	4	12	12	131
2	Damoh	647	6	19	1	18	..	56	17	1	93	2	..
3	Jubbulpore	1,268	58	28	15	225	30	512	66	3	18	39	19
	Jubbulpore City	*518*	*5*	*11*	*1*	*1*	..	*355*	*2*	..	..	..	..
4	Mandla	243	8	..	2	10	..	6	1	..	..	10	3
5	Seoni	798	1	11	4	91	..	28	23	..	4	..	1
	Nerbudda Division	*4,773*	*43*	*167*	*16*	*372*	*2*	*92*	*15*	..	*15*	*10*	*16*
6	Narsinghpur	785	10	9	3	68	..	16	1	..	4	1	..
7	Hoshangabad	932	8	45	2	53	..	43	3	..	..	1	..
8	Nimar	1,106	3	45	2	63	..	8	8	..	10	8	16
9	Betul	801	17	5	..	53	1	7	3	..	..	..	..
10	Chhindwara	1,149	5	63	9	135	1	18	..	..	1	..	..
	Nagpur Division	*9,871*	*174*	*223*	*35*	*1,390*	*44*	*207*	*12*	*12*	*2*	*13*	..
11	Wardha	1,192	5	36	..	128	1	6	3	..	..	5	..
12	Nagpur	3,168	50	57	6	157	..	153	9	8	2	5	..
	Nagpur City	*892*	*38*	*26*	*3*	*10*	..	*24*	*8*	*1*	*2*	..	..
13	Chanda	2,124	24	41	4	135	9	21	..	4	..	1	..
14	Bhandara	2,284	87	63	11	564	32	26	..	..	..	1	..
15	Balaghat	1,103	8	26	14	406	2	1	..	..	..	1	..
	Chhattisgarh Division	*2,076*	*129*	*310*	*32*	*708*	*4*	*43*	*43*	*8*	..	*20*	*11*
16	Raipur	725	93	113	15	248	3	25	22	6	..	16	11
17	Bilaspur	890	28	45	3	371	1	9	13	..	..	3	..
18	Drug	461	8	152	14	89	..	9	8	2	..	1	..
	Berar	**7,732**	**121**	**399**	**46**	**552**	**11**	**226**	**56**	..	**17**	**6**	**3**
19	Amraoti	2,374	29	79	6	223	..	33	17	..	8	5	2
20	Akola	1,943	24	37	4	114	1	19	26	..	7	1	..
21	Buldana	1,628	28	60	8	124	1	43	13	..	2	..	1
22	Yeotmal	1,787	40	223	28	91	9	131	..	..	..	..	..
	Central Provinces States	**1,270**	**61**	**148**	**52**	**229**	**8**	**72**	**31**	**10**	**2**	**3**	..
23	Makrai	38	..	..	..	..	..	..	..	..	..	..	..
24	Bastar	189	5	24	36	16	..	20	26	10	2	3	..
25	Kanker	39	1	5	9	11	..	..	..	..	..	..	..
26	Nandgaon	221	..	13	..	13	4	..	..	..	..	..	..
27	Khairagarh	89	2	22	1	18	..	..	1	..	..	..	..
28	Chhuikhadan	25	..	..	..	..	..	..	..	..	..	..	..
29	Kawardha	68	1	..	..	4	..	..	..	..	..	..	..
30	Sakti	34	..	1	..	..	..	..	..	..	..	..	..
31	Raigarh	161	4	36	5	44	..	2	..	..	..	..	..
32	Sarangarh	79	..	40	..	46	..	..	..	..	..	..	..
33	Chhangbhakar	11	..	..	..	2	..	..	..	..	..	..	..
34	Korea	50	1	..	..	3	4	..	..	..	..	..	..
35	Surguja	117	..	7	1	45	..	46	..	..	..	..	..
36	Udaipur	40	..	..	..	6	..	..	..	..	..	..	..
37	Jashpur	109	47	..	..	21	..	4	4	..	..	..	..

Livelihood—General Distribution—*contd.* TABLE X

supply of material substances—*contd.*

industries—*concld*						Sub-class IV.—Transport.												
100.—Scavenging.						Total sub-class IV.						Order 18.—Transport by air. Total order 18.						Serial No.
Total earners (principal occupations).		Total working dependants.		Total following occupation as subsidiary to other.		Total earners (principal occupations).		Total working dependants.		Total following occupation as subsidiary to other.		Total earners (principal occupations).		Total working dependants.		Total following occupation as subsidiary to other.		
Males	Females.	Males	Females.	Males	Females.	Males.	Females.	Males.	Females.	Males.	Females.	Males	Females.	Males	Females.	Males	Females.	
714	715	716	717	718	719	720	721	722	723	724	725	726	727	728	729	730	731	
7,000	**5,533**	**122**	**592**	**216**	**219**	**87,617**	**12,757**	**2,123**	**1,868**	**16,244**	**1,005**	..	..	..	..	..	..	
6,725	**5,224**	**119**	**518**	**201**	**213**	**81,814**	**11,033**	**1,385**	**1,105**	**14,970**	**838**	..	..	..	..	..	..	
5,734	**4,428**	**103**	**494**	**184**	**202**	**62,690**	**10,140**	**1,112**	**989**	**12,803**	**804**	..	..	..	..	..	..	
2,279	*1,566*	*44*	*169*	*95*	*66*	*16,966*	*1,933*	*481*	*272*	*4,363*	*240*	..	..	..	..	..	..	
691	464	22	58	5	8	4,530	560	40	57	381	11	..	..	..	..	..	..	1
373	347	8	33	30	24	900	75	1	60	392	4	..	..	..	..	..	..	2
1,098	655	7	71	59	32	7,660	454	415	128	2,558	180	..	..	..	..	..	..	3
698	*288*	*2*	*14*	*7*	..	*3,765*	*76*	*15*	*16*	*128*	*4*	..	..	..	..	..	..	
1	..	1	..	1	..	2,453	402	16	11	715	10	..	..	..	..	..	..	4
116	100	6	7	..	2	1,423	442	9	16	317	35	..	..	..	..	..	..	5
1,502	*1,148*	*25*	*180*	*61*	*37*	*15,989*	*2,667*	*106*	*175*	*3,914*	*115*	..	..	..	..	..	..	
375	223	..	35	14	6	1,440	203	11	31	477	58	..	..	..	..	..	..	6
737	533	10	53	36	11	6,045	347	61	33	1,373	15	..	..	..	..	..	..	7
318	215	15	35	10	9	3,962	468	16	29	415	2	..	..	..	..	..	..	8
10	95	..	12	1	11	1,945	1,029	2	44	1,212	30	..	..	..	..	..	..	9
62	82	..	45	..	..	2,597	620	16	38	437	10	..	..	..	..	..	..	10
1,382	*1,062*	*16*	*60*	*7*	*3*	*17,733*	*1,591*	*223*	*98*	*2,372*	*86*	..	..	..	..	..	..	
194	223	1	..	5	2	2,474	106	124	3	234	3	..	..	..	..	..	..	11
883	556	12	14	..	..	9,157	907	8	17	619	5	..	..	..	..	..	..	12
501	*257*	*10*	*13*	..	..	*6,360*	*717*	*5*	*10*	*35*	*1*	..	..	..	..	..	..	
88	81	..	1	..	..	2,371	173	9	14	659	25	..	..	..	..	..	..	13
122	122	2	9	2	1	2,556	241	41	13	504	35	..	..	..	..	..	..	14
95	80	1	36	..	..	1,175	164	41	51	356	18	..	..	..	..	..	..	15
571	*652*	*18*	*85*	*21*	*96*	*12,002*	*3,949*	*302*	*444*	*2,154*	*363*	..	..	..	..	..	..	
271	318	2	18	3	91	5,763	2,355	256	263	836	84	..	..	..	..	..	..	16
185	210	9	39	14	5	4,938	1,413	21	52	1,068	269	..	..	..	..	..	..	17
115	124	7	28	4	..	1,301	181	25	129	250	10	..	..	..	..	..	..	18
991	**796**	**16**	**24**	**17**	**11**	**19,124**	**893**	**273**	**116**	**2,167**	**34**	..	..	..	..	..	..	
456	401	5	3	2	..	4,992	192	149	39	673	22	..	..	..	..	..	..	19
237	179	2	5	..	10	5,027	254	42	7	485	4	..	..	..	..	..	..	20
194	138	5	3	..	..	5,674	138	20	34	729	3	..	..	..	..	..	..	21
104	78	4	13	15	1	3,431	309	62	36	280	5	..	..	..	..	..	..	22
275	**309**	**3**	**74**	**15**	**6**	**5,803**	**1,724**	**738**	**763**	**1,274**	**167**	..	..	..	..	..	..	
24	5	..	..	3	..	43	6	..	..	12	..	..	..	..	..	..	..	23
31	20	1	2	..	..	505	88	7	26	172	..	..	..	..	..	..	..	24
24	13	..	..	..	..	444	2	75	10	97	2	..	..	..	..	..	..	25
65	42	2	5	..	3	567	27	16	51	108	41	..	..	..	..	..	..	26
13	5	..	..	..	..	968	271	..	2	92	..	..	..	..	..	..	..	27
7	..	..	..	..	..	93	..	..	..	40	..	..	..	..	..	..	..	28
28	28	..	..	..	..	89	74	..	..	75	15	..	..	..	..	..	..	29
8	11	..	3	..	..	937	690	452	366	268	103	..	..	..	..	..	..	30
50	126	..	34	..	1	1,283	418	108	243	224	3	..	..	..	..	..	..	31
8	56	..	29	..	2	200	48	74	38	42	2	..	..	..	..	..	..	32
2	..	..	..	..	..	1	..	..	..	..	..	..	..	..	..	..	..	33
4	..	..	..	..	..	84	..	..	..	6	1	..	..	..	..	..	..	34
2	1	..	1	..	..	275	9	6	2	68	..	..	..	..	..	..	..	35
3	1	..	..	..	..	120	11	..	..	10	..	..	..	..	..	..	..	36
6	1	..	..	12	..	194	80	..	25	60	..	..	..	..	..	..	..	37

TABLE X Occupation or means of

Serial No.	District, City or State.	Class B.—Preparation and supply / Sub-class IV.— / Order 19.—Transport / Total order 19. Total earners (principal occupations). Males.	Females.	Total working dependants. Males.	Females.	Total following occupation as subsidiary to other. Males.	Females.
1	2	732	733	734	735	736	737
	Central Provinces and Berar	**2,919**	**1,003**	**63**	**13**	**471**	**79**
	C. P. British Districts and Berar	**2,774**	**1,003**	**29**	**13**	**453**	**79**
	C. P. British Districts	**2,708**	**1,003**	**28**	**13**	**382**	**79**
	Jubbulpore Division	*190*	*65*	*3*	*3*	*36*	*1*
1	Saugor	8	..	..	..	3	..
2	Damoh	6	1	..	..	2	1
3	Jubbulpore	115	32	2	2	16	..
	Jubbulpore City	6	..	..	..	..	..
4	Mandla	26	..	..	..	8	..
5	Seoni	35	32	1	1	7	..
	Nerbudda Division	***247***	***6***	***13***	***1***	***31***	***3***
6	Narsinghpur	23	..	2	..	3	3
7	Hoshangabad	146	..	9	..	18	..
8	Nimar	64	3	2	1	10	..
9	Betul	6	3	..	..	..	..
10	Chhindwara	8	..	..	..	..	..
	Nagpur Division	***295***	***11***	***2***	***6***	***118***	***6***
11	Wardha	9	4	..	..	6	1
12	Nagpur	83	..	..	3	16	..
	Nagpur City	..	..	..	..	..	..
13	Chanda	75	2	2	1	41	5
14	Bhandara	46	1	..	..	30	..
15	Balaghat	82	4	..	2	25	..
	Chhattisgarh Division	*1,976*	*921*	*10*	*3*	*197*	*69*
16	Raipur	404	98	6	3	35	2
17	Bilaspur	1,255	757	4	..	146	66
18	Drug	317	66	..	..	16	1
	Berar	**66**	..	**1**	.	**71**	..
19	Amraoti	13	..	..	..	18	..
20	Akola	1	..	..	..	..	..
21	Buldana	1	..	..	..	6	..
22	Yeotmal	51	..	1	..	47	..
	Central Provinces States	**145**	..	**34**	..	**18**	..
23	Makrai	1	..	..	..	1	..
24	Bastar	4	..	..	..	2	..
25	Kanker	110	..	34	..	10	..
26	Nandgaon	..	..	..	..	..	..
27	Khairagarh	..	..	..	..	..	..
28	Chhuikhadan	27	..	..	..	..	..
29	Kawardha	..	..	..	..	..	..
30	Sakti	..	..	..	..	..	..
31	Raigarh	3	..	..	..	1	..
32	Sarangarh	..	..	..	..	..	..
33	Changbhakar	..	..	..	..	..	..
34	Korea	..	..	..	..	..	..
35	Surguja	..	..	..	..	1	..
36	Udaipur	..	..	..	..	..	..
37	Jashpur	..	..	..	..	3	..

of material substances—*contd.*

Transport—*contd.*

by water

102.—Ship owners, boat owners and their employees, officers, mariners, etc., ship brokers, boatmen and towmen.						103.—Persons (other than labourers) employed in harbours, docks, rivers and canals including pilots.						Serial No.
Total earners (principal occupations).		Total working dependants.		Total following occupation as subsidiary to other.		Total earners (principal occupations).		Total working dependants.		Total following occupation as subsidiary to other.		
Males.	Females.	Males.	Females.	Males.	Females	Males.	Females.	Males	Females.	Males	Females	
738	739	740	741	742	743	744	745	746	747	748	749	
736	**12**	**54**	**5**	**270**	**2**	**935**	**69**	**5**	**4**	**38**	**3**	
621	**12**	**20**	**5**	**254**	**2**	**905**	**69**	**5**	**4**	**36**	**3**	
556	**12**	**19**	**5**	**183**	**2**	**904**	**69**	**5**	**4**	**36**	**3**	
42	..	*2*	*1*	*29*	*1*	*148*	*65*	*1*	*2*	*7*	..	
7	..	..	..	3	..	1	..	..	..	..	..	1
..	..	..	..	1	1	6	1	..	..	1	..	2
10	..	1	..	13	..	105	32	1	2	3	..	3
..	..	..	..	..	..	*6*	..	..	..	..	..	
25	..	..	..	8	..	1	..	..	..	..	..	4
..	..	1	1	4	..	35	32	..	..	3	..	5
215	*6*	*11*	*1*	*22*	..	*7*	..	..	..	*1*	*3*	
11	..	..	..	2	..	1	..	..	..	1	3	6
131	..	9	..	10	..	1	..	..	..	..	..	7
64	3	2	1	10	..	..	..	..	..	..	..	8
6	3	..	..	..	..	..	..	..	..	..	..	9
3	..	..	..	..	..	5	..	..	..	..	..	10
171	*6*	*2*	*3*	*104*	*1*	*114*	*4*	..	*2*	*14*	..	
9	4	..	..	6	1	..	..	..	..	..	..	11
66	..	..	3	16	..	9	..	..	..	..	..	12
..	..	..	..	..	..	..	..	..	..	..	..	
47	2	2	..	39	..	27	..	..	..	2	..	13
38	..	..	..	30	..	7	..	..	..	..	..	14
11	..	..	..	13	..	71	4	..	2	12	..	15
128	..	*4*	..	*28*	..	*635*	..	*4*	..	*14*	..	
93	..	4	..	11	..	274	..	..	..	4	..	16
33	..	..	..	15	..	187	..	4	..	10	..	17
2	..	..	..	2	..	174	..	..	..	..	..	18
65	..	**1**	..	**71**	..	**1**	..	..	..	..	..	
13	..	..	..	18	..	..	..	..	..	..	..	19
..	..	..	..	..	..	1	..	..	..	..	..	20
1	..	..	..	6	..	..	..	..	..	..	..	21
51	..	1	..	47	..	..	..	..	..	..	..	22
115	..	**34**	..	**16**	..	**30**	..	..	..	**2**	..	
..	..	..	..	..	..	1	..	..	..	..	..	23
2	..	..	..	1	..	2	..	..	..	..	..	24
110	..	34	..	10	..	..	..	..	..	..	..	25
..	..	..	..	..	..	..	..	..	..	..	..	26
..	..	..	..	..	..	..	..	..	..	..	..	27
..	..	..	..	..	..	27	..	..	..	..	..	28
..	..	..	..	..	..	..	..	..	..	..	..	29
..	..	..	..	..	..	..	..	..	..	..	..	30
3	..	..	..	1	..	..	..	..	..	..	..	31
..	..	..	..	..	..	..	..	..	..	..	..	32
..	..	..	..	..	..	..	..	..	..	..	..	33
..	..	..	..	..	..	..	..	..	..	..	..	34
..	..	..	..	1	..	..	..	..	..	..	..	35
..	..	..	..	..	..	..	..	..	..	..	..	36
..	..	..	..	3	..	..	..	..	..	..	..	37

TABLE X **Occupation or means of**

Serial No.	Class .. / Sub-class .. / Order .. / Sub-order .. / Group ..	Class B.—Preparation and supply / Sub-class IV.— / Order 19.—Transport by water—*concld.* / 104.—Labourers employed on harbours, docks, rivers and canals.					
	District, City or State.	Total earners (principal occupations).		Total working dependants		Total following occupation as subsidiary to other	
		Males.	Females.	Males	Females	Males.	Females.
1	2	750	751	752	753	754	755
	Central Provinces and Berar	**1,248**	**922**	**4**	**4**	**163**	**74**
	C. P. British Districts and Berar	**1,248**	**922**	**4**	**4**	**163**	**74**
	C. P. British Districts	**1,248**	**922**	**4**	**4**	**163**	**74**
	Jubbulpore Division	..	..	..	..	..	..
1	Saugor	..	..	..		..	..
2	Damoh	..					..
3	Jubbulpore	..	..	..	..		..
	Jubbulpore City	..	..	..		..	..
4	Mandla	..	..	..			..
5	Seoni	..	..	..	..		..
	Nerbudda Division	*25*	..	*2*	..	*8*	..
6	Narsinghpur	11	..	2	..	..	..
7	Hoshangabad	14	..	..	..	8	
8	Nimar	..	..	..	..	..	..
9	Betul	..	..	..	..	..	..
10	Chhindwara	..	..	..	..	..	..
	Nagpur Division	*10*	*1*	..	*1*	..	*5*
11	Wardha	..	..	..	..	..	..
12	Nagpur	8	..	..	..	..	..
	Nagpur City	..	..	..	..	..	..
13	Chanda	1	..	..	1	..	5
14	Bhandara	1	1	..	..	..	..
15	Balaghat	..	..	..	..	..	..
	Chhattisgarh Division	*1,213*	*921*	*2*	*3*	*155*	*69*
16	Raipur	37	98	2	3	20	2
17	Bilaspur	1,035	757	..	..	121	66
18	Drug	141	66	..	..	14	1
	Berar	..	..	..	..	..	..
19	Amraoti	..	..	..	..	..	..
20	Akola	..	..	..	..	..	..
21	Buldana	..	..	..	..	..	..
22	Yeotmal	..	..	..	..	..	..
	Central Provinces States	..	..	..	..	..	..
23	Makrai	..	..	..	..	..	..
24	Bastar	..	..	..	..	..	..
25	Kanker	..	..	..	..	..	..
26	Nandgaon	..	..	..	..	..	..
27	Khairagarh	..	..	..	..	..	..
28	Chhuikhadan	..	..	..	..	..	..
29	Kawardha	..	..	..	..	..	..
30	Sakti	..	..	..	..	..	..
31	Raigarh	..	..	..	..	..	..
32	Sarangarh	..	..	..	..	..	..
33	Changbhakar	..	..	..	..	..	..
34	Korea	..	..	..	..	..	..
35	Surguja	..	..	..	..	..	..
36	Udaipur	..	..	..	..	..	..
37	Jashpur	..	..	..	..	..	..

Livelihood—General Distribution—*contd.*

TABLE X

of material substances—*contd.*

Transport—*contd*

Order 20—Transport by road.

Total order 20.						105.—Persons (other than labourers) employed on the construction and maintenance of roads and bridges.						Serial No.
Total earners (principal occupations).		Total working dependants.		Total following occupation as subsidiary to other		Total earners (principal occupations).		Total working dependants		Total following occupation as subsidiary to other		
Males	Females	Males	Females.	Males	Females	Males	Females	Males	Females.	Males	Females	
756	757	758	759	760	761	762	763	764	765	766	767	
48,015	**9,709**	**1,802**	**1,816**	**14,732**	**745**	**2,883**	**152**	**19**	**30**	**214**	**36**	
43,642	**8,282**	**1,133**	**1,053**	**13,498**	**619**	**2,736**	**148**	**19**	**28**	**211**	**36**	
28,588	**7,642**	**876**	**939**	**11,449**	**586**	**1,923**	**134**	**6**	**28**	**170**	**36**	
8,291	*1,621*	*463*	*265*	*4,113*	*207*	*593*	*22*	*1*	..	*39*	*1*	
1,148	160	39	55	309	11	38	3	1	..	3	..	1
397	65	1	60	378	2	32	2	..	..	4	1	2
4,187	338	400	125	2,429	180	453	16	..	..	14	..	3
1,946	*52*	*9*	*15*	*127*	*4*	*146*	*4*	..	..	*2*	..	
1,744	391	16	11	698	10	57	..	..	..	17	..	4
815	317	7	14	299	4	13	1	..	..	1	..	5
6,744	*2,162*	*67*	*148*	*3,498*	*66*	*528*	*62*	*4*	*26*	*75*	*7*	
514	58	3	6	285	20	4	1	..	..	..	..	6
2,028	233	35	32	1,269	13	92	15	..	26	4	6	7
2,171	337	12	28	353	1	52	9	1	..	4	..	8
694	972	1	44	1,170	22	82	22	..	..	2	1	9
1,337	562	16	38	421	10	298	15	3	..	65	..	10
7,641	*1,194*	*67*	*85*	*2,147*	*73*	*623*	*41*	*1*	*2*	*44*	*3*	
1,177	55	9	3	209	2	52	2	..	..	5	2	11
3,681	650	6	11	573	5	241	1	..	..	1	..	12
2,469	*480*	*3*	*9*	*18*	*1*	*154*	*1*	..	..	*1*	..	
1,088	163	7	13	605	19	188	3	1	..	7	..	13
1,086	188	34	9	444	29	34	1	..	..	9	1	14
609	138	11	49	316	18	108	34	..	2	22	..	15
5,912	*2,665*	*279*	*441*	*1,691*	*240*	*179*	*9*	..	..	*12*	*25*	
3,975	2,136	239	260	747	76	83	5	..	..	3	..	16
1,216	417	15	52	724	156	59	4	..	..	6	25	17
721	112	25	129	220	8	37	..	..	..	3	..	18
15,054	**640**	**257**	**114**	**2,049**	**33**	**813**	**14**	**13**	..	**41**	..	
3,560	165	148	38	641	22	71	11	2	..	7	..	19
3,650	193	40	6	465	3	92	2	..	..	..	..	20
5,005	130	20	34	718	3	18	..	1	..	..	..	21
2,836	152	49	36	225	5	632	1	10	..	34	..	22
4,373	**1,427**	**669**	**763**	**1,234**	**126**	**147**	**4**	..	**2**	**3**	..	
35	6	..	..	11	..	..	..	..	..	..	..	23
451	88	7	26	169	..	61	..	..	2	..	..	24
311	2	41	10	87	2	7	..	..	..	2	..	25
340	21	16	51	108	..	24	4	..	..	..	..	26
445	97	..	2	88	..	6	..	..	..	..	..	27
57	..	..	..	40	..	18	..	..	..	..	..	28
80	74	..	..	75	15	12	..	..	..	1	..	29
909	646	452	366	266	103	..	..	..	..	..	..	30
931	345	100	243	210	3	8	..	..	..	..	..	31
196	48	47	38	42	2	1	..	..	..	..	..	32
1	..	..	..	..	..	..	..	..	..	..	..	33
75	..	..	..	5	1	..	..	..	..	..	..	34
256	9	6	2	67	..	3	..	..	..	..	..	35
108	11	..	..	10	..	5	..	..	..	..	..	36
178	80	..	25	56	..	2	..	..	..	..	..	37

TABLE X | **Occupation or means of**

Serial No.	Class .. / Sub-class .. / Order .. / Sub-order .. / Group ..	Class B.—Preparation and supply / Sub-class IV.— / Order 20.—Transport / 106.—Labourers employed on roads and bridges.					
	District, City or State.	Total earners (principal occupations).		Total working dependants.		Total following occupation as subsidiary to other.	
		Males	Females.	Males	Females.	Males.	Females.
1	2	768	769	770	771	772	773
	Central Provinces and Berar ..	**9,973**	**7,174**	**823**	**1,620**	**1,830**	**573**
	C. P. British Districts and Berar ..	**7,465**	**5,768**	**225**	**875**	**1,266**	**448**
	C. P. British Districts ..	**6,306**	**5,335**	**216**	**832**	**1,164**	**424**
	Jubbulpore Division ..	*1,625*	*1,142*	*41*	*237*	*292*	*157*
1	Saugor ..	251	209	16	55	..	8
2	Damoh ..	56	60	..	59	19	..
3	Jubbulpore ..	544	249	19	99	193	142
	Jubbulpore City ..	*100*	*3*	..	..	*1*	..
4	Mandla ..	461	319	5	10	37	4
5	Seoni ..	313	305	1	14	43	3
	Nerbudda Division ..	*2,261*	*1,831*	*16*	*121*	*193*	*41*
6	Narsinghpur ..	95	38	..	6	59	18
7	Hoshangabad ..	915	141	12	6	56	..
8	Nimar ..	648	307	..	27	20	1
9	Betul ..	200	945	..	44	39	14
10	Chhindwara ..	403	400	4	38	19	8
	Nagpur Division ..	*736*	*587*	*12*	*65*	*153*	*50*
11	Wardha ..	51	31	..	..	8	..
12	Nagpur ..	240	188	..	1	7	..
	Nagpur City ..	*67*	*52*	..	..	..	..
13	Chanda ..	102	102	3	9	26	8
14	Bhandara ..	147	171	..	8	23	26
15	Balaghat ..	196	95	9	47	89	16
	Chhattisgarh Division ..	*1,684*	*1,775*	*147*	*409*	*526*	*176*
16	Raipur ..	1,189	1,350	122	245	274	55
17	Bilaspur ..	275	319	8	40	239	114
18	Drug ..	220	106	17	124	13	7
	Berar ..	**1,159**	**433**	**9**	**43**	**102**	**24**
19	Amraoti ..	245	111	9	35	56	19
20	Akola ..	382	147	..	..	38	..
21	Buldana ..	441	67	..	..	4	1
22	Yeotmal ..	91	108	..	8	4	4
	Central Provinces States ..	**2,508**	**1,406**	**598**	**745**	**564**	**128**
23	Makrai ..	..	6	..	..	..	..
24	Bastar ..	92	85	..	24	..	..
25	Kanker ..	54	2	2	10	1	2
26	Nandgaon ..	77	15	12	51	..	..
27	Khairagarh ..	319	91	..	2	6	..
28	Chhuikhadan ..	29	..	..	..	12	..
29	Kawardha ..	48	72	..	..	20	15
30	Sakti ..	906	646	452	366	266	103
31	Raigarh ..	544	344	93	236	171	3
32	Sarangarh ..	174	48	39	38	42	2
33	Changbhakar ..	..	..	..	..	..	..
34	Korea ..	1	..	..	..	..	..
35	Surguja ..	52	9	..	2	23	..
36	Udaipur ..	83	11	..	..	2	..
37	Jashpur ..	129	77	..	16	21	..

of material substances—*contd.*

Transport—*contd.*

by road—*contd.*

107.—Owners, managers and employees (excluding personal servants) connected with mechanically driven vehicles (including trams).						108.—Owners, managers and employees (excluding personal servants) connected with other vehicles.						Serial No.
Total earners (principal occupations).		Total working dependants.		Total following occupation as subsidiary to other.		Total earners (principal occupations).		Total working dependants.		Total following occupation as subsidiary to other.		
Males.	Females.	Males	Females.	Males.	Females.	Males.	Females.	Males.	Females.	Males.	Females.	
774	775	776	777	778	779	780	781	782	783	784	785	
4,844	**5**	**71**		**161**	..	**17,433**	**186**	**384**	**46**	**10,337**	**78**	
4,713	**5**	**70**	.	**157**	..	**16,397**	**174**	**330**	**37**	**9,832**	**78**	
2,399	**4**	**12**	.	**73**	..	**11,396**	**121**	**213**	**28**	**8,621**	**70**	
459	*1*	*1*		*12*	..	*3,440*	*39*	*79*	*9*	*3,073*	*37*	
78	..	..	..	2	..	495	3	22	..	295	2	1
[illegible]	.	..	..	2	..	257	3	1	1	337	1	2
300	.	1	..	7	..	1,853	24	40	7	1,741	32	3
270	..	..	..	*1*	..	*920*	*8*	*1*	..	*101*	*1*	
22	..	..	.		..	506	2	10	1	453	1	4
56	1	..	..	1	..	329	7	6	..	247	1	5
485	*1*	*2*	.	*19*	..	*2,241*	*19*	*42*	..	*2,854*	*14*	
15	1	1	..	1	..	191	1	1	..	185	2	6
101	..	..	..	..	..	608	4	23	..	961	5	7
220	..	1	.	8	.	727	4	10	..	304	..	8
65	..	..	..	7	.	299	5	1	..	1,119	6	9
84	..	..	..	3	..	416	5	7	..	285	1	10
1,098	*1*	*7*	..	*26*	..	*3,136*	*29*	*28*	*3*	*1,780*	*10*	
159	..	3	..	13	..	397	2	6	1	158	..	11
600	1	1	..	5	.	1,575	10	4	..	546	2	12
461	*1*	*1*	..	*5*	..	*922*	*5*	*1*	..	*10*	..	
106	..	..	.	2	..	565	9	2	2	556	4	13
184	.	3	..	4	..	372	5	16	..	326	2	14
49	..	..	..	2	.	227	3	..	..	194	2	15
357	*1*	*2*	.	*16*	..	*2,579*	*34*	*64*	*16*	*914*	*9*	
179	.	..	..	6	..	1,697	16	54	14	367	1	16
115	1	1	..	6	...	557	15	4	2	383	8	17
63	.	1	..	4		325	3	6	.	164	..	18
2,814	**1**	**58**	.	**84**	..	**5,001**	**53**	**117**	**9**	**1,211**	**8**	
740	.	37	..	26	..	1,476	19	50	1	464	3	19
794	1	15	..	25	..	1,590	18	24	6	378	3	20
377	.	2	..	24	.	615	7	8	1	203	1	21
403	..	4	.	9	..	1,320	9	35	1	166	1	22
131	..	**1**	..	**4**	..	**1,036**	**12**	**54**	**9**	**505**	..	
3	..	..	..	..	..	27	.	.	..	11	..	23
29	..	.	..	..	..	193	2	5		146	..	24
10	..	1	..	2	..	227	..	29	.	63	..	25
52	..	..	.	..	..	172	2	4	.	107	..	26
22	..	.	..	..	..	25	5	..	.	61	..	27
..	..	..	..	..	..	10	..	..	..	28	..	28
..	..	..	..	..	..	12		..	..	34	..	29
3	..	..	..	..	..	..	.	..	.		..	30
3	..	..	..	..	..	274	..	7	.	22	..	31
2	..	..	..	..	..	19	.	8	.	..	..	32
..	..	..	..	..	..	1	.	..	..	..	..	33
..	..	..	..	..	..	25	..	..	..	1	..	34
3	..	..	..	2	..	22	..	1	..	..	..	35
3	..	..	..	..	..	..	..	..	.	..	..	36
1	..	..	..	..	..	29	3	..	9	32	..	37

TABLE X — Occupation or means of

Serial No.	Class ..	Class B.—Preparation and supply					
	Sub-class ..	Sub-class IV.					
	Order ..	Order 20 —Transport					
	Sub-order ..						
	Group ..	109.—Palkibearers and owners, etc.					
	District, City or State.	Total earners (principal occupations).		Total working dependants.		Total following occupation as subsidiary to other.	
		Males	Females.	Males.	Females.	Males	Females.
1	2	786	787	788	789	790	791
	Central Provinces and Berar ..	268	1	12	..	202	1
	C. P. British Districts and Berar ..	254	1	12	..	163	1
	C. P. British Districts	217	1	11	..	122	1
	Jubbulpore Division	*33*	..	..	..	*9*	..
1	Saugor	3	..	..	..	5	..
2	Damoh	..	..	..	..	..	..
3	Jubbulpore	18	..	..	..	..	..
	Jubbulpore City	*18*	..	..	..	..	..
4	Mandla	..	..	..	..	..	..
5	Seoni	12	..	..	..	4	..
	Nerbudda Division	*2*	*1*	..	..	..	..
6	Narsinghpur	..	..	..	..	..	..
7	Hoshangabad	..	1	..	..	..	..
8	Nimar	..	..	..	..	..	..
9	Betul	2	..	..	..	..	..
10	Chhindwara	..	..	..	..	..	..
	Nagpur Division	*4*	..	..	..	*1*	..
11	Wardha	..	..	..	..	1	..
12	Nagpur	4	..	..	..	..	..
	Nagpur City	*4*	..	..	..	..	..
13	Chanda	..	..	..	..	..	..
14	Bhandara	..	..	..	..	..	..
15	Balaghat	..	..	..	..	..	..
	Chhattisgarh Division	*178*	..	*11*	..	*112*	*1*
16	Raipur	90	..	10	..	14	..
17	Bilaspur	43	..	..	..	64	..
18	Drug	45	..	1	..	34	1
	Berar	37	..	1	..	41	..
19	Amraoti	11	..	..	..	29	..
20	Akola	4	..	1	..	8	..
21	Buldana	..	..	..	..	..	..
22	Yeotmal	22	..	..	..	4	..
	Central Provinces States	14	..	..	..	39	..
23	Makrai	..	..	..	..	..	..
24	Bastar	..	..	..	..	..	..
25	Kanker	..	..	..	..	..	..
26	Nandgaon	14	..	..	..	..	..
27	Khairagarh	..	..	..	..	21	..
28	Chhuikhadan	..	..	..	..	..	..
29	Kawardha	..	..	..	..	6	..
30	Sakti	..	..	..	..	..	..
31	Raigarh	..	..	..	..	12	..
32	Sarangarh	..	..	..	..	..	..
33	Changbhakar	..	..	..	..	..	..
34	Korea	..	..	..	..	..	..
35	Surguja	..	..	..	..	..	..
36	Udaipur	..	..	..	..	..	..
37	Jashpur	..	..	..	..	..	..

of material substances—*contd*

Transport—*contd*

by road—*concld.*

110.—Pack elephant, camel, mule, ass and bullock owners and drivers.						111.—Porters and messengers						Serial No.
Total earners (principal occupations)		Total working dependants.		Total following occupation as subsidiary to other.		Total earners (principal occupations).		Total working dependants.		Total following occupation as subsidiary to other		
Males	Females	Males	Females.	Males.	Females.	Males	Females	Males	Females	Males	Females	
792	793	794	795	796	797	798	799	800	801	802	803	
1,360	**86**	**93**	**29**	**496**	**5**	**11,254**	**2,105**	**400**	**91**	**1,492**	**52**	
1,107	**83**	**77**	**22**	**425**	**4**	**10,970**	**2,103**	**400**	**91**	**1,444**	**52**	
1,030	**79**	**77**	**22**	**416**	**4**	**5,317**	**1,968**	**341**	**29**	**883**	**51**	
758	*65*	*25*	*15*	*283*	*2*	*1,383*	*352*	*316*	*4*	*405*	*10*	
53	11	..	..	3	1	230	234	..	..	1	..	1
40	..	..	..	15	..	9	..	..	..	1	..	2
177	23	25	15	137	..	842	76	315	4	337	6	3
7	..	*7*	*15*	*17*	..	*485*	*37*	*1*	..	*5*	*3*	
485	31	..	..	127	1	213	39	1	..	64	4	4
3	..	..	..	1	..	89	3	..	..	2	..	5
31	*4*	..	*1*	*39*	*1*	*1,196*	*244*	*3*	..	*318*	*3*	
20	4	..	..	32	..	189	13	1	..	8	..	6
6	..	.	..	5	1	306	72	..	..	243	1	7
1	..	.	1		..	523	17	..	..	17	..	8
1	..	..	.	..	..	45	..	..	.	3	1	9
3	..	..	.	2	..	153	142	2	.	47	1	10
39	*8*	*2*	..	*11*	..	*2,005*	*528*	*17*	*15*	*132*	*10*	
9	2	..	.	2	..	509	18	..	2	22	..	11
4	..	.	.		..	1,017	450	1	10	14	3	12
1	..	..	..	.	..	*860*	*421*	*1*	*9*	*2*	*1*	
1	..	..	..	..	..	126	49	1	2	14	7	13
1	..	..	..	.	..	348	11	15	1	82	..	14
24	6	2	..	9	..	5	.	..	.	.	..	15
202	*2*	*50*	*6*	*83*	*1*	*733*	*844*	*5*	*10*	*28*	*28*	
160	1	48	..	78	1	577	764	5	1	5	19	16
37	1	2	1	5	..	130	77	..	9	21	9	17
5	..	..	5	..	.	26	3	..	..	2	..	18
77	**4**	..	.	**9**	..	**5,653**	**135**	**59**	**62**	**561**	**1**	
29	1	..		8	.	988	23	50	2	51	..	19
24	3	.	..	..	..	764	22	..	..	16	..	20
2	..	..	..	1	..	3,555	56	9	33	486	1	21
22	..	..	..	..	..	346	34	..	27	8	..	22
253	**3**	**16**	**7**	**71**	**1**	**284**	**2**	..	..	**48**	..	
1	..	..	..	..	..	4	..	..	..	.	..	23
32	1	2	..	4	..	44	..	..	..	19	..	24
5	..	9	..	18	.	8	..	..	..	1	..	25
..	..	..	..	..	.	1	..	..	..	1	..	26
..	..	..	.	.	.	73	1	..	..	..	..	27
..	..	..	..	.	..	..	..	..	..	..	..	28
4	2	.	..	..	.	4	..	..	..	14	..	29
..	..	..	..	..	..	..	..	.	.	..	..	30
..	..	..	7	.	..	*102*	*1*	..	..	5	..	31
..	..	..	..	..	..	..	..	..	..	..	.	32
..	..	..	..	..	..	..	..	..	..	..	..	33
40	..	..	..	2	1	9	..	..	..	2	..	34
143	..	5	..	36	..	33	..	..	..	6	..	35
17	..	..	..	8	..	..	..	..	..	..	..	36
11	..	..	..	3	..	6	..	..	..	..	..	37

TABLE X — Occupation or means of

Serial No.	Class / Sub-class / Order / Sub-order / Group	Class B.—Preparation and supply					
		Sub-class IV.—					
		Order 21. —Transport					
		Total order 21.					
	District, City or State	[illegible]		[illegible] working dependants		Total following occupation as subsidiary to other.	
		Males	Females	Males	Females	Males.	Females.
1	2	804	805	806	807	808	809
	Central Provinces and Berar	**33,691**	**2,037**	**216**	**39**	**935**	**181**
	C. P. British Districts and Berar	**32,608**	**1,740**	**208**	**39**	**918**	**140**
	C. P. British Districts	**29,175**	**1,490**	**205**	**37**	**911**	**139**
	Jubbulpore Division	*7,885*	*245*	*14*	*4*	*201*	*32*
1	Saugor	3,268	99	1	2	69	..
2	Damoh	456	9		..	10	1
3	Jubbulpore	3,096	33	13	1	108	..
	Jubbulpore City	*1,639*	*23*	*6*	*1*	*1*	..
4	Mandla	584	11			6	..
5	Seoni	481	93	..	1	8	31
	Nerbudda Division	*8,454*	*499*	*26*	*26*	*372*	*46*
6	Narsinghpur	871	145	6	25	187	35
7	Hoshangabad	3,666	114	17	1	83	2
8	Nimar	1,605	128	2	..	51	1
9	Betul	1,162	54	1	..	37	8
10	Chhindwara	1,150	58	..	..	14	..
	Nagpur Division	*9,088*	*383*	*153*	*7*	*97*	*7*
11	Wardha	1,201	46	115	..	16	..
12	Nagpur	5,045	255	2	3	29	..
	Nagpur City	*3,628*	*235*	*2*	*1*	*17*	..
13	Chanda	1,107	8	..	..	11	1
14	Bhandara	1,312	52	6	4	30	6
15	Balaghat	423	22	30	..	11	..
	Chhattisgarh Division	*3,748*	*363*	*12*	..	*241*	*54*
16	Raipur	1,211	121	11	..	53	47
17	Bilaspur	2,363	239	1	..	175	6
18	Drug	174	3	..	..	13	1
	Berar	**3,433**	**250**	**3**	**2**	**7**	**1**
19	Amraoti	1,174	26	1	1	2	..
20	Akola	1,201	60	2	1	3	1
21	Buldana	593	8	..	..	1	..
22	Yeotmal	465	156	..	..	1	..
	Central Provinces States	**1,083**	**297**	**8**	..	**17**	**41**
23	Makrai	4	..	..	..	..	..
24	Bastar	..	..	..	..	..	..
25	Kanker	..	..	..	..	..	..
26	Nandgaon	206	6	..	..	..	41
27	Khairagarh	503	174	..	..	4	..
28	Chhuikhadan	..	..	..	..	..	..
29	Kawardha	..	..	..	..	..	..
30	Sakti	28	44	..	..	2	..
31	Raigarh	332	73	8	..	11	..
32	Sarangarh	..	..	..	..	..	..
33	Changbhakar	..	..	..	..	..	..
34	Korea	6	..	..	..	..	..
35	Surguja	..	..	..	..	..	..
36	Udaipur	..	..	..	..	..	..
37	Jashpur	4	..	..	..	..	..

of material substances—*contd.*

Transport—*contd.*

by rail.

112.—Railway employees of all kinds other than porters and coolies.						113.—Labourers employed on railway construction and maintenance and coolies and porters employed on railway premises						Serial No.
Total earners (principal occupations).		Total working dependants.		Total following occupation as subsidiary to other.		Total earners (principal occupations)		Total working dependants.		Total following occupation as subsidiary to other		
Males.	Females.	Males	Females.	Males	Females	Males.	Females	Males	Females	Males	Females	
810	811	812	813	814	815	816	817	818	819	820	821	
17,484	**412**	**154**	**9**	**375**	**10**	**16,207**	**1,625**	**62**	**30**	**560**	**171**	
17,173	**412**	**146**	**9**	**362**	**10**	**15,435**	**1,328**	**62**	**30**	**556**	**130**	
15,266	**405**	**144**	**9**	**357**	**10**	**13,909**	**1,085**	**61**	**28**	**554**	**129**	
3,320	*19*	*6*	..	*112*	..	*4,559*	*226*	*8*	*4*	*80*	*32*	
1,240	2	1	..	68	..	2,028	97	..	2	1	.	1
22	..	..	..	..	..	434	9	.	.	10	1	2
1,661	17	5	..	41	..	1,435	16	8	1	67	..	3
1,420	*11*	*5*	..	*1*	..	*219*	*12*	*4*	*1*	.	.	
259	..	..	..	1	..	325	11	.	..	5	..	4
144	..	..	..	2	..	337	93	.	1	6	31	5
4,155	*119*	*12*	*2*	*65*	*2*	*4,299*	*380*	*14*	*24*	*307*	*44*	
270	8	..	1	..	..	601	137	6	24	187	35	6
2,152	62	12	1	50	2	1,514	52	5	..	33	.	7
749	16	..	..	1	..	856	112	2	..	50	1	8
419	30	..	..	1	..	743	24	1	..	36	8	9
565	3	..	...	13	..	585	55	.	..	1	..	10
6,353	*242*	*125*	*7*	*71*	*7*	*2,735*	*141*	*28*	.	*26*		
733	17	115	..	9	.	468	29		.	7	.	11
3,726	171	2	3	18	.	1,319	84	.	..	11	..	12
2,789	*156*	*2*	*1*	*12*	..	*839*	*79*		..	*5*	.	
565	6	..	..	6	1	542	2	.		5	..	13
1,084	32	3	4	27	6	228	20	3		3	.	14
245	16	5	..	11	...	178	6	25	.	.	..	15
1,432	*25*	*1*	..	*109*	*1*	*2,316*	*338*	*11*	..	*132*	*53*	
235	..	..	..	7	1	976	121	11		46	5	16
1,116	24	1	..	102	.	1,247	215	.	.	73	47	17
81	1	..	..	.	.	93	2	.	..	13	1	18
1,907	**7**	**2**	..	**5**	..	**1,526**	**243**	**1**	**2**	**2**	**1**	
777	2	1	..	1		397	24	.	1	1		19
497	3	1	..	2	.	704	57	1	1	1	1	20
528	2	..	..	1	..	65	6	.			.	21
105	..	..	.	1	..	360	156	.	..	.	.	22
311	..	**8**	.	**13**	.	**772**	**297**	.	.	**4**	**41**	
4	..	..	.	..	..	.	.	.		.	..	23
..	.	..	..	..	..		.	.			.	24
..	..	..	..	..	..	.	..	.			.	25
75	.	..	..	.	.	131	6	.			41	26
109	.	..	..	.	..	394	174	.		4	.	27
.	.	..	.	..	.	.	.	..	.		.	28
.	..	..	..	..	..	.	.	.		.	..	29
2	..	.	.	2	..	26	44		.	.	.	30
111	..	8	.	11	..	221	73			.		31
.	..	..	..	..	.		..	.			..	32
.		..	..	..	..	.		..	.	.	...	33
6	..	..	..	..	..	.		.	.		..	34
..	..	..	..	..	..	.	.	.	.	.	..	35
.		..		..	..	.		.	..	.		36
4	.	..	..	..	..	...	.	.	.		..	37

TABLE X — Occupation or means of

	Class ..		Class B — Preparation and supply				
	Sub-class		Sub-class IV.—				
	Order		Order 22 - Post office, Telegraph				
	Sub-order .		Total order 22				
Serial No.	Group						
	District, City or State.	Total earners (principal occupations)		Total working dependants.		Total following occupation as subsidiary to other.	
		Males.	Females	Males	Females.	Males.	Females.
1	2	822	823	824	825	826	827
	Central Provinces and Berar	**2,992**	**8**	**42**		**106**	..
	C. P. British Districts and Berar	**2,790**	**8**	**15**	.	**101**	..
	C. P. British Districts	**2,219**	**5**	**3**		**61**	..
	Jubbulpore Division	*600*	*2*	*1*	..	*13*	..
1	Saugor	106	1	..	..	.	..
2	Damoh	41	..	..	..	2	..
3	Jubbulpore	262	1	.		5	..
	Jubbulpore City	*174*	*1*	..	..	..	..
4	Mandla	99	.		.	3	..
5	Seoni	92	..	1	..	3	..
	Nerbudda Division	*544*		.	.	*13*	..
6	Narsinghpur	32	.	..	.	2	..
7	Hoshangabad	205	.	.	.	3	..
8	Nimar	122	.	.		1	..
9	Betul	83	.			5	..
10	Chhindwara	102	.		..	2	..
	Nagpur Division	*709*	*3*	*1*	..	*10*	..
11	Wardha	87	1	.		3	..
12	Nagpur	348	2	..		1	..
	Nagpur City	*263*	*2*	.	..	.	..
13	Chanda	101	..	..		2	..
14	Bhandara	112		1	..	.	..
15	Balaghat	61		..		4	..
	Chhattisgarh Division	*366*	.	*1*	..	*25*	..
16	Raipur	173		.	..	1	..
17	Bilaspur	104	.	1	..	23	..
18	Drug	89	..	..	..	1	..
	Berar	**571**	**3**	**12**	..	**40**	..
19	Amraoti	245	1	..	..	12	..
20	Akola	175	1	..	.	17	..
21	Buldana	72	.	..	..	4	..
22	Yeotmal	79	1	12	..	7	..
	Central Provinces States	**202**	..	**27**	.	**5**	..
23	Makrai	3	..	..	..	.	..
24	Bastar	50	..	..	..	1	..
25	Kanker	23	..	.	..	.	..
26	Nandgaon	21	..	..	..	..	..
27	Khairagarh	20	..	..	..	.	..
28	Chhuikhadan	9	..	..	..	..	..
29	Kawardha	9	..	..	..	..	..
30	Sakti	..	..	..	..	..	..
31	Raigarh	17	.	..	..	2	..
32	Sarangarh	4	.	27	..	..	..
33	Changbhakar	..	..	..	..	..	..
34	Korea	3	..	..	..	1	..
35	Surguja	19	..	..	..	..	..
36	Udaipur	12	..	..	..	..	..
37	Jashpur	2	..	..	..	1	..

Livelihood—General Distribution—*contd.* TABLE X

of material substances—*contd*

Transport—*concld.* Sub-class V.—Trade.

and Telephone services. Total sub-class V.

114.—Post office, Telegraph and Telephone services.

Total earners (principal occupations)		Total working dependants.		Total following occupation as subsidiary to other.		Total earners (principal occupations).		Total working dependants.		Total following occupation as subsidiary to other.		Serial No.
Males.	Females.	Males.	Females.	Males.	Females.	Males	Females	Males.	Females	Males	Females.	
828	829	830	831	832	833	834	835	836	837	838	839	
2,992	**8**	**42**	..	**106**	..	**222,212**	**101,096**	**8,095**	**28,459**	**65,768**	**23,449**	
2,790	**8**	**15**	..	**101**	..	**209,178**	**93,803**	**7,074**	**22,841**	**61,367**	**22,087**	
2,219	**5**	**3**	..	**61**	..	**157,490**	**84,080**	**5,241**	**19,719**	**45,831**	**19,341**	
600	*2*	*1*	..	*13*	..	*43,542*	*20,175*	*1,301*	*4,516*	*11,903*	*3,693*	
106	1	..	..	..	..	10,906	4,792	315	1,357	2,212	732	1
41	..	..	..	2	..	6,174	2,826	319	667	2,175	617	2
262	1	..	..	5	..	13,704	7,252	519	1,832	4,437	1,585	3
174	*1*	..	..	..	..	*5,899*	*1,385*	*40*	*121*	*189*	*24*	
99	..	..	..	3	..	6,075	2,485	60	276	1,420	488	4
92	..	1	..	3	..	6,683	2,820	88	384	1,659	271	5
544	..	..	..	*13*	..	*38,459*	*16,401*	*1,395*	*4,229*	*11,140*	*5,476*	
32	..	..	..	2	..	6,311	3,675	147	1,045	1,648	927	6
205	..	..	..	3	..	9,746	4,792	330	974	2,759	843	7
122	..	..	..	1	..	9,201	1,687	513	500	2,626	110	8
83	..	..	..	5	..	4,762	3,811	45	733	1,780	2,702	9
102	..	..	..	2	..	8,439	2,436	360	977	2,327	894	10
709	*3*	*1*	..	*10*	..	*52,416*	*27,420*	*1,206*	*4,971*	*12,322*	*5,247*	
87	1	..	..	3	..	8,104	2,002	112	276	1,732	267	11
348	2	..	..	1	..	18,226	6,804	319	856	3,136	1,187	12
263	*2*	..	..	..	..	*7,032*	*1,805*	*202*	*115*	*293*	*26*	
101	..	..	..	2	..	7,775	6,369	149	1,459	2,839	1,943	13
112	..	1	..	..	..	12,539	9,098	324	1,028	3,003	1,508	14
61	..	..	..	4	..	5,772	3,147	302	1,352	1,612	342	15
366	..	*1*	..	*25*	..	*23,073*	*20,084*	*1,339*	*6,003*	*10,466*	*4,925*	
173	..	..	..	1	..	11,558	11,411	384	1,906	4,494	2,484	16
104	..	1	..	23	..	7,750	5,796	425	1,741	4,864	2,154	17
89	..	..	..	1	..	3,765	2,877	530	2,356	1,108	287	18
571	**3**	**12**	..	**40**	..	**51,688**	**9,723**	**1,833**	**3,122**	**15,536**	**2,746**	
245	1	..	..	12	..	16,389	3,118	607	1,187	6,897	960	19
175	1	..	..	17	..	15,210	2,108	393	527	3,483	683	20
72	..	..	..	4	..	8,391	2,294	420	468	3,092	846	21
79	1	12	..	7	..	11,698	2,203	413	940	2,064	257	22
202	..	**27**	..	**5**	..	**13,034**	**7,293**	**1,021**	**5,618**	**4,401**	**1,362**	
3	..	..	..	..	..	335	122	.	64	74	13	23
50	..	..	..	1	..	1,770	870	197	771	463	71	24
23	..	..	..	..	..	916	505	136	644	279	535	25
21	..	..	..	..	..	1,712	947	102	243	238	53	26
20	..	..	..	..	..	781	589	95	97	123	53	27
9	..	..	..	..	..	201	195	15	194	77	10	28
9	..	..	..	..	..	473	779	1	20	591	487	29
..	..	..	..	..	..	82	117	1	7	12	1	30
17	..	..	..	2	..	1,794	1,163	160	727	450	93	31
4	..	27	..	..	..	518	615	114	215	369	9	32
..	..	..	..	..	..	119	28	6	10	23	2	33
3	..	..	..	1	..	458	52	..	2	133	2	34
19	..	..	..	..	..	2,367	491	170	2,291	1,115	28	35
12	..	..	..	..	..	216	135	3	3	106	1	36
12	..	..	..	1	..	1,292	685	21	330	348	4	37

TABLE X | **Occupation or means of**

Serial No.	Class ..	Class B.—Preparation and supply					
	Sub-class ..	Sub-class V.—					
	Order ..	Order 23.—Banks, establishments					
	Sub-order ..	Total order 23					
	Group ..						
	District, City or State.	Total earners (principal occupations).		Total working dependants.		Total following occupation as subsidiary to other.	
		Males.	Females.	Males.	Females.	Males.	Females.
1	2	840	841	842	843	844	845
	Central Provinces and Berar	**20,228**	**1,211**	**457**	**95**	**8,257**	**411**
	C. P. British Districts and Berar	**19,480**	**1,152**	**432**	**86**	**8,043**	**398**
	C. P. British Districts	**14,916**	**951**	**296**	**62**	**4,717**	**202**
	Jubbulpore Division	*5,284*	*379*	*70*	*22*	*1,036*	*63*
1	Saugor	1,339	87	9	3	240	33
2	Damoh	866	50	2	..	286	5
3	Jubbulpore	1,635	151	54	7	284	16
	Jubbulpore City	*835*	*94*	..	*1*	*27*	*4*
4	Mandla	876	52	5	12	70	4
5	Seoni	568	39	..	..	156	5
	Nerbudda Division	*4,145*	*288*	*147*	*16*	*1,624*	*55*
6	Narsinghpur	593	82	2	15	185	11
7	Hoshangabad	1,242	81	20	..	398	15
8	Nimar	1,131	58	48	..	461	8
9	Betul	427	27	1	1	276	9
10	Chhindwara	752	40	76	..	304	12
	Nagpur Division	*4,465*	*180*	*50*	*23*	*1,606*	*42*
11	Wardha	589	26	4	2	322	..
12	Nagpur	1,395	62	1	6	549	21
	Nagpur City	*360*	*24*	..	*2*	*44*	*2*
13	Chanda	785	21	4	..	383	9
14	Bhandara	1,111	18	34	2	247	9
15	Balaghat	585	53	7	13	105	3
	Chhattisgarh Division	*1,022*	*104*	*29*	*1*	*451*	*42*
16	Raipur	455	40	6	..	104	18
17	Bilaspur	477	50	18	1	301	22
18	Drug	90	14	5	..	46	2
	Berar	**4,564**	**201**	**136**	**24**	**3,326**	**196**
19	Amraoti	967	64	21	12	987	48
20	Akola	1,836	72	22	3	986	30
21	Buldana	1,005	45	76	9	904	104
22	Yeotmal	756	20	17	..	449	14
	Central Provinces States	**748**	**59**	**25**	**9**	**214**	**13**
23	Makrai	12	2	..	..	11	..
24	Bastar	131	10	1	..	2	..
25	Kanker	15	2	..	..	3	..
26	Nandgaon	40	6	3	..	10	..
27	Khairagarh	37	4	5	..	..	..
28	Chhuikhadan	13	..	3	..	7	..
29	Kawardha	23	2	..	1	39	2
30	Sakti	..	..	..	..	..	..
31	Raigarh	39	12	1	..	4	1
32	Sarangarh	24	..	..	..	4	..
33	Changbhakar	..	..	..	..	..	..
34	Korea	11	1	..	..	2	..
35	Surguja	380	15	11	8	130	10
36	Udaipur	18	..	..	..	..	..
37	Jashpur	5	5	1	..	2	..

of material substances—*contd.*

Trade—*contd.*

credit exchange and insurance. Order 24.—Brokerage, commission and export.

115.—Bank managers, money lenders, exchange and insurance agents, money changers and brokers and their employees.						Total order 24.						Serial No.
Total earners (principal occupations).		Total working dependants.		Total following occupation as subsidiary to other.		Total earners (principal occupations).		Total working dependants.		Total following occupation as subsidiary to other.		
Males.	Females.	Males.	Females.	Males.	Females.	Males.	Females.	Males.	Females.	Males.	Females.	
846	847	848	849	850	851	852	853	854	855	856	857	
20,228	**1,211**	**457**	**95**	**8,257**	**411**	**3,245**	**84**	**71**	**1**	**671**	**2**	
19,480	**1,152**	**432**	**86**	**8,043**	**398**	**3,047**	**83**	**71**	**1**	**651**	**2**	
14,916	**951**	**296**	**62**	**4,717**	**202**	**2,023**	**76**	**60**	..	**475**	**1**	
5,284	*379*	*70*	*22*	*1,036*	*63*	*476*	*14*	*10*	..	*196*	*1*	
1,339	87	9	3	240	33	146	..	2	..	117	..	1
866	50	2	..	286	5	19	..	..	..	34	..	2
1,635	151	54	7	284	16	293	13	8	..	42	1	3
835	*94*	..	*1*	*27*	*4*	*157*	*4*	..	..	*4*	*1*	
876	52	5	12	70	4	18	1	..	..	1	..	4
568	39	..	..	156	5	..	..	..	..	2	..	5
4,145	*288*	*147*	*16*	*1,624*	*55*	*434*	*7*	*9*	..	*49*	..	
593	82	2	15	185	11	45	..	..	..	3	..	6
1,242	81	20	..	398	15	112	..	..	..	10	..	7
1,131	58	48	..	461	8	213	..	2	..	29	..	8
427	27	1	1	276	9	24	4	..	..	5	..	9
752	40	76	..	304	12	40	3	7	..	2	..	10
4,465	*180*	*50*	*23*	*1,606*	*42*	*713*	*11*	*6*	..	*105*	..	
589	26	4	2	322	..	55	1	1	..	11	..	11
1,395	62	1	6	549	21	419	9	4	..	36	..	12
360	*24*	..	*2*	*44*	*2*	*313*	*8*	*2*	..	*27*	..	
785	21	4	..	383	9	99	1	..	..	36	..	13
1,111	18	34	2	247	9	123	..	1	..	14	..	14
585	53	7	13	105	3	17	..	..	..	8	..	15
1,022	*104*	*29*	*1*	*451*	*42*	*400*	*44*	*35*	..	*125*	..	
455	40	6	..	104	18	242	41	..	..	83	..	16
477	50	18	1	301	22	41	3	..	..	15	..	17
90	14	5	..	46	2	117	..	35	..	27	..	18
4,564	**201**	**136**	**24**	**3,326**	**196**	**1,024**	**7**	**11**	**1**	**176**	**1**	
967	64	21	12	987	48	357	..	2	..	64	1	19
1,836	72	22	3	986	30	310	2	3	1	57	..	20
1,005	45	76	9	904	104	27	5	..	..	7	..	21
756	20	17	..	449	14	330	..	6	..	48	..	22
748	**59**	**25**	**9**	**214**	**13**	**198**	**1**	..	..	**20**	..	
12	2	..	..	11	..	..	..	..	..	2	..	23
131	10	1	..	2	..	..	..	..	..	1	..	24
15	2	..	1	3	..	..	..	..	..	..	..	25
40	6	3	..	10	..	80	..	..	..	13	..	26
37	4	5	..	..	..	2	..	..	..	..	..	27
13	..	3	..	7	..	1	..	..	..	..	..	28
23	2	..	..	39	2	2	..	..	..	2	..	29
..	..	..	..	..	..	..	..	..	..	..	..	30
39	12	1	..	4	1	57	..	..	..	1	..	31
24	..	..	..	4	..	1	..	..	..	..	..	32
..	..	..	..	..	..	..	..	..	..	..	..	33
11	1	..	..	2	..	6	..	..	..	..	..	34
380	15	11	8	130	10	28	..	..	..	..	..	35
18	..	..	..	..	..	20	1	..	..	1	..	36
5	5	1	..	2	..	1	..	..	..	..	..	37

TABLE X

Serial No.	Class ..	Class B.—Preparation and supply					
	Sub-class ..	Sub-class V.—					
	Order ..	Order 24.—Brokerage, commission and export—*concld.*					
	Sub-order ..						
	Group ..	116.—Brokers commission agents, and commercial travellers, ware house owners and employees.					
	District, City or State	Total earners (principal occupations).		Total working dependants.		Total following occupation as subsidiary to other.	
		Males.	Females	Males.	Females	Males.	Females.
1	2	858	859	860	861	862	863
	Central Provinces and Berar ..	**3,245**	**84**	**71**	**1**	**671**	**2**
	C. P. British Districts and Berar ..	**3,047**	**83**	**71**	**1**	**651**	**2**
	C. P. British Districts	**2,023**	**76**	**60**	..	**475**	**1**
	Jubbulpore Division	*476*	*14*	*10*	..	*196*	*1*
1	Saugor	146	..	2	..	117	..
2	Damoh	19	..	..	..	34	..
3	Jubbulpore	293	13	8	..	42	1
	Jubbulpore City	*157*	*4*	..	..	*4*	*1*
4	Mandla	18	1	..	..	1	..
5	Seoni	..	..	..	..	2	..
	Nerbudda Division	*434*	*7*	*9*	..	*49*	..
6	Narsinghpur	45	..	..	..	3	..
7	Hoshangabad	112	..	..	..	10	..
8	Nimar	213	..	2	..	29	..
9	Betul	24	4	..	..	5	..
10	Chhindwara	40	3	7	..	2	..
	Nagpur Division	*713*	*11*	*6*	..	*105*	..
11	Wardha	55	1	1	..	11	..
12	Nagpur .. .	419	9	4	..	36	..
	Nagpur City	*313*	*8*	*2*	..	*27*	..
13	Chanda	99	1	..	..	36	..
14	Bhandara	123	..	1	..	14	..
15	Balaghat	17	..	..	..	8	..
	Chhattisgarh Division	*400*	*44*	*35*	..	*125*	..
16	Raipur	242	41	..	..	83	..
17	Bilaspur	41	3	..	..	15	..
18	Drug	117	..	35	..	27	..
	Berar	**1,024**	**7**	**11**	**1**	**176**	**1**
19	Amraoti	357	..	2	..	64	1
20	Akola	310	2	3	1	57	..
21	Buldana	27	5	..	..	7	..
22	Yeotmal	330	..	6	..	48	..
	Central Provinces States	**198**	**1**	..	..	**20**	..
23	Makrai	..	..	..	..	2	..
24	Bastar	..	..	..	..	1	..
25	Kanker	..	..	..	..	..	..
26	Nandgaon	80	..	..	..	13	..
27	Khairagarh	2	..	.	..	..	..
28	Chhuikhadan . ..	1	..	..	..	..	..
29	Kawardha	2	..	..	..	2	..
30	Sakti	..	..	..	..	..	..
31	Raigarh	57	..	..	..	1	..
32	Sarangarh	1	..	..	..	..	..
33	Changbhakar	..	..	..	..	..	..
34	Korea	6	..	..	..	..	..
35	Surguja	28	..	..	..	..	..
36	Udaipur	20	1	..	..	1	..
37	Jashpur	1	..	..	..	..	..

of material substances—*contd.*

Trade— *contd*

Order 25.—Trade in textiles.

Total order 25.						117 - Trade in piece goods, wool, cotton, silk hair and other textiles.						
Total earners (principal occupations)		Total working dependants.		Total following occupation as subsidiary to other.		Total earners (principal occupations).		Total working dependants.		Total following occupation as subsidiary to other.		Serial No.
Males	Females	Males	Females	Males	Females	Males.	Females	Males.	Females	Males	Females.	
864	865	866	867	868	869	870	871	872	873	874	875	
21,690	**1,569**	**696**	**987**	**5,064**	**427**	**21,690**	**1,569**	**696**	**987**	**5,064**	**427**	
20,676	**1,419**	**592**	**752**	**4,695**	**411**	**20,676**	**1,419**	**592**	**752**	**4,695**	**411**	
14,830	**1,216**	**351**	**681**	**3,021**	**389**	**14,830**	**1,216**	**351**	**681**	**3,021**	**389**	
3,393	*195*	*76*	*72*	*679*	*23*	*3,393*	*195*	*76*	*72*	*679*	*23*	
816	32	23	52	127	.	816	32	23	52	127	..	1
149	17	7	.	27	10	149	17	7	..	27	10	2
1,014	41	27	13	172	3	1,014	41	27	13	172	3	3
436	*6*	*4*	*1*	*10*	..	*436*	*6*	*4*	*1*	*10*	..	
642	15	2		198	10	642	15	2	.	198	10	4
772	90	17	7	155	.	772	90	17	7	155	..	5
3,934	*203*	*116*	*141*	*633*	*18*	*3,934*	*203*	*116*	*141*	*633*	*18*	
356	14	8	3	61	2	356	14	8	3	61	2	6
1,038	25	28	55	70	2	1,038	25	28	55	70	2	7
774	11	23	11	91	2	774	11	23	11	191	2	8
536	32	1	17	64	3	536	32	1	17	64	3	9
1,230	121	56	55	247	9	1,230	121	56	55	247	9	10
5,667	*620*	*79*	*222*	*1,228*	*172*	*5,667*	*620*	*79*	*222*	*1,228*	*172*	
1,284	58	15	9	346	16	1,284	58	15	9	346	16	11
1,887	248	25	128	388	23	1,887	248	25	128	388	23	12
549	*34*	*13*	*5*	*25*	..	*549*	*34*	*13*	*5*	*25*	..	
562	132	12	58	216	85	562	132	12	58	216	85	13
1,169	122	14	16	203	47	1,169	122	14	16	203	47	14
765	60	13	11	75	1	765	60	13	11	75	1	15
1,836	*198*	*80*	*246*	*481*	*176*	*1,836*	*198*	*80*	*246*	*481*	*176*	
966	88	28	8	270	134	966	88	28	8	270	134	16
506	96	3	29	154	42	506	96	3	29	154	42	17
364	14	49	209	57	..	364	14	49	209	57	..	18
5,846	**203**	**241**	**71**	**1,674**	**22**	**5,846**	**203**	**241**	**71**	**1,674**	**22**	
1,928	57	85	5	590	9	1,928	57	85	5	590	9	19
1,717	37	53	4	380	3	1,717	37	53	4	380	3	20
954	51	45	9	357	4	954	51	45	9	357	4	21
1,247	58	58	53	347	6	1,247	58	58	53	347	6	22
1,014	**150**	**104**	**235**	**369**	**16**	**1,014**	**150**	**104**	**235**	**369**	**16**	
31				1		31	..	..	..	1	..	23
249	3	24	13	26		249	3	24	13	26	..	24
59	49	9	38	6	5	59	49	9	38	6	5	25
107	8	21			.	107	8	21	..	..	..	26
37	6	4		2	.	37	6	4	.	2	..	27
20		3				20	..	3	..	..	..	28
39	27		10	4	4	39	27	..	10	4	4	29
		.		.	.	.	..	..	..	..	..	30
54	11		35	55	.	54	11	..	35	55	..	31
52	2	28	14	39	.	52	2	28	14	39	..	32
10	1	4	2	2	..	10	1	4	2	2	..	33
33				6	.	33	..	..	.	6	..	34
192	7	11	88	214	7	192	7	11	88	214	7	35
3	.			1	.	3	..	..	..	1	..	36
128	36	..	35	13	..	128	36	..	35	13	..	37

TABLE X

Occupation or means of

Serial No.	Class .. / Sub-class .. / Order .. / Sub-order .. / Group ..	Class B.—Preparation and supply — Sub-class V.— — Order 26.—Trade in skins, — Total order 26.					
	District, City or State.	Total earners (principal occupations) Males	Total earners (principal occupations) Females	Total working dependants. Males	Total working dependants. Females	Total following occupation as subsidiary to other. Males	Total following occupation as subsidiary to other. Females
1	2	876	877	878	879	880	881
	Central Provinces and Berar ..	**2,273**	**368**	**31**	**166**	**423**	**27**
	C. P. British Districts and Berar ..	**2,179**	**342**	**26**	**137**	**383**	**27**
	C. P. British Districts	**1,590**	**324**	**24**	**129**	**352**	**26**
	Jubbulpore Division	*382*	*60*	*1*	*1*	*110*	..
1	Saugor	73	1	.	.	55	..
2	Damoh	1	..	.	..	..	..
3	Jubbulpore	265	53	1	1	48	..
	Jubbulpore City	*80*	*45*	.	.	*3*	..
4	Mandla	29	5	..		2	..
5	Seoni . ..	14	1			5	..
	Nerbudda Division	*556*	*67*	*12*	*38*	*74*	*23*
6	Narsinghpur	17	..	.		9	..
7	Hoshangabad ..	227	17	2	15	33	21
8	Nimar . ..	170	10	8	4	22	..
9	Betul .	11	21			2	1
10	Chhindwara . .	131	19	2	19	8	1
	Nagpur Division	*330*	*83*	*5*	*53*	*108*	*1*
11	Wardha . ..	18	2	.	1	2	..
12	Nagpur . .	88	7	..	1	25	..
	Nagpur City	*2*	*2*	.	.	..	
13	Chanda ..	70	4	3	..	40	..
14	Bhandara . ..	55	56	.	.	5	..
15	Balaghat .. .	99	14	2	51	36	1
	Chhattisgarh Division	*322*	*114*	*6*	*37*	*60*	*2*
16	Raipur .. .	210	83	2	35	28	..
17	Bilaspur .. .	84	7	..	2	22	2
18	Drug	28	24	4	..	10	..
	Berar	**589**	**18**	**2**	**8**	**31**	**1**
19	Amraoti	212	4	1	8	4	1
20	Akola	103	1	1	..	9	..
21	Buldana	66	5	..	..	7	..
22	Yeotmal	208	8	..	..	11	..
	Central Provinces States	**94**	**26**	**5**	**29**	**40**	..
23	Makrai	..	10	..	17	3	..
24	Bastar	15	1	..	8	3	..
25	Kanker	1	..	..	..	1	..
26	Nandgaon	35	8	1	..	7	..
27	Khairagarh	.	..	..	..	..	..
28	Chhuikhadan	8	1	..	2	2	..
29	Kawardha	7	..	..	..	6	..
30	Sakti	.	..	..	..	..	..
31	Raigarh	14	1	..	..	1	..
32	Sarangarh	4	1	4	..	11	..
33	Changbhakar	..	..	..	..	..	..
34	Korea	3	2	..	..	1	..
35	Surguja	7	2	..	2	5	..
36	Udaipur	.	..	..	..	..	..
37	Jashpur	..	..	..	..	..	..

of material substances—*contd.*

Trade—*contd.*

leather and furs.

118.—Trade in skins, leather, furs, feathers, horn, etc., and articles made from those.

Order 27.—Trade in wood.

Total order 27.

Total earners (principal occupations). Males	Total earners (principal occupations). Females	Total working dependants. Males	Total working dependants. Females	Total following occupation as subsidiary to other. Males	Total following occupation as subsidiary to other. Females	Total earners (principal occupations). Males	Total earners (principal occupations). Females	Total working dependants. Males	Total working dependants. Females	Total following occupation as subsidiary to other. Males	Total following occupation as subsidiary to other. Females	Serial No.
882	883	884	885	886	887	888	889	890	891	892	893	
2,273	**368**	**31**	**166**	**423**	**27**	**8,630**	**9,166**	**390**	**1,397**	**5,704**	**3,611**	
2,179	**342**	**26**	**137**	**383**	**27**	**8,312**	**8,760**	**372**	**1,325**	**5,565**	**3,012**	
1,590	**324**	**24**	**129**	**352**	**26**	**7,634**	**8,717**	**283**	**1,206**	**4,542**	**2,937**	
382	*60*	*1*	*1*	*110*	..	*3,789*	*4,706*	*141*	*731*	*1,800*	*1,291*	
73	1		.	55	.	1,043	1,390	38	266	296	263	1
1	..	..	..	..	.	342	622	3	45	403	297	2
265	53	1	1	48	..	1,140	1,700	72	376	790	515	3
80	*45*	..	..	*3*	..	*109*	*32*	*1*	*2*	*10*	..	
29	3	..	.	2	..	851	936	26	27	133	204	4
14	1	...	..	5	..	413	58	2	17	178	12	5
556	*67*	*12*	*38*	*74*	*23*	*2,164*	*2,809*	*118*	*275*	*1,858*	*1,100*	
17	..	..	..	9	..	632	822	6	126	407	527	6
227	17	2	15	33	21	226	1,150	52	43	198	183	7
170	10	8	4	22	..	901	452	37	50	822	44	8
11	21	..	..	2	1	120	243	11	23	214	178	9
131	19	2	19	8	1	285	142	12	33	217	168	10
330	*83*	*5*	*53*	*108*		*457*	*150*	.	*6*	*575*	*9*	
18	2	..	1	2		40	8	..	1	44	1	11
88	7	..	1	25	.	81	46	.	..	88	2	12
2	*2*	..	..	..	..	*11*	*5*	..	..	*3*	*1*	
70	4	3	.	40	.	119	9	..	..	176	..	13
55	56	..	.	5	.	64	16	..	5	132	1	14
99	14	2	51	36	1	153	71	.	.	135	5	15
322	*114*	*6*	*37*	*60*	*2*	*1,224*	*1,052*	*24*	*194*	*309*	*537*	
210	83	2	35	28	..	[illegible]	669	11	53	171	427	16
84	7	..	2	22	2	370	332	8	120	107	97	17
28	24	4	..	10	.	59	51	5	21	31	13	18
589	**18**	**2**	**8**	**31**	**1**	**678**	**43**	**89**	**119**	**1,023**	**75**	
212	4	1	8	4	1	531	17	76	51	928	65	19
103	1	1	.	9	.	94	22	11	32	51	10	20
66	5	..	..	7	.	33	4	..	36	43	..	21
208	8	..		11		20	.	2	..	1	..	22
94	**26**	**5**	**29**	**40**	.	**318**	**406**	**18**	**72**	**139**	**599**	
..	10	..	17	3		58	21	..	..	8	6	23
15	1	..	8	3		30	9	4	33	.	.	24
1	..	..	..	1		16	.	8	.	49	477	25
35	8	1	..	7	.	2	..	.	..		.	26
..	..	..	..	.	..		.	.	..	..	.	27
8	1	..	2	2	.		27	..	.		1	28
7	..	..	..	6	.	11	23	.	.	46	91	29
..	.	..	.	.	..		.	..	.		..	30
14	1	.	..	1		103	107	2	12	26	24	31
4	1	4	..	11	.	37	26	.	2			32
..	.	..	..				.		.			33
3	2	..	..	1	.	4	2	.	.	1		34
7	2	.	2	5	..	50	48	4	18	1	.	35
..	..	..	..	.		4	9					36
..	.	..	..	.	.	3	134	.	7	8		37

TABLE X | **Occupation or means of**

Serial No.	District, City or State.	Class B.—Preparation and supply / Sub-class V.— / Order 27.—Trade / 119.—Trade in wood (not firewood). Total earners (principal occupations). Males.	Females.	Total working dependants. Males.	Females.	Total following occupation as subsidiary to other. Males.	Females.
1	2	894	895	896	897	898	899
	Central Provinces and Berar	**4,618**	**6,618**	**231**	**736**	**3,693**	**2,474**
	C. P. British Districts and Berar	**4,638**	**6,447**	**231**	**722**	**3,620**	**2,353**
	C. P. British Districts	**4,390**	**6,430**	**203**	**671**	**3,518**	**2,342**
	Jubbulpore Division	*2,208*	*3,728*	*96*	*536*	*1,546*	*1,211*
1	Saugor	698	1,242	28	173	251	247
2	Damoh	342	496	3	36	397	254
3	Jubbulpore	845	1,456	63	318	690	505
	Jubbulpore City	*95*	*31*	*1*	*2*	*9*	..
4	Mandla	123	510	..	6	84	196
5	Seoni	200	24	2	3	124	9
	Nerbudda Division	*1,491*	*2,429*	*101*	*82*	*1,576*	*1,083*
6	Narsinghpur	321	578	6	48	353	516
7	Hoshangabad	174	1,138	48	16	190	181
8	Nimar	867	406	36	11	812	41
9	Betul	55	216	11	5	177	178
10	Chhindwara	74	91	..	2	44	167
	Nagpur Division	*260*	*48*	..	*6*	*303*	*7*
11	Wardha	33	8	..	1	43	1
12	Nagpur	40	2	..	..	39	1
	Nagpur City	*7*	*1*	..	..	*1*	*1*
13	Chanda	95	..	..	..	62	..
14	Bhandara	38	..	..	5	39	..
15	Balaghat	54	38	..	..	120	5
	Chhattisgarh Division	*431*	*225*	*6*	*47*	*93*	*41*
16	Raipur	143	44	5	..	17	..
17	Bilaspur	267	176	1	47	75	41
18	Drug	21	5	..	..	1	..
	Berar	**248**	**17**	**28**	**51**	**102**	**11**
19	Amraoti	117	1	15	..	49	2
20	Akola	81	14	11	15	39	9
21	Buldana	31	2	..	36	13	..
22	Yeotmal	19	..	2	..	1	..
	Central Provinces States	**180**	**171**	..	**14**	**73**	**121**
23	Makrai	55	21	..	..	7	6
24	Bastar	13	..	..	..	..	..
25	Kanker	..	..	..	..	..	..
26	Nandgaon	1	..	..	..	..	..
27	Khairagarh	..	..	..	..	..	..
28	Chhuikhadan	..	14	..	..	..	..
29	Kawardha	..	..	..	..	43	91
30	Sakti	..	..	..	..	..	..
31	Raigarh	96	95	..	4	21	24
32	Sarangarh	..	..	..	..	..	..
33	Changbhakar	..	..	..	..	..	..
34	Korea	4	2	..	..	1	..
35	[illegible]	11	39	..	10	1	..
36		..	..	..	..	..	..
37		..	..	..	..	..	..

of material substances—*contd.*

Trade—*contd.*

in wood—*contd.*

120.—Trade in barks.						121.—Trade in bamboos and canes.						Serial No.
Total earners (principal occupations).		Total working dependants		Total following occupation as subsidiary to other		Total earners (principal occupations).		Total working dependants.		Total following occupation as subsidiary to other.		
Males.	Females.	Males.	Females.	Males.	Females.	Males	Females.	Males.	Females.	Males.	Females	
900	901	902	903	904	905	906	907	908	909	910	911	
19	**6**	..	**76**	**8**	**4**	**3,306**	**1,675**	**146**	**394**	**1,776**	**206**	
12	**6**	..	**76**	**8**	**4**	**3,210**	**1,600**	**132**	**350**	**1,771**	**206**	
12	**6**	..	**76**	**8**	**4**	**2,781**	**1,574**	**71**	**282**	**851**	**142**	
1	*6*	..	*76*	*2*	*4*	*1,389*	*936*	*45*	*116*	*202*	*69*	
1	6	..	76	..	4	323	137	10	17	30	12	1
..	..	..	..	..	..	..	126	..	9	6	43	2
..	..	..	..	2	..	268	231	9	56	85	9	3
..	..	..	..	..	..	..	..	..	..	*1*	..	
..	..	..	..	..	..	700	411	26	21	43	5	4
..	..	..	..	..	..	98	31	..	13	38	..	5
11	..	..	..	*6*	..	*532*	*265*	*9*	*71*	*217*	*9*	
..	..	..	..	..	..	304	183	..	40	29	8	6
11	..	..	..	6	..	20	1	..	..	..	..	7
..	..	..	..	..	..	4	7	..	..	1	..	8
..	..	..	..	..	..	28	23	..	..	17	..	9
..	..	..	..	..	..	176	51	9	31	170	1	10
..	..	..	..	..	..	*131*	*56*	..	..	*252*	*2*	
..	..	..	..	..	..	7	..	..	..	1	..	11
..	..	..	..	..	..	35	35	..	..	46	1	12
..	..	..	..	..	..	*1*	..	..	..	..	..	
..	..	..	..	..	..	18	8	..	..	114	..	13
..	..	..	..	..	..	5	1	..	..	90	1	14
..	..	..	..	..	..	66	12	..	..	1	..	15
..	..	..	..	..	..	*729*	*317*	*17*	*95*	*180*	*62*	
..	..	..	..	..	..	609	133	6	5	132	1	16
..	..	..	..	..	..	97	152	6	72	23	49	17
..	..	..	..	..	..	23	32	5	18	25	12	18
..	..	..	..	..	..	**429**	**26**	**61**	**68**	**920**	**64**	
..	..	..	..	..	..	414	16	61	51	879	63	19
..	..	..	..	..	..	12	8	..	17	12	1	20
..	..	..	..	..	..	2	2	..	..	29	..	21
..	..	..	..	..	..	1	..	..	..	..	..	22
7	..	..	..	..	..	**96**	**75**	**14**	**44**	**5**	..	
..	..	..	..	..	..	..	..	..	..	..	..	23
..	..	..	..	..	..	16	9	4	31	..	..	24
..	..	..	..	..	..	..	..	6	..	..	..	25
..	..	..	..	..	..	..	..	..	..	..	..	26
..	..	..	..	..	..	..	..	..	..	..	..	27
..	..	..	..	..	..	..	..	..	..	..	..	28
..	..	..	..	..	..	11	2	..	..	..	..	29
..	..	..	..	..	..	..	..	..	..	..	..	30
..	..	..	..	..	..	3	1	..	..	..	..	31
..	..	..	..	..	..	37	26	..	..	..	..	32
..	..	..	..	..	..	..	..	..	..	..	..	33
..	..	..	..	..	..	..	..	..	..	..	..	34
7	..	..	..	..	..	29	9	4	8	..	..	35
..	..	..	..	..	..	..	..	..	..	..	..	36
..	..	..	..	..	..	..	28	..	5	5	..	37

TABLE X — Occupation or means of

Serial No.	Class ..	Class B.—Preparation and supply					
	Sub-class ..	Sub-class V.—					
	Order ..	Order 27.—Trade in wood—*concld.*					
	Sub-order ..						
	Group ..	122.—Trade in thatches and other forest produce.					
	District, City or State.	Total earners (principal occupations).		Total working dependants		Total following occupation as subsidiary to other.	
		Males.	Females.	Males.	Females.	Males.	Females.
1	2	912	913	914	915	916	917
	Central Provinces and Berar ..	**487**	**867**	**13**	**191**	**227**	**927**
	C. P. British Districts and Berar ..	**452**	**707**	**9**	**177**	**166**	**449**
	C. P. British Districts	**451**	**707**	**9**	**177**	**165**	**449**
	Jubbulpore Division	*191*	*36*	..	*3*	*50*	*7*
1	Saugor	21	5	..	..	15	..
2	Damoh	..	..	..	..	..	..
3	Jubbulpore	27	13	..	2	13	1
	Jubbulpore City	*14*	*1*	..	..	..	..
4	Mandla	28	15	..	..	6	3
5	Seoni	115	3	..	1	16	3
	Nerbudda Division	*130*	*115*	*8*	*122*	*59*	*8*
6	Narsinghpur	7	61	..	38	25	3
7	Hoshangabad	21	11	4	27	2	2
8	Nimar	30	39	1	39	9	3
9	Betul	37	4	..	18	20	..
10	Chhindwara	35	..	3	..	3	..
	Nagpur Division	*66*	*46*	..	..	*20*	..
11	Wardha	..	..	..	..	..	..
12	Nagpur	6	9	..	..	3	..
	Nagpur City	*3*	*4*	..	..	*2*	..
13	Chanda	6	1	..	..	..	..
14	Bhandara	21	15	..	..	3	..
15	Balaghat	33	21	..	..	14	..
	Chhattisgarh Division	*64*	*510*	*1*	*52*	*36*	*434*
16	Raipur	43	492	..	48	22	426
17	Bilaspur	6	4	1	1	9	7
18	Drug	15	14	..	3	5	1
	Berar	**1**	..	..	..	**1**	..
19	Amraoti	..	..	..	..	..	..
20	Akola	1	..	..	..	..	..
21	Buldana	..	..	..	..	1	..
22	Yeotmal	..	..	..	..	..	..
	Central Provinces States	**35**	**160**	**4**	**14**	**61**	**478**
23	Makrai	3	..	..	..	1	..
24	Bastar	1	..	..	2	..	..
25	Kanker	16	..	2	..	49	477
26	Nandgaon	1	..	..	..	..	..
27	Khairagarh	..	..	..	..	..	..
28	Chhuikhadan	..	13	..	..	..	1
29	Kawardha	..	21	..	..	3	..
30	Sakti	..	..	..	..	..	..
31	Raigarh	4	11	2	8	5	..
32	Sarangarh	..	..	..	2	..	..
33	Changbhakar	..	..	..	..	..	..
34	Korea	..	..	..	..	..	..
35	Surguja	3	..	..	..	..	..
36	Udaipur	4	9	..	..	..	..
37	Jashpur	3	106	..	2	3	..

of material substances—*contd.*

Trade—*contd.*

Order 28.—Trade in metals.

Total order 28.						123.—Trade in metals, machinery, knives, tools, etc.						Serial No.
Total earners (principal occupations).		Total working dependants.		Total following occupation as subsidiary to other.		Total earners (principal occupations).		Total working dependants.		Total following occupation as subsidiary to other.		
Males.	Females.	Males.	Females.	Males.	Females.	Males.	Females.	Males.	Females.	Males.	Females.	
918	919	920	921	922	923	924	925	926	927	928	929	
1,243	**63**	**19**	**254**	**176**	**9**	**1,243**	**63**	**19**	**254**	**176**	**9**	
1,110	**56**	**19**	**6**	**175**	**9**	**1,110**	**56**	**19**	**6**	**175**	**9**	
978	**53**	**14**	**2**	**166**	**9**	**978**	**53**	**14**	**2**	**166**	**9**	
475	*13*	*2*	..	*34*	..	*475*	*13*	*2*	..	*34*	..	
272	..	2	..	14	..	272	..	2	..	14	..	1
1	..	..	..	..	..	1	..	..	..	..	..	2
86	11	..	..	10	..	86	11	..	..	10	..	3
40	*8*	..	..	*1*	..	*40*	*8*	..	..	*1*	..	
113	2	..	..	9	..	113	2	..	..	9	..	4
3	..	..	..	1	..	3	..	..	..	1	..	5
196	*5*	*5*	..	*40*	..	*196*	*5*	*5*	..	*40*	..	
..	..	..	..	..	..	..	..	..	..	..	..	6
9	2	..	..	4	..	9	2	..	..	4	..	7
57	1	..	..	..	..	57	1	..	..	..	..	8
28	..	..	..	1	..	28	..	..	..	1	..	9
102	2	5	..	35	..	102	2	5	..	35	..	10
104	*22*	..	..	*24*	*5*	*104*	*22*	..	..	*24*	*5*	
16	..	..	..	2	..	16	..	..	..	2	..	11
31	4	..	..	2	..	31	4	..	..	2	..	12
28	*4*	..	..	*1*	..	*28*	*4*	..	..	*1*	..	
20	18	..	..	11	5	20	18	..	..	11	5	13
11	..	..	..	1	..	11	..	..	..	1	..	14
26	..	..	..	8	..	26	..	..	..	8	..	15
203	*13*	*7*	*2*	*68*	*4*	*203*	*13*	*7*	*2*	*68*	*4*	
54	2	..	2	1	4	54	2	..	2	1	4	16
131	11	..	..	61	..	131	11	..	..	61	..	17
18	..	7	..	6	..	18	..	7	..	6	..	18
132	**3**	**5**	**4**	**9**	..	**132**	**3**	**5**	**4**	**9**	..	
36	..	3	..	4	..	36	..	3	..	4	..	19
33	1	2	..	4	..	33	1	2	..	4	..	20
5	..	..	2	..	..	5	..	..	2	..	..	21
58	2	..	2	1	..	58	2	..	2	1	..	22
133	**7**	..	**243**	**1**	..	**133**	**7**	..	**248**	**1**	..	
..	..	..	..	..	..	..	..	..	..	..	..	23
1	..	..	..	..	..	1	..	..	..	..	..	24
..	..	..	5	..	..	..	..	..	5	..	..	25
8	..	..	..	..	..	8	..	..	..	..	..	26
..	..	..	..	..	..	..	..	..	..	..	..	27
..	..	..	..	..	..	..	..	..	..	..	..	28
..	..	..	..	1	..	..	..	..	..	1	..	29
..	..	..	..	..	..	..	..	..	..	..	..	30
124	..	..	..	..	..	124	..	..	..	..	..	31
..	1	..	1	..	..	..	1	..	1	..	..	32
..	..	..	..	..	..	..	..	..	..	..	..	33
..	..	..	..	..	..	..	..	..	..	..	..	34
..	..	..	..	..	..	..	..	..	..	..	..	35
..	..	..	..	..	..	..	..	..	..	..	..	36
..	6	..	242	..	..	..	6	..	242	..	..	37

TABLE X — Occupation or means of

Serial No.	Class / Sub-class / Order / Sub-order / Group — District, City or State	Class B.—Preparation and supply — Sub-class V.— — Order 29.—Trade in — Total order 29. — Total earners (principal occupations). Males.	Females.	Total working dependants. Males.	Females.	Total following occupation as subsidiary to other. Males.	Females.
1	2	930	931	932	933	934	935
	Central Provinces and Berar ..	**2,048**	**1,148**	**77**	**511**	**273**	**84**
	C. P. British Districts and Berar ..	**2,022**	**1,144**	**77**	**498**	**272**	**84**
	C. P. British Districts	**1,734**	**1,024**	**60**	**236**	**245**	**74**
	Jubbulpore Division	*704*	*559*	*29*	*128*	*145*	*22*
1	Saugor	372	275	15	78	26	1
2	Damoh	138	189	11	12	1	9
3	Jubbulpore	6	..	..	..	..	..
	Jubbulpore City	*6*	..	..	..	..	..
4	Mandla	10	3	..	..	3	..
5	Seoni	178	92	3	38	115	12
	Nerbudda Division	*738*	*210*	*30*	*83*	*56*	*5*
6	Narsinghpur	302	30	22	22	31	..
7	Hoshangabad	72	68	..	6	4	5
8	Nimar	52	7	4	..	10	..
9	Betul	215	70	..	24	11	..
10	Chhindwara	97	35	4	31	..	..
	Nagpur Division	*281*	*181*	*1*	*7*	*22*	*1*
11	Wardha	1	11	..	..	1	1
12	Nagpur	107	75	..	3	13	..
	Nagpur City	*1*	*9*	..	*2*	..	..
13	Chanda	123	55	1	4	4	..
14	Bhandara	50	40	..	..	4	..
15	Balaghat	..	..	..	..	..	..
	Chhattisgarh Division	*11*	*74*	..	*18*	*22*	*46*
16	Raipur	..	..	..	..	..	..
17	Bilaspur	6	74	..	18	22	46
18	Drug	5	..	..	..	..	..
	Berar	**288**	**120**	**17**	**262**	**27**	**10**
19	Amraoti	28	9	..	6	13	4
20	Akola	176	64	15	37	13	6
21	Buldana	8	2	..	2	..	..
22	Yeotmal	76	45	2	217	1	..
	Central Provinces States	**26**	**4**	..	**13**	**1**	..
23	Makrai	25	4	..	13	..	..
24	Bastar	1	..	..	..	..	..
25	Kanker	..	..	..	..	..	..
26	Nandgaon	..	..	..	..	..	..
27	Khairagarh	..	..	..	..	1	..
28	Chhuikhadan	..	..	..	..	..	..
29	Kawardha	..	..	..	..	..	..
30	Sakti	..	..	..	..	..	..
31	Raigarh	..	..	..	..	..	..
32	Sarangarh	..	..	..	..	..	..
33	Changbhakar	..	..	..	..	..	..
34	Korea	..	..	..	..	..	..
35	Surguja	..	..	..	..	..	..
36	Udaipur	..	..	..	..	..	..
37	Jashpur	..	..	..	..	..	..

of material substances—*contd.*

Trade—*contd*

pottery, bricks and tiles — 124.—Trade in pottery, bricks and tiles

Order 30.—Trade in chemical products. — **Total order 30.**

Total earners (principal occupations)		Total working dependants		Total following occupation as subsidiary to other		Total earners (principal occupations).		Total working dependants.		Total following occupation as subsidiary to other.		Serial No.
Males	Females	Males	Females.	Males.	Females	Males.	Females.	Males.	Females.	Males.	Females.	
936	937	938	939	940	941	942	943	944	945	946	947	
2,048	**1,148**	**77**	**511**	**273**	**84**	**10,680**	**8,471**	**366**	**2,249**	**3,779**	**1,596**	
2,022	**1,144**	**77**	**498**	**272**	**84**	**10,356**	**8,338**	**358**	**2,169**	**3,668**	**1,588**	
1,734	**1,024**	**60**	**236**	**245**	**74**	**7,920**	**7,285**	**263**	**1,785**	**3,192**	**1,469**	
704	*559*	*29*	*128*	*145*	*22*	*2,103*	*1,939*	*64*	*433*	*905*	*209*	
372	275	15	78	26	1	399	810	12	126	134	81	1
138	189	11	12	1	9	114	151	14	1	94	51	2
6				.	..	757	514	28	177	393	56	3
6		.		.	..	*182*	*55*	*3*	*6*	*7*	*1*	
10	3	..		3		162	76	4	22	58	8	4
178	92	3	38	115	12	671	388	6	107	226	13	5
738	*210*	*30*	*83*	*56*	*5*	*2,327*	*1,356*	*125*	*743*	*543*	*62*	
302	30	22	22	31	.	364	239	22	146	69	10	6
72	68	.	6	4	5	494	205	22	51	125	18	7
52	7	4	.	10	..	538	151	45	67	94	4	8
215	70	.	24	11	..	390	358	5	97	60	5	9
97	35	4	31	..	..	541	403	31	382	195	25	10
281	*181*	*1*	*7*	*22*	*1*	*2,844*	*3,199*	*62*	*594*	*883*	*475*	
1	11	..	.	1	1	432	212	3	29	43	28	11
107	75	..	3	13	..	673	1,145	26	90	109	119	12
1	*9*	..	*2*	.	..	*196*	*225*	*22*	*15*	*15*	*2*	
123	35	1	4	4	..	397	529	7	114	131	106	13
50	40	..	..	4	.	972	944	17	88	327	184	14
.	.	.	.	..	..	370	369	9	273	273	38	15
11	*74*	.	*18*	*22*	*46*	*646*	*791*	*12*	*15*	*861*	*723*	
.	.	.		.		377	647	3	8	643	694	16
6	74	..	15	22	46	137	49	7	2	204	23	17
5	.				..	132	95	2	5	14	6	18
288	**120**	**17**	**262**	**27**	**10**	**2,436**	**1,053**	**95**	**384**	**476**	**119**	
28	9	.	6	13	4	837	528	31	107	200	40	19
176	64	15	37	13	6	584	170	7	15	113	22	20
8	2	.	.		.	408	151	17	82	103	26	21
76	25	2	217	1		607	204	40	180	60	31	22
26	**4**		**13**	**1**	..	**324**	**133**	**8**	**80**	**111**	**8**	
25	4		13	.	.	2	3	.	10	..	..	23
1	..		.	.	.	15	20	..	1	.	..	24
.	..				.	115	26	7	3	88	3	25
.	..	.		1	..	61	38	..	..	1	..	26
..	.			.	..	52	4		..	1	..	27
..	..	..	.		..	..	4	.	..	.	..	28
..	..	.		..		7	7	..	..	1	5	29
..	.	.	.	..	.	..	..		..	..		30
..	..	..		..		24	14	1	2	5	..	31
..	..	.	.	.	.	2	..	..	.	1	..	32
..	.	.		..	..	..		..	.	..	..	33
..	..	..	.	.	..	6	7	.	..	3	..	34
..	..	..		..	.	24	7	.	64	7	..	35
.	.	..	.	..	.	16	.	..	..	..	..	36
..	..	..	..	..	.	..	3		..	4	..	37

Serial No.	Class .. / Sub-class .. / Order .. / Sub-order .. / Group ..	Class B.—Preparation and supply / Sub-class V.— / Order 30.—Trade in chemical products—concld. / 125.—Drugs, dyes, paints, petroleum, explosive, etc.					
	District, City or State.	Total earners (principal occupations).		Total working dependants.		Total following occupation as subsidiary to other.	
		Males.	Females.	Males.	Females.	Males.	Females.
1	2	948	949	950	951	952	953
	Central Provinces and Berar	**10,680**	**8,471**	**366**	**2,249**	**3,779**	**1,596**
	C. P. British Districts and Berar ..	**10,356**	**8,338**	**358**	**2,169**	**3,668**	**1,588**
	C. P. British Districts	**7,920**	**7,285**	**263**	**1,785**	**3,192**	**1,469**
	Jubbulpore Division	*2,103*	*1,939*	*64*	*433*	*905*	*209*
1	Saugor	399	810	12	126	134	81
2	Damoh	114	151	14	1	94	51
3	Jubbulpore	757	514	28	177	393	56
	Jubbulpore City	*182*	*55*	*3*	*6*	*7*	*1*
4	Mandla	162	76	4	22	58	8
5	Seoni	671	388	6	107	226	13
	Nerbudda Division	*2,327*	*1,356*	*125*	*743*	*543*	*62*
6	Narsinghpur	364	239	22	146	69	10
7	Hoshangabad	494	205	22	51	125	18
8	Nimar	538	151	45	67	94	4
9	Betul	390	358	5	97	60	5
10	Chhindwara	541	403	31	382	195	25
	Nagpur Division	*2,844*	*3,199*	*62*	*594*	*883*	*475*
11	Wardha	432	212	3	29	43	28
12	Nagpur	673	1,145	26	90	109	119
	Nagpur City	*196*	*225*	*22*	*15*	*15*	*2*
13	Chanda	397	529	7	114	131	106
14	Bhandara	972	944	17	88	327	184
15	Balaghat	370	369	9	273	273	38
	Chhattisgarh Division	*646*	*791*	*12*	*15*	*861*	*723*
16	Raipur	377	647	3	8	643	694
17	Bilaspur	137	49	7	2	204	23
18	Drug	132	95	2	5	14	6
	Berar	**2,436**	**1,053**	**95**	**384**	**476**	**119**
19	Amraoti	837	528	31	107	200	40
20	Akola	584	170	7	15	113	22
21	Buldana	408	151	17	82	103	26
22	Yeotmal	607	204	40	180	60	31
	Central Provinces States	**324**	**133**	**8**	**80**	**111**	**8**
23	Makrai	2	3	..	10	..	..
24	Bastar	15	20	..	1	..	..
25	Kanker	115	26	7	3	88	3
26	Nandgaon	61	38	..	..	1	..
27	Khairagarh	52	4	..	..	1	..
28	Chhuikhadan	..	4	..	..	..	..
29	Kawardha	7	7	..	..	1	5
30	Sakti	..	..	..	..	..	..
31	Raigarh	24	14	1	2	5	..
32	Sarangarh	2	..	..	..	1	..
33	Changbhakar	..	..	..	..	..	..
34	Korea	6	7	..	..	3	..
35	Surguja	24	7	..	64	7	..
36	Udaipur	16	..	..	..	..	..
37	Jashpur	..	3	..	..	4	..

of material substances—*contd.*

Trade—*contd.*

Order 31.—**Hotels, cafes, restaurants, etc.**

Total order 31.						126.—Vendors of wine, liquors, ærated water and ice.						Serial No.
Total earners (principal occupations).		Total working dependants.		Total following occupation as subsidiary to other.		Total earners (principal occupations).		Total working dependants.		Total following occupation as subsidiary to other.		
Males.	Females.	Males.	Females.	Males.	Females.	Males.	Females.	Males.	Females.	Males.	Females.	
954	955	956	957	958	959	960	961	962	963	964	965	
5,498	**531**	**135**	**455**	**752**	**79**	**2,333**	**232**	**93**	**393**	**501**	**20**	
4,869	**393**	**82**	**77**	**551**	**70**	**1,751**	**102**	**43**	**15**	**302**	**12**	
3,483	**295**	**45**	**63**	**451**	**42**	**1,381**	**91**	**31**	**14**	**237**	**11**	
728	*43*	*5*	*8*	*80*	*4*	*234*	*6*	..	*1*	*26*	*4*	
89	28	..	7	11	1	18	..	..	..	..	1	1
25	..	..	..	12	..	5	..	..	..	..	..	2
477	10	1	..	19	..	141	2	..	..	5	..	3
302	*6*	*1*	..	*14*	..	*45*	..	..	..	..	..	
87	3	..	1	26	1	42	2	..	1	10	1	4
50	2	4	..	12	2	28	2	..	..	11	2	5
611	*135*	*3*	*31*	*116*	*33*	*259*	*12*	*2*	*3*	*46*	*2*	
13	2	..	..	..	..	11	1	..	..	..	.	6
191	117	..	27	44	31	45	4	..	..	5	..	7
231	8	1	2	31	..	82	3	..	2	10	..	8
85	2	..	2	25	1	58	2	..	1	19	1	9
91	6	2	..	16	1	63	2	2	..	12	1	10
1,886	*81*	*27*	*20*	*201*	*2*	*719*	*42*	*21*	*6*	*117*	*2*	
225	11	..	..	39	..	139	6	..	..	35	..	11
546	36	13	8	20	..	170	10	11	1	19	.	12
277	*18*	*11*	*1*	*3*	..	*82*	*7*	*11*	..	*3*	..	
281	15	6	1	41	..	254	12	6	1	41	..	13
761	11	6	2	88	..	110	7	2	2	9	..	14
73	8	2	9	13	2	46	7	2	2	13	2	15
258	*36*	*10*	*4*	*54*	*3*	*169*	*31*	*8*	*4*	*48*	*3*	
102	22	1	1	19	2	76	19	1	1	15	2	16
102	8	6	1	21	1	55	7	6	1	19	1	17
54	6	3	2	14	..	38	5	1	2	14	..	18
1,386	**98**	**37**	**14**	**100**	**28**	**370**	**11**	**12**	**1**	**65**	**1**	
471	59	12	5	31	13	90	4	4	..	19	1	19
464	11	3	..	35	..	92	1	2	..	19	..	20
144	11	12	..	11	1	46	4	..	..	8	..	21
307	17	10	9	23	14	142	2	6	1	19	..	22
629	**138**	**53**	**378**	**201**	**9**	**582**	**130**	**50**	**378**	**199**	**8**	
3	..	..	..	..	..	3	..	..	..	..	..	23
224	36	33	107	107	3	221	36	33	107	107	3	24
76	52	3	258	7	4	76	52	3	258	7	4	25
46	8	1	1	6	1	18	6	..	1	6	1	26
7	2	..	4	..	..	7	2	..	4	..	..	27
..	..	..	..	..	..	..	..	..	..	..	..	28
12	6	..	1	4	..	10	6	..	1	4	..	29
2	2	..	..	5	..	1	2	..	..	5	..	30
53	14	16	5	24	..	49	14	14	5	24	..	31
17	3	..	..	14	..	17	3	..	..	14	..	32
..	..	..	..	..	1	..	..	..	..	..	..	33
19	..	..	..	..	..	19	..	..	..	..	..	34
89	9	..	2	15	..	81	3	..	2	13	..	35
8	..	..	..	4	..	8	..	..	..	4	..	36
73	6	..	..	15	..	72	6	..	..	15	..	37

TABLE X

Occupation or means of

Serial No.	Class ..	Class B.—Preparation and supply					
	Sub-class ..	Sub-class V.—					
	Order ..	Order 31.—Hotels,					
	Sub-order ..						
	Group ..	127.—Owners and managers of hotels, cook shops, sarais, etc. (and employees).					
	District, City or State.	Total earners (principal occupations).		Total working dependants		Total following occupation as subsidiary to other.	
		Males.	Females.	Males	Females.	Males.	Females.
1	2	966	967	968	969	970	971
	Central Provinces and Berar ..	**2,926**	**229**	**41**	**51**	**226**	**48**
	C. P. British Districts and Berar ..	**2,879**	**221**	**38**	**51**	**224**	**47**
	C. P. British Districts	**1,894**	**180**	**14**	**43**	**189**	**31**
	Jubbulpore Division	*347*	*13*	*5*	*1*	*50*	..
1	Saugor	40	5	..	1	11	..
2	Damoh	20	..	..	..	12	..
3	Jubbulpore	225	7	1	..	10	..
	Jubbulpore City	*196*	*5*	*1*	..	*10*	..
4	Mandla	40	1	..	..	16	..
5	Seoni	22	..	4	..	1	..
	Nerbudda Division	*309*	*123*	*1*	*28*	*49*	*31*
6	Narsinghpur	..	1	..	..	..	..
7	Hoshangabad	133	113	..	27	34	31
8	Nimar	122	5	1	..	5	..
9	Betul	27	..	..	1	6	..
10	Chhindwara	27	4	..	..	4	..
	Nagpur Division	*1,153*	*39*	*6*	*14*	*84*	..
11	Wardha	86	5	..	..	4	..
12	Nagpur	376	26	2	7	1	..
	Nagpur City	*195*	*11*	..	*1*	..	..
13	Chanda	27	3	..	..	..	..
14	Bhandara	651	4	4	..	79	..
15	Balaghat	13	1	..	7	..	..
	Chhattisgarh Division	*85*	*5*	*2*	..	*6*	..
16	Raipur	26	3	..	..	4	..
17	Bilaspur	43	1	..	..	2	..
18	Drug	16	1	2	..	..	..
	Berar	**985**	**41**	**24**	**8**	**35**	**16**
19	Amraoti	375	9	8	..	12	1
20	Akola	372	10	1	..	16	..
21	Buldana	98	7	12	..	3	1
22	Yeotmal	140	15	3	8	4	14
	Central Provinces States	**47**	**8**	**3**	..	**2**	**1**
23	Makrai	..	..	..	..	..	..
24	Bastar	3	..	..	..	..	..
25	Kanker	..	..	..	..	..	..
26	Nandgaon	28	2	1	..	..	..
27	Khairagarh	..	..	..	..	..	..
28	Chhuikhadan	..	..	..	..	..	..
29	Kawardha	2	..	..	..	..	..
30	Sakti	1	..	..	..	..	..
31	Raigarh	4	..	2	..	..	..
32	Sarangarh	..	..	..	..	..	..
33	Changbhakar	..	..	..	..	..	1
34	Korea	..	..	..	..	..	..
35	Surguja	8	6	..	..	2	..
36	Udaipur	..	..	..	..	..	..
37	Jashpur	1	..	..	..	..	..

of material substances—*contd*

Trade—*contd.*

cafes, restaurants, etc—*concld.*

128.—Hawkers of drink and food stuffs.						Order 32.—Other trade in food stuffs. Total order 32.						Serial No.
Total earners (principal occupations).		Total working dependants.		Total following occupation as subsidiary to other.		Total earners (principal occupations)		Total working dependants		Total following occupation as subsidiary to other.		
Males.	Females	Males.	Females.	Males	Females	Males	Females	Males	Females	Males	Females.	
972	973	974	975	976	977	978	979	980	981	982	983	
239	**70**	**1**	**11**	**25**	**11**	**103,952**	**62,721**	**4,287**	**16,726**	**31,013**	**13,373**	
239	**70**	**1**	**11**	**25**	**11**	**97,439**	**58,484**	**3,768**	**14,761**	**28,753**	**13,018**	
208	**24**	..	**6**	**25**	..	**74,841**	**53,297**	**2,957**	**13,048**	**23,512**	**11,991**	
147	*24*	..	*6*	*4*	..	*19,753*	*10,819*	*653*	*2,780*	*5,532*	*1,969*	
31	23	..	6	..	..	4,079	1,367	203	767	795	348	1
..	..	..	..	..	..	3,840	1,523	167	588	1,175	206	2
111	1	..	..	4	..	6,318	4,293	214	1,087	2,208	943	3
61	*1*	..	..	*4*	..	*3,033*	*1,002*	*31*	*96*	*92*	*17*	
5	..	..	..	..	..	2,283	1,196	21	151	670	256	4
..	..	..	..	..	..	3,233	1,940	48	187	684	216	5
43	..	..	..	*21*	..	*17,768*	*10,165*	*726*	*2,403*	*5,394*	*3,898*	
2	..	..	..	..	..	2,782	2,220	83	656	743	344	6
13	..	..	..	5	..	5,099	2,745	184	519	1,606	506	7
27	..	..	..	16	..	3,811	829	293	340	857	41	8
..	..	..	..	..	..	2,239	2,957	24	502	1,032	2,335	9
1	..	..	..	..	..	3,837	1,414	142	386	1,156	672	10
14	..	..	..	..	..	*25,926*	*19,621*	*769*	*3,580*	*6,050*	*3,558*	
..	..	..	..	..	..	4,118	1,399	74	191	756	161	11
..	..	..	..	..	..	8,151	4,110	162	455	1,407	468	12
..	..	..	..	..	..	*2,638*	*1,071*	*93*	*55*	*91*	*18*	
..	..	..	..	..	..	3,981	4,676	75	1,134	1,504	1,573	13
..	..	..	..	..	..	6,650	7,065	203	853	1,575	1,073	14
14	..	..	..	..	..	3,016	2,371	255	947	808	283	15
4	..	..	..	..	..	*11,404*	*12,692*	*809*	*4,285*	*6,536*	*2,566*	
..	..	..	..	..	..	5,562	7,020	247	1,404	2,657	878	16
4	..	..	..	..	..	3,806	3,672	227	1,026	3,139	1,536	17
..	..	..	..	..	..	2,036	2,000	335	1,855	740	152	18
31	**46**	**1**	**5**	..	**11**	**22,598**	**5,187**	**811**	**1,713**	**5,241**	**1,027**	
6	46	..	5	..	11	7,878	1,771	290	824	2,156	221	19
..	..	..	..	..	..	6,103	1,005	155	294	1,166	351	20
..	..	..	..	..	..	3,635	1,159	161	238	1,062	300	21
25	..	1	..	..	..	4,982	1,252	205	357	857	155	22
..	..	..	..	..	..	**6,513**	**4,237**	**519**	**1,965**	**2,260**	**355**	
..	..	..	..	..	..	187	77	..	24	43	6	23
..	..	..	..	..	..	625	596	72	482	251	56	24
..	..	..	..	..	..	492	215	95	244	112	32	25
..	..	..	..	..	..	998	664	64	216	163	37	26
..	..	..	..	..	..	530	391	85	84	102	7	27
..	..	..	..	..	..	132	121	6	188	66	7	28
..	..	..	..	..	..	293	414	1	7	140	129	29
..	..	..	..	..	..	54	13	1	1	7	1	30
..	..	..	..	..	..	771	617	37	333	265	60	31
..	..	..	..	..	..	182	432	61	108	270	8	32
..	..	..	..	..	..	35	13	1	3	12	1	33
..	..	..	..	..	..	130	4	..	..	62	..	34
..	..	..	..	..	..	1,055	189	73	234	516	8	35
..	..	..	..	..	..	120	118	3	3	89	1	36
..	..	..	..	..	..	909	373	20	38	162	2	37

Serial No.	Class .. / Sub-class .. / Order .. / Sub-order .. / Group .. — District, City or State.	Class B.—Preparation and supply / Sub-class V.— / Order 32.—Other trade / 129.—Grain and pulse dealers. Total earners (principal occupations). Males.	Total earners (principal occupations). Females.	Total working dependants. Males.	Total working dependants. Females.	Total following occupation as subsidiary to other. Males.	Total following occupation as subsidiary to other. Females.
1	2	984	985	986	987	988	989
	Central Provinces and Berar ..	**16,126**	**13,673**	**484**	**2,271**	**4,469**	**1,745**
	C. P. British Districts and Berar ..	**14,673**	**12,535**	**363**	**2,068**	**4,103**	**1,644**
	C. P. British Districts	**12,140**	**11,641**	**274**	**1,859**	**3,525**	**1,515**
	Jubbulpore Division	*3,664*	*803*	*61*	*153*	*819*	*61*
1	Saugor	594	93	19	12	82	1
2	Damoh	1,384	18	26	4	363	1
3	Jubbulpore	858	282	8	30	152	41
	Jubbulpore City	*356*	*95*	*2*	*5*	*10*	*2*
4	Mandla	480	199	2	36	122	9
5	Seoni	348	211	6	71	100	9
	Nerbudda Division	*3,306*	*1,497*	*82*	*288*	*805*	*94*
6	Narsinghpur	429	111	3	22	63	9
7	Hoshangabad	1,153	402	36	60	176	57
8	Nimar	498	269	17	108	98	1
9	Betul	477	299	2	39	187	14
10	Chhindwara	749	416	24	59	281	13
	Nagpur Division	*2,850*	*5,481*	*68*	*765*	*910*	*657*
11	Wardha	450	148	4	15	88	9
12	Nagpur	936	827	34	137	219	69
	Nagpur City	*300*	*55*	*26*	*3*	*22*	..
13	Chanda	385	862	1	98	191	177
14	Bhandara	814	2,823	29	334	251	349
15	Balaghat	265	821	..	181	161	53
	Chhattisgarh Division	*2,320*	*4,060*	*63*	*653*	*991*	*703*
16	Raipur	1,121	2,002	22	196	238	239
17	Bilaspur	940	1,317	24	362	692	435
18	Drug	259	741	17	95	61	29
	Berar	**2,533**	**694**	**89**	**209**	**578**	**129**
19	Amraoti	770	114	34	20	220	8
20	Akola	801	187	16	62	133	30
21	Buldana	502	141	23	46	93	44
22	Yeotmal	460	252	16	81	132	47
	Central Provinces States	**1,453**	**1,138**	**121**	**203**	**366**	**101**
23	Makrai	17	3	..	..	10	2
24	Bastar	140	176	25	46	23	44
25	Kanker	156	51	29	4	46	6
26	Nandgaon	209	211	9	34	49	1
27	Khairagarh	134	63	31	6	47	2
28	Chhuikhadan	42	26	..	12	9	..
29	Kawardha	111	114	1	..	21	2
30	Sakti	21	5	1	1	7	1
31	Raigarh	367	274	10	26	44	39
32	Sarangarh	6	171	..	..	2	2
33	Changbhakar	1	..	..	..	..	..
34	Korea	3	..	..	..	..	..
35	Surguja	123	36	15	74	58	2
36	Udaipur	27	1	..	..	32	..
37	Jashpur	96	7	..	..	18	..

Livelihood—General Distribution—*contd.* **TABLE X**

of material substances—*contd.*

Trade—*contd.*

in food stuffs—*contd.*

130.—Dealers in sweetmeats, sugar and spices. Total earners (principal occupations). Males.	Females.	Total working dependants. Males.	Females	Total following occupation as subsidiary to other. Males	Females.	131.—Dealers in dairy products, eggs and poultry. Total earners (principal occupations). Males.	Females	Total working dependants. Males.	Females.	Total following occupation as subsidiary to other. Males.	Females.	Serial No.
990	991	992	993	994	995	996	997	998	999	1000	1001	
6,825	**1,917**	**171**	**421**	**1,105**	**360**	**5,411**	**4,548**	**192**	**1,274**	**2,131**	**701**	
6,602	**1,691**	**163**	**360**	**1,047**	**355**	**5,082**	**4,472**	**180**	**1,268**	**2,020**	**692**	
4,781	**1,507**	**127**	**305**	**744**	**336**	**3,816**	**3,542**	**132**	**967**	**1,718**	**611**	
1,188	*369*	*44*	*59*	*77*	*135*	*1,643*	*1,089*	*88*	*281*	*863*	*126*	
442	101	16	25	24	108	486	256	19	94	305	31	1
102	18	18	2	5	..	235	104	1	29	186	36	2
404	119	4	25	13	11	713	578	67	106	281	44	3
221	*36*	*1*	*7*	*1*	..	*369*	*120*	*2*	*2*	*13*	..	
114	47	5	1	11	2	186	100	..	46	59	8	4
126	84	1	6	24	14	23	51	1	6	32	7	5
1,209	*200*	*40*	*66*	*159*	*34*	*857*	*781*	*23*	*277*	*459*	*209*	
190	63	11	23	18	4	103	120	5	29	41	27	6
264	41	5	19	24	..	252	164	7	34	108	28	7
449	18	17	10	74	5	312	183	10	107	143	12	8
162	31	..	..	18	1	109	229	1	95	101	12	9
144	47	7	14	25	24	81	85	..	12	66	130	10
1,715	*663*	*34*	*117*	*382*	*135*	*1,234*	*1,361*	*20*	*154*	*336*	*208*	
326	47	10	3	43	7	341	372	6	37	74	58	11
553	103	4	23	62	6	634	498	11	48	139	100	12
212	*26*	*2*	*1*	*3*	..	*251*	*123*	*9*	*5*	*2*	*1*	
274	161	13	28	154	73	105	298	..	59	46	41	13
389	147	6	15	78	20	113	67	3	3	64	8	14
173	205	1	48	45	29	41	126	..	7	13	1	15
669	*275*	*9*	*63*	*126*	*32*	*82*	*311*	*1*	*255*	*60*	*68*	
267	170	..	24	44	25	7	26	..	7	7	1	16
201	82	7	26	66	7	52	65	1	59	50	55	17
201	23	2	13	16	..	23	220	..	189	3	12	18
1,821	**184**	**36**	**55**	**303**	**19**	**1,266**	**930**	**48**	**301**	**302**	**81**	
522	64	12	13	109	5	411	234	27	177	158	25	19
466	35	10	12	73	5	355	217	2	46	64	20	20
174	24	2	13	52	3	266	155	5	52	30	20	21
659	61	12	17	69	6	234	324	14	26	50	16	22
223	**226**	**8**	**61**	**58**	**5**	**329**	**76**	**12**	**6**	**111**	**9**	
15	3	..	..	4	1	4	..	..	..	..	..	23
18	14	..	18	3	2	..	3	..	5	..	..	24
..	1	..	..	1	..	30	4	12	..	..	..	25
26	52	8	21	6	1	8	1	..	..	2	..	26
12	28	..	..	2	..	1	..	..	..	..	..	27
13	14	..	6	..	1	6	1	..	..	31	..	28
20	14	..	..	..	..	7	28	..	1	34	8	29
17	1	..	..	..	..	..	1	..	..	..	..	30
10	15	..	2	4	..	..	..	..	..	..	..	31
..	2	..	1	1	..	..	..	..	..	..	..	32
..	..	..	..	2	..	..	..	..	..	..	..	33
10	..	..	..	..	..	2	..	..	..	..	..	34
34	2	..	10	10	..	65	1	..	..	7	1	35
41	75	..	3	25	..	..	17	..	..	12	..	36
7	5	..	..	..	..	206	20	..	..	25	..	37

TABLE X — **Occupation or means of**

Serial No.	Class ..	Class B.—Preparation and supply					
	Sub-class ..	Sub-class V.—					
	Order ..	Order 32.—Other trade					
	Sub-order ..						
	Group ..	132.—Dealers in animals for food.					
	District, City or State.	Total earners (principal occupations).		Total working dependants.		Total following occupation as subsidiary to other.	
		Males.	Females.	Males.	Females.	Males.	Females.
1	2	1002	1003	1004	1005	1006	1007
	Central Provinces and Berar ..	**540**	**74**	**7**	**5**	**94**	**58**
	C. P. British Districts and Berar ..	**535**	**73**	**7**	**5**	**88**	**58**
	C. P. British Districts	**385**	**45**	**5**	**5**	**56**	**20**
	Jubbulpore Division	*91*	*31*	..	..	*15*	*20*
1	Saugor	9	3	..	..	3	..
2	Damoh	3	1	..	..	..	..
3	Jubbulpore	74	3	..	..	8	13
	Jubbulpore City	*2*	..	..	..	..	..
4	Mandla	3	2	..	..	..	3
5	Seoni	2	22	..	..	4	4
	Nerbudda Division	*150*	*4*	*5*	*1*	*21*	..
6	Narsinghpur	16	..	..	..	3	..
7	Hoshangabad	84	..	5	..	5	..
8	Nimar	33	..	..	..	10	..
9	Betul	9	4	..	..	..	..
10	Chhindwara	8	..	..	1	3	..
	Nagpur Division	*130*	*9*	..	*4*	*15*	..
11	Wardha	2	5	..	1	1	..
12	Nagpur	114	2	..	2	11	..
	Nagpur City	*72*	..	..	..	*2*	..
13	Chanda	9	..	..	..	3	..
14	Bhandara	3	1	..	..	..	..
15	Balaghat	2	1	..	1	..	..
	Chhattisgarh Division .. .	*14*	*1*	..	..	*5*	..
16	Raipur	1	..	..	..	..	..
17	Bilaspur	12	1	..	..	3	..
18	Drug	1	.	..	..	2	..
	Berar	**150**	**28**	**2**	..	**32**	**38**
19	Amraoti	49	3	..	..	2	..
20	Akola	41	21	..	..	9	..
21	Buldana	48	4	2	..	19	..
22	Yeotmal	12	.	..	..	2	38
	Central Provinces States	**5**	**1**	..	..	**6**	..
23	Makrai	5	1	..	..	1	..
24	Bastar	.	..	..	..	..	..
25	Kanker	..	..	..	..	..	..
26	Nandgaon	..	..	..	..	..	..
27	Khairagarh	..	..	..	..	..	..
28	Chhuikhadan	..	..	..	..	..	..
29	Kawardha	..	..	..	..	5	..
30	Sakti	..	..	..	..	..	..
31	Raigarh	..	..	..	..	..	..
32	Sarangarh	..	..	..	..	..	..
33	Changbhakar	..	..	..	..	..	..
34	Korea	..	..	..	..	..	..
35	Surguja	..	..	..	..	..	..
36	Udaipur	..	..	..	..	..	..
37	Jashpur	..	..	..	..	..	..

of material substances—*contd*

Trade—*contd.*

in food stuffs—*contd.*

133.—Dealers in fodder for animals.						134.—Dealers in other food stuffs.						Serial No.
Total earners (principal occupations).		Total working dependants.		Total following occupation as subsidiary to other.		Total earners (principal occupations).		Total working dependants.		Total following occupation as subsidiary to other.		
Males.	Females.	Males.	Females.	Males.	Females.	Males.	Females.	Males.	Females.	Males.	Females.	
1008	1009	1010	1011	1012	1013	1014	1015	1016	1017	1018	1019	
3.863	**10,547**	**263**	**1,567**	**2,104**	**5,201**	**65,198**	**30,262**	**2,854**	**10,715**	**19,496**	**5,110**	
3,410	**10.421**	**236**	**1,543**	**1,986**	**5,153**	**61,722**	**27,916**	**2,524**	**9,131**	**18,067**	**4,927**	
2,875	**9,823**	**214**	**1.340**	**1,616**	**4,825**	**46,439**	**25,214**	**1,923**	**8,214**	**14,705**	**4,545**	
1,150	*3,138*	*66*	*333*	*502*	*923*	*11,619*	*5,288*	*379*	*1,950*	*3,154*	*690*	
365	519	3	97	52	122	2,100	886	140	538	320	84	1
43	236	6	59	53	17	2,038	1,139	116	494	566	150	2
530	985	55	154	276	439	3,675	2,309	72	770	1,455	390	3
40	*79*	*3*	*35*	*13*	..	*1,931*	*670*	*18*	*47*	*53*	*15*	
58	383	1	11	53	188	1,361	435	13	57	411	45	4
154	1,015	1	12	68	157	2.445	519	38	91	402	21	5
1,033	*4,576*	*58*	*648*	*943*	*3,092*	*10,532*	*3,020*	*500*	*1,115*	*2,871*	*465*	
330	1,009	10	195	106	180	1,626	906	51	385	466	123	6
430	1,315	6	160	238	213	2,803	806	122	242	1,055	208	7
39	39	..	..	64	14	2,379	315	247	114	440	9	8
157	1,885	5	287	434	2,262	1,183	491	15	80	279	45	9
77	328	37	6	101	423	2,541	502	65	294	631	80	10
415	*1,310*	*11*	*313*	*104*	*775*	*17,196*	*10,508*	*399*	*2,026*	*3,884*	*1,746*	
132	28	..	8	13	17	2,667	785	50	124	501	69	11
163	283	..	9	37	120	5,435	2,359	113	232	888	170	12
119	*128*	..	*4*	*21*	*4*	*1,634*	*732*	*56*	*42*	*38*	*13*	
18	628	1	259	30	471	2,952	2,672	50	686	995	800	13
16	256	1	19	7	151	4,774	3,657	143	469	1,096	526	14
86	115	9	18	17	16	1,368	1,035	43	515	404	181	15
277	*799*	*79*	*46*	*57*	*35*	*7,092*	*6,398*	*645*	*3,123*	*4,796*	*1,644*	
148	343	66	1	28	12	3,534	4,002	151	1,072	2,090	562	16
125	433	13	44	38	23	2,188	1,577	180	510	2,108	975	17
4	23	..	1	1	..	1,370	819	314	1,541	598	107	18
535	**598**	**22**	**203**	**370**	**328**	**15,283**	**2,702**	**601**	**917**	**3,362**	**382**	
265	175	16	179	229	73	5,507	1,163	197	434	1,332	106	19
186	19	2	3	74	163	3,992	513	118	170	749	130	20
44	358	3	8	59	82	2,414	472	126	119	728	113	21
40	46	1	13	8	10	3,370	554	160	194	553	33	22
453	**126**	**27**	**24**	**118**	**48**	**3,476**	**2,346**	**330**	**1,584**	**1,429**	**183**	
16	52	..	19	2	3	128	16	..	5	26	..	23
5	3	..	..	1	..	393	364	43	404	170	10	24
..	.	..	..	..	..	253	154	54	240	48	26	25
2	54	..	..	10	..	738	326	47	158	95	35	26
5	..	..	..	..	..	294	281	49	67	45	5	27
17	..	..	..	9	..	47	80	6	170	16	6	28
42	3	..	..	37	45	87	238	..	6	38	67	29
..	..	..	..	..	..	16	3	..	..	..	..	30
13	..	..	..	..	..	316	229	24	266	198	20	31
..	..	..	..	..	..	128	181	54	87	237	6	32
..	..	..	..	..	..	19	11	..	1	7	1	33
4	..	..	..	..	..	108	4	..	..	62	..	34
333	14	27	5	59	..	464	128	31	143	355	4	35
12	..	..	..	..	..	38	22	2	..	16	1	36
4	..	..	..	..	..	447	309	20	37	116	2	37

TABLE X — Occupation or means of

Serial No.	Class .. / Sub-class .. / Order .. / Sub-order .. / Group ..	Class B.—Preparation and / Sub-class V.— / Order 32.—Other trade / 135.—Dealers in tobacco.					
	District, City or State.	Total earners (principal occupations).		Total working dependants.		Total following occupation as subsidiary to other.	
		Males.	Females.	Males.	Females.	Males.	Females.
1	2	1020	1021	1022	1023	1024	1025
	Central Provinces and Berar ..	**5,317**	**1,672**	**299**	**465**	**1,410**	**197**
	C. P. British Districts and Berar ..	**4,808**	**1,350**	**279**	**380**	**1,259**	**188**
	C. P. British Districts ..	**3,940**	**1,303**	**272**	**352**	**992**	**138**
	Jubbulpore Division	*308*	*96*	*12*	*4*	*78*	*14*
1	Saugor	76	8	6	1	8	2
2	Damoh	28	5	..	..	2	2
3	Jubbulpore	46	17	5	2	8	5
	Jubbulpore City	*107*	*2*	*5*	..	*2*	..
4	Mandla	76	28	..	..	11	1
5	Seoni	82	38	1	1	49	4
	Nerbudda Division	*577*	*79*	*17*	*5*	*78*	*3*
6	Narsinghpur	57	9	3	2	1	..
7	Hoshangabad	91	13	3	2	..	..
8	Nimar	87	4	2	..	20	..
9	Betul	132	17	1	1	13	1
10	Chhindwara	210	36	8	..	44	2
	Nagpur Division	*2,242*	*285*	*234*	*199*	*393*	*37*
11	Wardha	173	14	4	3	29	1
12	Nagpur	284	38	..	4	44	3
	Nagpur City	*45*	*7*	..	..	*3*	..
13	Chanda	214	55	10	3	77	11
14	Bhandara	518	113	19	13	76	19
15	Balaghat	1,053	65	201	176	167	3
	Chhattisgarh Division	*813*	*843*	*9*	*144*	*443*	*84*
16	Raipur	461	477	6	104	244	39
17	Bilaspur	201	196	2	24	149	41
18	Drug	151	170	1	16	50	4
	Berar	**868**	**47**	**7**	**28**	**267**	**50**
19	Amraoti	321	18	3	1	101	4
20	Akola	206	13	3	1	53	3
21	Buldana	159	4	..	..	75	38
22	Yeotmal	182	12	1	26	38	5
	Central Provinces States	**509**	**322**	**20**	**85**	**151**	**9**
23	Makrai	2	2	..	..	..	..
24	Bastar	64	35	3	7	48	..
25	Kanker	50	5	..	..	8	..
26	Nandgaon	8	20	..	3	..	..
27	Khairagarh	82	19	5	11	8	..
28	Chhuikhadan	6	..	..	..	1	..
29	Kawardha	18	16	..	..	5	7
30	Sakti	..	3	..	..	..	..
31	Raigarh	55	99	3	39	19	1
32	Sarangarh	40	78	7	20	27	..
33	Changbhakar	15	2	1	2	3	..
34	Korea	3	..	..	..	..	..
35	Surguja	25	8	..	2	25	1
36	Udaipur	2	3	1	..	4	..
37	Jashpur	139	32	..	1	3	..

supply of material substances—*contd.*

Trade—*contd.*

in food stuffs—*concld.*

136.—Dealers in opium.						137.—Dealers in ganja.						Serial No.
Total earners (principal occupations).		Total working dependants.		Total following occupation as subsidiary to other.		Total earners (principal occupations).		Total working dependants.		Total following occupation as subsidiary to other.		
Males.	Females.	Males.	Females.	Males.	Females.	Males.	Females.	Males.	Females.	Males.	Females.	
1026	1027	1028	1029	1030	1031	1032	1033	1034	1035	1036	1037	
379	11	8	4	89	1	293	17	9	4	115	..	
332	9	7	2	75	1	275	17	9	4	108	..	
224	6	4	2	57	1	241	16	6	4	99	..	
56	..	..	..	*11*	..	*34*	*5*	*3*	..	*13*	..	
..	..	..	..	..	..	7	1	..	..	1	..	1
2	..	..	..	..	..	5	2	..	..	..	..	2
4	..	..	..	5	..	14	..	3	..	10	..	3
..	..	..	..	..	..	*7*	..	..	..	..	..	
3	..	..	..	2	..	2	2	..	..	1	..	4
47	..	..	..	4	..	6	..	..	..	1	..	5
59	*3*	..	*1*	*7*	*1*	*45*	*5*	*1*	*2*	*51*	..	
17	2	..	..	1	1	14	..	..	..	44	..	6
16	1	..	..	..	..	6	3	..	2	..	..	7
8	..	..	1	4	..	6	1	..	..	4	..	8
6	..	..	..	..	..	4	1	..	..	..	..	9
12	..	..	..	2	..	15	..	1	..	3	..	10
67	*2*	*1*	..	*19*	..	*67*	*2*	*2*	*2*	*7*	..	
15	..	..	..	5	..	12	..	..	..	2	..	11
14	..	..	..	5	..	18	..	..	..	2	..	12
3	..	..	..	..	..	*2*	..	..	..	..	..	
17	..	..	..	6	..	7	..	..	1	2	..	13
11	1	1	..	2	..	12	..	1	..	1	..	14
10	1	..	..	1		18	2	1	1	..	..	15
42	*1*	*3*	*1*	*20*	..	*95*	*4*	..	..	*28*	..	
14	..	2	..	2	..	9	..	..	..	4	..	16
14	1	..	1	9	..	73	..	..	..	24	..	17
14	..	1	..	9	..	13	4	..	..	..	..	18
108	3	3	..	18	..	34	1	3	..	9	..	
27	..	1	..	3	..	6	..	..	..	2	..	19
37	..	1	..	7	..	19	..	3	..	4	..	20
27	..	..	..	4	..	1	1	..	..	2	..	21
17	3	1	..	4	..	8	..	..	..	1	..	22
47	2	1	2	14	..	18	..	..	..	7	..	
..	..	..	..	..	..	..	..	..	..	..	..	23
5	1	1	2	6	..	..	..	..	..	..	..	24
2	..	..	..	7	..	1	..	..	..	2	..	25
3	..	..	..	..	..	4	..	..	..	1	..	26
..	..	..	..	..	..	2	..	..	..	..	..	27
1	..	..	..	..	..	..	..	..	..	..	..	28
5	1	..	..	..	..	3	..	..	..	..	..	29
..	..	..	..	..	..	..	..	..	..	..	..	30
9	..		..	..	..	1	..	..	..	..	..	31
7	..		..		..		..	..	..	3	..	32
..	..	..	..	..	..	..	..	..	..	..	..	33
..		..	..	..	..	..	..	..	..	..	..	34
11	..	..	..	1	..	..	..	..	..	1	..	35
..	..	..	..	..		..	..	..	..	..	..	36
4	..	..	..	..	..	6	..	..	..	..	..	37

TABLE X

Occupation or means of

Serial No.	Class .. / Sub-class / Order .. / Sub-order .. / Group ..	Class B.—Preparation and / Sub-class V.— / Order 33.— / Total order 33.					
	District, City, or State.	Total earners (principal occupations).		Total working dependants.		Total following occupation as subsidiary to other.	
		Males.	Females.	Males.	Females.	Males.	Females.
1	2	1038	1039	1040	1041	1042	1043
	Central Provinces and Berar ..	**5,511**	**831**	**188**	**174**	**775**	**80**
	C. P. British Districts and Berar ..	**5,465**	**722**	**184**	**162**	**748**	**78**
	C. P. British Districts ..	**4,252**	**516**	**160**	**84**	**641**	**61**
	Jubbulpore Division	*1,637*	*82*	*106*	*23*	*448*	*5*
1	Saugor	786	50	2	18	306	3
2	Damoh	222	..	99	..	59	..
3	Jubbulpore ..	112	6	5	1	16	..
	Jubbulpore City ..	*96*	*4*	..	..	*1*	..
4	Mandla	313	21	..	4	44	..
5	Seoni ..	204	5	..	..	23	2
	Nerbudda Division	*1,186*	*68*	*16*	*2*	*76*	*2*
6	Narsinghpur	249	13	2	..	21	1
7	Hoshangabad	36	4	..	..	22	..
8	Nimar	281	10	9	..	15	1
9	Betul	242	16	2	..	2	..
10	Chhindwara	378	25	3	2	16	..
	Nagpur Division	*1,255*	*246*	*32*	*39*	*90*	*34*
11	Wardha	136	30	1	2	14	1
12	Nagpur	564	60	27	9	45	2
	Nagpur City	*169*	*12*	*22*	..	*6*	..
13	Chanda	228	110	3	12	19	2
14	Bhandara	307	36	..	16	12	27
15	Balaghat	20	10	1	..	..	2
	Chhattisgarh Division	*174*	*120*	*6*	*20*	*27*	*20*
16	Raipur	84	71	..	5	3	12
17	Bilaspur	59	36	1	10	21	8
18	Drug	31	13	5	5	3	..
	Berar	**1,213**	**206**	**24**	**78**	**107**	**17**
19	Amraoti	321	47	3	18	21	9
20	Akola	438	67	18	16	48	3
21	Buldana	221	41	3	20	24	3
22	Yeotmal	233	51	..	24	14	2
	Central Provinces States	**46**	**109**	**4**	**12**	**27**	**2**
23	Makrai	1	..	..	..	..	..
24	Bastar	1	4	..	..	..	..
25	Kanker	..	..	..	..	..	..
26	Nandgaon	4	2	3	..	2	1
27	Khairagarh	1	..	..	..	1	..
28	Chhuikhadan	..	..	..	..	..	..
29	Kawardha	7	64	..	..	1	..
30	Sakti	..	..	..	..	..	..
31	Raigarh	20	4	1	1	5	..
32	Sarangarh	4	..	..	1	..	..
33	Changbhakar	..	..	..	..	..	..
34	Korea	1	..	..	..	..	..
35	Surguja	5	10	..	7	15	..
36	Udaipur	2	..	..	..	3	..
37	Jashpur	..	25	..	3	..	1

supply of material substances—*contd.*

Trade—*contd.*

Trade in clothing and other toilet articles.						Order 34.—Trade in furniture.						Serial No.
138.—Trade in ready-made clothing and other of dress and the toilet (hats, umbrellas, socks, ready-made shoes, perfumes etc.)						Total order 34.						
Total earners (principal occupations).		Total working dependants.		Total following occupation as subsidiary to other.		Total earners (principal occupations).		Total working dependants.		Total following occupation as subsidiary to other.		
Males.	Females.	Males.	Females.	Males.	Females.	Males.	Females.	Males.	Females	Males.	Females	
1044	1045	1046	1047	1048	1049	1050	1051	1052	1053	1054	1055	
5,511	**831**	**188**	**174**	**775**	**80**	**3,436**	**814**	**74**	**566**	**673**	**136**	
5,465	**722**	**184**	**162**	**748**	**78**	**3,109**	**705**	**42**	**326**	**535**	**113**	
4,252	**516**	**160**	**84**	**641**	**61**	**2,533**	**636**	**30**	**321**	**477**	**93**	
1,637	82	106	23	448	5	887	174	11	157	27[illegible]	3	
786	50	2	18	306	3	57	10	..	3	10	..	1
222	..	99	..	59	..	23	51	1	14	3	2	2
112	6	5	1	16	..	355	30	5	96	76	1	3
96	4	..	..	1	..	26	..	..	..	..	..	
313	21	..	4	44	..	327	80	1	44	161	..	4
204	5	..	..	23	2	125	3	4	..	26	..	5
1,186	68	16	2	76	2	933	101	5	89	95	16	
249	13	2	..	21	1	542	61	..	53	53	12	6
36	4	..	..	22	..	42	29	4	26	5	4	7
281	10	9	..	15	1	143	4	..	1	6	..	8
242	16	2	..	2	..	51	2	..	..	11	..	9
378	25	3	2	16	..	155	5	1	9	20	..	10
1,255	246	32	39	90	34	406	102	7	4	30	6	
136	30	1	2	14	1	49	4	1	..	12	1	11
564	60	27	9	45	2	145	26	..	4	2	..	12
169	12	22	..	6	..	116	19	..	4	1	..	
228	110	3	12	19	2	34	57	..	..	..	1	13
307	36	..	16	12	27	102	13	2	..	6	4	14
20	10	1	..	..	2	76	2	4	..	10	..	15
174	120	6	20	27	20	307	259	7	71	76	68	
84	71	..	5	3	12	147	126	3	12	29	64	16
59	36	1	10	21	8	105	119	..	56	40	4	17
31	13	5	5	3	..	55	14	4	3	7	..	18
1,213	**206**	**24**	**78**	**107**	**17**	**576**	**69**	**12**	**5**	**58**	**20**	
321	47	3	18	21	9	113	29	..	..	22	2	19
438	67	18	16	48	3	234	27	..	5	12	17	20
221	41	3	20	24	3	43	6	6	..	20	1	21
233	51	..	24	14	2	186	7	6	..	4	..	22
46	**109**	**4**	**12**	**27**	**2**	**327**	**109**	**32**	**240**	**138**	**23**	
1	..	..	..	..	..	7	3	..	..	..	..	23
1	4	..	..	..	..	64	22	19	13	13	3	24
..	..	..	..	..	..	59	7	..	74	..	10	25
4	2	3	..	2	1	27	19	3	9	5	8	26
1	..	..	..	1	..	..	..	..	..	..	..	27
..	..	..	..	..	..	..	..	..	..	..	..	28
7	64	..	..	1	..	2	22	..	..	1	1	29
..	..	..	..	..	..	..	..	..	..	..	..	30
20	4	1	1	5	..	30	8	1	58	9	..	31
4	..	..	1	..	..	1	12	..	6	1	1	32
..	..	..	..	..	..	9	..	..	..	..	..	33
1	..	..	..	..	..	9	..	..	..	5	..	34
5	10	..	7	15	..	32	12	9	80	44	..	35
2	..	..	..	3	..	1	..	..	..	..	..	36
..	25	..	3	..	1	80	4	..	..	60	..	37

TABLE X — Occupation or means of

Serial No.	Class ..	Class B.—Preparation and					
	Sub-class ..	Sub-class V.—					
	Order ..	Order 34.—Trade					
	Sub-order ..						
	Group ..	193.—Trade in furniture, carpets, curtains and beddings.					
	District, City, or State.	Total earners (principal occupations).		Total working dependants.		Total following occupation as subsidiary to other.	
		Males.	Females.	Males.	Females.	Males.	Females.
1	2	1056	1057	1058	1059	1060	1061
	Central Provinces and Berar	**462**	**148**	**5**	**15**	**134**	**13**
	C. P. British Districts and Berar	**433**	**127**	**4**	**15**	**125**	**10**
	C. P. British Dsitricts	**247**	**119**	**1**	**12**	**100**	**8**
	Jubbulpore Division	*114*	*21*	*1*	*2*	*38*	*1*
1	Saugor	31	10	..	..	5	..
2	Damoh	23	5	1	..	3	..
3	Jubbulpore	41	4	..	..	19	1
	Jubbulpore City	..	..	..	..	..	..
4	Mandla	15	2	..	2	10	..
5	Seoni	4	..	..	..	1	..
	Nerbudda Division	*69*	*3*	..	*4*	*39*	..
6	Narsinghpur	12	1	..	..	17	..
7	Hoshangabad	..	..	..	4	..	..
8	Nimar	1	..	..	..	5	..
9	Betul	31	2	..	..	8	..
10	Chhindwara	25	..	..	..	9	..
	Nagpur Division	*47*	*63*	..	*1*	*12*	*4*
11	Wardha	3	2	..	..	11	1
12	Nagpur	17	10	..	1	1	..
	Nagpur City	*13*	*3*	..	*1*	*1*	..
13	Chanda	..	47	..	..	..	1
14	Bhandara	27	4	..	..	..	2
15	Balaghat	..	..	..	..	..	..
	Chhattisgarh Division	*17*	*32*	..	*5*	*11*	*3*
16	Raipur	3	29	..	..	2	2
17	Bilaspur	11	3	..	5	9	1
18	Drug	3	..	..	..	..	..
	Berar	**186**	**8**	**3**	**3**	**25**	**2**
19	Amraoti	54	4	..	..	15	2
20	Akola	98	3	..	3	8	..
21	Buldana	..	1	..	..	1	..
22	Yeotmal	34	..	3	..	1	..
	Central Provinces States	**29**	**21**	**1**	..	**9**	**3**
23	Makrai	1	..	..	..	..	..
24	Bastar	..	16	..	..	..	3
25	Kanker	..	..	..	..	..	..
26	Nandgaon	..	..	..	..	1	..
27	Khairagarh	..	..	..	..	..	..
28	Chhuikhadan	..	..	..	..	..	..
29	Kawardha	2	3	..	..	..	..
30	Sakti	..	..	..	..	..	..
31	Raigarh	23	2	1	..	8	..
32	Sarangarh	..	..	..	..	..	..
33	Changbhakar	..	..	..	..	..	..
34	Korea	3	..	..	..	..	..
35	Surguja	..	..	..	..	..	..
36	Udaipur	..	..	..	..	..	..
37	Jashpur	..	..	..	..	..	..

supply of material substances—*contd.*

Trade—*contd.*

in furniture—*concld.*						**Order 35.—Trade in building materials.**						
						Total order 35.						
140.—Hardware, cooking utensils, porcelain, crockery, glassware bottles, articles for gardening, etc.												**Serial No.**
Total earners (*principal* occupations).		Total working dependants.		Total following occupation as subsidiary to other.		Total earners (*principal* occupations).		Total working dependants.		Total following occupation as subsidiary to other.		
Males.	Females.	Males.	Females.	Males.	Females.	Males.	Females.	Males.	Females.	Males.	Females.	
1062	1063	1064	1065	1066	1067	1068	1069	1070	1071	1072	1073	
2,974	**666**	**69**	**551**	**539**	**123**	**523**	**79**	**16**	**30**	**76**	**20**	
2,676	**578**	**38**	**311**	**410**	**103**	**511**	**70**	**15**	**22**	**67**	**19**	
2,286	**517**	**29**	**309**	**377**	**85**	**260**	**31**	**4**	**13**	**48**	**17**	
773	*153*	*10*	*155*	*238*	*2*	*24*	*2*	*3*	..	*3*	..	
26	..	..	3	5	..	6	..	..	..	..	..	1
..	46	..	14	..	2	11	2	3	..	1	..	2
314	26	5	96	57	..	7	..	..	..	1	..	3
26	..	..	..	..	..	*4*	..	..	..	..	..	
312	78	1	42	151	..	..	..	..	..	..	..	4
121	3	4	..	25	..	..	..	..	..	1	..	5
864	*98*	*5*	*85*	*56*	*16*	*107*	*3*	..	..	*15*	..	
530	60	..	53	36	12	1	..	..	..	..	..	6
42	29	4	22	5	4	94	..	..	..	15	..	7
142	4	..	1	1	..	4	..	..	..	..	..	8
20	..	..	..	3	..	4	..	..	..	..	..	9
130	5	1	9	11	..	4	3	..	..	..	..	10
359	*39*	*7*	*3*	*18*	*2*	*52*	*10*	*1*	*8*	*13*	*1*	
46	2	1	..	1	..	1	..	..	..	4	..	11
128	16	..	3	1	..	32	9	1	8	1	..	12
103	*16*	..	*3*	..	..	*16*	..	*1*	..	..	..	
34	10	..	..	..	..	2	..	..	..	2	1	13
75	9	2	..	6	2	10	1	..	..	6	..	14
76	2	4	..	10	..	7	..	..	..	..	..	15
290	*227*	*7*	*66*	*65*	*65*	*77*	*16*	..	*5*	*17*	*16*	
144	97	3	12	27	62	74	9	..	..	..	..	16
94	116	..	51	31	3	2	3	..	5	2	..	17
52	14	4	3	7	..	1	4	..	..	15	16	18
390	**61**	**9**	**2**	**33**	**18**	**251**	**39**	**11**	**9**	**19**	**2**	
59	25	..	..	7	..	61	7	..	..	7	2	19
136	24	..	2	4	17	41	2	2	..	5	..	20
43	5	6	..	19	1	20	24	..	9	7	..	21
152	7	3	..	3	..	129	6	9	..	..	..	22
298	**88**	**31**	**240**	**129**	**20**	**12**	**9**	**1**	**8**	**9**	**1**	
6	3	..	..	..	..	..	..	..	..	..	..	23
64	6	19	13	13	..	..	..	..	..	..	..	24
59	7	..	74	..	10	1	..	..	..	..	..	25
27	19	3	9	4	8	2	..	..	..	3	..	26
..	..	..	..	..	..	..	..	..	..	..	..	27
..	..	..	..	..	..	..	..	..	..	..	..	28
..	19	..	..	1	1	..	..	..	..	..	..	29
..	..	..	..	..	..	..	..	..	..	..	..	30
13	6	..	58	1	..	2	6	..	3	2	1	31
1	12	..	6	1	1	2	2	1	5	4	..	32
9	..	..	..	..	..	..	..	..	..	..	..	33
6	..	..	..	5	..	5	..	..	..	..	..	34
32	12	9	80	44	..	..	1	..	..	..	..	35
1	..	..	..	..	..	..	..	..	..	..	..	36
80	4	..	..	60	..	..	..	..	..	..	..	37

TABLE X — Occupation or means of

Serial No.	Class .. / Sub-class .. / Order .. / Sub-order .. / Group ..	Class B.—Preparation and / Sub-class V.— / Order 35.—Trade in building materials—*concld.* / 141.—Trade in building materials other than bricks, tiles and woody materials.					
	District, City, or State.	Total earners (principal occupations).		Total working dependants.		Total following occupation as subsidiary to other.	
		Males.	Females.	Males.	Females.	Males.	Females.
1	2	1074	1075	1076	1077	1078	1079
	Central Provinces and Berar ..	**523**	**79**	**16**	**30**	**76**	**20**
	C. P. British Districts and Berar ..	**511**	**70**	**15**	**22**	**67**	**19**
	C. P. British Districts ..	**260**	**31**	**4**	**13**	**48**	**17**
	Jubbulpore Division	*24*	*2*	*3*	..	*3*	..
1	Saugor ..	6	..	..	..	..	..
2	Damoh ..	11	2	3	..	1	..
3	Jubbulpore	7	..	..	..	1	..
	Jubbulpore City	*4*	..	..	..	..	..
4	Mandla	..	..	..	..	..	..
5	Seoni	..	..	..	..	1	....
	Nerbudda Division	*107*	*3*	..	..	*15*	..
6	Narsinghpur	1	..	..	..	..	..
7	Hoshangabad	94	..	..	..	15	..
8	Nimar	4	..	..	..	..	..
9	Betul	4	..	..	..	..	..
10	Chhindwara	4	3	..	..	..	..
	Nagpur Division	*52*	*10*	*1*	*8*	*13*	*1*
11	Wardha	1	..	..	..	4	..
12	Nagpur	32	9	1	8	1	..
	Nagpur City	*16*	..	*1*	..	..	..
13	Chanda	2	..	..	..	2	1
14	Bhandara	10	1	..	..	6	..
15	Balaghat	7	..	..	..	..	..
	Chhattisgarh Division	*77*	*16*	..	*5*	*17*	*16*
16	Raipur	74	9	..	..	..	..
17	Bilaspur	2	3	..	5	2	..
18	Drug	1	4	..	..	15	16
	Berar	**251**	**39**	**11**	**9**	**19**	**2**
19	Amraoti	61	7	.	..	7	2
20	Akola	41	2	2	..	5	..
21	Buldana	20	24	..	9	7	..
22	Yeotmal	129	6	9	..	..	..
	Central Provinces States	**12**	**9**	**1**	**8**	**9**	**1**
23	Makrai	..	..	..	..	..	..
24	Bastar	..	..	..	..	..	..
25	Kanker	1	..	..	..	..	..
26	Nandgaon	2	..	..	..	3	..
27	Khairagarh	..	..	..	..	..	..
28	Chhuikhadan	..	..	..	..	..	..
29	Kawardha	..	..	..	..	..	..
30	Sakti	..	..	..	..	..	..
31	Raigarh	2	6	..	3	2	1
32	Sarangarh	2	2	1	5	4	..
33	Changbhakar	..	..	..	..	..	..
34	Korea	..	..	..	..	..	..
35	Surguja	5	1	..	..	..	..
36	Udaipur	..	..	..	..	..	..
37	Jashpur	.	..	..	..	..	..

supply of material substances—*contd.*

Trade—*contd.*

Order 36.—Trade in means of transport.

Total order 36.						142.—Dealers and hirers in mechanical transport, motors, cycles, etc.						Serial No.
Total earners (principal occupations.)		Total working dependants.		Total following occupation as subsidiary to other.		Total earners (principal occupations).		Total working dependants.		Total following occupation as subsidiary to other.		
Males.	Females.	Males.	Females.	Males.	Females.	Males.	Females.	Males.	Females.	Males.	Females.	
1080	1081	1082	1083	1084	1085	1086	1087	1088	1089	1090	1091	
2,898	**111**	**22**	**63**	**1,080**	**189**	**316**	**7**	..	**1**	**16**	**7**	
2,761	**107**	**22**	**62**	**969**	**186**	**312**	**7**	..	**1**	**16**	**7**	
2,277	**72**	**16**	**61**	**756**	**184**	**282**	**3**	..	..	**16**	**7**	
1,001	*29*	*7*	..	*193*	*2*	*118*	..	..	..	*4*	..	
578	11	4	..	29	..	12	..	..	..	..	..	1
69	13	..	..	47	1	4	..	..	..	..	..	2
202	4	3	..	54	1	100	..	..	..	4	..	3
115	..	..	..	*4*	..	*94*	..	..	..	*4*	..	
83	1	..	..	22	..	1	..	..	..	..	..	4
69	..	..	..	41	..	1	..	..	..	..	..	5
467	**22**	..	*59*	*236*	*171*	**56**	**3**	..	..	**2**	*1*	
62	4	..	..	24	1	..	..	..	..	..	1	6
135	4	..	5	88	..	10	..	..	..	..	..	7
98	3	..	..	32	..	34	1	..	..	2	..	8
90	8	..	54	47	170	2	..	..	..	..	..	9
82	3	..	..	45	..	10	2	..	..	..	..	10
500	*19*	*1*	*1*	*241*	*11*	*84*	..	..	..	*6*	*6*	
30	1	..	..	26	6	3	..	..	..	2	6	11
159	1	1	..	58	4	62	..	..	..	3	..	12
64	..	..	..	*5*	..	*61*	..	..	..	*3*	..	
38	13	..	..	49	1	1	..	..	..	1	..	13
141	1	..	1	47	..	16	..	..	..	..	..	14
132	3	..	..	61	..	2	..	..	..	..	..	15
309	*2*	*8*	*1*	*86*	..	*24*	..	..	..	*4*	..	
89	..	6	..	19	..	15	..	..	..	4	..	16
146	1	..	..	50	..	5	..	..	..	..	..	17
74	1	2	1	17	..	4	..	..	..	..	..	18
484	**35**	**6**	**1**	**213**	**2**	**30**	**4**	..	**1**	..	..	
164	12	..	1	45	..	1	4	..	1	..	..	19
141	10	1	..	105	..	16	..	..	..	..	..	20
146	3	2	..	61	..	3	..	..	..	..	..	21
33	10	3	..	2	..	10	..	..	..	..	..	22
137	**4**	..	**1**	**111**	**3**	**4**	..	..	..	..	..	
1	..	..	..	..	1	..	..	..	..	..	..	23
19	1	..	..	1	..	..	..	..	..	..	..	24
..	..	..	..	..	..	..	..	..	..	..	..	25
26	..	..	..	1	..	4	..	..	..	..	..	26
6	..	..	..	..	..	..	..	..	..	..	..	27
6	..	..	..	..	..	..	..	..	..	..	..	28
31	3	..	..	34	2	..	..	..	..	..	..	29
1	..	..	1	..	..	..	..	..	..	..	..	30
..	..	..	..	1	..	..	..	..	..	..	..	31
..	..	..	..	..	..	..	..	..	..	..	..	32
..	..	..	..	..	..	..	..	..	..	..	..	33
..	..	..	..	..	..	..	..	..	..	..	..	34
12	..	..	..	1	..	..	..	..	..	..	..	35
..	..	..	..	4	..	..	..	..	..	..	..	36
35	..	..	..	69	..	..	..	..	..	..	..	37

TABLE X

Occupation or means of

Serial No.	District, City, or State.	Class B.—Preparation and; Sub-class V.—; Order 36.—Trade; 145.—Dealers and hirers in other carriages, carts, boats, etc.: Total earners (principal occupations). Males.	Total earners (principal occupations). Females.	Total working dependants. Males.	Total working dependants. Females.	Total following occupation as subsidiary to other. Males.	Total following occupation as subsidiary to other. Females.
1	2	1092	1093	1094	1095	1096	1097
	Central Provinces and Berar	29	2	..	3	6	..
	C. P. British Districts and Berar	29	2	..	3	6	..
	C. P. British Districts	21	2	..	3	5	..
	Jubbulpore Division	..	..	..	..	..	..
1	Saugor	..	..	..	..	..	..
2	Damoh	..	..	..	..	..	..
3	Jubbulpore	..	..	..	..	..	..
	Jubbulpore City	..	..	..	..	..	..
4	Mandla	..	..	..	..	..	..
5	Seoni	..	..	..	..	..	..
	Nerbudda Division	..	2	..	3	..	..
6	Narsinghpur	..	..	..	..	..	..
7	Hoshangabad	..	2	..	3	..	..
8	Nimar	..	..	..	..	..	..
9	Betul	..	..	..	..	..	..
10	Chhindwara	..	..	..	..	..	..
	Nagpur Division	15	..	..	..	1	..
11	Wardha	1	..	..	..	1	..
12	Nagpur	1	..	..	..	..	..
	Nagpur City	..	..	..	..	..	..
13	Chanda	2	..	..	..	..	..
14	Bhandara	11	..	..	..	..	..
15	Balaghat	..	..	..	..	..	..
	Chhattisgarh Division	6	..	..	..	4	..
16	Raipur	6	..	..	..	3	..
17	Bilaspur	..	..	..	..	1	..
18	Drug	..	..	..	..	..	..
	Berar	8	..	..	..	1	..
19	Amraoti	8	..	..	..	..	..
20	Akola	..	..	..	..	..	..
21	Buldana	..	..	..	..	1	..
22	Yeotmal	..	..	..	..	..	..
	Central Provinces States	..	..	..	..	..	..
23	Makrai	..	..	..	..	..	..
24	Bastar	..	..	..	..	..	..
25	Kanker	..	..	..	..	..	..
26	Nandgaon	..	..	..	..	..	..
27	Khairagarh	..	..	..	..	..	..
28	Chhuikhadan	..	..	..	..	..	..
29	Kawardha	..	..	..	..	..	..
30	Sakti	..	..	..	..	..	..
31	Raigarh	..	..	..	..	..	..
32	Sarangarh	..	..	..	..	..	..
33	Changbhakar	..	..	..	..	..	..
34	Korea	..	..	..	..	..	..
35	Surguja	..	..	..	..	..	..
36	Udaipur	..	..	..	..	..	..
37	Jashpur	..	..	..	..	..	..

Livelihood—General Distribution—*contd.*　　　　**TABLE X**

supply of material substances—*contd.*

Trade—*contd.*

in means of transport—*concld.* 144.—Dealers and hirers of elephants, camels, horses, cattle asses, mules, etc.						Order 37.—Trade in fuel. Total order 37.						
Total earners (principal occupations).		Total working dependants.		Total following occupation as subsidiary to other.		Total earners (principal occupations).		Total working dependants.		Total following occupation as subsidiary to other.		Serial No.
Males.	Females.	Males.	Females.	Males.	Females.	Males.	Females.	Males.	Females.	Males.	Females.	
1098	1099	1100	1101	1102	1103	1104	1105	1106	1107	1108	1109	
2,553	**102**	**22**	**59**	**1,058**	**182**	**3,482**	**5,714**	**293**	**3,067**	**3,289**	**2,750**	
2,420	**98**	**22**	**58**	**947**	**179**	**3,081**	**4,921**	**208**	**1,110**	**2,876**	**2,454**	
1,974	**67**	**16**	**58**	**735**	**177**	**1,755**	**3,571**	**168**	**870**	**880**	**1,280**	
883	*29*	*7*	..	*189*	*2*	*94*	*153*	*6*	*45*	*87*	*61*	
566	11	4	..	29	..	6	29	..	2	23	1	1
65	13	..	..	47	1	..	22	..	..	3	22	2
102	4	3	..	50	1	70	73	4	43	60	29	3
21	..	..	..	..	..	*11*	*44*	..	*12*	*3*	..	
82	1	..	..	22	..	14	14	1	..	..	5	4
68	..	..	..	41	..	4	15	1	..	1	4	5
411	*17*	..	*56*	*234*	*170*	*411*	*387*	*2*	*223*	*78*	*78*	
62	4	..	..	24	..	27	29	1	7	..	8	6
125	2	..	2	88	..	52	238	1	177	64	57	7
64	2	..	..	30	..	5	26	..	13	..	10	8
88	8	..	54	47	170	1	4	..	..	1	..	9
72	1	..	..	45	..	326	90	..	26	13	3	10
401	*19*	*1*	*1*	*234*	*5*	*747*	*1,287*	*41*	*220*	*516*	*844*	
26	1	..	..	23	..	145	103	..	20	22	38	11
96	1	1	..	55	4	375	349	4	79	157	526	12
3	..	..	..	*2*	..	*211*	*41*	*2*	*1*	*7*	..	
35	13	..	..	48	1	54	355	11	107	80	126	13
114	1	..	1	47	..	171	480	26	14	257	144	14
130	3	..	..	61	..	2	..	..	..	..	..	15
279	*2*	*8*	*1*	*78*	..	*503*	*1,744*	*119*	*382*	*199*	*297*	
68	..	6	..	12	..	323	1,318	9	83	88	135	16
141	1	..	..	50	..	147	331	109	276	97	114	17
70	1	2	1	16	..	33	95	1	23	14	48	18
446	**31**	**6**	..	**212**	**2**	**1,326**	**1,350**	**40**	**240**	**1,996**	**1,174**	
155	8	..	..	45	..	327	279	19	97	1,523	524	19
125	10	1	..	105	2	388	402	11	77	186	224	20
143	3	2	..	60	..	338	387	8	14	268	400	21
23	10	3	..	2	..	273	282	2	52	19	26	22
133	**4**	..	**1**	**111**	**3**	**401**	**793**	**85**	**1,957**	**413**	**296**	
1	..	..	..	..	1	2	..	..	..	..	..	23
19	1	..	..	1	..	44	26	..	5	10	9	24
..	..	..	..	..	..	..	29	..	..	..	..	25
22	..	..	..	1	..	18	123	4	12	18	5	26
6	..	..	..	..	..	26	81	..	..	14	46	27
6	..	..	..	..	..	5	23	..	..	..	..	28
31	3	..	..	34	2	12	151	..	1	308	235	29
1	..	..	1	..	..	..	..	..	..	..	..	30
..	..	..	..	1	..	59	84	55	123	15	..	31
..	..	..	..	..	..	55	90	7	49	10	..	32
..	..	..	..	..	..	..	..	..	..	..	..	33
..	..	..	..	..	..	28	..	..	2	3	..	34
12	..	..	..	1	..	145	130	19	1,761	35	..	35
..	..	..	..	4	..	..	..	..	..	..	..	36
35	..	..	..	69	..	7	56	..	4	..	1	37

TABLE X — Occupation or means of

Serial No.	Class .. / Sub-class .. / Order .. / Sub-order .. / Group ..	Class B.—Preparation and / Sub-class V.— / Order 37.—Trade in fuel—*concld.* / 145.—Dealers in fire-wood, charcoal, coal, cowdung, etc.					
	District, City or State.	Total earners (principal occupations).		Total working dependants.		Total following occupation as subsidiary to other.	
		Males.	Females	Males.	Females.	Males.	Females.
1	2	1110	1111	1112	1113	1114	1115
	Central Provinces and Berar	**3,482**	**5,714**	**293**	**3,067**	**3,289**	**2,750**
	C. P. British Districts and Berar	**3,081**	**4,921**	**208**	**1,110**	**2,876**	**2,454**
	C. P. British Districts	**1,755**	**3,571**	**168**	**870**	**880**	**1,280**
	Jubbulpore Division	*94*	*153*	*6*	*45*	*87*	*61*
1	Saugor	6	29	..	2	23	1
2	Damoh	..	22	..	..	3	22
3	Jubbulpore	70	73	4	43	60	29
	Jubbulpore City	*11*	*44*	..	*12*	*3*	..
4	Mandla	14	14	1	..	..	5
5	Seoni	4	15	1	..	1	4
	Nerbudda Division	*411*	*387*	*2*	*223*	*78*	*78*
6	Narsinghpur	27	29	1	7	..	8
7	Hoshangabad	52	238	1	177	64	57
8	Nimar	5	26	..	13	..	10
9	Betul	1	4	..	..	1	..
10	Chhindwara	326	90	..	26	13	3
	Nagpur Division	*747*	*1,287*	*41*	*220*	*516*	*844*
11	Wardha	145	103	..	20	22	38
12	Nagpur	375	349	4	79	157	536
	Nagpur City	*211*	*41*	*2*	*1*	*7*	..
13	Chanda	54	355	11	107	80	126
14	Bhandara	171	480	26	14	257	144
15	Balaghat	2	..	..	..	..	..
	Chhattisgarh Division	*503*	*1,744*	*119*	*382*	*199*	*297*
16	Raipur	323	1,318	9	83	88	135
17	Bilaspur	147	331	109	276	97	114
18	Drug	33	95	1	23	14	48
	Berar	**1,326**	**1,350**	**40**	**240**	**1,996**	**1,174**
19	Amraoti	327	279	19	97	1,523	524
20	Akola	388	402	11	77	186	224
21	Buldana	338	387	8	14	268	400
22	Yeotmal	273	282	2	52	19	26
	Central Provinces States	**401**	**793**	**85**	**1,957**	**413**	**296**
23	Makrai	2	..	..	..	..	..
24	Bastar	44	26	..	5	10	9
25	Kanker	..	29	..	..	..	..
26	Nandgaon	18	123	4	12	18	5
27	Khairagarh	26	81	..	..	14	46
28	Chhuikhadan	5	23	..	..	..	..
29	Kawardha	12	151	..	1	308	235
30	Sakti	..	..	..	..	..	..
31	Raigarh	59	84	55	123	15	..
32	Sarangarh	55	90	7	49	10	..
33	Changbhakar	..	..	..	..	..	..
34	Korea	28	..	..	2	3	..
35	Surguja	145	130	19	1,761	35	..
36	Udaipur	..	..	..	..	..	..
37	Jashpur	7	56	..	4	..	1

Livelihood—General Distribution—*contd.*

TABLE X

supply of material substances—*contd.*

Trade—*contd.*

Order 38.—Trade in articles of luxury and those pertaining to letters and the arts and sciences.

Total order 38.						146.—Dealers in precious stones, jewellery (real and imitation), clocks, optical instruments, etc.						Serial No.
Total earners (principal occupations).		Total working dependants		Total following occupation as subsidiary to other		Total earners (principal occupations).		Total working dependants.		Total following occupation as subsidiary to other.		
Males.	Females	Males.	Females.	Males.	Females	Males.	Females.	Males.	Females.	Males.	Females.	
1116	1117	1118	1119	1120	1121	1122	1123	1124	1125	1126	1127	
11,548	**5,155**	**357**	**1,195**	**1,509**	**426**	**2,040**	**254**	**64**	**24**	**248**	**11**	
11,092	**4,623**	**331**	**969**	**1,448**	**404**	**1,993**	**253**	**64**	**24**	**245**	**11**	
7,606	**3,859**	**259**	**858**	**1,151**	**370**	**1,482**	**195**	**54**	**15**	**192**	**11**	
1,964	*779*	*111*	*105*	*313*	*37*	*319*	*20*	*6*	*4*	*40*	..	
460	139	3	34	15	1	95	3	..	4	5	..	1
265	117	12	7	14	14	9	5	..	..	3	..	2
620	271	93	21	238	17	142	4	5	..	22	..	3
230	*48*	..	*3*	*5*	*1*	*61*	*1*	..	..	..	..	
257	72	..	15	22	..	69	6	..	..	7	..	4
362	180	3	28	24	5	4	2	1	..	3	..	5
2,055	*518*	*68*	*82*	*142*	*14*	*487*	*41*	*44*	*4*	*35*	*9*	
303	149	1	17	26	11	32	7	..	2	8	8	6
463	87	16	18	16	..	171	12	11	1	6	..	7
673	112	42	12	42	..	183	3	33	1	13	..	8
292	51	..	4	26	..	78	10	..	..	6	..	9
324	119	9	31	32	3	23	9	..	..	2	1	10
2,578	*844*	*33*	*98*	*266*	*30*	*369*	*117*	..	*7*	*32*	*1*	
574	94	3	7	41	9	89	7	..	..	4	1	11
821	175	15	28	80	2	133	13	..	3	23	..	12
406	*42*	*11*	*6*	*16*	..	*57*	*8*	..	..	..	..	
342	228	2	21	38	5	42	56	..	..	2	..	13
492	240	8	24	37	12	91	35	..	4	1	..	14
349	107	5	18	70	2	14	6	..	..	2	..	15
1,009	*1,718*	*47*	*573*	*430*	*289*	*307*	*17*	*4*	..	*85*	*1*	
546	806	25	222	126	46	269	2	3	..	85	1	16
206	507	9	159	237	229	5	6	..	..	..	..	17
257	405	13	192	67	14	33	9	1	..	..	..	18
3,486	**764**	**72**	**111**	**297**	**34**	**511**	**58**	**10**	**9**	**53**	..	
1,052	168	27	29	105	17	124	3	2	..	18	..	19
969	155	13	33	71	6	207	35	5	1	14	..	20
733	348	21	30	79	2	36	9	2	8	8	..	21
732	93	11	19	42	9	144	11	1	..	13	..	22
456	**532**	**26**	**226**	**61**	**22**	**47**	**1**	..	..	**3**	..	
5	2	..	..	5	..	..	..	..	..	..	..	23
37	29	2	20	11	..	4	..	..	..	1	..	24
16	65	6	15	5	3	..	..	..	..	..	..	25
53	48	..	3	3	..	37	1	..	..	..	..	26
16	91	1	9	..	..	..	..	..	..	..	..	27
14	9	3	1	2	..	1	..	..	..	..	..	28
5	55	..	..	3	18	..	..	..	..	2	..	29
1	18	..	2	..	..	..	..	..	..	..	..	30
189	109	14	143	7	..	5	..	..	..	..	..	31
27	35	..	28	3	..	..	..	..	..	..	..	32
7	2	..	..	2	..	..	..	..	..	..	..	33
25	13	..	4	..	1	..	..	..	..	..	..	34
29	32	..	..	17	..	..	..	..	..	..	..	35
15	6	..	..	2	..	..	..	..	..	..	..	36
17	18	..	1	1	..	..	..	..	..	..	..	37

TABLE X — Occupation or means of

Serial No.	District, City or State.	Total earners (principal occupations). Males.	Total earners (principal occupations). Females.	Total working dependants. Males.	Total working dependants. Females.	Total following occupation as subsidiary to other. Males.	Total following occupation as subsidiary to other. Females.
	Class ..	Class B.—Preparation and					
	Sub-class ..	Sub-class V.—					
	Order ..	Order 38.—Trade in articles of luxury and those					
	Sub-order ..						
	Group ..	147.—Dealers in common bangles, bead necklaces, fans, small articles, toys, hunting and fishing tackle, flowers, etc					
1	2	1128	1129	1130	1131	1132	1133
	Central Provinces and Berar ..	**8,822**	**4,846**	**272**	**1,165**	**1,139**	**413**
	C. P. British Districts and Berar .	**8,432**	**4,315**	**246**	**942**	**1,095**	**391**
	C. P. British Districts ..	**5,837**	**3,639**	**193**	**841**	**881**	**359**
	Jubbulpore Division ..	*1,600*	*757*	*104*	*100*	*259*	*37*
1	Saugor ..	343	136	3	30	8	1
2	Damoh ..	255	112	12	7	11	14
3	Jubbulpore ..	469	266	87	20	205	17
	Jubbulpore City ..	*169*	*46*	..	*2*	*4*	*1*
4	Mandla ..	177	65	..	15	15	..
5	Seoni ..	356	178	2	28	20	5
	Nerbudda Division ..	*1,498*	*473*	*24*	*78*	*93*	*5*
6	Narsinghpur ..	265	140	1	15	17	3
7	Hoshangabad ..	273	74	5	17	8	..
8	Nimar ..	460	109	9	11	20	..
9	Betul ..	210	41	..	4	20	..
10	Chhindwara ..	290	109	9	31	28	2
	Nagpur Division ..	*2,095*	*715*	*25*	*91*	*219*	*29*
11	Wardha ..	474	87	3	7	34	8
12	Nagpur .	613	160	8	25	50	2
	Nagpur City ..	*288*	*32*	*5*	*6*	*14*	..
13	Chanda ..	293	171	2	21	35	5
14	Bhandara ..	384	203	7	20	32	12
15	Balaghat ..	331	94	5	18	68	2
	Chhattisgarh Division ..	*644*	*1,694*	*40*	*572*	*310*	*288*
16	Raipur ..	261	804	22	222	40	45
17	Bilaspur ..	166	496	8	158	205	229
18	Drug ..	217	394	10	192	65	14
	Berar ..	**2,595**	**676**	**53**	**101**	**214**	**32**
19	Amraoti ..	816	157	23	29	75	17
20	Akola ..	667	107	5	32	51	6
21	Buldana ..	601	332	17	22	62	2
22	Yeotmal ..	511	80	8	18	26	7
	Central Provinces States ..	**390**	**531**	**26**	**223**	**44**	**22**
23	Makrai ..	5	2	..	..	5	..
24	Bastar ..	33	29	2	20	10	..
25	Kanker .	16	65	6	15	5	3
26	Nandgaon ..	11	47	..	3	3	..
27	Khairagarh ..	16	91	1	9	..	..
28	Chhuikhadan ..	13	9	3	1	2	..
29	Kawardha ..	5	55	..	..	1	18
30	Sakti ..	..	18	..	2	..	..
31	Raigarh ..	179	109	14	140	7	..
32	Sarangarh ..	22	35	..	28	3	..
33	Changbhakar ..	7	2	..	..	2	..
34	Korea ..	25	13	..	..	..	1
35	Surguja ..	27	32	..	4	3	..
36	Udaipur ..	14	6	..	..	2	..
37	Jashpur ..	17	18	..	1	1	..

supply of material substances—*contd.*

Trade—*contd.*

pertaining to letters and the arts and sciences—*concld.* | **Order 39.—Trade of other sorts.**

148.—Publishers, booksellers, stationers, dealers in music, pictures, musical instruments and curiosities.						Total order 39.						Serial No.
Total earners (principal occupations).		Total working dependants.		Total following occupation as subsidiary to other.		Total earners (principal occupations).		Total working dependants.		Total following occupation as subsidiary to other.		
Males.	Females.	Males.	Females.	Males.	Females.	Males.	Females.	Males.	Females.	Males.	Females.	
1134	*1135*	*1136*	*1137*	*1138*	*1139*	*1140*	*1141*	*1142*	*1143*	*1144*	*1145*	
686	**55**	**21**	**6**	**122**	**2**	**15,327**	**3,060**	**616**	**523**	**2,254**	**229**	
667	**55**	**21**	**3**	**108**	**2**	**13,669**	**2,484**	**475**	**378**	**1,968**	**214**	
287	**25**	**12**	**2**	**78**	..	**8,858**	**2,157**	**251**	**300**	**1,205**	**196**	
45	*2*	*1*	*1*	*14*	..	*848*	*229*	*6*	*11*	*66*	*3*	
22	..	..	..	2		385	63	2	1	14	..	1
1	..	..	..	..	..	89	69	..	..	16	..	2
9	1	1	1	11	..	347	82	4	10	26	3	3
..	*1*	..	*1*	*1*	..	*237*	*37*		..	*8*	..	
11	1	..	..	..	..	10	8			1	..	4
2		..	..	1	..	17	7	..		9	..	5
70	*4*	..	..	*14*	..	*427*	*57*	*13*	*44*	*111*	*1*	
6	2	..	..	1	..	23	10	..	..	16	..	6
19	1	..	..	2	..	214	20	1	32	57	1	7
30	..	..	..	9	..	119	5	1	..	14	..	8
4	..	..	..	..	..	7	16	1	9	3	..	9
11	1	..	..	2	..	64	6	10	3	21	..	10
114	*12*	*8*	..	*15*	..	*4,215*	*764*	*92*	*96*	*364*	*56*	
11	..	..	..	3	..	391	42	10	14	47	5	11
75	2	7	..	7	..	2,752	442	40	37	156	10	12
61	*2*	*6*	..	*2*	..	*1,675*	*291*	*25*	*24*	*49*	*3*	
7	1	..	..	1	..	640	146	25	8	109	29	13
17	2	1	..	4	..	350	55	13	7	42	7	14
4	7	..	..	..	..	82	79	4	30	10	5	15
58	*7*	*3*	*1*	*35*	..	*3,368*	*1,107*	*140*	*149*	*664*	*136*	
16	..	..	..	1	..	1,532	469	43	73	253	70	16
35	5	1	1	32	..	1,425	477	37	36	371	30	17
7	2	2	..	2	..	411	141	60	40	40	36	18
380	**30**	**9**	**1**	**30**	**2**	**4,811**	**327**	**224**	**78**	**763**	**18**	
112	8	2	..	12	..	1,106	67	37	24	197	4	19
95	13	3	..	6	..	1,579	60	76	10	242	9	20
96	7	2	..	9	..	605	52	69	17	139	5	21
77	2	2	1	3	2	1,521	148	42	27	185	..	22
19	..	..	**3**	**14**	..	**1,658**	**576**	**141**	**145**	**286**	**15**	
..	..	..	..	..	..	1	..	..	..	1	..	23
..	..	..	..	..	..	314	113	42	89	38	..	24
5	..	..	..	..	..	66	60	8	7	8	1	25
..	..	..	..	..	..	205	23	2	2	5	1	26
..	..	..	..	..	..	67	10	..	..	3	..	27
..	..	..	..	..	..	2	10	..	3	..	2	28
1	..	..	..	..	..	22	5	..	..	1	..	29
5	..	..	..	..	..	24	84	..	3	..	..	30
5	..	..	3	..	..	249	176	32	12	30	7	31
..	..	..	..	..	..	110	11	13	1	12	..	32
..	..	..	..	..	..	58	12	1	5	7	..	33
2	..	..	..	..	..	178	23	..	..	50	1	34
1	..	..	..	14	..	319	29	43	23	115	3	35
..	..	..	..	..	..	9	1	..	..	2	..	36
..	..	..	..	..	..	34	19	..	..	14	..	37

TABLE X — Occupation or means of

Serial No.	Class .. / Sub-class .. / Order .. / Sub-order .. / Group ..	Class B.—Preparation and / Sub-class V.— / Order 39.—Trade / 149.—Dealers in rags, stable refuse, etc.					
	District, City or State.	Total earners (principal occupations).		Total working dependants.		Total following occupation as subsidiary to other.	
		Males.	Females.	Males.	Females.	Males.	Females.
1	2	1146	1147	1148	1149	1150	1151
	Central Provinces and Berar ..	6	22	..	38	2	2
	C. P. British Districts and Berar ..	6	22	..	38	2	2
	C. P. British Districts	2	21	..	38	..	2
	Jubbulpore Division	..	..	..	*1*	..	..
1	Saugor	..	..	..	..	..	..
2	Damoh	..	..	..	..	..	..
3	Jubbulpore	..	..	..	1	..	..
	Jubbulpore City	..	..	..	..	..	..
4	Mandla	..	..	..	..	..	..
5	Seoni	..	..	..	..	..	..
	Nerbudda Division	..	*18*	..	*32*	..	..
6	Narsinghpur	..	1	..	..	..	..
7	Hoshangabad	..	17	..	32	..	..
8	Nimar	..	..	..	..	..	..
9	Betul	..	..	..	..	..	..
10	Chhindwara	..	..	..	..	..	..
	Nagpur Division	*1*	*2*	..	*5*	..	*2*
11	Wardha	..	..	..	..	..	..
12	Nagpur	1	..	..	..	..	..
	Nagpur City	..	..	..	..	..	..
13	Chanda	..	..	..	..	..	1
14	Bhandara	..	..	..	..	..	..
15	Balaghat	..	2	..	5	..	1
	Chhattisgarh Division	*1*	*1*	..	..	..	..
16	Raipur	1	..	..	..	..	..
17	Bilaspur	..	1	..	..	..	..
18	Drug	..	..	..	..	..	..
	Berar	4	1	..	..	2	..
19	Amraoti	..	..	..	..	..	..
20	Akola	..	..	..	..	..	..
21	Buldana	1	..	..	..	2	..
22	Yeotmal	3	1	..	..	..	..
	Central Provinces States	..	..	..	..	..	..
23	Makrai	..	..	..	..	..	..
24	Bastar	..	..	..	..	..	..
25	Kanker	..	..	..	..	..	..
26	Nandgaon	..	..	..	..	..	..
27	Khairagarh	..	..	..	..	..	..
28	Chhuikhadan	..	..	..	..	..	..
29	Kawardha	..	..	..	..	..	..
30	Sakti	..	..	..	..	..	..
31	Raigarh	..	..	..	..	..	..
32	Sarangarh	..	..	..	..	..	..
33	Changbhakar	..	..	..	..	..	..
34	Korea	..	..	..	..	..	..
35	Surguja	..	..	..	..	..	..
36	Udaipur	..	..	..	..	..	..
37	Jashpur	..	..	..	..	..	..

supply of material substances—*contd.*

Trade—*contd.*

of other sorts—*contd.*

150.—General store-keepers and shopkeepers otherwise unspecified.						151.—Itinerant traders, pedlars and hawkers (of other than food, etc.)						Serial No.
Total earners (principal occupations).		Total working dependants.		Total following occupation as subsidiary to other.		Total earners (principal occupations).		Total working dependants.		Total following occupation as subsidiary to other.		
Males.	Females.	Males.	Females.	Males.	Females.	Males.	Females.	Males.	Females.	Males.	Females.	
1152	1153	1154	1155	1156	1157	1158	1159	1160	1161	1162	1163	
13,535	**2,242**	**571**	**363**	**1,766**	**199**	**1,054**	**517**	**31**	**69**	**293**	**18**	
12,135	**1,808**	**440**	**244**	**1,512**	**187**	**824**	**378**	**21**	**43**	**266**	**15**	
7,525	**1,517**	**222**	**179**	**812**	**170**	**821**	**377**	**18**	**43**	**266**	**15**	
598	*33*	*3*	*3*	*34*	*2*	*91*	*51*	*2*	*4*	*5*	*1*	
336	1	..	..	11	..	18	5	2	..	1	..	1
..	..	..	..	..	..	4	3	..	..	..	..	2
251	32	3	3	18	2	64	35	..	4	3	1	3
207	*18*	..	..	*7*	..	*20*	*5*	..	..	..	..	
..	..	..	..	..	..	5	8	..	..	1	..	4
11	..	..	..	5	..	..	..	..	..	..	..	5
208	*6*	*7*	*3*	*47*	..	*70*	*7*	*1*	..	*1*	..	
..	..	..	..	..	..	1	..	..	..	..	..	6
157	..	..	..	36	..	36	..	1	..	..	..	7
2	..	..	..	..	..	29	1	..	..	..	..	8
..	..	..	..	..	..	2	6	..	..	..	..	9
49	6	7	3	11	..	2	..	..	..	1	..	10
4,083	*667*	*87*	*64*	*340*	*47*	*1*	*46*	..	*4*	*2*	..	
382	31	10	13	42	2	..	..	..	..	..	..	11
2,726	435	39	36	156	10	..	..	..	..	..	..	12
1,671	*291*	*25*	*24*	*49*	*3*	..	..	..	..	..	..	
635	146	25	8	103	28	..	..	..	..	..	..	13
340	55	13	7	39	7	..	..	..	..	..	..	14
..	..	..	..	..	..	1	46	..	4	2	..	15
2,636	*811*	*125*	*109*	*391*	*121*	*659*	*273*		*35*	*258*	*14*	
1,243	348	42	52	194	66	257	101	1	16	53	3	16
1,113	386	35	31	170	19	288	108	2	5	192	11	17
280	77	48	26	27	36	114	64	12	14	13	..	18
4,610	**291**	**218**	**65**	**700**	**17**	**3**	**1**	**3**	..	..	..	
1,073	61	33	16	173	4	2	..	3	..	..	..	19
1,523	55	75	10	223	9	..	1	..	..	..	..	20
582	52	69	17	128	4	..	..	..	..	..	..	21
1,432	123	41	22	176	..	1	..	..	..	..	..	22
1,400	**434**	**131**	**119**	**254**	**12**	**230**	**139**	**10**	**26**	**27**	**3**	
..	..	..	..	..	..	1	..	..	..	..	..	23
267	58	41	72	31	..	44	55	1	17	7	..	24
20	26	4	4	5	..	41	34	4	3	3	1	25
168	1	1	..	..	..	34	21	1	2	5	1	26
25	..	..	..	3	..	42	10	..	..	..	..	27
..	2	..	2	..	1	2	8	..	1	..	1	28
..	..	..	..	..	..	14	5	..	..	1	..	29
24	84	..	3	..	..	..	..	..	..	..	..	30
200	173	31	9	20	7	42	3	1	3	6	..	31
109	11	10	1	11	..	1	..	3	..	1	..	32
58	12	1	5	7	..	..	..	..	..	..	..	33
178	23	..	..	50	1	..	..	..	..	..	..	34
318	29	43	23	113	3	1	..	..	..	2	..	35
9	1	..	..	1	..	..	..	..	..	1	..	36
24	14	..	..	13	..	8	3	..	..	1	..	37

TABLE X — Occupation or means of

Serial No.	Class ..	Class B.—Preparation and supply of material substances—*concld.*					
	Sub-class ..	Sub-class V.—Trade—*concld.*					
	Order ..	Order 39.—Trade of other sorts—*concld.*					
	Sub-order ..						
	Group ..	152.—Other trades (including farmers of pounds, tools and markets)					
	District, City, or State.	Total earners (principal occupations).		Total working dependants		Total following occupation as subsidiary to other.	
		Males.	Females.	Males.	Females.	Males.	Females.
1	2	1164	1165	1166	1167	1168	1169
	Central Provinces and Berar ..	**732**	**279**	**14**	**53**	**193**	**10**
	C. P. British Districts and Berar ..	**704**	**276**	**14**	**53**	**188**	**10**
	C. P. British Districts ..	**510**	**242**	**11**	**40**	**127**	**9**
	Jubbulpore Division ..	*159*	*145*	*1*	*3*	*27*	..
1	Saugor	31	57	..	1	2	..
2	Damoh	85	66	..	..	16	..
3	Jubbulpore	32	15	1	2	5	..
	Jubbulpore City	*10*	*14*	..	..	*1*	..
4	Mandla	5	..	..	..	..	..
5	Seoni	6	7	..	..	4	..
	Nerbudda Division	*149*	*26*	*5*	*9*	*63*	*1*
6	Narsinghpur	22	9	..	..	16	..
7	Hoshangabad	21	3	..	..	21	1
8	Nimar	88	4	1	..	14	..
9	Betul	5	10	1	9	3	..
10	Chhindwara	13	..	3	..	9	..
	Nagpur Division	*130*	*49*	*5*	*23*	*22*	*7*
11	Wardha	9	11	..	1	5	3
12	Nagpur	25	7	1	1	..	..
	Nagpur City	*4*	..	..	..	..	..
13	Chanda	5	..	..	..	6	..
14	Bhandara	10	..	..	..	3	..
15	Balaghat	81	31	4	21	8	4
	Chhattisgarh Division	*72*	*22*	..	*5*	*15*	*1*
16	Raipur	31	20	..	5	6	1
17	Bilaspur	24	2	..	..	9	..
18	Drug	17	..	..	..	..	..
	Berar	**194**	**34**	**3**	**13**	**61**	**1**
19	Amraoti	31	6	1	8	24	..
20	Akola	56	4	1	..	19	..
21	Buldana	22	..	..	..	9	1
22	Yeotmal	85	24	1	5	9	..
	Central Provinces States	**28**	**3**	..	..	**5**	..
23	Makrai	..	..	..	..	1	..
24	Bastar	3	..	..	..	..	..
25	Kanker	5	..	..	..	..	..
26	Nandgaon	3	1	..	..	..	..
27	Khairagarh	..	..	..	..	..	..
28	Chhuikhadan	..	..	..	..	..	..
29	Kawardha	8	..	..	..	..	..
30	Sakti	..	..	..	..	..	..
31	Raigarh	7	..	..	..	4	..
32	Sarangarh	..	..	..	..	..	..
33	Changbhakar	..	..	..	..	..	..
34	Korea	..	..	..	..	..	..
35	Surguja	..	..	..	..	..	..
36	Udaipur	..	..	..	..	..	..
37	Jashpur	2	2	..	..	..	..

Class C.—Public administration and liberal arts.												
Total class C.						Sub-class VI.—Public Force.						
						Total sub-class VI.						Serial No.
Total earners (principal occupations).		Total working dependants		Total following occupation as subsidiary to other.		Total earners (principal occupations).		Total working dependants.		Total following occupation as subsidiary to other.		
Males.	Females.	Males.	Females.	Males.	Females	Males.	Females.	Males.	Females	Males	Females.	
1170	1171	1172	1173	1174	1175	1176	1177	1178	1179	1180	1181	
152,691	**14,057**	**2,300**	**1,572**	**28,072**	**1,570**	**43,949**	**261**	**344**	**218**	**5,417**	**42**	
141,325	**13,384**	**2,103**	**1,515**	**25,248**	**1,534**	**40,018**	**226**	**329**	**210**	**4,424**	**36**	
105,588	**11,145**	**1,617**	**1,205**	**18,379**	**1,262**	**33,173**	**163**	**304**	**37**	**3,865**	**21**	
24,783	*3,078*	*485*	*415*	*4,594*	*366*	*9,822*	*63*	*13*	*2*	*858*	*5*	
5,571	1,010	54	215	685	191	2,136	10	..	..	74	..	1
2,830	369	59	102	609	58	824	..	1	1	62	1	2
10,207	1,109	175	56	1,698	70	4,388	46	9	1	357	3	3
5,818	*800*	*24*	*11*	*53*	*3*	*2,978*	*32*	.	..	*6*	..	
2,826	129	13	10	1,009	14	1,190	5	1	..	224	1	4
3,349	461	184	32	593	33	1,284	2	2	..	141	..	5
23,948	*2,080*	*532*	*230*	*3,523*	*258*	*8,667*	*14*	*222*	*2*	*548*	..	
2,905	301	22	43	581	78	644	2	3	..	39	..	6
6,062	430	190	36	770	92	2,113	1	27	..	56	..	7
5,146	361	97	37	662	12	1,382	3	1	2	135	..	8
5,213	466	6	68	689	35	3,082	1	2	..	130	..	9
4,622	522	217	46	821	41	1,446	7	189	..	188	..	10
38,332	*3,425*	*301*	*326*	*4,423*	*394*	*8,867*	*47*	*35*	*5*	*847*	*4*	
6,517	376	18	9	649	49	1,536	6	3	..	65	..	11
16,050	1,547	98	114	911	109	3,344	16	12	1	126	..	12
6,699	*766*	*44*	*74*	*122*	*1*	*705*	*5*	..	..	*7*	..	
6,043	786	83	122	1,508	119	1,557	6	15	4	270	3	13
5,812	377	46	28	559	92	1,362	5	4	..	166	1	14
3,910	339	56	53	796	25	1,068	14	1	..	220	..	15
18,525	*2,562*	*299*	*234*	*5,839*	*244*	*5,817*	*39*	*34*	*28*	*1,612*	*12*	
8,330	1,125	103	131	2,396	81	2,375	9	14	11	730	4	16
5,742	738	88	64	2,646	148	1,639	20	6	9	669	3	17
4,453	699	108	39	797	15	1,803	10	14	8	213	5	18
35,737	**2,239**	**486**	**310**	**6,869**	**272**	**6,845**	**63**	**25**	**173**	**559**	**15**	
10,550	860	134	61	2,516	139	1,436	24	9	7	217	2	19
10,207	551	86	35	2,082	*56*	2,111	4	4	..	154	1	20
7,583	319	105	23	1,201	26	1,277	5	..	..	100	..	21
7,397	509	161	191	1,070	51	2,021	30	12	166	88	12	22
11,366	**673**	**197**	**57**	**2,824**	**36**	**3.931**	**35**	**15**	**8**	**993**	**6**	
235	6	..	..	22	..	60	..	..	..	6	..	23
1,344	70	9	5	482	1	330	3	1	..	262	..	24
481	19	17	10	71	7	245	2	5	8	46	..	25
1,403	174	38	1	200	16	473	2	3	..	89	6	26
990	97	17	12	108	1	503	..	..	..	61	..	27
318	23	1	..	37	1	162	7	..	..	11	..	28
576	33	1	..	65	6	321	1	1	..	11	..	29
194	5	21	..	65	..	60	..	..	..	22	..	30
1,288	62	22	22	282	1	560	1	..	..	110	..	31
870	11	21	..	260	..	440	..	..	..	111	..	32
36	..	..	..	17	..	7	..	..	..	5	..	33
882	97	..	..	117	..	54	1	..	..	58	..	34
1,742	31	46	3	583	1	475	18	5	..	89	..	35
309	9	..	.	120	..	72	..	..	..	20	..	36
698	36	4	4	395	2	169	..	..	..	92	..	37

TABLE X

Occupation or means of

Serial No.	Class .. / Sub-class .. / Order .. / Sub-order .. / Group ..	Class C.—Public administration — Sub-class VI.— — Order — Total order 40.					
	District, City, or State.	Total earners (principal occupations).		Total working dependants.		Total following occupation as subsidiary to other.	
		Males.	Females.	Males.	Females.	Males.	Females.
1	2	1182	1183	1184	1185	1186	1187
	Central Provinces and Berar ..	**3,685**	**31**	..	..	**8**	..
	C. P. British Districts and Berar ..	**3,685**	**31**	..	..	**8**	..
	C. P. British Districts ..	**3,676**	**31**	..	..	**8**	..
	Jubbulpore Division	*2,232*	*31*	..	...	*6*	..
1	Saugor	107	..	..	...	1	..
2	Damoh	...	...	..	...	..	..
3	Jubbulpore	2,123	31	..	...	5	..
	Jubbulpore City	*2,104*	*31*	..	..	*5*	..
4	Mandla	2	..	..	..	..	..
5	Seoni	..	..	..	..	..	..
	Nerbudda Division	*524*	..	..	..	*2*	..
6	Narsinghpur	5	..	..	..	1	..
7	Hoshangabad	501	..	..	..	..	..
8	Nimar	12	..	..	..	..	..
9	Betul	3	..	..	..	1	..
10	Chhindwara	3	..	..	..	..	..
	Nagpur Division	*913*	..	..	...	..	..
11	Wardha	...	..	..	..	..	..
12	Nagpur	907	..	..	..	..	..
	Nagpur City	*9*	..	..	..	..	..
13	Chanda	2	..	..	..	..	..
14	Bhandara	3	..	..	..	..	..
15	Balaghat	1	..	..	..	..	..
	Chhattisgarh Division	*7*	..	..	..	..	..
16	Raipur	3	..	..	..	..	..
17	Bilaspur	4	..	..	...	..	..
18	Drug	..	..	..	..	..	..
	Berar	**9**	..	..	..	..	..
19	Amraoti	1	..	..	..	..	..
20	Akola	6	..	..	..	..	..
21	Buldana	..	..	..	..	..	..
22	Yeotmal	2	..	..	..	..	..
	Central Provinces States	..	..	..	..	..	..
23	Makrai	..	..	..	..	..	..
24	Bastar	..	..	..	..	..	..
25	Kanker	..	..	..	..	..	..
26	Nandgaon	..	..	..	..	..	..
27	Khairagarh	..	..	..	..	..	..
28	Chhuikhadan	..	..	..	..	..	..
29	Kawardha	..	..	..	..	..	..
30	Sakti	..	..	..	..	..	..
31	Raigarh	..	..	..	..	..	..
32	Sarangarh	..	..	..	..	..	..
33	Changbhakar	..	..	..	..	..	..
34	Korea	..	..	..	..	..	..
35	Surguja	..	..	..	..	..	..
36	Udaipur	..	..	..	..	..	..
37	Jashpur	..	..	..	..	..	..

and liberal arts—*contd.*

Public Force—*contd.*

40.—Army.

153.—Army (Imperial).						154.—Army (Indian States).						Serial No.
Total earners (principal occupations).		Total working dependants.		Total following occupation as subsidiary to other.		Total earners (principal occupations.)		Total working dependants		Total following occupation as subsidiary to other.		
Males.	Females.	Males.	Females	Males.	Females.	Males.	Females.	Males.	Females.	Males.	Females.	
1188	1189	1190	1191	1192	1193	1194	1195	1196	1197	1198	1199	
3,684	**31**	..	..	**8**	..	**1**	..	..	..	..	..	
3,684	**31**	..	..	**8**	..	**1**	..	..	..	..	..	
3,675	**31**	..	..	**8**	..	**1**	..	..	..	..	..	
2,232	*31*	..	..	*6*	..	..	..	..	..	..	..	
107	..	..	..	1	..	..	..	..	..	..	..	1
..	..	..	..	..	..	..	..	..	..	..	..	2
2,123	31	..	..	5	..	..	..	..	..	..	..	3
2,104	*31*	..	..	*5*	..	..	..	..	..	..	..	
2	..	..	..	..	..	..	..	..	..	..	..	4
..	..	..	..	..	..	..	..	..	..	..	..	5
523	..	..	..	*2*	..	*1*	..	..	..	..	..	
5	..	..	..	1	..	..	..	..	..	..	..	6
500	..	..	..	..	..	1	..	..	..	..	..	7
12	..	..	..	..	..	..	..	..	..	..	..	8
3	..	..	..	1	..	..	..	..	..	..	..	9
3	..	..	..	..	..	..	..	..	..	..	..	10
913	..	..	..	..	..	..	..	..	..	..	..	
..	..	..	..	..	..	..	..	..	..	..	..	11
907	..	..	..	..	..	..	..	..	..	..	..	12
9	..	..	..	..	..	..	..	..	..	..	..	
2	..	..	..	..	..	..	..	..	..	..	..	13
3	..	..	..	..	..	..	..	..	..	..	..	14
1	..	..	..	..	..	..	..	..	..	..	..	15
7	..	..	..	..	..	..	..	..	..	..	..	
3	..	..	..	..	..	..	..	..	..	..	..	16
4	..	..	..	..	..	..	..	..	..	..	..	17
..	..	..	..	..	..	..	..	..	..	..	..	18
9	..	..	..	..	..	..	..	..	..	..	..	
1	..	..	..	..	..	..	..	..	..	..	..	19
6	..	..	..	..	..	..	..	..	..	..	..	20
..	..	..	..	..	..	..	..	..	..	..	..	21
2	..	..	..	..	..	..	..	..	..	..	..	22
..	..	..	..	..	..	..	..	..	..	..	..	
..	..	..	..	..	..	..	..	..	..	..	..	23
..	..	..	..	..	..	..	..	..	..	..	..	24
..	..	..	..	..	..	..	..	..	..	..	..	25
..	..	..	..	..	..	..	..	..	..	..	..	26
..	..	..	..	..	..	..	..	..	..	..	..	27
..	..	..	..	..	..	..	..	..	..	..	..	28
..	..	..	..	..	..	..	..	..	..	..	..	29
..	..	..	..	..	..	..	..	..	..	..	..	30
..	..	..	..	..	..	..	..	..	..	..	..	31
..	..	..	..	..	..	..	..	..	..	..	..	32
..	..	..	..	..	..	..	..	..	..	..	..	33
..	..	..	..	..	..	..	..	..	..	..	..	34
..	..	..	..	..	..	..	..	..	..	..	..	35
..	..	..	..	..	..	..	..	..	..	..	..	36
..	..	..	..	..	..	..	..	..	..	..	..	37

TABLE X — Occupation or means of

Serial No.	Class / Sub-class / Order / Sub-order / Group	Class C.—Public administration, Sub-class VI.—, Order 41.—Navy. Total order 41.						Order 42.— Total order 42.					
	District, City or State.	Total earners (principal occupations). Males.	Total earners (principal occupations). Females.	Total working dependants. Males.	Total working dependants. Females.	Total following occupation as subsidiary to other. Males.	Total following occupation as subsidiary to other. Females.	Total earners (principal occupations). Males.	Total earners (principal occupations). Females.	Total working dependants. Males.	Total working dependants. Females.	Total following occupation as subsidiary to other. Males.	Total following occupation as subsidiary to other. Females.
1	2	1200	1201	1202	1203	1204	1205	1206	1207	1208	1209	1210	1211
	C ntral Provinces and Berar	..	..	..	..	..	..	4	..	..	..	..	..
	C. P. British Districts and Berar.	..	..	..	..	..	..	4	..	..	..	..	..
	C. P. British Districts	..	..	..	..	..	..	4	..	..	..	..	..
	Jubbulpore Division	..	..	..	..	..	..	2	..	..	..	..	..
1	Saugor	..	..	..	..	..	..	..	..	..	..	..	..
2	Damoh	..	..	..	..	..	..	..	..	..	..	..	..
3	Jubbulpore	..	..	..	..	..	..	2	..	..	..	..	..
	Jubbulpore City	..	..	..	..	..	..	..	..	..	..	..	..
4	Mandla	..	..	..	..	..	..	..	..	..	..	..	..
5	Seoni	..	..	..	..	..	..	..	..	..	..	..	..
	Nerbudda Division	..	..	..	..	..	..	2	..	..	..	..	..
6	Narsinghpur	..	..	..	..	..	..	..	..	..	..	..	..
7	Hoshangabad	..	..	..	..	..	..	2	..	..	..	..	..
8	Nimar	..	..	..	..	..	..	..	..	..	..	..	..
9	Betul	..	..	..	..	..	..	..	..	..	..	..	..
10	Chhindwara	..	..	..	..	..	..	..	..	..	..	..	..
	Nagpur Division	..	..	..	..	..	..	..	..	..	..	..	..
11	Wardha	..	..	..	..	..	..	..	..	..	..	..	..
12	Nagpur	..	..	..	..	..	..	..	..	..	..	..	..
	Nagpur City	..	..	..	..	..	..	..	..	..	..	..	..
13	Chanda	..	..	..	..	..	..	..	..	..	..	..	..
14	Bhandara	..	..	..	..	..	..	..	..	..	..	..	..
15	Balaghat	..	..	..	..	..	..	..	..	..	..	..	..
	Chhattisgarh Division	..	..	..	..	..	..	..	..	..	..	..	..
16	Raipur	..	..	..	..	..	..	..	..	..	..	..	..
17	Bilaspur	..	..	..	..	..	..	..	..	..	..	..	..
18	Drug	..	..	..	..	..	..	..	..	..	..	..	..
	Berar	..	..	..	..	..	..	..	..	..	..	..	..
19	Amraoti	..	..	..	..	..	..	..	..	..	..	..	..
20	Akola	..	..	..	..	..	..	..	..	..	..	..	..
21	Buldana	..	..	..	..	..	..	..	..	..	..	..	..
22	Yeotmal	..	..	..	..	..	..	..	..	..	..	..	..
	Central Provinces States	..	..	..	..	..	..	..	..	..	..	..	..
23	Makrai	..	..	..	..	..	..	..	..	..	..	..	..
24	Bastar	..	..	..	..	..	..	..	..	..	..	..	..
25	Kanker	..	..	..	..	..	..	..	..	..	..	..	..
26	Nandgaon	..	..	..	..	..	..	..	..	..	..	..	..
27	Khairagarh	..	..	..	..	..	..	..	..	..	..	..	..
28	Chhuikhadan	..	..	..	..	..	..	..	..	..	..	..	..
29	Kawardha	..	..	..	..	..	..	..	..	..	..	..	..
30	Sakti	..	..	..	..	..	..	..	..	..	..	..	..
31	Raigarh	..	..	..	..	..	..	..	..	..	..	..	..
32	Sarangarh	..	..	..	..	..	..	..	..	..	..	..	..
33	Changbhakar	..	..	..	..	..	..	..	..	..	..	..	..
34	Korea	..	..	..	..	..	..	..	..	..	..	..	..
35	Surguja	..	..	..	..	..	..	..	..	..	..	..	..
36	Udaipur	..	..	..	..	..	..	..	..	..	..	..	..
37	Jashpur	..	..	..	..	..	..	..	..	..	..	..	..

and liberal arts—*contd.*																		
Public Force—*contd.*																		
Air Force.						Order 43.—Police.												Serial No.
						Total order 43.												
156.—Air Force.												157.—Police.						
Total earners (principal occupations).		Total working dependants.		Total following occupation as subsidiary to other.		Total earners (principal occupations.)		Total working dependants.		Total following occupation as subsidiary to other.		Total earners (principal occupations.)		Total working dependants.		Total following occupation as subsidiary to other.		
Males.	Females.	Males.	Females.	Males.	Females.	Males.	Females.	Males	Females.	Males.	Females.	Males.	Females.	Males.	Females.	Males.	Females.	
1212	1213	1214	1215	1216	1217	1218	1219	1220	1221	1222	1223	1224	1225	1226	1227	1228	1229	
4	..	..	..	..	..	40,260	230	344	218	5,409	42	13,327	1	26	2	203	..	
4	..	..	..	..	..	36,329	195	329	210	4,416	36	12,099	1	19	2	160	..	
4	..	..	..	..	..	29,493	132	304	37	3,857	21	10,156	1	18	2	135	..	
2	..	..	..	..	..	7,588	32	13	2	852	5	2,764	..	2	..	49	..	
..	..	..	..	..	..	2,029	10	..	..	73	..	970	..	..	..	..	..	1
..	..	..	..	..	..	824	..	1	1	62	1	237	..	..	..	..	..	2
2	..	..	..	..	..	2,263	15	9	1	352	3	1,051	..	..	..	34	..	3
..	..	..	..	..	..	874	1	..	..	1	..	850	..	..	..	..	..	
..	..	..	..	..	..	1,188	5	1	..	224	1	293	..	..	..	2	..	4
..	..	..	..	..	..	1,284	2	2	..	141	..	213	..	2	..	13	..	5
2	..	..	..	..	..	8,141	14	222	2	546	..	4,023	..	1	2	26	..	
..	..	..	..	..	..	639	2	3	..	38	..	135	..	..	..	2	..	6
2	..	..	..	..	..	1,610	1	27	..	56	..	693	..	1	..	7	..	7
..	..	..	..	..	..	1,370	3	1	2	135	..	419	..	..	2	6	..	8
..	..	..	..	..	..	3,079	1	2	..	129	..	2,301	..	..	..	8	..	9
..	..	..	..	..	..	1,443	7	189	..	188	..	475	..	..	..	3	..	10
..	..	..	..	..	..	7,954	47	35	5	847	4	2,074	1	1	..	31	..	
..	..	..	..	..	..	1,536	6	3	..	65	..	341	..	..	..	..	..	11
..	..	..	..	..	..	2,437	16	12	1	126	..	971	..	..	..	19	..	12
..	..	..	..	..	..	696	5	..	..	7	..	671	..	..	..	5	..	
..	..	..	..	..	..	1,555	6	15	4	270	3	292	..	..	..	1	..	13
..	..	..	..	..	..	1,359	5	4	..	166	1	265	..	1	..	..	..	14
..	..	..	..	..	..	1,067	14	1	..	220	..	205	1	..	..	11	..	15
..	..	..	..	..	..	5,810	39	34	28	1,612	12	1,295	..	14	..	29	..	
..	..	..	..	..	..	2,372	9	14	11	730	4	662	..	13	..	20	..	16
..	..	..	..	..	..	1,635	20	6	9	669	3	320	..	1	..	9	..	17
..	..	..	..	..	..	1,803	10	14	8	213	5	313	..	..	..	..	..	18
..	..	..	..	..	..	6,836	63	25	173	559	15	1,943	..	1	..	25	..	
..	..	..	..	..	..	1,435	24	9	7	217	2	591	..	1	..	4	..	19
..	..	..	..	..	..	2.105	4	4	..	154	1	608	..	..	..	2	..	20
..	..	..	..	..	..	1,277	5	..	..	100	..	361	..	..	..	..	..	21
..	..	..	..	..	..	2,019	30	12	166	88	12	383	..	..	..	19	..	22
..	..	..	..	..	..	3,931	35	15	8	993	6	1,228	..	7	..	43	..	
..	..	..	..	..	..	60	..	..	..	6	..	25	..	..	..	..	..	23
..	..	..	..	..	..	330	3	1	..	262	..	161	..	..	..	..	..	24
..	..	..	..	..	..	245	1	5	8	46	..	59	..	2	..	2	..	25
..	..	..	..	..	..	473	2	3	..	89	6	121	..	..	..	..	..	26
..	..	..	..	..	..	503	1	..	..	61	..	116	..	..	..	..	..	27
..	..	..	..	..	..	162	7	..	..	11	..	41	..	..	..	1	..	28
..	..	..	..	..	..	321	1	1	..	11	..	59	..	..	..	1	..	29
..	..	..	..	..	..	60	..	..	..	22	..	44	..	..	..	..	..	30
..	..	..	..	..	..	560	1	..	..	110	..	133	..	..	..	7	..	31
..	..	..	..	..	..	440	..	..	..	111	..	42	..	..	..	6	..	32
..	..	..	..	..	..	7	..	..	..	5	..	..	..	..	..	..	..	33
..	..	..	..	..	..	54	1	..	..	58	..	12	..	..	..	..	..	34
..	..	..	..	..	..	475	18	5	..	89	..	265	..	5	..	16	..	35
..	..	..	..	..	..	72	..	..	..	20	..	52	..	..	..	1	..	36
..	..	..	..	..	..	169	..	..	..	92	..	98	..	..	..	9	..	37

TABLE X — Occupation or means of

Serial No.	Class ..	Class C.—Public administration					
	Sub-class ..	Sub-class VI.—Public force—*concld.*					
	Order ..	Order 43.—Police—*concld.*					
	Sub-order ..						
	Group ..	158.—Village watchmen.					
	District, City or State.	Total earners (principal occupations).		Total working dependants.		Total following occupation as subsidiary to other.	
		Males.	Females.	Males.	Females.	Males.	Females.
1	2	1230	1231	1232	1233	1234	1235
	Central Provinces and Berar ..	**26,933**	**229**	**318**	**216**	**5,206**	**42**
	C. P. British Districts and Berar ..	**24,230**	**194**	**310**	**208**	**4,256**	**36**
	C. P. British Districts ..	**19,337**	**131**	**286**	**35**	**3,722**	**21**
	Jubbulpore Division ..	*4,824*	*32*	*11*	*2*	*803*	*5*
1	Saugor	1,059	10	..	..	73	..
2	Damoh ..	587	..	1	1	62	1
3	Jubbulpore	1,212	15	9	1	318	3
	Jubbulpore City ..	*24*	*1*	..	..	*1*	..
4	Mandla	895	5	1	..	222	1
5	Seoni	1,071	2	..	..	128	..
	Nerbudda Division ..	*4,118*	*14*	*221*	..	*520*	..
6	Narsinghpur	504	2	3	..	36	..
7	Hoshangabad	917	1	26	..	49	..
8	Nimar	951	3	1	..	129	..
9	Betul	778	1	2	..	121	..
10	Chhindwara	968	7	189	..	185	..
	Nagpur Division	*5,880*	*46*	*34*	*5*	*816*	*4*
11	Wardha	1,195	6	3	..	65	..
12	Nagpur	1,466	16	12	1	107	..
	Nagpur City	*25*	*5*	..	..	*2*	..
13	Chanda	1,263	6	15	4	269	3
14	Bhandara	1,094	5	3	..	166	1
15	Balaghat	862	13	1	..	209	..
	Chhattisgarh Division	*4,515*	*39*	*20*	*28*	*1,583*	*12*
16	Raipur . ..	1,710	9	1	11	710	4
17	Bilaspur	1,315	20	5	9	660	3
18	Drug	1,490	10	14	8	213	5
	Berar	**4,893**	**63**	**24**	**173**	**534**	**15**
19	Amraoti	844	24	8	7	213	2
20	Akola	1,497	4	4	..	152	1
21	Buldana	916	5	..	..	100	..
22	Yeotmal ..	1,636	30	12	166	69	12
	Central Provinces States	**2,703**	**35**	**8**	**8**	**950**	**6**
23	Makrai	35	..	..	..	6	..
24	Bastar	169	3	1	..	262	..
25	Kanker	186	1	3	8	44	..
26	Nandgaon	352	2	3	..	89	6
27	Khairagarh	387	1	..	..	61	..
28	Chhuikhadan	121	7	..	..	10	..
29	Kawardha	262	1	1	..	10	..
30	Sakti	16	..	..	..	22	..
31	Raigarh	427	1	..	..	103	..
32	Sarangarh	398	..	..	..	105	..
33	Changbhakar	7	..	..	..	5	..
34	Korea	42	1	..	..	58	..
35	Surguja	210	18	..	..	73	..
36	Udaipur	20	..	..	..	19	..
37	Jashpur	71	..	..	..	83	..

and liberal arts—*contd.*

Sub-class VII.—Public administration.

Total sub-class VII.						Order 44.—Public administration. Total order 44.						Serial No.
Total earners (principal occupations).		Total working dependants.		Total following occupation as subsidiary to other.		Total earners (principal occupations).		Total working dependants.		Total following occupation as subsidiary to other.		
Males.	Females.	Males.	Females.	Males.	Females.	Males.	Females.	Males.	Females.	Males.	Females.	
1236	1237	1238	1239	1240	1241	1242	1243	1244	1245	1246	1247	
41,813	**2,079**	**352**	**134**	**6,975**	**53**	**41,813**	**2,079**	**352**	**134**	**6,975**	**53**	
38,506	**1,945**	**327**	**134**	**6,584**	**53**	**38,506**	**1,945**	**327**	**134**	**6,584**	**53**	
28,084	**1,678**	**225**	**126**	**3,986**	**39**	**28,084**	**1,678**	**225**	**126**	**3,986**	**39**	
6,019	*690*	*118*	*60*	*953*	*14*	*6,019*	*690*	*118*	*60*	*953*	*14*	
1,320	43	..	1	48	3	1,320	43	..	1	48	3	1
843	45	34	48	196	2	843	45	34	48	196	2	2
2,293	455	4	4	337	3	2,293	455	4	4	337	3	3
1,202	*361*	..	*3*	*7*	..	*1,202*	*361*	..	*3*	*7*	..	
831	43	2	4	271	5	831	43	2	4	271	5	4
732	104	78	3	101	1	732	104	78	3	101	1	5
6,286	*411*	*55*	*57*	*1,064*	*11*	*6,286*	*411*	*55*	*57*	*1,064*	*11*	
905	69	4	15	130	1	905	69	4	15	130	1	6
1,501	98	9	5	215	6	1,501	98	9	5	215	6	7
1,605	74	36	17	246	2	1,605	74	36	17	246	2	8
921	43	..	8	290	1	921	43	..	8	290	1	9
1,354	127	6	12	183	1	1,354	127	6	12	183	1	10
11,257	*513*	*38*	*9*	*797*	*5*	*11,257*	*513*	*38*	*9*	*797*	*5*	
1,159	9	3	..	65	..	1,159	9	3	..	65	..	11
5,813	361	4	5	126	1	5,813	361	4	5	126	1	12
3,514	*315*	*4*	*5*	*25*	..	*3,514*	*315*	*4*	*5*	*25*	..	
1,548	76	5	..	382	..	1,548	76	5	..	382	..	13
1,876	30	3	4	61	..	1,876	30	3	4	61	..	14
861	37	23	..	163	4	861	37	23	..	163	4	15
4,522	*64*	*14*	..	*1,172*	*9*	*4,522*	*64*	*14*	..	*1,172*	*9*	
2,195	24	12	..	616	4	2,195	24	12	..	616	4	16
1,340	32	1	..	404	5	1,340	32	1	..	404	5	17
987	8	1	..	152	..	987	8	1	..	152	..	18
10,422	**267**	**102**	**8**	**2,598**	**14**	**10,422**	**267**	**102**	**8**	**2,598**	**14**	
2,934	32	19	..	798	4	2,934	32	19	..	798	4	19
2,927	135	11	1	814	7	2,927	135	11	1	814	7	20
2,406	44	11	4	461	1	2,406	44	11	4	461	1	21
2,155	56	61	3	525	2	2,155	56	61	3	525	2	22
3,307	**134**	**25**	..	**391**	..	**3,307**	**134**	**25**	..	**391**	..	
132	2	..	..	14	..	132	2	..	..	14	..	23
732	26	7	..	193	..	732	26	7	..	193	..	24
108	..	..	..	4	..	108	..	..	..	4	..	25
356	11	5	..	6	..	356	11	5	..	6	..	26
96	1	..	..	6	..	96	1	..	..	6	..	27
69	1	..	..	3	..	69	1	..	..	3	..	28
31	..	..	..	6	..	31	..	..	..	6	..	29
18	..	..	..	19	..	18	..	..	..	19	..	30
241	6	2	..	6	..	241	6	2	..	6	..	31
111	..	1	..	..	..	111	..	1	..	..	..	32
12	..	..	..	2	..	12	..	..	..	2	..	33
631	80	..	..	31	..	631	80	..	..	31	..	34
578	..	10	..	46	..	578	..	10	..	46	..	35
70	6	..	..	12	..	70	6	..	..	12	..	36
122	1	..	..	43	..	122	1	..	..	43	..	37

TABLE X — Occupation or means of

Serial No.	Class .. / Sub-class .. / Order .. / Sub-order .. / Group ..	Class C.—Public administration / Sub-class VII.— / Order 44.— / 159.—Service of the State.					
	District, City or State.	Total earners (principal occupations).		Total working dependants.		Total following occupation as subsidiary to other.	
		Males.	Females.	Males.	Females.	Males.	Females.
1	2	1248	1249	1250	1251	1252	1253
	Central Provinces and Berar ..	**24,076**	**384**	**171**	**57**	**1,085**	**10**
	C. P. British Districts and Berar ..	**23,942**	**382**	**171**	**57**	**1,071**	**10**
	C. P. British Districts ..	**18,962**	**326**	**112**	**57**	**769**	**9**
	Jubbulpore Division	*4,435*	*171*	*97*	*54*	*243*	*5*
1	Saugor	936	12	..	..	22	3
2	Damoh	715	45	34	48	153	..
3	Jubbulpore	1,614	75	2	2	47	1
	Jubbulpore City	*717*	*52*	..	*1*	*3*	..
4	Mandla	626	6	2	1	18	..
5	Seoni	544	33	59	3	3	1
	Nerbudda Division	*4,282*	*35*	*3*	*1*	*187*	*2*
6	Narsinghpur	753	14	..	1	88	1
7	Hoshangabad ..	1,045	5	1	..	23	..
8	Nimar	1,113	9	2	..	52	1
9	Betul	653	3	..	..	11	..
10	Chhindwara	718	4	..	..	13	..
	Nagpur Division	*7,928*	*98*	*10*	*2*	*148*	*1*
11	Wardha	564	2	1	..	6	..
12	Nagpur	4,342	60	1	2	39	..
	Nagpur City	*2,660*	*55*	*1*	*2*	*11*	..
13	Chanda	1,032	23	1	..	51	..
14	Bhandara	1,499	7	2	..	22	..
15	Balaghat ..	491	6	5	..	30	1
	Chhattisgarh Division	*2,317*	*22*	*2*	..	*191*	*1*
16	Raipur	1,013	4	..	..	91	..
17	Bilaspur	854	13	1	..	35	1
18	Drug	450	5	1	..	65	..
	Berar	**4,980**	**56**	**59**	..	**302**	**1**
19	Amraoti	1,495	16	6	..	48	..
20	Akola	1,330	17	2	..	125	..
21	Buldana	1,159	7	2	..	59	1
22	Yeotmal	996	16	49	..	70	..
	Central Provinces States	**134**	**2**	..	..	**14**	..
23	Makrai	116	2	..	..	14	..
24	Bastar	5	..	..	..	..	..
25	Kanker	..	..	..	..	..	..
26	Nandgaon	..	..	..	..	..	..
27	Khairagarh	..	..	..	..	..	..
28	Chhuikhadan	..	..	..	..	..	..
29	Kawardha	..	..	..	..	..	..
30	Sakti	8	..	..	..	..	..
31	Raigarh	..	..	..	..	..	..
32	Sarangarh	5	..	..	..	..	..
33	Changbhakar	..	..	..	..	..	..
34	Korea	..	..	..	..	..	..
35	Surguja	..	..	..	..	..	..
36	Udaipur	..	..	..	..	..	..
37	Jashpur	..	..	..	..	..	..

Livelihood—General Distribution—*contd.* **TABLE X**

and liberal arts—*contd.*

Public administration—*contd.*

Public administration—*contd*

160.—Service of Indian and Foreign States.						161.—Municipal and other local (not village) service.						Serial No.
Total earners (principal occupations).		Total working dependants.		Total following occupation as subsidiary to other.		Total earners (principal occupations).		Total working dependants.		Total following occupation as subsidiary to other.		
Males.	Females.	Males.	Females.	Males.	Females.	Males.	Females.	Males.	Females	Males.	Females.	
1254	1255	1256	1257	1258	1259	1260	1261	1262	1263	1264	1265	
2,769	110	24	..	108	..	7,280	1,553	79	73	235	24	
217	10	..	..	6	..	7,132	1,521	79	73	229	24	
216	10	..	..	6	..	5,860	1,332	71	68	170	24	
1	2	..	..	4	..	1,499	514	1	6	32	8	
1	..	..	..	4	..	362	31	..	1	4	..	1
..	..	..	..	..	..	119	..	..	..	9	2	2
..	2	..	..	..	..	649	375	1	2	12	1	3
..	2	..	..	..	..	476	304	..	2	3	..	
..	..	..	..	..	..	193	37	..	3	5	5	4
..	..	..	..	..	..	176	71	..	..	2	—	5
8	..	..	..	..	..	1,574	375	48	56	63	8	
4	..	..	..	..	..	132	55	2	14	7	..	6
3	..	..	..	..	..	371	93	8	5	18	6	7
1	..	..	..	..	..	369	64	33	17	14	..	8
..	..	..	..	..	..	199	40	..	8	3	1	9
..	..	..	..	..	..	503	123	5	12	21	1	10
55	3	..	..	..	..	2,243	407	22	6	69	4	
..	..	..	..	..	..	338	7	..	..	10	..	11
49	3	..	..	..	..	1,152	298	3	3	17	1	12
19	3	..	..	..	..	817	257	3	3	14	..	
2	..	..	..	..	..	270	53	2	..	28	..	13
..	..	..	..	..	..	188	18	..	3	4	..	14
4	..	..	..	..	..	295	31	17	..	10	3	15
152	5	..	..	2	..	544	36	..	..	6	4	
131	..	..	..	1	..	346	19	..	..	3	2	16
20	5	..	..	1	..	90	14	..	..	2	2	17
1	..	..	..	..	..	108	3	..	..	1	..	18
1	..	..	..	..	..	1,272	189	8	5	59	..	
..	..	..	..	..	..	361	10	3	..	23	..	19
..	..	..	..	..	..	434	111	1	..	18	..	20
1	..	..	..	..	..	258	37	4	3	13	..	21
..	..	..	..	..	..	219	31	..	2	5	..	22
2,552	100	24	..	102	..	148	32	..	..	6	..	
9	..	..	..	..	..	3	..	..	..	..	..	23
593	5	7	..	12	..	19	21	..	..	..	..	24
79	..	..	..	1	..	13	..	..	..	3	..	25
227	3	5	..	3	..	45	8	..	..	3	..	26
36	1	..	..	..	..	..	..	..	..	..	..	27
46	1	..	..	..	..	2	..	..	..	..	..	28
8	..	..	..	..	..	..	..	..	..	..	..	29
1	..	..	..	..	..	..	..	..	..	..	..	30
121	3	2	..	1	..	62	3	..	..	..	..	31
100	..	1	..	..	..	..	..	..	..	..	..	32
12	..	..	..	2	..	..	..	..	..	..	..	33
625	80	..	..	31	..	..	..	..	..	..	..	34
569	..	9	..	45	..	..	..	..	..	..	..	35
43	6	..	..	..	..	1	..	..	..	..	..	36
83	1	..	..	7	..	3	..	..	..	..	..	37

TABLE X — Occupation or means of

Serial No.	District, City or State	Total earners (principal occupations) Males	Total earners (principal occupations) Females	Total working dependants Males	Total working dependants Females	Total following occupation as subsidiary to other Males	Total following occupation as subsidiary to other Females
	Class ..	Class C.—Public administration					
	Sub-class ..	Sub-class VII.—Public administration—*concld.*					
	Order ..	Order 44.—Public administration—*concld.*					
	Sub-order						
	Group ..	162.—Village officials and servants other than watchmen					
1	2	1266	1267	1268	1269	1270	1271
	Central Provinces and Berar ..	**7,688**	**32**	**78**	**4**	**5,547**	**19**
	C. P. British Districts and Berar ..	**7,215**	**32**	**77**	**4**	**5,278**	**19**
	C. P. British Districts ..	**3,046**	**10**	**42**	**1**	**3,041**	**6**
	Jubbulpore Division ..	*84*	*3*	*20*	..	*674*	*1*
1	Saugor	21	..	..	..	18	..
2	Damoh	9	..	..	..	34	..
3	Jubbulpore	30	3	1	..	278	1
	Jubbulpore City	*9*	*3*	..	..	*1*	..
4	Mandla	12	..	..	..	248	..
5	Seoni	12	..	19	..	96	..
	Nerbudda Division	*422*	*1*	*4*	..	*814*	*1*
6	Narsinghpur	20	..	2	..	35	..
7	Hoshangabad	81	..	..	..	174	..
8	Nimar	120	1	1	..	180	1
9	Betul	68	..	..	..	276	..
10	Chhindwara	133	..	1	..	149	..
	Nagpur Division	*1,031*	*5*	*6*	*1*	*580*	..
11	Wardha	257	..	2	..	49	..
12	Nagpur	270	..	..	..	70	..
	Nagpur City	*18*	..	..	..	..	..
13	Chanda	244	..	2	..	303	..
14	Bhandara	189	5	1	1	35	..
15	Balaghat	71	..	1	..	123	..
	Chhattisgarh Division	*1,509*	*1*	*12*	..	*973*	*4*
16	Raipur .	705	1	12	..	521	2
17	Bilaspur .. .	376	..	..	..	366	2
18	Drug	428	..	..	..	86	..
	Berar .. .	**4,169**	**22**	**35**	**3**	**2,237**	**13**
19	Amraoti	1,078	6	10	..	727	4
20	Akola	1,163	7	8	1	671	7
21	Buldana	988	..	5	1	389	..
22	Yeotmal	940	9	12	1	450	2
	Central Provinces States	**473**	..	**1**	..	**269**	..
23	Makrai	4	..	..	..	..	..
24	Bastar	115	..	..	..	181	..
25	Kanker	16	..	..	..	..	..
26	Nandgaon	84	..	..	..	..	..
27	Khairagarh	60	..	..	..	6	..
28	Chhuikhadan	21	..	..	..	3	..
29	Kawardha	23	..	..	..	6	..
30	Sakti	9	..	..	..	19	..
31	Raigarh	58	..	..	..	5	..
32	Sarangarh ..	6	..	..	..	..	..
33	Changbhakar . ..	..	..	..	..	..	..
34	Korea . ..	6	..	..	..	..	..
35	Surguja .. .	9	..	1	..	1	..
36	Udaipur .. .	26	..	..	..	12	..
37	Jashpur . ..	36	..	..	..	36	..

Livelihood—General Distribution—*contd.*

and liberal arts—*contd.*

Sub-class VIII.—Professions and liberal arts.

Total Sub-class VIII.						Order 45.—Religion. Total order 45.						Serial No.
Total earners (principal occupations).		Total working dependants.		Total following occupation as subsidiary to other.		Total earners (principal occupations).		Total working dependants.		Total following occupation as subsidiary to other.		
Males.	Females.	Males.	Females.	Males.	Females.	Males	Females	Males.	Females.	Males.	Females.	
1272	1273	1274	1275	1276	1277	1278	1279	1280	1281	1282	1283	
66,929	**11,717**	**1,604**	**1,220**	**15,680**	**1,475**	**21,593**	**1,947**	**744**	**237**	**5,523**	**160**	
62,801	**11,213**	**1,447**	**1,171**	**14,2+0**	**1,445**	**20,213**	**1,858**	**685**	**210**	**5,001**	**150**	
44,331	**9,304**	**1,086**	**1,042**	**10,528**	**1,202**	**13,807**	**1,403**	**477**	**166**	**4,100**	**134**	
8,942	*2,325*	*354*	*353*	*2,785*	*347*	*3,198*	*203*	*81*	*25*	*1,366*	*19*	
2,115	957	54	214	563	188	1,000	57	31	7	265	4	1
1,163	324	24	53	351	55	640	15	15	1	233	1	2
3,526	608	162	51	1,004	64	1,079	96	28	8	708	13	3
1,638	*407*	*24*	*8*	*40*	*3*	*374*	*60*	*6*	*1*	*13*	*1*	
805	81	10	6	514	8	204	15	1	6	61	..	4
1,333	355	104	29	351	32	275	20	6	5	99	1	5
8,995	*1,655*	*255*	*171*	*1,911*	*247*	*2,587*	*258*	*160*	*8*	*493*	*22*	
1,356	230	15	28	412	77	682	61	11	1	208	6	6
2,448	331	154	31	499	86	934	32	129	3	139	5	7
2,159	284	60	18	281	10	507	70	15	3	48	..	8
1,210	422	4	60	269	34	184	50	..	1	38	11	9
1,822	388	22	34	450	40	280	45	5	..	60	..	10
18,208	*2,865*	*228*	*312*	*2,779*	*385*	*5,237*	*536*	*96*	*67*	*745*	*39*	
3,822	361	12	9	519	49	1,049	104	10	..	151	7	11
6,893	1,170	82	108	659	108	1,895	74	29	43	180	5	12
2,480	*446*	*40*	*69*	*90*	*1*	*777*	*25*	*10*	*31*	*18*	..	
2,938	704	63	118	856	116	1,416	326	37	20	185	22	13
2,574	342	39	24	332	91	534	23	19	..	89	5	14
1,981	288	32	53	413	21	343	9	1	4	140	..	15
8,186	*2,459*	*251*	*206*	*3,055*	*223*	*2,785*	*406*	*140*	*66*	*1,496*	*54*	
3,760	1,092	77	120	1,050	73	1,245	193	27	36	432	7	16
2,763	686	81	55	1,573	140	1,046	161	40	28	813	45	17
1,663	681	93	31	432	10	494	52	73	2	251	2	18
18,470	**1,909**	**359**	**129**	**3,712**	**243**	**6,406**	**455**	**208**	**44**	**901**	**16**	
6,180	804	106	54	1,501	133	1,707	168	64	22	274	9	19
5,169	412	71	34	1,114	48	1,845	114	44	4	179	2	20
3,900	270	94	19	640	25	1,744	34	54	16	306	3	21
3,221	423	88	22	457	37	1,110	139	46	2	142	2	22
4,128	**504**	**157**	**49**	**1,440**	**30**	**1,380**	**89**	**59**	**27**	**522**	**10**	
43	4	..	..	2	..	17	..	..	..	1	..	23
282	41	1	5	27	1	74	13	..	3	20	..	24
128	18	12	2	21	7	35	4	11	2	9	7	25
574	161	30	1	105	10	173	30	4	1	66	1	26
391	95	17	12	41	1	132	5	3	..	27	1	27
87	15	1	..	23	1	14	..	1	..	19	1	28
224	32	..	..	48	6	127	10	..	..	40	..	29
116	5	21	..	24	..	59	2	..	..	..	..	30
487	55	20	22	166	1	204	3	15	18	103	..	31
319	11	20	..	149	..	99	..	18	..	85	..	32
17	..	..	..	10	..	8	..	..	..	3	..	33
197	16	..	..	28	..	85	..	..	..	7	..	34
689	13	31	3	448	1	104	..	7	..	35	..	35
167	3	..	..	88	..	71	2	..	..	8	..	36
407	35	4	4	260	2	178	20	..	3	99	..	37

TABLE X

Occupation or means of

Serial No.	Class .. / Sub-class .. / Order .. / Sub-order .. / Group ..	Class C.—Public administration; Sub-class VIII.—Professions; Order 45.—; 163.—Priests, ministers, etc.					
	District, City or State.	Total earners (principal occupations).		Total working dependants.		Total following occupation as subsidiary to other.	
		Males.	Females.	Males.	Females.	Males.	Females.
1	2	1284	1285	1286	1287	1288	1289
	Central Provinces and Berar ..	**13,212**	**1,075**	**353**	**77**	**2,725**	**55**
	C. P. British Districts and Berar ..	**13,106**	**1,054**	**353**	**74**	**2,668**	**55**
	C. P. British Districts ..	**7,742**	**691**	**178**	**40**	**1,892**	**44**
	Jubbulpore Division ..	*2,033*	*86*	*54*	*7*	*1,083*	*10*
1	Saugor	690	30	20	..	227	2
2	Damoh	462	..	7	..	189	..
3	Jubbulpore ..	639	39	21	1	600	8
	Jubbulpore City	*226*	*21*	*2*	*1*	*11*	*1*
4	Mandla	115	11	..	6	19	..
5	Seoni	127	6	6	..	48	..
	Nerbudda Division	*1,268*	*44*	*48*	*1*	*286*	*2*
6	Narsinghpur ..	375	13	5	..	124	1
7	Hoshangabad ..	541	15	29	..	72	..
8	Nimar	104	1	9	..	11	..
9	Betul	82	11	..	1	26	1
10	Chhindwara ..	166	4	5	..	53	..
	Nagpur Division	*4,254*	*473*	*75*	*27*	*497*	*28*
11	Wardha	906	94	9	..	117	2
12	Nagpur	1,496	53	18	5	143	5
	Nagpur City	*659*	*13*	*2*	*1*	*13*	..
13	Chanda	1,308	308	36	19	133	21
14	Bhandara	342	11	12	..	33	..
15	Balaghat	202	7	..	3	71	..
	Chhattisgarh Division	*187*	*88*	*1*	*5*	*26*	*4*
16	Raipur	99	28	..	3	22	3
17	Bilaspur	38	33	..	..	1	..
18	Drug	50	27	1	2	3	1
	Berar .. .	**5,364**	**363**	**175**	**34**	**776**	**11**
19	Amraoti	1,264	129	48	15	223	7
20	Akola	1,514	84	39	1	132	1
21	Buldana	1,616	22	49	16	286	2
22	Yeotmal	970	128	39	2	135	1
	Central Provinces States	**106**	**21**	..	**3**	**57**	..
23	Makrai	10	..	..	..	..	..
24	Bastar	32	12	..	3	1	..
25	Kanker	..	..	..	..	..	..
26	Nandgaon	8	9	..	..	..	..
27	Khairagarh	..	..	..	..	..	..
28	Chhuikhadan ..	..	..	..	..	..	..
29	Kawardha	..	..	..	..	..	..
30	Sakti ..	20	..	..	..	..	..
31	Raigarh	..	..	..	..	..	..
32	Sarangarh	..	..	..	..	..	..
33	Changbhakar	..	..	..	..	..	..
34	Korea	..	..	..	..	..	..
35	Surguja	..	..	..	..	..	..
36	Udaipur	..	..	..	..	..	..
37	Jashpur	36	..	..	..	56	..

Livelihood—General Distribution—*contd.*

TABLE X

and liberal arts—*contd.*

and liberal arts—*contd.*

Religion—*contd.*

164.—Monks, nuns, religious mendicants.						165.—Other religious workers.						Serial No.
Total earners (principal occupations).		Total working dependants.		Total following occupation as subsidiary to other.		Total earners (principal occupations).		Total working dependants.		Total following occupation as subsidiary to other.		
Males.	Females.	Males.	Females.	Males.	Females.	Males.	Females.	Males.	Females.	Males.	Females.	
1290	1291	1292	1293	1294	1295	1296	1297	1298	1299	1300	1301	
2,004	**423**	**31**	**40**	**328**	**40**	**4,010**	**294**	**202**	**81**	**1,865**	**46**	
1,628	**372**	**28**	**37**	**267**	**40**	**3,171**	**280**	**152**	**61**	**1,476**	**36**	
1,525	**347**	**25**	**35**	**256**	**40**	**2,645**	**231**	**132**	**53**	**1,395**	**33**	
217	*10*	*2*	*3*	*18*	*1*	*182*	*45*	*1*	*6*	*16*	*1*	
13	1	..	..	..	..	33	18	..	2	..	..	1
1	..	..	..	..	..	22	8	..	..	5	..	2
169	2	2	3	10	1	91	17	1	1	5	..	3
54	*2*	*1*	..	..	..	*53*	*9*	..	..	*1*	..	
19	1	..	..	6	..	10	..	..	..	1	..	4
15	6	..	..	2	..	26	2	..	3	5	1	5
600	*130*	*8*	*4*	*47*	*17*	*211*	*54*	*4*	*1*	*40*	..	
72	34	..	1	..	4	26	8	3	..	2	..	6
187	10	4	1	25	3	54	..	..	..	7	..	7
266	49	4	2	13	..	99	14	1	1	24	..	8
70	31	..	..	9	10	6	2	..	..	1	..	9
5	6	..	..	..	..	26	30	..	..	6	..	10
48	*10*	*1*	..	*16*	*3*	*360*	*16*	*4*	*13*	*62*	*1*	
1	2	..	..	..	..	51	4	..	..	17	1	11
23	..	..	..	6	..	189	9	4	13	27	..	12
11	..	..	..	..	..	*29*	*1*	*2*	*13*	*3*	..	
10	2	..	..	8	1	41	3	..	..	7	..	13
11	6	1	..	2	2	74	..	..	..	10	..	14
3	..	..	..	..	..	5	..	..	..	1	..	15
660	*197*	*14*	*28*	*175*	*19*	*1,892*	*116*	*123*	*33*	*1,277*	*31*	
309	101	3	1	6	1	813	62	24	32	404	3	16
311	80	8	27	156	18	687	46	32	1	655	27	17
40	16	3	..	13	..	392	8	67	..	218	1	18
103	**25**	**3**	**2**	**11**	..	**526**	**49**	**20**	**8**	**81**	**3**	
27	..	..	..	..	..	333	31	15	7	47	2	19
53	21	2	2	11	..	109	7	1	1	27	1	20
4	..	..	..	..	..	15	8	..	..	2	..	21
19	4	1	..	..	..	69	3	4	..	5	..	22
376	**51**	**3**	**3**	**61**	..	**839**	**14**	**50**	**20**	**389**	**10**	
1	..	..	..	..	..	..	..	..	..	..	..	23
..	..	..	..	..	..	40	..	..	..	18	..	24
22	..	1	..	2	..	7	4	10	2	5	7	25
48	19	..	..	4	..	99	..	4	..	62	1	26
19	..	..	..	9	..	113	5	3	..	18	1	27
..	..	..	..	..	..	13	..	..	..	19	1	28
79	8	..	..	18	..	48	2	..	..	21	..	29
39	2	..	..	..	..	..	..	..	..	..	..	30
3	..	2	..	..	..	199	3	13	18	103	..	31
13	..	..	..	12	..	86	..	18	..	73	..	32
..	..	..	..	..	..	8	..	..	..	3	..	33
27	..	..	..	1	..	57	..	..	..	6	..	34
17	..	..	..	4	..	85	..	2	..	22	..	35
47	2	..	..	5	..	6	..	..	..	3	..	36
61	20	..	3	6	..	78	..	..	..	36	..	37

TABLE X Occupation or means of

Serial No.	Class ..	Class C.—Public administration					
	Sub-class ..	Sub-class VIII.—Professions					
	Order ..	Order 45.—Religion—*concld.*					
	Sub-order ..						
	Group ..	166.—Servants in religious edifices, burial and burning grounds, pilgrim conductors, circumciers, etc.					
	District, City or State.	Total earners (principal occupations).		Total working dependants.		Total following occupation as subsidiary to other.	
		Males.	Females.	Males.	Females.	Males.	Females.
1	2	1302	1303	1304	1305	1306	1307
	Central Provinces and Berar ..	**2,367**	**155**	**158**	**39**	**605**	**19**
	C. P. British Districts and Berar ..	**2,308**	**152**	**152**	**38**	**590**	**19**
	C. P. British Districts	**1,895**	**134**	**142**	**38**	**557**	**17**
	Jubbulpore Division	*766*	*62*	*24*	*9*	*249*	*7*
1	Saugor	264	8	11	5	38	2
2	Damoh	155	7	8	1	39	1
3	Jubbulpore	180	38	4	3	93	4
	Jubbulpore City	*41*	*28*	*3*	..	*1*	..
4	Mandla	60	3	1	..	35	..
5	Seoni	107	6	..	..	44	..
	Nerbudda Division	*508*	*30*	*100*	*2*	*120*	*3*
6	Narsinghpur	209	6	3	..	82	1
7	Hoshangabad	152	7	96	2	35	2
8	Nimar	38	6	1	..	..	..
9	Betul	26	6	..	..	2	..
10	Chhindwara	83	5	..	..	1	..
	Nagpur Division . ..	*575*	*37*	*16*	*27*	*170*	*7*
11	Wardha	91	4	1	..	17	4
12	Nagpur	187	12	7	25	4	..
	Nagpur City	*78*	*11*	*6*	*17*	*2*	..
13	Chanda . ..	57	13	1	1	37	..
14	Bhandara	107	6	6	..	44	3
15	Balaghat	133	2	1	1	68	..
	Chhattisgarh Division	*46*	*5*	*2*	..	*18*	..
16	Raipur	24	2	..	..	..	..
17	Bilaspur	10	2	..	..	1	..
18	Drug	12	1	2	..	17	..
	Berar	**413**	**18**	**10**	..	**33**	**2**
19	Amraoti	83	8	1	..	4	..
20	Akola	169	2	2	..	9	..
21	Buldana	109	4	5	..	18	1
22	Yeotmal	52	4	2	..	2	1
	Central Provinces States	**59**	**3**	**6**	**1**	**15**	..
23	Makrai	6	..	..	..	1	..
24	Bastar	2	1	..	..	1	..
25	Kanker	6	..	..	..	2	..
26	Nandgaon	18	2	..	1	..	..
27	Khairagarh	..	..	..	..	..	..
28	Chhuikhadan	1	..	1	..	..	..
29	Kawardha	..	..	..	..	1	..
30	Sakti	..	..	..	..	..	..
31	Raigarh	2	..	..	..	..	..
32	Sarangarh	..	..	..	..	..	..
33	Changbhakar	..	..	..	..	..	..
34	Korea	1	..	..	..	..	..
35	Surguja	2	..	5	..	9	..
36	Udaipur	18	..	..	..	..	..
37	Jashpur	3	..	..	..	1	..

and liberal arts—*contd.*

and liberal arts—*contd.*

Order 46.—Law.

Total order 46.						167.—Lawyers of all kinds, including quazis, law-agents and mukhtiars.						Serial No.
Total earners (principal occupations).		Total working dependants.		Total following occupation as subsidiary to other.		Total earners (principal occupations).		Total working dependants.		Total following occupation as subsidiary to other.		
Males	Females	Males	Females.	Males	Females.	Males	Females.	Males.	Females.	Males.	Females.	
1308	1309	1310	1311	1312	1313	1314	1315	1316	1317	1318	1319	
4,478	**68**	**73**	**72**	**742**	**14**	**2,691**	**67**	**47**	**70**	**531**	**13**	
4,357	**68**	**61**	**72**	**724**	**14**	**2,617**	**67**	**47**	**70**	**521**	**13**	
3,224	**38**	**49**	**72**	**604**	**11**	**2,095**	**37**	**43**	**70**	**498**	**11**	
680	..	*2*	..	*167*	*1*	*440*	..	*2*	..	*158*	*1*	
120	..	..	..	5	..	81	..	..	..	4	..	1
29	..	..	..	3	..	16	..	..	..	3	..	2
375	..	1	.	39	1	237	..	1	..	38	1	3
157	..	..	..	*1*	..	*47*	..	..	..	*1*	..	
64	..	1	..	92	..	33	..	1	..	87	..	4
92	..	..	..	28	..	73	..	..	..	26	..	5
1,170	*8*	*41*	..	*257*	..	*861*	*7*	*40*	..	*237*	..	
150	1	..	..	67	..	122	1	..	..	60	..	6
216	2	14	..	17	.	134	1	14	..	12	..	7
297	2	26	..	15	.	193	2	26	..	13	..	8
291	3	..	.	100	..	262	3	.	..	99	..	9
216	..	1	..	58	..	150	..	..	..	53	..	10
857	*30*	*3*	*72*	*89*	*10*	*480*	*30*	..	*70*	*41*	*10*	
164	..	..	2	8	..	78	..	..	..	2	..	11
309	1	3	.	38	..	187	1	..	..	10	..	12
208	*1*	*3*	..	*5*	..	*129*	*1*	..	..	*4*	..	
61	29	..	70	1	10	22	29	.	70	..	10	13
121	..	..	..	4	..	46	.	..	..	1	..	14
202	..	..	..	38	..	147	..	..	..	28	..	15
517	..	*3*	..	*91*	..	*314*	..	*1*	..	*62*	..	
210	..	1	..	39	..	100	..	..	..	19	..	16
206	..	2	..	37	..	148	..	1	..	31	..	17
101	..	..	..	15	..	66	..	..	..	12	..	18
1,133	**30**	**12**	..	**120**	**3**	**522**	**30**	**4**	..	**23**	**2**	
351	29	5	..	38	1	164	29	3	..	4	..	19
380	1	1	..	35	..	178	1	1	..	4	..	20
249	..	4	..	29	2	107	..	..	..	5	2	21
153	..	2	..	18	..	73	..	..	..	10	..	22
121	..	**12**	..	**18**	..	**74**	..	..	..	**10**	..	
4	..	..	..	..	..	4	..	..	..	..	..	23
12	..	..	..	1	..	8	..	..	..	..	..	24
1	..	..	..	..	..	..	..	..	..	..	..	25
35	..	..	..	2	..	27	..	..	..	1	..	26
15	..	12	..	..	..	8	..	..	..	..	..	27
7	..	..	..	3	..	3	..	..	..	2	..	28
7	..	..	..	4	..	3	..	..	..	3	..	29
6	..	..	..	..	..	6	..	..	..	..	..	30
26	..	..	..	4	..	11	..	..	..	2	..	31
..	..	..	..	1	..	..	..	..	..	1	..	32
..	..	..	..	..	..	..	..	..	..	..	..	33
3	..	..	..	1	..	..	..	..	..	1	..	34
3	..	..	..	1	..	3	..	..	..	..	..	35
1	..	..	..	1	..	1	..	..	..	..	..	36
1	..	..	..	..	..	..	..	..	..	..	..	37

TABLE X Occupation or means of

Serial No.	Class ..	Class C.—Public administration					
	Sub-class ..	Sub-class VIII.—Professions					
	Order ..	Order 46.—Law—*concld.*					
	Sub-order ..						
	Group ..	168.—Lawyers, clerks, petition-writers, etc.					
	District, City or State.	Total earners (principal occupations).		Total working dependants.		Total following occupation as subsidiary to other.	
		Males.	Females	Males.	Females	Males.	Females.
1	2	1320	1321	1322	1323	1324	1325
	Central Provinces and Berar	**1,787**	**1**	**26**	**2**	**211**	**1**
	C. P. British Districts and Berar ..	**1,740**	**1**	**14**	**2**	**203**	**1**
	C. P. British Districts	**1,129**	**1**	**6**	**2**	**106**	..
	Jubbulpore Division	***240***	..	..	..	***9***	..
1	Saugor	39	..	..	..	1	..
2	Damoh	13	..	..	..	..	..
3	Jubbulpore	138	..	..	..	1	..
	Jubbulpore City	***110***	..	..	..	..	..
4	Mandla	31	..	..	..	5	..
5	Seoni	19	..	..	..	2	..
	Nerbudda Division	***309***	***1***	***1***	..	***20***	.
6	Narsinghpur	28	..	..	..	7	..
7	Hoshangabad	82	1	..	..	5	..
8	Nimar	104	..	..	..	2	..
9	Betul	29	..	..	..	1	..
10	Chhindwara	66	..	1	..	5	..
	Nagpur Division	***377***	..	***3***	***2***	***48***	..
11	Wardha	86	..	..	2	6	..
12	Nagpur	122	..	3	..	28	..
	Nagpur City	***71***	..	***3***	..	***1***	..
13	Chanda	39	..	.	..	1	..
14	Bhandara	75	..	..	..	3	..
15	Balaghat	55	..	..	..	10	..
	Chhattisgarh Division	***203***	..	***2***	..	***29***	..
16	Raipur	110	..	1	..	20	..
17	Bilaspur	58	..	1	..	6	..
18	Drug	35	..	..	..	3	..
	Berar	**611**	..	**8**	..	**97**	**1**
19	Amraoti	187	..	2	..	34	1
20	Akola	202	..	.	..	31	..
21	Buldana	142	..	4	..	24	..
22	Yeotmal	80	..	2	..	8	..
	Central Provinces States	**47**	..	**12**	..	**8**	..
23	Makrai	..	..	..	..	..	..
24	Bastar	4	..	.	..	1	..
25	Kanker	1	..	..	..	..	..
26	Nandgaon	8	..	..	..	1	..
27	Khairagarh ..	7	..	12	..	..	..
28	Chhuikhadan	4	..	..	..	1	..
29	Kawardha	4	..	..	..	1	..
30	Sakti	..	..	..	..	..	..
31	Raigarh	15	..	..	..	2	..
32	Sarangarh	..	..	..	..	..	..
33	Changbhakar	..	..	..	..	..	..
34	Korea	3	..	..	..	..	..
35	Surguja	..	..	..	..	1	..
36	Udaipur ..	.	..	..	..	1	..
37	Jashpur	1	..	..	..	..	..

and liberal arts—*contd.*

and liberal arts—*contd.*

Order 47.—Medicine.

Total order 47.						169.—Registered medical practitioners including oculists.						Serial No.
Total earners (principal occupations).		Total working dependants		Total following occupation as subsidiary to other.		Total earners (principal occupations)		Total working dependants.		Total following occupation as subsidiary to other.		
Males.	Females.	Males.	Females.	Males.	Females	Males	Females	Males.	Females.	Males.	Females.	
1326	1327	1328	1329	1330	1331	1332	1333	1334	1335	1336	1337	
4,989	**6,228**	**39**	**726**	**877**	**1,161**	**968**	**78**	**2**	.	**89**	**1**	
4,699	**5,991**	**38**	**719**	**822**	**1,152**	**901**	**75**	**2**	..	**75**	**1**	
3,655	**5,302**	**29**	**667**	**631**	**967**	**567**	**58**	..	..	**58**	..	
1,374	*1,360*	*19*	*317*	*81*	*312*	*85*	*8*	..	..	*3*	..	
164	586	3	202	28	178	15	3	..	..	1	..	1
85	267	9	52	5	50	1	..	..	..	..	..	2
953	222	7	39	36	48	30	2	..	.	2	..	3
513	*139*	..	*3*	*5*	..	*19*	*1*	..		..	..	
104	11	..	..	7	5	13	1	..	.	.	..	4
68	274	..	24	5	31	26	2	..	..	..	..	5
592	*805*	*2*	*111*	*109*	*211*	*120*	*7*	..	..	*4*	..	
125	84	..	24	28	69	59	..	.	.	1	..	6
180	173	..	26	32	81	17	6	..	..	2	..	7
149	70	2	5	18	8	18	..	..	..	..	..	8
71	212	..	27	14	14	15	1	..	..	1	..	9
67	266	..	29	17	39	11	..	..	..	..	..	10
1,212	*1,732*	*8*	*142*	*359*	*316*	*188*	*30*	..	..	*14*	..	
226	171	..	6	55	35	35	6	..	..	2	..	11
556	806	2	40	81	100	121	18	..	..	10	..	12
311	*236*	..	*16*	*11*	*1*	*49*	*16*	..	..	*1*	..	
208	265	3	24	170	78	10	4	..	..	2	..	13
177	263	2	24	33	83	22	2	..	..	..	..	14
45	227	1	48	20	20	..	..	..	..	..	..	15
477	*1,405*	..	*97*	*82*	*128*	*174*	*13*	..	..	*37*	..	
251	525	..	50	25	47	103	3	..	..	14	..	16
151	335	..	18	53	74	49	9	..	..	22	..	17
75	545	..	29	4	7	22	1	..	..	1	..	18
1,044	**689**	**9**	**52**	**191**	**185**	**334**	**17**	**2**	..	**17**	**1**	
400	368	3	20	100	109	103	6	1	..	1	..	19
327	116	3	16	39	35	132	6	1	..	6	..	20
157	56	..	2	24	16	53	3	..	..	5	..	21
160	149	3	14	28	25	46	2	..	..	5	1	22
290	**237**	**1**	**7**	**55**	**9**	**67**	**3**	..	..	**14**	..	
4	4	..	..	1	..	..	.	..	..	..	..	23
37	14	..	1	1	..	9	..	..	..	..	..	24
16	5	..	..	..	..	6	..	..	..	..	..	25
36	95	..	..	1	1	8	..	..	..	1	..	26
19	57	..	1	1	..	6	..	..	..	..	..	27
7	11	..	..	1	..	1	..	..	..	..	..	28
9	22	..	..	1	6	1	..	..	..	..	..	29
10	2	..	..	..	..	3	..	..	..	..	..	30
65	15	..	4	25	..	14	2	..	..	2	..	31
36	1	1	..	10	..	1	..	..	..	..	..	32
..	..	..	..	1	..	..	..	..	..	..	..	33
5	1	..	..	..	..	1	..	..	..	..	..	34
23	7	..	1	11	..	15	1	..	..	10	..	35
7	1	..	..	..	..	1	..	..	..	..	..	36
16	2	..	..	2	2	1	..	..	..	1	..	37

TABLE X

Occupation or means of

Serial No.	Class ..	Class C.—Public administration					
	Sub-class ..	Sub-class VIII.—Professions					
	Order ..	Order 47.—					
	Sub-order ..						
	Group ..	170.—Other persons practising the healing arts without being registered.					
	District, City or State.	Total earners (principal occupations).		Total working dependants.		Total following occupation as subsidiary to other.	
		Males.	Females.	Males.	Females.	Males.	Females.
1	2	1338	1339	1340	1341	1342	1343
	Central Provinces and Berar ..	**1,987**	**179**	**23**	**14**	**642**	**20**
	C. P. British Districts and Berar ..	**1,896**	**176**	**22**	**13**	**605**	**20**
	C. P. British Districts	**1,420**	**113**	**17**	**8**	**442**	**7**
	Jubbulpore Division	*340*	*34*	*9*	..	*69*	*2*
1	Saugor	97	28	2	..	19	..
2	Damoh	41	2	..	..	5	..
3	Jubbulpore	146	3	7	..	33	1
	Jubbulpore City	*86*	*2*	..	..	*4*	..
4	Mandla	51	..	..	..	7	..
5	Seoni	5	1	..	..	5	1
	Nerbudda Division	*213*	*10*	*2*	..	*84*	..
6	Narsinghpur	34	..	..	..	26	..
7	Hoshangabad	61	..	..	..	20	..
8	Nimar	74	5	2	..	10	..
9	Betul	25	3	..	..	11	..
10	Chhindwara	19	2	..	..	17	..
	Nagpur Division	*740*	*40*	*6*	*8*	*246*	*5*
11	Wardha	131	4	..	1	53	2
12	Nagpur	315	18	2	7	65	2
	Nagpur City	*181*	*7*	..	*6*	*6*	*1*
13	Chanda	156	15	1	..	77	1
14	Bhandara	99	2	2	..	31	..
15	Balaghat	59	1	1	..	20	..
	Chhattisgarh Division	*127*	*29*	..	..	*43*	..
16	Raipur	67	17	..	..	11	..
17	Bilaspur	49	11	..	..	29	..
18	Drug	11	1	..	..	3	..
	Berar	**476**	**63**	**5**	**5**	**163**	**13**
19	Amraoti	230	50	1	2	95	2
20	Akola	119	5	2	1	30	..
21	Buldana	51	4	..	2	15	10
22	Yeotmal	76	4	2	..	23	1
	Central Provinces States	**91**	**3**	**1**	**1**	**37**	..
23	Makrai	2	..	..	..	1	..
24	Bastar	8	3	..	..	1	..
25	Kanker	3	..	..	..	..	..
26	Nandgaon	5	..	..	..	..	..
27	Khairagarh	4	..	..	1	1	..
28	Chhuikhadan	3	..	..	..	1	..
29	Kawardha	5	..	..	..	1	..
30	Sakti	..	..	..	..	..	..
31	Raigarh	29	..	..	..	20	..
32	Sarangarh	31	..	1	..	10	..
33	Changbhakar	..	..	..	..	1	..
34	Korea	..	..	..	..	..	..
35	Surguja	1	..	..	..	..	..
36	Udaipur	..	..	..	..	..	..
37	Jashpur	..	..	..	..	1	..

and liberal arts—*contd.*

and liberal arts—*contd.*

Medicine—*contd.*

171.—Dentists.						172.—Midwives, vaccinators, compounders, nurses, masseurs, etc.						Serial No.
Total earners (principal occupations).		Total working dependants.		Total following occupation as subsidiary to other.		Total earners (principal occupations).		Total working dependants.		Total following occupation as subsidiary to other		
Males.	Females	Males.	Females.	Males.	Females.	Males.	Females.	Males.	Females.	Males.	Females.	
1344	1345	1346	1347	1348	1349	1350	1351	1352	1353	1354	1355	
20	**3**	..	..	**2**	**5**	**1,580**	**5,965**	**13**	**712**	**143**	**1,135**	
20	**3**	..	..	**2**	**5**	**1,458**	**5,734**	**13**	**706**	**139**	**1,126**	
19	**3**	..	..	**?**	**5**	**1,237**	**5,125**	**11**	**659**	**128**	**955**	
6	..	..	..	*1*	*5*	*567*	*1,316*	*10*	*317*	*8*	*305*	
..	..	..	..	1	..	32	553	1	202	7	178	1
1	.	..	..	..	5	42	265	9	52	..	45	2
1	.	..	..	..	..	422	217	..	39	1	47	3
1	..	..	..	..	..	*403*	*136*	..	*3*	*1*	..	
..	..	..	..	..	..	38	10	..	..	..	5	4
4	..	..	..	..	..	33	271	..	24	..	30	5
2	*3*	..	..	..	..	*241*	*784*	..	*111*	*20*	*211*	
..	..	..	..	..	..	32	83	..	24	1	69	6
..	..	..	..	..	..	91	167	..	26	10	81	7
..	..	..	..	..	..	57	65	..	5	8	8	8
..	..	..	..	..	..	28	208	..	27	1	14	9
2	3	..	..	..	..	33	261	..	29	..	39	10
10	..	..	..	*1*	..	*262*	*1,662*	*1*	*134*	*98*	*311*	
8	..	..	..	..	..	51	161	..	5	..	33	11
2	..	..	.	1	.	110	770	..	33	5	98	12
2	..	..	..	*1*	..	*73*	*213*	..	*10*	*3*	..	
..	..	..	..	.	..	39	246	1	24	91	77	13
..	..	..	..	..	..	56	259	..	24	2	83	14
..	..	..	..	..	..	6	226	..	48	.	20	15
1	..	..	..	..	..	*167*	*1,363*	..	*97*	*2*	*128*	
..	..	..	..	..	.	76	505	..	50	..	47	16
..	..	..	..	..	.	52	315	..	18	2	74	17
1	..	..	..	.	..	39	543	..	29	..	7	18
1	..	..	.	..	..	**221**	**609**	**2**	**47**	**11**	**171**	
..	..	..	..	.	.	66	312	1	18	4	107	19
1	..	..	..	..	..	71	105	..	15	3	35	20
..	..	..	.	..	..	51	49	..	..	4	6	21
..	..	..	..	..	..	33	143	1	14	..	23	22
..	..	..	..	..	.	**122**	**231**	..	**6**	**4**	**9**	
..	..	..	..	..	..	2	4	..	..	..	..	23
..	..	..	..	..	..	19	11	..	1	..	..	24
..	..	..	..	..	..	6	5	..	..	..	..	25
..	..	..	.	.	..	21	95	..	..	.	1	26
..	..	.	.	..	..	9	57	..	..	..	..	27
..	..		..	..	..	2	11	..	..	..	..	28
..	..	..	..	..	..	2	22	..	..	..	6	29
..	..	..	..	.	..	7	2	..	..	..	..	30
..	.	..	..	..	..	19	13	..	4	3	..	31
..	..	..	..	..	..	4	1	..	..	..	..	32
..	..	..	..	..	..	..	..	..	..	..	..	33
..	..	..	..	..	..	4	1	..	..	..	..	34
..	..	..	..	..	..	7	6	..	1	1	..	35
..	..	..	..	..	..	6	1	..	..	..	..	36
..	..	..	..	..	..	14	2	..	..	..	2	37

TABLE X — **Occupation or means of**

Serial No.	District, City or State.	Class C.—Public administration / Sub-class VIII.—Professions / Order 47.—Medicine—*concld.* / Group 173.—Veterinary Surgeons. Total earners (principal occupations). Males	Females.	Total working dependants. Males	Females.	Total following occupation as subsidiary to other. Males.	Females.
1	2	1356	1357	1358	1359	1360	1361
	Central Provinces and Berar	**434**	3	1	..	1	..
	C. P. British Districts and Berar	**424**	3	1	..	1	..
	C. P. British Districts	**412**	3	1	..	1	..
	Jubbulpore Division	*376*	*2*	..	..	..	..
1	Saugor	20	2	..	..	..	..
2	Damoh	..	..	..	..	..	..
3	Jubbulpore	354	..	..	..	..	..
	Jubbulpore City	*4*	..	..	..	..	..
4	Mandla	2	..	..	..	..	..
5	Seoni	..	..	..	..	..	..
	Nerbudda Division	*16*	*1*	..	..	*1*	..
6	Narsinghpur	..	1	..	..	..	..
7	Hoshangabad	11	..	..	..	..	..
8	Nimar	..	..	..	..	..	..
9	Betul	3	..	..	..	1	..
10	Chhindwara	2	..	..	..	..	..
	Nagpur Division	*12*	..	*1*	..	..	..
11	Wardha	1	..	..	..	..	..
12	Nagpur	8	..	..	..	..	..
	Nagpur City	*6*	..	..	..	..	..
13	Chanda	3	..	1	..	..	..
14	Bhandara	..	..	..	..	..	..
15	Balaghat	..	..	..	..	..	..
	Chhattisgarh Division	*8*	..	..	..	..	..
16	Raipur	5	..	..	..	..	..
17	Bilaspur	1	..	..	..	..	..
18	Drug	2	..	..	..	..	..
	Berar	**12**	..	..	..	..	..
19	Amraoti	1	..	..	..	..	..
20	Akola	4	..	..	..	..	..
21	Buldana	2	..	..	..	..	..
22	Yeotmal	5	..	..	..	..	..
	Central Provinces States	**10**	..	..	..	..	..
23	Makrai	..	..	..	..	..	..
24	Bastar	1	..	..	..	..	..
25	Kanker	1	..	..	..	..	..
26	Nandgaon	2	..	..	..	..	..
27	Khairagarh	..	..	..	..	..	..
28	Chhuikhadan	1	..	..	..	..	..
29	Kawardha	1	..	..	..	..	..
30	Sakti	..	..	..	..	..	..
31	Raigarh	3	..	..	..	..	..
32	Sarangarh	..	..	..	..	..	..
33	Changbhakar	..	..	..	..	..	..
34	Korea	..	..	..	..	..	..
35	Surguja	..	..	..	..	..	..
36	Udaipur	..	..	..	..	..	..
37	Jashpur	1	..	..	..	..	..

and liberal arts—*contd.*												
and liberal arts—*contd.*												
Order 48.—Instruction.												Serial No.
Total order 48.						174.—Professors and teachers of all kinds.						
Total earners (principal occupations).		Total working dependants.		Total following occupation as subsidiary to other.		Total earners (principal occupations).		Total working dependants.		Total following occupation as subsidiary to other.		
Males.	Females.	Males.	Females.	Males	Females.	Males.	Females.	Males.	Females.	Males.	Females.	
1362	1363	1364	1365	1366	1367	1368	1369	1370	1371	1372	1373	
17,049	**1,839**	**177**	**24**	**806**	**26**	**16,324**	**1,638**	**162**	**21**	**767**	**21**	
15,887	**1,748**	**175**	**24**	**714**	**26**	**15,200**	**1,559**	**160**	**21**	**676**	**21**	
10,717	**1,309**	**137**	**19**	**485**	**20**	**10,111**	**1,162**	**123**	**17**	**450**	**17**	
2,288	*441*	*115*	*6*	*66*	*2*	*2,096*	*392*	*106*	*5*	*65*	*2*	
470	122	8	1	5	..	429	101	8	1	4	..	1
320	17	..	..	4	1	278	12	..	..	4	1	2
806	221	101	4	48	1	715	207	92	3	48	1	3
400	*169*	..	*4*	*3*	*1*	*332*	*158*	..	*3*	*3*	*1*	
292	37	3	..	5	..	275	32	3	..	5	..	4
400	44	3	1	4	..	399	40	3	1	4	..	5
2,382	*247*	*14*	*5*	*103*	*4*	*2,296*	*197*	*11*	*4*	*82*	*1*	
335	51	3	..	13	1	329	44	3	..	13	1	6
736	49	7	..	11	..	687	42	4	..	11	..	7
666	73	4	3	57	..	650	47	4	2	36	..	8
217	34	..	2	5	3	214	32	..	2	5	..	9
428	40	..	..	17	..	416	32	..	..	17	..	10
3,631	*364*	*8*	*2*	*155*	..	*3,401*	*337*	*6*	*2*	*149*	..	
778	46	1	..	33	..	661	40	1	..	32	..	11
1,211	205	5	2	58	..	1,150	196	4	2	57	..	12
511	*161*	*4*	*2*	*20*	..	*458*	*160*	*3*	*2*	*19*	..	
458	36	..	..	9	..	455	32	..	..	9	..	13
703	29	1	..	39	..	691	23	..	..	36	..	14
481	48	1	..	16	..	444	46	1	..	15	..	15
2,416	*257*	..	*6*	*161*	*14*	*2,318*	*236*	..	*6*	*154*	*14*	
1,224	113	..	5	59	12	1,167	100	..	5	54	12	16
684	94	..	1	81	2	656	90	..	1	79	2	17
508	50	..	..	21	..	495	46	..	..	21	..	18
5,170	**439**	**38**	**5**	**229**	**6**	**5,089**	**397**	**37**	**4**	**226**	**4**	
1,547	195	7	4	82	..	1,525	180	7	3	81	..	19
1,513	109	3	..	58	1	1,470	95	3	..	56	..	20
1,253	73	26	..	50	1	1,245	63	25	..	50	..	21
857	62	2	1	39	4	849	59	2	1	39	4	22
1,162	**91**	**2**	..	**92**	..	**1,124**	**79**	**2**	..	**91**	..	
18	..	..	..	..	..	18	..	..	..	..	..	23
93	14	..	..	..	..	88	13	..	..	..	..	24
71	9	..	..	2	..	69	9	..	..	2	..	25
219	30	2	..	9	..	217	21	2	..	9	..	26
133	6	..	..	4	..	125	6	..	..	4	..	27
59	4	..	..	..	..	55	4	..	..	..	..	28
81	..	..	..	3	..	78	..	..	..	3	..	29
25	1	..	..	8	..	25	1	..	..	8	..	30
108	8	..	..	11	..	102	7	..	..	10	..	31
95	8	..	..	10	..	90	7	..	..	10	..	32
..	..	..	..	..	..	..	..	..	..	..	..	33
24	..	..	..	1	..	24	..	..	..	1	..	34
59	1	..	..	4	..	57	1	..	..	4	..	35
53	..	..	..	18	..	52	..	..	..	18	..	36
124	10	..	..	22	..	124	10	..	..	22	..	37

Serial No.	Class ..	Class C.—Public administration					
	Sub-class ..	Sub-class VIII.—Professions					
	Order ..	Order 48.—Instruction—*concld.*					
	Sub-order ..						
	Group ..	175.—Clerks and servants connected with education.					
	District, City or State.	Total earners (principal occupations).		Total working dependants.		Total following occupation as subsidiary to other	
		Males	Females	Males.	Females	Males.	Females.
1	2	1374	1375	1376	1377	1378	1379
	Central Provinces and Berar ..	**725**	**201**	**15**	**3**	**39**	**5**
	C. P. British Districts and Berar ..	**687**	**189**	**15**	**3**	**38**	**5**
	C. P. British Districts ..	**606**	**147**	**14**	**2**	**35**	**3**
	Jubbulpore Division ..	*192*	*49*	*9*	*1*	*1*	..
1	Saugor ..	41	21	..	..	1	..
2	Damoh ..	42	5	..	..	..	..
3	Jubbulpore ..	91	14	9	1	..	..
	Jubbulpore City ..	*68*	*11*	..	*1*	..	..
4	Mandla ..	17	5	..	..	..	..
5	Seoni ..	1	4	..	..	..	..
	Nerbudda Division ..	*86*	*50*	*3*	*1*	*21*	*3*
6	Narsinghpur ..	6	7	..	..	..	..
7	Hoshangabad ..	19	7	3	..	..	..
8	Nimar ..	16	26	..	1	21	..
9	Betul ..	3	2	..	..	..	3
10	Chhindwara ..	12	8	..	..	..	..
	Nagpur Division ..	*230*	*27*	*2*	..	*6*	..
11	Wardha ..	117	6	..	..	1	..
12	Nagpur ..	61	9	1	..	1	..
	Nagpur City ..	*53*	*1*	*1*	..	*1*	..
13	Chanda ..	3	4	..	..	..	..
14	Bhandara ..	12	6	1	..	3	..
15	Balaghat ..	37	2	..	..	1	..
	Chhattisgarh Division ..	*98*	*21*	..	..	*7*	..
16	Raipur ..	57	13	..	..	5	..
17	Bilaspur ..	28	4	..	..	2	..
18	Drug ..	13	4	..	..	..	..
	Berar ..	**81**	**42**	**1**	**1**	**3**	**2**
19	Amraoti ..	22	15	..	1	1	..
20	Akola ..	43	14	..	..	2	1
21	Buldana ..	8	16	1	..	..	1
22	Yeotmal ..	8	3	..	..	..	..
	Central Provinces States ..	**38**	**12**	..	..	**1**	..
23	Makrai ..	..	..	..	..	..	..
24	Bastar ..	3	1	..	..	..	..
25	Kanker ..	2	..	..	..	..	..
26	Nandgaon ..	2	9	..	..	..	..
27	Khairagarh ..	8	..	..	..	..	..
28	Chhuikhadan ..	4	..	..	..	..	..
29	Kawardha ..	3	..	..	..	..	..
30	Sakti ..	..	..	..	..	..	..
31	Raigarh ..	6	1	..	..	1	..
32	Sarangarh ..	5	1	..	..	..	..
33	Changbhakar ..	..	..	..	..	..	..
34	Korea ..	..	..	..	..	..	..
35	Surguja ..	2	..	..	..	..	..
36	Udaipur ..	1	..	..	..	..	..
37	Jashpur ..	..	..	..	..	..	..

Livelihood—General Distribution—*contd.* **TABLE X**

and liberal arts—*contd.*

and liberal arts—*contd.*

Order 49.—Letters, arts and sciences (other than 44).												Serial No.
Total order 49.						176.—Public scribes, stenographers, etc.						
Total earners (principal occupations).		Total working dependants.		Total following occupation as subsidiary to other.		Total earners (principal occupations).		Total working dependants.		Total following occupation as subsidiary to other.		
Males.	Females.	Males.	Females.	Males.	Females.	Males.	Females.	Males.	Females.	Males.	Females.	
1380	1381	1382	1383	1384	1385	1386	1387	1388	1389	1390	1391	
18,820	**1,635**	**571**	**161**	**7,732**	**114**	**13**	..	..	..	**1**	..	
17,645	**1,548**	**488**	**146**	**6,979**	**103**	**13**	..	..	..	**1**	..	
12,928	**1,252**	**396**	**118**	**4,708**	**70**	**6**	..	..	..	..	..	
1,402	*321*	*137*	*5*	*1,103*	*13*	*1*	..	..	..	..	..	
361	192	12	4	260	6	..	..	..	..	..	..	1
89	25	..	..	106	3	..	..	..	..	..	..	2
313	69	25	..	173	1	1	..	..	..	..	..	3
194	*39*	*18*	..	*18*	*1*	*1*	..	..	..	..	..	
141	18	5	..	349	3	..	..	..	..	..	..	4
498	17	95	1	215	..	..	..	..	..	..	..	5
2,264	*337*	*38*	*47*	*949*	*10*	..	..	..	..	..	..	
64	33	1	3	96	1	..	..	..	..	..	..	6
382	75	4	2	300	..	..	..	..	..	..	..	7
540	69	13	7	143	2	..	..	..	..	..	..	8
447	123	4	30	112	6	..	..	..	..	..	..	9
831	37	16	5	298	1	..	..	..	..	..	..	10
7,271	*203*	*113*	*29*	*1,431*	*20*	*3*	..	..	..	..	..	
1,605	40	1	1	272	7	..	..	..	..	..	..	11
2,922	84	43	23	302	3	3	..	..	..	..	..	12
681	*23*	*23*	*20*	*36*	..	*3*	..	..	..	..	..	
795	48	25	4	491	6	..	..	..	..	..	..	13
1,039	27	17	..	167	3	..	..	..	..	..	..	14
910	4	29	1	199	1	..	..	..	..	..	..	15
1,991	*391*	*108*	*37*	*1,225*	*27*	*2*	..	..	..	..	..	
830	261	49	29	495	7	2	..	..	..	..	..	16
676	96	39	8	589	19	..	..	..	..	..	..	17
485	34	20	..	141	1	..	..	..	..	..	..	18
4,717	**296**	**92**	**28**	**2,271**	**33**	**7**	..	..	..	**1**	..	
2,175	44	27	8	1,007	14	1	..	..	..	..	..	19
1,104	72	20	14	803	10	4	..	..	..	1	..	20
497	107	10	1	231	3	2	..	..	..	..	..	21
941	73	35	5	230	6	..	..	..	..	..	..	22
1,175	**87**	**83**	**15**	**753**	**11**	..	..		..	..	..	
..	..	..	..	..	..	..	..	..	..	..	..	23
66	..	1	1	5	1	..	..	..	..	..	..	24
5	..	1	..	10	..	..	..	..	..	..	..	25
111	6	24	..	27	8	..	..	..	..	..	..	26
92	27	2	11	9	..	..	..	..	..	..	..	27
..	..	..	..	..	..	..	..	..	..	..	..	28
..	..	..	..	..	..	..	..	..	..	..	..	29
16	..	21	..	16	..	..	..	..	..	..	..	30
84	29	5	..	23	1	..	..	..	..	..	..	31
89	2	1	..	43	..	..	..	..	..	..	..	32
9	..	..	..	6	..	..	..	..	..	..	..	33
80	15	..	..	19	..	..	..	..	..	..	..	34
500	5	24	2	397	1	..	..	..	..	..	..	35
35	..	..	..	61	..	..	..	..	..	..	..	36
88	3	4	1	137	..	..	..	..	..	..	..	37

TABLE X Occupation or means of

Serial No.	Class .. / Sub-class .. / Order .. / Sub-order .. / Group ..	Class C.—Public administration / Sub-class VIII.—Professions / Order 49.—Letters, arts and / 177.—Architects, surveyors, engineers and their employees (not being state servants).					
	District, City or State.	Total earners (principal occupations).		Total working dependants.		Total following occupation as subsidiary to other.	
		Males.	Females.	Males.	Females.	Males.	Females.
1	2	1392	1393	1394	1395	1396	1397
	Central Provinces and Berar ..	**214**	**3**	..	..	**15**	..
	C. P. British Districts and Berar ..	**209**	**3**	..	..	**15**	..
	C. P. British Districts	**196**	**3**	..	..	**15**	..
	Jubbulpore Division	*36*	..	..	..	*4*	..
1	Saugor	10	..	..	..	..	..
2	Damoh	..	..	..	..	..	..
3	Jubbulpore	8	..	..	..	..	..
	Jubbulpore City	*7*	..	..	..	..	..
4	Mandla	3	..	..	..	..	..
5	Seoni	15	..	..	..	4	..
	Nerbudda Division	*29*	*2*	..	..	*4*	..
6	Narsinghpur	3	..	..	..	..	..
7	Hoshangabad	12	..	..	..	4	..
8	Nimar	..	..	..	..	..	..
9	Betul	2	..	..	..	..	..
10	Chhindwara	12	2	..	..	..	..
	Nagpur Division	*67*	*1*	..	..	..	..
11	Wardha	8	..	..	..	..	..
12	Nagpur	41	..	..	..	..	..
	Nagpur City	*24*	..	..	..	..	..
13	Chanda	3	..	..	..	..	..
14	Bhandara	5	1	..	..	..	..
15	Balaghat	10	..	..	..	..	..
	Chhattisgarh Division	*64*	..	..	..	*7*	..
16	Raipur	59	..	..	..	7	..
17	Bilaspur	4	..	..	..	..	..
18	Drug	1	..	..	..	..	..
	Berar	**13**	..	..	..	..	..
19	Amraoti	3	..	..	..	..	..
20	Akola	6	..	..	..	..	..
21	Buldana	3	..	..	..	..	..
22	Yeotmal	1	..	..	..	..	..
	Central Provinces States	**5**	..	..	..	..	..
23	Makrai	..	..	..	..	..	..
24	Bastar	5	..	..	..	..	..
25	Kanker	..	..	..	..	..	..
26	Nandgaon	..	..	..	..	..	..
27	Khairagarh	..	..	..	..	..	..
28	Chhuikhadan	..	..	..	..	..	..
29	Kawardha	..	..	..	..	..	..
30	Sakti	..	..	..	..	..	..
31	Raigarh	..	..	..	..	..	..
32	Sarangarh	..	..	..	..	..	..
33	Changbhakar	..	..	..	..	..	..
34	Korea	..	..	..	..	..	..
35	Surguja	..	..	..	..	..	..
36	Udaipur	..	..	..	..	..	..
37	Jashpur	..	..	..	..	..	..

and liberal arts—*contd.*

and liberal arts—*contd.*

sciences (other than 44)—*contd.*

178.—Authors, editors, journalists and photographers.						179.—Artists, sculptors and image makers.						Serial No.
Total earners (principal occupations).		Total working dependants.		Total following occupation as subsidiary to other.		Total earners (principal occupations).		Total working dependants.		Total following occupation as subsidiary to other.		
Males.	Females.	Males.	Females.	Males.	Females.	Males.	Females.	Males.	Females.	Males.	Females.	
1398	1399	1400	1401	1402	1403	1404	1405	1406	1407	1408	1409	
172	8	7	..	22	1	546	54	6	29	88	..	
172	8	7	..	21	1	489	53	6	29	84	..	
133	8	7	..	12	..	348	27	..	17	71	..	
18	2	5	..	..	..	105	5	..	2	14	..	
4	..	..	..	..	..	10	2	..	2	4	..	1
..	..	..	..	..	..	48	3	..	..	10	..	2
13	2	5	..	..	..	20	..	..	..	..	..	3
13	..	5	..	..	..	13	..	..	..	..	..	
1	..	..	..	..	..	..	..	..	..	..	..	4
..	..	..	..	..	..	27	..	..	..	..	..	5
43	5	1	..	3	..	19	..	..	..	26	..	
3	3	..	..	..	..	..	..	..	..	..	..	6
6	1	..	..	..	..	..	..	..	..	..	..	7
30	1	1	..	2	..	8	..	..	..	24	..	8
..	..	..	..	1	..	10	..	..	..	2	..	9
4	..	..	..	..	..	1	..	..	..	..	..	10
51	1	1	..	6	..	178	22	..	15	4	..	
8	..	..	..	2	..	29	7	..	1	1	..	11
31	1	1	..	1	..	128	12	..	14	2	..	12
27	..	..	..	..	..	110	8	..	13	1	..	
7	..	..	..	..	..	18	2	..	..	..	..	13
3	..	..	..	3	..	3	1	..	..	1	..	14
2	..	..	..	..	..	..	..	..	..	..	..	15
21	..	..	..	3	..	46	..	..	..	27	..	
13	..	..	..	..	..	21	..	..	..	8	..	16
5	..	..	..	3	..	18	..	..	..	5	..	17
3	..	..	..	..	..	7	..	..	..	14	..	18
39	..	..	..	9	1	141	26	6	12	13	..	
15	..	..	..	3	1	74	8	2	4	6	..	19
8	..	..	..	2	..	36	9	3	8	5	..	20
5	..	..	..	4	..	11	5	1	..	1	..	21
11	..	..	..	..	..	20	4	..	..	1	..	22
..	..	..	..	1	..	57	1	..	..	4	..	
..	..	..	..	..	..	..	..	..	..	..	..	23
..	..	..	..	..	..	..	..	..	..	1	..	24
..	..	..	..	..	..	..	..	..	..	..	..	25
..	..	..	..	1	..	4	..	..	..	..	..	26
..	..	..	..	..	..	1	..	..	..	..	..	27
..	..	..	..	..	..	..	..	..	..	..	..	28
..	..	..	..	..	..	..	..	..	..	..	..	29
..	..	..	..	..	..	..	..	..	..	..	..	30
..	..	..	..	..	..	10	..	..	..	3	..	31
..	..	..	..	..	..	2	..	..	..	..	..	32
..	..	..	..	..	..	..	..	..	..	..	..	33
..	..	..	..	..	..	11	1	..	..	..	..	34
..	..	..	..	..	..	25	..	..	..	..	..	35
..	..	..	..	..	..	..	..	..	..	..	..	36
..	..	..	..	..	..	4	..	..	..	..	..	37

TABLE X — Occupation or means of

Serial No.	Class ..	Class C.—Public administration					
	Sub-class ..	Sub-class VIII.—Professions					
	Order ..	Order 49.—Letters, arts					
	Sub-order ..						
	Group ..	180.—Scientists (astronomers, botanists, etc.)					
	District, City or State.	Total earners (principal occupations).		Total working dependants.		Total following occupation as subsidiary to other.	
		Males.	Females.	Males.	Females.	Males.	Females.
1	2	1410	1411	1412	1413	1414	1415
	Central Provinces and Berar ..	44	9	..	..	1	8
	C. P. British Districts and Berar ..	44	9	..	..	1	..
	C. P. British Districts	44	9	..	..	1	..
	Jubbulpore Division	37	..	..	..	1	..
1	Saugor	31	..	..	..	1	..
2	Damoh	..	..	..	..	..	..
3	Jubbulpore	3	..	..	..	..	..
	Jubbulpore City	3	..	..	..	..	..
4	Mandla	..	..	..	..	..	..
5	Seoni	3	..	..	..	..	..
	Nerbudda Division	5	9	..	..	..	..
6	Narsinghpur	..	..	..	..	..	..
7	Hoshangabad	1	9	..	..	..	..
8	Nimar	..	..	..	..	..	..
9	Betul	4	..	..	..	..	..
10	Chhindwara	..	..	..	..	..	..
	Nagpur Division	..	..	..	..	..	..
11	Wardha	..	..	..	..	..	..
12	Nagpur	..	..	..	..	..	..
	Nagpur City	..	..	..	..	..	..
13	Chanda	..	..	..	..	..	..
14	Bhandara	..	..	..	..	..	..
15	Balaghat	..	..	..	..	..	..
	Chhattisgarh Division	2	..	..	..	..	..
16	Raipur	2	..	..	..	..	..
17	Bilaspur	..	..	..	..	..	..
18	Drug	..	..	..	..	..	..
	Berar	..	..	..	..	..	..
19	Amraoti	..	..	..	..	..	..
20	Akola	..	..	..	..	..	..
21	Buldana	..	..	..	..	..	..
22	Yeotmal	..	..	..	..	..	..
	Central Provinces States	..	..	..	..	..	8
23	Makrai	..	..	..	..	..	..
24	Bastar	..	..	..	..	..	..
25	Kanker	..	..	..	..	..	..
26	Nandgaon	..	..	..	..	..	8
27	Khairagarh	..	..	..	..	..	..
28	Chhuikhadan	..	..	..	..	..	..
29	Kawardha	..	..	..	..	..	..
30	Sakti	..	..	..	..	..	..
31	Raigarh	..	..	..	..	..	..
32	Sarangarh	..	..	..	..	..	..
33	Changbhakar	..	..	..	..	..	..
34	Korea	..	..	..	..	..	..
35	Surguja	..	..	..	..	..	..
36	Udaipur	..	..	..	..	..	..
37	Jashpur	..	..	..	..	..	..

Livelihood—General Distribution—*contd.*

TABLE X

and liberal arts—*contd.*

and liberal arts—*contd.*

and sciences (other than 44)—*contd.*

181.—Horoscope casters, astrologers, fortune-tellers, wizards, witches, and mediums.						182.—Musicians (composers and performers other than military) actors, dancers, etc.						Serial No.
Total earners (principal occupations).		Total working dependants.		Total following occupation as subsidiary to other.		Total earners (principal occupations).		Total working dependants.		Total following occupation as subsidiary to other.		
Males.	Females.	Males.	Females.	Males.	Females	Males.	Females.	Males.	Females.	Males.	Females.	
1416	1417	1418	1419	1420	1421	1422	1423	1424	1425	1426	1427	
590	**117**	**8**	**35**	**308**	**4**	**16,217**	**1,317**	**512**	**87**	**7,252**	**96**	
521	**117**	**6**	**35**	**196**	**4**	**15,207**	**1,240**	**447**	**72**	**6,616**	**93**	
424	**113**	**6**	**35**	**178**	**4**	**11,109**	**1,009**	**362**	**56**	**4,396**	**61**	
40	*3*	*1*	..	*19*	*1*	*1,089*	*305*	*130*	*3*	*1,063*	*12*	
..	..		..	..	..	288	190	12	2	255	6	1
..	..	..	..	..	..	27	22	..		94	3	2
4	1	..	..	4	..	224	60	19	..	169	1	3
..	..	..	..	*1*	..	*122*	*39*	*13*	..	*17*	*1*	
18	2	1	..	9	1	115	16	4	..	340	2	4
18	..	..	..	6	..	435	17	95	1	205	..	5
182	*103*	*4*	*34*	*92*	*2*	*1,918*	*184*	*33*	*13*	*822*	*3*	
..	4	..	..	..	..	53	25	1	3	96	1	6
3	..	..	..		..	316	65	4	2	296	..	7
34	..	..		2	..	457	68	12	7	115	2	8
58	89	3	30	22	1	371	5	1	..	86	..	9
87	10	1	4	68	1	721	21	15	1	229	..	10
109	*6*	..	..	*13*	..	*6,550*	*158*	*96*	*10*	*1,390*	*20*	
16	2	..	..	..	..	1,461	31	1	..	269	7	11
36	3	..	..	9	..	2,573	68	29	9	276	3	12
9	..	..	..	*1*	..	*437*	*15*	*10*	*7*	*27*	..	
3	..	..	..	3	..	709	35	20	..	488	6	13
51	1	..	..	1	..	916	20	17	..	159	3	14
3	..	..	..	..	..	891	4	29	1	198	1	15
93	*1*	*1*	*1*	*54*	*1*	*1,552*	*362*	*103*	*30*	*1,121*	*26*	
28	1	1	..	26	..	550	250	45	29	446	7	16
10	..	..	1	12	1	606	87	39	1	564	18	17
55	..	..	..	16	..	396	25	19	..	111	1	18
97	**4**	..	..	**18**		**4,098**	**231**	**85**	**16**	**2,220**	**32**	
21	2	..	..	12	..	1,981	33	24	4	983	13	19
35	..	..	..	3	..	902	57	17	6	791	10	20
13	2	..	..	1	..	438	92	9	1	225	3	21
28	..	..	..	2	..	777	49	35	5	221	6	22
69	..	**2**	..	**112**	..	**1,010**	**77**	**65**	**15**	**636**	**3**	
..	..	..	..	..	..	..	..	..	..	..	..	23
1	..	..	..	..	..	58	..	1	1	4	1	24
..	..	..	..	..	..	2	..	..	..	10	..	25
..	..	..	..	6	..	103	3	9	..	20	..	26
..	..	..	..	..	..	90	27	2	11	9	..	27
..	..	..	..	..	..	..	..	..	..	..	..	28
..	..	..	..	..	..	..	..	..	..	..	..	29
..	..	..	..	..	..	16	..	21	..	16	..	30
2	..	..	..	..	..	66	23	5	..	20	1	31
40	..	..	..	21	..	47	2	1	..	22	..	32
..	..	..	..	..	..	9	..	..	..	6	..	33
2	..	..	..	4	..	57	14	..	..	15	..	34
14	..	2	..	26	..	461	5	22	2	371	1	35
..	..	..	..	..	..	35	..	..	..	61	..	36
10	..	..	..	55	..	66	3	4	1	82	..	37

TABLE X — Occupation or means of

Serial No.	District, City or State.	Class C.—Public administration; Sub-class VIII.—Professions; Order 49.—Letters, arts; 183.—Managers and employees of places of public entertainments, race courses, societies, clubs, etc. — Total earners (principal occupations).		Total working dependants.		Total following occupation as subsidiary to other.	
		Males.	Females.	Males.	Females.	Males.	Females.
1	2	1428	1429	1430	1431	1432	1433
	Central Provinces and Berar	410	57	21	..	30	5
	C. P. British Districts and Berar	410	57	6	..	30	5
	C. P. British Districts	231	42	6	..	22	5
	Jubbulpore Division	*33*	*6*	..	..	..	..
1	Saugor	..	..	..	..	..	..
2	Damoh	..	..	..	..	..	..
3	Jubbulpore	32	6	..	..	..	..
	Jubbulpore City	*29*	..	..	..	..	..
4	Mandla	1	..	..	..	..	..
5	Seoni	..	..	..	..	..	..
	Nerbudda Division	*40*	*30*	..	..	*1*	*5*
6	Narsinghpur	1	1	..	..	..	..
7	Hoshangabad	33	..	..	..	..	..
8	Nimar	4	..	..	..	..	..
9	Betul	1	29	..	..	..	5
10	Chhindwara	1	..	..	..	1	..
	Nagpur Division	*93*	*1*	*6*	..	*10*	..
11	Wardha	4	..	..	..	..	..
12	Nagpur	73	..	6	..	9	..
	Nagpur City	*58*	..	*6*	..	*3*	..
13	Chanda	5	1	..	..	..	..
14	Bhandara	7	..	..	..	..	..
15	Balaghat	4	..	..	..	1	..
	Chhattisgarh Division	*65*	*5*	..	..	*11*	..
16	Raipur	42	5	..	..	8	..
17	Bilaspur	5	..	..	..	3	..
18	Drug	18	..	..	..	..	..
	Berar	179	15	..	..	8	..
19	Amraoti	25	1	..	..	1	..
20	Akola	69	2	..	..	1	..
21	Buldana	4	1	..	..	..	..
22	Yeotmal	81	11	..	..	6	..
	Central Provinces States	..	..	15	..	..	..
23	Makrai	..	..	..	..	..	..
24	Bastar	..	..	..	..	..	..
25	Kanker	..	..	..	..	..	..
26	Nandgaon	..	..	15	..	..	..
27	Khairagarh	..	..	..	..	..	..
28	Chhuikhadan	..	..	..	..	..	..
29	Kawardha	..	..	..	..	..	..
30	Sakti	..	..	..	..	..	..
31	Raigarh	..	..	..	..	..	..
32	Sarangarh	..	..	..	..	..	..
33	Changbhakar	..	..	..	..	..	..
34	Korea	..	..	..	..	..	..
35	Surguja	..	..	..	..	..	..
36	Udaipur	..	..	..	..	..	..
37	Jashpur	..	..	..	..	..	..

and liberal arts—*concld.* and liberal arts—*concld.* and sciences (other than 44)—*concld.* 184.—Conjurors, acrobats, recitors, exhibitors of curiosities and wild animals, etc.						Class D.—Miscellaneous. Total class D.						
Total earners (principal occupations).		Total working dependants.		Total following occupation as subsidiary to other.		Total earners (principal occupations)		Total working dependants.		Total following occupation as subsidiary to other.		Serial No.
Males.	Females.	Males.	Females.	Males.	Females.	Males.	Females.	Males.	Females.	Males.	Females.	
1434	1435	1436	1437	1438	1439	1440	1441	1442	1443	1444	1445	
614	**70**	**17**	**10**	**15**	..	**205,344**	**121,157**	**8,027**	**27,734**	**21,639**	**6,473**	
580	**61**	**16**	**10**	**15**	..	**189,287**	**110,660**	**7,456**	**26,366**	**20,189**	**6,326**	
437	**41**	**15**	**10**	**13**	..	**134,621**	**83,764**	**4,067**	**14,478**	**16,706**	**5,194**	
43	..	*1*	..	*2*	..	*32,328*	*22,873*	*927*	*3,474*	*3,773*	*1,192*	
18	..	..	..	..	..	5,111	2,943	171	1,035	588	146	1
14	..	..	..	2	..	2,085	1,708	113	472	669	218	2
8	..	1	..	..	..	20,743	15,313	562	1,704	2,097	669	3
6	..	..	..	..	..	*9,403*	*3,276*	*266*	*203*	*133*	*14*	
3	..	..	..	..	..	1,836	883	41	103	176	35	4
..	..	..	..	..	..	2,553	2,026	40	160	243	124	5
28	*4*	..	..	*1*	..	*20,778*	*9,101*	*656*	*3,878*	*3,345*	*646*	
4	..	..	..	..	..	3,107	2,431	113	601	507	169	6
11	..	..	..	..	..	7,112	3,208	272	742	1,608	318	7
7	..	..	..	..	..	5,861	1,363	138	208	615	31	8
1	..	..	..	1	..	2,276	776	84	2,126	370	35	9
5	4	..	..	..	..	2,422	1,323	49	201	245	93	10
220	*14*	*10*	*4*	*8*	..	*51,292*	*26,817*	*1,498*	*5,083*	*4,716*	*1,643*	
79	..	..	..	..	..	4,646	1,981	107	75	362	130	11
37	..	7	..	5	..	24,177	11,087	291	654	973	274	12
13	..	*7*	..	*4*	..	*15,533*	*6,490*	*185*	*254*	*258*	*18*	
50	10	3	4	..	..	8,444	5,302	473	2,798	1,698	615	13
54	4	..	..	3	..	11,528	7,418	569	1,046	1,410	580	14
..	..	..	..	..	..	2,497	1,029	58	510	273	44	15
146	*23*	*4*	*6*	*2*	..	*30,223*	*24,973*	*986*	*2,043*	*4,872*	*1,713*	
113	5	3	..	..	..	12,613	10,014	442	529	962	206	16
28	9	..	6	2	..	14,214	10,570	427	1,154	3,432	1,413	17
5	9	1	..	..	..	3,396	4,389	117	360	478	94	18
143	**20**	**1**	..	**2**	..	**54,666**	**26,896**	**3,389**	**11,888**	**3,483**	**1,132**	
55	..	1	..	2	..	13,633	3,976	760	1,036	1,030	257	19
44	4	..	..	..	..	14,055	5,327	587	963	797	189	20
21	7	..	..	..	..	9,216	3,530	259	310	691	179	21
23	9	..	..	..	..	17,762	14,063	1,783	9,579	965	507	22
34	**9**	**1**	..	..	..	**16,057**	**10,497**	**571**	**1,368**	**1,450**	**147**	
..	..	..	..	..	..	142	35	8	..	8	..	23
2	..	..	..	..	..	2,454	1,320	212	148	148	11	24
3	..	1	..	..	..	1,392	380	32	24	82	48	25
4	3	..	..	..	..	1,504	1,128	12	133	58	9	26
1	..	..	..	..	..	1,368	1,121	16	5	33	1	27
..	..	..	..	..	..	371	549	3	44	45	24	28
..	..	..	..	..	..	417	761	1	8	55	35	29
..	..	..	..	..	..	363	189	..	..	34	2	30
6	6	..	..	..	..	2,050	1,619	101	235	210	1	31
..	..	..	..	..	..	882	360	41	150	55	1	32
..	..	..	..	..	..	669	601	11	..	75	4	33
10	..	..	..	..	..	967	928	5	5	55	5	34
..	..	..	..	..	..	2,503	1,098	98	532	348	4	35
..	..	..	..	..	..	350	64	19	..	27	..	36
8	..	..	..	..	..	625	344	12	84	217	2	37

TABLE X

Occupation or means of

Serial No.	Class .. / Sub-class .. / Order .. / Sub-order .. / Group ..	Class D.—					
		Sub-class IX.—Persons					
		Total sub-class IX.					
	District, City or State.	Total earners (principal occupations).		Total working dependants.		Total following occupation as subsidiary to other.	
		Males.	Females	Males.	Females.	Males.	Females.
1	2	1446	1447	1448	1449	1450	1451
	Central Provinces and Berar ..	**4,347**	**696**	**83**	**372**	**427**	**40**
	C. P. British Districts and Berar ..	**4,283**	**674**	**81**	**372**	**420**	**40**
	C. P. British Districts	**3,346**	**554**	**76**	**366**	**320**	**25**
	Jubbulpore Division	*907*	*208*	*20*	*112*	*97*	*6*
1	Saugor	276	40	2	6	28	2
2	Damoh	36	7	..	1	11	1
3	Jubbulpore	489	114	13	32	39	2
	Jubbulpore City	*416*	*84*	*8*	*9*	*24*	*1*
4	Mandla	38	23	1	..	8	..
5	Seoni	68	24	4	73	11	1
	Nerbudda Division	*757*	*126*	*31*	*155*	*72*	*10*
6	Narsinghpur	112	15	1	31	6	..
7	Hoshangabad	211	47	9	4	17	7
8	Nimar	177	37	..	15	16	3
9	Betul	97	23	19	105	15	..
10	Chhindwara	160	4	2	..	18	..
	Nagpur Division	*1,266*	*191*	*24*	*99*	*67*	*6*
11	Wardha	121	23	..	2	12	3
12	Nagpur	795	117	11	12	26	..
	Nagpur City	*664*	*112*	*11*	*1*	*11*	..
13	Chanda	129	8	3	..	14	..
14	Bhandara	87	16	3	2	4	1
15	Balaghat	134	27	7	83	11	2
	Chhattisgarh Division	*416*	*29*	*1*	..	*84*	*3*
16	Raipur	282	21	..	..	70	..
17	Bilaspur	103	2	1	..	8	..
18	Drug	31	6	..	..	6	3
	Berar	**937**	**120**	**5**	**6**	**100**	**15**
19	Amraoti	263	48	1	2	21	4
20	Akola	364	45	1	2	37	6
21	Buldana	161	15	1	1	24	3
22	Yeotmal	149	12	2	1	18	2
	Central Provinces States	**64**	**22**	**2**	..	**7**	..
23	Makrai	24	9	..	..	1	..
24	Bastar	8	12	1	..	3	..
25	Kanker	1	..	1	..	1	..
26	Nandgaon	4	..	..	..	2	..
27	Khairagarh	7	..	..	..	..	..
28	Chhuikhadan	..	..	..	..	..	..
29	Kawardha	..	..	..	..	..	..
30	Sakti	..	..	..	..	..	..
31	Raigarh	15	..	..	..	..	..
32	Sarangarh	..	..	..	..	..	..
33	Changbhakar	..	..	..	..	..	..
34	Korea	..	1	..	..	..	..
35	Surguja	..	..	..	..	..	..
36	Udaipur	1	..	..	..	..	..
37	Jashpur	4	..	..	..	..	..

Miscellaneous—*contd.*

living on their income.

Order 50.—Persons living principally on their income.												
Total order 50.						185.—Proprietors (other than of agricultural land), fund and scholarships holders and pensioners.						Serial No.
Total earners (principal occupations).		Total working dependants.		Total following occupation as subsidiary to other.		Total earners (principal occupations).		Total working dependants.		Total following occupation as subsidiary to other.		
Males.	Females	Males	Females.	Males.	Females.	Males.	Females.	Males.	Females.	Males	Females.	
1452	1453	1454	1455	1456	1457	1458	1459	1460	1461	1462	1463	
4,347	696	83	**372**	**427**	**40**	**4,347**	**696**	**83**	**372**	**427**	**40**	
4,283	674	81	**372**	**420**	**40**	**4,283**	**674**	**81**	**372**	**420**	**40**	
3,346	554	76	**366**	**320**	**25**	**3,346**	**554**	**76**	**366**	**320**	**25**	
907	*208*	*20*	*112*	*97*	*6*	*907*	*208*	*20*	*112*	*97*	*6*	
276	40	2	6	28	2	276	40	2	6	28	2	1
36	7	..	1	11	1	36	7	..	1	11	1	2
489	114	13	32	39	2	489	114	13	32	39	2	3
416	*84*	*8*	*9*	*24*	*1*	*416*	*84*	*8*	*9*	*24*	*1*	
38	23	1	..	8	..	38	23	1	..	8	..	4
68	24	4	73	11	1	68	24	4	73	11	1	5
757	*126*	*31*	*155*	*72*	*10*	*757*	*126*	*31*	*155*	*72*	*10*	
112	15	1	31	6	..	112	15	1	31	6	..	6
211	47	9	4	17	7	211	47	9	4	17	7	7
177	37	..	15	16	3	177	37	..	15	16	3	8
97	23	19	105	15	..	97	23	19	105	15	..	9
160	4	2	..	18	..	160	4	2	..	18	..	10
1,266	*191*	*24*	*99*	*67*	*6*	*1,266*	*191*	*24*	*99*	*67*	*6*	
121	23	..	2	12	3	121	23	..	2	12	3	11
795	117	11	12	26	..	795	117	11	12	26	..	12
664	*112*	*11*	*1*	*11*	..	*664*	*112*	*11*	*1*	*11*	..	
129	8	3	..	14	..	129	8	3	..	14	..	13
87	16	3	2	4	1	87	16	3	2	4	1	14
134	27	7	83	11	2	134	27	7	83	11	2	15
416	*29*	*1*	..	*84*	*3*	*416*	*29*	*1*	..	*84*	*3*	
282	21	..	..	70	..	282	21	..	..	70	..	16
103	2	1	..	8	..	103	2	1	..	8	..	17
31	6	..	..	6	3	31	6	..	..	6	3	18
937	**120**	**5**	**6**	**100**	**15**	**937**	**120**	**5**	**6**	**100**	**15**	
263	48	1	2	21	4	263	48	1	2	21	4	19
364	45	1	2	37	6	364	45	1	2	37	6	20
161	15	1	1	24	3	161	15	1	1	24	3	21
149	12	2	1	18	2	149	12	2	1	18	2	22
64	**22**	**2**	..	**7**	..	**64**	**22**	**2**	..	**7**	..	
24	9	..	..	1	..	24	9	..	..	1	..	23
8	12	1	..	3	..	8	12	1	..	3	..	24
1	..	1	..	1	..	1	..	1	..	1	..	25
4	..	..	..	2	..	4	..	..	..	2	..	26
7	..	..	..	..	..	7	..	..	..	..	..	27
..	..	..	..	..	..	..	..	..	..	..	..	28
..	..	..	..	..	..	..	..	..	..	..	..	29
..	..	..	..	..	..	..	..	..	..	..	..	30
15	..	..	..	..	..	15	..	..	..	..	..	31
..	..	..	..	..	..	..	..	..	..	..	..	32
..	..	..	..	..	..	..	..	..	..	..	..	33
..	1	..	..	..	..	..	1	..	..	..	..	34
..	..	..	..	..	..	..	..	..	..	..	..	35
1	..		..	..		1	..	..	..	..	..	36
4	..	..	..	..	..	4	..	..	..	..	..	37

TABLE X — Occupation or means of

Class D.— Sub-class X.— Total sub-class X.

Serial No.	District, City or State.	Total earners (principal occupations). Males.	Total earners (principal occupations). Females.	Total working dependants. Males.	Total working dependants. Females.	Total following occupation as subsidiary to other. Males.	Total following occupation as subsidiary to other. Females.
1	2	1464	1465	1466	1467	1468	1469
	Central Provinces and Berar	**61,167**	**34,767**	**1,543**	**10,833**	**5,758**	**2,050**
	C. P. British Districts and Berar	**54,471**	**29,369**	**1,448**	**10,031**	**5,214**	**1,972**
	C. P. British Districts	**42,404**	**26,708**	**1,180**	**8,963**	**4,748**	**1,760**
	Jubbulpore Division	*10,432*	*7,472*	*279*	*2,144*	*1,446*	*548*
1	Saugor	2,436	1,858	58	924	293	83
2	Damoh	1,054	1,270	84	462	334	164
3	Jubbulpore	5,894	3,226	86	661	716	236
	Jubbulpore City	*3,487*	*924*	*15*	*30*	*38*	*9*
4	Mandla	557	442	20	41	47	25
5	Seoni	491	676	31	56	56	40
	Nerbudda Division	*8,441*	*4,587*	*296*	*2,958*	*800*	*327*
6	Narsinghpur	1,254	1,499	78	498	212	118
7	Hoshangabad	3,294	1,435	112	223	307	122
8	Nimar	2,515	345	22	104	197	4
9	Betul	502	301	47	1,952	21	14
10	Chhindwara	876	1,007	37	181	63	69
	Nagpur Division	*13,276*	*4,950*	*491*	*2,887*	*1,428*	*524*
11	Wardha	1,955	606	3	24	170	84
12	Nagpur	6,537	2,218	133	302	454	143
	Nagpur City	*3,925*	*1,346*	*60*	*72*	*31*	*7*
13	Chanda	1,535	801	91	1,695	283	142
14	Bhandara	2,480	964	249	559	469	131
15	Balaghat	769	361	15	307	52	24
	Chhattisgarh Division	*10,255*	*9,699*	*114*	*974*	*1,074*	*361*
16	Raipur	5,341	4,809	26	285	411	125
17	Bilaspur	3,565	2,386	69	537	564	217
18	Drug	1,349	2,504	19	152	99	19
	Berar	**12,067**	**2,661**	**268**	**1,068**	**466**	**212**
19	Amraoti	3,815	791	89	346	105	93
20	Akola	3,268	634	57	318	127	38
21	Buldana	2,031	425	71	95	143	36
22	Yeotmal	2,953	811	51	309	91	45
	Central Provinces States	**6,696**	**5,398**	**95**	**802**	**544**	**78**
23	Makrai	19	15	..	..	1	..
24	Bastar	1,220	454	14	121	19	3
25	Kanker	647	277	18	9	30	23
26	Nandgaon	594	915	3	12	6	3
27	Khairagarh	704	1,049	3	5	21	1
28	Chhuikhadan	207	113	..	18	34	5
29	Kawardha	255	604	..	8	33	35
30	Sakti	72	36	..	..	..	2
31	Raigarh	936	1,045	23	181	117	1
32	Sarangarh	302	282	2	147	23	1
33	Changbhakar	192	60	..	..	26	1
34	Korea	334	29	4	..	13	..
35	Surguja	794	261	28	293	159	3
36	Udaipur	170	31	..	..	4	..
37	Jashpur	250	227	..	8	58	..

Miscellaneous—*contd*

Domestic service—*contd.*

Order 51.—Domestic service. Total order 51.						186.—Private motor drivers and cleaners.						Serial No.
Total earners (principal occupations).		Total working dependants.		Total following occupation as subsidiary to other.		Total earners (principal occupations).		Total working dependants.		Total following occupation as subsidiary to other.		
Males.	Females.	Males.	Females.	Males.	Females.	Males.	Females.	Males.	Females.	Males.	Females.	
1470	1471	1472	1473	1474	1475	1476	1477	1478	1479	1480	1481	
61,167	**34,767**	**1,543**	**10,833**	**5,758**	**2,050**	**418**	**10**	**2**	..	**63**	..	
54,471	**29,369**	**1,448**	**10,031**	**5,214**	**1,972**	**265**	**4**	**2**	..	**9**	..	
42,404	**26,708**	**1,180**	**8,963**	**4,748**	**1,760**	**163**	**4**	..	..	**5**	..	
10,432	*7,472*	*279*	*2,144*	*1,446*	*548*	*32*	*4*	..	..	*1*	..	
2,436	1,858	58	924	293	83	..	4	..	..	..	..	1
1,054	1,270	84	462	334	164	..	..	..	..	..	..	2
5,894	3,226	86	661	716	236	16	..	..	..	..	..	3
3,487	*924*	*15*	*30*	*38*	*9*	*16*	..	..	..	..	..	
557	442	20	41	47	25	6	..	..	..	..	..	4
491	676	31	56	56	40	10	..	..	..	1	..	5
8,441	*4,587*	*296*	*2,958*	*800*	*327*	*102*	..	..	..	*3*	..	
1,254	1,499	78	498	212	118	..	..	..	..	..	..	6
3,294	1,435	112	223	307	122	81	..	..	..	3	..	7
2,515	345	22	104	197	4	16	..	..	..	..	..	8
502	301	47	1,952	21	14	4	..	..	..	..	..	9
876	1,007	37	181	63	69	1	..	..	..	..	..	10
13,276	*4,950*	*491*	*2,887*	*1,428*	*524*	*2*	..	..	..	..	..	
1,955	606	3	24	170	84	1	..	..	..	..	..	11
6,537	2,218	133	302	454	143	1	..	..	..	..	..	12
3,925	*1,346*	*60*	*72*	*31*	*7*	..	..	..	..	..	..	
1,535	801	91	1,695	283	142	..	..	..	..	..	..	13
2,480	964	249	559	469	131	..	..	..	..	..	..	14
769	361	15	307	52	24	..	..	..	..	..	..	15
10,255	*9,699*	*114*	*974*	*1,074*	*361*	*27*	..	..	..	*1*	..	
5,341	4,809	26	285	411	125	25	..	..	..	1	..	16
3,565	2,386	69	537	564	217	2	..	..	..	..	..	17
1,349	2,504	19	152	99	19	..	..	..	..	..	..	18
12,067	**2,661**	**268**	**1,068**	**466**	**212**	**102**	..	**2**	..	**4**	..	
3,815	791	89	346	105	93	1	..	..	..	..	..	19
3,268	634	57	318	127	38	7	..	..	..	..	..	20
2,031	425	71	95	143	36	94	..	2	..	4	..	21
2,953	811	51	309	91	45	..	..	..	..	..	..	22
6,696	**5,398**	**95**	**802**	**544**	**78**	**153**	**6**	..	..	**54**	..	
19	15	..	..	1	..	..	..	..	..	..	..	23
1,220	454	14	121	19	3	5	..	..	..	..	..	24
547	277	18	9	30	23	5	..	..	..	1	..	25
594	915	3	12	6	3	60	..	..	..	..	..	26
704	1,049	3	5	21	1	..	..	..	..	..	..	27
207	113	..	18	34	5	12	..	..	..	..	..	28
255	604	..	8	33	35	3	3	..	..	..	..	29
72	36	..	..	..	2	1	..	..	..	..	..	30
936	1,045	23	181	117	1	23	..	..	..	4	..	31
302	282	2	147	23	1	..	..	..	..	..	..	32
192	60	..	..	26	1	..	..	..	..	..	..	33
334	29	4	..	13	..	4	..	..	..	..	..	34
794	261	28	293	159	3	25	3	..	..	49	..	35
170	31	..	..	4	..	3	..	..	..	..	..	36
250	227	..	8	58	..	12	..	..	..	..	..	37

Serial No.	Class ..	Class D.—					
	Sub-class ..	Sub-class X.—Domestic service—*concld.*					
	Order ..	Order 51.—Domestic service—*concld.*					
	Sub-order ..						
	Group ..	187.—Other domestic service.					
	District, City or State.	Total earners (principal occupations).		Total working dependants.		Total following occupation as subsidiary to other.	
		Males.	Females.	Males.	Females.	Males.	Females.
1	2	1482	1483	1484	1485	1486	1487
	Central Provinces and Berar	**60,749**	**34,757**	**1,541**	**10,833**	**5,695**	**2,050**
	C. P. British Districts and Berar	**54,206**	**29,365**	**1,446**	**10,031**	**5,205**	**1,972**
	C. P. British Districts	**42,241**	**26,704**	**1,180**	**8,963**	**4,743**	**1,760**
	Jubbulpore Division	*10,400*	*7,468*	*279*	*2,144*	*1,445*	*548*
1	Saugor	2,436	1,854	58	924	293	83
2	Damoh	1,054	1,270	84	462	334	164
3	Jubbulpore	5,878	3,226	86	661	716	236
	Jubbulpore City	*3,471*	*924*	*15*	*30*	*38*	*9*
4	Mandla	551	442	20	41	47	25
5	Seoni	481	676	31	56	55	40
	Nerbudda Division	*8,339*	*4,587*	*296*	*2,958*	*797*	*327*
6	Narsinghpur	1,254	1,499	78	498	212	118
7	Hoshangabad	3,213	1,435	112	223	304	122
8	Nimar	2,499	345	22	104	197	4
9	Betul	498	301	47	1,952	21	14
10	Chhindwara	875	1,007	37	181	63	69
	Nagpur Division	*13,274*	*4,950*	*491*	*2,887*	*1,428*	*524*
11	Wardha	1,954	606	3	24	170	84
12	Nagpur	6,536	2,218	133	302	454	143
	Nagpur City	*3,925*	*1,346*	*60*	*72*	*31*	*7*
13	Chanda	1,535	801	91	1,695	283	142
14	Bhandara	2,480	964	249	559	469	131
15	Balaghat	769	361	15	307	52	24
	Chhattisgarh Division	*10,228*	*9,699*	*114*	*974*	*1,073*	*361*
16	Raipur	5,316	4,809	26	285	410	125
17	Bilaspur	3,563	2,386	69	537	564	217
18	Drug	1,349	2,504	19	152	99	19
	Berar	**11,965**	**2,661**	**266**	**1,068**	**462**	**212**
19	Amraoti	3,814	791	89	346	105	93
20	Akola	3,261	634	57	318	127	38
21	Buldana	1,937	425	69	95	139	36
22	Yeotmal	2,953	811	51	309	91	45
	Central Provinces States	**6,543**	**5,392**	**95**	**802**	**490**	**78**
23	Makrai	19	15	..	..	1	..
24	Bastar	1,215	454	14	121	19	3
25	Kanker	642	277	18	9	29	23
26	Nandgaon	534	915	3	12	6	3
27	Khairagarh	704	1,049	3	5	21	1
28	Chhuikhadan	195	113	..	18	34	5
29	Kawardha	252	601	..	8	33	35
30	Sakti	71	36	..	..	..	2
31	Raigarh	913	1,045	23	181	113	1
32	Sarangarh	302	282	2	147	23	1
33	Changbhakar	192	60	..	..	26	1
34	Korea	330	29	4	..	13	..
35	Surguja	769	258	28	293	110	3
36	Udaipur	167	31	..	..	4	..
37	Jashpur	238	227	..	8	58	..

Miscellaneous—*contd.*

Sub-class XI.—Insufficiently described occupations.

Total sub-class XI.						Order 52.—General terms which do not indicate a definite occupation. Total order 52.						Serial No.
Total earners (principal occupations).		Total working dependants.		Total following occupation as subsidiary to other.		Total earners (principal occupations).		Total working dependants.		Total following occupation as subsidiary to other.		
Males.	Females.	Males.	Females.	Males.	Females.	Males.	Females.	Males.	Females.	Males.	Females.	
1488	1489	1490	1491	1492	1493	1494	1495	1496	1497	1498	1499	
95,113	**65,682**	**3,389**	**14,711**	**9,740**	**3,302**	**95,113**	**65,682**	**3,389**	**14,711**	**9,740**	**3,302**	
90,118	**62,520**	**3,247**	**14,347**	**9,222**	**3,264**	**90,118**	**62,520**	**3,247**	**14,347**	**9,222**	**3,264**	
60,783	**42,873**	**1,146**	**4,046**	**7,507**	**2,573**	**60,783**	**42,873**	**1,146**	**4,046**	**7,507**	**2,573**	
14,689	*12,434*	*174*	*1,038*	*1,019*	*417*	*14,689*	*12,434*	*174*	*1,038*	*1,019*	*417*	
998	462	26	58	38	6	998	462	26	58	38	6	1
1	5	..	..	..	2	1	5	..	..	..	2	2
12,603	10,956	143	906	923	359	12,603	10,956	143	906	923	359	3
5,171	*2,122*	*37*	*154*	*70*	*3*	*5,171*	*2,122*	*37*	*154*	*70*	*3*	
197	69	1	50	18	1	197	69	1	50	18	1	4
890	942	4	24	40	49	890	942	4	24	40	49	5
4,063	*2,450*	*97*	*600*	*1,277*	*178*	*4,063*	*2,450*	*97*	*600*	*1,277*	*178*	
719	514	..	20	31	10	719	514	..	20	31	10	6
874	1,118	59	475	880	147	874	1,118	59	475	880	147	7
1,361	643	32	83	235	17	1,361	643	32	83	235	17	8
853	173	5	22	98	4	853	173	5	22	98	4	9
256	2	1	..	33	..	256	2	1	..	33	..	10
29,609	*18,091*	*581*	*1,767*	*2,657*	*964*	*29,609*	*18,091*	*581*	*1,767*	*2,657*	*964*	
1,230	711	9	26	76	22	1,230	711	9	26	76	22	11
14,563	7,780	101	285	264	89	14,563	7,780	101	285	264	89	12
10,386	*4,631*	*85*	*167*	*89*	*5*	*10,386*	*4,631*	*85*	*167*	*89*	*5*	
5,930	3,852	267	1,000	1,351	439	5,930	3,852	267	1,000	1,351	439	13
7,400	5,525	202	402	855	403	7,400	5,525	202	402	855	403	14
486	223	2	54	111	11	486	223	2	54	111	11	15
12,422	*9,898*	*294*	*641*	*2,554*	*1,014*	*12,422*	*9,898*	*294*	*641*	*2,554*	*1,014*	
4,045	2,891	32	4	212	16	4,045	2,891	32	4	212	16	16
7,797	6,299	173	450	2,104	970	7,797	6,299	173	450	2,104	970	17
580	708	89	187	238	28	580	708	89	187	238	28	18
29,335	**19,647**	**2,101**	**10,301**	**1,715**	**691**	**29,335**	**19,647**	**2,101**	**10,301**	**1,715**	**691**	
5,943	1,843	265	592	485	85	5,943	1,843	265	592	485	85	19
7,195	3,411	268	538	274	95	7,195	3,411	268	538	274	95	20
4,363	2,156	59	147	267	84	4,363	2,156	59	147	267	84	21
11,834	12,237	1,509	9,024	689	427	11,834	12,237	1,509	9,024	689	427	22
4,995	**3,162**	**142**	**364**	**518**	**38**	**4,995**	**3,162**	**142**	**364**	**518**	**38**	
10	..	..	..	..	..	10	..	..	..	..	..	23
843	655	77	16	104	7	843	655	77	16	104	7	24
452	..	..	..	21	..	452	..	..	..	21	..	25
605	19	1	111	44	6	605	19	1	111	44	6	26
78	65	..	..	..	..	78	65	..	..	..	..	27
48	215	2	23	4	19	48	215	2	23	4	19	28
30	6	..	..	..	..	30	6	..	..	..	..	29
37	..	..	..	..	..	37	..	..	..	..	..	30
534	297	30	7	32	..	534	297	30	7	32	..	31
186	..	10	..	7	..	186	..	10	..	7	..	32
429	514	..	..	42	3	429	514	..	..	42	3	33
535	859	1	2	35	3	535	859	1	2	35	3	34
1,007	521	21	178	98	..	1,007	521	21	178	98	..	35
46	11	..	..	2	..	46	11	..	..	2	..	36
155	..	..	27	129	..	155	..	..	27	129	..	37

TABLE X **Occupation or means of**

Serial No.	District, City or State.	Total earners (principal occupations). Males.	Total earners (principal occupations). Females.	Total working dependants. Males.	Total working dependants. Females.	Total following occupation as subsidiary to other. Males.	Total following occupation as subsidiary to other. Females.
	Class ..	Class D.—					
	Sub-class ..	Sub-class XI.— Insufficiently					
	Order ..	Order 52.—General terms which do					
	Sub-order ..						
	Group ..	188.—Manufacturers, business men and contractors otherwise unspecified.					
1	2	1500	1501	1502	1503	1504	1505
	Central Provinces and Berar ..	**2,300**	**103**	**70**	**16**	**333**	**11**
	C. P. British Districts and Berar ..	**2,102**	**100**	**69**	**16**	**261**	**11**
	C. P. British Districts	**1,715**	**98**	**67**	**15**	**228**	**11**
	Jubbulpore Division	*400*	*10*	*8*	..	*54*	*1*
1	Saugor	56	1	5	..	5	..
2	Damoh	..	..	..	..	..	..
3	Jubbulpore	306	5	3	..	31	1
	Jubbulpore City	*242*	*4*	*2*	..	*10*	..
4	Mandla	32	2	..	..	14	..
5	Seoni	6	2	..	..	4	..
	Nerbudda Division	*145*	*9*	*19*	*6*	*15*	..
6	Narsinghpur	14	..	..	..	7	..
7	Hoshangabad	46	4	1	..	..	..
8	Nimar	57	5	18	6	5	..
9	Betul	3	..	..	..	..	..
10	Chhindwara	25	..	..	..	3	..
	Nagpur Division	*697*	*35*	..	..	*56*	..
11	Wardha	42	..	..	..	4	..
12	Nagpur	431	33	..	..	9	..
	Nagpur City	*278*	*8*	..	..	*6*	..
13	Chanda	136	1	..	..	24	..
14	Bhandara	81	1	..	..	17	..
15	Balaghat	7	..	..	..	2	..
	Chhattisgarh Division	*473*	*44*	*40*	*9*	*103*	*10*
16	Raipur	200	16	20	..	52	1
17	Bilaspur	245	28	9	9	49	9
18	Drug	28	..	11	..	2	..
	Berar	**387**	**2**	**2**	**1**	**33**	..
19	Amraoti	99	1	..	..	4	..
20	Akola	143	..	1	..	16	..
21	Buldana	67	..	..	..	4	..
22	Yeotmal	78	1	1	1	9	..
	Central Provinces States	**198**	**3**	**1**	..	**72**	..
23	Makrai	..	..	..	..	..	..
24	Bastar	67	..	1	..	50	..
25	Kanker	23	..	..	..	1	..
26	Nandgaon	12	..	..	..	..	..
27	Khairagarh	..	..	..	..	..	..
28	Chhuikhadan	..	..	..	..	1	..
29	Kawardha	..	..	..	..	..	..
30	Sakti	4	..	..	..	..	..
31	Raigarh	6	2	..	..	..	..
32	Sarangarh	3	..	..	..	2	..
33	Changbhakar	..	..	..	..	6	..
34	Korea	23	1	..	..	9	..
35	Surguja	24	..	..	..	3	..
36	Udaipur	5	..	..	..	..	..
37	Jashpur	31	..	..	..	..	..

Miscellaneous—*contd.*

described occupations—*contd.*

not indicate a definite occupation—*contd.*

189.—Cashiers, accountants, book-keepers, clerks and other employees in unspecified offices and warehouses and shops.						190.—Mechanics otherwise unspecified.						Serial No.
Total earners (principal occupations).		Total working dependants.		Total following occupation as subsidiary to other.		Total earners (principal occupations).		Total working dependants.		Total following occupation as subsidiary to other.		
Males.	Females.	Males.	Females.	Males.	Females.	Males.	Females.	Males.	Females.	Males.	Females.	
1506	1507	1508	1509	1510	1511	1512	1513	1514	1515	1516	1517	
9,177	**648**	**154**	**25**	**699**	**56**	**965**	**4**	**6**	**1**	**22**	..	
8,175	**644**	**143**	**23**	**474**	**56**	**930**	**4**	**6**	**1**	**21**	..	
5,298	**605**	**49**	**18**	**326**	**55**	**434**	..	**4**	**1**	**7**	..	
515	*463*	*1*	*1*	*25*	*18*	*40*	..	..	..	*3*	..	
11	1	..	..	2	..	1	..	..	..	..	..	1
1	..	..	..	..	..	..	..	..	..	..	..	2
402	461	1	1	20	18	32	..	..	..	3	..	3
253	*71*	..	*1*	*4*	..	*20*	..	..	..	..	..	
56	1	..	..	1	..	..	..	..	..	..	..	4
45	..	..	..	2	..	7	..	..	..	..	..	5
558	*4*	*2*	..	*67*	*28*	*50*	..	..	..	..	..	
20	1	..	..	1	..	1	..	..	..	..	..	6
146	..	1	..	23	28	16	..	..	..	..	..	7
176	2	..	..	6	..	8	..	..	..	..	..	8
63	1	..	..	20	..	..	..	..	..	..	..	9
153	..	1	..	17	..	25	..	..	..	..	..	10
3,022	*65*	*26*	*17*	*111*	*1*	*304*	..	*4*	*1*	*4*	..	
260	..	..	..	6	..	31	..	1	..	..	..	11
2,229	58	7	15	52	..	215	..	3	1	3	..	12
775	*16*	*2*	..	*3*	..	*182*	..	*3*	..	*1*	..	
313	7	7	2	14	1	35	..	..	..	..	..	13
170	..	11	..	26	..	22	..	..	..	1	..	14
50	..	1	..	13	..	1	..	..	..	..	..	15
1,203	*73*	*20*	..	*123*	*8*	*40*	..	..	..	..	..	
503	28	12	..	15	2	2	..	..	..	..	..	16
600	40	..	..	86	6	35	..	..	..	..	..	17
100	5	8	..	22	..	3	..	..	..	..	..	18
2,877	**39**	**94**	**5**	**148**	**1**	**496**	**4**	**2**	..	**14**	..	
668	21	26	3	78	..	185	1	..	..	8	..	19
790	4	6	..	22	1	200	2	..	..	2	..	20
259	4	10	1	12	..	63	1	2	..	4	..	21
1,160	10	52	1	36	..	48	..	..	..	..	..	22
1,002	**4**	**11**	**2**	**225**	..	**35**	..	..	..	**1**	..	
9	..	..	..	..	..	1	..	..	..	..	..	23
69	..	..	..	1	..	1	..	..	..	..	..	24
9	..	..	..	2	..	1	..	..	..	..	..	25
18	..	..	..	..	..	2	..	..	..	1	..	26
11	1	..	..	..	..	29	..	..	..	..	..	27
11	..	..	..	..	..	..	..	..	..	..	..	28
..	..	..	..	..	..	..	..	..	..	..	..	29
6	..	..	..	..	..	..	..	..	..	..	..	30
114	..	..	..	15	..	..	..	..	..	..	..	31
62	..	6	..	3	..	..	..	..	..	..	..	32
6	..	..	..	..	..	..	..	..	..	..	..	33
24	..	..	..	..	..	..	..	..	..	..	..	34
590	3	5	2	94	..	1	..	..	..	..	..	35
11	..	..	..	1	..	..	..	..	..	..	..	36
62	..	..	..	109	..	..	..	..	..	..	..	37

Serial No.	Class / Sub-class / Order / Sub-order / Group — District, City or State.	Class D.— Sub-class XI.—Insufficiently described occupations—*concld.* Order 52.—General terms which do not indicate a definite occupations—*concld.* 191.—Labourers and workmen otherwise unspecified.					
		Total earners (principal occupation).		Total working dependants.		Total following occupation as subsidiary to other.	
		Males.	Females.	Males.	Females.	Males.	Females.
1	2	1518	1519	1520	1521	1522	1523
	Central Provinces and Berar	**82,671**	**64,927**	**3,159**	**14,669**	**8,686**	**3,235**
	C. P. British Districts and Berar	**78,911**	**61,772**	**3,029**	**14,307**	**8,466**	**3,197**
	C. P. British Districts	**53,336**	**42,170**	**1,026**	**4,012**	**6,946**	**2,507**
	Jubbulpore Division	*13,734*	*11,961*	*165*	*1,037*	*937*	*398*
1	Saugor	930	460	21	58	31	6
2	Damoh	..	5	..	..	..	2
3	Jubbulpore	11,863	10,490	139	905	869	340
	Jubbulpore City	*4,656*	*2,047*	*35*	*153*	*56*	*3*
4	Mandla	109	66	1	50	3	1
5	Seoni	832	940	4	24	34	49
	Nerbudda Division	*3,310*	*2,437*	*76*	*594*	*1,195*	*150*
6	Narsinghpur	684	513	..	20	23	10
7	Hoshangabad	666	1,114	57	475	857	119
8	Nimar	1,120	636	14	77	224	17
9	Betul	787	172	5	22	78	4
10	Chhindwara	53	2	..	..	13	..
	Nagpur Division	*25,586*	*17,991*	*551*	*1,749*	*2,486*	*963*
11	Wardha	897	711	8	26	66	22
12	Nagpur	11,688	7,689	91	269	200	89
	Nagpur City	*9,151*	*4,607*	*80*	*167*	*79*	*5*
13	Chanda	5,446	3,844	260	998	1,313	438
14	Bhandara	7,127	5,524	191	402	811	403
15	Balaghat	428	223	1	54	96	11
	Chhattisgarh Division	*10,706*	*9,781*	*234*	*632*	*2,328*	*996*
16	Raipur	3,340	2,847	..	4	145	13
17	Bilaspur	6,917	6,231	164	441	1,969	955
18	Drug	449	703	70	187	214	28
	Berar	**25,575**	**19,602**	**2,003**	**10,295**	**1,520**	**690**
19	Amraoti	4,991	1,820	239	589	395	85
20	Akola	6,062	3,405	261	538	234	94
21	Buldana	3,974	2,151	47	146	247	84
22	Yeotmal	10,548	12,226	1,456	9,022	644	427
	Central Provinces States	**3,760**	**3,155**	**130**	**362**	**220**	**38**
23	Makrai	..	..	..	..	..	..
24	Bastar	706	655	76	16	53	7
25	Kanker	419	..	..	..	18	..
26	Nandgaon	573	19	1	111	43	6
27	Khairagarh	38	64	..	..	..	..
28	Chhuikhadan	37	215	2	23	3	19
29	Kawardha	30	6	..	..	..	..
30	Sakti	27	..	..	..	..	..
31	Raigarh	414	295	30	7	17	..
32	Sarangarh	121	..	4	..	2	..
33	Changbhakar	423	514	..	..	36	3
34	Korea	488	858	1	2	26	3
35	Surguja	392	518	16	176	1	..
36	Udaipur	30	11	..	..	1	..
37	Jashpur	62	..	..	27	20	..

Miscellaneous—*contd.*

Sub-class XII.—Unproductive.						Order 53.—Inmates of jails, asylums and alms-houses.						
Total sub-class XII.						Total order 53.						Serial No.
Total earners (principal occupations).		Total working dependants.		Total following occupation as subsidiary to other.		Total earners (principal occupations).		Total working dependants.		Total following occupation as subsidiary to other.		
Males.	Females.	Males.	Females.	Males.	Females.	Males.	Females.	Males.	Females.	Males.	Females.	
1524	1525	1526	1527	1528	1529	1530	1531	1532	1533	1534	1535	
44,717	**20,012**	**3,012**	**1,818**	**5,714**	**1,081**	..	..	**1,850**	**22**	..	..	
40,415	**18,097**	**2,680**	**1,616**	**5,333**	**1,050**	..	..	**1,664**	**21**	..	..	
28,088	**13,629**	**1,665**	**1,103**	**4,131**	**836**	..	..	**1,045**	**14**	..	..	
6,300	*2,759*	*454*	*180*	*1,211*	*221*	..	..	*260*	..	..	..	
1,401	583	85	47	229	55	..	..	..		..	..	1
994	426	29	9	324	51	..	..	..	..	..	..	2
1,757	1,017	320	105	419	72	..	..	259		..	..	3
329	*146*	*206*	*10*	*1*	*1*	..	..	*200*	..	..	..	
1,044	349	19	12	103	9	..	..	1	..	..	..	4
1,104	384	1	7	136	34	..	..	..	..	..	..	5
7,517	*1,938*	*232*	*165*	*1,196*	*131*	..	..	*85*	*5*	..	..	
1,022	403	34	52	258	41	..	..	..	..	..	..	6
2,733	608	92	40	404	42	..	..	36	3	..	..	7
1,808	338	84	6	167	7	..	..	49	..	..	..	8
824	279	13	47	236	17	..	..	..	2	..	..	9
1,130	310	9	20	131	24	..	..	..	..	..	..	10
7,141	*3,585*	*402*	*330*	*564*	*149*	..	..	*275*	*9*	..	..	
1,340	641	95	23	104	21	..	..	73	..	..	..	11
2,282	972	46	55	229	42	..	..	25	..	..	..	12
558	*401*	*29*	*14*	*127*	*6*	..	..	*25*	..	..	..	
850	641	112	103	50	34	..	..	90	6	..	..	13
1,561	913	115	83	82	45	..	..	87	3	..	..	14
1,108	418	34	66	99	7	..	..	..	..	..	..	15
7,130	*5,347*	*577*	*428*	*1,160*	*335*	..	..	*425*	..	..	..	
2,945	2,293	384	240	269	65	..	..	367	..		..	16
2,749	1,883	184	167	756	226	..	..	58	..	..	..	17
1,436	1,171	9	21	135	44	..	..	..	..	..	..	18
12,327	**4,468**	**1,015**	**513**	**1,202**	**214**	..	..	**619**	**7**	..	..	
3,612	1,294	405	96	419	75	..	..	288	..	..	..	19
3,228	1,237	261	105	359	50	..	..	183	..	..	..	20
2,661	934	128	67	257	56	..	..	79	..	..	..	21
2,826	1,003	221	245	167	33	..	..	69	7	..	..	22
4,302	**1,915**	**332**	**202**	**381**	**31**	..	..	**186**	**1**	..	..	
89	11	8	..	6	..	..	..	..	..	..	..	23
383	199	120	11	22	1	..	..	114	1	..	..	24
292	103	13	15	30	25	..	..	..	..	..	..	25
301	194	8	10	6	..	..	..	..		..	..	26
579	7	13	..	12	..	..	..	..	..	..	..	27
116	221	1	3	7	..	..	..	..	..	..	..	28
132	151	1	..	22	..	..	..	..		..	..	29
254	153	..	..	34	..	..	..	..	..	..	..	30
565	277	48	47	61	..	..	..	..	..	..	..	31
394	78	29	3	25	..	..	..	..	..	..	..	32
48	27	11	..	7	..	..	..	11	..	..	..	33
98	39	..	3	7	2	..	..	..	..	..	..	34
702	316	49	61	91	1	..	..	37		..	..	35
133	22	19	..	21	..	..	..	16	..	..	..	36
216	117	12	49	30	2	..	..	8	..	..	..	37

TABLE X — Occupation or means of

Serial No.	Class .. / Sub-class .. / Order .. / Sub-order .. / Group .. / District, City or State.	Class D.— Sub-class XII.— Order 53.—Inmates of jails, asylums and alms-houses—*concld.* 192.—Inmates of jails, asylums and alms-houses—*concld.* Total earners (principal occupations). Males.	Females.	Total working dependants. Males.	Females.	Total following occupation as subsidiary to other. Males.	Females.
1	2	1536	1537	1538	1539	1540	1541
	Central Provinces and Berar	*1,663	*117	1,850	22	..	..
	C. P. British Districts and Berar	*1,563	*114	1,664	21	..	..
	C. P. British Districts	*1,429	*114	1,045	14	..	..
	Jubbulpore Division	**806*	**22*	*260*	..	..	..
1	Saugor	..	..	..	..	..	..
2	Damoh	..	..	..	..	..	..
3	Jubbulpore	*806	*22	259	..	..	..
	Jubbulpore City	**522*	**22*	*200*	.	..	..
4	Mandla	..	..	1	..	.	..
5	Seoni	..	..	..	..	..	..
	Nerbudda Division	**118*	**1*	*85*	*5*	..	..
6	Narsinghpur	..	..	..	..	..	..
7	Hoshangabad	*4	..	36	3	..	..
8	Nimar	..	..	49	..	..	..
9	Betul	*114	*1	..	2	..	..
10	Chhindwara	..	..	..	..	..	..
	Nagpur Division	**376*	**91*	*275*	*9*	..	..
11	Wardha	*1	..	73	..	..	..
12	Nagpur	*375	*91	25	..	..	..
	Nagpur City	**375*	**91*	*25*	..	..	..
13	Chanda	..	..	90	6	..	..
14	Bhandara	..	..	87	3	..	..
15	Balaghat	..	..	..	..	..	..
	Chhattisgarh Division	**129*	..	*425*	..	..	..
16	Raipur	*96	..	367	..	..	..
17	Bilaspur	*32	..	58	..	..	..
18	Drug	*1	..	.	.	.	..
	Berar	*134	..	619	7	..	..
19	Amraoti	*48	..	288	..	..	..
20	Akola	..	..	183	..	..	..
21	Buldana	*86	..	79	..	..	..
22	Yeotmal	..	..	69	7	..	..
	Central Provinces States	*100	*3	186	1	..	..
23	Makrai	..	..	..	..	..	..
24	Bastar	..	..	114	1	..	..
25	Kanker	..	..	.	..	..	..
26	Nandgaon	..	.	..	..	..	..
27	Khairagarh	.	..	..	..	..	..
28	Chhuikhadan	..	.	..	..	..	..
29	Kawardha	..	..	.	..	..	..
30	Sakti	*9	..	..	..	..	..
31	Raigarh	..	..	..	..	..	..
32	Sarangarh	*14	..	..	..	..	..
33	Changbhakar	..	..	11	..	..	..
34	Korea	..	..	..	..	..	..
35	Surguja	.	..	37	..	..	..
36	Udaipur	*1	..	16	..	..	..
37	Jashpur	*76	*3	8	..	..	..

* The figures of persons undergoing simple imprisonment (and also of lunatics in the case of Nagpur District and City) appearing in columns 1536 and 1537 are excluded from the total of Principal Earners shown in columns 4 and 5 and included in the total of non-working dependants (columns 8 and 9); persons undergoing rigorous imprisonment are entered in columns 1538 and 1539, and have also been included in the grand total of working dependants (columns 6 and 7).

Miscellaneous—*contd.*

Unproductive—*contd*

Order 54 —Beggars, vagrants prostitutes.

Total order 54..						193.—Beggars and vagrants.						Serial No.
Total earners (principal occupations).		Total working dependants		Total following occupation as subsidiary to other		Total earners (principal occupations).		Total working dependants.		Total following occupation as subsidiary to other.		
Males.	Females.	Males.	Females.	Males.	Females	Males	Females.	Males.	Females	Males	Females.	
1542	1543	1544	1545	1546	1547	1548	1549	1550	1551	1552	1553	
44,582	**20,012**	**1,145**	**1,791**	**5,713**	**1,081**	**44,505**	**18,591**	**1,143**	**1,761**	**5,711**	**1,027**	
40,282	**18,097**	**999**	**1,590**	**5,332**	**1,050**	**40,207**	**16,701**	**997**	**1,560**	**5,330**	**996**	
27,998	**13,629**	**607**	**1,087**	**4,130**	**836**	**27,929**	**13,122**	**605**	**1,071**	**4,128**	**825**	
6,241	*2.759*	*194*	*180*	*1,211*	*221*	*6,212*	*2,709*	*194*	*179*	*1,211*	*221*	
1,389	583	85	47	229	55	1,389	575	85	47	229	55	1
994	426	29	9	324	51	990	424	29	9	324	51	2
1,757	1,017	61	105	419	72	1,732	977	61	104	419	72	3
329	*146*	*6*	*10*	*1*	*1*	*328*	*107*	*6*	*9*	*1*	*1*	
998	349	18	12	103	9	998	349	18	12	103	9	4
1,103	384	1	7	136	34	1,103	384	1	7	136	34	5
7,494	*1,938*	*141*	*158*	*1,195*	*131*	*7,461*	*1,839*	*141*	*158*	*1,194*	*124*	
1,005	403	34	52	258	41	982	402	34	52	258	41	6
2,732	608	55	37	403	42	2,722	608	55	37	402	40	7
1,807	338	30	4	167	7	1,807	242	30	4	167	2	8
824	279	13	45	236	17	824	279	13	45	236	17	9
1,126	310	9	20	131	24	1,126	308	9	20	131	24	10
7,135	*3,585*	*120*	*321*	*564*	*149*	*7,129*	*3,382*	*120*	*310*	*564*	*148*	
1,339	641	15	23	104	21	1.338	606	15	23	104	21	11
2,278	972	21	55	229	42	2,273	862	21	55	229	42	12
558	*401*	*4*	*14*	*127*	*6*	*554*	*304*	*4*	*14*	*127*	*6*	
849	641	22	97	50	34	849	594	22	86	50	33	13
1,561	913	28	80	82	45	1,561	902	28	80	82	45	14
1,108	418	34	66	99	7	1,108	418	34	66	99	7	15
7,128	*5,347*	*152*	*428*	*1,160*	*335*	*7,127*	*5,192*	*150*	*424*	*1,159*	*332*	
2,944	2,293	17	240	269	65	2,944	2,239	17	237	269	65	16
2,748	1,883	126	167	756	226	2,747	1,813	124	166	755	223	17
1,436	1.171	9	21	135	44	1,436	1,140	9	21	135	44	18
12,284	**4.468**	**392**	**503**	**1,202**	**214**	**12,278**	**3,579**	**392**	**489**	**1,202**	**171**	
3,609	1,294	115	94	419	75	3.605	975	115	90	419	56	19
3,199	1,237	76	105	359	50	3,199	1,029	76	103	359	34	20
2,661	934	49	67	257	56	2,661	703	49	61	257	49	21
2,815	1,003	152	237	167	33	2,813	872	152	235	167	32	22
4,300	**1,915**	**146**	**201**	**381**	**31**	**4,298**	**1,890**	**146**	**201**	**381**	**31**	
89	11	8	..	6	..	89	11	8	..	6	..	23
381	199	6	10	22	1	381	199	6	10	22	1	24
292	103	13	15	30	25	292	103	13	15	30	25	25
301	194	8	10	6	.	301	194	8	10	6	..	26
579	7	13	..	12	..	579	7	13	..	12	..	27
116	221	1	3	7	..	116	221	1	3	7	..	28
132	151	1	..	22	..	132	138	1	..	22	..	29
254	153	..	..	34	..	254	153	..	..	34	..	30
565	277	48	47	61	..	565	274	48	47	61	..	31
394	78	29	3	25	..	394	69	29	3	25	..	32
48	27	..	..	7	..	48	27	..	..	7	..	33
98	39	..	3	7	2	96	39	..	3	7	2	34
702	316	12	61	9	1	702	316	12	61	91	1	35
133	22	3	..	21	..	133	22	3	..	21	..	36
216	117	4	49	30	2	216	117	4	49	30	2	37

TABLE X — Occupation or means of

Serial No.	Class .. / Sub-class .. / Order .. / Sub-order .. / Group ..	Class D.— Sub-class XII.— Order 54.—Beggars, vagrants, prostitutes—*concld.* 194.—Procurers and prostitutes.					
	District, City or State.	Total earners (principal occupations).		Total working dependants.		Total following occupation as subsidiary to other.	
		Males.	Females.	Males.	Females.	Males.	Females.
1	2	1554	1555	1556	1557	1558	1559
	Central Provinces and Berar ..	**77**	**1,421**	**2**	**30**	**2**	**54**
	C. P. British Districts and Berar ..	**75**	**1,396**	**2**	**30**	**2**	**54**
	C. P. British Districts ..	**69**	**507**	**2**	**16**	**2**	**11**
	Jubbulpore Division ..	*29*	*50*	..	*1*	..	..
1	Saugor	..	8	..	..	..	..
2	Damoh	4	2	..	..	..	..
3	Jubbulpore	25	40	..	1	..	..
	Jubbulpore City	*1*	*39*	..	*1*	..	..
4	Mandla	..	.	..	..	..	..
5	Seoni	..	..	..	..	..	..
	Nerbudda Division	*33*	*99*	..	..	*1*	*7*
6	Narsinghpur	23	1	..	..	..	..
7	Hoshangabad	10	..	..	..	1	2
8	Nimar	..	96	..	..	..	5
9	Betul	..	..	..	..	..	..
10	Chhindwara	..	2	..	..	..	..
	Nagpur Division	*6*	*203*	..	*11*	..	*1*
11	Wardha	1	35	..	..	..	..
12	Nagpur	5	110	..	..	..	..
	Nagpur City	*4*	*97*	..	..	..	..
13	Chanda	..	47	..	11	..	1
14	Bhandara	..	11	..	..	..	..
15	Balaghat	..	..	..	..	..	..
	Chhattisgarh Division	*1*	*155*	*2*	*4*	*1*	*3*
16	Raipur	..	54	..	3	..	..
17	Bilaspur	1	70	2	1	1	3
18	Drug	..	31	..	..	..	..
	Berar	**6**	**889**	..	**14**	..	**43**
19	Amraoti	4	319	..	4	..	19
20	Akola	..	208	..	2	..	16
21	Buldana	..	231	..	6	..	7
22	Yeotmal	2	131	..	2	..	1
	Central Provinces States	**2**	**25**	..	..	..	..
23	Makrai	..		..	..	..	..
24	Bastar						
25	Kanker	..	..	..	..	..	..
26	Nandgaon	..	..	..	..	..	..
27	Khairagarh	..	..	..	..	..	..
28	Chhuikhadan	..	..	..	..	..	..
29	Kawardha	..	13	.	..	..	..
30	Sakti	..	..	..	..	..	..
31	Raigarh	..	3	..	..	..	..
32	Sarangarh	..	9	..	..	..	..
33	Changbhakar	..	..	..	..	..	..
34	Korea	2	..	..	..	..	..
35	Surguja	..	..	..	..	..	..
36	Udaipur	..	..	..	..	..	..
37	Jashpur	..	..	..	..	..	..

Livelihood—General Distribution—*concld.* **TABLE X**

Miscellaneous—*concld.*

Unproductive—*concld.*

Order 55.—Other unclassified non-productive industries.

Total order 55.						195.—Other unclassified non-productive industries.						Serial No.
Total earners (principal occupations).		Total working dependants.		Total following occupation as subsidiary to other.		Total earners (principal occupations).		Total working dependants.		Total following occupation as subsidiary to other.		
Males.	Females.	Males.	Females.	Males.	Females.	Males.	Females.	Males.	Females	Males.	Females	
1560	1561	1562	1563	1564	1565	1566	1567	1568	1569	1570	1571	
135	..	17	5	1	..	(a) 135	..	(b) 17	(c) 5	1	..	
133	..	17	5	1	..	133	..	17	5	1	..	
90	..	13	2	1	..	90	..	13	2	1	..	
59	..	..	..	..	..	*59*	..	..	..	..	..	
12	..	..	..	..	..	12	..	..	..	..	..	1
..	..	..	..	..	..	..	..	..	..	..	..	2
..	..	..	..	..	..	..	..	..	..	..	..	3
..	..	..	..	..	..	..	..	..	..	..	..	
46	..	..	..	..	..	46	..	..	..	..	..	4
1	..	..	..	..	..	1	..	..	..	..	..	5
23	..	6	2	*1*	..	*23*	..	6	2	*1*	..	
17	..	..	..	..	..	17	..	..	..	..	..	6
1	..	1	..	1	..	1	..	1	..	1	..	7
1	..	5	2	..	..	1	..	5	2	..	..	8
..	..	..	..	..	..	..	..	..	..	..	..	9
4	..	..	..	..	..	4	..	..	..	..	..	10
6	..	7	..	..	..	*6*	..	7	..	..	..	
1	..	7	..	..	..	1	..	7	..	..	..	11
4	..	..	..	..	..	4	..	..	..	..	..	12
..	..	..	..	..	..	..	..	..	..	..	..	
1	..	..	..	..	..	1	..	..	..	..	..	13
..	..	..	..	..	..	..	..	..	..	..	..	14
..	..	..	..	..	..	..	..	..	..	..	..	15
2	..	..	..	..	..	*2*	..	..	..	..	..	
1	..	..	..	..	..	1	..	..	..	..	..	16
1	..	..	..	..	..	1	..	..	..	..	..	17
..	..	..	..	..	..	..	..	..	..	..	..	18
43	..	4	3	..	..	43	..	4	3	..	..	
3	..	2	2	..	..	3	..	2	2	..	..	19
29	..	2	..	..	..	29	..	2	..	..	..	20
..	..	..	..	..	..	..	..	..	..	..	..	21
11	..	..	1	..	..	11	..	..	1	..	..	22
2	..	..	..	..	..	2	..	..	..	..	..	
..	..	..	..	..	..	..	..	..	..	..	..	23
2	..	..	..	..	..	2	..	..	..	..	..	24
..	..	..	..	..	..	..	..	..	..	..	..	25
..	..	..	..	..	..	..	..	..	..	..	..	26
..	..	..	..	..	..	..	..	..	..	..	..	27
..	..	..	..	..	..	..	..	..	..	..	..	28
..	..	..	..	..	..	..	..	..	..	..	..	29
..	..	..	..	..	..	..	..	..	..	..	..	30
..	..	..	..	..	..	..	..	..	..	..	..	31
..	..	..	..	..	..	..	..	..	..	..	..	32
..	..	..	..	..	..	..	..	..	..	..	..	33
..	..	..	..	..	..	..	..	..	..	..	..	34
..	..	..	..	..	..	..	..	..	..	..	..	35
..	..	..	..	..	..	..	..	..	..	..	..	36
..	..	..	..	..	..	..	..	..	..	..	..	37

(a) Inc udes 43 congressmen. Includes 4 congressmen. (c) Includes 2 congressmen

TABLE XI

Occupation by Caste, Tribe or Race.

1. This table is important as indicating the extent to which traditional occupations are being abandoned.

2. The information given in the corresponding Table XXI of 1921 has been modified, but sub-classes of occupations have been divided under the same minor heads as then.

3. The number of persons in each caste agrees with that shown in Table XVII except in respect of caste returns by Indian Christians. The latter in this table are not included in the figures of the castes to which they originally belonged.

TABLE XI

Occupation by Caste,

Caste, tribe or race.	Traditional occupation.	Population dealt with					Number of earners whose traditional caste occupation was returned as their			
		Earners.		Working dependants.		Non-working dependants.	Principal means of livelihood.		Subsidiary means of livelihood.	
		Males.	Females.	Males	Females.	Both sexes.	Males.	Females.	Males.	Females.
1	2	3	4	5	6	7	8	9	10	11
Ahir										
Province ..	Graziers ..	231,566	101,362	29,113	76,597	379,456	62,840	8,439	10,001	1,365
Andh Berar ..	Agriculturists ..	18,568	15,070	711	1,609	22,561	16,498	13,935	48	42
Bahna ..	Cotton-carders ..	8,005	3,254	565	1,593	16,271	1,556	418	390	61
Nerbudda Valley ..	..	4,815	2,059	345	878	9,977	1,130	271	285	40
Seoni ..	..	522	224	43	151	872	80	35	28	6
Nagpur ..	..	1,366	618	45	153	2,890	172	82	25	5
Chhindwara ..	..	1,302	353	132	411	2,532	174	30	52	10
Baiga ..	Agriculturists ..	7,157	2,736	491	2,107	15,752	4,038	120	101	92
Jubbulpore ..	..	774	404	55	354	1,078	429	18	92	92
Mandla ..	..	4,932	1,701	233	1,240	11,832	2,919	76	5	..
Balaghat ..	..	1,451	631	203	513	2,842	690	26	4	..
Bairagi										
Province ..	Devotees ..	11,199	3,402	1,011	2,353	20,508	2,020	428	475	76
Balahi ..	Cotton-weavers ..	15,627	9,901	1,210	4,086	21,669	597	57	64	159
Hoshangabad ..	..	6,451	4,078	295	1,191	8,299	330	15	50	..
Nimar ..	..	8,537	5,306	915	2,660	12,783	246	36	14	9
Makrai ..	..	639	517	..	235	587	21	6	..	150
Bania										
Province ..	Traders ..	68,521	10,949	3,527	3,555	147,108	36,149	4,105	3,685	224
Banjara ..	Pack-bullock carriers ..	45,203	31,058	3,580	10,216	62,104	1,166	1,712	294	125
Plateau Division ..	..	2,004	859	139	510	2,965	275	23	25	..
Maratha Division ..	..	34,571	26,520	2,289	6,394	44,648	362	1,386	30	47
Chhattisgarh Administra-clutive Division.	..	2,604	1,711	257	898	3,911	228	234	127	53
Chhattisgarh States (excluding Bastar.)	..	511	236	134	240	986	67	43	72	25
Nimar ..	..	4,690	1,459	573	1,777	8,148	18	15	12	..
Bastar ..	..	823	273	188	397	1,446	216	11	28	..
Barhai										
Province ..	Carpenters ..	35,274	12,632	1,475	4,168	58,415	25,444	546	2,310	34
Basor										
Nerbudda Valley ..	Bamboo-workers ..	9,348	5,779	327	1,502	14,774	6,300	3,244	587	248
Beldar ..	Earth-workers ..	1,648	924	58	256	2,629	771	302	20	3
Saugor ..	..	160	64	7	39	289	47	15	..	..
Jubbulpore ..	..	345	117	9	56	507	98	20	2	..
Nimar ..	..	360	208	29	87	597	256	124	4	..
Wardha ..	..	590	406	12	58	835	265	78	6	..
Nagpur ..	..	193	129	1	16	401	105	65	8	3
Bhaina Bilaspur ..	Agriculturists ..	4,672	3,091	147	778	6,543	3,530	2,138	8	8
Bharia-Bhumia	Agriculturists ..	11,148	8,174	476	2,043	16,509	2,993	330	129	8
Jubbulpore ..		8,484	6,946	124	648	12,804	1,511	272	115	8
Narsinghpur ..		673	393	60	198	821	210	8	12	..
Chhindwara ..		1,991	835	292	1,197	2,884	1,272	50	2	..

Number of working dependants following the traditional occupation of their caste.		Number of earners returning their traditional occupation as their principal means of livelihood who had some subsidiary occupation.		Recorded principal occupation of earners, other than traditional occupation of caste (by sub-classes). I.—Exploitation of animals and vegetation. Income from rent of land.		Cultivators of all kinds.		Agents and managers of landed estates, planters, forest officers and their clerks, rent collectors, etc.		Field labourers wood cutters, etc.		Raisers of live-stock, milkmen and herdsmen.	
Males.	Females.	Males.	Females.	Males.	Females.	Males.	Females.	Males.	Females.	Males.	Females.	Males	Females.
12	13	14	15	16	17	18	19	20	21	22	23	24	25
9,807	7,703	4,537	816	1,010	274	93,372	15,666	623	394	51,446	57,072	1,775	2,545
494	1,152	162	40	..	..	..	..	8	..	960	575	397	2
39	**146**	**579**	**99**	**63**	**11**	**2,181**	**193**	**46**	**1**	**1,928**	**2,034**	**141**	**44**
22	85	480	77	16	8	1,323	162	25	1	1,286	1,225	108	40
1	15	39	12	2	1	186	12	1	..	111	145	6	1
5	23	33	10	22	1	263	5	11	..	273	423	14	1
11	23	27	..	23	1	409	14	9	..	258	241	13	2
358	**1,014**	**248**	**12**	**9**	**1**	..	..	**97**	**2**	**2,382**	**2.209**	**77**	**5**
23	9	78	2	9	..	..	..	85	2	89	145	10	2
193	727	91	1	..	..	..	..	11	..	1,807	1,538	40	1
142	278	79	9	..	1	..	..	1	..	486	526	27	2
126	142	214	12	204	36	4,550	824	21	38	719	852	54	20
19	**96**	**69**	**11**	**136**	**10**	**3,044**	**66**	**417**	**3**	**9,152**	**9,487**	**515**	**6**
1	4	37	5	9	6	584	19	2	3	4,592	3,913	275	1
17	7	32	1	20	4	2,460	44	1	..	4,512	5,071	240	5
1	85	..	5	107	..	..	3	414	..	48	503	..	..
1,450	604	4,572	261	1,541	350	13,323	1,441	447	64	4,082	3,540	188	29
332	**303**	**139**	**458**	**721**	**78**	**16,194**	**2,844**	**62**	**473**	**22,247**	**24,039**	**1,864**	**90**
4	2	10	2	12	7	652	44	6	..	594	613	89	9
180	93	65	425	693	60	11,425	2,338	23	472	18,951	21,237	1,486	66
32	108	40	25	3	2	1,059	309	4	1	753	711	62	13
9	35	3	..	7	..	218	21	1	..	110	68	4	..
76	..	7	5	4	9	2,676	97	15	..	1,696	1,278	129	1
31	65	14	1	2	..	164	35	13	..	143	132	94	1
525	196	3,329	44	229	71	4,152	708	69	1	3,136	10,540	383	35
167	708	1,725	555	..	2	414	45	..	..	1,360	1,589	209	10
24	**62**	**62**	**36**	**30**	**10**	**144**	**45**	**46**	..	**238**	**376**	**5**	**11**
..	5	2	..	25	..	..	4	36	..	2	42	..	..
3	..	2	9	..	..	15	3	5	..	23	..	..	2
17	47	34	9	..	..	16	..	..	..	40	63	..	1
3	7	14	4	4	7	86	36	5	..	154	227	4	7
1	3	10	14	1	3	27	2	..	..	19	44	1	1
152	733	107	100	16	..	21	1	62	..	792	879	57	1
67	**1,558**	**521**	**33**	**5**	**1**	..	..	**52**	**229**	**5,696**	**5,324**	**271**	**123**
39	299	352	29	4	1	..	..	51	3	4,878	4,640	175	6
2	87	100	3	..	..	..	..	..	225	290	94	10	..
26	1,172	69	1	1	..	..	..	1	1	528	590	86	117

Caste, tribe or race.	Traditional occupation.	Recorded principal occupation of earners, — I.—Exploitation of animals and vegetation. — Fishing and hunting.		II.—Exploitation of minerals. — Owners, managers, clerks, etc.		II.—Exploitation of minerals. — Labourers.		III.— Owners, managers, clerks, etc.	
		Males.	Females.	Males.	Females.	Males.	Females.	Males.	Females.
1	2	26	27	28	29	30	31	32	33
Ahir									
Province	Graziers	31	..	16	2	764	255	33	8
Andh									
Berar	Agriculturists	2	..	..	..	..	..	6	..
Bahna	Cotton carders	2	7	1	..	64	9	..	..
Nerbudda Valley		1	7	1	..	18	..	..	..
Seoni		..	..	..	..	..	..	..	..
Nagpur		1	..	..	..	1	..	..	..
Chhindwara		..	..	..	..	45	9	..	..
Baiga	Agriculturists	..	..	..	..	..	7	..	..
Jubbulpore		..	..	..	..	..	2	..	..
Mandla		..	..	..	..	..	5	..	..
Balaghat		..	..	..	..	..	..	..	..
Bairagi									
Province	Devotees	..	..	3	..	8	..	3	1
Balahi	Cotton-weavers	..	..	..	6	2	..	1	9
Hoshangabad		..	..	..	..	1	..	1	..
Nimar		..	..	..	6	..	..	..	9
Makrai		..	..	..	..	1	..	..	..
Bania									
Province	Traders	2	1	47	..	66	15	218	7
Banjara	Pack-bullock carriers	17	25	..	2	22	4	12	..
Plateau Division		3	..	..	..	15	2	..	..
Maratha Division		..	22	..	..	4	2	11	..
Chhattisgarh Administrative Division.		..	3	..	2	..	..	..	..
Chhattisgarh States (excluding Bastar).		..	..	..	..	..	..	..	..
Nimar		1	..	..	..	3	..	1	..
Bastar		13	..	..	..	..	..	..	..
Barhai									
Province	Carpenters	18	2	2	..	83	12	7	..
Basor									
Nerbudda Valley	Bamboo-workers	..	..	..	..	21	..	2	..
Beldar	Earth-workers	1	1	..	..	1	3	28	..
Saugor		..	..	..	..	..	..	27	..
Jubbulpore		1	..	..	..	..	..	..	..
Nimar		..	..	..	..	..	..	..	..
Wardha		..	1	..	..	..	..	1	..
Nagpur		..	..	..	..	1	3	..	..
Bhaina									
Bilaspur	Agriculturists	..	1	..	..	5	..	..	..
Bharia-Bhumia	Agriculturists	..	..	..	..	108	51	..	..
Jubbulpore		..	..	..	..	88	45	..	..
Narsinghpur		..	..	..	..	..	..	..	..
Chhindwara		..	..	..	..	20	6	..	..

other than traditional occupation of caste (by sub-classes)—*contd.*

Industry.		IV.—Transport.				V.—Trade.		VI.—Public Force.				VII.—Public Administration.	
Artisans and other workmen.		Owners, managers, ships' officers, etc.		Labourers, boatmen, carters, palki-bearers, etc.				Commissioned and gazetted officers.		Others.		Gazetted officers.	
Males.	Females.	Males.	Females.	Males.	Females.	Males.	Females.	Males.	Females.	Males.	Females.	Males.	Females.
34	35	36	37	38	39	40	41	42	43	44	45	46	47
2,145	894	46	10	3,335	330	2,800	2,849	4	..	706	3	7	..
90	2	6	..	18	..	50	14	..	..	5	..	..	..
391	**173**	**4**	..	**230**	**16**	**769**	**197**	..	..	**35**	**5**	..	..
299	155	3	..	151	2	111	79	..	..	22	5	..	..
..	3	..	..	22	1	77	16	..	..	2	..	..	..
79	11	..	..	14	13	377	67	..	..	10	..	..	..
13	4	1	..	43	..	204	35	..	..	1	..	..	..
223	**25**	..	**8**	**45**	**3**	**173**	**245**	..	..	**6**	..	..	..
23	2	..	8	16	..	74	140	..	..	..	..	..	..
29	17	..	..	26	2	39	46	..	..	5	..	..	..
171	6	..	..	3	1	60	59	..	..	1	..	..	..
98	53	3	4	80	18	239	128	4	..	26	..	2	
126	**14**	..	**95**	**130**	**13**	**109**	**35**	..	..	**1,039**	**1**	..	—
14	14	..	..	34	..	37	33	..	..	370	1	..	..
111	..	..	95	96	13	71	..	..	..	640	..	..	..
1	..	..	..	..	..	1	2	..	..	29	..	..	..
2,704	304	135	1	577	21	..	..	8	..	121	1	53	1
472	**316**	**9**	..	**238**	**47**	**1,018**	**548**	..	..	**16**	..	..	..
54	113	4	..	54	1	141	23	..	..	1	..	..	..
381	134	..	..	114	6	300	64	..	..	1	..	..	..
10	37	5	..	11	2	365	327	..	..	4	..	..	..
7	26	..	..	10	4	67	65	..	..	4	..	..	..
12	1	..	..	49	25	7	..	..	..	6	..	..	..
8	5	..	..	..	9	138	69	..	..	..	..	..	..
597	141	10	..	155	6	217	137	17	..	11	..	6	..
111	27	1	..	93	7	71	89	..	..	203	..	..	..
133	**25**	**1**	..	**39**	**13**	**95**	**53**	..	..	**7**	..	..	..
..	..	1	..	18	..	..	3	..	..	1	..	..	..
57	14	..	..	16	1	57	35	..	..	6	..	..	..
26	5	..	..	2	12	11	..	..	..	..	..	..	..
39	3	..	..	1	..	12	11	..	..	..	..	..	..
11	3	..	..	2	..	15	4	..	..	..	..	..	..
11	1	..	..	13	1	10	5	..	..	2	..	..	..
195	**50**	**1**	..	**60**	**6**	**230**	**395**	..	..	**14**	..	..	..
163	42	..	..	40	1	81	308	..	..	9	..	..	..
9	4	..	..	..	..	143	59	..	..	1	..	..	..
23	4	1	..	..	5	6	28	..	..	4	..	..	..

Caste, tribe or race.	Traditional occupation.	Recorded principal occupation of earners, VII.—Public Administration—concld. Others. Males.	Females.	VIII.—Professions and Liberal Arts. Religious. Males	Females.	Lawyers, doctors and teachers. Males	Females.	Others. Males.	Females.
1	2	48	49	50	51	52	53	54	55
Ahir									
Province	Graziers ..	1,234	46	43	1	275	28	290	23
Andh									
Berar	Agriculturists ..	19	..	2	..	9	..	..	4
Bahna	Cotton-carders ..	64	..	2	..	40	..	6	1
Nerbudda Valley.. ..	..	14	..	1	..	13	..	2	1
Seoni	..	3	..	..	..	12	..	1	..
Nagpur	..	16	..	1	..	7	..	2	..
Chhindwara	..	31	..	..	..	8	..	1	..
Baiga	Agriculturists ..	6	..	14	..	..	..	1	1
Jubbulpore ..	..	..	..	..	..	..	..	..	..
Mandla	..	6	..	4	..	..	..	1	1
Balaghat	..	..	..	10	..	..	..	..	..
Bairagi									
Province	Devotees ..	70	..	328	33	101	10	48	..
Balahi	Cotton-weavers ..	67	5	3	..	2	2	9	16
Hoshangabad	..	49	..	1	..	..	..	..	14
Nimar	..	18	4	2	..	2	2	9	..
Makrai	..	..	1	..	..	..	..	..	2
Bania									
Province	Traders ..	558	12	284	13	745	72	167	16
Banjara .. .	Pack-bullock carriers ..	54	6	5	1	17	..	8	3
Plateau Division	..	..	..	..	1	..	..	..	1
Maratha Division ..	..	47	1	4	..	16	..	2	2
Chhattisgarh Administrative Division.	..	5	5	..	..	..	..	5	..
Chhattisgarh States (excluding Bastar)	..	1	..	..	..	1	..	..	..
Nimar	..	..	..	1	..	..	..	1	..
Bastar	..	1	..	..	..	..	..	..	..
Barhai									
Province	Carpenters ..	57	2	10	1	56	4	31	6
Basor									
Nerbudda Valley ..	Bamboo-workers ..	88	..	..	..	1	13	134	474
Beldar	Earth-workers ..	5	2	..	..	6	..	3	..
Saugor	..	..	..	..	..	..	..	..	..
Jubbulpore	..	2	..	..	..	..	..	..	..
Nimar .. .	..	..	2	..	..	1	..	3	..
Wardha	..	2	..	..	..	2	..	..	..
Nagpur ..	..	1	..	..	..	3	..	..	..
Bhaina									
Bilaspur	Agriculturists ..	..	..	..	..	..	..	..	..
Bharia-Bhumia ..	Agriculturists ..	4	..	..	1	..	..	1	2
Jubbulpore	..	1	..	..	1	..	..	..	..
Narsinghpur	..	..	..	..	..	..	..	..	..
Chhindwara	..	3	..	..	..	..	..	1	2

Tribe or Race—*contd.*

TABLE XI

other than traditional occupation of caste (by sub-classes)—*concld.*

IX.—Persons living on their income.		X.—Domestic service.		XI.—Insufficiently described occupations.				XII.—Unproductive.			
				Contractors, clerks, cashiers, etc., otherwise unspecified.		Labourers unspecified.		Beggars and prostitutes.		Other unclassified non-productive industries.	
Males.	Females.	Males.	Females.	Males.	Females.	Males.	Females.	Males.	Females.	Males.	Females.
56	57	58	59	60	61	62	63	64	65	66	67
102	136	5,056	9,796	364	53	2,743	2,122	506	416	..	..
..	..	53	7	..	22	415	505	30	4	..	..
4	1	178	28	35	3	240	105	25	8	..	..
3	1	96	19	20	2	164	78	8	3	..	..
..	..	10	3	1	..	8	5	..	2	..	..
..	..	29	2	5	..	52	9	17	3	..	..
1	..	43	4	9	1	16	13	..	..	..	..
..	..	25	20	1	..	55	86	5	4	..	..
..	..	1	15	..	..	38	69	..	1	..	..
..	..	24	5	1	..	16	6	4	3	..	..
..	..	..	..	..	..	1	11	1	..	..	..
20	2	195	32	9	2	48	44	2,346	877	..	..
81	10	25	21	59	3	91	39	22	3	..	..
80	1	..	21	58	..	14	34	..	3	..	..
1	9	8	..	1	3	77	5	22	..	..	..
..	..	17	..	..	..	..	..	..	..	..	..
1,229	178	3,460	291	1,241	16	749	344	427	127	..	..
8	3	213	64	180	13	511	737	149	53	..	..
..	..	13	9	79	1	7	10	5	2	..	..
3	..	139	25	100	12	425	671	84	22	..	..
2	3	24	19	1	..	38	20	25	23	..	..
3	..	9	..	..	..	..	3	2	6	..	..
..	..	4	..	..	..	40	33	27	..	..	..
..	..	24	11	..	..	1	..	6	..	..	..
15	*8*	*140*	*59*	*77*	*6*	*272*	*259*	*80*	*88*	..	..
3	..	97	178	103	2	91	77	46	22	..	..
1	..	17	19	6	..	68	61	3	3	..	..
1	..	1	..	1	..	..	..	..	..	..	..
..	..	9	5	3	..	52	36	1	1	..	..
..	..	2	..	1	..	1	1	1	..	..	..
..	..	3	14	..	..	11	20	1	2	..	..
..	..	2	..	1	..	4	4	..	..	..	..
..	..	107	17	1	..	41	44	4	3	..	..
..	..	47	70	97	3	1,372	1,577	2	12	..	..
..	..	43	54	96	3	1,344	1,560	..	10	..	..
..	..	..	..	..	..	8	3	2	..	..	..
..	..	4	16	1	..	20	14	..	2	..	..

TABLE XI

Occupation by Caste,

Caste, tribe or race.	Traditional occupation.	Population dealt with. — Earners. — Males.	Earners. — Females.	Working dependants. — Males.	Working dependants. — Females	Non-working dependants. — Both sexes.	Number of earners whose traditional caste occupation was returned as their Principal means of livelihood. — Males.	Principal means of livelihood. — Females.	Subsidiary means of livelihood. — Males.	Subsidiary means of livelihood. — Females.
1	2	3	4	5	6	7	8	9	10	11
Bhil										
Nimar ..	Agriculturists ..	7,114	4,202	1,116	2,873	9,688	2,646	256	7	4
Bhilala ..	Agriculturists ..	4,826	1,620	467	1,706	7,212	2,713	106	6	..
Hoshangabad ..	..	804	372	59	155	1,156	193	13	1	..
Nimar ..	..	4,022	1,248	408	1,551	6,056	2,520	93	5	..
Bhoyar ..	Agriculturists ..	20,646	8,978	1,558	7,999	31,329	15,008	4,616	22	..
Betul ..	..	8,089	2,906	145	805	14,391	5,275	126	8	..
Chhindwara ..	..	7,127	1,661	1,212	5,877	10,174	4,655	224	12	..
Wardha ..	..	4,228	3,586	170	1,211	5,033	3,937	3,466	1	..
Nagpur ..	..	1,202	825	31	106	1,731	1,141	800	1	..
Bhunjia										
Raipur ..	Agriculturists ..	2,248	1,110	146	603	3,151	1,235	108	60	57
Binjhwar ..	Agriculturists ..	15,933	7,934	1,253	4,929	23,756	7,806	2,173	75	20
Bhandara	..	1,089	814	94	219	1,521	652	612	21	9
Balaghat ..	..	2,754	2,017	86	633	2,769	438	248	16	..
Raipur ..	..	8,827	3,562	1,014	3,694	12,126	3,976	401	16	6
Bilaspur	..	3,263	1,541	59	383	7,340	2,740	912	22	5
Brahman										
Province	Priests ..	155,221	18,950	7,797	8,141	327,640	15,545	1,170	4,420	201
Chadar ..	Village watchmen ..	8,121	3,900	413	1,170	12,802	1,298	5	118	1
Saugor ..	..	4,424	1,852	245	659	7,102	748	1	64	..
Damoh ..	..	2,107	1,261	59	241	3,119	264	..	25	1
Narsinghpur ..	..	831	423	85	176	1,288	134	2	3	..
Jubbulpore ..	..	759	364	24	94	1,293	152	2	26	..
Chamar										
Province ..	Leather-workers ..	173,608	97,015	4,892	49,541	290,611	39,654	5,000	8,214	800
Dahayat										
Jubbulpore	Village watchmen ..	2,634	1,157	124	527	4.336	595	10	148	..
Darsi—										
Province ..	Tailors ..	15,772	4,599	584	2,088	28,186	11,229	1,992	629	135
Deswali ..	Agriculturists ..	2,046	565	306	623	3,421	1,167	84	61	4
Hoshangabad ..	..	1,372	339	232	424	2,342	688	33	52	4
Nimar ..	..	674	226	74	199	1,079	479	51	9	..
Dhanuk										
Narsinghpur ..	Labourers ..	1,463	1,089	164	425	2,045	548	542	11	3
Dhanwar										
Bilaspur ..	Agriculturists ..	3,300	1,704	185	558	7,024	1,847	614	59	97
Dhimar										
Province ..	Water-bearers ..	98,146	65,928	4,663	16,521	137,558	8,136	8,122	1,921	777
Dhobi										
Province ..	Washermen ..	53,651	31,212	4,883	15,658	82,190	18,628	12,857	5,439	1,909

Tribe or Race—*contd.*

TABLE XI

Number of working dependants following the traditional occupation of their caste.		Number of earners returning their traditional occupation as their principal means of livelihood who had some subsidiary occupation.		Recorded principal occupation of earners, other than traditional occupation of caste (by sub-classes). I—Exploitation of animals and vegetation. Income from rent of land.		Cultivators of all kinds.		Agents and managers of landed estates, planters, forest officers and their clerks, rent collectors, etc.		Field labourers wood cutters, etc.		Raisers of live-stock, milkmen, and herdsmen.	
Males.	Females.	Males.	Females.	Males.	Females.	Males.	Females.	Males.	Females.	Males.	Females.	Males.	Females.
12	13	14	15	16	17	18	19	20	21	22	23	24	25
590	1,356	41	5	1	..	..	..	2	..	4,107	3,913	172	2
275	**869**	**49**	**1**	**38**	**17**	..	..	**8**	..	**1,795**	**1,477**	**139**	**1**
27	35	7	1	18	9	..	..	1	..	488	337	45	..
248	834	42	..	20	8	..	..	7	..	1,307	1,140	94	1
575	**5,321**	**412**	**16**	**68**	**47**	**1**	..	**45**	..	**4,202**	**4,084**	**638**	**33**
29	547	124	8	62	40	..	..	13	..	2,094	2,684	391	4
399	3,971	247	8	4	7	1	..	9	..	2,102	1,400	129	..
118	770	36	..	..	..	..	..	22	..	..	..	105	29
29	33	5	..	2	..	..	..	1	..	6	..	13	..
40	202	168	13	4	..	..	..	..	..	874	878	36	30
1,001	**1,899**	**878**	**197**	**29**	**5**	**10**	..	**3**	..	**6,361**	**4,977**	**351**	**12**
49	185	65	56	..	..	10	..	..	..	31	51	89	5
19	60	71	62	1	..	..	..	..	..	1,400	1,339	83	4
903	1,477	459	3	25	3	..	..	3	..	4,510	3,002	159	3
30	177	283	76	3	2	..	..	..	..	420	585	20	..
549	285	2,403	109	4,849	1,147	49,675	5,652	2,291	41	9,325	4,094	588	62
17	**14**	**566**	..	**38**	**6**	**1,758**	**144**	**48**	..	**3,890**	**3,473**	**403**	**13**
1	..	334	..	6	1	1,061	56	8	..	2,000	1,690	290	5
1	..	92	..	3	2	359	24	..	..	1,221	1,151	84	4
10	14	60	..	1	2	151	14	3	..	412	365	29	1
5	..	80	..	28	1	187	50	37	..	257	267	..	3
1,696	4,109	9,282	1,079	1,989	249	64,102	14,674	901	109	49,295	66,814	3,643	175
14	5	354	4	..	1	805	120	25	1	76 5	724	33	3
420	1,071	892	194	71	15	1,619	228	34	2	1,220	2,007	113	3
196	**447**	**104**	**2**	**67**	**21**	..	..	**15**	..	**526**	**433**	**109**	**3**
173	262	93	2	65	16	..	..	15	..	386	264	74	3
23	185	11	..	2	5	..	..	..	..	140	169	35	..
22	141	50	43	1	4	449	26	..	..	339	340	26	1
152	408	242	67	2	..	..	..	..	6	788	794	3	2
306	1,637	2,118	1,614	307	63	20,865	4,201	387	413	19,367	30,082	2,957	193
1,050	5,177	5,090	2,552	201	92	16,670	3,882	53	21	13,571	13,126	993	45

TABLE XI — **Occupation by Caste,**

Caste, tribe or race.	Traditional occupation.	Recorded principal occupation of earners. I.—Exploitation of animals and vegetation. Fishing and hunting. Males.	Females.	II.—Exploitation of minerals. Owners, managers, clerks, etc. Males.	Females.	Labourers. Males.	Females.	III.— Owners, managers, clerks, etc. Males.	Females.
1	2	26	27	28		30	31	32	33
Bhil									
Nimar	Agriculturists ..	15	1	..	1	2	..	..	..
Bhilala	Agriculturists ..	..	..	..	..	..	1	..	..
Hoshangabad	..	..	..	..	..	..	1	..	..
Nimar	..	..	..	..	..	..	..	..	..
Bhoyar	Agriculturists ..	1	..	..	..	32	9	..	..
Betul	..	..	..	..	..	1	..	..	..
Chhíndwára	..	1	..	..	..	29	8	..	..
Wardha	..	..	..	..	..	..	..	..	..
Nagpur	..	..	..	..	..	2	1	..	..
Bhunjia									
Raipur	Agriculturists ..	..	2	..	..	1	..	..	..
Binjhwar	Agriculturists ..	537	215	..	..	40	23	1	..
Bhandara	..	41	6	..	..	..	2	..	..
Balaghat	..	488	209	..	..	34	21	..	..
Raipur	..	4	..	..	..	6	..	1	..
Bilaspur	..	4	..	..	..	..	..	..	..
Brahman									
Province	Priests ..	11	..	92	1	503	25	837	
Chadar ..	Village watchmen ..	29	..	..	..	1	..	..	..
Saugor	..	..	..	..	..	..	..	..	..
Damoh	..	..	..	..	..	1	..	..	..
Narsinghpur	..	..	..	..	..	..	..	..	..
Jubbulpore	..	29	..	..	..	..	..	..	..
Chamar									
Province	Leather-workers ..	18	58	1	2	408	253	669	89
Dahayat									
Jubbulpore	Village watchmen ..	..	..	3	..	39	12	..	..
Dazri									
Province	Tailors ..	2	..	4	..	17	1	7	..
Deswali	Agriculturists ..	..	..	..	..	..	..	..	..
Hoshangabad	..	..	..	..	..	..	..	..	..
Nimar	..	..	..	..	..	..	..	..	..
Dhanuk									
Narsinghpur	Labourers ..	..	..	..	..	..	..	..	..
Dhanwar									
Bilaspur	Agriculturists ..	93	29	..	..	..	..	..	..
Dhimar									
Province	Water-bearers ..	30,476	5,041	409	3	430	143	9	36
Dhobi									
Province	Washermen ..	15	15	..	..	91	16	99	2

other than traditional occupation of caste (by sub-classes)—*contd.*

Industry.		IV.—Transport.				V.—Trade.		VI.—Public Force.				VII.—Public Administration.	
Artisans, and other workmen.		Owners, managers, ships' officers, etc.		Labourers, boatmen, carters, palki bearers, etc.				Commissioned and gazetted officers.		Others.		Gazetted Officers.	
Males.	Females.	Males.	Females.	Males.	Females.	Males.	Females.	Males.	Females.	Males.	Females.	Males.	Females.
34	35	36	37	38	39	40	41	42	43	44	45	46	47
18	1	..	..	6	..	38	13	..	..	84	..	..	.
29	1	..	..	8	1	19	2	..	..	5	..	..	..
8	..	..	..	8	1	9	1	..	..	..	..	..	..
21	1	..	..	..	..	10	1	..	..	5	..	..	..
100	17	2	..	128	13	117	24	..	..	16	..	..	..
26	2	2	..	67	..	20	13	..	..	7	..	..	..
28	2	..	..	55	..	40	5	..	..	9	..	..	..
31	6	..	..	1	13	49	4	..	..	..	..	..	..
1	7	..	..	5	..	8	2	..	..	..	..	..	..
14	1	..		3	1	61	56	..	..	3	..	..	..
144	93	1		44	16	218	226	..	..	37	18	1	..
84	26	..	..	73	12	37	32	..	..	1	..	..	..
51	..	1	..	7	..	165	137	..	..	7	18	..	..
8	67	..	..	6	..	12	55	..	..	26	..	..	..
1	..	..	.	8	4	4	2	..	..	3	..	1	..
5,606	410	1,606	2	4,403	49	12,046	1,107	266	..	3,357	3	538	3
242	90	8	3	106	4	106	62	..	..	6	1	..	.
135	24	..	2	64	..	34	38	..	..	3	1	..	..
39	30	8	1	20	1	48	14	..	..	2	..	..	..
56	28	..	..	11	3	19	5	..	..	..	..	..	..
12	8	..	..	11	..	5	5	..	..	1	..	..	..
2,178	1,064	3	..	2,992	698	1,367	1,590	..	..	181	4	..	..
212	47	..	..	29	11	10	10	..	..	14	2	..	..
222	59	15	..	73	1	577	96	1	..	18	..	2	..
12	6	..	..	56	..	13	..	..	..	3	..	..	..
9	6	..	..	53	..	12	..	..	..	2	..	..	..
3	..	..	..	3	..	1	..	..	..	1	..	..	..
3	5	..	..	5	..	77	167	..	..	..	..	..	..
315	101	..	2	..	..	75	100	..	..	..	..	..	..
2,454	3,541	146	14	1,642	153	5,256	10,767	..	40	76	..	3	..
566	190	75	..	480	71	429	137	1	..	63	1	2	..

TABLE XI — **Occupation by Caste,**

Caste, tribe or race.	Traditional occupation.	Recorded principal occupation of earners, VII.—Public Administration—concld. Others. Males.	Females.	VIII.—Professions and Liberal Arts. Religious. Males.	Females.	Lawyers, doctors and teachers. Males.	Females.	Others. Males.	Females.
1	2	48	49	50	51	52	53	54	55
Bhil									
Nimar	Agriculturists	..	..	..	1	..	..	1	1
Bhilala	Agriculturists	1	..	4	..	4	..	6	..
Hoshangabad		..	..	..	..	1	..	5	..
Nimar		1	..	4	..	3	..	1	..
Bhoyar	Agriculturists	62	..	..	..	16	..	16	1
Betul		31	..	..	..	3	..	1	1
Chhindwara		8	..	..	..	6	..	11	..
Wardha		23	..	..	..	4	..	4	..
Nagpur		..	..	..	..	3	..	..	..
Bhunjia									
Raipur	Agriculturists	2	..	..	..	..	..	2	15
Binjhwar	Agriculturists	18	1	23	2	2	..	2	1
Bhandara		4	1	..	..	..	..	1	1
Balaghat		1	..	22	1	2	..	..	..
Raipur		12	..	1	1	..	..	1	..
Bilaspur		1	..	..	..	..	..	..	..
Brahman									
Province	Priests	9,509	85	1,269	153	6,807	303	1,461	99
Chadar	Village watchmen	17	..	..	..	3	..	4	3
Saugor		12	..	..	..	3	..	3	3
Damoh		2	..	..	..	..	..	1	..
Narsinghpur		1	..	..	..	..	..	..	..
Jubbulpore		2	..	..	..	..	..	..	..
Chamar									
Province	Leather-workers	102	33	4	..	14	43	237	722
Dahayat									
Jubbulpore	Village watchmen	8	1	1	..	8	..	1	1
Darzi									
Province	Tailors	96	1	11	..	87	11	29	3
Deswali	Agriculturists	4	..	1	..	..	..	1	..
Hoshangabad		4	..	1	..	..	..	1	..
Nimar		..	..	..	..	..	..	..	..
Dhanuk									
Narsinghpur	Labourers	..	..	..	..	..	..	..	..
Dhanwar									
Bilaspur	Agriculturists	..	1	1	..	..	..	7	1
Dhimar									
Province	Water-bearers	630	49	30	2	104	22	313	55
Dhobi									
Province	Washermen	132	1	12	..	108	2	128	20

other than traditional occupation of caste (by sub-classes)—*concld.*

IX.—Persons living on their income.		X.—Domestic Service.		XI.—Insufficiently described occupations.				XII.—Unproductive.			
				Contractors, Clerks, Cashiers, etc., otherwise unspecified.		Labourers unspecified.		Beggars and prostitutes.		Other unclassified non-productive industries.	
Males.	Females.	Males.	Females.	Males.	Females.	Males.	Females.	Males.	Females.	Males.	Females
56	57	58	59	60	61	62	63	64	65	66	67
..	..	15	2	..	..	1	7	6	4	..	..
..	2	52	2	4	2	..	7	1	1	..	..
..	..	24	2	4	..	..	7	..	1	..	..
..	2	28	..	..	2	..	..	1	..	..	..
3	..	74	42	11	21	87	60	19	11	..	.
..	..	40	5	2	21	49	8	5	2	..	..
3	..	13	10	9	..	13	..	2	5	..	..
..	..	18	27	..	..	24	37	10	4	..	..
..	..	3	..	..	..	1	15	2	..	..	..
1	1	4	10	1	1	.	2	7	5	..	..
4	2	161	63	11	13	92	81	37	13	..	..
2	1	35	10	11	13	67	42	1	..	..	..
..	..	36	32	..	.	17	7	1	1	..	..
1	..	41	4	..	..	1	15	34	11	..	..
1	1	49	17	..	..	7	71	1	1	..	..
1,968	232	11,124	1,108	3,745	75	2,167	576	5,628	2,549	5	..
5	..	46	7	2	1	96	81	15	7	..	..
3	..	33	4	..	1	17	21	4	5	..	..
1	..	3	..	1	..	41	32	9	2	..	..
..	..	9	1	..	..	3	2	2	..	..	..
1	..	1	2	1	..	35	26	..	..	..	..
49	85	1,660	535	241	40	3,409	4,487	491	291	..	..
1	..	59	5	11	..	202	202	2	7	..	..
14	8	148	38	42	9	78	104	43	21	..	..
..	..	17	10	..	..	51	7	4	1	..	..
..	..	11	10	..	..	51	7	..	..	..	..
..	..	6	..	..	..	..	..	4	1	..	..
	1	14	2	..	..	..	..	1	1	..	..
..	..	55	10	1	..	83	41	2	3	..	..
56	22	1,657	1,122	332	75	1,870	1,519	234	250	..	..
34	2	519	91	67	6	423	338	291	297	..	..

TABLE XI — **Occupation by Caste,**

Caste, tribe or race.	Traditional occupation.	Population dealt with. — Earners. — Males.	Population dealt with. — Earners. — Females.	Population dealt with. — Working dependants. — Males.	Population dealt with. — Working dependants. — Females.	Population dealt with. — Non-working dependants. — Both sexes.	Number of earners whose traditional caste occupation was returned as their — Principal means of livelihood. — Males.	Number of earners whose traditional caste occupation was returned as their — Principal means of livelihood. — Females.	Number of earners whose traditional caste occupation was returned as their — Subsidiary means of livelihood. — Males.	Number of earners whose traditional caste occupation was returned as their — Subsidiary means of livelihood. — Females.
1	2	3	4	5	6	7	8	9	10	11
Ganda ..	Cotton-weavers ..	**47,337**	**19,674**	**6,776**	**18,805**	**81,191**	**7,014**	**2,334**	**3,095**	**401**
Chhattisgarh Administrative Division.	..	30,792	15,497	3,045	10,425	48,786	3,259	2,079	1,934	343
Chhattisgarh States	..	12,811	3,701	2,987	6,121	25,102	2,155	127	646	48
Surguja ..	..	914	197	268	592	1,637	311	9	46	4
Jashpur ..	..	2,820	279	476	1,667	5,666	1,289	119	469	6
Ghasia ..	Labourers ..	**8,979**	**5,725**	**731**	**2,115**	**16,346**	**3,991**	**3,461**	**115**	**55**
Chhattisgarh Administrative Division.		6,430	4,501	326	1,251	10,886	2,752	2,690	91	42
Chhattisgarh States	.. ..	2,549	1,224	405	864	5,460	1,239	771	24	13
Golar—										
Yoetmal ..	Graziers ..	525	608	15	74	946	319	51	..	..
Gond—										
Province ..	Agriculturists ..	638,946	343,121	75,368	236,698	966,985	379,141	122,245	4,807	:6,523
Gosain .	Devotees ..	**6,377**	**2,266**	**513**	**1,263**	**11,329**	**1,066**	**183**	**160**	**4**
Balaghat ..	..	489	93	26	167	837	26	7	5	..
Narsinghpur	..	431	116	56	96	701	43	2	9	1
Jubbulpore ..	..	503	147	34	115	965	32	14	21	..
Hoshangabad ..	..	803	196	57	97	1,418	146	12	18	..
Nagpur ..	..	928	426	12	52	1,410	346	36	38	..
Wardha ..	..	580	251	4	23	766	129	24	8	1
Bhandara ..	..	483	316	128	104	620	105	32	13	1
Raipur ..	..	798	233	52	291	1,242	156	37	20	..
Bilaspur ..	..	957	393	53	167	2,375	49	19	14	1
Drug ..	..	405	95	91	151	995	34	..	14	..
Gowari—										
Maratha Division	Graziers ..	54,301	40,067	2,500	9,278	57,409	8,614	1,583	159	114
Halba ..	Agriculturists ..	**9,002**	**4,571**	**2,094**	**3,828**	**14,702**	**5,240**	**1,307**	**100**	**99**
Raipur ..	..	1,844	1,658	61	78	2,427	984	634	..	..
Chanda ..	..	1,022	569	113	223	1,360	797	439	35	30
Bastar ..	..	3,962	1,114	1,221	2,120	7,735	2,438	150	20	33
Kanker ..	..	2,174	1,230	699	1,407	3,180	1,021	84	45	36
Kahar ..	Palki-bearers ..	**5,149**	**2,851**	**409**	**1,195**	**8,087**	**51**	**21**	**8**	**2**
Narsinghpur ..	..	548	236	78	254	937	..	..	1	..
Hoshangabad ..	..	2,211	1,296	128	338	3,534	6	18	..	2
Nimar ..	..	957	543	107	221	1,599	1	..	7	..
Bilaspur ..	.	1,433	776	96	382	2,017	44	3	..	..
Kalar—										
Province ..	Distillers ..	59,688	23,079	8,702	21,940	105,756	1,988	253	700	57
Katia ..	Spinners ..	**11,510**	**5,353**	**995**	**4,437**	**16,458**	**476**	**129**	**82**	**27**
Plateau Division ..	..	8,231	3,354	785	4,027	11,346	311	54	78	24
Narsinghpur ..	..	513	299	34	73	901	43	26	1	3
Hoshangabad ..	..	2,766	1,700	176	337	4,211	122	49	3	..
Kawar ..	Agriculturists ..	**44,090**	**16,095**	**10,826**	**23,402**	**86,858**	**34,198**	**6,849**	**329**	**1,341**
Chanda ..		550	274	16	81	914	503	258	..	..
Chhattisgarh Administrative Division.	..	27,200	11,204	3,872	12,204	53,403	22,094	5,775	289	1,217
Chhattisgarh States ..	..	16,340	4,617	6,938	11,117	32,541	11,601	816	40	124

Number of working dependants following the traditional occupation of their caste.		Number of earners returning their traditional occupation as their principal means of livelihood who had some subsidiary occupation.		Recorded principal occupation of earners, other than traditional occupation of caste (by sub-classes). I—Exploitation of animals and vegetation. Income from rent of land.		Cultivators of all kinds.		Agents and managers of landed estates, planters, forest officers and their clerks, rent collectors, etc.		Field labourers wood cutters, etc.		Raisers of live-stock, milkmen, and herdsmen.	
Males.	Females.	Males.	Females.	Males.	Females.	Males.	Females.	Males.	Females.	Males.	Females.	Males.	Females.
12	13	14	15	16	17	18	19	20	21	22	23	24	25
1,541	**4,225**	**1,464**	**266**	**66**	**20**	**17,593**	**2,840**	**27**	..	**14,375**	**12,403**	**1,934**	**491**
689	1,994	542	261	29	16	12,059	2,452	17	..	9,837	9,635	1,236	285
506	1,390	320	3	4	1	3,946	340	8	..	4,208	2,625	661	91
178	77	43	..	31	..	418	37	2	..	99	53	22	93
168	764	559	2	2	3	1,170	11	..	..	231	90	15	22
187	**334**	**142**	**171**	**21**	**1**	**2,559**	**590**	**16**	**12**	**28**	**74**	**115**	**6**
57	120	104	148	21	..	2,000	565	16	12	..	25	77	6
130	214	38	23	..	1	559	25	..	..	28	49	38	..
3	..	31	..	16	..	60	4	..	..	78	548	..	..
51,472	132,553	27,553	5,699	1,077	473	..	..	1,566	527	198,267	194,958	23,269	1,500
31	**8**	**116**	**26**	**138**	**32**	**2,396**	**434**	**101**	**5**	**692**	**1,152**	**67**	**8**
..	..	11	1	12	4	134	6	2	..	36	16	2	..
1	3	11	1	16	1	205	11	..	..	116	83	3	..
3	.	1	3	4	..	299	50	8	..	54	50	8	..
..	..	13	3	22	9	266	3	2	..	156	142	22	1
1	2	24	4	15	..	178	13	16	..	51	327	15	1
..	1	5	5	12	3	80	7	6	..	55	191	6	..
10	1	20	2	11	4	135	69	2	..	63	168	3	..
3	1	21	2	9	6	335	60	54	..	45	59	4	..
12	..	4	5	30	1	586	188	1	5	86	98	2	6
1	..	6	..	7	4	178	27	10	..	30	18	2	..
584	158	279	115	504	38	9,480	2,056	269	..	28,415	33,357	1,763	60
1,432	**2,429**	**384**	**109**	**10**	**7**	..	..	**36**	..	**2,817**	**2,700**	**171**	**84**
21	252	43	6	1	..	..	..	2	..	619	964	71	8
50	203	208	93	..	..	..	..	5	..	9	8	30	1
917	1,283	89	8	9	1	..	..	24	..	1,150	726	37	75
444	691	44	2	..	6	..	..	5	..	1,039	1,002	33	..
..	**13**	..	**5**	**14**	**10**	**1,577**	**509**	**40**	**4**	**1,253**	**1,050**	**134**	**1**
..	..	..	..	5	4	194	12	..	..	199	103	18	..
..	12	..	5	3	4	430	42	32	4	507	461	99	1
..	..	..	..	2	2	107	5	8	..	191	226	15	..
..	1	..	..	4	..	846	450	..	..	356	260	2	..
291	381	274	40	849	143	32,154	5,413	375	9	13,283	14,754	762	36
32	**137**	**110**	**51**	**163**	**16**	**5,082**	**183**	**66**	**6**	**3,264**	**4,457**	**412**	**19**
18	117	47	25	146	11	4,310	160	52	..	1,975	2,807	212	12
12	1	5	..	5	1	105	13	..	..	208	213	2	3
2	19	58	26	12	4	667	10	14	6	1,081	1,437	198	4
7,392	**13,404**	**2,665**	**336**	**100**	**4**	**187**	**54**	**6**	..	**7,838**	**8,543**	**417**	**23**
14	81	31	..	..	..	..	..	..	..	..	..	..	1
3,111	8,117	823	257	58	4	187	6	6	..	4,067	4,976	217	19
4,267	5,206	1,811	79	42	..	..	48	..	..	3,771	3,567	200	3

TABLE XI **Occupation by Caste,**

Caste, tribe or race.	Traditional occupation.	I.—Exploitation of animals and vegetation. Fishing and hunting. Males.	I.—Fishing and hunting. Females.	Recorded principal occupation of earners, II.—Exploitation of minerals. Owners, managers, clerks, etc. Males.	II.—Owners, managers, clerks, etc. Females.	II.—Labourers. Males.	II.—Labourers. Females.	III.— Owners, managers, clerks, etc. Males.	III.— Owners, managers, clerks, etc. Females.
1	2	26	27	28	29	30	31	32	33
Ganda	Cotton-weavers ..	13	19	..	..	46	18	..	..
Chhattisgarh Administrative Division.	..	4	16	..	..	33	12	..	..
Chhattisgarh States ..	..	9	3	..	..	13	4	..	..
Surguja	..	..	..	..	..	..	2	..	..
Jashpur	..	..	..	..	..	..	..	..	..
Ghasia	Labourers ..	6	13	1	..	5	2	30	..
Chhattisgarh Administrative Division.	..	6	13	1	..	5	2	28	..
Chhattisgarh States ..	..	..	..	..	..	..	..	2	..
Golar—									
Yeotmal	Graziers ..	..	..	..	..	..	..	..	..
Gond—									
Province	Agriculturists ..	571	70	208	4	2,868	1,697	107	5
Gosain	Devotees ..	..	1	..	..	7	..	..	..
Balaghat ..	..	..	..	..	..	4	..	..	..
Narsinghpur	..	..	..	..	..	..	..	..	..
Jubbulpore	..	..	..	..	..	..	..	..	..
Hoshangabad	..	..	..	..	..	..	..	..	..
Nagpur	..	..	..	..	..	3	..	..	..
Wardha	..	..	..	..	..	..	..	..	..
Bhandara	..	..	..	..	..	..	..	..	..
Raipur	..	..	..	..	..	..	..	..	..
Bilaspur	..	..	..	..	..	..	..	..	..
Drug	..	..	1	..	..	..	..	..	..
Gowari—									
Maratha Division ..	Graziers ..	14	1	..	5	198	54	13	..
Halba	Agriculturists ..	4	..	..	4	..	..	..	..
Raipur	..	..	..	..	..		..	..	..
Chanda	..	..	..	..	..	..	..	..	..
Bastar	..	4	..	..	4	..	..	..	..
Kanker	..	..	..	..	..	..	..	..	..
Kahar	Palki bearers ..	846	33	8	..	48	1	1	..
Narsinghpur	..	9	..	..	..	..	..	..	..
Hoshangabad	..	358	6	..	..	48	1	1	..
Nimar	..	372	3	..	..	..	..	..	..
Bilaspur	..	107	24	8	..	..	..	..	..
Kalar—									
Province ..	Distillers ..	19	1	6	..	189	70	29	1
Katia	Spinners ..	2	..	..	7	186	63	..	20
Plateau Division	..	1	..	..	..	181	63	..	..
Narsinghpur	..	1	..	..	..	..	..	..	..
Hoshangabad	..	..	..	..	7	5	..	..	20
Kawar	Agriculturists ..	80	3	1	100	..	..	3	..
Chanda	..	24	..	1	..	..	..	..	..
Chhattisgarh Administrative Division.	..	47	3	..	100	..	..	..	..
Chhattisgarh States ..	..	9	..	..	..	..	..	3	..

other than traditional occupation of caste (by sub-classes)—*contd.*

Industry.		IV.—Transport.				V.—Trade.		VI.—Public Force.				VII.—Public Administration.	
Artisans and other workmen.		Owners, managers, ships' officers, etc.		Labourers, boatmen, carters, palki bearers, etc.				Commissioned and gazetted officers.		Others.		Gazetted officers.	
Males.	Females.	Males.	Females.	Males.	Females.	Males.	Females.	Males.	Females.	Males.	Females.	Males.	Females.
34	35	36	37	38	39	40	41	42	43	44	45	46	47
213	65	..	2	515	203	411	334	14	21	1,787	7	..	..
141	51	..	2	282	62	304	261	..	21	1,072	4	..	..
70	14	..	..	232	141	103	60	14	..	698	3	..	..
2	..	..	..	..	..	..	..	..	..	15	..	..	..
..	..	..	..	1	..	4	13	..	..	2	..	..	..
393	365	12	1	138	4	608	809	..	..	83	1	..	..
218	284	12	..	117	1	394	656	..	..	56	1	..	..
175	81	..	1	21	3	214	153	..	..	27	..	..	..
26	..	..	..	..	..	2	..	..	..	..	..	..	..
6,058	3,197	120	7	4,465	1,028	3,819	6,303	17	..	639	8	1	..
80	20	3	..	38	2	309	61	..	..	19	..	1	..
7	..	..	..	..	..	28	..	..	..	8	..	..	..
..	3	3	..	3	..	5	..	..	..	..	..	..	..
15	2	..	..	5	..	5	1	..	..	2	..	..	..
8	1	..	..	16	..	17	5	..	..	3	..	..	..
14	..	..	..	4	..	62	20	..	..	2	..	..	..
15	2	..	..	2	..	96	6	..	..	..	..	..	..
13	8	..	..	..	..	43	4	..	..	2	..	..	..
6	4	..	..	3	..	37	18	..	..	2	..	1	..
1	..	..	..	4	2	12	6	..	..	..	..	..	..
1	..	..	..	1	..	4	1	..	..	..	..	..	..
1,347	869	16	..	373	21	431	208	..	..	26	..	1	..
253	138	1	..	31	14	71	142	..	..	43	3	..	..
98	1	..	..	3	..	14	32	..	..	3	..	..	..
96	92	..	..	4	8	4	9	..	..	..	..	..	..
59	36	1	..	21	6	32	45	..	..	32	3	..	..
..	9	..	..	3	..	21	56	..	..	8	..	..	..
50	13	3	19	95	5	438	661	2	..	13	..	..	..
..	..	..	..	2	..	50	38	..	..	..	..	..	..
27	2	1	19	57	..	199	337	..	..	10	..	..	..
10	10	1	..	27	5	181	265	..	..	1	..	..	..
13	1	1	..	9	..	8	21	2	..	2	..	..	..
1,465	358	31	3	831	24	4,091	1,163	12	..	163	..	2	..
228	13	4	13	283	81	278	110	..	..	534	..	..	..
73	6	3	..	134	15	156	102	..	..	395	..	..	..
32	7	1	..	16	..	30	8	..	..	25	..	..	..
123	..	..	13	133	66	92	..	..	..	114	..	..	..
111	30	10	9	140	13	223	289	..	..	57	5	..	..
6	..	..	..	..	..	1	..	..	..	..	..	..	..
43	26	..	9	40	9	109	140	..	..	5	5	..	..
62	4	10	..	100	4	113	149	..	..	52	..	..	..

TABLE XI — **Occupation by Caste,**

Caste, tribe or race.	Traditional occupation.	Recorded principal occupation of earners,							
		VII.—Public Administration—*concld.*		VIII.—Professions and Liberal Arts.					
		Others.		Religious.		Lawyers, doctors and teachers.		Others.	
		Males.	Females.	Males.	Females.	Males.	Females.	Males.	Females.
1	2	48	49	50	51	52	53	54	55
Ganda	**Cotton-weavers** ..	**407**	**5**	**13**	..	**45**	..	**1,175**	**116**
Chhattisgarh Administrative Division. ..		288	4	4	..	36	..	913	81
Chhattisgarh States		92	1	..	..	5	..	258	35
Surguja		..	..	..	..	..	..	4	..
Jashpur		27	..	9	..	4	..	..	..
Ghasia	**Labourers** ..	**18**	**1**	..	..	**7**	**8**	**76**	**64**
Chhattisgarh Administrative Division. ..		13	1	..	..	6	6	57	54
Chhattisgarh States		5	..	..	..	1	2	19	10
Golar—									
Yeotma	Graziers ..	4	..	..	..	..	..	4	..
Gond—									
Province	Agriculturists ..	1,249	59	188	23	311	24	394	162
Gosain	**Devotees** ..	**67**	**14**	**198**	**27**	**51**	**3**	**6**	**1**
Balaghat		8	12	18	..	16	..	1	..
Narsinghpur		1	..	1	4	2	..	..	..
Jubbulpore		1	..	8	..	1	..	..	1
Hoshangabad		1	..	6	1	2	..	..	..
Nagpur		6	2	71	10	6	1	..	..
Wardha		5	..	16	1	8	..	2	..
Bhandara		28	..	15	8	5	2	..	..
Raipur		13	..	5	..	6	..	2	..
Bilaspur		2	..	41	..	3	..	1	..
Drug		2	..	17	3	2	..	..	..
Gowari—									
Maratha Division ..	Graziers ..	200	7	18	..	52	4	57	11
Halba	**Agriculturists** ..	**55**	..	..	..	**17**	..	**11**	**2**
Raipur		3	..	..	..	2	..	2	..
Chanda		5	..	..	..	1	..	2	..
Bastar		40	..	..	..	8	..	7	2
Kanker		7	..	..	..	6	..	..	..
Kahar	**Palki bearers** ..	**27**	..	**1**	..	**5**	..	**4**	..
Narsinghpur		1	..	..	..	..	..	..	..
Hoshangabad		19	..	..	..	1	..	4	..
Nimar		3	..	1	..	1	..	..	..
Bilaspur		4	..	..	..	3	..	..	..
Kalar—									
Province	Distillers ..	352	1	16	1	305	13	76	12
Katia	**Spinners** ..	**153**	**3**	**3**	..	**22**	..	**5**	..
Plateau Division		97	1	2	..	11	..	4	..
Narsinghpur		13	..	..	..	4	..	..	..
Hoshangabad		43	2	1	..	7	..	1	..
Kawar	**Agriculturists** ..	**17**	..	**4**	..	**22**	..	**11**	**1**
Chanda		..	..	..	..	1	..	..	..
Chhattisgarh Administrative Division. ..		14	..	2	..	4	..	11	1
Chhattisgarh States		3	..	2	..	17	..	..	..

other than traditional occupation of caste (by sub-classes)—*concld.*

IX.—Persons living on their income.		X.—Domestic service.		XI.—Insufficiently described occupations.				XII.—Unproductive.			
				Contractors, clerks, cashiers, etc., otherwise unspecified.		Labourers unspecified.		Beggars and prostitutes.		Other unclassified non-productive industries.	
Males.	Females.	Males.	Females.	Males.	Females.	Males.	Females.	Males.	Females.	Males.	Females.
56	57	58	59	60	61	62	63	64	65	66	67
30	4	1,019	344	10	1	385	271	245	176	..	..
14	3	769	134	5	..	327	257	163	122	..	..
16	1	192	203	..	..	55	13	72	39	..	..
..	..	1	..	5	..	1	..	3	3	..	..
..	..	57	7	..	1	2	1	7	12	..	..
83	21	733	211	..	..	..	10	56	71	..	..
57	2	557	118	..	..	..	9	37	56	..	..
26	19	176	93	..	..	..	1	19	15	..	..
..	..	..	..	..	..	15	5	1	..	..	..
244	88	5,173	2,175	937	335	7,196	7,474	1,061	759	..	..
8	1	109	19	21	8	54	34	946	261	..	..
1	..	9	..	..	..	..	..	177	48	..	..
1	..	2	1	..	..	2	1	28	10	..	..
1	..	7	..	1	..	16	13	36	16	..	..
1	..	14	5	..	..	5	3	116	14	..	..
1	..	28	3	12	..	10	7	88	6	..	..
1	..	5	..	1	8	10	2	131	7	..	..
..	..	4	1	6	..	6	4	42	16	..	..
1	..	15	..	1	..	..	3	103	46	..	..
1	1	20	9	..	..	2	1	116	57	..	..
..	..	5	..	..	..	3	..	109	41	..	..
18	8	803	428	322	22	1,172	1,268	195	67	..	..
2	8	104	81	16	..	92	64	28	17	..	..
2	..	16	12	..	..	15	3	9	4	..	..
..	..	19	1	16	..	33	11	1	..	..	..
..	8	50	11	..	..	44	38	6	9	..	..
..	..	19	57	..	..	..	12	12	4	..	..
7	..	442	495	4	..	81	28	5	1	..	..
1	..	51	75	..	..	17	4	1	..	..	..
5	..	358	390	2	..	43	11	1	..	..	..
1	..	20	23	2	..	12	4	1	..	..	..
..	..	13	7		..	9	9	2	1	..	..
67	19	1,166	131	484	67	822	526	151	81	..	..
3	29	117	35	3	49	216	113	10	7	..	..
2	..	46	33	2	11	110	83	8	6	..	..
1	..	2	2	1	..	23	25	1	1	..	..
..	29	69	..	..	48	83	5	1	..	..	..
2	..	380	31	6	17	128	86	149	38	..	..
..	..	1	..	3	..	10	15	..	..	..	..
1	..	121	20	1	17	116	69	57	25	..	..
1	..	258	11	2	..	2	2	92	13	..	..

TABLE XI — **Occupation by Caste,**

Caste, tribe or race.	Traditional occupation.	Population dealt with. Earners. Males.	Population dealt with. Earners. Females.	Population dealt with. Working dependants. Males.	Population dealt with. Working dependants. Females.	Population dealt with. Non-working dependants. Both sexes.	Number of earners whose traditional caste occupation was returned as their Principal means of livelihood. Males.	Principal means of livelihood. Females.	Subsidiary means of livelihood. Males.	Subsidiary means of livelihood. Females.
1	2	3	4	5	6	7	8	9	10	11
Kayasth—										
Province ..	Writers ..	10,970	1,111	394	460	25,892	1,092	11	30	..
Kewat ..	Boatmen ..	**4,019**	**2,690**	**139**	**696**	**4,863**	**19**	**1**	**5**	**59**
Jubbulpore ..	..	1,863	1,161	44	350	2,441	14	1	4	..
Narsinghpur ..	..	82	35	11	29	121	..	..	..	..
Chanda ..	..	2,074	1,494	84	317	2,301	5	..	1	59
Khangar ..	Village watchmen ..	**3,433**	**1,318**	**115**	**428**	**5,690**	**352**	**1**	**66**	..
Saugor ..	..	1,832	595	69	236	3,050	265	..	28	..
Damoh ..	..	569	295	11	65	814	60	..	35	..
Narsinghpur ..	..	262	118	7	27	456	11	..	..	..
Jubbulpore ..	..	770	310	28	100	1,370	16	1	3	..
Kol ..	Agriculturists ..	**23,417**	**19,224**	**710**	**2,067**	**31,217**	**5,446**	**1,357**	**207**	**92**
Jubbulpore ..	..	17,691	15,853	629	1,593	22,061	3,627	1,263	201	92
Mandla ..	..	3,271	2,678	3	13	4,959	500	16	4	..
Chhota Nagpur States ..	..	2,455	693	78	461	4,197	1,319	78	2	..
Koli—										
Berar ..	Fisherman ..	12,209	9,013	601	1,298	14,948	171	225	24	7
Kolta— Raigarh ..	Agriculturists ..	2,793	418	1,670	2,624	6,712	2,447	178	9	1
Komti— Chanda ..	Traders ..	988	137	20	50	2,351	712	84	69	5
Kori—										
Nerbudda Valley	Cotton-weavers ..	9,172	4,333	287	1,224	13,548	2,525	602	194	64
Korku ..	Agriculturists ..	**39,028**	**16,052**	**7,224**	**23,237**	**59,962**	**25,094**	**3,829**	**1,489**	**1,324**
Hoshangabad ..	..	6,710	2,991	577	2,010	9,726	2,967	87	14	1
Nimar ..	..	12,863	4,596	3,381	9,566	21,766	6,835	151	1,200	1,239
Betul ..	..	11,125	4,640	682	6,758	14,259	7,804	137	10	6
Amraoti ..	..	8,330	3,825	2,584	4,903	14,211	7,488	3,454	265	78
Koshti ..	Cotton-weavers ..	**45,067**	**14,298**	**3,536**	**19,994**	**74,013**	**33,888**	**8,615**	**2,311**	**586**
Jubbulpore ..	..	401	109	13	47	764	225	39	2	1
Seoni ..	..	362	58	38	284	456	289	23	..	..
Chhindwara ..	..	1,043	115	118	655	2,065	917	81	3	..
Nimar ..	..	234	141	64	29	439	120	10	1	..
Maratha Division	..	31,765	10,422	1,289	11,127	49,248	24,361	6,232	347	99
Chhattisgarh Administrative Division.	..	11,262	3,453	2,014	7,852	21,041	7,976	2,230	1,958	486
Kumhar—										
Province ..	Potters ..	38,308	17,013	3,617	13,160	59,211	24,736	10,781	3,721	762
Kumbi ..	Agriculturists ..	**394,392**	**210,413**	**28,661**	**72,793**	**566,792**	**323,486**	**178,569**	**2,986**	**680**
Maratha Division	..	361,987	201,797	25,376	59,272	517,308	301,507	177,690	2,863	626
Chhindwara ..	..	9,170	1,792	813	5,220	13,748	6,905	490	27	2
Nimar ..	..	4,901	817	1,638	3,362	7,829	3,243	122	30	1
Betul ..	..	18,334	6,007	834	4,939	27,907	11,831	267	66	51
Kurmi ..	Agriculturists ..	**85,970**	**27,235**	**11,069**	**37,166**	**153,064**	**63,096**	**11,623**	**870**	**720**
Nerbudda Valley ..	..	34,650	8.211	3,270	10,558	60,243	4,059	1,959	295	189
Plateau Division ..	..	5,337	1,487	559	2,173	9,865	2,796	489	60	4
Chhattisgarh Administrative Division.	..	41,806	15,071	6,255	23,285	74,097	32,920	7,952	493	512
Chhattisgarh States ..	..	4,177	2,466	985	1,150	8,859	3,321	1,223	22	15

Number of working dependents following the traditional occupation of their caste.		Number of earners returning their traditional occupation as their principal means of livelihood who had some subsidiary occupation.		Recorded principal occupation of earners, other than traditional occupation of caste (by sub-classes). I—Exploitation of animals and vegetation. Income from rent of land.		Cultivators of all kinds.		Agents and managers of landed estates, planters, forest officers and their clerks, rent collectors, etc.		Field labourers, wood cutters, etc.		Raisers of live-stock, milkmen and herdsmen.	
Males.	Females.	Males	Females.	Males.	Females.	Males.	Females.	Males.	Females.	Males.	Females.	Males.	Females.
12	13	14	15	16	17	18	19	20	21	22	23	24	25
17	6	83	1	341	69	2,592	374	343	18	637	342	23	3
..	**60**	**5**	..	**6**	**1**	**1,096**	**216**	**28**	..	**942**	**1,531**	**151**	**2**
..	..	1	..	..	1	660	96	26	..	668	806	48	1
..	..	..	..	1	.	20		.	..	46	26	2	..
..	60	4	..	5	..	416	120	2	..	228	699	101	1
1	..	**101**	..	**10**	**15**	**1,077**	**87**	**46**	**255**	**1,133**	**778**	**144**	**2**
1	..	82	..	4	..	516	20	17	2	638	508	99	2
..	..	12	..	..	9	141	..	3	253	238	..	39	..
..	..	1	..	3	4	60	5	1	..	97	84	3	..
..	..	6	..	3	2	360	62	25	..	160	186	3	..
94	**966**	**985**	**121**	**3**	**1**	**12**	**3**	**47**	**1**	**11,043**	**12,822**	**650**	**91**
45	615	912	119	3	1	..	..	47	1	8,066	10,157	382	89
1	6	57	2	..	..	..	..	..	..	2,234	2,220	191	..
48	345	16	..	..	..	12	3	..	..	743	445	77	2
43	97	43	25	253	13	3,027	358	33	1	7,353	7,960	243	3
1,180	1,842	24	37	10	..	..	..	..	..	281	204	10	..
13	4	153	12	30	4	149	16	11	..	12	21	3	..
97	581	485	156	47	..	718	129	270	4	1,549	1,891	153	14
3,278	**12,342**	**5,265**	**506**	**31**	**18**	..	..	**59**	**105**	**11,215**	**11,195**	**1,468**	**52**
75	782	953	61	14	4	..	..	5	..	3,180	2,788	358	14
1,064	6,089	550	2	7	10	..	..	19	..	5,314	4,405	558	8
230	1,593	1,379	53	10	4	..	..	26	11	2,632	3,989	402	25
1,909	3,878	2,383	390	..	.	.	.	9	94	89	13	150	5
3,100	**11,960**	**2,297**	**549**	**504**	**29**	**4,151**	**1,053**	**88**	.	**2,654**	**3,539**	**129**	**6**
..	26	5	1	..	..	10	4	..	..	3	2	..	..
31	264	.	..	..	..	2	..	.	..	6	15	..	..
110	621	50	1	5	..	19	.	2	..	25	18	1	..
..	12	30	10	..	..	18	40	23	..	11	51	..	..
1,022	7,512	884	292	464	28	1,403	194	63	..	2,423	3,193	110	4
1,937	3,525	1,328	245	35	1	2,699	815	...	...	186	260	18	2
1,826	7,636	3,806	884	139	47	7,508	890	34	13	3,341	4,252	345	71
17,525	**51,317**	**16,735**	**5,609**	**264**	**212**	..	.	**1,322**	**20**	**24,942**	**22,703**	**12,245**	**1,535**
15,590	41,867	15,358	5,560	28	41	..	..	960	15	18,187	15,605	11,364	1,524
577	4,507	335	15	6	6	..	..	17	..	1,383	1,223	134	1
1,038	2,843	117	..	26	21	..	..	14	..	809	509	40	4
320	2,100	925	34	204	144	..	..	331	5	4,563	5,366	707	6
8,244	**28,244**	**4,490**	**408**	**1,388**	**358**	**20**	**108**	**945**	**4**	**14,722**	**13 873**	**1,223**	**94**
2,233	7,512	2,067	101	623	225	..	..	900	3	5,866	5,448	944	81
369	1,346	323	130	28	26	..	..	28	..	1,820	815	86	2
5,003	18,573	2,029	169	679	77	..	.	13	1	6,532	6,578	136	10
639	813	71	8	58	30	20	108	4	..	504	1,032	57	1

TABLE XI

Caste, tribe or race.	Traditional occupation.	Recorded principal occupation of earners,							
		I.—Exploitation of animals and vegetation.		II.—Exploitation of minerals.				III.—	
		Fishing and hunting.		Owners, managers, clerks, etc.		Labourers.		Owners, managers, clerks, etc.	
		Males	Females.	Males.	Females.	Males.	Females.	Males.	Females.
1	2	26	27	28	29	30	31	32	33
Kayasth—									
Province	Writers	5	..	16	1	58	1	66	..
Kewat	Boatmen	1,260	534	1	..	35	3	..	..
Jubbulpore	..	7	..	1	..	35	3	..	..
Narsinghpur	..	..	..	..	..	..	..	..	..
Chanda	..	1,253	534	..	..	..	..	..	..
Khangar	Village watchmen	..	..	..	..	4	..	34	..
Saugor	..	..	..	..	..	..	..	34	..
Damoh	..	..	..	..	..	..	..	..	..
Narsinghpur	..	..	..	..	..	..	..	..	..
Jubbulpore	..	..	..	..	..	4	..	..	..
Kol	Agriculturists	..	..	..	..	1,341	572	..	461
Jubbulpore	..	..	..	..	..	1,341	572	..	455
Mandla	..	..	..	..	..	..	..	..	6
Chhota Nagpur States	..	..	..	..	..	..	..	..	..
Koli—									
Berar	Fishermen	11	2	..	..	3	..	8	..
Kolta—									
Raigarh	Agriculturists	2	..	..	..	..	..	..	..
Komti—									
Chanda	Traders	..	..	..	..	..	..	..	..
Kori—									
Nerbudda Valley	Cotton-weavers	..	..	7	1	55	57	90	..
Korku	Agriculturists	10	..	..	10	9	2	..	53
Hosnangabad	..	1	..	..	..	4	..	..	..
Nimar	..	6	..	..	..	5	..	..	..
Betul	..	1	..	..	10	..	2	..	53
Amraoti	..	2	..	..	..	..	..	..	..
Koshti	Cotton-weavers	..	..	1	..	19	10	31	2
Jubbulpore	..	..	..	..	..	..	..	..	..
Seoni	..	..	..	..	..	..	..	..	..
Chhindwara	..	..	..	..	..	..	..	..	..
Nimar	..	..	..	..	..	..	..	..	..
Maratha Division	..	..	..	1	..	18	10	9	..
Chhattisgarh Administrative Division.	..	.	..	..	..	1	..	22	2
Kumhar—									
Province	Potters	5	..	2	..	47	6	15	1
Kunbi	Agriculturists	233	7	83	..	313	78	149	172
Maratha Division	..	232	7	82	..	253	76	140	172
Chhindwara	..	1	..	..	..	55	1	..	..
Nimar	..	..	..	..	..	..	..	4	..
Betul	..	..	..	1	..	5	1	5	..
Kurmi	Agriculturists	67	1	20	..	104	24	211	..
Nerbudda Valley	..	65	..	19	..	39	16	199	..
Plateau Division	..	..	..	..	..	58	8	1	..
Chhattisgarh Administrative Division.	..	1	..	..	..	7	..	2	..
Chhattisgarh States	..	1	1	1	..	..	..	9	..

other than traditional occupation of caste (by sub-classes)—*contd.*

Industry.		IV.—Transport.				V.—Trade.		VI.—Public Force.				VII.—Public Administration.	
Artisans and other workmen.		Owners, managers, ships' officers, etc.		Labourers, boatmen, carters, palki-bearers, etc.				Commissioned and gazetted officers.		Others.		Gazetted officers.	
Males.	Females.	Males.	Females.	Males.	Females.	Males.	Females.	Males.	Females.	Males.	Females.	Males.	Females.
34	35	36	37	38	39	40	41	42	43	44	45	46	47
325	46	154	1	428	2	746	70	40	1	316	1	47	..
96	17	7	..	46	24	64	110	..	..	8	..	..	..
87	11	7	..	37	24	40	41	..	..	7	..	..	..
..	..	..	..	..	..	13	9	..	..	..	..	..	..
9	6	..	..	9	..	11	60	..	..	1	..	..	..
87	33	115	..	94	12	26	53	..	..	42	..	..	..
5	14	112	..	24	6	..	21	..	..	12	..	..	..
11	3	..	..	11	3	..	..	..	..	17	..	..	..
12	4	..	..	26	1	11	19	..	..	4	..	..	..
59	12	3	..	33	2	15	13	..	..	9	..	..	..
913	31	6	164	483	325	233	292	..	..	19	..	..	..
798	2	..	147	394	262	161	1	..	..	11	..	..	..
104	28	6	17	77	54	46	288	..	..	8	..	..	..
11	1	..	..	12	9	26	3	..	..	..	..	..	..
315	43	31	63	109	68	159	23	..	..	7	3	..	..
3	..	..	..	..	1	12	30	..	..	8	..	..	..
5	..	..	1	5	..	..	..	..	..	4	..	..	..
1,134	335	35	1	739	123	290	224	..	..	132	8	..	..
174	20	4	..	78	33	327	93	..	..	24	..	..	..
16	6	..	..	30	11	4	23	..	..	7	..	..	..
33	..	3	..	14	..	8	1	..	..	10	..	..	..
117	14	1	..	12	10	34	3	..	..	7	..	..	..
8	..	..	..	22	12	281	66	..	..	..	..	..	..
780	159	10	12	177	8	1,348	242	5	..	21	..	2	..
103	39	..	..	2	..	12	11	..	..	3	..	..	..
..	..	..	..	8	1	21	5	..	..	2	..	..	..
3	..	1	..	1	..	59	14	..	..	..	..	..	..
1	..	1	..	12	..	28	10	..	..	..	..	..	..
650	120	8	..	128	7	1,072	160	5	..	16	..	2	..
23	..	..	12	26	..	156	42	..	..	..	..	..	..
654	213	18	..	184	30	512	251	2	..	18	1	..	..
6,756	1,071	90	2	3,042	101	5,144	779	15	..	392	3	31	..
6,356	948	64	..	2,585	86	4,776	696	15	..	360	3	29	..
120	3	1	..	102	1	146	48	..	..	11	..	..	..
168	106	2	..	241	6	146	12	..	..	3	..	..	..
112	14	23	2	114	8	76	23	..	..	18	..	2	..
357	150	209	2	738	37	560	323	3	1	125	..	..	..
143	80	188	2	397	20	127	86	..	..	34	..	..	..
51	5	1	..	126	4	75	73	..	..	32	..	..	..
132	58	14	..	162	10	323	128	2	..	46	..	..	..
31	7	6	..	53	3	35	36	1	1	13	..	..	..

TABLE XI — **Occupation by Caste,**

Caste, tribe or race.	Traditional occupation.	VII.—Public Administration. *concld* Others.		VIII.—Professions and Liberal Arts. Religious.		Lawyers, doctors and teachers.		Others.	
		Males.	Females.	Males.	Females.	Males.	Females.	Males.	Females.
1	2	48	49	50	51	52	53	54	55
Kayasth—									
Province ..	.. Writers ..	1,643	13	31	6	624	32	149	8
Kewat ..	.. Boatmen ..	7	..	..	..	1	..	..	3
Jubbulpore ..	..	2	..	..	..	1	..	..	..
Narsinghpur ..	..	..	..	..	..	..	..	..	..
Chanda ..	..	5	..	..	..	..	..	..	3
Khangar ..	.. Village watchmen ..	33	1	9	..	11	..	11	2
Saugor ..	..	17	1	6	..	3	..	7	1
Damoh ..	..	5	..	3	..	..	..	2	..
Narsinghpur ..	..	6	..	..	..	5	..	2	..
Jubbulpore ..	..	5	..	..	..	3	..	..	1
Kol ..	.. Agriculturists ..	48	1	1	13	3	..	1	..
Jubbulpore ..	..	17	..	..	1	2	..	..	..
Mandla ..	..	30	1	..	12	1	..	1	..
Chhota Nagpur States	..	1	..	1	..	..	..	..	..
Koli—									
Berar ..	.. Fishermen ..	98	..	1	..	57	..	12	6
Kolta—									
Raigarh ..	.. Agriculturists ..	1	..	..	..	3	..	..	..
Komti— Chanda ..	.. Traders ..	6	..	..	..	9	..	..	..
Kori—									
Nerbudda Valley	.. Cotton-weavers ..	72	5	5	..	9	3	16	..
Korku ..	.. Agriculturists ..	81	6	1	..	2	..	..	4
Hoshangabad ..	..	..	..	..	..	1	..	..	..
Nimar ..	..	9	..	..	..	1	..	..	4
Betul ..	..	6	1	1	..	..	..	..	..
Amraoti ..	..	66	5	..	..	..	..	..	..
Koshti ..	.. Cotton-weavers ..	156	3	18	1	152	2	20	6
Jubbulpore ..	..	..	..	..	..	3	..	..	..
Seoni ..	..	8	..	..	..	1	..	1	..
Chhindwara ..	..	3	..	1	..	4	1	..	..
Nimar ..	..	..	..	..	..	2	..	..	..
Maratha Division	..	118	3	17	1	112	1	19	4
Chhattisgarh Administrative Division.	..	27	..	..	..	30	..	..	2
Kumhar—									
Province ..	.. Potters ..	81	3	6	9	40	3	29	9
Kunbi ..	.. Agriculturists ..	2,545	32	153	9	1,450	25	368	47
Maratha Division	..	2,356	25	145	9	1,370	24	335	44
Chhindwara ..	..	98	..	3	..	37	..	13	..
Nimar ..	..	28	2	3	..	15	1	2	..
Betul ..	..	63	5	2	..	28	..	18	3
Kurmi ..	.. Agriculturists ..	295	2	15	1	195	7	45	9
Nerbudda Valley	..	70	..	13	1	65	..	14	7
Plateau Division ..	..	52	..	..	..	18	3	3	1
Chhattisgarh Administrative Division.	..	161	1	2	..	106	2	21	1
Chhattisgarh States	..	12	1	..	..	6	2	7	..

Recorded principal occupation of earners,

other than traditional occupation of caste (by sub-classes)—*concld.*

IX.—Persons living on their income.		X.—Domestic Service.		XI.—Insufficiently described occupations.				XII.—Unproductive.			
				Contractors, Clerks, Cashiers, etc., otherwise unspecified.		Labourers unspecified.		Beggars and prostitutes.		Other unclassed non-productive industries.	
Males.	Females.	Males.	Females.	Males.	Females.	Males.	Females.	Males	Females.	Males.	Females.
56	57	58	59	60	61	62	63	64	65	66	67
173	16	753	32	236	3	100	51	32	10	..	..
1	..	**48**	**69**	**11**	..	**189**	**173**	**3**	**6**	..	..
..	..	45	31	11	..	166	144	1	2	..	..
..	..	..	..	..	..	..	..	..	..	..	..
1	..	3	38	..	..	23	29	2	4	..	..
51	..	**29**	**4**	**46**	**28**	**58**	**43**	**21**	**4**	..	..
44	..	1	..	23	..	5	18	..	2	..	..
3	..	1	1	13	..	4	25	18	1	..	..
1	..	6	..	5	..	7	..	2	1	..	..
3	..	21	3	5	28	42	..	1	..	..	..
10	**89**	**369**	**100**	**741**	**1**	**1,957**	**2,806**	**91**	**94**	..	..
9	89	241	89	739	..	1,778	2,637	75	87	..	..
1	..	53	11	2	1	10	17	7	7	..	..
..	..	75	..	..	..	169	152	9	..	..	..
4	..	118	9	13	..	158	207	25	29	..	..
2	1	10	..	..	..	..	1	4	3	..	..
..	5	24	5	1	1	11	..	6	..	..	..
19	2	451	37	86	19	729	859	41	19	..	..
..	**18**	**186**	**47**	**42**	**7**	**214**	**551**	**9**	**9**	..	..
..	..	60	26	..	..	62	26	1	6	..	..
..	..	27	9	..	..	9	8	5	..	..	..
..	18	21	5	1	..	50	357	..	1	..	..
..	..	78	7	41	7	93	160	3	2	..	..
14	**4**	**249**	**123**	**153**	**22**	**371**	**359**	**126**	**103**	..	..
..	..	1	..	16	..	22	12	1	2	..	..
..	..	4	..	..	..	20	14	..	..	..	..
..	..	..	..	..	..	..	..	2	1	..	..
..	..	4	20	1	10	13	..	..	..	..	..
10	4	225	95	136	12	285	276	110	78	..	..
4	..	15	8	..	..	31	57	13	22	..	..
15	2	185	61	41	4	294	302	57	64	..	..
189	**44**	**4,131**	**559**	**1,922**	**144**	**4,235**	**3,976**	**892**	**325**	..	..
167	44	3,880	524	1,886	142	4,043	3,816	867	306	..	..
8	..	80	6	21	1	20	..	9	12	..	..
3	..	65	9	3	..	81	22	5	3	..	..
11	..	106	20	12	1	91	138	11	4	..	..
157	**17**	**664**	**110**	**342**	**10**	**347**	**394**	**122**	**87**	..	..
113	2	289	30	319	3	136	231	28	17	..	..
9	3	81	26	10	1	41	29	21	2	..	..
32	11	266	46	10	3	169	129	70	64	..	..
3	1	28	8	3	3	1	5	3	4	..	..

Caste, tribe or race.	Traditional occupation.	Population dealt with.					Number of earners whose traditional caste occupation was returned as their			
		Earners.		Working dependants.		Non-working dependants.	Principal means of livelihood.		Subsidiary means of livelihood.	
		Males.	Females.	Males.	Females.	Both sexes.	Males.	Females.	Males.	Females.
1	2	3	4	5	6	7	8	9	10	11
Lodhi—										
Province	Agriculturists	87,425	29,500	13,723	39,583	148,341	62,575	10,105	488	756
Lohar—										
Province	Ironsmiths	58,269	23,408	5,367	15,358	100,531	32,567	1,860	4,768	309
Madgi—										
Chanda	Leather-workers	1,936	903	55	235	2,343	1,128	99	13	41
Majhwar	Labourers	**2,482**	**180**	**224**	**335**	**5,969**	**386**	**136**	**22**	..
Surguja		1,264	168	224	335	3,445	284	136	22	..
Udaipur		1,218	12	..	..	2,524	102	..	..	..
Mala—										
Chanda	Labourers	..	..	..	..	..	..	..	..	..
Mali—										
Province	Vegetable and fruit growers.	184,562	95,335	18,820	59,524	268,325	8,149	6,437	6,533	1,930
Mana—										
Nagpur Division (excluding Balaghat).	Agriculturists	15,982	12,045	361	1,423	19,568	13,834	11,599	52	6
Mang—										
Maratha Division	Native musicians	29,659	26,353	793	2,276	35,334	7,229	552	2,667	101
Maratha—										
Province	Soldiers	85,700	33,275	6,470	12,821	148,920	217	1,075	33	44
Mehra or Mahar—										
Province	Cotton-weavers	401,334	303,539	21,529	68,970	511,980	29,962	7,657	4,626	1,070
Mehtar	Scavengers	**5,622**	**3,829**	**156**	**375**	**9,220**	**4,500**	**3,323**	**73**	**31**
Nerbudda Valley		4,087	2,608	132	318	6,745	3,229	2,212	66	31
Nagpur		1,286	963	16	45	2,179	1,127	890	7	..
Raipur		249	258	8	12	296	144	221	..	..
Mhali—										
Maratha Division	Barbers	19,959	9,707	704	3,145	28,513	14,540	219	1,265	9
Nai—										
Province	Barbers	39,116	11,458	2,929	10,396	69,354	25,610	1,199	5,888	97
Oraon (Hindu and Tribal)	Agriculturists	**23,066**	**3,901**	**6,306**	**11,256**	**55,472**	**20,608**	**2,240**	**69**	..
Raigarh		1,461	210	945	1,300	4,054	1,067	11	26	..
Chhota Nagpur States		21,605	3,691	5,361	9,956	51,418	19,541	2,229	43	.
Oraon (Christian)—										
Jashpur		11,817	419	2,347	5,077	27,819	11,016	157	32	.
Paik—										
Raipur	Soldiers	1,287	816	256	315	2,027	20	..	104	..

Number of working dependants following the traditional occupation of their caste.		Number of earners returning their traditional occupation as their principal means of livelihood who had some subsidiary occupation.		Recorded principal occupation of earners, other than traditional occupation of caste (by sub-classes). I.—Exploitation of animals and vegetation. Income from rent of land.		Cultivators of all kinds.		Agents and managers of landed estates, planters, forest officers and their clerks, rent collectors, etc		Field labourers wood cutters, etc.		Raisers of live-stock, milkmen, and herdsmen.	
Males.	Females.	Males.	Females.	Males.	Females.	Males.	Females.	Males.	Females.	Males.	Females.	Males.	Females.
12	13	14	15	16	17	18	19	20	21	22	23	24	25
9,090	25,577	4,493	425	802	321	..	..	120	8	16,792	17,129	1,968	61
1,922	3,023	6,632	260	238	63	11,819	2,720	81	58	6,913	16,888	911	248
17	9	426	49	1	..	74	32	8	10	107	597	48	1
7	60	7	..	33	..	1,422	28	..	..	279	12	253	..
7	60	4	..	..	..	946	28	..	..	..	..	1	..
..	..	3	..	33	..	476	..	..	..	279	12	252	..
..	..	..	..	..	..	..	..	..	..	..	..	..	..
1,707	4,585	1,054	999	1,940	653	91,412	13,241	403	84	66,801	70,397	2,881	265
167	807	393	241	..	..	..	..	49	1	75	193	1,308	6
76	38	2,633	143	44	4	1,033	288	21	217	15,410	18,883	946	27
47	38	36	432	1,293	590	37,407	3,913	441	135	27,679	23,296	1,045	51
2,032	9,092	5,603	2,149	3,293	422	89,825	16,700	497	119	187,354	242,276	12,749	478
77	181	347	130	..	11	80	18	5	..	200	131	39	1
68	170	342	110	..	11	77	16	5	..	192	113	39	1
8	6	4	2	..	..	3	..	..	..	..	1	..	..
1	5	1	18	..	..	..	2	..	..	8	17	..	..
177	46	2,977	23	120	44	2,702	907	55	1	1,326	7,694	315	8
1,034	1,079	5,608	94	135	69	9,685	1,981	41	5	1,802	5,680	220	6
3,584	5,079	383	3	17	11	1	..	26	..	1,991	716	112	376
733	1,092	101	..	..	..	..	..	..	..	220	71	3	1
2,851	3,987	282	3	17	11	1	..	26	..	1,771	645	109	375
1,508	4,155	410	6	3	3	..	..	3	..	529	164	21	4
..	..	4	..	3	3	773	342	18	..	319	386	7	..

TABLE XI — **Occupation by Caste,**

Caste, tribe or race.	Traditional occupation.	Recorded principal occupation of earners, I.—Exploitation of animals and vegetation. Fishing and hunting. Males.	Fishing and hunting. Females.	II.—Exploitation of minerals. Owners, managers, clerks, etc. Males.	Owners, managers, clerks, etc. Females.	Labourers. Males.	Labourers. Females.	III.— Owners, managers, clerks, etc. Males.	Owners, managers, clerks, etc. Females.
1	2	26	27	28	29	30	31	32	33
Lodhi—									
Province ..	... Agriculturists ..	25	..	51	.	464	140	6	..
Lohar—									
Province ..	.. Ironsmiths ..	8	11	11	..	236	71	30	6
Madgi—									
Chanda ..	.. Leather workers ..	..	..	2	..	339	59	..	..
Majhwar ..	.. Labourers ..	..	..	..	..	..	..	6	..
Surguja ..	.. ..	..	..	..	..	..	..	..	..
Udaipur ..	.. ..	..	..	..	..	..	..	6	..
Mala—									
Chanda ..	.. Labourers ..	..	..	..	..	..	..	..	..
Mali—									
Province ..	... Vegetable and fruit growers.	79	5	..	..	179	96	53	..
Mana—									
Nagpur Division (excluding Balaghat).	Agriculturists ..	6	...	..	..	19	..	..	..
Mang—									
Maratha Division	Native musicians ..	7	..	..	..	11	5	11	9
Maratha—									
Province ..	.. Soldiers ..	5	..	57	..	307	54	167	7
Mehra or Mahar—									
Province ..	.. Cotton-weavers ..	91	7	16	2	1,439	793	175	52
Mehtar ..	.. Scavengers ..	6	..	..	..	6	1	..	..
Nerbudda Valley	.. .	6	..	..	..	5	..	..	..
Nagpur ..	.. ..	..	..	..	..	1	1	..	..
Raipur ..	.. ..	..	..	..	..	..	..	..	..
Mhali—									
Maratha Division	.. Barbers ..	..	..	..	..	27	6	2	..
Nai—									
Province ..	.. Barbers ..	2	..	3	..	32	7	16	..
Oraon (Hindu and Tribal)	.. Agriculturists ..	..	..	..	..	..	23	1	109
Raigarh ..	.. ..	..	..	..	..	..	23	..	..
Chhota Nagpur States	.. ..	..	..	..	..	..	..	1	109
Oraon (Christian)—									
Jashpur ..	.. ..	..	..	..	..	..	..	..	.
Paik—									
Raipur ..	.. Soldiers ..	..	..	..	..	..	..	..	..

other than traditional occupation of caste (by sub-classes)—*contd.*

Industry		IV.—Transport.				V.—Trade.		VI.—Public Force.				VII.—Public Administration.	
Artisans and other workmen.		Owners, managers, ships' officers, etc.		Labourers, boatmen, carters, palki-bearers, etc.				Commissioned and gazetted officers.		Others.		Gazetted officers.	
Males.	Females.	Males.	Females.	Males.	Females.	Males.	Females.	Males.	Females.	Males.	Females.	Males.	Females.
34	35	36	37	38	39	40	41	42	43	44	45	46	47
1,281	413	42	2	779	43	692	321	5	..	50	2	2	..
3,241	402	16	3	489	69	465	236	2	..	41	..	3	..
11	6	..	..	4	..	12	2	..	..	3	..	..	..
92	4	..	..	..	..	3	..	..	..	..	..	..	..
27	4	..	..	..	..	1	..	..	..	..	..	..	..
65	..	..	..	..	..	2	..	..	..	..	..	..	..
..	..	..	..	..	..	..	..	..	..	..	..	..	..
2,771	452	42	4	1,068	80	2,944	1,576	3	..	172	2	11	..
261	45	..	13	19	..	140	27	2	..	15	..	..	..
2,025	2,673	..	..	287	114	511	902	1	..	67	..	..	..
3,969	1,568	124	..	1,988	59	2,369	391	16	..	736	1	50	..
25,923	17,379	288	5	6,273	.,171	8,788	3,246	7	..	7,031	95	5	2
75	39	10	..	162	39	41	11	..	..	1	..	..	..
63	35	10	..	156	38	35	11	..	..	..	..	..	..
12	4	..	..	5	1	6	..	..	..	1	..	..	..
..	..	..	..	1	..	..	..	..	..	..	..	..	..
161	436	3	..	42	1	161	73	4	..	15	..	1	..
199	575	12	..	137	8	208	305	6	..	90	2	..	..
8	33	..	..	43	22	80	149	..	..	4	1	..	..
..	..	..	..	38	22	60	62	..	..	1	..	..	..
8	33	..	..	5	..	20	87	..	..	3	1	..	..
39	47	..	..	12	2	5	14	..	..	17	..	..	..
15	..	..	..	4	..	38	85	..	..	..	..	..	..

TABLE XI

Occupation by Caste,

Caste, tribe or race.	Traditional occupation.	Recorded principal occupation of earners, VII.—Public Administration—*concld.* Others. Males.	Females.	VIII.—Professions and Liberal Arts. Religious. Males.	Females.	Lawyers, doctors, and teachers. Males.	Females.	Others. Males.	Females.
1	2	48	49	50	51	52	53	54	55
Lodhi—									
Province	Agriculturists ..	130	4	9	4	57	11	25	8
Lohar—									
Province	Ironsmiths ..	103	4	8	..	74	4	52	3
Madgi—									
Chanda	Leather workers ..	3	..	..	..	..	1	4	1
Majhwar ..	Labourers	..	..	..	..	..	..	..	..
Surguja		..	..	..	..	..	..	..	..
Udaipur		..	..	..	..	..	..	..	..
Mala—									
Chanda ..	Labourers ..	..	..	..	..	..	..	..	..
Mali—									
Province ..	Vegetable and fruit growers.	549	13	76	17	602	14	170	59
Mana—									
Nagpur Division (excluding Balaghat).	Agriculturists ..	28	..	9	..	12	..	8	
Mang—									
Maratha Division ..	Native musicians ..	313	19	4	2	4	26	167	1,259
Maratha—									
Province ..	Soldiers ..	1,489	27	129	7	720	32	312	82
Mehra or Mahar—									
Province .	Cotton-weavers ..	8,904	19	180	143	378	35	822	469
Mehtar ..	Scavengers ..	**131**	**8**	**5**	**1**	..	..	**69**	**61**
Nerbudda Valley ..	..	..	..	5	1	..	..	69	61
Nagpur ..	..	53	6	..	..	..	..	..	..
Raipur .	..	78	2	..	..	..	..	..	..
Mhali—									
Maratha Division ..	Barbers ..	53	5	8	..	68	..	21	65
Nai—									
Province .	Barbers .	110	5	22	..	126	13	43	46
Oraon (Hindu and Tribal) .	Agriculturists ..	**2**	.	..	..	**3**	..	**1**	..
Raigarh .	..	..	..	..	..	..	..	..	..
Chhota Nagpur States	..	2	..	..	..	3	..	1	..
Oraon (Christian)—									
Jashpur ..	..	20	1	62	..	67	9	..	..
Paik—									
Raipur ..	Soldiers ..	5	..	..	..	..	..	..	..

other than traditional occupation of caste (by sub-classes)—*concld.*

IX.—Persons living on their income.		X.—Domestic Service.		XI.—Insufficiently described occupations.				XII.—Unproductive.			
				Contractors, Clerks, Cashiers, etc., otherwise unspecified.		Labourers unspecified.		Beggars and prostitutes.		Other unclassified non-productive industries.	
Males.	Females.	Males.	Females	Males.	Females.	Males.	Females.	Males.	Females.	Males.	Females.
56	57	58	59	60	61	62	63	64	65	66	67
31	36	542	107	107	4	788	706	82	75	..	..
14	14	347	139	80	25	427	495	93	89	..	..
..	..	6	..	2	..	177	87	7	8	..	..
1	..	4	..	..	..	3	..	..	..	..	..
1	..	1	..	..	..	3	..	..	.	..	..
..	..	3	..	..		..	..	..	..	..	
..	..	..	..	..	..	..	..	..	..	..	..
57	19	1,694	428	349	25	1,772	1,275	385	193	..	..
3	..	94	74	18	1	62	70	20	16	..	.
15	26	138	188	30	8	667	617	718	534	..	.
174	37	1,589	479	415	10	2,470	1,234	532	227	..	.
248	61	3,525	998	1,205	767	9,694	9,509	2,662	1,134	..	.
3	1	178	119	41	22	56	36	14	7	..	
3	1	106	62	38	20	39	22	10	4	..	.
..	..	58	44	3	2	17	14	..	..	..	.
..	..	14	13	..	.	..	..	4	3	..	.
..											
14	5	143	46	25	4	112	181	41	12	..	.
41	11	370	1,206	63	7	104	262	39	71	..	..
2	103	113	63	10	2	37	37	7	16	..	..
2	..	66	4	..	2	2	14	2	..	..	..
..	103	47	59	10	..	35	23	5	16	..	..
..	..	22	16	..	..	..	..	1	2	..	..
..	..	78	..	..	..	..	..	7	..	..	..

TABLE XI — Occupation by Caste,

Caste, tribe or race.	Traditional occupation.	Population dealt with. Earners. Males.	Earners. Females.	Working dependants. Males.	Working dependants. Females.	Non-working dependants. Both sexes.	Number of earners whose traditional caste occupation was returned as their Principal means of livelihood. Males.	Principal means of livelihood. Females.	Subsidiary means of livelihood. Males.	Subsidiary means of livelihood. Females.
1	2	3	4	5	6	7	8	9	10	11
Panka ..	Cotton-weavers ..	**46,536**	**22,039**	**4,579**	**15,659**	**84,179**	**4,792**	**915**	**3,050**	**238**
Mandla ..	..	4,621	1,380	163	917	11,958	315	1	99	..
Seoni ..	..	514	338	62	177	667	3	..	1	..
Balaghat ..	..	923	365	74	213	1,702	2	3	3	..
Chhattisgarh Administrative Division.	..	31,869	17,249	2,363	9,841	52,729	2,818	801	2,285	213
Chhattisgarh States	..	8,609	2,707	1,917	4,511	17,123	1,654	110	662	25
Rajput—										
Province ..	Soldiers ..	149,346	39,549	16,560	54,325	246,280	2,130	..	124	..
Sawara or Saonr	Agriculturists ..	**24,411**	**12,031**	**2,069**	**6,556**	**39,992**	**8,313**	**1,671**	**83**	**113**
Saugor ..	..	6,784	4,683	124	646	9,630	579	520	16	3
Damoh ..	..	2,086	1,627	30	166	2,559	270	22	3	32
Chhattisgarh Administrative Division.	..	10,721	4,731	982	3,982	17,820	5,346	893	42	75
Chhattisgarh States ..	..	4,820	990	933	1,762	9,983	2,118	236	22	3
Sunar—										
Province ..	Goldsmiths ..	41,453	9,291	2,412	4,970	84,415	27,735	41	3,390	37
Teli—										
Province ..	Oil-pressers ..	276,175	135,567	39,265	115,665	456,184	15,142	11,384	6,480	1,615
Waddar—										
Yeotmal ..	Earth-workers ..	1,747	1,304	96	609	2,662	730	372	19	17
Wanjari—										
Berar ..	Carriers ..	13,046	7,836	1,638	3,304	20,084	141	122	2	..
Europeans—										
Province ..	..	3,577	328	7	34	1,704	..	..	..	..
Anglo-Indians—										
Province ..	..	1,207	200	7	539	3,112	..	..	..	..
Indian Christians (excluding Oraon Christians of Jashpur— Province ..	..	10,167	4,082	480	1,245	27,838	..	..	..	..

Number of working dependants following the traditional occupation of their caste.		Number of earners returning their traditional occupation as their principal means of livelihood who had some subsidiary occupation.		Recorded principal occupation of earners, other than traditional occupation of caste (by sub-classes). I—Exploitation of animals and vegetation. Income from rent of land.		Cultivators of all kinds.		Agents and managers of landed estates, planters, forest officers and their clerks, rent collectors, etc.		Field labourers, wood cutters, etc.		Raisers of live-stock, milkmen and herdsmen.	
Males.	Females.	Males.	Females.	Males.	Females.	Males.	Females.	Males.	Females.	Males.	Females.	Males.	Females.
12	13	14	15	16	17	18	19	20	21	22	23	24	25
828	**2,822**	**588**	**90**	**128**	**20**	**22,852**	**6.003**	**142**	..	**11,111**	**12,979**	**525**	**30**
12	24	23	..	1	..	2,144	54	21	..	1,238	1,240	91	10
1	2	..	..	2	2	154	4	2	..	208	314	18	1
4	35	1	..	16	..	439	17	51	..	254	301	10	..
432	1,456	406	88	43	14	16,954	5,701	58	..	7,449	9,234	267	16
379	1,305	158	2	66	4	3,161	227	10	..	1,962	1,890	139	3
516	..	243	..	3,462	807	88,296	12,736	1,666	1,076	25,308	21,155	3,076	195
1,638	**3,612**	**461**	**167**	**65**	**1**	..	**5**	**45**	**7**	**13,955**	**9,172**	**915**	**88**
54	127	49	..	1	..	..	..	23	3	5,208	3,662	507	57
7	126	123	5	1	..	..	..	1	4	1,656	1,396	100	22
859	2,010	190	154	56	1	..	5	2	..	4,782	3,486	181	9
718	1,349	99	8	7	..	..	..	19	..	2,309	628	127	..
939	325	4,117	49	390	103	6,545	1,307	128	79	2,802	5,952	215	139
1,856	6,586	3,475	1,599	2,623	370	149,699	27,621	1,147	116	73,821	85,703	5,408	1,017
17	77	33	25	..	2	79	77	..	..	270	563	52	3
139	1	1	..	796	157	4,721	701	49	6	5,915	6,430	451	23
..	..	..	..	..	1	6	1	30	..	..	..	..	..
..	..	..	..	2	4	8	..	7	1	3	..	..	..
..	..	..	..	11	2	1,663	118	102	2	1,706	1,517	59	7

TABLE XI **Occupation by Caste,**

Caste, tribe or race.	Traditional occupation.	Record principal occupation of earners, I.—Exploitation of animals and vegetation—*concld.* Fishing and hunting. Males.	Females.	II.—Exploitation of minerals. Owners, managers, clerks, etc. Males.	Females.	Labourers. Males.	Females.	III.— Owners, managers, clerks, etc. Males.	Females.
1	2	26	27	28	29	30	31	32	33
Panka	Cotton-weavers ..	4	1	12	6	15	5	7	5
Mandla	..	..	..	12	..	..	..	1	..
Seoni	..	..	..	..	..	..	..	..	..
Balaghat	..	1	1	..	..	3	5	..	..
Chhattisgarh Administrative Division.	..	3	..	..	6	12	..	..	5
Chhattisgarh States ..	..	..	..	..	..	..	..	6	..
Rajput—									
Province	Soldiers ..	128	4	36	1	178	84	161	11
Sawara or Saonr ..	*Agriculturists* ..	15	..	..	..	12	50	..	..
Saugor	..	..	..	..	..	..	..	..	..
Damoh	..	..	..	..	..	4	50	..	..
Chhattisgarh Administrative Division.	..	4	..	..	..	1	..	..	..
Chhattisgarh States ..	..	11	..	..	..	7	..	..	..
Sunar—									
Province	Goldsmiths ..	2	..	6	..	49	1	18	..
Teli—									
Province	Oil-pressers ..	33	442	27	..	320	109	43	4
Waddar—									
Yeotmal	Earth-workers ..	..	..	..	..	32	..	..	..
Wanjari—									
Berar	Carriers ..	..	..	..	..	..	..	3	..
Europeans—									
Province	..	..	..	26	..	..	..	114	2
Anglo-Indians—									
Province	..	..	..	12	..	2	..	5	2
Indian Christians (excluding Oraon Christians of Jashpur)—									
Province	..	37	..	18	8	104	3	36	..

other than traditional occupation of caste (by sub-classes)—*contd.*

Industry.		IV.—Transport.				V.—Trade.		VI.—Public Force.				VII.—Public Administration.	
Artisans and other workmen.		Owners, managers, ships' officers, etc.		Labourers, boatmen, carters, palki-bearers, etc.				Commissioned and gazetted officers.		Others.		Gazetted officers.	
Males.	Females.	Males.	Females.	Males.	Females.	Males.	Females.	Males.	Females.	Males.	Females.	Males.	Females.
34	35	36	37	38	39	40	41	42	43	44	45	46	47
385	**244**	**2**	..	**605**	**232**	**473**	**542**	..	**1**	**2,824**	**17**	..	..
38	3	..	..	20	..	46	34	..	..	433	4	..	..
11	1	1	..	14	..	4	1	..	..	71	..	..	..
11	1	..	..	14	3	9	15	..	..	75	1	..	..
206	184	1	..	323	73	272	371	..	..	1,705	10	..	..
119	55	..	..	234	156	142	121	..	1	540	2	..	..
4,398	769	222	7	2,948	126	4,377	826	41	..	1,970	2	75	4
84	**71**	..	.	**109**	**34**	**355**	**645**	..	..	**41**	**1**	..	..
27	14	..	..	73	31	251	341	..	..	7	..	..	..
5	6	..	..	4	.	7	98	..	..	..	..	..	..
42	49	..	..	15	..	52	122	..	..	8	..	..	..
10	2	..	..	17	3	45	84	.	..	26	1	..	..
762	*214*	*27*	..	*202*	*15*	*1,271*	*346*	*1*	..	*54*	*1*	*12*	.
5,322	1,665	154	5	2,997	238	9,376	3,015	8	..	464	1	2	..
329	13	..	..	28	25	120	18	..	..	..	..	..	..
308	93	..	2	59	1	108	7	..	..	2	1	..	..
19	16	144	4	52	..	25	3	169	1	2,081	1	92	3
71	7	418	3	268	2	17	5	19	1	19	2	40	..
1,327	*157*	*213*	5	*730*	25	*210*	65	*10*	..	*221*	2	33	7

TABLE XI

Occupation by Caste,

Caste, tribe or race.	Traditional occupation.	Recorded principal occupation of earners, VII.—Public Administration—*concld.* Others.		VIII.—Professions and Liberal Arts. Religious		Lawyers, doctors and teachers.		Others.	
		Males.	Females.	Males.	Females.	Males.	Females.	Males.	Females
1	2	48	49	50	51	52	53	54	55
Panka ..	Cotton-weavers ..	**683**	**7**	**13**	**1**	**88**	**4**	**47**	**10**
Mandla ..	..	130	..	4	..	6	..	..	1
Seoni ..	..	9	..	2	..	..	..	..	..
Balaghat ..	..	2	..	..	..	3	..	2	3
Chhattisgarh Administrative Division.	..	382	7	4	1	67	3	38	2
Chhattisgarh States ..	..	160	..	3	..	12	1	7	4
Rajput—									
Province	Soldiers ..	2,076	31	102	5	960	55	344	29
Sawara or Saonr ..	Agriculturists ..	**23**	..	**6**	..	**7**	**2**	**3**	**2**
Saugor	..	3	..	..	..	..	..	..	2
Damoh	..	1	..	..	..	..	2	..	..
Chhattisgarh Administrative Division.	..	15	..	1	..	2	..	..	..
Chhattisgarh States ..	..	4	..	5	..	5	..	3	..
Sunar—									
Province	Goldsmiths ..	181	4	15	3	262	34	54	11
Teli—									
Province ..	Oil-pressers ..	745	37	45	6	693	23	389	14
Waddar—									
Yeotmal	Earth-workers ..	..	..	..	..	..	..	36	..
Wanjari—									
Berar	Carriers ..	23	2	..	..	19	1	..	2
Europeans—									
Province	..	574	5	84	128	42	100	7	29
Anglo-Indians—									
Province	..	76	16	11	10	47	89	9	34
Indian Christians (excluding Oraon Christians of Jashpur)—									
Province	..	322	30	455	293	673	660	209	254

Tribe or Race—*concld.* **TABLE XI**

other than traditional occupation of caste (by sub-classes)—*concld.*

IX.—Persons living on their income.		X.—Domestic service.		XI.—Insufficiently described occupations.				Unproductive.			
				Contractors, clerks, cashiers, etc., otherwise unspecified.		Labourers unspecified.		Beggars and prostitutes.		Other unclassified non-productive industries.	
Males.	Females.	Males.	Females.	Males.	Females	Males.	Females.	Males.	Females.	Males.	Females.
56	57	58	59	60	61	62	63	64	65	66	67
31	**10**	**948**	**223**	**18**	**1**	**543**	**468**	**288**	**315**	..	..
..	..	65	14	..	..	25	3	31	16	..	..
..	..	2	9	..	..	3	..	10	6	..	..
..	..	11	6	..	..	3	..	17	9	..	..
27	9	590	141	12	1	479	444	159	226	..	..
4	1	280	53	6	..	33	21	71	58	..	..
311	71	3,645	468	984	31	1,707	848	445	208	..	..
14	**5**	**164**	**70**	**3**	..	**199**	**142**	**83**	**65**	..	..
1	..	30	12	..	..	69	31	5	10	..	..
..	..	8	5	..	..	28	20	1	2	..	..
6	4	82	27	3	..	93	91	30	44	..	..
7	1	44	26	..	.	9	..	47	9	..	..
33	24	328	165	97	30	187	340	75	72	..	..
332	124	2,292	629	862	37	3,676	2,471	555	536	..	..
..	42	..	..	..	21	58	168	13	..	..	..
1	9	95	18	11	13	297	231	47	17	..	..
42	17	54	11	13	6	3	..	..	..	..	..
57	7	87	12	24	9	5	..	..	1	..	..
91	21	1,496	638	132	2	291	265	18	7	.	..

TABLE XIII*

Literacy by Religion and Age.

1. This Table, like Table VII, is divided into three parts. Part A shows the extent of literacy in the Province as a whole amongst the total population and for each religion returned. Part B gives details for the districts for the total district population and for each main religion, and Part C gives similar details for Cities.

2. Columns 6, 7 and 8 of the Table show the number of persons literate in their vernacular. The number of persons literate in English has also been shown. Some of these have returned English as their only language, while others are also literate in a vernacular and have accordingly been entered twice—once in the column referring to the vernacular, and again in the column "Literate in English". The latter columns must, therefore, be left out of account in calculating the total number of literate persons. Returns of literacy for children under five years of age have been ignored.

3. An Appendix showing the number of those literate in Urdu and Hindi and the number of those educated up to the Primary Certificate Standard is printed at the end of the Table.

4. The following statement shows literacy among Indian Christians (other than Oraons). Details by sect are not available :—

Total.	Literate.		Illiterate.		Literate in English.	
	Males.	Females.	Males.	Females.	Males.	Females.
43,774	8,632	7,497	13,013	14,632	3,736	2,634

*Table XII not Printed

TABLE XIII

Literacy by Religion and Age.

Part A.—Provincial Summary.

Religion.	Age.	Population. Total. Persons.	Population. Total. Males.	Population. Total. Females.	Population. Literate. Persons.	Population. Literate. Males.	Population. Literate. Females.	Population. Illiterate. Persons.	Population. Illiterate. Males.	Population. Illiterate. Females.	Literate in English. Persons.	Literate in English. Males.	Literate in English. Females.
1	2	3	4	5	6	7	8	9	10	11	12	13	14
ALL RELIGIONS	*Total* ..	*17,990,937*	*8,997,205*	*8,993,731*	*913,428*	*833,479*	*79,919*	*17,077,509*	*8,163,724*	*8,913,785*	*93,636*	*84,104*	*9,532*
	0—5 ..	2,875,090	1,408,399	1,466,691	..	..	..	2,875,090	1,408,399	1,466,691	..	..	..
	5—10 ..	2,303,905	1,175,395	1,128,510	60,359	50,565	9,794	2,243,546	1,124,830	1,118,716	3,577	2,678	899
	10—15 ..	2,039,504	1,051,893	987,611	98,360	84,910	13,450	1,941,144	966,983	974,161	7,735	6,388	1,347
	15—20 ..	1,599,713	779,121	820,592	132,179	118,208	13,971	1,467,534	660,913	806,621	15,662	13,916	1,746
	20 and over	9,172,725	4,582,395	4,590,330	622,530	579,796	42,734	8,550,195	4,002,599	4,547,596	66,662	61,122	5,540
HINDU	*Total* ..	*15,126,624*	*7,557,449*	*7,569,175*	*756,811*	*702,108*	*54,703*	*11,369,813*	*6,855,341*	*7,514,472*	*63,793*	*60,769*	*3,024*
	0—5 ..	2,388,008	1,170,134	1,217,874	..	..	..	2,388,008	1,170,134	1,217,874	..	..	..
	5—10 ..	1,925,032	982,118	942,914	48,956	42,126	6,830	1,876,076	939,992	936,084	1,695	1,468	227
	10—15 .	1,714,665	884,662	830,003	81,188	71,833	9,355	1,633,477	812,829	820,648	5,050	4,587	463
	15—20 ..	1,346,827	656,866	689,961	109,312	99,862	9,450	1,237,515	557,004	680,511	11,038	10,352	686
	20 and over	7,752,092	3,863,669	3,888,423	517,355	488,287	29,068	7,234,737	3,375,382	3,859,355	46,010	44,362	1,648
SIKH	*Total* ..	*4,520*	*3,003*	*1,517*	*1,731*	*1,515*	*216*	*2,789*	*1,488*	*1,301*	*489*	*456*	*33*
	0—5 ..	597	314	283	..	..	..	597	314	283	..	..	..
	5—10 ..	452	256	196	83	55	28	369	201	168	19	15	4
	10—15 ..	432	278	154	113	82	31	319	196	123	24	20	4
	15—20 ..	568	398	170	267	230	37	301	168	133	71	64	7
	20 and over	2,471	1,757	714	1,268	1,148	120	1,203	609	594	375	357	18
JAIN	*Total* ..	*79,855*	*41,416*	*38,439*	*25,583*	*22,306*	*3,277*	*54,272*	*19,110*	*35,162*	*1,472*	*1,438*	*34*
	0—5 ..	11,499	5,712	5,787	..	..	..	11,499	5,712	5,787	..	..	..
	5—10 ..	9,330	4,818	4,512	1,612	1,209	403	7,718	3,609	4,109	43	34	9
	10—15 ..	8,686	4,589	4,099	2,652	2,071	581	6,036	2,518	3,518	131	125	6
	15—20 ..	7,770	4,083	3,687	3,611	3,007	604	4,159	1,076	3,083	277	273	4
	20 and over	42,568	22,214	20,354	17,708	16,019	1,689	24,860	6,195	18,665	1,021	1,006	15
BUDDHIST	*Total* ..	*69*	*44*	*25*	*33*	*28*	*5*	*36*	*16*	*20*	*13*	*12*	*1*
	0—5 ..	12	6	6	..	..	..	12	6	6	..	..	..
	5—10 ..	6	4	2	1	1	..	5	3	2	..	..	..
	10—15 ..	5	4	1	1	1	..	4	3	1	..	..	..
	15—20 ..	14	8	6	7	6	1	7	2	5	1	1	..
	20 and over	32	22	10	24	20	4	8	2	6	12	11	1

Literacy by Religion and Age. TABLE XIII

Part A.—Provincial Summary—*concld.*

Religion.	Age.	Population.									Literate in English.		
		Total.			Literate.			Illiterate.					
		Persons.	Males.	Females.	Persons.	Males.	Females.	Persons.	Males.	Females.	Persons.	Males.	Females.
1	2	3	4	5	6	7	8	9	10	11	12	13	14
ZOROASTRIAN	*Total* ..	*2,109*	*1,119*	*990*	*1,622*	*920*	*702*	*487*	*199*	*288*	*1,240*	*776*	*464*
	0—5 ..	258	121	137	..	..	..	258	121	137	..	..	..
	5—10 ..	231	105	126	153	73	80	78	32	46	87	43	44
	10—15 ..	198	92	106	150	66	84	48	26	22	97	36	61
	15—20 ..	168	77	91	154	74	80	14	3	11	132	66	66
	20 and over	1,254	724	530	1,165	707	458	89	17	72	924	631	293
MUSLIM	*Total* ..	*706,108*	*370,633*	*335,475*	*93,580*	*83,727*	*9,853*	*612,528*	*286,906*	*325,622*	*11,279*	*10,970*	*309*
	0—5 ..	110,476	54,446	56,030	..	..	..	110,476	54,446	56,030	..	..	..
	5—10 ..	92,966	47,938	45,028	6,474	5,329	1,145	86,492	42,609	43,883	553	526	27
	10—15 ..	81,904	43,009	38,895	9,848	8,262	1,586	72,056	34,747	37,309	906	869	37
	15—20 .	66,693	34,620	32,073	13,473	11,652	1,821	53,220	22,968	30,252	1,797	1,737	60
	20 and over	354,069	190,620	163,449	63,785	58,484	5,301	290,284	132,136	158,148	8,023	7,838	185
CHRISTIAN	*Total* ..	*102,285*	*52,540*	*49,745*	*26,434*	*15,631*	*10,803*	*75,851*	*36,909*	*38,942*	*15,145*	*9,508*	*5,637*
	0—5 ..	18,484	9,207	9,277	..	..	..	18,484	9,207	9,277	..	..	..
	5—10 ..	14,357	7,343	7,014	2,558	1,287	1,271	11,799	6,056	5,743	1,159	576	583
	10—15 ..	12,657	6,501	6,156	3,555	1,791	1,764	9,102	4,710	4,392	1,503	732	771
	15—20 ..	9,882	4,979	4,903	4,302	2,392	1,910	5,580	2,587	2,993	2,312	1,394	918
	20 and over	46,905	24,510	22,395	16,019	10,161	5,858	30,886	14,349	16,537	10,171	6,806	3,365
JEW	*Total* ..	*153*	*88*	*65*	*104*	*64*	*40*	*49*	*24*	*25*	*85*	*57*	*28*
	0—5 ..	30	15	15	..	..	..	30	15	15	..	..	..
	5—10 ..	25	14	11	22	14	8	3	..	3	18	13	5
	10—15 ..	19	14	5	16	12	4	3	2	1	13	9	4
	15—20 ..	18	12	6	15	9	6	3	3	..	12	8	4
	20 and over	61	33	28	51	29	22	10	4	6	42	27	15
TRIBAL	*Total* ..	*1,969,214*	*970,911*	*998,303*	*7,530*	*7,180*	*350*	*1,961,684*	*963,731*	*997,953*	*120*	*118*	*2*
	0—5 ..	345,726	168,444	177,282	..	..	..	345,726	168,444	177,282	..	..	..
	5—10 ..	261,506	132,799	128,707	500	471	29	261,006	132,328	128,678	3	3	..
	10—15 ..	220,936	112,744	108,192	837	792	45	220,099	111,952	108,147	11	10	1
	15—20 ..	167,773	78,078	89,695	1,038	976	62	166,735	77,102	89,633	22	21	1
	20 and over	973,273	478,846	494,427	5,155	4,941	214	968,118	473,905	494,213	84	84	..

TABLE XIII

Saugor
Damoh.]

Literacy by Religion and Age.

Part B.—Details for Districts.

District.	Age.	Population.									Literate in English.		
		Total.			Literate.			Illiterate.					
		Persons.	Males.	Females.	Persons.	Males.	Females.	Persons.	Males.	Females.	Persons.	Males.	Females.
1	2	3	4	5	6	7	8	9	10	11	12	13	14
SAUGOR	ALL RELIGIONS ..	*544,589*	*280,385*	*264,204*	*34,277*	*30,918*	*3,359*	*510,312*	*249,467*	*260,845*	*3,002*	*2,641*	*361*
	0—5 ..	77,870	39,309	38,561	..	..	..	77,870	39,309	38,561	..	..	..
	5—10 ..	70,718	37,218	33,500	1,971	1,570	401	68,747	35,648	33,099	94	65	29
	10—15 ..	66,274	35,637	30,637	3,425	2,857	568	62,849	32,780	30,069	198	153	45
	15—20 ..	55,506	29,086	26,420	4,835	4,301	534	50,671	24,785	25,886	404	358	46
	20 and over ..	274,221	139,135	135,086	24,046	22,190	1,856	250,175	116,945	133,230	2,306	2,065	241
	HINDUS ..	*480,121*	*247,101*	*233,020*	*24,782*	*22,974*	*1,808*	*455,339*	*224,127*	*231,212*	*1,762*	*1,720*	*42*
	0—5 ..	68,341	34,544	33,797	..	..	..	68,341	34,544	33,797	..	..	..
	5—10 ..	62,403	32,878	29,525	1,401	1,163	238	61,002	31,715	29,287	37	36	1
	10—15 ..	58,687	31,600	27,087	2,491	2,157	334	56,196	29,443	26,753	115	109	6
	15—20 ..	49,245	25,857	23,388	3,497	3,210	287	45,748	22,647	23,101	255	246	9
	20 and over ..	241,445	122,222	119,223	17,393	16,444	949	224,052	105,778	118,274	1,355	1,329	26
	JAINS ..	*17,136*	*8,910*	*8,226*	*5,058*	*4,309*	*749*	*12,078*	*4,601*	*7,477*	*83*	*82*	*1*
	0—5 ..	2,555	1,308	1,247	..	..	..	2,555	1,308	1,247	..	..	..
	5—10 ..	2,101	1,102	999	275	185	90	1,826	917	909	2	2	..
	10—15 ..	1,881	1,010	871	496	370	126	1,385	640	745	7	7	..
	15—20 ..	1,594	848	746	728	602	126	866	246	620	13	13	..
	20 and over ..	9,005	4,642	4,363	3,559	3,152	407	5,446	1,490	3,956	61	60	1
	MUSLIMS ..	*25,746*	*13,655*	*12,091*	*3,074*	*2,888*	*186*	*22,672*	*10,767*	*11,905*	*433*	*428*	*5*
	0—5 ..	4,009	1,966	2,043	..	..	..	4,009	1,966	2,043	..	..	..
	5—10 ..	3,404	1,799	1,605	177	160	17	3,227	1,639	1,588	6	5	1
	10—15 ..	3,105	1,685	1,420	288	262	26	2,817	1,423	1,394	21	19	2
	15—20 ..	2,605	1,377	1,228	431	402	29	2,174	975	1,199	59	58	1
	20 and over ..	12,623	6,828	5,795	2,178	2,064	114	10,445	4,764	5,681	347	346	1
	CHRISTIANS ..	*1,930*	*994*	*936*	*1,188*	*620*	*568*	*742*	*374*	*368*	*636*	*346*	*290*
	0—5 ..	310	161	149	..	..	..	310	161	149	..	..	..
	5—10 ..	243	130	113	106	55	51	137	75	62	47	21	26
	10—15 ..	219	101	118	134	58	76	85	43	42	51	16	35
	15—20 ..	198	90	108	161	76	85	37	14	23	69	35	34
	20 and over ..	960	512	448	787	431	356	173	81	92	469	274	195
	TRIBALS ..	*19,415*	*9,583*	*9,832*	*40*	*38*	*2*	*19,375*	*9,545*	*9,830*	..	..	..
	0—5 ..	2,623	1,316	1,307	..	..	..	2,623	1,316	1,307	..	..	..
	5—10 ..	2,537	1,295	1,242	4	4	..	2,533	1,291	1,242	..	..	..
	10—15 ..	2,359	1,229	1,130	5	5	..	2,354	1,224	1,130	..	..	..
	15—20 ..	1,843	901	942	4	3	1	1,839	898	941	..	..	..
	20 and over ..	10,053	4,842	5,211	27	26	1	10,026	4,816	5,210	..	..	..
DAMOH	ALL RELIGIONS ..	*305,568*	*154,791*	*150,777*	*20,087*	*18,557*	*1,530*	*285,481*	*136,234*	*149,247*	*1,093*	*1,054*	*39*
	0—5 ..	45,795	23,005	22,790	..	..	..	45,795	23,005	22,790	..	..	..
	5—10 ..	36,744	19,138	17,606	1,143	966	177	35,601	18,172	17,429	25	24	1
	10—15 ..	35,526	19,055	16,471	2,173	1,913	260	33,353	17,142	16,211	77	75	2
	15—20 ..	30,796	15,827	14,969	3,127	2,857	270	27,669	12,970	14,699	166	159	7
	20 and over ..	156,707	77,766	78,941	13,644	12,821	823	143,063	64,945	78,118	825	796	29
	HINDUS ..	*265,708*	*134,626*	*131,082*	*15,861*	*14,814*	*1,047*	*249,847*	*119,812*	*130,035*	*806*	*796*	*10*
	0—5 ..	39,691	19,880	19,811	..	..	..	39,691	19,880	19,811	..	..	..
	5—10 ..	31,866	16,603	15,263	842	720	122	31,024	15,883	15,141	19	18	1
	10—15 ..	31,032	16,649	14,383	1,680	1,490	190	29,352	15,159	14,193	66	65	1
	15—20 ..	27,149	13,948	13,201	2,505	2,317	188	24,644	11,631	13,013	123	121	2
	20 and over ..	135,970	67,546	68,424	10,834	10,287	547	125,136	57,259	67,877	598	592	6
	MUSLIMS ..	*10,516*	*5,439*	*5,077*	*1,420*	*1,313*	*107*	*9,096*	*4,126*	*4,970*	*166*	*165*	*1*
	0—5 ..	1,706	871	835	..	..	..	1,706	871	835	..	..	..
	5—10 ..	1,339	704	635	89	74	15	1,250	630	620	2	2	..
	10—15 ..	1,217	659	558	152	136	16	1,065	523	542	9	9	..
	15—20 ..	992	533	459	205	191	14	787	342	445	23	22	1
	20 and over ..	5,262	2,672	2,590	974	912	62	4,288	1,760	2,528	132	132	..
	TRIBALS ..	*21,331*	*10,555*	*10,776*	*220*	*216*	*4*	*21,111*	*10,339*	*10,772*	..	..	..
	0—5 ..	3,185	1,616	1,569	..	..	..	3,185	1,616	1,569	..	..	..
	5—10 ..	2,594	1,333	1,261	13	12	1	2,581	1,321	1,260	..	..	..
	10—15 ..	2,357	1,225	1,132	30	29	1	2,327	1,196	1,131	..	..	..
	15—20 ..	1,914	937	977	42	41	1	1,872	896	976	..	..	..
	20 and over ..	11,281	5,444	5,837	135	134	1	11,146	5,310	5,836	..	..	..

Literacy by Religion and Age.

TABLE XIII

Part B.—Details for Districts—*contd.*

[Jubbulpore Mandla.

District.	Age.	Population. Total Persons	Total Males	Total Females	Literate. Persons.	Literate. Males.	Literate. Females.	Illiterate. Persons.	Illiterate. Males	Illiterate. Females	Literate in English. Persons.	Literate in English. Males.	Literate in English. Females.
1	2	3	4	5	6	7	8	9	10	11	12	13	14
JUBBULPORE	ALL RELIGIONS ..	*773,811*	*391,649*	*382,162*	*67,799*	*59,260*	*8,539*	*706,012*	*332,389*	*373,623*	*12,702*	*10,588*	*2,114*
	0—5 ..	120,210	59,237	60,973	..	..	..	120,210	59,237	60,973	..	..	..
	5—10 ..	94,476	48,875	45,601	4,575	3,497	1,078	89,901	45 378	44,523	629	408	221
	10—15 ..	85,795	45,356	40,439	6,967	5,599	1,368	78,828	39,757	39,071	1,062	725	337
	15—20 ..	76,421	39,241	37,180	9,802	8,362	1,440	66,619	30,879	35,740	1,988	1,611	377
	20 and over ..	396,909	198 940	197,969	46,455	41,802	4,653	350,454	157 138	193,316	9,023	7,844	1,179
	HINDUS ..	*697,355*	*350,708*	*346,617*	*49,803*	*45,299*	*4,501*	*617,552*	*305,409*	*312,113*	*5,712*	*5,368*	*344*
	0—5 ..	108,938	53,690	55,248	..	..	..	108,938	53,690	55,248	..	..	..
	5—10 ..	85,387	44,215	41,172	3,205	2,647	558	82,182	41,568	40,614	196	165	31
	10—15 ..	77,455	40,982	36,473	5,097	4,397	700	72,358	36,585	35,773	440	381	59
	15—20 ..	68,403	34,827	33,576	7,143	6,366	777	61,260	28,461	32,799	923	843	80
	20 and over ..	357,172	176,994	180,178	34,358	31,889	2,469	322,814	145,105	177,709	4,153	3,979	174
	MUSLIMS ..	*47,614*	*25,763*	*21,851*	*8,982*	*7,653*	*1,329*	*38,632*	*18,110*	*20,522*	*1,742*	*1,689*	*53*
	0—5 ..	7,349	3,606	3,743	..	..	..	7,349	3,606	3,743	..	..	..
	5—10 ..	5,834	3,055	2,779	670	486	184	5,164	2,569	2,595	47	45	2
	10—15 ..	5,179	2,821	2,358	916	703	213	4,263	2,118	2,145	108	101	7
	15—20 ..	4,816	2,633	2,183	1,299	1,075	224	3,517	1,558	1,959	262	250	12
	20 and over ..	24,436	13,648	10,788	6,097	5,389	708	18,339	8,259	10,080	1,325	1,293	32
	CHRISTIANS ..	*7,697*	*4,494*	*3,203*	*5,739*	*3,584*	*2,155*	*1,958*	*910*	*1,048*	*4,786*	*3,155*	*1,631*
	0—5 ..	812	426	386	..	..	..	812	426	386	..	..	..
	5—10 ..	770	347	423	486	218	268	284	129	155	351	174	177
	10—15 ..	819	343	476	624	261	363	195	82	113	464	208	256
	15—20 ..	985	585	400	855	508	347	130	77	53	729	453	276
	20 and over ..	4,311	2,793	1,518	3,774	2,597	1,177	537	196	341	3,242	2,320	922
	TRIBALS ..	*13,261*	*6,405*	*6,856*	*118*	*103*	*15*	*13,143*	*6,302*	*6,841*	*1*	*1*	..
	0—5 ..	2,034	986	1,048	..	..	..	2,034	986	1,048	..	..	..
	5—10 ..	1,673	841	832	6	4	2	1 667	837	830	..	..	..
	10—15 ..	1,523	763	760	8	6	2	1,515	757	758	..	..	..
	15—20 ..	1,278	623	655	11	10	1	1,267	613	654	..	..	..
	20 and over ..	6,753	3,192	3,561	93	83	10	6,660	3,109	3,551	1	1	..
MANDLA	ALL RELIGIONS ..	*445,766*	*221,359*	*224,107*	*13,238*	*12,017*	*1,221*	*432,528*	*209,342*	*223,186*	*1,220*	*1,147*	*73*
	0—5 ..	77,630	38,146	39,484	..	..	..	77,630	38,146	39,484	..	..	..
	5—10 ..	57,426	29,643	27,783	682	546	136	56,744	29,097	27,647	15	10	5
	10—15 ..	49,733	25,671	24,062	1,295	1,080	215	48,438	24,591	23,847	56	51	5
	15—20 ..	41,283	19,450	21,833	1,961	1,737	224	39,322	17,713	21,609	185	176	9
	20 and over ..	219,694	108,449	111,245	9,300	8,654	646	210,394	99,795	110,599	964	910	54
	HINDUS ..	*237,934*	*118,713*	*119,221*	*10,702*	*9,863*	*839*	*227,232*	*108,850*	*118,382*	*910*	*894*	*16*
	0—5 ..	41,185	20,339	20,846	..	..	..	41,185	20,339	20,846	..	..	..
	5—10 ..	30,405	15,645	14,760	513	418	95	29,892	15,227	14,665	4	3	1
	10—15 ..	26,758	13,782	12,976	1,009	856	153	25,749	12,926	12,823	42	41	1
	15—20 ..	22,680	10,878	11,802	1,568	1,410	158	21,112	9,468	11,644	154	150	4
	20 and over ..	116,906	58,069	58,837	7,612	7,179	433	109,294	50,890	58,404	710	700	10
	MUSLIMS ..	*6,866*	*3,667*	*3,199*	*1,225*	*1,083*	*142*	*5,641*	*2,584*	*3,057*	*188*	*183*	*5*
	0—5 ..	1,103	559	544	..	..	..	1,103	559	544	..	..	..
	5—10 ..	822	459	363	82	69	13	740	390	350	5	4	1
	10—15 ..	718	398	320	141	116	25	577	282	295	10	9	1
	15—20 ..	675	361	314	191	165	26	484	196	288	22	22	..
	20 and over ..	3,548	1,890	1,658	811	733	78	2,737	1,157	1,580	151	148	3
	TRIBALS ..	*199,310*	*98,123*	*101,187*	*622*	*618*	*4*	*198,688*	*97,505*	*101,183*	..	..	..
	0—5 ..	35,065	17,099	17,966	..	..	..	35,065	17,099	17,966	..	..	..
	5—10 ..	25,976	13,425	12,551	32	32	..	25,944	13,393	12,551	..	..	..
	10—15 ..	22,066	11,396	10,670	62	62	..	22,004	11,334	10,670	..	..	..
	15—20 ..	17,761	8,123	9,638	94	94	..	17,667	8,029	9,638	..	..	..
	20 and over ..	98,442	48,080	50,362	434	430	4	98,008	47,650	50,358	..	..	..

TABLE XIII

Seoni
Narsinghpur.]

Literacy by Religion and Age.

Part B.—Details for Districts—*contd.*

District.	Age.	Population.									Literate in English.		
		Total.			Literate.			Illiterate.					
		Persons.	Males.	Females.	Persons.	Males.	Females.	Persons.	Males.	Females.	Persons.	Males.	Females.
1	2	3	4	5	6	7	8	9	10	11	12	13	14
SEONI	ALL RELIGIONS ..	*393,732*	*192,471*	*201,261*	*16,889*	*15,386*	*1,503*	*376,843*	*177,085*	*199,758*	*938*	*878*	*60*
	0—5 ..	62,107	30,129	31,978	..	..	..	62,107	30,129	31,978	..	..	..
	5—10 ..	46,995	23,883	23,112	878	715	163	46,117	23,168	22,949	18	14	4
	10—15 ..	42,264	21,818	20,446	1,633	1,393	240	40,631	20,425	20,206	67	56	11
	15—20 ..	36,142	17,507	18,635	2,372	2,115	257	33,770	15,392	18,378	133	120	13
	20 and over ..	206,224	99,134	107,090	12,006	11,163	843	194,218	87,971	106,247	720	688	32
	HINDUS ..	*215,865*	*106,813*	*109,052*	*12,779*	*11,860*	*919*	*203,086*	*94,953*	*108,133*	*613*	*595*	*18*
	0—5 ..	34,600	16,953	17,647	..	..	..	34,600	16,953	17,647	..	..	..
	5—10 ..	26,293	13,355	12,938	636	538	98	25,657	12,817	12,840	10	9	1
	10—15 ..	23,702	12,205	11,497	1,187	1,049	138	22,515	11,156	11,359	42	37	5
	15—20 ..	19,972	9,912	10,060	1,784	1,631	153	18,188	8,281	9,907	87	82	5
	20 and over ..	111,298	54,388	56,910	9,172	8,642	530	102,126	45,746	56,380	474	467	7
	MUSLIMS	*18,506*	*9,152*	*9,354*	*2,276*	*2,043*	*233*	*16,230*	*7,109*	*9,121*	*171*	*169*	*2*
	0—5 ..	3,085	1,514	1,571	..	..	..	3,085	1,514	1,571	..	..	..
	5—10 ..	2,361	1,224	1,137	112	91	21	2,249	1,133	1,116	3	3	..
	10—15 ..	2,026	1,058	968	221	187	34	1,805	871	934	10	9	1
	15—20 ..	1,718	829	889	326	285	41	1,392	544	848	17	16	1
	20 and over ..	9,316	4,527	4,789	1,617	1,480	137	7,699	3,047	4,652	141	141	..
	TRIBALS ..	*157,194*	*75,407*	*81,787*	*814*	*783*	*31*	*156,380*	*74,624*	*81,756*	*5*	*5*	..
	0—5 ..	24,102	11,502	12,600	..	..	..	24,102	11,502	12,600	..	..	..
	5—10 ..	18,061	9,154	8,907	35	33	2	18,026	9,121	8,905	..	..	..
	10—15 ..	16,270	8,421	7,849	77	74	3	16,193	8,347	7,846	1	1	..
	15—20 ..	14,234	6,664	7,570	110	107	3	14,124	6,557	7,567	2	2	..
	20 and over ..	84,527	39,666	44,861	592	569	23	83,935	39,097	44,838	2	2	..
NARSINGHPUR	ALL RELIGIONS ..	*321,481*	*161,417*	*160,064*	*23,533*	*21,590*	*1,943*	*297,948*	*139,827*	*158,121*	*1,332*	*1,288*	*44*
	0—5 ..	48,214	23,949	24,265	..	..	..	48,214	23,949	24,265	..	..	..
	5—10 ..	39,979	20,781	19,198	1,612	1,391	221	38,367	19,390	18,977	30	29	1
	10—15 ..	37,292	19,606	17,686	2,644	2,304	340	34,648	17,302	17,346	102	98	4
	15—20 ..	30,027	15,193	14,834	3,260	2,925	335	26,767	12,268	14,499	268	257	1,1
	20 and over ..	165,969	81,888	84,081	16,017	14,970	1,047	149,952	66,918	83,034	932	904	28
	HINDUS ..	*264,233*	*133,214*	*131,019*	*20,712*	*19,180*	*1,532*	*243,521*	*114,034*	*129,487*	*1,024*	*1,001*	*23*
	0—5 ..	39,834	19,937	19,897	..	..	..	39,834	19,937	19,897	..	..	..
	5—10 ..	33,121	17,275	15,846	1,382	1,201	181	31,739	16,074	15,665	23	22	1
	10—15 ..	30,805	16,241	14,564	2,287	2,010	277	28,518	14,231	14,287	80	76	4
	15—20 ..	24,629	12,517	12,112	2,847	2,598	249	21,782	9,919	11,863	219	211	8
	20 and over ..	135,844	67,244	68,600	14,196	13,371	825	121,648	53,873	67,775	702	692	10
	MUSLIMS ..	*11,404*	*5,802*	*5,602*	*1,561*	*1,378*	*183*	*9,843*	*4,424*	*5,419*	*191*	*191*	..
	0—5 ..	1,780	871	909	..	..	..	1,780	871	909	..	..	..
	5—10 ..	1,480	784	696	120	103	17	1,360	681	679	4	4	..
	10—15 ..	1,381	742	639	201	174	27	1,180	568	612	16	16	..
	15—20 ..	1,113	589	524	241	198	43	872	391	481	31	31	..
	20 and over ..	5,650	2,816	2,834	999	903	96	4,651	1,913	2,738	140	140	..
	TRIBALS ..	*42,890*	*20,845*	*22,045*	*152*	*146*	*6*	*42,738*	*20,699*	*22,039*	..	..	..
	0—5 ..	6,104	2,895	3,209	..	..	..	6,104	2,895	3,209	..	..	..
	5—10 ..	4,994	2,516	2,478	8	8	..	4,986	2,508	2,478	..	..	..
	10—15 ..	4,765	2,437	2,328	16	16	..	4,749	2,421	2,328	..	..	..
	15—20 ..	4,022	1,947	2,075	24	22	2	3,998	1,925	2,073	..	..	..
	20 and over ..	23,005	11,050	11,955	104	100	4	22,901	10,950	11,951	..	..	..

Literacy by Religion and Age.

Part B.—Details for Districts—*contd.*

TABLE XIII

[Hoshangabad
[Nimar.

District.	Age.	Population. Total. Persons.	Total. Males.	Total. Females.	Literate. Persons.	Literate. Males	Literate. Females.	Illiterate Persons	Illiterate Males	Illiterate Females.	Literate in English. Persons.	Literate in English. Males.	Literate in English. Females.
1	2	3	4	5	6	7	8	9	10	11	12	13	14
HOSHANGABAD	**ALL RELIGIONS**	*486,630*	*248,226*	*238,404*	*40,134*	*37,430*	*2,704*	*446,496*	*210,796*	*235,700*	*4,365*	*4,072*	*293*
	0—5	72,165	35,725	36,440	..	..	..	72,165	35,725	36,440	..	..	..
	5—10	58,956	30,926	28,030	2,210	1,951	259	56,746	28,975	27,771	116	104	12
	10—15	54,350	28,829	25,521	3,846	3,433	413	50,504	25,396	25,108	318	294	24
	15—20	44,397	22,447	21,950	5,396	4,926	470	39,001	17,521	21,480	679	639	40
	20 and over	256,762	130,299	126,463	28,682	27,120	1,562	228,080	103,179	124,901	3,252	3,035	217
	HINDUS	*413,303*	*210,899*	*202,404*	*34,179*	*32,370*	*1,809*	*379,124*	*178,529*	*200,595*	*3,112*	*3,047*	*65*
	0—5	61,142	30,390	30,752	..	..	..	61,142	30,390	30,752	..	..	..
	5—10	50,092	26,343	23,749	1,895	1,690	205	48,197	24,653	23,544	91	86	5
	10—15	46,359	24,604	21,755	3,315	3,005	310	43,044	21,599	21,445	263	252	11
	15—20	37,782	19,132	18,650	4,589	4,267	322	33,193	14,865	18,328	529	516	13
	20 and over	217,928	110,430	107,498	24,380	23,408	972	193,548	87,022	106,526	2,229	2,193	36
	MUSLIMS	*23,475*	*12,368*	*11,107*	*3,767*	*3,427*	*340*	*19,708*	*8,941*	*10,767*	*505*	*501*	*4*
	0—5	3,483	1,693	1,790	..	..	..	3,483	1,693	1,790	..	..	..
	5—10	2,992	1,566	1,426	204	169	35	2,788	1,397	1,391	6	6	..
	10—15	2,667	1,428	1,239	337	284	53	2,330	1,144	1,186	21	20	1
	15—20	2,192	1,168	1,024	530	470	60	1,662	698	964	73	71	2
	20 and over	12,141	6,513	5,628	2,696	2,504	192	9,445	4,009	5,436	405	404	1
	TRIBALS	*45,450*	*22,567*	*22,883*	*142*	*134*	*8*	*45,308*	*22,433*	*22,875*	*1*	*1*	..
	0—5	6,903	3,339	3,564	..	..	..	6,903	3,339	3,564	..	..	..
	5—10	5,340	2,746	2,594	8	7	1	5,332	2,739	2,593	..	..	..
	10—15	4,845	2,547	2,298	16	14	2	4,829	2,533	2,296	..	..	..
	15—20	4,017	1,924	2,093	21	19	2	3,996	1,905	2,091	..	..	..
	20 and over	24,345	12,011	12,334	97	94	3	24,248	11,917	12,331	1	1	..
NIMAR	**ALL RELIGIONS**	*466,931*	*242,042*	*224,889*	*36,271*	*33,374*	*2,897*	*430,660*	*208,668*	*221,992*	*3,550*	*3,304*	*246*
	0—5	71,762	35,465	36,297	..	..	..	71,762	35,465	36,297	..	..	..
	5—10	58,388	30,403	27,985	2,145	1,820	325	56,243	28,583	27,660	91	75	16
	10—15	53,491	27,841	25,650	3,622	3,142	480	49,869	24,699	25,170	276	244	32
	15—20	46,016	22,576	23,440	5,060	4,527	533	40,956	18,049	22,907	618	560	58
	20 and over	237,274	125,757	111,517	25,444	23,885	1,559	211,830	101,872	109,958	2,565	2,425	140
	HINDUS	*372,583*	*193,412*	*179,171*	*28,283*	*26,604*	*1,679*	*344,300*	*166,808*	*177,492*	*2,427*	*2,355*	*72*
	0—5	55,909	27,711	28,198	..	..	..	55,909	27,711	28,198	..	..	..
	5—10	45,820	23,907	21,913	1,541	1,333	208	44,279	22,574	21,705	51	45	6
	10—15	42,365	22,072	20,293	2,680	2,383	297	39,685	19,689	19,996	163	150	13
	15—20	36,838	18,139	18,699	3,927	3,613	314	32,911	14,526	18,385	398	379	19
	20 and over	191,651	101,583	90,068	20,135	19,275	860	171,516	82,308	89,208	1,815	1,781	34
	MUSLIMS	*50,925*	*26,839*	*24,086*	*6,199*	*5,427*	*772*	*44,726*	*21,412*	*23,314*	*673*	*650*	*23*
	0—5	7,996	3,974	4,022	..	..	..	7,996	3,974	4,022	..	..	..
	5—10	6,922	3,627	3,295	473	399	74	6,449	3,228	3,221	20	19	1
	10—15	6,209	3,275	2,934	735	620	115	5,474	2,655	2,819	68	64	4
	15—20	4,933	2,491	2,442	885	749	136	4,048	1,742	2,306	141	134	7
	20 and over	24,865	13,472	11,393	4,106	3,659	447	20,759	9,813	10,946	444	433	11
	CHRISTIANS	*4,928*	*2,486*	*2,442*	*655*	*390*	*265*	*4,273*	*2,096*	*2,177*	*277*	*167*	*110*
	0—5	828	405	423	..	..	..	828	405	423	..	..	..
	5—10	673	334	339	59	35	24	614	299	315	12	7	5
	10—15	631	323	308	101	57	44	530	266	264	32	20	12
	15—20	520	249	271	115	55	60	405	194	211	57	30	27
	20 and over	2,276	1,175	1,101	380	243	137	1,896	932	964	176	110	66
	TRIBALS	*35,429*	*17,659*	*17,770*	*72*	*67*	*5*	*35,357*	*17,592*	*17,765*	..	..	..
	0—5	6,613	3,177	3,436	..	..	..	6,613	3,177	3,436	..	..	..
	5—10	4,611	2,342	2,269	8	8	..	4,603	2,334	2,269	..	..	..
	10—15	3,957	1,987	1,970	9	8	1	3,948	1,979	1,969	..	..	..
	15—20	3,439	1,539	1,900	9	9	..	3,430	1,530	1,900	..	..	..
	20 and over	16,809	8,614	8,195	46	42	4	16,763	8,572	8,191	..	..	..

TABLE XIII

Betul
Chhindwara.]

Literacy by Religion and Age.

Part B.—Details for Districts—*contd.*

District.	Age.	Population. Total. Persons.	Total. Males.	Total. Females.	Literate. Persons.	Literate. Males.	Literate. Females.	Illiterate. Persons.	Illiterate. Males.	Illiterate. Females.	Literate in English. Persons.	Literate in English. Males.	Literate in English. Females.
1	2	3	4	5	6	7	8	9	10	11	12	13	14
BETUL	ALL RELIGIONS ..	*406,252*	*201,114*	*205,138*	*13,816*	*12,975*	*871*	*392,406*	*188,139*	*204,267*	*1,152*	*1,085*	*67*
	0—5 ..	69,438	34,275	35,163	..	..	..	69,438	34,275	35,163	..	..	..
	5—10 ..	52,980	26,861	26,119	694	610	84	52,286	26,251	26,035	23	21	2
	10—15 ..	47,402	24,180	23,222	1,187	1,057	130	46,215	23,123	23,092	59	55	4
	15—20 ..	36,181	17,408	18,773	1,707	1,549	158	34,474	15,859	18,615	136	129	7
	20 and over ..	200,251	98,390	101,861	10,258	9,759	499	189,993	88,631	101,362	934	880	54
	HINDUS ..	*275,093*	*136,689*	*138,404*	*11,487*	*10,947*	*540*	*263,606*	*125,742*	*137,864*	*804*	*800*	*4*
	0—5 ..	45,355	22,254	23,101	..	..	..	45,355	22,254	23,101	..	..	..
	5—10 ..	35,041	17,768	17,273	591	530	61	34,450	17,238	17,212	18	18	..
	10—15 ..	31,994	16,506	15,488	1,009	918	91	30,985	15,588	15,397	49	49	..
	15—20 ..	24,660	12,066	12,594	1,394	1,302	92	23,266	10,764	12,502	98	98	..
	20 and over ..	138,043	68,095	69,948	8,493	8,197	296	129,550	59,898	69,652	639	635	4
	MUSLIMS ..	*7,037*	*3,644*	*3,393*	*1,338*	*1,227*	*111*	*5,699*	*2,417*	*3,282*	*157*	*150*	*7*
	0—5 ..	1,101	541	560	..	..	..	1,101	541	560	..	..	..
	5—10 ..	877	428	449	53	43	10	824	385	439	2	2	..
	10—15 ..	760	371	389	91	77	14	669	294	375	7	5	1
	15—20 ..	653	333	320	172	149	23	481	184	297	23	22	1
	20 and over ..	3,646	1,971	1,675	1,022	958	64	2,624	1,013	1,611	125	120	5
	TRIBALS ..	*121,883*	*59,642*	*62,241*	*225*	*223*	*2*	*121,658*	*59,419*	*62,239*	*20*	*20*	...
	0—5 ..	22,637	11,308	11,329	..	..	..	22,637	11,308	11,329	..	..	..
	5—10 ..	16,788	8,523	8,265	16	16	..	16,772	8,507	8,265	..	..	..
	10—15 ..	14,413	7,185	7,228	21	21	..	14,392	7,164	7,228	..	..	..
	15—20 ..	10,651	4,912	5,739	29	29	..	10,622	4,883	5,739	2	2	..
	20 and over ..	57,394	27,714	29,680	159	157	2	57,235	27,557	29,678	18	18	..
CHHINDWARA	ALL RELIGIONS ..	*573,272*	*285,007*	*288,265*	*25,051*	*23,483*	*1,568*	*548 221*	*261,524*	*286,697*	*1,748*	*1,611*	*137*
	0—5 ..	97,007	47,210	49,797	..	..	..	97,007	47,210	49,797	..	..	..
	5—10 ..	72,096	36,558	35,538	2,255	2,090	165	69,841	34,468	35,373	39	33	6
	10—15 ..	63,002	32,439	30,563	2,252	2,001	251	60,750	30,438	30,312	114	105	9
	15—20 ..	50,272	24,383	25,889	3,206	2,936	270	47,066	21,447	25,619	231	207	24
	20 and over ..	290,895	144,417	146,478	17,338	16,456	882	273,557	127,961	145,596	1,364	1,266	98
	HINDUS ..	*349,600*	*175,768*	*173,832*	*20,171*	*19,187*	*984*	*329,429*	*156,581*	*172,848*	*1,165*	*1,118*	*47*
	0—5 ..	58,562	28,648	29,914	..	..	..	58,562	28,648	29,914	..	..	..
	5—10 ..	44,170	22,491	21,679	1,967	1,864	103	42,203	20,627	21,576	24	22	2
	10—15 ..	38,723	20,066	18,657	1,770	1,611	159	36,953	18,455	18,498	79	73	6
	15—20 ..	30,586	15,142	15,444	2,522	2,363	159	28,064	12,779	15,285	159	150	9
	20 and over ..	177,559	89,421	88,138	13,912	13,349	563	163,647	76,072	87,575	903	873	30
	MUSLIMS ..	*20,183*	*10,550*	*9,633*	*3,807*	*2,586*	*221*	*17,376*	*7,964*	*9,412*	*263*	*257*	*6*
	0—5 ..	3,364	1,662	1,702	..	..	..	3,364	1,662	1,702	..	..	..
	5—10 ..	2,583	1,323	1,260	151	123	28	2,432	1,200	1,232	5	4	1
	10—15 ..	2,186	1,145	1,041	247	212	35	1,939	933	1,006	14	12	2
	15—20 ..	1,825	960	865	393	357	36	1,432	603	829	33	32	1
	20 and over ..	10,225	5,460	4,765	2,016	1,894	122	8,209	3,566	4,643	211	209	2
	TRIBALS ..	*290,173*	*96,986*	*103,187*	*721*	*708*	*13*	*199,452*	*96,278*	*103,174*	*9*	*9*	..
	0—5 ..	34,592	16,644	17,948	.	.	..	34,592	16,644	17,948	..	..	..
	5—10 ..	24,920	12,527	12,393	40	139	1	24,880	12,488	12,392	..	..	..
	10—15 ..	21,689	11,016	10,673	64	61	3	21,625	10,955	10,670	..	..	..
	15—20 ..	17,523	8,111	9,412	79	77	2	17,444	8,034	9,410	2	2	..
	20 and over ..	101,449	48,688	52,761	538	531	7	100,911	48,157	52,754	7	7	--

Literacy by Religion and Age.

Part B.—Details for Districts—*contd.*

TABLE XIIa

[Wardha. Nagpur.]

District.	Age	Population. Total Persons.	Total Males.	Total Females	Literate Persons.	Literate Males.	Literate Females.	Illiterate Persons.	Illiterate Males	Illiterate Females.	Literate in English. Persons.	Literate in English. Males.	Literate in English. Females.
1	2	3	4	5	6	7	8	9	10	11	12	13	14
WARDHA	**ALL RELIGIONS** ..	*516,266*	*261,391*	*254,872*	*34,972*	*32,204*	*2,768*	*481,294*	*229,190*	*252,104*	*3,816*	*3,655*	*161*
	0—5 ..	77,141	38,111	39,030	..	..	..	77,141	38,111	39,030	..	..	..
	5—10 ..	63,745	32,088	31,657	2,756	2,155	601	60,989	29,933	31,056	157	138	19
	10—15 ..	58,532	29,641	28,891	4,540	3,834	706	53,992	25,807	28,185	436	404	32
	15—20 ..	45,901	22,275	23,626	4,884	4,481	403	41,017	17,794	23,223	661	628	33
	20 and over ..	270,947	139,279	131,668	22,792	21,734	1,058	248,155	117,545	130,610	2,562	2,485	77
	HINDUS ..	*452,285*	*229,234*	*223,051*	*31,064*	*28,650*	*2,414*	*421,221*	*200,584*	*220,637*	*3,245*	*3,131*	*114*
	0—5 ..	67,537	33,358	34,179	..	..	..	67,537	33,358	34,179	..	..	..
	5—10 ..	55,812	28,182	27,630	2,477	1,916	561	53,335	26,266	27,069	122	106	16
	10—15 ..	51,470	26,127	25,343	4,121	3,481	640	47,349	22,646	24,703	386	358	28
	15—20 ..	40,388	19,596	20,792	4,378	4,043	335	36,010	15,553	20,457	599	573	26
	20 and over ..	237,078	121,971	115,107	20,088	19,210	878	216,990	102,761	114,229	2,138	2,094	44
	MUSLIMS ..	*20,928*	*11,046*	*9,882*	*2,733*	*2,611*	*122*	*18,192*	*8,432*	*9,760*	*262*	*259*	*3*
	0—5 ..	3,299	1,671	1,628	..	..	..	3,299	1,671	1,628	..	..	..
	5—10 ..	2,735	1,343	1,392	171	151	20	2,564	1,192	1,372	27	27	..
	10—15 ..	2,390	1,201	1,189	261	235	26	2,129	966	1,163	35	34	1
	15—20 ..	1,927	1,026	901	317	300	17	1,610	726	884	27	26	1
	20 and over ..	10,577	5,805	4,772	1,987	1,928	59	8,590	3,877	4,713	173	172	1
	TRIBALS	*39,789*	*19,408*	*20,381*	*251*	*246*	*5*	*39,538*	*19,162*	*20,376*	*6*	*5*	*1*
	0—5 ..	5,857	2,856	3,001	..	..	..	5,857	2,856	3,001	..	..	..
	5—10 ..	4,812	2,349	2,463	23	22	1	4,789	2,327	2,462	1	1	..
	10—15 ..	4,331	2,126	2,205	42	40	2	4,289	2,086	2,203	3	2	1
	15—20 ..	3,260	1,491	1,769	43	41	2	3,217	1,450	1,767	2	2	..
	20 and over ..	21,529	10,586	10,943	143	143	..	21,386	10,443	10,943	..	..	..
NAGPUR	**ALL RELIGIONS** ..	*940,049*	*481,246*	*458,803*	*88,380*	*75,450*	*12,930*	*851,669*	*405,796*	*445,873*	*20,646*	*17,524*	*3,122*
	0—5 ..	138,995	68,894	70,101	..	..	..	138,995	68,894	70,101	..	..	..
	5—10 ..	116,156	59,071	57,085	6,897	5,336	1,561	109,259	53,735	55,524	1,019	665	354
	10—15 ..	105,604	54,256	51,348	10,462	8,522	1,940	95,142	45,734	49,408	1,748	1,332	416
	15—20 ..	84,826	42,498	42,328	13,094	10,951	2,143	71,732	31,547	40,185	3,579	3,047	532
	20 and over ..	491,468	256,527	237,941	57,927	50,641	7,286	436,541	205,886	230,655	14,300	12,480	1,820
	HINDUS ..	*862,519*	*439,201*	*423,318*	*71,794*	*62,921*	*8,873*	*790,725*	*376,280*	*414,445*	*13,873*	*12,681*	*1,192*
	0—5 ..	128,274	63,594	64,680	..	..	..	128,274	63,594	64,680	..	..	..
	5—10 ..	106,543	54,185	52,358	5,383	4,378	1,005	101,160	49,807	51,353	384	304	80
	10—15 ..	96,805	49,704	47,101	8,603	7,284	1,319	88,202	42,420	45,782	1,072	921	151
	15—20 ..	77,206	38,333	38,873	10,718	9,213	1,505	66,488	29,120	37,368	2,542	2,280	262
	20 and over ..	453,691	233,385	220,306	47,090	42,046	5,044	406,601	191,339	215,262	9,875	9,176	699
	MUSLIMS ..	*53,809*	*29,366*	*24,443*	*8,903*	*7,395*	*1,508*	*44,906*	*21,971*	*22,935*	*1,391*	*1,295*	*96*
	0—5 ..	7,617	3,767	3,850	..	..	..	7,617	3,767	3,850	..	..	..
	5—10 ..	6,857	3,485	3,372	696	518	178	6,161	2,967	3,194	59	50	9
	10—15 ..	6,164	3,196	2,968	968	736	232	5,196	2,460	2,736	100	92	8
	15—20 ..	5,143	2,815	2,328	1,257	982	275	3,886	1,833	2,053	232	215	17
	20 and over ..	28,028	16,103	11,925	5,982	5,159	823	22,046	10,944	11,102	1,000	938	62
	TRIBALS ..	*9,784*	*4,972*	*4,812*	*91*	*88*	*3*	*9,693*	*4,884*	*4,809*	*4*	*4*	..
	0—5 ..	1,414	700	714	..	..	..	1,414	700	714	..	..	..
	5—10 ..	1,132	579	553	6	5	1	1,126	574	552	1	1	..
	10—15 ..	1,031	531	500	10	9	1	1,021	522	499	1	1	..
	15—20 ..	854	415	439	17	16	1	837	399	438	2	2	..
	20 and over ..	5,353	2,747	2,606	58	58	..	5,295	2,689	2,606	..	..	..
	CHRISTIANS ..	*8,558*	*4,810*	*3,748*	*5,394*	*3,354*	*2,040*	*3,164*	*1,456*	*1,768*	*4,504*	*2,946*	*1,558*
	0—5 ..	1,052	526	526	..	..	..	1,052	526	526	..	..	..
	5—10 ..	1,030	523	507	644	331	313	386	192	194	509	278	231
	10—15 ..	1,035	531	504	666	351	315	369	180	189	495	279	216
	15—20 ..	1,064	629	435	829	530	299	235	99	136	690	473	217
	20 and over ..	4,377	2,601	1,776	3,255	2,142	1,113	1,122	459	663	2,810	1,916	894

TABLE XIII Literacy by Religion and Age.

Chanda
Bhandara

Part B.—Details for Districts—*contd.*

District.	Age	Population.									Literate in English.		
		Total.			Literate.			Illiterate.					
		Persons.	Males	Females	Persons	Males.	Females	Persons.	Males	Females	Persons.	Males.	Females.
1	2	3	4	5	6	7	8	9	10	11	12	13	14
CHANDA	ALL RELIGIONS ..	*759,695*	*381,201*	*378,494*	*26,621*	*24,757*	*1,864*	*733,074*	*355,417*	*376,527*	*2,311*	*2,136*	*175*
	0—5 ..	120,355	58,756	61,599	..	..	..	120,355	58,756	61,599	..	..	..
	5—10 ..	100,063	50,225	49,838	1,791	1,558	233	98,272	48,667	49,605	72	50	22
	10—15 ..	89,270	44,971	44,299	2,937	2,622	315	86,333	42,349	43,984	207	173	34
	15—20 ..	67,024	31,930	35,094	3,676	3,334	342	63,348	28,596	34,752	369	333	36
	20 and over .	382,983	195,322	187,661	18,217	17,243	974	364,766	178,079	186,687	1,663	1,580	83
	HINDUS ..	*630,517*	*317,050*	*313,467*	*22,711*	*21,313*	*1,398*	*607,806*	*295,737*	*312,069*	*1,788*	*1,751*	*37*
	0—5 .	99,383	48,592	50,791	..	..	..	99,383	48,592	50,791	..	..	..
	5—10 ..	82,896	41,859	41,037	1,529	1,360	169	81,367	40,499	40,868	44	42	2
	10—15 .	74,458	37,893	36,565	2,526	2,297	229	71,932	35,596	36,336	152	147	5
	15—20	55,221	26,439	28,782	3,125	2,874	251	52,096	23,565	28,531	283	277	6
	20 and over	318,559	162,267	156,292	15,531	14,782	749	303,028	147,485	155,543	1,309	1,285	24
	MUSLIMS .	*13,556*	*7,045*	*6,511*	*2,403*	*2,245*	*158*	*11,153*	*4,800*	*6,353*	*187*	*185*	*2*
	0—5 .	1,842	917	925	..	..	..	1,842	917	925	..	..	..
	5—10 ..	1,713	866	847	134	113	21	1,579	753	826	2	1	1
	10—15 ..	1,582	797	785	221	191	30	1,361	606	755	7	6	1
	15—20 ..	1,290	671	619	320	293	27	970	378	592	23	23	..
	20 and over ..	7,129	3,794	3,335	1,728	1,648	80	5,401	2,146	3,255	155	155	..
	TRIBALS ..	*113,327*	*55,916*	*57,411*	*529*	*513*	*16*	*112,798*	*55,403*	*57,395*	*13*	*13*	..
	0—5 .	18,818	9,096	9,722	..	..	..	18,818	9,096	9,722	..	..	..
	5—10 .	15,147	7,347	7,800	36	32	4	15,111	7,315	7,796	..	..	..
	10—15 ..	12,931	6,125	6,806	51	49	2	12,880	6,076	6,804	2	2	..
	15—20 ..	10,252	4,686	5,566	67	65	2	10,185	4,621	5,564	2	2	..
	20 and over ..	56,179	28,662	27,517	375	367	8	55,804	28,295	27,509	9	9	..
BHANDARA	ALL RELIGIONS .	*824,496*	*408,799*	*415,697*	*33,435*	*31,090*	*2,345*	*791,061*	*377,709*	*413,352*	*1,976*	*1,860*	*116*
	0—5 .	126,074	61,843	64,231	..	..	..	126,074	61,841	64,231	..	..	..
	5—10 ..	102,136	52,074	50,062	2,477	2,181	296	99,659	49,893	49,766	68	59	9
	10—15 .	92,619	47,254	45,365	3,745	3,362	383	88,874	43,892	44,982	169	156	13
	15—20 ..	71,303	34,909	36,394	4,701	4,288	413	66,602	30,621	35,981	315	284	31
	20 and over .	432,364	212,719	219,645	22,512	21,259	1,253	409,852	191,460	218,392	1,424	1,361	63
	HINDUS	*767,373*	*380,517*	*386,856*	*29,449*	*27,532*	*1,917*	*737,924*	*352,985*	*384,939*	*1,590*	*1,513*	*77*
	0—5 .	117,786	57,848	59,938	..	..	..	117,786	57,848	59,938	..	..	..
	5—10 .	95,445	48,765	46,680	2,207	1,967	240	93,238	46,798	46,440	51	44	7
	10—15	86,492	44,177	42,315	3,306	3,002	304	83,186	41,175	42,011	139	128	11
	15—20	66,276	32,428	33,848	4,108	3,776	332	62,168	28,652	33,516	250	228	22
	20 and over	401,374	197,299	204,075	19,828	18,787	1,041	381,546	178,512	203,034	1,150	1,113	37
	MUSLIMS .	*15,484*	*8,134*	*7,350*	*2,801*	*2,542*	*259*	*12,683*	*5,592*	*7,091*	*199*	*197*	*2*
	0—5 .	2,305	1,149	1,156	..	..	..	2,305	1,149	1,156	..	..	..
	5—10 .	1,912	969	943	176	139	37	1,736	830	906	6	6	..
	10—15	1,696	878	818	283	233	50	1,413	645	768	18	17	1
	15—20 .	1,430	755	675	415	368	47	1,015	387	628	44	43	1
	20 and over	8,141	4,383	3,758	1,927	1,802	125	6,214	2,581	3,633	131	131	..
	TRIBALS .	*39,600*	*19,156*	*20,444*	*661*	*591*	*70*	*38,939*	*18,565*	*20,374*	*38*	*38*	..
	0—5 ..	5,681	2,699	2,982	..	..	..	5,681	2,699	2,982	..	..	..
	5—10 .	4,517	2,218	2,299	48	41	7	4,469	2,177	2,292	..	..	..
	10—15 .	4,191	2,085	2,106	93	80	13	4,098	2,005	2,093	3	3	..
	15—20 .	3,401	1,630	1,771	111	96	15	3,290	1,534	1,756	3	3	..
	20 and over ..	21,810	10,524	11,286	409	374	35	21,401	10,150	11,251	32	32	..

Literacy by Religion and Age.

Part B.—Details for Districts—*contd.*

TABLE XIII

[Balaghat
Raipur.

District.	Age.	Population. Total. Persons.	Total. Males	Total. Females	Literate. Persons	Literate. Males.	Literate. Females	Illiterate. Persons.	Illiterate. Males.	Illiterate. Females.	Literate in English. Persons.	Literate in English. Males.	Literate in English. Females.
1	2	3	4	5	6	7	8	9	10	11	12	13	14
BALAGHAT	ALL RELIGIONS ..	*561,602*	*276,898*	*284,704*	*24,704*	*23,408*	*1,296*	*536,898*	*253,490*	*283,408*	*1,197*	*1,118*	*79*
	0—5 ..	80,808	39,753	41,055	..	..	..	80,808	39,753	41,055	..	..	..
	5—10 ..	69,921	35,331	34,590	1,573	1,413	160	68,348	33,918	34,430	49	43	6
	10—15 ..	65,995	33,587	32,408	2,608	2,394	214	63,387	31,193	32,194	112	101	11
	15—20 ..	51,725	25,377	26,348	3,394	3,180	214	48,331	22,197	26,134	180	160	20
	20 and over ..	293,153	142,850	150,303	17,129	16,421	708	276,024	126,429	149,595	856	814	42
	HINDUS ..	*481,520*	*237,728*	*243,792*	*21,036*	*20,147*	*889*	*460,484*	*217,581*	*242,903*	*873*	*851*	*22*
	0—5 ..	69,736	34,416	35,320	..	..	..	69,736	34,416	35,320	..	..	..
	5—10 ..	60,122	30,368	29,754	1,288	1,177	111	58,834	29,191	29,643	37	35	2
	10—15 ..	56,907	28,945	27,962	2,181	2,035	146	54,726	26,910	27,816	89	86	3
	15—20 ..	44,487	21,882	22,605	2,904	2,766	138	41,583	19,116	22,467	131	127	4
	20 and over ..	250,268	122,117	128,151	14,663	14,169	494	235,605	107,948	127,657	616	603	13
	MUSLIMS ..	*11,121*	*5,485*	*5,636*	*2,028*	*1,830*	*198*	*9,093*	*3,655*	*5,438*	*163*	*161*	*2*
	0—5 ..	1,619	816	803	..	..	..	1,619	816	803	..	..	..
	5—10 ..	1,404	722	682	112	88	24	1,292	634	658	4	3	1
	10—15 ..	1,253	637	616	182	149	33	1,071	488	583	6	6	..
	15—20 ..	1,011	501	510	272	237	35	739	264	475	19	19	..
	20 and over ..	5,834	2,809	3,025	1,462	1,356	106	4,372	1,453	2,919	134	133	1
	TRIBALS ..	*67,404*	*32,884*	*34,520*	*978*	*966*	*12*	*66,426*	*31,918*	*34,508*	*11*	*11*	..
	0—5 ..	9,193	4,398	4,795	..	..	..	9,193	4,398	4,795	..	..	..
	5—10 ..	8,205	4,137	4,068	110	109	1	8,095	4,028	4,067	1	1	..
	10—15 ..	7,659	3,910	3,749	153	151	2	7,506	3,759	3,747	1	1	..
	15—20 ..	6,068	2,918	3,150	118	115	3	5,950	2,803	3,147	2	2	..
	20 and over ..	36,279	17,521	18,758	597	591	6	35,682	16,930	18,752	7	7	..
RAIPUR	ALL RELIGIONS ..	*1,527,573*	*739,950*	*787,623*	*47,700*	*43,513*	*4,187*	*1,479,873*	*696,437*	*783,436*	*4,021*	*3,676*	*345*
	0—5 ..	244,813	118,808	126,005	..	..	..	244,813	118,808	126,005	..	..	..
	5—10 ..	196,535	100,388	96,147	2,906	2,493	413	193,629	97,895	95,734	117	100	17
	10—15 ..	169,211	87,712	81,499	4,845	4,207	638	164,366	83,505	80,861	342	294	48
	15—20 ..	129,212	61,362	67,850	6,706	5,959	747	122,506	55,403	67,103	635	561	74
	20 and over ..	787,802	371,680	416,122	33,243	30,854	2,389	754,559	340,826	413,733	2,927	2,721	206
	HINDUS ..	*1,403,879*	*679,436*	*724,443*	*39,723*	*37,124*	*2,599*	*1,364,156*	*642,312*	*721,844*	*2,633*	*2,553*	*80*
	0—5 ..	226,125	109,827	116,298	..	..	..	226,125	109,827	116,298	..	..	..
	5—10 ..	180,513	92,130	88,383	2,339	2,081	258	178,174	90,049	88,125	71	66	5
	10—15 ..	155,369	80,406	74,963	3,919	3,555	364	151,450	76,851	74,599	209	200	9
	15—20 ..	118,543	56,259	62,284	5,470	5,058	412	113,073	51,201	61,872	381	368	13
	20 and over ..	723,329	340,814	382,515	27,995	26,430	1,565	695,334	314,384	380,950	1,972	1,919	53
	MUSLIMS ..	*19,992*	*10,251*	*9,741*	*4,296*	*3,765*	*531*	*15,696*	*6,486*	*9,210*	*653*	*625*	*28*
	0—5 ..	2,683	1,322	1,361	..	..	..	2,683	1,322	1,361	..	..	..
	5—10 ..	2,332	1,210	1,122	282	231	51	2,050	979	1,071	20	18	2
	10—15 ..	2,139	1,143	996	425	344	81	1,714	799	915	44	41	3
	15—20 ..	1,918	982	936	583	493	90	1,335	489	846	94	90	4
	20 and over ..	10,920	5,594	5,326	3,006	2,697	309	7,914	2,897	5,017	495	476	19
	CHRISTIANS ..	*5,980*	*2,980*	*3,000*	*2,087*	*1,186*	*901*	*3,893*	*1,794*	*2,099*	*613*	*393*	*220*
	0—5 ..	919	455	464	..	..	..	919	455	464	..	..	..
	5—10 ..	771	385	386	189	101	88	582	284	298	18	9	9
	10—15 ..	769	391	378	364	192	172	405	199	206	82	47	35
	15—20 ..	691	330	361	448	229	219	243	101	142	143	88	55
	20 and over ..	2,830	1,419	1,411	1,086	664	422	1,744	755	989	370	249	121
	TRIBALS ..	*95,393*	*45,951*	*49,439*	*702*	*654*	*48*	*94,691*	*45,300*	*49,391*	*2*	*2*	..
	0—5 ..	14,764	7,056	7,708	..	..	..	14,764	7,056	7,708	..	..	..
	5—10 ..	12,660	6,527	6,133	38	33	5	12,622	6,494	6,128	..	..	..
	10—15 ..	10,702	5,643	5,059	63	55	8	10,639	5,588	5,051	..	..	..
	15—20 ..	7,812	3,654	4,158	83	74	9	7,729	3,580	4,149	..	..	..
	20 and over ..	49,455	23,074	26,381	518	492	26	48,937	22,582	26,355	2	2	..

TABLE XIII

Bilaspur, Drug and Amraoti.

Literacy by Religion and Age.

Part B.—Details for Districts—*contd.*

District.	Age.	Population. Total. Persons.	Total. Males.	Total. Females.	Literate. Persons.	Literate. Males.	Literate. Females.	Illiterate. Persons.	Illiterate. Males.	Illiterate. Females.	Literate in English. Persons	Literate in English. Males.	Literate in English. Females.
1	2	3	4	5	6	7	8	9	10	11	12	13	14
BILASPUR	ALL RELIGIONS ..	*1,100,248*	*683,925*	*716,323*	*43,374*	*38,948*	*4,426*	*1,356,874*	*644,972*	*711,902*	*3,513*	*2,857*	*656*
	0—5 ..	232,350	113,516	118,834	..	..	..	232,350	113,516	118,834	..	..	..
	5—10 ..	187,554	95,094	92,460	3,205	2,650	555	184,349	92,444	91,905	165	96	69
	10—15 ..	159,057	81,629	77,428	4,657	3,951	706	154,400	77,678	76,722	304	192	112
	15—20 ..	120,483	56,734	63,749	5,905	5,181	724	114,578	51,553	63,025	527	400	127
	20 and over .	700,804	336,947	363,857	29,607	27,166	2,441	671,197	309,781	361,416	2,517	2,169	348
	HINDUS .	*1,326,399*	*657,789*	*669,610*	*37,237*	*34,349*	*2,888*	*1,269,662*	*602,940*	*666,722*	*2,050*	*1,955*	*95*
	0—5 .	216,108	105,708	110,400	..	..	..	216,706	105,708	110,400	..	..	..
	5—10 ..	175,151	88,762	86,389	2,708	2,755	353	172,443	86,407	86,036	71	65	6
	10—15 ..	148,723	76,247	72,476	3,951	3,517	434	144,772	72,730	72,042	148	135	13
	15—20 ..	112,390	52,908	59,482	5,001	4,558	443	107,389	48,350	59,039	295	275	20
	20 and over ..	654,527	313,664	340,863	25,577	23,919	1,658	628,950	289,745	339,205	1,536	1,480	56
	MUSLIMS ..	*15,673*	*7,105*	*9,178*	*3,398*	*3,076*	*322*	*15,275*	*6,119*	*8,856*	*399*	*390*	*9*
	0—5 ..	2,709	1,275	1,434	.		..	2,709	1,275	1,434	..	..	..
	5—10	2,202	1,119	1,083	201	175	26	2,001	944	1,057	10	10	..
	10—15 .	1,960	1,032	928	304	264	40	1,656	766	888	24	24	..
	15—20 .	1,789	877	912	473	403	70	1,316	474	842	54	51	3
	20 and over .	10,013	5,192	4,821	2,420	2,234	186	7,593	2,958	4,635	311	305	6
	CHRISTIANS .	*5,216*	*2,459*	*2,757*	*2,238*	*1,080*	*1,158*	*2,978*	*1,379*	*1,599*	*1,012*	*468*	*544*
	0—5 ..	777	384	393	..	..	..	777	384	393	..	..	..
	5—10 ..	676	330	346	256	91	165	420	239	181	81	19	62
	10—15 ..	634	291	343	352	128	224	282	163	119	129	31	98
	15—20 ..	551	248	303	365	165	200	186	83	103	169	68	101
	20 and over ..	2,578	1,206	1,372	1,265	696	569	1,313	510	803	633	350	283
	TRIBAL	*68,672*	*34,231*	*34,441*	*178*	*178*	..	*68,494*	*34,053*	*34,441*	..	..	..
	0—5 .	12,624	6,083	6,541	..	..	..	12,624	6,083	6,541	..	..	..
	5—10 ..	9,432	4,831	4,601	10	10	..	9,422	4,821	4,601	..	..	..
	10—15 ..	7,663	4,015	3,648	18	18	..	7,645	3,997	3,648	..	..	..
	15—20 ..	5,679	2,660	3,019	29	29	..	5,650	2,631	3,019	..	..	..
	20 and over .	33,274	16,642	16,632	121	121	..	33,153	16,521	16,632	..	..	..
DRUG	ALL RELIGIONS ..	*817,924*	*390,367*	*427,557*	*22,983*	*21,449*	*1,534*	*794,941*	*365,918*	*426,023*	*927*	*867*	*60*
	0—5 ..	134,332	64,540	69,792		.	.	134,332	64,540	69,792	..	..	..
	5—10 ..	98,785	50,696	48,089	1,179	1,025	154	97,606	49,671	47,935	24	22	2
	10—15 ..	86,152	44,389	41,763	2,057	1,822	235	84,095	42,567	41,528	61	57	4
	15—20 ..	68,142	32,106	36,036	3,178	2,889	289	64,964	29,217	35,747	128	120	8
	20 and over ..	430,513	198,636	231,877	16,569	15,713	856	413,944	182,923	231,021	714	668	46
	HINDUS .	*794,949*	*378,958*	*415,991*	*20,619*	*19,640*	*979*	*774,330*	*359,318*	*415,012*	*701*	*685*	*16*
	0—5 .	130,646	62,736	67,910	..	..	..	130,646	62,736	67,910	.	..	..
	5—10 .	95,845	49,184	46,661	1,004	915	89	94,841	48,269	46,572	19	19	..
	10—15 ..	83,640	43,099	40,541	1,801	1,669	132	81,839	41,430	40,409	51	50	1
	15—20 .	66,195	31,181	35,014	2,824	2,664	160	63,371	28,517	34,854	103	101	2
	20 and over ..	418,623	192,758	225,865	14,990	14,392	598	403,633	178,366	225,267	528	515	13
	TRIBALS ..	*12,158*	*6,140*	*6,018*	*37*	*24*	*13*	*12,121*	*6,116*	*6,005*	..	..	..
	0—5	2,172	1,046	1,126	.	..	.	2,172	1,046	1,126	..	..	..
	5—10 .	1,742	907	837	2	2	...	1,740	905	835	..	..	..
	10—15 ..	1,423	737	686	3	1	2	1,420	736	684	..	..	..
	15—20 ..	954	458	496	7	3	4	947	455	492	..	..	..
	20 and over .	5,867	2,992	2,875	25	18	7	5,842	2,974	2,868	..	..	..
AMRAOTI	ALL RELIGIONS	*941,601*	*485,595*	*455,011*	*85,012*	*78,090*	*6,922*	*856,592*	*407,505*	*449,089*	*7,806*	*7,247*	*559*
	0—5 ..	139,442	69,040	70,402	..			139,442	69,040	70,402	..	..	..
	5—10 ..	114,417	57,557	56,860	5,636	4,724	912	108,781	52,833	55,948	177	130	47
	10—15 .	105,271	53,330	51,941	9,700	8,375	1,325	95,571	44,955	50,616	583	477	106
	15—20	87,214	43,411	43,803	13,074	11,784	1,290	74,140	31,627	42,513	1,528	1,397	131
	20 and over ..	495,260	262,255	233,005	56,602	53,207	3,395	438,658	209,048	229,610	5,518	5,243	275
	HINDUS .	*835,409*	*430,034*	*405,375*	*72,706*	*67,159*	*5,547*	*762,703*	*362,875*	*399,828*	*6,219*	*5,899*	*320*
	0—5 ..	122,697	60,777	61,920	..		.	122,697	60,777	61,920	..	..	..
	5—10 ..	100,274	50,302	49,972	4,834	4,082	752	95,440	46,220	49,220	113	88	25
	10—15 .	92,532	46,758	45,774	8,368	7,285	1,083	84,164	39,473	44,691	435	369	66
	15—20 ..	76,999	38,201	38,798	11,250	10,208	1,042	65,749	27,993	37,756	1,238	1,152	86
	20 and over ..	442,907	233,996	208,911	48,254	45,584	2,670	394,653	188,412	206,241	4,433	4,290	143

Literacy by Religion and Age.

TABLE XIII

Part B.—Details for Districts—*contd.*

District.	Age.	Population. Total. Persons.	Population. Total. Males.	Population. Total. Females.	Population. Literate. Persons.	Population. Literate. Males.	Population. Literate. Females.	Population. Illiterate. Persons.	Population. Illiterate. Males.	Population. Illiterate. Females.	Literate in English. Persons.	Literate in English. Males.	Literate in English. Females.
1	2	3	4	5	6	7	8	9	10	11	12	13	14
AMRAOTI—concld	MUSLIMS ..	*86,498*	*45,714*	*40,784*	*9,639*	*8,888*	*751*	*76,859*	*36,826*	*40,033*	*1,001*	*991*	*10*
	0—5 ..	13,701	6,793	6,908	..	..	..	13,701	6,793	6,908	..	..	..
	5—10 ..	11,660	6,055	5,605	609	524	85	11,051	5,531	5,520	35	34	1
	10—15 ..	10,387	5,483	4,904	1,030	898	132	9,357	4,585	4,772	90	88	2
	15—20 ..	8,327	4,346	3,981	1,441	1,301	140	6,886	3,045	3,841	202	199	3
	20 and over ..	42,423	23,037	19,386	6,559	6,165	394	35,864	16,872	18,992	674	670	4
	TRIBALS ..	*11,871*	*5,810*	*6,061*	*39*	*38*	*1*	*11,832*	*5,772*	*6,060*	*1*	*1*	..
	0—5 ..	1,964	932	1,032	..	..	..	1,964	932	1,032	..	..	..
	5—10 ..	1,556	737	819	2	2	..	1,554	735	819	..	..	..
	10—15 ..	1,465	649	816	5	4	1	1,460	645	815	..	..	..
	15—20 ..	1,091	479	612	7	7	..	1,084	472	612	1	1	..
	20 and over ..	5,795	3,013	2,782	25	25	..	5,770	2,988	2,782	..	..	..
	JAINS ..	*5,052*	*2,587*	*2,465*	*1,623*	*1,458*	*165*	*3,429*	*1,129*	*2,300*	*141*	*138*	*3*
	0—5 ..	679	332	347	..	..	..	679	332	347	..	..	..
	5—10 ..	559	276	283	102	81	21	457	195	262	4	3	1
	10—15 ..	528	268	260	163	133	30	365	135	230	11	10	1
	15—20 ..	601	350	251	225	194	31	376	156	220	25	25	..
	20 and over ..	2,685	1,361	1,324	1,133	1,050	83	1,552	311	1,241	101	100	1
	CHRISTIANS ..	*2,554*	*1,319*	*1,235*	*893*	*473*	*420*	*1,661*	*846*	*815*	*371*	*168*	*203*
	0—5 ..	370	190	180	..	..	..	370	190	180	..	..	..
	5—10 ..	355	175	180	81	31	50	274	144	130	23	4	19
	10—15 ..	340	160	180	126	52	74	214	108	106	42	8	34
	15—20 ..	282	126	156	141	68	73	141	58	83	53	15	38
	20 and over ..	1,207	668	539	545	322	223	662	346	316	253	141	112
AKOLA	ALL RELIGIONS ..	*876,362*	*448,896*	*427,466*	*68,921*	*63,785*	*5,136*	*807,441*	*385,111*	*422,330*	*6,087*	*5,810*	*277*
	0—5 ..	132,089	64,213	67,876	..	..	..	132,089	64,213	67,876	..	..	..
	5—10 ..	110,246	55,669	54,577	4,393	3,722	671	105,853	51,947	53,906	134	114	20
	10—15 ..	99,015	50,325	48,690	7,575	6,640	935	91,440	43,685	47,755	427	392	35
	15—20 ..	79,184	38,656	40,528	10,381	9,450	931	68,803	29,206	39,597	1,061	1,008	53
	20 and over ..	455,828	240,033	215,795	46,572	43,973	2,599	409,256	196,060	213,196	4,465	4,296	169
	HINDUS ..	*778,451*	*397,460*	*380,991*	*57,742*	*53,829*	*3,913*	*720,709*	*343,631*	*377,078*	*4,882*	*4,678*	*204*
	0—5 ..	116,148	56,380	59,768	..	..	..	116,148	56,380	59,768	..	..	..
	5—10 ..	96,794	48,801	47,993	3,636	3,120	516	93,158	45,681	47,477	102	88	14
	10—15 ..	87,436	44,304	43,132	6,399	5,659	740	81,037	38,645	42,392	339	308	31
	15—20 ..	70,271	34,072	36,199	8,820	8,100	720	61,451	25,972	35,479	859	812	47
	20 and over ..	407,802	213,903	193,899	38,887	36,950	1,937	368,915	176,953	191,962	3,582	3,470	112
	JAINS ..	*6,866*	*3,535*	*3,331*	*2,061*	*1,880*	*181*	*4,805*	*1,655*	*3,150*	*213*	*213*	..
	0—5 ..	1,039	501	538	..	..	..	1,039	501	538	..	..	..
	5—10 ..	852	452	400	126	102	24	726	350	376	2	2	..
	10—15 ..	787	424	363	211	180	31	576	244	332	25	25	..
	15—20 ..	635	322	313	279	250	29	356	72	284	53	53	..
	20 and over ..	3,553	1,836	1,717	1,445	1,348	97	2,108	488	1,620	133	133	..
	MUSLIMS ..	*89,185*	*46,903*	*42,282*	*8,431*	*7,619*	*812*	*80,754*	*39,284*	*41,470*	*746*	*736*	*10*
	0—5 ..	14,571	7,189	7,382	..	..	..	14,571	7,189	7,382	..	..	..
	5—10 ..	12,338	6,274	6,064	554	451	103	11,784	5,823	5,961	17	16	1
	10—15 ..	10,569	5,463	5,106	877	736	141	9,692	4,727	4,965	47	46	1
	15—20 ..	8,119	4,166	3,953	1,191	1,037	154	6,928	3,129	3,799	115	113	2
	20 and over ..	43,588	23,811	19,777	5,809	5,395	414	37,779	18,416	19,363	567	561	6
	CHRISTIANS ..	*1,321*	*726*	*595*	*584*	*389*	*195*	*737*	*337*	*400*	*194*	*143*	*51*
	0—5 ..	227	106	121	..	..	..	227	106	121	..	..	..
	5—10 ..	203	113	90	69	46	23	134	67	67	12	7	5
	10—15 ..	169	105	64	81	60	21	88	45	43	15	12	3
	15—20 ..	114	71	43	84	60	24	30	11	19	32	29	3
	20 and over ..	608	331	277	350	223	127	258	108	150	135	95	40

TABLE XIII — Buldana, Yeotmal.

Literacy by Religion and Age.

Part B.—Details for Districts—*concld.*

District.	Age.	Population. Total. Persons.	Total. Males.	Total. Females.	Literate. Persons.	Literate. Males.	Literate. Females.	Illiterate. Persons.	Illiterate. Males.	Illiterate. Females.	Literate in English. Persons.	Literate in English. Males.	Literate in English. Females.
1	2	3	4	5	6	7	8	9	10	11	12	13	14
BULDANA	ALL RELIGIONS ..	*766,584*	*388,966*	*377,618*	*59,346*	*55,658*	*3,688*	*707,238*	*333,308*	*373,930*	*3,870*	*3,693*	*177*
	0—5 ..	118,383	57,693	60,690	..	..	..	118,383	57,693	60,690	..	..	..
	5—10 ..	100,528	50,547	49,981	4,192	3,708	484	96,336	46,839	49,497	119	103	16
	10—15 ..	90,686	46,252	44,434	7,377	6,675	702	83,309	39,577	43,732	373	349	24
	15—20 ..	70,071	34,412	35,659	9,321	8,641	680	60,750	25,771	34,979	709	677	32
	20 and over ..	386,916	200,062	186,854	38,456	36,634	1,822	348,460	163,428	185,032	2,669	2,564	105
	HINDUS ..	*689,152*	*348,531*	*340,621*	*51,554*	*48,531*	*3,023*	*637,598*	*300,000*	*337,598*	*3,169*	*3,041*	*128*
	0—5 ..	105,473	51,410	54,063	..	..	..	105,473	51,410	54,063	..	..	..
	5—10 ..	89,523	44,877	44,646	3,642	3,250	392	85,881	41,627	44,254	89	75	14
	10—15 ..	81,150	41,239	39,911	6,446	5,879	567	74,704	35,360	39,344	296	274	22
	15—20 ..	62,885	30,752	32,133	8,155	7,601	554	54,730	23,151	31,579	576	551	25
	20 and over ..	350,121	180,253	169,868	33,311	31,801	1,510	316,810	148,452	168,358	2,208	2,141	67
	JAINS ..	*4,547*	*2,400*	*2,147*	*1,449*	*1,323*	*126*	*3,098*	*1,077*	*2,021*	*83*	*82*	*1*
	0—5 ..	642	317	325	..	..	..	642	317	325	..	..	..
	5—10 ..	525	274	251	77	65	12	448	209	239	5	4	1
	10—15 ..	496	264	232	141	121	20	355	143	212	7	7	..
	15—20 ..	447	229	218	205	180	25	242	49	193	20	20	..
	20 and over ..	2,437	1,316	1,121	1,026	957	69	1,411	359	1,052	51	51	..
	MUSLIMS	*71,766*	*37,474*	*34,292*	*5,930*	*5,602*	*328*	*65,836*	*31,872*	*33,964*	*473*	*465*	*8*
	0—5	12,068	5,864	6,204	..	..	..	12,068	5,864	6,204	..	..	..
	5—10 ..	10,325	5,319	5,006	435	384	51	9,890	4,935	4,955	22	21	1
	10—15 ..	8,896	4,687	4,209	727	658	69	8,169	4,029	4,140	58	58	..
	15—20 ..	6,615	3,378	3,237	889	832	57	5,726	2,546	3,180	92	91	1
	20 and over ..	33,862	18,226	15,636	3,879	3,728	151	29,983	14,498	15,485	301	295	6
YEOTMAL	ALL RELIGIONS ..	*857,288*	*436,124*	*421,164*	*41,192*	*37,639*	*3,553*	*816,096*	*398,485*	*417,611*	*4,001*	*3,853*	*148*
	0—5 ..	137,177	66,545	70,632	..	..	..	137,177	66,545	70,632	..	..	..
	5—10 ..	110,121	55,094	55,027	3,067	2,619	448	107,054	52,475	54,579	331	323	8
	10—15 ..	98,703	49,477	49,226	4,785	4,155	630	93,918	45,322	48,596	483	459	24
	15—20 ..	76,884	36,858	40,026	6,668	5,893	775	70,216	30,965	39,251	788	751	37
	20 and over ..	434,403	228,150	206,253	26,672	24,972	1,700	407,731	203,178	204,553	2,399	2,320	79
	HINDUS ..	*763,475*	*387,945*	*375,530*	*33,274*	*30,891*	*2,383*	*730,201*	*357,054*	*373,147*	*2,881*	*2,789*	*92*
	0—5 ..	121,803	58,963	62,840	..	..	..	121,803	58,963	62,840	..	..	..
	5—10 ..	97,687	48,749	48,938	2,187	1,864	323	95,500	46,885	48,615	86	80	6
	10—15 ..	87,906	43,946	43,960	3,677	3,237	440	84,229	40,709	43,520	286	270	16
	15—20 ..	68,553	32,754	35,799	5,292	4,804	488	63,261	27,950	35,311	580	557	23
	20 and over ..	387,526	203,533	183,993	22,118	20,986	1,132	365,408	182,547	182,861	1,929	1,882	47
	MUSLIMS ..	*52,231*	*27,457*	*24,774*	*6,195*	*5,372*	*823*	*46,036*	*22,085*	*23,951*	*917*	*915*	*2*
	0—5 ..	8,601	4,258	4,343	..	..	..	8,601	4,258	4,343	..	..	..
	5—10 ..	7,220	3,705	3,515	739	660	79	6,481	3,045	3,436	239	239	..
	10—15 ..	6,233	3,225	3,008	892	763	129	5,341	2,462	2,879	178	178	..
	15—20 ..	4,860	2,484	2,376	1,123	895	228	3,737	1,589	2,148	167	166	1
	20 and over .	25,317	13,785	11,532	3,441	3,054	387	21,876	10,731	11,145	333	332	1
	TRIBALS .	*36,739*	*18,251*	*18,488*	*170*	*104*	*66*	*36,569*	*18,147*	*18,422*	*4*	*3*	*1*
	0—5 .	6,072	3,006	3,066	..	..	..	6,070	3,006	3,066	..	..	..
	5—10 ..	4,614	2,358	2,256	14	12	2	4,602	2,346	2,254	..	..	..
	10—15 .	3,998	2,022	1,976	19	18	1	3,979	2,004	1,975	..	..	..
	15—20 .	2,985	1,368	1,617	30	20	10	2,955	1,348	1,607	3	2	1
	20 and over .	19,070	9,497	9,573	107	54	53	18,963	9,443	9,520	1	1	..

Literacy by Religion and Age.

Part B.—Details for Central Provinces States.

TABLE XIII

District or state.	Age.	Population									Literate in English.		
		Total.			Literate.			Illiterate.					
		Persons.	Males.	Females.	Persons.	Males.	Females.	Persons.	Males.	Females.	Persons.	Males.	Females.
1	2	3	4	5	6	7	8	9	10	11	12	13	14
C. P. STATES	ALL RELIGIONS ..	*2,483,214*	*1,235,385*	*1,247,829*	*45,663*	*42,498*	*3,165*	*2,437,551*	*1,192,887*	*1,244,664*	*2,363*	*2,140*	*223*
	0—5 ..	450,941	220,237	230,704	.	..	..	450,941	220,237	230,704	..	..	..
	5—10 ..	344,941	177,276	167,665	2,122	1,825	297	342,819	175,451	167,368	65	52	13
	10—15 ..	284,259	148,637	135,622	4.028	3,572	456	280,231	145,065	135,166	161	146	15
	15—20 ..	200,754	95,536	105,218	6,471	5,942	529	194,283	89,594	104,689	374	334	40
	20 and over ..	1,202,319	593,699	608,620	33.042	31,159	1,883	1,169,277	562,540	606,737	1,763	1,608	155
	HINDUS ..	*1,788,401*	*886,123*	*902,278*	*39,143*	*36,924*	*2,219*	*1,749,258*	*849,199*	*900,059*	*1,554*	*1,548*	*6*
	0—5 ..	312,733	152,179	160,554	..	..	..	312,733	152,179	160,554	..	..	..
	5—10 ..	243,829	125,474	118,355	1,749	1,557	192	242,080	123,917	118,163	33	32	1
	10—15 ..	203,897	107,110	96,787	3,365	3,057	308	200,532	104,053	96,479	109	108	1
	15—20 ..	145,469	69.643	75,826	5,491	5,120	371	139,978	64.523	75,455	256	255	1
	20 and over ..	882,473	431,717	450,756	28,538	27,190	1,348	853,935	404.527	449,408	1,156	1,153	3
	MUSLIMS .	*23,254*	*11,733*	*11,521*	*3,065*	*2,754*	*311*	*20,189*	*8,979*	*11,210*	*275*	*267*	*8*
	0—5 ..	3,409	1,617	1,792	..	..	..	3,409	1,617	1,792	..	..	..
	5—10 ..	2,809	1,470	1,339	176	135	41	2,633	1,335	1,298	8	6	2
	10—15 ..	2,446	1,298	1,148	269	221	48	2,177	1,077	1,100	12	12	..
	15—20 ..	2,073	1,007	1,066	384	348	36	1,689	659	1,030	33	33	..
	20 and over ..	12,517	6,341	6,176	2,236	2,050	186	10,281	4,291	5,990	222	216	6
	CHRISTIANS ..	*51,701*	*26,102*	*25,599*	*1,841*	*1,331*	*510*	*49,860*	*24,771*	*25,089*	*438*	*258*	*180*
	0—5 ..	11,257	5,620	5,637	..	..	..	11,257	5,620	5,637	..	..	..
	5—10 ..	7,924	4,130	3,794	114	63	51	7,810	4,067	3,743	22	14	8
	10—15 ..	6,438	3,437	3,001	246	163	83	6,192	3,274	2,918	33	21	12
	15—20 ..	4,231	2,075	2,156	372	271	101	3,859	1,804	2,055	66	35	31
	20 and over ..	21,851	10,840	11,011	1,109	834	275	20,742	10,006	10,736	317	188	129
	TRIBALS ..	*617,599*	*310,156*	*307,443*	*761*	*736*	*25*	*616,838*	*309,420*	*307,418*	*5*	*5*	..
	0—5 ..	123,219	60,657	62,562	..	..	..	123,219	60,657	62,562	..	..	..
	5—10 ..	90,125	46,069	44,056	41	40	1	90,084	46,029	44,055	..	..	..
	10—15 ..	71,240	36.662	34,578	71	70	1	71,169	36,592	34,577	2	2	..
	15—20 ..	48,738	22,673	26,065	103	99	4	48,635	22,574	26,061	1	1	..
	20 and over ..	284,277	144,095	140,182	546	527	19	283,731	143,568	140,163	2	2	..

TABLE XIII

Jubbulpore]
Nagpur.

Literacy by Religion and Age.

Part C.—Details for Cities.

City.	Age.	Population. Total. Persons.	Total. Males.	Total. Females.	Literate. Persons.	Literate. Males.	Literate. Females.	Illiterate. Persons.	Illiterate. Males.	Illiterate. Females.	Literate in English. Persons.	Literate in English. Males.	Literate in English. Females.
1	2	3	4	5	6	7	8	9	10	11	12	13	14
JUBBULPORE	ALL RELIGIONS ..	124,382	69,258	55,124	30,745	24,714	6,031	93,637	44,544	49,093	10,555	8,802	1,753
	0—5 ..	17,666	8,659	9,007	..	..	..	17,666	8,659	9,007	..	..	..
	5—10 ..	13,574	7,284	6,290	2,436	1,662	774	11,138	5,622	5,516	560	373	187
	10—15 ..	12,578	6,943	5,635	3,276	2,339	937	9,302	4,604	4,698	891	642	249
	15—20 ..	12,986	7,239	5,747	4,555	3,567	988	8,431	3,672	4,759	1,620	1,344	276
	20 and over ..	67,578	39,133	28,445	20,478	17,146	3,332	47,100	21,987	25,113	7,484	6,443	1,041
	HINDUS ..	85,539	47,124	38,415	17,569	14,685	2,884	67,970	32,439	35,531	4,293	4,010	283
	0—5 ..	12,139	5,909	6,230	..	..	..	12,139	5,909	6,230	..	..	..
	5—10 ..	9,130	4,970	4,160	1,382	1,007	375	7,748	3,963	3,785	165	138	27
	10—15 ..	8,421	4,693	3,728	1,917	1,464	453	6,504	3,229	3,275	357	308	49
	15—20 ..	8,690	4,696	3,994	2,604	2,093	511	6,086	2,603	3,483	689	622	67
	20 and over ..	47,159	26,856	20,303	11,666	10,121	1,545	35,493	16,735	18,758	3,082	2,942	140
	MUSLIMS ..	29,022	16,187	12,835	6,585	5,462	1,123	22,437	10,725	11,712	1,492	1,443	49
	0—5 ..	4,433	2,184	2,249	..	..	..	4,433	2,184	2,249	..	..	..
	5—10 ..	3,518	1,857	1,661	526	374	152	2,992	1,483	1,509	43	41	2
	10—15 ..	3,165	1,741	1,424	705	528	177	2,460	1,213	1,247	101	94	7
	15—20 ..	3,035	1,714	1,321	972	781	191	2,063	933	1,130	232	221	11
	20 and over ..	14,871	8,691	6,180	4,382	3,779	603	10,489	4,912	5,577	1,116	1,087	29
	CHRISTIANS ..	6,724	4,132	2,592	5,069	3,356	1,713	1,655	776	879	4,360	3,020	1,340
	0—5 ..	708	364	344	..	..	..	708	364	344	..	..	..
	5—10 ..	634	309	325	420	206	214	214	103	111	319	171	148
	10—15 ..	656	312	344	507	247	260	149	65	84	385	206	179
	15—20 ..	831	552	279	717	482	235	114	70	44	628	439	189
	20 and over ..	3,895	2,595	1,300	3,425	2,421	1,004	470	174	296	3,028	2,204	824
NAGPUR	ALL RELIGIONS ..	215,165	116,403	98,762	46,840	35,807	11,033	168,325	80,596	87,729	16,912	14,068	2,844
	0—5 ..	28,206	14,140	14,066	..	..	..	28,206	14,140	14,066	..	..	..
	5—10 ..	24,545	12,792	11,753	3,932	2,649	1,283	20,613	10,143	10,470	871	578	293
	10—15 ..	23,167	12,345	10,822	5,726	4,127	1,599	17,441	8,218	9,223	1,473	1,111	362
	15—20 ..	22,531	11,971	10,560	7,495	5,659	1,836	15,036	6,312	8,724	2,985	2,480	505
	20 and over ..	116,716	65,155	51,561	29,687	23,372	6,315	87,029	41,783	45,246	11,583	9,899	1,684
	HINDUS ..	176,237	95,077	81,160	35,541	28,106	7,435	140,696	66,971	73,725	11,719	10,557	1,162
	0—5 ..	23,124	11,647	11,477	..	..	..	23,124	11,647	11,477	..	..	6
	5—10 ..	19,814	10,370	9,444	2,753	1,939	814	17,061	8,431	8,630	337	258	79
	10—15 ..	18,694	9,997	8,697	4,330	3,263	1,067	14,364	6,734	7,630	900	751	149
	15—20 ..	18,524	9,787	8,737	5,864	4,613	1,251	12,660	5,174	7,486	2,223	1,971	252
	20 and over ..	96,081	53,276	42,805	22,594	18,291	4,303	73,487	34,985	38,502	8,259	7,577	682
	MUSLIMS ..	28,042	15,628	12,414	5,693	4,304	1,389	22,349	11,324	11,025	1,180	1,088	92
	0—5 ..	3,673	1,800	1,873	..	..	..	3,673	1,800	1,873	..	..	..
	5—10 ..	3,416	1,744	1,672	504	342	162	2,912	1,402	1,510	55	47	8
	10—15 ..	3,158	1,660	1,498	672	461	211	2,486	1,199	1,287	94	86	8
	15—20 ..	2,805	1,580	1,225	859	607	252	1,946	973	973	213	196	17
	20 and over ..	14,990	8,844	6,146	3,658	2,894	764	11,332	5,950	5,382	818	759	59
	CHRISTIANS ..	6,449	3,359	3,090	4,024	2,258	1,766	2,425	1,101	1,324	3,229	1,898	331
	0—5 ..	866	440	426	..	..	..	866	440	426	..	..	..
	5—10 ..	834	435	399	548	297	251	286	138	148	424	248	1,176
	10—15 ..	845	444	401	564	305	259	281	139	142	407	240	167
	15—20 ..	740	366	374	572	296	276	168	70	98	446	245	201
	20 and over ..	3,164	1,674	1,490	2,340	1,360	980	824	314	510	1,952	1,165	787

APPENDIX TO TABLE XIII

NUMBER EDUCATED UP TO THE PRIMARY CERTIFICATE STANDARD AND TOTAL NUMBER LITERATE IN HINDI AND URDU

Serial No.	District or State.	Educated to Primary Certificate* Standard.			Literate in Hindi.			Literate in Urdu.		
		Persons.	Males.	Females.	Persons.	Males.	Females.	Persons.	Males.	Females.
	1	2	3	4	5	6	7	8	9	10
	Central Provinces and Berar	**364,723**	**341,012**	**23,711**	**380,950**	**349,864**	**31,086**	**44,247**	**37,489**	**6,758**
	C. P. British Districts and Berar.	**341,254**	**319,066**	**22,188**	**337,350**	**309,066**	**28,284**	**43,600**	**37,036**	**6,564**
	Jubbulpore Division ..	*53,652*	*48,706*	*4,946*	*100,422*	*89,991*	*10,431*	*7,312*	*5,713*	*1,599*
1	Saugor ..	11,544	10,615	929	24,039	21,534	2,505	563	455	108
2	Damoh ..	10,246	9,705	541	12,940	11,771	1,169	276	211	65
3	Jubbulpore ..	18,344	15,591	2,753	42,033	37,251	4,782	5,291	4,150	1,141
4	Mandla ..	6,340	5,998	342	8,488	7,633	855	260	158	102
5	Seoni ..	7,178	6,797	381	12,922	11,802	1,120	922	739	183
	Nerbudda Division ..	*45,514*	*43,251*	*2,263*	*92,291*	*85,876*	*6,415*	*5,518*	*4,456*	*1,062*
6	Narsinghpur ..	7,712	7,168	544	18,374	16,806	1,568	230	143	87
7	Hoshangabad ..	12,937	12,349	588	33,957	31,994	1,963	731	616	115
8	Nimar ..	7,773	7,283	490	20,677	19,031	1,646	3,508	2,852	656
9	Betul ..	7,287	7,031	256	8,168	7,665	503	208	145	63
10	Chhindwara ..	9,805	9,420	385	11,115	10,380	735	841	700	141
	Nagpur Division ..	*78,011*	*71,755*	*6,256*	*30,979*	*28,693*	*2,286*	*9,568*	*8,249*	*1,319*
11	Wardha ..	15,209	14,504	705	1,415	1,290	125	1,590	1,518	72
12	Nagpur ..	35,250	30,902	4,348	5,958	5,406	552	4,311	3,418	893
13	Chanda ..	6,886	6,514	372	1,278	1,144	134	1,316	1,205	111
14	Bhandara ..	10,487	9,955	532	5,968	5,329	639	1,495	1,373	122
15	Balaghat ..	10,179	9,880	299	16,360	15,524	836	856	735	121
	Chhattisgarh Division ..	*58,531*	*54,846*	*3,685*	*105,871*	*97,474*	*8,397*	*3,392*	*2,742*	*650*
16	Raipur ..	24,756	23,261	1,495	42,947	39,818	3,129	2,099	1,657	442
17	Bilaspur ..	18,992	17,465	1,527	40,503	36,650	3,853	1,066	914	152
18	Drug ..	14,783	14,120	663	22,421	21,006	1,415	227	171	56
	Berar ..	**105,546**	**100,508**	**5,038**	**7,787**	**7,032**	**755**	**17,810**	**15,876**	**1,934**
19	Amraoti ..	37,601	35,493	2,108	4,244	3,850	394	6,665	6,088	577
20	Akola ..	30,340	28,798	1,542	1,023	949	74	3,369	2,951	418
21	Buldana ..	24,796	23,894	902	1,741	1,537	204	3,770	3,537	233
22	Yeotmal ..	12,809	12,323	486	779	696	83	4,006	3,300	706
	Central Provinces States ..	**23,469**	**21,946**	**1,523**	**43,600**	**40,798**	**2,802**	**647**	**453**	**194**
23	Makrai ..	25	25	.	958	953	5	13	..	13
24	Bastar ..	1,498	1,338	160	3,785	3,374	411	101	77	24
25	Kanker ..	976	931	45	2,417	2,229	188	23	16	7
26	Nandgaon ..	6,384	5,850	534	7,817	7,259	558	221	151	70
27	Khairagarh ..	2,596	2,456	140	3,287	3,108	179	106	67	39
28	Chhuikhadan ..	1,139	1,076	63	1,291	1,214	77	..	..	..
29	Kawardha ..	1,192	1,167	25	1,652	1,569	83	13	8	5
30	Sakti ..	1,138	1,099	39	1,783	1,701	82	1	..	1
31	Raigarh ..	3,522	3,394	128	8,418	7,938	480	76	47	29
32	Sarangarh ..	3,382	3,094	288	4,457	4,086	371	5	5	..
33	Changbhakar ..	5	5	..	103	95	8	5	5	..
34	Korea ..	172	167	5	658	631	27	28	25	3
35	Surguja ..	191	183	8	3,177	3,013	164	38	37	1
36	Udaipur ..	499	493	6	984	941	43	7	5	2
37	Jashpur ..	750	668	82	2,813	2,687	126	10	10	..

* These figures include those literate in English.

TABLE XIV

Literacy by selected castes.

1. This table, like Table VIII, deals not with the whole population, but with certain selected castes in certain districts where they are specially numerous.

2. The figures do not agree with Table VIII as the population dealt with is of seven years and over : the caste strength can be verified by adding the figures in age group 0—6 of Table VIII.

TABLE XIV Literacy by selected castes.

Caste, tribe or race.	Locality.	Population. (7 years and over). Total. Persons.	Total. Males.	Total. Females.	Literate. Persons	Literate. Males.	Literate. Females.	Illiterate. Persons.	Illiterate. Males.	Illiterate. Females.	Literate in English. Persons.	Literate in English. Males.	Literate in English. Females.
1	2	3	4	5	6	7	8	9	10	11	12	13	14
Ahir ..	Province ..	(a) 647,095	322,772	324,323	11,181	10,580	601	635,914	312,192	323,722	405	397	8
(Hindu)		643,459	321,065	322,394	11,166	10,570	596	632,293	310,495	321,798	404	396	8
(Tribal)		3,625	1,704	1,921	10	10	..	3,615	1,694	1,921	1	1	..
Andh ..	Berar ..	45,359	23,339	22,020	484	466	18	44,875	22,873	22,002	3	3	..
Baiga ..	*Total* ..	*21,308*	*10,693*	*10,615*	*459*	*459*	..	*20,849*	*10,234*	*10,615*	*68*	*68*	..
(Hindu)		6,184	3,045	3,139	447	447	..	5,737	2,598	3,139	68	68	..
	Jubbulpore ..	1,778	878	900	435	435	..	1,343	443	900	68	68	..
	Mandla ..	4,170	2,050	2,120	12	12	..	4,158	2,038	2,120	..	..	..
	Balaghat ..	236	117	119	..	..	..	236	117	119	..	..	..
(Tribal)		15,124	7,648	7,476	12	12	..	15,112	7,636	7,476	..	..	..
	Jubbulpore ..	251	118	133	..	..	..	251	118	133	..	..	..
	Mandla ..	10,882	5,534	5,348	8	8	..	10,874	5,526	5,348	..	.	..
	Balaghat ..	3,991	1.996	1,995	4	4	..	3,987	1,992	1,995	..	..	..
Bairagi	Province ..	(b) 31,654	16,071	15,583	4,377	4,048	329	27,277	12,023	15,254	47	47	..
Balahi ..	*Total* ..	*44,078*	*22,138*	*21,940*	*561*	*554*	*7*	*43,517*	*21,584*	*21,933*	*3*	..	*3*
(Hindu)	Hoshangabad ..	16,518	8,189	8,329	178	178	..	16,340	8,011	8,329	..	..	..
	Nimar ..	24,025	12,177	11,848	16	314	2	23,709	11,863	11,846	..	..	..
	Makrai ..	1,595	794	801	20	20	..	1,575	774	801	..	..	..
(Christian)	Nimar ..	1,940	978	962	47	42	5	1,893	936	957	3	..	3
Bania ..	Province ..	191,777	101,257	90,520	67,197	60,540	6,657	124,580	40,717	83,863	4,779	4,682	97
Banjara ..	*Total* ..	*117,729*	*59,520*	*58,209*	*1,442*	*1,356*	*86*	*116,287*	*58,164*	*58,123*	*31*	*31*	...
(Hindu and Tribal.)		117,643	59,472	58,171	1,441	1,355	86	116,202	58,117	58,085	31	31	..
	Plateau Division	5,072	2,607	2,465	67	64	3	5,005	2,543	2,462	..	..	..
	Maratha Division	87,794	44,159	43,635	1,020	946	74	86,774	43,213	43,561	27	27	..
	Chhattisgarh Administrative Division.	7,587	3,573	4,014	110	102	8	7,477	3,471	4,006	2	2	..
	8 States of Chhattisgarh Plain Division.	1,729	830	899	38	38	..	1,691	792	899	1	1	..
	Nimar ..	12,956	7,052	5,904	194	193	1	12,762	6,859	5,903	1	1	..
	Bastar ..	2,505	1,251	1,254	12	12	..	2,493	1,239	1,254	..	..	..
(Muslim)		86	48	38	1	1	..	85	47	38	..	..	..
	Plateau Division	6	3	3	..	..	..	6	3	3	..	..	..
	Maratha Division	..	..	..	..	..	..	..	..	..	..	..	..
	Chhattisgarh Administrative Division.	..	..	..	..	..	..	..	..	..	..	..	..
	Nimar	80	45	35	1	1	..	79	44	35	..	..	..
	Bastar ..	..	..	..	..	..	..	..	..	..	..	..	..

(a) Includes 11 Christians—3 males, 8 females ; (b) Includes 1 Christian male.

Caste, tribe or race.	Locality.	Population (7 years and over). Total. Persons.	Males.	Females.	Literate. Persons.	Males.	Females.	Illiterate. Persons.	Males.	Females.	Literate in English. Persons.	Males.	Females.
1	2	3	4	5	6	7	8	9	10	11	12	13	14
Barhai ..	Province ..	(c) 91,233	47,911	43,322	9,774	9,470	304	81,459	38,441	43,018	248	243	5
Basor ..	Nerbudda Valley	(d) 25,017	12,646	12,371	200	198	2	24,817	12,448	12,369	1	1	..
Beldar ..	*Total* ..	*4,501*	*2,214*	*2,287*	*302*	*289*	*13*	*4,199*	*1,925*	*2,274*	*17*	*17*	..
	Saugor ..	463	225	238	29	28	1	434	197	237	1	1	..
	Jubbulpore ..	866	451	415	29	28	1	837	423	414	3	3	..
	Nimar ..	1,016	493	523	9	7	2	1,007	486	521	..	..	..
	Wardha ..	1,563	774	789	151	146	5	1,412	628	784	7	7	..
	Nagpur ..	593	271	322	84	80	4	509	191	318	6	6	..
Bharia-Bhumia.	*Total* ..	*29,585*	*14,191*	*15,394*	*113*	*103*	*10*	*29,472*	*14,088*	*15,384*	..	..	..
(Hindu)		23,333	11,108	12,225	102	93	9	23,231	11,015	12,216	..	..	..
	Jubbulpore ..	22,505	10,705	11,800	97	88	9	22,408	10,617	11,791	..	..	..
	Narsinghpur ..	741	359	382	4	4	..	737	355	382	..	..	..
	Chhindwara ..	87	44	43	1	1	..	86	43	43	..	..	..
(Tribal)		6,252	3,083	3,169	11	10	1	6,241	3,073	3,168	..	..	..
	Jubbulpore ..	18	8	10	1	1	..	17	7	10	..	..	..
	Narsinghpur ..	875	500	375	..	..	..	875	500	375	..	..	..
	Chhindwara ..	5,359	2,575	2,784	10	9	1	5,349	2,566	2,783	..	..	..
Bhil ..	Nimar ..	(e) 19,903	10,054	9,849	58	58	..	19,845	9,996	9,849	..	..	..
Bhilala ..	*Total* ..	*12,743*	*6,662*	*6,081*	*323*	*320*	*3*	*12,420*	*6,342*	*6,078*	*2*	*2*	..
	Hoshangabad ..	2,089	1,053	1,036	68	67	1	2,021	986	1,035	1	1	..
	Nimar ..	10,654	5,609	5,045	255	253	2	10,399	5,356	5,043	1	1	..
Bhulia ..	Raipur ..	3,330	1,625	1,705	61	60	1	3,269	1,565	1,704	..	..	..
Bohra ..	Nimar ..	2,157	1,036	1,121	1,178	806	372	979	230	749	231	226	5
Bhoyar ..	*Total* ..	*54,967*	*27,145*	*27,822*	*1,802*	*1,789*	*13*	*53,165*	*25,356*	*27,809*	*13*	*13*	..
	Betul ..	20,552	10,095	10,457	482	477	5	20,070	9,618	10,452	8	8	..
	Chhindwara ..	20,270	10,021	10,249	796	791	5	19,474	9,230	10,244	4	4	..
	Wardha ..	11,071	5,459	5,612	447	444	3	10,624	5,015	5,609	1	1	..
	Nagpur ..	3,074	1,570	1,504	77	77	..	2,997	1,493	1,504	..	..	..
Brahmin ..	Province ..	(f) 428,734	233,389	195,345	159,514	135.679	23,835	269,220	97,710	171,510	33,411	31,398	2,013
Chadar ..	*Total* ..	*21,711*	*10,939*	*10,772*	*545*	*530*	*15*	*21,166*	*10,409*	*10,757*	*6*	*6*	..
	Saugor ..	11,787	5,988	5,799	236	228	8	11,551	5,760	5,791	3	3	..
	Jubbulpore ..	1,995	1,015	980	85	83	2	1,910	932	978	1	1	..
	Damoh ..	5,656	2,806	2,850	137	133	4	5,519	2,673	2,846	.	..	..
	Narsinghpur ..	2,273	1,130	1,143	87	86	1	2,186	1,044	1,142	2	2	..
Chamar ..	Province ..	(g) 482,918	240,020	242,898	3,937	3,795	142	478,981	236,225	242,756	71	70	1
Dahayat ..	Jubbulpore ..	7,053	3,473	3,580	524	520	4	6,529	2,953	3,576	32	32	..

(c) Includes 17 Christians—7 males, 10 females ; (d) Includes 2 Christians—1 male, 1 female ; (e) Includes 38 Muslims—23 males, 15 females ; (f) Includes 13 Christians—8 males, 5 females ; (g) Includes 21 Christians—11 males, 10 females.

TABLE XIV Literacy by selected castes—*contd.*

Caste, tribe or race.	Locality.	Population (7 years and over). Total. Persons.	Total. Males.	Total. Females.	Literate. Persons.	Literate. Males.	Literate. Females.	Illiterate. Persons.	Illiterate. Males.	Illiterate. Females.	Literate in English. Persons.	Literate in English. Males.	Literate in English. Females.
1	2	3	4	5	6	7	8	9	10	11	12	13	14
Darzi ..	Province ..	41,672	21,483	20,189	7,680	7,244	436	33,992	14,239	19,753	313	311	2
Deswali ..	*Total* ..	*5,776*	*2,991*	*2,785*	*250*	*249*	*1*	*5,526*	*2,742*	*2,784*	*2*	*2*	..
	Hoshangabad ..	3,868	2,005	1,863	158	158	..	3,710	1,847	1,863	2	2	..
	Nimar ..	1,908	986	922	92	91	1	1,816	895	921	..	..	..
Dhimar ..	Province ..	(h)254,628	127,198	127,430	4,412	4,139	273	250,216	123,059	127,157	144	121	23
Dhobi ..	Province ..	(i) 149,010	73,504	75,506	4,827	4,588	239	144,183	68,916	75,267	95	93	2
Dohor ..	Buldana ..	2,245	1,155	1,090	61	60	1	2,184	1,095	1,089	..	..	..
Dom ..	Province ..	5,263	2,651	2,612	109	105	4	5,154	2,546	2,608	..	..	..
Ganda ..	*Total* ..	*(j) 135,486*	*65,413*	*70,073*	*1,159*	*1,115*	*44*	*134,327*	*64,298*	*70,029*	..	..	..
	Chhattisgarh Administrative Division.	84,668	40,249	44,419	690	664	26	83,978	39,585	44,393	..	..	..
	9 States of Chhattisgarh Plain Division.	39,735	19,646	20,089	366	348	18	39,369	19,298	20,071	..	..	..
	Surguja ..	2,662	1,342	1,320	4	4	..	2,658	1,338	1,320	..	..	..
	Jashpur ..	8,421	4,176	4,245	99	99	..	8,322	4,077	4,245	..	..	..
Ghasia ..	*Total* ..	*(k) 26,910*	*12,668*	*14,242*	*242*	*233*	*9*	*26,668*	*12,435*	*14,233*	..	..	..
	Chhattisgarh Administrative Division.	18,719	8,825	9,894	182	175	7	18,537	8,650	9,887	..	..	..
	9 States of Chhattisgarh Plain Division.	8,191	3,843	4,348	60	58	2	8,131	3,785	4,346	..	..	..
Gond ..	Province ..	(l) 1,792,809	876,331	916,478	15,508	14,703	805	1,777,301	861,628	915,673	310	289	21
(Hindu)		824,425	401,843	422,582	10,303	9,669	634	814,122	392,174	421,948	260	240	20
(Tribal)		968,361	474,477	493,884	5,200	5,031	169	963,161	469,446	493,715	49	48	1
Gosain ..	*Total* ..	*17,619*	*8,860*	*8,759*	*2,174*	*2,011*	*163*	*15,445*	*6,849*	*8,596*	*52*	*50*	*2*
	Balaghat ..	1,307	672	635	210	204	6	1,097	468	629	4	2	2
	Narsinghpur ..	1,145	601	544	101	99	2	1,044	502	542	4	4	..
	Jubbulpore ..	1,407	716	691	218	210	8	1,189	506	683	3	3	..
	Hoshangabad ..	2,089	1,105	984	178	176	2	1,911	929	982	1	1	..
	Nagpur ..	2,307	1,209	1,098	363	358	5	1,944	851	1,093	13	13	..
	Wardha ..	1,333	695	638	209	197	12	1,124	498	626	6	6	..
	Bhandara ..	1,260	622	638	245	175	70	1,015	447	568	3	3	..
	Raipur ..	2,147	1,052	1,095	331	306	25	1,816	746	1,070	13	13	..
	Bilaspur ..	3,186	1,516	1,670	221	197	24	2,965	1,319	1,646	5	5	..
	Drug ..	1,438	672	766	98	89	9	1,340	583	757	..	..	..
Gowari ..	Maratha Division	132,185	66,473	65,712	1,864	1,738	126	130,321	64,735	65,586	76	46	30
Halba ..	*Total* ..	*26,850*	*13,667*	*13,183*	*905*	*877*	*28*	*25,945*	*12,790*	*13,155*	*6*	*6*	..
	Chanda ..	2,666	1,433	1,233	75	72	3	2,591	1,361	1,230	..	..	..
	Raipur ..	4,736	2,246	2,490	310	296	14	4,426	1,950	2,476	3	3	..
	Bastar ..	12,546	6,575	5,971	332	325	7	12,214	6,250	5,964	3	3	..
	Kanker ..	6,902	3,413	3,489	188	184	4	6,714	3,229	3,485	..	..	..

(h) Includes 2 Christian males ; (i) Includes 10 Christians—5 males, 5 females ; (j) Includes 26 Muslims—13 males, 13 females and 134 Christians—76 males, 58 females ; (k) Includes 13 Christian males ; (l) Includes 19 Christians—8 males, 11 females, and 4 Muslims—3 males, 1 female.

Literacy by selected castes—*contd.*

TABLE XIV

Caste, tribe or race.	Locality.	Population (7 years and over). Total. Persons.	Total. Males.	Total. Females.	Literate. Persons.	Literate. Males.	Literate. Females.	Illiterate. Persons.	Illiterate. Males.	Illiterate. Females.	Literate in English. Persons.	Literate in English. Males.	Literate in English. Females.
1	2	3	4	5	6	7	8	9	10	11	12	13	14
Kahar	Total	10,128	5,192	4,936	229	229	..	9,899	4,963	4,936	6	6	..
	Narsinghpur	1,589	817	772	19	19	..	1,570	798	772	..	..	..
	Hoshangabad	5,834	2,966	2,868	130	130	..	5,704	2,836	2,868	4	4	..
	Nimar	2,705	1,409	1,296	80	80	..	2,625	1,329	1,296	2	2	..
Kalar	Province	(m)175,884	87,615	88,269	16,677	15,809	868	159,207	71,806	87,401	710	611	99
Katia	Total	30,381	15,081	15,300	969	902	67	29,412	14,179	15,233	33	33	..
	Plateau Division	21,791	10,786	11,005	629	582	47	21,162	10,204	10,958	22	22	..
	Narsinghpur	1,230	589	641	80	75	5	1,150	514	636	2	2	..
	Hoshangabad	7,360	3,706	3,654	260	245	15	7,100	3,461	3,639	9	9	..
Kawar (Hindu).	Total	142,137	69,880	72,257	1,387	1,361	26	140,750	68,519	72,231	2	2	..
	Chhattisgarh Administrative Division.	83,339	40,629	42,710	820	810	10	82,519	39,819	42,700	1	1	..
	9 States of Chhattisgarh Plain Division.	57,340	28,506	28,834	561	546	15	56,779	27,960	28,819	1	1	..
	Chanda	1,458	745	713	6	5	1	1,452	740	712	..	..	..
Kayasth	Province	(n)31,753	16,838	14,915	14,789	12,021	2,768	16,964	4,817	12,147	4,153	3,833	320
Kewat	Total	9,713	4,938	4,775	89	86	3	9,624	4,852	4,772	2	2	..
	Jubbulpore	4,554	2,324	2,230	66	64	2	4,488	2,260	2,228	2	2	..
	Narsinghpur	221	113	108	2	2	..	219	111	108	..	..	..
	Chanda	4,938	2,501	2,437	21	20	1	4,917	2,481	2,436	..	..	..
Khangar	Total	9,052	4,614	4,438	607	579	28	8,445	4,035	4,410	29	29	..
	Saugor	4,746	2,459	2,287	225	210	15	4,521	2,249	2,272	13	13	..
	Damoh	1,479	737	742	107	104	3	1,372	633	739	1	1	..
	Jubbulpore	2,114	1,062	1,052	195	189	6	1,919	873	1,046	8	8	..
	Narsinghpur	713	356	357	80	76	4	633	280	353	7	7	..
Khatik	Jubbulpore	1,564	760	804	93	84	9	1,471	676	795	3	3	..
Kol	Total	59,313	29,275	30,038	222	214	8	59,091	29,061	30,030	3	3	..
(Hindu)		48,500	23,669	24,831	216	208	8	48,284	23,461	24,823	3	3	..
	Jubbulpore	44,984	21,880	23,104	181	175	6	44,803	21,705	23,098	3	3	..
	Mandla	1,870	951	919	22	20	2	1,848	931	917	..	..	..
	Chhota Nagpur States.	1,646	838	808	13	13	..	1,633	825	808	..	..	..
(Tribal)		10,813	5,606	5,207	6	6	..	10,807	5,600	5,207	..	..	..
	Jubbulpore	70	38	32	..	..	..	70	38	32	..	..	..
	Mandla	6,393	3,253	3,140	6	6	..	6,387	3,247	3,140	..	..	..
	Chhota Nagpur States.	4,350	2,315	2,035	..	..	..	4,350	2,315	2,035	..	..	..
Koli	Berar	30,512	15,706	14,806	1,877	1,850	27	28,635	13,856	14,779	18	18	..
Kolta	Raigarh	11,406	5,657	5,749	629	617	12	10,777	5,040	5,737	3	3	..
Komti	Chanda	2,955	1,433	1,522	974	941	33	1,981	492	1,489	63	63	..
Kori	Nerbudda Valley	(o)23,280	11,711	11,569	1,010	964	46	22,270	10,747	11,523	42	42	..

(*m*) Includes 3 Christian males; (*n*) Includes 1 Christian male; (*o*) Includes 1 Christian male.

TABLE XIV Literacy by selected castes—*contd.*

Caste, tribe or race.	Locality.	Population (7 years and over). Total. Persons.	Total. Males.	Total. Females.	Literate. Persons.	Literate. Males.	Literate. Females.	Illiterate. Persons.	Illiterate. Males.	Illiterate. Females.	Literate in English. Persons.	Literate in English. Males.	Literate in English. Females.
1	2	3	4	5	6	7	8	9	10	11	12	13	14
Korku ..	*Total* ..	*(p)109,878*	*55,010*	*54,868*	*188*	*173*	*15*	*109,690*	*54,837*	*54,853*	*8*	*8*	..
(Hindu)		57,177	28,818	28,359	106	100	6	57,071	28,718	28,353	8	8	..
	Hoshangabad ..	9,535	4,802	4,733	15	15	..	9,520	4,787	4,733	..	..	..
	Nimar ..	19,865	9,910	9,955	13	13	..	19,852	9,897	9,955	2	2	..
	Betul ..	5,629	2,747	2,882	6	6	..	5,623	2,741	2,882	..	..	..
	Amraoti ..	22,148	11,359	10,789	72	66	6	22,076	11,293	10,783	6	6	..
(Tribal)		52,686	26,186	26,500	77	73	4	52,609	26,113	26,496	..	..	..
	Hoshangabad ..	7,766	4,011	3,755	11	10	1	7,755	4,001	3,754	..	..	..
	Nimar ..	19,391	9,720	9,671	42	39	3	19,349	9,681	9,668	..	..	..
	Betul ..	22,527	10,995	11,532	24	24	..	22,503	10,971	11,532	..	..	..
	Amraoti ..	3,002	1,460	1,542	..	..	..	3,002	1,460	1,542	..	..	..
Kumhar ..	Province ..	(q)104,456	53,198	51,258	4,034	3,847	187	100,422	49,351	51,071	93	90	3
Kunbi ..	*Total* ..	*(r)1,041,493*	*534,421*	*507,072*	*79,361*	*76,988*	*2,373*	*962,132*	*457,433*	*504,699*	*2,837*	*2,733*	*104*
	Maratha Division	954,683	490,333	464,350	73,758	71,456	2,302	880,925	418,877	462,048	2,668	2,566	102
	Chhindwara ..	24,822	12,602	12,220	1,648	1,641	7	23,174	10,961	12,213	41	41	..
	Nimar ..	15,355	8,165	7,190	1,899	1,856	43	13,456	6,309	7,147	84	82	2
	Betul ..	46,633	23,321	23,312	2,056	2,035	21	44,577	21,286	23,291	44	44	..
Kurmi ..	*Total* ..	*251,870*	*124,878*	*126,992*	*15,993*	*15,535*	*458*	*235,877*	*109,343*	*126,534*	*342*	*341*	*1*
	Nerbudda Valley	95,827	49,295	46,532	7,497	7,365	132	88,330	41,930	46,400	154	154	..
	Plateau Division	15,559	7,462	8,097	1,378	1,339	39	14,181	6,123	8,058	54	54	..
	Chhattisgarh Administrative Division.	126,445	61,465	64,980	6,118	5,854	264	120,327	55,611	64,716	109	108	1
	9 States of Chhattisgarh Plain Division.	14,039	6,656	7,383	1,000	977	23	13,039	5,679	7,360	25	25	..
Lodhi ..	Province ..	(s)256,099	127,500	128,599	11,425	11,019	406	244,674	116,481	128,193	156	151	5
Lohar ..	Province ..	(t)161,491	81,616	79,875	12,325	11,988	337	149,166	69,628	79,538	206	199	7
Madgi ..	Chanda ..	4,339	2,402	1,937	29	29	..	4,310	2,373	1,937	9	9	..
Mali ..	Province ..	(u)505,224	253,939	251,285	24,056	23,392	664	481,168	230,547	250,621	919	909	10
Mana ..	Nagpur Division	39,722	19,691	20,031	797	784	13	38,925	18,907	20,018	16	15	1
Mang ..	Maratha Plain Division.	(v)73,720	36,587	37,133	772	742	30	72,948	35,845	37,103	18	18	..
Maratha ..	Province ..	(w)236,968	120,857	116,111	30,790	28,519	2,271	206.178	92,338	113,840	2,524	2,443	81
Mehra or Mahar. (Hindu)	Province ..	1,037,529	514,736	522,793	30,151	28,815	1,336	1,007,378	485,921	521,457	1,171	1,153	18
(Christian)		500	309	191	98	90	8	402	219	183	18	14	4
Mehtar ..	*Total* ..	*(x) 15,174*	*7,933*	*7,241*	*535*	*504*	*31*	*14,639*	*7,429*	*7,210*	*3*	*2*	*1*
	Nerbudda Valley	11,038	5,814	5,224	308	295	13	10,730	5,519	5,211	..	..	..
	Nagpur ..	3,449	1,806	1,643	219	201	18	3,230	1,605	1,625	2	1	1
	Raipur ..	687	313	374	8	8	..	679	305	374	1	1	..
Mhali ..	Maratha Division	50,601	26,150	24,451	4,000	3,911	89	46,601	22,239	24,362	145	145	..
Nai ..	Province ..	(y)107,304	53,822	53,482	7,495	7,134	361	99,809	46,688	53,121	245	237	8
Oraon ..	*Total* ..	*105,160*	*53,978*	*51,182*	*1,214*	*1,138*	*76*	*103,946*	*52,840*	*51,106*	*8*	*8*	..

(p) Includes 15 Christians—6 males, 9 females; (q) Includes 2 Christian males; (r) Includes 5 Christian males;
(s) Includes 4 Christian males; (t) Includes 263 Christians—130 males, 133 females; and 49 Muslims—19 males, 30 females;
(u) Includes 3 Christians—1 male, 2 females; (v) Includes 31 Christians—13 males, 18 females; (w) Includes 3 Christians—1 male, 2 females;
(x) Includes 23 Christians—14 males, 9 females; and 171 Muslims—83 males, 88 females;
(y) Includes 3 Christian males and 81 Muslims—40 males, 41 females.

Literacy by selected castes—*concld.*

Caste, tribe or race.	Locality.	Population (7 years and over).									Literate in English.		
		Total.			Literate.			Illiterate.					
		Persons.	Males.	Females.	Persons.	Males.	Females.	Persons.	Males.	Females.	Persons.	Males.	Females.
1	2	3	4	5	6	7	8	9	10	11	12	13	14
Oraon—*concld* (Hindu and Tribal.)	..	71,076	36,668	34,408	276	271	5	70,800	36,397	34,403	1	1	..
	Raigarh ..	5,872	2,953	2,919	36	35	1	5,836	2,918	2,918	..	..	..
	Chhota Nagpur States.	65,204	33,715	31,489	240	236	4	64,964	33,479	31,485	1	1	..
(Christian)		34,084	17,310	16,774	938	867	71	33,146	16,443	16,703	7	7	..
	Raigarh ..	26	13	13	1	1	..	25	12	13	..	..	..
	Jashpur ..	34,058	17,297	16,761	937	866	71	33,121	16,431	16,690	7	7	..
Panka	*Total* ..	(x) *138,774*	*66,750*	*72,024*	*3,295*	*3,206*	*89*	*135,479*	*63,544*	*71,935*	*19*	*19*	..
	Mandla ..	14,869	7,318	7,551	359	353	6	14,510	6,965	7,545	2	2	..
	Seoni ..	1,355	660	695	28	27	1	1,327	633	694	..	..	..
	Balaghat ..	2,649	1,288	1,361	146	142	4	2,503	1,146	1,357	3	3	..
	Chhattisgarh Administrative Division.	91,793	43,921	47,872	2,257	2,197	60	89,536	41,724	47,812	12	12	..
	9 States of Chhattisgarh Plain Division.	28,108	13,563	14,545	505	487	18	27,603	13,076	14,527	2	2	..
Rajput (Hindu).	Province ..	(a[1])414,198	212,338	201,860	47,315	44,380	2,935	366,883	167,958	198,925	3,637	3,509	128
(Muslim)		164	143	21	78	75	3	86	68	18	22	19	3
Sawara or Saonr. (Hindu)	*Total* ..	*66,241*	*32,353*	*33,888*	*651*	*546*	*105*	*65,590*	*31,807*	*33,783*	*11*	*11*	..
	Saugor ..	17,419	8,693	8,726	29	28	1	17,390	8,665	8,725	2	2	..
	Damoh ..	4,931	2,445	2,486	80	21	59	4,851	2,424	2,427	..	..	..
	Chhattisgarh Administrative Division. ..	29,235	14,154	15,081	312	289	23	28,923	13,865	15,058	1	1	..
	9 States of Chhattisgarh Plain Division.	14,656	7,061	7,595	230	208	22	14,426	6,853	7,573	8	8	..
Satnami ..	Province .	(a[2])283,373	136,565	146,808	1,377	1,340	37	281,996	135,225	146,771	8	8	..
Sunar ..	Province ..	114,805	58,473	56,332	25,724	24,322	1,402	89,081	34,151	54,930	905	896	9
Teli ..	Province ..	(a[3])811,706	397,910	413,796	42,247	40,814	1,433	769,459	357,096	412,363	900	884	16
(Muslim)		100	33	67	8	8	..	92	25	67	..	..	..
Waddar ..	Yeotmal ..	4,790	2,167	2,623	12	11	1	4,778	2,156	2,622	1	1	..
Wanjari ..	Berar ..	35,416	17,993	17,423	1,339	1,279	60	34,077	16,714	17,363	37	37	..
Indian Christians (excluding those who returned their original caste).	Province ..	32,310	15,809	16,501	15,888	8,445	7,443	16,422	7,364	9,058	6,322	3,701	2,621

(x) Includes 7 Christians—2 males, 5 females ; (a[1]) Includes 22 Christians—9 males, 13 females ; (a[2]) Includes 8 Christians—4 males, 4 females ; (a[3]) Includes 19 Christians—13 males, 6 females.

TABLE XV.—Part I

Language

In part I of this table, the languages have been arranged according to their family affinity, the classification having been based on Sir George Grierson's revised scheme. The arrangement of columns is as follows :—

A—Vernaculars of India—

(i) Aryan sub-family of Indo-European family ..	Columns 5 to 67.
(ii) Dravidian family	Columns 68 to 103.
(iii) Austro-Asiatic sub-family of Austric family—Munda branch	Columns 104 to 118.
(iv) Unclassed languages—	
(a) Gipsy	Columns 119 to 121
(b) Others	Columns 122 to 124
B.—Vernaculars of Asiatic countries beyond India ..	Columns 125 to 127
C.—European languages	Columns 128 to 133

2. Hindi has, at this census, been divided into Western and Eastern Hindi. Hindustani, which includes all language returns of Urdu, Hindustani and Hindi unspecified, except in the Mandla and Jubbulpore districts and Changbhakar state, appears as a dialect of Western Hindi. Eastern Hindi includes Chhattisgarhi, Awadhi, Bagheli and other minor dialects detailed in the appendix. According to the figures of the Linguistic survey 99 per cent of the population of Mandla and Jubbulpore and 95 per cent of the population of Changbhakar speaks the Bagheli dialect of Eastern Hindi, but as no special instructions were issued for recording dialects, Hindi (Unspecified) was generally returned as the mother-tongue in those units. Against them, therefore, the proportion of Hindi speakers reported at the Linguistic survey to use the Bagheli dialect has been shown under Eastern Hindi. It may also be assumed that the number of Eastern Hindi speakers is considerably greater than that actually returned in the units in Chhattisgarh.

3. Sanskrit, Lahnda (Western Punjabi), Konkani, Khandesi and languages of the Pahari group have, at this census, been treated as independent languages of the Aryan sub-family and shown in column 65.

4. The appendix at the end of the table has been made considerably fuller than that of the last census and all returns of languages having no local importance, together with minor dialects, sub-dialects and forms of languages have been shown therein.

TABLE XV

PART I.—

Serial number.	District or State.	Population.			A—Vernaculars of India (i)					
					Total Western Hindi.			Dialect included in Western Hindi		
								Hindustani.		
		Persons.	Males.	Females.	Persons.	Males.	Females.	Persons.	Males.	Females.
	1	2	3	4	5	6	7	8	9	10
	Central Provinces and Berar.	**17,990,937**	**8,997,203**	**8,993,734**	**5,605,461**	**2,826,577**	**2,778,884**	**5,601,063**	**2,824,347**	**2,776,716**
	C. P. British Districts and Berar.	**15,507,723**	**7,761,818**	**7,745,905**	**4,825,293**	**2,432,735**	**2,392,558**	**4,820,895**	**2,430,505**	**2,390,390**
	C. P. British Districts	**12,065,885**	**6,002,239**	**6,063,646**	**4,432,936**	**2,223,199**	**2,209,737**	**4,431,133**	**2,222,233**	**2,208,900**
	Jubbulpore Division ..	*2,463,466*	*1,240,655*	*1,222,811*	*1,135,040*	*578,200*	*556,840*	*1,135,031*	*578,193*	*556,838*
1	Saugor ..	544,589	280,385	264,204	540,520	278,073	262,447	540,519	278,072	262,447
2	Damoh ..	305,568	154,791	150,777	303,836	153,913	149,923	303,836	153,913	149,923
3	Jubbulpore ..	773,811	391,649	382,162	7,556	3,814	3,742	7,549	3,809	3,740
4	Mandla ..	445,766	221,359	224,407	3,399	1,691	1,708	3,399	1,691	1,708
5	Seoni ..	393,732	192,471	201,261	279,729	140,709	139,020	279,728	140,708	139,020
	Nerbudda Division ..	*2,254,566*	*1,137,806*	*1,116,760*	*1,378,590*	*699,387*	*679,203*	*1,378,138*	*699,092*	*679,046*
6	Narsinghpur ..	321,481	161,417	160,064	319,949	160,590	159,359	319,949	160,590	159,359
7	Hoshangabad ..	486,630	248,226	238,404	432,516	219,870	212,646	432,507	219,865	212,642
8	Nimar ..	466,931	242,042	224,889	173,911	92,382	81,529	173,550	92,168	81,382
9	Betul ..	406,252	201,114	205,138	150,661	75,207	75,454	150,594	75,140	75,454
10	Chhindwara ..	573,272	285,007	288,265	301,553	151,338	150,215	301,538	151,329	150,209
	Nagpur Division ..	*3,602,108*	*1,809,541*	*1,792,567*	*650,771*	*332,052*	*318,719*	*649,448*	*331,396*	*318,052*
11	Wardha ..	516,266	261,394	254,872	38,040	21,132	16,908	37,706	20,971	16,735
12	Nagpur ..	940,049	481,246	458,803	142,916	77,932	64,984	142,116	77,527	64,589
13	Chanda ..	759,695	381,204	378,491	23,311	12,719	10,592	23,130	12,632	10,498
14	Bhandara ..	824,496	408,799	415,697	131,003	63,950	67,053	130,995	63,947	67,048
15	Balaghat ..	561,602	276,898	284,704	315,501	156,319	159,182	315,501	156,319	159,182
	Chhattisgarh Division ..	*3,745,715*	*1,814,237*	*1,931,508*	*1,268,535*	*613,560*	*654,975*	*1,268,516*	*613,552*	*654,964*
16	Raipur ..	1,527,573	739,950	787,623	48,552	25,981	22,571	48,545	25,977	22,568
17	Bilaspur ..	1,400,248	683,920	716,328	437,513	214,650	222,863	437,501	214,646	222,855
18	Drug ..	817,924	390,367	427,557	782,470	372,929	409,541	782,470	372,929	409,541
	Berar ..	**3,441,838**	**1,759,579**	**1,682,259**	**392,357**	**209,536**	**182,821**	**389,762**	**208,272**	**181,490**
19	Amraoti ..	941,604	485,593	456,011	130,824	70,651	60,173	130,063	70,307	59,756
20	Akola ..	876,362	448,896	427,466	111,820	60,366	51,454	111,576	60,244	51,332
21	Buldana ..	766,584	388,966	377,618	85,443	44,640	40,803	84,712	44,263	40,449
22	Yeotmal ..	857,288	436,124	421,164	64,270	33,879	30,391	63,411	33,458	29,953
	Central Provinces States.	**2,483,214**	**1,235,385**	**1,247,829**	**780,168**	**393,842**	**386,326**	**780,168**	**393,842**	**386,326**
23	Makrai ..	15,516	7,900	7,616	11,457	5,700	5,757	11,457	5,700	5,757
24	Bastar ..	524,721	263,248	261,473	9,861	5,309	4,552	9,861	5,309	4,552
25	Kanker ..	136,101	67,132	68,969	73,224	35,963	37,261	73,224	35,963	37,261
26	Nandgaon ..	182,380	87,886	94,494	18,143	9,301	8,842	18,143	9,301	8,842
27	Khairagarh ..	157,400	75,647	81,753	3,100	1,573	1,527	3,100	1,573	1,527
28	Chhuikhadan ..	31,668	15,238	16,430	31,310	15,046	16,264	31,310	15,046	16,264
29	Kawardha ..	72,820	35,098	37,722	323	204	119	323	204	119
30	Sakti ..	48,489	23,571	24,918	829	460	369	829	460	369
31	Raigarh ..	277,569	136,723	140,846	2,734	1,589	1,145	2,734	1,589	1,145
32	Sarangarh ..	128,967	62,443	66,524	372	194	178	372	194	178
33	Changbhakar ..	23,322	11,987	11,335	323	157	166	323	157	166
34	Korea ..	90,886	46,748	44,138	81,811	42,082	39,729	81,811	42,082	39,729
35	Surguja ..	501,939	254,923	247,016	443,593	224,467	219,126	443,593	224,467	219,126
36	Udaipur ..	97,738	49,425	48,313	307	213	94	307	213	94
37	Jashpur ..	193,698	97,416	96,282	102,781	51,584	51,197	102,781	51,584	51,197

Indo-European Family—Aryan Sub-Family.

Total Rajasthani.			Dialects included in Rajasthani.									Gujarati.			
			Marwari.			Nimari (Gurvi).			Labhani or Banjari (Naiki).						
Persons.	Males.	Females.	Persons.	Males.	Females.	Persons.	Males.	Females.	Persons.	Males.	Females.	Persons.	Males.	Females.	Serial number.
11	12	13	14	15	16	17	18	19	20	21	22	23	24	25	
346,548	**183,422**	**163,126**	**95,890**	**54,257**	**41,633**	**108,743**	**55,210**	**53,533**	**120,354**	**63,057**	**57,297**	**57,311**	**33,348**	**23,963**	
336,648	**178,179**	**158,469**	**90,764**	**51,429**	**39,335**	**108,743**	**55,210**	**53,533**	**115,580**	**60,642**	**54,938**	**56,249**	**32,686**	**23,563**	
194,667	**101,797**	**92,870**	**44,910**	**25,532**	**19,378**	**108,136**	**54,881**	**53,255**	**26,412**	**13,709**	**12,703**	**28,253**	**16,696**	**11,557**	
4,518	*2,232*	*2,286*	*3,435*	*1,773*	*1,662*	*17*	*8*	*9*	*1,065*	*450*	*615*	*2,282*	*1,345*	*937*	
511	305	206	313	214	99	..	..	..	197	90	107	524	295	229	1
672	336	336	667	334	333	..	..	..	5	2	3	524	255	269	2
695	342	353	676	332	344	17	8	9	2	2	..	929	584	345	3
1,212	616	596	1,039	529	510	..	..	..	173	87	86	160	114	46	4
1,428	633	795	740	364	376	..	..	..	688	269	419	145	97	48	5
142,961	*74,102*	*68,859*	*17,770*	*10,071*	*7,699*	*108,111*	*54,865*	*53,246*	*16,839*	*9,041*	*7,798*	*12,169*	*6,619*	*5,550*	
506	267	239	503	267	236	..	..	..	3	..	3	104	69	35	6
10,677	6,025	4,652	10,588	5,977	4,611	61	32	29	25	14	11	855	521	334	7
28,981	66,386	62,595	5,659	3,297	2,362	108,033	54,828	53,205	15,051	8,138	6,913	10,600	5,665	4,935	8
821	434	387	167	97	70	17	5	12	637	332	305	326	194	132	9
1,976	990	986	853	433	420	...	..	..	1,123	557	566	284	170	114	10
33,402	*18,146*	*15,256*	*15,173*	*8,980*	*6,193*	*8*	*8*	..	*3,678*	*1,860*	*1,818*	*10,363*	*6,550*	*3,813*	
20,759	10,805	9,954	4,830	2,728	2,102	8	8	..	1,467	822	645	1,749	1,044	705	11
4,272	2,312	1,960	3,727	2,053	1,674	..	..	..	476	218	258	3,624	1,872	1,752	12
2,404	1,246	1,158	1,147	671	476	..	..	..	1,237	565	672	1,294	812	482	13
5,012	3,331	1,681	4,957	3,302	1,655	..	..	..	55	29	26	3,449	2,669	780	14
955	452	503	512	226	286	..	..	..	443	226	217	247	153	94	15
13,786	*7,317*	*6,469*	*8,532*	*4,708*	*3,824*	..	..	..	*4,830*	*2,358*	*2,472*	*3,439*	*2,182*	*1,257*	
8,506	4,400	4,106	4,452	2,443	2,009	..	..	..	4,054	1,957	2,097	2,256	1,389	867	16
3,419	1,873	1,546	2,524	1,399	1,125	..	..	..	775	400	375	881	612	269	17
1,861	1,044	817	1,556	866	690	..	..	..	1	1	..	302	181	121	18
141,981	**76,382**	**65,599**	**45,854**	**25,897**	**19,957**	**607**	**329**	**278**	**89,168**	**46,933**	**42,235**	**27,996**	**15,990**	**12,006**	
18,082	9,594	8,488	11,690	6,338	5,352	310	183	127	780	391	389	7,376	4,190	3,186	19
35,184	19,255	15,929	15,389	9,113	6,276	7	6	1	19,702	10,082	9,620	10,132	5,912	4,220	20
19,128	10,778	8,350	11,268	6,339	4,929	289	140	149	6,637	3,831	2,806	6,526	3,597	2,929	21
69,587	36,755	32,832	7,507	4,107	3,400	1	..	1	62,049	32,629	29,420	3,962	2,291	1,671	22
9,900	**5,243**	**4,657**	**5,126**	**2,828**	**2,298**	..	..	..	**4,774**	**2,415**	**2,359**	**1,062**	**662**	**400**	
117	69	48	110	62	48	..	..	..	7	7	..	6	4	2	23
2,968	1,544	1,424	89	55	34	..	..	..	2,879	1,489	1,390	121	83	38	24
442	226	216	274	145	129	..	..	..	168	81	87	123	87	36	25
1,425	833	592	1,425	833	592	..	..	..	..	..	..	172	117	55	26
970	503	467	970	503	467	..	..	..	..	..	..	97	48	49	27
98	51	47	98	51	47	..	..	..	..	..	..	..	..	..	28
146	71	75	146	71	75	..	..	..	..	..	..	10	7	3	29
8	6	2	8	6	2	..	..	..	..	..	..	2	1	1	30
2,364	1,228	1,136	1,530	822	708	..	..	..	834	406	428	317	189	128	31
365	196	169	123	87	36	..	..	..	242	109	133	26	17	9	32
66	35	31	63	32	31	..	..	..	3	3	..	..	..	..	33
47	33	14	47	33	14	..	..	..	..	..	..	9	9	..	34
89	51	38	75	45	30	..	..	..	14	6	8	151	86	65	35
730	362	368	168	83	85	..	..	..	562	279	283	19	8	11	36
65	35	30	..	..	..	..	..	..	65	35	30	9	6	3	37

TABLE XV — PART I.—

A.—Vernaculars of India (i)

Serial number.	District or State.	Total Bhili. Persons.	Total Bhili. Males.	Total Bhili. Females.	Dialect included in Bhili. Pardhi. Persons.	Pardhi. Males.	Pardhi. Females.	Punjabi. Persons.	Punjabi. Males.	Punjabi. Females.	Bengali. Persons.	Bengali. Males.	Bengali. Females.
	1	26	27	28	29	30	31	32	33	34	35	36	37
	Central Provinces and Berar.	**30,756**	**15,397**	**15,359**	**3,496**	**1,782**	**1,714**	**10,130**	**7,372**	**2,758**	**5,907**	**3,326**	**2,581**
	C. P. British Districts and Berar.	**30,732**	**15,383**	**15,349**	**3,472**	**1,768**	**1,704**	**9,760**	**7,126**	**2,634**	**5,335**	**3,011**	**2,324**
	C. P. British Districts	**26,151**	**13,032**	**13,119**	**846**	**433**	**413**	**8,965**	**6,591**	**2,374**	**5,268**	**2,971**	**2,297**
	Jubbulpore Division ..	*21*	*10*	*11*	*21*	*10*	*11*	*2,343*	*1,724*	*619*	*1,377*	*752*	*625*
1	Saugor ..	12	7	5	12	7	5	350	252	98	55	34	21
2	Damoh ..	..	..	..	..	..	..	50	32	18	42	17	25
3	Jubbulpore ..	2	2	..	2	2	..	1,711	1,287	424	1,059	587	472
4	Mandla ..	..	..	..	..	..	..	147	90	57	148	79	69
5	Seoni ..	7	1	6	7	1	6	85	63	22	73	35	38
	Nerbudda Division ..	*25,348*	*12,599*	*12,749*	*168*	*83*	*85*	*1,439*	*1,086*	*353*	*492*	*291*	*201*
6	Narsinghpur ..	..	..	..	..	..	..	45	27	18	35	23	12
7	Hoshangabad ..	38	21	17	38	21	17	645	497	148	175	98	77
8	Nimar ..	25,308	12,578	12,730	130	62	68	270	208	62	105	62	43
9	Betul ..	2	..	2	..	..	..	126	97	29	35	23	12
10	Chhindwara ..	..	..	..	..	..	..	353	257	96	142	85	57
	Nagpur Division ..	*555*	*288*	*267*	*549*	*282*	*267*	*3,708*	*2,838*	*870*	*1,945*	*1,151*	*794*
11	Wardha ..	293	153	140	293	153	140	52	35	17	23	18	5
12	Nagpur ..	118	54	64	113	49	64	1,665	1,296	369	1,545	916	629
13	Chanda ..	143	80	63	143	80	63	86	50	36	81	48	33
14	Bhandara ..	1	1	..	..	..	..	1,742	1,350	392	190	117	73
15	Balaghat ..	..	..	..	..	..	..	163	107	56	106	52	54
	Chhattisgarh Division ..	*227*	*135*	*92*	*108*	*58*	*50*	*1,475*	*943*	*532*	*1,454*	*777*	*677*
16	Raipur ..	110	58	52	83	43	40	951	599	352	651	338	313
17	Bilaspur ..	100	66	34	8	4	4	420	283	137	655	356	299
18	Drug ..	17	11	6	17	11	6	104	61	43	148	83	65
	Berar ..	**4,581**	**2,351**	**2,230**	**2,626**	**1,335**	**1,291**	**795**	**535**	**260**	**67**	**40**	**27**
19	Amraoti ..	2,001	1,026	975	1,160	594	566	183	102	81	38	27	11
20	Akola ..	751	355	396	609	288	321	227	173	54	21	11	10
21	Buldana ..	1,032	529	503	332	162	170	149	113	36	2	1	1
22	Yeotmal ..	797	441	356	525	291	234	236	147	89	6	1	5
	Central Provinces States.	**24**	**14**	**10**	**24**	**14**	**10**	**370**	**246**	**124**	**572**	**315**	**257**
23	Makrai ..	..	..	..	..	..	..	20	14	6	..	..	..
24	Bastar ..	..	..	..	..	..	..	7	5	2	54	31	23
25	Kanker ..	..	..	..	..	..	..	3	3	..	45	27	18
26	Nandgaon ..	..	..	..	..	..	..	18	13	5	44	28	16
27	Khairagarh ..	24	14	10	24	14	10	49	35	14	73	29	44
28	Chhuikhadan ..	..	..	..	..	..	..	5	5	..	3	2	1
29	Kawardha ..	..	..	..	..	..	..	3	3	..	..	..	..
30	Sakti ..	..	..	..	..	..	..	11	8	3	6	3	3
31	Raigarh ..	..	..	..	..	..	..	139	72	67	167	78	89
32	Sarangarh ..	..	..	..	..	..	..	2	2	..	28	19	9
33	Changbhakar ..	..	..	..	..	..	..	..	..	..	..	..	..
34	Korea ..	..	..	..	..	..	..	28	21	7	19	19	..
35	Surguja ..	..	..	..	..	..	..	83	63	20	52	31	21
36	Udaipur ..	..	..	..	..	..	..	..	..	..	26	12	14
37	Jashpur ..	..	..	..	..	..	..	2	2	..	55	36	19

Indo-European family—Aryan Sub-family—*contd.*

Bihari.			Total Oriya.			Dialect included in Oriya.			Total Eastern Hindi.			Dialect included in Eastern Hindi.			
						Bhatri.						Chhattisgarhi.			
Persons.	Males.	Females.	Persons.	Males.	Females.	Persons.	Males.	Females.	Persons.	Males.	Females.	Persons.	Males.	Females.	Serial number.
38	39	40	41	42	43	44	45	46	47	48	49	50	51	52	
278	**194**	**84**	**385,651**	**189,447**	**196,204**	**45,847**	**22,909**	**22,938**	**4,107,757**	**2,007,183**	**2,100,574**	**3,011,124**	**1,456,490**	**1,554,634**	
268	**184**	**84**	**263,133**	**128,750**	**134,383**	**17**	**6**	**11**	**3,239,030**	**1,585,999**	**1,653,031**	**2,148,507**	**1,038,268**	**1,110,239**	
268	**184**	**84**	**262,948**	**128,709**	**134,239**	**17**	**6**	**11**	**3,238,617**	**1,585,791**	**1,652,826**	**2,148,506**	**1,038,267**	**1,110,239**	
1	*1*	..	*459*	*249*	*210*	..	..	..	*1,083,763*	*544,442*	*539,321*	*34*	*30*	*4*	
..	..	..	3	3	..	..	..	..	..	..	..	..	..	..	1
..	..	..	2	1	1	..	..	..	1	1	..	..	..	..	2
1	1	..	411	205	206	..	..	..	747,305	377,026	370,279	34	30	4	3
..	..	..	39	38	1	..	..	..	336,451	167,412	169,039	..	..	..	4
..	..	..	4	2	2	..	..	..	6	3	3	..	..	..	5
1	*1*	..	*26*	*20*	*6*	..	..	..	*253*	*131*	*122*	*12*	*6*	*6*	
..	..	..	11	6	5	..	..	..	..	..	..	..	..	..	6
1	1	..	5	5	..	..	..	..	147	74	73	4	4	..	7
..	..	..	2	2	..	..	..	..	43	26	17	4	..	4	8
..	..	..	5	5	..	..	..	..	..	..	..	..	..	..	9
..	..	..	3	2	1	..	..	..	63	31	32	4	2	2	10
127	*100*	*27*	*692*	*433*	*259*	..	..	..	*23,018*	*11,342*	*11,676*	*16,877*	*8,355*	*8,522*	
..	..	..	30	30	..	..	..	..	273	147	126	7	6	1	11
..	..	..	263	111	152	..	..	..	2,607	1,359	1,248	2,440	1,275	1,165	12
125	98	27	45	32	13	..	..	..	3,470	1,801	1,669	1,926	1,056	870	13
2	2	..	67	38	29	..	..	..	8,969	4,275	4,694	4,814	2,262	2,552	14
..	..	..	287	222	65	..	..	..	7,699	3,760	3,939	7,690	3,556	3,934	15
139	*82*	*57*	*261,771*	*128,007*	*133,764*	*17*	*6*	*11*	*2,131,583*	*1,029,876*	*1,101,707*	*2,131,583*	*1,029,876*	*1,101,707*	
128	76	52	238,232	116,496	121,736	..	..	..	1,207,261	580,188	627,073	1,207,261	580,188	627,073	16
11	6	5	23,321	11,394	11,927	..	..	..	923,903	449,536	474,367	923,903	449,536	474,367	17
..	..	..	218	117	101	17	6	11	419	152	267	419	152	267	18
..	..	..	**185**	**41**	**144**	..	..	..	**413**	**208**	**205**	**1**	**1**	..	
..	..	..	22	14	8	..	..	..	110	60	50	1	1	..	19
..	..	..	2	2	..	..	..	..	130	65	65	..	..	..	20
..	..	..	..	..	..	..	..	..	143	69	74	..	..	..	21
..	..	..	161	25	136	..	..	..	30	14	16	..	..	..	22
10	**10**	..	**122,518**	**60,697**	**61,821**	**45,830**	**22,903**	**22,927**	**868,727**	**421,184**	**447,543**	**862,617**	**418,222**	**444,395**	
..	..	..	..	..	..	..	..	..	..	..	..	..	..	..	23
..	..	..	48,129	24,038	24,091	45,830	22,903	22,927	12,945	6,891	6,054	12,945	6,891	6,054	24
..	..	..	86	37	49	..	..	..	11,074	4,400	6,674	11,074	4,400	6,674	25
..	..	..	19	13	6	..	..	..	154,845	73,767	81,078	154,845	73,767	81,078	26
..	..	..	74	39	35	..	..	..	149,467	71,769	77,698	149,467	71,769	77,698	27
..	..	..	..	..	..	..	..	..	15	7	8	15	7	8	28
..	..	..	4	4	..	..	..	..	72,089	34,695	37,394	72,089	34,695	37,394	29
..	..	..	58	26	32	..	..	..	47,166	22,845	24,321	47,166	22,845	24,321	30
1	1	..	33,368	16,172	17,196	..	..	..	228,580	112,312	116,268	228,580	112,312	116,268	31
..	..	..	25,271	12,634	12,637	..	..	..	100,725	48,207	52,518	100,725	48,207	52,518	32
..	..	..	..	..	..	..	..	..	6,127	2,974	3,153	17	12	5	33
..	..	..	15	9	6	..	..	..	8,190	4,172	4,018	8,190	4,172	4,018	34
..	..	..	619	314	305	..	..	..	1,129	506	623	1,129	506	623	35
9	9	..	4,204	2,090	2,114	..	..	..	76,375	38,639	37,736	76,375	38,639	37,736	36
..	..	..	10,671	5,321	5,350	..	..	..	..	..	..	..	..	..	37

A.—Vernaculars of India (i) Indo-European family—Aryan

Serial number.	District or State.	Total Marathi.			Dialects included in Marathi.								
					Halbi.			Koshti.			C. P. Dialects.		
		Persons.	Males.	Females.	Persons.	Males.	Females.	Persons.	Males.	Females.	Persons.	Males.	Females.
	1	53	54	55	56	57	58	59	60	61	62	63	64
	Central Provinces and Berar.	**5,617,544**	**2,822,000**	**2,795,544**	**174,681**	**88,609**	**86,072**	**11,555**	**7,726**	**3,829**	**18,236**	**8,784**	**9,452**
	C. P. British Districts and Berar.	**5,432,265**	**2,728,270**	**2,703,995**	**3,340**	**1,703**	**1,637**	**11,555**	**7,726**	**3,829**	**18,110**	**8,717**	**9,393**
	C. P. British Districts ..	**2,759,990**	**1,378,466**	**1,381,524**	**3,030**	**1,555**	**1,475**	**11,469**	**7,677**	**3,792**	**17,534**	**8,435**	**9,099**
	Jubbulpore Division ..	*24,401*	*12,179*	*12,222*	..	..	..	*1*	*1*	..	*1*	*1*	..
1	Saugor ..	1,552	809	743	..	..	..	..	..	..	..	..	..
2	Damoh ..	346	185	161	..	..	..	..	..	..	..	..	..
3	Jubbulpore ..	3,367	1,962	1,405	..	..	..	1	1	..	1	1	..
4	Mandla ..	676	338	338	..	..	..	..	..	..	..	..	..
5	Seoni ..	18,460	8,885	9,575	..	..	..	..	..	..	..	..	..
	Nerbudda Division ..	*276,574*	*138,824*	*137,750*	*63*	*30*	*33*	..	..	..	*2,726*	*1,363*	*1,363*
6	Narsinghpur ..	490	263	227	..	..	..	..	..	..	..	..	..
7	Hoshangabad ..	4,389	2,290	2,099	..	..	..	..	..	..	462	226	236
8	Nimar ..	69,915	35,827	34,088	63	30	33	..	..	..	60	33	27
9	Betul ..	97,621	48,383	49,238	..	..	..	..	..	..	..	..	..
10	Chhindwara ..	104,159	52,061	52,098	..	..	..	..	..	..	2,204	1,104	1,100
	Nagpur Division ..	*2,431,243*	*1,213,687*	*1,217,556*	*2,872*	*1,478*	*1,394*	*11,468*	*7,676*	*3,792*	*5,475*	*2,448*	*3,027*
11	Wardha ..	400,131	200,592	199,539	98	50	48	985	506	479	513	248	265
12	Nagpur ..	712,533	359,047	353,486	1,010	527	483	8,567	6,004	2,563	17	10	7
13	Chanda ..	548,011	274,689	273,322	1,757	899	858	1,510	958	552	4,933	2,182	2,751
14	Bhandara ..	610,140	300,269	309,871	7	2	5	406	208	198	8	5	3
15	Balaghat ..	160,428	79,090	81,338	..	..	..	..	..	..	4	3	1
	Chhattisgarh Division ..	*27,772*	*13,776*	*13,996*	*95*	*47*	*48*	..	..	..	*9,332*	*4,623*	*4,709*
16	Raipur ..	14,380	7,120	7,260	3	3	..	..	..	..	9,332	4,623	4,709
17	Bilaspur ..	4,114	2,052	2,062	..	..	..	..	..	..	..	..	..
18	Drug ..	9,278	4,604	4,674	92	44	48	..	..	..	..	..	..
	Berar ..	**2,672,275**	**1,349,804**	**1,322,471**	**310**	**148**	**162**	**86**	**49**	**37**	**576**	**282**	**294**
19	Amraoti ..	721,528	369,101	352,427	250	118	132	11	9	2	277	140	137
20	Akola ..	707,549	357,038	350,511	..	..	..	..	..	..	103	53	50
21	Buldana ..	647,098	325,475	321,623	20	11	9	..	..	..	12	11	1
22	Yeotmal ..	596,100	298,190	297,910	40	19	21	75	40	35	184	78	106
	Central Provinces States	**185,279**	**93,730**	**91,549**	**171,341**	**86,906**	**84,435**	..	..	..	**126**	**67**	**59**
23	Makrai ..	61	35	26	..	..	..	..	..	..	..	..	..
24	Bastar ..	175,463	88,892	86,571	171,293	86,884	84,409	..	..	..	44	18	26
25	Kanker ..	1,016	579	437	48	22	26	..	..	..	43	20	23
26	Nandgaon ..	5,544	2,701	2,843	..	..	..	..	..	..	..	..	..
27	Khairagarh ..	[illegible],238	1,018	1,220	..	..	..	..	..	..	..	..	..
28	Chhuikhadan ..	236	126	110	..	..	..	..	..	..	..	..	..
29	Kawardha ..	170	79	91	..	..	..	..	..	..	..	..	..
30	Sakti ..	130	73	57	..	..	..	..	..	..	..	..	..
31	Raigarh ..	326	161	165	..	..	..	..	..	..	..	..	..
32	Sarangarh ..	24	16	8	..	..	..	..	..	..	..	..	..
33	Changbhakar ..	..	..	..	..	..	..	..	..	..	..	..	..
34	Korea ..	8	6	2	..	..	..	..	..	..	..	..	..
35	Surguja ..	46	34	12	..	..	..	..	..	..	39	29	10
36	Udaipur ..	11	5	6	..	..	..	..	..	..	..	..	..
37	Jashpur ..	6	5	1	..	..	..	..	..	..	..	..	..

Sub-family—*concld.* Other Aryan languages of Sub-family. Persons.	Males.	Females.	A.—Vernaculars of India—(ii) Dravidian family. Total Gondi. Persons.	Males.	Females.	Dialects included in Gondi. Mari. Persons.	Males.	Females.	Parji (Dhurwa) Persons.	Males.	Females.	Koya. Persons.	Males.	Females.	Serial number
65	66	67	68	69	70	71	72	73	74	75	76	77	78	79	
6,035	**4,474**	**1,561**	**1,280,421**	**628,834**	**651,587**	**150,837**	**75,285**	**75,552**	**12,363**	**6,255**	**6,108**	**7,027**	**3,441**	**3,586**	
5,826	**4,358**	**1,468**	**946,702**	**461,855**	**484,847**	**28,032**	**13,937**	**14,095**	**2**	**2**	..	**855**	**417**	**438**	
4,398	**3,313**	**1,085**	**863,854**	**419,083**	**444,771**	**28,031**	**13,937**	**14,094**	**2**	**2**	..	**701**	**334**	**367**	
876	*707*	*169*	*199,422*	*93,347*	*106,075*	..	..	..	*2*	*2*	..	..	..	..	
258	202	56	62	28	34	..	..	..	..	..	..	..	..	..	1
27	23	4	2	1	1	..	..	..	..	..	..	..	..	..	2
462	373	89	3,374	994	2,380	..	..	..	2	2	..	..	..	..	3
52	41	11	103,180	50,791	52,389	..	..	..	..	..	..	..	..	..	4
77	68	9	92,804	41,533	51,271	..	..	..	..	..	..	..	..	..	5
1,481	*1,102*	*379*	*293,054*	*142,589*	*150,465*	..	..	..	..	..	..	..	..	..	
24	19	5	271	124	147	..	..	..	..	..	..	..	..	..	6
316	255	61	23,399	11,526	11,873	..	..	..	..	..	..	..	..	..	7
589	370	219	9,023	4,596	4,427	..	..	..	..	..	..	..	..	..	8
69	64	5	118,769	58,051	60,718	..	..	..	..	..	..	..	..	..	9
483	394	89	141,592	68,292	73,300	..	..	..	..	..	..	..	..	..	10
1,738	*1,260*	*478*	*345,462*	*170,566*	*174,896*	*28,031*	*13,937*	*14,094*	..	..	..	*701*	*334*	*367*	
227	101	126	48,718	24,076	24,642	..	..	..	..	..	..	..	..	..	11
1,156	892	264	52,139	25,759	26,380	..	..	..	..	..	..	..	..	..	12
88	53	35	109,822	53,807	56,015	28,031	13,937	14,094	..	..	..	701	334	367	13
231	183	48	60,078	30,937	29,141	..	..	..	..	..	..	..	..	..	14
36	31	5	74,705	35,987	38,718	..	..	..	..	..	..	..	..	..	15
303	*244*	*59*	*25,916*	*12,581*	*13,335*	..	..	..	..	..	..	..	..	..	
120	99	21	2,610	1,314	1,296	..	..	..	..	..	..	..	..	..	16
132	105	27	421	224	197	..	..	..	..	..	..	..	..	..	
51	40	11	22,885	11,043	11,842	..	..	..	..	..	..	..	..	..	18
1,428	**1,045**	**383**	**82,848**	**42,772**	**40,076**	**1**	..	**1**	..	..	..	**154**	**83**	**'1**	
229	173	56	20,333	10,012	10,321	..	..	..	..	..	..	154	83	71	19
448	348	100	1,485	836	649	1	..	1	..	..	..	..	..	..	20
187	113	74	283	141	142	..	..	..	..	..	..	..	..	..	21
564	411	153	60,747	31,783	28,964	..	..	..	..	..	..	..	..	..	22
209	**116**	**93**	**333,719**	**166,979**	**166,740**	**122,805**	**61,348**	**61,457**	**12,361**	**6,253**	**6,108**	**6,172**	**3,024**	**3,148**	
..	..	..	1,073	570	503	..	..	..	..	..	..	..	..	..	23
8	5	3	262,988	130,436	132,552	122,805	61,348	61,457	12,361	6,253	6,108	6,172	3,024	3,148	24
1	1	..	50,087	25,809	24,278	..	..	..	..	..	..	..	..	..	25
14	10	4	1,859	943	916	..	..	..	..	..	..	..	..	..	26
25	14	11	747	329	418	..	..	..	..	..	..	..	..	..	27
..	..	..	..	..	..	..	..	..	..	..	..	..	..	..	28
..	..	..	71	31	40	..	..	..	..	..	..	..	..	..	29
..	..	..	11	7	4	..	..	..	..	..	..	..	..	..	30
7	6	1	165	73	92	..	..	..	..	..	..	..	..	..	31
..	..	..	26	15	11	..	..	..	..	..	..	..	..	..	32
..	..	..	16,663	8,746	7,917	..	..	..	..	..	..	..	..	..	33
34	27	7	29	20	9	..	..	..	..	..	..	..	..	..	34
76	31	45	..	..	..	..	..	..	..	..	..	..	..	..	35
9	1	8	..	..	..	..	..	..	..	..	..	..	..	..	36
35	21	14	..	..	..	..	..	..	..	..	..	..	..	..	37

A.—Vernaculars of India—

Serial number.	District or State.	Kurukh or Oraon (Dhangari).			Kolami.			Telugu.			Total Kanarese.			Dialect in Golari
		Persons.	Males.	Females.	Persons.	Males.	Females.	Persons.	Males.	Females.	Persons.	Males.	Females.	Persons.
	1	80	81	82	83	84	85	86	87	88	89	90	91	92
	Central Provinces and Berar.	**142,323**	**73,120**	**69,203**	**28,362**	**15,232**	**13,130**	**142,430**	**73,182**	**69,248**	**9,132**	**4.485**	**4,647**	**3,530**
	C. P. British Districts and Berar.	**2,456**	**1,170**	**1,286**	**28,362**	**15,232**	**13,130**	**130.393**	**67,228**	**63,165**	**9,126**	**4,481**	**4,645**	**3,530**
	C. P. British Districts.	**2,456**	**1.170**	**1,286**	**2,609**	**1,398**	**1,211**	**84,007**	**42,910**	**41,097**	**7,830**	**3,755**	**4,075**	**3,529**
	Jubbulpore Division ..	..	..	..	..	..	..	*949*	*491*	*458*	*820*	*395*	*425*	*429*
1	Saugor ..	..	..	.	..	..	..	41	24	17	1	1	..	..
2	Damoh ..	..	..	.	..	..	..	12	5	7	..	.	..	..
3	Jubbulpore ..	..	..	..	..	..	..	733	378	355	16	9	7	..
4	Mandla ..	..	..	..	..	..	..	130	66	64	..	..	..	..
5	Seoni ..	..	..	..	..	..	..	33	18	15	803	385	418	429
	Nerbudda Division ..	..	..	..	..	..	..	*1,043*	*548*	*495*	*93*	*55*	*38*	*9*
6	Narsinghpur ..	..	..	..	..	..	..	22	13	9	..	.	..	..
7	Hoshangabad ..	..	..	..	..	..	..	154	86	68	31	22	9	..
8	Nimar ..	..	..	..	..	..	..	601	316	285	49	23	26	..
9	Betul ..	..	..	..	.	.	..	58	27	31	..	..	..	..
10	Chhindwara ..	..	..	..	..	..	..	208	106	102	13	10	3	9
	Nagpur Division ..	..	..	..	*2,609*	*1,398*	*1,211*	*79,991*	*40,829*	*39,162*	*6,897*	*3,293*	*3,604*	*3,091*
11	Wardha ..	..	..	..	2,520	1,352	1,168	2,320	1,356	964	14	9	5	1
12	Nagpur ..	..	..	..	..	..	..	9,173	4,855	4,318	578	310	268	299
13	Chanda ..	..	..	..	89	46	43	66,779	33,843	32.936	3,318	1,549	1,769	17
14	Bhandara ..	..	..	..	..	..	..	1,521	687	834	1,817	850	967	1,785
15	Balaghat ..	..	..	..	..	..	..	198	88	110	1,170	575	595	989
	Chhattisgarh Division	*2,456*	*1,170*	*1,286*	..	..	..	*2,024*	*1,042*	*982*	*20*	*12*	*8*	..
16	Raipur ..	313	148	165	..	..	..	1.020	498	522	..	..	..	..
17	Bilaspur ..	2.143	1,022	1.121	..	..	..	964	519	445	.	..	..	..
18	Drug ..	..	..	..	..	..	..	40	25	15	20	12	8	..
	Berar ..	..	..	..	**25,753**	**13,834**	**11,919**	**46,386**	**24,318**	**22,068**	**1,296**	**726**	**570**	**1**
19	Amraoti ..	..	..	..	106	51	55	2,722	1,389	1,333	333	173	160	1
20	Akola ..	..	..	..	..	..	..	5,111	2,710	2,401	353	202	151	..
21	Buldana ..	..	..	..	..	..	..	4,001	2,176	1,825	441	252	189	..
22	Yeotmal ..	..	..	..	25,647	13,783	11,864	34,552	18,043	16,509	169	99	70	..
	Central Provinces States.	**139,867**	**71,950**	**67,917**	..	..	..	**12,037**	**5,954**	**6,083**	**6**	**4**	**2**	..
23	Makrai ..	..	..	..	..	..	..	..	..	..	..	..	..	..
24	Bastar .	..	..	..	..	..	..	11,662	5,762	5,900	..	..	..	..
25	Kanker ..	..	..	..	..	..	..	..	..	..	..	..	..	..
26	Nandgaon ..	.	..	..	..	..	..	155	82	73	6	4	2	..
27	Khairagarh .	.	..	.	..	..	..	145	74	71	..	..	..	..
28	Chhuikhadan ..	..	.	.	..	..	..	..	..	..	..	..	..	..
29	Kawardha ..	..	..	..	..	..	..	4	4	..	..	..	..	.
30	Sakti ..	182	93	89	..	..	..	10	4	6	..	..	..	..
31	Raigarh ..	6,520	3,447	3,073	..	..	..	60	27	33	..	..	..	..
32	Sarangarh ..	1,411	758	653	..	..	..	..	.	..	..	..	..	..
33	Changbhakar ..	.	..	..	..	..	..	..	..	..	..	..	..	..
34	Korea ..	689	345	344	..	..	..	..	..	.	..	..	..	..
35	Surguja ..	44,856	23,556	21,300	..	..	.	..	..	..	..	..	..	..
36	Udaipur ..	14,363	7,318	7,045	..	..	..	..	..	..	..	..	..	..
37	Jashpur ..	71,846	36,453	35,413	..	..	..	1	1	..	..	..	..	..

(ii) Dravidian family—*concld.*											A.—Vernaculars of India—(iii) Austric family (Austro-Asiatic sub-family) Munda branch.						
included Kanarese.		Total Tamil.			Dialect included in Tamil.			Other languages of Dravidian family.			Total Kherwari.			Dialect included in Kherwari.			
or Holia.					Kaikadi.									Korwa.			
Males.	Females.	Persons.	Males.	Females.	Persons.	Males.	Females.	Persons.	Males.	Females.	Persons.	Males.	Females.	Persons.	Males.	Females.	Serial number.
93	94	95	96	97	98	99	100	101	102	103	104	105	106	107	108	109	
1,717	**1,813**	**9,754**	**5,351**	**4,403**	**1,786**	**917**	**869**	**4,235**	**2,125**	**2,110**	**12,134**	**6,003**	**6,131**	**9,651**	**4,793**	**4,858**	
1,717	**1,813**	**9,540**	**5,243**	**4,297**	**1,785**	**916**	**869**	**4,222**	**2,118**	**2,104**	**1,525**	**737**	**788**	..	..	..	
1,717	**1,812**	**8,264**	**4,544**	**3,720**	**1,110**	**562**	**548**	**4,190**	**2,102**	**2,088**	**1.524**	**736**	**788**	..	..	..	
207	*222*	*1,992*	*1,158*	*834*	..	..	..	*51*	*38*	*13*	*4*	*1*	*3*	..	..	..	
..	..	53	34	19	..	..	..	..	..	..	..	..	..	..	..	..	1
..	..	6	1	5	..	..	..	2	2	..	4	1	3	..	..	..	2
..	..	1,808	1,061	747	..	..	..	47	34	13	..	..	..	..	..	..	3
..	..	67	32	35	..	..	..	1	1	..	..	..	..	..	..	..	4
207	222	58	30	28	..	..	..	1	1	..	..	..	..	..	..	..	5
7	*2*	*1,557*	*799*	*758*	*1,074*	*551*	*523*	*3,933*	*1,939*	*1,994*	*1*	..	*1*	..	..	..	
..	..	6	3	3	..	..	..	..	..	..	..	..	..	..	..	..	6
..	..	146	79	67	..	..	..	10	6	4	..	..	..	..	..	..	7
..	..	1,283	651	632	1,074	551	523	..	..	..	1	..	1	..	..	..	8
..	..	42	21	21	..	..	..	1	1	..	..	..	..	..	..	..	9
7	2	80	45	35	..	..	..	3,922	1,932	1,990	..	..	..	..	..	..	10
1,503	*1,588*	*4,017*	*2,220*	*1,797*	*36*	*11*	*25*	*205*	*124*	*81*	*68*	*44*	*24*	..	..	..	
..	1	77	40	37	..	..	..	2	2	..	..	..	..	..	..	..	11
159	140	3,380	1,903	1,477	..	..	..	74	47	27	68	44	24	..	..	..	12
8	9	344	169	175	19	10	9	127	75	52	..	..	..	..	..	..	13
834	951	177	82	95	16	..	16	2	..	2	..	..	..	..	..	..	14
502	487	39	26	13	1	1	..	..	..	..	..	..	..	..	..	..	15
..	..	*698*	*367*	*331*	..	..	..	*1*	*1*	..	*1,451*	*691*	*760*	..	..	..	
..	..	293	158	135	..	..	..	1	1	..	1,170	555	615	..	..	..	16
..	..	350	174	176	..	..	..	..	..	..	281	136	145	..	..	..	17
..	..	55	35	20	..	..	..	..	..	..	..	..	..	..	..	..	18
..	**1**	**1,276**	**699**	**577**	**675**	**354**	**321**	**32**	**16**	**16**	**1**	**1**	..	..	..	..	
..	1	411	238	173	160	75	85	9	5	4	1	1	..	..	..	..	19
..	..	688	366	322	460	250	210	9	2	7	..	..	..	..	..	..	20
..	..	129	66	63	53	29	24	10	8	2	..	..	..	..	..	..	21
..	..	48	29	19	2	..	2	4	1	3	..	..	..	..	..	..	22
..	..	**214**	**108**	**106**	**1**	**1**	..	**13**	**7**	**6**	**10,609**	**5,266**	**5,343**	**9,651**	**4,793**	**4,858**	
..	..	..	..	..	..	..	..	..	..	..	..	..	..	..	..	..	23
..	..	20	9	11	..	..	..	8	4	4	..	..	..	..	..	..	24
..	..	..	..	..	..	..	..	..	..	..	..	..	..	..	..	..	25
..	..	105	55	50	..	..	..	..	..	..	..	..	..	..	..	..	26
..	..	68	34	34	..	..	..	..	..	..	..	..	..	..	..	..	27
..	..	1	1	..	1	1	..	..	..	..	..	..	..	..	..	..	28
..	..	..	..	..	..	..	..	..	..	..	..	..	..	..	..	..	29
..	..	..	..	..	..	..	..	..	..	..	21	12	9	..	..	..	30
..	..	..	..	..	..	..	..	5	3	2	24	12	12	..	..	..	31
..	..	15	7	8	..	..	..	..	..	..	206	99	107	..	..	..	32
..	..	..	..	..	..	..	..	..	..	..	143	75	68	..	..	..	33
..	..	..	..	..	..	..	..	..	..	..	..	..	..	..	..	..	34
..	..	..	..	..	..	..	..	..	..	..	4,874	2,572	2,302	4,830	2,548	2,282	35
..	..	5	2	3	..	..	..	..	..	..	1,175	510	666	954	400	554	36
..	..	..	..	..	..	..	..	..	..	..	4,165	1,986	2,179	3,867	1,845	2,022	37

Serial number.	District or State.	A.—Vernaculars of India—(iii) Austric family (Austro-Asiatic sub-family) Munda branch—*contd.* Korku. Persons.	Korku. Males.	Korku. Females.	Kharia. Persons.	Kharia. Males.	Kharia. Females.	Other languages of the Munda branch. Persons.	Other languages of the Munda branch. Males.	Other languages of the Munda branch. Females.	(iv) Un- Gipsy languages. Persons.	Gipsy languages. Males.	Gipsy languages. Females.
	1	110	111	112	113	114	115	116	117	118	119	120	121
	Central Provinces and Berar.	**161,975**	**81,204**	**80,771**	**9,076**	**4,528**	**4,548**	**463**	**229**	**234**	**4,059**	**1,982**	**2,077**
	C. P. British Districts and Berar.	**152,838**	**76,492**	**76,346**	**1,194**	**641**	**553**	..	..	..	**4,043**	**1,976**	**2,072**
	C. P. British Districts	**114,712**	**57,231**	**57,481**	**1,194**	**641**	**553**	..	..	..	**1,114**	**533**	**581**
	Jubbulpore Division ..	*2*	*2*	..	..	..	..	..	..	..	*4*	*2*	*2*
1	Saugor ..	..	..	..	..	..	..	..	..	..	1	..	1
2	Damoh ..	..	..	..	..	..	..	..	..	..	..	..	..
3	Jubbulpore ..	..	..	..	..	..	..	..	..	..	3	2	1
4	Mandla ..	2	2	..	..	..	..	..	..	..	..	..	..
5	Seoni ..	..	..	..	..	..	..	..	..	..	..	..	..
	Nerbudda Division ..	*114,442*	*57,068*	*57,374*	..	..	..	..	..	..	*106*	*48*	*58*
6	Narsinghpur ..	..	..	..	..	..	..	..	..	..	..	..	..
7	Hoshangabad ..	12,550	6,512	6,038	..	..	..	..	..	..	5	2	3
8	Nimar ..	46,010	22,817	23,193	..	..	..	..	..	..	101	46	55
9	Betul ..	37,579	18,534	19,045	..	..	..	..	..	..	..	..	..
10	Chhindwara ..	18,303	9,205	9,098	..	..	..	..	..	..	..	..	..
	Nagpur Division ..	*5*	*1*	*4*	..	..	..	..	..	..	*1,004*	*483*	*521*
11	Wardha ..	5	1	4	..	..	..	..	..	..	990	477	513
12	Nagpur ..	..	..	..	..	..	..	..	..	..	..	..	..
13	Chanda ..	..	..	..	..	..	..	..	..	..	10	3	7
14	Bhandara ..	..	..	..	..	..	..	..	..	..	..	..	..
15	Balaghat ..	..	..	..	..	..	..	..	..	..	4	3	1
	Chhattisgarh Division ..	*263*	*160*	*103*	*1,194*	*641*	*553*	..	..	..	..	..	..
16	Raipur ..	..	..	..	703	353	350	..	..	..	..	..	..
17	Bilaspur ..	263	160	103	491	288	203	..	..	..	..	..	..
18	Drug ..	..	..	..	..	..	..	..	..	..	..	..	..
	Berar ..	**38,126**	**19,261**	**18,865**	..	..	..	..	..	..	**2,934**	**1,443**	**1,491**
19	Amraoti ..	35,400	17,871	17,529	..	..	..	..	..	..	1,379	668	711
20	Akola ..	1,419	737	682	..	..	..	..	..	..	811	403	408
21	Buldana ..	1,307	653	654	..	..	..	..	..	..	461	232	249
22	Yeotmal ..	..	..	..	..	..	..	..	..	..	263	140	123
	Central Provinces States.	**9,137**	**4,712**	**4,425**	**7,882**	**3,887**	**3,995**	**463**	**229**	**234**	**11**	**6**	**5**
23	Makrai ..	2,782	1,508	1,274	..	..	..	..	..	..	..	..	..
24	Bastar ..	..	..	..	..	..	..	451	220	231	..	..	..
25	Kanker ..	..	..	..	..	..	..	..	..	..	..	..	..
26	Nandgaon ..	..	..	..	..	..	..	..	..	..	..	..	..
27	Khairagarh ..	..	..	..	..	..	..	..	..	..	..	..	..
28	Chhuikhadan ..	..	..	..	..	..	..	..	..	..	..	..	..
29	Kawardha ..	..	..	..	..	..	..	..	..	..	..	..	..
30	Sakti ..	..	..	..	52	32	20	..	..	..	..	..	..
31	Raigarh ..	..	..	..	2,792	1,353	1,439	..	..	..	..	..	..
32	Sarangarh ..	..	..	..	496	279	217	..	..	..	..	..	..
33	Changbhakar ..	..	..	..	..	..	..	..	..	..	..	..	..
34	Korea ..	..	..	..	..	..	..	1	1	..	..	..	..
35	Surguja ..	*6,355	3,204	3,151	..	..	..	8	5	3	..	..	..
36	Udaipur ..	..	..	..	504	256	248	..	..	..	..	..	..
37	Jashpur ..	..	..	..	4,038	1,967	2,071	3	3	..	11	6	5

* This is almost certainly a sub-dialect of Korwa. Crooke held Korwas and Korkus to be branches of the same tribe, but, although both languages belong to the Munda branch, Grierson has stated that the two tribes and languages are now distinct. See Part I of the Report

...classed languages.			B.—Vernaculars of Asiatic Countries beyond India.			C.—European languages.						
Others.			All families.			English.			Other European languages.			
Persons.	Males.	Females.	Persons.	Males.	Females.	Persons.	Males.	Females.	Persons.	Males.	Females.	Serial number.
122	123	124	125	126	127	128	129	130	131	132	133	
8	**4**	**4**	**1,173**	**757**	**416**	**11,529**	**7,177**	**4,352**	**485**	**250**	**235**	
7	**3**	**4**	**1,156**	**749**	**407**	**11,141**	**6,972**	**4,169**	**474**	**240**	**234**	
3	**3**	..	**761**	**523**	**238**	**10,499**	**6,649**	**3,850**	**407**	**212**	**195**	
..	..	..	*53*	*36*	*17*	*5,078*	*3,340*	*1,738*	*10*	*4*	*6*	
..	..	..	2	..	2	644	318	326	..	..	..	1
..	..	..	1	1	..	41	17	24	..	..	..	2
..	..	..	41	30	11	4,291	2,958	1,333	..	..	..	3
..	..	..	9	5	4	83	39	44	10	4	6	4
..	..	..	..	..	..	19	8	11	..	..	..	5
..	..	..	*60*	*48*	*12*	*843*	*497*	*346*	*100*	*53*	*47*	
..	..	..	1	1	..	17	12	5	..	..	..	6
..	..	..	11	3	8	516	308	208	44	25	19	7
..	..	..	21	18	3	101	56	45	17	13	4	8
..	..	..	8	7	1	111	57	54	18	9	9	9
..	..	..	19	19	..	98	64	34	21	6	15	10
..	..	..	*486*	*342*	*144*	*3,548*	*2,267*	*1,281*	*254*	*127*	*127*	
..	..	..	7	5	2	33	16	17	3	3	..	11
..	..	..	373	274	99	3,316	2,141	1,175	249	122	127	12
..	..	..	72	39	33	74	43	31	2	2	..	13
..	..	..	32	22	10	63	36	27	..	..	..	14
..	..	..	2	2	..	62	31	31	..	..	..	15
3	*3*	..	*162*	*97*	*65*	*1,030*	*545*	*485*	*13*	*28*	*15*	
..	..	..	59	38	21	[illegible]	119	103	35	22	13	16
3	3	..	90	51	39	765	404	361	8	6	2	17
..	..	..	13	8	5	43	22	21	..	..	..	18
4	..	**4**	**395**	**226**	**169**	**642**	**323**	**319**	**67**	**28**	**39**	
..	..	..	42	24	18	416	203	213	59	20	39	19
4	..	4	90	46	44	125	66	59	3	3	..	20
..	..	..	177	96	81	44	24	20	3	3	..	21
..	..	..	86	60	26	57	30	27	2	2	..	22
1	**1**	..	**17**	**8**	**9**	**388**	**205**	**183**	**11**	**10**	**1**	
..	..	..	..	..	..	..	..	..	..	..	..	23
..	..	..	..	..	..	36	19	17	..	..	..	24
..	..	..	..	..	..	..	..	..	..	..	..	25
..	..	..	6	3	3	25	16	9	..	..	..	26
..	..	..	2	1	1	319	166	153	2	1	1	27
..	..	..	..	..	..	..	..	..	..	..	..	28
..	..	..	..	..	..	..	..	..	..	..	..	29
..	..	..	3	1	2	..	..	..	..	..	..	30
..	..	..	..	..	..	..	..	..	..	..	..	31
..	..	..	..	..	..	..	..	..	..	..	..	32
..	..	..	..	..	..	..	..	..	..	..	..	33
..	..	..	..	..	..	6	4	2	..	..	..	34
..	..	..	6	3	3	2	..	2	..	..	..	35
..	..	..	..	..	..	..	..	..	..	..	..	36
1	1	..	..	..	..	..	..	..	9	9	..	37

APPENDIX TO TABLE XV, PART I

Details of languages and dialects not separately shown in the table.

Languages.	Males.	Females.	Persons.	Locality.
1	2	3	4	5
LANGUAGES OF INDO-EUROPEAN FAMILY AND ARYAN SUB-FAMILY INCLUDED IN COLUMN 65				
1 Pashto (including Afgani, Kabuli and Rohilli).	1,868	345	2,213	Saugor (124), Damoh (24), Jubbulpore (329), Mandia (40), Seoni (65), Narsinghpur (12), Hoshangabad (83), Nimar (71), Betul (13), Chhindwara (408), Wardha (15), Nagpur (232), Chanda (27), Bhandara (38), Balaghat (31), Raipur (60), Bilaspur (66), Drug (38), Amraoti (69), Akola (123), Buldana (94), Yeotmal (202), Bastar (3), Kanker (1), Nandgaon (9), Korea (14), Surguja (22).
2 Balochi (including)— ..	67	32	99	Jubbulpore (2), Narsinghpur (5), Nimar (60), Amraoti (4), Akola (27), Yeotmal (1).
Makrani.	4	1	5	Narsinghpur (5)
3 Kashmiri ..	..	4	4	Amraoti (1), Buldana (3).
4 Sanskrit ..	5	..	5	Jubbulpore (2), Mandla (1), Akola (1), Buldana (1).
5 Lahnda or Western Punjabi (including Peshawari, Multani and Kohati).	173	155	328	Damoh (1), Jubbulpore (1), Nimar (280), Chhindwara (1), Nagpur (39), Amraoti (6).
6 Sindhi including— ..	1,491	430	1,921	Saugor (10), Jubbulpore (38), Mandla (8), Seoni (4), Narsinghpur (7), Hoshangabad (89), Nimar (88), Betul (37), Chhindwara (10), Wardha (53), Nagpur (530), Chanda (59), Bhandara (137), Balaghat (5), Raipur (15), Bilaspur (49), Drug (9), Amraoti (73), Akola (262), Buldana, (85) Yeotmal (352), Korea (1).
(a) Balai ..	1	..	1	Hoshangabad (1).
(b) Kachhi ..	1,400	390	1,790	Saugor (10), Jubbulpore (26), Mandla (8), Seoni (4), Narsinghpur (7), Hoshangabad (88), Nimar (84), Betul (37), Chhindwara (9), Wardha (53), Nagpur (481), Chanda (38), Bhandara (137), Balaghat (5), Bilaspur (36), Drug (8), Amraoti (73), Akola (261), Buldana (85), Yeotmal (339), Korea (1).
7 Konkani including— ..	276	206	482	Jubbulpore (10), Mandla (3), Hoshangabad (58), Nimar (11), Betul (18), Chhindwara, (9) Wardha (12), Nagpur (287), Chanda (2), Bhandara (1), Raipur (5), Amraoti (48), Akola (6), Buldana (3), Yeotmal (9).
Goanese ..	154	91	245	Mandla (3), Hoshangabad (35), Nimar (6), Betul (18), Wardha (6), Nagpur (138), Chanda (2), Bhandara (1), Raipur (4), Amraoti (20), Akola (1), Buldana (3), Yeotmal (8).
8 Khandesi (including Aherani)	25	13	38	Nimar (13), Wardha (19), Amraoti (6).
9 Eastern Pahari (Naipali or Gorkhiya).	400	235	635	Saugor (122), Damoh (2 [illegible] ngabad (68), Nimar (3), Chhindwar [illegible] Raipur (37), Bilaspur (11), Drug ([illegible] (5), Nandgaon (5), Khairagarh [illegible] urguja (54), Udaipur (9), Jashpur (35).
10 Central Pahar (Dosandhi) including—	129	127	256	Saugor (2), Jubbulpore (1), Hoshangabad (18), Nimar (22), Chhindwara (41), Wardha (128), Nagpur (27), Raipur (3), Bilaspur (6), Amraoti (8).
Garhwali ..	128	127	255	Saugor (2), Jubbulpore (1), Hoshangabad (18), Nimar (22), Chhindwara (41), Wardha (128), Nagpur (27), Raipur (3), Bilaspur (6), Amraoti (7).
11 Pahari (Unspecified) ..	40	14	54	Jubbulpore (1), Nimar (41), Betul (1), Akola (10), Buldana (1).
DIALECTS OF WESTERN HINDI INCLUDED IN COLUMN 5				
1 Bundeli (Bundelkhandi) including— ..	1,518	1,493	3,011	Saugor (1), Jubbulpore (1), Hoshangabad (2), Nimar (339), Chhindwara (15), Wardha (247), Nagpur (800), Chanda (52), Bhandara (8), Raipur (6), Bilaspur (1), Amraoti (569), Buldana (708), Yeotmal (172), Akola (90).
(a) Kirari ..	81	98	179	Nagpur (85), Amraoti (94).
(b) Raghubans ..	5	2	7	Nagpur (7).
(c) Lodhi ..	557	566	1,123	Wardha (247), Nagpur (650), Bhandara (8), Amraoti (54), Yeotmal (164).
(d) Gawlainee (Goulani) ..	150	208	358	Amraoti (358).
(e) Dhamdi ..	26	26	52	Chanda (52).
2 Brajbhasha ..	228	242	470	Nimar (6), Chanda (22), Akola (81), Yeotmal (361).
3 Kanauji ..	62	65	127	Chanda (127).

APPENDIX TO TABLE XV, PART I

Details of languages and dialects not separately shown in the table—*contd.*

Languages.	Males.	Females.	Persons	Locality.
1	2	3	4	5
DIALECTS OF WESTERN HINDI INCLUDED IN COLUMN 5—*concld.*				
4 Deshwali or Hariani (Bangaru) ..	3	..	3	Hoshangabad (3).
5 Jatu ..	13	3	16	Nimar (16).
6 Pardeshi ..	283	259	542	Wardha (47), Amraoti (160), Akola (65), Buldana (23), Yeotmal (247).
FORMS OF WESTERN HINDI INCLUDED IN COLUMN 5				
1 Purbhai ..	8	8	16	Amraoti (16).
2 Chhatrapuri ..	2	2	4	Amraoti (4).
3 Kalari ..	23	13	36	Wardha (23), Amraoti (12), Yeotmal (1).
4 Chhatri ..	7	14	21	Wardha (17), Chanda (4).
5 Bhat ..	17	61	78	Yeotmal (78).
OTHER LANGUAGE NAMES RETURNED, WHICH HAVE BEEN CLASSED AS WESTERN HINDI AND INCLUDED IN COLUMN 5				
1 Bhangi ..	..	4	4	Akola (4)
2 Gosavi ..	2	2	4	Akola (4).
3 Bijnori ..	1	..	1	Raipur (1).
4 Dhalia ..	4	7	11	Bilaspur (11)
5 Gareli ..	1	..	1	Seoni (1).
DIALECTS OF RAJASTHANI INCLUDED IN COLUMN 11				
1 Malvi (Bhopali and Bharni) includes—	7,229	7,206	14,435	Saugor (1), Hoshangabad (3), Nimar (239), Wardha (14,085), Nagpur (56), Chanda (14), Amraoti (28), Akola (7), Buldana (2).
(*a*) Patvi (Patwekari) ..	42	43	85	Nagpur (49), Chanda (14), Amraoti (22).
(*b*) Bhoyari ..	7,046	7,039	14,085	Wardha (14,085).
2 Central Eastern Dialect (Sipari)	4	2	6	Chanda (6).
3 Gujar ..	12	11	23	Amraoti (7), Akola (16).
FORMS OF RAJASTHANI INCLUDED IN COLUMN 11				
1 Rajhadi ..	552	538	1,090	Amraoti (1,090).
2 Jata ..	2	..	2	Drug (2)
SUB-DIALECT OF MARWARI INCLUDED IN COLUMN 14				
1 Bagri ...	7	..	7	Mandla (7).
FORMS OF MARWARI INCLUDED IN COLUMN 14				
1 Maheswari ..	14	8	22	Chhindwara (2), Bhandara (7), Akola (13).
2 Mewadi ..	68	10	78	Nimar (15), Nagpur (12), Chanda (1), Amraoti (2), Akola (43), Yeotmal (5)
FORMS OF NIMADI INCLUDED IN COLUMN 17				
1 Balahi ..	42	..	42	Amraoti (42).
DIALECTS OF GUJARATI INCLUDED IN COLUMN 23				
1 Kathiawari ..	154	93	247	Jubbulpore (2), Wardha (16), Nagpur (1), Chanda (2), Bhandara (6), Raipur (5), Amraoti (47), Akola (87), Buldana (1), Yeotmal (80).
2 Parsi ..	171	141	312	Jubbulpore (4), Nimar (37), Chhindwara (5), Wardha (3), Nagpur (47), Balaghat (3), Amraoti (25), Akola (25), Buldana (7), Yeotmal (3), Nandgaon (3), Surguja (150).
3 Memani ..	51	49	100	Jubbulpore (4), Hoshangabad (38), Nagpur (6), Yeotmal (48), Nandgaon (4).
4 Nagari ..	5	..	5	Hoshangabad (4), Akola (1).
5 Ghisadi ..	93	69	162	Amraoti (2), Akola (48), Buldana (44), Yeotmal (68).

APPENDIX TO TABLE XV, PART I

Details of language and dialects not separately shown in the table—*contd.*

Languages.	Males.	Females.	Persons.	Locality.
1	2	3	4	5
FORMS OF GUJARATI INCLUDED IN COLUMN 23				
1 Jaini ..	3	1	4	Buldana (4).
DIALECTS OF BHILI INCLUDED IN COLUMN 26				
1 Panchali ..	62	64	126	Amraoti (4), Akola (49), Buldana (41), Yeotmal (32).
2 Moghia (Baori) ..	17	19	36	Nimar (36).
3 Kotali ..	14	17	31	Nimar (31).
FORMS OF BHILI INCLUDED IN COLUMN 26				
1 Mankari ..	359	335	694	Amraoti (694).
FORMS OF PARDHI INCLUDED IN COLUMN 29				
1 Bahelia ..	3	3	6	Raipur (6)
2 Takankari ..	112	110	222	Amraoti (222).
3 Takari ..	262	266	528	Amraoti (161), Akola (293), Buldana (74).
4 Kachpardhi ..	26	19	45	Buldana (45).
DIALECTS OF PUNJABI INCLUDED IN COLUMN 32				
1 Dogra ..	8	..	8	Buldana (8)
2 Rathauri ..	13	17	30	Balaghat (30).
FORM OF BENGALI INCLUDED IN COLUMN 35				
1 Triholi ..	..	1	1	Nimar (1).
DIALECTS OF BIHARI INCLUDED IN COLUMN 38				
1 Maithili ..	12	13	25	Hoshangabad (1), Raipur (23), Raigarh (1).
2 Kurmari (Magahi) ..	98	27	125	Chanda (125).
FORMS OF ORIYA INCLUDED IN COLUMN 41				
1 Vadyani (Vadi) ..	18	127	145	Yeotmal (142), Jashpur (3).
2 Goria ..	5	3	8	Raipur (8).
3 Turiya, Turi (Tiwar, Tirra, Tirhora).	534	640	1,174	Raipur (66), Bilaspur (41), Raigarh (1), Sarangarh (206), Surguja (27), Jashpur (833).
4 Handoli ..	2	3	5	Raipur (5).
DIALECTS OF EASTERN HINDI INCLUDED IN COLUMN 47				
1 Broken dialects of the South including—				
(a) Ojhi ..	176	177	353	Hoshangabad (134), Chhindwara (59), Wardha (107), Bhandara (39), Balaghat (8), Yeotmal (6).
2 Awadhi (Purbi) or Kosali including— ..	1,062	1,151	2,213	Damoh (1), Hoshangabad (9), Nimar (31), Wardha (79), Nagpur (24), Chanda (1,544), Bhandara (200), Amraoti (82), Akola (100), Buldana (143).
(a) Pardeshi ..	28	22	50	Nagpur (24), Chanda (23), Bhandara (3).
(b) Nunia	166	159	325	Amraoti (82), Akola (100), Buldana (143).
3 Powari ..	2,045	2,182	4,227	Seoni (6), Wardha (80), Nagpur (143), Bhandara (3,916), Balaghat (1), Amraoti (27), Akola (30), Yeotmal (24).
BROKEN DIALECTS OF CHHATTISGARHI INCLUDED IN COLUMN 50				
1 Baigani ..	1,811	1,830	3,641	Mandla (7), Balaghat (3,634).
2 Sadari ..	85	98	183	Raipur (183).
3 Binjhwari ..	1,126	1,213	2,339	Raipur (1,838), Surguja (501).
4 Pando ..	240	262	502	Udaipur (502)
5 Bhuihari ..	3	25	28	Korea (28).
6 Bholoo ..	1	1	2	Drug (2).

APPENDIX TO TABLE XV, PART I

Details of languages and dialects not separately shown in the table—*contd.*

Languages.	Males.	Females.	Persons.	Locality.
1	2	3	4	5
FORM OF CHHATTISGARHI				
1 Dangcharha ..	39	48	87	Raipur (17), Bilaspur (70).
OTHER LANGUAGE RETURNS CLASSED AS CHHATTISGARHI AND INCLUDED IN COLUMN 50				
1 Chamari ..	2	3	5	Bhandara (5).
DIALECTS OF MARATHI INCLUDED IN COLUMN 53				
1 Poonekari or Deshi ..	2	..	2	Nagpur (2).
2 Parbhani ..	81	57	138	Wardha (1), Yeotmal (137).
3 Ghatoli ..	1	..	1	Akola (1)
4 Dakhani ..	63	60	123	Saugor (5), Nimar (16), Wardha (4), Chanda (15), Akola (7), Yeotmal (76).
FORMS OF MARATHI INCLUDED IN COLUMN 53				
1 Dohori ..	1,637	1,587	3,224	Nagpur (2,707), Akola (353), Buldana (164).
FORMS OF HALBI INCLUDED IN COLUMN 56				
1 Chandori ..	63	55	118	Bastar (118).
2 Muria ..	1,580	1,356	2,936	Chanda (8), Raipur (3), Amraoti (250), Bastar (2,675).
3 Adkuri ..	81	44	125	Bastar (125).
4 Bastari ..	133	136	269	Chanda (177). Drug (92)
5 Mirgani ..	142	163	305	Bastar (305).
SUB-DIALECTS OF KOSHTI SHOWN IN COLUMN 59				
1 Rangari	1	..	1	Jubbulpore (1).
CENTRAL PROVINCES AND BERAR DIALECTS OF MARATHI INCLUDED IN COLUMN 62				
1 Berari ..	60	61	121	Nimar (60), Bastar (44), Kanker (17).
2 Dhangari ..	11	8	19	Amraoti (19).
3 Zadpi or Dzadpi ..	23	28	51	Wardha (1), Amraoti (2), Akola (20), Yeotmal (28).
4 Govari ..	183	291	474	Chanda (434), Bhandara (5), Balaghat (1), Akola (19), Yeotmal (15).
5 Mahari ..	12	7	19	Chanda (10), Raipur (9).
6 Katia ..	1,338	1,340	2,678	Hoshangabad (462), Chhindwara (2,204), Nagpur (12).
7 Kamari ..	3,521	3,658	7,179	Raipur (7,179).
8 Kohli (Kunbau) ..	3	..	3	Balaghat (3).
BROKEN CENTRAL PROVINCES AND BERAR DIALECTS OF MARATHI INCLUDED IN COLUMN 62				
1 Bhunjia ..	1,121	1,055	2,176	Raipur (2,137), Surguja (39).
2 Nahari ..	19	15	34	Jubbulpore (1), Raipur (7), Kanker (26).
MIXED DIALECT OF MARATHI INCLUDED IN COLUMN 53				
1 Burdi ..	24	20	44	Chanda (44).
DIALECT OF MIXED MARATHI AND BAGHELI INCLUDED IN COLUMN 62				
1 Kewati or Dhiorboli ..	1,984	2,458	4,442	Chanda (4,442).
OTHER LANGUAGE NAMES WHICH HAVE BEEN CLASSED AS MARATHI AND INCLUDED IN COLUMN 62				
1 Gondhali ..	2	1	3	Akola (1), Yeotmal (2).
2 Sarodi ..	3	4	7	Yeotmal (7).
3 Pardhani (other than Gondi Pardhani).	11	17	28	Yeotmal (28).
4 Andhi ..	32	28	60	Nagpur (5), Akola (41), Yeotmal (14).

APPENDIX TO TABLE XV, PART I

Details of languages and dialects not separately shown in the table—*contd.*

Languages.		Males.	Females.	Persons	Locality.
1		2	3	4	5
OTHER LANGUAGE NAMES WHICH HAVE BEEN CLASSED AS MARATHI AND INCLUDED IN COLUMN 62—*concld.*					
5 Chitarkathi	..	4	7	11	Akola (11).
6 Bawani	..	144	137	281	Chanda (38), Amraoti (243).
7 Dhidasi	..	3	1	4	Akola (4)
8 Marari	..	263	287	550	Wardha (512), Chanda (9), Bhandara (3), Amraoti (13), Yeotmal (13).
9 Hatkari	..	7	14	21	Yeotmal (21)
10 Ramdasi	..	20	31	51	Yeotmal (51)
11 Gurao	..	2	1	3	Buldana (3)
12 Lohari	..	9	..	9	Buldana (9)
13 Otkari	..	9	3	12	Akola (7), Yeotmal (5).
DIALECTS OF GONDI INCLUDED IN COLUMN 68					
1 Gotte (Gaita, Gayeti)	..	1,174	1,326	2,500	Raipur (13), Bastar (2,487).
FORMS OF GONDI INCLUDED IN COLUMN 68					
1 Pardhani	..	46	102	148	Wardha (8), Chanda (1), Yeotmal (139).
2 Pathri	..	60	68	128	Bastar (128).
DIALECT OF KURUKH OR ORAON INCLUDED IN COLUMN 80					
1 Mirdahi	..	418	400	818	Raipur (212), Raigarh (606).
DIALECTS OF TELUGU INCLUDED IN COLUMN 86					
1 Vadari	..	153	161	314	Nimar (7), Wardha (9), Chanda (23), Amraoti (23), Akola (68), Buldana (17), Yeotmal (167).
2 Komti	..	5	4	9	Buldana (9)
FORMS OF TELUGU INCLUDED IN COLUMN 86					
1 Kapewari	..	12	..	12	Chanda (12).
2 Madgi	..	2	1	3	Chanda (3)
Cuttacki	..	2	3	5	Raipur (1), Bastar (4).
4 Andhra	..	3	9	12	Hoshangabad (2), Nimar (4), Betul (6).
DIALECTS OF TAMIL INCLUDED IN COLUMN 95					
1 Yerukul	..	9	9	18	Chanda (6), Bastar (12)
2 Buragandi	..	73	95	168	Nimar (168).
OTHER LANGUAGES OF THE DRAVIDIAN FAMILY INCLUDED IN COLUMN 101					
* 1 Malayalam or	..	182	101	283	Damoh (2), Jubbulpore (21), Mandla (1), Seoni (1), Hoshangabad (7), Chhindwara (37), Wardha (2), Nagpur (55), Chanda (127), Amraoti (8), Akola (8), Buldana (10), Yeotmal (4).
Malabari	..	38	14	52	Jubbulpore (26), Hoshangabad (3), Betul (1), Nagpur (17), Bhandara (2), Raipur (1), Amraoti (1), Akola (1).
2 Coorgi	..	6	4	10	Nagpur (2), Bastar (8).
3 Bharia	..	1,896	1,989	3,885	Chhindwara (3,885).
DIALECTS OF KHERWARI INCLUDED IN COLUMN 104					
1 Koda	.	537	570	1,107	Nagpur (68), Raipur (1,039).
2 Santali	..	2	4	6	Damoh (4), Nimar (1), Amraoti (1).
3 Kol (Koli or Kolah)		93	87	180	Raipur (13), Changbhakar (143), Raigarh (24).
4 Birhor and Birhole	..	119	121	240	Surguja (44), Udaipur (137), Jashpur (59).
5 Munda	..	271	299	570	Raipur (118), Bilaspur (5), Sakti (21), Sarangarh (206), Jashpur (220).
6 Mundhari	.	9	10	19	Jashpur (19).

* The number of persons speaking these languages comes to 4,230 which differs from the total figure given in column 101 on page 345 of this Table by 5. This difference is due to the fact that five persons in Raigarh State returned their mother-tongue as "Dravidian". These figures have been included in the total shown in the Table but could not be classified and shown here.

APPENDIX TO TABLE XV, PART I

Details of languages and dialects not separately shown in the table—*contd.*

Language.	Males.	Females.	Persons.	Locality.
1	2	3	4	5
FORMS OF KHERWARI INCLUDED IN COLUMN 104				
1 Mahto ..	10	6	16	Bilaspur (16).
FORMS OF KORWA INCLUDED IN COLUMN 107				
1 Biyadha ..	11	10	21	Udaipur (14), Jashpur (7).
FORMS OF KORKU INCLUDED IN COLUMN 110				
1 Muwasi ..	7,870	7,781	15,651	Chhindwara (15,651).
2 Nihali ..	579	617	1,196	Nimar (407), Amraoti (174), Buldana (615).
LANGUAGES AND DIALECTS OF THE MUNDA BRANCH INCLUDED IN COLUMN 116				
1 Gadaba ..	221	231	452	Bastar (451), Korea (1).
2 Chick ..	5	3	8	Surguja (8)
3 Nagasia ..	3	..	3	Jashpur (3)
GIPSY LANGUAGES INCLUDED IN COLUMN 119				
1 Beldari ..	1,203	1,272	2,475	Nimar (70), Wardha (336), Amraoti (604), Akola (760), Buldana (446), Yeotmal (259).
2 Bhamti ..	4	14	18	Wardha (10), Akola (8).
3 Kolhati ..	12	24	36	Chanda (10), Amraoti (14), Akola (10), Buldana (1), Yeotmal (1).
4 Lad ..	6	5	11	Buldana (11).
5 Ladsee ..	698	703	1,401	Wardha (644), Amraoti (757)
6 Gopali ..	2	1	3	Yeotmal (3).
7 Tirguli ..	28	30	58	Amraoti (4), Akola (31), Buldana (23).
8 Arbani ..	7	6	13	Saugor (1), Jubbulpore (3), Hoshangabad (5), Balaghat (4).
9 Chitodi* ..	14	17	31	Nimar (31).
10 Domra ..	6	5	11	Jashpur (11).
11 Khadi ..	2	..	2	Akola (2).

* Shown as Gipsy language in 1921 Report. Language of same name appears in survey as mixture of Gujrati and Marathi.

Language.	Males.	Females.	Persons.	Locality.
OTHER LANGUAGE RETURNS INCLUDED IN COLUMN 122				
1 Nadir ..	3	..	3	Bilaspur (3).
2 Michal ..	1	..	1	Jashpur (1).
3 Patharkari ..	..	4	4	Akola (4).
OTHER VERNACULARS OF ASIA INCLUDED IN COLUMN 125				
1 Arabic ..	337	110	447	Saugor (2), Damoh (1), Jubbulpore (9), Mandla (9), Narsinghpore (1), Hoshangabad (3), Nimar (5), Betul (7), Chhindwara (2), Wardha (6), Nagpur (317), Chanda (1), Bhandara (3), Balaghat (2), Raipur (4), Bilaspur (12), Drug (1), Amraoti (21), Akola (13), Buldana (18), Yeotmal (3), Nandgaon (1), Khairagarh (1), Surguja (5).
2 Japanese ..	7	1	8	Nimar (2), Wardha (1), Amraoti (3), Akola (2)
3 Chinese ..	17	10	27	Jubbulpore (18), Hoshangabad (1), Nagpur (5), Sakti (3).
4 Mongolian ..	4	5	9	Hoshangabad (4), Nagpur (5).
5 Persian (including Irani) ..	387	283	670	Jubbulpore (10), Nimar (11), Betul (1), Chhindwara (17), Nagpur (45), Chanda (70), Bhandara (29), Raipur (55), Bilaspur (78), Drug (12), Amraoti (18), Akola (75), Buldana (159), Yeotmal (83), Nandgaon (5), Khairagarh (1), Surguja (1).
6 Singhalese ..	3	4	7	Jubbulpore (4), Hoshangabad (3).
7 Turkish ..	2	2	4	Nimar (3), Chanda (1).
8 Hebrew ..	..	1	1	Nagpur (1).

APPENDIX TO TABLE XV PART I

Details of languages and dialects not separately shown in the table—*concld.*

Language.	Males.	Females.	Persons.	Locality.
1	2	3	4	5
				OTHER NON-ASIATIC LANGUAGES INCLUDED IN COLUMN 131
1 French ..	31	74	105	Mandla (6), Hoshangabad (4), Nimar (6), Chhindwara (4), Nagpur (47), Bilaspur (3), Amraoti (26), Yeotmal (1), Khairagarh (2), Jashpur (6).
2 Portuguese ..	180	128	308	Mandla (4), Hoshangabad (36), Nimar (6), Betul (5), Chhindwara (5), Wardha (3), Nagpur (189), Chanda (2), Raipur (23), Bilaspur (1), Amraoti (29), Akola (3), Buldana (1), Yeotmal (1).
3 German ..	24	12	36	Hoshangabad (4), Nimar (5), Nagpur (7), Raipur (12), Bilaspur (4), Amraoti (3), Buldana (1).
4 Greek ..	3	2	5	Nagpur (3), Amraoti (1), Buldana (1).
5 Italian ..	1	1	2	Nagpur (2).
6 Swedish ..	8	16	24	Betul (11), Chhindwara (12), Nagpur (1).
7 Finnish ..	..	1	1	Betul (1).
8 Flemish ..	3	..	3	Jashpur (3).
9 Dutch ..	..	1	1	Betul (1).

TABLE XV—PART II

Bi-lingualism

This part of Table XV appears for the first time at the 1931 Census. It shows figures of those who daily or very commonly use some language other than their mother-tongue. Details have been given only for the following ten important vernaculars of the province:—

(1) Hindustani.
(2) Marathi.
(3) Bhili.
(4) Oriya.
(5) Gondi.
(6) Telugu.
(7) Kurukh or Oraon.
(8) Kherwari.
(9) Korku.
(10) Kharia.

Figures of Western and Eastern Hindi and Rajasthani have been amalgamated to economise space, as these three languages are closely allied. They appear together under the heading "Hindustani".

2. Gujarati is an important mother-tongue only in Akola and Nimar districts of this Province. Figures of bi-lingualism in respect of this language are considerable in the areas noted below :—

Area of bi-lingualism.	Number speaking mother-tongue Gujarati.	Percentage on population.	Number speaking — Subsidiary languages. Hindustani.	Percentage.	Marathi.	Percentage.
Akola, Akot, Balapur and Murtizapur taluqs.	8,987	1.5	691	7.6	4,330	48.2
Burhanpur tahsil ..	7,873	5.4	1,904	24·2	158	2
Khandwa tahsil ..	2,609	1.1	1,831	70.2	..	..

3. Statistics have been shown against areas of bi-lingualism. In some cases it has been possible to amalgamate homogeneous districts or tracts. In others separate figures have been given for tahsils and zamindaris. The details of the table are illustrated in the linguistic map published with Part I of the Report.

4. There were no special instructions issued for recording cases of tri-lingualism or poly-lingualism at the census. The numbers of those who did return two subsidiary languages are given below :—

Locality.	Persons.	Males.	Females.
Jubbulpore Division	230	197	33
Nerbudda Division	188	156	32
Nagpur Division	689	523	166
Chhattisgarh Division	5	5	..
Berar	209	184	25
C. P. States	..	..	..

More than two subsidiary languages were returned by 9 men and 1 woman only in the Jubbulpore District. Detailed figures have been preserved in a manuscript register.

5. Against serial No. 47 figures for the Chandrapur-Padampur estate have been shown. The people of the Padampur tract of the estate are nearly all Oriya speaking but separate figures for other languages were not available for this tract. Comparative figures for the principal languages are given below :—

	1 Padampur.	2 Chandrapur.
Hindustani	.. 2,623	62,660
Oriya	.. 20,962	884

TABLE XV—PART II

Bi-lingualism

Serial No.	Area of Bi-lingualism. District or State.	Area of Bi-lingualism. Tahsil or Zamindari.	Mother-tongue— Number of persons speaking mother-tongue. Males.	Number of persons speaking mother-tongue. Females.	Subsidiary Marathi. Males.	Subsidiary Marathi. Females.
	1	2	3	4	5	6
1	Saugor, Damoh, Jubbulpore and Narsinghpur.	..	974,667	946,884	233	114
2	Mandla ..	Mandla	54,389	55,086	5	4
3		Dindori	69,066	70,388	..	1
4		Niwas	46,264	45,869	4	3
5	Seoni ..	Seoni	85,452	81,424	124	82
6		Lakhnadon	55,893	58,394	2	1
7	Hoshangabad (excluding Sohagpur).		157,855	151,526	128	73
8	Hoshangabad ..	Sohagpur	68,114	65,845	7	3
9	Nimar ..	Khandwa	101,765	93,813	79	41
10		Burhanpur	25,576	22,225	562	367
11		Harsud	31,453	28,103	17	4
12	Betul ..	Betul	26,166	25,814	231	292
13		Multai	39,275	40,178	2,246	1,524
14		Bhainsdehi	10,200	9,849	224	256
15	Chhindwara ..	Chhindwara Khalsa	68,764	66,891	220	114
16		Chhindwara Zamindari	7,987	7,660	8	11
17		Amarwara Khalsa	44,956	46,787	17	23
18		Amarwara Zamindari	11,080	11,331	1	..
19		Sausar	19,572	18,564	8,975	7,368
20	Wardha ..	Wardha and Hinganghat	15,544	11,980	5,688	4,278
21		Arvi	16,540	15,008	10,637	9,423
22	Nagpur ..	Nagpur	51,129	39,613	11,459	6,552
23		Ramtek	9,860	9,510	5,566	5,496
24		Umrer	3,383	3,067	1,640	1,549
25		Katol and Saoner	17,231	16,002	10,569	9,639
26	Chanda ..	Warora	3,847	3,246	2,166	1,894
27		Brahmapuri	1,477	1,331	955	807
28		Chanda	4,349	3,337	1,657	1,475
29		Garchiroli Khalsa	1,725	1,600	1,263	1,227
30		Garchiroli Zamindari	3,243	2,863	542	521
31		Sironcha Khalsa	360	311	4	2
32		Ahiri Zamindari	765	731	110	41
33	Bhandara ..	Bhandara	14,483	15,363	6,569	7,448
34		Gondia	50,616	51,420	16,071	14,442
35		Sakoli Khalsa	3,811	2,416	1,569	925
36		Sakoli Zamindari	2,646	4,229	846	1,513
37	Balaghat ..	Balaghat	54,386	55,459	127	116
38		Baihar Khalsa	31,446	30,846	48	34
39		Baihar Zamindari	5,373	5,381	..	..
40		Waraseoni	69,326	71,938	2,625	2,239
41	Raipur (excluding 5 Zamindaris).		503,908	544,395	204	36
42		Deori and Kauria Zamindaris ..	20,360	21,107	..	..
43		Khariyar Zamindari	19,199	20,444	2	..
44		Phuljhar Zamindari	44,725	44,589	..	..
45		Bindra Nawagarh Zamindari ..	22,377	23,215	3	..
46	Bilaspur (excluding Chandrapur-Padampur estate.)		634,762	665,790	56	51
47		Chandrapur-Padampur Estate ..	31,297	32,986	..	..
48	Drug ..	Drug, Bemetara and Sanjari Khalsa ..	335,317	370,403	158	143
49		Sanjari Zamindari	38,808	40,222	8,143	5,206
50	Amraoti ..	Amraoti and Ellichpur	44,965	37,892	8,065	5,156
51		Chandur	10,610	9,465	5,210	4,060
52		Morsi	9,822	8,451	3,973	2,761
53		Daryapur	10,189	8,682	2,203	1,880
54		Melghat	4,719	4,221	135	30
55	Akola ..	Akola, Akot, Balapur and Murtizapur ..	56,595	46,804	12,112	6,365
56		Basim and Mangrulpir	23,091	20,644	10,497	7,676
57	Buldana ..	Chikhli	11,484	11,230	5,031	3,330
58		Jalgaon	6,558	6,015	2,753	2,035
59		Khamgaon and Malkapur	25,613	23,114	5,699	4,935
60		Mehkar	11,432	8,868	7,580	4,655
61	Yeotmal ..	Darwha and Pusad	47,834	42,538	27,456	24,203
62		Yeotmal	10,362	8,700	6,330	4,236
63		Kelapur	9,302	8,380	6,624	5,942
64		Wun	3,150	3,621	1,367	1,387
65	Central Provinces States ..	Makrai	5,769	5,805	..	..
66		Bastar	13,744	12,030	3,226	2,611
67		Kanker	40,589	44,151	33	67
68		Kawardha	34,970	37,588	..	..
69		Sakti	23,311	24,692	5	5
70		Raigarh	115,129	118,549	..	..
71		Sarangarh	48,597	52,865	..	1
72		Korea	46,287	43,761	1	..
73		Surguja	225,024	219,787	..	..
74		Udaipur	39,214	38,198	..	..
75		Jashpur	51,619	51,227	..	..
76		Changbhakar	3,166	3,350	..	..
77		Khairagarh, Nandgaon and Chhuikhadan ..	172,850	186,523	..	..

Bi-lingualism.

TABLE XV

Hindi and Rajasthani.

Languages.

Gondi.		Telugu.		Oriya.		Korku.		Kherwari.		Kurukh Oraon.		Serial No.
Males.	Females.	Males.	Females.	Males.	Females.	Males.	Females.	Males.	Females.	Males.	Females.	
7	8	9	10	11	12	13	14	15	16	17	18	
1,309	66	21	17	8	1	..	..	1	..	..	..	1
65	76	6	2	..	..	..	..	..	..	..	..	2
..	..	..	..	..	..	..	..	..	..	..	..	3
5	28	..	..	..	..	..	..	..	..	..	..	4
6,849	178	..	..	..	..	..	..	..	..	..	..	5
10	19	..	..	..	..	..	..	..	..	..	..	6
51	37	1	1	..	..	13	4	..	..	..	..	7
33	31	..	..	..	..	..	..	..	..	..	..	8
5	1	6	1	..	..	3	..	9	5	..	..	9
..	..	4	12	..	..	169	174	32	28	..		10
29	19	..	..	..	..	46	44	..	..	..	..	11
197	97	1	..	..	..	2	6	..	..	..	..	12
406	300	..	..	..	..	..	..	..	..	..	..	13
273	226	..	..	..	..	128	129	..	..	..	..	14
336	261	3	..	..	..	3	..	..	..	..	..	15
55	57	..	..	..	..	..	3	..	..	..	..	16
20	40	..	..	..	..	..	..	..	..	..	..	17
..	..	..	..	..	..	..	..	..	..	..	..	18
193	125	..	..	..	..	..	..	..	..	..	..	19
..	..	9	1	..	..	..	..	..	..	..	..	20
..	..	..	..	..	..	..	..	..	..	..	..	21
..	..	5	8	..	..	..	..	..	..	..	..	22
..	..	..	..	..	..	..	..	..	..	..	..	23
..	..	..	..	..	..	..	..	..	..	..	..	24
..	..	..	..	..	..	..	..	..	..	..	..	25
..	..	12	4	..	..	..		..	..	..	..	26
1	1	1	4	..	..	..	..	..	..	..	..	27
..	..	69	60	..	..	..	..	..		..	..	28
5	5	5	11	..	..	..	..	..	..	..	..	29
24	32	3	6	..	..	..	..	..	..	..	..	30
20	9	231	202	..	..	..	..	..	..	..	..	31
158	149	87	101	..	..	..	..	..	..	..	..	32
..	..	..	..	..	..	..	..	..	..	..	..	33
18	10	..	..	..	..	..	..	..	..	..	..	34
41	9	..	..	..	..	..	..	..	..	..	..	35
..	19	..	..	..	..	..	..	..	..	..	..	36
8	11	1	..	..	..	..	..	..	..	..	..	37
28	523	..	..	..	..		..	..	..	..	..	38
..	..	..	..	..	..	..	..	..	..	..	..	39
4	4	..	..	..	..	..	..	..	..	..	..	40
25	13	2	15	314	324	..	..	..	..	..	..	41
..	1	..	..	150	179	..	..	..		..	..	42
..	..	1	..	1,749	1,793	..	..	..	..	..	..	43
..	..	..	..	1,983	2,318	..	..	..	..	..	..	44
..	..	..	..	167	265	..	..	..	..	..	..	45
95	95	5	3	17	2	..	..	..	..	..	..	46
..	..	..	..	1,149	998	..	..	..	..	..	..	47
18	31	..	..	17	..	..	..	..	..	..	..	48
55	62	..	..	1	2	..	..	..	..	..	..	49
..	..	..	..	..	..	..	9	..	..	..	..	50
..	..	..	..	..	..	81	..	..	..	..	..	51
..	..	..	..	..	..	..	..	..	..	..	..	52
..	..	..	..	..	..	..	..	..	..	..	..	53
..	1	..	..	..	..	65	85	..	..	..	..	54
..	..	10	160	..	..	..	..	..	..	..	..	55
..	..	2	..	..	..	..	..	..	..	..	..	56
..	..	4	..	..	..	..	..	..	..	..	..	57
..	..	..	..	..	..	..	..	..	..	..	..	58
..	..	3	..	..	..	..	..	..	..	..	..	59
..	..	..	..	..	..	..	..	..	..	..	..	60
..	..	27	4	..	..	..	..	..	..	..	..	61
..	..	..	..	..	..	..	..	..	..	..	..	62
55	3	125	163	..	..	..	..	..	..	..	..	63
..	..	96	78	..	..	..	..	..	..	..	..	64
..	..	..	..	..	..	..	..	..	..	..	..	65
911	625	296	242	115	102	..	..	..	..	..	..	66
938	1,137	..	..	..	..	..	..	..	..	..	..	67
..	..	..	..	..	..	..	..	..	..	..	..	68
..	..	..	..	..	..	..	..	..	..	..	..	69
..	..	..	..	164	90	..	..	..	..	..	..	70
..	..	..	..	197	105	..	..	..	..	..	..	71
..	..	..	..	..	..	..	..	..	..	42	41	72
..	..	..	..	..	..	..	..	..	..	4,578	8,464	73
..	..	..	..	218	150	..	..	..	..	..	..	74
..	..	..	..	..	..	..	..	..	..	2,847	2,232	75
..	..	..	..	..	..	..	..	..	..	..	..	76
..	..	..	..	..	..	..	..	11	14	..	..	77

TABLE XV **PART II.—**

Serial No.	Area of Bi-lingualism. District or State.	Tahsil or Zamindari.	Number of persons speaking mother-tongue. Males.	Females.	Mother-tongue—Subsidiary: Hindustani. Males.	Females.	Gondi. Males.	Females.
	1	2	19	20	21	22	23	24
1	Saugor Damoh, Jubbulpore and Narsinghpur.		3,219	2,536	2,408	1,818	..	..
2	Mandla ..	Mandla ..	304	311	272	274	..	..
3		Dindori ..	28	26	15	16	..	..
4		Niwas	6	1	6	1	..	..
5	Seoni ..	Seoni	8,843	9,536	7,112	7,788	17	..
6		Lakhnadon	42	39	41	38	..	..
7	Hoshangabad (excluding Sohagpur).		2,112	1,973	1,568	1,411	..	4
8	Hoshangabad ..	Sohagpur	178	126	165	104	..	..
9	Nimar ..	Khandwa	3,643	3,020	2,218	1,745	..	..
10		Burhanpur	31,919	30,850	5,377	1,794	..	..
11		Harsud	265	218	236	193	..	..
12	Betul ..	Betul	8,943	9,182	7,061	6,983	28	31
13		Multai	29,411	29,784	14,613	8,980	5	..
14		Bhainsdehi . ..	10,029	10,272	7,251	5,173	14	3
15	Chhindwara ..	Chhindwara Khalsa ..	10,105	9,737	7,452	5,415	1	..
16		Chhindwara Zamindari ..	449	394	358	312	..	..
17		Amarwara Khalsa ..	533	591	450	487	..	..
18		Amarwara Zamindari ..	7	..	..	..	..	..
19		Sausar	40,967	41,376	18,095	10,997	44	10
20	Wardha ..	Wardha and Hinganghat ..	140,345	140,479	1,394	487	..	1
21		Arvi	60,247	59,060	536	154	..	1
22	Nagpur ..	Nagpur	127,010	121,736	14,474	9,848	..	..
23		Ramtek	49,173	49,113	195	81	..	..
24		Umrer	70,155	71,667	249	127	..	..
25		Katol and Saoner ..	112,709	110,970	787	307	..	..
26	Chanda ..	Warora	80,409	79,432	36	5	..	..
27		Brahmapuri	70,468	71,412	24	5	..	..
28		Chanda	67,005	66,806	180	92	..	4
29		Garchiroli Khalsa ..	44,225	43,905	14	6	18	11
30		Garchiroli Zamindari ..	8,192	7,424	226	115	13	65
31		Sironcha Khalsa ..	1,431	1,457	49	17	..	..
32		Ahiri Zamindari ..	2,959	2,886	45	23	839	777
33	Bhandara ..	Bhandara	104,706	104,070	623	182	2	..
34		Gondia	95,108	102,989	12,152	15,041	14	..
35		Sakoli Khalsa	76,466	81,169	5,883	2,619	23	8
36		Sakoli Zamindari ..	23,989	21,643	48	47	..	5
37	Balaghat ..	Balaghat	32,129	33,275	9,630	7,876	7	13
38		Baihar Khalsa	2,947	2,753	2,773	2,602	..	..
39		Baihar Zamindari ..	237	190	180	153	..	..
40		Waraseoni	43,777	45,120	18,987	11,892	27	11
41	Raipur (excluding 5 Zamindaris).		3,291	3,329	2,896	2,769	..	..
42		Deori and Kauria Zamindaris ..	14	27	7	21	..	..
43		Khariar Zamindari ..	1,262	1,316	179	185	..	..
44		Phuljhar Zamindari ..	13	14	12	11	..	..
45		Bindra-Nawagarh Zamindari ..	2,540	2,574	1,766	1,705	..	..
46	Bilaspur (excluding Chandrapur-Padampur Estate.	..	2,052	2,062	1,665	1,470	..	..
47		Chandrapur-Padampur Estate ..	..	..	..	..	..	..
48	Drug ..	Drug, Bemetara and Sanjari Khalsa.	1,658	1,678	1,559	1,502	..	..
49		Sanjari Zamindari ..	2,946	2,996	2,713	2,824	..	..
50	Amraoti ..	Amraoti and Ellichpur ..	144,372	136,122	13,394	5,615	2	..
51		Chandur	91,916	88,699	99	26	4	5
52		Morsi	71,968	68,743	272	152	..	6
53		Daryapur ..	59,220	57,369	231	741	..	..
54		Melghat	1,625	1,494	727	687	7	..
55	Akola ..	Akola, Akot, Balapur and Murtizapur.	234,653	228,501	3,854	1,221	..	..
56		Basim and Mangrulpir ..	122,385	122,010	472	219	..	..
57	Buldana ..	Chikhli ..	71,683	70,713	2,200	542	..	..
58		Jalgaon ..	41,858	41,526	95	305	..	..
59		Khamgaon and Malkapur ..	140,521	135,881	6,819	13,558	..	..
60		Mehkar	71,413	73,503	120	55	..	..
61	Yeotmal .	Darwha and Pusad ..	141,832	142,047	386	156	10	17
62		Yeotmal . ..	58,421	56,991	3,775	69	..	..
63		Kelapur	47,756	46,977	172	169	20	18
64		Wun	50,181	51,895	65	87	..	..
65	Central Provinces States ..	Makrai	35	26	34	25	..	..
66		Bastar	88,892	86,571	4,393	3,399	11,310	9,381
67		Kanker	579	437	417	373	..	..
68		Kawardha ..	79	91	79	88	..	..
69		Sakti	73	57	73	57	..	..
70		Raigarh	161	165	148	151	..	..
71		Sarangarh	16	8	16	8	..	..
72		Korea	6	2	6	2	..	..
73		Surguja	34	12	34	12	..	..
74		Udaipur	5	6	4	5	..	..
75		Jashpur ..	5	1	1	..	..	..
76		Changbhakar	..	..	..	..	..	..
77		Khairagarh, Nandgaon and Chhuikhadan.	3,845	4,173	3,779	4,107	..	..

Marathi. Languages.						Mother-tongue—Bhili.						
Oriya.		Telugu.		Korku.		Number of persons speaking mother-tongue.		Subsidiary Languages. Hindustani.		Marathi.		Serial No.
Males.	Females.	Males.	Females.	Males.	Females.	Males.	Females.	Males.	Females.	Males.	Females.	
25	26	27	28	29	30	31	32	33	34	35	36	
..	..	..	2	..	..	9	5	2	..	..	..	1
..	..	..	..	..	..	..	..	..	..	..	..	2
..	..	..	..	..	..	..	..	..	..	..	..	3
..	..	..	..	..	..	..	..	..	..	..	..	4
..	..	..	..	..	..	1	6	1	6	..	..	5
..	..	..	..	..	..	..	..	..	..	..	..	6
..	..	..	..	2	..	21	17	11	11	..	..	7
..	..	..	..	..	..	..	..	..	..	..	..	8
..	..	..	..	..	..	10,549	10,730	8,793	8,725	..	..	9
..	..	..	..	..	..	2,013	1,981	781	584	160	158	10
..	..	..	..	..	..	16	19	8	13	..	..	11
..	..	..	..	..	..	..	2	..	..	..	..	12
..	..	..	..	..	..	..	..	..	..	..	..	13
..	..	..	..	..	..	..	..	..	..	..	..	14
..	..	..	..	..	..	..	..	..	..	..	..	15
..	..	..	..	..	..	..	..	..	..	..	..	16
..	..	..	..	..	..	..	..	..	..	..	..	17
..	..	..	..	..	..	..	..	..	..	..	..	18
..	..	..	..	..	..	..	..	..	..	..	..	19
..	..	..	..	..	..	126	115	..	..	92	83	20
..	..	..	..	..	..	27	25	..	..	21	20	21
..	..	..	..	..	..	35	52	13	..	9	21	22
..	..	..	..	..	..	..	..	..	..	..	..	23
..	..	..	..	..	..	..	..	..	..	..	..	24
..	..	..	..	..	..	19	12	..	..	19	12	25
..	..	4	10	..	..	68	54	..	..	46	54	26
..	..	17	23	..	..	..	..	..	..	..	..	27
..	..	143	116	..	..	12	9	..	..	9	7	28
..	..	73	23	..	..	..	..	..	..	..	..	29
..	..	2	1	..	..	..	..	..	..	..	..	30
..	..	1,104	1,158	..	..	..	..	..	..	..	..	31
..	..	738	689	..	..	..	..	..	..	..	..	32
..	..	..	1	..	..	1	..	1	..	..	..	33
..	..	..	..	..	..	..	..	..	..	..	..	34
..	..	..	..	..	..	..	..	..	..	..	..	35
..	..	..	..	..	..	..	..	..	..	..	..	36
..	..	..	..	..	..	..	..	..	..	..	..	37
..	..	..	..	..	..	..	..	..	..	..	..	38
..	..	..	..	..	..	..	..	..	..	..	..	39
..	..	..	..	..	..	..	..	..	..	..	..	40
..	..	..	..	..	..	43	40	43	39	..	..	41
..	..	..	..	..	..	..	..	..	..	..	..	42
431	483	..	..	..	..	15	12	13	10	..	..	43
..	..	..	..	..	..	..	..	..	..	..	..	44
56	72	..	..	..	..	..	..	..	..	..	..	45
..	..	..	..	..	..	66	34	66	33	..	..	46
..	..	..	..	..	..	..	..	..	..	..	..	47
..	..	..	..	..	..	11	6	11	6	..	..	48
..	..	..	..	..	..	..	..	..	..	..	..	49
..	..	12	18	..	..	783	730	123	40	477	519	50
..	..	..	..	..	..	168	172	..	..	103	138	51
..	..	..	..	..	..	70	68	..	..	49	39	52
..	..	..	..	..	..	5	5	..	..	..	3	53
..	..	..	..	2	20	..	..	..	..	..	..	54
..	..	..	..	..	..	269	310	..	..	230	240	55
..	..	..	..	..	..	86	86	1	1	49	61	56
..	..	1	..	..	..	272	243	8	11	224	197	57
..	..	8	..	..	..	25	33	13	20	7	..	58
..	..	..	..	..	..	227	227	4	6	197	189	59
..	..	..	..	..	..	5	..	..	..	2	..	60
..	..	37	36	..	..	203	184	..	..	168	156	61
..	..	..	5	..	..	169	124	..	..	166	119	62
..	..	275	270	..	..	49	31	..	..	47	31	63
..	..	35	15	..	..	20	17	..	..	20	17	64
..	..	..	..	..	..	..	..	..	..	..	..	65
4,214	4,092	1,148	1,345	..	..	..	..	..	..	..	..	66
..	..	..	..	..	..	..	..	..	..	..	..	67
..	..	..	..	..	..	..	..	..	..	..	..	68
..	..	..	..	..	..	..	..	..	..	..	..	69
..	..	..	..	..	..	..	..	..	..	..	..	70
..	..	..	..	..	..	..	..	..	..	..	..	71
..	..	..	..	..	..	..	..	..	..	..	..	72
..	..	..	..	..	..	..	..	..	..	..	..	73
..	..	..	..	..	..	..	..	..	..	..	..	74
..	..	..	..	..	..	..	..	..	..	..	..	75
..	..	..	..	..	..	..	..	..	..	..	..	76
..	..	..	..	..	..	14	10	14	10	..	..	77

Serial No.	Area of Bi-lingualism. District or State.	Area of Bi-lingualism. Tahsil or Zamindari.	Mother-tongue—Oriya. Number of persons speaking mother-tongue. Males.	Number of persons speaking mother-tongue. Females.	Subsidiary Languages. Hindustani. Males.	Hindustani. Females.	Marathi. Males.	Marathi. Females.	Gondi. Males.	Gondi. Females.	Telugu. Males.	Telugu. Females.	Kurukh or Oraon. Males.	Kurukh or Oraon. Females.
	1	2	37	38	39	40	41	42	43	44	45	46	47	48
1	Saugor, Damoh, Jubbulpore and Narsinghpur.	..	215	212	180	188	..	..	..	..	..	..	..	..
2	Mandla ..	Mandla ..	3	1	2	..	..	..	..	..	..	..	..	..
3		Dindori ..	35	..	14	..	..	..	..	..	..	..	..	..
4		Niwas ..	..	..	..	..	..	..	..	..	..	..	..	..
5	Seoni ..	Seoni ..	2	2	1	..	..	..	..	..	..	..	..	..
6		Lakhnadon ..	..	..	..	..	..	..	..	..	..	..	..	..
7	Hoshangabad (excluding Sohagpur).	..	3	..	3	..	..	..	..	..	..	..	..	..
8	Hoshangabad ..	Sohagpur ..	2	..	2	..	..	..	..	..	..	..	..	..
9	Nimar ..	Khandwa ..	1	..	1	..	..	..	..	..	..	..	..	..
10		Burhanpur ..	1	..	1	..	..	..	..	..	..	..	..	..
11		Harsud ..	..	..	..	..	..	..	..	..	..	..	..	..
12	Betul ..	Betul ..	5	..	5	..	..	..	..	..	..	..	..	..
13		Multai ..	..	..	..	..	..	..	..	..	..	..	..	..
14		Bhainsdehi ..	..	..	..	..	..	..	..	..	..	..	..	..
15	Chhindwara ..	Chhindwara Khalsa	1	1	..	1	..	..	..	..	..	..	..	..
16		Chhindwara Zamindari	..	..	..	..	..	..	..	..	..	..	..	..
17		Amarwara Khalsa	..	..	..	..	..	..	..	..	..	..	..	..
18		Amarwara Zamindari	..	..	..	..	..	..	..	..	..	..	..	..
19		Sausar ..	1	..	..	..	..	..	..	..	..	..	..	..
20	Wardha ..	Wardha and Hinganghat	30	..	30	..	..	..	..	..	..	..	..	..
21		Arvi ..	..	..	..	..	..	..	..	..	..	..	..	..
22	Nagpur ..	Nagpur ..	96	92	68	59	19	19	..	..	..	5	..	..
23		Ramtek ..	15	13	15	11	..	..	..	..	..	..	..	..
24		Umrer ..	..	..	..	..	..	..	..	..	..	..	..	..
25		Katol and Saoner	..	47	..	..	..	..	..	..	..	..	..	..
26	Chanda ..	Warora ..	12	..	..	..	12	..	..	..	..	..	..	..
27		Brahmapuri ..	2	..	..	..	..	..	..	..	..	..	..	..
28		Chanda ..	..	..	..	..	..	..	..	..	..	..	..	..
29		Garchiroli Khalsa	..	..	..	..	..	..	..	..	..	..	..	..
30		Garchiroli Zamindari	..	..	..	..	..	..	..	..	..	..	..	..
31		Sironcha Khalsa	..	..	..	..	..	..	..	..	..	..	..	..
32		Ahiri Zamindari	18	13	..	..	..	..	14	10	..	..	..	..
33	Bhandara ..	Bhandara ..	26	17	9	..	..	..	..	..	..	..	..	..
34		Gondia ..	1	5	1	3	..	..	..	..	..	..	..	..
35		Sakoli Khalsa ..	11	7	2	..	..	..	..	..	..	..	..	..
36		Sakoli Zamindari	..	..	..	..	..	..	..	..	..	..	..	..
37	Ba aghat ..	Balaghat ..	49	57	39	43	..	..	..	..	..	..	..	..
38		Baihar Khalsa ..	158	5	153	5	5	..	..	..	..	..	..	..
39		Baihar Zamindari	..	..	..	..	..	..	..	..	..	..	..	..
40		Waraseoni ..	15	3	15	3	..	..	..	..	..	..	..	..
41	Raipur (excluding 5 Zamindaris).	..	2,110	1,977	1,433	1,334	..	..	..	..	1	..	..	..
42		Deori and Kauria Zamindaris ..	2,328	2,442	1,574	2,046	..	..	..	..	..	..	..	..
43		Khariar Zamindari	58,162	59,560	2,356	2,193	..	..	..	..	..	..	..	..
44		Phuljhar Zamindari	35,511	38,521	4,134	4,087	..	..	..	..	..	..	..	..
45		Bindra-Nawagarh Zamindari	18,385	19,236	2,209	1,996	..	..	..	..	..	..	..	..
46	Bilaspur (excluding Chandrapur-Padampur Estate).		799	676	478	208	..	..	..	..	..	..	..	..
47		Chandrapur-Padampur Estate ..	10,595	11,251	390	566	..	..	..	..	..	..	..	..
48	Drug ..	Drug, Bemetara and Sanjari Khalsa	74	48	62	45	..	..	..	..	..	..	..	..
49		Sanjari Zamindari ..	43	53	43	53	..	..	..	..	..	..	..	..
50	Amraoti	Amraoti and Ellichpur ..	1	..	..	..	..	..	..	..	..	..	..	..
51		Chandur ..	..	..	..	..	..	..	..	..	..	..	..	..
52		Morsi ..	..	..	..	..	..	..	..	..	..	..	..	..
53		Daryapur ..	13	8	..	..	..	2	..	..	..	..	..	..
54		Melghat ..	..	..	..	..	..	..	..	..	..	..	..	..
55	Akola ..	Akola, Akot, Balapur and Murtizapur.	2	..	1	..	..	..	..	..	..	..	..	..
56		Basim and Mangrulpir ..	..	..	..	..	..	..	..	..	..	..	..	..
57	Buldana ..	Chikhli ..	..	..	..	..	..	..	..	..	..	..	..	..
58		Jalgaon ..	..	..	..	..	..	..	..	..	..	..	..	..
59		Khamgaon and Malkapur ..	..	..	..	..	..	..	..	..	..	..	..	..
60		Mehkar ..	..	..	..	..	..	..	..	..	..	..	..	..
61	Yeotmal ..	Darwha and Pusad ..	..	..	..	..	..	..	..	..	..	..	..	..
62		Yeotmal ..	..	..	..	..	..	..	..	..	..	..	..	..
63		Kelapur ..	..	..	..	..	..	..	..	..	..	..	..	..
64		Wun ..	25	136	..	..	..	121	..	..	..	..	..	..
65	Central Provinces States ..	Makrai ..	..	..	..	..	..	..	..	..	..	..	..	..
66		Bastar ..	24,038	24,091	251	333	5,555	5,184	775	865	4	2	..	..
67		Kanker ..	37	49	31	43	..	..	..	..	..	..	..	..
68		Kawardha ..	4	..	4	..	..	..	..	..	..	..	..	..
69		Sakti ..	26	32	26	21	..	..	..	..	..	..	..	..
70		Raigarh ..	16,172	17,196	8,531	6,515	..	..	..	..	..	..	..	..
71		Sarangarh ..	12,634	12,637	3,210	2,593	..	..	..	..	..	..	..	..
72		Korea ..	9	6	9	6	..	..	..	..	..	..	..	..
73		Surguja ..	314	305	243	237	..	..	..	..	..	..	..	..
74		Udaipur ..	2,090	2,114	1,642	1,587	..	..	..	..	..	..	..	..
75		Jashpur ..	5,321	5,350	4,224	3,390	..	..	..	..	..	..	4	1
76		Changbhakar ..	..	..	..	..	..	..	..	..	..	..	..	..
77		Khairagarh, Nandgaon and Chhuikhadan.	52	41	29	21	..	..	..	..	..	..	..	..

Number of persons speaking mother-tongue.		Mothertongue—Gondi. Subsidiary Languages. Hindustani.		Marathi.		Oriya.		Telugu.		Korku.		Serial No.
Males.	Females.	Males.	Females.	Males.	Females.	Males.	Females.	Males.	Females.	Males.	Females.	
49	50	51	52	53	54	55	56	57	58	59	60	
1,147	2,562	1,065	1,100	..	..	..	..	..	..	..	..	1
39,115	40,236	31,741	31,475	..	..	..	..	..	..	..	..	2
84	77	84	77	..	..	..	..	..	..	..	..	3
11,592	12,076	8,833	9,247	..	..	..	..	..	..	..	..	4
27,637	37,222	22,418	31,199	2	38	..	..	..	..	..	..	5
13,896	14.049	10,809	11,824	..	..	..	..	..	..	..	..	6
10,557	11,019	8,793	9,036	..	..	..	..	..	..	..	..	7
969	854	955	842	..	..	..	..	..	.	..	..	8
1,294	1,264	1,006	877	..	..	..	..	..	..	..	..	9
507	453	213	178	7	5	..	..	..	..	31	27	10
2,795	2,710	2,344	2,236	..	..	..	..	..	..	8	7	11
28,674	30,058	22,932	23,742	1	9	..	..	..	..	..	..	12
14,605	15,743	10,311	10,703	149	173	..	..	..	..	..	..	13
14,772	14,917	10,114	11,016	29	11	..	..	..	..	..	..	14
27,398	29,393	22,961	23,456	..	1	..	..	..	..	..	..	15
9,555	9,998	7,471	7,836	..	..	..	..	..	..	..	..	16
4,354	4,792	3,657	4,134	..	..	..	..	..	..	..	..	17
3,820	4,261	2,921	3,232	..	..	..	..	..	..	..	..	18
23,165	24,856	11,159	11,906	5,672	5,912	..	..	..	..	..	..	19
13,680	14,270	4	12	11,643	12,675	..	..	..	..	..	..	20
10,396	10,372	14	3	9,087	9,012	..	..	..	..	..	..	21
6,919	7,248	563	497	5,064	5,347	..	..	..	..	..	..	22
8,019	7,985	1,443	1,042	4,804	4,548	..	..	..	..	..	..	23
2,524	2,756	..	..	2,487	2,728	.	..	..	..	..	..	24
8,297	8,391	60	242	7,568	7,348	..	..	..	..	..	..	25
2,670	2,472	..	..	2,633	2,466	..	..	..	..	..	..	26
2,121	2,325	..	..	2,075	2,292	..	..	..	..	..	..	27
9,860	10,006	17	8	9,155	9,274	..	..	42	40	..	..	28
6,947	7,678	14	15	4,738	5,159	..	..	26	262	..	..	29
15,074	16,352	1,079	1,037	9,150	8,461	..	..	2	..	..	..	30
3,190	2,972	89	86	26	25	..	..	2,254	1,984	..	..	31
13,945	14,210	12	4	214	152	..	..	2,416	2,450	..	..	32
6,073	6,412	97	79	5,124	5,469	..	..	..	..	..	..	33
16,708	13,894	835	603	12,581	8,693	..	..	..	..	..	..	34
2,843	2,284	17	15	2,437	2,125	..	..	..	..	..	..	35
5,313	6.551	40	80	4,646	5,475	..	..	..	..	..	..	36
9,981	10,752	7,864	8,344	125	157	..	..	..	..	..	..	37
8,527	9,363	7,821	8,884	..	..	..	..	..	..	..	..	38
796	744	617	622	..	..	..	..	..	..	..	..	39
16,683	17,859	9,691	8,831	899	922	..	..	..	..	..	..	40
680	661	545	568	1	..	1	6	..	..	..	..	41
142	131	128	113	..	..	11	12	..	..	..	..	42
18	17	2	2	..	..	3	1	..	..	..	..	43
105	113	44	76	..	..	30	30	..	..	..	..	44
369	374	369	373	..	..	..	..	..	..	..	..	45
224	197	201	139	..	..	..	..	..	..	..	..	46
..	..	..	..	..	..	..	..	..	..	..	..	47
924	965	859	818	..	..	..	..	..	..	..	..	48
10,119	10,877	8,882	5.554	..	..	..	..	..	..	..	..	49
1,614	1,689	195	259	1,050	1,087	..	..	..	..	..	..	50
3,493	3,657	5	7	2,920	3,165	..	..	..	..	..	..	51
3,434	3,426	21	..	2,889	2,940	..	..	..	..	..	..	52
87	76	7	8	72	55	..	..	..	..	..	..	53
1,384	1,473	821	1,114	190	146	..	..	..	..	20	37	54
750	572	6	13	577	432	..	..	..	..	..	..	55
86	77	..	..	70	61	..	..	..	..	..	..	56
43	50	..	..	34	38	..	..	..	..	..	..	57
89	87	36	30	22	28	...	..	..	..	..	..	58
7	5	1	..	4	3	..	..	..	..	..	..	59
2	..	..	..	1	..	..	..	..	..	..	..	60
3,061	2,374	26	29	2,536	1,928	..	..	..	..	..	..	61
7,454	7,020	4	1	6,284	5,878	..	..	..	..	..	..	62
14,210	14,703	92	115	10,600	12,623	..	..	27	226	..	..	63
7,058	4,867	22	7	5,796	3,805	..	..	..	..	..	..	64
570	503	487	503	..	..	..	..	..	..	..	..	65
130,436	132,552	1,595	1,442	27,980	26,818	362	302	4,612	4,960	..	..	66
25,809	24,278	17,781	13,613	..	..	..	..	..	..	..	..	67
31	40	19	19	..	..	..	..	..	..	..	..	68
7	4	..	..	..	..	..	..	..	..	..	..	69
73	92	67	91	..	..	..	..	..	..	..	..	70
15	11	15	11	..	..	..	..	..	..	..	..	71
20	9	20	8	..	..	..	..	..	..	..	..	72
..	..	..	..	..	..	..	..	..	..	..	..	73
..	..	..	..	..	..	..	..	..	..	..	..	74
..	..	..	..	..	..	..	..	..	..	..	..	75
8,746	7,917	110	59	..	..	..	..	..	..	..	..	76
1,272	1,334	1,234	1,322	..	..	..	..	..	..	..	..	77

Serial No.	Area of Bi-lingualism.		Mother-tongue—			
			Number of persons speaking mother-tongue.		Subsidiary Hindustani.	
	District or State.	Tahsil or Zamindari.	Males.	Females.	Males.	Females.
	1	2	61	62	63	64
1	Saugor, Damoh, Jubbulpore and Narsinghpur.	.. ..	420	388	304	286
2	Mandla ..	Mandla	66	64	66	64
3		Dindori	..	..	..	..
4		Niwas	..	..	..	..
5	Seoni ..	Seoni	11	7	7	5
6		Lakhnadon	7	8	2	1
7	Hoshangabad (excluding Sohagpur).	.. ..	68	52	37	28
8	Hoshangabad ..	Sohagpur	18	16	18	15
9	Nimar ..	Khandwa	211	197	138	133
10		Burhanpur	89	72	18	14
11		Harsud	16	16	6	9
12	Betul ..	Betul	21	23	15	17
13		Multai	5	6	4	2
14		Bhainsdehi	1	2	1	1
15	Chhindwara ..	Chhindwara Khalsa	83	85	54	52
16		Chhindwara Zamindari	1	..	1	..
17		Amarwara Khalsa	2	4	2	3
18		Amarwara Zamindari	..	..	..	..
19		Sausar	20	13	13	9
20	Wardha ..	Wardha and Hinganghat	1,248	876	124	76
21		Arvi	108	88	14	1
22	Nagpur ..	Nagpur	4,440	3,910	2,218	2,055
23		Ramtek	120	148	25	26
24		Umrer	167	148	8	3
25		Katol and Saoner	128	112	21	11
26	Chanda ..	Warora	753	716	23	..
27		Brahmapuri	2,302	2,456	8	13
28		Chanda	12,165	11,304	374	117
29		Garchiroli Khalsa	4,596	4,517	16	..
30		Garchiroli Zamindari	271	391	4	..
31		Sironcha Khalsa	11,189	11,238	23	13
32		Ahiri Zamindari	2,567	2,314	51	10
33	Bhandara ..	Bhandara	253	265	18	15
34		Gondia	348	515	153	213
35		Sakoli Khalsa	68	54	27	6
36		Sakoli Zamindari	18	..	2	..
37	Balaghat ..	Balaghat	47	75	18	35
38		Baihar Khalsa	..	..	..	..
39		Baihar Zamindari	..	..	..	..
40		Waraseoni	41	35	25	17
41	Raipur (excluding 5 Zamindaris).	.. ..	452	488	376	316
42		Deori and Kauria Zamindaris ..	2	4	1	3
43		Khariar Zamindari ..	19	9	11	7
44		Phuljhar Zamindari	12	7	10	6
45		Bindra-Nawagarh	13	14	3	..
46	Bilaspur (excluding Chandrapur-Padampur Estate).	Bilaspur	519	445	294	326
47		Chandrapur-Padampur Estate ..	..	..	..	..
48	Drug ..	Drug, Bemetara and Sanjari Khalsa ..	23	14	21	14
49		Sanjari Zamindari	2	1	2	1
50	Amraoti ..	Amraoti and Ellichpur	1,125	1,082	408	503
51		Chandur	81	97	9	17
52		Morai	65	60	..	19
53		Daryapur	87	83	3	3
54		Melghat	31	11	21	8
55	Akola ..	Akola, Akot, Balapur and Murtizapur ..	1,581	1,463	309	179
56		Basim and Mangrulpir	1,129	938	80	82
57	Buldana ..	Chikhli	788	748	106	114
58		Jalgaon	62	59	..	1
59		Khamgaon and Malkapur	407	428	56	40
60		Mehkar	919	590	11	..
61	Yeotmal ..	Darwha and Pusad	3,371	2,533	47	64
62		Yeotmal	493	589	113	30
63		Kelapur	8,777	8,728	3	122
64		Wun	5,402	4,659	..	26
65	Central Provinces States ..	Makrai	..	..	..	..
66		Bastar	5,762	5,900	319	387
67		Kanker	..	..	..	..
68		Kawardha	4	..	4	..
69		Sakti	4	6	3	5
70		Raigarh	27	33	26	30
71		Sarangarh	..	..	..	..
72		Korea	..	..	..	..
73		Surguja	..	..	..	..
74		Udaipur	..	..	..	..
75		Jashpur	1	..	..	..
76		Changbhakar	..	..	..	..
77		Khairagarh, Nandgaon and Chhuikhadan ..	156	144	144	137

Telugu. Languages. Marathi. Males.	Telugu. Languages. Marathi. Females.	Telugu. Languages. Gondi. Males.	Telugu. Languages. Gondi. Females.	Mother-tongue—Kurukh or Oraon. Number of persons speaking mother-tongue. Males.	Mother-tongue—Kurukh or Oraon. Number of persons speaking mother-tongue. Females.	Mother-tongue—Kurukh or Oraon. Subsidiary Languages. Hindustani. Males.	Mother-tongue—Kurukh or Oraon. Subsidiary Languages. Hindustani. Females.	Mother-tongue—Kurukh or Oraon. Subsidiary Languages. Oriya. Males.	Mother-tongue—Kurukh or Oraon. Subsidiary Languages. Oriya. Females.	Serial No.
65	66	67	68	69	70	71	72	73	74	
11	13	..	..	..	..	..	..	..	..	1
..	..	..	..	..	..	..	..	..	..	2
..	..	..	..	..	..	..	..	..	..	3
..	..	..	..	..	..	..	..	..	..	4
1	1	..	..	..	..	..	..	..	..	5
..	..	..	..	..	..	..	..	..	..	6
1	..	..	..	..	..	..	..	..	..	7
..	..	..	..	..	..	..	..	..	..	8
1	30	..	..	..	..	..	..	..	..	9
46	38	..	..	..	..	..	..	..	..	10
..	..	..	..	..	..	..	..	..	..	11
3	2	..	..	..	..	..	..	..	..	12
..	..	..	..	..	..	..	..	..	..	13
..	..	..	..	..	..	..	..	..	..	14
..	..	..	..	..	..	..	..	..	..	15
..	..	..	..	..	..	..	..	..	..	16
..	..	..	..	..	..	..	..	..	..	17
..	..	..	..	..	..	..	..	..	..	18
7	2	..	..	..	..	..	..	..	..	19
858	649	..	..	..	..	..	..	..	..	20
75	73	..	..	..	..	..	..	..	..	21
997	863	..	..	..	..	..	..	..	..	22
84	74	..	..	..	..	..	..	..	..	23
142	124	..	..	..	..	..	..	..	..	24
97	82	..	..	..	..	..	..	..	..	25
512	622	..	..	..	..	..	..	..	..	26
2,225	2,367	..	..	..	..	..	..	..	..	27
9,249	8,993	..	2	..	..	..	..	..	..	28
3,154	2,965	1	..	..	..	..	..	..	..	29
229	331	1	..	..	..	..	..	..	..	30
103	57	..	..	..	..	..	..	..	..	31
200	62	101	90	..	..	..	..	..	..	32
127	216	..	..	..	..	..	..	..	..	33
3	1	..	..	..	..	..	..	..	..	34
21	37	..	..	..	..	..	..	..	..	35
16	..	..	..	..	..	..	..	..	..	36
9	29	..	..	..	..	..	..	..	..	37
..	..	..	..	..	..	..	..	..	..	38
..	..	..	..	..	..	..	..	..	..	39
4	3	..	..	..	..	..	..	..	..	40
..	..	..	..	36	45	36	45	..	..	41
..	..	..	..	49	54	39	52	..	..	42
..	..	..	..	17	21	..	..	4	13	43
..	..	..	..	46	45	22	35	11	7	44
..	..	..	..	..	..	..	..	..	..	45
22	2	..	..	1,022	1,121	795	883	5	58	46
..	..	..	..	..	..	..	..	..	..	47
..	..	..	..	..	..	..	..	..	..	48
..	..	..	..	..	..	..	..	..	..	49
328	178	..	..	..	..	..	..	..	..	50
64	69	..	..	..	..	..	..	..	..	51
48	29	..	..	..	..	..	..	..	..	52
54	50	..	..	..	..	..	..	..	..	53
..	1	..	..	..	..	..	..	..	..	54
660	504	..	..	..	..	..	..	..	..	55
632	500	..	..	..	..	..	..	..	..	56
456	419	..	..	..	..	..	..	..	..	57
31	26	..	..	..	..	..	..	..	..	58
206	259	..	..	..	..	..	..	..	..	59
610	411	..	..	..	..	..	..	..	..	60
2,460	1,862	..	..	..	..	..	..	..	..	61
293	390	..	..	..	..	..	..	..	..	62
2,557	4,010	..	..	..	..	..	..	..	..	63
2,324	1,511	..	..	..	..	..	..	..	..	64
..	..	..	..	..	..	..	..	..	..	65
256	124	586	462	..	..	..	..	..	..	66
..	..	..	..	..	..	..	..	..	..	67
..	..	..	..	..	..	..	..	..	..	68
..	..	..	..	93	89	84	73	..	..	69
..	..	..	..	3,447	3,073	2,684	1,882	..	..	70
..	..	..	..	758	653	544	535	23	31	71
..	..	..	..	345	344	345	344	..	..	72
..	..	..	..	23,556	21,300	21,049	19,810	..	..	73
..	..	..	..	7,318	7,045	5,099	4,758	..	..	74
..	..	..	..	36.433	35,413	19,535	21,329	71	68	75
..	..	..	..	..	..	..	..	..	..	76
..	..	..	..	..	..	..	..	..	..	77

TABLE XV

PART II.—

Serial No.	Area of Bi-lingualism. District or State.	Area of Bi-lingualism. Tahsil or Zamindari.	Mother-tongue—Kherwari. Number of persons speaking mother-tongue. Males.	Females.	Subsidiary Languages. Hindustani. Males.	Females.	Oriya. Males.	Females.	Mother-tongue— Number of persons speaking mother-tongue. Males.	Females.
	1	2	75	76	77	78	79	80	81	82
1	Saugor, Damoh, Jubbulpore and Narsinghpur.	..	1	3	..	..	..	..	..	..
2	Mandla ..	Mandla	..	..	..	..	..	..	..	..
3		Dindori	..	..	..	..	..	..	1	..
4		Niwas	..	..	..	..	..	..	1	..
5	Seoni ..	Seoni	..	..	..	..	..	..	..	..
6		Lakhnadon	..	..	..	..	..	..	..	..
7	Hoshangabad (excluding Sohagpur).	.. ..	..	..	..	..	..	..	6,018	5,602
8	Hoshangabad ..	Sohagpur	..	..	..	..	..	..	494	436
9	Nimar ..	Khandwa	..	1	..	..	..	..	2,078	2,072
10		Burhanpur	..	..	..	..	..	..	9,892	10,102
11		Harsud	..	..	..	..	..	..	10,847	11,019
12	Betul ..	Betul	..	..	..	..	..	..	6,383	6,443
13		Multai	..	..	..	..	..	..	684	647
14		Bhainsdehi	..	..	..	..	..	..	11,467	11,955
15	Chhindwara ..	Chhindwara Khalsa ..	..	..	..	..	..	..	4,190	4,278
16		Chhindwara Zamindari ..	..	..	..	..	..	..	3,605	3,472
17		Amarwara Khalsa ..	..	..	..	..	..	..	..	..
18		Amarwara Zamindari ..	..	..	..	..	..	..	..	..
19		Sausar	..	..	..	..	..	..	1,410	1,348
20	Wardha ..	Wardha and Hinganghat ..	..	..	..	..	..	..	..	..
21		Arvi	..	..	..	..	..	..	1	4
22	Nagpur ..	Nagpur	44	24	44	24	..	..	..	..
23		Ramtek	..	..	..	..	..	..	..	..
24		Umrer	..	..	..	..	..	..	..	..
25		Katol and Saoner ..	..	..	..	..	..	..	..	..
26	Chanda ..	Warora	..	..	..	..	..	..	..	..
27		Brahmapuri	..	..	..	..	..	..	..	..
28		Chanda ..	..	..	..	..	..	..	..	..
29		Garchiroli Khalsa ..	..	..	..	..	..	..	..	..
30		Garchiroli Zamindari ..	..	..	..	..	..	..	..	..
31		Sironcha Khalsa ..	..	..	..	..	..	..	..	..
32		Ahiri Zamindari ..	..	..	..	..	..	..	..	..
33	Bhandara ..	Bhandara	..	..	..	..	..	..	..	..
34		Gondia	..	..	..	..	..	..	..	..
35		Sakoli Khalsa	..	..	..	..	..	..	..	..
36		Sakoli Zamindari ..	..	..	..	..	..	..	..	..
37	Balaghat ..	Balaghat	..	..	..	..	..	..	..	..
38		Baihar Khalsa . ..	..	..	..	..	..	..	..	..
39		Baihar Zamindari ..	..	..	..	..	..	..	..	..
40		Waraseoni	..	..	..	..	..	..	..	..
41	Raipur (excluding 5 Zamindaris).	..	16	22	11	17	4	4	..	..
42		Deori and Kauria Zamindari ..	..	..	..	..	..	..	..	..
43		Khariar Zamindari ..	191	226	18	23	24	165	..	..
44		Phulihar Zamindari ..	348	367	88	111	110	102	..	..
45		Bindra-Nawagarh Zamindari ..	..	..	..	..	..	..	..	..
46	Bilaspur (excluding Chandrapur-Padampur Estate)	Bilaspur ..	136	145	20	17	100	124	160	103
47		Chandrapur-Padampur Estate ..	..	..	..	..	..	..	..	..
48	Drug ..	Drug, Bemetara and Sanjari Khalsa	..	..	..	..	..	..	..	..
49		Sanjari Zamindari ..	..	..	..	..	..	..	..	..
50	Amraoti .	Amraoti and Ellichpur ..	..	..	..	..	..	..	1,239	1,255
51		Chandur	..	..	..	..	..	..	..	..
52		Morsi	..	..	..	..	..	..	57	28
53		Daryapur	..	..	..	..	..	..	14	13
54		Melghat	1	..	..	..	..	..	16,561	16,233
55	Akola ..	Akola, Akot, Balapur and Murtizapur.	..	..	..	..	..	..	737	682
56		Basim and Mangrulpir ..	..	..	..	..	..	..	..	..
57	Buldana ..	Chikhli	..	..	..	..	..	..	..	..
58		Jalgaon	..	..	..	..	..	..	653	653
59		Khamgaon and Malkapur ..	..	..	..	..	..	..	..	1
60		Mehkar	..	..	..	..	..	..	..	..
61	Yeotmal .	Darwha and Pusad ..	..	..	..	..	..	..	..	..
62		Yc tnial	..	..	..	..	..	..	..	..
63		Kelapur	..	..	..	..	..	..	..	..
64		Wun	..	..	..	..	..	..	..	..
65	Central Provinces States.	Makrai	..	..	..	..	..	..	1,508	1,274
66		Bastar	..	..	..	..	..	..	..	..
67		Kanker	..	..	..	..	..	..	..	..
68		Kawardha	..	..	..	..	..	..	..	..
69		Sakti	12	9	7	..	..	..	..	..
70		Raigarh	12	12	12	12	..	..	..	..
71		'arangarh	99	107	99	104	..	..	..	..
72		Korea	..	..	..	..	..	..	..	..
73		Surguja	2,572	2,302	2,170	1,817	..	..	*3,204	*3,151
74		Udaipur	510	666	316	435	..	..	..	..
75		Jashpur	1,986	2,179	1,379	1,507	21	18	..	..
76		Changbhakar	75	68	3	2	..	..	..	..
77		Khairagarh, Nandgaon and Chhuikhadan.	..	..	..	..	..	..	..	..

*This is almost certainly a Sub-dialect of Korwa. Crooke held Korwas and Korkus to be branches of the same tribe, but, although both

Korku.								Mother-tongue—Kharia.						
Subsidiary languages								Number of persons speaking mother-tongue.		Subsidiary Languages.				Serial No.
Hindustani.		Marathi.		Gondi.		Telugu.				Hindustani.		Oriya.		
Males.	Females.	Males.	Females.	Males.	Females.	Males.	Females.	Males.	Females.	Males.	Females.	Males.	Females.	
83	84	85	86	87	88	89	90	91	92	93	94	95	96	
..	..	..	..	..	..	..	..	..	..	..	..	..	..	1
..	..	..	..	..	..	..	..	..	..	..	..	..	..	2
..	..	..	..	1	..	..	..	..	..	..	..	..	..	3
..	..	..	..	1	..	..	..	..	..	..	..	..	..	4
..	..	..	..	..	..	..	..	..	..	..	..	..	..	5
..	..	..	..	..	..	..	..	..	..	..	..	..	..	6
4,765	4,391	..	..	..	..	..	..	..	..	..	..	..	..	7
494	430	..	..	..	..	..	..	..	..	..	..	..	..	8
1,498	1,441	..	..	..	..	..	..	..	..	..	..	..	..	9
4,107	2,425	..	..	..	..	..	..	..	..	..	..	..	..	10
8,565	8,457	..	..	2	1	..	..	..	..	..	..	..	..	11
4,926	4,916	..	..	..	5	..	..	..	..	..	..	..	..	12
513	483	10	11	..	..	..	..	..	..	..	..	..	..	13
7,882	8,194	9	2	1	..	..	..	..	..	..	..	..	..	14
2,956	3,155	..	..	1	4	158	..	..	..	..	..	..	..	15
2,697	2,507	..	..	..	..	..	..	..	..	..	..	..	..	16
..	..	..	..	..	..	..	..	..	..	..	..	..	..	17
..	..	..	..	..	..	..	..	..	..	..	..	..	..	18
1,082	1,019	45	37	7	..	..	..	..	..	..	..	..	..	19
..	..	..	..	..	..	..	..	..	..	..	..	..	..	20
..	..	..	1	..	..	..	..	..	..	..	..	..	..	21
..	..	..	..	..	..	..	..	..	..	..	..	..	..	22
..	..	..	..	..	..	..	..	..	..	..	..	..	..	23
..	..	..	..	..	..	..	..	..	..	..	..	..	..	24
..	..	..	..	..	..	..	..	..	..	..	..	..	..	25
..	..	..	..	..	..	..	..	..	..	..	..	..	..	26
..	..	..	..	..	..	..	..	..	..	..	..	..	..	27
..	..	..	..	..	..	..	..	..	..	..	..	..	..	28
..	..	..	..	..	..	..	..	..	..	..	..	..	..	29
..	..	..	..	..	..	..	..	..	..	..	..	..	..	30
..	..	..	..	..	..	..	..	..	..	..	..	..	..	31
..	..	..	..	..	..	..	..	..	..	..	..	..	..	32
..	..	..	..	..	..	..	..	..	..	..	..	..	..	33
..	..	..	..	..	..	..	..	..	..	..	..	..	..	34
..	..	..	..	..	..	..	..	..	..	..	..	..	..	35
..	..	..	..	..	..	..	..	..	..	..	..	..	..	36
..	..	..	..	..	..	..	..	..	..	..	..	..	..	37
..	..	..	..	..	..	..	..	..	..	..	..	..	..	38
..	..	..	..	..	..	..	..	..	..	..	..	..	..	39
..	..	..	..	..	..	..	..	..	..	..	..	..	..	40
..	..	..	..	..	..	..	..	28	16	28	26	..	..	41
..	..	..	..	..	..	..	..	..	..	..	..	..	..	42
..	..	..	..	..	..	..	..	33	35	..	..	..	..	43
..	..	..	..	..	..	..	..	292	299	136	137	..	..	44
..	..	..	..	..	..	..	..	..	..	..	..	..	..	45
160	82	..	..	..	..	..	..	288	203	53	61	5	118	46
..	..	..	..	..	..	..	..	..	..	..	..	..	..	47
..	..	..	..	..	..	..	..	..	..	..	..	..	..	48
..	..	..	..	..	..	..	..	..	..	..	..	..	..	49
383	361	487	558	..	..	..	..	..	..	..	..	..	..	50
..	..	..	..	..	..	..	..	..	..	..	..	..	..	51
..	..	44	25	..	..	..	..	..	..	..	..	..	..	52
..	..	1	5	..	..	..	..	..	..	..	..	..	..	53
8,869	7,712	61	19	..	..	..	..	..	..	..	..	..	..	54
200	140	126	68	..	..	..	..	..	..	..	..	..	..	55
..	..	..	..	..	..	..	..	..	..	..	..	..	..	56
124	124	271	263	..	..	..	..	..	..	..	..	..	..	57
..	..	..	..	..	..	..	..	..	..	..	..	..	..	58
..	..	..	1	..	..	..	..	..	..	..	..	..	..	59
..	..	..	..	..	..	..	..	..	..	..	..	..	..	60
..	..	..	..	..	..	..	..	..	..	..	..	..	..	61
..	..	..	..	..	..	..	..	..	..	..	..	..	..	62
..	..	..	..	..	..	..	..	..	..	..	..	..	..	63
..	..	..	..	..	..	..	..	..	..	..	..	..	..	64
1,096	1,002	..	..	..	..	..	..	..	..	..	..	..	..	65
..	..	..	..	..	..	..	..	..	..	..	..	..	..	66
..	..	..	..	..	..	..	..	..	..	..	..	..	..	67
..	..	..	..	..	..	..	..	..	..	..	..	..	..	68
..	..	..	..	..	..	..	..	32	20	32	20	..	..	69
..	..	..	..	..	..	..	..	1,353	1,439	1,042	1,044	4	2	70
..	..	..	..	..	..	..	..	279	217	279	202	..	..	71
..	..	..	..	..	..	..	..	..	..	..	..	..	..	72
3,174	3,129	..	..	..	..	..	..	..	..	..	..	..	..	73
..	..	..	..	..	..	..	..	256	248	184	180	..	..	74
..	..	..	..	..	..	..	..	1,967	2,071	1,227	1,242	196	208	75
..	..	..	..	..	..	..	..	..	..	..	..	..	..	76
..	..	..	..	..	..	..	..	..	..	..	..	..	..	77

languages belong to the Munda branch, Grierson has stated that the two tribes and languages are now distinct. See Part I of the Report.

TABLE XVI

Religion

1. The few persons who returned themselves as Brahmos by religion have been included with the Hindu totals in columns 14, 15 and 16. Foot-notes show the districts in which they were enumerated.

2. Jains and Buddhists returned as Hindus are not included in the Hindu total but have been shown separately, Jains in columns 23, 24 and 25 and Buddhists in the foot-notes to columns 21 and 22.

3. In accordance with the orders contained in Government of India, Home Department, Resolution No. F. 45-43-31-Public, dated the 30th April 1931, the table showing the territorial distribution of the Christian population by race and sect has been abandoned and the figures of Christians have been classified as follows :—

Sect.	Persons.	Males.	Females.
Roman Catholics	55,964	28,763	27,201
Romo Syrians	*Nil.*	*Nil.*	*Nil.*
Other Syrians	14	9	5
Others	46,307	23,768	22,539

In "Others" are included members of the Anglican Communion and of all sects found in the Province which are not shown separately above.

4. No Indefinite Beliefs were returned at the Census.

TABLE XVI

Religion.

Serial number.	District or State.	Total population. Persons.	Total population. Males.	Total population. Females.	HIN — Brahmanic. Persons.	Brahmanic. Males.	Brahmanic. Females.	Satnamis. Persons.	Satnamis. Males.	Satnamis. Females.
	1	2	3	4	5	6	7	8	9	10
	Central Provinces and Berar.	**17,990,937**	**8,997,203**	**8,993,734**	**14,632,833**	**7,317,829**	**7,315,004**	**491,933**	**238,568**	**253,365**
	C. P. British Districts and Berar.	**15,507,723**	**7,761,818**	**7,745,905**	**12,903,044**	**6,460,354**	**6,442,690**	**433,328**	**209,924**	**223,404**
	C. P. British Districts	**12,065,885**	**6,002,239**	**6,063,646**	**9,837,195**	**4,896,739**	**4,940,456**	**433,290**	**209,893**	**223,397**
	Jubbulpore Division ..	*2,463,466*	*1,240,655*	*1,222,811*	*1,887,317*	*953,119*	*934,198*	*9,326*	*4,649*	*4,677*
1	Saugor	544,589	280,385	264,204	480,058	247,074	232,984	24	9	15
2	Damoh ..	305,568	154,791	150,777	265,542	134,545	130,997	150	70	80
3	Jubbulpore ..	773,811	391,649	382,162	690,091	347,080	343,011	6,983	3,465	3,518
4	Mandla ..	445,766	221,359	224,407	235,790	117,630	118,160	2,144	1,083	1,061
5	Seoni ..	393,732	192,471	201,261	215,836	106,790	109,046	25	22	3
	Nerbudda Division ..	*2,254,566*	*1,137,806*	*1,116,760*	*1,673,971*	*849,516*	*824,455*	*481*	*270*	*211*
6	Narsinghpur ..	321,481	161,417	160,064	264,189	133,188	131,001	4	4	..
7	Hoshangabad ..	486,630	248,226	238,404	412,864	210,633	202,231	332	203	129
8	Nimar ..	466,931	242,042	224,889	372,499	193,350	179,149	4	3	1
9	Betul ..	406,252	201,114	205,138	274,839	136,586	138,253	126	54	72
10	Chhindwara ..	573,272	285,007	288,265	349,580	175,759	173,821	15	6	9
	Nagpur Division ..	*3,602,108*	*1,809,541*	*1,792,567*	*3,193,459*	*1,603,317*	*1,590,172*	*477*	*273*	*204*
11	Wardha ..	516,266	261,394	254,872	452,219	229,200	223,019	58	30	28
12	Nagpur ..	940,049	481,246	458,803	862,152	438,967	423,185	194	134	60
13	Chanda ..	759,695	381,204	378,491	630,452	317,023	313,429	18	9	9
14	Bhandara ..	824,496	408,799	415,697	767,247	380,442	386,805	106	57	49
15	Balaghat ..	561,602	276,898	284,704	481,419	237,685	243,734	101	43	58
	Chhattisgarh Division ..	*3,745,745*	*1,814,237*	*1,931,508*	*3,082,418*	*1,490,787*	*1,591,631*	*423,006*	*204,701*	*218,305*
16	Raipur ..	1,527,573	739,950	787,623	1,229,166	594,665	634,501	174,528	84,646	89,882
17	Bilaspur ..	1,400,248	683,920	716,328	1,162,911	567,642	595,269	143,928	69,614	74,314
18	Drug ..	817,924	390,367	427,557	690,341	328,480	361,861	104,550	50,441	54,109
	Berar ..	**3,441,838**	**1,759,579**	**1,682,259**	**3,065,849**	**1,563,615**	**1,502,234**	**38**	**31**	**7**
19	Amraoti ..	941,604	485,[illegible]93	456,011	835,398	430,026	405,372	..	.	..
20	Akola ..	876,362	448,896	427,466	778,363	397,416	380,947	..	..	..
21	Buldana ..	766,584	388,966	377,618	688,623	348,233	340,390	38	31	7
22	Yeotmal ..	857,288	436,124	421,164	763,465	387,940	375,525	..	..	..
	C. P. States ..	**2,483,214**	**1,235,385**	**1,247,829**	**1,729,789**	**857,475**	**872,314**	**58,605**	**28,644**	**29,961**
23	Makrai ..	15,516	7,900	7,616	9,965	5,040	4,925	27	5	22
24	Bastar ..	524,721	263,248	261,473	158,051	79,478	78,573	774	393	381
25	Kanker ..	136,101	67,132	68,969	61,141	29,954	31,187	645	348	297
26	Nandgaon ..	182,380	87,886	94,494	160,039	77,111	82,928	16,772	7,933	8,839
27	Khairagarh ..	157,400	75,647	81,753	138,531	66,425	72,106	15,595	7,587	8,008
28	Chhuikhadan ..	31,668	15,238	16,430	28,252	13,632	14,620	2,402	1,138	1,264
29	Kawardha ..	72,820	35,098	37,722	61,563	29,502	32,061	9,944	4,968	4,976
30	Sakti ..	48,489	23,571	24,918	45,735	22,166	23,569	2,128	1,089	1,039
31	Raigarh ..	277,569	136,723	140,846	266,917	131,388	135,529	8,567	4,263	4,304
32	Sarangarh ..	128,967	62,443	66,524	128,258	62,071	66,187	285	153	132
33	Changbhakar ..	23,322	11,987	11,335	6,879	3,594	3,282	133	77	56
34	Korea ..	90,886	46,748	44,138	25,063	13,137	11,926	560	300	260
35	Surguja ..	501,939	254,923	247,016	432,628	219,808	212,820	185	83	102
36	Udaipur ..	97,738	49,425	48,313	80,203	40,597	39,606	556	290	266
37	Jashpur ..	193,698	97,416	96,282	126,567	63,572	62,995	32	17	15

DUS												
Aryas.			Total Hindus.			Sikhs.			Buddhists.			Serial number.
Persons.	Males.	Females.	Persons.	Males.	Females.	Persons.	Males.	Females.	Persons.	Males.	Females.	
11	12	13	14	15	16	17	18	19	20	21	22	
1,842	**1,049**	**793**	**15,126,624**	**7,557,449**	**7,569,175**	**4,520**	**3,003**	**1,517**	**69**	**44**	**25**	
1,836	**1,046**	**790**	**13,338,223**	**6,671,326**	**6,666,897**	**4,241**	**2,828**	**1,413**	**66**	**43**	**23**	
1,236	**722**	**514**	**10,271,736**	**5,107,356**	**5,164,380**	**3,788**	**2,566**	**1,222**	**61**	**39**	**22**	
340	*193*	*147*	*1,896,983*	*957,961*	*939,022*	*982*	*716*	*266*	*25*	*18*	*7*	
39	18	21	480,121	247,101	233,020	122	84	38	..	..	..	1
16	11	5	265,708	134,626	131,082	18	15	3	..	..	..	2
281	163	118	697,355	350,708	346,647	772	581	191	25	(a) 18	(b) 7	3
..	..	..	237,934	118,713	119,221	62	31	31	..	..	..	4
4	1	3	215,865	106,813	109,052	8	5	3	..	..	..	5
360	*196*	*164*	*1 674,812*	*849,982*	*824,830*	*1,076*	*679*	*397*	*6*	*2*	*4*	
40	22	18	264,233	133,214	131,019	6	5	1	..	..	..	6
107	63	44	413,303	210,899	202,404	255	200	55	5	1	4	7
80	59	21	372,583	193,412	179,171	691	393	298	1	1	..	8
128	49	79	275,093	136,689	138,404	52	37	15	..	..	..	9
5	3	2	349,600	175,768	173,832	72	44	28	..	..	..	10
240	*140*	*100*	*3,191,214*	*1,603,730*	*1,590,484*	*871*	*599*	*272*	*19*	*13*	*6*	
8	4	4	452,285	229,234	223,051	25	15	10	16	(c) 11	(d) 5	11
173	100	73	862,519	439,201	423,318	677	481	196	3	2	1	12
39	18	21	630,517	317,050	(e) 313,467	15	10	5	..	..	..	13
20	18	2	767,373	380,517	386,856	84	47	37	..	..	..	14
..	..	..	481,520	237,728	243,792	70	46	24	..	..	..	15
296	*193*	*103*	*3,505,727*	*1,695,683*	*1,810,044*	*859*	*572*	*287*	*11*	*6*	*5*	
182	123	59	1,403,879	(f) 679,436	(g) 724,443	557	377	180	..	..	..	16
56	33	23	1,306,899	637,289	(h) 669,610	241	152	89	11	6	5	17
58	37	21	794,949	378,958	415,991	61	43	18	..	..	..	18
600	**324**	**276**	**3,066,487**	**1,563,970**	**1,502,517**	**453**	**262**	**191**	**5**	**4**	**1**	
11	8	3	835,409	430,034	405,375	91	56	35	2	1	1	19
88	44	44	778,451	397,460	380,991	82	48	34	2	2	..	20
491	267	224	689,152	348,531	340,621	135	78	57	1	1	..	21
10	5	5	763,475	387,945	375,530	145	80	65	..	..	..	22
6	**3**	**3**	**1,788,401**	**886,123**	**902,278**	**279**	**175**	**104**	**3**	**1**	**2**	
..	..	..	9,992	5,045	4,947	4	4	..	..	..	..	23
..	..	..	158,825	79,871	78,954	..	..	..	..	..	..	24
..	..	..	61,786	30,302	31,484	..	..	..	..	..	..	25
..	..	..	176,811	85,044	91,767	10	7	3	..	..	..	26
6	3	3	154,135	(i) 74,016	80,117	18	13	5	..	..	..	27
..	..	..	30,654	14,770	15,884	..	..	..	..	..	..	28
..	..	..	71,507	34,470	37,037	4	3	1	..	..	..	29
..	..	..	47,863	23,255	24,608	10	7	3	3	1	2	30
..	..	..	275,484	135,651	139,833	150	82	68	..	..	..	31
..	..	..	128,543	62,224	66,319	1	1	..	..	..	..	32
..	..	..	7,009	3,671	3,338	..	..	..	..	..	..	33
..	..	..	25,623	13,437	12,186	3	3	..	..	..	..	34
..	..	..	432,813	219,891	212,922	79	55	24	..	..	..	35
..	..	..	80,759	40,887	39,872	..	..	..	..	..	..	36
..	..	..	126,599	63,589	63,010	..	..	..	..	..	..	37

(a) Includes 7 and (b) 5 returned as Hindus; (c) Includes 9 and (d) 5 returned as Hindus; (e) Includes 8 Brahmos; (f) Includes 2 and (g) 1 Brahmo; (h) Includes 4 Brahmos; (i) Includes 1 Brahmo.

TABLE XVI — Religion—*contd.*

Serial number.	District or State.	Jains. Returned as Hindus. Persons.	Males.	Females.	Jains. Others. Persons.	Males.	Females.	Tribal Religion. Persons.	Males.	Females.
	1	23	24	25	26	27	28	29	30	31
	Central Provinces and Berar.	**3,800**	**2,043**	**1,757**	**76,055**	**39,373**	**36,682**	**1,969,214**	**970,911**	**998,303**
	C. P. British Districts and Berar.	**3,729**	**2,001**	**1,728**	**74,166**	**38,332**	**35,834**	**1,351,615**	**660,755**	**690,860**
	C. P. British Districts	**3,024**	**1,603**	**1,421**	**54,469**	**28,170**	**26,299**	**1,302,463**	**636,433**	**666,030**
	Jubbulpore Division ..	*324*	*201*	*123*	*33,648*	*17,381*	*16,267*	*410,511*	*200,073*	*210,438*
1	Saugor ..	..	..	..	17,136	8,910	8,226	19,415	9,583	9,832
2	Damoh ..	..	..	..	7,478	3,825	3,653	21,331	10,555	10,776
3	Jubbulpore ..	324	201	123	6,468	3,320	3,148	13,261	6,405	6,856
4	Mandla ..	..	..	..	784	415	369	199,310	98,123	101,187
5	Seoni ..	..	..	..	1,782	911	871	157,194	75,407	81,787
	Nerbudda Division ..	*75*	*46*	*29*	*10,013*	*5,156*	*4,857*	*445,825*	*217,699*	*228,126*
6	Narsinghpur ..	..	..	..	2,654	1,376	1,278	42,890	20,845	22,045
7	Hoshangabad ..	20	12	8	1,831	942	889	45,450	22,567	22,883
8	Nimar ..	..	..	..	2,204	1,164	1,040	35,429	17,659	17,770
9	Betul ..	..	..	..	1,331	674	657	121,883	59,642	62,241
10	Chhindwara ..	55	34	21	1,993	1,000	993	200,173	96,986	103,187
	Nagpur Division ..	*2,395*	*1,233*	*1,162*	*7,552*	*3,861*	*3,691*	*269,904*	*132,336*	*137,568*
11	Wardha ..	60	40	20	2,839	1,448	1,391	39,789	19,408	20,381
12	Nagpur ..	938	493	445	2,683	1,334	1,349	9,784	4,972	4,812
13	Chanda ..	278	154	124	724	393	331	113,327	55,916	57,411
14	Bhandara ..	1,119	546	573	441	233	208	39,600	19,156	20,444
15	Balaghat ..	..	..	..	865	453	412	67,404	32,884	34,520
	Chhattisgarh Division ..	*230*	*123*	*107*	*3,256*	*1,772*	*1,484*	*176,223*	*86,325*	*89,898*
16	Raipur ..	95	50	45	1,638	882	756	95,393	45,954	49,439
17	Bilaspur ..	85	48	37	435	234	201	68,672	34,231	34,441
18	Drug ..	50	25	25	1,183	656	527	12,158	6,140	6,018
	Berar ..	**705**	**398**	**307**	**19,697**	**10,162**	**9,535**	**49,152**	**24,322**	**24,830**
19	Amraoti ..	187	99	88	4,865	2,488	2,377	11,871	5,810	6,061
20	Akola ..	206	119	87	6,660	3,416	3,244	370	180	190
21	Buldana ..	76	45	31	4,471	2,355	2,116	172	81	91
22	Yeotmal ..	236	135	101	3,701	1,903	1,798	36,739	18,251	18,488
	C. P. States ..	**71**	**42**	**29**	**1,889**	**1,041**	**848**	**617,599**	**310,156**	**307,443**
23	Makrai ..	..	..	..	54	26	28	4,438	2,311	2,127
24	Bastar ..	..	..	..	134	78	56	361,920	181,390	180,530
25	Kanker ..	..	..	..	155	79	76	73,462	36,385	37,077
26	Nandgaon ..	71	42	29	784	445	339	1,805	915	890
27	Khairagarh ..	..	..	..	414	230	184	..	..	..
28	Chhuikhadan ..	..	..	..	151	79	72	5	5	..
29	Kawardha ..	..	..	..	125	61	64	94	50	44
30	Sakti ..	..	..	..	2	2	..	198	89	109
31	Raigarh ..	..	..	..	46	28	18	..	.	..
32	Sarangarh ..	..	..	..	2	2	..	..	..	..
33	Changbhakar ..	..	..	.	..	..	..	16,240	8,271	7,969
34	Korea ..	..	..	..	..	..	..	64,193	32,709	31,484
35	Surguja ..	.	..	..	22	11	11	61,960	31,327	30,633
36	Udaipur ..	..	..	..	..	..	..	16,708	8,404	8,304
37	Jashpur ..	.	..	..	.	..	..	16,576	8,300	8,276

Zoroastrians.			Muslims.			Christians.			Jews.			Serial number.
Persons.	Males.	Females.	Persons.	Males.	Females.	Persons.	Males.	Females.	Persons.	Males.	Females.	
32	33	34	35	36	37	38	39	40	41	42	43	
2,109	**1,119**	**990**	**706,108**	**370,633**	**335,475**	**102,285**	**52,540**	**49,745**	**153**	**88**	**65**	
2,092	**1,107**	**985**	**682,854**	**358,900**	**323,954**	**50,584**	**26,438**	**24,146**	**153**	**88**	**65**	
1,849	**969**	**880**	**383,174**	**201,352**	**181,822**	**45,189**	**23,673**	**21,516**	**132**	**78**	**54**	
367	*184*	*183*	*109,248*	*57,676*	*51,572*	*11,305*	*6,401*	*4,904*	*73*	*44*	*29*	
119	58	61	25,746	13,655	12,091	1,930	994	936	..	..	..	1
12	5	7	10,516	5,439	5,077	503	325	178	2	1	1	2
224	116	108	47,614	25,763	21,851	7,697	4,494	3,203	71	43	28	3
..	..	..	6,866	3,667	3,199	810	410	400	..	..	..	4
12	5	7	18,506	9,152	9,354	365	178	187	..	..	..	5
296	*157*	*139*	*113,024*	*59,203*	*53,821*	*9,433*	*4,879*	*4,554*	*6*	*3*	*3*	
..	..	..	11,404	5,802	5,602	294	175	119	..	..	..	6
90	41	49	23,475	12,368	11,107	2,201	1,196	1,005	..	..	..	7
170	88	82	50,925	26,839	24,086	4,928	2,486	2,442	..	..	..	8
10	10	..	7,037	3,644	3,393	846	418	428	..	..	..	9
26	18	8	20,183	10,550	9,633	1,164	604	560	6	3	3	10
1,139	*607*	*532*	*114,898*	*61,076*	*53,822*	*11,081*	*6,064*	*5,017*	*35*	*22*	*13*	
42	20	22	20,928	11,046	9,882	278	170	108	4	2	2	11
1,047	567	480	53,809	29,366	24,443	8,558	4,810	3,748	31	20	11	12
35	13	22	13,556	7,045	6,511	1,243	623	620	..	..	..	13
..	..	..	15,484	8,134	7,350	395	166	229	..	..	..	14
15	7	8	11,121	5,485	5,636	607	295	312	..	..	..	15
47	*21*	*26*	*46,004*	*23,397*	*22,607*	*13,370*	*6,329*	*7,041*	*18*	*9*	*9*	
30	14	16	19,992	10,251	9,741	5,980	2,980	3,000	9	6	3	16
7	3	4	18,673	9,495	9,178	5,216	2,459	2,757	9	3	6	17
10	4	6	7,339	3,651	3,688	2,174	890	1,284	..	..	..	18
243	**138**	**105**	**299,680**	**157,548**	**142,132**	**5,395**	**2,765**	**2,630**	**21**	**10**	**11**	
127	72	55	86,498	45,714	40,784	2,554	1,319	1,235	..	..	..	19
71	36	35	89,185	46,903	42,282	1,321	726	595	14	6	8	20
33	21	12	71,766	37,474	34,292	778	380	398	..	..	..	21
12	9	3	52,231	27,457	24,774	742	340	402	7	4	3	22
17	**12**	**5**	**23,254**	**11,733**	**11,521**	**51,701**	**26,102**	**25,599**	..	..	..	
..	..	..	1,027	514	513	1	..	1	..	..	..	23
2	1	1	1,967	988	979	1,873	920	953	..	..	..	24
..	..	..	674	353	321	24	13	11	..	..	..	25
3	2	1	2,512	1,268	1,244	384	163	221	..	..	..	26
5	2	3	2,403	1,177	1,226	427	209	218	..	..	..	27
..	..	..	857	383	474	1	1	..	..	..	..	28
..	..	..	1,083	512	571	7	2	5	..	..	..	29
1	1	..	400	210	190	12	6	6	..	..	..	30
3	3	..	1,743	891	852	143	68	75	..	..	..	31
2	2	..	330	165	165	89	49	40	..	..	..	32
..	..	..	73	45	28	..	..	..	..	..	..	33
..	..	..	1,056	592	464	11	7	4	..	..	..	34
1	1	..	7,035	3,625	3,410	29	13	16	..	..	..	35
..	..	..	271	134	137	..	..	..	..	..	..	36
..	..	..	1,823	876	947	48,700	24,651	24,049	..	..	..	37

TABLE XVII

Race, Tribe or Caste

1. This table shows for the Province and for each district or State in which they were returned the total population and the religion of those castes or tribes which are of considerable importance in their own locality. If a district is not mentioned under the name of a caste or tribe, it means that no members of that caste or tribe were returned there. Where various religions are professed by a caste or tribe separate figures have been given for each.

2. Audhelias, Chauhans, Dewars and Kamars are shown for the Chhattisgarh Division and Central Provinces States only. It is exceptional for these four castes or tribes to be found elsewhere.

3. The statistics of Indian Christians, apart from those shown in this table as returning their original caste or tribe, will be found in Tables VIII, XI and XIV.

TABLE XVII Race, Tribe or Caste.

Tribe or caste with religion and locality.	Persons.	Males	Females.
1	2	3	4
AHIR, HINDU			
Central Provinces and Berar ..	**813,535**	**404,826**	**408,709**
Saugor	27,311	14,505	12,806
Damoh ..	13,629	7,164	6,465
Jubbulpore	35,496	18,234	17,262
Mandla	32,247	16,149	16,098
Seoni	29,040	14,273	14,767
Narsinghpur	21,443	10,965	10,478
Hoshangabad ..	11,053	5,667	5,386
Nimar	11,553	6,162	5,391
Betul	17,697	9,025	8,672
Chhindwara ..	43,977	22,042	21,935
Wardha	4,694	2,420	2,274
Nagpur ..	5,647	3,092	2,555
Chanda	3,364	1,687	1,677
Bhandara ..	2,992	1,298	1,694
Balaghat	10,498	5,271	5,227
Raipur ..	161,406	78,401	83,005
Bilaspur	125,300	61,877	63,423
Drug	74,007	35,365	38,642
Berar ..	*19,882*	*10,529*	*9,353*
Amraoti	8,480	4,492	3,988
Akola	4,393	2,332	2,061
Buldana	1,803	944	859
Yeotmal	5,206	2,761	2,445
Central Provinces States ..	*162,299*	*80,700*	*81,599*
Makrai ..	7	4	3
Bastar	21,110	10,709	10,401
Kanker	7,653	3,977	3,676
Nandgaon	17,998	8,624	9,374
Khairagarh	14,237	6,801	7,436
Chhuikhadan	2,876	1,451	1,425
Kawardha	5,240	2,483	2,757
Sakti	4,259	2,098	2,161
Raigarh	23,857	11,352	12,505
Sarangarh	10,479	5,060	5,419
Changbhakar	2,017	1,089	928
Korea	4,233	2,281	1,952
Surguja	24,722	12,709	12,013
Udaipur	8,533	4,353	4,180
Jashpur	15,078	7,709	7,369
AHIR TRIBAL RELIGIONS			
Central Provinces and Berar ..	**4,559**	**2,164**	**2,395**
Damoh	7	5	2
Jubbulpore	7	4	3
Mandla	23	15	8
Seoni	1,032	489	543
Narsinghpur	5	3	2
Hoshangabad	45	24	21
Nimar	1	1	
Chhindwara	2,866	1,317	1,549
Chanda	4	3	1
Balagaht	9	4	5
Raipur	204	104	100
Bilaspur	65	31	34
Drug	28	18	10
Berar	*29*	*28*	*1*
Amraoti	29	28	1
Central Provinces States ..	*234*	*118*	*116*
Bastar	4	3	1
Kanker	31	25	6
Changbhakar	91	50	41
Korea	87	34	53
Surguja	21	6	15

Tribe or caste with religion and locality.	Persons.	Males.	Females.
1	2	3	4
AHIR, CHRISTIAN			
Central Provinces and Berar ..	**11**	**3**	**8**
Drug	4	2	2
Berar	*5*	*1*	*4*
Amraoti ..	5	1	4
Central Provinces States	*2*	..	*2*
Khairagarh	1	..	1
Kawardha	1	..	1
ANDH, HINDU			
Central Provinces and Berar ..	**58,549**	**29,820**	**28,729**
Chanda	30	19	11
Berar ..	*58,519*	*29,801*	*28,718*
Amraoti	22	13	9
Akola	23,118	11,246	11,872
Buldana	4,680	2,367	2,313
Yeotmal	30,699	16,175	14,524
AUDHELIA, HINDU			
Chhattisgarh Division	*749*	*444*	*305*
Bilaspur ..	749	444	305
BAHNA, HINDU			
Central Provinces and Berar ..	**1,108**	**528**	**580**
Chanda ..	1	1	..
Raipur	713	343	370
Bilaspur	44	25	19
Drug	108	45	63
Berar ..	*8*	*4*	*4*
Amraoti	6	2	4
Yeotmal	2	2	..
Central Provinces States ..	*234*	*110*	*124*
Nandgaon ..	22	9	13
Chhuikhadan	1	1	..
Sakti	208	99	109
Udaipur	3	1	2
BAHNA, MUSLIM			
Central Provinces and Berar ..	**37,549**	**18,977**	**18,572**
Saugor	2,748	1,467	1,281
Damoh	3,117	1,560	1,557
Jubbulpore	4,865	2,395	2,470
Mandla	435	220	215
Seoni	1,812	897	915
Narsinghpur	2,744	1,377	1,367
Hoshangabad	2,536	1,250	1,286
Nimar	1,997	989	1,008
Betul ..	399	212	187
Chhindwara	4,730	2,447	2,283
Wardha	782	436	346
Nagpur	5,072	2,529	2,543
Chanda	329	159	170
Bhandara	1,488	723	765
Balaghat	798	379	419

Tribe or caste with religion and locality.	Persons.	Males.	Females.
1	2	3	4
BAHNA, MUSLIM—*concld.*			
Berar	*3,612*	*1,897*	*1,715*
Amraoti	2,393	1,246	1,147
Akola	187	123	64
Buldana	479	246	233
Yeotmal	553	282	271
Central Provinces States	*55*	*40*	*15*
Makrai	67	33	34
Bastar	14	4	10
Korea	4	3	1
BAIGA, HINDU			
Central Provinces and Berar	**14,288**	**7,046**	**7,242**
Jubbulpore	2,340	1,173	1,167
Mandla	5,507	2,704	2,803
Seoni	1	1	..
Chhindwara	48	35	13
Nagpur	3	3	..
Balaghat	238	119	119
Raipur	270	137	133
Bilaspur	1,397	646	751
Drug	42	23	19
Berar	*1*	..	*1*
Yeotmal	1	..	1
Central Provinces States	*4,441*	*2,205*	*2,236*
Bastar	389	197	192
Kanker	55	28	27
Kawardha	3,043	1,500	1,543
Raigarh	791	398	393
Changbhakar	32	14	18
Surguja	34	18	16
Udaipur	97	50	47
BAIGA, TRIBAL RELIGIONS			
Central Provinces and Berar	**22,798**	**11,389**	**11,409**
Jubbulpore	325	150	175
Mandla	14,431	7,266	7,165
Seoni	658	319	339
Chhindwara	4	2	2
Balaghat	5,402	2,663	2,739
Raipur	116	56	60
Bilaspur	1,007	508	499
Drug	213	113	100
Central Provinces States	*642*	*312*	*330*
Bastar	8	5	3
Kanker	365	162	203
Kawardha	31	19	12
Changbhakar	130	60	70
Korea	108	66	42
BAIRAGI, HINDU			
Central Provinces and Berar	**38,473**	**19,407**	**19,066**
Saugor	790	429	361
Damoh	309	176	133
Jubbulpore	1,467	781	686
Mandla	510	283	227
Seoni	274	130	144
Narsinghpur	790	433	357
Hoshangabad	2,127	1,170	957
Nimar	584	340	244
Betul	126	58	68
Chhindwara	476	244	232
BAIRAGI, HINDU—*concld.*			
Wardha	148	80	68
Nagpur	519	280	239
Chanda	106	56	50
Bhandara	866	239	627
Balaghat	430	218	212
Raipur	6,643	3,288	3,355
Bilaspur	9,199	4,497	4,702
Drug	2,960	1,457	1,503
Berar	*1,245*	*728*	*517*
Amraoti	449	270	179
Akola	406	220	186
Buldana	296	183	113
Yeotmal	94	55	39
Central Provinces States	*8,904*	*4,520*	*4,384*
Makrai	18	8	10
Bastar	542	279	263
Kanker	116	69	47
Nandgaon	1,580	837	743
Khairagarh	1,004	515	489
Chhuikhadan	513	258	255
Kawardha	338	165	173
Sakti	622	311	311
Raigarh	1,628	804	824
Sarangarh	1,046	515	531
Changbhakar	12	5	7
Korea	118	72	46
Surguja	880	433	447
Udaipur	343	178	165
Jashpur	144	71	73
BAIRAGI, CHRISTIAN			
Central Provinces and Berar	**1**	**1**	..
Central Provinces States	*1*	*1*	..
Bastar	1	1	..
BALAHI, HINDU			
Central Provinces and Berar	**54,230**	**27,163**	**27,067**
Jubbulpore	92	5	87
Mandla	19	..	19
Hoshangabad	20,307	10,041	10,266
Nimar	30,191	15,241	14,950
Nagpur	87	42	45
Chanda	2	1	1
Raipur	28	15	13
Bilaspur	3	1	2
Berar	*1,523*	*835*	*688*
Amraoti	1,523	835	688
Central Provinces States	*1,978*	*982*	*996*
Makrai	1,978	982	996
BALAHI, TRIBAL RELIGIONS			
Central Provinces and Berar	**35**	**21**	**14**
Hoshangabad	7	3	4
Nimar	10	4	6
Berar	*18*	*14*	*4*
Amraoti	18	14	
BALAHI, CHRISTIAN			
Central Provinces and Berar	**2,517**	**1,258**	**1,259**
Nimar	2,517	1,258	1,259

TABLE XVII Race, Tribe or Caste—*contd.*

Tribe or caste with religion and locality.	Persons.	Males.	Females.
1	2	3	4
BANIA, HINDU			
Central Provinces and Berar ..	**153,768**	**80,715**	**73,053**
Saugor	4,317	2,184	2,133
Damoh	3,550	1,841	1,709
Jubbulpore	12,924	6,556	6,368
Mandla	1,795	924	871
Seoni	1,867	973	894
Narsinghpur	6,220	3,278	2,942
Hoshangabad	6,000	3,184	2,816
Nimar	10,393	5,521	4,872
Betul	1,101	528	573
Chhindwara	2,954	1,533	1,421
Wardha	5,379	2,806	2,564
Nagpur	6,598	3,659	2,939
Chanda	1,988	1,056	932
Bhandara	4,673	2,596	2,077
Balaghat	1,861	981	880
Raipur	6,394	3,335	3,059
Bilaspur	9,996	4,964	5,032
Drug	2,338	1,161	1,177
Berar	*51,453*	*27,313*	*24,140*
Amraoti	11,641	6,037	5,604
Akola	16,004	8,628	7,376
Buldana	12,799	6,660	6,139
Yeotmal	11,009	5,988	5,021
Central Provinces States ..	*11,976*	*6,322*	*5,654*
Makrai	336	178	158
Bastar	179	106	73
Kanker	179	110	69
Nandgaon	993	510	483
Khairagarh	905	487	418
Chhuikhadan	135	58	77
Kawardha	868	388	480
Sakti	481	266	215
Raigarh	2,365	1,251	1,114
Sarangarh	503	255	248
Changbhakar	204	110	94
Korea	594	398	196
Surguja	3,617	1,862	1,755
Udaipur	187	110	77
Jashpur	430	233	197
BANIA, JAIN			
Central Provinces and Berar ..	**79,855**	**41,416**	**38,439**
Saugor	17,136	8,910	8,226
Damoh	7,478	3,825	3,653
Jubbulpore	6,792	3,521	3,271
Mandla	784	415	369
Seoni	1,782	911	871
Narsinghpur	2,654	1,376	1,278
Hoshangabad	1,851	954	897
Nimar	2,204	1,164	1,040
Betul	1,331	674	657
Chhindwara	2,048	1,034	1,014
Wardha	2,899	1,488	1,411
Nagpur	3,621	1,827	1,794
Chanda	1,002	547	455
Bhandara	1,560	779	781
Balaghat	865	453	412
Raipur	1,733	932	801
Bilaspur	520	282	238
Drug	1,233	681	552
Berar	*20,402*	*10,560*	*9,842*
Amraoti	5,052	2,587	2,465
Akola	6,866	3,535	3,331
Buldana	4,547	2,400	2,147
Yeotmal	3,937	2,038	1,899
Central Provinces States ..	*1,960*	*1,083*	*877*
Makrai	54	26	28
Bastar	134	78	56
Kanker	155	79	76
BANIA, JAIN—*concld.*			
Nandgaon	855	487	368
Khairagarh	414	230	184
Chhuikhadan	151	79	72
Kawardha	125	61	64
Sakti	2	2	..
Raigarh	46	28	18
Sarangarh	2	2	..
Surguja	22	11	11
BANIA, TRIBAL RELIGIONS			
Central Provinces and Berar ..	**37**	**24**	**13**
Bilaspur	1	1	..
Central Provinces States ..	*36*	*23*	*13*
Korea	36	23	13
BANIA, CHRISTIAN			
Central Provinces and Berar ..	**1**	**1**	..
Narsinghpur	1	1	..
BANJARA, HINDU			
Central Provinces and Berar ..	**154,226**	**77,901**	**76,325**
Saugor	85	62	23
Damoh	696	373	323
Jubbulpore	205	114	91
Mandla	1,807	926	881
Seoni	1,613	749	864
Narsinghpur	126	77	49
Hoshangabad	1,018	561	457
Nimar	16,542	8,932	7,610
Betul	765	389	376
Chhindwara	2,275	1,213	1,062
Wardha	1,281	664	617
Nagpur	1,986	983	1,003
Chanda	932	467	465
Bhandara	345	176	169
Balaghat	623	328	295
Raipur	5,312	2,502	2,810
Bilaspur	3,273	1,545	1,728
Drug	85	42	43
Berar	*109,032*	*54,734*	*54,293*
Amraoti	1,089	616	473
Akola	25,659	12,977	12,682
Buldana	20,178	9,907	10,271
Yeotmal	62,106	31,234	30,872
Central Provinces States ..	*6,225*	*3,064*	*3,161*
Makrai ..	61	39	22
Bastar	3,127	1,555	15,721
Kanker	439	209	230
Nandgaon	48	20	28
Khairagarh	1	..	1
Kawardha	11	8	3
Sakti	11	7	4
Raigarh	1,172	572	600
Sarangarh	425	202	223
Korea	15	9	6
Surgúja	142	69	73
Udaipur	686	314	372
Jashpur	87	60	27

Tribe or caste with religion and locality.	Persons.	Males.	Females.
1	2	3	4
BANJARA, TRIBAL RELIGIONS			
Central Provinces and Berar ..	**1,007**	**486**	**521**
Mandla	5	3	2
Chhindwara	4	2	2
Chanda	193	88	105
Raipur	710	334	376
Bilaspur	1	..	1
Berar	*30*	*10*	*20*
Amraoti	30	10	20
Central Provinces States ..	*64*	*49*	*15*
Korea	64	49	15
BANJARA, MUSLIM			
Central Provinces and Berar ..	**120**	**64**	**56**
Jubbulpore . ..	6	6	..
Hoshangabad . ..	1	..	1
Nimar	105	54	51
Betul	8	4	4
BARHAI, HINDU			
Central Provinces and Berar ..	**111,952**	**58,078**	**53,874**
Saugor	5,466	2,919	2,547
Damoh	4,266	2,113	2,153
Jubbulpore	6,245	3,241	3,004
Mandla	307	159	148
Seoni	1,222	618	604
Narsinghpur	5,377	2,723	2,654
Hoshangabad	7,608	3,922	3,686
Nimar	3,388	1,817	1,571
Betul . ..	3,327	1,742	1,585
Chhindwara	4,185	2,143	2,042
Wardha	9,479	4,794	4,685
Nagpur	15,147	7,653	7,494
Chanda	5,623	2,843	2,780
Bhandara	5,373	2,855	2,518
Balaghat . ..	831	446	385
Raipur	357	188	169
Bilaspur ..	479	191	288
Drug	54	29	25
Berar	*32,635*	*17,377*	*15,258*
Amraoti	12,367	6,362	6,005
Akola . ..	5,802	3,085	2,717
Buldana	5,341	2,801	2,540
Yeotmal . ..	9,125	5,129	3,996
Central Provinces States ..	*583*	*305*	*278*
Makrai . ..	135	67	66
Bastar ..	4	3	1
Kanker . .	5	5	..
Nandgaon ..	50	35	15
Khairagarh . ..	39	18	21
Kawardha ..	6	..	6
Sakti . ..	53	29	[illegible]
Raigarh	26	18	8
Sarangarh . ..	2	..	2
Changbhakar . ..	3	3	..
Korea . ..	9	7	2
Surguja . ..	237	112	125
Jashpur	14	8	6
BARHAI, TRIBAL RELIGIONS			
Central Provinces and Berar ..	**12**	**6**	**6**
Bilaspur	12	6	6

Tribe or caste with religion and locality.	Persons.	Males.	Females.
1	2	3	4
BARHAI, CHRISTIAN			
Central Provinces and Berar ..	**26**	**13**	**13**
Berar	*26*	*13*	*13*
Amraoti	3	1	2
Akola ..	16	9	7
Buldana	7	3	4
BASOR, HINDU			
Central Provinces and Berar ..	**52,130**	**26,150**	**25,980**
Saugor	9,588	4,940	4,648
Damoh	7,172	3,676	3,496
Jubbulpore	8,723	4,383	4,340
Mandla	2,200	1,083	1,117
Seoni	1,822	906	916
Narsinghpur	3,099	1,550	1,549
Hoshangabad	2,736	1,380	1,356
Nimar	358	186	172
Betul	940	449	491
Chhindwara	1,402	690	712
Wardha	375	202	173
Nagpur	1,512	776	736
Chanda	2,601	1,369	1,232
Bhandara	1,410	572	838
Balaghat	772	386	386
Raipur	1,088	492	596
Bilaspur	1,519	749	770
Drug	1,386	627	759
Berar ..	*1,935*	*1,018*	*917*
Amraoti	884	458	426
Akola	187	95	92
Buldana	130	61	69
Yeotmal	734	404	330
Central Provinces States ..	*1,492*	*716*	*776*
Makrai	51	24	27
Bastar	12	8	4
Kanker	87	41	46
Nandgaon	357	176	181
Khairagarh	244	110	134
Chhuikhadan . ..	84	41	43
Kawardha . ..	43	19	24
Sakti	51	75	76
Raigarh	378	186	192
Changbhakar	64	28	36
Korea	8	1	7
Udaipur	2	2	..
Jashpur	11	5	6
BASOR, TRIBAL RELIGIONS			
Central Provinces and Berar ..	**2,849**	**1,363**	**1,486**
Damoh	2	1	1
Mandla	1,360	643	717
Seoni	2	..	2
Narsinghpur	1	1	..
Wardha	87	41	46
Chanda	404	197	207
Bhandara	660	316	344
Raipur	1	..	1
Bilaspur . .	49	22	27
Central Provinces States ..	*283*	*142*	*141*
Bastar .. .	3	2	1
Changbhakar	191	93	98
Korea	89	47	42
BASOR, CHRISTIAN			
Central Provinces and Berar ..	**8**	**4**	**4**
Saugor . ..	1	..	1
Damoh	1	1	..
Chhindwara	6	3	3

TABLE XVII Race, Tribe or Caste—*contd.*

Tribe or caste with religion and locality.	Persons.	Males.	Females.
1	2	3	4
BEDAR, HINDU			
Central Provinces and Berar ..	**1,139**	**619**	**520**
Nimar	92	89	3
Betul	2	2	..
Nagpur	27	18	9
Berar	*1,018*	*510*	*508*
Amraoti	258	124	134
Akola	136	69	67
Buldana	96	56	40
Yeotmal	528	261	267
BELDAR, HINDU			
Central Provinces and Berar ..	**25,972**	**12,596**	**13,376**
Saugor	559	266	293
Damoh	390	198	192
Jubbulpore	1,034	524	510
Mandla	10	7	3
Seoni	111	49	62
Narsinghpur	164	84	80
Hoshangabad	564	283	281
Nimar	1,281	612	669
Betul	130	79	51
Chhindwara	216	98	118
Wardha	1,901	946	955
Nagpur	740	343	397
Chanda	1,080	526	554
Bhandara	395	23	277
Balaghat	32	10	22
Raipur	1,585	735	850
Bilaspur	586	243	343
Drug	190	88	102
Berar	*14,222*	*7,057*	*7,165*
Amraoti	2,609	1,317	1,292
Akola	3,754	1,849	1,905
Buldana	3,497	1,731	1,766
Yeotmal	4,362	2,160	2,202
Central Provinces States ..	*872*	*420*	*452*
Makrai	12	8	4
Bastar	4	2	2
Kanker	21	14	7
Nandgaon	738	348	390
Chhuikhadan	42	22	20
Sarangarh	6	1	5
Changbhakar	14	7	7
Korea	7	2	5
Udaipur	8	6	2
Jashpur	20	10	10
BELDAR, TRIBAL RELIGIONS			
Central Provinces and Berar ..	**20**	**13**	**7**
Chhindwara	1	1	..
Bilaspur	7	3	4
Central Provinces States ..	*12*	*9*	*3*
Korea	12	9	3
BHAINA, HINDU			
Central Provinces and Berar ..	**16,836**	**8,195**	**8,641**
Mandla	812	372	440
Bhandara	1	1	..
Raipur	202	90	112
Bilaspur	11,416	5,649	5,767
Central Provinces States ..	*4,405*	*2,083*	*2,322*
Raigarh	2,265	1,061	1,204
Sarangarh	1,062	506	556
Jashpur	1,078	516	562
BHAINA, TRIBAL RELIGIONS			
Central Provinces and Berar ..	**4,043**	**2,032**	**2,011**
Mandla	201	105	96
Bilaspur	3,815	1,912	1,903
Central Provinces States ..	*27*	*15*	*12*
Korea	27	15	12
BHAMTA, HINDU			
Central Provinces and Berar ..	**4,336**	**2,131**	**2,205**
Nimar	8	6	2
Betul	5	5	..
Chhindwara	23	9	14
Wardha	1,176	593	583
Nagpur	777	379	398
Chanda	434	211	223
Bhandara	7	3	4
Berar	*1,906*	*925*	*981*
Amraoti	546	274	272
Akola	576	290	286
Buldana	8	5	3
Yeotmal	776	356	420
BHATTRA, HINDU			
Central Provinces and Berar ..	**650**	**331**	**319**
Raipur	351	185	166
Drug	45	16	29
Berar	*2*	*2*	..
Yeotmal	2	2	..
Central Provinces States ..	*252*	*128*	*124*
Bastar	26	15	11
Sakti	164	81	83
Surguja	4	3	1
Udaipur	48	24	24
Jashpur	10	5	5
BHATTRA, TRIBAL RELIGIONS			
Central Provinces and Berar ..	**36,597**	**18,327**	**18,270**
Raipur	12	7	5
Central Provinces States ..	*36,585*	*18,320*	*18,265*
Bastar	36,585	18,320	18,265
BHARIA—BHUMIA, HINDU			
Central Provinces and Berar ..	**36,650**	**17,550**	**19,100**
Saugor	1	1	..
Damoh	442	194	248
Jubbulpore	28,985	13,877	15,108
Mandla	12	4	8
Seoni	297	152	145
Narsinghpur	992	481	511
Hoshangabad	81	46	35
Nimar	3	2	1
Betul	1	1	..
Chhindwara	106	53	53
Nagpur	4	4	..
Bhandara	314	57	257
Balaghat	124	55	69
Raipur	11	6	5
Bilaspur	3,398	1,669	1,729
Drug	134	69	65

Tribe or caste with religion and locality.	Persons.	Males.	Females.
1	2	3	4
BHARIA—BHUMIA, HINDU —concld.			
Berar	*250*	*120*	*130*
Akola	250	120	130
Central Provinces States ..	*1,495*	*759*	*736*
Changbhakar	66	32	34
Surguja	1,171	587	584
Jashpur	258	140	118
BHARIA—BHUMIA, TRIBAL RELIGIONS			
Central Provinces and Berar ..	**18,691**	**9,095**	**9,596**
Damoh	317	154	163
Jubbulpore	21	10	11
Mandla	1,469	715	754
Seoni	1,239	595	644
Narsinghpur	1,153	640	513
Hoshangabad	677	337	340
Chhindwara	7,093	3,462	3,631
Balaghat	66	33	33
Bilaspur	5,928	2,788	3,140
Drug	701	339	362
Central Provinces States ..	*27*	*22*	*5*
Bastar	2	2	..
Korea	17	17	..
Surguja	8	3	5
BHIL, HINDU			
Central Provinces and Berar ..	**29,760**	**14,927**	**14,833**
Saugor	9	4	5
Jubbulpore	11	8	3
Hoshangabad	27	13	14
Nimar	24,637	12,367	12,270
Chhindwara	1	1	..
Wardha	13	9	4
Nagpur	9	7	2
Bhandara	10	6	4
Berar	*5,021*	*2,499*	*2,522*
Amraoti	94	49	45
Akola	1,064	547	517
Buldana	1,155	582	573
Yeotmal	2,708	1,321	1,387
Central Provinces States ..	*22*	*13*	*9*
Surguja	22	13	9
BHIL, TRIBAL RELIGIONS			
Central Provinces and Berar ..	**405**	**226**	**179**
Mandla	4	1	3
Narsinghpur	1	1	..
Nimar	310	173	137
Berar	*90*	*51*	*39*
Amraoti	34	26	8
Akola	18	10	8
Buldana	38	15	23
BHIL, MUSLIM			
Central Provinces and Berar ..	**160**	**89**	**71**
Nimar	46	28	18
Berar	*114*	*61*	*53*
Amraoti	22	11	11
Buldana	92	50	42

Tribe or caste with religion and locality.	Persons.	Males.	Females.
1	2	3	4
BHILALA, HINDU			
Central Provinces and Berar ..	**15,906**	**8,219**	**7,687**
Jubbulpore	13	7	6
Hoshangabad	2,546	1,249	1,297
Nimar	13,285	6,928	6,357
Betul	9	5	4
Central Provinces States ..	*53*	*30*	*23*
Makrai	53	30	23
BHOYAR, HINDU			
Central Provinces and Berar ..	**74,646**	**36,812**	**37,834**
Narsinghpur	..	..	..
Betul	26,336	12,884	13,452
Chhindwara	26,051	12,863	13,188
Wardha	14,228	7,030	7,198
Nagpur	3,895	1,989	1,906
Bhandara	60	27	33
Bilaspur	327	172	155
Berar	*862*	*430*	*432*
Amraoti	57	33	24
Buldana	805	397	408
Central Provinces States ..	*2,886*	*1,416*	*1,470*
Sakti	163	87	76
Raigarh	740	375	365
Sarangarh	1,137	525	612
Korea	1	1	..
Surguja	750	385	365
Udaipur	95	43	52
BHOYAR, TRIBAL RELIGIONS			
Central Provinces and Berar ..	**369**	**181**	**188**
Central Provinces States ..	*369*	*181*	*188*
Korea	369	181	188
BHUINHAR, HINDU			
Central Provinces and Berar ..	**20,939**	**10,647**	**10,292**
Wardha	2	2	..
Raipur	27	11	16
Bilaspur	318	142	176
Central Provinces States ..	*20,592*	*10,492*	*10,100*
Raigarh	2,794	1,305	1,489
Surguja	10,791	5,572	5,219
Udaipur	860	434	426
Jashpur	6,147	3,181	2,966
BHUINHAR, TRIBAL RELIGIONS			
Central Provinces and Berar ..	**4,689**	**2,434**	**2,255**
Bilaspur	903	475	428
Central Provinces States ..	*3,786*	*1,959*	*1,827*
Changbhakar	492	251	241
Korea	3,143	1,629	1,314
Surguja	151	79	72

TABLE XVII Race, Tribe or Caste—*contd.*

Tribe or caste with religion and locality.	Persons.	Males.	Females.
1	2	3	4
BHULIA, HINDU			
Central Provinces and Berar	**6,888**	**3,567**	**3,321**
Nagpur	3	1	2
Chanda	13	10	3
Raipur	4,128	2,077	2,051
Bilaspur	1,572	917	655
Drug	11	4	7
Berar	*2*	*2*	..
Yeotmal	2	2	..
Central Provinces States	*1,159*	*556*	*603*
Bastar	2	1	1
Raigarh	962	456	506
Sarangarh	195	99	96
BHUNJIA, HINDU			
Central Provinces and Berar	**3,318**	**1,647**	**1,671**
Saugor	2	1	1
Jubbulpore	67	36	31
Seoni	6	3	3
Nimar	40	23	17
Betul	12	6	6
Chhindwara	10	..	10
Wardha	25	14	11
Nagpur	136	71	65
Chanda	3	2	1
Raipur	2,063	1,000	1,063
Bilaspur	99	53	46
Drug	8	5	3
Berar	*23*	*5*	*18*
Amraoti	1	1	..
Akola	3	3	..
Buldana	3	..	3
Yeotmal	16	1	15
Central Provinces States	*824*	*428*	*396*
Nandgaon	35	16	19
Raigarh	10	4	6
Korea	6	3	3
Surguja	761	399	362
Jashpur	12	6	6
BHUNJIA, TRIBAL RELIGIONS			
Central Provinces and Berar	**5,195**	**2,586**	**2,609**
Raipur	5,195	2,586	2,609
BINJHWAR, HINDU			
Central Provinces and Berar	**61,581**	**30,482**	**31,099**
Saugor	2	2	..
Seoni	165	72	93
Nagpur	89	42	47
Chanda	273	116	157
Bhandara	3,737	1,842	1,895
Balaghat	8,237	4,005	4,232
Raipur	23,839	11,692	12,147
Bilaspur	12,317	6,268	6,049
Berar	*269*	*110*	*129*
Amraoti	25	18	7
Akola	211	107	104
Yeotmal	33	15	18
Central Provinces States	*12,653*	*6,303*	*6,350*
Sakti	76	41	35
Raigarh	250	135	115
Sarangarh	6,975	3,400	3,575
Surguja	5,352	2,727	2,625

Tribe or caste with religion and locality.	Persons	Males.	Females.
1	2	3	4
BINJHWAR, TRIBAL RELIGIONS			
Central Provinces and Berar	**5,680**	**2,786**	**2,894**
Balaghat	22	22	..
Raipur	5,384	2,638	2,746
Bilaspur	269	122	147
Central Provinces States	*5*	*4*	*1*
Surguja	2	2	..
Udaipur	3	2	1
BOHRA, MUSLIM			
Central Provinces and Berar	**7,926**	**4,305**	**3,621**
Saugor	175	57	118
Damoh	30	22	8
Jubbulpore	555	335	220
Mandla	6	4	2
Seoni	51	34	17
Narsinghpur	31	21	10
Hoshangabad	471	268	203
Nimar	2,613	1,206	1,407
Betul	117	65	52
Chhindwara	39	24	15
Wardha	372	220	152
Nagpur	667	364	303
Chanda	118	54	64
Bhandara	171	93	78
Balaghat	36	12	24
Raipur	349	197	152
Bilaspur	298	177	121
Drug	96	55	41
Berar	*1,611*	*1,023*	*588*
Amraoti	632	443	189
Akola	328	182	146
Buldana	333	187	146
Yeotmal	318	211	107
Central Provinces States	*120*	*74*	*46*
Bastar	2	1	1
Kanker	18	8	10
Nandgaon	48	30	18
Khairagarh	13	7	6
Raigarh	31	22	9
Sarangarh	8	6	2
BRAHMAN, HINDU			
Central Provinces and Berar	**517,745**	**277,925**	**239,820**
Saugor	41,161	21,931	19,230
Damoh	21,381	11,318	10,063
Jubbulpore	65,121	34,347	30,774
Mandla	8,865	4,761	4,104
Seoni	8,264	4,304	3,960
Narsinghpur	22,396	11,679	10,717
Hoshangabad	34,668	18,266	16,402
Nimar	18,499	10,535	7,964
Betul	5,345	2,930	2,415
Chhindwara	10,456	5,625	4,831
Wardha	15,339	8,682	6,657
Nagpur	37,838	21,494	16,344
Chanda	7,614	3,969	3,645
Bhandara	8,561	4,638	3,923
Balaghat	4,985	2,702	2,283
Raipur	27,622	14,253	13,369
Bilaspur	37,177	18,805	18,372
Drug	15,172	7,609	7,563
Berar	*103,328*	*57,218*	*46,110*
Amraoti	29,849	16,695	13,154
Akola	29,851	16,669	13,182
Buldana	24,535	13,234	11,301
Yeotmal	19,093	10,620	8,473

Tribe or caste with religion and locality.	Persons.	Males	Females.
1	2	3	4
BRAHMAN, HINDU—*concld.*			
Central Provinces States ..	*23,953*	*12,859*	*11,094*
Makrai	1,066	540	526
Bastar .. .	2,969	1,495	1,474
Kanker	827	436	391
Nandgaon	2,887	1,588	1,299
Khairagarh	2,516	1,300	1,216
Chhuikhadan	393	213	180
Kawardha	1,187	620	567
Sakti	539	269	270
Raigarh	4,009	2,127	1,882
Sarangarh	1,829	945	884
Changbhakar	402	230	172
Korea	1,094	689	405
Surguja . .	3,321	1,843	1,478
Udaipur	352	208	144
Jashpur	562	356	206
BRAHMAN, TRIBAL RELIGIONS			
Central Provinces and Berar ..	**4**	**2**	**2**
Bilaspur	3	1	2
Central Provinces States .	*1*	*1*	..
Changbhakar .. .	1	1	..
BRAHMAN, CHRISTIAN			
Central Provinces and Berar ..	**16**	**9**	**7**
Narsinghpur	1	1	..
Nimar	5	4	1
Nagpur	1	..	1
Drug	1	..	1
Berar	*6*	*3*	*3*
Amraoti	6	3	3
Central Provinces States ..	*2*	*1*	*1*
Bastar	2	1	1
CHADAR, HINDU			
Central Provinces and Berar ..	**26,986**	**13,685**	**13,301**
Saugor	14,282	7,300	6,982
Damoh	6,787	3,407	3,380
Jubbulpore	2,534	1,270	1,264
Mandla	57	31	26
Seoni	233	117	116
Narsinghpur	2,803	1,415	1,388
Hoshangabad	73	39	34
Chhindwara	9	6	3
Nagpur	7	5	2
Bhandara	2	1	1
Central Provinces States ..	*199*	*94*	*105*
Bastar	199	94	105
CHAMAR, HINDU			
Central Provinces and Berar ..	**615,596**	**305,633**	**309,963**
Saugor	78,946	40,015	38,931
Damoh	41,591	20,583	21,008
Jubbulpore	44,842	22,537	22,305
Mandla . ..	4,646	2,324	2,322
Seoni	5,502	2,750	2,752
Narsinghpur	19,081	9,583	9,498
Hoshangabad	26,079	13,253	12,826
Nimar	7,409	3,892	3,517
Betul	4,099	2,078	2,021
Chhindwara	9,290	4,581	4,709
Wardha	3,569	1,831	1,738
Nagpur	10,053	5,074	4,979
Chanda	3,853	1,928	1,925
Bhandara	6,790	3,594	3,196
Balaghat	4,151	2,067	2,084
Raipur	91,956	44,426	47,530
Bilaspur	117,978	57,566	60,412
Drug	9,496	4,575	4,921
CHAMAR, HINDU—*concld.*			
Berar	*38,645*	*19,742*	*18,903*
Amraoti	8,811	4,499	4,312
Akola	10,958	5,665	5,293
Buldana	11,795	6,013	5,782
Yeotmal	7,081	3,565	3,516
Central Provinces States ..	*87,620*	*43,234*	*44,386*
Makrai	490	244	246
Bastar . ..	1,959	999	960
Kanker ..	372	201	171
Nandgaon ..	17,144	8,113	9,031
Khairagarh	16,552	8,060	8,492
Chhuikhadan	2,638	1,255	1,383
Kawardha	10,262	5,102	5,160
Sakti	2,940	1,575	1,365
Raigarh . ..	9,897	4,908	4,989
Sarangarh	12,392	6,244	6,148
Changhhakar . ..	602	328	274
Korea . ..	2,083	1,039	1,044
Surguja . ..	8,913	4,439	4,474
Udaipur	966	509	457
Jashpur	410	218	192
CHAMAR, TRIBAL RELIGIONS			
Central Provinces and Berar ..	**71**	**47**	**24**
Damoh	2	1	1
Mandla	33	24	9
Seoni	20	12	8
Chhindwara	7	4	3
Drug	1	1	..
Central Provinces States ..	*8*	*5*	*3*
Korea	8	5	3
CHAMAR, CHRISTIAN			
Central Provinces and Berar ..	**25**	**13**	**12**
Nagpur . ..	2	1	1
Raipur	8	6	2
Bilaspur	15	6	9
CHAUHAN, HINDU			
Chhattisgarh Division .	*5,061*	*2,353*	*2,708*
Raipur ..	949	419	530
Bilaspur	2,086	1,005	1,081
Drug	2,026	929	1,097
Central Provinces States .	*745*	*369*	*376*
Kanker . .	24	24	..
Nandgaon . ..	118	56	62
Khairagarh . ..	186	85	101
Kawardha	299	145	154
Raigarh . .	112	54	58
Korea	5	5	..
Surguja	1	.	1
DAHAYAT, HINDU			
Central Provinces and Berar ..	**13,219**	**6,495**	**6,724**
Damoh	833	409	424
Jubbulpore	8,778	4,311	4,467
Mandla	84	44	40
Seoni	323	154	169
Narsinghpur . ..	163	82	81
Hoshangabad	4	2	2
Chhindwara	168	86	82
Nagpur	12	5	7
Bhandara	8	6	2
Balaghat	8	3	5
Raipur . ..	1	1	..
Bilaspur	2,779	1,365	1,414

TABLE XVII Race, Tribe or Caste—*contd.*

Tribe or caste with religion and locality.	Persons.	Males.	Females.
1	2	3	4
DAHAYAT, HINDU—*concld.*			
Central Provinces States	*58*	*27*	*31*
Kawardha	58	27	31
DAHAYAT, TRIBAL RELIGIONS			
Central Provinces and Berar ..	**180**	**92**	**88**
Mandla	53	27	26
Balaghat	7	3	4
Bilaspur .. .	120	62	58
DARZI, HINDU			
Central Provinces and Berar .	**51,213**	**26,198**	**25,015**
Saugor	2,889	1,469	1,420
Damoh	2,096	1,064	1,032
Jubbulpore	5,114	2,615	2,499
Mandla	993	503	490
Seoni	1,140	585	555
Narsinghpur	2,110	1,025	1,085
Hoshangabad	1,903	943	960
Nimar .. .	2,066	1,116	950
Betul	497	278	219
Chhindwara	1,127	576	551
Wardha	2,826	1,440	1,386
Nagpur	4,013	2,029	1,984
Chanda	3,314	1,684	1,630
Bhandara	3,093	1,593	1,500
Balaghat	968	499	469
Raipur	745	373	372
Bilaspur	1,819	873	946
Drug	252	117	135
Berar	*13,049*	*6,783*	*6,266*
Amraoti	3,901	2,016	1,885
Akola	2,634	1,371	1,263
Buldana	3,366	1,746	1,620
Yeotmal	3,148	1,650	1,498
Central Provinces States ..	*1,109*	*633*	*566*
Makrai	60	26	34
Bastar	24	11	13
Kanker	5	2	3
Nandgaon	131	70	61
Khairagarh	217	114	103
Chhuikhadan	20	9	11
Kawardha	100	58	42
Sakti	26	17	9
Raigarh	158	87	71
Sarangarh	112	59	53
Changbhakar	21	11	10
Korea	47	34	13
Surguja	271	130	141
Jashpur .. .	7	5	2
DARZI, MUSLIM			
Central Provinces and Berar ..	**16**	**12**	**4**
Saugor	1	1	..
Jubbulpore	9	6	3
Hoshangabad ..	6	5	1
DESWALI, HINDU			
Central Provinces and Berar ..	**8,126**	**4,126**	**4,000**
Saugor	2	2	..
Jubbulpore	3	3	..
Narsinghpur	3	..	3
Hoshangabad	4,709	2,405	2,304
Nimar	2,252	1,149	1,103
Betul	3	1	2
Raipur	191	97	94
Bilaspur	356	191	165

Tribe or caste with religion and locality.	Persons.	Males.	Females.
1	2	3	4
DESWALI, HINDU—*concld.*			
Berar	*17*	*6*	*11*
Akola	17	6	11
Central Provinces States ..	*590*	*272*	*318*
Makrai	412	210	202
Sakti	40	18	22
Raigarh	27	12	15
Surguja	111	32	79
DESWALI, TRIBAL RELIGINOS			
Central Provinces and Berar ..	**2**	**1**	**1**
Raipur	2	1	1
DEWAR, HINDU			
Chhattisgarh Division ..	*1,523*	*696*	*827*
Raipur	541	241	300
Bilaspur	700	324	376
Drug	282	131	151
Central Provinces States ..	*1,027*	*461*	*566*
Nandgaon	87	35	52
Khairagarh	140	62	78
Chhuikhadan	237	117	120
Sakti	123	57	66
Raigarh	227	101	126
Sarangarh	155	61	94
Surguja	58	28	30
DEWAR, TRIBAL RELIGIONS			
Chhattisgarh Division ..	*263*	*121*	*142*
Raipur	255	118	137
Drug	8	3	5
DHANUK, HINDU			
Central Provinces and Berar ..	**6,894**	**3,371**	**3,523**
Saugor	3	2	1
Jubbulpore	49	31	18
Narsinghpur	5,186	2,534	2,652
Hoshangabad	744	351	393
Nimar	851	412	439
Betul	3	1	2
Chhindwara	26	21	5
Raipur	32	19	13
DHANWAR, HINDU			
Central Provinces and Berar ..	**19,343**	**9,635**	**9,708**
Jubbulpore .. .	1	1	..
Raipur	904	462	442
Bilaspur . ..	9,229	4,588	4,641
Drug	20	10	10
Berar	*5,[illegible]*	*2,620*	*2,579*
Buldana	5,199	2,620	2,579
Central Provinces States ..	*3,990*	*1,954*	*2,036*
Khairagarh	15	6	9
Sakti	291	142	149
Raigarh .. .	2,828	1,374	1,454
Sarangarh	94	39	55
Surguja	431	226	205
Udaipur	331	167	164

Tribe or caste with religion and locality.	Persons.	Males.	Females
1	2	3	4
DHANWAR, TRIBAL RELIGIONS			
Central Provinces and Berar ..	4,612	2,317	2,295
Raipur	34	21	13
Bilaspur	3,542	1,780	1,762
Central Provinces States ..	*1,036*	*516*	*520*
Bastar	7	5	2
Korea	1,022	510	512
Udaipur	7	1	6
DHIMAR, HINDU			
Central Provinces and Berar ..	322,816	161,062	161,754
Saugor	11,598	5,888	5,710
Damoh	10,364	5,248	5,116
Jubbulpore	36,002	17,742	18,260
Mandla	12,251	6,034	6,217
Seoni	6,034	2,965	3,069
Narsinghpur	13,939	6,911	7,028
Hoshangabad	8,579	4,502	4,077
Nimar	1,421	804	617
Betul	2,876	1,407	1,469
Chhindwara	7,748	3,850	3,898
Wardha	13,587	6,854	6,733
Nagpur	23,568	11,870	11,698
Chanda	38,563	19,331	19,232
Bhandara	43,529	21,504	22,025
Balaghat	13,184	6,532	6,652
Raipur	21,182	10,229	10,953
Bilaspur	10,661	5,299	5,362
Drug	6,929	3,288	3,641
Berar	*38,561*	*19,768*	*18,793*
Amraoti	14,629	7,404	7,225
Akola	6,000	3,087	2,913
Buldana	2,542	1,321	1,221
Yeotmal	15,390	7,956	7,434
Central Provinces States ..	*2,240*	*1,036*	*1,204*
Makrai	142	76	66
Bastar	95	44	51
Kanker	442	140	302
Nandgaon	718	353	365
Khairagarh	407	217	190
Chhuikhadan	5	5	..
Kawardha	37	17	20
Sakti	81	35	46
Raigarh	28	14	14
Sarangarh	32	13	19
Changbhakar	190	87	103
Korea	49	25	24
Jashpur	14	10	4
DHIMAR, CHRISTIAN			
Central Provinces and Berar ..	2	2	..
Narsinghpur	1	1	..
Nimar	1	1	..
DHOBI, HINDU			
Central Provinces and Berar ..	187,277	92,082	95,195
Saugor	8,248	4,278	3,970
Damoh	4,805	2,381	2,424
Jubbulpore	10,220	5,129	5,091
Mandla	1,898	952	946
Seoni	3,821	1,864	1,957
Narsinghpur	4,876	2,506	2,370
Hoshangabad	6,025	2,795	3,230
Nimar	2,297	1,169	1,128
Betul	1,992	996	996
Chhindwara	3,870	1,886	1,984
Wardha	4,991	2,544	2,447
Nagpur	9,092	4,583	4,509
Chanda	5,641	2,860	2,781
Bhandara	5,024	2,439	2,585
Balaghat	1,893	931	962
Raipur	18,682	8,891	9,791
Bilaspur	29,294	14,086	15,208
Drug	14,034	6,640	7,394

Tribe or caste with religion and locality.	Persons.	Males.	Females.
1	2	3	4
DHOBI, HINDU—*concld.*			
Berar	*28,494*	*14,463*	*14,031*
Amraoti	9,104	4,689	4,415
Akola	7,715	3,931	3,784
Buldana	5,001	2,519	2,482
Yeotmal	6.674	3,324	3,350
Central Provinces States ..	*22,080*	*10,689*	*11,391*
Makrai	109	55	54
Bastar	1,272	627	645
Kanker	764	349	415
Nandgaon	3,069	1,424	1,645
Khairagarh	3,184	1,605	1,579
Chhuikhadan ..	577	272	305
Kawardha ..	1,186	577	609
Sakti	1,689	858	831
Raigarh	3,253	1,575	1,678
Sarangarh	2,839	1,285	1,554
Changbhakar	15	9	6
Korea	153	82	71
Surguja	2,723	1,336	1,387
Udaipur	550	279	271
Jashpur	697	356	341
DHOBI, TRIBAL RELIGIONS			
Central Provinces and Berar ..	286	145	141
Raipur	7	4	3
Bilaspur	6	3	3
Central Provinces States ..	*273*	*138*	*135*
Korea	273	138	135
DHOBI, MUSLIM			
Central Provinces and Berar ..	31	13	18
Jubbulpore	6	3	3
Hoshangabad	1	1	..
Nimar	24	9	15
DHOBI, CHRISTIAN			
Central Provinces and Berar ..	12	5	7
Betul	5	3	2
Bilaspur	2	..	2
Central Provinces States ..	*5*	*2*	*3*
Kawardha	5	2	3
DOHOR, HINDU			
Central Provinces and Berar ..	6,616	3,331	3,285
Wardha	190	97	93
Nagpur	22	12	10
Berar	*6,404*	*3,222*	*3,182*
Amraoti	1,796	911	885
Akola	1,544	774	770
Buldana	2,976	1,523	1,453
Yeotmal	88	14	74
DOHOR, TRIBAL RELIGIONS			
Central Provinces and Berar ..	116	52	64
Central Provinces States ..	*116*	*52*	*64*
Kanker	116	52	64

Tribe or caste with religion and locality.	Persons.	Males.	Females
1	2	3	4
DOM, HINDU			
Central Provinces and Berar	**6,399**	**3,095**	**3,304**
Saugor	106	51	55
Jubbulpore	3,748	1,790	1,958
Mandla	418	202	216
Seoni	30	14	16
Hoshangabad	42	22	20
Chanda	13	5	8
Bhandara	11	6	5
Raipur	277	131	146
Berar	*15*	*8*	*7*
Akola	15	8	7
Central Provinces States	*1,739*	*866*	*873*
Khairagarh	80	46	34
Raigarh	18	7	11
Surguja	180	97	83
Udaipur	274	134	140
Jashpur	1,187	582	605
FAKIR, MUSLIM			
Central Provinces and Berar	**10,524**	**5,296**	**5,228**
Saugor	193	104	89
Damoh	323	159	164
Jubbulpore	829	424	405
Mandla	38	24	14
Seoni	416	204	212
Narsinghpur	133	71	62
Hoshangabad	1,092	559	533
Nimar	81	38	43
Betul	115	54	61
Chhindwara	864	429	435
Wardha	464	229	235
Nagpur	407	229	178
Chanda	56	31	25
Bhandara	152	85	67
Balaghat	129	66	63
Raipur	62	26	36
Bilaspur	137	45	92
Drug	52	34	18
Berar	*4,607*	*2,297*	*2,310*
Amraoti	2,132	1,056	1,076
Akola	1,124	593	531
Buldana	821	395	426
Yeotmal	530	253	277
Central Provinces States	*374*	*188*	*186*
Makrai	35	21	14
Bastar	1	..	1
Kanker	3	2	1
Khairagarh	6	3	3
Korea	3	3	..
Surguja	99	50	49
Jashpur	227	109	118
GADABA, HINDU			
Central Provinces and Berar	**4**	**2**	**2**
Central Provinces States	*4*	*2*	*2*
Bastar	4	2	2
GADABA, TRIBAL RELIGIONS			
Central Provinces and Berar	**391**	**185**	**206**
Central Provinces States	*391*	*185*	*206*
Bastar	391	185	206
GADABA, CHRISTIAN			
Central Provinces and Berar	**3**	..	**3**
Central Provinces States	*3*	..	*3*
Bastar	3	..	3

Tribe or caste with religion and locality.	Persons.	Males.	Females.
1	2	3	4
GANDA, HINDU			
Central Provinces and Berar	**173,784**	**84,503**	**89,281**
Jubbulpore	3	3	..
Chhindwara	1	1	..
Chanda	141	69	72
Balaghat	152	88	64
Raipur	70,829	34,193	36,636
Bilaspur	30,676	14,765	15,911
Drug	6,602	3,103	3,499
Berar	*1*	*1*	..
Amraoti	1	1	..
Central Provinces States	*65,379*	*32,280*	*33,099*
Bastar	5,353	2,605	2,748
Kanker	4,494	2,155	2,339
Nandgaon	1,016	498	518
Khairagarh	1,056	461	595
Chhuikhadan	135	68	67
Kawardha	502	237	265
Sakti	2,599	1,254	1,345
Raigarh	21,822	10,901	10,921
Sarangarh	13,178	6,486	6,692
Surguja	3,571	1,813	1,758
Udaipur	745	377	368
Jashpur	10,908	5,425	5,483
GANDA, TRIBAL RELIGIONS			
Central Provinces and Berar	**1,146**	**564**	**582**
Raipur	328	176	152
Bilaspur	100	53	47
Drug	10	3	7
Central Provinces States	*708*	*332*	*376*
Bastar	194	87	107
Kanker	373	177	196
Korea	104	54	50
Surguja	37	14	23
GANDA, CHRISTIAN			
Central Provinces and Berar	**447**	**228**	**219**
Raipur	142	72	70
Drug	1	..	1
Central Provinces States	*304*	*156*	*148*
Raigarh	58	22	36
Sarangarh	65	36	29
Jashpur	181	98	83
GHASIA, HINDU			
Central Provinces and Berar	**45,566**	**21,858**	**23,708**
Jubbulpore	61	44	17
Mandla	132	63	69
Seoni	14	8	6
Hoshangabad	3	2	1
Chhindwara	1	1	..
Nagpur	14	5	9
Chanda	18	9	9
Bhandara	8	4	4
Balaghat	158	83	75
Raipur	8,365	3,998	4,367
Bilaspur	13,461	6,378	7,083
Drug	1,514	672	842
Berar	*1*	*1*	..
Amraoti	1	1	..

Tribe or caste with religion and locality.	Persons.	Males.	Females.
1	2	3	4
GHASIA, HINDU—*concld.*			
Central Provinces States ..	*21,816*	*10,590*	*11,226*
Bastar	2,277	1,105	1,172
Kanker	593	280	313
Nandgaon	366	176	190
Khairagarh	232	91	141
Chhuikhadan	54	25	29
Kawardha	211	98	113
Sakti . ..	757	327	430
Raigarh	3,776	1,800	1,976
Sarangarh	2,234	1,020	1,214
Changbhakar	99	50	49
Korea	1	1	..
Surguja	8,245	4,148	4,097
Udaipur	1,134	569	565
Jashpur	1,837	900	937
GHASIA, TRIBAL RELIGIONS			
Central Provinces and Berar ..	**1,551**	**809**	**742**
Raipur	35	22	13
Bilaspur	19	9	10
Central Provinces States ..	*1,497*	*778*	*719*
Bastar	2	1	1
Changbhakar	13	5	8
Korea	1,456	762	694
Surguja	26	10	16
GHASIA, CHRISTIAN			
Central Provinces and Berar ..	**13**	**13**	..
Raipur	13	13	..
GOLAR, HINDU			
Central Provinces and Berar ..	**6,909**	**3,504**	**3,405**
Seoni . ..	26	10	16
Hoshangabad	380	202	178
Nimar	30	16	14
Betul	1,035	669	366
Chhindwara . ..	11	7	4
Chanda	2,513	1,217	1,296
Bhandara	182	92	90
Balaghat	486	217	269
Bilaspur	3	.	3
Berar .. .	*2,172*	*1,010*	*1,132*
Amraoti .. .	4	2	2
Yeotmal	2,168	1,038	1,130
Central Provinces States ..	*71*	*31*	*37*
Bastar	71	34	37
GOLAR, TRIBAL RELIGIONS			
Central Provinces and Berar ..	**87**	**41**	**46**
Hoshangabad	36	15	21
Chanda . ..	2	2	..
Central Provinces States ..	*19*	*24*	*25*
Makrai	49	24	25

Tribe or caste with religion and locality.	Persons.	Males.	Females.
1	2	3	4
GOND, HINDU			
Central Provinces and Berar ..	**1,036,673**	**504,710**	**531,963**
Saugor	11,384	5,662	5,722
Damoh . ..	6,802	3,394	3,408
Jubbulpore	81,359	39,805	41,554
Mandla	59,736	29,171	30,565
Seoni	253	119	134
Narsinghpur	2,166	1,051	1,115
Hoshangabad	15,537	7,643	7,894
Nimar	2,903	1,504	1,399
Betul	22,320	10,900	11,420
Chhindwara	1,871	968	903
Wardha .. .	11,985	5,935	6,050
Nagpur	43,347	21,546	21,801
Chanda	25,302	12,569	12,733
Bhandara	41,681	20,565	21,116
Balaghat	44,115	21,827	22,288
Raipur	165,426	80,281	85,145
Bilaspur	123,950	59,407	64,543
Drug . ..	104,523	49,037	55,486
Berar	*61,605*	*31,819*	*32,786*
Amraoti	16,115	8,071	8,044
Akola	3,575	1,811	1,764
Buldana .. .	261	92	169
Yeotmal . ..	44,654	21,845	22,809
Central Provinces States ..	*207,408*	*101,507*	*105,901*
Makrai	109	54	55
Bastar . .	4,981	2,545	2,436
Kanker	9,107	4,526	4,581
Nandgaon	23,912	11,339	12,573
Khairagarh	22,790	10,819	11,971
Chhuikhadan	4,392	2,031	2,361
Kawardha	10,835	5,205	5,630
Sakti	8,246	3,569	4,677
Raigarh	29,305	14,261	15,044
Sarangarh	4,069	1,967	2,102
Changbhakar	92	51	41
Korea	325	176	149
Surguja	73,798	37,159	36,639
Udaipur	11,438	5,692	5,746
Jashpur	4,009	2,113	1,896

Tribe or caste with religion and locality.	Persons.	Males.	Females.
GOND, TRIBAL RELIGIONS			
Central Provinces and Berar ..	**1,224,441**	**599,456**	**624,985**
Saugor	19,365	9,558	9,807
Dam[illegible]	20,562	10,180	10,382
Jubb[illegible]pore	12,723	6,146	6,577
Mandla	159,400	78,180	81,220
Seoni	135,678	65,064	70,614
Narsinghpur	40,078	19,348	20,730
Hoshangabad	33,083	16,317	16,766
Nimar	7,504	3,804	3,700
Betul .. .	89,282	43,602	45,680
Chhindwara	174,933	84,674	90,259
Wardha .. .	31,210	15,258	15,952
Nagpur . ..	9,655	4,925	4,730
Chanda . ..	70,056	34,652	35,404
Bhandara	36,608	17,719	18,889
Balaghat . ..	57,904	28,270	29,634
Raipur	73,849	35,278	38,571
Bilaspur	48,410	24,255	24,155
Drug	11,106	5,623	5,483
Berar	*31,147*	*15,420*	*15,727*
Amraoti	7,438	3,656	3,782
Akola	231	106	125
Buldana ..	119	64	55
Yeotmal	23,359	11,594	11,765
Central Provinces States ..	*161,8[illegible]*	*81,183*	*80,705*
Makrai	995	515	480
Bastar	19,426	9,789	9,637
Kanker	70,89[illegible]	35,190	35,706
Nandgaon . .	1,796	910	886

Tribe or caste with religion and locality.	Persons.	Males.	Females.
1	2	3	4
GOND, TRIBAL RELIGIONS —*concld.*			
Chhuikhadan	5	5	..
Kawardha	63	31	32
Sakti	198	89	109
Changbhakar	7,403	3,676	3,727
Korea	32,224	16,458	15,766
Surguja	28,882	14,520	14,362
GOND, MUSLIM			
Central Provinces and Berar ..	**4**	**3**	**1**
Hoshangabad	1	..	1
Nimar	3	3	..
GOND, CHRISTIAN			
Central Provinces and Berar ..	**20**	**9**	**11**
Jubbulpore	1	1	..
Narsinghpur	1	1	..
Nimar	1	..	1
Chhindwara	4	3	1
Raipur	1	..	1
Bilaspur	1	1	..
Drug	3	2	1
Berar	*1*	*1*	..
Amraoti	1	1	..
Central Provinces States ..	*7*	..	*7*
Khairagarh	7	..	7
GOSAIN, HINDU			
Central Provinces and Berar ..	**42,240**	**21,432**	**20,808**
Saugor	488	260	228
Damoh	287	167	120
Jubbulpore	1,764	887	877
Mandla	389	203	186
Seoni	856	439	417
Narsinghpur	1,400	741	659
Hoshangabad	2,571	1,337	1,234
Nimar	1,114	576	538
Betul	1,073	417	656
Chhindwara	898	469	429
Wardha	1,624	832	792
Nagpur	2,828	1,471	1,357
Chanda	610	302	308
Bhandara	1,651	828	823
Balaghat	1,612	809	803
Raipur	2,613	1,283	1,330
Bilaspur	3,945	1,900	2,045
Drug	1,737	812	925
Berar	*11,631*	*6,119*	*5,512*
Amraoti	2,860	1,563	1,297
Akola	3,339	1,789	1,550
Buldana	2,773	1,432	1,341
Yeotmal	2,659	1,335	1,324
Central Provinces States ..	*3,149*	*1,580*	*1,569*
Makrai	1	1	..
Kanker	130	62	68
Nandgaon	129	68	61
Khairagarh	331	162	169
Chhuikhadan	26	16	10
Kawardha	75	35	40
Sakti	348	163	185
Raigarh	48	26	22
Sarangarh	56	24	32
Korea	58	20	38
Surguja	1,449	729	720
Udaipur	33	21	12
Jashpur	465	253	212

Tribe or caste with religion and locality.	Persons.	Males.	Females.
1	2	3	4
GOSAIN, TRIBAL RELIGIONS			
Central Provinces and Berar ..	**3**	**2**	**1**
Raipur	3	2	1
GOWARI, HINDU			
Central Provinces and Berar ..	**175,708**	**87,956**	**87,752**
Jubbulpore	11	3	8
Mandla	7	6	1
Seoni	5,418	2,661	2,757
Nimar	24	13	11
Betul	5,493	2,562	2,931
Chhindwara	2,781	1,384	1,397
Wardha	17,539	8,896	8,643
Nagpur	21,960	11,020	10,940
Chanda	10,913	5,508	5,405
Bhandara	43,928	22,071	21,857
Balaghat	35,181	17,363	17,818
Raipur	10	6	4
Bilaspur	12	7	5
Berar	*32,343*	*16,410*	*15,933*
Amraoti	12,712	6,457	6,255
Akola	2,272	1,201	1,071
Buldana	200	108	92
Yeotmal	17,159	8,644	8,515
Central Provinces States ..	*88*	*46*	*42*
Bastar	10	7	3
Surguja	78	39	39
GOWARI, TRIBAL RELIGIONS			
Central Provinces and Berar ..	**2,286**	**1,093**	**1,193**
Seoni	394	180	214
Chanda	1,532	760	772
Balaghat	103	46	57
Raipur	201	99	102
Berar	*56*	*8*	*48*
Amraoti	56	8	48
GUJAR, HINDU			
Central Provinces and Berar ..	**59,995**	**31,409**	**28,586**
Saugor	454	270	184
Damoh	60	32	28
Jubbulpore	127	61	66
Mandla	6	5	1
Seoni	165	93	72
Narsinghpur	3,711	2,236	1,475
Hoshangabad	24,501	12,885	11,616
Nimar	27,723	14,116	13,607
Betul	28	19	9
Chhindwara	987	514	473
Wardha	84	47	37
Nagpur	82	38	44
Chanda	1	1	..
Bhandara	159	70	89
Raipur	2	2	..
Bilaspur	45	22	23
Berar	*819*	*449*	*370*
Amraoti	583	318	265
Akola	77	47	30
Buldana	142	72	70
Yeotmal	17	12	5
Central Provinces States ..	*1,041*	*549*	*492*
Makrai	1,030	549	481
Kawardha	11	..	11

Tribe or caste with religion and locality.	Persons.	Males.	Females.
1	2	3	4
GUJAR, MUSLIM			
Central Provinces and Berar ..	**33**	**28**	**5**
Jubbulpore	32	27	5
Mandla	1	1	..
HALBA, HINDU			
Central Provinces and Berar ..	**120,025**	**58,732**	**61,293**
Jubbulpore	34	18	16
Seoni	698	362	336
Nimar	246	120	126
Chhindwara	9	6	3
Wardha	1,227	653	574
Nagpur	523	260	263
Chanda	3,280	1,734	1,546
Bhandara	19,233	9,723	9,510
Balaghat	1,553	741	812
Raipur	6,049	2,880	3,169
Bilaspur	160	75	85
Drug	55,338	26,249	29,089
Berar	*3,890*	*1,954*	*1,936*
Amraoti	2,321	1,159	1,162
Akola	482	231	251
Buldana	20	13	7
Yeotmal	1,067	551	516
Central Provinces States ..	*27,785*	*13,957*	*13828*
Bastar	16,148	8,287	7,861
Kanker	8,686	4,257	4,429
Nandgaon	2,859	1,359	1,500
Khairagarh	36	20	16
Chhuikhadan	1	1	..
Surguja	55	33	22
HALBA, TRIBAL RELIGIONS			
Central Provinces and Berar ..	**36**	**25**	**11**
Chanda	7	5	2
Raipur	19	12	7
Drug	2	1	1
Central Provinces States ..	*8*	*7*	*1*
Bastar	4	4	..
Kanker	4	3	1
HALBA, CHRISTIAN			
Central Provinces and Berar ..	**13**	**9**	**4**
Drug	7	7	..
Central Provinces States ..	*6*	*2*	*4*
Khairagarh	6	2	4
HOLIA, HINDU			
Central Provinces and Berar ..	**4,785**	**2,400**	**2,385**
Seoni	915	442	473
Chhindwara	13	7	6
Nagpur	498	260	238
Bhandara	2,278	1,146	1,132
Balaghat	1,081	545	536
HOLIA, TRIBAL RELIGIONS			
Central Provinces and Berar ..	**80**	**11**	**69**
Bhandara	80	11	69

Tribe or caste with religion and locality.	Persons.	Males.	Females.
1	2	3	4
JANGAM, HINDU			
Central Provinces and Berar ..	**2,765**	**1,418**	**1,347**
Hoshangabad	106	88	18
Nimar	47	24	23
Betul	46	19	27
Chhindwara	25	16	9
Wardha	316	145	171
Nagpur	136	62	74
Chanda	303	151	152
Bhandara	12	6	6
Raipur	1	1	..
Berar ..	*1,764*	*901*	*863*
Amraoti	321	161	160
Akola	445	218	227
Buldana	198	97	101
Yeotmal	800	425	375
Central Provinces States ..	*9*	*5*	*4*
Makrai	4	2	2
Bastar	5	3	2
KAHAR, HINDU			
Central Provinces and Berar ..	**29,302**	**14,807**	**14,495**
Saugor	28	19	9
Damoh	11	6	5
Jubbulpore	494	256	238
Mandla	12	8	4
Seoni	860	421	439
Narsinghpur	2,053	1,029	1,024
Hoshangabad	7,507	3,759	3,748
Nimar	3,427	1,722	1,705
Betul	58	28	30
Chhindwara	233	129	104
Wardha	294	150	144
Nagpur	1,625	861	764
Chanda	343	182	161
Bhandara	2,064	1,065	999
Balaghat	922	441	481
Raipur	872	415	457
Bilaspur	4,704	2,348	2,356
Drug	81	31	50
Berar	*1,079*	*550*	*529*
Amraoti	435	222	213
Akola	221	127	94
Buldana	55	40	15
Yeotmal	368	161	207
Central Provinces States ..	*2,635*	*1,387*	*1,248*
Makrai	96	43	53
Bastar	48	23	25
Kanker	191	101	90
Nandgaon	152	76	76
Khairagarh	23	9	14
Kawardha	26	14	12
Raigarh	216	109	107
Sarangarh	503	260	243
Changbhakar	1	1	..
Korea	163	92	71
Surguja	1,003	551	452
Udaipur	72	30	42
Jashpur	141	78	63
KAHAR, TRIBAL RELIGION			
Central Provinces and Berar ..	**9**	**4**	**5**
Central Provinces States ..	*9*	*4*	*5*
Korea	9	4	5

Tribe or caste with religion and locality.	Persons.	Males.	Females.
1	2	3	4
KAIKARI, HINDU			
Central Provinces and Berar ..	**2,211**	**1,111**	**1,100**
Nimar	54	24	30
Wardha	15	8	7
Chanda	14	7	7
Bhandara	36	20	16
Raipur	1	1	..
Berar	*2,091*	*1,051*	*1,040*
Amraoti	390	186	204
Akola	1,100	556	544
Buldana	519	261	258
Yeotmal	82	48	34
KALAR, HINDU			
Central Provinces and Berar ..	**219,056**	**108,593**	**110,463**
Saugor	2,230	1,122	1,108
Damoh	2,369	1,169	1,200
Jubbulpore	6,800	3,436	3,364
Mandla	1,409	700	709
Seoni	5,553	2,747	2,806
Narsinghpur	3,073	1,583	1,490
Hoshangabad	4,210	2,143	2,067
Nimar	2,336	1,173	1,163
Betul	3,638	1,817	1,821
Chhindwara	8,803	4,485	4,318
Wardha	3,766	1,953	1,813
Nagpur	10,247	5,278	4,969
Chanda	8,216	4,202	4,014
Bhandara	26,286	12,958	13,328
Balaghat	15,941	7,786	8,155
Raipur	20,157	9,679	10,478
Bilaspur	13,191	6,422	6,769
Drug	15,466	7,508	7,958
Berar	*19,707*	*10,034*	*9,673*
Amraoti	8,314	4,225	4,089
Akola	4,192	2,154	2,038
Buldana	1,693	898	795
Yeotmal	5,508	2,757	2,751
Central Provinces States ..	*45,658*	*22,398*	*23,260*
Makrai	80	36	44
Bastar	14,295	7,148	7,147
Kanker	7,337	3,513	3,824
Nandgaon	3,921	1,847	2,074
Khairagarh	3,872	1,901	1,971
Chhuikhadan	588	293	295
Kawardha	1,596	783	813
Sakti	810	374	436
Raigarh	5,679	2,789	2,890
Sarangarh	2,295	1,080	1,215
Changbhakar	55	22	33
Korea	893	456	437
Surguja	3,558	1,814	1,744
Udaipur	439	217	222
Jashpur	240	125	115
KALAR, TRIBAL, RELIGION			
Central Provinces and Berar ..	**109**	**60**	**49**
Raipur	22	14	8
Bilaspur	12	5	7
Central Provinces States ..	*75*	*41*	*31*
Kanker	7	2	5
Nandgaon	3	2	1
Changbhakar	3	2	1
Korea	54	30	24
Surguja	8	5	3

Tribe or caste with religion and locality.	Persons.	Males.	Females.
1	2	3	4
KALAR, CHRISTIAN			
Central Provinces and Berar ..	**3**	**3**	..
Drug	2	2	..
Central Provinces States ..	*1*	*1*	..
Chhuikhadan	1	1	..
KAMAR, HINDU			
Chhattisgarh Division ..	*3,291*	*1,624*	*1,667*
Raipur	3,291	1,624	1,667
Central Provinces States ..	*3*	*3*	..
Bastar	2	2	..
Raigarh	1	1	..
KAMAR, TRIBAL RELIGIONS			
Chhattisgarh Division ..	*5,953*	*2,940*	*3,013*
Raipur	5,953	2,940	3,013
Central Provinces States ..	*202*	*110*	*92*
Bastar	183	99	84
Kanker	19	11	8
KANJAR, HINDU			
Central Provinces and Berar ..	**1,301**	**619**	**682**
Saugor	167	89	78
Damoh	91	47	44
Jubbulpore	328	147	181
Mandla	5	..	5
Seoni	1	1	..
Narsinghpur	99	53	46
Hoshangabad	234	160	74
Nimar	58	27	31
Betul	12	12	..
Chhindwara	69	24	45
Nagpur	23	6	17
Bilaspur	88	36	52
Berar	*115*	*12*	*103*
Amraoti	112	10	102
Akola	3	2	1
Central Provinces States ..	*11*	*5*	*6*
Udaipur	11	5	6
KAPEWAR, HINDU			
Central Provinces and Berar ..	**10,408**	**5,131**	**5,277**
Wardha	88	41	47
Nagpur	85	43	42
Chanda	6,526	3,249	3,277
Bhandara	4	1	3
Raipur	5	2	3
Berar	*3,346*	*1,623*	*1,723*
Akola	1	1	..
Yeotmal	3,345	1,622	1,723
Central Provinces States ..	*354*	*172*	*182*
Bastar	352	172	180
Sakti	2	..	2

Tribe or caste with religion and locality.	Persons.	Males.	Females.
1	2	3	4
KAPEWAR, TRIBAL RELIGIONS			
Central Provinces and Berar ..	4	4	
Chanda	4	4	
KATIA, HINDU			
Central Provinces and Berar	**45,497**	**22,259**	**23,238**
Saugor	95	64	31
Jubbulpore	54	35	19
Mandla	2,466	1,182	1,284
Seoni	9,273	4,539	4,734
Narsinghpur . .	1,820	887	933
Hosbangabad	9,190	4,532	4,658
Nimar	259	139	120
Betul	3,137	1,539	1,598
Chhindwara	12,856	6,387	6,469
Nagpur . ..	59	40	19
Bhandara	507	107	400
Balaghat	4,365	2,101	2,264
Raipur	86	52	34
Bilaspur	879	448	431
Drug . ..	220	96	124
Berar	*2*	*2*	..
Amraoti	2	2	..
Central Provinces States ..	*229*	*109*	*120*
Bastar	2	1	1
Kawardha	226	107	119
Sarangarh	1	1	..
KATIA, TRIBAL RELIGIONS			
Central Provinces and Berar ..	**11**	**6**	**5**
Mandla	2	1	1
Seoni	8	5	3
Chhindwara	1	..	1
KAWAR, HINDU			
Central Provinces and Berar ..	**275,965**	**136,538**	**139,427**
Saugor	1	1	..
Jubbulpore	36	25	11
Seoni	18	18	..
Hoshangabad	4	4	.
Betul	7	4	3
Chhindwara	31	25	6
Wardha	1	..	1
Nagpur	4	3	1
Chanda	1,831	952	879
Bhandara	1,382	753	629
Raipur	31,709	15,235	16,474
Bilaspur	69,488	34,244	35,244
Drug	6,123	2,898	3,225
Berar	*1*	*1*	..
Amraoti . ..	1	1	..
Central Provinces States ..	*165,329*	*82,375*	*82,954*
Bastar . ..	199	103	96
Kanker	120	77	43
Nandgaon	10,247	4,768	5,479
Khairagarh	7,438	3,447	3,991
Chhuikhadan	251	129	122
Kawardha	121	98	23
Sakti	4,626	2,252	2,374
Raigarh	48,110	24,213	23,897
Sarangarh	441	219	222
Changbhakar	429	222	207
Korea	170	81	89
Surguja	48,307	24,095	24,212
Udaipur	32,735	16,485	16,250
Jashpur	12,135	6,186	5,949

Tribe or caste with religion and locality.	Persons.	Males.	Females.
	2	3	4
KAWAR, TRIBAL RELIGIONS			
Central Provinces and Berar ..	**11,191**	**5,694**	**5,497**
Chanda ..	4	..	4
Raipur . ..	264	142	122
Bilaspur . ..	298	151	147
Drug	1	..	1
Central Provinces States ..	*10,624*	*5,401*	*5,223*
Changbhakar . ..	1,723	914	809
Korea	8,819	4,448	4,371
Surguja	82	39	43
KAYASTH, HINDU			
Central Provinces and Berar ..	**38,827**	**20,331**	**18,496**
Saugor	4,794	2,550	2,244
Damoh	2,735	1,416	1,319
Jubbulpore	6,498	3,508	2,990
Mandla . ..	868	456	412
Seoni . ..	1,743	842	901
Narsinghpur	4,035	2,049	1,986
Hoshangabad . ..	1,662	909	753
Nimar	742	408	334
Betul	235	124	111
Chhindwara . ..	1,212	637	575
Wardha	218	133	85
Nagpur	1,956	1,028	928
Chanda	196	111	85
Bhandara	625	195	430
Balaghat ..	717	405	312
Raipur	1,947	1,011	936
Bilaspur	2,010	1,089	921
Drug . ..	852	458	394
Berar . ..	*1,442*	*734*	*708*
Amraoti	782	371	411
Akola ..	338	189	149
Buldana .. .	183	100	83
Yeotmal	139	74	65
Central Provinces States .	*4,340*	*2,268*	*2,072*
Makrai . ..	5	3	2
Bastar . ..	441	215	226
Kanker . ..	215	89	126
Nandgaon . ..	791	409	382
Khairagarh	556	286	270
Chhuikhadan . ..	163	85	78
Kawardha . ..	304	159	145
Sakti . ..	65	32	33
Raigarh . ..	876	429	447
Sarangarh	112	58	54
Changbhakar ..	19	10	9
Korea . ..	118	72	46
Surguja . ..	465	291	174
Udaipur . ..	72	40	32
Jashpur . ..	138	90	48
KAYASTH, CHRISTIAN			
Central Provinces and Berar ..	**2**	**2**	..
Drug . ..	2	2	..
KEWAT, HINDU			
Central Provinces and Berar ..	**196,954**	**95,219**	**101,735**
Saugor	188	103	85
Damoh	265	140	125
Jubbulpore	5,859	2,972	2,887
Mandla	120	77	43
Seoni	253	106	147
Narsinghpur . ..	278	144	134

TABLE XVII Race, Tribe or Caste—*contd.*

Tribe or caste with religion and locality.	Persons.	Males.	Females.
1	2	3	4
KEWAT, HINDU—*concld.*			
Hoshangabad	101	54	47
Nimar	24	12	12
Betul	1	1	..
Chhindwara	35	20	15
Wardha	7	5	2
Nagpur	148	78	70
Chanda	6,270	3,124	3,146
Bhandara	393	142	251
Balaghat	720	345	375
Raipur	61,215	29,355	31,860
Bilaspur	49,901	24,042	25,859
Drug	35,285	17,067	18,218
Berar	*486*	*284*	*202*
Amraoti	60	42	18
Akola	67	52	15
Buldana	344	178	166
Yeotmal	15	12	3
Central Provinces States	*35,405*	*17,148*	*18,257*
Bastar	1,767	896	871
Kanker	2,355	1,137	1,218
Nandgaon	7,047	3,285	3,762
Khairagarh	5,011	2,409	2,602
Chhuikhadan	1,003	485	518
Kawardha	1,419	651	768
Sakti	1,745	868	877
Raigarh	6,383	3,103	3,280
Sarangarh	4,971	2,405	2,566
Changbhakar	168	80	88
Korea	462	232	230
Surguja	2,584	1,342	1,242
Udaipur	270	143	127
Jashpur	220	112	108
KEWAT, TRIBAL RELIGIONS			
Central Provinces and Berar	**74**	**30**	**44**
Raipur	59	23	36
Central Provinces States	*15*	*7*	*8*
Changbhakar	4	2	2
Korea	11	5	6
KEWAT, CHRISTIAN			
Central Provinces and Berar	**7**	**2**	**5**
Drug	5	2	3
Central Provinces States	*2*	*..*	*2*
Khairagarh	2	..	2
KHANGAR, HINDU			
Central Provinces and Berar	**12,326**	**6,284**	**6,042**
Saugor	5,782	2,955	2,827
Damoh	1,754	870	884
Jubbulpore	2,578	1,298	1,280
Mandla	85	57	28
Seoni	19	6	13
Narsinghpur	870	423	447
Hoshangabad	412	168	244
Nimar	94	54	40
Betul	16	4	12
Chhindwara	61	39	22
Wardha	4	2	2
Nagpur	55	33	22
Bhandara	10	6	4
Balaghat	24	..	24
Raipur	7	6	1
Bilaspur	6	2	4
Drug	14	6	8
KHANGAR, HINDU—*concld.*			
Berar	*533*	*353*	*180*
Amraoti	432	296	136
Akola	66	31	35
Buldana	2	2	..
Yeotmal	33	24	9
Central Provinces States	*2*	*2*	*..*
Khairagarh	2	2	..
KHARIA, HINDU			
Central Provinces and Berar	**12,341**	**5,938**	**6,403**
Jubbulpore	1	1	..
Seoni	3	2	1
Chhindwara	648	307	341
Raipur	911	446	465
Bilaspur	1,444	687	757
Drug	124	54	70
Central Provinces States	*9,210*	*4,441*	*4,769*
Sakti	109	60	49
Raigarh	4,192	2,011	2,181
Sarangarh	856	374	482
Surguja	241	122	119
Udaipur	6	5	1
Jashpur	3,806	1,869	1,937
KHARIA, TRIBAL RELIGIONS			
Central Provinces and Berar	**590**	**307**	**283**
Raipur	115	76	39
Central Provinces States	*475*	*231*	*244*
Korea	3	1	2
Udaipur	465	226	239
Jashpur	7	4	3
KHARIA, CHRISTIAN			
Central Provinces and Berar	**335**	**173**	**162**
Central Provinces States	*335*	*173*	*162*
Jashpur	335	173	162
KHATIK, HINDU			
Central Provinces and Berar	**18,623**	**9,322**	**9,301**
Saugor	788	389	399
Damoh	348	173	175
Jubbulpore	1,763	861	902
Mandla	69	29	40
Seoni	82	37	45
Narsinghpur	206	94	112
Hoshangabad	264	116	148
Nimar	36	21	15
Betul	197	95	102
Chhindwara	350	188	162
Wardha	917	457	460
Nagpur	1,735	888	847
Chanda	398	193	205
Bhandara	550	229	321
Balaghat	84	50	34
Raipur	19	8	11
Bilaspur	137	83	54
Drug	17	7	10
Berar	*6,453*	*3,195*	*3,258*
Amraoti	4,399	2,159	2,240
Akola	922	476	446
Buldana	337	168	169
Yeotmal	795	392	403

Tribe or caste with religion and locality.	Persons.	Males	Females.
1	2	3	4
KHATIK, HINDU—*concld*			
Central Provinces States ..	*4,210*	*2,209*	*2,001*
Bastar ..	28	20	8
Khairagarh ..	31	16	15
Raigarh ..	22	10	12
Korea ..	3	2	1
Surguja ..	331	165	166
Udaipur ..	3,795	1,996	1,799
KHATIK, TRIBAL RELIGIONS			
Central Provinces and Berar ..	**1**	**1**	..
Central Provinces States ..	*1*	*1*	..
Korea ..	1	1	..
KHATIK, MUSLIM			
Central Provinces and Berar ..	**1,782**	**926**	**856**
Chhindwara ..	30	14	16
Wardha ..	63	29	34
Nagpur ..	102	65	37
Berar ..	*1,587*	*818*	*769*
Amraoti ..	442	241	201
Akola ..	376	182	194
Buldana ..	625	317	308
Yeotmal ..	144	78	66
KOL, HINDU			
Central Provinces and Berar ..	**75,757**	**37,312**	**38,445**
Saugor ..	101	45	56
Damoh ..	31	17	14
Jubbulpore ..	57,743	28,215	29,528
Mandla ..	2,444	1,244	1,200
Seoni ..	188	101	87
Narsinghpur ..	585	252	333
Hoshangabad ..	609	308	301
Nimar ..	15	9	6
Betul ..	22	12	10
Chhindwara ..	1,692	906	786
Wardha ..	238	119	119
Nagpur ..	1,903	925	978
Chanda ..	8	5	3
Bhandara ..	1,775	891	884
Balaghat ..	1,968	958	1,010
Raipur ..	258	129	129
Bilaspur ..	2,482	1,266	1,216
Berar ..	*1,113*	*592*	*521*
Amraoti ..	246	137	109
Akola ..	59	41	18
Buldana ..	128	71	57
Yeotmal ..	680	343	337
Central Provinces States ..	*2,582*	*1,318*	*1,264*
Khairagarh ..	168	90	78
Sakti ..	173	102	71
Raigarh ..	103	38	65
Changbhakar ..	86	43	43
Surguja ..	2,052	1,045	1,007
KOL, TRIBAL RELIGIONS			
Central Provinces and Berar ..	**15,799**	**8,130**	**7,669**
Damoh ..	30	15	15
Jubbulpore ..	84	45	39
Mandla ..	8,480	4,296	4,184
Seoni ..	52	32	20
Narsinghpur ..	85	68	17
Chhindwara ..	68	33	35
Balaghat ..	87	70	17
Raipur ..	124	63	61
Bilaspur ..	1,039	509	530
KOL, TRIBAL RELIGIONS—*concld*			
Berar ..	*4*	*2*	*2*
Akola ..	4	2	2
Central Provinces States ..	*5,746*	*2,997*	*2,749*
Changbhakar ..	4,522	2,382	2,140
Korea ..	1,214	609	605
Surguja ..	6	3	3
Udaipur ..	4	3	1
KOLAM, HINDU			
Central Provinces and Berar ..	**19,374**	**9,762**	**9,612**
Betul ..	1	1	..
Wardha ..	2,034	1,061	973
Nagpur ..	3	1	2
Chanda ..	151	69	82
Berar ..	*17,185*	*8,630*	*8,555*
Amraoti ..	103	48	55
Akola ..	1	1	..
Yeotmal ..	17,081	8,581	8,500
KOLAM, TRIBAL RELIGIONS			
Central Provinces and Berar ..	**12,389**	**6,225**	**6,164**
Wardha ..	59	36	23
Berar ..	*12,330*	*6,189*	*6,141*
Yeotmal ..	12,330	6,189	6,141
KOLI, HINDU			
Central Provinces and Berar ..	**43,129**	**21,996**	**21,133**
Saugor ..	44	43	1
Jubbulpore ..	4	3	1
Hoshangabad ..	156	73	83
Nimar ..	3,352	1,726	1,626
Chhindwara ..	86	49	37
Wardha ..	449	220	229
Nagpur ..	242	129	113
Chanda ..	397	217	180
Bhandara ..	206	63	143
Bilaspur ..	124	55	69
Berar ..	*38,069*	*19,418*	*18,651*
Amraoti ..	9,446	4,916	4,530
Akola ..	11,196	5,684	5,512
Buldana ..	12,362	6,280	6,082
Yeotmal ..	5,065	2,538	2,527
KOLI, TRIBAL RELIGIONS			
Central Provinces and Berar ..	**1**	..	**1**
Chanda ..	1	..	1
KOLTA, HINDU			
Central Provinces and Berar ..	**45,454**	**22,268**	**23,186**
Betul ..	2	2	..
Raipur ..	17,028	8,296	8,732
Bilaspur ..	7,336	3,605	3,731
Central Provinces States ..	*21,088*	*10,365*	*10,723*
Raigarh ..	14,217	6,973	7,244
Sarangarh ..	5,995	2,931	3,064
Surguja ..	336	183	153
Udaipur ..	536	276	260
Jashpur ..	4	2	2

TABLE XVII Race, Tribe or Caste—*contd.*

Tribe or caste with religion and locality.	Persons.	Males.	[illegible]
1	2	3	
KOLTA, TRIBAL RELIGIONS			
Central Provinces and Berar ..	39	20	9
Raipur	23	17	6
Central Provinces States ..	6	3	3
Nandgaon	6	3	3
KOMTI, HINDU			
Central Provinces and Berar ..	11,702	5,552	6,150
Jubbulpore	26	14	12
Wardha	568	281	287
Nagpur	257	136	121
Chanda	3,546	1,719	1,827
Bhandara	463	84	379
Raipur ..	1	1	..
Berar	6,797	3,294	3,503
Amraoti	267	123	144
Akola	254	119	135
Buldana	78	34	44
Yeotmal	6,198	3,018	3,180
Central Provinces States ..	44	23	21
Bastar	43	22	21
Jashpur	1	1	..
KORI, HINDU			
Central Provinces and Berar ..	34,987	18,072	16,915
Saugor	7,551	3,849	3,702
Damoh	3,129	1,482	1,647
Jubbulpore	11,298	5,605	5,693
Mandla	249	135	114
Seoni	313	155	158
Narsinghpur	2,687	1,266	1,421
Hoshangabad	1,492	772	720
Nimar	2,407	1,271	1,136
Betul . ..	'04	61	43
Chhindwara	501	317	184
Wardha	212	128	84
Nagpur	1,407	761	646
Chanda	68	45	23
Bhandara	74	14	60
Balaghat	42	19	23
Raipur ..	157	76	81
Bilaspur . ..	821	418	403
Drug	18	6	12
Berar	1,326	1,[illegible]92	534
Amraoti	917	586	331
Akola	318	180	138
Buldana	526	490	36
Yeotmal	65	36	29
Central Provinces States ..	631	400	231
Nandgaon ..	12	9	3
Khairagarh ..	3	3	..
Korea	18	11	7
Surguja	598	377	221
KORI, TRIBAL RELIGIONS			
Central Provinces and Berar ..	6	6	..
Central Provinces States ..	6	6	..
Korea	6	6	..

Tribe or caste, with religion and locality.	Persons.	Males.	Females.
1	2	3	4
KORI, CHRISTIAN			
Central Provinces and Berar ..	1	1	..
Hoshangabad	1	1	..
KORKU, HINDU			
Central Provinces and Berar ..	94,549	47,454	47,095
Jubbulpore	9	8	1
Hoshangabad	12,149	6,127	6,022
Nimar ..	26,284	13,092	13,192
Betul	7,492	3,683	3,809
Chhindwara	13,557	6,744	6,813
Wardha	560	281	279
Nagpur . ..	25	18	7
Bhandara . ..	25	13	12
Raipur . ..	7	7	..
Bilaspur	22	8	14
Berar	32,409	16,454	15,955
Amraoti ..	29,870	15,103	14,767
Akola . ..	1,794	943	851
Buldana	745	408	337
Central Provinces States ..	2,010	1,019	991
Bastar . ..	21	12	9
Surguja	*1,989	1,007	982
KORKU, TRIBAL RELIGIONS			
Central Provinces and Berar ..	82,051	40,767	41,284
Narsinghpur	1	1	..
Hoshangabad .. .	9,865	5,012	4,853
Nimar	25,888	12,849	13,039
Betul .	2 ,972	14,732	15,240
Chhindwara	5,401	2,728	2,673
Wardha	131	69	62
Nagpur . .	7	3	4
Bhandara . ..	41	23	18
Berar . .	4,036	1,955	2,081
Amraoti . .	3,983	1,925	2,058
Akola . ..	53	30	23
Central Provinces States ..	6,709	3,395	3,314
Makrai	2,703	1,401	1,302
Korea	*32	14	18
Surguja	*3,974	1,980	1,994
KORKU, CHRISTIAN			
Central Provinces and Berar ..	16	6	10
Berar . ..	16	6	10
Amraoti . ..	16	6	10
KORWA, HINDU			
Central Provinces and Berar ..	18,925	9,384	9,541
Raipur ..	2	2	..
Bilaspur	370	175	195
Central Provinces States ..	18,553	9,207	9,346
Sakti	74	37	37
Korea	5	2	3
Surguja	10,788	5,398	5,390
Jashpur	7,686	3,770	3,916

* Probably a sub-tribe of Korwas. Crooke held Korwas and Korkus to be branches of the same tribe. See part I of this Report.

Tribe or caste with religion and locality.	Persons.	Males.	Females.
1	2	3	4
KORWA, TRIBAL RELIGIONS			
Central Provinces and Berar	**7,586**	**3,650**	**3,936**
Raipur	12	6	6
Central Provinces States	*7,574*	*3,644*	*3,930*
Korea	8	3	5
Surguja	2,667	1,350	1,317
Udaipur	976	414	562
Jashpur	3,923	1,877	2,046
KORWA, CHRISTIAN			
Central Provinces and Berar	**65**	**29**	**36**
Central Provinces States	*65*	*29*	*36*
Jashpur	65	29	36
KOSHTI, HINDU			
Central Provinces and Berar	**171,297**	**85,954**	**85,343**
Saugor	772	380	392
Damoh	182	85	97
Jubbulpore	1,334	704	630
Mandla	382	213	169
Seoni	1,198	610	588
Narsinghpur	449	197	252
Hoshangabad	145	81	64
Nimar	907	468	439
Betul	276	128	148
Chhindwara	3,996	2,029	1,967
Wardha	7,487	3,775	3,712
Nagpur	47,149	23,822	23,327
Chanda	13,566	7,120	6,446
Bhandara	18,752	9,770	8,982
Balaghat	4,391	2,139	2,252
Raipur	16,514	8,002	8,512
Bilaspur	14,901	7,247	7,654
Drug	14,207	6,844	7,363
Berar	*12,506*	*6,443*	*6,063*
Amraoti	6,777	3,500	3,277
Akola	1,956	1,019	937
Buldana	735	373	362
Yeotmal	3,038	1,551	1,487
Central Provinces States	*12,183*	*5,897*	*6,286*
Bastar	2,614	1,282	1,332
Kanker	511	262	249
Nandgaon	3,706	1,693	2,013
Khairagarh	2,020	998	1,022
Chhuikhadan	511	256	255
Kawardha	319	150	169
Sakti	858	445	413
Raigarh	1,084	533	551
Sarangarh	529	257	272
Surguja	13	13	..
Udaipur	18	8	10
KOSHTI, TRIBAL RELIGIONS			
Central Provinces and Berar	**25**	**15**	**10**
Central Provinces States	*25*	*15*	*10*
Kanker	25	15	10
KOSHTI, CHRISTIAN			
Central Provinces and Berar	**1**	..	**1**
Drug	1	..	1
KOYA, HINDU			
Central Provinces and Berar	**1**	**1**	..
Berar	*1*	*1*	..
Akola	1	1	..

Tribe or caste with religion and locality.	Persons.	Males.	Females.
1	2	3	4
KOYA, TRIBAL RELIGIONS			
Central Provinces and Berar	**9,988**	**4,761**	**5,227**
Central Provinces States	*9,988*	*4,761*	*5,227*
Bastar	9,988	4,761	5,227
KUMHAR, HINDU			
Central Provinces and Berar	**130,210**	**65,842**	**64,368**
Saugor	8,245	4,143	4,102
Damoh	4,849	2,372	2,477
Jubbulpore	10,443	5,207	5,236
Mandla	2,049	1,046	1,003
Seoni	2,218	1,097	1,121
Narsinghpur	3,546	1,807	1,739
Hoshangabad	5,052	2,520	2,532
Nimar	4,095	2,124	1,971
Betul	1,393	739	654
Chhindwara	2,831	1,484	1,347
Wardha	2,514	1,307	1,207
Nagpur	4,338	2,172	2,166
Chanda	3,682	1,868	1,814
Bhandara	3,331	1,684	1,647
Balaghat	1,861	949	912
Raipur	13,128	6,393	6,735
Bilaspur	8,867	4,376	4,491
Drug	4,803	2,305	2,498
Berar	*23,284*	*12,303*	*10,981*
Amraoti	7,169	3,965	3,204
Akola	6,904	3,625	3,279
Buldana	5,080	2,598	2,482
Yeotmal	4,131	2,115	2,016
Central Provinces States	*19,681*	*9,946*	*9,735*
Makrai	95	42	53
Bastar	2,955	1,473	1,482
Kanker	835	411	424
Nandgaon	798	415	383
Khairagarh	617	298	319
Chhuikhadan	288	153	135
Kawardha	249	114	135
Sakti	295	148	147
Raigarh	2,304	1,160	1,144
Sarangarh	976	470	506
Changbhakar	109	56	53
Korea	446	213	233
Surguja	6,667	3,518	3,149
Udaipur	711	352	359
Jashpur	2,336	1,123	1,213
KUMHAR, TRIBAL RELIGIONS			
Central Provinces and Berar	**1,099**	**476**	**623**
Damoh	4	3	1
Seoni	3	2	1
Chhindwara	19	8	11
Raipur	431	201	230
Bilaspur	12	8	4
Central Provinces States	*630*	*254*	*376*
Kanker	169	33	136
Changbhakar	3	1	2
Korea	455	217	238
Surguja	3	3	..
KUMHAR, CHRISTIAN			
Central Provinces and Berar	**2**	**2**	..
Nagpur	1	1	..
Central Provinces States	*1*	*1*	..
Jashpur	1	1	..

TABLE XVII Race, Tribe or Caste—*contd.*

Tribe or caste with religion and locality.	Persons.	Males.	Females.
1	2	3	4
KUNBI, HINDU			
Central Provinces and Berar	**1,281,172**	**654,171**	**627,001**
Saugor	157	91	66
Jubbulpore	287	181	106
Mandla	2,613	1,578	1,035
Seoni	250	114	136
Narsinghpur	938	495	443
Hoshangabad	249	144	105
Nimar	18,547	9,837	8,710
Betul	58,021	29,034	28,987
Chhindwara	30,743	15,435	15,308
Wardha	93,107	47,204	45,903
Nagpur	176,279	89,934	86,345
Chanda	125,474	64,887	60,587
Bhandara	102,729	51,301	51,428
Balaghat	14,527	7,152	7,375
Raipur	734	362	372
Bilaspur	166	76	90
Drug	65	38	27
Berar	*653,624*	*335,050*	*318,574*
Amraoti	187,696	97,686	90,010
Akola	136,324	70,030	66,294
Buldana	202,186	102,101	100,085
Yeotmal	127,418	65,233	62,185
Central Provinces States	*2,662*	*1,258*	*1,404*
Makrai	1	1	..
Bastar	216	104	112
Nandgaon	792	352	440
Khairagarh	257	137	120
Korea	207	107	100
Surguja	1,189	557	632
KUNBI, TRIBAL RELIGIONS			
Central Provinces and Berar	7	6	1
Bilaspur	7	6	1
KUNBI, CHRISTIAN			
Central Provinces and Berar	5	5	..
Wardha	1	1	..
Berar	*4*	*4*	..
Amraoti	4	4	..
KURMI, HINDU			
Central Provinces and Berar	**317,396**	**156,548**	**160,848**
Saugor	23,454	12,331	11,123
Damoh	20,887	10,966	9,921
Jubbulpore	33,030	16,561	16,469
Mandla	4,986	2,120	2,866
Seoni	8,487	4,241	4,246
Narsinghpur	4,762	2,373	2,389
Hoshangabad	20,923	10,601	10,322
Nimar	13,410	6,658	6,752
Betul	2,549	1,231	1,318
Chhindwara	3,399	1,664	1,735
Wardha	130	64	66
Nagpur	284	173	111
Chanda	489	240	249
Bhandara	319	30	289
Balaghat	497	294	203
Raipur	55,599	27,097	28,502
Bilaspur	64,329	31,272	33,057
Drug	40,584	19,277	21,307
Berar	*506*	*353*	*153*
Amraoti	286	196	90
Akola	74	49	25
Buldana	4	3	1
Yeotmal	142	105	37
KURMI, HINDU—*concld.*			
Central Provinces States	*18,772*	*9,002*	*9,770*
Makrai	466	236	230
Bastar	438	207	231
Kanker	143	78	65
Nandgaon	644	332	312
Khairagarh	1,699	852	847
Chhuikhadan	359	165	194
Kawardha	7,398	3,434	3,964
Sakti	1,545	765	780
Raigarh	3,564	1,730	1,834
Sarangarh	1,847	829	1,018
Korea	47	31	16
Surguja	497	275	222
Udaipur	72	43	29
Jashpur	53	25	28
KURMI, TRIBAL RELIGIONS			
Central Provinces and Berar	3	2	1
Raipur	2	1	1
Central Provinces States	*1*	*1*	..
Korea	1	1	..
LODHI, HINDU			
Central Provinces and Berar	**318,572**	**158,670**	**159,902**
Saugor	34,319	17,594	16,725
Damoh	39,451	19,646	19,805
Jubbulpore	46,048	22,836	23,212
Mandla	6,598	3,245	3,353
Seoni	6,383	3,215	3,168
Narsinghpur	29,265	14,846	14,419
Hoshangabad	10,759	5,387	5,372
Nimar	3,192	1,701	1,491
Betul	231	119	112
Chhindwara	15,521	7,751	7,770
Wardha	1,044	530	514
Nagpur	9,256	4,652	4,604
Chanda	370	215	155
Bhandara	16,669	8,406	8,263
Balaghat	38,806	19,088	19,718
Raipur	1,385	710	675
Bilaspur	8,091	3,830	4,261
Drug	13,132	6,306	6,826
Berar	*1,924*	*1,118*	*806*
Amraoti	805	475	330
Akola	585	370	215
Buldana	19	12	7
Yeotmal	515	261	254
Central Provinces States	*36,128*	*17,475*	*18,653*
Makrai	20	9	11
Bastar	16	6	10
Nandgaon	5,955	2,948	3,007
Khairagarh	21,850	10,511	11,339
Chhuikhadan	6,134	2,971	3,163
Kawardha	2,071	991	1,080
Sakti	38	16	22
Changbhakar	19	6	13
Korea	18	16	2
Surguja	7	1	6
LODHI, CHRISTIAN			
Central Provinces and Berar	5	5	—
Nimar	5	5	..

Tribe or caste with religion and locality.	Persons.	Males.	Females.
1	2	3	4
LOHAR, HINDU			
Central Provinces and Berar ..	**197,609**	**99,365**	**98,244**
Saugor	8,588	4,485	4,103
Damoh	3,709	1,913	1,796
Jubbulpore .. .	10,901	5,592	5,309
Mandla	5,620	2,766	2,854
Seoni	5,111	2,507	2,604
Narsinghpur	3,408	1,759	1,649
Hoshangabad	5,197	2,707	2,490
Nimar	2,441	1,292	1,149
Betul	4,742	2,391	2,351
Chhindwara . ..	8,190	4,067	4,123
Wardha	4,054	2,136	1,918
Nagpur	12,251	6,202	6,049
Chanda . .	12,400	6,290	6,110
Bhandara	17,102	9,012	8,090
Balaghat	8,839	4,296	4,534
Raipur	16,455	7,939	8,516
Bilaspur	12,244	5,942	6,302
Drug	10,034	4,773	5,261
Berar .. .	*18,560*	*9,763*	*8,797*
Amraoti	5,285	2,775	2,510
Akola	3,265	1,855	1,410
Buldana . ..	3,045	1,556	1,489
Yeotmal	6,965	3,577	3,388
Central Provinces States ..	*27,772*	*13,533*	*14,239*
Makrai	98	40	58
Bastar	2,332	1,208	1,124
Kanker	919	379	540
Nandgaon	2,655	1,013	1,642
Khairagarh	1,584	743	841
Chhuikhadan	372	182	190
Kawardha	577	275	302
Sakti	247	110	137
Raigarh	2,665	1,294	1,371
Sarangarh	884	432	452
Changbhakar	83	47	36
Korea	652	325	327
Surguja	9,096	4,617	4,479
Udaipur	1,606	829	777
Jashpur	4,002	2,039	1,963
LOHAR, TRIBAL RELIGIONS			
Central Provinces and Berar ..	**5,259**	**2,625**	**2.634**
Damoh	1	..	1
Mandla	26	12	14
Seoni	829	403	426
Narsinghpur	4	2	2
Hoshangabad	19	12	7
Nimar	2	2	
Chhindwara	416	172	244
Raipur	222	106	116
Drug	10	6	4
Berar	2	2	..
Amraoti	2	2	
Central Provinces States ..	*3,728*	*1,908*	*1,820*
Bastar	2,017	1,034	983
Kanker	1,143	579	564
Changbhakar	4	2	2
Korea	532	278	254
Surguja	32	15	17
LOHAR, MUSLIM			
Central Provinces and Berar ..	**65**	**22**	**43**
Seoni	4	2	2
Hoshangabad	34	18	16
Nimar	27	2	25
LOHAR, CHRISTIAN			
Central Provinces and Berar ..	**370**	**182**	**188**
Saugor . ..	1	..	1
Damoh	1	1	..
Nagpur .. .	1	1	..
Raipur	6	..	6
Drug .. .	1	1	..
Berar . ..	*22*	*11*	*11*
Akola	22	11	11
Central Provinces States ..	*338*	*168*	*170*
Surguja	1	.	1
Jashpur . ..	337	168	169
MADGI, HINDU			
Central Provinces and Berar ..	**10,186**	**5,300**	**4,886**
Wardha	9	6	3
Nagpur . ..	12	7	5
Chanda	5,468	2,969	2,499
Bhandara . ..	60	28	32
Berar	*4,517*	*2,231*	*2,286*
Amraoti	2	2	..
Akola	3	2	1
Yeotmal .. .	4,512	2,227	2,285
Central Provinces States ..	*120*	*59*	*61*
Sakti	120	59	61
MADGI, TRIBAL RELIGIONS			
Central Provinces and Berar ..	**4**	**4**	..
Chanda	4	4	..
MAJHWAR, HINDU			
Central Provinces and Berar ..	**18,940**	**9,720**	**9,220**
Raipur	650	334	316
Bilaspur	8,411	4,239	4,172
Central Provinces States ..	*9,879*	*5,147*	*4,732*
Raigarh	669	341	328
Surguja	5,436	2,757	2,679
Udaipur	3,754	2,036	1,718
Jashpur	20	13	7
MAJHWAR, TRIBAL RELIGIONS			
Central Provinces and Berar ..	**170**	**85**	**85**
Bilaspur	170	85	85
MALA, HINDU			
Central Provinces and Berar ..	**11,921**	**5,947**	**5,974**
Saugor	18	11	7
Jubbulpore	885	481	404
Seoni	5	3	2
Hoshangabad	30	16	14
Nimar	53	33	20
Betul	4	2	2
Chhindwara	10	3	7
Nagpur . ..	15	6	9
Balaghat	43	20	23
Raipur	83	42	41
Bilaspur	12	8	4
Drug	15	4	11
Central Provinces State ..	*10,748*	*5,318*	*5,430*
Bastar	10,667	5,281	5,386
Khairagarh	56	27	29
Raigarh	25	10	15

TABLE XVII — Race, Tribe or Caste—*contd.*

Tribe or caste with religion and locality.	Persons.	Males.	Females.
1	2	3	4
MALA, TRIBAL RELIGIONS			
Central Provinces and Berar	**12**	**3**	**9**
Central Provinces States	*12*	*3*	*9*
Bastar	12	3	9
MALI, HINDU			
Central Provinces and Berar	**626,525**	**313,163**	**313,362**
Saugor	1,138	577	561
Damoh	440	214	226
Jubbulpore	997	504	493
Mandla	5,868	2,889	2,979
Seoni	13,829	6,737	7,092
Narsinghpur	123	68	55
Hoshangabad	4,370	2,198	2,172
Nimar	10,325	5,426	4,899
Betul	5,982	2,987	2,995
Chhindwara	10,187	5,147	5,040
Wardha	21,363	10,917	10,446
Nagpur	34,074	17,366	16,708
Chanda	38,438	19,204	19,234
Bhandara	26,053	12,972	13,081
Balaghat	66,435	32,251	34,184
Raipur	57,479	27,827	29,652
Bilaspur	49,407	24,456	24,951
Drug	28,638	13,601	15,037
Berar	*208,833*	*107,090*	*101,743*
Amraoti	76,315	39,646	36,669
Akola	47,061	23,902	23,159
Buldana	55,401	28,141	27,260
Yeotmal	30,056	15,401	14,655
Central Provinces States	*42,546*	*20,732*	*21,814*
Makrai	148	71	77
Bastar	5,634	2,870	2,764
Kanker	4,153	2,008	2,145
Nandgaon	5,660	2,703	2,957
Khairagarh	5,242	2,490	2,752
Chhuikhadan	1,462	661	801
Kawardha	6,340	3,095	3,245
Sakti	3,123	1,555	1,568
Raigarh	4,237	2,068	2,169
Sarangarh	6,267	3,047	3,220
Korea	20	17	3
Surguja	225	137	88
Udaipur	28	6	22
Jashpur	7	4	3
MALI, TRIBAL RELIGIONS			
Central Provinces and Berar	**41**	**22**	**19**
Raipur	3	2	1
Bilaspur	6	2	4
Central Provinces States	*32*	*18*	*14*
Kanker	32	18	14
MALI, CHRISTIAN			
Central Provinces and Berar	**3**	**1**	**2**
Nimar	1	..	1
Chhindwara	1	1	..
Central Provinces States	*1*	..	*1*
Khairagarh	1	..	1

Tribe or caste with religion and locality.	Persons.	Males.	Females.
1	2	3	4
MANA, HINDU			
Central Provinces and Berar	**57,457**	**28,606**	**28,851**
Saugor	60	33	27
Mandla	3	3	..
Hoshangabad	135	71	64
Nimar	4	2	2
Betul	3	2	1
Chhindwara	9	6	3
Wardha	3,457	1,778	1,679
Nagpur	4,651	2,308	2,343
Chanda	38,648	19,081	19,567
Bhandara	2,621	1,287	1,334
Balaghat	5,329	2,615	2,714
Berar	*2,537*	*1,420*	*1,117*
Amraoti	372	189	183
Buldana	299	299	..
Yeotmal	1,866	932	934
MANA, TRIBAL RELIGIONS			
Central Provinces and Berar	**16**	**11**	**5**
Chanda	2	2	..
Central Provinces States	*14*	*9*	*5*
Korea	14	9	5
MANG, HINDU			
Central Provinces and Berar	**101,189**	**49,918**	**51,271**
Saugor	2	2	..
Jubbulpore	59	34	25
Seoni	81	37	44
Narsinghpur	65	33	32
Hoshangabad	487	192	295
Nimar	1,262	649	613
Betul	1,449	713	736
Chhindwara	1,692	827	865
Wardha	7,337	3,680	3,657
Nagpur	9,182	4,523	4,659
Chanda	935	459	476
Bhandara	3,374	1,800	1,574
Balaghat	248	95	153
Raipur	1,323	607	716
Bilaspur	302	154	148
Drug	5	4	1
Berar	*73,339*	*36,088*	*37,251*
Amraoti	15,821	8,136	7,685
Akola	24,864	12,038	12,826
Buldana	18,688	9,120	9,568
Yeotmal	13,966	6,794	7,172
Central Provinces States	*47*	*21*	*26*
Makrai	17	8	9
Bastar	11	7	4
Nandgaon	19	6	13
MANG, CHRISTIAN			
Central Provinces and Berar	**37**	**16**	**21**
Berar	*37*	*16*	*21*
Buldana	31	14	17
Yeotmal	6	2	4

Race, Tribe or Caste—*contd.*

TABLE XVII

Tribe or caste with religion and locality.	Persons.	Males.	Females.
1	2	3	4
MARATHA, HINDU			
Central Provinces and Berar	**287,186**	**145,575**	**141,611**
Saugor	249	138	111
Damoh	149	83	66
Jubbulpore	755	411	344
Mandla	58	25	33
Seoni	7,903	3,878	4,025
Narsinghpur	105	60	45
Hoshangabad	1,406	734	672
Nimar	5,561	2,888	2,673
Betul	1,292	599	693
Chhindwara	12,500	6,278	6,222
Wardha	8,778	4,474	4,304
Nagpur	9,958	5,081	4,877
Chanda	1,434	754	680
Bhandara	985	406	579
Balaghat	182	104	78
Raipur	3,227	1,531	1,696
Bilaspur	2,516	1,318	1,198
Drug	659	307	352
Berar	*229,025*	*116,288*	*112,737*
Amraoti	30,081	15,524	14,557
Akola	109,055	55,586	53,469
Buldana	49,669	25,169	24,500
Yeotmal	40,220	20,009	20,211
Central Provinces States	*444*	*218*	*226*
Makrai	46	24	22
Bastar	39	21	18
Kanker	27	19	8
Nandgaon	251	119	132
Khairagarh	28	4	24
Chhuikhadan	2	2	..
Sakti	13	3	10
Raigarh	18	10	8
Korea	11	11	..
Udaipur	9	5	4
MARATHA, CHRISTIAN			
Central Provinces and Berar	**3**	**1**	**2**
Nimar	3	1	2
MARIA, HINDU			
Central Provinces and Berar	**572**	**325**	**247**
Jubbulpore	203	105	98
Betul	1	1	..
Chanda	274	162	112
Bilaspur	6	5	1
Central Provinces States	*88*	*52*	*36*
Bastar	70	39	31
Khairagarh	18	13	5
MARIA, TRIBAL RELIGIONS			
Central Provinces and Berar	**180,523**	**90,343**	**90,180**
Chanda	34,502	16,966	17,536
Central Provinces States	*146,021*	*73,377*	*72,644*
Bastar	146,000	73,367	72,633
Changbhakar	21	10	11

Tribe or caste with religion and locality.	Persons.	Males.	Females.
1	2	3	4
MEHRA, HINDU			
Central Provinces and Berar	**1,306,878**	**645,896**	**660,982**
Saugor	296	159	137
Damoh	1,716	826	890
Jubbulpore	15,854	7,816	8,038
Mandla	15,809	7,943	7,866
Seoni	14,107	7,001	7,106
Narsinghpur	17,949	8,307	9,642
Hoshangabad	14,554	7,232	7,322
Nimar	8,303	4,194	4,109
Betul	40,487	19,867	20,620
Chhindwara	30,118	14,975	15,143
Wardha	80,780	39,994	40,786
Nagpur	164,837	82,360	82,477
Chanda	104,774	51,809	52,965
Bhandara	150,595	73,181	77,414
Balaghat	59,367	29,001	30,366
Raipur	10,917	5,228	5,689
Bilaspur	7,083	3,484	3,599
Drug	20,167	9,657	10,510
Berar	*497,901*	*247,251*	*250,650*
Amraoti	148,266	73,753	74,513
Akola	148,027	73,559	74,468
Buldana	106,919	53,209	53,710
Yeotmal	94,689	46,730	47,959
Central Provinces States	*51,264*	*25,611*	*25,653*
Bastar	31,963	16,090	15,873
Kanker	1,960	906	1,054
Nandgaon	8,665	4,417	4,248
Khairagarh	5,293	2,544	2,749
Chhuikhadan	895	428	467
Kawardha	800	396	404
Sakti	68	33	35
Raigarh	1,181	574	607
Sarangarh	225	95	130
Korea	4	4	..
Surguja	48	24	24
Udaipur	162	100	62
MEHRA, TRIBAL RELIGIONS			
Central Provinces and Berar	**451**	**242**	**209**
Damoh	1	..	1
Jubbulpore	2	1	1
Mandla	3	1	2
Seoni	3	1	2
Narsinghpur	2	..	2
Hoshangabad	1	..	1
Chhindwara	1	1	..
Balaghat	4	4	..
Raipur	55	27	28
Bilaspur	11	8	3
Drug	3	2	1
Berar	*3*	*3*	..
Amraoti	2	2	..
Yeotmal	1	1	..
Central Provinces States	*362*	*194*	*168*
Bastar	237	128	109
Kanker	114	58	56
Korea	11	8	3
MEHRA, MUSLIM			
Central Provinces and Berar	**23**	**14**	**9**
Seoni	6	4	2
Nimar	17	10	7

TABLE XVII Race, Tribe or Caste—*contd.*

Tribe or caste with religion and locality.	Persons.	Males.	Females.
1	2	3	4
MEHRA, CHRISTIAN			
Central Provinces and Berar	**610**	**369**	**241**
Nagpur	4	3	1
Chanda	16	7	9
Raipur	5	3	2
Berar	*421*	*265*	*156*
Amraoti	283	190	93
Akola	138	75	63
Central Provinces States	*164*	*91*	*73*
Bastar	164	91	73
MEHTAR, HINDU			
Central Provinces and Berar	**31,895**	**16,219**	**15,676**
Saugor	2,662	1,384	1,278
Damoh	1,567	804	763
Jubbulpore	3,312	1,774	1,538
Mandla	331	171	160
Seoni	587	282	305
Narsinghpur	1,415	726	689
Hoshangabad	2,878	1,500	1,378
Nimar	1,775	938	837
Betul	435	237	198
Chhindwara	1,054	510	544
Wardha	980	494	486
Nagpur	4,489	2,314	2,175
Chanda	750	408	342
Bhandara	1,033	367	666
Balaghat	362	159	203
Raipur	823	392	431
Bilaspur	1,532	714	818
Drug	533	252	281
Berar	*4,408*	*2,346*	*2,062*
Amraoti	1,479	780	699
Akola	1,383	731	652
Buldana	881	478	403
Yeotmal	665	357	308
Central Provinces States	*969*	*447*	*522*
Makrai	66	31	35
Bastar	178	82	96
Kanker	40	18	22
Nandgaon	180	98	82
Khairagarh	108	37	71
Chhuikhadan	28	15	13
Kawardha	86	41	45
Sakti	20	8	12
Raigarh	140	61	79
Sarangarh	50	21	29
Changbhakar	3	2	1
Korea	25	10	15
Surguja	45	23	22
MEHTAR, TRIBAL RELIGIONS			
Central Provinces and Berar	**28**	**9**	**19**
Bilaspur	24	5	19
Central Provinces States	*4*	*4*	..
Korea	4	4	..
MEHTAR, MUSLIM			
Central Provinces and Berar	**228**	**108**	**120**
Saugor	71	36	35
Jubbulpore	39	20	19
Mandla	6	4	2
Narsinghpur	1	1	..
Hoshangabad	103	44	59
Nimar	1	1	..
Wardha	7	2	5
MEHTAR, CHRISTIAN			
Central Provinces and Berar	**31**	**18**	**13**
Jubbulpore	3	2	1
Narsinghpur	23	14	9
Drug	4	1	3
Central Provinces States	*1*	*1*	..
Bastar	1	1	..
MHALI, HINDU			
Central Provinces and Berar	**62,256**	**32,021**	**30,235**
Chhindwara	2	2	..
Wardha	6,702	3,476	3,226
Nagpur	11,022	5,468	5,554
Chanda	6,657	3,328	3,329
Bhandara	9,501	4,772	4,729
Balaghat	5,941	2,915	3,026
Bilaspur	46	24	22
Berar	*22,205*	*11,948*	*10,257*
Amraoti	5,598	3,025	2,573
Akola	5,517	2,915	2,602
Buldana	3,970	2,113	1,857
Yeotmal	7,120	3,895	3,225
Central Provinces States	*180*	*88*	*92*
Surguja	116	55	61
Udaipur	57	31	26
Jashpur	7	2	5
MHALI, TRIBAL RELIGIONS			
Central Provinces and Berar	**12**	**4**	**8**
Bilaspur	12	4	8
MOCHI, HINDU			
Central Provinces and Berar	**6,848**	**3,477**	**3,371**
Saugor	284	141	143
Damoh	59	29	30
Jubbulpore	722	337	385
Mandla	47	23	24
Seoni	5	3	2
Narsinghpur	31	21	10
Hoshangabad	324	165	159
Nimar	640	353	287
Chhindwara	18	12	6
Wardha	263	148	115
Nagpur	542	249	293
Chanda	54	35	19
Bhandara	68	39	29
Balaghat	45	24	21
Raipur	295	160	135
Bilaspur	252	113	139
Drug	628	324	304
Berar	*1,902*	*982*	*920*
Amraoti	418	214	204
Akola	982	521	461
Buldana	167	87	80
Yeotmal	335	160	175
Central Provinces States	*669*	*319*	*350*
Makrai	18	7	11
Bastar	39	19	20
Kanker	25	14	11
Nandgaon	343	167	176
Khairagarh	225	106	119
Raigarh	13	3	10
Surguja	6	3	3

Tribe or caste with religion and locality.	Persons.	Males.	Females.
1	2	3	4
MOCHI, MUSLIM			
Central Provinces and Berar ..	9	9	..
Jubbulpore	9	9	..
MOCHI, CHRISTIAN			
Central Provinces and Berar ..	1	1	..
Drug	1	1	..
MURIA, HINDU			
Central Provinces and Berar ..	2,052	812	1,240
Saugor	218	128	90
Damoh	237	119	118
Narsinghpur	671	340	331
Hoshangabad	30	13	17
Nimar	11	6	5
Chhindwara	2	1	1
Nagpur	8	6	2
Bhandara	276	..	276
Balaghat	13	13	..
Raipur	9	6	3
Bilaspur	184	..	184
Berar	*53*	*35*	*18*
Amraoti	16	6	10
Akola	24	19	5
Yeotmal	13	10	3
Central Provinces States ..	*340*	*145*	*195*
Bastar	44	15	29
Surguja	135	48	87
Jashpur	161	82	79
MURIA, TRIBAL RELIGIONS			
Central Provinces and Berar ..	124,998	62,670	62,328
Bilaspur	29	16	13
Drug	20	9	11
Central Provinces States ..	*124,949*	*62,645*	*62,304*
Bastar	124,949	62,645	62,304
NAGARCHI, HINDU			
Central Provinces and Berar ..	4,745	2,451	2,294
Mandla	106	48	58
Seoni	713	345	368
Chhindwara	414	198	216
Nagpur	123	64	59
Bhandara	1,353	798	555
Balaghat	1,621	789	832
Raipur	34	22	12
Bilaspur	37	15	22
Drug	265	134	131
Berar	*11*	*7*	*4*
Amraoti	11	7	4
Central Provinces States ..	*68*	*31*	*37*
Nandgaon	29	12	17
Khairagarh	20	12	8
Chhuikhadan ..	19	7	12
NAGARCHI, TRIBAL RELIGIONS			
Central Provinces and Berar ..	1,622	788	834
Seoni	1,069	512	557
Narsinghpur	16	8	8
Chhindwara	537	268	269

Tribe or caste with religion and locality.	Persons.	Males.	Females.
1	2	3	4
NAGASIA, HINDU			
Central Provinces and Berar ..	48,144	23,923	24,221
Bhandara	13	8	5
Balaghat	111	67	44
Raipur	203	98	105
Bilaspur	597	301	296
Central Provinces States ..	*47,220*	*23,449*	*23,771*
Khairagarh	1	1	..
Sakti	174	86	88
Raigarh	2,768	1,342	1,426
Surguja	23,999	11,988	12,011
Udaipur	4,680	2,265	2,414
Jashpur	15,598	7,766	7,832
NAGASIA, TRIBAL RELIGIONS			
Central Provinces and Berar ..	518	258	260
Bilaspur	198	97	101
Central Provinces States ..	*320*	*161*	*159*
Korea	1	1	..
Surguja	319	160	159
NAGASIA, CHRISTIAN			
Central Provinces and Berar ..	24	15	9
Central Provinces States ..	*24*	*15*	*9*
Jashpur	24	15	9
NAI, HINDU			
Central Provinces and Berar ..	133,135	66,745	66,390
Saugor	12,356	6,378	5,978
Damoh	6,305	3,167	3,138
Jubbulpore	11,609	5,907	5,702
Mandla	1,847	942	905
Seoni	4,494	2,264	2,230
Narsinghpur	6,113	3,076	3,037
Hoshangabad	7,796	3,980	3,816
Nimar	5,058	2,748	2,310
Betul	3,852	1,900	1,952
Chhindwara	6,045	3,035	3,010
Wardha	453	221	232
Nagpur	1,241	744	497
Chanda	209	57	152
Bhandara	814	487	327
Raipur	14,002	6,923	7,079
Bilaspur	14,057	6,821	7,236
Drug	8,867	4,284	4,583
Berar	*15,011*	*7,648*	*7,363*
Amraoti	5,368	2,790	2,578
Akola	3,801	2,045	1,756
Buldana	4,569	2,272	2,297
Yeotmal	1,273	541	732
Central Provinces States ..	*13,006*	*6,163*	*6,843*
Makrai	227	117	110
Bastar	396	180	216
Kanker	658	348	310
Nandgaon	2,350	1,113	1,237
Khairagarh	2,074	1,012	1,062
Chhuikhadan	449	210	239
Kawardha	790	342	448
Sakti	672	283	389
Raigarh	1,497	739	758
Sarangarh	735	326	409
Changbhakar	51	27	24
Korea	318	166	152
Surguja	2,342	1,079	1,263
Udaipur	111	58	53
Jashpur	336	163	173

Tribe or caste with religion and locality.	Persons	Males	Females.
1	2	3	4
NAI, TRIBAL RELIGIONS			
Central Provinces and Berar ..	**15**	**6**	**9**
Raipur	3	1	2
Bilaspur	1	1	..
Central Provinces States ..	*11*	*4*	*7*
Kanker	3	..	3
Changbhakar	1	1	..
Korea	7	3	4
NAI, MUSLIM			
Central Provinces and Berar ..	**103**	**50**	**53**
Saugor . ..	4	1	3
Jubbulpore .. .	56	29	27
Seoni .. .	4	1	3
Hoshangabad	8	8	.
Nimar	31	11	20
NAI, CHRISTIAN			
Central Provinces and Berar ..	**3**	**3**	..
Damoh	2	2	..
Nimar	1	1	..
OJHA, HINDU			
Central Provinces and Berar ..	**2,937**	**1,536**	**1,401**
Saugor	3	3	..
Jubbulpore .. .	11	7	4
Mandla	301	139	162
Seoni	144	71	73
Narsinghpur	22	14	8
Hoshangabad	116	62	54
Nimar	125	59	66
Betul	759	390	369
Chhindwara	71	30	41
Wardha	121	65	56
Nagpur	60	30	30
Chanda	24	17	7
Bhandara	673	369	304
Balaghat	178	92	86
Raipur	137	77	60
Bilaspur	30	21	9
Drug	48	30	18
Central Provinces States ..	*114*	*60*	*54*
Bastar	64	31	33
Kanker	42	24	18
Raigarh	8	5	3
OJHA, TRIBAL RELIGIONS			
Central Provinces and Berar ..	**2,169**	**1,048**	**1,121**
Mandla	120	52	68
Seoni	544	251	293
Narsinghpur	190	94	96
Hoshangabad .. .	249	121	128
Nimar	238	119	119
Chhindwara	421	184	237
Balaghat	227	139	88
Raipur	125	60	65
Central Provinces States ..	*55*	*28*	*27*
Makrai . ..	26	15	11
Kanker	29	13	16
ORAON, HINDU			
Central Provinces and Berar ..	**55,310**	**27,887**	**27,423**
Chhindwara	5	3	2
Raipur	1,775	830	945
Bilaspur	4,093	1,999	2,094
Drug	56	28	28

Tribe or caste with religion and locality.	Persons	Males.	Females.
1	2	3	4
ORAON, HINDU—*contd.*			
Central Provinces States ..	*49,381*	*25,027*	*24,354*
Sakti	434	268	166
Raigarh .. .	7,970	3,813	4,157
Sarangarh . .	1,181	523	658
Korea	13	8	5
Surguja	27,946	14,423	13,523
Jashpur	11,837	5,992	5,845
ORAON, TRIBAL RELIGIONS			
Central Provinces and Berar ..	**53,256**	**27,081**	**26,175**
Raipur	111	62	49
Bilaspur . ..	910	470	440
Central Provinces States . ..	*52,235*	*26,549*	*25,686*
Korea	1,426	721	705
Surguja	24,044	12,217	11,827
Udaipur	14,336	7,303	7,033
Jashpur . ..	12,429	6,308	6,121
ORAON, CHRISTIAN			
Central Provinces and Berar ..	**47,517**	**24,047**	**23,470**
Central Provinces States ..	*47,517*	*24,047*	*23,470*
Raigarh	38	18	20
Jashpur	47,479	24,029	23,450
PAIK, HINDU			
Central Provinces and Berar ..	**4,709**	**2,396**	**2,313**
Bhandara	1	1	..
Raipur	4,698	2,391	2,307
Central Provinces States ..	*10*	*4*	*6*
Sarangarh	10	4	6
PAIK, TRIBAL RELIGIONS			
Central Provinces and Berar ..	**3**	**1**	**2**
Raipur	3	1	2
PANKA, HINDU			
Central Provinces and Berar ..	**221,753**	**107,782**	**113,971**
Saugor . ..	12	5	7
Damoh	599	324	275
Jubbulpore	2,061	991	1,070
Mandla	13,656	6,753	6,903
Seoni	1,756	854	902
Betul	2	2	..
Chhindwara	16	8	8
Nagpur .. .	71	32	39
Chanda .. .	14	9	5
Bhandara .. .	436	39	397
Balaghat .. .	3,276	1,608	1,668
Raipur	29,874	14,149	15,675
Bilaspur	71,749	34,755	36,994
Drug	12,453	5,744	6,709
Berar	*16*	*6*	*10*
Amraoti	2	2	..
Buldana	8	4	4
Yeotmal	6	..	6

Tribe or caste with religion and locality.	Persons	Males.	Females.
1	2	3	4
PANKA, HINDU—*concld.*			
Central Provinces States	*85,812*	*42,503*	*43,309*
Bastar	3,597	1,772	1,825
Kanker	1,325	590	735
Nandgaon	2,610	1,227	1,383
Khairagarh	2.448	1,119	1,329
Chhuikhadan	642	288	354
Kawardha	1,767	843	924
Sakti	3,229	1,528	1,701
Raigarh	13,097	6,485	6,612
Sarangarh	6,152	2,996	3,156
Changbhakar	1,189	592	597
Korea	7,030	3,517	3,513
Surguja	38,411	19,425	18,986
Udaipur	2,777	1,360	1,417
Jashpur	1,538	761	777
PANKA, TRIBAL RELIGIONS			
Central Provinces and Berar ..	**5,615**	**2,769**	**2,846**
Mandla	5,383	2,646	2,737
Seoni	2	1	1
Balaghat	1	1	..
Raipur	1	1	..
Bilaspur	24	12	12
Central Provinces States ..	*204*	*108*	*96*
Changbhakar	14	7	7
Korea	141	74	67
Surguja	49	27	22
PANKA, CHRISTIAN			
Central Provinces and Berar ..	**8**	**2**	**6**
Balaghat	4	1	3
Raipur	4	1	3
PARDHAN, HINDU			
Central Provinces and Berar ..	**63,743**	**31.490**	**32,253**
Jubbulpore	1,652	813	839
Mandla	5,756	3,075	2,681
Seoni	26	13	13
Narsinghpur	123	61	62
Hoshangabad	804	392	412
Nimar	34	13	21
Betul	657	327	330
Chhindwara	375	195	180
Wardha	1,409	693	716
Nagpur	6,187	3,009	3,178
Chanda	16,450	8,058	8,392
Bhandara	1,056	494	562
Balaghat	965	477	488
Raipur	842	386	456
Bilaspur	2,446	1,155	1,291
Drug	409	175	234
Berar	*21,991*	*10,899*	*11,092*
Amraoti	310	158	152
Akola	241	124	117
Buldana	16	6	10
Yeotmal	21,424	10,611	10.813
Central Provinces States ..	*2,561*	*1,255*	*1,306*
Bastar	1,169	589	580
Kanker	150	92	58
Nandgaon	123	56	67
Khairagarh	105	41	64
Kawardha	90	39	51
Sakti	13	..	13
Raigarh	155	73	82
Korea	4	3	1
Surguja	657	318	339
Udaipur	83	40	43
Jashpur	12	4	8

Tribe or caste with religion and locality.	Persons.	Males.	Females
1	2	3	4
PARDHAN, TRIBAL RELIGIONS			
Central Provinces and Berar ..	**55,811**	**26,820**	**28,991**
Jubbulpore	48	17	31
Mandla	6,637	3,319	3,318
Seoni	15,589	7,505	8,084
Narsinghpur	1,347	677	670
Hoshangabad	1,288	630	658
Nimar	83	38	45
Betul	2,629	1,308	1,321
Chhindwara	8,322	4,075	4,247
Wardha	7,102	3,206	3,896
Nagpur	122	44	78
Chanda	4.793	2,321	2,472
Bhandara	1,818	926	892
Balaghat	3,299	1,505	1,794
Raipur	122	59	63
Bilaspur	207	92	115
Drug	24	9	15
Berar	*1,200*	*534*	*666*
Amraoti	219	111	108
Yeotmal	981	423	558
Central Provinces States ..	*1,181*	*555*	*626*
Makrai	91	54	37
Bastar	521	237	284
Kanker	69	27	42
Changbhakar	40	19	21
Korea	420	199	221
Surguja	40	19	21
PARDHAN, CHRISTIAN			
Central Provinces and Berar ..	**1**	..	**1**
Chhindwara	1	..	1
PARDHI, HINDU			
Central Provinces and Berar ..	**14,756**	**7.625**	**7,131**
Saugor	236	101	135
Damoh	7	7	..
Jubbulpore	69	29	40
Mandla	11	7	4
Seoni	121	45	76
Narsinghpur	41	27	14
Hoshangabad	359	191	168
Nimar	549	266	283
Betul	2	2	..
Chhindwara	14	7	7
Wardha	361	172	189
Nagpur	466	236	230
Chanda	468	356	112
Balaghat	184	88	96
Raipur	544	262	282
Bilaspur	354	154	200
Drug	498	254	244
Berar	*9,810*	*5,081*	*4,729*
Amraoti	3,612	1,861	1,751
Akola	1,967	1,040	927
Buldana	2,934	1,499	1,435
Yeotmal	1,297	681	616
Central Provinces States ..	*662*	*340*	*322*
Bastar	120	58	62
Nandgaon	160	94	66
Khairagarh	214	101	113
Chhuikhadan	106	49	57
Kawardha	34	22	12
Surguja	25	13	12
Jashpur	3	3	..

Tribe or caste with religion and locality	Persons.	Males.	Females.
1	2	3	4
PARDHI, TRIBAL RELIGIONS			
Central Provinces and Berar ..	871	635	236
Mandla	35	16	19
Hoshangabad	48	26	22
Nimar	41	19	22
Wardha	506	445	61
Chanda	10	8	2
Bilaspur	37	16	21
Drug	11	4	7
Berar	*15*	*15*	..
Yeotmal	15	15	..
Central Provinces States ..	*168*	*86*	*82*
Makrai	54	30	24
Bastar	114	56	58
PARJA, HINDU			
Central Provinces and Berar ..	43	23	20
Drug	34	15	19
Central Provinces States ..	*9*	*8*	*1*
Bastar	9	8	1
PARJA, TRIBAL RELIGIONS			
Central Provinces and Berar ..	**17,559**	**8,820**	**8,739**
Central Provinces States ..	*17,559*	*8,820*	*8,739*
Bastar	17,559	8,820	8,739
RAJJHAR, HINDU			
Central Provinces and Berar ..	**7,778**	**3,830**	**3,948**
Jubbulpore	176	133	43
Mandla	442	243	199
Seoni	1,046	512	534
Narsinghpur	545	267	278
Hoshangabad ..	1,313	631	682
Nimar	17	9	8
Betul	1,234	592	642
Chhindwara	1,502	721	781
Wardha	25	11	14
Nagpur	44	19	25
Bhandara	6	..	6
Balaghat	40	22	18
Bilaspur	61	26	35
Berar	*876*	*420*	*456*
Amraoti	692	335	357
Akola	171	85	86
Yeotmal	13	..	13
Central Provinces States ..	*451*	*224*	*227*
Kawardha	19	7	12
Korea	274	138	136
Jashpur	158	79	79
RAJJHAR, TRIBAL RELIGIONS			
Central Provinces and Berar ..	**2,699**	**1,370**	**1,329**
Central Provinces States ..	*2,699*	*1,370*	*1,329*
Korea	2,699	1,370	1,329
RAJPUT, HINDU			
Central Provinces and Berar ..	**505,117**	**257,652**	**247,465**
Saugor	23,037	12,164	10,873
Damoh	7,732	4,065	3,667
Jubbulpore	21,980	11,827	10,153
Mandla	1,946	1,080	866
Seoni	35,359	17,588	17,771
Narsinghpur	12,343	6,192	6,151
Hoshangabad	55,429	28,278	27,151
Nimar	36,046	18,879	17,167
Betul	8,010	4,095	3,915
Chhindwara	12,906	6,571	6,335
Wardha	3,948	2,184	1,764
Nagpur	12,048	6,650	5,398
Chanda	2,256	1,237	1,019
Bhandara	80,454	40,111	40,343
Balaghat	82,875	41,369	41,506
Raipur	9,188	4,676	4,512
Bilaspur	21,887	10,729	11,158
Drug	7,849	3,772	4,077
Berar	*50,195*	*26,177*	*24,018*
Amraoti	13,667	7,396	6,271
Akola ..	9,327	5,058	4,269
Buldana	19,575	9,664	9,911
Yeotmal	7,626	4,059	3,567
Central Provinces States ..	*19,629*	*10,008*	*9,621*
Makrai	1,498	769	729
Bastar	2,970	1,461	1,509
Kanker	1,032	517	515
Nandgaon	2,293	1,178	1,115
Khairagarh	3,197	1,639	1,558
Chhuikhadan	276	145	131
Kawardha	365	193	172
Sakti	216	108	108
Raigarh	1,058	516	542
Sarangarh	498	220	278
Changbhakar	316	171	145
Korea	526	323	203
Surguja	3,491	1,824	1,667
Udaipur	399	209	190
Jashpur	1,494	735	759
RAJPUT, TRIBAL RELIGIONS			
Central Provinces and Berar ..	**762**	**418**	**344**
Raipur ..	18	7	11
Central Provinces States ..	*744*	*411*	*333*
Bastar	297	175	122
Changbhakar	361	189	172
Korea	4	1	3
Surguja	82	46	36
RAJPUT, MUSLIM			
Central Provinces and Berar ..	**181**	**151**	**30**
Saugor	3	3	..
Jubbulpore	171	144	27
Hoshangabad	2	1	1
Nimar	5	3	2
RAJPUT, CHRISTIAN			
Central Provinces and Berar ..	**27**	**10**	**17**
Saugor	2	2	..
Nimar	2	2	..
Nagpur	1	1	..
Bilaspur ..	16	5	11
Berar	*5*	..	*5*
Amraoti	5	..	5
Central Provinces States ..	*1*	..	*1*
Kawardha	1	..	1

Tribe or caste with religion and locality	Persons.	Males.	Females.
1	2	3	4
SATNAMI, HINDU			
Central Provinces and Berar ..	**351,559**	**169,258**	**182,301**
Jubbulpore	57	32	25
Wardha .. .	39	18	21
Nagpur . ..	184	57	127
Bhandara	106	57	49
Raipur . .	114,461	54,753	59,708
Bilaspur ..	131,159	63,370	67,789
Drug	103,828	50,075	53,753
Berar ..	[illegible]	[illegible]	[illegible]
Akola	7	3	4
Yeotmal	1	1	.
Central Provinces States ..	*1,717*	[illegible]	[illegible]
Bastar . ..	17	9	8
Kanker .. .	482	241	[illegible]
Sakti	1,158	612	546
Surguja	60	30	30
SATNAMI, TRIBAL RELIGIONS			
Central Provinces and Berar .	**5**	**3**	**2**
Bilaspur	5	3	2
SATNAMI, CHRISTIAN			
Central Provinces and Berar ..	**9**	**4**	**5**
Bilaspur	6	2	4
Drug .. .	3	2	1
SAUNTA, HINDU			
Central Provinces and Berar ..	**6,369**	**3,183**	**3,186**
Jubbulpore	1	1	..
Bilaspur	168	89	79
Central Provinces States ..	*6,200*	*3,093*	*3,107*
Surguja	6,143	3,060	3,083
Jashpur	57	33	24
SAUNTA, TRIBAL RELIGIONS			
Central Provinces and Berar ..	**682**	**343**	**339**
Bilaspur	536	264	272
Central Provinces States ..	*146*	*79*	*67*
Surguja	146	79	67
SAWARA OR SAONR, HINDU			
Central Provinces and Berar ..	**84,971**	**41,620**	**43,351**
Saugor	21,817	10,834	10,983
Damoh	6,124	3,023	3,101
Hoshangabad	498	244	254
Betul	8	4	4
Chhindwara	28	19	9
Nagpur	4	3	1
Raipur	28,038	13,712	14,326
Bilaspur	9,535	4,575	4,960
Berar	*7*	*7*	..
Amraoti	3	3	..
Buldana	4	4	..
Central Provinces States ..	*18,912*	*9,199*	*9,713*
Bastar	321	146	175
Sakti	398	193	205
Raigarh	8,098	3,886	4,212
Sarangarh	9,671	4,757	4,914
Surguja	68	31	37
Udaipur	197	113	84
Jashpur	159	73	86

Tribe or caste with religion and locality	Persons	Males	Females.
1	2	3	4
SAWARA OR SAONR, TRIBAL RELIGIONS			
Central Provinces and Berar ..	**1,057**	**527**	**530**
Saugor	50	25	25
Damoh . ..	344	167	177
Raipur	663	335	328
SUNAR, HINDU			
Central Provinces and Berar	**142,540**	**72,549**	**69,991**
Saugor	5,116	2,728	2,388
Damoh . .	2,618	1,330	1,288
Jubbulpore . .	7,974	4,022	3,952
Mandla	1,681	841	840
Seoni .	4,343	2,155	2,158
Narsinghpur	4,170	2,153	2,017
Hoshangabad . ..	3,961	2,092	1,869
Nimar .	5,037	2,757	2,280
Betul .	3,786	1,892	1,694
Chhindwara .	[illegible]	2,816	2,734
Wardha .	5,176	2,571	2,605
Nagpur . ..	11,486	5,716	5,770
Chanda . .	5,512	2,760	2,752
Bhandara .	12,506	6,430	6,076
Balaghat .	7,776	3,903	3,873
Raipur ..	6,790	3,321	3,469
Bilaspur . ..	6,306	3,251	3,055
Drug	3,792	1,802	1,990
Berar	*33,499*	[illegible]	*16,255*
Amraoti . .	11,912	6,160	5,752
Akola	8,702	4,476	4,226
Buldana ..	7,496	3,924	3,572
Yeotmal ..	5,589	2,984	2,605
Central Provinces States ..	*5,108*	*2,502*	*2,606*
Makrai	111	61	50
Bastar	876	428	448
Kanker .. .	320	156	164
Nandgaon . ..	1,063	497	566
Khairagarh .. .	575	285	290
Chhuikhadan	121	56	65
Kawardha . ..	220	113	107
Sakti . ..	70	40	30
Raigarh	581	273	308
Sarangarh . ..	353	181	172
Changbhakar	25	18	7
Korea	71	42	29
Surguja . ..	662	356	306
Udaipur .. .	45	26	19
Jashpur .. .	105	60	45
SUNAR, TRIBAL RELIGIONS			
Central Provinces and Berar ..	**1**	**1**	..
Drug	1	1	..
TELI, HINDU			
Central Provinces and Berar ..	**1,022,447**	**501,754**	**520,693**
Saugor	12,366	6,377	5,989
Damoh	6,310	3,132	3,178
Jubbulpore . ..	17,133	8,468	8,665
Mandla	13,808	6,925	6,883
Seoni	8,104	4,029	4,075
Narsinghpur	7,329	3,705	3,624
Hoshangabad	8,911	4,571	4,340
Nimar	7,256	3,605	3,651
Betul	10,798	5,241	5,557
Chhindwara	19,381	9,682	9,699
Wardha	55,823	27,914	27,909
Nagpur	79,942	40,317	39,625
Chanda	43,174	21,365	21,809
Bhandara	56,448	28,188	28,260
Balaghat	11,344	5,627	5,717
Raipur	211,605	101,196	110,409
Bilaspur	100,999	49,247	51,752
Drug	155,519	73,690	81,829

TABLE XVII Race, Tribe or Caste—*concld.*

Tribe or caste with religion and locality	Persons.	Males.	Females.
1	2	3	4
TELI, HINDU —*concld.*			
Berar	*82,222*	*42,684*	*39,538*
Amraoti	33,929	17,527	16,402
Akola . ..	14,926	7,818	7,108
Buldana	12,661	6,398	6,263
Yeotmal	20,706	10,941	9,765
Central Provinces States ..	*113,975*	*55,791*	*58,184*
Makrai	186	87	99
Bastar . ..	1,538	849	689
Kanker	4,590	2,237	2,353
Nandgaon	39,049	19,085	19,964
Khairagarh . ..	23,139	10,884	12,255
Chhuikhadan	4,021	1,953	2,068
Kawardha	9,439	4,604	4,835
Sakti	2,942	1,516	1,426
Raigarh	11,277	5,640	5,637
Sarangarh	7,602	3,732	3,870
Changbhakar	124	62	62
Korea	1,887	994	893
Surguja	7,322	3,717	3,605
Udaipur	308	154	154
Jashpur	551	277	274
TELI, TRIBAL RELIGIONS			
Central Provinces and Berar ..	**289**	**149**	**140**
Raipur	26	11	15
Bilaspur	8	3	5
Drug	1	..	1
Central Provinces States ..	*254*	*135*	*119*
Bastar	24	12	12
Kanker	19	1	18
Changbhakar	4	2	2
Korea	207	120	87
TELI, MUSLIM			
Central Provinces and Berar ..	**120**	**35**	**85**
Saugor	1	1	..
Jubbulpore	4	4	..
Hoshangabad	8	6	2
Nimar	105	22	83
Balaghat	2	2	..
TELI, CHRISTIAN			
Central Provinces and Berar ..	**25**	**14**	**11**
Narsinghpur	1	1	..
Chhindwara	1	1	..
Raipur	2	..	2
Drug	14	9	5
Central Provinces States ..	*7*	*3*	*4*
Khairagarh	7	3	4
WADDAR, HINDU			
Central Provinces and Berar ..	**13,171**	**6,281**	**6,890**
Jubbulpore	11	11	..
Wardha	463	237	226
Nagpur	233	113	120
Chanda	210	113	97
Berar	*12,254*	*5,807*	*6,447*
Amraoti	430	210	220
Akola	2,117	1,063	1,054
Buldana	3,289	1,583	1,706
Yeotmal	6,418	2,951	3,467
WANJARI, HINDU			
Central Provinces and Berar ..	**48,860**	**24,693**	**24,167**
Wardha	1,679	879	800
Nagpur	194	98	96
Chanda	1,045	519	526
Bhandara	34	22	12
Berar	*45,908*	*23,175*	*22,733*
Amraoti	2,886	1,446	1,440
Akola	14,660	7,505	7,155
Buldana	12,426	6,348	6,078
Yeotmal	15,936	7,876	8,060
CASTE NIL, (HINDU EXCLUDING ARYAS AND BRAHMOS)			
Central Provinces and Berar ..	**2,847**	**1,505**	**1,342**
Saugor	28	11	17
Damoh	9	7	2
Jubbulpore	1,286	699	587
Mandla	8	8	..
Seoni	26	24	2
Narsinghpur	27	13	14
Hoshangabad	25	16	9
Nimar	13	2	11
Betul	24	16	8
Chhindwara	34	20	14
Wardha	5	2	3
Nagpur	2	2	..
Chanda	130	59	71
Bhandara	6	4	2
Balaghat	88	37	51
Raipur	151	87	64
Bilaspur	760	385	375
Drug	77	39	38
Berar	*18*	*7*	*11*
Amraoti	18	7	11
Central Provinces States ..	*130*	*67*	*63*
Bastar	7	7	..
Nandgaon	55	31	24
Khairagarh	30	11	19
Chhuikhadan	1	1	..
Raigarh	14	3	11
Sarangarh	4	3	1
Korea	2	2	..
Surguja	16	8	8
Jashpur	1	1	..

TABLE XVIII

Variation of population of selected tribes

1. The Table, which has been prepared at this Census for the first time, is presented in two parts (i) for British districts with an appendix showing figures by tahsils and taluqs and (ii) for the Central Provinces States. In Part A plus and minus figures, as far as they are available have been shown for the period 1881 to 1931. In part B they are shown for 1891 to 1931. For the appendix, only figures for 1921 and 1931 are forthcoming.

2. Figures for the first three decades 1881—1901 are not available for the districts of Berar as they have undergone changes in composition from time to time. The variations have therefore been shown only on the Divisional totals.

3. The Drug district was formed from portions of Bilaspur and Raipur after 1901, and so the statistics for those two districts in the period 1881 to 1901 include the figures for Drug which it has been impossible to separate.

4. Details for religion are not forthcoming prior to 1911 and variations of total figures only can be shown for the earlier decades. Figures were not tabulated by sex in 1891 ; thus males and females are shown together under that year.

5. Separate figures for the Chhota Nagpur States were not abstracted before 1911. This accounts for blanks and marked variations against them.

6. Blanks under any year indicate either that figures are not available or that there was a nil return. The entries in columns 8 to 12 show when the latter is the case.

7. Figures for the thirty principal primitive tribes of the Province have been included. Agarias do not appear because the statistics abstracted were unreliable as they were confused with Agharias both at Enumeration and Tabulation. The following tribes found in the Chhota Nagpur States were also omitted either because they have not appeared in previous Census Reports or because they are of small numerical importance:—Khond, Rautia, Birhul, Pando Kharia and one or two others which are mentioned in part I of the report. 1931 figures for Kharias can be found in Table XVII.

TABLE XVIII—PART A

Variation of Population

Tribe and locality.	Persons.						Variation		
	1931.	1921.	1911.	1901.	1891.	1881.	1921 to 1931.	1911 to 1921.	1901 to 1911.
1	2	3	4	5	6	7	8	9	10
ANDH									
Central Provinces and Berar ..	**58,549**	**52,414**	**52,378**	**39,679**	**43,602**	**37,010**	**+6,135**	**+36**	**+12,699**
Hindu	58,549	52,414	52,378	..	..	..	+6,135	+36	..
Chhindwara District ..	..	*133*	..	..	..	..	*—133*	*+133*	..
Hindu	..	133	..	..	..	..	—133	+133	..
Wardha District	..	*19*	*1*	..	..	..	*—19*	*+18*	..
Hindu	..	19	1	..	..	..	—19	+18	..
Nagpur District	..	*51*	..	..	..	..	*—51*	*+51*	..
Hindu	..	51	..	..	..	..	—51	+51	..
Chanda District	*30*	*3*	*1*	..	..	..	*+27*	*+2*	..
Hindu	30	3	1	..	..	..	+27	+2	..
Bhandara District .	..	*103*	..	..	..	..	*—103*	*+103*	..
Hindu	..	103	..	..	..	..	—103	+103	..
Berar	**58,519**	**52,105**	**52,376**	**39,679**	**43,602**	**37,010**	**+6,414**	**—271**	**+12,697**
Hindu	58,519	52,105	52,376	..	..	..	+6,414	—271	..
Amraoti District ..	*22*	*2*	*1*	..	..	..	*+20*	*+1*	..
Hindu	22	2	1	..	..	..	+20	+1	..
Akola District	*23,118*	*19,960*	*19,540*	..	..	..	*+3,158*	*+420*	..
Hindu	23,118	19,960	19,540	..	..	..	+3,158	+420	..
Buldana District	*4,680*	*4,362*	*4,392*	..	..	..	*+318*	*—30*	..
Hindu .. .	4,680	4,362	4,392	.	.	..	+318	—30	..
Yeotmal District	*30,699*	*27,781*	*28,443*	..	..	..	*+2,918*	*—662*	..
Hindu .. .	30,699	27,781	28,443	..	..	..	+2,918	—662	..
BAIGA									
Central Provinces and Berar ..	**32,003**	**25,078**	**27,274**	**23,471**	**21,336**	**38,883**	**+6,925**	**—2,196**	**+3,803**
Hindu	9,847	3,307	1,125	..	..	..	+6,540	+2,182	..
Tribal	22,156	21,771	26,149	..	..	..	+385	—4,378	..
Saugor District	..	*1*	..	*1*	..	*23*	*—1*	*+1*	*—1*
Hindu .. .	.	1	..	..	..	..	—1	+1	..
Damoh District .. .	..	..	..	*37*	*9*	*25*	..	..	*—37*
Jubbulpore District .	*2,665*	*2,639*	*2,226*	*1,826*	*2,329*	*1,320*	*+26*	*+413*	*+400*
Hindu .. .	2,340	549	89	..	..	..	+1,791	+460	..
Tribal	325	2,090	2,137	..	..	..	—1,765	—47	..
Mandla District .. .	*19,938*	*16,302*	*18,684*	*13,875*	*13,935*	*11,493*	*+3,636*	*—2,382*	*+4,809*
Hindu .	3,507	1,547	205	..	..	..	+3,960	+1,342	..
Tribal	14,431	14,755	18,479	..	..	..	—324	—3,724	..
Seoni District . .	*659*	*344*	*964*	*644*	*213*	*598*	*+315*	*—620*	*+320*
Hindu ..	1	23	18	..	..	..	—22	—55	..
Tribal .. .	658	321	886	..	..	..	+337	—565	..
Narsinghpur District ..	..	*106*	*9*	..	..	..	*—106*	*+97*	*+9*
Hindu ..	.	..	9	..	..	.	..	—9	..
Tribal	.	106	..	..	..	..	—106	+106	..
Hoshangabad District ..	..	..	..	..	*3*	..	..	..	..
Nimar District	..	..	..	..	*1*		..	..	..

of Selected Tribes.

TABLE XVIII—PART A

(Increase + Decrease —).		Net variation, 1881 to 1931 (Increase + Decrease —).	Males					Females.				
1891 to 1901.	1881 to 1891.		1931.	1921.	1911.	1901.	1881.	1931.	1921	1911.	1901	1881.
11	12	13	14	15	16	17	18	19	20	21	22	23
—3,923	**+6,592**	**+21,539**	**29,820**	**25,815**	**25,563**	**19,318**	**18,699**	**28,729**	**26,599**	**26,815**	**20,361**	**18,311**
..	..	..	29,820	25,815	25,563	..	..	28,729	26,599	26,815	..	..
..	..	..	..	*69*	..	..	..	..	*64*	..	..	..
..	..	..	..	69	..	..	..	..	64	..	..	..
..	..	..	..	*10*	*1*	..	..	..	*9*	..	..	..
..	..	..	..	10	1	..	..	..	9	..	..	..
..	..	..	..	*28*	..	..	..	..	*23*	..	..	..
..	..	..	..	28	..	..	..	..	23	..	..	..
..	..	..	*19*	*2*	*1*	..	..	*11*	*1*	..	..	..
..	..	..	19	2	1	..	..	11	1	..	..	..
..	..	..	..	*1*	..	..	..	..	*102*	..	..	..
..	..	..	..	1	..	..	..	..	102	..	..	..
—3,923	**+6,592**	**+21,509**	**29,801**	**25,705**	**25,561**	**19,318**	**18,699**	**28,718**	**26,400**	**26,815**	**20,361**	**18,311**
..	..	..	29,801	25,705	25,561	..	..	28,718	26,400	26,815	..	..
..	..	..	*13*	*1*	..	..	..	*9*	*1*	*1*	..	..
..	..	..	13	1	..	..	..	9	1	1	..	..
..	..	..	*11,246*	*9,756*	*9,504*	..	..	*11,872*	*10,204*	*10,036*	..	..
..	..	..	11,246	9,756	9,504	..	..	11,872	10,204	10,036	..	..
..	..	..	*2,367*	*2,130*	*2,091*	..	..	*2,313*	*2,232*	*2,301*	..	..
..	..	..	2,367	2,130	2,091	..	..	2,313	2,232	2,301	..	..
..	..	..	*16,175*	*13,818*	*13,966*	..	..	*14,524*	*13,963*	*14,477*	..	..
..	..	..	16,175	13,818	13,966	..	..	14,524	13,963	14,477	..	..
+2,135	**—17,547**	**—6,880**	**15,918**	**12,410**	**13,480**	**11,364**	**19,689**	**16,085**	**12,668**	**13,794**	**12,107**	**19,194**
.. ..	.. ..	.. ..	4,841 11,077	1,536 10,874	536 12,944	.. ..	.. ..	5,006 11,079	1,771 10,897	589 13,205	.. ..	.. ..
+1	*—23*	*—23*	..	*1*	..	..	*11*	..	..	..	*1*	*12*
..	..	..	..	1	..	..	..	..	..	..	..	..
+28	*—16*	*—25*	..	..	..	*18*	*16*	..	..	..	*19*	*9*
—503	*+1,009*	*+1,345*	*1,323*	*1,222*	*1,099*	*822*	*673*	*1,342*	*1,417*	*1,127*	*1,004*	*647*
.. ..	.. ..	.. ..	1,173 150	253 969	48 1,051	.. ..	.. ..	1,167 175	296 1,121	41 1,086	.. ..	.. ..
—60	*+2,442*	*+8,445*	*9,970*	*8,188*	*9,311*	*6,802*	*5,902*	*9,968*	*8,114*	*9,373*	*7,073*	*5,591*
.. ..	.. ..	.. ..	2,704 7,266	792 7,396	99 9,212	.. ..	.. ..	2,803 7,165	755 7,359	106 9,267	.. ..	.. ..
+431	*—385*	*+61*	*320*	*71*	*445*	*298*	*318*	*339*	*273*	*519*	*346*	*280*
.. ..	.. ..	.. ..	1 319	8 63	30 415	.. ..	.. ..	.. 339	15 258	48 471	.. ..	.. ..
..	..	..	..	*54*	*6*	..	..	..	*52*	*3*	..	..
.. ..	.. ..	.. ..	.. ..	.. 54	6 ..	.. ..	.. ..	.. ..	.. 52	3 ..	.. ..	.. ..
—3	*+3*	..	..	..	..	..	..	..	..	..	..	..
—1	*—5*	*—6*	..	..	..	..	*5*	..	..	..	..	*1*

Tribe and Locality.	Persons. 1931	1921.	1911.	1901.	1891.	1881.	Variation 1921 to 1931.	1911 to 1921.	1901 to 1911.
1	2	3	4	5	6	7	8	9	10
BAIGA—*concld.*									
Chhindwara District ..	*52*	*20*	*4*	*720*	..	..	*+32*	*+16*	*−716*
Hindu ..	48	20	..	..	..	..	+28	+20	..
Tribal ..	4	..	4	..	..	..	+4	−4	..
Nagpur District ..	*3*	*3*	.	*1*	..	*4*	..	*+3*	*−1*
Hindu ..	3	..	.	..	.	..	+3	..	..
Tribal ..	..	3	.	..	..	..	3	+3	..
Chanda District ..	..	.	..	*1*	..	*41*	..	..	*−1*
Bhandara District	..	*5*	..	*138*	..	*1,887*	*−5*	*+5*	*−138*
Tribal	..	5	..	..	..	..	−5	+5	..
Balaghat District	*5,640*	*5,051*	*5,070*	*3,442*	*3,863*	*7,737*	*+589*	*−19*	*+1,628*
Hindu	238	965	460	..	..	..	−727	+505	..
Tribal ..	5,402	4,086	4,610	..	..	..	+1,316	−524	..
Raipur District ..	*386*	..	*159*	*70*	*189*	*7,316*	*+386*	*−159*	*+89*
Hindu	270	..	141	..	..	..	+270	−141	..
Tribal	116	..	18	..	..	.	+116	−18	..
Bilaspur District ..	*2,404*	*405*	*157*	*2,716*	*794*	*8,433*	*+1,999*	*+248*	*−2,559*
Hindu ..	1,397		142	..	..	..	+1,397	−142	..
Tribal ..	1,007	405	15	..	..	..	+602	+390	..
Drug District ..	*255*	*201*	*1*	..	..	..	*+54*	*+200*	*+1*
Hindu ..	42	201	1	..	..	..	−159	+200	..
Tribal ..	213	..	..	..	..	..	+213	..	..
Berar ..	**1**	**1**	..	..	..	..	..	**+1**	..
Hindu ..	1	1	..	..	..	..	..	+1	..
Buldana District ..	.	*1*	..	..	..	..	*−1*	*+1*	..
Hindu ..	..	1	..	..	..	..	−1	+1	..
Yeotmal District ..	*1*	..	..	..	..	..	*+1*	..	..
Hindu ..	1	..	..	.	..	..	+1	..	..
BHAINA									
Central Provinces and Berar ..	**16,447**	**11,523**	**14,522**	**7,454**	**12,413**	..	**+4,924**	**−2,999**	**+7,068**
Hindu ..	12,431	11,523	14,522	..	..	..	+908	−2,999	..
Tribal ..	4,016	..	..	..	..	..	+4,016	..	..
Saugor District ..	..	..	..	..	*1*	..	..	..	..
Mandla District ..	*1,013*	..	*968*	*662*	*617*	..	*+1,013*	*−968*	*+306*
Hindu ..	812	..	968	.	..	..	+812	−968	..
Tribal ..	201	..	..	..	..	..	+201	..	..
Betul District ..	..	..	*1*	..	..	..	..	*−1*	*+1*
Hindu ..	.	.	1	..	..	..	..	−1	..
Bhandara District	*1*	..	..	..	..	..	*+1*	..	..
Hindu ..	1	..	..	..	.	..	+1	..	..
Raipur District ..	*202*	..	*231*	*27*	*49*	..	*+202*	*−231*	*+204*
Hindu ..	202	..	231	..	..	..	+202	−231	..
Bilaspur District ..	*15,231*	*11,523*	*13,322*	*6,765*	*11,716*	..	*+3,708*	*−1,799*	*+6,557*
Hindu ..	11,416	11,523	13,322	..	..	..	−107	−1,799	..
Tribal ..	3,815	..	..	..	..	..	+3,815	..	..

(Increase + Decrease —).			Males.					Females.				
1891 to 1901.	1881 to 1891.	Net variation 1881 to 1931 (Increase + Decrease —).	1931	1921.	1911.	1901.	1881.	1931.	1921.	1911.	1901.	1881.
11	12	13	14	15	16	17	18	19	20	21	22	23
+720	..	+52	37	6	3	311	..	15	14	1	409	..
..	..	..	35	6	..	..	.	13	14	..	..	..
..	.	..	2	..	3		..	2	.	1	..	..
+1	−4	−1	3	2	..	1	1	..	1	..	..	3
..	..	..	3	.	.	..	..	..	..	..	..	..
..	..	..	..	2	..	.	..	..	1	.	..	..
+1	−41	−41	..	..	..	..	22	..	..	..	1	19
+138	−1,887	−1,887	..	2	.	68	927	..	3	..	70	960
..	..	..	..	2	..	..	..	..	3	..	..	..
−421	−3,874	−2,097	2,782	2,631	2,465	1,710	3,773	2,858	2,420	2,605	1,732	3,964
..	..	..	119	475	219	..	..	119	490	241	..	..
..	..	..	2,663	2,156	2,246	..	..	2,739	1,930	2,364	..	..
—119	−7,127	−6,930	193	..	81	35	3,823	193	..	78	34	3,493
..	..	..	137	..	71	..	..	133	..	70	..	..
..	..	..	56	..	10	..	..	60	..	8	..	..
+1,922	−7,639	−6,029	1,154	232	70	1,298	4,218	1,250	173	87	1,418	4,215
..	..	..	646	..	63	..	..	751	..	79	..	..
..	..	..	508	232	7	..	..	499	173	8	..	..
..	..	+255	136	..	..	.	..	119	201	1	..	..
..	..	..	23	..	.	.	.	19	201	1	..	..
..	..	..	113	..	..	.	..	100	..	..	..	..
..	..	+ 1	..	1	.	.	.	1	..	..	..	..
..	..	..	..	1	.	.	..	1	.	..	..	..
..	..	..	..	1	..	..	..	..	..	..	..	..
..	..	..	..	1	..	..	..	..	..	..	..	..
.	..	+1	..	..	..	.	..	1	.	..	..	..
..	..	..	..	..	..	..	.	1	..	..	..	..
−4,959	..	..	8,129	6,437	7,132	3,578	.	8,318	5,086	7,390	3,876	..
.	..	..	6,112	6 437	7,132	..	..	6,319	5,086	7,390	..	..
..	..	..	2,017	..	.	.	.	1,999	..	..	..	..
—1	.	..	..	..	..	..	..	.	..	..	..	..
+15	..	..	477	..	462	269	..	536	..	506	393	..
..	..	.	372	..	462	..	..	440	..	506	..	..
.	..	..	105	..	..	..	..	96	..	..	..	..
..	..	..	..	..	.	.	..	..	..	1	..	..
..	..	..	..	..	..	..	..	..	..	1	..	..
..	..	..	1	.	.	.		..	..	..	..	..
.	..	..	1		.	..	..	..	..	..	..	..
—22	..	..	90	.	127	14	..	112	..	104	13	..
..	..	.	90	..	127	.	..	112	..	104	..	..
−4,951	..	.	7,551	6,437	6,543	3,295	..	7,670	5,086	6,779	3,470	..
..	..	.	5,649	6,437	6,543	..	..	5,767	5,086	6,779	..	.
..	..	..	1,912	..	.	..	..	1,903	..	..	..	..

TABLE XVIII—PART A

Tribe and locality.	Persons. 1931	1921	1911	1901	1891	1881.	1921 to 1931	1911 to 1921.	Variation 1901 to 1911.
1	2	3	4	5	6	7	8	9	10
BHARIA—BHUMIA									
Central Provinces and Berar ..	**53,819**	**48,657**	**50,125**	**33,512**	**48,202**	**29,529**	**+5,162**	**−1,468**	**+16,613**
Hindu	35,155	40,291	21,970	..	..	..	−5,136	+18,321	..
Tribal	18,664	8,366	28,155	..	..	..	+10,298	−19,789	..
Saugor District	*1*	..	*9*	*20*	*15*	*2*	*+1*	*−9*	*−11*
Hindu .. .	1	..	9	..	..	..	+1	−9	..
Damoh District	*759*	*1,016*	*1,575*	*503*	*1,242*	*342*	*−287*	*−529*	*+1,072*
Hindu .. .	442	575	1,234	..	..	..	−133	−659	..
Tribal	317	471	341	..	..	..	−154	+130	..
Jubbulpore District ..	*29,006*	*26,303*	*26,982*	*21,831*	*26,541*	*14,665*	*+2,703*	*−679*	*+5,151*
Hindu	28,985	26,192	15,624	..	..	..	+2,793	+10,568	..
Tribal .. .	21	111	11,358	..	..	..	−90	−11,247	..
Mandla District	*1,481*	*1,331*	*1,664*	*1,157*	*1,283*	*1,363*	*+150*	*−333*	*+507*
Hindu	12	648	80	..	..	..	−636	+568	..
Tribal ..	1,469	683	1,584	..	..	..	+786	−901	..
Seoni District	*1,536*	*1,407*	*1,832*	*1,647*	*1,670*	*1,864*	*+129*	*−425*	*+185*
Hindu ..	297	352	359	..	..	..	−55	−7	..
Tribal	1,239	1,055	1,473	..	..	..	+184	−418	..
Narsinghpur District .	*2,115*	*1,954*	*2,514*	*2,674*	*2,494*	*1,805*	*+191*	*−590*	*−130*
Hindu	992	1,281	232	..	..	..	−289	+1,049	..
Tribal .. .	1,153	673	2,312	..	..	..	+480	−1,639	..
Hoshangabad District ..	*758*	*507*	*789*	*644*	*911*	*888*	*+251*	*−282*	*+145*
Hindu	81	193	47	..	..	..	−112	+146	..
Tribal . ..	677	314	742	..	..	..	+363	−428	..
Nimar District	*3*	..	..	*5*	..	..	*+3*	..	*−5*
Hindu	3	..	..	.	..	..	+3	..	..
Betul District	*1*	*1,596*	*178*	*5*	*51*	*58*	*−1,595*	*+1,418*	*+173*
Hindu	1	1,596	166	..	..	..	−1,595	+1,430	..
Tribal	..	..	12	..	..	..	..	−12	..
Chhindwara District ..	*7,199*	*6,524*	*7,737*	*3,658*	*6,801*	*6,380*	*+675*	*−1,213*	*+4,079*
Hindu	106	3,746	434	..	..	..	−3,640	+3,312	..
Tribal	7,093	2,778	7,303	..	..	..	+4,315	−4,525	..
Nagpur District	*4*	*142*	*3*	..	*148*	*44*	*−138*	*+139*	*+3*
Hindu	4	142	3	..	..	..	−138	+139	..
Chanda District	..	..	..	..	*11*	*44*	..	..	..
Bhandara District ..	*314*	*61*	*87*	*1*	..	*1*	*+253*	*−26*	*+86*
Hindu	314	61	87	..	..	..	+253	−26	..
Balaghat District ..	*190*	*474*	*75*	..	*17*	*46*	*−284*	*+399*	*+75*
Hindu	124	412	75	..	..	..	−288	+337	..
Tribal	66	62	..	..	..	..	+4	+62	..
Raipur District	*11*	..	*9*	*51*	*755*	*482*	*+11*	*−9*	*−42*
Hindu	11	..	8	..	..	..	+11	−8	..
Tribal	..	..	1	..	..	..	..	−1	..
Bilaspur District	*9,326*	*7,312*	*5,641*	*1,316*	*6,263*	*1,545*	*+2,014*	*+671*	*+5,325*
Hindu ..	3,398	5,093	3,612	..	..	..	−1,695	+1,481	..
Tribal	5,928	2,219	3,029	..	..	..	+3,709	−810	..

(Increase + Decrease —).			Males.					Females.				
1891 to 1901.	1881 to 1891.	Net variation 1881 to 1931 (Increase + Decrease —)	1931.	1921.	1911.	1901.	1881.	1931.	1921.	1911.	1901.	1881.
11	12	13	14	15	16	17	18	19	20	21	22	23
—14,690	**+18,673**	**+24,290**	**25,864**	**24,431**	**24,168**	**16,094**	**14,406**	**27,955**	**24,226**	**25,957**	**17,418**	**15,123**
..	..	..	16,791	20,177	10,620	..	.	18,364	20,114	11,350	..	..
..	..	..	9,073	4,254	13,548	..	..	9,591	4,112	14,607	..	..
+5	*+13*	*—1*	*1*	.	*8*	*10*	*2*	..	..	*1*	*10*	..
..	..	..	1	.	8	..	..	..	..	1	..	..
—739	*+900*	*+117*	*348*	*541*	*768*	*242*	*165*	*411*	*505*	*807*	*261*	*177*
..	..	..	194	298	600	..	.	248	277	634	..	..
..	..	..	154	243	168	..	..	163	228	173	..	..
—4,710	*+11,876*	*+14,341*	*13,887*	*12,658*	*12,882*	*10,501*	*7,035*	*15,119*	*13,645*	*11,100*	*11,327*	*,630*
..	..	..	13,877	12,605	7,518	..	..	15,108	13,587	8,106	..	..
..	..	..	10	53	5,364	..	..	11	58	5,994	..	..
—126	*—80*	*+118*	*719*	*665*	*828*	*563*	*702*	*762*	*666*	*836*	*594*	*661*
..	..	..	4	343	40	..	..	8	305	40	..	..
..	..	..	715	322	788	..	..	754	361	796	..	..
—23	*—194*	*—328*	*747*	*680*	*877*	*807*	*905*	*789*	*727*	*955*	*840*	*959*
..	..	..	152	186	174	..	..	145	166	185	..	..
..	..	..	595	494	703	..	..	644	561	770	..	..
+180	*+689*	*+340*	*1,121*	*968*	*1,230*	*1,190*	*915*	*1,024*	*986*	*1,314*	*1,484*	*890*
..	..	..	481	632	113	.	..	511	649	119	..	..
..	..	..	640	336	1,117	..	.	513	337	1,195	..	..
—267	*+23*	*—130*	*383*	*237*	*392*	*334*	*426*	*375*	*270*	*397*	*310*	*462*
..	..	..	46	.	22	..	..	35	193	25	..	..
..	..	..	337	237	370	.	..	340	77	372	..	..
+5	..	*+3*	*2*	..	..	*3*	..	*1*	..	..	*2*	..
..	..	..	2	..	..	..	.	1	..	..	..	..
—46	*—7*	*—57*	*1*	*1,570*	*109*	*1*	*31*	..	*26*	*69*	*4*	*27*
..	..	..	1	1,570	104	..	..	..	26	62	..	..
..	..	..	..	..	5	..	..	..	...	7	..	..
—3,143	*+421*	*+819*	*3,515*	*2,969*	*3,752*	*1,771*	*3,116*	*3,684*	*3,555*	*3,985*	*1,887*	*3,264*
..	..	..	53	1,657	214	..	..	53	2,089	220	..	..
..	..	..	3,462	1,312	3,538	..	.	3,631	1,466	3,765	..	..
—148	*+104*	*—40*	*4*	*73*	..	..	*27*	...	*69*	*3*	..	*17*
..	..	..	4	73	.	..	..	..	69	3	.	..
—11	*—33*	*—44*	..	..	.	..	*22*	..	..	..	..	*22*
+1	*—1*	*+313*	*57*	*31*	*46*	..	*1*	*257*	*30*	*41*	*1*	..
..	..	..	57	31	46	..	...	257	30	41	..	..
—17	*—29*	*+144*	*88*	*372*	*39*	..	*22*	*102*	*102*	*36*	..	*24*
..	..	..	55	311	39	..	.	69	101	36	..	..
..	..	..	33	61	..	..	..	33	1	..	..	..
—705	*+273*	*—471*	*6*	..	*5*	*20*	*255*	*5*	..	*4*	*31*	*227*
..	..	..	6	..	4	..	..	5	..	4	..	..
..	..	..	..	..	1	..	..	..	..	..	..	..
—4,947	*+4,718*	*+7,781*	*4,457*	*3,667*	*3,232*	*649*	*782*	*4,869*	*3,645*	*3,409*	*667*	*763*
..	..	..	1,669	2,471	1,738	..	...	1,729	2,622	1,874	..	..
..	..	..	2,788	1,196	1,494	..	..	3,140	1,023	1,535	..	..

Tribe and locality.	Persons. 1931.	1921.	1911.	1901.	1891.	1881.	Variation 1921 to 1931.	1911 to 1921.	1901 to 1911.
1	2	3	4	5	6	7	8	9	10
BHARIA—BHUMIA—*concld.*									
Drug District	*835*	..	..	..	..	..	*+835*	..	..
Hindu	134	..	..	..	..	..	+134	..	..
Tribal	701	..	..	..	..	..	+701	..	..
Berar	**250**	..	..	..	..	..	**+250**	..	..
Hindu	250	..	..	..	..	..	+250	..	..
Akola District	*250*	..	..	..	..	..	*+250*	..	..
Hindu	250	..	..	..	..	..	+250	..	..
*** BHATTRA**									
Central Provinces and Berar ..	**410**	..	..	..	**97**	..	..	..	..
Hindu	398	..	..	..	..	..	..	..	..
Tribal	12	..	..	..	..	..	..	..	..
Raipur District	*363*	..	..	..	*97*	..	..	..	..
Hindu	351	..	..	..	..	..	..	..	..
Tribal	12	..	..	..	..	..	..	..	..
Drug District	*45*	..	..	..	..	..	..	..	..
Hindu	45	..	..	..	..	..	..	..	..
Berar ..	**2**	..	..	..	..	..	..	..	..
Hindu ..	2	..	..	..	..	..	..	..	..
Yeotmal District	*2*	..	..	..	..	..	..	..	..
Hindu	2	..	..	..	..	..	..	..	..
BHIL									
Central Provinces and Berar ..	**30,303**	**24,865**	**27,621**	**28,416**	**27,888**	**41,868**	**+5,438**	**−2,756**	**−795**
Hindu	29,738	24,720	24,580	..	..	..	+5,018	+140	..
Tribal	405	..	..	..	..	..	+405	..	..
Muslim	160	145	3,041	..	..	..	+15	−2,896	..
Saugor District .. .	*9*	..	*73*	*45*	*4*	..	+9	−73	+28
Hindu	9	..	73	.	..	..	+9	−73	..
Damoh District	..	..	*1*	*6*	*117*	..	..	−1	−5
Hindu .. .	..	-	1	..	..	..	..	−1	..
Jubbulpore District .	*11*	*23*	*2*	*18*	*7*	*126*	−12	+21	−16
Hindu .. .	11	23	3	...	..	..	−12	+21	..
Mandla District .. .	*4*	..	..	..	*6*	..	+4	..	..
Tribal	4	..	.	..	.	.	+4	..	..
Seoni District	..	..	*5*	*9*	..	.	..	−5	−4
Hindu .. .	..	..	5	.	..	.	..	−5	..
Narsinghpur District .	*1*	..	.	.	..	*17*	+1	.	..
Tribal	1	..	..	..	.	.	+1	..	..
Hoshangabad District ..	*27*	..	*37*	*165*	*60*	*6,604*	+27	−37	−68
Hindu .. .	27	..	37	..	..	.	+27	−37	..
Nimar District	*24,993*	*21,634*	*23,761*	*22,323*	*21,460*	*23,619*	+3,359	−2,127	+1,438
Hindu	24,637	21,634	22,282	..	..	.	+3,003	−648	..
Tribal	310	..	.	..	..	.	+310	..	..
Muslim	46	.	1,479	..	.	.	+46	−1,479	..

* From 1901—1921 the figures of Bhattras were included under Gonds.

(Increase + Decrease —).			Males					Females.				
1891 to 1901.	1881 to 1891.	Net variation 1881 to 1931 (Increase + Decrease —).	1931.	1921.	1911.	1901.	1881.	1931.	1921.	1911	1901.	1881.
11	12	13	14	15	16	17	18	19	20	21	22	23
..	..	+835	*108*	..	..	..	..	*427*	.	..	..	..
..	..	..	69	..		..	..	65	..	..	..	..
..	..	.	339	.		.	..	362	..	.	..	..
..	..	+250	**120**	..	..	..	..	**130**	..	..	..	..
..	..	.	120	.	.	.	.	130	..	..	..	..
..	..	*+250*	*120*	.	..	..	.	*130*	..	.	..	..
..	..	..	120	.	.	..	..	130	..	..	..	..
..	..	..	**210**	..	..	..	..	**200**	..	..	..	..
..	..	..	203	.	..	..	..	195	..	..	..	..
..	..	..	7	..	..	..	..	5	..	..	..	..
..	..	..	*19*[illegible]	..	..	..	..	*171*	..	..	..	..
..	..	..	185	..	..	..	..	166	..	.	..	..
..	..		7	.	..	..	.	5	..	..	..	..
..	..	..	*16*	..	..	..	..	*29*	..	..	..	..
..	..	..	16	.	..	..	..	29	..	..	..	..
..	..	..	**2**	..	.	..	..	..	..	..	..	..
..	..	..	2	..	..	..	..	..	..	..	..	..
..	..	..	*2*	..	..	..	..	..	..	..	..	..
..	..	..	2	..	..	..	..	..	..	..	..	..
+528	**−13,980**	**—11,565**	**15,229**	**12,273**	**13,704**	**14,049**	**21,003**	**15,074**	**12,592**	**13,917**	**14,367**	**20,865**
..	..	.	14,914	12,201	12,200	..	..	14,824	12,519	12,380	..	..
..	..	..	226	..	..	..	..	179	..	..	..	..
..	..	.	89	72	1,504	..	..	71	73	1,537	..	..
+41	*+4*	*+9*	*4*	.	*41*	*23*	..	*5*	..	*32*	*22*	..
..	..	..	4	..	41	..	..	5	..	32	..	..
—111	*+117*	.	..	..	*1*	*6*	..	..	..	..	..	..
..	..	..	..	..	1	..	..	..	..	..	..	..
+11	*—119*	*—115*	*8*	*1*	*1*	*18*	*93*	*3*	*22*	*1*	..	*33*
..	..	..	8	1	1	..	..	3	22	1	..	..
—6	*+6*	*+4*	*1*	..	..	..	..	*3*	..	..	..	..
..	..	..	1	..	..	..	..	3	..	..	..	..
+9	..	..	..	..	..	*7*	..	..	..	*5*	*2*	..
..	..	..	..	..	..	..	..	..	..	5	..	..
..	*—17*	*—16*	*1*	..	..	.	*10*	..	..	..	..	*7*
..	..	..	1	..	[illegible]	..	..	..	..	..	..	..
+45	*—6,544*	*—6,577*	*13*	..	*20*	*53*	*3,280*	*14*	..	*17*	*52*	*3,324*
..	..	..	13	..	20	..	..	14	..	17	..	—
+863	*—71,59*	*—3,626*	*12,568*	*10,662*	*21,806*	*11,041*	*14,422*	*12,425*	*10,972*	*11,955*	*11,282*	*14,197*
..	..	..	12,367	10,662	11,046	..	..	12,270	10,972	11,236	..	..
..	..	..	173	..	..	..	..	137	..	..	..	..
..	..	..	28	..	760	..	..	18	..	719	..	

Tribe and locality.	Persons. 1931.	1921.	1911.	1901.	1891.	1881.	Variation 1921 to 1931.	1911 to 1921.	1901 to 1911.
1	2	3	4	5	6	7	8	9	10
BHIL—*concld.*									
Betul District ..	..	..	*30*	*29*	..	*1,095*	..	*−30*	*+1*
Hindu ..	..	..	30	..	..	..	..	−30	..
Chhindwara District	*1*	..	*3*	*1*	*1*	*47*	*+1*	*−3*	*+2*
Hindu ..	1	..	3	..	..	..	+1	−3	..
Wardha District ..	*13*	..	*1*	*144*	*20*	..	*−13*	*−1*	*−143*
Hindu ..	13	.	1	..	.	.	+13	−1	..
Nagpur District ..	*9*	*6*	*21*	*32*	*2*	*35*	*+3*	*−18*	*−8*
Hindu .	9	6	24	..	..	..	−3	−18	..
Bhandhara District	*10*	..	..	..	..	*13*	*+10*	..	..
Hindu ..	10			..	..	.	+10	..	..
Raipur District	.	.	*5*	..	..	*3*	..	*−5*	*+5*
Hindu ..	.		5	..	..		..	−5	..
Bilaspur District ..	.	..	..	..	*8*	*1*	..	..	..
Berar ..	**5,225**	**3,202**	**3,679**	**5,704**	**6,194**	**5,308**	**+2,023**	**−477**	**−2,025**
Hindu ..	5,021	3,057	2,117	..	..	..	+1,964	+940	..
Tribal ..	90	.	.	..	.	..	+90	..	..
Muslim ..	114	145	1,562	..	..	..	−31	−1,417	..
Amraoti District ..	*150*	*188*	*910*	..	..	..	*−38*	*−722*	..
Hindu ..	94	188	130	..	..	..	−94	+58	..
Tribal ..	34	..	..	..	..	..	+34	..	..
Muslim ..	22	..	780	..	..	..	+22	−780	..
Akola District ..	*1,082*	*767*	*181*	..	..	..	*+315*	*+586*	..
Hindu ..	1,064	767	181	..	..	..	+297	+586	..
Tribal ..	18	.	..	..	..	..	+18	..	..
Buldana District ..	*1,285*	*1,087*	*1,647*	..	.	..	*+198*	*−560*	..
Hindu .	1,155	942	865	..	.	..	+213	+77	..
Tribal ..	38	..	..	..	..	..	+38	..	..
Muslim	92	145	782	..	.	..	−53	−637	..
Yeotmal District ..	*2,708*	*1,160*	*941*	..	..	..	*+1,548*	*+219*	..
Hindu ..	2,708	1,160	941	..	..	..	+1,548	+219	..
BHUINHAR									
Central Provinces and Berar ..	**1,250**	**660**	**1,811**	..	**504**	..	**+590**	**−1,151**	..
Hindu ..	347	613	1,788	..	..	..	−266	−1,175	..
Tribal ..	903	47	23	..	..	..	+856	+24	..
Saugor District ..	..	*48*	.	..	*12*	..	*−48*	*+48*	..
Hindu .	..	48	..	..	..	..	−48	+48	..
Jubbulpore District	..	..	*2*	..	..	..	..	*−2*	..
Hindu ..	..	..	2	..	..	..	..	−2	..
Mandla District ..	..	*14*	..	..		..	*−14*	*+14*	..
Hindu ..	..	5	..	..	..	..	−5	+5	..
Tribal	..	9	..	..	..	..	−9	+9	..
Seoni District	..	..	..	..	*5*	..	..	..	..
Nimar District ..	..	*45*	..	..	..	..	*−45*	*+45*	..
Hindu .	..	45	..	..	..	..	−45	+45	..

(Increase + Decrease −).			Males.					Females.				
1891 to 1901.	1881 to 1891.	Net variation 1881 to 1931 (Increase + Decrease −).	1931.	1921.	1911.	1901.	1881.	1931.	1921.	1911.	1901.	1881.
11	12	13	14	15	16	17	18	19	20	21	22	23
+29	*−1,095*	*−1,095*	..	..	*28*	*28*	*513*	..	..	*2*	*1*	*552*
..	..	..	..	..	28	..	..	..	..	2	..	..
..	*−1*[illegible]	*−46*	*1*	..	*3*	*1*	*23*	..	..	..	..	*24*
..	..	..	1	..	3	..	..	..	..	..	..	..
+115	*+29*	*+13*	*9*	..	*1*	*71*	..	*4*	..	..	*73*	..
.	.	..	9	..	1	..	..	4	..	..	..	..
+30	*−33*	*−26*	*7*	*2*	*17*	*24*	*35*	*2*	*4*	*7*	*8*	..
..	..	..	7	2	17	..	..	2	4	7	..	..
..	*−13*	*−3*	*6*	..	..	..	*5*	*4*	..	..	..	*8*
..	.	..	6	..	..	..	..	4	..	..	..	..
..	*−3*	*−3*	..	..	*5*	..	*2*	..	..	..	..	*1*
..	..	..	..	..	5	..	..	..	..	..	..	..
−8	*+7*	*−1*	..	.	.	..	*1*	..	..	..	..	..
−490	***+886***	***−83***	***2,611***	**1,608**	**1,781**	**2,777**	**2,589**	**2,614**	**1,594**	**1,898**	**2,927**	**2,719**
..	..		2,499	1,536	1,037	..	.	2,522	1,521	1,080	..	..
..	..	..	51		..	..	..	39		..	..	..
..	..	..	61	72	744	..	.	53	73	818	..	..
..	..	..	*86*	*96*	*447*	..	..	*64*	*92*	*463*	..	..
..	..	..	49	96	55	.	.	45	92	75	..	..
..	..	.	26	.	.	..	..	8	.	.	..	..
..	.	..	*11*	..	*392*	..	..	11	..	388	..	..
..	..	..	*557*	*375*	*91*	..	..	*525*	*392*	*90*	..	..
..	..	..	547	375	91	.	.	517	392	90	..	..
..	..	..	10	..	..	..	..	8	..	..	..	..
..	..	..	*647*	*555*	*783*	.	..	*638*	*532*	*864*	..	..
..	..	..	582	483	431	.	..	573	459	434	..	..
..	..	..	*15*	..	..	..	..	*23*	..	..	..	..
..	..	..	50	72	352	..	..	42	73	430	..	..
..	..	..	*1,321*	*582*	*460*	..	..	*1,387*	*578*	*481*	..	..
..	..	..	1,321	582	460	..	..	.387	578	481	..	.
..	..	..	**630**	**582**	**997**	..	..	**620**	**78**	**814**	..	..
..	..	..	155	555	984	..	..	192	58	804	..	..
..	..	..	475	*27*	13	..	..	428	20	10	..	..
..	..	..	...	*23*	..	..	..	..	*25*	..	..	..
..		..	..	23	.	..	..	..	25	..	..	..
..	..	..	..	..	*2*	..	..	..	..	..	..	..
..	..	..	..	..	2	..	..	..	..	..	..	..
..	..	..	..	*4*	..	..	..	..	*10*	..	..	..
..	..	..	..	1	..	..	..	..	4	..	..	..
..	..	..	..	3	..	..	..	..	6	..	..	..
..	..	..	..	..	..	..	..	..	..	..	..	..
..	..	..	..	*16*	.	..	..	..	*29*	..	..	..
..	..	..	..	16	..	..	..	..	29	..	..	..

Tribe and locality.	Persons.						Variation		
	1931	1921.	1911.	1901.	1891.	1881.	1921 to 1931.	1911 to 1921.	1901 to 1911.
1	2	3	4	5	6	7	8	9	10
BHUINHAR—*concld.*									
Chhindwara District ..	..	..	*6*	..	..	..	..	*−6*	..
Hindu ..	..	..	6	..	..	..	..	−6	..
Wardha District ..	*2*	*15*	..	..	..	..	*−13*	*+15*	..
Hindu ..	2	15	..	..	..	..	−13	+15	..
Chanda District ..	..	..	*122*	..	..	..	..	*−122*	..
Hindu ..	..	..	122	..	..	..	..	−122	..
Balaghat District ..	..	..	*6*	..	..	..	..	*−6*	..
Hindu ..	..	..	6	..	..	..	..	−6	..
Raipur District ..	*27*	..	*3*	..	..	..	*+27*	*−3*	..
Hindu ..	27	..	3	..	..	..	+27	−3	..
Bilaspur District ..	*1,221*	*538*	*1,650*	..	*487*	..	*+683*	*−1,112*	..
Hindu ..	318	500	1,627	..	..	..	−182	−1,127	..
Tribal ..	903	38	23	..	..	..	+865	+15	..
Berar ..	..	..	**22**	..	..	..	..	**−22**	..
Hindu ..	..	..	22	..	..	..	..	−22	..
Amraoti District ..	..	..	*15*	..	..	..	..	*−15*	..
Hindu ..	..	..	15	..	..	..	..	−15	..
Yeotmal District ..	..	..	*7*	..	..	..	..	*−7*	..
Hindu ..	..	..	7	..	..	..	..	−7	..
BHUNJIA									
Central Provinces and Berar ..	**7,689**	**6,376**	**6,913**	**3,013**	**6,187**	..	**+1,313**	**−537**	**+3,900**
Hindu ..	2,494	6,376	6,913	..	..	..	−3,882	−537	..
Tribal ..	5,195	..	..	..	..	..	+5,195	..	..
Saugor District ..	*2*	..	..	..	..	..	*+2*	..	..
Hindu ..	2	..	..	..	..	..	+2	..	..
Jubbulpore District ..	*67*	..	..	..	..	..	*+67*	..	..
Hindu ..	67	..	..	..	..	..	+67	..	..
Seoni District ..	*6*	..	..	..	..	..	*+6*	..	..
Hindu ..	6	..	..	..	..	..	+6	..	..
Hoshangabad District ..	..	..	..	..	*1*	..	..	..	..
Nimar District ..	*40*	..	..	..	..	..	*+40*	..	..
Hindu ..	40	..	..	..	..	..	+40	..	..
Betul District ..	*12*	..	..	..	..	..	*+12*	..	..
Hindu ..	12	..	..	..	..	..	+12	..	..
Chhindwara District ..	*10*	..	..	..	..	..	*+10*	..	..
Hindu ..	10	..	..	..	..	..	+10	..	..
Wardha District ..	*25*	..	..	..	..	..	*+25*	..	..
Hindu ..	25	..	..	..	..	..	+25	..	..
Nagpur District ..	*136*	..	..	..	..	..	*+136*	..	..
Hindu ..	136	..	..	..	..	..	+136	..	..
Chanda District ..	*3*	..	..	..	..	..	*+3*	..	..
Hindu ..	3	..	..	..	..	..	+3	..	..

(Increase + Decrease −).			Males.					Females.				
1891 to 1901.	1881 to 1891.	Net variation 1881 to 1931. (Increase + Decrease −.)	1931.	1921.	1911.	1901.	1881.	1931.	1921.	1911.	1901.	1881.
11	12	13	14	15	16	17	18	19	20	21	22	23
..	..	..	..	..	*3*	..	..	..	..	*3*	..	..
..	..	..	..	..	3	..	..	..	..	3	..	..
..	..	..	*2*	*15*	..	..	..	..	..	..	..	..
..	..	..	2	15	..	..	..	..	..	..	..	..
..	..	..	..	..	*115*	..	..	..	..	*7*	..	..
..	..	..	..	..	115	..	..	..	..	7	..	..
..	..	..	..	..	*4*	..	..	..	..	*2*	..	..
..	..	..	..	..	4	..	..	..	..	2	..	..
..	..	..	*11*	..	*2*	..	..	*16*	..	*1*	..	..
..	..	..	11	..	2	..	..	16	..	1	..	..
..	..	..	*617*	*524*	*861*	..	..	*604*	*14*	*789*	..	..
..	..	..	142	500	848	..	..	176	..	779	..	..
..	..	..	475	24	13	..	..	428	14	10	..	..
..	..	..	..	..	10	..	..	..	..	12	..	..
..	..	..	..	..	10	..	..	..	..	12	..	..
..	..	..	..	..	*6*	..	..	..	..	*9*	..	..
..	..	..	..	..	6	..	..	..	..	9	..	..
..	..	..	..	..	*4*	..	..	..	..	*3*	..	..
..	..	..	..	..	4	..	..	..	..	3	..	..
−3,174	..	..	**3,805**	**3,016**	**3,463**	**1,451**	..	**3,884**	**3,360**	**3,450**	**1,562**	..
..	..	..	1,219	3,016	3,463	..	..	1,275	3,360	3,450	..	..
..	..	..	2,586	..	..	..	..	2,609	..	..	..	..
..	..	..	*1*	..	..	..	..	*1*	..	..	..	..
..	..	..	1	..	..	..	..	1	..	..	..	..
..	..	..	*36*	..	..	..	..	*31*	..	..	..	..
..	..	..	36	..	..	..	..	31	..	..	..	..
..	..	..	*3*	..	..	..	..	*3*	..	..	..	..
..	..	..	3	..	..	..	..	3	..	..	..	..
−1	*+1*	..	..	..	..	..	..	..	..	..	..	..
..	..	..	*23*	..	..	..	..	*17*	..	..	..	..
..	..	..	23	..	..	..	..	17	..	..	..	..
..	..	..	*6*	..	..	..	..	*6*	..	..	..	..
..	..	..	6	..	..	..	..	6	..	..	..	..
..	..	..	..	..	..	..	..	*10*	..	..	..	..
..	..	..	..	..	..	..	..	10	..	..	..	..
..	..	..	*14*	..	..	..	..	*11*	..	..	..	..
..	..	..	14	..	..	..	..	11	..	..	..	..
..	..	..	*71*	..	..	..	..	*65*	..	..	..	..
..	..	..	71	..	..	..	..	65	..	..	..	..
..	..	..	*2*	..	..	..	..	*1*	..	..	..	..
..	..	..	2	..	..	..	..	1	..	..	..	..

TABLE XVIII—PART A

Variation of Population

Tribe and locality.	Persons.						Variation (Increase +		
	1931.	1921.	1911.	1901.	1891.	1881.	1921 to 1931.	1911 to 1921.	1901 to 1911.
1	2	3	4	5	6	7	8	9	10
BHUNJIA—*concld.*									
Raipur District ..	*7,258*	*6,376*	*6,913*	*3,013*	*6,186*	..	*+882*	*−537*	*+3,900*
Hindu ..	2,063	6,376	6,913	..	..	..	−4,313	−537	..
Tribal ..	5,195	..	..	..	..	..	+5,195	..	..
Bilaspur District ..	*99*	..	..	..	..	..	*+99*	..	..
Hindu ..	99	..	..	..	..	..	+99	..	..
Drug District ..	*8*	..	..	..	..	..	*+8*	..	..
Hindu ..	8	..	..	..	..	..	+8	..	..
Berar ..	**23**	..	..	..	..	..	**+23**	..	..
Hindu ..	23	..	..	..	..	..	+23	..	..
Amraoti District ..	*1*	..	..	..	..	..	*+1*	..	..
Hindu ..	1	..	..	..	..	..	+1	..	..
Akola District ..	*3*	..	..	..	..	..	*+3*	..	..
Hindu ..	3	..	..	..	..	..	+3	..	..
Buldana District ..	*3*	..	..	..	..	..	*+3*	..	..
Hindu ..	3	..	..	..	..	..	+3	..	..
Yeotmal District ..	*16*	..	..	..	..	..	*+16*	..	..
Hindu ..	16	..	..	..	..	..	+16	..	..
BINJHWAR									
Central Provinces and Berar ..	**54,603**	**28,284**	**47,582**	**12,625**	**26,948**	..	**+26,319**	**−19,298**	**+34,957**
Hindu ..	48,928	27,360	42,897	..	..	..	+21,568	−15,537	..
Tribal ..	5,675	924	4,685	..	..	..	+4,751	−3,761	..
Saugor District ..	*2*	..	..	..	..	..	*+2*	..	..
Hindu ..	2	..	..	..	..	..	+2	..	..
Jubbulpore District	..	..	..	..	*196*	..	..	..	..
Mandla District ..	..	..	*19*	*8*	*3,280*	..	..	*−19*	*+11*
Hindu ..	..	..	19	..	..	..	..	−19	..
Seoni District ..	*165*	*229*	*246*	*168*	*659*	..	*−64*	*−17*	*+78*
Hindu ..	165	229	246	..	..	..	−64	−17	..
Narsinghpur District	..	..	..	*23*	..	..	..	..	*−23*
Hoshangabad District	..	*21*	..	..	..	..	*−21*	*+21*	..
Hindu ..	..	21	..	..	..	..	−21	+21	..
Betul District ..	..	..	*3*	..	..	..	..	*−3*	*+3*
Hindu ..	..	..	3	..	..	..	..	−3	+3
Chhindwara District	..	*3*	..	..	..	..	*−3*	*+3*	..
Hindu ..	..	3	..	..	..	..	−3	+3	..
Wardha District ..	..	..	*5*	..	..	..	..	*−5*	*+5*
Hindu ..	..	..	5	..	..	..	..	−5	+5
Nagpur District ..	*89*	*101*	*125*	..	..	..	*−12*	*−24*	*+125*
Hindu ..	89	101	125	..	..	..	−12	−24	+125
Chanda District ..	*273*	*248*	*386*	..	..	..	*+25*	*−138*	*+386*
Hindu ..	273	248	386	..	..	..	+25	−138	+386

Decrease —).			Males.					Females.				
1891 to 1901.	1881 to 1891.	Net variation 1881 to 1931. (Increase + Decrease —).	1931.	1921.	1911.	1901	1881.	1931.	1921.	1911	1901.	1881.
11	12	13	14	15	16	17	18	19	20	21	22	23
—3,173	..	..	*3,586*	*3,016*	*3,463*	*1,451*	..	*3,672*	*3,360*	*3,450*	*1,62*	..
..	..	..	1,000	3,016	3,463	..	..	1,063	3,360	3.450	..	..
..	..	..	2,586	..	..	..	..	2,609	..	.	..	..
..	..	..	*53*	..	..	..	..	*46*	..	..	..	..
..	..	..	53	..	..	..	..	46	..	..	..	..
..	..	..	*5*	..	..	..	..	*3*	..	..	..	..
..	..	..	5	...	..	..	..	3	..	..	..	..
..	..	..	*5*	..	..	..	..	*18*	..	..	..	..
..	..	..	5	..	.		..	18	..	..	..	..
..	..	..	*1*	..	..	..	..	..	..	..	..	..
..	..	..	1	..			..	..	..	..	..	..
..	..	..	*3*	..	..	..	..	..	..	..	..	..
..	..	..	3	..	..	..	..	..	..	..	..	..
..	..	..	..	..	..	..	..	*3*	..	..	..	..
..	..	..	..	..	..	..	..	3	..	..	..	..
..	..	..	*1*	..	..	..	..	*15*	..	..	..	..
..	..	..	1	.	..	..	..	15	..	..	..	..
—14,323	..	..	**26,961**	**13,990**	**23,446**	**6,145**	..	**27,642**	**14,294**	**24,136**	**6,480**	..
..	..	..	24,179	13,531	21,129	..	..	24,749	13,829	21,768	..	..
..	..	..	2,782	59	2,317		..	2,893	465	2,368	..	..
..	..	..	*2*	..	..	.	..	..	..	..	..	..
..	..	..	2	..	..	..	..	..	..	..	..	..
—196	..	..	..	..	..	..	..	..	..	..	..	..
—3,272	..	..	..	..	*10*	*5*	..	..	..	*9*	*3*	..
..	..	..	..	..	10	..	..	..	..	9	..	..
—491	..	..	*72*	*106*	*109*	*72*	..	*93*	*123*	*137*	*96*	..
..	..	..	72	106	109	..	.	93	123	137	.	.
+23	..	..	..	..	..	*10*	..	..	..	..	*13*	.
..	..	..	..	*12*	..	..	..	..	*9*	..	..	..
..	..	..	..	12	..	..	..	..	9	..	..	..
	..	..	..	..	*3*	..	..	..	..	..	..	..
..	..	..	..	..	3	..	..	..	..	..	..	..
..	..	..	..	*3*	..	..	..	..	..	..	..	..
..	..	..	..	3	..	..	..	..	..	..	..	..
..	..	..	..	..	*3*	..	.	..	..	2	..	..
..	..	..	..	..	3	..	..	..	..	*2*	..	..
..	..	..	*42*	*40*	*59*	..	..	*47*	*61*	*66*	..	..
..	..	..	42	40	59	..	..	47	61	66	..	..
..	..	..	*116*	*111*	*199*	..	..	*157*	*137*	*187*	..	..
..	..	..	116	111	199	..	.	157	137	187	..	..

TABLE XVIII—PART A

Tribe and locality.	Persons.						Variation (Increase+		
	1931.	1921.	1911.	1901.	1891.	1881.	1921 to 1931.	1911 to 1921.	1901 to 1911.
1	2	3	4	5	6	7	8	9	10
BINJHWAR—*concld.*									
Bhandara District ..	*3,737*	*3,977*	*5,413*	..	..	..	*−240*	*−1,436*	*+5,413*
Hindu	3,737	3,977	5,413	..	..	..	−240	−1,436	+5,413
Balaghat District ..	*8,259*	*6,271*	*6,005*	*2,593*	*3,449*	..	*+1,988*	*+266*	*+3,412*
Hindu	8,237	6,271	6,004	..	..	..	+1,966	+267	..
Tribal	22	..	1	..	..	..	+22	−1	..
Raipur District	*29,223*	*5,378*	*24,358*	*7,508*	*9,822*	..	*+23,845*	*−18,980*	*+16,850*
Hindu	23,839	5,378	19,714	..	..	..	+18,461	−14,336	..
Tribal	5,384	..	4,644	..	..	..	+5,384	−4,644	..
Bilaspur	*12,586*	*11,792*	*10,792*	*2,325*	*10,542*	..	*+794*	*+1,000*	*+8,467*
Hindu	12,317	10,868	10,752	..	..	..	+1,449	+116	..
Tribal	269	924	40	..	..	..	−655	+884	..
Drug District	..	..	*1*	..	..	..	..	*−1*	*+1*
Hindu	..	..	1	..	..	..	..	−1	+1
Berar	**269**	**264**	**229**	..	..	..	**+5**	**+35**	**+229**
Hindu	269	264	229	..	..	..	+5	+35	..
Amraoti District	*25*	*109*	*130*		..	..	*−84*	*−21*	..
Hindu	25	109	130	..	..	..	−84	−21	..
Akola District	*211*	*87*	*99*	..	..	..	*+124*	*−12*	..
Hindu	211	87	99	..	..	..	+124	−12	..
Yeotmal District	*33*	*68*	..	..	..	..	*−35*	*+68*	..
Hindu	33	68	..	..	..	..	−35	+68	..
DHANWAR									
Central Provinces and Berar ..	**18,929**	**12,046**	**11,188**	**8,397**	**9,280**	..	**+6,883**	**+858**	**+2,791**
Hindu	15,353	9,358	10,092	..	..	..	+5,995	−734	..
Tribal	3,576	2,688	1,096	..	..	..	+888	+1,592	..
Saugor District	..	*7*	..	..	..	..	*−7*	*+7*	..
Hindu	..	7	..	..	..	..	−7	+7	..
Jubbulpore District ..	*1*	*420*	..	..	..	..	*−419*	*+420*	..
Hindu	1	420	..	..	..	..	−419	+420	..
Mandla District	..	..	*7*	..	..	..	..	*−7*	*+7*
Hindu	..	..	6	..	..	..	..	−6	+6
Tribal	..	..	1	..	..	..	..	−1	+1
Hoshangabad District ..	..	..	*7*	..	..	..	..	*−7*	*+7*
Hindu	..	..	7	..	..	..	..	−7	+7
Nimar District	..	..	*1*	..	..	..	..	*−1*	*+1*
Hindu	..	..	1	..	..	..	..	−1	+1
Nagpur District	..	..	..	*3*	..	..	..	..	*−3*
Raipur District	*938*	*801*	*751*	*509*	*109*	..	*+137*	*+50*	*+242*
Hindu	904	801	751	..	..	..	+103	+50	..
Tribal	34	..	..	..	..	..	+34	..	..
Bilaspur District	*12,771*	*10,639*	*10,416*	*7,885*	*9,171*	..	*+2,132*	*+223*	*+2,531*
Hindu	9,229	7,951	9,321	..	..	..	+1,278	−1,370	..
Tribal	3,542	2.688	1,095	..	..	..	+854	+1,593	..
Drug District	*20*	*179*	*6*	..	..	..	*−159*	*+173*	*+6*
Hindu	20	179	6	..	..	..	−159	+173	..

[illegible] Decrease —).		Net variation 1881 to 1931 (Increase + Decrease —).	Males.					Females.				
1891 to 1901.	1881 to 1891.		1931.	1921.	1911.	1901.	1881.	1931.	1921.	1911.	1901.	1881.
11	12	13	14	15	16	17	18	19	20	21	22	23
..	..	..	1,842	2,028	2,641	..	..	1,895	1,949	2,772	..	..
..	..	..	1,842	2,028	2,641	..	..	1,895	1,949	2,772	..	..
−856	..	..	4,027	2,863	2,840	1,190	..	4,232	3,408	3,165	1,403	..
..	..	..	4,005	2,863	2,840	..	..	4,232	3,408	3,164	..	..
..	..	..	22	..	..	..	..	..	..	1	..	..
−1,314	..	..	14,330	2,497	12,082	3,707	..	14,893	2,881	12,276	3,801	..
..	..	..	11,692	2,497	9,790	..	..	12,147	2,831	9,924	..	..
..	..	..	2,638	..	2,292	..	..	2,746	..	2,352	..	..
−8,217	..	..	6,390	6,203	5,390	1,161	..	[illegible]	5,589	5,402	1,164	..
..	..	..	6,268	5,744	5,365	..	..	6,049	5,124	5,387	..	..
..	..	..	122	459	25	..	..	147	465	15	..	..
..	..	..	..	..	1	..	..	..	..	..	..	..
..	..	..	..	..	1	..	..	..	..	..	..	..
..	..	..	140	127	109	..	..	129	137	120	..	..
..	..	..	140	127	109	..	..	129	137	120	..	..
..	..	..	18	52	66	..	..	7	57	64	..	..
..	..	..	18	52	66	..	..	7	57	64	..	..
..	..	..	107	42	43	..	..	104	45	56	..	..
..	..	..	107	42	43	..	..	104	45	56	..	..
..	..	..	15	33	..	..	..	18	35	..	..	..
..	..	..	15	33	..	..	..	[illegible]	35	..	..	..
−883	..	..	9,482	6,078	5,426	3,979	..	9,447	5,968	5,762	4,418	..
..	..	..	7,681	4,667	4,924	..	..	7,672	4,691	5,168	..	..
..	..	..	1,801	1,411	502	..	..	1,775	1,277	594	..	..
..	..	..	..	3	..	..	..	..	4	..	..	..
..	..	..	..	3	..	..	..	..	4	..	..	..
..	..	..	1	176	..	..	..	..	244	..	..	..
..	..	..	1	176	..	..	..	..	244	..	..	..
..	..	..	..	..	4	..	..	..	..	3	..	..
..	..	..	..	..	3	..	..	..	..	3	..	..
..	..	..	..	..	1	..	..	..	..	..	..	..
..	..	..	..	..	7	..	..	..	..	..	..	..
..	..	..	..	..	7	..	..	..	..	..	..	..
..	..	..	..	..	1	..	..	..	..	..	..	..
..	..	..	..	..	1	..	..	..	..	..	..	..
+3	..	..	..	..	..	..	..	..	..	..	3	..
+400	..	..	483	388	362	248	..	455	413	389	261	..
..	..	..	462	388	362	..	..	442	413	389	..	..
..	..	..	21	..	..	..	..	13	..	..	..	..
−1,286	..	..	6,368	5,430	5,047	3,731	..	6,403	5,209	5,369	4,154	..
..	..	..	4,588	4,019	4,546	..	..	4,641	3,932	4,775	..	..
..	..	..	1,780	1,411	501	..	..	1,762	1,277	594	..	..
..	..	..	10	81	5	..	..	10	98	1	..	..
..	..	..	10	81	5	..	..	10	98	1	..	..

TABLE XVIII—PART A

Variation of Population

Tribe and locality.	Persons. 1931.	1921.	1911.	1901.	1891.	1881.	Variation (Increase + 1921 to 1931.	1911 to 1921.	1901 to 1911.
1	2	3	4	5	6	7	8	9	10
DHANWAR—*concld.*									
Berar	**5,199**	..	..	..	..	..	**+5,199**	..	..
Hindu	5,199	..	..	..	..	..	+5,199	..	..
Buldana District ..	5,199	..	..	..	..	..	+5,199	..	..
Hindu	5,199	..	..	..	..	..	+5,199	..	..
GADBA									
Central Provinces and Berar ..	..	..	..	..	..	..	..	..	..
GOND									
Central Provinces and Berar ..	**1,891,835**	(a) **1,714,898**	**1,755,141**	**1,523,170**	**1,666,764**	**1,542,921**	**+176,937**	**−40,243**	**+231,971**
Hindu	829,265	364,843	322,137	..	..	..	+464,422	+42,706	..
Tribal	1,062,553	1,350,055	1,433,004	..	..	..	−287,502	−82,949	..
Muslim	4	..	..	..	..	..	+4	..	..
Christian	13	..	..	..	..	..	+13	..	..
Saugor District	*30,749*	*29,041*	*30,048*	*21,546*	*30,065*	*29,395*	*+1,708*	*−1,067*	*+8,502*
Hindu	11,384	18,442	6,476	..	..	..	−7,058	+11,966	..
Tribal	19,365	10,599	23,572	..	..	..	+8,766	−12,973	..
Damoh District	*27,364*	*22,061*	*31,507*	*27,521*	*30,709*	*33,157*	*+5,303*	*−9,446*	*+3,986*
Hindu	6,802	16,526	21,756	..	..	..	−9,724	−5,230	..
Tribal	20,562	5,535	9,751	..	..	..	+15,027	−4,216	..
Jubbulpore District ..	*94,083*	*91,254*	*89,086*	*78,689*	*94,048*	*83,459*	*+2,829*	*+2,168*	*+10,397*
Hindu	81,359	41,615	25,685	..	..	..	+39,744	+15,930	..
Tribal	12,723	49,639	63,401	..	..	..	−36,916	−13,762	..
Christian	1	..	..	..	..	..	+1	..	..
Mandla District	*219,136*	*185,784*	*191,466*	*159,949*	*174,977*	*162,360*	*+33,352*	*−5,682*	*+31,517*
Hindu	59,736	2,569	603	..	..	..	+57,167	+1,966	..
Tribal	159,400	183,215	190,863	..	..	..	−23,815	−7,648	..
Seoni District	*135,931*	*120,698*	*139,921*	*130,392*	*143,320*	*134,289*	*+15,233*	*−19,223*	*+9,529*
Hindu	253	1,008	725	..	..	..	−755	+283	..
Tribal	135,678	119,690	139,196	..	..	..	+15,988	−19,506	..
Narsinghpur District ..	*42,245*	*42,238*	*37,075*	*34,797*	*41,683*	*44,020*	*+7*	*+5,163*	*+2,278*
Hindu	2,166	9,965	8,439	..	..	..	−7,799	+1,526	..
Tribal	40,078	32,273	28,636	..	..	..	+7,805	+3,637	..
Christian	1	..	..	..	..	..	+1	..	..
Hoshangabad District ..	*48,621*	*45,439*	*46,796*	*48,788*	*61,069*	*59,020*	*+3,182*	*−1,357*	*−1,992*
Hindu	15,537	11,731	8,499	..	..	..	+3,806	+3,232	..
Tribal	33,083	33,708	38,297	..	..	..	−625	−4,589	..
Muslim	1	..	..	..	..	..	+1	..	..
Nimar District	*10,411*	*7,846*	*8,221*	*4,310*	*1,589*	*748*	*+2,565*	*−375*	*+3,911*
Hindu	2,903	6,798	3,761	..	..	..	−3,895	+3,037	..
Tribal	7,504	1,048	4,460	..	..	..	+6,456	−3,412	..
Muslim	3	..	..	..	..	..	+3	..	..
Christian	1	..	..	..	..	..	+1	..	..
Betul District	*111,602*	*99,742*	*105,151*	*82,513*	*92,201*	*87,128*	*+11,860*	*−5,409*	*+22,638*
Hindu	22,320	4,891	1,876	..	..	..	+17,429	+3,015	..
Tribal	89,282	94,851	103,275	..	..	..	−5,569	−8,424	..
Chhindwara District ..	*176,808*	*149,114*	*159,979*	*137,111*	*139,305*	*126,762*	*+27,694*	*−10,865*	*+22,868*
Hindu	1,871	16,853	1,225	..	..	..	−14,982	+15,628	..
Tribal	174,933	132,261	158,754	..	..	..	+42,672	−26,493	..
Christian	4	..	..	..	..	..	+4	..	..
Wardha District	*43,195*	*37,074*	*40,694*	*40,339*	*37,677*	*41,244*	*+6,121*	*−3,620*	*+355*
Hindu	11,985	..	789	..	..	..	+11,985	−789	..
Tribal	31,210	37,074	39,905	..	..	..	−5,864	−2,831	..

(a) From 1901—1921 the figures of Marias, Murias, Bhattras and Parjas were included with Gonds.

of Selected Tribes.

TABLE XVIII—PART A

Decrease —).			Males.					Females.				
1891 to 1901.	1881 to 1891.	Net variation 1881 to 1931 (Increase + Decrease —).	1931.	1921.	1911.	1901.	1881.	1931.	1921.	1911.	1901.	1881
11	12	13	14	15	16	17	18	19	20	21	22	23
..	..	..	**2,620**	..	..	..	..	**2,579**	..	..	..	..
..	..	..	2,620	..	..	..	..	2,579	..	..	..	..
..	..	..	2,620	..	..	..	..	2,579	..	..	..	..
..	..	..	2,620	..	..	..	..	2,579	..	..	..	..
..	..	..	..	..	..	..	..	..	..	..	..	..
−143,594	**+123,843**	**+348,914**	**921,488**	**827,599**	**850,876**	**733,194**	**766,550**	**970,347**	**887,299**	**904,265**	**789,976**	**776,371**
..	..	..	403,203	171,698	156,259	..	..	426,062	193,145	165,878	..	..
..	..	..	518,273	655,901	694,617	..	..	544,280	694,154	738,387	..	..
..	..	..	3	..	..	..	..	1	..	..	..	..
..	..	..	9	..	..	..	..	4	..	..	..	..
−8,519	*+670*	*+1,354*	*15,220*	*14,351*	*14,745*	*10,376*	*14,963*	*15,529*	*14,690*	*15,303*	*11,170*	*14,432*
..	..	..	5,662	9,067	3,253	..	..	5,722	9,375	3,223	..	..
..	..	..	9,558	5,284	11,492	..	..	9,807	5,315	12,080	..	..
−3,188	*—2,448*	*—5,793*	*13,574*	*11,126*	*15,519*	*13,447*	*16,666*	*13,790*	*10,935*	*15,988*	*14,074*	*16,491*
..	..	..	3,394	8,358	10,729	..	..	3,408	8,168	11,027	..	..
..	..	..	10,180	2,768	4,790	..	..	10,382	2.767	4,961	..	..
−15,359	*+10,589*	*+10,624*	*45,952*	*44,766*	*43,594*	*37,870*	*41,603*	*48,131*	*46,488*	*45,492*	*40,819*	*41,856*
..	..	..	39,805	20,438	12,665	..	..	41,554	21,177	13,020	..	..
..	..	..	6,146	24,328	30,929	..	..	6,577	25,311	32,472	..	..
..	..	..	1	..	..	..	..	..	..	..	..	..
·15,028	*+12,617*	*+56,776*	*107,351*	*91,335*	*93,489*	*77,822*	*81,893*	*111,785*	*94,449*	*97,977*	*82,127*	*80,467*
..	..	..	29,171	1,359	323	..	..	30,565	1,210	280	..	..
..	..	..	78,180	89,976	93,166	..	..	81,220	93,239	97,697	..	..
−12,928	*+9,031*	*+1,642*	*65,183*	*56,913*	*67,241*	*62,498*	*66,891*	*70,748*	*63,785*	*72,680*	*67,894*	*67,398*
..	..	..	119	528	339	..	..	134	480	386	..	..
..	..	..	65,064	56,385	66,902	..	..	70,614	63,305	72,294	..	..
−6,886	*−2,337*	*−1,775*	*20,400*	*20,547*	*17,722*	*16,573*	*21,853*	*21,845*	*21,691*	*19,353*	*18,224*	*22,167*
..	..	..	1,051	4,820	4,132	..	..	1,115	5,145	4,307	..	..
..	..	..	19,348	15,727	13,590	..	..	20,730	16,546	15,046	..	..
..	..	..	1	..	..	..	..	..	..	..	..	..
−12,281	*+2,049*	*—10,399*	*23,960*	*21,909*	*22,517*	*23,086*	*29,259*	*24,661*	*23,530*	*24,279*	*25,702*	*29,761*
..	..	..	7,643	5,483	4,090	..	..	7,894	6,248	4,409	..	..
..	..	..	16,317	16,426	18,427	..	..	16,766	17,282	19,870	..	..
..	..	..	..	..	..	..	..	1	..	..	..	..
+2,721	*+841*	*+9,663*	*5,311*	*4,073*	*4,205*	*2,343*	*414*	*5,100*	*3,773*	*4,016*	*1,967*	*334*
..	..	..	1,504	3,521	1,978	..	..	1,399	3,277	1,783	..	..
..	..	..	3,804	552	2,227	..	..	3,700	496	2,233	..	..
..	..	..	3	..	..	..	..	..	..	..	..	..
..	..	..	..	..	..	..	..	1	..	..	..	..
−9,688	*+5,073*	*+24,474*	*54,502*	*48,987*	*51,188*	*40,021*	*43,673*	*57,100*	*50,755*	*53,963*	*42,492*	*43,455*
..	..	..	10,900	2,440	1,017	..	..	11,420	2,451	859	..	..
..	..	..	43,602	46,547	50,171	..	..	45,680	48,304	53,104	..	..
−2,194	*+12,543*	*+50,046*	*85,645*	*72,600*	*77,338*	*66,602*	*62,748*	*91,163*	*76,514*	*82,641*	*70,509*	*64,014*
..	..	..	968	8,768	625	..	..	903	8,085	600	..	..
..	..	..	84,674	63,832	76,713	..	..	90,259	68,429	82,041	..	..
..	..	..	3	..	..	..	..	1	..	..	..	..
+2,662	*—3,567*	*+1,951*	*21,193*	*18,479*	*20,095*	*19,779*	*20,415*	*22,002*	*18,595*	*20,599*	*20,560*	*20,829*
..	..	..	5,935	..	421	..	..	6,050	..	368	..	..
..	..	..	15,258	18,479	19,674	..	..	15,952	18,595	20,231	..	..

Tribe and locality.	Persons. 1931.	1921.	1911.	1901.	1891.	1881.	Variation (Increase + 1921 to 1931.	1911 to 1921.	1901 to 1911.
1	2	3	4	5	6	7	8	9	10
GOND—*concld.*									
Nagpur District	*53,002*	*46,241*	*48,991*	*45,660*	*42,026*	*41,825*	*+6,761*	*+2,750*	*−3,331*
Hindu	43,347	11	16,172	..	..	..	+43,336	−16,161	..
Tribal	9,655	46,230	32,819	..	..	..	−36,575	+13,411	..
Chanda District	*95,358*	*110,977*	*115,732*	*135,034*	*118,256*	*106,508*	*−15,619*	*−4,755*	*−19,302*
Hindu ..	25,302	8	12,511	..	..	..	+25,294	−12,503	..
Tribal ..	70,056	110,969	103,221	..	..	..	−40,913	+7,748	..
Bhandara District ..	*78,289*	*73,547*	*75,871*	*70,147*	*88,768*	*83,129*	*+4,742*	*−2,324*	*+5,724*
Hindu	41,681	..	7,911	..	..	..	+41,681	−7,911	..
Tribal	36,608	73,547	67,960	..	..	..	−36,939	+5,587	..
Balaghat District ..	*102,019*	*88,832*	*79,158*	*73,400*	*87,758*	*82,925*	*+13,187*	*+9,674*	*+5,758*
Hindu	44,115	26,092	5,748	..	..	..	+18,023	+20,344	..
Tribal	57,904	62,740	73 410	..	..	..	−4,836	−10,670	..
Raipur District	*239,276*	*221,577*	*211,392*	*215,639*	*249,571*	*229,447*	*+17,699*	*+10,185*	*−4,247*
Hindu	165,426	85,396	52,015	..	..	..	+80,030	+33,381	..
Tribal	73,849	136,181	159,377	..	..	..	−62,332	−23,196	..
Christian	1	..	..	..	..	..	+1	..	..
Bilaspur District	*172,361*	*152,169*	*139,267*	*143,055*	*152,815*	*132,688*	*+20,192*	*+12,902*	*−3,788*
Hindu	123,950	92,198	93,249	..	..	..	+31,752	−1,051	..
Tribal	48,410	59,971	46,018	..	..	..	−11,561	+13,953	..
Christian	1	..	..	..	..	..	+1	..	..
Drug District	*115,632*	*104,679*	*115,445*	..	..	..	*+10,953*	*−10,766*	*+115,445*
Hindu	104,523	30,740	24,199	..	..	..	+73,783	+6,541	..
Tribal	11,106	73,939	91,246	..	..	..	−62,833	−17,307	..
Christian	3	..	..	..	..	..	+3	..	..
Berar	**95,753**	**86,585**	**89,341**	**74,280**	**80,927**	**64,817**	**+9,168**	**−2,756**	**+15,061**
Hindu	64,605	..	30,498	..	..	..	+64,605	−30,498	..
Tribal	31,147	86,585	58,843	..	..	..	−55,438	+27,742	..
Christian	1	..	..	..	..	..	+1	..	..
Amraoti District	*23,554*	*21,017*	*24,079*	..	..	..	*+2,537*	*−3,062*	..
Hindu	16,115	..	9,337	..	..	..	+16,115	−9,337	..
Tribal	7,438	21,017	14,742	..	..	..	−13,579	+6,275	..
Christian	1	..	..	..	..	..	+1	..	..
Akola District	*3,806*	*3,260*	*4,187*	..	..	..	*+546*	*−927*	..
Hindu	3,575	..	3,323	..	..	..	+3,575	−3,323	..
Tribal	231	3,260	864	..	..	..	−3,029	+2,396	..
Buldana District	*380*	*911*	*497*	..	..	..	*−531*	*+514*	..
Hindu	261	..	404	..	..	..	+261	−404	..
Tribal	119	911	93	..	..	..	−792	+818	..
Yeotmal District	*68,013*	*61,397*	*60,578*	..	..	..	*+6,616*	*+819*	..
Hindu	44,654	..	17,434	..	..	..	+44,654	−17,434	..
Tribal	23,359	61,397	43,144	..	..	..	−38,038	+18,253	..
HALBA									
Central Provinces and Berar ..	**92,275**	**83,941**	**73,420**	**63,795**	**75,277**	**47,240**	**+8,334**	**+10,521**	**+9,625**
Hindu	92,240	83,941	73,420	..	..	..	+8,299	+10,521	..
Tribal	28	..	..	..	..	..	+28	..	..
Christian	7	..	..	..	..	..	+7	..	..
Saugor District	..	*2*	*57*	..	..	*2*	*−2*	*−55*	*+57*
Hindu	..	2	57	..	..	..	−2	−55	..
Jubbulpore District ..	*34*	*57*	*4*	..	..	..	*−23*	*+53*	*+4*
Hindu	34	57	4	..	..	..	−23	+53	..

Decrease —).		Net variation 1881 to 1931 (Increase + Decrease —).	Males.					Females.				
1891 to 1901	1881 to 1891		1931.	1921.	1911.	1901.	1881.	1931.	1921.	1911.	1901.	1881.
11	12	13	14	15	16	17	18	19	20	21	22	23
+3,634	+201	+11,177	26,471	22,899	24,383	22,602	20,868	26,531	23,342	24,608	23,058	20,967
..	..	..	21,546	9	8,062	..	..	21,801	2	8,110	..	..
..	..	..	4,925	22,890	16,321	..	..	4,730	23,340	16,498	..	..
+16,778	+11,748	—11,150	47,221	54,650	56,811	66,072	53,189	48,137	56,327	58,921	68,962	53,319
..	..		12,569	3	6,086	..	.	12,733	5	6,425	..	..
..	..	..	34,652	54,647	50,725	..	..	35,404	56,322	52,496	..	..
—18,621	+5,639	—4,840	38,284	35,304	36,217	32,326	40,573	40,005	38,243	39,654	37,821	42,556
..	..	..	20,565	.	3,746	..	..	21,116	..	4,165	..	..
..	..	..	17,719	35,304	32,471	..	..	18,889	38,243	35,489	..	..
—14,358	+4,833	+19,094	50,097	44,009	38,361	35,132	41,027	51,922	44,823	40,797	38,268	41,898
..	..	..	21,827	13,512	2,817	..	..	22,288	12,580	2,931	..	..
..	..	..	28,270	30,497	35,544	..	..	29,634	32,243	37,866	..	..
—33,932	+20,124	+9,829	115,559	101,691	101,000	102,112	112,986	123,717	119,886	110,392	113,527	116,461
..	..	..	80,281	36,683	24,711	..	..	85,145	48,713	27,304	..	..
..	..	..	35,278	65,008	76,289	..	..	38,571	71,173	83,088	..	..
..	..	..	..	..	..	..	..	1	..	..	..	..
—9,760	+20,127	+39,673	83,663	71,916	67,183	68,018	64,751	88,698	80,253	72,084	75,037	67,937
..	..	..	59,407	42,765	44,842	..	..	64,543	49,433	48,407	..	..
..	..	..	24,255	29,151	22,341	..	..	24,155	30,820	23,677	..	..
..	..	..	1	..	..	..	..	..	..	..	..	..
..	..	+115,632	54,662	49,249	55,062	..	..	60,970	55,430	60,383	..	..
..	..	..	49,037	13,944	11,342	..	..	55,486	16,796	12,857	..	..
..	..	..	5,623	35,305	43,720	..	..	5,483	38,634	47,526	..	..
..	..	.	2	..	..	..	..	1	..	..	..	..
—6,647	+16,110	+30,936	47,240	42,795	44,206	36,515	32,778	48,513	43,790	45,135	37,765	32,039
..	..	..	31,819	..	15,081	..	.	32,786	..	15,417	..	..
..	..	..	15,420	42,795	29,125	..	..	15,727	43,790	29,718	..	..
..	..	..	1	.	..	..	.	..	..	.	..	..
..	..	..	11,728	10,374	12,008	..	..	11,826	10,643	12,071	..	..
..	..	.	8,071	.	4,658	..	..	8,044	.	4,679	..	..
..	..	.	3,656	10,374	7,350	..	.	3,782	10,643	7,392	..	..
..	..	..	1	.		..	..	..	..	..	..	..
..	..	..	1,917	1,679	2,144	..	..	1,889	1,581	2,013	..	..
..	..	..	1,811	..	1,692	..	..	1,764	..	1,631	..	..
..	..	..	106	1,679	452	..	..	125	1,581	412	..	..
..	..	..	156	436	265	..	..	224	475	232	..	..
..	..	.	92	..	213	..	..	169	.	191	..	..
..	..	..	64	436	52	..	.	55	475	41	..	..
..	..	..	33,439	30,306	29,789	..	..	34,574	31,091	30,789	..	..
..	..	..	21,845	..	8,518	..	.	22,809	.	8,916	..	..
..	..	..	11,594	30,306	21,271	..	..	11,765	31,091	21,873	..	..
—11,482	+28.037	+45,035	44,800	40,328	35,545	30,329	23,427	47,475	43,613	37,875	33,466	23,813
..	..	..	44,775	40,328	35,545	..	..	47,465	43,613	37,875	..	..
..	..	..	18	..	..	..	..	10	..	..	..	..
..	..	..	7	..	..	..	..	..	.	.	..	..
..	—2	—2	..	2	26	..	2	..	..	31	..	..
..	..	..	..	2	26	..	..	..	.	31	..	..
..	..	+34	18	5	3	..	..	16	52	1	..	..
..	..	..	18	5	3	..	..	16	52	1	..	..

TABLE XVIII—PART A — Variation of Population

Tribe and locality.	Persons.						Variation (Increase +		
	1931.	1921.	1911.	1901.	1891.	1881.	1921 to 1931.	1911 to 1921.	1901 to 1911.
1	2	3	4	5	6	7	8	9	10
Halba—*concld.*									
Mandla District ..	..	2	7	..	..	..	−2	−5	..
Hindu ..	..	2	7	..	..	..	−2	−5	..
Seoni District ..	698	836	809	503	689	651	−138	+27	+306
Hindu ..	698	836	809	..	..	..	−138	+27	..
Hoshangabad District	..	113	..	..	..	..	−113	+113	..
Hindu ..	..	113	..	..	..	..	−113	+113	..
Nimar District ..	246	348	267	31	26	8	−102	+81	+236
Hindu ..	246	348	267	..	..	..	−102	+81	..
Betul District ..	..	..	1	..	..	..	..	−1	+1
Hindu ..	..	..	1	..	..	..	..	−1	..
Chhindwara District	9	..	1	..	13	..	+9	−1	+1
Hindu ..	9	..	1	..	..	..	+9	−1	..
Wardha District ..	1,227	1,038	734	593	129	45	+189	+304	+141
Hindu ..	1,227	1,038	734	..	..	..	+189	+304	..
Nagpur District ..	523	409	683	480	71	64	+114	−274	+203
Hindu ..	523	409	683	..	..	..	+114	−274	..
Chanda District ..	3,287	2,604	2,419	6,153	7,199	2,147	+683	+185	−3,734
Hindu ..	3,280	2,604	2,419	..	..	..	+676	+185	..
Tribal ..	7	..	..	..	..	..	+7	..	..
Bhandara District	19,233	18,240	9,837	17,068	18,425	12,105	+993	+8,403	−7,231
Hindu ..	19,233	18,240	9,837	..	..	..	+993	+8,403	..
Balaghat District	1,553	1,421	1,298	1,281	1,433	1,412	+132	+123	+17
Hindu ..	1,553	1,421	1,298	..	..	..	+132	+123	..
Raipur District ..	6,068	4,457	4,499	37,672	47,273	30,776	+1,611	−42	−33,173
Hindu ..	6,049	4,457	4,499	..	..	..	+1,592	−42	..
Tribal ..	19		.	..	..	..	+19	..	..
Bilaspur District ..	160	203	1	14	19	..	−43	+202	−13
Hindu ..	160	203	1	..	..	..	−43	+202	..
Drug District ..	55,347	50,827	49,199	..	..	..	+4,520	+1,628	+49,199
Hindu ..	55,338	50,827	49,199	..	..	..	+4,511	+1,628	..
Tribal ..	2	..	..	..	..	..	+2	..	..
Christian ..	7	..	..	..	..	..	+7	..	..
Berar ..	3,890	3,384	3,604	..	..	..	+506	−220	..
Hindu ..	3,890	3,384	3,604	..	..	..	−506	−220	..
Amraoti District ..	2,321	2,000	2,201	..	..	..	+321	−201	..
Hindu ..	2,321	2,000	2,201	..	..	..	+321	−201	..
Akola District ..	482	468	403	..	..	..	+14	+65	..
Hindu ..	482	468	403	..	..	..	+14	+65	..
Buldana District ..	20	26	24	..	..	..	−6	+2	..
Hindu ..	20	26	24	..	..	..	−6	+2	..
Yeotmal District ..	1,067	890	976	..	..	..	−177	−86	..
Hindu ..	1,067	890	976	..	..	..	+177	−86	..

of Selected Tribes. **TABLE XVIII—PART A**

Decrease −).			Males.					Females.				
1891 to 1901.	1881 to 1891.	Net variation 1881 to 1931 (Increase + Decrease −).	1931	1921.	1911.	1901.	1881.	1931.	1921.	1911.	1901.	1881.
11	12	13	14	15	16	17	18	19	20	21	22	23
..	..	..	..	*2*	*3*	.	..	..	..	*4*	..	..
..	..	..	..	2	3	..	..	..	.	4	..	..
−186	*+38*	*+47*	*362*	*401*	*396*	*225*	*319*	*336*	*435*	*413*	*278*	*332*
..	.	..	362	401	396	..	..	336	435	413	..	..
..	..	..	..	*113*	..	..	..	..	..	..	..	..
..	..	..	..	113	.	..	..	...	..	..	..	..
+5	*+18*	*+238*	*120*	*167*	*127*	*13*	*3*	*126*	*181*	*140*	*18*	*5*
..	..	..	120	167	127	..	..	126	181	140	..	..
..	..	..	.	.	*1*	..	..	..	..	..	..	..
..	..	..	..	..	1	..	..	..	..	.	..	..
−13	*+13*	*+9*	*6*	..	*1*	..	..	*3*	..	..	..	..
..	..	..	6	.	1	..	..	3	..	..	..	..
+464	*+84*	*+1,182*	*653*	*507*	*388*	*306*	*24*	*574*	*531*	*346*	*287*	*21*
..	..	..	653	507	388	..	..	574	531	346	..	..
+409	*+7*	*+459*	*260*	*210*	*331*	*246*	*56*	*263*	*199*	*352*	*234*	*8*
..	..	..	260	210	331	.	..	263	199	352	..	..
−1,046	*+5,052*	*+1,140*	*1,739*	*1,200*	*1,222*	*3,131*	*1,085*	*1,548*	*1,404*	*1,197*	*3,022*	*1,062*
..	..	..	1,734	1,200	1,222	.	..	1,546	1,404	1,197	..	..
..	..	..	5	..	..	..	..	2	..	..	..	..
−1,357	*+6,320*	*+7,128*	*9,723*	*8,789*	*4,891*	*7,902*	*5,792*	*9,510*	*9,451*	*4,946*	*9,166*	*6,313*
..	..	..	9,723	8,789	4,891	...	..	9,510	9,451	4,946	..	..
−152	*−9*	*+111*	*741*	*592*	*618*	*610*	*683*	*812*	*829*	*680*	*671*	*759*
..	..	..	741	592	618	..	...	812	829	680	..	..
−9,601	*+16,497*	*−24,708*	*2,892*	*2,429*	*2,186*	*17,889*	*15,463*	*3,176*	*2,028*	*2,313*	*19,783*	*15,313*
..	..	..	2,880	2,429	2,186	..	..	3,169	2,028	2,313	..	..
..	..	..	12	.	..	..	..	7	..	.	..	..
−5	*+19*	*+160*	*75*	*95*	*1*	*7*	..	*85*	*108*	..	*7*	..
..	..	..	75	95	1	..	..	85	108	..	..	..
..	..	*+55,347*	*26,257*	*24,091*	*23,566*	..	..	*29,090*	*26,736*	*25,633*	..	..
..	..	..	26,249	24,091	23,566	..	..	29,089	26,736	25,633	..	..
..	..	..	1	..	..	..	..	1	..	..	..	..
..	..	..	7	..	..	..	..	.	..	..	..	..
..	..	..	**1,954**	**1,725**	**1,785**	..	..	**1,936**	**1,659**	**1,819**	..	..
..	.	..	1,954	1,725	1,785	..	..	1,936	1,659	1,819	..	..
..	..	...	*1,159*	*1,017*	*1,066*	..	..	*1,162*	*983*	*1,135*	..	..
..	..	..	1,159	1,017	1,066	..	..	1,162	983	1,135	..	..
..	..	..	*231*	*243*	*211*	..	..	*251*	*225*	*192*	..	..
..	..	..	231	243	211	..	..	251	225	192	..	..
..	..	..	*13*	*14*	*14*	.	..	*7*	*12*	*10*	..	..
..	..	..	13	14	14	..	.	7	12	10	..	..
..	..	..	*551*	*451*	*494*	..	..	*516*	*439*	*482*	..	..
..	..	..	551	451	494	..	..	516	439	482	..	..

Tribe and locality.	Persons.						Variation (Increase +		
	1931.	1921.	1911.	1901.	1891.	1881.	1921 to 1931.	1911 to 1921.	1901 to 1911.
1	2	3	4	5	6	7	8	9	10
KAMAR									
Chhattisgarh Division	**9,244**	..	**7,186**	**505**	**5,228**	..	..	..	**+6,681**
Hindu ..	*3,291*	..	..	..	.	..	..	..	..
Tribal ..	5,953	..	7,186	..	..	..	..	..	..
Raipur District ..	*9,244*	..	*7,185*	*505*	*5,205*	..	..	..	*+6,680*
Hindu ..	3,291	..	..	..	..	..	..	..	..
Tribal ..	5,953	.	7,185	..	..	..	..	..	..
Bilaspur District ..	..	..	*1*	..	*23*	..	..	..	*+1*
Tribal ..	..	..	1	..	..	..	..	..	..
KAWAR									
Central Provinces and Berar ..	**111,203**	**90,063**	**90,501**	**71,999**	**71,154**	**73,822**	**+21,140**	**−438**	**+18,502**
Hindu ..	110,636	90,022	90,454	..	..	..	+20,614	−432	..
Tribal ..	567	41	47	..	..	..	+526	−6	..
Saugor District ..	*1*	*2*	*2*	..	*2*	*5*	*−1*	..	*+2*
Hindu ..	1	2	2	..	..	..	−1	..	..
Jubbulpore District	*36*	.	*18*	..	..	*33*	*+36*	*−18*	*+18*
Hindu ..	36	..	18	..	..	..	+36	−18	..
Mandla District ..	..	..	*5*	*56*	*12*	*1*	..	*−5*	*−51*
Hindu ..	..	..	5	..	..	..	..	−5	..
Seoni District ..	*18*	*89*	*8*	..	*11*	*49*	*−71*	*+81*	*+8*
Hindu .	18	89	8	..	..	..	−71	+81	..
Narsinghpur District	..	*11*	..	..	..	*15,903*	*−11*	*+11*	..
Hindu ..	.	11	..	..	..	..	−11	+11	..
Hoshangabad District	*4*	..	..	..	*1*	*97*	*+4*	..	..
Hindu ..	4	..	..	..	..	..	+4	..	..
Nimar District ..	..	..	..	..	..	*1*	..	..	..
Betul District ..	*7*	..	..	*30*	*89*	*70*	*+7*	..	*−30*
Hindu ..	7	..	..	.	..	..	+7	..	..
Chhindwara District	*31*	*41*	..	..	..	*4*	*−10*	*+41*	..
Hindu ..	31	41	..	..	..	..	−10	+41	..
Wardha District ..	*1*	..	..	..	..	*5*	*+1*	..	..
Hindu ..	1	..	..	..	..	..	+1	..	..
Nagpur District ..	*4*	..	*22*	*15*	*27*	*42*	*+4*	*−22*	*+7*
Hindu ..	4	..	22	..	..	..	+4	−22	..
Chanda District ..	*1,835*	*1,494*	*1,447*	*3,558*	*3,860*	*2,238*	*+341*	*+47*	*−2,111*
Hindu ..	1,831	1,494	1,447	.	..	..	+337	+47	..
Tribal ..	4	..	.	..	.	.	+4	..	..
Bhandara District	*1,382*	*1,959*	*940*	*956*	*625*	*81*	*−577*	*+1,019*	*−16*
Hindu ..	1,382	1,959	940	..	..	..	−577	+1,019	..
Balaghat District	..	*2,071*	*1*	*43*	*30*	*36*	*−2,071*	*+2,070*	*−42*
Hindu ..	..	2,071	..	..	..	..	−2,071	+2,071	..
Tribal ..	..	..	1	..	..	..	..	−1	..

(Increase + Decrease —).			Males.					Females.				
1891 to 1901.	1881 to 1891.	Net variation 1881 to 1931 (Increase + Decrease —)	1931.	1921.	1911.	1901.	1881.	1931.	1921.	1911.	1901.	1881.
11	12	13	14	15	16	17	18	19	20	21	22	23
—4,723	..	..	4,564	..	3,432	245	..	4,680	..	3,754	260	..
..	..	..	1,624	..	..	..	.	1,667	..	..	..	..
..	..	..	2,940	.	3,432	.	.	3,013	..	3,754	..	..
—4,700	..	..	4,564	..	3,432	245	..	4,680	..	3,753	260	..
..	..	..	1,624	..	..	..	..	1,667	..	..	..	..
..	..	..	2,940	..	3,432	..	..	3,013	..	3,753	..	..
—23	.	..	..	..	..	..	..	..	..	1	..	..
..	..	..	..		..	..	..	..	..	1	..	..
+845	-2,668	+37,381	54,456	44,937	44,464	35,174	37,021	56,747	45,126	46,037	36,825	36,801
..	..	..	54,163	44,911	44,430	..	..	56,473	45,111	46,024	..	..
..	..	..	293	26	34	..	.	274	15	13	..	..
—2	—3	—4	1	2	2	..	1	..	..	..	..	4
..	..	..	1	2	2	..	..	..	..	..	.	..
..	—33	+3	25	..	10	..	15	11	..	8	..	18
..	..	..	25	..	10	..	..	11	..	8	..	..
+44	+11	—1	..	..	3	26	1	..	..	2	30	..
..	..	..	..	..	3	..	..	..	..	2	..	..
—11	—38	—31	18	45	2	..	27	..	44	6	..	22
..	..	..	18	45	2	..	..	..	44	6	..	..
..	-15,903	—15,903	..	5	..	..	8,172	..	6	..	..	[illegible],731
..	..	..	..	5	..	..	..	..	6	..	..	..
—1	—96	—95	4	..	..	..	58	..	..	..	..	39
..	..	..	4	..	..	..	.	..	..	..	..	..
..	—1	—1	..	..	..	..	1	..	..	..	..	..
—59	+15	—63	4	..	..	15	41	3	..	..	15	29
..	..	..	4	..	.	..	..	3	..	..	..	..
..	—4	+27	25	41	..	..	3	6	..	..	..	1
..	..	..	25	41	..	..	..	6	..	..	..	..
..	—5	—4	..	..	..	..	2	1	..	..	..	3
..	..	..	..	..	..	..	..	1	..	..	..	..
—12	—15	—38	3	..	12	5	19	1	..	10	10	23
..	..	..	3	..	12	..	..	1	..	10	..	..
—302	+1,622	—403	952	735	751	1,676	1,108	883	759	696	1,882	1,130
..	..	..	952	735	751	..	..	879	759	696	..	..
..	..	..	..	..	..	..	..	4	..	..	..	..
+331	+544	+1,301	753	913	466	469	43	629	1,046	474	487	38
..	..	..	753	913	466	..	..	629	1,046	474	..	..
+13	—6	—36	..	1,168	1	23	21	..	903	..	20	15
..	..	..	..	1,168	..	..	..	.	903	..	..	..
..	..	..	..	..	1	..	..	..	..	..	..	..

Tribe and locality.	Persons. 1931.	1921.	1911.	1901.	1891.	1881.	Variation 1921 to 1931.	1911 to 1921.	1901 to 1911.
1	2	3	4	5	6	7	8	9	10
KAWAR—*concld.*									
Raipur District	*31,973*	*27,308*	*27,817*	*25,776*	*22,195*	*19,333*	*+4,665*	*−509*	*+2,041*
Hindu	31,709	27,308	27,783	..	..	..	+4,401	−475	..
Tribal	264	..	34	..	..	..	+264	−34	..
Bilaspur District	*69,786*	*51,206*	*53,944*	*41,565*	*44,302*	*35,924*	*+18,580*	*−2,738*	*+12,379*
Hindu	69,488	51,165	53,934	..	..	..	+18,323	−2,769	..
Tribal	298	41	10	..	..	..	+257	+31	..
Drug District	*6,124*	*5,870*	*6,297*	..	..	..	*+254*	*−427*	*+6,297*
Hindu	6,123	5,870	6,295	..	..	..	+253	−425	..
Tribal	1	..	2	..	..	..	+1	−2	..
Berar	1	12	..	..	..	..	−11	+12	..
Hindu	1	12	..	..	..	..	−11	+12	..
Amraoti District	*1*	*12*	..	..	..	..	*−11*	*+12*	..
Hindu	1	12	..	..	..	..	−11	+12	..
KOL									
Central Provinces and Berar ..	**83,228**	**90,884**	**76,485**	**55,363**	**74,757**	**57,420**	**−7,656**	**+14,399**	**+21,122**
Hindu	73,175	86,669	57,821	..	..	..	−13,494	+28,848	..
Tribal	10,053	4,215	18,664	..	..	..	+5,838	−14,449	..
Saugor District	*101*	..	*12*	*13*	*123*	*64*	*+101*	*−12*	*−1*
Hindu	101	..	12	..	..	..	+101	−12	..
Damoh District	*61*	*726*	*115*	*76*	*206*	*349*	*−665*	*+611*	*+39*
Hindu	31	607	101	..	..	..	−576	+506	..
Tribal	30	119	14	..	..	..	−89	+105	..
Jubbulpore District ..	*57,827*	*63,491*	*52,326*	*46,130*	*61,705*	*46,383*	*−5,664*	*+11,165*	*+6,196*
Hindu	57,743	61,517	40,734	..	..	..	−3,774	+20,783	..
Tribal	84	1,974	11,592	..	..	..	−1,890	−9,618	..
Mandla District	*10,924*	*9,739*	*10,104*	*7,352*	*8,313*	*7,308*	*+1,185*	*−365*	*+2,752*
Hindu	2,444	9,041	3,707	..	..	..	−6,597	+5,334	..
Tribal	8,480	698	6,397	..	..	..	+7,782	−5,699	..
Seoni District	*240*	*304*	*315*	*209*	*636*	*279*	*−64*	*−11*	*+106*
Hindu	188	241	125	..	..	..	−53	+116	..
Tribal	52	63	190	..	..	..	−11	−127	..
Narsinghpur District ..	*670*	*1,119*	*644*	*479*	*666*	*897*	*−449*	*+475*	*+165*
Hindu	585	950	631	..	..	..	−365	+319	..
Tribal	85	169	13	..	..	..	−84	+156	..
Hoshangabad District ..	*609*	*317*	*410*	*66*	*267*	*375*	*+292*	*−93*	*+344*
Hindu	609	172	367	..	..	..	+437	−195	..
Tribal	..	145	43	..	..	..	−145	+102	..
Nimar District	*15*	*2,315*	*150*	*78*	*12*	*99*	*−2,300*	*+2,165*	*+72*
Hindu	15	2,310	150	..	..	..	−2,295	+2,160	..
Tribal	..	5	..	..	..	..	−5	+5	..
Betul District	*22*	*472*	*2,347*	*5*	*4*	..	*−450*	*−1,875*	*+2,342*
Hindu	22	472	2,344	..	..	..	−450	−1,872	..
Tribal	..	..	3	..	..	..	..	−3	..
Chhindwara District ..	*1,760*	*1,174*	*3,947*	*30*	*564*	*3*	*+586*	*−2,773*	*+3,917*
Hindu	1,692	1,160	3,566	..	..	..	+532	−2,406	..
Tribal	68	14	381	..	..	..	+54	−367	..

(Increase + Decrease —).			Males.					Females.				
1891 to 1901.	1881 to 1891.	Net variation 1881 to 1931 (Increase + Decrease —).	1931.	1921.	1911.	1901.	1881.	1931.	1921.	1911.	1901.	1881.
11	12	13	14	15	16	17	18	19	20	21	22	23
+3,581	*+2,862*	*+12,640*	*15,377*	*12,765*	*13,326*	*12,274*	*9,475*	*16,596*	*14,543*	*14,491*	*13,502*	*9,858*
..	..	..	15,235	12,765	13,302	..	..	16,474	14,543	14,481	..	..
..	..	..	142	..	24	..	..	122	..	10	..	..
—2,737	*+8,378*	*+33,862*	*34,395*	*26,592*	*26,856*	*20,686*	*18,034*	*35,391*	*24,614*	*27,088*	*20,879*	*17,890*
..	..	..	34,244	26,566	26,849	..	..	35,244	24,599	27,085	..	..
..	..	..	151	26	7	..	..	147	15	3	..	..
..	..	*+6,124*	*2,898*	*2,659*	*3,035*	..	..	*3,226*	*3,211*	*3,262*	..	..
..	..	..	2,898	2,659	3,033	..	..	3,225	3,211	3,262	..	..
..	..	..	..	..	2	..	..	1	..	..	..	..
..	..	*+1*	*1*	*12*	..	..	..	..	..	..	..	..
..	..	..	1	12	..	..	..	..	..	..	..	..
..	..	*+1*	*1*	*12*	..	..	..	..	..	..	..	..
..	..	...	1	12	..	..	..	..	..	..	..	..
—19,394	**+17,337**	**+25,808**	**41,127**	**47,382**	**37,758**	**26,418**	**28,468**	**42,101**	**43,502**	**38,727**	**28,945**	**28,952**
..	..	..	35,994	45,334	28,884	..	..	37,181	41,335	28,937	..	..
..	..	..	5,133	2,048	8,874	..	..	4,920	2,167	9,790	..	..
—110	*+59*	*+37*	*45*	..	*10*	*11*	*32*	*56*	..	*2*	*2*	*32*
..	..	..	45	..	10	..	..	56	..	2	..	..
—130	*—143*	*—288*	*32*	*435*	*71*	*38*	*190*	*29*	*291*	*44*	*38*	*159*
..	..	..	17	338	60	..	..	14	269	41	..	..
..	..	..	15	97	11	..	..	15	22	3	..	..
—15,575	*+15,322*	*+11,444*	*28,260*	*30,409*	*24,813*	*21,857*	*22,671*	*29,567*	*33,082*	*27,513*	*24,273*	*23,712*
..	..	..	28,215	29,460	19,542	..	..	29,528	32,057	21,192	..	..
..	..	..	45	949	5,271	..	..	39	1,025	6,321	..	..
—961	*+1,005*	*+3,616*	*5,540*	*4,824*	*5,023*	*3,556*	*3,747*	*5,384*	*4,915*	*5,081*	*3,796*	*3,561*
..	..	..	1,244	4,502	1,855	.	..	1,200	4,539	1,852	..	..
..	..	..	4,296	322	3,168	..	..	4,184	376	3,229	..	..
—427	*+357*	*—39*	*133*	*141*	*173*	*107*	*156*	*107*	*160*	*142*	*102*	*123*
.	..	..	101	107	75	..	..	87	134	50	..	..
..	..	..	32	37	98	..	..	20	26	92	..	..
—187	*—231*	*—227*	*320*	*541*	*332*	*270*	*460*	*350*	*578*	*312*	*209*	*437*
..	..	..	252	460	326	..	..	3	490	305	..	..
..	..	..	68	81	6	..	..	17	88	7	..	..
—201	*—108*	*+234*	*308*	*91*	*195*	*25*	*240*	*301*	*226*	*215*	*41*	*135*
..	..	..	308	91	168	..	..	301	81	199	..	..
..	..	..	..	...	27	..	..	..	145	16	..	..
+66	*—87*	*—84*	*9*	*1,043*	*49*	*46*	*58*	*6*	*1,272*	*101*	*32*	*41*
..	..	..	9	1,040	49	..	..	6	1,270	101	..	..
..	..	..	..	3	..	..	..	..	2	..	..	..
+1	*+4*	*+22*	*12*	*310*	*1,399*	*5*	..	*10*	*162*	*948*	..	..
..	..	..	12	310	1,397	..	..	10	162	947	..	..
..	..	..	..	..	2	..	..	..	..	1	..	..
—534	*+561*	*+1,757*	*939*	*760*	*2,482*	*19*	*3*	*821*	*414*	*1,465*	*11*	..
..	..	..	906	760	2,209	..	..	786	400	1,357	..	..
..	..		33	..	273	..	..	35	14	108	..	..

Tribe and locality.	Persons.						Variation		
	1931.	1921.	1911.	1901.	1891.	1881.	1921 to 1931.	1911 to 1921.	1901 to 1911.
1	2	3	4	5	6	7	8	9	10
KOL—*concld.*									
Wardha District ..	*238*	*29*	*38*	..	..	..	*+209*	*−9*	*+38*
Hindu ..	238	8	38	..	..	..	+230	−30	..
Tribal ..	..	21	..	..	..	..	−21	+21	..
Nagpur District ..	*1,903*	*728*	*322*	..	*4*	*2*	*+1,175*	*+406*	*+322*
Hindu ..	1,903	..	322	..	..	..	+1,903	−322	..
Tribal ..	..	728	..	..	..	..	−728	+728	..
Chanda District ..	*8*	..	*611*	..	*12*	*161*	*+8*	*−611*	*+611*
Hindu ..	8	..	611	..	..	..	+8	−611	..
Bhandara District ..	*1,775*	*260*	*840*	..	*17*	*107*	*+1,515*	*−580*	*+840*
Hindu ..	1,775	260	840	..	..	..	+1,515	−580	..
Balaghat District ..	*2,055*	*2,592*	*1,420*	*46*	*222*	*27*	*−537*	*+1,172*	*+1,374*
Hindu ..	1,968	2,578	1,405	..	..	..	−610	+1,173	..
Tribal ..	87	14	15	..	..	..	+73	−1	..
Raipur District ..	*382*	*7,036*	*150*	*79*	*264*	*101*	*−6,654*	*+6,886*	*+71*
Hindu ..	258	7,036	146	..	..	..	−6,778	+6,890	..
Tribal ..	124	..	4	..	..	..	+124	−4	..
Bilaspur District ..	*3,521*	*265*	*2,531*	*800*	*1,731*	*1,265*	*+3,256*	*−2,266*	*+1,731*
Hindu ..	2,482	..	2,519	..	..	..	+2,482	−2,519	..
Tribal ..	1,039	265	12	..	..	..	+774	+253	..
Drug District ..	..	*19*	*33*	..	..	..	*−19*	*−14*	..
Hindu ..	..	19	33	..	..	..	−19	−14	+33
Berar ..	**1,117**	**298**	**170**	..	**11**	..	**+819**	**+128**	**+170**
Hindu ..	1,113	298	170	..	..	..	+815	+128	..
Tribal ..	4	..	..	..	..	..	+4	..	..
Amraoti District ..	*246*	*144*	*120*	..	..	..	*+102*	*+24*	*+120*
Hindu ..	246	144	120	..	..	..	+102	+24	..
Akola District ..	*63*	..	*50*	..	..	..	*+63*	*−50*	*+50*
Hindu ..	59	..	50	..	..	..	+59	−50	..
Tribal ..	4	..	..	..	..	..	+4	..	..
Buldana District ..	*128*	*154*	..	..	..	..	*−26*	*+154*	..
Hindu ..	128	154	..	..	..	..	−26	+154	..
Yeotmal District ..	*680*	..	..	..	..	..	*+680*	..	..
Hindu ..	680	..	..	..	..	..	+680	..	..
KOLAM									
Central Provinces and Berar ..	**31,763**	**23,721**	**24,976**	**15,799**	**19,318**	**12,163**	**+8,042**	**−1,255**	**+9,177**
Hindu ..	19,374	..	..	..	..	..	..	..	..
Tribal ..	12,389	23,721	24,976	..	..	..	..	..	..
Saugor District ..	..	..	..	..	*2*	..	..	..	..
Betul District ..	*1*	..	..	..	..	..	*+1*	..	..
Hindu ..	1	..	..	..	..	..	+1	..	..
Wardha District ..	*2,093*	*1,808*	*2,084*	..	*1,902*	..	*+285*	*−276*	..
Hindu ..	2,034	..	..	..	..	..	+2,034	..	..
Tribal ..	59	1,808	2,084	..	..	..	−1,749	−276	..
Nagpur District ..	*3*	*8*	*57*	..	..	..	*−5*	*−49*	..
Hindu ..	3	..	..	..	..	..	+3	..	..
Tribal ..	..	8	57	..	..	..	−8	−49	..

(Increase + Decrease —). 1891 to 1901.	1881 to 1891.	Net variation 1881 to 1931 (Increase + Decrease —).	Males. 1931.	1921.	1911.	1901.	1881.	Females. 1931.	1921.	1911.	1901.	1881.
11	12	13	14	15	16	17	18	19	20	21	22	23
..	..	+238	119	19	13	..	..	119	10	25	..	..
..	..	..	119	8	13	..	..	119	..	25	..	..
..	..	..	..	11	..	..	..	..	10	..	..	..
—4	+2	+1,901	925	372	187	..	1	978	356	135	..	1
..	..	..	925	..	187	..	..	978	..	135	..	..
..	..	..	..	372	..	..	..	..	356	..	..	..
—12	—149	—153	5	..	320	..	77	3	..	291	..	84
..	..	..	5	..	320	..	..	3	..	291	..	..
—17	—90	+1,668	891	131	445	..	66	884	129	395	..	41
..	..	..	891	131	445	..	..	884	129	395	..	..
—176	+195	+2,028	1,028	1,256	738	21	15	1,027	1,336	682	25	12
..	..	..	958	1,245	729	..	..	1,010	1,333	676	..	..
..	..	..	70	11	9	..	..	17	3	6	..	..
—185	+163	+281	192	6,692	78	48	54	190	344	72	31	47
..	..	..	129	6,692	76	..	..	129	344	70	..	..
..	..	..	63	..	2	..	..	61	..	2	..	..
—931	+466	+2,256	1,775	165	1,298	415	698	1,746	100	1,233	385	567
..	..	..	1,266	..	1,291	..	..	1,216	..	1,228	..	..
..	..	..	509	165	7	..	..	530	100	5	..	..
..	..	..	..	19	15	..	..	..	..	18	..	..
..	..	..	..	19	15	..	..	..	..	18	..	..
—11	+11	+1,117	594	171	117	..	..	523	127	53	..	..
..	..	..	592	171	117	..	..	521	127	53	..	..
..	..	..	2	..	..	..	..	2	..	..	..	..
..	..	+246	137	84	71	..	..	109	60	49	..	..
..	..	..	137	84	71	..	..	109	60	49	..	..
..	..	+63	43	..	46	..	..	20	..	4	..	..
..	..	..	41	..	46	..	..	18	..	4	..	..
..	..	..	2	..	..	..	..	2	..	..	..	..
..	..	+128	71	87	..	..	..	57	67	..	..	..
..	..	..	71	87	..	..	..	57	67	..	..	..
..	..	+680	343	..	..	..	..	337	..	..	..	..
..	..	..	343	..	..	..	..	337	..	..	..	..
—3,519	+7,155	+19,600	15,987	11,925	12,331	7,735	6,118	15,776	11,796	12,645	8,064	6,045
..	..	..	9,762	..	..	..	..	9,612	..	..	..	..
..	..	..	6,225	11,925	12,331	..	..	6,164	11,796	12,645	..	..
..	..	..	..	..	..	..	..	..	..	..	..	..
..	..	+1	1	..	..	..	..	..	..	..	..	..
..	..	..	1	..	..	..	..	..	..	..	..	..
..	..	+2,093	1,097	911	1,047	..	..	996	897	1,037	..	..
..	..	..	1,061	..	..	..	..	973	..	..	..	..
..	..	..	36	911	1,047	..	..	23	897	1,037	..	..
..	..	+3	1	8	35	..	..	2	..	22	..	..
..	..	..	1	..	..	..	..	2	..	..	..	..
..	..	..	..	8	35	..	..	..	..	22	..	..

Tribe and locality.	Persons. 1931.	1921.	1911.	1901.	1891.	1881.	Variation 1921 to 1931.	1911 to 1921.	1901 to 1911.
1	2	3	4	5	6	7	8	9	10
KOLAM—concld.									
Chanda District	151	18	..	..	..	..	+133	+18	..
Hindu	151	..	..	..	..	..	+151	..	..
Tribal	..	18	..	..	..	..	-18	+18	..
Bhandara District	..	4	..	..	..	..	-4	+4	..
Tribal	..	4	..	..	..	..	-4	+4	..
Berar	29,515	21,883	22,835	15,799	17,414	12,163	+7,632	-952	+7,036
Hindu	17,185	..	..	..	..	..	+17,185	..	..
Tribal	12,330	21,883	22,835	..	..	..	-9,553	-952	..
Amraoti District	103	..	120	..	..	..	+103	-120	..
Hindu	103	..	..	..	..	..	+103	..	..
Tribal	..	..	120	..	..	..	..	-120	..
Akola District	1	1	10	..	..	..	..	-9	..
Hindu	1	..	..	..	..	..	+1	..	..
Tribal	..	1	10	..	..	..	-1	-9	..
Buldana District	..	1	..	..	..	..	-1	+1	..
Tribal	..	1	..	..	..	..	-1	+1	..
Yeotmal District	29,411	21,881	22,705	..	..	..	+7,530	-824	..
Hindu	17,081	..	..	..	..	..	+17,081	..	..
Tribal	12,330	21,881	22,705	..	..	..	-9,551	-824	..
KOLI									
Central Provinces and Berar	43,130	40,866	36,146	28,038	32,628	30,398	+2,264	+4,720	+8,108
Hindu	43,129	40,866	36,146	..	..	..	+2,263	+4,720	..
Tribal	1	..	..	..	..	..	+1	..	..
Saugor District	44	..	5	..	..	..	+44	-5	..
Hindu	44	..	5	..	..	..	+44	-5	..
Jubbulpore District	4	..	..	..	..	..	+4	..	..
Hindu	4	..	..	..	..	..	+4	..	..
Narsinghpur District	..	11	..	..	..	..	-11	+11	..
Hindu	..	11	..	..	..	..	-11	+11	..
Hoshangabad District	156	77	..	..	..	..	+79	+77	..
Hindu	156	77	..	..	..	..	+79	+77	
Nimar District	3,352	2,864	2,461	..	..	..	+488	+403	..
Hindu	3,352	2,864	2,461	..	..	..	+488	+403	..
Chhindwara District	86	348	..	..	..	..	-262	+348	..
Hindu	86	348	..	..	..	..	-262	+348	..
Wardha District	449	351	253	..	..	..	+98	+98	..
Hindu	449	351	253	..	..	..	+98	+98	..
Nagpur District	242	1,520	..	..	..	..	-1,278	+1,520	..
Hindu	242	1,520	..	..	..	..	-1,278	+1,520	..
Chanda District	398	470	..	..	..	..	-72	+470	..
Hindu	397	470	..	..	..	..	-73	+470	..
Tribal	1	..	..	..	..	..	+1	..	..
Bhandara District	206	297	71	..	..	..	-91	+226	..
Hindu	206	297	71	..	..	..	-91	+226	..

(Increase + Decrease —).		Net variation 1881 to 1931 (Increase + Decrease —).	Males.					Females.				
1891 to 1901.	1881 to 1891.		1931.	1921.	1911.	1901.	1881.	1931.	1921.	1911.	1901.	1881.
11	12	13	14	15	16	17	18	19	20	21	22	23
..	..	+151	69	9	..	..	..	82	9	..	..	..
..	..	..	69	..	..	..	..	82	..	..	..	..
..	..	..	..	9	..	..	..	..	9	..	..	..
..	..	..	..	..	..	..	..	..	4	..	..	..
..	..	..	..	..	..	..	..	..	4	..	..	..
−1,615	+5,251	+17,352	14,819	10,997	11,249	7,735	6,118	14,696	10,886	11,586	8,064	6,045
..	..	..	8,630	..	..	..	..	8,555	..	..	..	..
..	..	..	6,189	10.997	11,249	..	..	6,141	10,886	11,586	..	..
..	..	..	48	..	61	..	..	55	..	59	..	..
..	..	..	48	..	..	..	..	55	..	..	..	..
..	..	..	..	..	61	..	..	..	..	59	..	..
..	..	..	1	..	..	..	..	..	1	10	..	..
..	..	..	1	..	..	..	..	..	..	..	..	..
..	..	..	..	..	..	..	..	..	1	10	..	..
..	..	..	..	..	..	..	..	..	1	..	..	..
..	..	..	..	..	..	..	..	..	1	..	..	..
..	..	..	14,770	10,997	11,188	..	..	14,641	10,884	11,517	..	..
..	..	..	8,581	..	..	..	..	8,500	..	..	..	..
..	..	..	6,189	10,997	11,188	..	..	6,141	10,884	11,517	..	..
−4,590	+2,230	+12,732	21,996	21,083	18,129	13,858	15,471	21,134	19,783	18,017	14,180	14,927
..	..	..	21,996	21,083	13,129	..	..	21,133	19,783	18,017	..	..
..	..	..	..	..	..	..	..	1	..	..	..	..
..	..	..	43	..	3	..	..	1	..	2	..	..
..	..	..	43	..	3	..	..	1	..	2	..	..
..	..	..	3	..	..	..	..	1	..	..	..	..
..	..	..	3	..	..	..	..	1	..	..	..	..
..	..	..	..	..	..	..	..	..	11	..	..	..
..	..	..	..	..	..	..	..	..	11	..	..	..
..	..	..	73	38	..	..	..	83	39	..	..	..
..	..	..	73	38	..	..	..	83	39	..	..	..
..	..	..	1,726	2,136	1,232	..	..	1,626	728	1,229	..	..
..	..	..	1,726	2,136	1,232	..	..	1,626	728	1,229	..	..
..	..	..	49	81	..	..	..	37	267	..	..	..
..	..	..	49	81	..	..	..	37	267	..	..	..
..	..	..	220	185	142	..	..	229	166	111	..	..
..	..	..	220	185	142	..	..	229	166	111	..	..
..	..	..	129	761	..	..	..	113	759	..	..	..
..	..	..	129	761	..	..	..	113	759	..	..	..
..	..	..	217	248	..	..	..	181	222	..	..	..
..	..	..	217	248	..	..	..	180	222	..	..	..
..	..	..	..	..	..	..	..	1	..	..	..	..
..	..	..	63	162	34	..	..	143	135	37	..	..
..	..	..	63	162	34	..	..	143	135	37	..	..

Tribe and locality.	Persons. 1931.	1921.	1911.	1901.	1891.	1881.	Variation 1921 to 1931	1911 to 1921.	1901 to 1911
1	2	3	4	5	6	7	8	9	10
KOLI—concld.									
Balaghat District	..	..	3	..	..	..	..	−3	..
Hindu	..	..	3	..	..		..	−3	..
Bilaspur District	*124*	*1,768*	..	..	..	..	*−1,644*	*+1,768*	..
Hindu	124	1,768	..	..	..	..	−1,644	+1,768	..
Berar ..	**38,069**	**33,160**	**33,353**	**28,038**	**32,628**	**30,398**	**+4,909**	**−193**	**+5,315**
Hindu	38,069	33,160	33,353	..	..	..	+4,909	−193	..
Amraoti District	*9,446*	*7,990*	*8,211*	..	..	..	*+1,456*	*−221*	..
Hindu	9,446	7,990	8,211	..	..	..	+1,456	−221	..
Akola District	*11,196*	*9,767*	*9,613*	..	..	..	*+1,429*	*+154*	..
Hindu	11,196	9,767	9,613	..	..	..	+1,429	+154	..
Buldana District	*12,362*	*11,076*	*11,549*	..	..	..	*+1,286*	*−473*	..
Hindu	12,362	11,076	11,549	..	..	..	+1,286	−473	..
Yeotmal District	*5,065*	*4,327*	*3,980*	..	..	..	*+738*	*+347*	..
Hindu	5,065	4,327	3,980	..	..	..	+738	+347	..
KORKU									
Central Provinces and Berar ..	**167,897**	**135,357**	**149,537**	**125,365**	**126,682**	**110,951**	**+32,540**	**−14,180**	**+24,172**
Hindu	92,539	46,098	84,727	..	..	..	+46.441	−38,629	..
Tribal	75,342	89,259	64,810	..	..	..	−13,917	+24,449	..
Christian	16	..	.	..	..	..	+16	..	..
Saugor District	.	*6*			*23*	*3*	*−6*	*6*	..
Tribal . ..	..	6	..	..	..	..	−6	+6	..
Damoh District	..	*889*	*23*	*343*	..	*47*	*−889*	*+866*	*−320*
Hindu	.	8	22	..	..		−8	−14	..
Tribal	..	881	1	..	..	..	−881	+880	..
Jubbulpore District	*9*	..	*9*	*59*	*7*	*3*	*+9*	*−9*	*−50*
Hindu . ..	9	..	8	..	..	..	+9	−8	..
Tribal	.	..	1	..	..	..	..	−1	..
Mandla District	.	*47*	..	*23*	..	..	*−47*	*+47*	*−23*
Hindu	..	8	..	..	..	..	−8	+8	..
Tribal	..	39	.	..	..	..	−39	+39	..
Seoni District		.	*1*	.	..	*4*	.	*−1*	*+1*
Hindu	..	...	1	..	..	..	..	−1	..
Narsinghpur District	*1*	..	..	*97*	..	*2*	*+1*	..	*−97*
Tribal	1	.	..	..	..	..	+1	..	..
Hoshangabad District	*22,014*	*20,783*	*20,204*	*22,571*	*36,772*	*28,458*	*+1,231*	*+579*	*−2,367*
Hindu	12,149	16,326	11,639	..	.	..	−4,177	+4,687	..
Tribal	9,865	4,457	8,565	..	..	..	+5,408	−4,108	..
Nimar District	*52,172*	*41,417*	*36,929*	*31,041*	*10,118*	*9,541*	*+10,755*	*+4,458*	*+5,888*
Hindu	26,284	28,450	34,640	..	..	..	−2,166	−6,190	..
Tribal	25,888	12,967	2,289	..	..	..	+12,921	+10,678	..
Betul District	*37,464*	*32,606*	*35,674*	*23,868*	*31,880*	*32,634*	*+4,858*	*−3,068*	*+11,806*
Hindu	7,492	512	25,857	..	..	..	+6,980	−25,345	..
Tribal	29,972	32,094	9,817	..	..	...	−2,122	+22,277	..

(Increase + Decrease —). 1891 to 1901.	1881 to 1891.	Net variation 1881 to 1931 (Increase + Decrease —).	Males. 1931.	1921.	1911	1901.	1881.	Females. 1931.	1921.	1911.	1901.	1881.
11	12	13	14	15	16	17	18	19	20	21	22	23
..	..	..		..	*2*	..	..	..	..	*1*	..	..
..	..	..	..	.	2	..	.	..	..	1	..	..
..	..	..	*55*	*924*	..	..	..	*69*	*844*	..	..	..
..	..	.	55	924	..	..	..	69	844	..	..	..
—4,590	**+2,230**	**+7,671**	**19,418**	**16,548**	**16,716**	**13,858**	**15,471**	**18,651**	**16,612**	**16,637**	**14,180**	**14,927**
..	..	.	19,418	16,548	16,716	.	..	18,651	16,612	16,637	..	..
..	..	..	*4,916*	*3,991*	*4,170*	..	..	*4,530*	*3,999*	*4,041*	..	..
..	..	..	4,916	3,991	4,170	..	..	4,530	3,999	4,041	..	..
..	..	.	*5,684*	*4,838*	*4,875*	.	..	*5,512*	*4,929*	*4,738*	..	.
..	..	..	5,684	4,838	4,875	..	..	5,512	4,929	4,738	..	..
..	.	..	*6,280*	*5,500*	*5,711*	.	..	*6,082*	*5,576*	*5,838*	..	..
..	..	..	6,280	5,500	5,711	..	..	6,082	5,576	5,838	..	..
..	..	..	*2,538*	*2,219*	*1,960*	..	..	*2,527*	*2,108*	*2,020*	..	..
..	..	..	2,538	2,219	1,960	..	.	2,527	2,108	2,020	..	.
—1,317	**+15,731**	**+56,946**	**83,813**	**66,413**	**74,110**	**61,602**	**56,391**	**84,084**	**68,944**	**75,427**	**63,763**	**54,560**
..	..	..	46,435	23,037	42,230	..	..	46,104	23,061	42,497	..	..
..	..	..	37,372	43,376	31,880	..	..	37,970	45,883	32,930	..	..
..	..	..	6	..	..	..	..	10	..	..	..	..
—23	*+20*	*—3*	..	*6*	..	..	*3*	..	..	..	..	..
..	..	..	..	6	..	..	..	..	..	..	..	..
+343	*—47*	*—47*		*405*	*11*	*162*	*27*	..	*484*	*12*	*181*	*20*
..	..	.	.	4	10	..	..	.	4	12	..	..
..	..	..	..	401	1	..	..	.	480	..	..	..
+52	*+4*	*+6*	*8*	..	*7*	*33*	*1*	*1*	..	*2*	*26*	*2*
..	..	..	8	..	6	..	..	1	..	2	..	..
..	..	.	..	..	1	..	..	..	..	..	..	..
+23	..	..	..	*33*	..	*9*	..	..	*14*	..	*14*	..
..	..	..	..	1	..	..	..	..	7	..	..	..
..	..	..	..	32	..	..	..	..	7	..	..	..
..	*—4*	*—4*	..	..	*1*	..	*2*	..	..	..	..	*2*
..	..	..	..	..	1	..	..		..	..	..	..
+97	*—2*	*—1*	*1*	..	..	*63*	*2*	..	..	..	*34*	..
..	..	..	1	..	..	..	..	..	..	..	..	..
—14,201	*+8,314*	*—6,441*	*11,139*	*10,583*	*10,014*	*10,969*	*14,317*	*10,875*	*10,200*	*10,190*	*11,602*	*14,111*
..	..	..	6,127	8,208	5,752	..	..	6,022	8,118	5,887	..	..
..	..	..	5,012	2,375	4,262	.	.	4,853	2,082	4,303	..	..
+20,923	*+577*	*+42,631*	*25,941*	*20,674*	*18,556*	*15,197*	*4,957*	*26,231*	*20,743*	*18,373*	*15,844*	*4,584*
..	..	.	13,092	14,153	17,379	..	.	13,192	14,297	17,261	..	..
..	..	.	12,849	6,521	1,177	..	..	13,039	6,446	1,112	..	..
—8,012	*—754*	*+4,830*	*18,415*	*15,256*	*17,620*	*11,167*	*16,595*	*19,049*	*17,350*	*18,054*	*12,401*	*16,039*
..	..	.	3,683	318	12,832	..	..	3,809	194	13,025	..	..
..	..	.	14,732	14,938	4,788	..	..	15,240	17,156	5,029	..	..

TABLE XVIII—PART A

Tribe and locality.	Persons. 1931.	1921.	1911.	1901.	1891.	1881.	Variation 1921 to 1931.	1911 to 1921.	1901 to 1911.
1	2	3	4	5	6	7	8	9	10
KORKU—*concld.*									
Chhindwara District	*18,958*	*4,367*	*16,423*	*18,771*	*12,559*	*11,081*	*+14,591*	*−12,056*	*−2,343*
Hindu	13,557	131	9,139	..	..	..	+13,426	−9,008	..
Tribal	5,401	4,236	7,284	..	..	..	+1,165	−3,048	..
Wardha District . ..	*691*	*1,150*	*660*	*501*	*21*	*627*	*−459*	*+490*	*+159*
Hindu	560	..	623	..	..	..	+560	−623	..
Tribal	131	1,150	37	..	..	..	−1,019	+1,113	..
Nagpur District . ..	*32*	*72*	*97*	*52*	*80*	*6*	*−10*	*−25*	*+45*
Hindu	25	3	88	..	..	..	+22	−85	..
Tribal	7	69	9	..	..	..	−62	+60	..
Chanda District	..	*30*	..	..	*6*	*3*	*−30*	*+30*	..
Hindu	..	2	..	..	..	..	−2	+2	..
Tribal		28	..	..	..	..	−28	+28	..
Bhandara District ..	*66*	..	.	*22*	*231*	*25*	*+66*	..	*−22*
Hindu	25	.	.	..	..	..	+25	..	..
Tribal	41	..	.	..	..	..	+41	..	..
Balaghat District	..	*57*	*2*	..	..	.	*−57*	*+55*	*+2*
Tribal . .	.	57	2	..	..	..	−57	+55	..
Raipur District	*7*	.	*1*	..	..	*37*	*+7*	*−1*	*+1*
Hindu	7	..	1	..	..	..	+7	−1	..
Bilaspur District	*22*	*40*	*13*	*53*	*4*	*30*	*−18*	*+27*	*−40*
Hindu	22	..	12	..	..	..	+22	−12	..
Tribal	..	40	1	..	..	..	−40	+39	..
Drug District .. .	..	*16*	..	..	..	..	*−16*	*+16*	..
Tribal	..	16	.	..	..	..	−16	+16	..
Berar	**36,461**	**33,877**	**39,501**	**27,964**	**34,981**	**28,450**	**+2,584**	**−5,624**	**+11,537**
Hindu	32,409	658	2,697	.	..	..	+31,751	−2,039	..
Tribal	4,036	33,219	36,804	..	..	..	−29,183	−3,585	..
Christian . .	16	..	..	.	..	..	+16	..	..
Amraoti District	*33,869*	*31,793*	*38,827*	..	..	..	*+2,076*	*−7,034*	..
Hindu	29,870	658	2,240	..	..	..	+29,212	−1,582	..
Tribal	3,983	31,135	36,587	..	..	..	−27,152	−5,452	..
Christian .. .	16	..	..	..	..	..	+16	..	..
Akola District .. .	*1,847*	*1,494*	*121*	..	..	..	*+353*	*+1,373*	..
Hindu .. .	1,794	.	119	..	..	..	+1,794	−119	..
Tribal .. .	53	1,494	2	..	..	..	−1,441	+1,492	..
Buldana District	*745*	*590*	*551*	..	..	..	*+155*	*+39*	..
Hindu	745	..	338	..	..	..	+745	−338	..
Tribal	..	590	213	..	..	..	−590	+377	..
Yeotmal District	..	..	*2*	..	..	..	..	*−2*	*+2*
Tribal .. .	...	..	2	.	..	..	..	−2	..
KORWA									
Central Provinces and Berar .	**384**	**444**	**876**	**105**	**439**	..	**−60**	**−432**	**+771**
Hindu . ..	372	439	870	..	..	..	−67	−431	..
Tribal	12	5	6	..	..	..	+7	−1	..
Jubbulpore District ..	..	..	*1*	..	..	..	..	*−1*	*+1*
Hindu	..	..	1	..	..	..	..	−1	..

(Increase + Decrease −).		Net variation 1881 to 1931 (Increase + Decrease −).	Males.					Females.				
1891 to 1931.	1881 to 1891.		1931.	1921.	1911.	1901.	1881.	1931.	1921.	1911.	1901.	1881.
11	12	13	14	15	16	17	18	19	20	21	22	23
+6,212	+1,478	+7,877	9,472	2,107	8,095	9,723	5,640	9,486	2,260	8,328	9,048	5,441
..	..	..	6,744	41	4,530	..	..	6,813	90	4,609	..	..
..	..	..	2,728	2,066	3,565	..	..	2,673	2,170	3,719	..	..
+480	−606	+64	350	196	332	243	320	341	954	328	258	307
..	..	..	281	..	312	..	..	279	..	311	..	..
..	..	..	69	196	20	..	..	62	954	17	..	..
−28	+74	+26	21	41	56	38	3	11	31	41	14	3
..	..	..	18	3	51	..	..	7	..	37	..	..
..	..	..	3	38	5	..	..	4	31	4	..	..
−6	+3	−3	..	13	..	..	2	..	17	..	..	1
..	..	..	..	..	..	..	..	..	2	..	..	..
..	..	..	..	13	..	..	..	..	15	..	..	..
−209	+206	+41	36	..	..	8	12	30	..	..	14	13
..	..	..	13	..	..	..	..	12	..	..	..	..
..	..	..	23	..	..	..	..	18	..	..	..	..
..	..	..	..	25	2	..	..	..	32	..	..	..
..	..	..	..	25	2	..	..	..	32	..	..	..
..	−37	−30	7	..	..	..	23	..	..	1	..	14
..	..	..	7	..	..	..	..	..	..	1	..	..
+49	−26	−8	8	18	5	28	14	14	22	8	25	16
..	..	..	8	..	4	..	..	14	..	8	..	..
..	..	..	..	18	1	..	..	..	22	..	..	..
..	..	..	..	8	..	..	..	..	8	..	..	..
..	..	..	..	8	..	..	..	..	8	..	..	..
−7,017	**+6,531**	**+8,011**	**18,415**	**17,048**	**19,411**	**13,662**	**14,443**	**18,046**	**16,829**	**20,090**	**14,302**	**14,007**
..	..	..	16,454	309	1,353	..	..	15,955	349	1,344	..	..
..	..	..	1,955	16,739	18,058	..	..	2,081	16,480	18,746	..	..
..	..	..	6	..	..	..	..	10	..	..	..	..
..	..	..	17,034	15,981	19,070	..	..	16,835	15,812	19,757	..	..
..	..	..	15,103	309	1,124	..	..	14,767	349	1,116	..	..
..	..	..	1,925	15,672	17,946	..	..	2,058	15,463	18,641	..	..
..	..	..	6	..	..	..	..	10	..	..	..	..
..	..	..	973	754	61	..	..	874	740	60	..	..
..	..	..	943	..	59	..	..	851	..	60	..	..
..	..	..	30	754	2	..	..	23	740	..	..	..
..	..	..	408	313	278	..	..	337	277	273	..	..
..	..	..	408	..	170	..	..	337	..	168	..	..
..	..	..	..	313	108	..	..	..	277	105	..	..
..	..	..	..	..	2	..	..	..	..	..	..	..
..	..	..	..	..	2	..	..	..	..	..	..	..
−334	..	..	**183**	**320**	**419**	**49**	..	**201**	**124**	**457**	**56**	..
..	..	..	177	317	417	..	..	195	122	453	..	..
..	..	..	6	3	2	..	..	6	2	4	..	..
..	..	..	..	..	..	..	..	..	..	1	..	..
..	..	..	..	..	..	..	..	..	..	1	..	..

Tribe and locality.	Persons. 1931.	1921.	1911.	1901.	1891.	1881.	Variation 1921 to 1931.	1911 to 1921.	1901 to 1911.
1	2	3	4	5	6	7	8	9	10
KORWA—*concld.*									
Betul District	..	..	*1*	..	..	..	..	*—1*	..
Hindu	..	..	1	..	..	..	..	—1	..
Raipur District	*14*	..	*9*	..	..	..	*+14*	*—9*	*+9*
Hindu	2	..	9	..	..	..	+2	—9	..
Tribal	12	..	..	..	..	..	+12	..	..
Bilaspur District	*370*	*444*	*864*	*105*	*439*	..	*—74*	*—420*	*+759*
Hindu	370	439	858	..	..	..	—69	—419	..
Tribal	..	5	6	..	..	..	—5	—1	..
Drug District	..	..	*1*	..	..	..	..	*—1*	*+1*
Hindu	..	..	1	..	..	..	..	—1	..
MAJHWAR									
Central Provinces and Berar	**9,231**	**7,136**	**6,473**	..	..	..	**+2,095**	**+663**	..
Hindu	9,061	6,791	6,349	..	..	..	+2,270	+442	..
Tribal	170	345	124	..	..	..	—175	+221	..
Jubbulpore District	..	..	*2*	..	..	..	..	*—2*	..
Hindu	..	..	2	..	..	..	..	—2	..
Raipur District	*650*	..	..	..	..	..	*+650*	..	..
Hindu	650	..	..	..	..	..	+650	..	..
Bilaspur District	*8,581*	*7,136*	*6,471*	..	..	..	*+1,445*	*+665*	..
Hindu	8,411	6,791	6,347	..	..	..	+1,620	..	..
Tribal	170	345	124	..	..	..	—175	..	..
MARIA									
Central Provinces and Berar	**34,986**	(*b*)..	..	..	**32,812**	**30,792**	..	..	..
Hindu	484	..	..	..	..	..	..	..	..
Tribal	34,502	..	..	..	..	..	..	..	..
Jubbulpore District	*203*	..	..	..	..	..	..	..	..
Hindu	203	..	..	..	..	..	..	..	..
Betul District	*1*	..	..	..	..	*1*	..	..	..
Hindu	1	..	..	..	..	..	..	..	..
Wardha District	..	..	..	..	*1*	..	..	..	..
Nagpur District	..	..	..	..	*22*	..	..	..	..
Chanda District	*34,776*	..	..	..	*32,783*	*30,586*	..	..	..
Hindu	274	..	..	..	..	..	..	..	..
Tribal	34,502	..	..	..	..	..	..	..	..
Bhandara District	..	..	..	..	..	*89*	..	..	..
Bilaspur District	*6*	..	..	..	*6*	*116*	..	..	..
Hindu	6	..	..	..	..	..	..	..	..
MURIA									
Central Provinces and Berar	**1,761**	..	..	..	**23**	**34**	..	..	..
Hindu	1,712	..	..	..	..	..	..	..	..
Tribal	49	..	..	..	..	..	..	..	..
Saugor District	*218*	..	..	..	..	..	..	..	..
Hindu	218	..	..	..	..	..	..	..	..

(*b*) Figures of Marias and Murias were included with Gonds from 1901—1921.

(Increase + Decrease −).		Net variation 1881 to 1931 (Increase + Decrease −).	Males.					Females.				
1891 to 1901.	1881 to 1891		1931.	1921.	1911.	1901.	1881.	1931.	1921.	1911	1901.	1881.
11	12	13	14	15	16	17	18	19	20	21	22	23
..	..	..	..	..	*1*	..	..	..	..	..	..	..
..	..	..	..	..	1	..	..	..	..	..	..	..
..	..	..	*8*	..	*9*	..	..	*6*	..	..	..	..
..	..	..	2	..	9	..	..	..	..	..	..	..
..	..	..	6	..	..	..	..	6	..	..	..	..
−334	..	..	*175*	*320*	*409*	*49*	..	*195*	*124*	*455*	*56*	..
..	..	..	*175*	*317*	*407*	..	..	*195*	122	451	..	..
..	..	..	..	3	2	..	..	..	2	4	..	..
..	..	..	..	..	..	..	..	..	..	*1*	..	..
..	..	..	..	..	..	..	..	..	..	1	..	..
..	..	..	**4,658**	**3,981**	**3,285**	..	..	**4,573**	**3,155**	**3,188**	..	..
..	..	..	4,573	3,789	3,224	..	..	4,488	3,002	3,125	..	..
..	..	..	85	192	61	..	..	85	153	63	..	..
..	..	..	..	..	..	..	..	..	..	*2*	..	..
..	..	..	..	..	..	..	..	..	..	2	..	..
..	..	..	*334*	..	..	..	..	*316*	..	..	..	..
..	..	..	334	..	..	..	..	316	..	..	..	..
..	..	..	*4,324*	*3,981*	*3,285*	..	..	*4,257*	*3,155*	*3,186*	..	..
..	..	..	4,239	3,789	3,224	..	..	4,172	3,002	3,123	..	..
..	..	..	85	192	61	..	..	85	153	63	..	..
..	**+2,020**	**+4,194**	**17,239**	..	..	..	**15,543**	**17,747**	..	..	..	**15,249**
..	..	..	273	..	..	..	..	211	..	..	..	..
..	..	..	16,966	..	..	..	..	17,536	..	..	..	..
..	..	*+203*	*105*	..	..	..	..	*98*	..	..	..	..
..	..	..	105	..	..	..	..	98	..	..	..	..
..	*−1*	..	*1*	..	..	..	*1*	..	..	..	..	..
..	..	..	1	..	..	..	..	..	..	..	..	..
..	+1	..	..	..	..	..	..	..	..	..	..	..
..	+22	..	..	..	..	..	..	..	..	..	..	..
..	*+2,197*	*+4,190*	*17,128*	..	..	..	*15,423*	*17,648*	..	..	..	*15,163*
..	..	..	162	..	..	..	..	112	..	..	..	..
..	..	..	16,966	..	..	..	..	17,536	..	..	..	..
..	*−89*	*−89*	..	..	..	..	*52*	..	..	..	..	*37*
..	*−110*	*—110*	*5*	..	..	..	*67*	*1*	..	..	..	*49*
..	..	..	5	..	..	..	..	1	..	..	..	..
..	**−11**	**+1,727**	**692**	..	..	..	**18**	**1,069**	..	..	..	**16**
..	..	..	667	..	..	..	..	1,045	..	..	..	..
..	..	..	25	..	..	..	..	24	..	..	..	..
..	..	*+218*	*128*	..	..	..	..	*90*	..	..	..	..
..	..	..	128	..	..	..	..	90	..	..	..	..

Tribe and locality.	Persons.						Variation		
	1931.	1921.	1911.	1901.	1891.	1881.	1921 to 1931.	1911 to 1921.	1901 to 1911.
1	2	3	4	5	6	7	8	9	10
MURIA—*concld.*									
Damoh District	*237*	..	..	..	..	..	..	..	..
Hindu	237	..	..	..	..	..	..	..	..
Jubbulpore District ..	..	..	..	..	*14*	..	..	..	..
Narsinghpur District ..	*671*	..	..	..	..	..	..	..	..
Hindu	671	..	..	..	..	..	..	..	..
Hoshangabad District ..	*30*	..	..	..	..	..	..	..	..
Hindu	30	..	..	..	..	..	..	..	..
Nimar District ..	*11*	..	..	..	..	..	..	..	..
Hindu	11	..	..	..	..	..	..	..	..
Chhindwara District ..	*2*	..	..	..	..	..	..	..	..
Hindu	2	..	..	..	..	..	..	..	..
Nagpur District	*8*	..	..	..	..	..	..	..	..
Hindu	8	..	..	..	..	..	..	..	..
Chanda District	..	..	..	..	..	*28*	..	..	..
Bhandara District ..	*276*	..	..	..	..	..	..	..	..
Hindu	276	..	..	..	..	..	..	..	..
Balaghat District	*13*	..	..	..	..	..	..	..	..
Hindu	13	..	..	..	..	..	..	..	..
Raipur District	*9*	..	..	..	*9*	..	..	..	..
Hindu	9	..	..	..	..	..	..	..	..
Bilaspur District	*213*	..	..	..	..	*6*	..	..	..
Hindu	184	..	..	..	..	..	..	..	..
Tribal	29	..	..	..	..	..	..	..	..
Drug District	*20*	..	..	..	..	..	..	..	..
Tribal	20	..	..	..	..	..	..	..	..
Berar	**53**	..	..	..	..	..	..	..	..
Hindu	53	..	..	..	..	..	..	..	..
Amraoti District	*16*	..	..	..	..	..	..	..	..
Hindu	16	..	..	..	..	..	..	..	..
Akola District	*24*	..	..	..	..	..	..	..	..
Hindu	24	..	..	..	..	..	..	..	..
Yeotmal District	*13*	..	..	..	..	..	..	..	..
Hindu	13	..	..	..	..	..	..	..	..
NAGARCHI									
Central Provinces and Berar ..	**6,299**	..	**6,148**	..	**6,326**	..	..	..	..
Hindu	4,677	..	6,148	..	..	..	..	..	..
Tribal	1,622	..	..	..	..	..	..	..	..
Jubbulpore District ..	..	..	*1*	..	..	..	..	..	..
Hindu	..	..	1	..	..	..	..	..	..
Mandla District ..	*106*	..	*155*	..	*169*	..	..	..	..
Hindu	106	..	155	..	..	..	..	..	..

(Increase + Decrease —). 1891 to 1901.	1881 to 1891.	Net variation 1881 to 1931 (Increase + Decrease —).	Males. 1931.	1921.	1911.	1901.	1881.	Females. 1931.	1921.	1911.	1901.	1881.
11	12	13	14	15	16	17	18	19	20	21	22	23
..	..	+237	119	..	..	..	.	118	..	.	..	..
..	..	..	110	..	..	..	..	118	..	.	..	..
..	+14	..	..	.	..	..	..	..	..	..	..	..
..	..	+671	340	..	..	..	..	331	..	..	..	..
..	..	..	340	..	..	..	..	331	..	..	..	..
..	..	+30	13	..	..	..	..	17	..	..	..	..
..	..	..	13	..	..	..	..	17	..	..	..	..
..	..	+11	6	..	..	..	..	5	..	..	..	..
..	..	..	6	..	..	..	..	5	..	..	..	..
..	..	+2	1	..	.	..	..	1	..	..	..	..
..	..	..	1	..	..	..	..	1	..	..	..	..
..	..	+8	6	..	..	..	..	2	..	..	..	..
..	..	..	6	..	..	.	..	2	..	..	..	..
..	−28	−28	..	..	..	..	15	..	..	..	..	13
..	..	+276	..	..	..	..	..	276	..	..	..	..
..	..	..	..	..	..	..	..	276	..	..	..	..
..	..	+13	13	..	..	..	..	..	..	..	..	..
..	..	..	13	..	..	..	..	..	..	..	..	..
−9	+9	+9	6	..	..	..	..	3	..	..	..	..
..	..	..	6	..	..	..	..	3	..	..	..	..
..	−6	+207	16	..	..	..	3	197	..	..	..	3
..	..	..	..	..		..	..	184	..	..	..	..
..	..	..	16	.	..	..	..	13	..	..	..	..
..	..	+20	9	..	..	..	..	11	..	..	..	..
..	..	..	9	..	..	..	..	11	..	..	..	..
..	..	+53	35	..	..	..	..	18	..	..	..	..
..	..	+53	35	..	..	..	..	18	..	..	..	..
..	..	+16	6	..	..	..	..	10	..	..	..	..
..	..	..	6	..	..	..	..	10	..	..	..	..
..	..	+24	19	..	..	..	..	5	..	..	..	..
..	..	..	19	..	..	..	..	5	..	..	..	..
..	..	+13	10	..	..	..	..	3	.	..	..	..
..	..	..	10	..	..	..	..	3	..	..	..	..
..	..	..	3,208	..	2,946	..	..	3,091	..	3,202	..	..
..	..	..	2,420	..	2,946	..	..	2,257	..	3,202	..	..
..	..	..	788	..	..	..	..	834	..	..	..	..
..	..	..	..	..	1	..	..	..	..	..	..	..
..	..	..	..	.	1	..	..	.	..	..	..	..
.	..	..	48	..	82	..	.	58	..	73	..	..
	..	.	48	..	82	..	..	58	.	73	..	..

TABLE XVIII—PART A

Variation of Population

Tribe and locality.	Persons.						Variation		
	1931.	1921.	1911.	1901.	1891.	1881.	1921 to 1931.	1911 to 1921.	1901 to 1911.
1	2	3	4	5	6	7	8	9	10
NAGARCHI—*concld.*									
Seoni District	*1,782*	..	*1,886*	..	*1,950*	..	..	..	..
Hindu	713	..	1,886	..	..	..	..	..	..
Tribal	1,069	..	..	..	..	..	..	..	..
Narsinghpur District	*16*	..	..	..	*5*	..	..	..	..
Tribal	16	..	..	..	..	..	..	..	..
Chhindwara District	*951*	..	*925*	..	*593*	..	..	..	..
Hindu	414	..	925	..	..	..	..	..	..
Tribal	537	..	..	..	..	..	..	..	..
Nagpur District	*123*	..	*140*	..	*100*	..	..	..	..
Hindu	123	..	140	..	..	..	..	..	..
Bhandara District	*1,353*	..	*1,136*	..	*1,168*	..	..	..	..
Hindu	1,353	..	1,136	..	..	..	..	..	..
Balaghat District	*1,621*	..	*1,579*	..	*2,044*	..	..	..	..
Hindu	1,621	..	1,579	..	..	..	..	..	..
Raipur District	*34*	..	*7*	..	*250*	..	..	..	..
Hindu	34	..	7	..	..	..	..	..	..
Bilaspur District	*37*	..	*60*	..	*47*	..	..	..	..
Hindu	37	..	60	..	..	..	..	..	..
Drug District	*265*	..	*259*	..	..	..	..	..	..
Hindu	265	..	259	..	..	..	..	..	..
Berar	**11**	..	..	..	..	..	..	..	..
Hindu	11	..	..	..	..	..	..	..	..
Amraoti District	*11*	..	..	..	..	..	..	..	..
Hindu	11	..	..	..	..	..	..	..	..
NAGASIA									
Central Provinces and Berar	**1,122**	**26**	**212**	..	..	..	**+1,096**	**−186**	..
Hindu	924	26	212	..	..	..	+898	−186	..
Tribal	198	..	..	..	..	..	+198	..	..
Jubbulpore District	..	*1*	..	..	..	..	*−1*	*+1*	..
Hindu	..	1	..	..	..	..	−1	+1	..
Wardha District	..	*13*	..	..	..	..	*−13*	*+13*	..
Hindu	..	13	..	..	..	..	−13	+13	..
Nagpur District	..	*4*	..	..	..	..	*−4*	*+4*	..
Hindu	..	4	..	..	..	..	−4	+4	..
Bhandara District	*13*	..	..	..	..	..	*+13*	..	..
Hindu	13	..	..	..	..	..	+13	..	..
Balaghat District	*111*	..	..	..	..	..	*+111*	..	..
Hindu	111	..	..	..	..	..	+111	..	..
Raipur District	*203*	..	..	..	..	..	*+203*	..	..
Hindu	203	..	..	..	..	..	+203	..	..
Bilaspur District	*795*	*8*	*212*	..	..	..	*+787*	*−204*	..
Hindu	597	8	212	..	..	..	+589	−204	..
Tribal	198	..	..	..	..	..	+198	..	..

(Increase + Decrease —). 1891 to 1901.	1881 to 1891.	Net variation 1881 to 1931 (Increase + Decrease —).	Males. 1931.	1921.	1911.	1901.	1881.	Females. 1931.	1921.	1911	1901	1881.
11	12	13	14	15	16	17	18	19	20	21	22	23
..	..	..	*857*	..	*893*	..	..	*925*	..	*993*	..	..
..	..	..	345	..	893	..	..	368	..	993	..	..
..	..	..	512	..	..	..	..	557	..	..	..	..
..	..	..	*8*	..	..	..	..	*8*	..	..	..	..
..	..	..	8	..		..	..	8	..	..	..	..
..	..	..	*466*	..	*452*	..	..	*485*	..	*473*	..	..
..	..	..	198	..	452	..	..	216	..	473	..	..
..	..	..	268	..	..	..	.	269	..	..	..	..
..	..	..	*64*	..	*61*	..	..	*59*	..	*79*	..	..
..	..	..	64	..	61	..	..	59	..	79	..	..
..	..	..	*798*	..	*565*	..	..	*555*	..	*571*	..	..
..	..	..	798	..	565	..	..	555	..	571	..	..
..	..	..	*789*	..	*752*	..	..	*832*	..	*827*	..	..
..	..	..	789	..	752	..	..	832	..	827	..	..
..	..	..	*22*	..	*3*	..	..	*12*	..	*4*	..	..
..	..	..	22	..	3	..	..	12	..	4	..	..
..	..	..	*15*	..	*27*	..	..	*22*	..	*33*	..	..
..	..	..	15	..	27	..	..	22	..	33	..	..
..	..	..	*134*	..	*110*	..	..	*131*	..	*149*	..	..
..	..	..	134	..	110	..	..	131	..	149	..	..
..	..	..	*7*	..	..	..	..	*4*	..	..	..	..
..	..	..	7	..	..	..	..	4	..	..	..	..
..	..	..	*7*	..	..	..	..	*4*	..	..	..	..
..	..	..	7	..	..	..	..	4	..	..	..	..
..	..	..	**571**	**14**	**112**	..	..	**551**	**12**	**100**	..	..
..	..	..	474	14	112	..	..	450	12	100	..	..
..	..	..	97	..	..	..	..	101	..	..	..	..
..	..	..	..	*1*	..	..	..	..	..	..	..	..
..	..	..	..	1	..	..	..	..	..	..	..	..
..	..	..	..	*8*	..	..	..	..	*5*	..	..	..
..	..	..	..	8	..	..	..	..	5	..	..	..
..	..	..	..	..	..	..	..	..	*4*	..	..	..
..	..	..	..	..	..	..	..	..	4	..	..	..
..	..	..	*8*	..	..	..	..	*5*	..	..	..	..
..	..	..	8	..	..	..	..	5	..	..	..	..
..	..	..	*67*	..	..	..	..	*44*	..	..	..	..
..	..	..	67	..	..	..	..	44	..	..	..	..
..	..	..	*98*	..	..	..	..	*105*	..	..	..	..
..	..	..	98	..	..	..	..	105	..	..	..	..
..	..	..	*398*	*5*	*112*	..	..	*397*	*3*	*100*	..	..
..	..	..	301	5	112	..	..	296	[illegible]	100	..	..
..	..	..	97	..	..	..	..	101	..	..	..	..

Tribe and locality.	Persons. 1931.	1921.	1911.	1901.	1891.	1881.	Variation 1921 to 1931.	1911 to 1921.	1901 to 1911.
1	2	3	4	5	6	7	8	9	10
ORAON									
Central Provinces and Berar ..	**6,950**	**176**	**4,328**	..	**1,151**	..	**+6,774**	**−4,152**	..
Hindu ..	5,929	174	4,231	..	..	..	..	..	..
Tribal ..	1,021	2	97	..	..	..	..	..	..
Jubbulpore District	..	..	..	..	*3*	..	..	..	..
Mandla District ..	..	..	..	..	*2*	..	..	..	..
Chhindwara District	*5*	..	..	..	..	..	*+5*	..	..
Hindu ..	5	..	..	..	..	..	+5	..	..
Raipur District ..	*1,886*	..	*1,443*	..	*24*	..	*+1,886*	*−1,443*	..
Hindu ..	1,775	..	1,398	..	..	..	+1,775	−1,398	..
Tribal ..	111	..	45	..	..	..	+111	−45	..
Bilaspur District ..	*5,003*	*176*	*2,876*	..	*1,122*	..	*+4,827*	*−2,700*	..
Hindu ..	4,093	174	2,824	..	..	..	..	..	..
Tribal ..	910	2	52	..	..	..	..	..	..
Drug District ..	*56*	..	*9*	..	..	..	*+56*	*−9*	..
Hindu ..	56	..	9	..	..	..	+56	−9	..
PARDHAN									
Central Provinces and Berar ..	**115,813**	**91,692**	**114,877**	**14,382**	**83,654**	**60,279**	**+24,121**	**−23,185**	**+100,495**
Hindu ..	61,182	17,914	22,756	..	..	..	+43,268	−4,842	..
Tribal ..	54,630	73,778	92,121	..	..	..	−19,148	−18,343	..
Christian ..	1	..	..	..	..	..	+1	..	..
Saugor District ..	..	..	*10*	..	*44*	*8*	..	*−10*	..
Hindu ..	..	..	10	..	..	..	..	−10	..
Damoh District ..	..	..	..	..	*27*	..	..	..	..
Jubbulpore District	*1,700*	*472*	*2,036*	..	*1,264*	*260*	*+1,228*	*−1,564*	..
Hindu ..	1,652	333	273	..	..	..	+1,319	+60	..
Tribal ..	48	139	1,763	..	..	..	−91	−1,624	..
Mandla District ..	*12,393*	*3,727*	*11,538*	..	*2,007*	*1,246*	*+8,666*	*−7,811*	..
Hindu ..	5,756	969	385	..	..	..	+4,787	+584	..
Tribal ..	6,637	2,758	11,153	..	..	..	+3,879	−8,395	..
Seoni District ..	*15,615*	*11,670*	*17,725*	..	*13,035*	*8,210*	*+945*	*−3,055*	..
Hindu ..	26	506	179	..	..	..	−480	+327	..
Tribal ..	15,589	14,164	17,546	..	..	..	+1,425	−3,382	..
Narsinghpur District	*1,470*	*1,990*	*1,887*	..	*3,395*	*820*	*−520*	*+103*	..
Hindu ..	123	753	188	..	..	..	−630	+565	..
Tribal ..	1,347	1,237	1,699	..	..	..	+110	−462	..
Hoshangabad District	*2,092*	*1,511*	*2,079*	..	*3,596*	*1,191*	*+551*	*−538*	..
Hindu ..	804	884	787	..	..	..	−80	+97	..
Tribal ..	1,288	657	1,292	..	..	..	+631	−635	..
Nimar District ..	*117*	*24*	*108*	..	..	*5*	*+93*	*−84*	*+108*
Hindu ..	34	18	59	..	..	..	+16	−41	..
Tribal ..	83	6	49	..	..	..	+77	−43	..
Betul District ..	*3,286*	*2,366*	*4,113*	..	*2,340*	*1,881*	*+920*	*−1,747*	*+4,113*
Hindu ..	657	63	198	..	..	..	+594	−135	..
Tribal ..	2,629	2,303	3,915	..	..	..	+326	−1,612	..

(Increase + Decrease −).		Net variation 1881 to 1931 (Increase + Decrease −).	Males.					Females.				
1891 to 1901.	1881 to 1891.		1931.	1921.	1911.	1901.	1881.	1931.	1921.	1911.	1901.	1881.
11	12	13	14	15	16	17	18	19	20	21	22	23
..	..	..	3,392	81	2,190	..	..	3,558	95	2,138	..	..
..	..	..	2,860	79	2,137	..	..	3,069	95	2,094	..	..
..	..	..	532	2	53	..	..	489	..	44	..	..
..	..	..	..	..	..	..	..	..	..	..	..	..
..	..	..	..	..	..	..	..	..	..	..	..	..
..	..	..	3	..	..	..	..	2	..	..	..	..
..	..	..	3	..	..	..	..	2	..	..	..	..
..	..	..	892	..	728	..	..	994	..	715	..	..
..	..	..	830	..	706	..	..	945	..	692	..	..
..	..	..	62	..	22	..	..	49	..	23	..	..
..	..	..	2,469	81	1,453	..	..	2,534	95	1,423	..	..
..	..	..	1,999	79	1,422	..	..	2,094	95	1,402	..	..
..	..	..	470	2	31	..	..	440	..	21	..	..
..	..	..	28	..	9	..	..	28	..	..	..	..
..	..	..	28	..	9	..	..	28	..	..	..	..
−69,272	+23,375	+55,534	**56,500**	**45,870**	**55,905**	**7,147**	**29,904**	**59,313**	**45,822**	**58,972**	**7,235**	**30,375**
..	..	..	30,235	8,863	11,026	..	..	30,947	9,051	11,730	..	..
..	..	..	26,265	37,007	44,879	..	..	28,365	36,771	47,242	..	..
..	..	..	..	..	..	..	..	1	..	..	..	..
−44	+36	−8	..	..	6	..	4	..	..	4	..	4
..	..	..	..	..	6	..	..	..	..	4	..	..
−27	+27	..	..	..	..	..	..	..	..	..	..	..
−1,264	+1,004	+1,440	830	222	983	..	144	870	250	1,053	..	116
..	..	..	813	169	133	..	..	839	164	140	..	..
..	..	..	17	53	850	..	..	31	86	913	..	..
−2,007	+761	+11,147	6,394	1,835	5,688	..	629	5,999	1,892	5,550	..	617
..	..	..	3,075	487	200	..	..	2,681	482	185	..	..
..	..	..	3,319	1,348	5,488	..	..	3,318	1,410	5,665	..	..
−13,035	+4,825	+7,405	7,518	7,931	8,413	..	4,041	8,097	6,739	9,312	..	4,169
..	..	..	13	266	89	..	..	13	240	90	..	..
..	..	..	7,505	7,665	8,324	..	..	8,084	6,499	9,222	..	..
−3,395	+2,575	+650	738	997	912	..	401	732	993	975	..	419
..	..	..	61	394	86	..	..	62	359	102	..	..
..	..	..	677	603	826	..	..	670	634	873	..	..
−3,596	+2,405	+901	1,022	732	971	..	578	1,070	809	1,108	..	613
..	..	..	392	438	367	..	..	412	446	420	..	..
..	..	..	630	294	604	..	..	658	363	688	..	..
..	−5	+112	51	16	57	..	3	66	8	51	..	2
..	..	..	13	10	30	..	..	21	8	29	..	..
..	..	..	38	6	27	..	..	45	..	22	..	..
−2,340	+459	+1,405	1,635	1,150	2,027	..	939	1,651	1,216	2,086	..	942
..	..	..	327	31	109	..	..	330	32	89	..	..
..	..	..	1,308	1,119	1,918	..	..	1,321	1,184	1,997	..	..

Tribe and locality.	Persons. 1931.	1921.	1911	1901.	1891.	1881.	Variation 1921 to 1931.	1911 to 1921.	1901 to 1911.
1	2	3	4	5	6	7	8	9	10
PARDHAN—*contd.*									
Chhindwara District ..	*8,698*	*7,010*	*9,161*	..	*4,293*	*7,597*	*+1,688*	*−2,121*	*+9,161*
Hindu ..	375	1,098	194	..	..	..	−723	+904	..
Tribal ..	8,322	5,942	8,967	..	..	..	+2,380	−3,025	..
Christian ..	1	..	..	..	..	..	+1	..	..
Wardha District ..	*8,511*	*7,534*	*8,330*	..	*5,150*	*1,699*	*+977*	*−796*	*+8,330*
Hindu ..	1,409	1,209	1,560	..	..	..	+200	−351	..
Tribal ..	7,102	6,325	6,770	..	..	..	+777	−445	..
Nagpur District ..	*6,309*	*5,573*	*6,500*	..	*5,159*	*1,952*	*+736*	*−927*	*+6,500*
Hindu ..	6,187	746	3,968	..	..	..	+5,441	−3,222	..
Tribal ..	122	4,827	2,532	..	..	..	−4,705	+2,295	..
Chanda District ..	*21,243*	*17,708*	*19,890*	..	*17,158*	*15,388*	*+3,535*	*−2,182*	*+19,890*
Hindu ..	16,450	2,710	1,500	..	..	..	+13,740	+1,210	..
Tribal ..	4,793	14 998	18,390	..	..	..	−10,205	−3,392	..
Bhandara District ..	*2,874*	*2,112*	*2,815*	..	*4,155*	*3,175*	*+762*	*−703*	*+2,815*
Hindu ..	1,056	399	570	..	..	..	+657	−171	..
Tribal ..	1,818	1,713	2,245	..	..	..	+105	−532	..
Balaghat District ..	*4,264*	*5,150*	*4,843*	..	*5,172*	*4,275*	*−886*	*+307*	*+4,843*
Hindu ..	965	2,743	305	..	..	..	−1,778	+2,438	..
Tribal ..	3,299	2,407	4,538	..	..	..	+892	−2,131	..
Raipur District ..	*964*	*87*	*1,280*	..	*834*	*1,086*	*+877*	*−1,193*	*+1,280*
Hindu ..	842	87	1,027	..	..	..	+755	−940	..
Tribal ..	122	..	253	..	..	..	+122	−253	..
Bilaspur District ..	*2,653*	*132*	*2,730*	..	*2,789*	*458*	*+2,521*	*−2,598*	*+2,730*
Hindu ..	2,446	59	2,175	..	..	..	+2,387	−2,116	..
Tribal ..	207	73	555	..	..	..	+134	−482	..
Drug District ..	*433*	*590*	*732*	..	..	..	*−157*	*−142*	*+732*
Hindu ..	409	558	613	..	..	..	−149	−55	..
Tribal ..	24	32	119	..	..	..	−8	−87	..
Berar ..	**23,191**	**20,976**	**19,100**	**14,382**	**12,936**	**11,028**	**+2,215**	**+1,876**	**+4,718**
Hindu ..	21,991	4,779	8,765	..	..	..	+17,212	−3,986	..
Tribal ..	1,200	16,197	10,335	..	..	..	−14,997	+5,862	..
Amraoti District ..	*529*	*687*	*897*	..	..	..	*−158*	*−210*	..
Hindu ..	310	40	469	..	..	..	+270	−429	..
Tribal ..	219	647	428	..	..	..	−428	+219	..
Akola District ..	*241*	*549*	*149*	..	..	..	*−308*	*+400*	..
Hindu ..	241	249	116	..	..	..	−8	+133	..
Tribal ..	..	300	33	..	..	..	−300	+267	..
Buldana District ..	*16*	*151*	..	..	..	..	*−135*	*+151*	..
Hindu ..	16	..	..	..	..	..	+16	..	..
Tribal ..	..	151	..	..	..	..	−151	+151	..
Yeotmal District ..	*22,405*	*19,589*	*18,051*	..	..	..	*+2,816*	*+1,535*	..
Hindu ..	21,424	4,490	8,180	..	..	..	+16,934	−3,690	..
Tribal ..	981	15,099	9,874	..	..	..	−14,118	+5,225	..
*** PARJA**									
Central Provinces and Berar ..	*34	..	..	..	..	..	..	..	..
Hindu ..	34	..	..	..	..	..	..	..	..
Drug District ..	*34*	..	..	..	..	..	..	..	..
Hindu ..	34	..	..	..	..	..	..	..	..

*Figures previously included with Gonds.

of Selected Tribes.

TABLE XVIII—PART A

(Increase + Decrease —). 1891 to 1901.	1881 to 1891.	Net variation 1881 to 1931 (Increase + Decrease —).	Males. 1931	1921.	1911.	1901.	1881.	Females. 1931.	1921.	1911.	1901.	1881.
11	12	13	14	15	16	17	18	19	20	21	22	23
—4,293	*—3,304*	*+1,101*	*4,270*	*3,387*	*4,512*	..	*3,748*	*4,428*	*3,653*	*4,649*	..	*3,829*
..	..	..	195	503	87	..	..	180	595	107	..	..
..	..	..	4,075	2,884	4,425	..	..	4,247	3,058	4,542	..	..
..	..	..	..	..	..	..	..	1	..	..	..	..
—5,150	*+3,451*	*+6,812*	*3,899*	*3,623*	*4,068*	..	*849*	*4,612*	*3,911*	*4,262*	..	*850*
..	..	..	693	580	748	..	..	716	629	812	..	..
..	..	..	3,206	3,043	3,320	..	..	3,896	3,282	3,450	..	..
—5,159	*+3,207*	*+4,357*	*3,053*	*2,752*	*3,216*	..	*977*	*3,256*	*2,821*	*3,284*	..	*975*
..	..	..	3,009	383	1,974	..	..	3,178	363	1,994	..	..
..	..	..	44	2,369	1,242	..	..	78	2,458	1,290	..	..
—17,458	*+2,070*	*+5,855*	*10,379*	*8,933*	*9,800*	..	*7,573*	*10,864*	*8,775*	*10,090*	..	*7,715*
..	..	..	8.058	1,476	760	..	..	8,392	1,234	740	..	..
..	..	..	2,321	7,457	9.040	..	..	2,472	7,541	9.350	..	..
—4,155	*+980*	*—301*	*1,420*	*1,131*	*1,359*	..	*1,507*	*1,454*	*981*	*1,456*	..	*1,668*
..	..	..	494	224	286	..	..	562	175	284	..	..
..	..	..	926	907	1,073	..	..	892	806	1,172	..	..
—5,172	*+897*	*—11*	*1.982*	*2,341*	*2,355*	..	*2,092*	*2,282*	*2,809*	*2,488*	..	*2,183*
..	..	..	477	1,209	163	..	..	488	1,534	142	..	..
..	..	..	1,505	1,132	2,192	..	..	1,794	1,275	2,346	..	..
—834	*—252*	*—122*	*445*	*49*	*610*	..	*525*	*519*	*38*	*670*	..	*561*
..	..	..	386	49	486	..	..	456	38	541	..	..
..	..	..	59	..	124	..	..	63	..	129	..	..
—2,789	*+2,331*	*+2,195*	*1,247*	*101*	*1,265*	..	*225*	*1,406*	*31*	*1,465*	..	*233*
..	..	..	1,155	59	986	..	..	1,291	..	1,189	..	..
..	..	..	92	42	279	..	..	115	31	276	..	..
..	..	*+433*	*184*	*286*	*334*	..	..	*249*	*304*	*398*	..	..
..	..	..	175	273	280	..	..	234	285	333	..	..
..	..	..	9	13	54	..	..	15	19	65	..	..
+1,446	**+1,908**	**+12,163**	**11,433**	**10,384**	**9,329**	**7,147**	**5,549**	**11,758**	**10,592**	**9,771**	**7,235**	**5,479**
..	..	..	10,899	2,312	4,236	..	..	11,092	2,467	4,529	..	..
..	..	..	534	8,072	5,093	..	..	666	8,125	5,242	..	..
..	..	..	*269*	*324*	*450*	..	..	*260*	*363*	*447*	..	..
..	..	..	158	18	243	..	..	152*	22	226	..	..
..	..	..	111	306	207	..	..	108	341	221	..	..
..	..	..	*124*	*256*	*47*	..	..	*117*	*293*	*102*	..	..
..	..	..	124	115	29	..	..	117	134	87	..	..
..	..	..	..	141	18	..	..	..	159	15	..	..
..	..	..	*6*	*67*	..	..	..	*10*	*84*	..	..	..
..	..	..	6	..	..	..	..	10	..	..	..	..
..	..	..	..	67	..	..	..	..	84	..	..	..
..	..	..	*11,034*	*9,737*	*8,832*	..	..	*11,371*	*9,852*	*9,222*	..	..
..	..	..	10,611	2,179	3,964	..	..	10,813	2,311	4,216	..	..
..	..	..	423	7,558	4,868	..	..	558	7,541	5,006	..	..
..	..	..	**15**	..	..	..	..	**19**	..	..	..	..
..	..	..	15	..	..	..	..	19	..	..	..	..
..	..	..	*15*	..	..	..	..	*19*	..	..	..	..
..	..	..	15	..	..	..	..	19	..	..	..	..

Tribe and locality.	Persons. 1931.	1921.	1911.	1901.	1891.	1881.	Variation 1921 to 1931.	1911 to 1921.	1901 to 1911.
1	2	3	4	5	6	7	8	9	10
SAUNTA									
Central Provinces and Berar ..	**705**	..	**642**	..	..	..	..	..	..
Hindu ..	169	..	424	..	..	..	..	..	..
Tribal ..	536	..	218	..	..	..	..	..	..
Jubbulpore District	*1*	..	..	..	..	..	..	..	..
Hindu ..	1	..	..	..	..	..	..	..	..
Bilaspur District ..	*701*	..	*642*	..	..	..	..	..	..
Hindu ..	168	..	424	..	..	..	..	..	..
Tribal ..	536	..	218	..	..	..	..	..	..
SAWARA OR SAONR									
Central Provinces and Berar ..	**67,116**	**55,703**	**56,913**	**25,531**	**31,768**	**25,834**	**+11,413**	**−1,210**	**+31,382**
Hindu ..	66,059	55,703	56,913	..	..	..	+10,356	−1,210	..
Tribal ..	1,057	..	..	..	..	..	+1,057	..	..
Saugor District ..	*21,867*	*20,400*	*18,527*	*12,891*	*18,448*	*16,109*	*+1,467*	*+1,873*	*+5,636*
Hindu ..	21,817	20,400	18,527	..	..	..	+1,417	+1,873	..
Tribal ..	50	..	..	..	..	..	+50	..	..
Damoh District ..	*6,468*	*4,991*	*6,705*	*3,896*	*4,753*	*3,466*	*+1,477*	*−1,714*	*+2,809*
Hindu ..	6,124	4,991	6,705	..	..	..	+1,133	−1,714	..
Tribal ..	344	..	..	..	..	..	+344	..	..
Jubbulpore District	..	..	*1,496*	*917*	*9*	*2*	..	*−1,496*	*+579*
Hindu ..	..	..	1,496	..	..	..	..	−1,496	..
Mandla District ..	..	..	*4*	*27*	*1*	..	..	*−4*	*−23*
Hindu ..	..	..	4	..	..	..	..	−4	..
Seoni District ..	..	..	..	*8*	..	..	..	..	*−8*
Narsinghpur District	..	..	*917*	*611*	*190*	*120*	..	*−917*	*+306*
Hindu ..	..	..	917	..	..	..	..	−917	..
Hoshangabad District	*498*	..	*303*	*634*	*553*	*894*	*+498*	*−303*	*−331*
Hindu ..	498	..	303	..	..	..	+498	−303	..
Nimar District ..	..	..	..	*16*	..	*1*	..	..	*−16*
Betul District ..	*8*	..	*43*	..	..	..	*+8*	*−43*	*+43*
Hindu ..	8	..	43	..	..	..	+8	−43	..
Chhindwara District	*28*	..	..	*2*	..	..	*+28*	..	*−2*
Hindu ..	28	..	..	..	..	..	+28	..	..
Nagpur District ..	*4*	..	..	..	..	..	*+4*	..	..
Hindu ..	4	..	..	..	..	..	+4	..	..
Chanda District ..	..	*1*	*1*	..	..	..	*−1*	..	*+1*
Hindu ..	..	1	1	..	..	..	−1	..	..
Bhandara District ..	..	..	..	*1*	..	..	..	..	*−1*
Balaghat District ..	..	..	..	*1*	..	..	..	..	*−1*
Raipur District ..	*28,701*	*25,353*	*21,702*	*5,358*	*5,916*	*3,849*	*+3,348*	*+3,651*	*+16,344*
Hindu ..	28,038	25,353	21,702	..	..	..	+2,685	+3,651	..
Tribal ..	663	..	..	..	..	..	+663	..	..

(Increase + Decrease —).		Net variation 1881 to 1931 (Increase + Decrease—).	Males.					Females.				
1891 to 1901.	1881 to 1891.		1931.	1921.	1911.	1901.	1881.	1931.	1921.	1911.	1901.	1881.
11	12	13	14	15	16	17	18	19	20	21	22	23
..	..	..	**354**	..	**327**	..	..	**351**	..	**315**	..	..
..	..	..	90	..	252	..	..	79	..	172	..	..
..	..	..	264	..	75	..	..	272	..	143	..	..
..	..	..	1	..	..	..	..	..	..	..	..	..
..	..	..	1	..	..	..	..	..	..	..	..	..
..	..	..	353	..	327	..	..	351	..	315	..	..
..	..	..	89	..	252	..	..	79	..	172	..	..
..	..	..	264	..	75	..	..	272	..	143	..	..
—6,237	**+5,934**	**+41,282**	**32,948**	**27,342**	**27,725**	**12,341**	**12,990**	**34,168**	**28,361**	**29,188**	**13,190**	**12,844**
..	..	..	32,421	27,342	27,725	..	..	33,638	28,361	29,188	..	..
..	..	..	527	..	..	..	..	530	..	..	..	..
—5,557	+2,339	+5,758	10,859	10,273	9,062	6,207	8,131	11,008	10,127	9,465	6,684	7,978
..	..	..	10,834	10,273	9,062	..	..	10,983	10,127	9,465	..	..
..	..	..	25	..	..	..	..	25	..	..	..	..
—857	+1,287	+3,002	3,190	2,475	3,243	1,885	1,741	3,278	2,516	3,462	2,011	1,725
..	..	..	3,023	2,475	3,243	..	..	3,101	2,516	3,462	..	..
..	..	..	167	..	..	..	..	177	..	..	..	..
+908	+7	—2	..	..	684	447	1	..	..	812	470	1
..	..	..	..	..	684	..	..	..	..	812	..	..
+26	+1	..	..	..	4	..	..	..	..	..	27	..
..	..	..	..	..	4	..	..	..	..	..	..	..
+8	..	..	..	..	..	4	..	..	..	..	4	—
+421	+70	—120	..	..	440	309	59	..	..	477	302	61
..	..	..	..	..	440	..	..	..	..	477	..	..
+81	—341	—396	244	..	160	297	419	254	..	143	337	475
..	..	..	244	..	160	..	..	254	..	143	..	..
+16	—1	—1	..	..	..	9	1	..	..	..	7	..
..	..	+8	4	..	22	..	..	4	..	21	..	..
..	..	..	4	..	22	..	..	4	..	21	..	..
+2	..	+28	19	..	..	2	..	9	..	..	..	..
..	..	..	19	..	..	..	..	9	..	..	..	..
..	..	+4	3	..	..	..	..	1	..	..	..	..
..	..	..	3	..	..	..	..	1	..	..	..	..
..	..	..	..	..	1	..	..	..	1	..	..	..
..	..	..	..	..	1	..	..	..	1	..	..	..
+1	..	..	..	..	..	..	..	..	..	..	1	..
+1	..	..	..	..	..	1	..	..	..	..	..	..
—558	—2,067	+24,852	14,047	12,231	10,631	2,629	1,973	14,654	13,122	11,071	2,729	1,876
..	..	..	13,712	12,231	10,631	..	..	14,326	13,122	11,071	..	..
..	..	..	335	..	..	..	..	328	..	..	..	..

TABLE XVIII—PART A

Variation of Population

Tribe and locality.	Persons. 1931.	1921.	1911.	1901.	1891.	1881.	Variation 1921 to 1931.	1911 to 1921.	1901 to 1911.
1	2	3	4	5	6	7	8	9	10
SAWARA OR SAONR—*concld.*									
Bilaspur District	9,535	4,958	7,206	1,169	1,898	1,393	+4,577	−2,248	+6,037
Hindu	9,535	4,958	7,206	..	..	..	+4,577	−2,248	..
Drug District	..	..	4	..	..	..	..	−4	+4
Hindu	..	..	4	..	..	..	..	−4	..
Berar	7	..	5	..	..	..	+7	−5	+5
Hindu	7	..	5	..	..	..	+7	−5	..
Amraoti District	3	..	5	..	..	..	+3	−5	+5
Hindu	3	..	5	..	..	..	+3	−5	..
Buldana District	4	..	..	..	..	..	+4	..	..
Hindu	4	..	..	..	..	..	+4	..	..

(Increase + Decrease −).		Net variation 1881 to 1931 (Increase + Decrease −).	Males.					Females.				
1891 to 1901.	1881 to 1891.		1931.	1921.	1911.	1901.	1881.	1931.	1921.	1911.	1901.	1881.
11	12	13	14	15	16	17	18	19	20	21	22	23
−729	+505	+8,142	4,575	2,363	3,476	551	665	4,960	2,595	3,730	618	728
..	..	..	4,575	2,363	3,476	..	..	4,960	2,595	3,730	..	..
..	..	..	..	..	2	..	..	..	..	2	..	..
..	..	..	..	..	2	..	..	..	..	2	..	..
..	..	+7	7	..	..	..	..	..	..	5	..	..
..	..	..	7	..	..	..	..	..	...	5	..	..
..	..	..	3	..	..	..	..	..	..	5	..	..
..	..	..	3	..	..	..	..	..	..	5	.	..
..	..	+4	4	..	..	..	..	..	..	..	..	..
..	..	..	4	..	..	..	..	..	..	..	..	..

APPENDIX TO TABLE XVIII—PART A

Variation of Population of Selected Tribes.

Tribe and Tahsil or Taluq.	1931 Persons.	1931 Males.	1931 Females.	1921 Persons.	1921 Males.	1921 Females.
1	2	3	4	5	6	7
ANDH						
Sausar	..	..	..	133	69	64
Wardha	..	..	..	14	7	7
Arvi	..	..	..	5	3	2
Nagpur	..	..	..	33	28	5
Umrer	..	..	..	14	..	14
Saoner	..	..	..	4	..	4
Warora	30	19	11	..	..	..
Garchiroli	..	..	..	3	2	1
Bhandara	..	..	..	103	1	102
Amraoti	7	6	1	..	..	..
Morsi	9	4	5	..	..	..
Chandur	3	1	2	..	..	..
Ellichpur	..	..	..	2	1	1
Daryapur	3	2	1	..	..	..
Akola	1,632	778	854	1,240	835	405
Akot	1	1	..	..	..	..
Balapur	3,621	1,759	1,862	2,730	1,645	1,085
Basim	10,737	5,270	5,467	10,535	4,690	5,845
Mangrulpir	6,956	3,338	3,618	5,345	2,536	2,809
Murtizapur	171	100	71	110	50	60
Chikhli	304	158	146	240	118	122
Mehkar	4,041	2,035	2,006	3,685	1,776	1,909
Khamgaon	335	174	161	437	236	201
Yeotmal	3,230	1,642	1,588	2,676	1,346	1,330
Kelapur	350	184	166	288	145	143
Darwha	8,035	4,991	3,044	10,261	5,020	5,041
Pusad	19,084	9,358	9,726	14,556	7,107	7,449
BAIGA						
Saugor	..	..	..	1	1	..
Jubbulpore	2,305	1,144	1,161	1,399	670	729
Sihora	316	151	165	1,166	511	655
Murwara	44	28	16	63	38	25
Patan	..	..	..	11	3	8
Mandla	7,193	3,594	3,599	6,135	3,041	3,094
Dindori	7,186	3,581	3,605	6,080	2,996	3,084
Niwas	5,559	2,795	2,764	4,087	2,151	1,936
Seoni	175	80	95	23	8	15
Lakhnadon	484	240	244	321	63	258
Gadarwara	..	..	..	106	54	52
Chhindwara	48	35	13	20	6	14
Amarwara	4	2	2	..	..	..
Nagpur	..	..	..	3	2	1
Saoner	3	3	..	..	..	..
Bhandara	..	..	..	5	2	3
Balaghat	762	355	407	1,087	659	428
Baihar	4,877	2,426	2,451	3,870	1,928	1,942
Waraseoni	1	1	..	94	44	50
Baloda Bazar	279	145	134	..	..	..
Dhamtari	107	48	59	..	..	..
Bilaspur	1,028	515	513	..	..	..
Mungeli	282	147	135	3	2	1
Janjgir	749	329	420	402	230	172
Katghora	345	163	182	..	..	..
Bemetara	220	117	103	201	..	201
Sanjari Balod	35	19	16	..	..	..
Mehkar	..	..	..	1	1	..
Wun	1	..	1	..	..	..
BHAINA						
Mandla	812	372	440	..	..	..
Dindori	201	105	96	..	..	..
Bhandara	1	1	..	..	..	..
Raipur	4	4	..	..	..	..
Mahasamund	170	75	95	..	..	..
Dhamtari	28	11	17	..	..	..
Bilaspur	10,905	5,443	5,462	7,739	4,525	3,214
Mungeli	4	3	1	..	..	..
Janjgir	4,094	2,000	2,094	3,435	1,740	1,695
Katghora	228	115	113	349	172	177
BHARIA-BHUMIA						
Banda	1	1	..	..	..	..
Damoh	317	154	163	282	131	151
Hatta	442	194	248	764	410	354
Jubbulpore	3,445	1,647	1,798	3,307	1,566	1,741
Sihora	8,942	4,226	4,716	10,943	5,375	5,568
Murwara	14,890	7,181	7,709	9,966	4,737	5,229
Patan	1,729	834	895	2,087	980	1,107
BHARIA-BHUMIA—*concld.*						
Mandla	1	..	1	41	24	17
Dindori	1,432	696	736	1,211	613	598
Niwas	48	23	25	79	28	51
Seoni	664	325	339	575	262	313
Lakhnadon	872	422	450	832	4,8	414
Narsinghpur	887	483	404	990	444	546
Gadarwara	1,258	638	620	964	524	440
Hoshangabad	4	3	1	356	163	193
Sohagpur	754	380	374	146	69	77
Burhanpur	3	2	1	..	..	..
Betul	..	..	..	501	501	..
Multai	1	1	..	30	4	26
Bhainsdehi	..	..	..	1,065	1,065	..
Chhindwara	4,806	2,364	2,442	4,116	1,917	2,199
Sausar	..	..	..	35	22	13
Amarwara	2,393	1,151	1,242	2,373	1,030	1,343
Nagpur	..	..	..	13	5	8
Ramtek	4	4	..	93	53	40
Saoner	..	..	..	36	15	21
Bhandara	314	57	257	61	31	30
Balaghat	46	19	27	160	160	..
Baihar	3	3	..	168	152	16
Waraseoni	141	66	75	146	60	86
Baloda Bazar	11	6	5	..	..	..
Bilaspur	4,894	2,402	2,492	4,448	2,137	2,311
Mungeli	3,683	1,680	2,003	1,877	1,115	762
Janjgir	271	141	130	277	119	158
Katghora	478	234	244	710	296	414
Bemetara	818	396	422	..	..	..
Sanjari Balod	17	12	5	..	..	..
Akot	250	120	130	..	..	..
***BHATTRA**						
Mahasamund	60	39	21	..	..	..
Baloda Bazar	303	153	150	..	..	..
Drug	24	7	17	..	..	..
Bemetara	21	9	12	..	..	..
Yeotmal	2	2	..	..	..	..
BHIL						
Saugor	9	4	5	..	..	..
Jubbulpore	8	5	3	3	1	2
Sihora	1	1	..	..	..	..
Murwara	2	2	..	19	..	19
Patan	..	..	..	1	..	1
Dindori	4	1	3	..	..	..
Narsinghpur	1	1	..	..	..	..
Hoshangabad	25	11	14	..	..	..
Sohagpur	1	1	..	..	..	..
Seoni-Malwa	1	1	..	..	..	..
Khandwa	22,379	11,230	11,149	20,534	10,396	10,138
Burhanpur	2,468	1,262	1,206	977	208	769
Harsud	146	76	70	123	58	65
Sausar	1	1	..	..	..	..
Wardha	13	9	4	..	..	..
Nagpur	..	..	..	6	2	4
Ramtek	9	7	2	..	..	..
Bhandara	2	2	..	..	..	..
Gondia	8	4	4	..	..	..
Amraoti	12	9	3	..	..	..
Morsi	2	..	2	..	..	..
Ellichpur	80	40	40	92	45	47
Daryapur	..	..	..	96	51	45
Melghat	56	37	19	..	..	..
Akola	63	45	18	..	..	..
Akot	755	376	379	435	213	222
Balapur	128	61	67	190	100	90
Basim	105	57	48	142	62	80
Mangrulpir	27	16	11	..	..	..
Murtizapur	4	2	2	..	..	..
Chikhli	956	481	475	551	287	264
Mehkar	41	19	22	188	86	102
Khamgaon	105	56	49	5	5	..
Jalgaon	34	16	18	195	91	104
Malkapur	149	75	74	148	86	62
Kelapur	56	27	29	69	36	33
Darwha	71	36	35	225	109	116
Pusad	2,581	1,258	1,323	866	437	429

*Figures for 1921 are not available; they were included under Gonds.

APPENDIX TO TABLE XVIII—PART A

Variation of Population of Selected Tribes.

Tribe and Tahsil or Taluq.	1931. Persons.	1931. Males.	1931. Females.	1921. Persons.	1921. Males.	1921. Females.
1	2	3	4	5	6	7
BHUINHAR						
Saugor	..	..	..	48	23	25
Mandla	..	..	..	14	4	10
Burhanpur	..	..	..	45	16	29
Wardha	..	..	..	15	15	..
Arvi	2	2	..	..	..	..
Raipur	21	9	12	..	..	..
Mahasamund	6	2	4	..	..	..
Bilaspur	179	85	94	110	110	..
Janjgir	206	91	115	390	390	..
Katghora	836	441	395	38	24	14
BHUNJIA						
Banda	2	1	1	..	..	..
Jubbulpore	64	34	30	..	..	..
Patan	3	2	1	..	..	..
Seoni	6	3	3	..	..	..
Burhanpur	11	7	4	..	..	..
Harsud	29	16	13	..	..	..
Betul	12	6	6	..	..	..
Chhindwara	10	..	10	..	..	..
Wardha	13	8	5	..	..	..
Arvi	5	2	3	..	..	..
Hinganghat	7	4	3	..	..	..
Nagpur	108	55	53	..	..	..
Ramtek	12	7	5	..	..	..
Katol	13	7	6	..	..	..
Saoner	3	2	1	..	..	..
Garchiroli	3	2	1	..	..	..
Raipur	110	53	57	5	3	2
Mahasamund	6,834	3,378	3,456	6,214	2,941	3,273
Baloda Bazar	32	12	20	32	16	16
Dhamtari	282	143	139	125	56	69
Bilaspur	51	30	21	..	..	..
Mungeli	8	4	4	..	..	..
Janjgir	40	19	21	..	..	..
Drug	8	5	3	..	..	..
Amraoti	1	1	..	..	..	..
Akot	3	3	..	..	..	..
Jalgaon	3	..	3	..	..	..
Darwha	2	1	1	..	..	..
Pusad	14	..	14	..	..	..
BINJHWAR						
Rehli	2	2	..	..	..	..
Seoni	165	72	93	229	106	123
Hoshangabad	..	..	..	21	12	9
Amarwara	..	..	..	3	3	..
Nagpur	..	..	..	1	1	..
Ramtek	89	42	47	86	34	52
Umrer	..	..	..	14	5	9
Chanda	35	13	22	11	..	11
Warora	26	11	15	1	..	1
Brahmapuri	141	57	84	148	70	78
Garchiroli	71	35	36	85	41	44
Sironcha	..	..	..	3	..	3
Bhandara	872	425	447	779	367	412
Gondia	2,260	1,119	1,141	2,630	1,372	1,258
Sakoli	605	298	307	568	289	279
Balaghat	4,490	2,211	2,279	2,775	1,093	1,682
Baihar	118	61	57	114	44	70
Waraseoni	3,651	1,755	1,896	3,382	1,726	1,656
Raipur	39	28	11	6	6	..
Mahasamund	24,336	11,943	12,393	3,748	867	2,881
Baloda Bazar	4,837	2,355	2,482	1,624	1,624	..
Dhamtari	11	4	7	..	..	..
Bilaspur	3,207	1,708	1,499	3,033	1,424	1,609
Janjgir	3,141	1,564	1,577	3,241	1,630	1,611
Mungeli	18	9	9	..	..	..
Katghora	6,220	3,109	3,111	5,518	3,149	2,369
Amraoti	7	7	..	..	..	..
Chandur	1	1	..	95	43	52
Ellichpur	17	10	7	13	8	5
Melghat	..	..	..	1	1	..
Akola	71	36	35	68	30	38
Akot	140	71	69	19	12	7
Yeotmal	..	..	..	26	13	13
Darwha	15	9	6	..	..	..
Pusad	..	..	..	42	20	22
Kelapur	18	6	12	..	..	..
DHANWAR						
Saugor	..	..	..	1	1	..
Khurai	..	..	..	6	2	4
Jubbulpore	1	1	..	420	176	244
Raipur	..	..	..	12	4	8
Mahasamund	19	11	8	75	40	35
Baloda Bazar	919	472	447	714	344	370
Bilaspur	2,621	1,275	1,346	1,887	919	968
Mungeli	17	12	5	1,382	40	1,342
Janjgir	2,241	1,097	1,144	2,439	1,237	1,202
Katghora	7,892	3,984	3,908	4,931	3,234	1,697
Drug	..	..	..	16	8	8
Bemetara	11	4	7	161	73	88
Sanjari Balod	9	6	3	2	..	2
Jalgaon	2,536	1,262	1,274	..	..	..
Malkapur	2,663	1,358	1,305	..	..	..
GADBA		Nil				
*** GOND**						
Saugor	5,155	2,536	2,619	4,828	2,443	2,385
Khurai	728	357	371	745	361	384
Rehli	22,457	11,112	11,345	21,435	10,522	10,913
Banda	2,409	1,215	1,194	2,033	1,025	1,008
Damoh	20,610	10,197	10,413	15,822	7,898	7,924
Hatta	6,754	3,375	3,379	6,239	3,228	3,011
Jubbulpore	39,345	19,537	19,808	37,109	18,258	18,851
Sihora	16,565	8,014	8,551	17,864	8,565	9,299
Murwara	17,197	8,361	8,836	13,613	6,644	6,969
Patan	20,976	10,040	10,936	22,668	11,299	11,369
Mandla	82,522	40,270	42,252	73,113	35,729	37,384
Dindori	68,486	33,424	35,062	57,064	28,025	29,039
Niwas	68,128	33,657	34,471	55,607	27,581	28,026
Seoni	72,950	34,813	38,137	69,490	33,341	36,149
Lakhnadon	62,981	30,370	32,611	51,208	23,572	27,636
Narsinghpur	24,413	11,708	12,705	24,507	11,992	12,515
Gadarwara	17,832	8,692	9,140	17,731	8,555	9,176
Hoshangabad	15,334	7,564	7,770	13,945	6,750	7,195
Harda	6,940	3,479	3,461	6,465	3,236	3,229
Sohagpur	20,496	10,049	10,447	19,373	9,188	10,185
Seoni-Malwa	5,851	2,868	2,983	5,656	2,735	2,921
Khandwa	3,642	1,825	1,817	2,881	1,552	1,329
Burhanpur	1,279	691	588	939	472	467
Harsud	5,490	2,795	2,695	4,026	2,049	1,977
Betul	56,585	27,601	28,984	50,307	25,019	25,288
Multai	28,231	13,777	14,454	25,146	12,224	12,922
Bhainsdehi	26,786	13,124	13,662	24,289	11,744	12,545
Chhindwara	85,462	41,672	43,790	72,291	35,787	36,504
Sausar	45,962	22,146	23,816	37,585	18,003	19,582
Amarwara	45,384	21,825	23,559	39,238	18,810	20,428
Wardha	16,171	7,846	8,325	14,397	7,396	7,001
Hinganghat	9,371	4,527	4,844	7,418	3,518	3,900
Arvi	17,653	8,820	8,833	15,259	7,565	7,694
Nagpur	15,842	7,943	7,899	12,928	6,423	6,505
Ramtek	15,829	7,955	7,874	14,020	6,918	7,102
Umrer	6,028	2,914	3,114	5,026	2,492	2,534
Katol	11,246	5,574	5,672	10,581	5,214	5,367
Saoner	4,057	2,085	1,972	3,686	1,852	1,834
Chanda	21,004	10,433	10,571	17,019	8,575	8,444
Warora	11,736	5,836	5,900	10,522	5,329	5,193
Brahmapuri	12,749	6,223	6,526	12,501	5,765	6,736
Garchiroli	33,606	16,638	16,968	43,848	21,588	22,260
Sironcha	16,263	8,091	8,172	27,087	13,393	13,694
Bhandara	15,958	7,855	8,103	13,487	6,564	6,923
Gondia	30,651	15,124	15,527	28,794	13,708	15,086
Sakoli	31,680	15,305	16,375	31,266	15,032	16,234
Balaghat	20,149	9,925	10,224	15,346	8,018	7,328
Baihar	48,510	24,066	24,444	41,058	20,367	20,691
Waraseoni	33,360	16,106	17,254	32,428	15,624	16,804
Raipur	12,237	5,901	6,336	9,478	4,193	5,285
Mahasamund	124,341	60,266	64,075	108,780	50,430	58,350
Baloda Bazar	39,959	18,943	21,016	37,330	17,604	19,726
Dhamtari	62,739	30,449	32,290	65,989	29,464	36,525
Bilaspur	83,768	40,675	43,093	79,604	37,881	41,723
Mungeli	26,215	12,283	13,932	18,327	8,527	9,800
Janjgir	23,490	11,078	12,412	25,561	12,147	13,414
Katghora	38,888	19,627	19,261	28,677	13,361	15,316
Drug	24,310	11,104	13,206	22,516	10,061	12,455
Bemetara	23,847	10,950	12,897	20,863	9,658	11,205
Sanjari Balod	67,475	32,608	34,867	61,300	29,530	31,770
Amraoti	2,695	1,303	1,392	1,956	969	987
Morsi	7,739	3,865	3,874	6,894	3,406	3,488
Chandur	7,860	3,902	3,958	7,648	3,735	3,913
Ellichpur	1,687	846	841	1,316	695	621

† figures include Marias, Murias, Bhattras and Parjas.

APPENDIX TO TABLE XVIII—PART A

Variation of Population of Selected Tribes.

Tribe and Tahsil or Taluq.	1931. Persons.	1931. Males.	1931. Females	1921. Persons.	1921. Males.	1921. Females.
1	2	3	4	5	6	7
GOND—*concld.*						
Daryapur ..	490	242	248	417	205	212
Melghat ..	3,183	1,570	1,613	2,786	1,364	1,422
Akola ..	1,276	651	625	1,080	520	560
Akot ..	896	449	447	716	375	341
Balapur ..	184	85	99	101	45	56
Basim ..	9	5	4	3	1	2
Mangrulpir ..	421	230	191	299	109	190
Murtizapur ..	1,020	497	523	1,061	629	432
Chikhli ..	111	62	49	114	51	63
Mehkar ..	37	16	21	219	109	110
Khamgaon ..	141	35	106	110	59	51
Jalgaon ..	85	40	45	388	173	215
Malkapur ..	6	3	3	80	44	36
Yeotmal ..	15,668	7,819	7,849	14,680	7,280	7,400
Kelapur ..	30,996	15,099	15,897	26,322	12,890	13,432
Wun ..	15,425	7,638	7,787	13,599	6,808	6,791
Darwha ..	6,465	2,638	3,827	6,338	3,097	3,241
Pusad ..	459	245	214	458	231	227
HALBA						
Saugor ..	..	..	..	2	2	..
Jubbulpore ..	22	10	12	57	5	52
Patan ..	12	8	4	..	..	..
Mandla ..	..	..	..	2	2	..
Seoni ..	698	362	336	836	401	435
Sohagpur ..	..	..	..	113	113	..
Khandwa ..	224	111	113	348	167	181
Burhanpur ..	12	3	9	..	..	..
Harsud ..	10	6	4	..	..	..
Chhindwara	9	6	3	..	..	..
Wardha ..	627	346	281	540	247	293
Arvi ..	250	130	120	185	101	84
Hinganghat ..	350	177	173	313	159	154
Nagpur ..	305	150	155	378	189	189
Ramtek ..	155	79	76	31	21	10
Saoner ..	63	31	32	..	..	..
Chanda ..	77	40	37	28	15	13
Warora ..	23	10	13	33	15	18
Brahmapuri	60	32	28	206	102	104
Garchiroli ..	2,575	1,367	1,208	2,126	1,052	1,074
Sironcha ..	552	290	262	211	16	195
Bhandara ..	110	64	46	104	47	57
Gondia ..	10,666	5,383	5,283	9,781	4,623	5,158
Sakoli ..	8,457	4,276	4,181	8,355	4,119	4,236
Balaghat ..	1,230	571	659	1,131	476	655
Baihar ..	..	..	..	142	57	85
Waraseoni ..	323	170	153	148	59	89
Raipur ..	26	19	7	64	36	28
Mahasamund	999	485	514	305	305	..
Baloda Bazar	30	17	13	..	..	..
Dhamtari ..	5,013	2,371	2,642	4,088	2,088	2,000
Bilaspur ..	40	17	23	..	..	..
Mungeli ..	51	23	28	..	..	..
Janjgir ..	69	35	34	152	80	72
Katghora ..	..	..	..	51	15	36
Drug ..	2,449	1,209	1,240	2,405	1,174	1,231
Bemetara ..	1	1	..	38	38	..
Sanjari Balod	52,897	25,047	27,850	48,384	22,879	25,505
Amraoti ..	99	50	49	135	66	69
Morsi ..	13	6	7	39	16	23
Chandur ..	545	267	278	430	213	217
Ellichpur ..	1,565	821	744	1,303	633	670
Daryapur ..	79	2	77	80	80	..
Melghat ..	20	13	7	13	9	4
Akola ..	204	104	100	290	195	95
Akot ..	140	63	77	75	30	45
Mangrulpir ..	1	1	..	..	..	..
Murtizapur ..	137	63	74	103	18	85
Khamgaon ..	4	4	..	4	3	1
Jalgaon ..	16	9	7	22	11	11
Yeotmal ..	386	188	198	364	180	184
Kelapur ..	139	74	65	149	76	73
Wun ..	..	..	..	26	2	24
Darwha ..	123	73	50	104	57	47
Pusad ..	419	216	203	247	136	111
KAMAR						
Raipur ..	46	19	27	..	..	..
Mahasamund	7,353	3,618	3,735	..	..	..
Baloda Bazar	2	..	2	..	..	..
Dhamtari ..	1,843	927	916	..	..	..
KAWAR						
Saugor ..	1	1	..	2	2	..
Jubbulpore ..	36	25	11	..	..	..
Seoni ..	18	18	..	89	45	44
Narsinghpur	..	..	..	11	5	6
Hoshangabad	2	2	..	..	..	..
Sohagpur ..	2	2	..	..	..	..
Betul ..	7	4	3	..	..	..
Chhindwara	20	14	6	21	21	..
Sausar ..	11	11	..	20	20	..
Hinganghat ..	1	..	1	..	..	..
Nagpur ..	3	2	1	..	..	..
Ramtek ..	1	1	..	..	..	..
Garchiroli ..	1,835	952	883	1,494	735	759
Bhandara ..	..	..	..	5	3	2
Gondia ..	160	130	30	206	84	122
Sakoli ..	1,222	623	599	1,748	826	922
Balaghat ..	..	..	..	2,022	1,156	866
Baihar ..	..	..	..	49	12	37
Raipur ..	484	268	216	82	38	44
Mahasamund	15,737	7,545	8,192	15,663	8,350	7,313
Baloda Bazar	9,930	4,850	5,080	6,728	2,090	4,638
Dhamtari ..	5,822	2,714	3,108	4,835	2,287	2,548
Bilaspur ..	9,017	4,315	4,702	7,057	3,682	3,375
Janjgir ..	10,424	5,079	5,345	11,015	5,487	5,528
Mungeli ..	261	120	141	233	112	121
Katghora ..	50,084	24,881	25,203	32,901	17,311	15,590
Drug ..	1,028	538	490	947	383	564
Bemetara ..	532	228	304	596	274	322
Sanjari Balod	4,564	2,132	2,432	4,327	2,002	2,325
Ellichpur ..	..	..	..	12	12	..
Melghat ..	1	1	..	..	..	..
KOL						
Saugor ..	101	45	56	..	..	..
Damoh ..	60	32	28	684	409	275
Hatta ..	1	..	1	42	26	16
Jubbulpore ..	11,894	5,863	6,031	17,829	8,819	9,010
Sihora ..	21,858	10,649	11,209	25,093	11,891	13,202
Murwara ..	21,998	10,751	11,247	15,392	7,528	7,864
Patan ..	2,077	997	1,080	5,177	2,171	3,006
Mandla ..	730	378	352	954	496	458
Dindori ..	8,465	4,287	4,178	7,117	3,535	3,582
Niwas ..	1,729	875	854	1,668	793	875
Seoni ..	169	97	72	191	81	110
Lakhnadon ..	71	36	35	113	63	50
Narsinghpur	649	310	339	762	355	407
Gadarwara ..	21	10	11	357	186	171
Hoshangabad	571	289	282	235	38	197
Harda ..	..	..	..	24	20	4
Sohagpur ..	34	18	16	58	33	25
Seoni-Malwa	4	1	3	..	..	..
Khandwa ..	8	5	3	279	153	176
Burhanpur ..	..	..	..	1,759	740	1,019
Harsud ..	7	4	3	277	150	127
Betul ..	1	1	..	..	..	..
Multai ..	20	10	10	472	310	162
Bhainsdehi ..	1	1	..	..	..	..
Chhindwara	1,658	885	773	915	501	414
Sausar ..	..	..	..	259	259	..
Amarwara ..	102	54	48	..	..	..
Wardha ..	120	65	55	8	8	..
Arvi ..	107	49	58	21	11	10
Hinganghat ..	11	5	6	..	..	..
Nagpur ..	403	203	200	95	51	44
Ramtek ..	1,411	684	727	633	321	312
Saoner ..	89	38	51	..	..	..
Chanda ..	8	5	3	..	..	..
Bhandara ..	1,728	866	862	260	131	129
Gondia ..	47	2[illegible]	22	..	..	..
Balaghat ..	477	229	248	1,221	513	708
Baihar ..	206	128	78	134	77	57
Waraseoni ..	1,372	671	701	1,237	666	571
Raipur ..	5	4	1	..	..	..
Mahasamund	374	185	189	6,992	6,648	344
Baloda Bazar	3	3	..	..	..	..
Dhamtari ..	..	..	..	44	44	..
Bilaspur ..	2,423	1,209	1,214	25	25	..
Mungeli ..	534	300	234	71	45	26
Janjgir ..	340	156	184	..	..	..
Katghora ..	224	110	114	169	95	74
Sanjari Balod	..	..	..	19	19	..
Amraoti ..	67	35	32	89	48	41

APPENDIX TO TABLE XVIII—PART A

Variation of Population of Selected Tribes.

Tribe and Tahsil or Taluq.	1931.			1921.		
	Persons.	Males.	Females.	Persons.	Males.	Females.
1	2	3	4	5	6	7
KOL— *concld.*						
Chandur ..	4	2	2	..	..	..
Ellichpur ..	3	1	2	15	15	..
Daryapur ..	4	4	..	..	..	..
Melghat ..	168	95	73	40	21	19
Akola ..	58	39	19	..	..	..
Balapur ..	4	3	1	..	..	..
Murtizapur ..	1	1	..	..	..	..
Khamgaon ..	128	71	57	113	61	52
Malkapur ..	..	..	..	41	26	15
Yeotmal ..	1	1	..	..	..	..
Darwha ..	446	217	229	..	..	..
Pusad ..	233	125	108	..	..	..
KOLAM						
Betul ..	1	1	..	..	..	..
Wardha ..	152	82	70	629	307	322
Arvi ..	1,878	977	901	1,179	604	575
Hinganghat ..	63	38	25	..	..	..
Nagpur ..	3	1	2	8	8	..
Warora ..	90	47	43	11	5	6
Sironcha ..	61	22	39	7	4	3
Bhandara ..	..	..	..	4	4	..
Chandur ..	103	48	55	..	..	..
Akola ..	1	1	..	1	..	1
Mehkar ..	..	..	..	1	..	1
Yeotmal ..	12,343	6,199	6,144	9,846	4,889	4,957
Kelapur ..	8,607	4,357	4,250	5,997	3,099	2,898
Wun ..	6,452	3,203	3,249	4,812	2,402	2,410
Darwha ..	1,507	747	760	1,226	607	619
Pusad ..	502	264	238	..	..	..
KOLI						
Khurai ..	44	43	1	..	..	..
Jubbulpore ..	3	2	1	..	..	..
Murwara ..	1	1	..	..	..	..
Narsinghpur	..	..	..	11	..	11
Hoshangabad	154	71	83	64	33	31
Harda ..	2	2	..	..	..	.
Seoni-Malwa	..	..	..	13	5	8
Khandwa ..	96	54	42	106	53	53
Burhanpur ..	3,256	1,672	1,584	2,758	2,083	675
Sausar ..	86	49	37	348	81	267
Wardha ..	210	107	103	185	94	91
Arvi ..	191	87	104	153	86	67
Hinganghat ..	48	26	22	13	5	8
Nagpur ..	179	92	87	222	139	83
Ramtek ..	19	10	9	940	420	520
Katol ..	16	12	4	106	64	42
Umrer ..	4	1	3	6	6	..
Saoner ..	24	14	10	246	132	114
Chanda ..	255	137	118	188	104	84
Warora ..	97	52	45	89	46	43
Brahmapuri	1	1	..	104	59	45
Garchiroli ..	39	23	16	89	39	50
Sironcha ..	6	4	2	..	..	..
Bhandara ..	65	63	2	..	..	..
Gondia ..	140	..	140	81	51	30
Sakoli ..	1	..	1	216	111	105
Janjgir ..	124	55	69	1,768	924	844
Amraoti ..	6.134	3,159	2,975	4,353	2,152	2,201
Morsi ..	22	13	9	52	44	8
Chandur ..	88	49	39	159	84	75
Ellichpur ..	220	105	115	169	90	79
Daryapur ..	2,921	1,563	1,358	3,257	1,621	1,636
Melghat .	61	27	34	..	..	..
Akola ..	3,875	1,992	1,883	3,535	1,805	1,730
Akot ..	4,619	2,333	2,286	3,935	1,976	1,959
Balapur ..	391	212	179	199	114	85
Basim ..	1,456	720	736	1,352	690	662
Mangrulpir ..	321	147	174	231	125	106
Murtizapur ..	534	280	254	515	128	387
Chikhli ..	2,485	1,266	1,219	2,302	1,144	1,158
Mehkar ..	613	344	269	706	348	358
Khamgaon ..	1,295	680	615	954	455	499
Jalgaon ..	2,099	1,040	1,059	2,234	1,127	1,107
Malkapur ..	5,870	2,950	2,920	4,880	2,426	2,454
Yeotmal ..	167	81	86	180	76	104
Kelapur ..	1,243	683	560	1,012	537	475
Wun ..	487	424	423	757	391	366
Darwha ..	906	452	454	862	434	428
Pusad ..	1,902	898	1,004	1,516	781	735
KORKU						
Rehli ..	..	..	..	6	6	..
Damoh ..	..	..	..	758	337	421
Hatta ..	..	..	..	131	68	63
Jubbulpore	9	8	1	..	..	..
Mandla ..	..	..	..	47	33	14
Narsinghpur	1	1	..	..	..	..
Hoshangabad	4,367	2,216	2,151	3,974	2,028	1,946
Sohagpur ..	1,748	923	825	1,132	664	468
Harda ..	12,641	6,343	6,298	12,373	6,230	6,143
Seoni-Malwa	3,258	1,657	1,601	3,304	1,661	1,643
Khandwa ..	8,018	4,090	3,928	7,028	3,562	3,466
Burhanpur ..	20,194	10,004	10,190	15,418	7,783	7,635
Harsud ..	23,960	11,847	12,113	18,671	9,329	9,342
Betul ..	12,856	6,410	6,446	11,407	5,302	6,105
Multai ..	1,362	700	662	1,308	689	619
Bhainsdehi ..	23,246	11,305	11,941	19,891	9,265	10,626
Chhindwara	16,207	8,148	8,059	2,869	1,352	1,517
Sausar ..	2,751	1,324	1,427	1,498	755	743
Wardha ..	2	..	2	769	13	756
Arvi ..	560	281	279	15	10	5
Hinganghat ..	129	69	60	366	173	193
Nagpur ..	20	15	5	33	20	13
Ramtek ..	2	2	..	7	3	4
Umrer ..	7	3	4	10	7	3
Saoner ..	3	1	2	22	11	11
Chanda ..	..	..	..	28	12	16
Warora ..	..	..	..	2	1	1
Bhandara ..	41	23	18	..	..	..
Sakoli ..	25	13	12	..	..	..
Balaghat ..	..	..	..	57	25	32
Raipur ..	7	7	..	..	..	..
Bilaspur ..	4	3	1	..	..	..
Mungeli ..	8	1	7	3	..	3
Janjgir ..	..	..	..	32	13	19
Katghora ..	10	4	6	5	5	..
Drug ..	..	..	..	12	4	8
Sanjari Balod	..	..	..	4	4	..
Amraoti ..	27	17	10	14	8	6
Morsi ..	471	254	217	477	220	257
Chandur ..	8	3	5	5	5	..
Ellichpur ..	3,068	1,523	1,545	2,688	1,357	1,331
Daryapur ..	22	6	16	328	176	152
Melghat ..	30,273	15,231	15,042	28,281	14,215	14,066
Akola ..	26	13	13	..	..	..
Akot ..	1,714	889	825	1,444	728	716
Balapur ..	35	35	..	..	..	..
Basim ..	1	..	1	..	..	..
Mangrulpir	71	36	35	50	26	24
Chikhli ..	3	3	..	..	..	..
Khamgaon ..	1	1	..	..	..	..
Jalgaon ..	741	404	337	590	313	277
KORWA						
Baloda Bazar	14	8	6	..	..	..
Janjgir ..	22	9	13	252	130	122
Katghora ..	348	166	182	192	190	2
MAJHWAR						
Raipur ..	4	4	..	..	..	..
Mahasamund	371	194	177	..	..	..
Baloda Bazar	275	136	139	..	..	..
Janjgir ..	1,566	776	790	97	47	50
Katghora ..	7,015	3,548	3,467	7,039	3,934	3,105
*** MARIA**						
Jubbulpore	103	54	49	..	..	..
Patan ..	100	51	49	..	..	..
Multai ..	1	1	..	..	..	..
Chanda ..	133	73	60	..	..	..
Brahmapuri	5	4	1	..	..	..
Garchiroli ..	15,573	7,470	8,103	..	..	..
Sironcha ..	19,065	9,581	9,484	..	..	..
Mungeli ..	6	5	1	..	..	..
***MURIA**						
Saugor ..	190	110	80	..	..	..
Rehli ..	28	18	10	..	..	..
Damoh ..	237	119	118	..	..	..
Narsinghpur	671	340	331	..	..	..

*Figures for 1921 are not available; they were included under Gonds.

APPENDIX TO TABLE XVIII—PART A

Variation of Population of Selected Tribes.

Tribe and Tahsil or Taluq.	1931.			1921.		
	Persons.	Males.	Females.	Persons.	Males.	Females.
1	2	3	4	5	6	7
***MURIA—concld.**						
Sohagpur ..	30	13	17	..	..	.
Khandwa ..	4	4	..	..	..	..
Burhanpur ..	7	2	5	..	..	..
Sausar ..	2	1	1	..	..	..
Nagpur ..	8	6	2	..	..	..
Gondia ..	276	..	276	..	..	..
Balaghat ..	13	13	..	..	..	..
Dhamtari ..	9	6	3	..	..	..
Bilaspur ..	9	5	4	..	..	..
Katghora ..	204	11	193	..	..	..
Sanjari Balod	20	9	11	..	..	..
Amraoti ..	16	6	10	..	..	..
Akot ..	17	15	2	..	..	..
Basim ..	7	4	3	..	..	..
***NAGARCHI.**						
Mandla ..	106	48	58	..	..	..
Seoni ..	949	458	491	..	..	..
Lakhnadon ..	833	399	434	..	..	..
Narsinghpur	16	8	8	..	..	..
Chhindwara	362	173	189	..	..	..
Amarwara ..	555	276	279	..	..	.
Sausar ..	34	17	17	..	..	..
Ramtek ..	123	64	59	..	..	..
Bhandara ..	158	80	78	..	..	..
Gondia ..	1,161	705	456	..	..	..
Sakoli ..	34	13	21	..	..	..
Balaghat ..	524	245	279	..	..	..
Baihar ..	304	171	133	..	..	..
Waraseoni ..	793	373	420	..	..	..
Raipur ..	10	6	4	..	..	..
Mahasamund	7	7	..	..	..	..
Dhamtari ..	17	9	8	..	..	..
Bilaspur ..	24	10	14	..	..	..
Mungeli ..	13	5	8	..	..	..
Drug ..	212	105	107	..	..	..
Bemetara ..	53	29	24	..	..	..
Chandur ..	11	7	4	..	..	..
NAGASIA						
Jubbulpore	..	..	..	1	1	..
Arvi ..	..	..	..	13	8	5
Nagpur ..	..	..	..	4	..	4
Sakoli ..	13	8	5	..	..	..
Baihar ..	19	19	..	..	..	..
Waraseoni ..	92	48	44	..	..	..
Raipur ..	80	38	42	..	..	..
Mahasamund	123	60	63	..	..	..
Janjgir ..	193	109	84	8	5	3
Bilaspur ..	198	97	101	..	..	..
Katghora ..	404	192	212	..	..	..
ORAON						
Amarwara ..	5	3	2	..	..	..
Raipur ..	20	16	4	..	..	..
Mahasamund	1,452	661	791	..	..	..
Baloda Bazar	414	215	199	..	..	..
Bilaspur ..	775	411	364	10	4	6
Janjgir ..	3,607	1,753	1,854	166	77	89
Katghora ..	621	305	316	..	..	..
Bemetara ..	54	27	27	..	..	..
Sanjari Balod	2	1	1	..	..	..
PARDHAN						
Jubbulpore	1,403	703	700	313	142	171
Sihora ..	180	80	100	..	..	..
Murwara ..	28	11	17	..	..	..
Patan ..	89	36	53	159	80	79
Mandla ..	5,877	3,126	2,751	3,693	1,802	1,891
Dindori ..	4,007	1,994	2,013	15	14	1
Niwas ..	2,509	1,274	1,235	19	19	..
Seoni ..	9,345	4,489	4,856	8,155	3,946	4,209
Lakhnadon ..	6,270	3,029	3,241	6,515	3,985	2,530
Narsinghpur	793	420	373	1,017	535	482
Gadarwara ..	677	318	359	873	462	411
Hoshangabad	766	375	391	511	216	295
Harda ..	197	96	101	102	45	57
Sohagpur ..	915	443	472	690	303	387
Seoni-Malwa	214	108	106	138	68	70
Khandwa ..	23	9	14	18	10	8
Burhanpur ..	7	2	5	..	..	..
Harsud ..	87	40	47	6	6	..
Betul ..	1,556	770	786	894	430	464
PARDHAN—concld.						
Multai ..	990	480	510	610	292	318
Bhainsdehi ..	740	385	355	862	428	434
Chhindwara	4,018	1,988	2,030	3,006	1,455	1,551
Amarwara ..	2,578	1,255	1,323	2,098	1,010	1,088
Sausar ..	2,102	1,028	1,074	1,936	922	1,014
Wardha ..	2,622	1,276	1,346	2,190	1,083	1,107
Arvi ..	3,833	1,882	1,951	3,684	1,728	1,956
Hinganghat ..	2,056	741	1,315	1,660	812	848
Nagpur ..	2,060	1,030	1,030	1,775	902	873
Ramtek ..	1,082	494	588	1,037	497	540
Umrer ..	1,127	536	591	883	449	434
Katol ..	1,510	733	777	1,359	641	718
Saoner ..	530	260	270	519	263	256
Chanda ..	6,441	3,183	3,258	5,488	2,771	2,717
Warora ..	4,667	2,267	2,400	3,807	1,796	2,011
Brahmapuri	4,449	2,143	2,306	3,383	1,864	1,519
Garchiroli ..	5,009	2,471	2,538	4,529	2,250	2,279
Sironcha ..	677	315	362	501	252	249
Bhandara ..	458	234	224	267	128	139
Gondia ..	1,691	852	839	1,002	562	440
Sakoli ..	725	334	391	843	441	402
Balaghat ..	1,625	780	845	2,066	679	1,387
Baihar ..	1,059	444	615	1,197	570	627
Waraseoni ..	1,580	758	822	1,887	1,092	795
Raipur ..	84	38	46	17	14	3
Mahasamund	526	244	282	24	16	8
Baloda Bazar	167	95	72	..	..	..
Dhamtari ..	187	68	119	46	19	27
Bilaspur ..	1,571	720	851	59	59	..
Mungeli ..	382	197	185	..	..	..
Janjgir ..	373	182	191	73	42	31
Katghora ..	327	148	179	..	..	..
Drug ..	37	16	21	..	..	..
Bemetara ..	55	23	32	..	..	..
Sanjari Balod	341	145	196	590	286	304
Amraoti ..	7	3	4	..	..	..
Morsi ..	105	58	47	218	100	118
Chandur ..	319	158	161	420	203	217
Ellichpur ..	78	39	39	47	21	26
Melghat ..	20	11	9	4	2	2
Akola ..	16	7	9	249	115	134
Akot ..	225	117	108	300	141	159
Chikhli ..	..	..	..	12	2	10
Khamgaon ..	..	..	..	6	2	4
Jalgaon ..	16	6	10	79	40	39
Malkapur	..	..	..	54	23	31
Yeotmal ..	3,271	1,610	1,661	2,773	1,372	1,401
Kelapur ..	8,796	4,369	4,427	7,996	3,934	4,062
Wun ..	8,120	4,035	4,085	7,114	3,601	3,513
Darwha ..	1,975	902	1,073	1,533	747	786
Pusad ..	243	118	125	173	83	90
***PARJA**						
Drug ..	34	15	19	..	..	..
SAUNTA						
Jubbulpore	1	1	..	..	..	..
Bilaspur ..	460	231	229	..	..	..
Janjgir ..	3	3	..	..	..	..
Katghora ..	241	119	122	..	..	..
SAWARA OR SAONR						
Saugor ..	5,603	2,799	2,804	6,670	3,306	3,364
Khurai ..	8,599	4,282	4,317	7,496	3,846	3,650
Rehli ..	1,807	869	938	1,877	895	982
Banda ..	5,858	2,909	2,949	4,357	2,226	2,131
Damoh ..	2,726	1,375	1,351	2,386	1,246	1,140
Hatta ..	3,742	1,815	1,927	2,605	1,229	1,376
Hoshangabad	498	244	254	..	..	..
Betul ..	8	4	4	..	..	..
Chhindwara	28	19	9	..	..	..
Ramtek ..	4	3	1	..	..	..
Chanda ..	..	..	..	1	..	1
Raipur ..	42	27	15	..	..	..
Mahasamund	26,935	13,198	13,737	24,361	11,695	12,666
Baloda Bazar	1,689	805	884	992	536	456
Dhamtari ..	35	17	18	..	..	..
Bilaspur ..	2	2	..	..	..	..
Janjgir ..	9,531	4,571	4,960	4,958	2,363	2,595
Katghora ..	2	2	..	..	..	..
Melghat ..	3	3	..	..	..	..
Khamgaon ..	4	4	..	..	..	..

*Figures for 1921 are not available; they were included under Gonds.

TABLE XVIII

PART B

Tribe and locality.	Persons. 1931.	1921.	1911.	1901.	1891.	Variation (Increase + Decrease —). 1921 to 1931.	1911 to 1921.	1901 to 1911.	1891 to 1901.
1	2	3	4	5	6	7	8	9	10
ANDH									
Central Provinces States	..	20	..	..	..	−20	+20	..	..
Hindu	..	20	..	..	..	−20	+20	..	..
Surguja	..	*20*	..	..	..	*−20*	*+20*	..	..
Hindu	..	20	..	..	..	−20	+20	..	..
BAIGA									
Central Provinces States	5,083	2,500	3,117	1,272	946	+2,583	−617	+1,845	+326
Hindu	4,441	245	762	..	..	+4,196	−517	..	..
Tribal	642	2,255	2,355	..	..	−1,613	−100	..	..
Makrai	..	..	*1*	..	..	..	*−1*	*+1*	..
Tribal	..	..	1	..	..	..	−1	+1	..
Bastar	*397*	*17*	*441*	*159*	*14*	*+380*	*−424*	*+282*	*+145*
Hindu	389	16	367	..	..	+373	−351	..	..
Tribal	8	1	74	..	..	+7	−73	..	..
Kanker	*420*	*106*	*402*	..	..	*+314*	*−296*	*+402*	..
Hindu	55	..	290	..	..	+55	−290	..	..
Tribal	365	106	112	..	..	+259	−6	..	..
Nandgaon	..	*55*	..	..	1	*−55*	*+55*	..	−1
Hindu	..	12	..	..	..	−12	+12	..	..
Tribal	..	43	..	..	..	−43	+43	..	..
Kawardha	*3,074*	*2,217*	*2,167*	*1,113*	*931*	*+857*	*+50*	*+1,054*	*+182*
Hindu	3,043	112	..	..	..	+2,931	+112	..	..
Tribal	31	2,105	2,167	..	..	−2,074	−62	..	..
Raigarh	*791*	*96*	*103*	..	..	*+695*	*−7*	*+103*	..
Hindu	791	96	103	..	..	+695	−7	..	..
Sarangarh	..	*9*	..	..	..	*−9*	*+9*	..	..
Hindu	..	9	..	..	..	−9	+9	..	..
Changbhakar	*162*	..	..	..	..	*+162*	..	..	..
Hindu	32	..	..	..	..	+32	..	..	..
Tribal	130	..	..	..	..	+130	..	..	..
Korea	*108*	..	..	..	..	*+108*	..	..	..
Tribal	108	..	..	..	..	+108	..	..	..
Surguja	*34*	..	..	..	..	*+34*	..	..	..
Hindu	34	..	..	..	..	+34	..	..	..
Udaipur	*97*	..	..	..	..	*+97*	..	..	..
Hindu	97	..	..	..	..	+97	..	..	..
Jashpur	..	..	*3*	..	..	..	*−3*	*+3*	..
Hindu	..	..	2	..	..	..	−2	..	..
Tribal	..	..	1	..	..	..	−1	..	..
BHAINA									
Central Provinces States	4,432	..	2,865	2,455	2,509	+4,432	−2,865	+410	−54
Hindu	4,405	..	2,865	..	..	+4,405	−2,865	..	..
Tribal	27	..	..	..	..	+27	..	..	..
Bastar	..	..	*7*	..	..	..	*−7*	*+7*	..
Hindu	..	..	7	..	..	..	−7	..	..

Net variation 1891 to 1931 (Increase + Decrease —).	Males.				Females.			
	1931.	1921.	1911.	1901.	1931.	1921.	1911.	1901.
11	12	13	14	15	16	17	18	19
..	..	**12**	..	..	..	**8**	..	..
..	..	12	..	..	..	8	..	..
..	..	*12*	..	..	..	*8*	..	..
..	..	12	..	..	..	8	..	..
+4,137	**2,517**	**1,286**	**1,565**	**648**	**2,566**	**1,214**	**1,552**	**624**
..	2,205	118	399	..	2,236	127	363	..
..	312	1,168	1,166	..	330	1,087	1,189	..
..	..	..	*1*	..	..	..	..	..
..	..	..	1	..	..	..	..	..
+383	*202*	*7*	*227*	*81*	*195*	*10*	*214*	*78*
..	197	7	193	..	192	9	174	..
..	5	..	34	..	3	1	40	..
+420	*190*	*15*	*200*	..	*230*	*91*	*202*	..
..	28	..	147	..	27	..	143	..
..	162	15	53	..	203	91	59	..
—1	..	*23*	..	..	..	*32*	..	..
..	..	..	..	..	..	12	..	..
..	..	23	..	..	..	20	..	..
+2,143	*1,519*	*1,187*	*1,077*	*567*	*1,555*	*1,030*	*1,090*	*546*
..	1,500	57	..	..	1,543	55	..	..
..	19	1,130	1,077	..	12	975	1,090	..
+191	*398*	*50*	*57*	..	*393*	*46*	*46*	..
..	398	50	57	..	393	46	46	..
..	..	*4*	..	..	..	*5*	..	..
..	..	4	..	..	..	5	..	..
+162	*74*	..	..	..	*88*	..	..	..
..	14	..	..	..	18	..	..	..
..	60	..	..	..	70	..	..	..
+108	*66*	..	..	..	*42*	..	..	..
..	66	..	..	..	42	..	..	..
+34	*18*	..	..	..	*16*	..	..	..
..	18	..	..	..	16	..	..	..
+97	*50*	..	..	..	*17*	..	..	..
..	50	..	..	..	47	..	..	..
..	..	..	*3*	..	..	..	..	..
..	..	..	2	..	..	..	..	..
..	..	..	1	..	..	..	..	..
+1,923	**2,098**	..	**1,357**	**1,156**	**2,334**	..	**1,508**	**1,299**
..	2,083	..	1,357	..	2,322	..	1,508	..
..	15	..	..	..	12	..	..	..
..	..	..	*7*	..	..	..	..	..
..	..	..	7	..	..	..	..	..

TABLE XVIII—PART B.

Tribe and locality.	Persons. 1931.	1921.	1911.	1901.	1891.	Variation (Increase + Decrease —). 1921 to 1931.	1911 to 1921.	1901 to 1911.	1891 to 1901.
1	2	3	4	5	6	7	8	9	10
BHAINA—*concld.*									
Kanker ..	..	..	*1*	..	..	..	..	..	..
Hindu ..	..	..	1	..	..	..	..	..	..
Kawardha ..	..	..	..	..	*43*	..	..	..	*—43*
Sakti ..	..	..	*19*	..	*109*	..	*—19*	*+19*	*—109*
Hindu ..	..	..	19	..	..	..	—19	..	..
Raigarh ..	*2,265*	..	*1,886*	*1,663*	*1,545*	*+2,265*	*—1,886*	*+223*	*+118*
Hindu ..	2,265	..	1,886	..	..	+2,265	—1,886	..	..
Sarangarh ..	*1,062*	..	*901*	*792*	*812*	*+1,062*	*—901*	*+109*	*—20*
Hindu ..	1,062	..	901	..	..	+1,062	—901	..	..
Korea ..	*27*	..	*51*	..	..	*+27*	*—51*	*+51*	..
Hindu ..	..	..	51	..	..	..	—51	..	..
Tribal ..	27	..	..	..	..	+27	..	..	..
Jashpur ..	*1,078*	..	..	..	..	*+1,078*	..	..	..
Hindu ..	1,078	..	..	..	..	+1,078	..	..	..
BHARIA-BHUMIA									
Central Provinces States ..	**1,522**	**3,395**	**881**	**49**	**992**	**—1,873**	**+2,514**	**+832**	**—943**
Hindu ..	1,495	3,393	832	..	..	—1,898	+2,561	..	..
Tribal ..	27	2	49	..	..	+25	—47	..	..
Bastar ..	*2*	..	*19*	..	*34*	*+2*	*—19*	*+19*	*—34*
Tribal ..	2	..	19	..	..	+2	—19	..	..
Kanker ..	..	..	*1*	..	..	..	*—1*	..	..
Hindu ..	..	..	1	..	..	..	—1	..	..
Khairagarh ..	..	*1,246*	..	*5*	..	*—1,246*	*+1,246*	*—5*	*+5*
Hindu ..	..	1,246	..	..	..	—1,246	+1,246	..	..
Kawardha ..	..	..	..	*44*	*958*	..	..	*—44*	*—914*
Raigarh ..	..	*404*	*692*	..	..	*—404*	*—288*	*+692*	..
Hindu ..	..	404	692	..	..	—404	—288	..	..
Sarangarh ..	..	..	*8*	..	..	..	*—8*	*+8*	..
Hindu ..	..	..	8	..	..	..	—8	..	..
Changbhakar ..	*66*	*94*	*122*	..	..	*—28*	*—28*	*+122*	..
Hindu ..	66	94	116	..	..	—28	—22	..	..
Tribal ..	..	..	6	..	..	..	—6	..	..
Korea ..	*17*	..	*32*	..	..	*+17*	*—32*	*+32*	..
Hindu ..	..	..	8	..	..	..	—8	..	..
Tribal ..	17	..	24	..	..	+17	—24	..	..
Surguja ..	*1,179*	*1,651*	*1*	..	..	*—472*	*+1,650*	*+1*	..
Hindu ..	1,171	1,649	1	..	..	—478	+1,648	..	..
Tribal ..	8	2	..	..	..	+6	+2	..	..
Udaipur ..	..	..	*2*	..	..	..	*—2*	*+2*	..
Hindu ..	..	..	2	..	..	..	—2	..	..
Jashpur ..	*258*	..	*4*	..	..	*+258*	*—4*	*+4*	..
Hindu ..	258	..	4	..	..	+258	—4	..	..

Net variation 1891 to 1931 (Increase + Decrease −).	Males.				Females.			
	1931.	1921.	1911.	1901.	1931.	1921.	1911.	1901.
11	12	13	14	15	16	17	18	19
..	..	..	1	..	..	..	..	..
..	..	..	1	..	..	..	..	..
−43	..	..	..	..	..	..	..	..
−109	..	..	..	..	..	..	19	..
..	..	..	..	..	..	..	19	..
+720	1,061	..	909	797	1,204	..	977	866
..	1,061	..	909	..	1,204	..	977	..
+250	506	..	415	359	556	..	486	433
..	506	..	415	..	556	..	486	..
+27	15	..	25	..	12	..	26	..
..	..	..	25	..	..	..	26	..
..	15	..	..	..	12	..	..	..
+1,078	516	..	..	..	562	..	..	..
..	516	..	..	..	562	..	..	..
+530	**781**	**1,767**	**420**	**23**	**741**	**1,628**	**461**	**26**
..	759	1,765	385	..	736	1,628	447	..
..	22	2	35	..	5	..	14	..
−32	2	..	13	..	..	..	6	..
..	2	..	13	..	..	..	6	..
..	..	..	1	..	..	..	..	..
..	..	..	1	..	..	..	..	..
..	..	746	..	3	..	500	..	2
..	..	746	..	..	..	500	..	..
−958	..	..	..	20	..	..	..	24
..	..	221	308	..	..	183	384	..
..	..	221	308	..	..	183	384	..
..	..	..	5	..	..	..	3	..
..	..	..	5	..	..	..	3	..
+66	32	35	66	..	34	59	56	..
..	32	35	63	..	34	59	53	..
..	..	..	3	..	..	..	3	..
+17	17	..	22	..	..	..	10	..
..	..	..	3	..	..	..	5	..
..	17	..	19	..	..	..	5	..
+1,179	590	765	1	..	589	886	..	..
..	587	763	1	..	584	886	..	..
..	3	2	..	..	5	..	..	..
..	..	..	2	..	..	..	..	..
..	..	..	2	..	..	..	..	..
+258	140	..	2	..	118	..	2	..
..	140	..	2	..	118	..	2	..

Tribe and locality.	Persons. 1931.	1921.	1911.	1901.	1891.	Variation (Increase + Decrease —). 1921 to 1931.	1911 to 1921.	1901 to 1911.	1891 to 1901.
1	2	3	4	5	6	7	8	9	10
***BHATTRA**									
Central Provinces States	**36,837**	..	..	..	**21,477**	..	..	..	..
Hindu	252	..	..	..	..	..	..	..	..
Tribal	36,585	..	..	..	..	..	..	..	..
Bastar	*36,611*	..	..	..	*21,477*	..	..	..	..
Hindu	26	..	..	..	..	..	..	..	..
Tribal	36,585	..	..	..	..	..	..	..	..
Sakti	*164*	..	..	..	..	..	..	..	..
Hindu	164	..	..	..	..	..	..	..	..
Surguja	*4*	..	..	..	..	..	..	..	..
Hindu	4	..	..	..	..	..	..	..	..
Udaipur	*48*	..	..	..	..	..	..	..	..
Hindu	48	..	..	..	..	..	..	..	..
Jashpur	*10*	..	..	..	..	..	..	..	..
Hindu	10	..	..	..	..	..	..	..	..
BHIL									
Central Provinces States	**22**	..	**164**	..	**307**	**+22**	**—164**	**+164**	**—307**
Hindu	22	..	164	..	..	..	..	..	..
Makrai	..	..	..	..	*2*	..	..	..	*—2*
Kanker	..	..	..	..	*302*	..	..	..	*—302*
Nandgaon	..	..	*12*	..	..	..	*—12*	*+12*	..
Hindu	..	..	12	..	..	..	—12	..	..
Khairagarh	..	..	..	..	*3*	..	..	..	*—3*
Raigarh	..	..	*7*	..	..	..	*—7*	*+7*	..
Hindu	..	..	7	..	..	..	—7	..	..
Korea	..	..	*4*	..	..	..	*—4*	*+4*	..
Hindu	..	..	4	..	..	..	—4	..	..
Surguja	*22*	..	*141*	..	..	*+22*	*—141*	*+141*	..
Hindu	22	..	141	..	..	+22	—141	..	..
BHUINHAR									
Central Provinces States	**24,378**	**11,330**	**25,809**	..	**2,466**	**+13,048**	**—14,479**	..	..
Hindu	20,592	9,137	14,682	..	..	+11,455	—5,545	..	..
Tribal	3,786	2,193	11,127	..	..	+1,593	—8,934	..	..
Bastar	..	..	*32*	..	..	..	*—32*	..	..
Hindu	..	..	32	..	..	..	—32	..	..
Sakti	..	*128*	*81*	..	*50*	*—128*	*+47*	..	..
Hindu	..	128	79	..	..	—128	+49	..	..
Tribal	..	..	2	..	..	..	—2	..	..
Raigarh	*2,794*	*790*	*2,258*	..	*2,415*	*+2,004*	*—1,468*	..	..
Hindu	2,794	790	2,252	..	..	+2,004	—1,462	..	..
Tribal	..	..	6	..	..	..	—6	..	..
Sarangarh	..	*82*	*22*	..	*1*	*—82*	*+60*	..	..
Hindu	..	82	22	..	..	—82	+60	..	..

*From 1901—1921 the figures for Bhattras were included under Gonds.

Net variation (1891 to 1931 Increase + Decrease −).	Males. 1931.	Males. 1921.	Males. 1911.	Males. 1901.	Females. 1931.	Females. 1921.	Females. 1911.	Females. 1901.
11	12	13	14	15	16	17	18	19
+15,360	18,448	..	..	..	18,389	..	..	..
..	128	..	..	..	124	..	..	..
..	18,320	.	.	..	18,265	..	..	..
+15,134	18,335	..	..	..	18,276	..	..	..
..	15	..	..	..	11	..	..	..
..	18,320	..	..	..	18,265	..	..	..
+164	81	..	..	..	83	..	..	..
..	81	..	..	..	83	..	..	..
+4	3	..	..	..	1	..	..	..
..	3	..	..	..	1	..	..	..
+48	24	..	..	..	24	..	..	..
..	24	..	..	..	24	..	..	..
+10	5	.	..	..	5	..	..	..
..	5	..	..	..	5	..	..	..
−285	13	..	64	..	9	..	100	..
..	13	..	64	..	9	..	100	..
−2	..	..	..	..	..	..	..	..
−302	..	..	..	..	..	..	..	..
..	..	..	7	..	..	..	5	..
..	..	..	7	..	..	..	5	..
−3	..	..	.	..	..	..	..	..
..	..	..	4	..	..	..	3	..
..	..	..	4	..	..	.	3	..
..	..	..	4	..	..	..	..	..
..	..	..	4	..	..	..	..	..
+22	13	..	49	..	9	..	92	..
..	13	..	49	..	9	..	92	..
+21,912	12,451	5,699	13,129	..	11,927	5,631	12,680	..
..	10,492	4,586	7,531	..	10,100	4,551	7,151	..
..	1,959	1,113	5,598	..	1,827	1,080	5,529	..
..	..	..	19	..	..	..	13	..
..	..	..	19	..	..	..	13	..
−50	..	55	37	..	..	73	44	..
..	..	55	35	..	..	73	44	..
..	..	..	2	..	..	..	..	..
+379	1,305	379	1,137	..	1,489	411	1,121	..
..	1,305	379	1,134	..	1,489	411	1,118	..
..	..	..	3	..	..	..	3	..
−1	..	46	6	..	..	36	16	..
..	..	46	6	..	..	36	16	..

TABLE XVIII—PART B

Tribe and locality.	Persons. 1931.	1921.	1911.	1901.	1891.	Variation (Increase + Decrease −). 1921 to 1931.	1911 to 1921.	1901 to 1911.	1891 to 1901.
1	2	3	4	5	6	7	8	9	10
BHUINHAR—*concld.*									
Changbhakar	*492*	*7*	*53*	..	..	*+485*	*−46*	..	..
Hindu	..	7	..	..	..	−7	+7	..	..
Tribal	492	..	53	..	..	+492	−53	..	..
Korea	*3,143*	*3,041*	*2,574*	..	..	*+102*	*+467*	..	..
Hindu	..	965	3	..	..	−965	+962	..	..
Tribal	3,143	2,076	2,571	..	..	+1,067	−495	..	..
Surguja	*10,942*	*1,369*	*12,581*	..	..	*+9,573*	*−11,212*	..	..
Hindu	10,791	1,288	5,628	..	..	+9,503	−4,340	..	..
Tribal	151	81	6,953	..	..	+70	−6,872	..	..
Udaipur	*860*	*180*	*891*	..	..	*+680*	*−711*	..	..
Hindu	860	180	16	..	..	+680	+164	..	..
Tribal	..	..	875	..	..	..	−875	..	..
Jashpur	*6,147*	*5,733*	*7,317*	..	..	*+414*	*−1,584*	..	..
Hindu	6,147	5,697	6,650	..	..	+450	−953	..	..
Tribal	..	36	667	..	..	−36	−631	..	..
BHUNJIA									
Central Provinces States	**824**	..	**8**	**73**	..	**+824**	**−8**	**−65**	**+73**
Hindu	824	..	8	..	..	+824	−8	..	..
Bastar	..	..	*7*	*58*	..	..	*−7*	*−51*	*+58*
Hindu	..	..	7	..	..	..	−7	..	..
Nandgaon	*35*	..	..	..	..	*+35*	..	..	..
Hindu	35	..	..	..	..	+35	..	..	..
Raigarh	*10*	..	..	*15*	..	*+10*	..	*−15*	*+15*
Hindu	10	..	..	..	..	+10	..	..	..
Korea	*6*	..	..	..	..	*+6*	..	..	..
Hindu	6	..	..	..	..	+6	..	..	..
Surguja	*761*	..	..	..	..	*+761*	..	..	..
Hindu	761	..	..	..	..	+761	..	..	..
Jashpur	*12*	..	*1*	..	..	*+12*	*−1*	*+1*	..
Hindu	12	..	1	..	..	+12	−1	..	..
BINJHWAR									
Central Provinces States	**12,658**	**7,831**	**11,151**	**6,415**	**6,915**	**+4,827**	**−3,320**	**+4,736**	**−500**
Hindu	12,653	7,831	9,965	..	..	+4,822	−2,134	..	..
Tribal	5	..	1,186	..	..	+5	−1,186	..	..
Makrai	..	*10*	..	..	..	*−10*	*+10*	..	..
Hindu	..	10	..	..	..	−10	+10	..	..
Bastar	..	*17*	..	*2*	..	*−17*	*+17*	*−2*	*+2*
Hindu	..	17	..	2	..	−17	+17	..	..
Nandgaon	..	*301*	..	..	*3*	*+301*	*−301*	..	*−3*
Hindu	..	301	..	..	..	+301	−301	..	..
Khairagarh	..	..	*3*	*2*	..	..	*−3*	*+1*	*+2*
Hindu	..	..	3	..	..	..	−3	..	..
Kawardha	..	..	*7*	*123*	*74*	..	*−7*	*−116*	*+49*
Hindu	..	..	7	..	..	..	−7	..	..

Net variation 1891 to 1931 (Increase + Decrease −).	Males.				Females.			
	1931.	1921.	1911.	1901.	1931.	1921.	1911.	1901.
11	12	13	14	15	16	17	18	19
+492	*251*	*5*	*26*	..	*241*	*2*	*27*	..
..	..	5	..	..	..	2	..	..
..	251	..	26	..	241	..	27	..
+3,143	*1,629*	*1,522*	*1,301*		*1,511*	*1,519*	*1,273*	..
..	..	510	1	..	..	455	2	..
..	1,629	1,012	1,300	..	1,514	1,064	1,271	..
+10,942	*5,651*	*737*	*6,511*	..	*5,291*	*632*	*6,070*	..
..	5,572	656	3,009	..	5,219	632	2,619	..
..	79	81	3,502	..	72	..	3,451	..
+860	*434*	*110*	*429*	..	*426*	*70*	*462*	..
..	434	110	8	..	426	70	8	..
..	.	..	421	..	..	..	454	..
+6,147	*3,181*	*2,845*	*3,663*	..	*2,966*	*2,858*	*3,654*	..
..	3,181	2,825	3,319	..	2,966	2,872	3,331	..
..	..	20	344	..	..	16	323	..
+824	**428**	..	**3**	**36**	**396**	..	**5**	**37**
..	428	..	3	..	396	..	5	..
..	..	..	*3*	*31*	..	..	*4*	*27*
..	..	..	3	..	..	..	4	..
+35	*16*	..	..	..	*19*	..	..	..
..	16	..	..	..	19	..	..	..
+10	*4*	..	..	*5*	*6*	..	..	*10*
..	4	.	..	..	6	.	..	..
+6	*3*	..	..	..	*3*	..	..	..
..	3	..	..	..	3	..	..	..
+761	*399*	..	..	..	*362*	..	..	..
..	399		..	..	362	..	..	..
+12	*6*	..	..	..	*6*	..	*1*	..
..	6	..	..	..	6	..	1	..
+5,743	**6,307**	**3,666**	**5,452**	**3,043**	**6,351**	**4,165**	**5,699**	**3,372**
..	6,303	3,666	4,881	..	6,350	4,165	5,084	..
..	4	..	571	..	1	..	615	..
..	..	..	..	..	..	*10*	..	..
..	..	..	..	..	..	10	..	..
..	.	..	..	..	..	*17*	..	*2*
..	..	.	.	..	..	17	..	2
−3	..	..		..	..	*301*	..	..
..	..			.	..	301	..	..
..	.	.	*2*	*1*	..	..	*1*	*1*
..	..	..	2	.	..	.	1	..
−74	..	..	*6*	*66*	..	..	*1*	*57*
..	..	.	6	..	..	..	1	..

TABLE XVIII—PART B

Tribe and locality.	Persons. 1931.	1921.	1911.	1901.	1891.	Variation (Increase + Decrease —). 1921 to 1931.	1911 to 1921.	1901 to 1911.	1891 to 1901.
1	2	3	4	5	6	7	8	9	10
BINJHWAR—*concld.*									
Sakti	*76*	..	*6*	..	*1*	*+76*	*—6*	*+6*	*—4*
Hindu	76	..	5	..	..	+76	—5	..	..
Tribal	..	..	1	..	..	..	—1	..	..
Raigarh	*250*	*13*	*553*	*476*	*125*	*+237*	*—510*	*+77*	*+351*
Hindu	250	13	51	..	..	+237	—38	..	..
Tribal	..	..	502	..	..	..	—502	..	..
Sarangarh	*6,975*	*6,995*	*6,764*	*5,812*	*6,709*	*—20*	*+231*	*+952*	*—897*
Hindu	6,975	6,995	6,744	..	..	—20	+251	..	..
Tribal	..	..	20	..	..	..	—20	..	..
Korea	..	..	*664*	..	..	..	*—664*	*+661*	..
Hindu	..	..	6	..	..	..	—6	..	..
Tribal	..	..	658	.	..	..	—658	..	..
Surguja	*5,354*	*216*	*3,138*	..	..	*+5,138*	*—2,922*	*+3,138*	..
Hindu	5,352	216	3,133	..	..	+5,136	—2,917	..	..
Tribal	2	..	5	..	..	+2	—5	..	..
Udaipur	*3*	*279*	..	..	..	*—276*	*+279*	..	..
Hindu	..	279	..	..	..	—279	+279	..	..
Tribal	3	.	..	..	..	+3	..	..	..
Jashpur	..	..	*16*	..	..	..	*—16*	*+16*	..
Hindu	..	..	16	.	..	..	—16	..	
DHANWAR									
Central Provinces States ..	**5,026**	**4,720**	**7,449**	**2,418**	**3,123**	**+306**	**—2,729**	**+5,031**	**—705**
Hindu .. .	3,990	4,343	4,165	..	..	—353	+178	..	..
Tribal . ..	1,036	377	3,284	.	..	+659	—2,907	.	..
Bastar	*7*	..	..	*30*	.	*+7*	..	*—30*	*+30*
Tribal .. .	7	..	..	.	.	+7	..	..	..
Nandgaon .. .	..	..	..	..	*6*	..	..	..	*—6*
Khairagarh	*15*	..	..	..	..	*+15*	.	.	..
Hindu .. .	15	..	.	..	.	+15	..	.	..
Kawardha	..	..	*1*	..	..	..	*—1*	*+1*	..
Hindu	..	.	1	..	..	.	—1	..	..
Sakti	*291*	*282*	*347*	*323*	*377*	*+9*	*—65*	*+24*	*—54*
Hindu .. .	291	282	336	.	..	+9	—54	..	..
Tribal	.	..	11	..	..	.	—11	.	..
Raigarh	*2,828*	*2,101*	*2,352*	*1,890*	*2,449*	*+727*	*—251*	*+462*	*—559*
Hindu	2,828	2,101	72	..	..	+727	+2,029	..	..
Tribal .. .	..	.	2,280	..	..	.	—2,280	..	..
Sarangarh	*94*	*122*	*106*	*175*	*291*	*—28*	*+16*	*—69*	*—116*
Hindu	94	122	100	..	..	—28	+22	..	..
Tribal	..	..	6	..	..	..	—6	..	..
Korea	*1,022*	*582*	*468*	..	..	*+440*	*+114*	*+468*	..
Hindu	..	294	..	..	..	—294	+294	..	..
Tribal .. .	1,022	288	468	..	..	+734	—180	..	..
Surguja	*431*	*1,621*	*3,626*	..	..	*—1,190*	*—2,005*	*+3,626*	..
Hindu	431	1,532	3,620	..	..	—1,101	—2,088	..	..
Tribal	..	89	6	..	..	—89	+83	..	..

Net variation 1891 to 1931 (Increase + Decrease −).	Males. 1931.	1921.	1911.	1901.	Females. 1931.	1921.	1911.	1901.
11	12	13	14	15	16	17	18	19
+72	41	..	1	..	35	..	5	..
..	41	..	1	..	35	..	4	..
..	..	..	..	..	..	..	1	..
+125	135	5	271	212	115	8	282	234
..	135	5	34	..	115	8	17	..
..	..	..	237	..	.	..	265	..
+266	3,400	3,396	3,248	2,734	3,575	3,599	3,576	3,078
..	3,400	3,396	3,239	..	3,575	3,599	3,505	..
..	..	..	9	..	..	..	11	..
..	..	..	326	..	..	..	338	..
..	..	..	5	..	..	..	1	..
.	..	..	321	..	..	..	337	..
+5,354	2,729	109	1,598	..	2,625	107	1,540	..
..	2,727	109	1,594	..	2,625	107	1,539	..
..	2	..	4	..	..	..	1	..
+3	2	156	..	..	1	123	..	..
..	..	156	.	..	..	123	..	..
..	2	..	..	..	1	..	..	..
..	..	..	..	..	..	..	16	..
..	..	..	..	..	..	..	16	..
+1,903	2,470	2,351	3,755	1,196	2,556	2,369	3,694	1,222
..	1,954	2,164	2,150	..	2,036	2,179	2,015	..
..	516	187	1,605	..	520	190	1,679	..
+7	5	..	..	14	2	..	..	16
..	5	..	..	..	2	..	..	..
−6	..	..	..	..	..	..	..	..
+15	6	..	..	..	9	..	..	..
..	6	..	.	..	9	..	..	..
..	.	..	1	..	..	..	..	..
..	..	..	1	..	..	..	..	..
−86	142	149	182	156	149	133	165	167
..	142	149	177	..	149	133	159	..
..	..	..	5	..	..	..	6	..
+379	1,374	1,033	1,133	945	1,454	1,068	1,219	945
..	1,374	1,033	35	..	1,454	1,068	37	..
..	..	..	1,098	..	..	..	1,182	..
−197	39	51	57	81	55	71	49	94
..	39	51	54	..	55	71	46	..
..	..	..	3	..	..	..	3	.
+1,022	510	295	233	..	512	287	235	..
..	..	153	..	..	..	141	..	..
..	510	142	233	..	512	146	235	.
+431	226	815	1,885	..	205	806	1,741	..
..	226	770	1,881	..	205	762	1,739	.
..	..	45	4	..	..	44	2	..

TABLE XVIII—PART B

Variation of Population

Tribe and locality.	Persons. 1931.	1921	1911.	1901.	1891.	Variation (Increase + Decrease —). 1921 to 1931.	1911 to 1921.	1901 to 1911.	1891 to 1901.
1	2	3	4	5	6	7	8	9	10
DHANWAR—*concld.*									
Udaipur	*338*	..	*513*	..	..	*—338*	*—513*	*+513*	..
Hindu	331			..	..	—331			..
Tribal	7	.	513	..	..	—7	—513	+513	..
Jashpur	..	*12*	*36*	..	..	*—12*	*—24*	*+36*	..
Hindu	.	12	36	..	..	—12	—24	..	..
GADABA									
Central Provinces States	**398**	..	..	**729**	**555**	..	..	..	**+174**
Hindu	4	..	.	..	..	..	.	..	..
Tribal	391	..	..	..	..	..	..	..	..
Christian	3	..	.	.	..	.	..	..	..
Bastar	*398*	..	.	*729*	*555*	.	..	..	*+174*
Hindu	4	.	.	..	..	..	..	..	..
Tribal	391	..	.	.	..	.	.	..	..
Christian	3	.	.	.	..	..	..	..	..
***GOND**									
Central Provinces States	**369,303**	**394,685**	**578,752**	**338,275**	**193,956**	**—25,382**	**—184,067**	**+240,477**	**+144,319**
Hindu	207,408	89,949	45,120	..	..	+117,459	+44,829	..	..
Tribal	161,888	304,736	533,632	.	..	—142,848	—226,896	..	..
Christian	7	..		.	..	+7	..	..	..
Makrai	*1,104*	*940*	*1,102*	*1,193*	*2,060*	*+164*	*—162*	*—91*	*—867*
Hindu	109	120	58	..	..	—11	+62	..	..
Tribal	995	820	1,044	..	..	+175	—224	..	..
Bastar	*24,407*	*107,503*	*285,519*	*204,841*	*13,683*	*—83,096*	*—178,016*	*+80,678*	*+191,158*
Hindu	4,981	5,809	2,315	..	..	—828	+3,494	..	..
Tribal	19,426	101,694	283,204	.	..	—82,268	—181,510	..	..
Kanker	*80,003*	*64,848*	*68,500*	*54,113*	*47,086*	*+15,155*	*—3,652*	*+14,387*	*+7,027*
Hindu	9,107	9,476	205	..	..	—369	+9,271	..	..
Tribal	70,896	55,372	68,295	..	..	+15,524	—12,923	..	..
Nandgaon	*25,708*	*19,059*	*26,044*	*18,541*	*36,740*	*+6,649*	*—6,985*	*+7,503*	*—18,199*
Hindu	23,912	2,573	369	..	..	+21,339	+2,204	..	..
Tribal	1,796	16,486	25,675	..	..	—14,690	—9,189	..	..
Khairagarh	*22,797*	*17,613*	*23,457*	*22,291*	*40,397*	*+5,184*	*—5,844*	*+1,166*	*—18,106*
Hindu	22,790	17,540	15,016	.	..	+5,250	+2,524	..	..
Tribal	..	73	8,441	..	..	—73	—8,368	..	..
Christian	7	..	..	..	..	+7	..	..	..
Chhuikhadan	*4,397*	*3,450*	*4,743*	*4,574*	*8,339*	*+947*	*—1,293*	*+169*	*—3,765*
Hindu	4,392	3,446	185	..	..	+946	+3,261	..	..
Tribal	5	4	4,558	.	..	+1	—4,554	..	..
Kawardha	*10,898*	*11,210*	*13,748*	*9,341*	*18,994*	*—312*	*—2,538*	*+4,407*	*—9,653*
Hindu	10,835	6,681	115	..	..	+4,154	+6,566	..	..
Tribal	63	4,529	13,633	..	..	—4,466	—9,104	..	..
Sakti	*8,444*	*6,448*	*5,424*	*3,904*	*4,495*	*+1,996*	*+1,024*	*+1,520*	*—591*
Hindu	8,246	1,508	1,466	..	..	+6,738	+42	..	..
Tribal	198	4,940	3,958	..	..	—4,742	+982	..	..
Raigarh	*29,305*	*26,751*	*23,208*	*16,392*	*17,962*	*+2,554*	*+3,543*	*+6,816*	*—1,570*
Hindu	29,305	19,587	18,923	..	..	+9,718	+664	..	..
Tribal	..	7,164	4,285	..	..	—7,164	+2,879	..	..
Sarangarh	*4,069*	*4,316*	*3,878*	*3,085*	*4,200*	*—247*	*+438*	*+793*	*—1,115*
Hindu	4,069	784	3,716	..	..	+3,285	—2,932	..	..
Tribal	..	3,532	162	..	..	—3,537	+3,370	..	..

*From 1901—1921 Marias, Murias, Bhattras and Parjas were included with Gonds

Net variation 1891 to 1931 (Increase + Decrease —).	Males.				Females.			
	1931.	1921.	1911.	1901.	1931.	1921.	1911.	1901.
11	12	13	14	15	16	17	18	19
+338	*168*	..	*262*	..	*170*	..	*251*	..
..	167	..	..	..	164	..	..	..
..	1	..	262	.	6	..	251	..
..	..	*8*	*2*	.	..	*4*	*34*	..
..	.	8	2	..	.	4	34	.
—157	**187**	..		**369**	**211**	..	.	**360**
..	2	.	..	..	2	.	..	..
..	185	..	.	..	206	..	..	..
..	..	.	..	.	3	..	.	..
—157	*187*	..	..	*369*	*211*	..	..	*360*
..	2	..	.	.	2	.	..	..
..	185	..	..	..	206	.	..	..
..	..	..	..		3	..	.	..
+175,347	**182,690**	**196,359**	**287,281**	**167,382**	**186,613**	**198.326**	**291,471**	**170,893**
..	101,507	44,277	21,723	..	105 901	45,672	23,397	..
..	81,183	152,082	265,558	.	80,705	152,654	268,074	..
..	..	..	..	..	7	..	..	..
—956	*569*	*483*	*545*	*620*	*535*	*457*	*557*	*573*
..	54	56	27	..	55	64	31	..
..	515	427	518	..	480	393	526	..
+10,724	*12,334*	*53,991*	*143,036*	*103,159*	*12,073*	*53,512*	*142,483*	*101,682*
..	2,545	2,867	1,285	..	2,436	2,942	1,030	..
..	9,789	51,124	141,751	..	9,637	50,570	141,453	..
+32,917	*39,716*	*32,613*	*34,057*	*27,232*	*40,287*	*32,235*	*34,443*	*26,881*
..	4,526	5,049	116	..	4,581	4,427	89	..
..	35,190	27,564	33,941	..	35,706	27,808	34,354	..
—11,032	*12,249*	*8,433*	*12,125*	*8,366*	*13,459*	*10,626*	*13,919*	*10,175*
..	11,339	1,003	180	..	12,573	1,570	189	..
..	910	7,430	11,945	..	886	9,056	13,730	..
—17,600	*10,819*	*7,913*	*10,834*	*10,105*	*11,978*	*9,700*	*12,623*	*12,186*
..	10,819	7,879	6,933	..	11,971	9,661	8,083	..
..	..	34	3,901	..	..	39	4.540	..
..	..	..	..	..	7	..	..	..
—3,942	*2,036*	*1,648*	*2,224*	*2,058*	*2,361*	*1,802*	*2,519*	*2,516*
..	2,031	1,646	91	..	2,361	1.800	94	..
..	5	2	2,133	.	..	2	2,425	..
—8,096	*5,236*	*5,638*	*6,597*	*4,444*	*5,662*	*5,572*	*7,151*	*4,897*
..	5,205	3,461	72	..	5,630	3,220	43	..
..	31	2,177	6,525	..	32	2,352	7,108	..
+3,949	*3,658*	*3,141*	*2,600*	*1,860*	*4,786*	*3,307*	*2,824*	*2,044*
..	3,569	792	691	..	4,677	716	775	..
..	89	2,349	1,909	..	109	2,591	2,049	..
+11,343	*14,261*	*13,142*	*11,254*	*8,069*	*15,044*	*13,609*	*11,954*	*8,323*
..	14,261	9,709	9,143	..	15,044	9,878	9,780	..
..	..	3,433	2,111	..	..	3,731	2,174	..
—131	*1,967*	*2,067*	*1,840*	*1,469*	*2,102*	*2,249*	*2,038*	*1,616*
..	1.967	383	1,765	..	2,102	401	1,951	..
..	..	1,684	75	..	..	1.848	87	..

Tribe and locality.	Persons. 1931.	1921.	1911.	1901.	1891	Variation (Increase + Decrease —). 1921 to 1931.	1911 to 1921.	1901 to 1911.	1891 to 1901.
1	2	3	4	5	6	7	8	9	10
GOND—*concld*									
Changbhakar	*7,195*	*7,419*	*7,964*	..	..	*+76*	*−545*	*+7,964*	..
Hindu	92	6,420	225	..	..	−6,328	+6,195	..	..
Tribal	7,403	999	7,739	..		+6,404	−6,740	..	..
Korea	*32,549*	*28,937*	*19,940*	..	..	*+3,612*	*+8,997*	*+19,940*	..
Hindu	325	1,074	135	..	..	−749	+939	..	..
Tribal	32,224	27,863	19,805	..	..	+4,361	+8,058	..	..
Surguja	*102,680*	*83,151*	*84,859*	..	..	*+19,529*	*−1,708*	*+84,859*	..
Hindu	73,798	2,858	832	..	..	+70,940	+2,026	..	..
Tribal	28,882	80,293	84,027	..	..	−51,411	−3,734	..	..
Udaipur	*11,438*	*9,281*	*6,607*	..	..	*+2,157*	*+2,674*	*+6,607*	..
Hindu	11,438	9,274	187	..	..	+2,164	+9,087	..	..
Tribal	..	7	6,420	..	..	−7	−6,413	..	..
Jashpur	*4,009*	*3,759*	*3,759*	..	..	*+250*	..	*+3,759*	..
Hindu	4,009	2,799	1,373	..	..	+1,210	+1,426	..	..
Tribal	..	960	2,386	..	..	−960	−1,426	..	..
HALBA									
Central Provinces States	**27,799**	**25,228**	**•26,791**	**22,794**	**22,194**	**+2,571**	**−1,563**	**+3,997**	**+600**
Hindu	27,785	25,228	26,791	..	..	+2,557	−1,563	..	..
Tribal	8	..	..	..	..	+8	..	..	..
Christian	6	..	..	..	..	+6	..	..	..
Bastar	*16,152*	*15,834*	*15,850*	*12,887*	*13,865*	*+318*	*−16*	*+2,963*	*−978*
Hindu	16,148	15,834	15,850	..	..	+314	−16	..	..
Tribal	4	..	..	..	..	+4	..	..	..
Kanker	*8,690*	*8,009*	*8,729*	*8,446*	*5,879*	*+681*	*−720*	*+283*	*+2,567*
Hindu	8,686	8,009	8,729	..	..	+677	−720	..	..
Tribal	4	..	..	..	..	+4	..	..	..
Nandgaon	*2,859*	*1,315*	*2,112*	*1,374*	*2,324*	*+1,544*	*−797*	*+738*	*−950*
Hindu	2,859	1,315	2,112	..	..	+1,544	−797	..	..
Khairagarh	*12*	..	*83*	*86*	*65*	*+42*	*−83*	*−3*	*+21*
Hindu	36	..	83	..	..	+36	−83	..	..
Christian	6	..	..	..	..	+6	..	..	..
Chhuikhadan	*1*	..	*2*	*1*	..	*+1*	*−2*	*+1*	*+1*
Hindu	1	..	2	..	..	+1	−2	..	..
Raigarh	..	*27*	..	..	..	*−27*	*+27*	..	..
Hindu	..	27	..	..	..	−27	+27	..	..
Sarangarh	..	..	*9*	..	*61*	..	*−9*	*+9*	*−61*
Hindu	..	..	9	..	..	..	−9	..	..
Surguja	*55*	*43*	*6*	..	..	*+12*	*+37*	*+6*	..
Hindu	55	43	6	..	..	+12	+37	..	..
KAMAR									
Central Provinces States	**205**	..	**252**	**71**	**369**	..	..	**+181**	**−298**
Hindu	3	..	252	..	..	..	..	..	..
Tribal	202	..	..	..	..	..	..	..	..
Bastar	*185*	..	*27*	*32*	*169*	..	..	*−5*	*−137*
Hindu	2	..	27	..	..	..	..	..	..
Tribal	183	..	..	..	..	..	..	..	..

Net variation 1891 to 1931 (*Increase* + Decrease —).	Males.				Females.			
	1931.	*1921.*	*1911.*	*1901.*	*1931.*	*1921.*	*1911.*	*1901.*
11	12	13	14	15	16	17	18	19
+7,495	*3,727*	*3,956*	*3,999*	..	*3,768*	*3,433*	*3,965*	..
..	51	3,483	125	..	41	2,937	100	..
..	3,676	503	3,874	..	3,727	496	3,865	..
+32,540	*16,631*	*14,704*	*10,085*	..	*15,915*	*14,233*	*9,855*	..
..	176	555	75	..	149	519	60	..
..	16,458	14,149	10,010	..	15,766	13,714	9,795	..
+102,680	*51,679*	*42,156*	*42,854*	..	*51,001*	*40,995*	*42,005*	..
..	37,159	1,442	441	..	36,639	1,416	391	..
..	14,520	40,714	42,413	..	14,362	39,579	41,614	..
+11,438	*5,692*	*4,568*	*3,371*	..	*5,746*	*4,713*	*3,236*	..
..	5,692	4,563	95	..	5,746	4,711	92	..
..	..	5	3,276	..	..	2	3,144	..
+4,009	*2,113*	*1,876*	*1,860*	..	*1,896*	*1,883*	*1,899*	..
..	2,113	1,389	684	..	1,896	1,410	689	..
..	..	487	1,176	..	..	473	1,210	..
+5,605	**13,966**	**12,941**	**13,291**	**11,300**	**13,833**	**12,287**	**13,500**	**11,494**
..	13,957	12,941	13,291	..	13,828	12,287	13,500	..
..	7	..	..	..	1	..	..	..
..	2	..	..	..	4	..	..	..
+2,287	*8,291*	*8,157*	*7,966*	*6,590*	*7,861*	*7,677*	*7,884*	*6,297*
..	8,287	8,157	7,966	..	7,861	7,677	7,884	..
..	4	..	..	..	..	..	..	..
+2,811	*4,260*	*3,933*	*4,276*	*4,042*	*4,430*	*4,076*	*4,453*	*4,404*
..	4,257	3,933	4,276	..	4,429	4,076	4,453	..
..	3	.	.	..	1	..	..	..
+535	*1,359*	*808*	*1,002*	*625*	*1,500*	*507*	*1,110*	*749*
..	1,359	808	1,002	..	1,500	507	1,110	..
—23	*22*	..	*36*	*42*	*20*	..	*47*	*44*
..	20	..	36	..	16	..	47	..
..	2	..	..	..	4	..	..	..
+1	*1*	..	*1*	*1*	..	..	*1*	..
..	1	..	1	..	..	..	1	..
..	..	*14*	..	..	..	*13*	..	..
..	..	14	..	..	..	13	..	..
—61	..	..	*9*	..	..	..	..	..
..	..	..	9	..	..	.	..	..
+55	*33*	*29*	*1*	..	*22*	*14*	*5*	..
..	33	29	1	..	22	14	5	..
—164	**113**	..	**110**	**37**	**92**	..	**142**	**34**
..	3	.	110	..	..	..	142	..
..	110	..	..	..	92	.	.	..
+16	*101*	..	*9*	*14*	*84*	.	*18*	*18*
..	2	..	9	.	.	..	18	..
..	99	..	..	..	84	..	..	..

TABLE XVIII—PART B

Variation of Population

Tribe and locality.	Persons.					Variation (Increase + Decrease—).			
	1931.	1921.	1911.	1901.	1891.	1921 to 1931.	1911 to 1921.	1901 to 1911.	1891 to 1901.
1	2	3	4	5	6	7	8	9	10
KAMAR—*concld.*									
Kanker	*19*	..	*225*	*39*	*187*	..	..	*+186*	*—148*
Hindu	..	..	225	..	..	..	..	..	..
Tribal	19	..	..	..	..	..	..	..	..
Rasiarh	*1*	..	..	..	*13*	..	..	..	*—13*
Hindu	1	..	..	..	..	..	..	..	..
KAWAR									
Central Provinces States ..	**175,953**	**132,004**	**138,911**	**46,247**	**52,431**	**+43,949**	**—6,907**	**+92,664**	**—6,184**
Hindu	165,329	131,652	110,421	..	..	+33,677	+21,231	..	..
Tribal	10,624	352	28,490	..	..	+10,272	—28,138	..	..
Bastar	*199*	*196*	*220*	*204*	*23*	*+3*	*—24*	*+16*	*+181*
Hindu	199	196	210	..	..	+3	—14	..	..
Tribal	..	..	10	..	..	..	—10	..	..
Kanker	*120*	*75*	*113*	*106*	*20*	*+45*	*—38*	*+7*	*+86*
Hindu	120	75	110	..	..	+45	—35	..	..
Tribal	..	..	3	..	..	..	—3	..	..
Nandgaon	*10,247*	*7,138*	*9,139*	*6,487*	*11,830*	*+3,109*	*—2,001*	*+2,652*	*—5,343*
Hindu	10,247	6,796	9,139	..	..	+3,451	—2,343	..	..
Tribal	..	342	..	..	..	—342	+342	..	..
Khairagarh	*7,438*	*6,114*	*7,244*	*5,988*	*8,977*	*+1,324*	*—1,130*	*+1,256*	*—2,989*
Hindu	7,438	6,114	7,238	..	..	+1,324	—1,124	..	..
Tribal	..	..	6	..	..	..	—6	..	..
Chhuikhadan	*251*	*175*	*317*	*208*	*491*	*+76*	*—142*	*+109*	*—283*
Hindu	251	175	317	..	..	+76	—142	..	..
Kawardha	*121*	..	*9*	*21*	*4*	*+121*	*—9*	*—12*	*+17*
Hindu	121	..	9	..	..	+121	—9	..	..
Sakti	*4,626*	*4,306*	*3,828*	*2,689*	*3,256*	*+320*	*+478*	*+1,139*	*—567*
Hindu	4,626	4,306	3,824	..	..	+320	+482	..	..
Tribal	..	..	4	..	..	..	—4	..	..
Raigarh	*48,110*	*42,570*	*36,788*	*30,180*	*27,435*	*+5,540*	*+5,782*	*+6,608*	*+2,745*
Hindu	48,110	42,570	36,770	..	..	+5,540	+5,800	..	..
Tribal	..	..	18	..	..	..	—18	..	..
Sarangarh	*441*	*445*	*410*	*364*	*395*	*—4*	*+35*	*+46*	*—31*
Hindu	441	445	410	..	..	—4	+35	..	..
Changbhakar	*2,152*	..	*2,117*	..	..	*+2,152*	*—2,117*	*+2,117*	..
Hindu	429	..	2,075	..	..	+429	—2,075	..	..
Tribal	1,723	..	42	..	..	+1,723	—42	..	..
Korea	*8,989*	*2,070*	*7,497*	..	..	*+6,919*	*—5,427*	*+7,497*	..
Hindu	170	2,068	64	..	..	—1,898	+2,004	..	..
Tribal	8,819	2	7,433	..	..	+8,817	—7,431	..	..
Surguja	*48,389*	*35,704*	*40,962*	..	..	*+12,685*	*—5,258*	*+40,962*	..
Hindu	48,307	35,704	40,859	..	..	+12,603	—5,155	..	..
Tribal	82	..	103	..	..	+82	—103	..	..
Udaipur	*32,735*	*24,177*	*21,262*	..	..	*+8,558*	*+2,915*	*+21,262*	..
Hindu	32,735	24,177	399	..	..	+8,558	+23,778	..	..
Tribal	..	..	20,863	..	..	..	—20,863	..	..
Jashpur	*12,135*	*9,034*	*9,005*	..	..	*+3,101*	*+29*	*+9,005*	..
Hindu	12,135	9,026	8,997	..	..	+3,109	+29	..	..
Tribal	..	8	8	..	..	—8	..	..	..

of Selected Tribes. **TABLE XVIII—PART B**

Net variation 1891 to 1931 (Increase + Decrease —).	Males. 1931.	Males. 1921.	Males. 1911.	Males. 1901.	Females. 1931.	Females. 1921.	Females. 1911.	Females. 1901.
11	12	13	14	15	16	17	18	19
+168	*11*	..	*101*	*23*	*8*	..	*124*	*16*
..	..	..	101	..	..	..	124	..
..	11	..	..	..	8	..	..	..
—12	*1*	..	..	..	..	..	..	..
..	1	..	..	..	..	..	..	..
+123,522	**87,776**	**65,234**	**69,099**	**22,357**	**88,177**	**66,770**	**69,812**	**23,890**
..	82,375	65,015	54,704	..	82,954	66,637	55,717	..
..	5,401	219	14,395	..	5,223	133	14,095	..
+176	*103*	*81*	*116*	*95*	*96*	*115*	*104*	*109*
..	103	81	110	..	96	115	100	..
..	..	.	6	..	.	..	4	..
+100	*77*	*32*	*51*	*60*	*43*	*43*	*59*	*46*
..	77	32	51	..	43	43	59	..
..	..	..	3	..	..	..	..	..
—1,583	*4,768*	*3,447*	*4,312*	*2,984*	*5,479*	*3,691*	*4,827*	*3,503*
..	4,768	3,234	4,312	..	5,479	3,562	4,827	..
..	..	213	..	..	..	129	.	..
—1,539	*3,447*	*2,788*	*3,393*	*2,725*	*3,991*	*3,326*	*3,851*	*3,263*
..	3,447	2,788	3,391	..	3,991	3,326	3,847	..
..	..	..	2	..	..	..	4	..
—240	*129*	*75*	*140*	*87*	*122*	*100*	*177*	*121*
..	129	75	140	..	122	100	177	..
+117	*98*	..	*5*	*20*	*23*	..	*4*	*1*
..	98	..	5		23	..	4	..
+1,370	*2,252*	*2,117*	*1,849*	*1,288*	*2,374*	*2,189*	*1,979*	*1,101*
..	2,252	2,117	1,845	.	2,374	2,189	1,979	..
..	..	.	4			..	..	..
+20,675	*24,213*	*21,081*	*18,006*	*[illegible]*	*23,897*	*21,489*	*18,782*	*15,252*
..	24,213	21,081	17,994	..	23,897	21,489	18,776	..
..	..	..	12	..	.	..	6	..
+46	*219*	*185*	*211*	*170*	*222*	*260*	*199*	*194*
..	219	185	211	.	222	260	199	..
+2,152	*1,136*	..	*1,092*	.	*1,016*	..	*1,025*	..
..	222	..	1,067	.	207	..	1,008	..
..	914	..	25	.	809	..	17	..
+8,989	*4,529*	*1,040*	*3,766*	..	*4,460*	*1,030*	*3,731*	..
..	81	1,039	37	..	89	1,029	27	..
..	4,448	1	3,729	..	4,371	1	3,704	..
+48,389	*24,134*	*18,456*	*20,769*	.	*24,255*	*17,246*	*20,193*	.
..	24,095	18,456	20,712	..	24,212	17,246	20,147	..
..	39	.	57	.	43	.	46	.
+32,735	*16,485*	*11,388*	*10,753*	..	*16,250*	*12,789*	*10,509*	..
..	16,485	11,388	198		16,250	12,789	201	..
..	..	..	10,555	.		.	10,308	.
+12,135	*6,186*	*4,544*	*4,633*	..	*[illegible]*	*4,490*	*4,372*	.
..	6,186	4,539	4,631	.	5,949	4,487	4,366	..
..	.	5	2		.	3	.	..

TABLE XVIII—PART B

Variation of Population

Tribe and locality.	Persons.					Variation (Increase+ Decrease—).			
	1931.	1921.	1911.	1901.	1891.	1921 to 1931.	1911 to 1921.	1901 to 1911.	1891 to 1901.
1	2	3	4	5	6	7	8	9	10
KOL									
Central Provinces States ..	**8 328**	**5,709**	**6,113**	**458**	**238**	**+2,619**	**−404**	**+5,655**	**+220**
Hindu ..	2,582	5,448	958	..	..	−2,866	+4,490	..	..
Tribal ..	5,746	261	5,155	..	..	+5,485	−4,894	..	..
Bastar ..	..	..	*59*	..	..	..	*−59*	*+59*	..
Hindu ..	..	..	59	..	..	..	−59	..	..
Khairagarh ..	*168*	..	*1*	..	*25*	*+168*	*−1*	*+1*	*−25*
Hindu ..	168	..	1	..	..	+168	−1	..	..
Kawardha ..	..	..	*3*	..	*2*	..	*−3*	*+3*	*−2*
Hindu ..	..	..	3	..	..	..	−3	..	..
Sakti ..	*173*	*8*	*5*	..	..	*+165*	*+3*	*+5*	..
Hindu ..	173	8	5	..	..	+165	+3	..	..
Raigarh ..	*103*	*252*	*1*	*438*	*123*	*−149*	*+251*	*−437*	*+315*
Hindu ..	103	252	1	..	..	−149	+251	..	..
Sarangarh ..	..	..	*1*	*20*	*88*	..	*−1*	*−19*	*−68*
Hindu ..	..	..	1	..	..	..	−1	..	..
Changbhakar ..	*4,608*	*4,378*	*4,968*	..	..	*+230*	*−590*	*+4,968*	..
Hindu ..	86	4,224	75	..	..	−4,138	+4,149	..	..
Tribal ..	4,522	154	4,893	..	..	+4,368	−4,739	..	..
Korea ..	*1,214*	*997*	*760*	..	..	*+217*	*+237*	*+760*	..
Hindu ..	..	917	557	..	..	−917	+360	..	..
Tribal ..	1,214	80	203	..	..	+1,134	−123	..	..
Surguja ..	*2,058*	*58*	*293*	..	..	*+2,000*	*−235*	*+293*	..
Hindu ..	2,052	41	255	..	..	+2,011	−214	..	..
Tribal ..	6	17	38	..	..	−11	−21	..	..
Udaipur ..	*4*	*10*	*21*	..	..	*−6*	*−11*	*+21*	..
Tribal ..	4	10	21	..	..	−6	−11	..	..
Jashpur ..	..	*6*	*1*	..	..	*−6*	*+5*	*+1*	..
Hindu ..	..	6	1	..	..	−6	+5	..	..
KOLAM ..	..	..	..	..	..	..	..	..	..
KOLI									
Central Provinces States ..	..	**183**	..	..	..	**−183**	**+183**	..	..
Hindu ..	..	183	..	..	..	−183	+183	..	..
Surguja ..	..	*183*	..	..	..	*−183*	*+183*	..	..
Hindu ..	..	183	..	..	..	−183	+183	..	..
KORKU									
Central Provinces States ..	**8,719**	**5,087**	**2,826**	**2,364**	**3,933**	**+3,636**	**+2,257**	**+462**	**−1,569**
Hindu ..	2,010	455	54	..	..	+1,555	+401	..	..
Tribal ..	6,709	4,632	2,772	..	..	+2,081	+1,856	..	..
Makrai ..	*2,703*	*2,326*	*2,756*	*2,280*	*3,933*	*+377*	*−430*	*+476*	*−1,653*
Hindu ..	..	221	26	..	..	−221	+195	..	..
Tribal ..	2,703	2,105	2,730	..	..	+598	−625	..	..
* *Bastar* ..	*21*	*295*	*69*	*5*	..	*−274*	*+226*	*+64*	*+5*
Hindu ..	21	179	27	..	..	−158	+152	..	..
Tribal ..	..	116	42	..	..	−116	+74	..	..
* *Kanker* ..	..	..	..	*6*	..	..	..	*−6*	*+6*

*Probably a sub-tribe of Korwas. Crooke held Korwas and Korkus to be branches of the same tribe. See Part I of this Report.

of Selected Tribes

TABLE XVIII—PART B

Net variation 1891 to 1931 (Increase + Decrease —).	Males.				Females.			
	1931.	1921.	1911.	1901.	1931.	1921.	1911.	1901.
11	12	13	14	15	16	17	18	19
+8,090	**4,315**	**3,033**	**8,099**	**224**	**4,013**	**2,676**	**3,014**	**234**
..	1,318	2,915	503	..	1,264	2,533	455	..
..	2,997	118	2,596	..	2,749	143	2,559	..
..	..	..	*43*	..	..	..	*16*	..
..	..	..	43	..	..	..	16	..
+143	*90*	..	*1*	..	*78*	..	..	..
..	90	..	1	..	78	..	..	..
—2	..	..	*2*	..	..	..	*1*	..
..	..	..	2	..	..	..	1	..
+173	*102*	..	*5*	..	*71*	*8*	..	..
..	102	..	5	..	71	8	..	..
—20	*38*	*122*	*1*	*214*	*65*	*130*	..	*224*
..	38	122	1	..	65	130	..	..
—88	..	..	*1*	*10*	..	..	..	*10*
..	..	..	1	..	..	..	..	..
+4,608	*2,425*	*2,340*	*2,495*	..	*2,185*	*2,038*	*2,473*	..
..	43	2,271	38	..	43	1,953	37	..
..	2,382	69	2,457	..	2,140	85	2,436	..
+1,214	*609*	*538*	*397*	..	*605*	*459*	*363*	..
..	..	496	284	..	..	421	273	..
..	609	42	113	..	605	38	90	..
+2,058	*1,048*	*27*	*148*	..	*1,010*	*31*	*145*	..
..	1,045	26	128	..	1,007	15	127	..
..	3	1	20	..	3	16	18	..
+4	*3*	*6*	*6*	..	*1*	*4*	*15*	..
..	3	6	6	..	1	4	15	..
..	..	..	..	..	..	*6*	*1*	..
..	..	..	..	..	..	6	1	..
..	..	..	..	..	..	..	..	..
..	..	**118**	..	..	..	**65**	..	..
..	..	118	..	..	..	65	..	..
..	..	*118*	..	..	..	*65*	..	..
..	..	118	..	..	..	65	..	..
+4,786	**4,414**	**2,727**	**1,449**	**1,205**	**4,305**	**2,360**	**1,377**	**1,159**
..	1,019	239	21	..	991	216	33	..
..	3,395	2,488	1,428	..	3,314	2,1[illegible]	1,344	..
—1,230	*1,401*	*1,211*	*1,413*	*1,165*	*1,302*	*1,115*	*1,343*	*1,115*
..	..	125	9	..	..	96	17	..
..	1,401	1,086	1,404	..	1,302	1,019	1,326	..
+21	*12*	*150*	*36*	*3*	*9*	*145*	*33*	*2*
..	12	84	12	..	9	95	15	..
..	..	66	24	..	..	50	18	..
..	..	..	..	*3*	..	..	..	3

Tribe and locality.	Persons.					Variation (Increase + Decrease—).			
	1931.	1921.	1911.	1901.	1891.	1921 to 1931.	1911 to 1921.	1901 to 1911.	1891 to 1901.
1	2	3	4	5	6	7	8	9	10
KORKU—*concld.*									
**Sakti*	..	..	..	*73*	..	..	..	*−73*	*+73*
**Korea*	*32*	..	*1*	..	..	*+32*	*−1*	*+1*	..
Hindu	..	..	1	..	..	..	−1	..	..
Tribal	32	..	..	..	..	+32	..	..	..
**Surguja*	*5,963*	*2,466*	..	..	..	*+3,497*	*+2,466*	..	..
Hindu	1,989	55	..	..	..	+1,934	+55	..	..
Tribal	3,974	2,411	..	..	..	+1,563	+2,411	..	..
KORWA									
Central Provinces States ..	**26,192**	**20,028**	**33,124**	**142**	**447**	**+6,164**	**−13,096**	**+ 32,982**	**−305**
Hindu	18,553	8,879	3,736	..	..	+9,674	+5,143	..	..
Tribal	7,574	11,149	29,388	..	..	−3,575	−18,239	..	..
Christian	65	..	..	..	..	+65	..	..	..
Kanker	..	*16*	..	..	..	*−16*	*+16*	..	..
Hindu	..	16	..	..	..	−16	+16	..	..
Sakti	*74*	*82*	*65*	..	*116*	*−8*	*+17*	*+65*	*−116*
Hindu	74	82	63	..	..	−8	+19	..	..
Tribal	..	..	2	..	..	..	−2	..	..
Raigarh	..	*317*	*363*	*130*	*331*	*−317*	*−46*	*+233*	*−201*
Hindu	..	317	35	..	..	−317	+282	..	..
Tribal	..	..	328	..	..	..	−328	..	..
Sarangarh	..	*41*	*4*	*12*	..	*−41*	*+37*	*−8*	*+12*
Hindu	..	41	4	..	..	−41	+37	..	..
Changbhakar	..	..	*407*	..	..	..	*−407*	*+407*	..
Hindu	..	..	407	..	..	..	−407	..	..
Korea	*13*	..	*37*	..	..	*+13*	*−37*	*+37*	..
Hindu	5	..	..	..	..	+5	..	..	..
Tribal	8	..	37	..	..	+8	−37	..	..
Surguja	*13,455*	*9,687*	*17,982*	..	..	*+3,768*	*−8,295*	*+17,982*	..
Hindu	10,788	2,198	583	..	..	+8,590	+1,615	..	..
Tribal	2,667	7,489	17,399	..	..	−4,822	−9,910	..	..
Udaipur	*976*	*476*	*770*	..	..	*+500*	*−294*	*+770*	..
Hindu	..	168	8	..	..	−168	+160	..	..
Tribal	976	308	762	..	..	+668	−454	..	..
Jashpur	*11,674*	*9,409*	*13,496*	..	..	*+2,265*	*−4,087*	*+13,496*	..
Hindu	7,686	6,057	2,636	..	..	+1,629	+3,421	..	..
Tribal	3,923	3,352	10,860	..	..	+571	−7,508	..	..
Christian	65	..	..	..	..	+65	..	..	..
MAJHWAR									
Central Provinces States ..	**9,879**	**3,063**	**7,737**	..	..	**+6,816**	**−4,674**	..	..
Hindu	9,879	3,063	3,500	..	..	+6,816	−437	..	..
Tribal	..	..	4,237	..	..	..	−4,237	..	..
Sakti	..	..	*73*	..	..	..	*−73*	..	..
Hindu	..	..	71	..	..	..	−71	..	..
Tribal	..	..	2	..	..	..	−2	..	..
Raigarh	*669*	..	*1,659*	..	..	*+669*	*−1,659*	..	..
Hindu	669	..	509	..	..	+669	−509	..	..
Tribal	..	..	1,150	..	..	..	−1,150	..	..

* Probably a sub-tribe of Korwas. Crooke held Korwas and Korkus to be branches of the same tribe. See Part I of this Report.

Net variation 1891 to 1931 (Increase + Decrease —).	Males. 1931.	Males. 1921.	Males. 1911.	Males. 1901.	Females. 1931.	Females. 1921.	Females. 1911.	Females. 1901.
11	12	13	14	15	16	17	18	19
..	..	..	..	34	..	..	..	39
+32	14	..	..	..	18	..	1	..
..	..	..	..	..	..	..	1	..
..	14	..	..	..	18	..	..	..
+5,963	2,987	1,366	..	..	2,976	1,100	..	..
..	1,007	30	..	..	982	25	..	..
..	1,980	1,336	..	..	1,994	1,075	..	..
+25,745	**12,880**	**9,607**	**16,745**	**65**	**13,312**	**10,421**	**16,379**	**77**
..	9,207	4,224	1,859	..	9,346	4,655	1,877	..
..	3,644	5,383	14,886	..	3,930	5,766	14,502	..
..	29	..	..	..	36	..	..	..
..	..	16	..	..	..	..	..	..
..	..	16	..	..	..	..	..	
−42	37	38	18	..	37	44	47	..
..	37	38	17	..	37	44	46	..
..	..	..	1	..	..	..	1	..
−331	..	142	174	62	..	175	189	68
..	..	142	17	..	..	175	18	..
..	..	..	157	..	..	..	171	..
..	..	15	'	3	..	26	3	9
..	..	15	1	..	..	26	3	..
..	..	..	210	..	..	..	197	..
..	..	..	210	..	..	..	197	..
+13	5	..	19	..	8	..	18	..
..	2	..	..	..	3	..	..	..
..	3	..	19	..	5	..	18	..
+13,455	6,748	4,480	9,205	..	6,707	5,207	8,777	..
..	5,398	947	309	..	5,390	1,251	274	..
..	1,350	3,533	8,896	..	1,317	3,956	8,503	..
+976	414	252	394	..	562	224	376	..
..	..	95	7	..	..	73	1	..
..	414	157	387	..	562	151	375	..
+11,674	5,676	4,664	6,724	..	5,998	4,745	6,772	..
..	3,770	2,971	1,298	..	3,916	3,086	1,538	..
..	1,877	1,693	5,426	..	2,046	1,659	5,434	..
..	29	..	..	..	36	..	..	..
..	**5,147**	**1,543**	**3,911**	..	**4,732**	**1,520**	**3,826**	..
..	5,147	1,543	1,745	..	4,732	1,520	1,755	..
..	..	..	2,166	..	..	..	2,071	..
..	..	..	37	..	..	..	36	..
..	..	..	36	..	..	..	35	..
..	..	..	1	..	..	..	1	..
..	341	..	829	..	328	..	830	..
..	341	..	254	..	328	..	255	..
..	..	..	575	..	..	..	575	..

Tribe and locality.	Persons.					Variation (Increase + Decrease —).			
	1931.	1921.	1911.	1901.	1891.	1921 to 1931.	1911 to 1921.	1901 to 1911.	1891 to 1901.
1	2	3	4	5	6	7	8	9	10
MAJHWAR—*concld.*									
Sarangarh	..	..	*338*	..	..	..	*—338*	..	..
Hindu	..	..	338	..	..	..	—338	..	..
Surguja	*5,436*	*3,063*	*2,789*	..	..	*+2,373*	*+274*	..	..
Hindu	5,436	3,063	2,578	..	..	+2,373	+485	..	..
Tribal	..	..	211	..	..	..	—211	..	..
Udaipur	*3,754*	..	*2,878*	..	..	*+3,754*	*—2,878*	..	..
Hindu	3,754	..	4	..	..	+3,754	—4	..	..
Tribal	..	..	2,874	..	..	..	—2,874	..	..
Jashpur	*20*	..	..	..	..	*+20*	..	..	..
Hindu	20	..	..	..	..	+20	..	..	..
* **MARIA**									
Central Provinces States ..	**146,109**	..	..	..	**25,855**	..	..	..	..
Hindu	88	..	..	..	..	..	..	..	..
Tribal	146,021	..	..	..	..	..	..	..	..
Bastar	*146,070*	..	..	..	*25,855*	..	..	..	..
Hindu	70	..	..	..	..	..	..	..	..
Tribal	146,000	..	..	..	..	..	..	..	..
Khairagarh	*18*	..	..	..	..	..	..	..	..
Hindu	18	..	..	..	..	..	..	..	..
Changbhakar	*21*	..	..	..	..	..	..	..	..
Tribal	21	..	..	..	..	..	..	..	..
* **MURIA**									
Central Provinces States ..	**125,289**	..	..	..	**54,048**	..	..	..	..
Hindu	340	..	..	..	..	..	..	..	..
Tribal	124,949	..	..	..	..	..	..	..	..
Bastar	*124,993*	..	..	..	*53,960*	..	..	..	..
Hindu	44	..	..	..	..	..	..	..	..
Tribal	124,949	..	..	..	..	..	..	..	..
Raigarh	..	..	..	..	*88*	..	..	..	..
Surguja	*135*	..	..	..	..	..	..	..	..
Hindu	135	..	..	..	..	..	..	..	..
Jashpur	*161*	..	..	..	..	..	..	..	..
Hindu	161	..	..	..	..	..	..	..	..
NAGARCHI									
Central Provinces States ..	**68**	..	**91**	..	..	..	..	..	..
Hindu	68	..	91	..	..	..	..	..	..
Nandgaon	*29*	..	*35*	..	..	..	..	..	..
Hindu	29	..	35	..	..	..	..	..	..
Khairagarh	*20*	..	*28*	..	..	..	..	..	..
Hindu	20	..	28	..	..	..	..	..	..
Chhuikhadan	*19*	..	*12*	..	..	..	..	..	..
Hindu	19	..	12	..	..	..	..	..	..

* **Figures of Marias and Murias from 1901—1921 were included with Gonds.**

Net variation 1891 to 1931 (Increase + Decrease —).	Males.				Females			
	1931.	1921.	1911.	1901	1931.	1921.	1911.	1901.
11	12	13	14	15	16	17	18	19
..	..	.	*164*	..	..	..	*174*	..
..	..	.	164	..	..	..	174	..
..	*2,757*	*1,543*	*1,404*	..	*2,679*	*1,520*	*1,385*	..
..	2,757	1,543	1,288	.	2,679	1,520	1,290	..
..	..	..	116	.	..	..	95	..
..	*2,036*	..	*1,477*	..	*1,718*	..	*1,401*	..
..	2,036	.	3	.	1,718	..	1	..
..	..	..	1,474	..	..	..	1,400	..
..	*13*	..	.	.	*7*	..	..	..
.	13	..	..	..	7	..	..	..
+120,254	**73,429**	..	..	..	**72,680**		..	..
..	52	..	..	.	36	..	..	..
..	73,377	.	..	.	72,644	..	.	..
+120,215	*73,406*	..	..	..	*72,664*	.	..	..
..	39	..	..	..	31	..	..	..
..	73,367	..	..	..	72,633	..	..	..
+18	*13*	..	..	..	*5*	..	..	.
..	13	..	..	.	5	..	..	..
+21	*10*	..	..	..	*11*	..	..	..
..	10	..	..	..	11	..	..	..
+71,241	**62,790**	..	..	..	**62,499**	..	..	..
..	145	.	..	..	195	..	..	..
..	62,645	.	..	..	62,304	..	..	..
+71,033	*62,660*	..	.	..	*62,333*	..	..	..
..	15	..	..	..	29	..	..	..
..	62,645	..	..	..	62,304	..	..	..
—88	..	.	..	..	..	..	..	..
+135	*48*	..	..	..	*87*	..	..	..
..	48	..	..	..	87	..	..	..
+161	*82*	.	..	.	*79*	..	..	..
..	82		..	..	79	..	..	..
+68	**31**	.	**45**	..	**37**	..	**46**	..
..	31	..	45	..	37	..	46	..
+29	*12*	..	*18*	.	*17*	.	*17*	..
..	12	..	18	..	17		17	.
+20	*12*	..	*15*	..	*8*		*13*	..
..	12	..	15	..	8	..	13	..
+19	*7*	..	*3*	..	*12*	..	*9*	..
..	7	..	3	..	12	.	9	..

Tribe and locality.	Persons.					Variation (Increase + Decrease −).			
	1931.	1921.	1911.	1901.	1891.	1921 to 1931.	1911 to 1921.	1901 to 1911.	1891 to 1901.
1	2	3	4	5	6	7	8	9	10
NAGARCHI—*concld.*									
Kawardha	..	..	*3*	..	..	..	..	..	..
Hindu	..	..	3	..	..	..	..	..	..
Korea	..	..	*10*	..	..	..	..	..	..
Hindu	..	..	10	..	..	..	..	..	..
Udaipur	..	..	*3*	..	..	..	..	..	..
Hindu	..	..	3	..	..	..	..	..	..
NAGASIA									
Central Provinces States	**47,564**	**14,766**	**43,953**	..	..	**+32,798**	**−29,187**	..	..
Hindu	47,220	14,719	39,674	..	..	+32,501	−24,955	..	..
Tribal	320	47	4,279	..	..	+273	−4,232	..	..
Christian	24	..	..	..	..	+24	..	..	..
Khairagarh	*1*	..	..	..	..	*+1*	..	..	..
Hindu	1	..	..	..	..	+1	..	..	..
Sakti	*174*	*153*	*109*	..	..	*+21*	*+44*	..	..
Hindu	174	153	109	..	..	+21	+44	..	..
Raigarh	*2,768*	*681*	*2,382*	..	..	*+2,087*	*−1,701*	..	..
Hindu	2,768	681	2,382	..	..	+2,087	−1,701	..	..
Sarangarh	..	..	*1*	..	..	..	*−1*	..	..
Hindu	..	..	1	..	..	..	−1	..	..
Korea	*1*	..	..	..	..	*+1*	..	..	..
Tribal	1	..	..	..	..	+1	..	..	..
Surguja	*24,318*	..	*22,066*	..	..	*+24,318*	*−22,066*	..	..
Hindu	23,999	..	21,123	..	..	+23,999	−21,123	..	..
Tribal	319	..	943	..	..	+319	−943	..	..
Udaipur	*4,680*	*557*	*3,317*	..	..	*+4,123*	*−2,760*	..	..
Hindu	4,680	557	4	..	..	+4,123	+553	..	..
Tribal	..	..	3,313	..	..	..	−3,313	..	..
Jashpur	*15,622*	*13,375*	*16,078*	..	..	*+2,247*	*−2,703*	..	..
Hindu	15,598	13,328	16,055	..	..	+2,270	−2,727	..	..
Tribal	..	47	23	..	..	−47	+24	..	..
Christian	24	..	..	..	..	+24	..	..	..
ORAON									
Central Provinces States	**149,133**	**73,905**	**78,494**	..	**4,605**	**+75,228**	**−4,589**	..	..
Hindu	49,381	17,799	549	..	..	+31,582	+17,250	..	..
Tribal	52,235	56,106	77,945	..	..	−3,871	−21,839	..	..
Christian	47,517	..	..	..	..	+47,517	..	..	..
Chhuikhadan	..	*6*	..	..	..	*−6*	*+6*	..	..
Hindu	..	6	..	..	..	−6	+6	..	..
Sakti	*434*	..	*409*	..	*695*	*+434*	*−409*	..	..
Hindu	434	..	86	..	..	+434	−86	..	..
Tribal	..	..	323	..	..	..	−323	..	..

Net variation 1891 to 1931 (Increase + Decrease —).	Males. 1931.	Males. 1921.	Males. 1911.	Males. 1901.	Females. 1931.	Females. 1921.	Females. 1911.	Females. 1901.
11	12	13	14	15	16	17	18	19
..	..	..	*2*	..	..	..	*1*	..
..	..	..	2	..	..	..	1	..
..	..	..	*6*	..	..	..	*4*	..
..	..	..	6	..	..	..	4	..
..	..	..	*1*	..	..	..	*2*	..
..	..	..	1	..	..	..	2	..
..	**23,625**	**7,180**	**22,095**	..	**23,939**	**7,586**	**21,858**	..
..	23,449	7,159	19,993	..	23,771	7,560	19,681	..
..	161	21	2,102	..	159	26	2,177	..
..	15	..	..	..	9	..	..	..
..	*1*	..	..	..	..	..	..	..
..	1	..	..	..	..	..	..	..
..	*86*	*81*	*63*	..	*88*	*72*	*46*	..
..	86	81	63	..	88	72	46	..
..	*1,342*	*290*	*1,235*	..	*1,426*	*391*	*1,147*	..
..	1,342	290	1,235	..	1,426	391	1,147	..
..	..	..	*1*	..	..	..	..	..
..	..	..	1	..	..	..	..	..
..	*1*	..	..	..	..	..	..	..
..	1	..	..	..	..	..	..	..
..	*12,148*	..	*11,138*	..	*12,170*	..	*10,928*	..
..	11,988	..	10,659	..	12,011	..	10,464	..
..	160	..	479	..	159	..	464	..
..	*2,266*	*295*	*1,615*	..	*2,414*	*262*	*1,702*	..
..	2,266	295	2	..	2,414	262	2	..
..	..	..	1,613	..	..	..	1,700	..
..	*7,781*	*6,514*	*8,043*	..	*7,841*	*6,861*	*8,035*	..
..	7,766	6,493	8,033	..	7,832	6,835	8,022	..
..	..	21	10	..	..	26	13	..
..	15	..	..	..	9	..	..	..
+144,528	**75,623**	**37,780**	**39,597**	..	**73,510**	**36,125**	**38,897**	..
..	25,027	9,033	260	..	24,354	8,766	289	..
..	26,549	28,747	39,337	..	25,686	27,359	38,608	..
..	24,047	..	..	..	23,470	..	..	..
..	..	*4*	..	..	..	*2*	..	..
..	..	4	..	..	..	2	..	..
—261	*268*	..	*207*	..	*166*	..	*202*	..
..	268	..	42	..	166	..	44	..
..	..	..	165	..	..	..	158	..

TABLE XVIII—PART B | Variation of Population.

Tribe and locality.	Persons. 1931.	1921.	1911.	1901.	1891.	Variation (Increase + Decrease —). 1921 to 1931.	1911 to 1921.	1901 to 1911.	1891 to 1901.
1	2	3	4	5	6	7	8	9	10
ORAON—*concld.*									
Raigarh	*8,008*	*4,981*	*6,108*	..	*3,886*	*+3,027*	*—1,127*	..	..
Hindu	7,970	1,719	42	..	..	+6,251	+1,677	..	..
Tribal	..	3,262	6,066	..	..	—3,262	—2,804	..	..
Christian	38	..	..	..	..	+38	..	..	..
Sarangarh	*1,181*	*990*	*931*	..	*24*	*+191*	*+59*	..	..
Hindu	1,181	981	67	..	..	+200	+914	..	..
Tribal	..	9	864	..	..	—9	—855	..	..
Korea	*1,439*	*1,070*	*635*	..	..	*+369*	*+435*	..	..
Hindu	13	708	1	..	..	—695	+707	..	..
Tribal	1,426	362	634	..	..	+1,064	—272	..	..
Surguja	*51,990*	*37,330*	*39,770*	..	..	*+14,660*	*—2,440*	..	..
Hindu	27,946	5,118	51	..	..	+22,828	+5,067	..	..
Tribal	24,044	32,212	39,719	..	..	—8,168	—7,507	..	..
Udaipur	*14,336*	*9,382*	*6,376*	..	..	*+4,954*	*+3,006*	..	..
Hindu	..	445	73	..	..	—445	+372	..	..
Tribal	14,336	8,937	6,303	..	..	+5,399	+2,634	..	..
Jashpur	*71,745*	*20,146*	*24,265*	..	..	*+51,599*	*—4,119*	..	..
Hindu	11,837	8,822	229	..	..	+3,015	+8,593	..	..
Tribal	12,429	11,324	24,036	..	..	+1,105	—12,712	..	..
Christian	47,479	..	..	..	..	+47,479	..	..	..
PARDHAN									
Central Provinces States ..	**3,742**	**4,126**	**3,753**	..	..	**—384**	**+373**	..	..
Hindu	2,561	2,093	2,414	..	..	+468	—321	..	..
Tribal	1,181	2,033	1,339	..	..	—852	+694	..	..
Makrai	*91*	*71*	*79*	..	..	*+20*	*—8*	..	..
Hindu	..	13	..	..	..	—13	+13	..	..
Tribal	91	58	79	..	..	+33	—21	..	..
Bastar	*1,690*	*971*	*605*	..	..	*+719*	*+366*	..	..
Hindu	1,169	920	431	..	..	+249	+489	..	..
Tribal	521	51	174	..	..	+470	—123	..	..
Kanker	*219*	*67*	*392*	..	..	*+152*	*—325*	..	..
Hindu	150	67	186	..	..	+83	—119	..	..
Tribal	69	..	206	..	..	+69	—206	..	..
Nandgaon	*123*	*1,917*	*154*	..	..	*—1,794*	*+1,763*	..	..
Hindu	123	314	112	..	..	—191	+202	..	..
Tribal	..	1,603	42	..	..	—1,603	+1,561	..	..
Khairagarh	*105*	*3*	*238*	..	..	*+102*	*—235*	..	..
Hindu	105	3	209	..	..	+102	—206	..	..
Tribal	..	..	29	..	..	..	—29	..	..
Kawardha	*90*	..	*215*	..	..	*+90*	*—215*	..	..
Hindu	90	..	213	..	..	+90	—213	..	..
Tribal	..	..	2	..	..	..	—2	..	..
Sakti	*13*	..	*335*	..	..	*+13*	*—335*	..	..
Hindu	13	..	88	..	..	+13	—88	..	..
Tribal	..	..	247	..	..	..	—247	..	..
Raigarh	*155*	*129*	*297*	..	..	*+26*	*—168*	..	..
Hindu	155	129	297	..	..	+26	—168	..	..
Sarangarh	..	..	*21*	..	..	..	*—21*	..	..
Hindu	..	..	21	..	..	..	—21	..	..

Net variation 1891 to 1931 (Increase + Decrease —).	Males. 1931.	Males. 1921.	Males. 1911.	Males. 1901.	Females. 1931.	Females. 1921.	Females. 1911.	Females. 1901.
11	12	13	14	15	16	17	18	19
+4,122	*3,831*	*2,518*	*3,004*	..	*4,177*	*2,163*	*3,104*	..
..	3,813	847	23	..	4,157	872	19	..
..	..	1,671	2,981	..	..	1,591	3,085	..
..	18	..	...	..	20	...	...	..
+1,157	*523*	*457*	*444*	..	*658*	*533*	*487*	..
..	523	456	33	..	658	525	34	..
..	..	1	411	..	..	8	453	..
+1,439	*729*	*558*	*327*	..	*710*	*512*	*308*	..
..	8	367	..	..	5	341	1	..
..	721	191	327	..	705	171	307	..
+51,990	*26,640*	*19,209*	*20,143*	..	*25,350*	*18,121*	*19,627*	..
..	14,423	2,670	24	..	13,523	2,448	27	..
..	12,217	16,539	20,119	..	11,827	15,673	19,600	..
+14,336	*7,303*	*4,790*	*3,230*	..	*7,033*	*4,592*	*3,146*	..
..	..	249	3	..	..	196	70	..
..	7,303	4,541	3,227	..	7,033	4,396	3,076	..
+71,745	*36,329*	*10,244*	*12,242*	..	*35,416*	*9,902*	*12,023*	..
..	5,992	4,440	135	..	5,845	4,382	94	..
..	6,308	5,804	12,107	..	6,121	5,520	11,929	..
..	24,029	..	...	..	23,450	...	..	..
+3,742	**1,810**	**2,352**	**1,806**	..	**1,932**	**1,774**	**1,947**	..
..	1,255	905	1,177	..	1,306	1.188	1,237	..
..	555	1,447	629	..	626	586	710	..
+91	*54*	*42*	*36*	..	*37*	*29*	*43*	..
..	..	9	..	..	..	4	..	..
..	54	33	36	..	37	25	43	..
+1,690	*826*	*489*	*290*	..	*804*	*482*	*315*	..
..	589	453	212	..	580	467	219	..
..	237	36	78	..	284	15	96	..
+219	*119*	*29*	*181*	..	*100*	*38*	*211*	..
..	92	29	82	..	58	38	104	..
..	27	..	99	..	42	..	107	..
+123	*56*	*1,206*	*68*	..	*67*	*711*	*86*	..
..	56	4	50	..	67	310	62	..
..	..	1,202	18	..	..	401	24	..
+105	*41*	*3*	*113*	..	*64*	..	*125*	..
..	41	3	101	..	64	..	108	..
..	..	..	12	..	..	..	17	..
+90	*39*	..	*89*	..	*51*	..	*126*	..
..	39	..	89	..	51	..	124	..
..	..	..	...	..	..	..	2	..
+13	..	..	*150*	..	*13*	..	*185*	..
..	..	..	43	..	13	..	45	..
..	..	..	107	..	..	..	140	..
+155	*73*	*53*	*156*	..	*82*	*76*	*141*	..
..	73	53	156	..	82	76	141	..
..	..	..	*15*	..	..	..	*6*	..
..	..	..	15	..	..	..	6	..

TABLE XVIII—PART B — **Variation of Population**

Tribe and locality.	Persons. 1931.	1921.	1911.	1901.	1891.	Variation (Increase + Decrease —). 1921 to 1931.	1911 to 1921.	1901 to 1911.	1891 to 1901.
1	2	3	4	5	6	7	8	9	10
PARDHAN—*concld.*									
Changbhakar	*40*	..	*56*	..	..	*+40*	*—56*	..	..
Hindu	..	..	41	..	..	..	—41	..	..
Tribal ..	40	..	15	..	..	+40	—15	..	..
Korea	*424*	*557*	*296*	..	..	*—133*	*+261*	..	..
Hindu	4	330	15	..	..	—326	+315	..	..
Tribal	420	227	281	..	..	+193	—54	..	..
Surguja	*697*	*407*	*994*	..	..	*+290*	*—587*	..	..
Hindu	657	317	789	..	..	+340	—472	..	..
Tribal	40	90	205	..	..	—50	—115	..	..
Udaipur ..	[illegible]	..	*59*	..	..	*+83*	*—59*	..	..
Hindu ..	83	..	..	..	..	+83	..	..	..
Tribal ..	..	..	59	..	..	..	—59	..	..
Jashpur	*12*	*4*	*12*	..	..	*+8*	*—8*	..	..
Hindu	12	..	12	..	..	+12	—12	..	..
Tribal	.	4	..	..	..	—4	+4	..	..
*** PARJA**									
Central Provinces States ..	**17,568**	..	..	..	**13,491**	..	..	..	..
Hindu	9	..	..	..	..	..	..	..	..
Tribal	17,559	..	..	..	..	..	..	..	..
Bastar	*17,568*	..	..	..	*13,467*	..	..	..	..
Hindu	9	..	..	..	..	..	..	..	..
Tribal	17,559	..	..	..	..	..	..	..	..
Raigarh	..	..	..	..	*1*	..	..	..	..
Sarangarh	.	..	..	..	*23*	..	..	..	..
SAUNTA									
Central Provinces States ..	**6,346**	**3,942**	**9,761**	..	**8**	**+2,404**	**—5,819**	..	..
Hindu	6,200	3,820	2,678	..	..	+2,380	+1,142	..	..
Tribal	146	122	7,083	..	..	+24	—6,961	..	..
Raigarh . ..	..	..	*6*	..	*8*	..	*—6*	..	..
Hindu	..	..	6	..	..	..	—6	..	..
Korea	..	..	*77*	.	..	..	*—77*	..	..
Tribal	..	..	77	..	..	..	—77	..	..
Surguja	*6,289*	*3,942*	*7,826*	..	..	*+2,347*	*—3,884*	..	..
Hindu . ..	6,143	3,820	2,597	..	..	+3,323	+1,223	..	..
Tribal	146	122	5,229	..	..	+24	—5,107	..	..
Udaipur .. .	..	..	*1,779*	..	..	..	*—1,779*	..	..
Hindu	..	..	7	..	..	..	—7	..	..
Tribal .. .	.	..	1,772	..	..	..	—1,772	..	..
Jashpur	*57*	..	*73*	..	..	*+57*	*—73*	..	..
Hindu	57	..	68	..	.	+57	—68	..	..
Tribal	..	..	5	..	..	.	—5	..	..

* From 1901—1921 figures for Parjas were included with Gonds.

Net variation 1891 to 1931 (Increase + Decrease −).	Males.				Females.			
	1931.	1921.	1911.	1901.	1931.	1921.	1911.	1901.
11	12	13	14	15	16	17	18	19
+40	*19*	..	*34*	..	*21*	..	*22*	..
..	..	..	26	..	..	..	15	..
..	19	..	8	..	21	..	7	..
+424	*202*	*279*	*143*	..	*22?*	*278*	*153*	..
..	3	164	7	..	1	166	8	..
..	199	115	136	..	221	112	145	..
+697	*337*	*247*	*495*	..	*360*	*160*	*499*	..
..	318	190	390	..	339	127	399	..
..	19	57	105	..	21	33	100	..
+83	*40*	..	*30*	..	*43*	..	*29*	..
..	40	..	..	..	43	..	..	..
..	..	..	30	..	..	..	29	..
+12	*4*	*4*	*6*	..	*8*	..	*6*	..
..	4	..	6	..	8	..	6	..
..	..	4	..	..	..	..	..	..
+4,077	**8,828**	..	..	..	**8,740**	..	..	..
..	8	..	..	..	1	..	..	..
..	8,820	..	..	..	8,739	..	..	..
+4,101	*8,828*	..	..	..	*8,740*	..	..	..
..	8	..	..	..	1	..	..	..
..	8,820	..	..	..	8,739	..	..	..
−1	..	..	..	..	..	..	..	..
−23	..	..	..	..	..	..	..	..
+6,338	**3,172**	**1,934**	**4,971**	..	**3,174**	**2,008**	**4,790**	..
..	3,093	1,876	1,351	..	3,107	1,944	1,327	..
..	79	58	3,620	..	67	64	3,463	..
−8	..	..	*1*	..	..	..	*5*	..
..	..	..	1	..	..	..	5	..
..	..	..	*41*	..	..	..	*36*	..
..	..	..	41	..	..	..	36	..
+6,289	*3,139*	*1,934*	*4,015*	..	*3,150*	*2,008*	*3,811*	..
..	3,060	1,876	1,305	..	3,083	1,944	1,292	..
..	79	58	2,710	..	67	64	2,519	..
..	..	..	*867*	..	..	..	*912*	..
..	..	..	2	..	..	..	5	..
..	..	..	865	..	..	..	907	..
+57	*33*	..	*47*	..	*24*	..	*26*	..
..	33	..	43	..	24	..	25	..
..	..	..	4	..	..	..	1	..

TABLE XVIII—PART B

Tribe and locality.	Persons.					Variation (Increase + Decrease −).			
	1931.	1921.	1911.	1901.	1891.	1921 to 1931.	1911 to 1921.	1901 to 1911.	1891 to 1901.
1	2	3	4	5	6	7	8	9	10
SAWARA OR SAONR									
Central Provinces States	**18,912**	**18,347**	**17,268**	**13,597**	**14,878**	**+565**	**+1,079**	**+3,671**	**−1,281**
Hindu	18,912	18,347	17,268	..	..	+565	+1,079	..	..
Bastar	*321*	*276*	*262*	*183*	*317*	*+45*	*+14*	*+79*	*−134*
Hindu	321	276	262	..	..	+45	+14	..	..
Kawardha . ..	..	..	..	..	*1*	..	..	..	..
Sakti	*398*	*162*	*198*	*110*	*134*	*+236*	*−36*	*+88*	*−24*
Hindu	398	162	198	..	..	+236	−36	..	..
Raigarh	*8,098*	*7,678*	*7,793*	*6,255*	*6,811*	*+420*	*−115*	*+1,538*	*−556*
Hindu	8,098	7,678	7,793	..	..	+420	−115	..	..
Sarangarh	*9,671*	*9,975*	*8,870*	*7,049*	*7,615*	*−304*	*+1,105*	*+1,821*	*−566*
Hindu	9,671	9,975	8,870	..	..	−304	+1,105	..	..
Surguja	*68*	*111*	*9*	..	..	*−43*	*+102*	*+9*	..
Hindu	68	111	9	..	..	−43	+102	..	..
Udaipur	*197*	..	*63*	..	..	*+197*	*−63*	*+63*	..
Hindu	197	..	63	..	..	+197	−63	..	..
Jashpur	*159*	*145*	*73*	..	..	*+14*	*+72*	*+73*	..
Hindu	159	145	73	..	..	+14	+72	..	..

Net variation 1891 to 1931 (Increase+ Decrease—).	Males.				Females.			
	1931.	1921.	1911.	1901.	1931.	1921.	1911.	1901.
11	12	13	14	15	16	17	18	19
+4,034	9,199	8,824	8,316	6,514	9,713	9,523	8,952	7,083
..	9,199	8,824	8,316	..	9,713	9,523	8,952	..
+4	146	125	118	87	175	151	144	96
..	146	125	118	..	175	151	144	..
−1	..	..	..	..	..	..	..	..
+264	193	12	93	45	205	150	105	65
..	193	12	93	..	205	150	105	..
+1,287	3,886	3,614	3,748	3,006	4,212	4,064	4,045	3,249
..	3,886	3,614	3,748	..	4,212	4,064	4,045	..
+2,056	4,757	4,855	4,284	3,376	4,914	5,120	4,586	3,673
..	4,757	4,855	4,284	..	4,914	5,120	4,586	..
+68	31	100	1	..	37	11	8	..
..	31	100	1	..	37	11	8	..
+197	113	..	38	..	84	..	25	..
..	113	..	38	..	84	..	25	..
+159	73	118	34	..	86	27	39	..
..	73	118	34	..	86	27	39	..

TABLE XIX

European and Allied Races and Anglo-Indians by Race and Age

1. The totals in columns 2, 3 and 4 are those for both Parts of the Table. In the 1921 Report these columns gave the figures for European and Allied Races only.

2. Only one Armenian was returned in the Province and is included in the figures against Saugor for females in the age period 14—16 under British Subjects.

TABLE XIX — European and Allied Races and Anglo-

Serial No.	Province, State or Agency.	Total.			A—European and Allied races												
					(a) British subjects.												
					All ages.			0—13.		14—16.		17—23.		24—33.		34—43.	
		Persons.	Males.	Females.	Persons.	Males.	Females.	Males.	Females.	Males.	Females.	Males.	Females.	Males.	Females.	Males.	Females.
	1	2	3	4	5	6	7	8	9	10	11	12	13	14	15	16	17
	Central Provinces and Berar ..	**10,715**	**6,689**	**4,026**	**5,124**	**3,815**	**1,309**	**985**	**348**	**98**	**105**	**539**	**107**	**907**	**248**	**435**	**230**
	C. P. British Districts and Berar	**10,313**	**6,474**	**3,839**	**5,075**	**3,782**	**1,293**	**980**	**345**	**96**	**105**	**538**	**104**	**904**	**244**	**428**	**227**
	C. P. British Districts ..	**9,843**	**6,296**	**3,547**	**5,006**	**3,745**	**1,261**	**979**	**339**	**95**	**105**	**535**	**101**	**893**	**236**	**419**	**219**
	Jubbulpore Division ..	*4,873*	*3,258*	*1,615*	*3,012*	*2,271*	*741*	*859*	*209*	*86*	*93*	*84*	*56*	*329*	*112*	*247*	*124*
1	Saugor	640	318	322	318	170	148	29	48	4	16	17	6	65	32	27	14
2	Damoh	30	13	17	2	2	..	..	..	..	..	..	..	2	..	..	..
3	Jubbulpore	4,056	2,851	1,205	2,650	2,074	576	826	160	82	77	67	50	253	73	211	107
	(Jubbulpore City)* ..	3,908	2,768	1,140	2,600	2,047	553	821	156	81	74	60	47	253	70	205	101
4	Mandla	114	62	52	23	16	7	4	..	..	..	..	..	4	2	5	2
5	Seoni	33	14	19	19	9	10	..	1	..	..	..	..	5	5	4	1
	Nerbudda Division	*834*	*487*	*347*	*428*	*270*	*158*	*44*	*40*	..	..	*22*	*15*	*108*	*45*	*59*	*27*
6	Narsinghpur	17	12	5	10	8	2	1	..	..	..	1	1	3	1	1	..
7	Hoshangabad ..	503	306	197	305	201	104	34	29	..	..	18	8	90	28	36	20
8	Nimar	102	57	45	37	25	12	4	2	..	..	1	4	8	2	7	1
9	Betul	111	56	55	22	7	15	1	1	..	..	..	1	..	6	5	4
10	Chhindwara	101	56	45	54	29	25	4	8	..	..	2	1	7	8	10	2
	Nagpur Division	*3,214*	*2,065*	*1,149*	*1,436*	*1,130*	*306*	*69*	*78*	*8*	*10*	*424*	*24*	*445*	*70*	*91*	*55*
11	Wardha	24	8	16	13	6	7	1	..	..	..	..	..	1	..	1	1
12	Nagpur	2,969	1,926	1,043	1,358	1,091	267	63	71	8	8	424	19	438	63	75	51
	(Nagpur City) *	1,804	967	837	314	169	145	27	24	2	6	5	14	32	28	34	30
13	Chanda	68	36	32	20	12	8	..	1	..	..	..	..	2	4	8	1
14	Bhandara	101	74	27	14	8	6	1	1	..	..	..	1	2	2	4	..
15	Balaghat	52	21	31	31	13	18	4	5	..	2	..	4	2	1	3	2
	Chhattisgarh Division ..	*922*	*486*	*436*	*130*	*74*	*56*	*7*	*12*	*1*	*2*	*5*	*6*	*11*	*9*	*22*	*13*
16	Raipur	164	89	75	56	34	22	2	4	..	2	2	1	7	5	13	6
17	Bilaspur	724	381	343	74	40	34	5	8	1	..	3	5	4	4	9	7
18	Drug	34	16	18	..	..	..	..	..	..	..	..	..	..	..	..	..
	Berar	**470**	**178**	**292**	**69**	**37**	**32**	**1**	**6**	**1**	..	**3**	**3**	**11**	**8**	**9**	**8**
19	Amraoti	289	85	204	44	25	19	..	5	1	..	3	2	8	4	6	5
20	Akola	97	49	48	18	7	11	1	1	..	..	..	1	1	2	1	3
21	Buldana	40	20	20	4	2	2	..	..	..	..	..	..	1	2	1	..
22	Yeotmal	44	24	20	3	3	..	..	..	..	..	..	..	1	..	1	..
	Central Provinces States ..	**402**	**215**	**187**	**49**	**33**	**16**	**5**	**3**	**2**	..	**1**	**3**	**3**	**4**	**7**	**3**
23	Makrai	..	..	..	..	..	..	..	..	..	..	..	..	..	..	..	..
24	Bastar	37	19	18	17	9	8	2	1	..	..	1	2	1	3	2	..
25	Kanker	..	..	..	..	..	..	..	..	..	..	..	..	..	..	..	..
26	Nandgaon	22	13	9	5	5	..	..	..	..	..	..	..	1	..	1	..
27	Khairagarh	321	166	155	20	15	5	3	2	2	..	..	..	1	..	2	3
28	Chhuikhadan	..	..	..	..	..	..	..	..	..	..	..	..	..	..	..	..
29	Kawardha	..	..	..	..	..	..	..	..	..	..	..	..	..	..	..	..
30	Sakti	..	..	..	..	..	..	..	..	..	..	..	..	..	..	..	..
31	Raigarh	..	..	..	..	..	..	..	..	..	..	..	..	..	..	..	..
32	Sarangarh ..	..	..	..	..	..	..	..	..	..	..	..	..	..	..	..	..
33	Changbhakar	..	..	..	..	..	..	..	..	..	..	..	..	..	..	..	..
34	Korea	11	7	4	6	4	2	..	..	..	..	..	1	..	1	2	..
35	Surguja	1	..	1	1	..	1	..	..	..	..	..	..	..	..	..	..
36	Udaipur	..	..	..	..	..	..	..	..	..	..	..	..	..	..	..	..
37	Jashpur	10	10	..	..	..	..	..	..	..	..	..	..	..	..	..	..

* Included in district figures.

Indians by Race and Age. **TABLE XIX**

(including Armenians).

44—53.		54 and over.		(b) Others.																	
				All ages.			0—13.		14—16.		17—23.		24—33.		34—43.		44—53.		54 and over.		
Males.	Females.	Males.	Females.	Persons.	Males.	Females.	Males.	Females.	Males.	Females.	Males.	Females.	Males.	Females.	Males.	Females.	Males.	Females.	Males.	Females.	Serial No.
18	19	20	21	22	23	24	25	26	27	28	29	30	31	32	33	34	35	36	37	38	
651	**147**	**200**	**124**	**526**	**234**	**292**	**40**	**37**	**6**	**8**	**10**	**25**	**53**	**66**	**65**	**72**	**31**	**40**	**29**	**44**	
643	**145**	**193**	**123**	**498**	**217**	**281**	**38**	**36**	**6**	**8**	**10**	**24**	**51**	**60**	**60**	**71**	**25**	**38**	**27**	**44**	
636	**142**	**188**	**119**	**406**	**182**	**224**	**36**	**27**	**6**	**7**	**9**	**21**	**47**	**50**	**41**	**51**	**20**	**29**	**23**	**39**	
530	*71*	*136*	*76*	*86*	*33*	*53*	*6*	*4*	..	*2*	*1*	*2*	*10*	*16*	*8*	*14*	*1*	*4*	*7*	*11*	
16	18	12	14	14	4	10	1	2	..	..	..	1	2	3	..	1	..	2	1	1	
.	..	..	..	11	4	7	1	..	..	..	..	1	..	1	2	5	1	..	..	..	1
513	50	122	59	53	23	30	4	2	..	1	1	..	8	9	6	7	..	1	4	10	2
509	46	118	59	53	23	30	4	2	..	1	1	..	8	9	6	7	..	1	4	10	3
1	1	2	2	7	1	6	..	..	..	1	..	..	..	3	..	1	..	1	1	..	4
..	2	..	1	1	1	..	..	..	..	..	..	..	..	..	..	..	..	..	1	..	5
23	*20*	*14*	*11*	*64*	*36*	*28*	*3*	..	..	..	*1*	*2*	*12*	*11*	*6*	*4*	*7*	*7*	*7*	*4*	
2	..	..	..	2	1	1	..	..	..	..	..	..	1	..	..	..	..	1	..	..	6
17	11	6	8	11	7	4	..	..	..	..	..	..	2	4	1	..	1	..	3	..	7
2	2	3	1	16	9	7	..	..	..	..	1	..	3	2	2	..	2	2	1	3	8
..	1	1	2	16	10	6	3	..	..	..	..	..	3	1	1	2	2	2	1	1	9
2	6	4	..	19	9	10	..	..	..	..	..	2	3	4	2	2	2	2	2	..	10
65	*44*	*28*	*25*	*130*	*59*	*71*	*6*	*9*	*4*	*2*	*7*	*7*	*14*	*11*	*14*	*13*	*7*	*9*	*7*	*20*	
1	5	2	1	..	..	..	..	..	..	..	..	..	..	..	..	..	..	..	..	..	
60	34	23	21	122	58	64	6	9	4	2	7	7	13	10	14	10	7	7	7	19	11
49	27	20	16	113	55	58	6	9	4	2	7	7	13	10	14	9	6	7	5	14	12
2	2	..	..	4	1	3	..	..	..	..	..	..	1	..	..	1	..	1	..	1	13
..	..	1	2	..	..	..	..	..	..	..	..	..	..	..	..	..	..	..	..	..	14
2	3	2	1	4	..	4	..	..	..	..	..	..	..	1	..	2	..	1	..	..	15
18	*7*	*10*	*7*	*126*	*54*	*72*	*21*	*14*	*2*	*3*	..	*10*	*11*	*12*	*13*	*20*	*5*	*9*	*2*	*4*	
9	1	1	3	57	24	33	11	3	..	2	..	5	5	4	5	13	2	5	1	1	16
9	6	9	4	41	19	22	5	6	2	..	..	5	2	4	7	4	2	2	1	1	17
..	..	..	..	28	11	17	5	5	..	1	..	..	4	4	1	3	1	2	.	2	18
7	**3**	**5**	**4**	**92**	**35**	**57**	**2**	**9**	..	**1**	**1**	**3**	**4**	**10**	**19**	**20**	**5**	**9**	**4**	**5**	
4	1	3	2	48	13	35	..	3	..	1	..	3	1	7	6	9	2	7	4	5	19
3	2	1	2	11	6	5	..	1	..	..	..	..	..	1	4	2	2	1	..	..	20
..	..	..	..	20	9	11	1	3	..	..	..	..	1	1	6	6	1	1	..	..	21
..	..	1	..	13	7	6	1	2	..	..	1	..	2	1	3	3	..	..	..	..	22
8	**2**	**7**	**1**	**28**	**17**	**11**	**2**	**1**	..	..	..	**1**	**2**	**6**	**5**	**1**	**6**	**2**	**2**	..	
.	..	.	..	..	..	..	..	..	..	..	..	..	..	..	..	..	..	..	..	..	23
2	1	1	1	7	4	3	2	1	..	..	..	..	..	1	1	..	..	1	1	..	24
..	..	..	..	..	..	..	..	..	..	..	..	..	..	..	..	..	..	..	..	..	25
3	..	..	..	11	4	7	..	..	..	..	..	1	2	4	1	1	1	1	..	..	26
2	..	5	..	1	..	1	..	..	..	..	..	..	..	1	..	..	..	..	..	..	27
..	..	..	..	..	..	..	..	..	..	..	..	..	..	..	..	..	..	..	..	..	28
..	..	..	..	..	..	..	..	..	..	..	..	..	..	..	..	..	..	..	..	..	29
..	..	..	..	..	..	..	..	..	..	..	..	..	..	..	..	..	..	..	..	..	30
..	..	..	..	..	..	..	..	..	..	..	..	..	..	..	..	..	..	..	..	..	31
..	..	..	..	..	..	..	..	..	..	..	..	..	..	..	..	..	..	..	..	..	32
..	..	..	..	..	..	..	..	..	..	..	..	..	..	..	..	..	..	..	..	..	33
1	..	1	..	..	..	..	..	..	..	..	..	..	..	..	..	..	..	..	..	..	34
..	1	..	..	..	..	..	..	..	..	..	..	..	..	..	..	..	..	..	..	..	35
..	..	..	..	..	..	..	..	..	..	..	..	..	..	..	..	..	..	..	..	..	36
..	..	..	..	9	9	..	..	..	..	..	..	..	..	..	3	..	5	..	1	..	37

B.—Anglo-

Serial No.	Province, State or Agency.	All ages. Persons.	All ages. Males.	All ages. Females.	0—3 Males.	0—3 Females.	4—6 Males.	4—6 Females.	7—13 Males.	7—13 Females.	14—16 Males.	14—16 Females.
	1	39	40	41	42	43	44	45	46	47	48	49
	Central Provinces and Berar.	**5,065**	**2,640**	**2,425**	**233**	**280**	**228**	**199**	**468**	**389**	**185**	**201**
	C. P. British Districts and Berar.	**4,740**	**2,475**	**2,265**	**212**	**257**	**213**	**183**	**445**	**371**	**177**	**194**
	C. P. British Districts ..	**4,431**	**2,369**	**2,062**	**200**	**244**	**201**	**167**	**430**	**320**	**174**	**170**
	Jubbulpore Division ..	*1,775*	*954*	*821*	*81*	*100*	*67*	*52*	*201*	*94*	*96*	*88*
1	Saugor	308	144	164	13	28	10	13	15	11	4	13
2	Damoh	17	7	10	2	1	..	1	1	..	..	..
3	Jubbulpore	1,353	754	599	60	63	47	36	179	76	92	74
	(Jubbulpore City)* ..	1,255	698	557	55	60	45	34	172	69	91	72
4	Mandla	84	45	39	6	6	9	2	5	7	..	1
5	Seoni	13	4	9		2	1	..	1	..	..	..
	Nerbudda Division ..	*342*	*181*	*161*	*12*	*25*	*16*	*18*	*15*	*20*	*5*	*8*
6	Narsinghpur ..	5	3	2	..	..	..	1	2	..	..	..
7	Hoshangabad ..	187	98	89	6	13	12	11	6	10	2	7
8	Nimar	49	23	26	3	5	..	5	2	3	2	1
9	Betul	73	39	34	3	7	3	1	4	6	1	..
10	Chhindwara	28	18	10	..	..	1	..	1	1	..	..
	Nagpur Division ..	*1,648*	*876*	*772*	*78*	*80*	*71*	*62*	*173*	*163*	*61*	*60*
11	Wardha	11	2	9	..	..	..	2	..	1	..	..
12	Nagpur	1,489	777	712	71	75	60	55	165	157	61	58
	(Nagpur City)* ..	1,377	743	634	71	70	59	51	155	111	58	49
13	Chanda	44	23	21	3	2	3	3	..	2	..	1
14	Bhandara	87	66	21	4	3	7	1	7	2	..	..
15	Balaghat	17	8	9	..	..	1	1	1	1	..	1
	Chhattisgarh Division ..	*666*	*358*	*308*	*29*	*39*	*47*	*35*	*41*	*43*	*12*	*14*
16	Raipur	51	31	20	1	6	..	1	..	..	1	1
17	Bilaspur	609	322	287	27	33	47	34	41	43	11	13
18	Drug	6	5	1	1	..	..	..	..	..	..	..
	Berar	**309**	**106**	**203**	**12**	**13**	**12**	**16**	**15**	**51**	**3**	**24**
19	Amraoti	197	47	150	2	5	7	11	7	47	2	24
20	Akola	68	36	32	6	5	4	4	6	4	1	..
21	Buldana	16	9	7	2	..	1	..	1	..	..	..
22	Yeotmal	28	14	14	2	3	..	1	1	..	..	..
	Central Provinces States ..	**325**	**165**	**160**	**21**	**23**	**15**	**16**	**23**	**18**	**8**	**7**
23	Makrai	..	..	..	..	..	..	..	..	..	..	..
24	Bastar	13	6	7	..	..	..	..	3	..	..	..
25	Kanker	..	..	..	..	..	..	..	..	..	..	..
26	Nandgaon	6	4	2	..	..	..	1	..	..	1	..
27	Khairagarh	300	151	149	21	23	15	15	20	18	7	7
28	Chhuikhadan ..	..	..	..	..	..	..	..	..	..	..	..
29	Kawardha	..	..	..	..	..	..	..	..	..	..	..
30	Sakti	..	..	..	..	..	..	..	..	..	..	..
31	Raigarh	..	..	..	..	..	..	..	..	..	..	..
32	Sarangarh	..	..	..	..	..	..	..	..	..	..	..
33	Changbhakar ..	..	..	..	..	..	..	..	..	..	..	..
34	Korea	5	3	2	..	..	..	..	..	..	..	..
35	Surguja	..	..	..	..	..	..	..	..	..	..	..
36	Udaipur	..	..	..	..	..	..	..	..	..	..	..
37	Jashpur	1	1	..	..	..	..	..	..	..	..	..

* Included in district figures.

Indians by Race and Age.

TABLE XIX

Indians.

17—19		20—29		30—39		40—49		50—59		60—69		70 and over.		
Males.	Females.	Males.	Females.	Males.	Fema	Males	Females.	Males.	Females.	Males.	Females.	Males	Femal..	Serial No.
50	51	52	53	54	55	56	57	58	59	60	61	62	63	64
180	**174**	**425**	**404**	**388**	**315**	**290**	**222**	**137**	**117**	**69**	**80**	**37**	**44**	
167	**160**	**390**	**369**	**357**	**300**	**280**	**202**	**130**	**113**	**67**	**76**	**37**	**40**	
165	**148**	**383**	**341**	**335**	**269**	**260**	**187**	**122**	**108**	**62**	**70**	**37**	**38**	
66	*59*	*148*	*143*	*109*	*107*	*101*	*76*	*45*	*52*	*21*	*28*	*19*	*22*	
13	13	35	36	26	13	17	12	9	12	1	6	1	7	1
..	1	..	4	2	2	2	..	..	..	..	..	..	1	2
47	42	102	94	77	80	77	60	35	40	20	20	18	14	3
43	37	94	87	66	72	69	55	29	38	17	19	17	14	
6	3	11	7	3	9	4	3	1	..	..	1	..	..	4
..	..	..	2	1	3	1	1	..	..	..	1	..	..	5
11	*8*	*30*	*25*	*47*	*24*	*23*	*12*	*9*	*11*	*10*	*6*	*3*	*4*	
..	..	..	..	..	1	1	..	..	..	.	..	..	..	6
6	3	18	13	26	12	11	5	3	9	7	5	1	1	7
1	1	2	2	6	5	4	2	1	..	1	1	1	1	8
3	3	7	6	13	4	2	3	3	2	..	..	..	2	9
1	1	3	4	2	2	5	2	2	..	2	..	1	..	10
57	*57*	*126*	*112*	*117*	*98*	*105*	*80*	*55*	*27*	*23*	*22*	*10*	*11*	
1	2	..	2	..	1	..	1	..	..	1	..	..	..	11
55	50	109	104	96	89	85	70	48	26	17	18	10	10	12
53	47	107	99	92	87	80	66	45	26	16	18	7	10	
..	2	4	2	3	4	7	3	1	..	2	1	..	1	13
1	2	13	3	16	3	10	4	6	1	2	2	..	..	14
..	1	..	1	2	1	3	2	..	..	1	1	..	..	15
31	*24*	*79*	*61*	*62*	*40*	*31*	*19*	*13*	*18*	*8*	*14*	*5*	*1*	
3	1	6	3	10	2	4	2	5	4	..	..	1	..	16
28	23	72	58	50	37	26	17	8	14	8	14	4	1	17
..	..	1	..	2	1	1	..	..	..	..	..	..	..	18
2	**12**	**7**	**28**	**22**	**31**	**20**	**15**	**8**	**5**	**5**	**6**	..	**2**	
1	11	4	21	12	17	8	7	2	2	2	3	..	2	19
1	1	..	5	4	9	8	2	4	1	2	1	..	..	20
..	..	..	..	2	2	1	3	2	..	..	2	..	..	21
..	..	3	2	4	3	3	3	..	2	1	..	..	..	22
13	**14**	**35**	**35**	**31**	**15**	**10**	**20**	**7**	**4**	**2**	**4**	..	**4**	
..	..	..	..	..	..	..	..	..	..	..	..	..	..	23
1	..	..	1	2	2	..	1	..	..	..	1	..	2	24
..	..	..	..	..	..	..	..	..	..	..	..	..	..	25
..	..	1	1	1	..	1	..	..	..	..	..	..	..	26
12	13	33	32	25	13	9	19	7	4	2	3	..	2	27
..	..	..	..	..	..	..	..	..	..	..	..	..	..	28
..	..	..	..	..	..	..	..	..	..	..	..	..	..	29
..	..	..	..	..	..	..	..	..	..	..	..	..	..	30
..	..	..	..	..	..	..	..	..	..	..	..	..	..	31
..	..	..	..	..	..	..	..	..	..	..	..	..	..	32
..	..	..	..	..	..	..	..	..	..	..	..	..	..	33
..	1	1	1	2	..	..	..	..	..	..	..	..	..	34
..	..	..	..	..	..	..	..	..	..	..	..	..	..	35
..	..	..	..	..	..	..	..	..	..	..	..	..	..	36
..	..	..	..	1	..	..	..	..	..	..	..	..	..	37

TABLE XX

Summary figures for districts and states

This table contains for easy reference a few of the salient figures for individual Districts or States. It corresponds to Table XXIII of 1921 which was not printed in the Central Provinces Report.

TABLE XX — Summary figures for

Serial number.	District or State.	Area in square miles.	Population, 1931. Persons.	Males.	Females.	Population 1921.	Percentage of variation. 1921-1931.	1911-1921.
	1	2	3	4	5	6	7	8
	Central Provinces and Berar ..	**131,095**	**17,990,937**	**8,997,203**	**8,993,734**	**15,979,660**	**+12.59**	**−0.34**
	C. P. British Districts and Berar	**99,920**	**15,507,723**	**7,761,818**	**7,745,905**	**13,912,760**	**+11.46**	**−0.02**
	C. P. British Districts ..	**82,153**	**12,065,885**	**6,002,239**	**6,063,646**	**10,837,444**	**+11.34**	**−0.19**
	Jubbulpore Division ..	*18,956*	*2,463,466*	*1,240,655*	*1,222,811*	*2,296,508*	*+7·27*	*−5.17*
1	Saugor	3,964	544,589	280,385	264,204	528,380	+3.07	−2.40
2	Damoh	2,807	305,568	154,791	150,777	287,126	+6.42	−13.78
3	Jubbulpore	3,912	773,811	391,649	382,162	745,685	+3.77	−0.02
4	Mandla	5,057	445,766	221,359	224,407	386,446	+15.35	−4.63
5	Seoni	3,216	393,732	192,471	201,261	348,871	+12.86	−11.93
	Nerbudda Division	*18,386*	*2,254,566*	*1,137,806*	*1,116,760*	*2,013,021*	*+12·00*	*−3 29*
6	Narsinghpur	1,978	321,481	161,417	160,064	315,162	+2.01	−3.22
7	Hoshangabad	3,693	486,630	248,226	238,404	445,733	+9.18	−2.54
8	Nimar	4,227	466,931	242,042	224,889	396,554	+17.75	+1.40
9	Betul	3,910	406,252	201,114	205,138	363,737	+11.69	−6.82
10	Chhindwara .. .	4,578	573,272	285,007	288,265	491,835	+16.56	−4.88
	Nagpur Division	*22,760*	*3,602,108*	*1,809,541*	*1,792,567*	*3,146,228*	*+14·49*	*+1·19*
11	Wardha	2,434	516,266	261,394	254,872	463,696	+11.34	+0.63
12	Nagpur ..	3,834	940,049	481,246	458,803	792,521	+18.61	−2.02
13	Chanda .. .	9,312	759,695	381,204	378,491	660,630	+15.00	−2.49
14	Bhandara	3,623	824,496	408,799	415,697	717,747	+14.87	+4.65
15	Balaghat	3,557	561,602	276,898	284,704	511,634	+9.77	+7.50
	Chhattisgarh Division ..	*22,051*	*3,745,745*	*1,814,237*	*1,931,508*	*3,381,687*	*+10·77*	*+4·16*
16	Raipur	9,717	1,527,573	739,950	787,623	1,392,768	+9.68	+6.27
17	Bilaspur	7,618	1,400,248	683,920	716,328	1,231,765	+13.68	+7.46
18	Drug	4,716	817,924	390,367	427,557	757,154	+8.03	−4.13
	Berar	**17,767**	**3,441,838**	**1,759,579**	**1,682,259**	**3,075,316**	**+11.92**	**+0.59**
19	Amraoti	4,691	941,604	485,593	456,011	827,867	+13.74	−5.17
20	Akola	4,091	876,362	448,896	427,466	794,847	+10.26	+1.12
21	Buldana	3,766	766,584	388,966	377,618	703,643	+8.95	+4.44
22	Yeotmal	5,219	857,288	436,124	421,164	748,959	+14.46	+3.38
	C. P. States	**31,175**	**2,483,214**	**1,235,385**	**1,247,829**	**2,066,900**	**+20·14**	**−2.37**
23	Makrai	155	15,516	7,900	7,616	12,803	+21.19	−14.77
24	Bastar	13,062	524,721	263,248	261,473	464,407	+12.99	+7.18
25	Kanker	1,431	136,101	67,132	68,969	124,928	+8.94	−1.76
26	Nandgaon	671	182,380	87,886	94,494	147,906	+23.31	−11.63
27	Khairagarh	931	157,400	75,647	81,753	124,008	+26.93	−20.24
28	Chhuikhadan	153	31,668	15,238	16,430	26,122	+21.23	−16.14
29	Kawardha	798	72,820	35,098	37,722	61,783	+17.86	−20.44
30	Sakti	138	48,489	23,571	24,918	41,554	+16.69	+20.28
31	Raigarh	1,486	277,569	136,723	140,846	241,634	+14.87	+10.41
32	Sarangarh	540	128,967	62,443	66,524	117,781	+9.50	+15.39
33	Changbhakar	906	23,322	11,987	11,335	21,826	+6.85	−10.63
34	Korea	1,631	90,886	46,748	44,138	79,189	+14.77	+27.50
35	Surguja	6,055	501,939	254,923	247,016	377,679	+32.90	−11.90
36	Udaipur	1,055	97,738	49,425	48,313	71,124	+37.42	+9.67
37	Jashpur	1,963	193,698	97,416	96,282	154,156	+25.65	−11.64

Number of persons per square mile in 1931.	1921.	Distribution by Religion: Hindus. Males.	Hindus. Females.	Muslims. Males.	Muslims. Females.	Christians. Males.	Christians. Females	Tribal. Males	Tribal. Females.	Jains. Males.	Jains. Females.	Others. Males.	Others. Females.	Serial number.
9	10	11	12	13	14	15	16	17	18	19	20	21	22	
137	**122**	**7,557,449**	**7,569,175**	**370,633**	**335,475**	**52,540**	**49,745**	**970,911**	**998,303**	**41,416**	**38,439**	**4,254**	**2,597**	
155	**139**	**6,671,326**	**6,666,897**	**358,900**	**323,954**	**26,438**	**24,146**	**660,755**	**690,860**	**40,333**	**37,562**	**4,066**	**2,486**	
147	**132**	**5,107,356**	**5,164,380**	**201,352**	**181,822**	**23,673**	**21,516**	**636,433**	**666,030**	**29,773**	**27,720**	**3,652**	**2,178**	
130	*121*	*957,961*	*939,022*	*57,676*	*51,572*	*6,401*	*4,904*	*200,073*	*210,438*	*17,582*	*16,390*	*962*	*485*	
137	133	247,101	233,020	13,655	12,091	994	936	9,583	9,832	8,910	8,226	142	99	1
109	102	134,626	131,082	5,439	5,077	325	178	10,555	10,776	3,825	3,653	21	11	2
198	191	350,708	346,647	25,763	21,851	4,494	3,203	6,405	6,856	3,521	3,271	758	334	3
88	76	118,713	119,221	3,667	3,199	410	400	98,123	101,187	415	369	31	31	4
122	108	106,813	109,052	9,152	9,354	178	187	75,407	81,787	911	871	10	10	5
123	*110*	*849,982*	*824,830*	*59,203*	*53,821*	*4,879*	*4,554*	*217,699*	*228,126*	*5,202*	*4,886*	*841*	*543*	
163	160	133,214	131,019	5,802	5,602	175	119	20,845	22,045	1,376	1,278	5	1	6
132	121	210,899	202,404	12,368	11,107	1,196	1,005	22,567	22,883	954	897	242	108	7
110	94	193,412	179,171	26,839	24,086	2,486	2,442	17,659	17,770	1,164	1,040	482	380	8
104	94	136,689	138,404	3,644	3,393	418	428	59,642	62,241	674	657	47	13	9
125	107	175,768	173,832	10,550	9,633	604	560	96,986	103,187	1,034	1,014	65	39	10
158	*138*	*1,603,730*	*1,590,484*	*61,076*	*53,822*	*6,064*	*5,017*	*132,336*	*137,568*	*5,094*	*4,853*	*1,241*	*823*	
212	191	229,234	223,051	11,046	9,882	170	108	19,408	20,381	1,488	1,411	48	39	11
245	207	439,201	423,318	29,366	24,443	4,810	3,748	4,972	4,812	1,827	1,794	1,070	688	12
82	71	317,050	313,467	7,045	6,511	623	620	55,916	57,411	547	455	23	27	13
228	198	380,517	386,856	8,134	7,350	166	229	19,156	20,444	779	781	47	37	14
158	144	237,728	243,792	5,485	5,636	295	312	32,884	34,520	453	412	53	32	15
179	*153*	[illegible]	[illegible]	*23,397*	*22,607*	*6,329*	*7,041*	*86,325*	*89,898*	*1,895*	*1,591*	*608*	*327*	
157	[illegible]	[illegible]	724,443	10,251	9,741	2,980	3,000	45,954	49,439	932	801	397	100	16
184	[illegible]	[illegible]	[illegible]	9,495	9,178	2,459	2,757	34,231	34,441	282	238	164	104	17
173	[illegible]	[illegible]	[illegible]	3,651	3,688	890	1,284	6,140	6,018	681	552	47	24	18
194	**173**	**1,563,970**	[illegible]	**157,548**	**142,132**	**2,765**	**2,630**	**24,322**	**24,830**	**10,560**	**9,842**	**414**	**308**	
201	176	436,034	405,375	45,714	40,784	1,319	1,235	5,810	6,061	2,587	2,465	129	91	19
214	194	397,460	380,991	46,903	42,282	726	595	180	190	3,535	3,331	92	77	20
204	187	348,531	340,621	37,474	34,292	380	398	81	91	2,400	2,147	100	69	21
164	144	387,945	375,530	27,457	24,774	340	402	18,251	18,488	2,038	1,899	93	71	22
80	**66**	**886,123**	**902,278**	**11,733**	**11,521**	**26,102**	**25,599**	**310,156**	**307,443**	**1,083**	**877**	**188**	**111**	
100	83	5,045	4,947	514	513	..	1	2,311	2,127	26	28	4	..	23
40	36	79,871	78,954	988	979	920	953	181,390	180,530	78	56	1	1	24
95	87	30,302	31,484	353	321	13	11	36,385	37,077	79	76	..	..	25
209	170	85,044	91,767	1,268	1,244	163	221	915	890	487	368	9	4	26
169	133	74,016	80,117	1,177	1,226	209	218	..	..	230	184	15	8	27
207	170	14,770	15,884	383	474	1	..	5	..	79	72	..	..	28
91	77	34,470	37,037	512	571	2	5	50	44	61	64	3	1	29
351	301	23,255	24,608	210	190	6	6	89	109	2	..	9	5	30
187	163	135,651	139,833	891	852	68	75	..	..	28	18	85	68	31
239	218	62,224	66,319	165	165	49	40	..	..	2	..	3	..	32
26	24	3,671	3,338	45	28	..	..	8,271	7,969	..	..	..	..	33
56	49	13,437	12,186	592	464	7	4	32,709	31,484	..	..	3	..	34
83	62	219,891	212,922	3,625	3,410	13	16	31,327	30,633	11	11	56	24	35
93	67	40,887	39,872	134	137	..	..	8,404	8,304	..	..	..	..	36
99	79	63,589	63,010	876	947	24,651	24,049	8,300	8,276	..	..	..	..	37

PROVINCIAL TABLE I

Area and Population of Tahsils, Cities and Large Towns

1. In this Table area and population of the Tahsils of the Central Provinces, the Taluks of Berar, and of two cities and twenty-three large towns are shown. The figures for Zamindaris are given separately under the Tahsil to which they belong. The figures of the cities and towns are shown above the Tahsil to which they belong and are not included in the Tahsil figures. Jubbulpore, Saugor and Kamptee Cantonments have been treated as separate towns.

2. Figures for Amraoti Camp and Ellichpur Camp in this table are included in those of the taluks in which they lie, but in Provincial Table II they have been added to those of Amraoti Town and Ellichpur Town. The inconsistency was unavoidable owing to the system of sorting Christian slips.

3. Statistics for the Central Provinces States have not been shown here because they are readily available in Tables I, II, and XX.

4. The population of the strictly military area of Saugor Cantonment (1,305 persons) has been included in the figure for Saugor Town instead of in that for the Cantonment. The correct figures are given below :—

		Persons.	Males.	Females.
Saugor Town	..	38,517	19,735	18,782
Saugor Cantonment	..	10,345	5,571	4,774

PROVINCIAL TABLE I.—Area and Population of Tahsils, Cities and large Towns.

Tahsil, Taluk Zamindari or Township	Area in square miles.	Number of Towns.	Number of Villages.	Number of occupied houses.	Population, 1931. Persons.	Population, 1931. Males.	Population, 1931. Females.	Population, 1921 (Both sexes).	Percentage of variation. 1921 to 1931.	Percentage of variation. 1911 to 1921.	Number of persons per square mile in 1931.
1	2	3	4	5	6	7	8	9	10	11	12
C. P. British Districts and Berar.	**99,920**	**112**	**39,762**	**3,168,788**	**15,507,723**	**7,761,818**	**7,745,905**	**13,912,760**	**+11.46**	**−.02**	**155**
C. P. British Districts.	**82,153**	**70**	**33,827**	**2,439,990**	**12,065,885**	**6,002,239**	**6,063,646**	**10,837,444**	**+11.34**	**−0.19**	**147**
Jubbulpore Division.	**18,956**	**13**	**8,992**	**517,616**	**2,463.466**	**1,240,655**	**1,222,811**	**2,296,508**	**+7.27**	**−5.17**	**130**
Saugor District ..	*3,964*	*6*	*1,860*	*107,656*	*544,589*	*280,355*	*264,204*	*528,380*	*+3·07*	*−2·40*	*137*
Saugor Town ..	..	1	..	8,175	39,822	20,723	19,099	28,571	+39 38	−18.08	
Saugor Cantonment.	..	1	..	1,987	9,040	4,583	4,457	10,748	−15.89	−2.57	178
Saugor Tahsil ..	1,064	..	492	22,561	140,788	71,825	68,963	147,712	−4.69	+2.02	
Khurai Tahsil ..	940	2	497	26,280	126,910	66,345	60,565	122,268	+3.80	+10·08	135
Rehli Tahsil ..	1,254	2	594	31,882	148,002	75,959	72,043	144,451	+2.46	−8.46	118
Banda Tahsil ..	706	..	277	16,771	80,027	40,950	39,077	74,630	+7.23	−8.80	113
Damoh District.	*2,807*	*1*	*1,148*	*68,0*[illegible]	*305,568*	*154,791*	*150,777*	*287,126*	*+6·42*	*−13·78*	*109*
Damoh Town ..	..	1	..	2,348	20,728	10,726	10,002	15,296	+35.51	−10.24	107
Damoh Tahsil ..	1,790	..	706	39,237	170,915	86,415	84,500	164,065	+4.18	−15.36	
Hatta Tahsil ..	1,017	..	442	26,480	113,925	57,650	56,275	107,765	+5.72	−11.77	112
Jubbulpore District	*3,912*	*4*	*2,382*	*169,520*	*773,811*	*391,649*	*382,162*	*745,685*	*+3·77*	*−0·02*	*198*
Jubbulpore City..	..	1	..	23,709	104,317	56,613	47,704	86,796	+20·19	+9.86	
Jubbulpore Cantonment.	..	1	..	3,160	20,065	12,645	7,420	21,997	−8.78	+1.64	269
Jubbulpore Tahsil	999	..	652	31,025	144,702	72,148	72,554	148,057	−2.27	+3.09	
Sihora Tahsil ..	1,181	1	739	42,871	196,536	97,080	99,456	205,551	−4.39	+0·33	166
Murwara Town	..	1	..	5,552	21,959	11,572	10,387	19,682	+11.57	+24.48	166
Murwara Tahsil..	1,190	..	534	39,441	175,620	86,451	89,169	148,707	+18.10	−10.36	
Patan Tahsil ..	542	..	457	23,762	110,612	55.140	55,472	114,895	−3.73	−0.14	204
Mandla District	*5,057*	*1*	*2,020*	*88,473*	*445,766*	*221,359*	*224,407*	*386,446*	*+15·35*	*−4 63*	*88*
Mandla Tahsil ..	1,725	1	726	37,913	190,109	94,184	95,925	170,239	+11.67	+0.55	110
Dindori Tahsil ..	1,944	..	660	28,551	139,798	69,278	70,520	119,774	+16.72	−7.59	72
Niwas Tahsil ..	1,388	..	634	22,009	115,859	57,897	57,962	96,433	+20.14	−9.30	83
Seoni District ..	*3,216*	*1*	*1,582*	*83,902*	*393,732*	*192,471*	*201,261*	*348,871*	*+12·86*	*−11 93*	*122*
Seoni Tahsil ..	1,756	1	782	52,524	251,304	122,555	128,749	227,051	+10.68	−5·98	143
Lakhnadon Tahsil	1,460	..	800	31,378	142,428	69,916	72,512	121,820	+16.92	−21.22	98
Nerbudda Division.	**18,386**	**18**	**6,650**	**482,879**	**2,254,566**	**1,137,806**	**1,116,760**	**2,013,021**	**+12.00**	**−3.29**	**123**
Narsinghpur District.	*1,978*	*3*	*992*	*69,732*	*321,481*	*161,417*	*160,064*	*315,162*	*+2.01*	*−3.22*	*163*
Narsinghpur Tahsil.	1,069	2	548	34,499	157,012	78,515	78,497	152,116	+3.22	−0.89	147
Gadarwara Tahsil	909	1	444	35,233	164,469	82,902	81,567	163,046	+0.87	−5.31	181
Hoshangabad District.	*3,693*	*8*	*1,335*	*123,351*	*486,630*	*248,226*	*238,404*	*445,733*	*+9·18*	*−2·54*	*132*
Hoshangabad Tahsil.	776	2	316	29,835	141,553	72,477	69,076	128,023	+10.57	− 0.11	182
Harda Tahsil ..	1,127	1	392	29,010	141,674	72,299	69,375	129,264	+9.60	−0.50	126
Sohagpur Tahsil	1,269	4	433	30,007	138,094	70,525	67,569	126,030	+9.57	−6.26	109
Seoni-Malwa Tahsil.	521	1	194	34,499	65,309	32,925	32,384	62,416	+4.63	−3.77	125
Nimar District ..	*4,227*	*2*	*1,141*	*92 101*	*466,931*	*242,042*	*224,889*	*396,554*	*+17·75*	*+1·40*	*110*
Khandwa Town..	..	1	..	7,206	34,622	19,060	15,562	26,802	+29.10	+24.06	
Khandwa Tahsil	1,871	..	501	37,420	199,342	102,402	96,940	178,324	+11 79	−2.94	125
Burhanpur Town	..	1	..	8,234	44,066	23,056	21,010	35,916	+22.69	+57.68	
Burhanpur Tahsil	1,138	..	284	20,818	101,175	51,967	49,208	88,316	+14.56	+3.96	128
Harsud Tahsil ..	1,218	..	356	18,423	87,726	45,557	42,169	67,196	+30.55	−13.85	72
Betul District ..	*3,910*	*2*	*1,252*	*77,449*	*406 252*	*201,114*	*205,138*	*363,737*	*+11·69*	*−6·82*	*104*
Betul Tahsil ..	1,598	2	497	28,362	142.106	70,435	71,670	129,052	+10.12	−14.24	89
Multai Tahsil ..	972	..	389	31,627	170,592	84,136	86,456	151,961	+12.26	−1.65	176
Bhainsdehi Tahsil	1,340	..	366	17,460	93,554	46,542	47,012	82,724	+13.09	−3·09	70
Chhindwara District.	*4,578*	*3*	*1,930*	*120,246*	*573,272*	*285,007*	*288,265*	*491,835*	*+16 56*	*−4·88*	*125*
Chhindwara Tahsil Khalsa.	1,174	1	662	44,820	222,076	111,340	110,736	187,511	+18.43	+38.64	189
Chhindwara Tahsil Zamindaris.	807	..	262	13,344	45,933	22,952	22,981	38,390	+19.65	−58 70	57
Amarwara Tahsil Khalsa.	693	..	348	20,855	102,143	49,905	52,238	90,637	+12.69	+41.14	147
Amarwara Tahsil Zamindaris.	790	..	236	6,777	31,558	15,473	16,085	26.852	+17.53	−63.31	40
Sausar Tahsil	1,114	2	422	34,450	171,562	85,337	86,225	148,445	+15.57	−2.00	154

Note —A reference is invited to paragraph 4 of the fly-sheet regarding the figures for Saugor Town and Saugor Cantonment.

PROVINCIAL TABLE I.—Area and Population of Tahsils, Cities and large Towns—*contd.*

Tahsil, Taluk Zamindari or Township.	Area in square miles	Number of Towns.	Number of Villages.	Number of occupied houses.	Population, 1931. Persons.	Population, 1931. Males.	Population, 1931. Females.	Population, 1921 (Both sexes).	Percentage of variation. 1921 to 1931.	Percentage of variation. 1911 to 1921	Number of persons per square mile in 1931.
1	2	3	4	5	6	7	8	9	10	11	12
Nagpur Division	**22,760**	**31**	**7,690**	**696,085**	**3,602,108**	**1,809,541**	**1,792,567**	**3,146,228**	**+14.49**	**+1.19**	**158**
Wardha District.	*2,434*	*7*	*939*	*108,224*	*516,266*	*261,394*	*254,872*	*463,696*	*+11·34*	*+0·63*	*212*
Wardha Tahsil ..	815	4	326	44,002	205,105	104,022	101,083	187,060	+9.65	+4.78	252
Arvi Tahsil ..	890	2	325	35,284	175,238	89,033	86,205	165,027	+6.19	−0.68	197
Hinganghat Town.	..	1	..	4,866	22,601	11,812	10,789	17,200	+31.40	+15.10 }	186
Hinganghat Tahsil.	729	..	288	24,072	113,322	56,527	56,795	94,409	+20.03	−6.66 }	
Nagpur District ..	*3,834*	*13*	*1,644*	*184,097*	*940,049*	*481,246*	*458,803*	*792,521*	*+18·61*	*−2·02*	*245*
Nagpur City ..	..	1	..	40,900	215,165	116,403	98,762	145,193	+48 19	+43.16 }	
Kamptee Town	..	1	..	4,670	20,787	10,806	9,981	17,531	+18 57	+17 90 }	
Kamptee Cantonment.	..	1	..	965	5,554	3,704	1,850	2,695	+106.09	+17.89 }	465
Nagpur Tahsil ..	811	..	365	28,204	135,533	67,774	67,759	115,895	+16.94	−11.24 }	
Ramtek Tahsil ..	897	1	381	26,463	134,663	67,573	67,090	122,817	+9.65	−15.38	150
Umrer Town .	..	1	..	3,358	17,913	8,857	9,056	15,061	+18.94	−14.57 }	
Umrer Tahsil ..	969	..	416	25,888	136,152	67,501	68,651	118,506	+14.89	−6.90 }	159
Katol Tahsil ..	614	3	277	28,593	148,588	74,912	73,676	136,691	+8.70	−4.11	242
Saoner Tahsil ..	543	5	205	25,056	125,694	63,716	61,978	118,132	+6 40	−7 08	231
Chanda District	*9,312*	*6*	*2,385*	*148,382*	*759,695*	*381,204*	*378,491*	*660,630*	*+15·00*	*−2·49*	*82*
Chanda Town ..	..	1	..	5,270	28,138	14,394	13,744	22,981	+22.44	+15.68 }	160
Chanda Tahsil ..	1,174	..	355	31,042	159,441	80,394	79,047	136,293	+16.98	+1.21 }	
Warora Tahsil ..	1,282	2	445	33,325	174,086	88,001	86,085	155,723	+11.79	−1.78	136
Brahmapuri Tahsil.	897	2	336	30,815	155,262	77,078	78,184	139,911	+10.97	−7 23	173
Garchiroli Tahsil Khalsa.	1,457	1	331	23,391	116,264	58,048	58,216	95,118	+22.23	−2.64	80
Garchiroli Tahsil Zamindaris.	1,413	..	463	10,447	53,826	26,791	27,035	49,376	+9.01	+6.93	38
Sironcha Tahsil Khalsa.	489	..	97	6,344	32,228	16,216	16,012	25,368	+27.04	−21.58	66
Ahiri Zamindari .	2,600	..	358	7,748	40,450	20,282	20,168	35,860	+12 80	−4.17	16
Bhandara District.	*3,623*	*1*	*1,498*	*154,070*	*824,496*	*408,799*	*415,697*	*717,747*	*+14 87*	*+4 65*	*228*
Bhandara Tahsil	967	3	462	46,402	252,315	125,954	126,361	216,923	+16.31	+0.59	261
Gondia Town ..	..	1	..	3,559	14,957	8,201	6,756	10,617	+40.88	+81.58 }	
Gondia Tahsil Khalsa.	386	..	157	17,005	96,121	47,348	48,573	78,567	+22 34	−3.33 }	288
Gondia Tahsil Zamindaris.	719	..	310	42,265	227,271	111,751	115,520	197,981	+14.79	+8.10	316
Sakoli Tahsil Khalsa.	734	..	340	33,350	169,400	83,370	86,030	155,705	+8.79	+13.60	231
Sakoli Tahsil Zamindaris.	817	..	229	11,489	64,432	31,975	32,457	57,954	+11.18	−7.86	79
Balaghat District.	*3,557*	*1*	*1,224*	*101,312*	*561,602*	*276,898*	*284,704*	*511,634*	*+9·77*	*+7 50*	*158*
Balaghat Tahsil Khalsa.	654	1	256	33,505	113,704	56,049	57,655	95,642	+18.89	−24.95	174
Balaghat Tahsil Zamindaris.	431	..	175	5,684	82,945	40,799	42,146	82,754	+0.23	+79.38	192
Baihar Tahsil Khalsa.	1,271	..	320	16,999	86,352	43,218	43,134	75,048	+15.06	−4.85	68
Baihar Tahsil Zamindaris.	285	..	67	2,486	12,740	6,416	6,324	11,390	+11.85	+45.48	45
Waraseoni Tahsil	916	..	406	42,638	265,861	130,416	135,445	246,800	+7.72	+14.45	290
Chhattisgarh Division.	**22,051**	**8**	**10,495**	**743,410**	**3,745,745**	**1,814,237**	**1,931,508**	**3,381,687**	**+10.77**	**+4.16**	**170**
Raipur District ..	*9,717*	*4*	*4,481*	*304,367*	*1,527,573*	*739,950*	*787,623*	*1,392,768*	*+9·68*	*+6·27*	*157*
Raipur Town ..	..	1	..	9,680	45,390	24,060	21,330	38,341	+18.39	+8.50 }	
Raipur Tahsil ..	1,115	1	541	53,653	252,026	120,085	131,941	235,158	+7.17	+0.1 }	267
Mahasamund Tahsil Khalsa.	610	..	279	24,467	106,852	51,663	55,189	103,129	+3.61	+0.18	175
Mahasamund Tahsil Zamindaris.	4,584	..	2,116	98,521	508,776	249,004	259,772	450,960	+12.82	+9.89	111
Baloda Bazar Tahsil Khalsa.	1,465	1	716	61,101	297,448	143,320	154,128	272,285	+9.24	+6.95	203
Baloda Bazar Tahsil Zamindaris	315	..	206	12,860	70,983	34,627	36,356	61,655	+15.13	+20.51	225
Dhamtari Tahsil.	1,628	1	623	44,085	246,098	117,191	128,907	231,240	+6.43	+4.52	151

PROVINCIAL TABLE I.—Area and Population of Tahsils, Cities and large Towns—*concld.*

Tahsil, Taluk, Zamindari or Township.	Area in square miles.	Number of Towns.	Number of Villages.	Number of occupied houses.	Population 1931. Persons.	Population 1931. Males.	Population 1931. Females.	Population 1921 (Both sexes).	Percentage of variation 1921 to 1931.	Percentage of variation 1911 to 1921.	Number of persons per square mile in 1931.
1	2	3	4	5	6	7	8	9	10	11	12
Bilaspur District ..	*7,618*	*3*	*3,439*	*271,514*	*1,400,248*	*683,920*	*716,328*	*1,231,765*	*+13·68*	*+7 46*	*184*
Bilaspur Town ..	..	1	..	6,829	31,374	16,366	15,008	24,295	+29.14	+22.38 }	287
Bilaspur Tahsil Khalsa.	1,135	..	600	63,965	293,883	141,464	152,419	325,383	−9.68	+29.09 }	
Bilaspur Tahsil Zamindaris.	1,073	..	309	24,428	119,771	59,929	59,842	49,222	+143.33	−47 50	112
Mungeli Tahsil Khalsa.	940	1	555	30,319	152,327	72,639	79,688	131,933	+15.46	−9. 13	162
Mungeli Tahsil Zamindaris.	512	..	382	14,316	72,271	34,636	37,635	59,788	+20.88	−14 16	141
Janjgir Tahsil Khalsa.	1,300	..	751	82,061	473,952	230,810	243,142	432,850	+9.50	+14.98	365
Janjgir Tahsil Zamindaris.	105	1	62	8,179	41,952	20,507	21,445	33,661	+24 63	+5.78	400
Katghora Tahsil Khalsa.	3	..	1	333	1,477	712	765	1,470	+0 48	+274.04	492
Katghora Tahsil Zamindaris.	2,550	..	779	41,084	213,241	106 857	106,384	173,163	+23.14	+10 25	84
Drug District ..	*4,716*	*1*	*2,575*	*167,529*	*817,924*	*390,367*	*427,557*	*757,154*	*+8·03*	*−4 13*	*173*
Drug Tahsil Khalsa.	994	1	570	54,957	259,796	123,792	136,004	254,503	+2.08	+8.37	261
Drug Tahsil Zamindaris.	140	..	55	4,948	24,178	11,671	12,507	20,828	+16.08	−19.79	173
Bemetara Tahsil Khalsa.	952	..	605	40,003	208,196	98,344	109,852	185,452	+12.26	−11.16	219
Bemetara Tahsil Zamindaris.	615	..	288	12,977	53,550	25,748	27,802	45,846	+16.80	−21.95	87
Sanjari Tahsil Khalsa.	891	..	468	33,592	166,096	78,873	87,223	155,355	+6.91	−2.26	186
Sanjari Tahsil Zamindaris	1,124	..	589	21,052	106,108	51,939	54,169	95,170	+11.49	−7.18	94
Berar ..	**17,767**	**42**	**5,935**	**728,798**	**3,441,838**	**1,759,579**	**1,682,259**	**3,075,316**	**+11.92**	**+0.59**	**194**
Amraoti District ..	*4,691*	*14*	*1,612*	*202,415*	*941,604*	*485,593*	*456,011*	*827,867*	*+13 74*	*—5 17*	*201*
Amraoti Town ..	..	1	..	10,873	46,832	25,746	21,086	40,694	+15.08	+18.74 }	323
Amraoti Taluk* ..	672	2	276	37,089	170,188	88,108	82,080	141,590	+20.20	−8 59 }	
Morsi Taluk ..	623	2	233	35,875	167,238	86,023	81,215	145,276	+15 12	−5 75	268
Chandur Taluk ..	855	1	316	47,055	209,558	106,914	102,644	193,457	+8.32	−5.22	245
Ellichpur Town ..	..	1	..	5,017	28,592	14,822	13,770	23,899	+19.64	+71.82 }	329
Ellichpur Taluk†	490	5	243	27,965	132,811	68,448	64,363	119,156	+11.46	−8 61 }	
Daryapur Taluk ..	505	2	241	29,922	138,538	71,141	67,397	122,514	+13 08	−5 67	274
Melghat Taluk ..	1,546	..	303	8,619	47,847	24,391	23,456	41,281	+15.91	−19.68	31
Akola District ..	*4,091*	*11*	*1,492*	*187,100*	*876,362*	*448,896*	*427,466*	*794,847*	*+10 26*	*+1 12*	*214*
Akola Town ..	..	1	..	8,694	47,632	26,401	21,231	37,864	+25.80	+46 61 }	250
Akola Taluk ..	739	1	297	30,689	136,793	70,018	66,775	125,844	+8 70	−3.85 }	
Akot Taluk ..	550	2	249	33,672	153,507	78,372	75,135	140,128	+9 54	−0 16	279
Balapur Taluk ..	530	3	157	24,192	112,492	56,975	55,517	106,741	+5.39	−0.66	212
Basim Taluk ..	1,046	1	318	39,658	194,084	98,285	95,799	170,996	+13.50	+3 25	186
Mangrulpir Taluk	616	1	204	20,514	98,618	49,730	48,888	93,391	+5.60	−0.57	160
Karanja Town ..	..	1	.	3,369	16,615	8,776	7,839	13,645	+21.77	+7.90 }	218
Murtizapur Taluk	610	1	267	26,312	116,621	60,339	56,282	106,238	+9.77	−2.83 }	
Buldana District	*3,766*	*9*	*1,206*	*160,225*	*766,584*	*388,966*	*377,618*	*703,643*	*+8·95*	*+4·44*	*204*
Chikhli Taluk ..	904	3	261	34,282	168,754	85,324	83,430	157,189	+7.35	+12.80	187
Mehkar Taluk ..	1,027	1	321	32,568	167,319	84,167	83,152	148,723	+12.50	+4.68	163
Khamgaon Town	..	1	..	3,591	23,462	13,113	10,349	19,962	+17.53	+97.19 }	
Shegaon Town ..	..	1	..	3,476	14,699	7,583	7,116	14,531	+1.16	+21.48 }	218
Khamgaon Taluk	710	..	213	26,809	116,270	58,801	57,469	111,376	+4 39	−6.65 }	
Jalgaon Taluk ..	474	1	171	22,286	98,882	49,935	48,947	95,195	+3 87	+3.71	209
Malkapur Town	..	1	..	3,642	17,565	9,350	8,215	14,947	+17.52	+2.63 }	272
Malkapur Taluk	651	1	240	33,571	159,633	80,693	78,940	141,720	+12.64	−3.40 }	
Yeotmal District ..	*5,219*	*8*	*1,625*	*179,058*	*857,288*	*436,124*	*421,164*	*748,959*	*+14·46*	*+3·38*	*164*
Yeotmal Town ..	..	1	..	4,516	20,967	11,434	9,533	17,238	+21.63	+27.45 }	1
Yeotmal Taluk ..	908	..	314	30,877	143,241	72,284	70,957	129,349	+10.74	−5 83 }	
Kelapur Taluk ..	1,086	2	333	36,748	167,162	84,416	82,746	148,703	+12.41	+13.68	154
Wun Taluk ..	862	1	300	28,425	135,291	68,848	66,443	119,267	+13.44	+10.36	157
Darwha Taluk ..	1,078	2	350	40,978	201,962	103,009	98,953	172,390	+17.15	−5.52	187
Pusad Taluk .	1,285	2	328	37,514	188,665	96,133	92,532	162,012	+16.45	+6. 46	147

* Includes figures for Amraoti Camp.
† Includes figures for Ellichpur Camp.

PROVINCIAL TABLE II

Population of Districts, Tahsils, Cities and large Towns by Religion and Literacy.

1. In this Table the population of the Tahsils and States of the Central Provinces, of the Taluks of Berar, of the two cities and of 20 large towns is shown by religion and literacy. Zoroastrians, Jews and Buddhists have been grouped together under the head "Others". Hindus have been shown in three classes—Brahmins, Depressed classes and Other Hindus.

2. The figures for Zamindari areas are given separately under the tahsils to which they belong. The figures for the cities and towns are shown above the tahsil in which they lie and are not included in the tahsil figures.

3. The age groups for the number of the total population literate have not been smoothed as in Imperial Tables VII and XIII and present the original crude figures collected at the Census.

4. Only the figures of those castes regarded as untouchable in each unit have been included in columns 10 and 11. Such castes vary from district to district. Lists of those held to be untouchable throughout the Province or the administrative divisions mentioned and throughout the States are given below. Other castes included in depressed classes in any particular unit are named in the Remarks column.

Castes held to be untouchable throughout the Central Provinces British districts and Berar :—

(*a*) 1. Mehra or Mahar (Somvansi—Manepwar).
2. Basor or Burud.
3. Mehtar or Bhangi.
4. Dom.
5. Chamar or Chambhar.
6. Satnami.
7. Mochi.
8. Ganda.
9. Mang.

Other castes held to be untouchable throughout the Jubbulpore and Nerbudda Divisions :—

(*a*) 1. Kori.
2. Mala.
(*a*) 3. Balahi.

Other castes held to be untouchable throughout the Nagpur and Berar Divisions :—

1. Madgi.
2. Balahi.
(*b*) 3. Pardhan.
4. Ghasia.
5. Katia.
6. Panka.
7. Khatik
(*b*) 8. Kaikari.
9. Dohor

Other castes held to be untouchable throughout the Chhattisgarh Division :—

1. Ghasia.
2. Katia.
3. Panka.
4. Dewar.

Caste held to be untouchable throughout the Central Provinces States :—

1. Mehtar.

The names of the other castes regarded as untouchable in each separate State appear at *the end of the Table.*

5. Statistics of literacy by caste (Table XIV) were as at the last Census tabulated only for units in which the caste concerned is important. Columns 12 and 13 therefore contain figures for the principal depressed castes only—and the literates among other untouchable castes of small numerical importance in a unit are included in columns 8 and 9. The error resulting is inconsiderable.

(*a*) Except in the Harda and Sohagpur tahsils of Hoshangabad district where these three castes are not regarded as untouchable.
(*b*) Except in Balaghat district where these two castes are not regarded as untouc able.

Serial number.	Tahsil, Taluk, Zamindari or Township.	Hindus.									
		Brahmins.				Other Hindus.				Depressed	
		Number of persons.		Number literate.		Number of persons.		Number literate.		Number of persons.	
		Males.	Females.	Males.	Females.	Males.	Females	Males.	Females.	Males.	Females.
	1	2	3	4	5	6	7	8	9	10	11
	Central Provinces and Berar.	**277,925**	**239,820**	**135,672**	**23,833**	**5,713,076**	**5,715,728**	**523,369**	**28,871**	**1,566,448**	**1,613,627**
	C. P. British Districts and Berar.	**265,066**	**228,726**	**130,534**	**23,366**	**4,964,683**	**4,952,405**	**492,704**	**27,178**	**1,441,577**	**1,485,766**
	C. P. British Districts	**207,848**	**182,616**	**97,364**	**15,977**	**3,794,580**	**3,835,065**	**336,850**	**20,230**	**1,104,928**	**1,146,699**
	JUBBULPORE DIVISION ..	76,661	68,131	31,209	3,628	706,088	697,448	69,380	5,323	175,212	173,443
	Saugor District ..	*21,931*	*19,230*	*7,362*	*768*	*155,482*	*146,570*	*11,561*	*992*	*69,688*	*67,220*
1	Saugor Town and Cantonment.	2,821	2,462	1,675	352	10,515	9,817	3,281	376	5,292	5,169
2	Saugor Tahsil ..	5,677	5,367	1,454	108	41,778	39,797	3,399	78	19,927	19,697
3	Khurai Tahsil ..	4,223	3,592	1,479	127	37,792	34,255	3,314	179	18,804	17,787
4	Rehli Tahsil ..	6,777	5,753	1,976	136	39,748	37,825	3,044	250	15,386	14,794
5	Banda Tahsil ..	2,433	2,056	778	45	25,649	24,876	1,523	109	10,279	9,773
	Damoh District ..	*11,318*	*10,063*	*4,325*	*444*	*86,145*	*83,321*	*9,768*	*576*	*37,163*	*37,698*
6	Damoh Town ..	1,289	1,051	777	172	4,857	4,549	1,381	201	1,806	1,864
7	Damoh Tahsil ..	5,143	4,542	1,790	122	45,532	44,084	4,698	234	20,819	21,051
8	Hatta Tahsil ..	4,886	4,470	1,758	150	35,756	34,688	3,689	141	14,538	14,783
	Jubbulpore District ..	*34,347*	*30,774*	*15,215*	*1,869*	*271,564*	*271,075*	*28,650*	*2,578*	*44,797*	*44,798*
9	Jubbulpore City and Cantonment.	7,548	5,371	4,559	1,180	29,923	24,306	9,276	1,664	9,653	8,738
10	Jubbulpore Tahsil ..	4,346	3,932	1,793	106	57,168	57,871	3,511	129	7,925	8,156
11	Sihora Tahsil ..	9,583	9,309	4,008	267	71,621	73,947	6,155	328	9,850	9,990
12	Murwara Town ..	1,370	1,005	738	117	7,029	6,337	1,634	165	1,023	1,035
13	Murwara Tahsil ..	7,435	7,601	3,061	119	65,653	67,580	5,109	189	8,531	9,002
14	Patan Tahsil ..	4,065	3,556	1,056	80	40,170	41,034	2,974	103	7,815	7,877
	Mandla District ..	*4,761*	*4,104*	*2,330*	*311*	*101,884*	*103,059*	*6,963*	*501*	*12,068*	*12,058*
15	Mandla Tahsil ..	2,795	2,410	1,497	246	54,624	55,982	4,305	343	5,216	5,434
16	Dindori Tahsil	941	732	360	16	17,920	17,863	1,200	36	2,752	2,581
17	Niwas Tahsil ..	1,025	962	473	49	29,340	29,214	1,458	122	4,100	4,043
	Seoni District ..	*4,304*	*3,960*	*1,977*	*236*	*91,013*	*93,423*	*9,429*	*676*	*11,496*	*11,669*
18	Seoni Tahsil ..	2,740	2,516	1,359	169	66,636	68,926	6,807	428	5,988	6,292
19	Lakhnadon Tahsil ..	1,564	1,444	618	67	24,377	24,497	2,622	248	5,508	5,377
	NERBUDDA DIVISION ..	49,035	42,329	25,203	2,996	672,956	653,157	79,566	3,490	127,991	129,344
	Narsinghpur District ..	*11,679*	*10,717*	*5,055*	*590*	*100,022*	*97,447*	*13,415*	*926*	*21,513*	*22,855*
20	Narsinghpur Tahsil ..	5,117	4,588	2,384	317	44,846	43,345	6,495	469	11,483	12,955
21	Gadarwara Tahsil ..	6,562	6,129	2,671	273	55,176	54,102	6,920	457	10,030	9,900
	Hoshangabad District ..	*18,266*	*16,402*	*9,374*	*949*	*166,902*	*160,209*	*22,136*	*854*	*25,731*	*25,793*
22	Hoshangabad Tahsil ..	5,790	5,129	2,999	301	43,738	41,173	6,088	203	10,991	11,146
23	Harda Tahsil ..	6,506	5,782	3,632	395	54,202	52,635	6,895	213	3,723	3,745
24	Sohagpur Tahsil ..	4,247	3,859	1,763	184	48,927	46,782	5,952	329	5,301	5,158
25	Seoni-Malwa Tahsil ..	1,723	1,632	980	69	20,035	19,619	3,201	109	5,716	5,744
	Nimar District ..	*10,535*	*7,964*	*6,102*	*813*	*155,968*	*145,425*	*19,805*	*857*	*26,909*	*25,782*
26	Khandwa Town ..	3,037	2,223	1,940	410	8,176	6,442	2,617	181	1,934	1,783
27	Khandwa Tahsil ..	3,626	2,757	2,112	141	73,245	69,537	9,847	280	14,228	14,004
28	Burhanpur Town	1,417	1,174	894	216	10,561	9,888	3,359	314	1,533	1,428
29	Burhanpur Tahsil ..	1,006	683	473	11	41,124	39,141	2,565	43	4,542	4,374
30	Harsud Tahsil ..	1,449	1,127	683	35	22,862	20,417	1,417	39	4,672	4,193
	Betul District ..	*2,930*	*2,415*	*1,778*	*244*	*108,813*	*110,280*	*8,723*	*275*	*24,946*	*25,709*
31	Betul Tahsil ..	1,695	1,370	982	147	32,227	32,522	2,892	167	6,610	6,862
32	Multai Tahsil ..	877	766	568	80	54,905	56,283	4,053	99	14,613	15,192
33	Bhainsdehi Tahsil ..	358	279	228	17	21,681	21,475	1,778	9	3,723	3,655
	Chhindwara District ..	*5,625*	*4,831*	*2,894*	*400*	*141,251*	*139,796*	*15,487*	*578*	*28,892*	*29,205*
34	Chhindwara Tahsil Khalsa	2,535	2,036	1,456	246	58,191	57,063	5,717	308	9,181	9,117
35	Chhindwara Tahsil Zamindaris.	137	80	81	7	7,897	7,345	294	7	1,288	1,295
36	Amarwara Tahsil Khalsa	1,633	1,613	670	50	26,499	27,273	3,363	75	5,526	5,838
37	Amarwara Tahsil Zamindaris.	102	87	56	5	2,479	2,371	354	2	1,451	1,390
38	Sausar Tahsil ..	1,218	1,015	631	92	46,185	45,744	5,759	186	11,444	11,565

Classes.		Jains.				Sikhs.				Muslims.				
Number literate.		Number of persons.		Number literate.		Number of persons.		Number literate.		Number of persons.		Number literate.		Serial number.
Males.	Females.	Males.	Females.	Males.	Females.	Males.	Females.	Males.	Females.	Males.	Females.	Males.	Females.	
12	13	14	15	16	17	18	19	20	21	22	23	24	25	
43,067	**1,999**	**41,416**	**38,439**	**22,306**	**3,277**	**3,003**	**1,517**	**1,515**	**216**	**370,633**	**335,475**	**83,727**	**9,853**	
41,946	**1,940**	**40,333**	**37,562**	**21,643**	**3,188**	**2,828**	**1,413**	**1,436**	**209**	**358,900**	**323,954**	**80,973**	**9,542**	
30,560	**1,411**	**29,773**	**27,720**	**15,937**	**2,629**	**2,566**	**1,222**	**1,330**	**192**	**201,352**	**181,822**	**53,492**	**6,828**	
4,221	166	17,582	16,390	9,156	1,683	716	266	501	75	57,676	51,572	14,980	1,997	
1,051	*48*	*3,910*	*3,226*	*4,309*	*749*	*84*	*38*	*45*	*13*	*13,655*	*12,091*	*2,888*	*186*	
257	15	963	792	511	130	44	23	25	11	5,265	4,885	1,410	117	1
281	9	1,982	1,849	964	110	7	1	7	..	2,221	2,023	290	7	2
251	10	2,017	1,962	1,011	232	33	14	16	2	2,833	2,361	666	49	3
140	3	2,271	2,061	1,048	180	..	..	..	..	2,569	2,141	370	9	4
122	11	1,677	1,562	775	97	..	..	..	..	767	681	152	4	5
721	*27*	*3,825*	*3,653*	*1,945*	*275*	*15*	*3*	*10*	*1*	*5,139*	*5,077*	*1,313*	*107*	
109	8	489	496	296	83	4	3	2	1	1,923	1,836	640	69	6
350	13	2,478	2,332	1,203	138	..	..	8	..	1,918	1,747	372	28	7
262	6	858	825	446	54	..	..	..	..	1,598	1,494	301	10	8
1,425	*57*	*3,521*	*3,271*	*2,065*	*385*	*581*	*191*	*421*	*50*	*25,763*	*21,851*	*7,653*	*1,329*	
850	40	990	873	678	177	533	155	391	38	16,187	12,835	5,462	1,123	9
97	6	333	362	216	40	4	1	4	..	1,593	1,441	306	17	10
147	5	534	524	292	68	3	4	3	3	2,738	2,767	577	51	11
35	2	273	210	189	22	14	15	9	6	1,742	1,393	601	75	12
217	2	242	237	141	39	17	12	9	2	2,003	1,928	502	41	13
79	2	1,149	1,065	549	39	10	4	5	1	1,500	1,487	205	22	14
570	*27*	*415*	*369*	*250*	*51*	*31*	*31*	*18*	*11*	*3,667*	*3,199*	*1,083*	*142*	
264	11	325	312	191	46	24	27	13	11	2,183	1,895	633	114	15
72	2	65	40	44	1	3	3	2	..	845	737	240	21	16
234	14	25	17	15	4	4	1	3	..	639	567	210	7	17
454	*7*	*911*	*871*	*587*	*223*	*5*	*3*	*4*	..	*9,152*	*9,354*	*2,043*	*233*	
326	6	456	421	329	149	1	2	1	..	6,187	6,244	1,504	174	18
128	1	455	450	258	74	4	1	3	..	2,965	3,110	539	59	19
3,519	58	5,202	4,886	3,148	454	679	397	242	33	59,203	53,821	14,045	1,627	
710	*16*	*1,376*	*1,278*	*771*	*167*	*5*	*1*	*3*	*1*	*5,802*	*5,602*	*1,378*	*183*	
416	12	897	852	500	106	4	1	2	1	3,699	3,545	900	112	20
294	4	479	426	271	61	1	..	1	..	2,103	2,057	478	71	21
860	*6*	*954*	*897*	*641*	*87*	*200*	*55*	*143*	*13*	*12,368*	*11,107*	*3,427*	*340*	
434	6	330	286	214	20	46	11	21	6	3,370	2,991	997	77	22
231	..	306	303	216	44	39	21	36	1	4,103	3,586	994	104	23
66	..	216	218	129	7	84	19	63	4	3,603	3,296	1,100	144	24
129	..	102	90	82	16	31	4	23	2	1,292	1,234	336	15	25
697	*9*	*1,164*	*1,040*	*772*	*111*	*393*	*298*	*41*	*7*	*26,839*	*24,086*	*5,427*	*772*	
147	3	323	265	232	56	16	5	9	3	5,166	4,406	1,457	181	26
272	3	297	255	215	20	10	8	8	4	5,416	4,869	1,075	63	27
90	2	145	117	90	15	..	..	..	..	9,328	8,347	2,300	513	28
123	..	204	189	113	13	1	..	..	..	5,030	4,776	282	1	29
65	1	195	214	122	7	366	285	24	..	1,899	1,688	313	14	30
446	*21*	*674*	*657*	*351*	*15*	*37*	*15*	*24*	*1*	*3,644*	*3,393*	*1,227*	*111*	
154	3	184	174	111	9	12	7	13	1	1,568	1,425	579	52	31
238	9	374	378	167	6	6	5	3	..	1,311	1,264	384	54	32
54	9	116	105	73	..	19	3	8	..	765	704	264	5	33
806	*6*	*1,034*	*1,014*	*613*	*74*	*44*	*28*	*31*	*11*	*10,550*	*9,633*	*2,586*	*221*	
197	4	443	416	279	36	42	28	29	11	5,109	4,548	1,397	131	34
21		38	37	17	9	..	..	..	..	260	226	57	1	35
159	..	347	358	198	24	2	..	2	..	1,837	1,788	330	39	36
55	..	15	15	16	1	..	..	..	..	286	268	112	1	37
374	2	191	188	103	4	..	..	..	..	3,058	2,803	690	49	38

PROVINCIAL TABLE II

Population of Tahsils, Cities and

Serial number.	Tahsil, Taluk, Zamindari or Township.	Christians.				Tribal Religion.				Others.		
		Number of persons.		Number literate.		Number of persons.		Number literate.		Number of persons.		Number
		Males.	Females.	Males.	Females.	Males.	Females.	Males.	Females.	Males.	Females.	Males.
	1	26	27	28	29	30	31	32	33	34	35	36
	Central Provinces and Berar.	**52,540**	**49,745**	**15,631**	**10,803**	**970,911**	**998,303**	**7,180**	**350**	**1,251**	**1,080**	**1,014**
	C. P. British Districts and Berar.	**26,438**	**24,146**	**14,300**	**10,293**	**660,755**	**690,860**	**6,444**	**325**	**1,238**	**1,073**	**1,003**
	C. P. British Districts ..	**23,673**	**21,516**	**13,098**	**9,299**	**636,433**	**666,030**	**6,296**	**257**	**1,086**	**956**	**884**
	JUBBULPORE DIVISION ..	6,401	4,904	4,748	3,077	200,073	210,438	1,758	56	246	219	187
	Saugor District ..	*994*	*936*	*620*	*568*	*9,583*	*9,832*	*38*	*2*	*58*	*61*	*41*
1	Saugor Town and Cantonment	397	400	254	283	..	..	..	..	9	8	6
2	Saugor Tahsil ..	192	196	97	83	41	33	..	..	..	..	..
3	Khurai Tahsil ..	367	316	242	188	227	225	3	..	49	53	35
4	Rehli Tahsil ..	20	13	17	8	9,188	9,456	35	2	..	..	..
5	Banda Tahsil ..	18	11	10	6	127	118	..	..	..	..	..
	Damoh District ..	*325*	*178*	*254*	*88*	*10,555*	*10,776*	*216*	*4*	*6*	*8*	*5*
6	Damoh Town ..	301	154	236	78	52	42	2	1	5	7	5
7	Damoh Tahsil ..	10	9	8	3	10,503	10,734	214	3	1	1	..
8	Hatta Tahsil ..	14	15	10	7	..	..	..	..	..	..	..
	Jubbulpore District ..	*4,494*	*3,203*	*3,584*	*2,155*	*6,405*	*6,856*	*103*	*15*	*177*	*143*	*137*
9	Jubbulpore City and Cantonment.	4,132	2,592	3,356	1,713	134	121	14	4	158	133	122
10	Jubbulpore Tahsil ..	124	116	79	85	644	671	2	..	11	4	7
11	Sihora Tahsil ..	6	3	4	2	2,744	2,912	46	10	1	..	1
12	Murwara Town ..	118	391	76	330	..	..	..	..	3	1	3
13	Murwara Tahsil ..	98	84	59	20	2,468	2,720	40	1	4	5	4
14	Patan Tahsil ..	16	17	10	5	415	432	1	..	..	..	..
	Mandla District ..	*410*	*400*	*185*	*174*	*98,123*	*101,187*	*618*	*4*	..	..	..
15	Mandla Tahsil ..	351	345	154	159	28,666	29,520	122	2	..	..	..
16	Dindori Tahsil ..	51	50	24	13	46,701	48,514	380	2	..	..	..
17	Niwas Tahsil ..	8	5	7	2	22,756	23,153	116	..	..	..	..
	Seoni District ..	*178*	*187*	*105*	*92*	*75,407*	*81,787*	*783*	*31*	*5*	*7*	*4*
18	Seoni Tahsil ..	160	167	92	81	40,382	44,174	553	19	5	7	4
19	Lakhnadon Tahsil ..	18	20	13	11	35,025	37,613	230	12	..	..	..
	NERBUDDA DIVISION ..	4,879	4,554	1,716	1,198	217,699	228,126	1,278	34	162	146	135
	Narsinghpur District ..	*175*	*119*	*112*	*54*	*20,845*	*22,045*	*146*	*6*	..	..	..
20	Narsinghpur Tahsil ..	134	90	96	44	12,335	13,121	90	4	..	..	..
21	Gadarwara Tahsil ..	41	29	16	10	8,510	8,924	56	2	..	..	..
	Hoshangabad District ..	*1,196*	*1,005*	*681*	*418*	*22,567*	*22,883*	*134*	*8*	*42*	*53*	*34*
22	Hoshangabad Tahsil ..	554	427	325	196	7,633	7,877	49	..	25	36	18
23	Harda Tahsil ..	115	100	83	56	3,292	3,191	4	..	13	12	13
24	Sohagpur Tahsil ..	409	371	240	144	7,734	7,861	68	8	4	5	3
25	Seoni-Malwa Tahsil ..	118	107	33	22	3,908	3,954	13	..	..	..	..
	Nimar District ..	*2,486*	*2,442*	*390*	*265*	*17,659*	*17,770*	*67*	*5*	*89*	*82*	*73*
26	Khandwa Town ..	365	381	222	216	5	6	1	..	38	51	28
27	Khandwa Tahsil ..	1,899	1,872	113	25	3,679	3,638	23	1	2	..	1
28	Burhanpur Town ..	21	26	16	13	6	1	..	..	45	29	40
29	Burhanpur Tahsil ..	58	44	18	10	..	..	..	..	2	1	2
30	Harsud Tahsil ..	143	119	21	1	13,969	14,125	43	4	2	1	2
	Betul District ..	*418*	*428*	*193*	*202*	*59,642*	*62,241*	*223*	*2*	*10*	..	*10*
31	Betul Tahsil ..	308	337	129	159	27,825	28,973	114	..	7	..	7
32	Multai Tahsil ..	81	67	46	28	11,966	12,501	71	2	3	..	3
33	Bhainsdehi Tahsil ..	29	24	18	15	19,851	20,767	38	..	..	..	..
	Chhindwara District ..	*604*	*560*	*340*	*259*	*96,986*	*103,187*	*708*	*13*	*21*	*11*	*18*
34	Chhindwara Tahsil Khalsa ..	431	393	260	191	35,393	37,124	268	5	15	11	13
35	Chhindwara Tahsil Zamindaris	53	52	18	20	13,279	13,946	99	..	..	..	..
36	Amarwara Tahsil Khalsa ..	82	90	42	38	13,977	15,278	102	5	..	..	..
37	Amarwara Tahsil Zamindaris	16	15	8	8	11,124	11,939	70	3	..	..	..
38	Sausar Tahsil ..	22	10	12	2	23,213	24,900	169	..	6	..	5

Illiterate.	Number literate in total population.								Literate in English.		Remarks see paragraph 4 on the fly-sheet.	Serial number.
	Aged 4—6.		Aged 7—13.		Aged 14—23.		Aged 24 and over.					
Females.	Males.	Females.	Males.	Females.	Males	Females.	Males.	Females.	Males.	Females.		
37	38	39	40	41	42	43	44	45	46	47	48	
747	**2,785**	**1,255**	**93,567**	**17,068**	**237,640**	**27,856**	**499,489**	**33,770**	**84,104**	**9,532**		
743	**2,718**	**1,238**	**90,077**	**16,525**	**225,750**	**26,802**	**472,438**	**32,219**	**81,964**	**9,309**		
662	**1,899**	**971**	**62,180**	**12,044**	**154,215**	**19,456**	**337,517**	**25,014**	**61.361**	**8,148**		
147	407	261	13,818	3,388	38,914	5,449	83,001	7,054	16,308	2,647		
33	*54*	*24*	*3,030*	*750*	*8,604*	*1,068*	*19,230*	*1,517*	*2,611*	*361*		
4	23	16	970	320	2,165	383	4,261	569	1,478	170	Panka, Katia, Khatik, Dhobi, Khangar, Chadar, Dhanuk. Kumhar	1
..	4	1	589	86	1,782	132	4,117	176	120	17		2
29	7	2	500	129	1,949	272	4,561	413	812	165		3
..	17	4	625	142	1,783	196	4,205	246	158	6		4
..	3	1	346	73	925	85	2.086	113	73	3		5
8	*31*	*7*	*1,921*	*336*	*5,881*	*540*	*10,724*	*647*	*1,054*	*39*		
7	2	4	540	125	1,054	196	1,852	295	682	37	Panka, Dhobi, Khangar, Chadar, Kumhar, Dahayat.	6
1	3	..	838	123	2,697	206	5,105	213	149	1		7
..	26	3	543	88	2,130	138	3.767	139	223	1		8
101	*285*	*213*	*6,424*	*1,736*	*16,728*	*2 893*	*35,825*	*3,697*	*10,588*	*2,114*		
93	203	171	2,913	1,205	7,129	1,973	14,463	2,683	8,802	1,753		9
4	11	2	667	76	1,788	126	3,549	183	407	50		10
..	29	13	1,108	147	3,194	248	6,902	326	279	7		11
..	9	14	362	169	929	311	1,985	223	722	250		12
4	25	9	928	69	2,455	150	5,734	189	295	52		13
..	8	4	446	70	1,233	85	3,192	93	83	2		14
..	*16*	*5*	*1,058*	*260*	*3,473*	*448*	*7,470*	*508*	*1,147*	*73*		
..	13	2	664	193	2,054	334	4,448	403	952	64	Nagarchi, Ojha.	15
..	1	2	160	16	699	29	1,462	44	102	7		16
..	2	1	234	51	720	85	1,560	61	93	2		17
5	*21*	*12*	*1,385*	*306*	*4,228*	*500*	*9,752*	*685*	*878*	*60*		
5	17	11	998	230	3,041	360	6,919	430	756	57	Nagarchi.	18
..	4	1	387	76	1,187	140	2,833	255	122	3		19
93	209	72	13,291	1,993	34,723	3,468	80,629	4,450	11,360	787		
	58	*5*	*2,664*	*430*	*5,851*	*648*	*13,017*	*860*	*1,288*	*44*		
..	35	3	1,420	242	3,083	373	6,345	447	892	38	Pardhi.	20
..	23	2	1,244	188	2,768	275	6,672	413	396	6		21
29	*44*	*17*	*3,812*	*526*	*9,849*	*895*	*23,725*	*1,266*	*4,072*	*295*		
17	5	..	1,048	146	3,027	271	7,065	409	1,713	125	Katia, Khatik, Dhobi, Kumhar, Ojha, Khangar.	22
10	19	6	1,415	176	3,212	289	7,458	352	1,203	70	*Nil.*	23
2	17	8	942	169	2,495	249	5,930	396	826	92	Rajjhar.	24
..	3	3	407	35	1,115	86	3,272	109	330	6	Katia, Dhobi, Kumhar, Khangar.	25
58	*55*	*32*	*3,527*	*580*	*9,053*	*1,069*	*20,739*	*1,216*	*3,304*	*241*		
37	17	18	803	233	1,930	452	3,903	384	1,648	189	Pardhan, Katia.	26
..	16	3	1,119	111	3,570	179	8,961	244	247	6		27
19	13	9	969	198	1,859	381	3,948	504	1,177	45		28
1	6	1	426	16	1,006	28	2,138	34	95	4		29
1	3	1	210	22	688	29	1,789	50	137	2		30
..	*12*	*2*	*1,194*	*162*	*3,098*	*317*	*8,671*	*390*	*1,085*	*67*		
..	3	1	531	88	1,261	205	3,186	244	603	29	Katia.	31
..	9	1	507	65	1,301	92	3,716	120	390	34		32
..	.	..	156	9	536	20	1,769	26	92	4		33
6	*40*	*16*	*2,094*	*295*	*6,872*	*539*	*14,477*	*718*	*1,611*	*137*		
6	23	15	944	163	2,588	342	6,061	418	1,267	109	Katia, Nagarchi, Khatik, Panka, Pardhan.	34
..	..	..	43	7	137	18	407	19	34	3		35
..	4	1	315	52	2,003	70	2,544	108	87	6		36
..	1	..	52	5	173	7	445	8	21	3		37
..	12	..	740	68	1,971	102	5,020	165	202	16		38

Serial number.	Tahsil, Taluk, Zamindari or Township.	Hindus									
		Brahmins.				Other Hindus.				Depressed	
		Number of persons.		Number literate.		Number of persons.		Number literate.		Number of persons.	
		Males.	Females.	Males.	Females.	Males.	Females.	Males.	Females.	Males.	Females.
	1	2	3	4	5	6	7	8	9	10	11
	NAGPUR DIVISION ..	41,485	32,852	24,013	7,271	1,202,256	1,188,957	121,148	7,295	359,989	368,675
	Wardha District ..	*8,682*	*6,657*	*4,704*	*1,249*	*172,924*	*168,139*	*22,247*	*1,087*	*47,628*	*48,255*
39	Wardha Tahsil ..	4,638	3,404	2,491	670	65,785	63,853	9,409	558	19,773	20,082
40	Arvi Tahsil ..	2,381	1,926	1,210	340	61,412	59,340	7,364	339	13,038	12,863
41	Hinganghat Town .. }	1,663									
42	Hinganghat Tahsil .. }		1,327	1,003	239	45,727	44,946	5,474	190	14,817	15,310
	Nagpur District ..	*21,494*	*16,344*	*13,072*	*4,406*	*318,255*	*307,317*	*43,917*	*4,257*	*99,452*	*99,657*
43	Nagpur City ..	15,525	11,204	9,717	3,716	59,459	50,733	16,359	3,577	20,093	19,223
44	Kamptee Town and Cantonment.	478	480	160	76	3,992	4,023	273	11	4,211	3,309
45	Nagpur Tahsil ..	845	642	422	75	48,906	48,626	3,511	50	16,159	16,833
46	Ramtek Tahsil ..	1,036	923	626	150	48,615	48,209	4,473	104	13,059	13,486
47	Umrer Town .. }	1,032									
48	Umrer Tahsil .. }		932	642	138	52,429	53,176	5,319	127	21,057	21,846
49	Katol Tahsil ..	1,402	1,208	804	133	56,900	56,048	6,549	205	13,630	13,640
50	Saoner Tahsil ..	1,176	955	701	118	47,954	46,502	7,433	183	11,243	11,320
	Chanda District ..	*3,969*	*3,645*	*2,208*	*602*	*245,753*	*241,665*	*16,996*	*698*	*67,328*	*68,157*
51	Chanda Town ..	1,181	1,094	795	289	8,885	8,483	2,586	257	2,823	2,737
52	Chanda Tahsil ..	528	448	306	68	56,659	55,607	2,957	74	18,128	18,057
53	Warora Tahsil ..	995	979	482	118	65,604	63,922	4,389	118	17,404	17,355
54	Brahmapuri Tahsil ..	584	596	371	82	52,891	52,383	3,999	68	15,670	17,084
55	Garchiroli Tahsil Khalsa	335	259	104	20	37,839	38,360	1,973	56	9,837	9,631
56	Garchiroli Tahsil Zamindaris.	37	15	14	2	8,117	7,391	420	15	1,599	1,506
57	Sironcha Tahsil Khalsa ..	249	217	97	14	11,175	11,258	361	29	804	808
58	Ahiri Zamindari ..	60	37	39	9	4,583	4,261	311	81	1,063	979
	Bhandara District ..	*4,638*	*3,923*	*2,385*	*730*	*267,375*	*269,111*	*21,169*	*683*	*108,504*	*113,822*
59	Bhandara Tahsil ..	2,137	1,996	1,309	397	79,807	79,290	6,980	276	35,532	36,640
60	Gondia Town .. }	1,222									
61	Gondia Tahsil Khalsa .. }		978	546	162	35,103	34,091	4,320	299	14,704	15,834
62	Gondia Tahsil Zamindaris	739	528	269	83	78,968	80,252	3,653	4	22,195	24,077
63	Sakoli Tahsil Khalsa ..	425	339	222	70	51,923	51,719	5,144	80	28,545	31,399
64	Sakoli Tahsil Zamindaris	115	82	39	18	21,574	23,759	1,072	24	7,528	5,872
	Balaghat District ..	*2,702*	*2,283*	*1,644*	*284*	*197,949*	*202,725*	*16,819*	*570*	*37,077*	*38,784*
65	Balaghat Tahsil Khalsa ..	1,154	967	775	203	40,085	41,257	4,424	240	6,699	7,035
66	Balaghat Tahsil Zamindaris	284	269	163	18	33,427	33,837	2,675	82	6,124	6,986
67	Baihar Tahsil Khalsa ..	274	166	172	13	29,550	29,590	2,869	79	3,838	3,735
68	Baihar Tahsil Zamindaris	17	6	6	..	4,925	4,939	162	26	381	344
69	Waraseoni Tahsil ..	973	875	528	50	89,962	93,102	6,689	143	20,035	20,684
	CHHATTISGARH DIVISION ..	40,667	39,304	16,939	2,082	1,213,280	1,295,503	66,756	4,122	441,736	475,237
	Raipur District ..	*14,253*	*13,369*	*6,700*	*797*	*496,986*	*528,771*	*27,432*	*1,701*	*168,197*	*182,303*
70	Raipur Town ..	3,253	2,626	2,073	418	13,015	11,637	3,691	474	3,144	2,816
71	Raipur Tahsil ..	2,504	2,621	975	97	80,056	87,417	4,789	208	35,801	40,200
72	Mahasamund Tahsil Khalsa.	1,142	1,054	592	48	34,033	36,398	2,417	112	11,723	12,593
73	Mahasamund Tahsil Zamindaris.	3,133	3,071	1,117	88	181,131	188,582	5,384	279	43,420	45,644
74	Baloda Bazar Tahsil Khalsa.	2,578	2,451	1,141	86	87,482	94,427	3,841	178	47,773	51,580
75	Baloda Bazar Tahsil Zamindaris.	272	240	114	9	22,245	23,397	915	26	9,797	10,300
76	Dhamtari Tahsil ..	1,371	1,306	688	51	79,024	86,913	6,395	424	16,539	19,170

Classes. Number literate. Males.	Classes. Number literate. Females.	Jains. Number of persons. Males.	Jains. Number of persons. Females.	Jains. Number literate. Males.	Jains. Number literate. Females.	Sikhs. Number of persons. Males.	Sikhs. Number of persons. Females.	Sikhs. Number literate. Males.	Sikhs. Number literate. Females.	Muslims. Number of persons. Males.	Muslims. Number of persons. Females.	Muslims. Number literate. Males.	Muslims. Number literate. Females.	Serial number.
12	13	14	15	16	17	18	19	20	21	22	23	24	25	
15,402	925	5,094	4,853	2,437	372	599	272	257	30	61,076	53,822	16,626	2,245	
1,699	*78*	*1,488*	*1,411*	*553*	*160*	*15*	*10*	*7*	*1*	*11,046*	*9,882*	*2,614*	*122*	
786	65	708	703	244	68	12	7	5	1	4,311	3,781	1,219	41	39
322	6	478	458	125	37	3	3	2	..	4,175	3,868	812	47	40
		207	187	159	53	..	..	..	..	1,466	1,263	333	28	41
591	7	95	63	25	2	..	..	..	..	1,094	970	250	6	42
5,932	*210*	*1,827*	*1,794*	*1,014*	*126*	*481*	*196*	*192*	*18*	*29,366*	*24,443*	*7,395*	*1,508*	
2,030	142	955	878	564	86	274	170	95	13	15,628	12,414	4,304	1,389	43
816	9	35	40	21	4	193	22	84	2	4,395	3,529	522	26	44
518	34	112	111	52	11	..	..	..	..	1,727	1,528	363	7	45
540	3	113	125	74	8	12	1	11	..	1,319	1,130	444	19	46
		9	12	7	..	..	..	..	..	440	420	215	5	47
819	9	201	234	72	4	..	..	..	..	1,013	915	303	13	48
481	10	295	289	154	11	2	3	2	3	2,671	2,476	597	31	49
728	3	107	105	70	2	..	..	..	..	2,173	2,031	647	18	50
2,109	*98*	*547*	*455*	*329*	*16*	*10*	*5*	*6*	*2*	*7,045*	*6,511*	*2,245*	*158*	
350	1	114	83	85	8	2	3	2	1	1,100	1,057	473	48	51
313	7	49	28	26	..	1	..	..	..	1,077	975	249	10	52
480	12	289	67	171	6	..	..	..	..	2,180	2,088	591	42	53
539	8	18	9	10	1	1	1	1	1	1,129	956	535	30	54
320	..	47	43	21	1	3	1	..	..	740	699	159	14	55
42	2	16	12	9	..	3	..	3	..	267	217	87	7	56
3	..	4	1	3	..	..	..	..	..	329	315	81	7	57
62	68	10	12	4	..	..	..	..	..	223	204	70	..	58
3,978	*504*	*779*	*781*	*257*	..	*47*	*37*	*32*	*5*	*8,134*	*7,350*	*2,542*	*259*	
1,398	44	217	200	55	..	6	9	5	1	3,369	3,076	996	66	59
		37	39	20	..	24	20	16	3	1,130	823	454	62	60
660	396	67	72	31	..	4	..	2	..	787	604	280	88	61
787	54	169	167	18	..	6	4	5	1	1,394	1,469	282	10	62
969	8	244	256	116	..	4	..	1	..	1,027	951	413	25	63
164	2	45	47	17	..	3	4	3	..	427	427	117	8	64
1,684	*35*	*453*	*412*	*284*	*70*	*46*	*24*	*20*	*4*	*5,485*	*5,636*	*1,830*	*198*	
253	9	145	114	84	14	10	12	5	3	1,832	1,848	729	121	65
335	1	..	..	..	..	9	3	4	..	461	492	149	11	66
305	3	8	10	4	1	18	7	4	..	454	391	195	20	67
19	..	..	..	..	..	..	..	..	..	22	30	8	..	68
772	22	300	288	196	55	9	2	7	1	2,716	2,875	749	46	69
7.418	262	1,895	1,591	1,196	120	572	287	330	54	23,397	22,607	7,841	959	
2,992	*101*	*932*	*801*	*570*	*69*	*377*	*180*	*196*	*22*	*10,251*	*9,741*	*3,765*	*531*	
140	3	274	222	190	33	68	40	30	10	3,798	3,429	1,792	407	70
697	29	143	125	75	6	49	35	28	5	1,134	1,167	345	17	71
204	2	73	65	50	2	26	4	5	..	643	583	191	18	72
336	25	81	71	53	6	167	74	90	5	1,839	1,886	520	37	73
786	13	109	81	73	9	41	7	26	2	1,172	1,080	397	6	74
169	..	..	..	..	..	..	..		..	233	275	81	2	75
660	29	252	237	129	13	26	20	17	..	1,432	1,321	439	44	76

Serial number.	Tahsil, Taluk, Zamindari or Township.	Christians.				Tribal Religion.				Others.		
		Number of persons.		Number literate.		Number of persons.		Number literate.		Number of persons.		Number.
		Males.	Females.	Males.	Females.	Males.	Females.	Males.	Females.	Males.	Females.	Males
	1	26	27	28	29	30	31	32	33	34	35	36
	NAGPUR DIVISION ..	6,064	5,017	4,089	2,561	132,336	137,568	2,404	106	642	551	533
	Wardha District .	*170*	*108*	*106*	*50*	*19,408*	*20,381*	*246*	*5*	*33*	*29*	*28*
39	Wardha Tahsil ..	151	87	92	37	8,616	9,140	111	3	28	26	25
40	Arvi Tahsil ..	..	..	..	..	7,544	7,746	102	2	2	1	..
41	Hinganghat Town ..	15	16	11	12	118	118	12	..	3	2	3
42	Hinganghat Tahsil ..	4	5	3	1	3,130	3,377	21	..	..	..	..
	Nagpur District ..	*4,810*	*3,748*	*3,354*	*2,040*	*4,972*	*4,812*	*88*	*3*	*589*	*492*	*486*
43	Nagpur City ..	3,359	3,090	2,258	1,766	572	591	32	3	538	459	448
44	Kamptee Town and Cantonment.	1,182	404	1,030	233	2	2	..	..	22	22	18
45	Nagpur Tahsil ..	24	19	3	6	..	..	..	..	1	..	1
46	Ramtek Tahsil ..	38	40	27	14	3,370	3,172	43	..	11	4	7
47	Umrer Town ..	11	12	8	6	..	..	..	..	1	1	1
48	Umrer Tahsil ..	159	155	10	6	3	4	..	..	3	..	3
49	Katol Tahsil ..	3	8	..	1	..	..	..	..	9	4	4
50	Saoner Tahsil ..	34	20	18	8	1,025	1,043	13	..	4	2	4
	Chanda District ..	*623*	*620*	*339*	*258*	*55,916*	*57,411*	*513*	*16*	*13*	*22*	*12*
51	Chanda Town ..	210	191	130	94	72	89	17	2	7	7	6
52	Chanda Tahsil ..	201	155	82	26	3,751	3,777	29	..	..	..	..
53	Warora Tahsil ..	45	37	28	11	1,478	1,422	24	..	6	15	6
54	Brahmapuri Tahsil ..	26	26	11	10	6,759	7,129	144	..	..	..	..
55	Garchiroli Tahsil Khalsa ..	4	4	2	2	9,243	9,219	102	7	..	..	..
56	Garchiroli Tahsil Zamindaris	..	..	..	..	16,752	17,894	138	4	..	..	..
57	Sironcha Tahsil Khalsa ..	110	184	71	103	3,545	3,229	17	2	..	..	..
58	Ahiri Zamindari ..	27	23	15	12	14,316	14,652	42	1	..	..	..
	Bhandara District ..	*166*	*229*	*136*	*94*	*19,156*	*20,444*	*591*	*70*	..	..	..
59	Bhandara Tahsil ..	81	157	71	68	4,805	4,993	48	..	..	..	..
60	Gondia Town ..	62	54	44	18	22	23	3	..	..	..	..
61	Gondia Tahsil Khalsa ..	5	7	7	4	2,582	2,784	272	66	..	..	..
62	Gondia Tahsil Zamindaris ..	7	3	7	3	8,273	9,020	207	2	..	..	..
63	Sakoli Tahsil Khalsa ..	5	4	4	1	1,197	1,362	19	1	..	..	..
64	Sakoli Tahsil Zamindaris ..	6	4	3	..	2,277	2,262	42	1	..	..	..
	Balaghat District ..	*295*	*312*	*154*	*119*	*32,884*	*34,520*	*966*	*12*	*7*	*8*	*7*
65	Balaghat Tahsil Khalsa ..	59	47	38	31	6,064	6,372	162	1	1	3	1
66	Balaghat Tahsil Zamindaris ..	12	9	3	4	482	550	7	..	..	..	..
67	Baihar Tahsil Khalsa ..	194	232	99	78	8,881	9,003	471	9	1	..	1
68	Baihar Tahsil Zamindaris ..	1	..	..	..	1,070	1,005	2	..	..	..	..
69	Waraseoni Tahsil ..	29	24	14	6	16,387	17,590	324	2	5	5	5
	CHHATTISGARH DIVISION ..	6,329	7,041	2,545	2,463	86,325	89,898	856	61	36	40	29
	Raipur District ..	*2,980*	*3,000*	*1,186*	*901*	*45,954*	*49,439*	*654*	*48*	*20*	*19*	*18*
70	Raipur Town ..	440	519	315	350	51	22	7	3	17	19	15
71	Raipur Tahsil ..	224	183	70	24	172	193	3	1	2	..	2
72	Mahasamund Tahsil Khalsa ..	89	48	59	25	3,934	4,444	85	..	..	..	..
73	Mahasamund Tahsil Zamindaris	819	854	101	62	18,414	19,590	199	27	..	..	..
74	Baloda Bazar Tahsil Khalsa ..	732	808	293	241	3,433	3,694	48	3	..	..	..
75	Baloda Bazar Tahsil Zamindaris	42	36	13	9	2,038	2,108	32	1	..	..	..
76	Dhamtari Tahsil ..	634	552	335	190	17,912	19,388	280	13	1	..	1

Number literate in total population.												
literate.	Aged 4—6.		Aged 7—13.		Aged 14—23.		Aged 24 and over.		Literate in English.		Remarks see paragraph 4 on the fly-sheet.	Serial number.
Females.	Males.	Females.	Males.	Females.	Males.	Females.	Males.	Females.	Males.	Females.		
37	38	39	40	41	42	43	44	45	46	47	48	
398	863	502	23,552	4,706	52,464	7,023	110,030	8,972	26,293	3,653		
16	*71*	*46*	*4,164*	*1,110*	*8,960*	*802*	*19,009*	*810*	*3,655*	*161*		
15	39	32	1,919	748	3,642	350	8,782	328	1,755	108		39
1	16	12	1,263	208	2,989	283	5,669	269	913	32		40
..	7	2	388	85	1,068	121	1,840	148	877	20		41
..	9	..	594	69	1,261	48	2,718	65	110	1		42
362	*414*	*338*	*9,842*	*2,442*	*21,899*	*4,286*	*43,295*	*5,864*	*17,524*	*3,122*		
341	340	301	4,615	1,961	11,319	3,668	19,533	5,103	14,068	2,844		43
16	10	15	280	132	927	76	1,707	154	1,290	231		44
..	4	2	521	40	1,367	72	2,978	69	218	3	Nagarchi.	45
1	19	8	743	71	1,488	98	3,995	122	443	16		46
1	8	1	329	26	604	43	1,275	70	270	5		47
..	5	1	722	37	1,299	64	3,157	67	129	7		48
2	6	4	1,231	109	2,250	145	5,104	138	367	7		49
1	22	6	1,401	66	2,645	120	5,546	141	739	9		50
16	*70*	*41*	*2,974*	*380*	*6,667*	*683*	*15,046*	*760*	*2,136*	*175*		
4	12	10	674	157	1,329	279	2,429	258	945	48		51
..	8	3	457	37	964	67	2,533	78	326	16		52
12	4	6	663	46	1,639	107	3,865	160	351	13		53
..	4	2	595	40	1,485	71	3,526	87	260	8		54
..	17	2	350	21	774	29	1,540	48	90	6		55
..	4	..	73	6	175	7	461	17	8	..		56
..	..	2	82	41	167	70	384	42	125	81		57
..	21	16	80	32	134	53	308	70	31	3		58
..	*244*	*58*	*3,872*	*471*	*8,578*	*825*	*18,396*	*991*	*1,860*	*116*		
..	59	17	1,343	167	3,204	301	6,256	367	1,208	78	Kori, Nagarchi, Holiya, Ojha, Dhobi, Dhimar, Kumhar, Khangar, Chadar, Jangam.	59
..	16	5	227	84	525	115	1,343	142	270	18		60
..	123	29	669	148	1,296	260	2,456	315	127	4		61
..	4	1	393	24	1,378	67	3,453	65	144	5		62
..	41	5	1,009	41	1,801	64	4,037	75	94	10		63
..	1	1	231	7	374	18	851	27	17	1		64
4	*64*	*19*	*2,700*	*303*	*6,360*	*427*	*14,284*	*547*	*1,118*	*79*		
2	10	12	783	156	1,767	192	3,911	264	759	34	Holiya, Nagarchi, Ojha, Mala, Kori.	65
..	2	2	299	37	962	35	2,073	42	39	5		66
..	41	3	872	37	1,132	76	2,075	87	135	37		67
..	..	..	16	..	47	4	134	22	..	..		68
2	11	2	730	73	2,452	120	6,091	132	185	3		69
24	**420**	**136**	**11,519**	**1,957**	**28,114**	**3,516**	**63,857**	**4,538**	**7,400**	**1,061**		
17	*132*	*29*	*4,715*	*762*	*11,916*	*1,498*	*26,750*	*1,898*	*3,676*	*345*		
17	25	10	1,113	368	2,413	658	4,702	679	2,373	273	Kori, Pardhan, Nagarchi, Dhobi.	70
..	11	5	649	40	1,792	118	4,532	224	282	6		71
..	20	1	448	29	958	75	2,177	102	143	7		72
..	8	4	729	97	2,206	155	4,857	273	214	11		73
..	18	3	681	72	1,852	236	4,054	227	163	19		74
..	7	1	186	9	408	21	723	16	20	1		75
..	13	5	909	147	2,287	235	5,705	377	481	28		76

PROVINCIAL TABLE II

Serial number.	Tahsil, Taluk, Zamindari or Township.	Hindus.									
		Brahmans.				Other Hindus.				Depressed	
		Number of persons.		Number literate.		Number of persons.		Number literate.		Number of persons.	
		Males.	Females.	Males.	Females.	Males.	Females.	Males.	Females.	Males.	Females.
	1	2	3	4	5	6	7	8	9	10	11
	Bilaspur District ..	*18,805*	*18,372*	*7,164*	*1,046*	*421,134*	*441,255*	*24,325*	*1,729*	*197,350*	*209,983*
77	Bilaspur Town ..	1,770	1,888	1,326	451	8,183	7,277	2,583	454	3,279	2,975
78	Bilaspur Tahsil Khalsa ..	5,393	5,576	1,660	159	87,085	93,594	4,028	294	46,310	50,579
79	Bilaspur Tahsil Zamindaris	1,247	978	446	29	36,886	37,069	1,620	129	7,330	7,520
80	Mungeli Tahsil Khalsa ..	2,363	2,271	898	115	43,813	47,980	2,060	193	23,743	26,337
81	Mungeli Tahsil Zamindaris	863	867	283	20	17,318	19,019	758	75	12,288	13,257
82	Janjgir Tahsil Khalsa ..	5,662	5,570	2,115	210	142,829	150,543	10,044	399	79,787	84,454
83	Janjgir Tahsil Zamindaris	750	593	151	25	13,882	14,803	1,123	85	5,243	5,332
84	Katghora Tahsil Khalsa	41	53	24	10	478	490	139	21	109	119
85	Katghora Tahsil Zamindaris.	716	576	261	27	70,660	70,480	1,970	79	19,261	19,410
	Drug District ..	*7,609*	*7,563*	*3,075*	*239*	*295,160*	*325,477*	*14,999*	*692*	*76,189*	*82,951*
86	Drug Tahsil Khalsa ..	2,798	2,779	1,319	124	90,807	101,448	6,136	283	28,434	30,189
87	Drug Tahsil Zamindaris	110	115	66	6	9,031	9,648	500	12	2,449	2,665
88	Bemetara Tahsil Khalsa	3,121	3,278	1,088	64	68,171	75,964	2,472	117	25,759	29,178
89	Bemetara Tahsil Zamindaris.	342	287	125	10	20,457	22,281	467	22	3,932	4,189
90	Sanjari Tahsil Khalsa ..	890	833	330	29	66,780	73,910	4,399	233	9,978	10,968
91	Sanjari Tahsil Zamindaris	348	271	147	6	39,914	42,226	1,025	25	5,637	5,762
	Berar ..	**57,218**	**46,110**	**33,170**	**7,389**	**1,170,103**	**1,117,340**	**155,854**	**6,948**	**336,649**	**339,067**
	Amraoti District ..	*16,695*	*13,154*	*9,726*	*2,684*	*320,530*	*299,744*	*53,692*	*2,739*	*92,809*	*92,477*
92	Amraoti Town (*a*) ..	5,139	4,145	3,399	1,442	15,757	12,564	5,331	716	3,547	3,444
93	Amraoti Taluk ..	2,084	1,512	1,101	183	49,664	46,248	10,107	387	21,796	21,486
94	Morsi Taluk ..	1,993	1,418	1,163	247	62,504	58,040	8,530	582	13,729	14,431
95	Chandur Taluk ..	2,876	2,131	1,515	258	73,660	70,821	10,554	401	22,221	22,245
96	Ellichpur Town (*b*) ..	1,669	1,290	1,058	323	9,744	9,036	2,787	79	2,637	2,307
97	Ellichpur Taluk ..	952	1,003	507	110	43,501	40,512	7,873	371	11,742	11,902
98	Daryapur Taluk ..	1,789	1,546	895	113	45,726	43,373	8,278	189	15,973	15,536
99	Melghat Taluk ..	193	109	88	8	19,974	19,150	232	14	1,164	1,126
	Akola District ..	*16,669*	*13,182*	*9,288*	*2,181*	*286,170*	*272,061*	*41,798*	*1,533*	*94,621*	*95,748*
100	Akola Town ..	4,554	2,755	3,252	997	11,793	9,631	3,529	392	5,265	3,204
101	Akola Taluk ..	1,209	1,459	125	116	46,073	42,875	6,877	202	17,509	17,896
102	Akot Taluk ..	3,289	3,046	1,743	316	53,389	50,899	9,382	348	12,712	12,632
103	Balapur Taluk ..	1,055	874	574	94	35,692	34,741	5,013	156	12,280	12,382
104	Basim Taluk ..	2,804	2,311	1,596	256	63,713	62,462	6,367	171	23,330	23,319
105	Mangrulpir Taluk ..	895	743	391	57	34,991	34,920	3,964	120	9,884	9,656
106 107	Karanja Town .. Murtizapur Taluk ..	2,863	1,994	1,607	345	40,519	36,533	6,666	144	15,641	16,659

(*a*) Includes figures for Amraoti Camp which in Provincial Table I have been included with the figures of Amraoti Taluk.
(*b*) Includes figures for Ellichpur Camp which in Provincial Table I have been included with the figures of Ellichpur Taluk.

Classes.		Jains.				Sikhs.				Muslims.				
Number literate.		Number of persons.		Number literate.		Number of persons.		Number literate.		Number of persons.		Number literate.		Serial number.
Males.	Females.	Males.	Females.	Males.	Females.	Males.	Females.	Males.	Females.	Males.	Females.	Males.	Females.	
12	13	14	15	16	17	18	19	20	21	22	23	24	25	
2,860	*113*	*287*	*238*	*151*	*21*	*152*	*89*	*106*	*31*	*9,495*	*9,178*	*3,076*	*322*	
269	35	6	7	3	1	56	24	41	12	2,265	1,948	1,001	122	77
510	17	2	2	..	..	47	28	31	10	1,844	1,795	504	82	78
117	5	87	80	39	1	18	11	15	5	949	875	334	39	79
289	8	62	44	37	6	9	7	8	1	755	805	266	22	80
83		14	14	6	1	13	13	6	2	438	524	82	6	81
1,291	35	106	90	62	12	7	2	4	1	1,940	1,981	499	30	82
106	7	3	1	2	..	2	4	1	..	361	328	122	8	83
8		..	..	..	..	..	..	..	..	64	78	35	1	84
187	6	2	..	2	..	..	..	..	..	879	844	233	12	85
1,566	*48*	*681*	*552*	*475*	*30*	*43*	*18*	*28*	*1*	*3,651*	*3,688*	*1,000*	*106*	
509	15	269	190	197	20	24	8	15	..	1,374	1,315	410	52	86
72	1	19	15	13	..	..	..	..	..	53	60	13	4	87
296	3	65	66	45	3	16	9	10	1	672	680	202	13	88
71	..	28	28	18	4	1	1	1	..	466	477	56	4	89
446	18	208	184	134	3	..	..	..	..	539	543	204	15	90
172	11	92	69	68	..	2	..	2	..	547	613	115	18	91
11,386	**529**	**10,560**	**9,842**	**5,706**	**559**	**262**	**191**	**106**	**17**	**157,548**	**142,132**	**27,481**	**2,714**	
3,741	*124*	*2,587*	*2,465*	*1,458*	*165*	*56*	*35*	*18*	*3*	*45,714*	*40,784*	*8,888*	*751*	
297	28	344	305	235	40	19	9	9	3	6,218	5,012	2,004	260	92
821	15	302	299	174	26	1	..	1	..	8,178	7,190	1,461	80	93
387	49	518	567	241	17	..	1	..	..	6,210	5,688	1,267	119	94
660	13	741	645	391	29	23	17	4	..	5,822	5,237	952	6/	95
125	5	137	117	88	25	11	7	4	..	5,720	5,414	1,157	90	96
466	5	237	254	132	10	..	..	..	..	5,753	5,237	828	31	97
975	9	297	278	186	18	2	1	..	..	7,042	6,457	1,075	99	98
10		11	..	11	..	..	..	..	..	771	549	144	5	99
2,743	*199*	*3,535*	*3,331*	*1,880*	*181*	*48*	*34*	*29*	*3*	*46,903*	*42,282*	*7,619*	*812*	
205	16	330	260	191	33	20	21	16	3	6,118	5,090	1,661	226	100
525	7	268	270	109	11	1	2	1	..	4,840	4,203	668	94	101
496	7	257	243	131	9	3	3	1	..	8,619	8,211	1,048	108	102
381	7	380	372	217	6	..	..	..	..	7,551	7,127	1,075	105	103
410	8	944	902	505	31	3	..	1	..	7.369	6,685	1,275	92	104
265	4	189	174	86	6	..	..	..	..	3,751	3,373	472	47	105
	..	625	613	367	57	5	..	2	..	2,838	2,536	557	80	106
461	150	542	497	274	28	16	8	8	..	5,817	5,057	863	60	107

PROVINCIAL TABLE II

Population of Tahsils, Cities and

Serial number.	Tahsil, Taluk, Zamindari or Township.	Christians.				Tribal Religion.				Others.		
		Number of persons.		Number literate.		Number of persons.		Number literate.		Number of persons.		Number.
		Males.	Females.	Males.	Females.	Males.	Females.	Males.	Females.	Males.	Females.	Males.
	1	26	27	28	29	30	31	32	33	34	35	36
	Bilaspur District ..	*2,459*	*2,757*	*1,080*	*1,158*	*34,231*	*34,441*	*178*	..	*12*	*15*	*8*
77	Bilaspur Town ..	773	872	467	549	23	3	1	..	11	14	7
78	Bilaspur Tahsil Khalsa ..	248	216	107	77	535	629	3	..	..	..	..
79	Bilaspur Tahsil Zamindaris ..	283	277	141	113	13,129	13,032	56	..	..	..	..
80	Mungeli Tahsil Khalsa ..	416	542	125	155	1,478	1,702	14	..	..	..	..
81	Mungeli Tahsil Zamindaris ..	57	46	15	4	3,644	3,894	1	..	1	1	1
82	Janjgir Tahsil Khalsa ..	343	349	129	186	136	153	..	..	..	..	..
83	Janjgir Tahsil Zamindaris ..	253	369	61	49	13	15	..	..	..	..	..
84	Katghora Tahsil Khalsa ..	6	4	2	1	14	21	..	..	..	..	..
85	Katghora Tahsil Zamindaris ..	80	82	33	24	15,259	14,992	103	..	..	..	..
	Drug District ..	*890*	*1,284*	*279*	*404*	*6,140*	*6,018*	*24*	*13*	*4*	*6*	*3*
86	Drug Tahsil Khalsa ..	49	33	26	13	33	36	..	..	4	6	3
87	Drug Tahsil Zamindaris ..	..	2	..	..	9	2	..	..	..	..	..
88	Bemetara Tahsil Khalsa ..	499	632	143	115	41	45	..	..	..	..	..
89	Bemetara Tahsil Zamindaris ..	7	6	5	4	515	533	..	..	..	..	..
90	Sanjari Tahsil Khalsa ..	269	567	76	251	209	218	1	..	..	..	..
91	Sanjari Tahsil Zamindaris ..	66	44	29	21	5,333	5,184	23	13	..	..	..
	Berar ..	**2,765**	**2,630**	**1,202**	**994**	**24,322**	**24,830**	**148**	**68**	**152**	**117**	**119**
	Amraoti District ..	*1,319*	*1,235*	*473*	*420*	*5,810*	*6,061*	*38*	*1*	*73*	*56*	*56*
92	Amraoti Town ..	214	359	109	209	2	1	..	..	15	5	14
93	Amraoti Taluk ..	171	163	96	67	362	384	8	..	41	40	29
94	Morsi Taluk ..	5	2	4	1	1,057	1,068	2	..	7	..	4
95	Chandur Taluk ..	34	17	19	5	1,537	1,530	21	1	..	1	..
96	Ellichpur Town ..	137	117	73	76	16	19	1	..	7	6	6
97	Ellichpur Taluk ..	309	192	75	12	696	720	3	..	2	..	2
98	Daryapur Taluk ..	301	198	61	6	11	8	..	..	..	..	..
99	Melghat Taluk ..	148	187	36	44	2,129	2,331	3	..	1	4	1
	Akola District ..	*726*	*595*	*389*	*195*	*180*	*190*	*6*	*1*	*44*	*43*	*33*
100	Akola Town ..	286	235	181	99	7	8	..	..	28	27	21
101	Akola Taluk ..	87	43	52	17	31	27	1	..	..	..	..
102	Akot Taluk ..	40	47	34	4	62	54	2	1	1	..	1
103	Balapur Taluk ..	4	1	3	..	12	20	1	..	1	..	1
104	Basim Taluk ..	118	112	49	47	2	2	2	..	2	6	1
105	Mangrulpir Taluk ..	6	6	3	3	14	16	..	..	..	..	..
106	Karanja Town ..	6	4	5	..	..	..	..	..	7	..	6
107	Murtizapur Taluk ..	179	147	62	25	52	63	..	..	5	10	5

literate.	Number literate in total population.								Literate in English.		Remarks see paragraph 4 on the fly-sheet.	Serial number.
	Aged 4—6.		Aged 7—13.		Aged 14—23.		Aged 24 and over.					
Females.	Males.	Females.	Males.	Females.	Males.	Females.	Males.	Females.	Males.	Females.		
37	38	39	40	41	42	43	44	45	46	47	48	
6	*233*	*57*	*4,858*	*930*	*10,416*	*1,439*	*23,431*	*1,970*	*2,857*	*655*		
5	53	35	818	332	1,701	531	3,126	731	2,018	534		77
..	24	5	767	113	1,717	247	4,335	274	298	35		78
..	34	12	342	75	760	101	1,632	133	120	..		79
..	22	12	546	120	882	161	2,247	207	183	11		80
1	1	..	128	15	314	30	792	64	40	2	Dhobi, Audhelia.	81
..	83	15	1,791	231	3,800	274	8,470	353	131	54		82
..	6	4	177	14	405	30	978	126	19	14		83
..	1	2	15	7	71	11	121	13	13	..		84
..	9	2	284	23	766	54	1,730	69	35	6		85
1	*55*	*20*	*1,936*	*265*	*5,782*	*579*	*13,676*	*670*	*867*	*60*		
1	26	10	900	76	2,520	172	5,169	250	579	23		86
..	..	..	57	7	180	6	427	10	14	1		87
..	3	2	273	57	1,082	116	2,898	141	113	14		88
..	3	..	39	3	185	16	516	25	32	3	Chauhan.	89
..	17	7	544	110	1,420	240	3,609	192	114	17		90
..	6	1	123	12	395	29	1,057	52	15	2		91
81	**819**	**267**	**27,897**	**4,481**	**71,535**	**7,346**	**134,921**	**7,205**	**20,603**	**1,161**		
35	*142*	*80*	*9,161*	*1,660*	*23,567*	*2,579*	*45,220*	*2,603*	*7,247*	*559*		
5	37	18	1,394	584	3,670	1,021	6,297	1,080	3,552	412		92
25	23	9	1,848	226	3,973	276	7,954	272	834	74		93
..	45	27	1,405	262	3,316	332	6,832	394	693	12		94
1	11	13	1,323	162	4,283	298	8,499	302	695	18		95
3	18	4	686	188	1,583	199	3,012	210	804	24	Bedar, Bahna, Kori.	96
..	5	2	1,267	145	2,922	219	5,692	173	220	4		97
..	1	6	1,189	84	3,692	200	6,588	144	395	6		98
1	2	1	49	9	128	34	346	28	54	9		99
31	*135*	*82*	*7,172*	*1,175*	*18,900*	*1,861*	*37,578*	*2,018*	*5,810*	*277*		
20	23	32	850	342	2,663	601	5,520	811	2,842	206		100
..	17	7	885	112	2,532	174	4,924	154	225	6		101
..	15	10	1,504	235	3,936	275	7,383	273	622	21		102
..	7	..	717	82	2,141	147	4,400	139	258	4		103
6	25	5	1,261	154	2,991	230	5,929	222	713	14	Bedar.	104
..	15	4	600	54	1,434	90	3,132	89	143	..		105
..	13	5	303	58	742	124	1,476	121	353	5		106
5	20	19	1,052	138	2,461	220	4,814	209	654	21		107

Serial number.	Tahsil, Taluk, Zamindari or Township.	Hindus.									
		Brahmans.				Other Hindus.				Depressed	
		Number of persons.		Number literate.		Number of persons.		Number literate.		Number of persons.	
		Males.	Females.	Males.	Females.	Males.	Females.	Males.	Females.	Males.	Females.
	1	2	3	4	5	6	7	8	9	10	11
	Buldana District	*13,234*	*11,301*	*8,514*	*1,540*	*257,381*	*251,553*	*37,192*	*1,374*	*77,916*	*77,767*
108	Chikhli Taluk	3,368	2,944	2,098	408	54,197	53,726	5,298	117	17,880	17,581
109	Mehkar Taluk	2,237	2,022	1,356	172	56,569	56,032	3,514	75	18,594	18,913
110	Khamgaon Town }										
111	Shegaon Town }	3,735	2,857	2,739	518	50,462	48,144	9,653	466	16,307	16,121
112	Khamgaon Taluk }										
113	Jalgaon Taluk	1,483	1,444	896	177	35,534	34,780	5,887	194	8,266	8,250
114	Malkapur Town }	2,411	2,034	1,425	265	60,619	58,871	12,840	522	16,869	16,902
115	Malkapur Taluk }										
	Yeotmal District	*10,620*	*8,473*	*5,642*	*984*	*306,022*	*293,982*	*23,172*	*1,302*	*71,303*	*73,075*
116	Yeotmal Town	1,861	1,311	1,281	238	6,169	5,206	1,729	442	1,661	1,650
117	Yeotmal Taluk	1,131	857	544	99	43,369	42,277	4,639	116	10,659	10,867
118	Kelapur Taluk	1,703	1,236	797	133	64,850	63,983	3,709	64	13,009	12,799
119	Wun Taluk	1,647	1,225	939	290	51,581	50,062	3,436	143	10,272	10,109
120	Darwha Taluk	2,067	2,083	1,039	85	72,519	67,656	5,468	453	18,399	20,084
121	Pusad Taluk	2,211	1,761	1,042	139	67,534	64,798	4,191	84	17,303	17,566
	Central Provinces States	**12,859**	**11,094**	**5,138**	**467**	**748,393**	**763,323**	**30,665**	**1,693**	**124,871**	**127,861**
122	Makrai	540	526	298	4	3,216	3,108	539	..	1,289	1,313
123	Bastar	1,495	1,474	471	66	55,593	54,668	2,378	166	22,783	22,812
124	Kanker	436	391	196	22	27,990	28,935	1,583	149	1,876	2,158
125	Nandgaon	1,588	1,299	932	95	67,162	72,979	5,227	288	16,294	17,489
126	Khairagarh	1,300	1,216	473	24	61,770	67,217	2,045	42	10,946	11,684
127	Chhuikhadan	213	180	119	12	12,676	13,649	911	57	1,881	2,055
128	Kawardha	620	567	236	17	26,173	28,522	1,107	50	7,677	7,948
129	Sakti	269	270	132	13	22,921	24,260	1,488	54	65	78
130	Raigarh	2,127	1,882	903	101	131,562	135,770	7,145	387	1,962	2,181
131	Sarangarh	945	884	462	56	44,472	48,131	3,413	290	16,807	17,304
132	Changbhakar	230	172	39	2	3,027	2,802	48	5	414	364
133	Korea	68[illegible]	405	201	5	8,180	7,202	377	27	4,568	4,579
134	Surguja	1,843	1,478	447	30	189,570	183,413	2,146	111	28,478	28,031
135	Udaipur	208	144	84	9	39,090	38,198	840	28	1,589	1,530
136	Jashpur	356	206	145	11	54,991	54,469	1,418	39	8,242	8,335

Classes.		Jains				Sikhs.				Muslims.				Serial number.
Number literate.		Number of persons.		Number literate.		Number of persons.		Number literate.		Number of persons.		Number literate.		
Males.	Females.	Males.	Females.	Males.	Females.	Males.	Females.	Males.	Females.	Males.	Females.	Males.	Females.	
12	13	14	15	16	17	18	19	20	21	22	23	24	25	
2,325	*109*	*2,400*	*2,147*	*1,323*	*126*	*78*	*57*	*33*	*6*	*37,474*	*34,292*	*5,602*	*328*	
584	14	673	564	310	15	2	..	..	..	8,895	8,381	1,275	90	108
407	34	707	631	408	34	12	5	3	..	6,002	5,496	746	34	109
		163	139	111	20	40	30	13	4	2,847	2,129	851	81	110
692	26	52	39	32	5	2	..	2	..	1,196	1,119	305	32	111
		243	204	120	2	2	2	1	1	4,369	3,988	663	31	112
553	32	28	35	23	4	11	6	7	..	4,585	4,398	482	25	113
589	3	237	210	170	31	8	11	6	..	3,396	3,049	506	27	114
		297	325	149	15	1	3	1	1	6,184	5,732	774	8	115
2,077	*97*	*2,038*	*1,899*	*1,045*	*87*	*80*	*65*	*26*	*5*	*27,457*	*24,774*	*5,372*	*823*	
429	22	101	97	63	9	3	..	3	..	1,376	1,054	575	109	116
450	5	402	417	241	15	..	..	..	..	3,055	2,757	441	33	117
149	1	257	229	130	6	50	41	10	5	3,157	2,828	671	35	118
206	7	174	137	107	14	3	..	1	..	2,412	2,180	515	38	119
503	21	548	531	254	23	8	2	6	..	9,027	8,128	2,248	563	120
340	11	556	488	250	20	16	22	6	..	8,430	7,827	922	45	121
1,121	**59**	**1,083**	**1877**	**663**	**89**	**175**	**104**	**79**	**7**	**11,733**	**11,521**	**2,754**	**311**	
24	..	26	28	21	1	4	..	4	..	514	513	121	14	122
70	5	78	56	52	3	..	..	..	..	988	979	395	64	123
64	5	79	76	38	1	..	..	..	..	353	321	118	13	124
454	25	487	368	298	66	7	3	.	..	1,268	1,244	495	77	125
71	1	230	184	138	4	13	5	10	2	1,177	1,226	320	36	126
37	..	79	72	50	6	..	..	..	..	383	474	96	2	127
95	4	61	64	47	6	3	1	2	..	512	571	126	11	128
..	..	2	..	2	..	7	3	1	..	210	190	69	11	129
12	..	28	18	15	2	82	68	38	4	891	852	289	50	130
172	19	2	..	2	..	1	..	1	..	165	165	34		131
3	..	..	..	..	..	..	..	..	..	45	28	4		132
..	..	..	..	..	..	3	..	1	..	592	464	94	6	133
9	..	11	11	..	..	55	24	22	1	3,625	3,410	415	19	134
3	..	..	..	..	..	..	..	..	..	134	137	28	5	135
107	..	..	..	..	..	..	..	..	..	876	947	150	3	136

Serial number.	Tahsil, Taluk, Zamindari or Township.	Christians.				Tribal Religion.				Others.		
		Number of persons.		Number literate.		Number of persons.		Number literate.		Number of persons.		Number.
		Males.	Females.	Males.	Females.	Males.	Females.	Males.	Females.	Males.	Females.	Males.
	1	26	27	28	29	30	31	32	33	34	35	36
	Buldana District ..	*380*	*398*	*151*	*194*	*81*	*91*	..	..	*22*	*12*	*18*
108	Chikhli Taluk ..	249	169	88	55	58	62	..	..	2	3	2
109	Mehkar Taluk ..	40	46	13	6	6	7	..	..	..	..	..
110	Khamgaon Taluk ..	39	139	21	110	..	..	..	..	12	8	9
111	Shegaon Town ..	10	7	7	6	..	..	..	..	8	1	7
112	Khamgaon Taluk ..	10	7	5	1	..	..	..	..	..	..	..
113	Jalgaon Taluk ..	11	12	5	7	17	22	..	..	..	..	..
114	Malkapur Town ..	14	16	8	9	..	..	..	..	..	..	..
115	Malkapur Taluk ..	7	2	4	..	..	..	..	..	..	..	..
	Yeotmal District ..	*340*	*402*	*189*	*185*	*18,251*	*18,488*	*104*	*66*	*13*	*6*	*12*
116	Yeotmal Town ..	158	118	113	63	95	91	8	..	10	6	9
117	Yeotmal Taluk ..	15	25	8	6	13,653	13,757	46	62	..	..	..
118	Kelapur Taluk ..	20	135	8	77	1,370	1,495	17	2	..	..	..
119	Wun Taluk ..	28	27	15	13	2,730	2,703	20	..	1	..	1
120	Darwha Taluk ..	56	42	24	19	384	427	13	2	1	..	1
121	Pusad Taluk ..	63	55	21	7	19	15	..	..	1	..	1
	Central Provinces States ..	**26,102**	**25,599**	**1,331**	**510**	**310,156**	**307,443**	**736**	**25**	**13**	**7**	**11**
122	Makrai ..	..	1	..	1	2,311	2,127	10	..	..	..	..
123	Bastar ..	920	953	179	190	181,390	180,530	199	4	1	1	1
124	Kanker ..	13	11	7	4	36,385	37,077	285	5	..	..	..
125	Nandgaon ..	163	221	90	109	915	890	9	..	2	1	1
126	Khairagarh ..	209	218	136	111	..	..	..	..	2	3	2
127	Chhuikhadan ..	1	..	1	..	5	..	..	..	..	..	..
128	Kawardha ..	2	5	..	1	50	44	..	..	..	..	..
129	Sakti ..	6	6	4	..	89	109	9	5	2	2	2
130	Raigarh ..	68	75	13	3	..	..	..	..	3	..	2
131	Sarangarh ..	49	40	6	7	..	..	..	..	2	..	2
132	Changbhakar ..	..	..	..	..	8,271	7,969	6	1	..	..	..
133	Korea ..	7	4	7	4	32,709	31,484	119	2	..	..	..
134	Surguja ..	13	16	1	4	31,327	30,633	57	2	1	..	1
135	Udaipur ..	..	..	..	..	8,404	8,304	18	6	..	..	..
136	Jashpur ..	24,651	24,049	887	76	8,300	8,276	24	..	..	..	..

Makrai.—Chamar, Mang, Balahi.
Bastar.—Mehra or Mahar, Ghasia, Chamar, Panka, Mangiya, Katia, Ganda, Chadar, Mochi, Satnami.
Kanker.—Mehra or Mahar, Ghasia, Chamar, Pardhan, Lohar (wade).
Nandgaon.—Mehra or Mahar, Ghasia, Chamar, Panka, Mang, Basor, Pardhan, Nagarchi, Ganda, Dhobi, Chauhan, Dewar.
Khairagarh.—Ghasia, Chamar, Mochi, Dom, Mehra or Mahar, Dewar.
Chhuikhadan.—Mehra or Mahar, Ghasia, Chamar, Basor, Dewar.
Kawardha.—Mehra or Mahar, Dhobi, Chauhan, Panka, Ganda, Katia, Kumhar, Chamar, Dhimar, Ghasia.
Sakti.—Dewar.
Raigarh.—Ghasia, Dewar.
Sarangarh.—Ganda, Ghasia, Panka, Chamar, Dewar.
Changbhakar.—Chamar, Basor, Kumhar.
Korea.—Basor, Chamar, Ghasia, Panka.
Surguja.—Ghasia, Chamar, Panka, Dom, Pardhan, Dewar.
Udaipur.—Chamar, Dom, Ganda, Ghasia.
Jashpur.—Ghasia, Chamar, Panka, Dom, Ganda, Dhobi.

literate.	Number literate in total population.										Remarks see paragraph 4 on the fly-sheet.	Serial number.
	Aged 4—6.		Aged 7—13.		Aged 14—23.		Aged 24 and over.		Literate in English.			
Females.	Males.	Females.	Males.	Females.	Males.	Females.	Males.	Females.	Males.	Females.		
37	38	39	40	41	42	43	44	45	46	47	48	
11	*111*	*37*	*7,191*	*891*	*17,280*	*1,357*	*31,076*	*1,403*	*3,693*	*177*		
3	20	9	1,151	146	3,298	293	5,186	254	681	48		108
..	11	1	822	85	2,005	119	3,609	150	272	5		109
7	15	11	539	210	1,357	312	2,746	340	1,134	77		110
1	6	2	347	41	625	92	1,325	85	411	12		111
..	18	3	1,063	61	2,441	87	4,749	67	107	2	Bedar, Dhimar, Dhobi, Khangar, Kori, Kumhar.	112
..	20	6	1,001	113	2,227	155	4,605	165	348	8		113
..	1	..	298	63	613	120	1,453	151	302	11		114
..	20	5	1,970	172	4,714	179	7,403	191	438	14		115
4	*431*	*68*	*4,373*	*755*	*11,788*	*1,549*	*21,047*	*1,181*	*3,853*	*148*		
4	23	11	707	237	1,375	324	2,105	315	1,224	73		116
..	8	4	722	92	1,857	109	3,782	131	199	5		117
..	3	1	585	90	1,628	138	3,275	94	320	22		118
..	30	10	497	133	1,334	183	3,379	209	761	20		119
..	316	38	977	122	3,530	692	4,733	314	1,032	22		120
..	51	4	885	81	2,064	103	3,773	118	317	6		121
4	**67**	**17**	**3,490**	**543**	**11,890**	**1,054**	**27,051**	**1,551**	**2,140**	**223**	Only Mehtars are regarded as untouchable throughout the States. The names of the other untouchable castes of each separate State are given below.	
..	2	..	131	4	281	8	603	8	37	..		122
1	12	5	354	112	1,223	170	2,156	212	208	44		123
..	..	..	195	35	651	57	1,445	107	155	..		124
1	4	..	642	125	2,231	282	4,629	254	426	34		125
2	10	5	246	34	876	60	2,063	123	374	118		126
..	1	..	91	18	359	32	763	27	6	..		127
..	..	..	103	7	515	35	995	47	61	..		128
..	..	..	116	10	520	32	1,071	41	13	..		129
..	12	2	726	80	2,068	162	5,611	303	323	8		130
..	..	..	265	54	1,134	122	2,693	196	162	7		131
..	..	..	7	..	18	..	75	8	3	..		132
..	2	1	72	8	227	16	498	19	104	4		133
..	24	4	278	32	673	36	2,123	95	175	5		134
..	..	..	60	3	238	9	675	36	32	1		135
..	..	..	204	21	876	33	1,651	75	61	2		136